Advanced Microprocessors and Peripherals

Third Edition

About the Authors

K M Bhurchandi received his BE and ME degrees in Electronics Engineering in 1990 and 1992, with distinction from Shri Guru Gobind Singhji Institute of Engineering and Technology, Nanded (formerly known as Shri Gobind Singhji College of Engineering and Technology), an autonomous institute under the aegis of Government of Maharashtra. He then went on to receive his PhD degree from Visvesvaraya Regional Engineering College, Nagpur under Nagpur University in 2004. He worked in many self-financed engineering institutes till he was promoted as a Professor. After around 18 years of teaching experience, he joined Visvesvaraya National Institute of Technology, Nagpur, in the Electronics Department where he is currently working as an Associate Professor since 2010. He has been working in the field of Signal and Image Processing, Computer Vision, Microprocessors and Computer Architectures, Embedded Systems, Automation and Instrumentation Systems. His interest areas include Automation, Heavy Weighing Systems and Color Image Processing and has completed a few academic, sponsored industrial and consultancy projects in these areas. He has authored more than 35 research papers for national, international conferences and journals with good impact factors. He is the Principal Investigator of a funded research project on Face Recognition. He is the coordinator of ATMEL and Texas Instruments embedded systems laboratories at Department of Electronics Engineering, VNIT, Nagpur. He has filed a patent application on 'Remote Monitoring of Energy meters using Communication Channels'. He is currently guiding six PhD. students.

A K Ray received his Bachelor's degree from Bengal Engineering College, Shibpur, followed by MTech and PhD degrees from Electronics and Electrical Communication Engineering Department of IIT Kharagpur. He joined Bengal Engineering and Science University, Shibpur, as a Vice Chancellor from March 2009. Prior to this, he was a Professor of Electronics and Electrical Communication Engineering and Head, School of Medical Science and Technology at IIT Kharagpur. Prof. Ray has successfully completed 17 research projects, sponsored by several agencies like Defence Research & Development Organization, Department of Atomic Energy, Department of Science and Technology, and so on. He was the Principal Investigator of research projects, sponsored by Intel Corporation during 1997 – 2004 and is the co-inventor of six US patents jointly with Intel Corporation and has filed three USA patents jointly with Texas Instruments. He has co-authored more than 100 research papers in International journals and Conferences. He has authored five books published by international publishing houses including one in Chinese. He has been serving as a member of the working committee of National Planning Commission on 'Technical Education'.

Advanced Microprocessors and Peripherals

Third Edition

K M Bhurchandi
Associate Professor
Department of Electronics Engineering
Visvesvaraya National Institute of Technology
Nagpur, Maharashtra

A K Ray
Vice Chancellor
Bengal Engineering and Science University, Shibpur, Kolkata
Professor, Electronics and ECE Department,
IIT Kharagpur, West Bengal

Tata McGraw Hill Education Private Limited

NEW DELHI

McGraw-Hill Offices

New Delhi New York St Louis San Francisco Auckland Bogotá Caracas
Kuala Lumpur Lisbon London Madrid Mexico City Milan Montreal
San Juan Santiago Singapore Sydney Tokyo Toronto

Tata McGraw-Hill

Published by Tata McGraw Hill Education Private Limited,
7 West Patel Nagar, New Delhi 110 008

Advanced Microprocessors and Peripherals, 3e

ISBN (13 digits): 978-1-25-902977-6
ISBN (10 digits): 1-25-902977-8

Vice President and Managing Director—McGraw-Hill Education: *Ajay Shukla*

Head—Publishing and Marketing, Higher Education: *Vibha Mahajan*

Publishing Manager—SEM & Tech. Ed.: *Shalini Jha*
Assistant Sponsoring Editor: *Smruti Snigdha*
Editorial Researcher: *Sourabh Maheshwari*
Executive—Editorial Services: *Sohini Mukherjee*
Senior Production Manager: *Satinder S. Baveja*
Production Executivee: *Anuj K Shriwastava*

Marketing Manager—Higher Education: *Vijay Sarathi*
Senior Product Specialist: *Tina Jajoriya*
Graphic Designer—Cover: *Meenu Raghav*

General Manager—Production: *Rajender P. Ghansela*
Manager—Production: *Reji Kumar*

Typeset at BeSpoke Integrated Solutions, Puducherry, India 605 008 and printed at Krishna Offset, 10/122, Vishnu Gali, Vishwas Nagar, DELHI-110032

Cover Printer: A. P. Offset
RALLCRBGDRAYR

To My parents—Smt. Malati and Shri Madhukar Bhurchandi
My wife—Minal, and son—Mandar.
All of them have sacrificed a lot of family time for this text.

—K M Bhurchandi

In memory of My parents—Smt. Parul Ray and Late Shri Shailendra Madhab Ray and to My wife—Supriya, and children—Aniruddha, Ananya

—A K Ray

Contents

Preface

We are very happy to witness the launch of this third edition of our work, which we are sure will generate a lot of interest amongst readers. Since the publication of the first edition of this book in 2000, followed by its second edition in 2006, the field of microprocessors and microcontrollers has undergone phenomenal developments. The Intel microprocessor family has evolved from those early days of 4-bit and 8-bit microprocessors through a long evolution of 16-bit, 32-bit microprocessors to Pentium and the advanced I-7 in addition to many variants of Pentium, Celeron and Itanium. The arena of multi-core processors has already begun. On the other hand, 8-bit microprocessors are mostly of academic interest only, and microcontrollers are widely used for small, dedicated hardware systems and embedded applications. In this background, we present a brief overview of microprocessors, starting from the basic concept of a microprocessor followed by the intermediate microprocessors, and concepts of microcontrollers and interfacing with microcontrollers.

A microprocessor is a programmable circuit that supports the execution of a set of instructions called an instruction set. Each instruction in the instruction set is represented by a predefined unique sequence of 1s and 0s called OPCODE (Operation Code). The data required for the execution of operation, i.e. operands are also expressed in 1s and 0s, i.e. binary form, and follows the opcode. Customarily, the opcode and operands are specified in instructions in the form of bytes. Thus, microprocessor instructions consist of opcode and operand bytes. A microprocessor can execute one instruction at a time. Hence, a task to be executed by a microprocessor is expressed in terms of a sequence of instructions called a 'program'. It is to be noted here that the microprocessor is a digital circuit and understands (accepts) the instructions or data expressed only in terms of 1s and 0s. For convenience of entering into a microprocessor-based system, it is customarily entered byte by byte. Thus, a microprocessor system program is a sequence of bytes expressed in hexadecimal system. These programs, expressed in terms of hexadecimal bytes, are called 'machine-language programs'. Thus, the types of circuits, systems and machines which are able to remember the sequence of instructions, the operands related to each instruction, can execute them and finally store the result of the complete execution are called 'programmable circuits or machines'. These are available in the form of crude microprocessor-based systems or advanced personal computers or more savvy laptops, notebooks and palmtops.

Intel Corporation has been one of the pioneers in the microprocessor industry right from its infant stage. Even today, they are one of the major players in the field though many have emerged. It is thus very natural and justified to start the introduction to the field using Intel's framework.

With the advent of the first 4-bit microprocessor 4004 from Intel Corporation in 1971, there has been a silent revolution in the domain of digital system design, which has shaken many facets of the current technological progress. In the last 40 years, the world has seen an evolution of microprocessors, whose impact on today's technological scenario is phenomenal.

This evolution was possible because of tremendous advances in semiconductor process technology. The first microprocessor 4004 contained only around thousand transistors, while the component density increased more than threefold in less than a decade's time. Immediately after the introduction of the 4004, Intel introduced the first 8-bit microprocessor 8008 in 1972; these processors were, however, not successful because of their inherent limitations. In 1974, Intel released the first general-purpose 8-bit microprocessor 8080. This CPU also was not functionally complete and the first 8-bit functionally complete CPU 8085 was introduced in 1977.

The 8085 CPU is still the most popular amongst all the 8-bit CPUs. The 8085 CPU houses an on-chip clock generator and provides good performance utilizing an optimum set of registers and a reasonably powerful ALU. The major limitations of these 8-bit microprocessors are their limited memory addressing capacity, slow speed of execution, limited number of general-purpose registers and non-availability of complex instructions and addressing modes. Another important point to be mentioned here is that 8085 does not support adequate pipelining or parallelism, which is so important for enhancing the speed of computation. For example, the non-availability of any instruction queue in an 8085 CPU leads to a situation where the fetching of opcode and operands along with the execution is compelled in an absolutely sequential manner.

The first 16-bit CPU from Intel was a result of the designers' efforts to produce a more powerful and efficient computing machine. The designers of 8086 CPU had taken note of the major limitations of the previous generations of the 8-bit CPUs. The 8086 contains a set of 16-bit general-purpose registers, supports a 16-bit ALU, a rich instruction set and provides a segmented memory-addressing scheme. The introduction of a set of segment registers for addressing the segmented memory in 8086 was indeed a major step in the process of evolution. All these features made this 16-bit processor a more efficient CPU, and thus it is termed the first member of Intel's advanced microprocessors family.

The development of the IBM PC started in July 1980, and precisely after one year, the first machine based on Intel 8088 CPU (which is functionally equivalent to 8086 but supports only 8-bit external data bus) with one or two floppy disk drives, a keyboard and a monochrome monitor was announced in August 1981. The machine operating system was an early version of the operating system MS-DOS from Microsoft. In March 1983, a new version of IBM PC called PC-XT was introduced with a 10-megabyte hard disk, one double-side double-density floppy disk drive, keyboard, monitor and an asynchronous communication adapter. In fact, the introduction of IBM PCs in 1980s had, to a large extent, produced a profound impact on the evolution of microprocessors. With the introduction of each new generation of microprocessors, the performance of Personal Computers have also been enriched. Rather the computational performance of PC machines and their state of art has improved due to the availability of high-speed advanced microprocessors.

The major limitation in 8086 was that it did not have memory management and protection capabilities, which was considered an extremely important feature, deemed to be an integral part of a CPU of the eighties. The 80286 was the first CPU to possess the ability of memory management, privilege and protection. However, the 80286 CPU also had a limitation on the maximum segment size supported by it (only 64 KB). Another limitation of 80286 was that once it was switched into protected mode, it was difficult to get it back to real mode. The only way of reverting it to the real mode was to reset the system.

In the mid-eighties, more computationally demanding problems necessitated the development of still faster CPUs. Thus appeared 80386, which was the first 32-bit CPU from Intel. The memory management capability of 80286 was enhanced to support huge virtual memory, paging and four levels of protection. The design of 80386 circumvented this problem. Moreover, the maximum segment size in 80386 was enhanced and this could be as large as 4 GB with 80386 supporting as many as 16384 segments. The 80386 along with its math coprocessor 80387, provided a high-speed environment even for graphical applications. Around the early nineties, the graphical displays, and interactive tools started becoming more and more popular. Soon, the operating system Windows 95 with graphical interface became a part of every machine. This lead to design of 80486 as a processor of similar capacity as 80386, but with an integrated math coprocessor. After getting integrated, the speed of execution of mathematical operations required for graphics applications enhanced threefold. In addition, for the first time an 8 KB four-way set associative code and data cache was introduced in 80486. A five-stage instruction pipelining was also introduced.

The earlier generation CPUs supported rather crude instruction sets. It was not expected that the programmers those days would write large machine-code programs. A single high-level instruction might be compiled into ten or even hundred machine-code operations. In the course of evolution, from the early 8-bit CPUs, the trend was to design CPUs that could support more and more complex instructions at the assembly-language level. Designers of Complex Instruction Set Computers (CISC) wanted to reduce this gap. The design and research efforts further led to the first virtually 64-bit processor: Pentium-I. The Pentium used to execute the computationally greedy applications with a 64-bit wide data bus. Thus, a family of operations like Single Instruction Multiple Data (SIMD) and Multiple Instructions Multiple Data (MIMD) emerged and became popular for multimedia applications. Hence, the developing technologies of fabrication and the demand for more and more computational power for advanced applications resulted in launching of many variations of Pentium either with higher clock speed or with special features like superscalar execution, multimedia extension, streaming SIMD extension and RISC features. To name a few Pentium variants, they are P-I, P-II, P-III, P-IV, Pentium PRO, and Pentium MMX, etc. Further, it was observed that whatever the technology of manufacture, a single processor core will always have upper limitation on its processing capability and higher degrees of parallelism may boost the processing power. Thus, multi-core processor architectures with instruction-level massive parallelism have been introduced and are popular in modern PCs.

Since the early days of microprocessor development, designers have tried to make them more powerful by designing more complex instructions. But then, some of these powerful instructions and addressing modes were hardly used by programmers. In fact, some of these instructions' logic took up a large part of the microprocessors' silicon chip. The Reduced Instruction Set Computer (RISC) designers observed that the data-movement type of machine instructions are frequently executed by the CPU. They have optimized CPUs to execute these instructions rapidly. RISC provided a regular set of instructions having the same format with a lot of pipelining. To improve the processor's performance, the possible ways are suggested below.

(a) Increasing the processor and system clock rate
(b) Optimizing and improving the instruction set
(c) Executing multiple instructions in one cycle and incorporating parallelism in the CPU architecture

The first option is applicable both to CISC and RISC processors. The second option is primarily for CISC but is applicable to RISC as well. The third option is more suited to RISC CPUs. Ever since the appearance of commercially available RISC CPUs, there has been a debate over the performance of RISC versus CISC. The RISC architects argue that their instructions may be executed in a single cycle and thus take less time than is taken by a CISC CPU. This is because of pipelining, reduction of instructions to a simple operation and synthesis of complex operations with compiler generated code sequences. When RISC machines first arrived in the market, CISC processors were performing at 6 to 10 cycles per instruction, while RISC CPUs could execute a set of simpler instructions in one cycle and offer better performance. Many CISC processors have subsequently used many features of RISC.

A processor without its memory and peripherals is hardly a useful component. Integrating a microprocessor with its peripherals to form a practical system requires a big circuit board and many soldered connections. Thus, microprocessor systems have disadvantages like big physical size, less reliability, no upgradability, high power consumption and high cost of product and maintenance. To pacify these disadvantages, Intel introduced its first 8-bit embedded microcontroller 8031 with 128 bytes on-chip RAM and capable of addressing program memory of 4 KB with on-chip ports, timers and a serial communication unit. Soon its on-chip EPROM version 8051 was introduced by ATMEL and it became so popular that it replaced most 8-bit microprocessors. It must be noted that microprocessors are implemented as

Von Neumann architecture while microcontrollers are implemented as Harvard architectures. Thus, the microcontroller is nothing but a microprocessor with on-chip integrated peripherals. Microcontroller-based systems have advantages like small size, low power consumption, portability, better upgradability, low cost of manufacturing and maintenance. Due to these advantages of embedded controllers and ARM processors, they have become very popular in dedicated small applications and embedded systems. It should, however, be noted that programming with microcontrollers and ARM using machine language is very tedious and prone to mistakes. The advanced embedded system design and programming tools for microcontrollers and ARM processors facilitate use of sophisticated debuggers, emulators, simulators along with the ease of high-level language programming like C, JAVA and operating systems like VXWORKS, EMBEDDED LINUX, etc.

Target Audience

This book is intended as a textbook on 'Advanced Microprocessors' which is a compulsory course at graduate and postgraduate levels in many science and engineering branches of studies, specially in Electronics, Electrical, Instrumentation, Physics and Computer Science disciplines. The book is suitable for a one-semester course on advanced microprocessors, their architectures, programming, hardware interfacing and applications. The book will primarily serve the needs of undergraduate students for CSE, IT, ECE, EE, EEE. It can also be used by polytechnic students doing diploma and DOEACC courses in computer sciences. The subject needs to have a very practical approach and a basic knowledge of C programming is required to understand the practical applications of the subject.

Objective of the Book

The purpose of our book is to provide readers with a good foundation on advanced microprocessors, their principles and practices. We have tried to keep an appropriate balance between the basic concepts and practical applications related to microprocessor technology. Thus, we have aimed at the following:

- To present fundamental concepts of advanced microprocessors and their architectures
- To enable students write efficient programs in assembly-level language of the 8086 family of microprocessors
- To make students aware of the techniques of interfacing between processors and peripheral devices so that they themselves can design and develop a complete microprocessor-based system
- To present the concepts of microcontroller and ARM architectures in a lucid manner
- To present a host of interesting applications involving microprocessors and microcontrollers

Salient Features

Some of the salient features of the book are listed below.

- Simple and easy-to-understand language
- Updated with crucial topics like ARM *Architecture, Serial communication Standard USB*
- New and updated chapters explaining *8051 Microcontrollers, Instruction set and Peripheral Interfacing along with Project(s) Design*
- Improved explanation and presentation of concept like 80286 and 80386 Descriptors, Addressing modes and 8051Stacks
- Explanation on latest real-life applications like *Hard drives, CDs, DVDs, Blue Ray Drives*

Web Supplements

There are a number of supplementary resources available on the Website http://www.mhhe.com//ray/microprocessors 3 and updated from time to time to support this book.

- 700 presentation slides for instructors and students.

Chapter Organisation

1. The book covers a wide range of microprocessors from 16-bit 8086 to Pentium in a lucid manner. The evolution from one processor architecture to another is evident as one goes through the chapters. A detailed description of each microprocessor has been presented in individual chapters. **Chapter 1** covers 8086/8088 architecture in adequate detail. **Chapter 9** covers 80286 along with its coprocessor. **Chapter 10** covers the microprocessor 80386 and its coprocessor 80387. This chapter also covers 80486, the integrated CPU with built-in math coprocessor in sufficient detail. Pentium, the latest in the Intel microprocessor family, has been briefly presented in **Chapter 11**. One of the most advanced microprocessors of Intel, Pentium IV is presented in **Chapter 12**. A few RISC architectures and their features have been presented in **Chapter 13**.

2. An important feature of the book is the inclusion of a number of interesting applications of microprocessors. An adequate account of each one of these applications has been presented in the book. An interesting application of microprocessors for controlling an aluminium smelter has been presented in **Chapter l4. Chapter 15** presents another interesting application in the area of pattern scanner design. Design of a microprocessor-based electronic weighing bridge has been elaborated in **Chapter 16.**

3. One of the major problems encountered by students is difficulty in writing assembly-language programs. In this book, a large number of assembly-language programs have been presented. They will enable students to write efficient codes on 16-bit or 32-bit platforms. **Chapter 2** covers the 8086 family instruction set and the assembler directives with necessary examples. The art of programming in 8086 assembly language has been elaborated with a large number of program examples in **Chapter 3**. A very important spectrum of programs involving stacks, subroutines, interrupts, macros and time delays has been discussed in adequate detail in **Chapter 4.**

4. A good account of a number of general peripheral devices like I/O ports, keyboards, displays, ADCs, DACs, stepper motors, etc., and their interfacing with 8086 has been elaborated in **Chapter 5**.

5. Some special dedicated peripherals like timer, USART, keyboard display interface, interrupt controllers, and DMA controllers, CRT controllers, floppy disk controllers, etc., have been discussed elaborately along with interfacing examples and programs in **chapters 6 and 7**. Detailed knowledge about these peripherals is extremely important for interfacing these devices with advanced CPUs and also for designing standalone microprocessor-based systems. Brief notes on high-capacity memory devices and a high-speed serial communication standard USB are presented at the end of the respective chapters.

6. The importance of multiprocessor-based system design cannot be underestimated in today's world. A full chapter has been devoted to presenting issues related to the multiprocessor-based system design. The co-processors like 8087, 8089, etc., along with their interfacing strategies have been presented in

Chapter 8 of the book. Design of an 8088 based multi-microprocessor system has been described in adequate detail in this chapter with an example.

7. In recent days, the importance of microcontrollers has increased manifold for small, dedicated system designs and embedded applications. Sensing the fact, the instruction set of MCS-51 family has been included in **Chapter 17** followed by a few simple programming examples. A full in-depth chapter on interfacing with MCS-51 microcontroller family has been included with adequate theory , significant number of interfacing, programming and project design examples as **Chapter 18.** Thus, though the core content of this book is weaved around advanced microprocessors and interfacing, this book presents microcontrollers and interfacing in significant details.

Like the earlier editions, this text very much maintains the apt balance between basic concepts and practical/real-life applications related to the subject technology.

Additional projects on microprocessors and microcontrollers will surely help students in grasping better practical applications of the subject!

Feedback

We firmly believe that, on the whole, this complete text will be very useful for the students, designers and general readers for their academic and technical ventures in the field of microprocessors and microcontrollers. Further suggestions for improvement will always be welcome.

KM Bhurchandi
AK Ray

Publisher's Note

Do you have any feedback? We look forward to receive your views and suggestions for improvement. The same can be sent to *tmh.csefeedback@gmail.com*, mentioning the title and authors' name in the subject line.

Pircay related issues, may also be reported.

Acknowledgements

Several individuals have contributed to prepare the manuscript of this book. The authors gratefully acknowledge contributions of each one of them.

At the outset, the authors would like to express their thanks to the faculty members of Indian Institute of Technology (IIT), Kharagpur and Visvesvaraya National Institute of Technology (VNIT), Nagpur. The authors would also like to convey their gratitude to numerous teachers and students - belonging to multiple sciences and engineering institutions from diverse parts of India as well as abroad - for their keen interest in this book. All of these in unison have encouraged and prompted the authors to undertake the publication of the third edition of this book.

In particular, Late Prof. G S Sanyal - Former Director and Advisor, IIT Kharagpur, Prof. A K Majumdar- Head, Department of Computer Science and Engineering, IIT Kharagpur, Dr. Tinku Acharya - CTO, Avisere Inc., USA have always shown their active interest in the publication of this book. We are thankful to them. The authors would also like to acknowledge Intel Corporation, USA for allowing them to use some of their product specifications for the book.

Some faculty members and students of IIT Kharagpur have contributed in various ways to enable completion of this work. The authors would like to acknowledge the services rendered by them. In particular, we thank Rajat Sethi of Computer Science and Engineering department of IIT Kharagpur, who has contributed in shaping the chapter on Pentium 4. Anoop C V, Rahul Gupta, U V Srinadh, Maj. Nilesh Ingle, Maj. Vivek Vaidyanathan of Electronics & ECE department, IIT Kharagpur have reviewed some of the chapters in the second edition and we thank them all.

We thank Prof. D Sarkar, A K Ghosh, Ananda Mitra and. S S Biswas for providing valuable inputs for the chapter on Microprocessor Based Aluminium Smelter Design, Prof B P Sandilya, Tamalika Chaira, D S Deshpande, Amit Chatterji, S Verma, S Sukumar, Mainak Chowdhary, Rajat Subhra Mukherji, Arnab Chakraborti, Abha Jain, Smarahara Mishra, Animesh Khemka and S Dihidar deserve special mention for going through parts of the manuscript. We acknowledge the help rendered by Kaushik Mallick Arumoy Mukherjee, Arindam Mandal, Rana Pratap Ghoshal and many others for their help in preparation of the manuscript.

Third Edition of this book has been carefully reviewed, improved and upgraded from the earlier two editions. We remain thankful to the contributors of the earlier editions : Prof. A.G.Kothari - VNIT, Nagpur, our erst while colleagues Prof. K K Bhoyar, Prof. Aniket Gokhale, Prof. D. P. Dave, Prof. Padma Rao and Prof. Rajesh Raut for their technical contributions towards the soul of this book.

Our heartiest thanks are due to Dr S S Gokhale - Director, VNIT, Nagpur for his encouragement, appreciation and support towards the work of this edition. We must also thank Prof. A G Keskar, a well known expert in the fields of microprocessors and embedded systems, for his contributions not only in terms of discussions on concepts and ideas related to the topics of this book but also in general as a friend, philosopher and a senior colleague at VNIT, Nagpur. We are especially thankful to Prof. Vishal Satpute, VNIT Nagpur, for his efforts and contribution towards the preparation of the power point presentation of the web course on Advanced Microprocessors. Herein we must express our gratitude towards Hemprasad Patil, Research Scholar and Krishnarao, Snehanshu Sahu and Padmsingh Kolhe, all final year students at Electronics Engineering department of VNIT Nagpur for their critical reviews of different topics.

We would also like to express our thanks to Prof. R M Patrikar, Prof. K D Kulat, Prof. A.S. Gandhi, Prof. R. B. Deshmukh, Prof. A G Kothari and Prof. S B Dhok - our colleagues at VNIT Nagpur for their support and appreciation.

At this juncture we gratefully thank the numerous reviewers commissioned by the publisher, who had sent useful comments and suggestions after going through the manuscript. Their names are given below:

Siddharth Chauhan	*National Institute of Technology, Hamirpur, Himachal Pradesh*
Kanchan Sharma	*Guru Gobind Singh Indraprastha University, New Delhi*
Madan Mohan Agarwal	*Birla Institute of Technology (BIT), Jaipur, Rajasthan*
Eldo P Elias	*M A College of Engineering, Kothamangalam, Kerala*
Sadanand Kulkarni	*KLE Society's College of Engineering and Technology, Belgaum, Karnataka*
C A Ghuge	*PE Society's Modern College of Engineering, Pune*

Our appreciation to the entire editorial team at Tata McGraw Hill – Ms. Vibha Mahajan, Ms. Shalini Jha, Ms. Smruti Snigdha, Mr. Sourabh Maheshwari, Ms. Sohini Mukherjee, Mr. Satinder Singh, and Mr. Anuj K. Shriwastava - without their efforts this edition would not have been in the form in which it is at present.

KM Bhurchandi
AK Ray

1 The Processors: 8086/8088—Architectures, Pin Diagrams and Timing Diagrams

INTRODUCTION

Intel introduced its first 4-bit microprocessor 4004 in 1971 and its 8-bit microprocessor 8008 in 1972. These microprocessors could not survive as general purpose microprocessors due to their design and performance limitations. The launch of the first general purpose 8-bit microprocessor 8080 in 1974 by Intel is considered to be the first major stepping stone towards the development of advanced microprocessors. The microprocessor 8085 followed 8080, with a few more added features to its architecture, which resulted in a functionally complete microprocessor. The main limitations of the 8-bit microprocessors were their low speed, low memory addressing capability, limited number of general purpose registers and a less powerful instruction set. All these limitations of the 8-bit microprocessors pushed the designers to build more powerful processors in terms of advanced architecture, more processing capability, larger memory addressing capability and a more powerful instruction set. The 8086 was a result of such developmental design efforts.

In the family of 16-bit microprocessors, Intel's 8086 was the first one to be launched in 1978. The introduction of the 16-bit processor was a result of the increasing demand for more powerful and high speed computational resources. The 8086 microprocessor has a much more powerful instruction set along with the architectural developments which imparts substantial programming flexibility and improvement in speed over the 8-bit microprocessors.

The peripheral chips designed earlier for 8085 were compatible with microprocessor 8086 with slight or no modifications. Though there is a considerable difference between the memory addressing techniques of 8085 and 8086, the memory interfacing technique is similar, but includes the use of a few additional signals. The clock requirements are also different as compared to 8085, but the overall minimal system organisation of 8086 is similar to that of a general 8-bit microprocessor. In this chapter, the architectures of 8086 and 8088 are discussed in adequate details along with the interfacing of the supporting chips with them to form a minimum system. The system organisation is also discussed in significant details for both the operating modes of 8086 and 8088, along with necessary timing diagrams.

1.1 REGISTER ORGANISATION OF 8086

8086 has a powerful set of registers known as *general purpose* and *special purpose registers*. All of them are 16-bit registers. The general purpose registers, can be used as either 8-bit registers or 16-bit registers. They may be either used for holding data, variables and intermediate results temporarily or for other purposes like a counter or for storing offset address for some particular addressing modes etc. The special purpose registers are used as segment registers, pointers, index registers or as offset storage registers for particular addressing modes. We will categorize the register set into four groups, as follows:

1.1.1 General Data Registers

Figure 1.1 shows the register organisation of 8086. The registers AX,BX,CX and DX are the general purpose 16-bit registers. AX is used as 16-bit *accumulator*, with the lower 8-bits of AX designated as AL and higher 8-bits as AH. AL can be used as an 8-bit accumulator for 8-bit operations. This is the most important general purpose register having multiple functions, which will be discussed later.

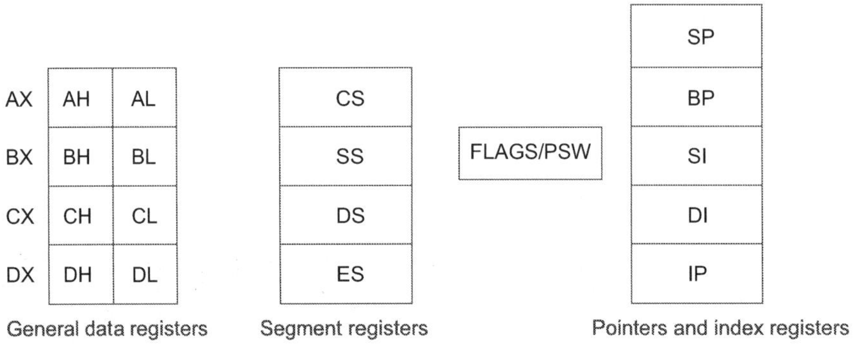

Fig. 1.1 *Register organisation of 8086*

Usually the letters L and H specify the lower and higher bytes of a particular register. For example, CH means the higher 8-bits of the CX register and CL means the lower 8-bits of the CX register. The letter X is used to specify the complete 16-bit register. The register CX is also used as a default counter in case of string and loop instructions. The register BX is used as an offset storage for forming physical addresses in case of certain addressing modes. DX register is a general purpose register which may be used as an implicit operand or destination in case of a few instructions. The detailed uses of these registers will be more clear when we discuss the addressing modes and the instruction set of 8086.

1.1.2 Segment Registers

Unlike 8085, the 8086 addresses a segmented memory. The complete 1 megabyte memory, which the 8086 addresses, is divided into 16 logical segments. Each segment thus contains 64 Kbytes of memory. There are four segment registers, viz. Code Segment Register (CS), Data Segment Register (DS), Extra Segment Register (ES) and Stack Segment Register (SS). The code segment register is used for addressing a memory location in the code segment of the memory, where the executable program is stored. Similarly, the data segment register points to the data segment of the memory, where the data is resided. The extra segment also refers to a segment which essentially is another data segment of the memory. Thus, the extra segment also contains data. The stack segment register is used for addressing stack segment of memory i.e. memory which is used to store stack data. The CPU uses the stack for temporarily storing important data, e.g. the contents of the CPU registers which will be required at a later stage. The stack grows down, i.e. the data is pushed onto the stack in the memory locations with decreasing addresses. When this information will be required by the CPU, they will be popped off from the stack. While addressing any location in the memory bank, the physical address is calculated from two parts, the first is *segment address* and the second is *offset*. The segment registers contain 16-bit segment base addresses, related to different segments. Any of the pointers and index registers or BX may contain the offset of the location to be addressed. The advantage of this scheme is that instead of maintaining a 20-bit register for a physical address, the processor just maintains two 16-bit registers which are within the word length capacity of the machine. Thus the CS, DS, SS and ES segment registers, respectively, contain the segment addresses for the code, data, stack and extra segments of memory. It may be noted that all these segments are the logical segments. They may or may not be physically separated. In other words, a single segment may require more than one memory chip or more than one segment may be accommodated in a single memory chip.

1.1.3 Pointers and Index Registers

The pointers contain offset within the particular segments. The pointers IP, BP and SP usually contain offsets within the code (JP), and stack (BP & SP) segments. The *index registers* are used as general purpose registers as well as for offset storage in case of indexed, based indexed and relative based indexed addressing modes. The register SI is generally used to store the offset of source data in data segment while the register DI is used to store the offset of destination in data or extra segment. The index registers are particularly useful for string manipulations.

1.1.4 Flag Register

The 8086 *flag register* contents indicate the results of computations in the ALU. It also contains some flag bits to control the CPU operations. Details of the flag register are discussed later in this chapter.

1.2 ARCHITECTURE

The architecture of 8086 provides a number of improvements over 8085 architecture. It supports a 16-bit ALU, a set of 16-bit registers and provides segmented memory addressing capability, a rich instruction set, powerful interrupt structure, fetched instruction queue for overlapped fetching and execution etc. The internal block diagram, shown in Fig.1.2, describes the overall organization of different units inside the chip.

The complete architecture of 8086 can be divided into two parts (a) Bus Interface Unit (BIU) and (b) Execution Unit (EU). *The bus interface unit contains the circuit for physical address calculations and a predecoding instruction byte queue (6 bytes long)*. The bus interface unit makes the system's bus signals available for external interfacing of the devices. In other words, this unit is responsible for establishing communications with external devices and peripherals including memory via the bus. As already stated, the 8086 addresses a segmented memory. The complete physical address which is 20-bits long is generated using segment and offset registers, each 16-bits long.

For generating a physical address from contents of these two registers, the content of a segment register also called as segment address is shifted left bit-wise four times and to this result, content of an offset register also called as offset address is added, to produce a 20-bit physical address. For example, if the segment address is 1005H and the offset is 5555H, then the physical address is calculated as below:

Segment address	⟶ 1005H	
Offset address	⟶ 5555H	
Segment address	⟶ 1005H ⟶	0001 0000 0000 0101
Shifted by 4 bit positions		⟶ 0001 0000 0000 0101 0000
	+	
Offset address		⟶ 0101 0101 0101 0101
Physical address		⟶ 0001 0101 0101 1010 0101
		1 5 5 A 5

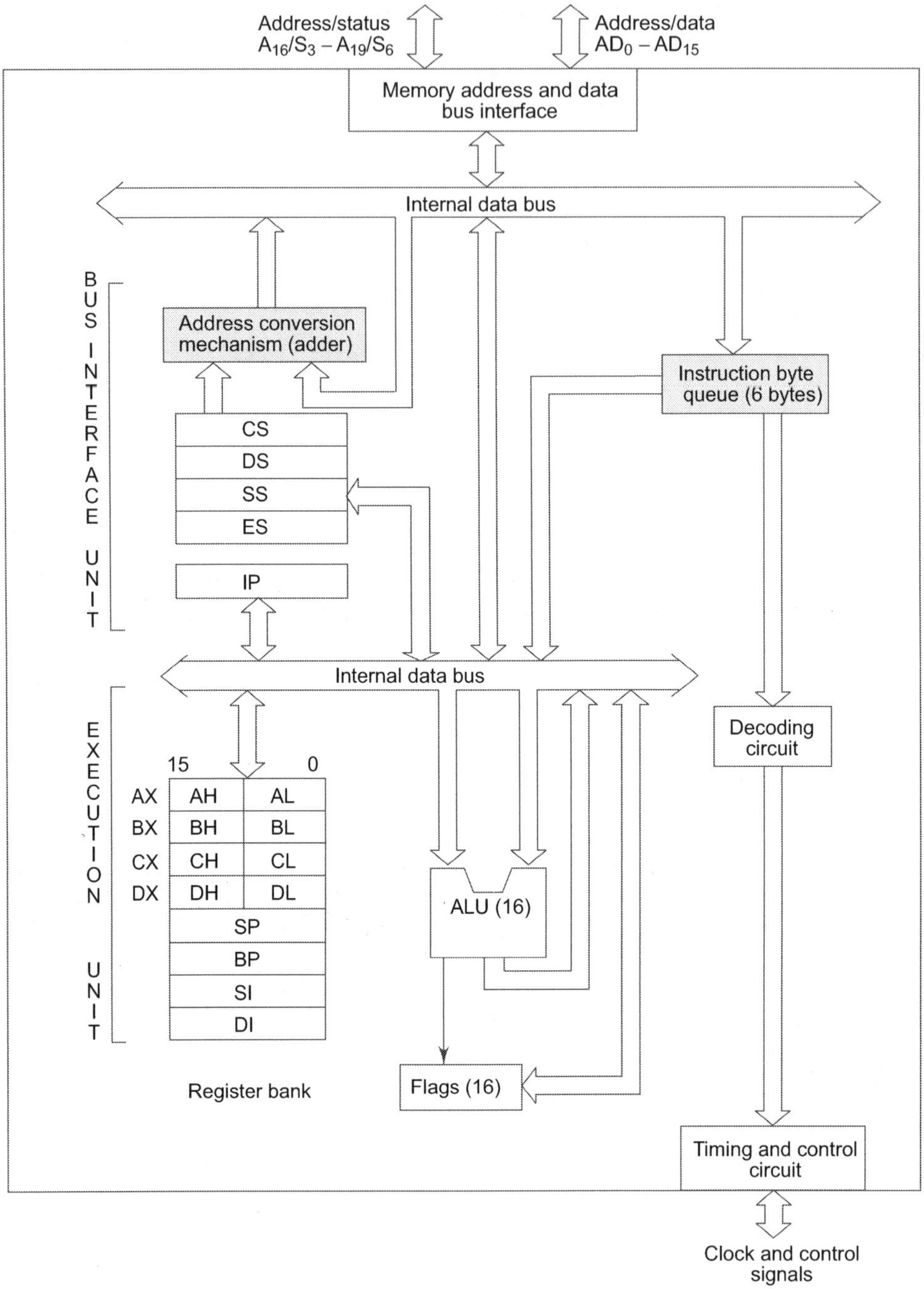

Fig. 1.2 *8086 Architecture*

Thus, the segment addressed by the segment value 1005H can have offset values from 0000H to FFFFH within it, i.e. maximum 64K locations may be accommodated in the segment. Thus, the segment register indicates the base address of a particular segment, while the offset indicates the distance of the required memory location in the segment from the base address. Since the offset is a 16-bit number, each segment can have a maximum of 64K locations. The bus interface unit has a separate adder to perform this procedure for obtaining a physical address while addressing memory. The segment address value is to be taken from an appropriate segment register depending upon whether code, data or stack are to be accessed, while the offset may be the content of IP, BX, SI, DI, SP, BP or an immediate 16-bit value, depending upon the addressing mode.

In case of 8085, once the opcode is fetched and decoded, the external bus remains free for some time, while the processor internally executes the instruction. This time slot is utilised in 8086 to achieve the overlapped fetch and execution cycles. While the fetched instruction is executed internally, the external bus is used to fetch the machine code of the next instruction and arrange it in a queue known as predecoded instruction byte queue. It is a 6 bytes long, first-in first-out structure. The instructions from the queue are taken for decoding sequentially. Once a byte is decoded, the queue is rearranged by pushing it out and the queue status is checked for the possibility of the next opcode fetch cycle. While the opcode is fetched by the Bus Interface Unit (BIU), the Execution Unit (EU) executes the previously decoded instruction concurrently. The BIU along with the Execution Unit (EU) thus forms a pipeline. The bus interface unit, thus manages the complete interface of execution unit with memory and I/O devices, of course, under the control of the timing and control unit.

The execution unit contains the register set of 8086 except segment registers and IP. It has a 16-bit ALU, able to perform arithmetic and logic operations. The 16-bit flag register reflects the results of execution by the ALU. The decoding unit decodes the opcode bytes issued from the instruction byte queue. The timing and control unit derives the necessary control signals to execute the instruction opcode received from the queue, depending upon the information made available by the decoding circuit. The execution unit may pass the results to the bus interface unit for storing them in memory.

1.2.1 Memory Segmentation

The memory in an 8086/8088 based system is organised as segmented memory. In this scheme, the complete physically available memory may be divided into a number of logical segments. Each segment is 64K bytes in size and is addressed by one of the segment registers. The 16-bit contents of the segment register actually point to the starting location of a particular segment. To address a specific memory location within a segment, we need an offset address. The offset address is also 16-bit long so that the maximum offset value can be FFFFH, and the maximum size of any segment is thus 64K locations. The physical address formation has been explained previously in Section 1.2.

To emphasize this segmented memory concept, we will consider an example of a housing colony containing say, 100 houses. The simplest method of numbering the houses will be to assign the numbers from 1 to 100 to each house sequentially. Suppose, now, if one wants to find out house number 67, then he will start from house number 1 and go on till he finds the house, numbered 67. Consider another case where the 100 houses are arranged in the 10 × 10 (rows × columns) pattern. In this case, to find out house number 67, one will directly go to the 6th row and then to the 7th column. In the second scheme, the efforts required for finding the same house will be too less. This second scheme in our example is analogous to the segmented memory scheme, where the addresses are specified in terms of segment addresses analogous to rows and offset addresses analogous to columns.

The CPU 8086 is able to address 1Mbytes of physical memory. The complete 1Mbytes memory can be divided into 16 segments, each of 64Kbytes size. The addresses of the segments may be assigned as 0000H to F000H respectively. The offset address values are from 0000H to FFFFH so that the physical addresses range from 00000H to FFFFFH. In the above said case, the segments are called non-overlapping segments. The non-overlapping segments are shown in Fig. 1.3(a). In some cases, however, the segments may be overlapping. Suppose a segment starts at a particular address and its maximum size can be 64Kbytes. But, if another segment starts before this 64Kbytes locations of the first segment, the two segments are said to be overlapping segments. The area of memory from the start of the second segment to the possible end of the first segment is called an overlapped segment area. Figure 1.3(b) explains the phenomenon more clearly. The locations lying in the overlapped area may be addressed by the same physical address generated from two different sets of segment and offset addresses. The main advantages of the segmented memory scheme are as follows:

1. Allows the memory capacity to be 1Mbytes although the actual addresses to be handled are of 16-bit size
2. Allows the placing of code, data and stack portions of the same program in different parts (segments) of memory, for data and code protection
3. Permits a program and/or its data to be put into different areas of memory each time the program is executed, i.e. provision for relocation is done.

In the Overlapped Area Locations Physical Address = $CS_1 + IP_1 = CS_2 + IP_2$, where '+' indicates the procedure of physical address formation.

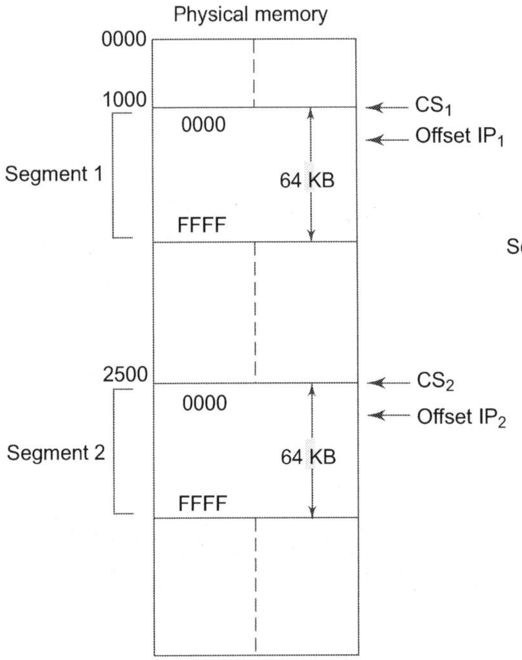

Fig. 1.3(a) *Non-overlapping Segments*

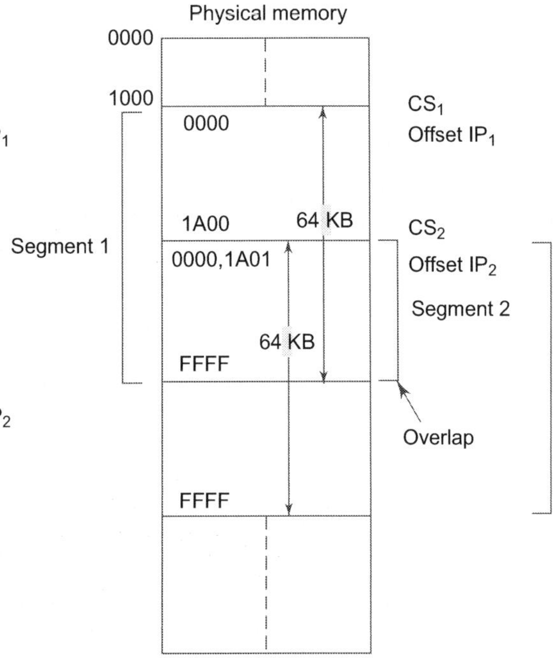

Fig. 1.3(b) *Overlapping Segments*

1.2.2 Flag Register

8086 has a 16-bit flag register which is divided into two parts, viz. (a) *condition code or status flags* and (b) *machine control flags*. The ***condition code flag register*** is the lower byte of the 16-bit flag register along with the *overflow flag*. This flag is identical to the 8085 flag register, with an additional overflow flag, which is not present in 8085. This part of the flag register of 8086 reflects the results of the operations performed by ALU. The *control flag register* is the higher byte of the flag register of 8086. It contains three flags, viz. *direction flag* (D), *interrupt flag* (I) and *trap flag* (T).

The complete bit configuration of 8086 flag register is shown in Fig. 1.4.

15	14	13	12	11	10	9	8	7	6	5	4	3	2	1	0
X	X	X	X	O	D	I	T	S	Z	X	Ac	X	P	X	Cy

O — Overflow flag
D — Direction flag
I — Interrupt flag
T — Trap flag
S — Sign flag
Z — Zero flag
Ac — Auxiliary carry flag
P — Parity flag
Cy — Carry flag
X — Not used

Fig. 1.4 *Flag Register of 8086*

The description of each flag bit is as follows:

S-Sign Flag This flag is set when the result of any computation is negative. For signed computations, the sign flag equals the MSB of the result.

Z-Zero Flag This flag is set if the result of the computation or comparison performed by the previous instruction/instructions is zero.

P-Parity Flag This flag is set to 1 if the lower byte of the result contains even number of 1s.

C-Carry Flag This flag is set when there is a carry out of MSB in case of addition or a borrow in case of subtraction. For example, when two numbers are added, a carry may be generated out of the most significant bit position. The carry flag, in this case, will be set to '1'. In case, no carry is generated, it will be '0'. Some other instructions also affect or use this flag and will be discussed later in this text.

T-Trap Flag If this flag is set, the processor enters the single step execution mode. In other words, a trap interrupt is generated after execution of each instruction. The processor executes the current instruction and the control is transferred to the Trap interrupt service routine.

I-Interrupt Flag If this flag is set, the maskable interrupts are recognised by the CPU, otherwise they are ignored.

D-Direction Flag This is used by string manipulation instructions. If this flag bit is '0', the string is processed beginning from the lowest address to the highest address, i.e. *autoincrementing mode*. Otherwise, the string is processed from the highest address towards the lowest address, i.e. *autodecrementing mode*. We will describe string manipulations later in chapter 2 in more detail.

AC-Auxiliary Carry Flag This is set if there is a carry from the lowest nibble, i.e. bit three, during addition or borrow for the lowest nibble, i.e. bit three, during subtraction.

O-Overflow Flag This flag is set if an overflow occurs, i.e. if the result of a signed operation is large enough to be accommodated in a destination register. For example, in case of the addition of two signed numbers, if the result overflows into the sign bit, i.e. the result is of more than 7-bits in size in case of 8-bit signed operations and more than 15-bits in size in case of 16-bit signed operations, then the overflow flag will be set.

1.3 SIGNAL DESCRIPTIONS OF 8086

The microprocessor 8086 is a 16-bit CPU available in three clock rates, i.e. 5, 8 and 10 MHz, packaged in a 40 pin CERDIP or plastic package. The 8086 operates in single processor or multiprocessor configurations to achieve high performance. The pin configuration is shown in Fig. 1.5. Some of the pins serve a particular function in minimum mode (single processor mode) and others function in maximum mode (multiprocessor mode) configuration.

The 8086 signals can be categorised in three groups. The first are the signals having common functions in minimum as well as maximum mode, the second are the signals which have special functions for minimum mode and the third are the signals having special functions for maximum mode.

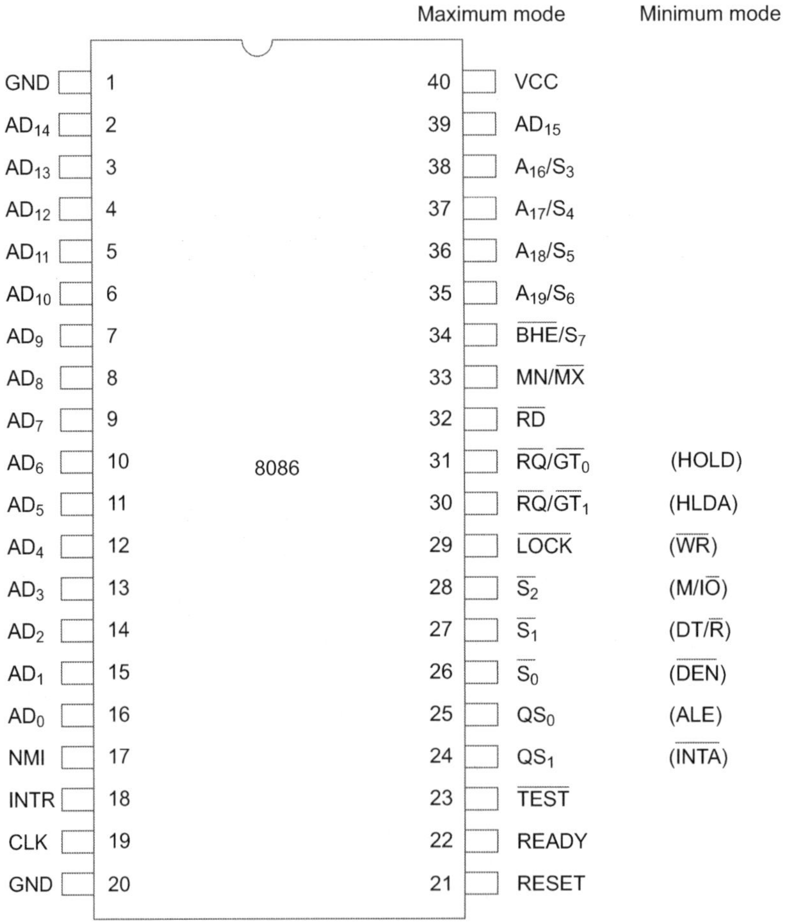

Fig. 1.5 *Pin Configuration of 8086*

The following signal descriptions are common for both the minimum and maximum modes.

AD_{15}-AD_0 These are the time multiplexed memory I/O address and data lines. Address remains on the lines during T_1 state, while the data is available on the data bus during T_2,T_3,T_w and T_4. Here T_1,T_2,T_3,T_4 and

T_w are the clock states of a machine cycle. T_w is a wait state. These lines are active high and float to a tristate during interrupt acknowledge and local bus hold acknowledge cycles.

$A_{19}/S_6, A_{18}/S_5, A_{17}/S_4, A_{16}/S_3$ These are the time multiplexed address and status lines. During T_1, these are the most significant address lines for memory operations. During I/O operations, these lines are low. During memory or I/O operations, status information is available on those lines for T_2, T_3, T_w and T_4. The status of the interrupt enable flag bit(displayed on S_5) is updated at the beginning of each clock cycle. The S_4 and S_3 together indicate which segment register is presently being used for memory accesses, as shown in Table 1.1. These lines float to tri-state off (tristated) during the local bus hold acknowledge. The status line S_6 is always low (logical). The address bits are separated from the status bits using latches controlled by the ALE signal.

Table 1.1 *Status*

S_4	S_3	*Indications*
0	0	Alternate Data
0	1	Stack
1	0	Code or none
1	1	Data

$\overline{BHE}/S_7$-Bus High Enable/Status The bus high enable signal is used to indicate the transfer of data over the higher order (D_{15}–D_8) data bus as shown in Table 1.2. It goes low for the data transfers over D_{15}–D_8 and is used to derive chip selects of odd address memory bank or peripherals. $\overline{BHE}$ is low during T_1 for read, write and interrupt acknowledge cycles, whenever a byte is to be transferred on the higher byte of the data bus. The status information is available during T_2, T_3 and T_4. The signal is active low and is tristated during 'hold'. It is low during T_1 for the first pulse of the interrupt acknowledge cycle. S_7 is not currently used.

Table 1.2 *Bus High Enable and A_0*

$\overline{BHE}$	A_0	*Indication*
0	0	Whole word (2 bytes)
0	1	Upper byte from or to odd address.
1	0	Lower byte from or to even address
1	1	None

$\overline{RD}$-Read Read signal, when low, indicates the peripherals that the processor is performing a memory or I/O read operation. $\overline{RD}$ is active low and shows the state for T_2, T_3, T_w of any read cycle. The signal remains tristated during the 'hold acknowledge'.

READY This is the acknowledgement from the slow devices or memory that they have completed the data transfer. The signal made available by the devices is synchronized by the 8284A clock generator to provide ready input to the 8086. The signal is active high.

INTR-Interrupt Request This is a level triggered input. This is sampled during the last clock cycle of each instruction to determine the availability of the request. If any interrupt request is pending, the processor enters the interrupt acknowledge cycle. This can be internally masked by resetting the interrupt enable flag. This signal is active high and internally synchronized.

$\overline{\text{TEST}}$ This input is examined by a 'WAIT' instruction. If the $\overline{\text{TEST}}$ input goes low, execution will continue, else, the processor remains in an idle state. The input is synchronized internally during each clock cycle on leading edge of clock.

NMI-Non-maskable Interrupt This is an edge-triggered input which causes a Type2 interrupt. The NMI is not maskable internally by software. A transition from low to high initiates the interrupt response at the end of the current instruction. This input is internally synchronized.

RESET This input causes the processor to terminate the current activity and start execution from FFFF0H. The signal is active high and must be active for at least four clock cycles. It restarts execution when the RESET returns low. RESET is also internally synchronised.

CLK-Clock Input The clock input provides the basic timing for processor operation and bus control activity. It's an asymmetric square wave with 33% duty cycle. The range of frequency for different 8086 versions is from 5MHz to 10MHz.

Vcc +5V power supply for the operation of the internal circuit.

GND ground for the internal circuit.

MN/$\overline{\text{MX}}$ The logic level at this pin decides whether the processor is to operate in either minimum (single processor) or maximum (multiprocessor) mode.

The following pin functions are for the minimum mode operation of 8086:

M/$\overline{\text{IO}}$ -Memory/IO This is a status line logically equivalent to $\overline{S_2}$ in the maximum mode. When it is low, it indicates the CPU is having an I/O operation, and when it is high, it indicates that the CPU is having a memory operation. This line becomes active in the previous T_4 and remains active till final T_4 of the current cycle. It is tristated during local bus "hold acknowledge".

$\overline{\text{INTA}}$ -Interrupt Acknowledge This signal is used as a read strobe for interrupt acknowledge cycles. In other words, when it goes low, it means that the processor has accepted the interrupt. It is active low during T_2, T_3 and T_W of each interrupt acknowledge cycle.

ALE-Address Latch Enable This output signal indicates the availability of the valid address on the address/data lines, and is connected to latch enable input of latches. This signal is active high and is never tristated.

DT/$\overline{\text{R}}$ -Data Transmit/Receive This output is used to decide the direction of data flow through the transreceivers (bidirectional buffers). When the processor sends out data, this signal is high and when the processor is receiving data, this signal is low. Logically, this is equivalent to $\overline{S_1}$ in maximum mode. Its timing is the same as M/$\overline{\text{I/O}}$. This is tristated during 'hold acknowledge'.

$\overline{\text{DEN}}$ -Data Enable This signal indicates the availability of valid data over the address/data lines. It is used to enable the transreceivers (bidirectional buffers) to separate the data from the multiplexed address/data signal. It is active from the middle of T_2 until the middle of T_4. $\overline{\text{DEN}}$ is tristated during 'hold acknowledge' cycle.

HOLD,HLDA-Hold/Hold Acknowledge When the HOLD line goes high, it indicates to the processor that another master is requesting the bus access. The processor, after receiving the HOLD request, issues the hold acknowledge signal on HLDA pin, in the middle of the next clock cycle after completing the current bus (instruction) cycle. At the same time, the processor floats the local bus and control lines. When the processor detects the HOLD line low, it lowers the HLDA signal. HOLD is an asynchronous input, and it should be externally synchronized.

If the DMA request is made while the CPU is performing a memory or I/O cycle, it will release the local bus during T_4 provided:

1. The request occurs on or before T_2 state of the current cycle
2. The current cycle is not operating over the lower byte of a word (or operating on an odd address)
3. The current cycle is not the first acknowledge of an interrupt acknowledge sequence
4. A Lock instruction is not being executed.

So far we have presented the pin descriptions of 8086 in minimum mode.

The following pin functions are applicable for maximum mode operation of 8086.

$\overline{S}_2$, $\overline{S}_1$, $\overline{S}_0$-Status Lines These are the status lines which indicate the type of operation, being carried out by the processor. These become active during T_4 of the previous cycle and remain active during T_1 and T_2 of the current bus cycle. The status lines return to passive state during T_3 of the current bus cycle so that they may again become active for the next bus cycle during T_4. Any change in these lines during T_3 indicates the starting of a new cycle, and return to passive state indicates end of the bus cycle. These status lines are encoded in Table 1.3.

Table 1.3

$\overline{S}_2$	$\overline{S}_1$	$\overline{S}_0$	*Indication*
0	0	0	Interrupt acknowledge
0	0	1	Read I/O port
0	1	0	Write I/O port
0	1	1	Halt
1	0	0	Code access
1	0	1	Read memory
1	1	0	Write memory
1	1	1	Passive

$\overline{\text{LOCK}}$ This output pin indicates that other system bus masters will be prevented from gaining the system bus, while the $\overline{\text{LOCK}}$ signal is low. The $\overline{\text{LOCK}}$ signal is activated by the 'LOCK' prefix instruction and remains active until the completion of the next instruction. This floats to tri-state off during "hold acknowledge". When the CPU is executing a critical instruction which requires the system bus, the LOCK prefix instruction ensures that other processors connected in the system will not gain the control of the bus. The 8086, while executing the prefixed instruction, asserts the bus lock signal output, which may be connected to an external bus controller.

QS_1, QS_0-Queue Status These lines give information about the status of the code-prefetch queue. These are active during the CLK cycle after which the queue operation is performed. These are encoded as shown in Table 1.4.

Table 1.4

QS_1	QS_0	*Indication*
0	0	No operation
0	1	First byte of opcode from the queue
1	0	Empty queue
1	1	Subsequent byte from the queue

This modification in a simple fetch and execute architecture of a conventional microprocessor offers an added advantage of *pipelined processing* of the instructions. The 8086 architecture has a 6-byte instruction prefetch queue. Thus even the largest (6-bytes) instruction can be prefetched from the memory and stored in the prefetch queue. This results in a faster execution of the instructions. In 8085, an instruction (opcode and operand) is fetched, decoded and executed and only after the execution of this instruction, the next one is fetched. By prefetching the instruction, there is a considerable speeding up in instruction execution in 8086. This scheme is known as *instruction pipelining*.

In the beginning, the CS:IP is loaded with the required address from which the execution is to be started. Initially, the queue will be empty and the microprocessor starts a fetch operation to bring one byte (the first byte) of instruction code, if the CS:IP address is odd or two bytes at a time, if the CS:IP address is even. The first byte is a complete opcode in case of some instructions (one byte opcode instruction) and it is a part of opcode, in case of other instructions (two byte long opcode instructions), the remaining part of opcode may lie in the second byte. But invariably the first byte of an instruction is an opcode. These opcodes along with data are fetched and arranged in the queue. When the first byte from the queue goes for decoding and interpretation, one byte in the queue becomes empty and subsequently the queue is updated. The microprocessor does not perform the next fetch operation till at least two bytes of the instruction queue are emptied. The instruction execution cycle is never broken for fetch operation. After decoding the first byte, the decoding circuit decides whether the instruction is of single opcode byte or double opcode byte. If it is single opcode byte , the next bytes are treated as data bytes depending upon the decoded instruction length, otherwise, the next byte in the queue is treated as the second byte of the instruction opcode. The second byte is then decoded in continuation with the first byte to decide the instruction length and the number of subsequent bytes to be treated as instruction data. The queue is updated after every byte is read from the queue but the fetch cycle is initiated by BIU only if at least two bytes of the queue are empty and the EU may be concurrently executing the fetched instructions.

The next byte after the instruction is completed is again the first opcode byte of the next instruction. A similar procedure is repeated till the complete execution of the program. The main point to be noted here is, that the fetch operation of the next instruction is overlapped with the execution of the current instruction. As shown in the architecture, there are two separate units, namely, the execution unit and the bus interface unit. While the execution unit is busy in executing an instruction, after it is completely decoded, the bus interface unit may be fetching the bytes of the next instruction from memory, depending upon the queue status. Figure 1.6 explains the queue operation.

$\overline{RQ}/\overline{GT}_0$, $\overline{RQ}/\overline{GT}_1$ -Request/Grant These pins are used by other local bus masters, in maximum mode, to force the processor to release the local bus at the end of the processor's current bus cycle. Each of the pins is bidirectional with $\overline{RQ}/\overline{GT}_0$ having higher priority than $\overline{RQ}/\overline{GT}_1$. $\overline{RQ}/\overline{GT}$ pins have internal pull-up resistors and may be left unconnected. The request/grant sequence is as follows:

1. A pulse one clock wide from another bus master requests the bus access to 8086.
2. During T_4 (current) or T_1 (next) clock cycle, a pulse one clock wide from 8086 to the requesting master, indicates that the 8086 has allowed the local bus to float and that it will enter the "hold acknowledge"

state in the next clock cycle. The CPU's bus interface unit is likely to be disconnected from the local bus of the system.

3. A one clock wide pulse from the another master indicates to 8086 that the 'hold' request is about to end and the 8086 may regain control of the local bus at the next clock cycle.

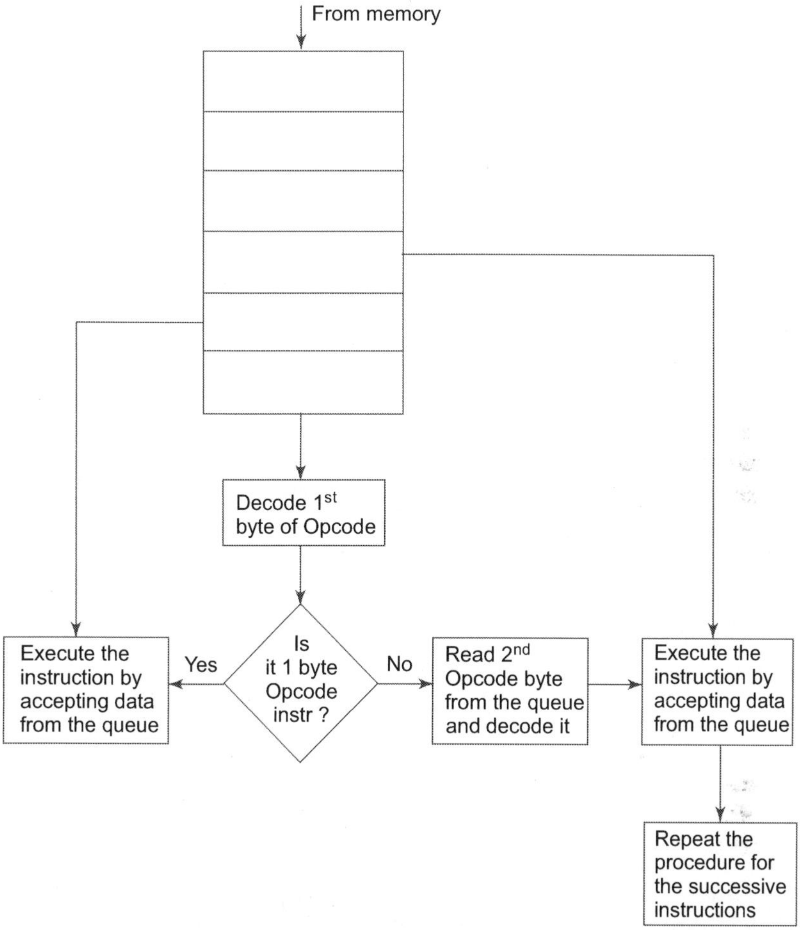

Fig. 1.6 *The Queue Operation*

Thus, each master to master exchange of the local bus is a sequence of 3 pulses. There must be at least one dead clock cycle after each bus exchange. The request and grant pulses are active low. For the bus requests those are received while 8086 is performing memory or I/O cycle, the granting of the bus is governed by the rules as discussed in case of HOLD, and HLDA in the minimum mode.

Until now, we have described the architecture and pin configuration of 8086. In the next section, we will study some operational features of 8086 based systems.

1.4 PHYSICAL MEMORY ORGANISATION

In an 8086 based system, the 1Mbytes memory is physically organised as an odd bank and an even bank, each of 512 Kbytes, addressed in parallel by the processor. Byte data with an even address is transferred on D_7-D_0, while the byte data with an odd address is transferred on $D_{15}-D_8$ buss lines. The processor provides two enable signals, $\overline{BHE}$ and A_0 for selection of either even or odd or both the banks. The instruction stream is fetched from memory as words and is addressed internally by the processor as necessary. In other words, if the processor fetches a word (consecutive two bytes) from memory, there are different possibilities, like:

1. Both the bytes may be data operands
2. Both the bytes may contain opcode bits
3. One of the bytes may be opcode while the other may be data

All the above possibilities are taken care of by the internal decoder circuit of the microprocessor. The opcodes and operands are identified by the internal decoder circuit which further derives the signals those act as input to the timing and control unit. The timing and control unit then derives all the signals required for execution of the instruction.

While referring to word data, the BIU requires one or two memory cycles, depending upon whether the starting byte is located at an even or odd address. It is always better to locate the word data at an even address. To read or write a complete word from/to memory, if it is located at an even address, only one read or write cycle is required. If the word is located at an odd address, the first read or write cycle is required for accessing the lower byte while the second one is required for accessing the upper byte. Thus, two bus cycles are required, if a word is located at an odd address. It should be kept in mind that while initialising the structures like stack they should be initialised at an even address for efficient operation.

8086 is a 16-bit microprocessor and hence can access two bytes of data in one memory or I/O read or write operation. But the commercially available memory chips are only byte size, i.e. they can store only one byte in a memory location. Obviously, to store 16-bit data, two successive memory locations are used and the lower byte of 16-bit data can be stored in the first memory location while the second byte is stored in the next location. In a sixteen bit read or write operation both of these bytes will be read or written in a single machine cycle.

A map of an 8086 memory system starts at 00000H and ends at FFFFFH. 8086 being a 16-bit processor is expected to access 16-bit data to / from 8-bit commerically available memory chips in parallel, as shown below in Fig. 1.7.

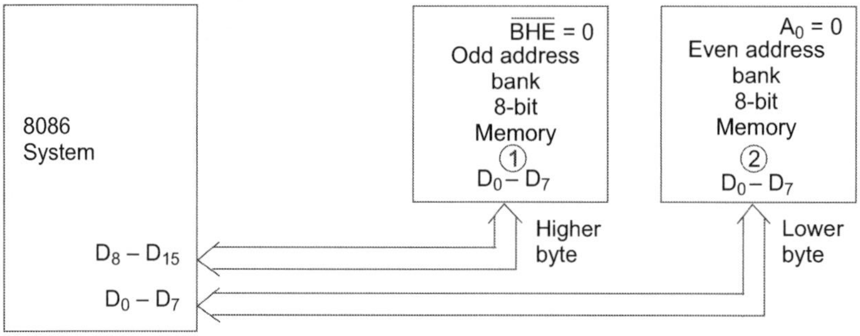

Fig. 1.7 *Physical Memory Organisation*

Thus, bits D_0–D_7 of a 16-bit data will be transferred over D_0–D_7 (lower byte) of 16-bit data bus to / from 8-bit memory (2) and bit D_8–D_{15} of the 16-bit data will be transferred over D_8–D_{15} (higher byte) of the 16-bit data bus of the microprocessor, to / from 8-bit memory (1). Thus to achieve 16-bit data transfer using 8-bit memories, in parallel, the map of the complete system byte memory addresses will obviously be divided into the two memory banks as shown in Fig. 1.7.

The lower byte of a 16-bit data is stored at the first address of the map 00000H and it is to be transferred over D_0–D_7 of the microprocessor bus so 00000H must be in 8-bit memory (2). Higher byte of the 16-bit data is stored in the next address 00001H; it is to be transferred over D_8–D_{15} of the microprocessor bus so the address 00001H must be in 8-bit memory (1) of Fig. 1.7. On similar lines, for the next 16-bit data stored in the memory, immediately after the previous one, the lower byte will be stored at the next address 00002H and it must be in 8-bit memory (2) while the higher byte will be stored at the next address 00003H that must be in 8-bit memory (1). Thus, if it is imagined that the complete memory map of 8086 is filled with 16-bit data, all the lower bytes (D_0–D_7) will be stored in the 8-bit memory bank (2) and all the higher bytes (D_8–D_{15}) will be stored in the 8-bit memory bank (1). Consequently, it can be observed that all the lower bytes have to be stored at even addresses and all the higher bytes have to be stored at odd addresses. Thus, the 8-bit memory bank (1) will be called an odd address bank and the 8-bit memory bank (2) will be called an even address bank. The complete memory map of 8086 system is thus divided into even and odd address memory banks.

If 8086 transfers a 16-bit data to / from memory, both of these banks must be selected for the 16-bit operation. However, to maintain an upward compatibility with 8085, 8086 must be able to implement 8-bit operations. In which case, two possibilities arise; the first being 8-bit operation with even memory bank, i.e. with an even address and the second one is 8-bit operation with odd address memory bank, i.e. with an odd address. The two signals A_0 and $\overline{BHE}$ solve the problem of selection of appropriate memory banks as presented in Table 1.2.

Certain locations in memory are reserved for specific CPU operations. The locations from FFFF0H to FFFFFH are reserved for operations including jump to initialisation programme and I/O-processor initialisation. The locations 00000H to 003FFH are reserved for *interrupt vector table*. The interrupt structure provides space for a total of 256 interrupt vectors. The vectors, i.e. CS and IP for each interrupt routine requires 4 bytes for storing it in the interrupt vector table. Hence, 256 types of interrupt require 256 C 4 = 03FFH (1Kbyte) locations for the complete interrupt vector table.

1.5 GENERAL BUS OPERATION

The 8086 has a combined address and data bus commonly referred to as a time multiplexed address and data bus. The main reason behind multiplexing address and data over the same pins is the maximum utilisation of processor pins and it facilitates the use of 40 pin standard DIP package. The bus can be demultiplexed using a few latches and transreceivers, whenever required. In the following text, we will discuss a general bus operation cycle.

Basically, all the processor bus cycles consist of at least four clock cycles. These are referred to as T_1, T_2,T_3 and T_4. The address is transmitted by the processor during T_1. It is present on the bus only for one cycle. During T_2, i.e. the next cycle, the bus is tristated for changing the direction of bus for the following data read cycle. The data transfer takes place during T_3 and T_4. In case, an addressed device is slow and shows 'NOT READY' status the wait states T_w are inserted between T_3 and T_4. These clock states during wait period are called *idle states* (T_i), *wait states* (T_w) or *inactive states*. The processor uses these cycles for internal housekeeping. The Address Latch Enable (ALE) signal is emitted during T_1 by the processor (minimum mode) or the bus controller (maximum mode) depending upon the status of the MN/$\overline{MX}$ input. The negative edge of this ALE pulse is used to separate the address and the data or status information. In maximum mode, the status lines $\overline{S_0}$, $\overline{S_1}$ and $\overline{S_2}$ are used to indicate the type of operation as discussed in the signal description section of this chapter. Status bits $\overline{S_3}$ to $\overline{S_7}$ are multiplexed with higher order address bits and the $\overline{BHE}$ signal. Address is valid during T_1 while the status bits S_3 to S_7 are valid during T_2 through T_4. Figure 1.8 shows a general bus operation cycle of 8086.

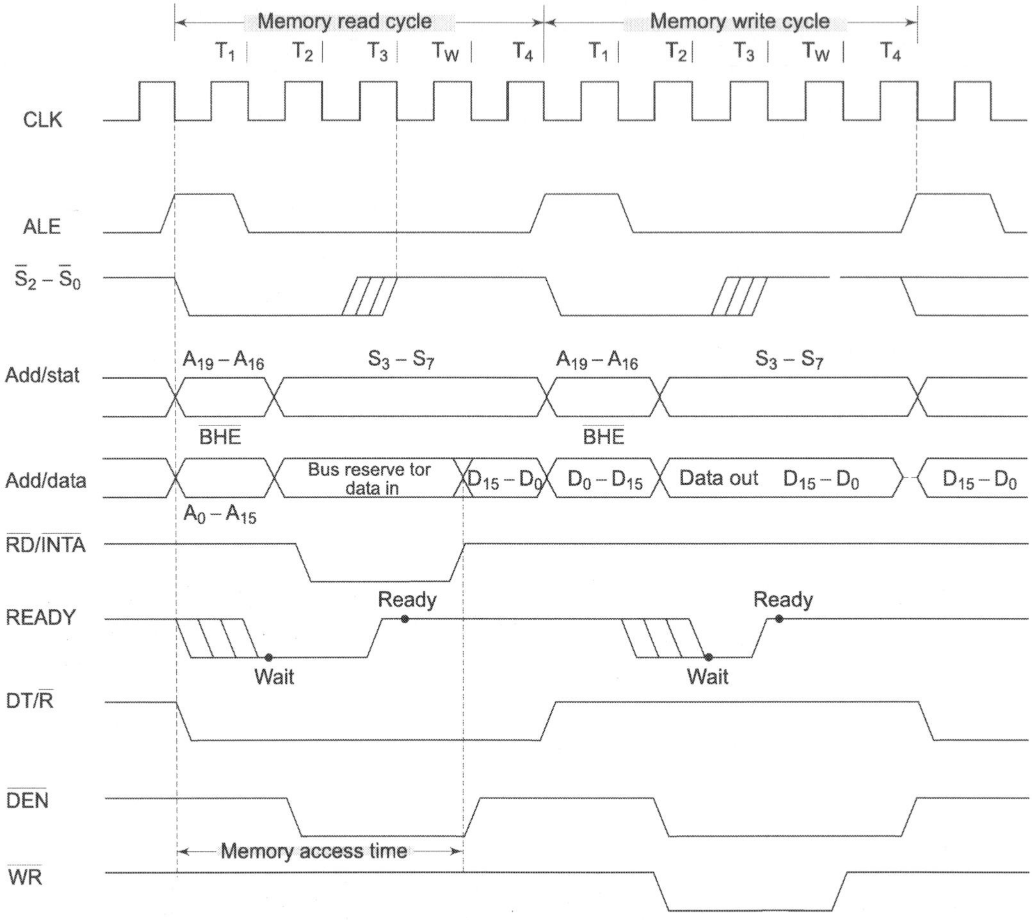

Fig. 1.8 *General Bus Operation Cycle of 8086*

1.6 I/O ADDRESSING CAPABILITY

The 8086/8088 processor can address up to 64K I/O byte registers or 32K word registers. The limitation is that the address of an I/O device must not be greater than 16 bits in size, this means that a maximum number of 2^{16}, i.e. 64Kbyte I/O devices may be accessed by the CPU. The I/O address appears on the address lines A_0 to A_{15} for one clock cycle (T_1). It may then be latched using the ALE signal. The upper address lines (A_{16}–A_{19}) are at logic 0 level during the I/O operations.

The 16-bit register DX is used as 16-bit I/O address pointer, with full capability to address up to 64K devices. In this case, the I/O ports are addressed in the same manner as memory locations in the based addressing mode using BX. In memory mapped I/O interfacing, the I/O device addresses are treated as memory locations in page 0, i.e. segment address 0000H. Even addressed bytes are transferred on D_7–D_0 and odd addressed bytes are transferred on D_8–D_{15} lines. While designing any 8-bit I/O system around 8086, care must be taken that all the byte registers in the system should be even addressed. Figure 1.9 shows 8086 IO addressing scheme.

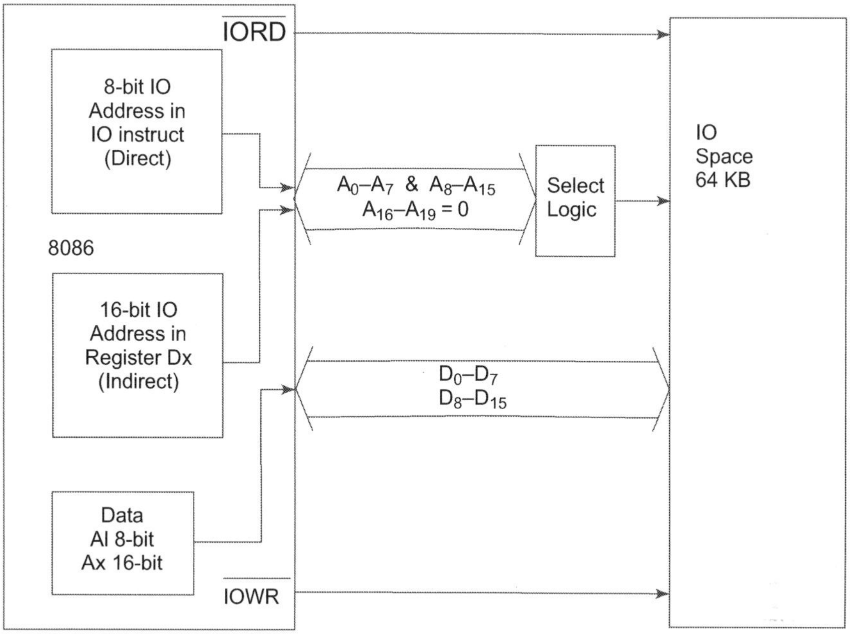

Fig. 1.9 *8086 IO Addressing*

1.7 SPECIAL PROCESSOR ACTIVITIES

1.7.1 Processor Reset and Initialisation

When logic 1 is applied to the RESET pin of the microprocessor, it is reset. It remains in this state till logic 0 is again applied to the RESET pin. The 8086 terminates the on-going operation on the positive edge of the reset signal. When the negative edge is detected, the reset sequence starts and is continued for nearly 10 clock cycles. During this period, all the internal register contents are set to 0000H except CS is set to value FFFFH . Thus, the execution starts again from the physical address FFFF0H. Due to this, the EPROM in an 8086 system is interfaced so as to have the physical memory locations FFFF0H to FFFFFH in it, i.e. at the end of the map.

For the reset signal to be accepted by 8086, it must be high for at least 4 clock cycles. From the instant the power is on, the reset pulse should not be applied to 8086 before 50 μs to allow proper initialisation of 8086. In the reset state, all 3-state outputs are tristated. Status signals are active in idle state for the first clock cycle after the reset becomes active, and then floats to tristate. The ALE and HLDA lines are driven low during the reset operation.

Non-maskable interrupt enable request, which appears before the second clock after the end of the reset operation, will not be served. For the NMI request to be served, it must appear after the second clock cycle during reset initialisation or later. If a HOLD request appears immediately after RESET, it will be immediately served after initialisation, before execution of any instruction.

1.7.2 HALT

When the processor executes a HLT instruction, it enters the 'halt' state. However, before doing so, it indicates that it is entering 'halt' state in two ways, depending upon whether it is in the minimum or maximum mode. When the processor is in minimum mode and wants to enter halt state, it issues an ALE pulse but does not issue any control signal. When the processor is in maximum mode and wants to enter the halt state, it puts the HALT status (011) on $\overline{S}_2$, $\overline{S}_1$ and $\overline{S}_0$ pins and then the bus controller issues an ALE pulse but no qualifying signal, i.e.

no appropriate address or control signals are issued to the bus. Only an interrupt request or reset will force the 8086 to come out of the 'halt' state. Even the HOLD request cannot force the 8086 out of 'halt' state.

1.7.3 TEST and Synchronisation with External Signals

Besides the interrupt, hold and general I/O capabilities, the 8086 has an extra facility of the $\overline{\text{TEST}}$ signal. When the CPU executes a WAIT instruction, the processor preserves the contents of the registers, before execution of the WAIT instruction, and the CPU waits for the $\overline{\text{TEST}}$ input pin to go low. If the $\overline{\text{TEST}}$ pin goes low, it continues further execution, otherwise, it keeps on waiting for the $\overline{\text{TEST}}$ pin to go low. For the $\overline{\text{TEST}}$ signal to be accepted, it must be low for at least 5 clock cycles. The activity of waiting does not consume any bus cycle. The processor remains in the idle state while waiting. While waiting, any 'HOLD' request from an external device may be served. If an interrupt occurs when the processor is waiting, it fetches the wait instruction once more, executes it, and then serves the interrupt. After returning from the interrupt, it fetches the wait instruction once more and continues in the 'wait' state.

Thus, the execution of the portion of a program which appears in the program after WAIT instruction can be synchronized with an external signal connected with the $\overline{\text{TEST}}$ input.

1.7.4 Deriving System Bus

The 8086 has a multiplexed 16-bit address / data bus (AD_0–AD_{15}) and a multiplexed 4-bit address / status bus A_{16}/S_3–A_{19}/S_6. The address can be latched using signal ALE, as shown in Fig. 1.10. Commercially available latch chips contain eight latches. Thus for demultiplexing twenty address lines one requires three latch chips like 74373. While demultiplexing the address bus, two of the three latch chips will be fully used and four latches of the third chip will be used. Figure 1.10 shows arrangement for latching the twenty bit address. Di indicate D inputs of latches and Q indicate the respective latch outputs.

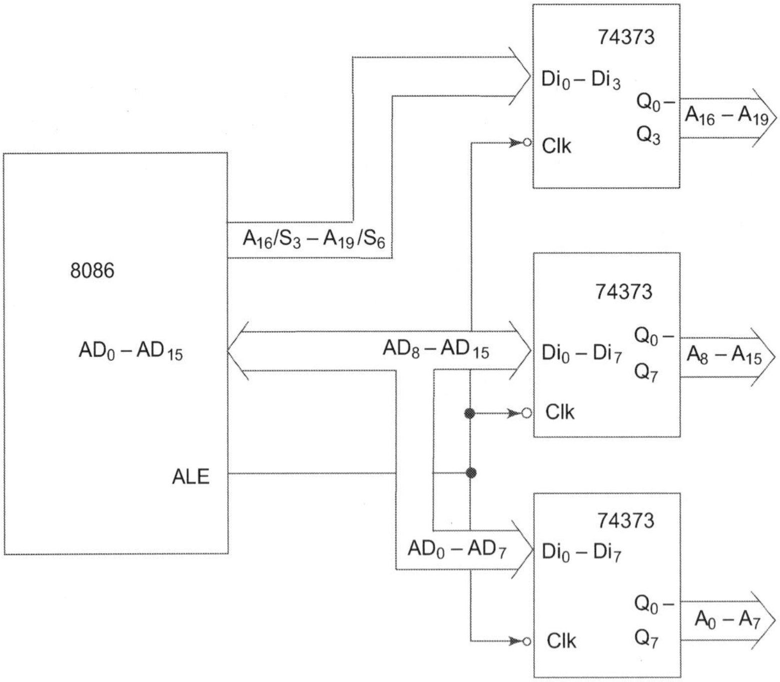

Fig. 1.10 *Latching 20-Bit Address of 8086*

8086 has multiplexed 16-bit data bus in the form of AD_0–AD_{15}. The data can be separated from the address and buffered using two bidirectional buffers 74245. It may be noted that the data can either be transferred from microprocessor to memory or from memory to microprocessor in case of write or read operations respectively hence bidirectional buffers are required for deriving the data bus. The signals $\overline{DNE}$ and DT / $\overline{R}$ indicate the presence of data on the bus and the direction of the data, i.e. to / from the microprocessor. They are used to drive the chip select (enable) and direction pins of the buffers as indicated below in Fig. 1.11.

If $\overline{DNE}$ is low it indicates that the data is available on the multiplexed bus and both the buffers (74245) are enabled to transfer data. When DIR pin goes high the data available at X pins of 74245 are transferred to Y pins, i.e. data is transmitted from microprocessor to either memory or IO device (write operation). If DIR pin goes low the data available at Y pins of 74245 is transferred to X pins, i.e. data is received by microprocessor from memory or IO device (read operation).

For deriving control bus from the available control signals $\overline{RD}$, $\overline{WR}$ and M / $\overline{IO}$ in case of minimum mode of operation any combinational logic circuit may be used as shown in Fig. 1.12 (a) and Fig. 1.12 (b).

In case of maximum mode of operation a chip bus controller derives all the control signals using status signals $\overline{S}_0$, $\overline{S}_1$ and $\overline{S}_2$.

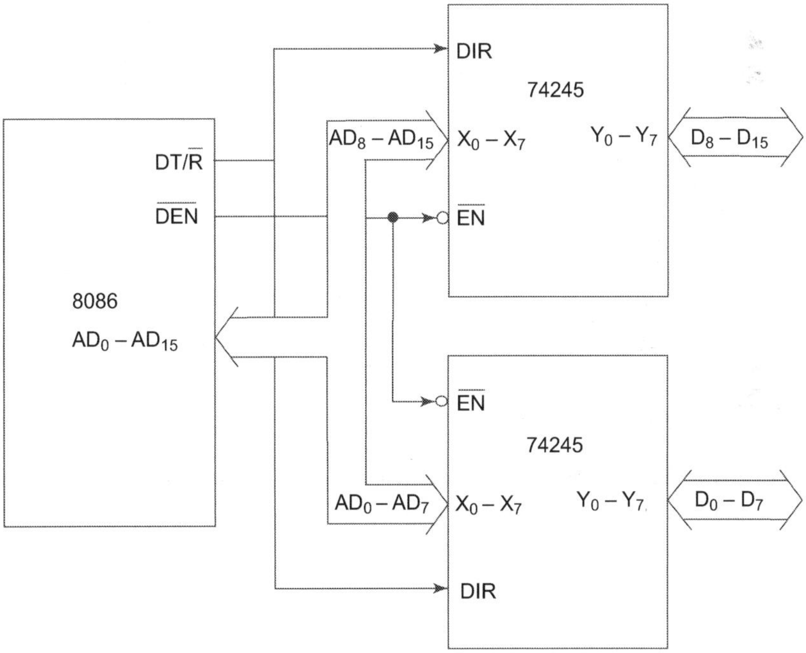

Fig. 1.11 *Buffering Data Bus of 8086*

1.8 MINIMUM MODE 8086 SYSTEM AND TIMINGS

In a minimum mode 8086 system, the microprocessor 8086 is operated in minimum mode by strapping its MN/ $\overline{MX}$ pin to logic 1. In this mode, all the control signals are given out by the microprocessor chip itself. There is a single microprocessor in the minimum mode system. The remaining components in the system are latches, transreceivers, clock generator, memory and I/O devices. Some type of chip selection logic may be required for selecting memory or I/O devices, depending upon the address map of the system.

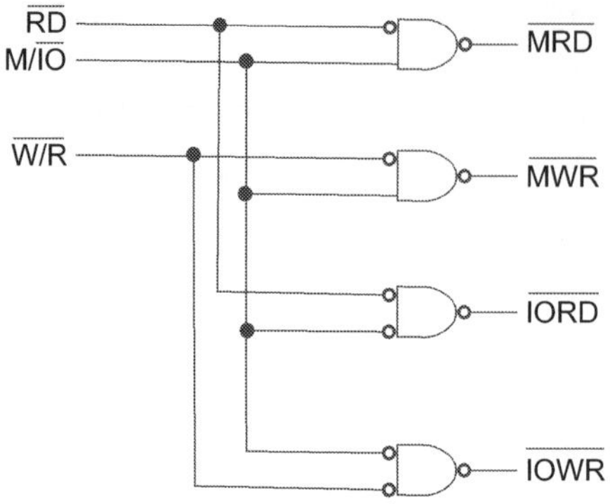

Fig. 1.12 (a) *Deriving 8086 Control Signals*

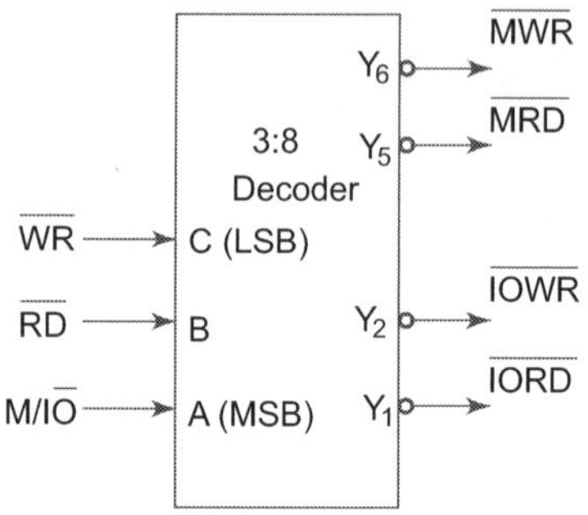

Fig. 1.12 (b) *Deriving 8086 Control Signals*

The latches are generally buffered output D-type flip-flops, like, 74LS373 or 8282. They are used for separating the valid address from the multiplexed address/data signals and are controlled by the ALE signal generated by 8086. Transreceivers are the bidirectional buffers and sometimes they are called data amplifiers. They are required to separate the valid data from the time multiplexed address/data signal. They are controlled by two signals, namely, $\overline{DEN}$ and DT/$\overline{R}$. The $\overline{DEN}$ signal indicates that the valid data is available on the data bus, while DT/$\overline{R}$ indicates the direction of data, i.e. from / to the processor. The system contains memory for the monitor and users program storage. Usually, EPROMS are used for monitor storage, while RAMs for users' program storage. A system may contain I/O devices for communication with the processor as well as some special purpose I/O devices. The clock generator (IC8284) generates the clock from the crystal oscillator and then shapes it to make it more precise so that it can be used as an accurate timing reference for the system. The clock generator also synchronizes some external signals with the system clock. The general system organisation is shown in Fig. 1.13. Since it has 20 address lines and 16 data lines, the 8086 CPU requires three octal address latches and two octal data buffers for the complete address and data separation.

The working of the minimum mode configuration system can be better described in terms of the timing diagrams rather than qualitatively describing the operations. The opcode fetch and read cycles are similar. Hence, the timing diagram can be categorized in two parts, the first is the timing diagram for *read cycle* and the second is the timing diagram for *write cycle*.

The read cycle begins in T_1 with the assertion of the Address Latch Enable (ALE) signal and M/$\overline{IO}$ signal. During the negative going edge of this signal, the valid address is latched on the local bus. The $\overline{BHE}$ and A_0 signals address low, high or both bytes. From T_1 to T_4, the M/$\overline{IO}$ signal indicates a memory or I/O operation. At T_2, the address is removed from the local bus and is sent to the output. The bus is then tristated. The Read ($\overline{RD}$) control signal is also activated in T_2. This signal causes the addressed device to enable its data bus drivers. After $\overline{RD}$ goes low, the valid data is available on the data bus. The addressed device will drive the READY line high. When the processor returns the read signal to high level, the addressed device will again tristate its bus drivers. CS logic indicates chip select logic and 'e' and 'O' sufixes indicate even and odd address memory banks.

A write cycle also begins with the assertion of ALE and the emission of the address. The M/$\overline{IO}$ signal is again asserted to indicate a memory or I/O operation. In T_2, after sending the address in T_1, the processor sends the data to be written to the addressed location. The data remains on the bus until the middle of T_4 state. The $\overline{WR}$ becomes active at the beginning of T_2 (unlike $\overline{RD}$ is somewhat delayed in T_2 to provide time for floating).

The $\overline{BHE}$ and A_0 signals are used to select the proper byte or bytes of memory or I/O word to be read or written as already discussed in the signal description section of this chapter.

The M/$\overline{IO}$, $\overline{RD}$ and $\overline{WR}$ signals indicate the types of data transfer as specified in Table 1.5.

Table 1.5

$M/\overline{IO}$	$\overline{RD}$	$\overline{DEN}$	*Transfer Type*
0	0	1	I/O read
0	1	0	I/O write
1	0	1	Memory read
1	1	0	Memory write

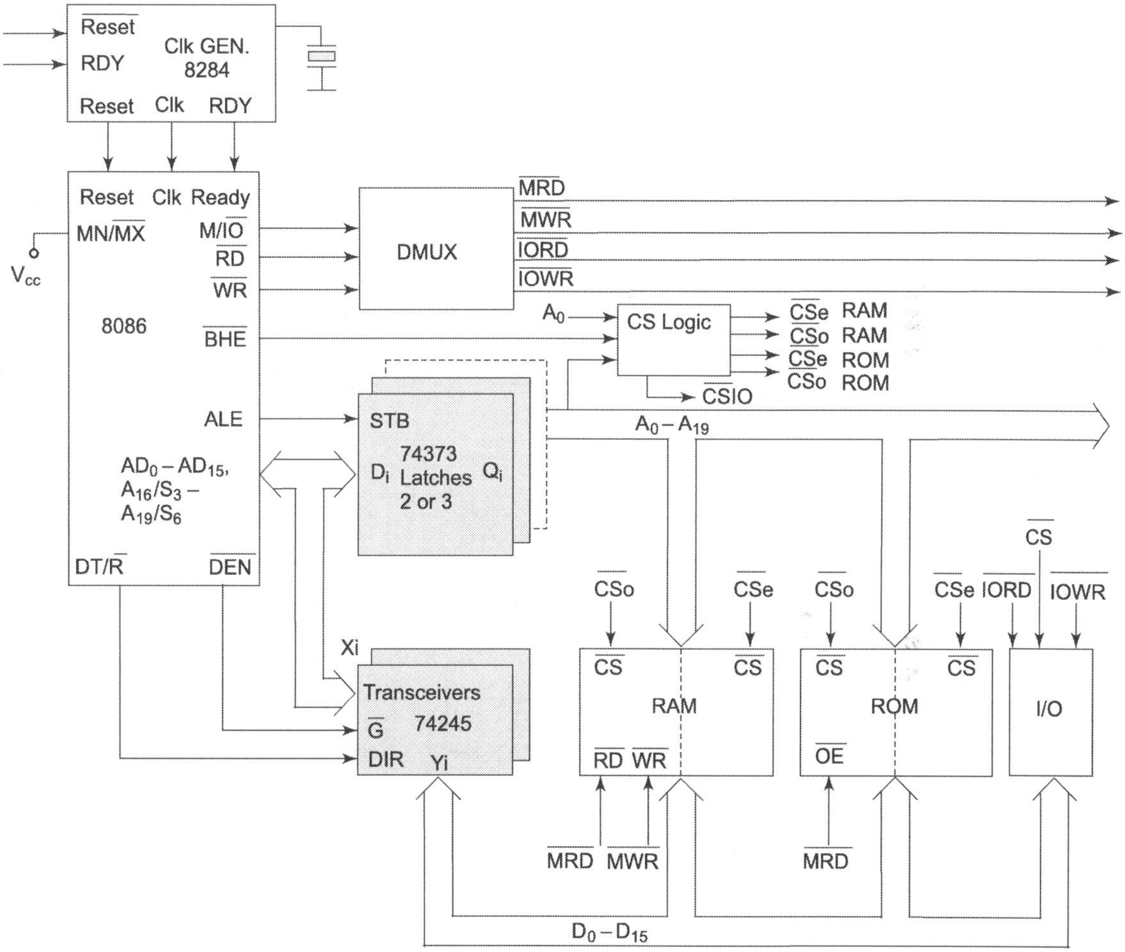

Fig. 1.13 *Minimum Mode 8086 System*

Figure 1.14(a) shows the read cycle while Fig. 1.14(b) shows the write cycle.

1.8.1 HOLD Response Sequence

The HOLD pin is checked at the end of each bus cycle. If it is received active by the processor before T_4 of the previous cycle or during T_1 state of the current cycle, the CPU activates HLDA in the next clock cycle and for the succeeding bus cycles, the bus will be given to another requesting master. The control of the bus is not regained by the processor until the requesting master does not drop the HOLD pin low. When the request is dropped by the requesting master, the HLDA is dropped by the processor at the trailing edge of the next clock, as shown in Fig. 1.14 (c). The other conditions have already been discussed in the signal description section for the HOLD and HLDA signals.

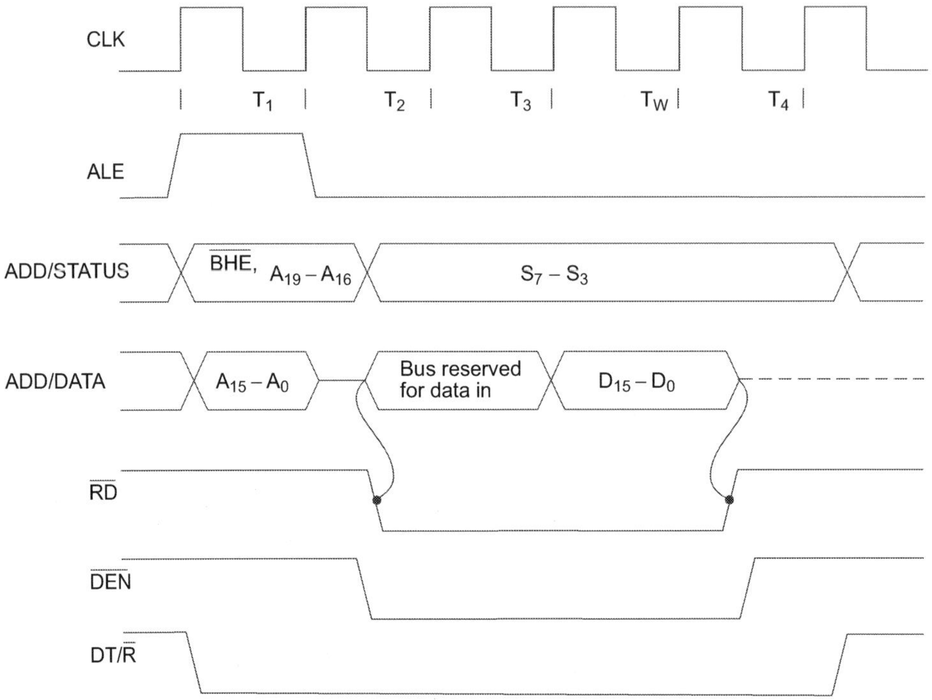

Fig. 1.14(a) *Read Cycle Timing Diagram for Minimum Mode*

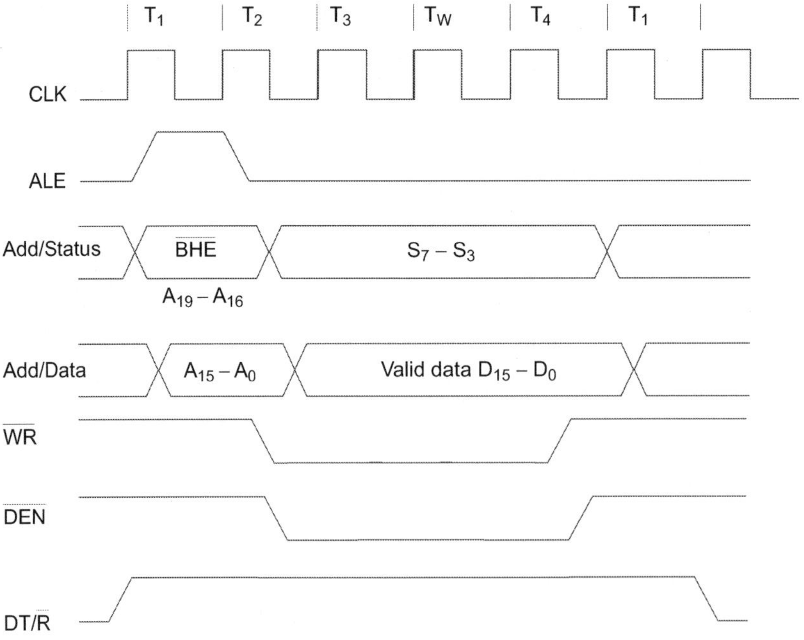

Fig. 1.14(b) *Write Cycle Timing Diagram for Minimum Mode Operation*

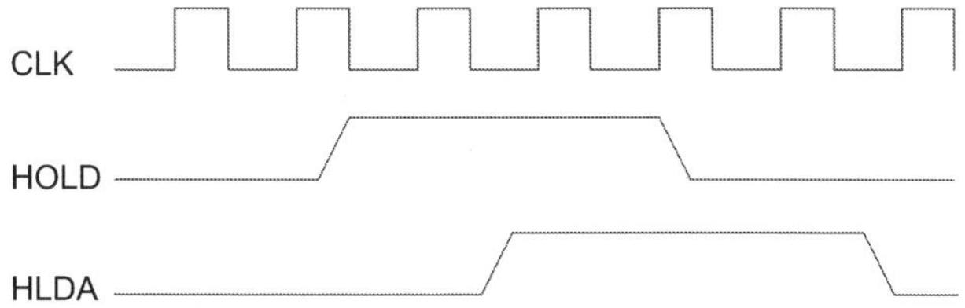

Fig. 1.14(c) *Bus Request and Bus Grant Timings in Minimum Mode System*

1.9 MAXIMUM MODE 8086 SYSTEM AND TIMINGS

In the maximum mode, the 8086 is operated by strapping the MN/$\overline{MX}$ pin to ground. In this mode, the processor derives the status signals $\overline{S_2}$, $\overline{S_1}$ and $\overline{S_0}$. Another chip called bus controller derives the control signals using this status information. In the maximum mode, there may be more than one microprocessor in the system configuration. The other components in the system are the same as in the minimum mode system. In this section, we will study the bus controller chip and its functions in brief. The functions of all the pins having special functions in maximum mode have already been discussed in the pin diagram section of this chapter.

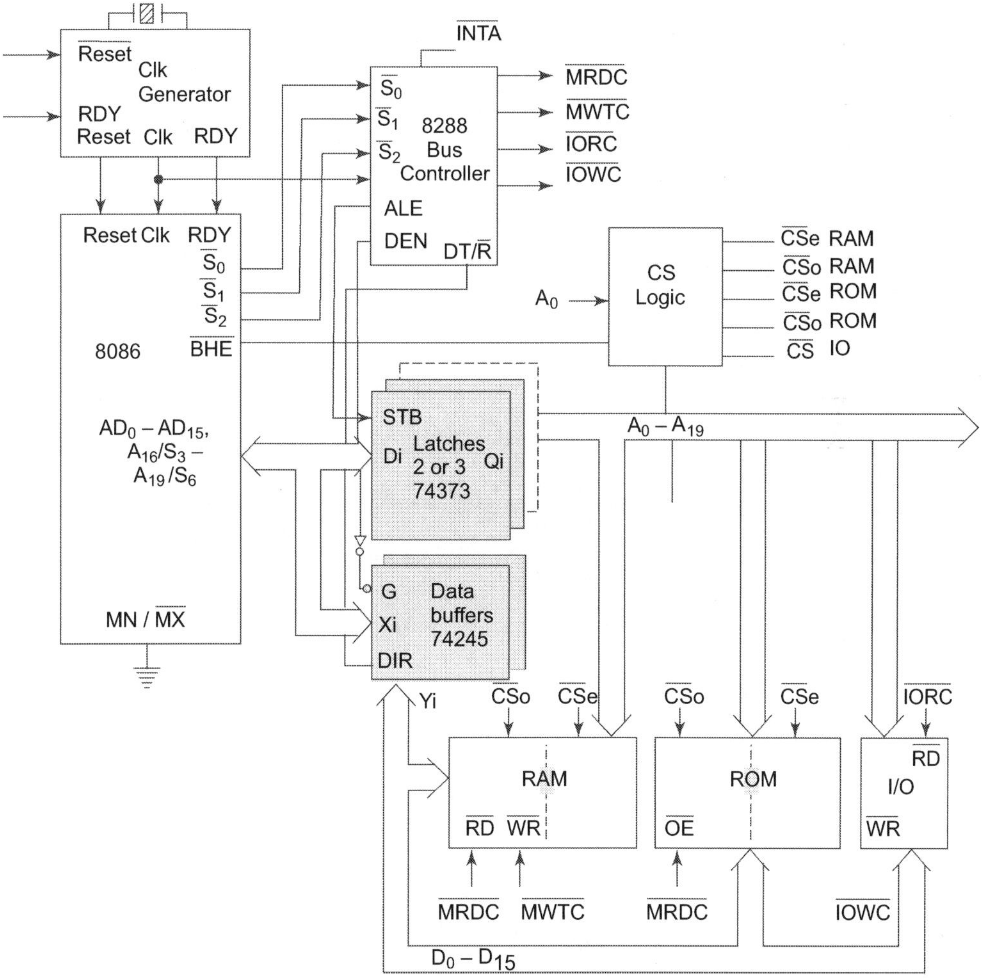

Fig. 1.15 *Maximum Mode 8086 System*

The basic functions of the bus controller chip IC8288, is to derive control signals like $\overline{RD}$ and $\overline{WR}$ (for memory and I/O devices), $\overline{DEN}$, DT/$\overline{R}$, ALE, etc. using the information made available by the processor on the status lines. The bus controller chip has input lines $\overline{S}_2$, $\overline{S}_1$ and $\overline{S}_0$ and CLK, which are driven by the CPU. It derives the outputs ALE, DEN, DT/$\overline{R}$, $\overline{MRDC}$, $\overline{MWTC}$, $\overline{AMWC}$, $\overline{IORC}$, $\overline{IOWC}$ and $\overline{AIOWC}$. The $\overline{AEN}$, IOB and CEN pins are specially useful for multiprocessor systems. $\overline{AEN}$ and IOB are generally grounded. CEN pin is usually tied to +5V. The significance of the MCE/$\overline{PDEN}$ output depends upon the status of the IOB pin. If IOB is grounded, it acts as master cascade enable to control cascaded 8259A, else it acts as peripheral data enable used in the multiple bus configurations. $\overline{INTA}$ pin is used to issue two interrupt acknowledge pulses to the interrupt controller or to an interrupting device.

$\overline{IORC}$, $\overline{IOWC}$ are I/O read command and I/O write command signals respectively. These signals enable an IO interface to read or write the data from or to the addressed port. The $\overline{MRDC}$, $\overline{MWTC}$ are memory read command and memory write command signals respectively and may be used as memory read and write signals. All these command signals instruct the memory to accept or send data to or from the bus. For both of these write command signals, the advanced signals namely $\overline{AIOWC}$ and $\overline{AMWTC}$ are available. They also serve the same purpose, but are activated one clock cycle earlier than the $\overline{IOWC}$ and $\overline{MWTC}$ signals, respectively. The maximum mode system is shown in Fig. 1.15.

The maximum mode system timing diagrams are also divided in two portions as read (input) and write (output) timing diagrams. The address/data and address/status timings are similar to the minimum mode. ALE is asserted in T_1, just like minimum mode. The only difference lies in the status signals used and the available control and advanced command signals. Figure 1.16 (a) shows the maximum mode timings for the read operation while the Fig. 1.16 (b) shows the same for the write operation. The CS Logic block represents chip select logic and the 'e' and 'O' suffixes indicate even and odd address memory bank.

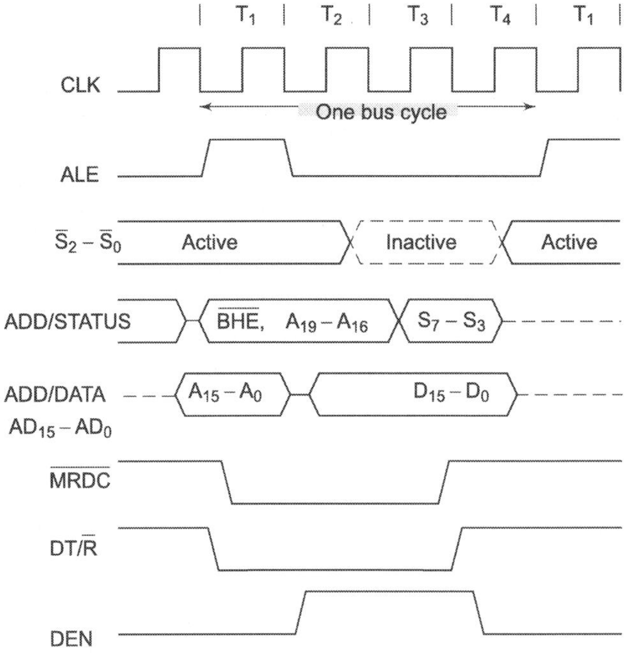

Fig. 1.16 (a) *Memory Read Timing in Maximum Mode*

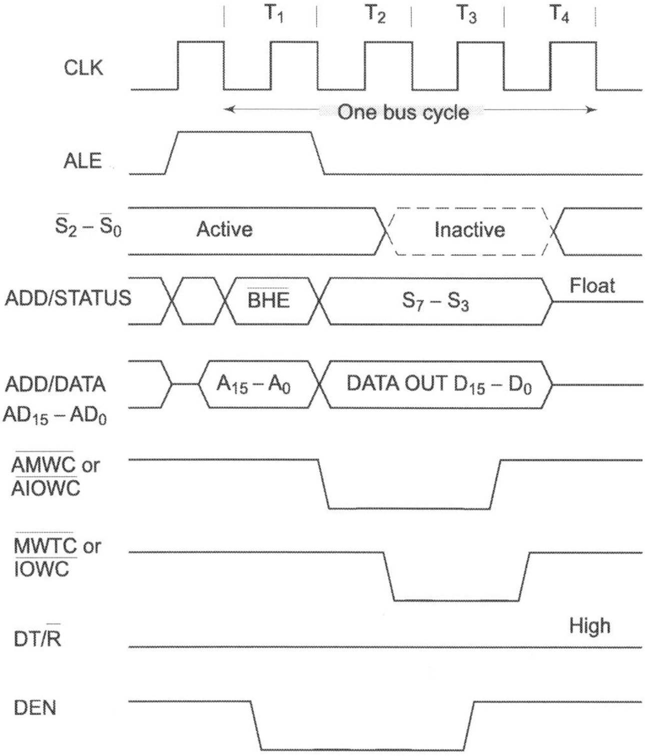

Fig. 1.16(b) *Memory Write Timing in Maximum Mode*

1.9.1 Timings for $\overline{RQ}/\overline{GT}$ Signals

The request/grant response sequence contains a series of three pulses as shown in the timing diagram Fig.1.16 (c). The request/grant pins are checked at each rising pulse of clock input. When a request is detected and if the conditions discussed in pin diagram section of this chapter for valid HOLD request are satisfied, the processor issues a grant pulse over the $\overline{RQ}/\overline{GT_0}$ pin immediately during the T_4 (current) or T_1 (next) state. When the requesting master receives this pulse, it accepts the control of the bus. The requesting master uses the bus till it requires. When it is ready to relinquish the bus, it sends a release pulse to the processor (host) using the $\overline{RQ}/\overline{GT}$ pin. This sequence is shown in Fig. 1.16 (c).

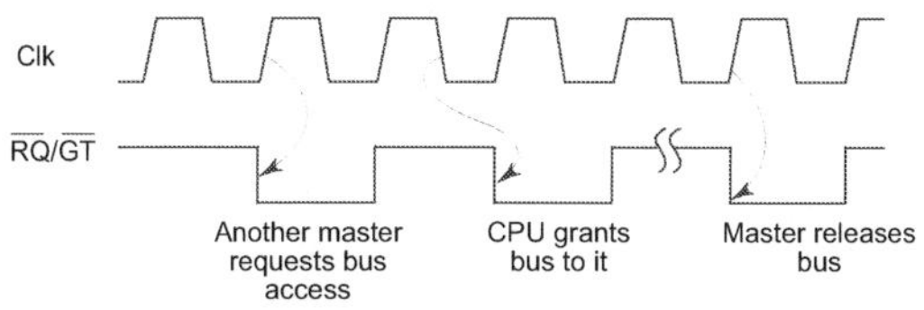

Fig. 1.16 (c) *$\overline{RQ}/\overline{GT}$ Timings in Maximum Mode*

1.10 THE PROCESSOR 8088

The launching of the processor 8086 is seen as a remarkable step in the development of high speed computing machines. Before the introduction of 8086, most of the circuits required for the different applications in computing and industrial control fields were already designed around the 8-bit processor 8085. The 8086 imparted tremendous flexibility in the programming as compared to 8085. So naturally, after the introduction of 8086, there was a search for a microprocessor chip which has the programming flexibility like 8086 and the external interface like 8085, so that all the existing circuits built around 8085 can work as before, with this new chip. The chip 8088 was a result of this demand. The microprocesser 8088 has all the programming facilities that 8086 has, along with some hardware features of 8086, like 1Mbyte memory addressing capability, operating modes (MN/$\overline{\text{MX}}$), interrupt structure etc. However, 8088, unlike 8086, has 8-bit data bus. This feature of 8088 makes the circuits, designed around 8085, compatible with 8088, with little or no modification.

All the peripheral interfacing schemes with 8088 are the same as those for the 8-bit pro-cessors. The memory and I/O addressing schemes are now exactly similar to 8085 schemes except for the increased memory (1Mbyte) and I/O (64Kbyte) capabilities. The architecture shows the developments in 8088 over 8086. The abilities and limitations of 8088 are same as 8086. In this section, we will discuss those properties of 8088 which are different from that of 8086 in some respects.

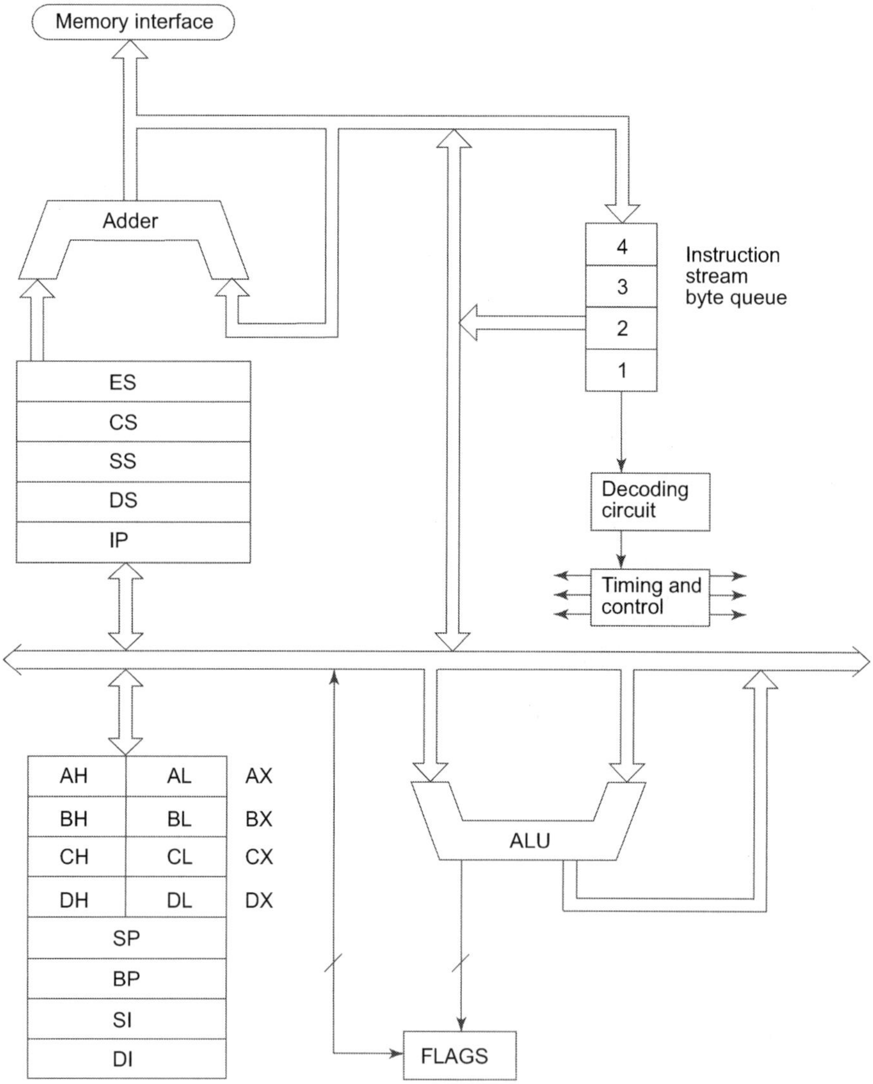

Fig. 1.17 *Architecture of 8088*

1.10.1 Architecture and Signal Description of 8088

The register set of 8088 is exactly the same as that of 8086. The architecture of 8088 is also similar to 8086 except for two changes; a) 8088 has 4-byte instruction queue and b) 8088 has 8-bit data bus. The function of each block is the same as in 8086. Figure 1.17 shows the 8088 architecture.

The addressing capability of 8088 is 1Mbyte, therefore, it needs 20 address bits, i.e. 20 addressing lines. While handling this 20-bit address, the segmented memory scheme is used and the complete physical address forming procedure is the same as explained in case of 8086. The memory organisation and addressing methods of 8088 and 8086 are similar. While physically interfacing memory to 8088, there is nothing like an even address bank or odd address bank. The complete memory is homogeneously addressed as a bank of 1Mbyte memory locations using the segmented memory scheme. This change in hardware is completely transparent to software. As a result of the modified data bus, the 8088 can access only a byte at a time. This fact reduces the speed of operation of 8088 as compared to 8086, but the 8088 can process the 16-bit data internally. On account of this change in bus structure, the 8088 has slightly different timing diagrams than 8086.

The pin diagram of 8088 is shown in Fig. 1.18. Most of the 8088 pins and their functions are exactly similar to the corresponding pins of 8086 . Hence the pins that have different functions or timings are discussed in this section. Amongst them are the pins that have a common function in minimum and maximum mode.

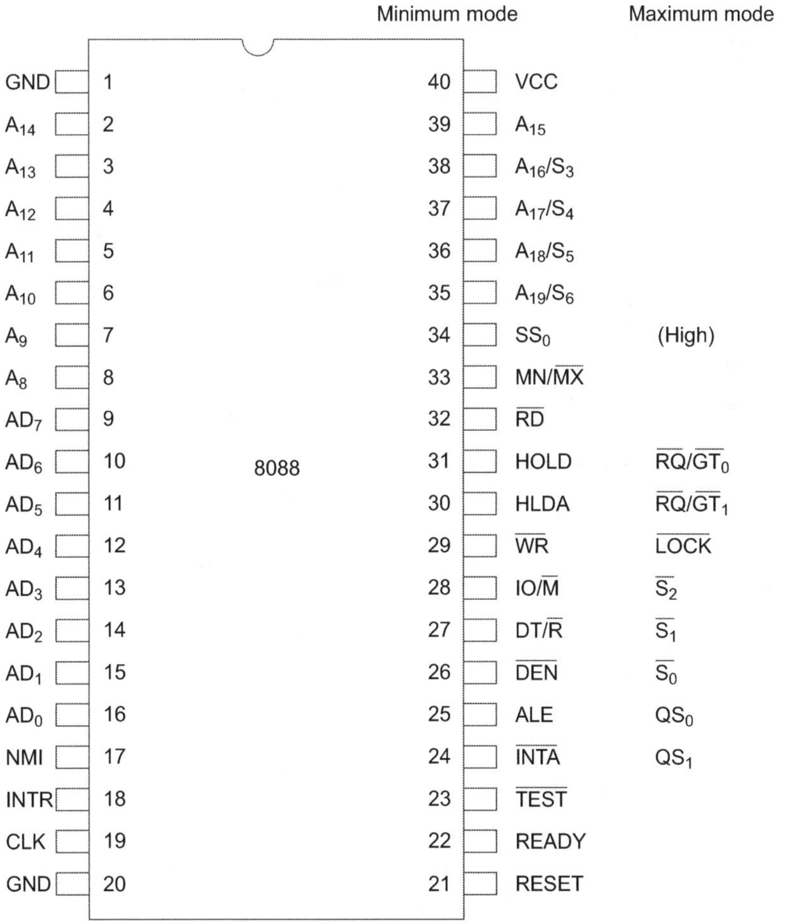

Fig. 1.18 *Pin Diagram of 8088*

AD_7–AD_0 (Address/Data) These lines constitute the address/data time multiplexed bus. During T_1 the bus is used for conducting addresses and during T_2, T_3, T_W and T_4 states these lines are used for conducting data. These are tristated during 'hold acknowledge' and 'interrupt acknowledge' cycles.

A_{15}–A_8 (Address Bus) These lines provide the address bits A_8 to A_{15} in the entire bus cycle. These need not be latched for obtaining a stable valid address. These are active high and are tristated during the 'acknowledge' cycles. Note that as the 8088 data bus is only of 8 bits, there is no need of the $\overline{BHE}$ signal.

$\overline{SS_0}$ A new pin $\overline{SS_0}$ is introduced in 8088 instead of $\overline{BHE}$ pin in 8086. In minimum mode, the pin $\overline{SS_0}$ is logically equivalent to the $\overline{S}_0$ in the maximum mode. In maximum mode it is always high.

$IO/\overline{M}$ This pin is similar to $M/\overline{IO}$ pin of 8086, but it offers an 8085 compatible, memory/ IO bus interface.

The signals $\overline{SS_0}$, $DT/\overline{R}$, $IO/\overline{M}$ can be decoded to interpret the activities of the microprocessor as given in Table 1.6, in the minimum mode.

In the maximum mode, the pin $\overline{SS_0}$ is permanently high. The functions and timings of other pins of 8088 are like that of 8086. Due to the difference in the bus structure, the timing diagrams are somewhat different.

Table 1.6

$IO/\overline{M}$	$DT/\overline{R}$	$\overline{SS}_0$	*Operation/Interpretation*
1	0	0	Interrupt Acknowledge
1	0	1	Read I/O port
1	1	0	Write I/O port
1	1	1	HALT
0	0	0	Code Access
0	0	1	Read memory
0	1	0	Write memory
0	1	1	Passive

1.10.2 Deriving 8088 Bus

As discussed earlier, 8088 is a microprocessor with an internal architecture, instruction set and memory addressing capability of 8086 but with the data bus of 8-bits like 8085. The 8-bit data bus makes 8088 compatible with the family of 8-bit peripherals designed around 8085.

For demultiplexing the bus, ALE signal is used to enable address latches. Usually three latch chips like 74373 are used for latching the twenty bit address while one bidirectional buffer chip (74245) is used for bufferring the 8-bit data bus. The $\overline{DEN}$ and $DT/\overline{R}$ signals are used for bufferring the data. The control bus may be derived exactly in the same way as that of 8086. The schematic diagram for deriving demultiplexed address/data bus is shown in Fig. 1.19, while the control bus can be derived as in Figs 1.20 (a) and 1.20 (b).

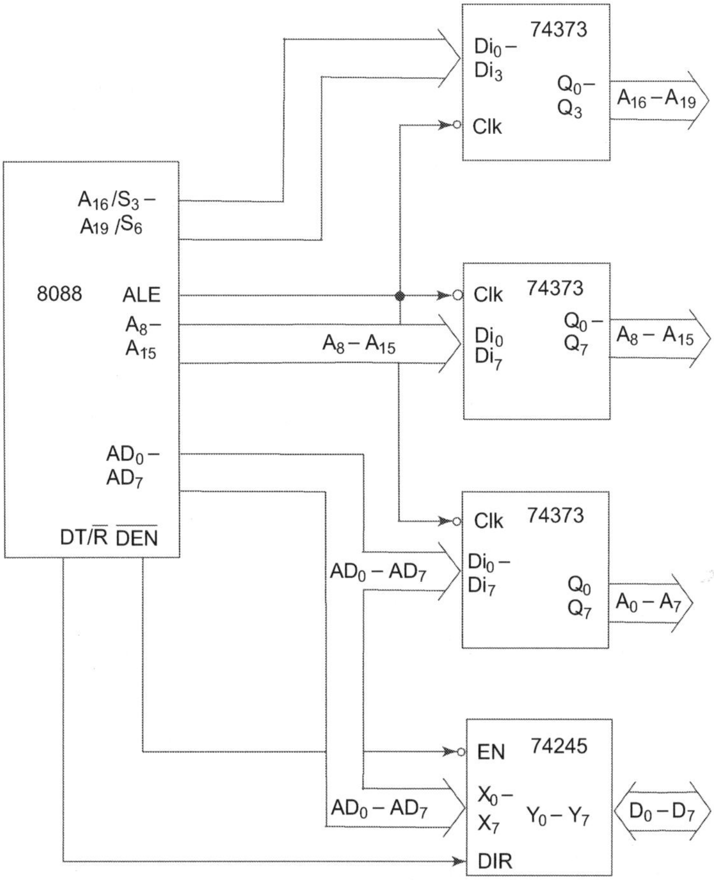

Fig. 1.19 *Deriving 8088 Address and Data Bus*

The minimum and maximum mode systems are also similar to the respective 8086 systems. The 8088 systems require only one data buffer due to the 8-bit data bus. The minimum and maximum mode systems of 8088 are shown in Figs 1.21 (a) and (b) respectively.

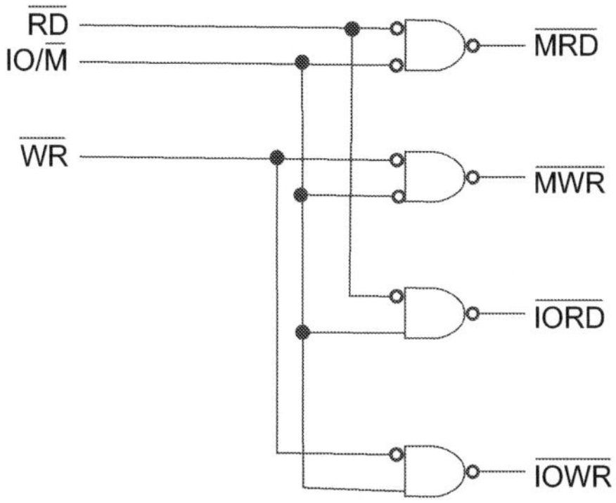

Fig. 1.20 (a) *Deriving 8088 Control Bus*

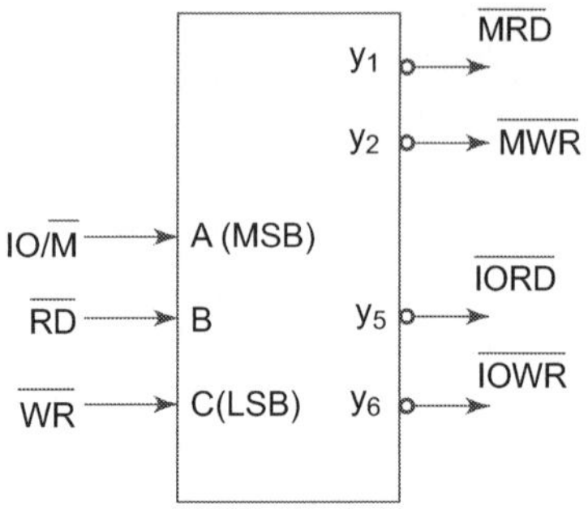

Fig. 1.20 (b) *Deriving 8088 Control Bus*

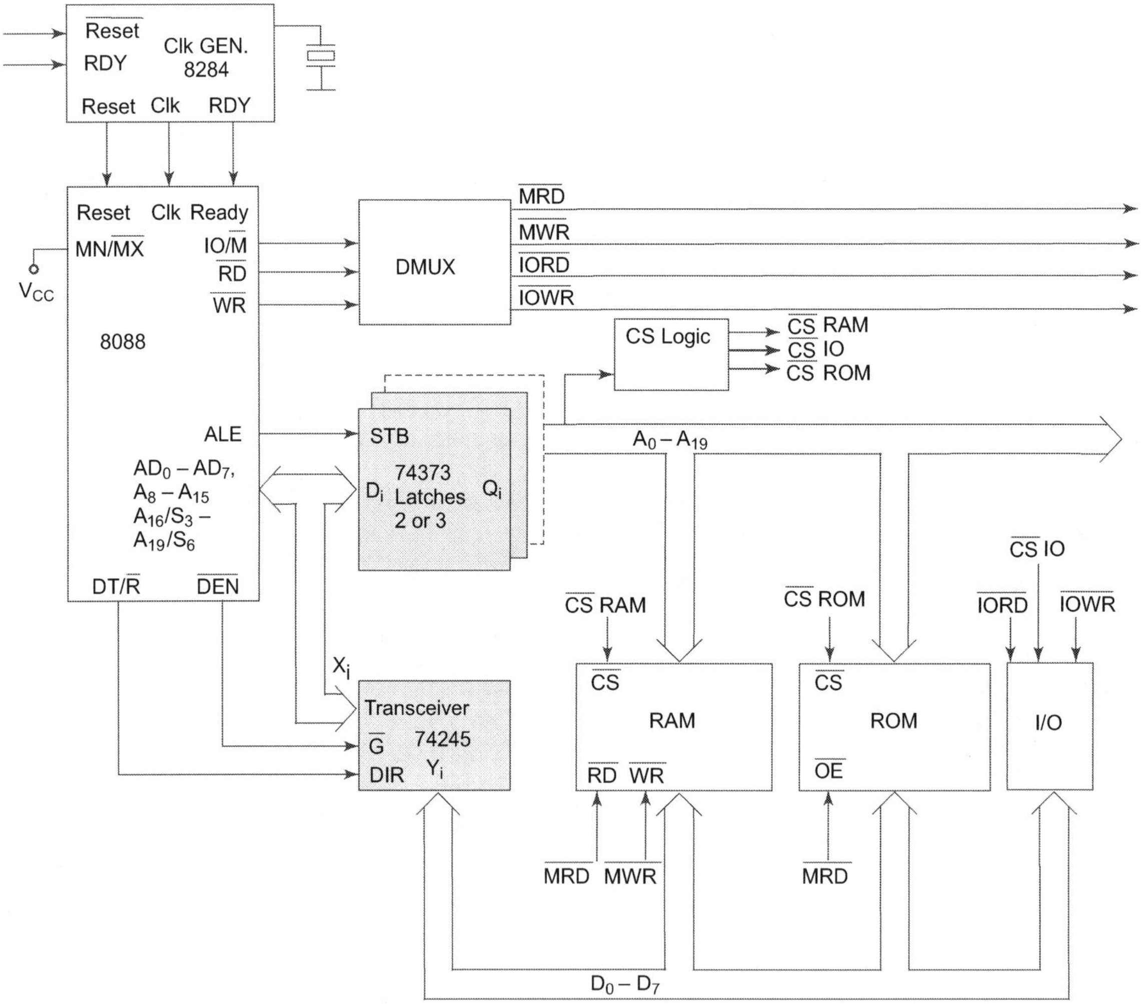

Fig. 1.21 (a) *Minimum Mode 8088 System*

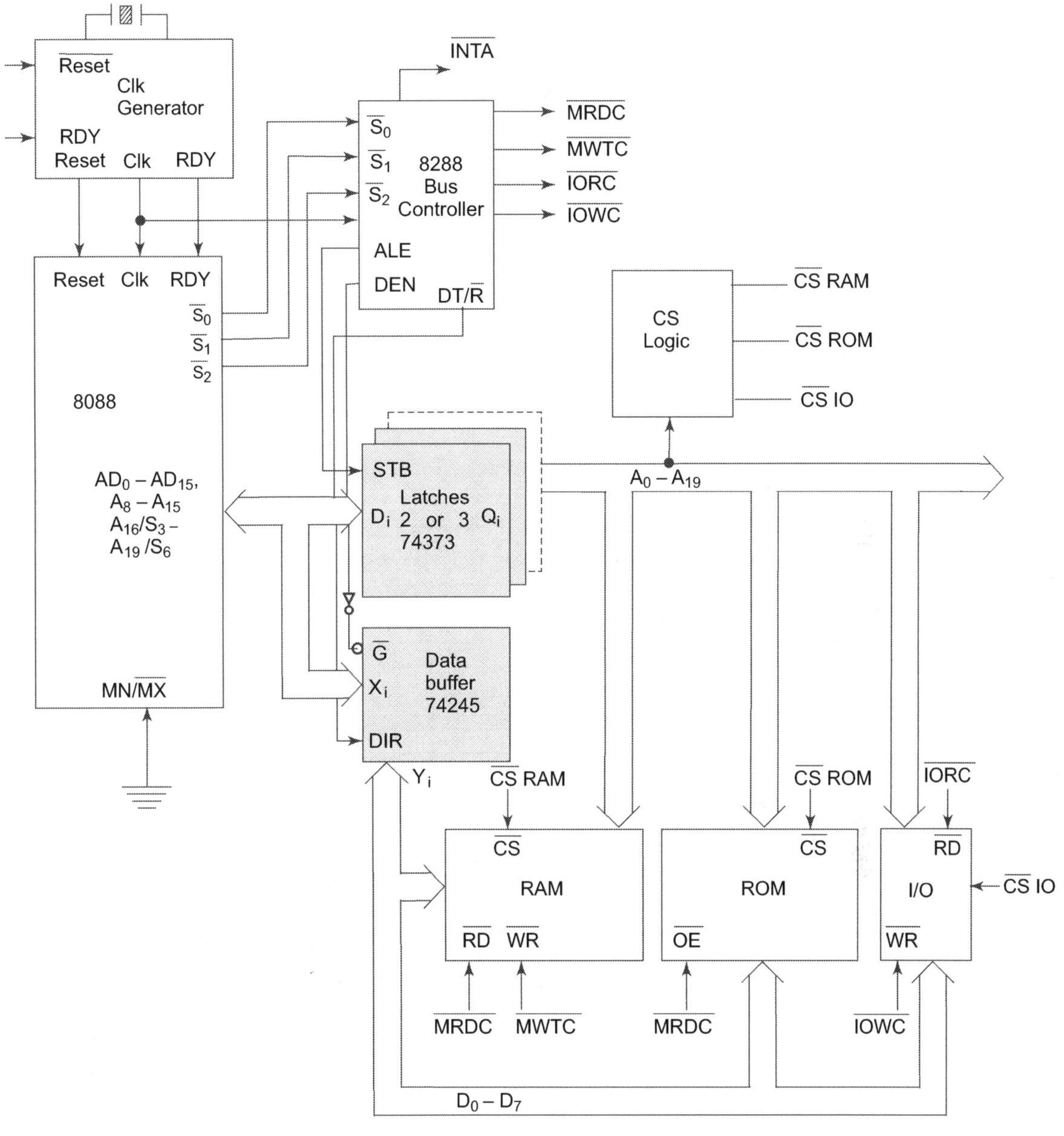

Fig. 1.21 (b) *Maximum Mode Minimum System of 8088*

1.10.3 General 8088 System Timing Diagram

The 8088 address/data bus is divided into three parts (a) the lower 8 address/data bits, (b) the middle 8 address bits, and (c) the upper 4 address/status bits. The lower 8 lines are time multiplexed for address and data. The upper 4 lines are time multiplexed for address and status. Each of the bus cycles contains T_1, T_2, T_3, T_w and T_4 states . The ALE signal goes high for one clock cycle in T_1. The trailing edge of ALE is used to latch the valid addresses available on the multiplexed lines. They remain valid on the bus for the next cycle (T_2). The middle 8 address bits are always present on the bus throughout the bus cycle. The lower order address bus is tristated after T_2 to change its direction for read data operation. The actual data transfer takes place during T_3 and T_4. Hence the data lines are valid in T_3 or T_4. The multiplexed bus is again tristated to be ready for the next bus cycle. The status lines are valid over the multiplexed address/status bus for T_2, T_3 and T_4 clock cycles.

In case of write cycle, the timing diagram is similar to the read cycle except for the validity of data. In write cycle, the data bits are available on the bus for T_2, T_3, T_w, and T_4. At the end of T_4, the bus is tristated. The other signals $\overline{RD}$, $\overline{WR}$, $\overline{INTA}$, $DT/\overline{R}$, $\overline{DEN}$ and READY are similar to the 8086 timing diagram. Figure 1.22 shows the details of read and write bus cycles of 8088.

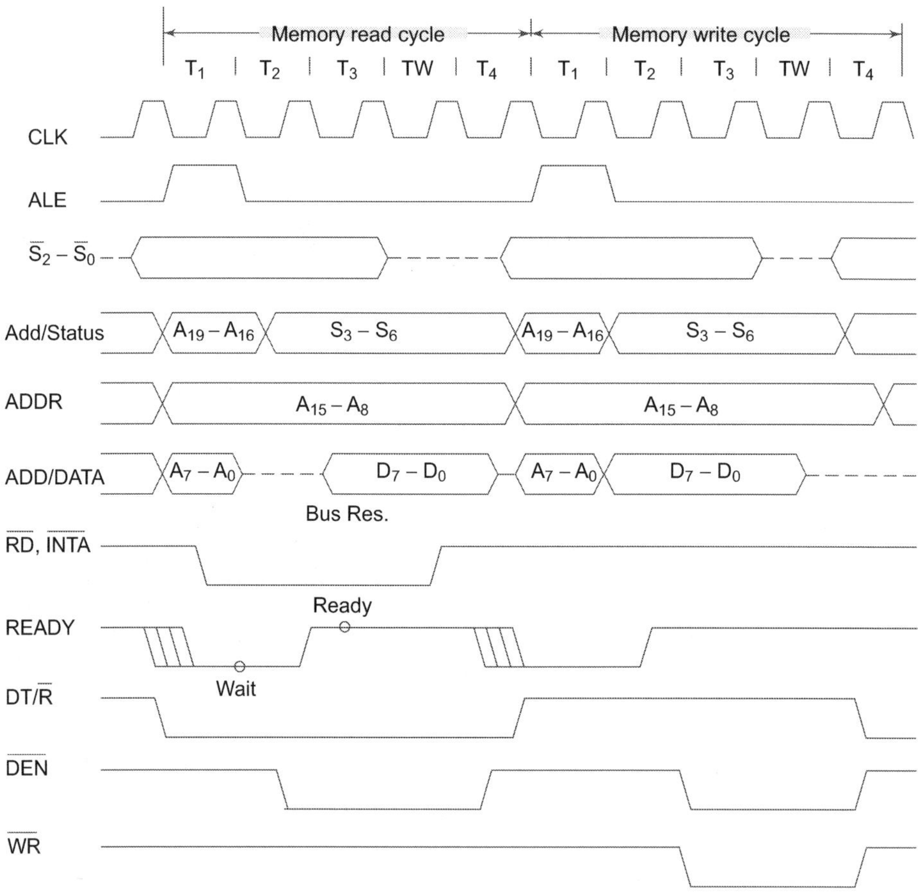

Fig. 1.22 *Read and Write Cycle Timing Diagram of 8088*

1.10.4 Comparison between 8086 and 8088

The 8088, with an 8-bit external data bus, has been designed for internal 16-bit processing capability. Nearly all the internal functions of 8088 are identical to 8086. The 8088 uses the external bus in the same way as 8086, but only 8 bits of external data are accessed at a time. While fetching or writing the 16-bit data, the task is performed in two consecutive bus cycles. As far as the software is concerned, the chips are identical, except in case of timings. The 8088, thus may take more time for execution of a particular task as compared to 8086.

All the changes in 8088 over 8086 are directly or indirectly related to the 8-bit, 8085 compatible data and control bus interface.

1. The predecoded code queue length is reduced to 4 bytes in 8088, whereas the 8086 queue contains 6 bytes. This was done to avoid the unnecessary prefetch operations and optimize the use of the bus by BIU while prefetching the instructions.
2. The 8088 bus interface unit will fetch a byte from memory to load the queue each time, if at least 1 byte is free. In case of 8086, at least 2 bytes should be free for the next fetch operation.
3. The overall execution time of the instructions in 8088 is affected by the 8-bit external data bus. All the 16-bit operations now require additional 4 clock cycles. The CPU speed is also limited by the speed of instruction fetches.

The pin assignments of both the CPUs are nearly identical, however, they have the following functional changes.

1. A_8–A_{15} already latched, all time valid address bus.
2. $\overline{BHE}$ has no meaning as the data bus is of 8-bits only.
3. $\overline{SS_0}$ provides the S_0 status information in minimum mode.
4. $\overline{IO}/M$ has been inverted to be compatible with 8085 bus structure.

SUMMARY

In this chapter, we have presented the internal architecture and signal descriptions of 8086. The functional details of the architecture, like register set, flags and segmented memory organisation are also discussed in significant details. Further, general bus cycle operations have been described with the help of timing diagrams. Then minimal 8086 systems have been presented for the minimum and maximum modes of operation. A software compatible processor-8088 has been discussed in the light of the modifications in it over 8086. To conclude with, the basic bus cycle operations and the timing diagrams of 8088 were discussed along with its comparison with 8086. This chapter has elaborated the architectural and functional concepts of the processors 8086 and 8088. The instruction set and programming techniques have been discussed in the following chapters.

EXERCISES

1.1 Draw and discuss the internal block diagram of 8086.
1.2 What do you mean by pipelined architecture? How is it implemented in 8086?
1.3 Explain the concept of segmented memory? What are its advantages?
1.4 Explain the physical address formation in 8086.
1.5 Draw the register organisation of 8086 and explain typical applications of each register.
1.6 Draw and discuss flag register of 8086 in brief.
1.7 Explain the function of the following signals of 8086.

(i) ALE (ii) DT/$\overline{R}$ (iii) $\overline{DEN}$ (iv) $\overline{LOCK}$
(v) $\overline{TEST}$ (vi) MN/$\overline{MX}$ (vii) $\overline{BHE}$ (viii) M/$\overline{IO}$
(ix) $\overline{RQ}$/$\overline{GT}$ (x) QS_0 (xi) READY (xii) NMI
(xiii) INTR (xiv) HOLD (xv) HLDA

1. 8 Explain the function of opcode prefetch queue in 8086.
1. 9 How does 8086 differentiate between an opcode and instruction data?
1. 10 Explain the physical memory organisation in an 8086 system.
1. 11 What is the maximum memory addressing and I/O addressing capability of 8086?
1. 12 Draw and discuss the read and write cycle timing diagrams of 8086 in minimum mode.
1. 13 Draw and discuss the read and write cycle timing diagram of 8086 in maximum mode.
1. 14 From which address the 8086 starts execution after reset?
1. 15 How will you synchronise an external phenomenon like energising a relay with a program segment execution?
1. 16 Draw and discuss a typical minimum mode 8086 system.
1. 17 Draw and discuss a typical maximum mode 8086 system. What is the use of a bus controller in maximum mode?
1. 18 Bring out the architectural and signal differences between 8086 and 8088.
1. 19 What may be the reason for developing an externally 8-bit processor like 8088 after the 8086, when a 16-bit processor had already been introduced?
1. 20 Explain the signal $\overline{SS_0}$ of 8088.
1. 21 Compare the bus interface of 8085 with 8088.
1. 22 Draw and discuss a typical minimum mode 8088 system.
1. 23 Draw and discuss a typical maximum mode 8088 system.
1. 24 Draw and discuss a general 8088 system timing diagram.
1. 25 What are the functions of the clock generator IC 8284, in the 8086/8088 systems?

2 8086/8088 Instruction Set and Assembler Directives

INTRODUCTION

In Chapter 1, we have discussed the 8086/8088 architecture, pin diagrams and timing diagrams of read and write cycles. This chapter aims at introducing the readers with the general instruction formats, different addressing modes supported by 8086/8088 along with 8086/8088 instruction set. Further, a few important and frequently used assembler directives and operators have also been discussed. Thus this chapter creates a background for 'assembly language programming using 8086/8088'. A number of assemblers are available for programming with 8086/8088. Each of them has slightly different syntax, directives and operators. However, most of them work on similar principles. The directives and operators considered here are available with MASM (Microsoft MACRO ASSEMBLER).

2.1 MACHINE LANGUAGE INSTRUCTION FORMATS

A machine language instruction format has one or more number of fields associated with it. The first field is called as *operation code field* or *opcode field*, which indicates the type of the operation to be performed by the CPU. The instruction format also contains other fields known as *operand fields*. The CPU executes the instruction using the information which reside in these fields.

There are six general formats of instructions in 8086 instruction set. The length of an instruction may vary from one byte to six bytes. The instruction formats are described as follows:

1. One byte Instruction This format is only one byte long and may have the implied data or register operands. The least significant 3-bits of the opcode are used for specifying the register operand, if any. Otherwise, all the 8-bits form an opcode and the operands are implied.

2. Register to Register This format is 2 bytes long. The first byte of the code specifies the operation code and width of the operand specified by w bit. The second byte of the code shows the register operands and R/M field, as shown below.

D_7 ... D_1	D_0
OP CODE	W

D7 D6	D5 D4 D3	D2 D1 D0
11	REG	R/M

The register represented by the REG field is one of the operands. The R/M field specifies another register or memory location, i.e. the other operand.

3. Register to/from Memory with no Displacement This format is also 2 bytes long and similar to the register to register format except for the MOD field as shown.

D_7 D_1	D_0	D7 D6	D5 D4 D3	D2 D1 D0
OP CODE	W	MOD	REG	R/M

The MOD field shows the mode of addressing. The MOD, R/M, REG and the W fields are decided in Table 2.2.

4. Register to/from Memory with Displacement This type of instruction format contains one or two additional bytes for displacement along with 2-byte the format of the register to/from memory without displacement. The format is as shown below.

D_7 D_0	D7 D6	D5 D4 D3	D2 D1 D0	D_7 D_0	D_7 D_0
OP CODE	MOD	REG	R/M	Lower Byte of Disp.	Higher Byte of Disp.

5. Immediate Operand to Register In this format, the first byte as well as the 3-bits from the second byte which are used for REG field in case of register to register format are used for opcode. It also contains one or two bytes of immediate data. The complete instruction format is as shown below.

D_7 D_0	D7 D6	D5 D4 D3	D2 D1 D0	D_7 D_0	D_7 D_0
OP CODE	11	OP-CODE	R/M	Lower Byte DATA	Higher Byte DATA

6. Immediate Operand to Memory with 16-bit Displacement This type of instruction format requires 5 or 6 bytes for coding. The first 2 bytes contain the information regarding OPCODE, MOD, and R/M fields. The remaining 4 bytes contain 2 bytes of displacement and 2 bytes of data as shown.

D_7 D_0	D7 D6	D5 D4 D3	D2 D1 D0	D_7 D_0
OP CODE	MOD	OP-CODE	R/M	Lower Byte of Disp.

D_7 D_0	D_7 D_0	D_7 D_0
Higher Byte of Disp.	Lower Byte of DATA	Higher Byte of DATA

The opcode usually appears in the first byte, but in a few instructions, a register destination is in the first byte and few other instructions may have their 3-bits of opcode in the second byte. The opcodes have the single bit indicators. Their definitions and significances are given as follows:

W-bit This indicates whether the instruction is to operate over an 8-bit or 16-bit data/operands. If W bit is 0, the operand is of 8-bits and if W is 1, the operand is of 16-bits.

D-bit This is valid in case of double operand instructions. One of the operands must be a register specified by the REG field. The register specified by REG is source operand if D = 0, else, it is a destination operand.

S-bit This bit is called as sign extension bit. The S bit is used along with W-bit to show the type of the operation. For, example

8-bit operation with 8-bit immediate operand is indicated by S = 0, W = 0;

16-bit operation with 16-bit immediate operand is indicated by S = 0, W = 1 and

16-bit operation with a sign extended immediate data is given by S = 1, W = 1

V-bit This is used in case of shift and rotate instructions. This bit is set to 0, if shift count is 1 and is set to 1, if CL contains the shift count.

Z-bit This bit is used by REP instruction to control the loop. If Z bit is equal to 1, the instruction with REP prefix is executed until the zero flag matches the Z bit.

The REG code of the different registers (either as source or destination operands) in the opcode byte are assigned with binary codes. The segment registers are only 4 in number hence 2 binary bits will be sufficient to code them. The other registers are 8 in number, so at least 3-bits will be required for coding them. To allow the use of 16-bit registers as two 8-bit registers they are coded with W bit as shown in Table 2.1.

Table 2.1 *Assignment of Codes with Different Registers*

W	*Register Address (code)*	*Registers*	*Segment 2 bit bit Register (code)*	*Segment Register*
0	000	AL		
0	001	CL	00	ES
0	010	DL	01	CS
0	011	BL	10	SS
0	100	AH	11	DS
0	101	CH		
0	110	DH		
0	111	BH		
1	000	AX		
1	001	CX		
1	010	DX		
1	011	BX		
1	100	SP		
1	101	BP		
1	110	SI		
1	111	DI		

Please note that usually all the addressing modes have DS as the default data segment. However, the addressing modes using BP and SP have SS as the default segment register.

To find out the MOD and R/M fields of a particular instruction, one should first decide the addressing mode of the instruction. The addressing mode depends upon the operands and suggests how the effective address may be computed for locating the operand, if it lies in memory. The different addressing modes of the 8086 instructions are listed in Table 2.2. The R/M column and addressing mode row element specifies the R/M field, while the addressing mode column specifies the MOD field.

Table 2.2 *Addressing Modes and the Corresponding MOD, REG and R/M Fields*

Operands	*Memory Operands* No Displacement	*Memory Operands* Displacement 8-bit	*Memory Operands* Displacement 16-bit	*Register Operands*	
MOD / *R/M*	*00*	*01*	*10*	*11*	
				W = 0	*W = 1*
000	(BX) + (SI)	(BX) + (SI) + D8	(BX) + (SI) + D16	AL	AX
001	(BX) + (DI)	(BX) + (DI) + D8	(BX) + (DI) + D16	CL	CX
010	(BP) + (SI)	(BP) + (SI) + D8	(BP) + (SI) + D16	DL	DX
011	(BP) + (DI)	(BP) + (DI) + D8	(BP) + (DI) + D16	BL	BX
100	(SI)	(SI) + D8	(SI) + D16	AH	SP
101	(DI)	(DI) + D8	(DI) + D16	CH	BP
110	D16	(BP) + D8	(BP) + D16	DH	SI
111	(BX)	(BX) + D8	(BX) + D16	BH	DI

Note: 1. D8 and D16 represent 8 and 16 bit displacements respectively.
2. The default segment for the addressing modes using BP and SP is SS. For all other addressing modes the default segments are DS or ES.

DS is the default data segment register when a data is to be referred as an operand. CS is the default code segment register for storing program codes (executable codes). SS is the default segment register for the stack data accesses and operations. ES is the default segment register for the destination data storage. All the segments available (defined in a particular program) can be read or written as data segments by newly defining the data segment as required. There is no physical difference in the memory structure or no physical separation between the segment areas. They may or may not overlap with each other. Chapter 3 on 'Assembly Language Programming' explains the coding procedure of the instructions with suitable examples.

2.2 ADDRESSING MODES OF 8086

Addressing mode indicates a way of locating data or operands. Depending upon the data types used in the instruction and the memory addressing modes, any instruction may belong to one or more addressing modes, or some instruction may not belong to any of the addressing modes. Thus the addressing modes describe the types of operands and the way they are accessed for executing an instruction. Here, we will present the addressing modes of the instructions depending upon their types. According to the flow of instruction execution, the instructions may be categorised as (i) Sequential control flow instructions and (ii) Control transfer instructions.

Sequential control flow instructions are the instructions which after execution, transfer control to the next instruction appearing immediately after it (in the sequence) in the program. For example, the arithmetic, logical, data transfer and processor control instructions are sequential control flow instructions. *The control transfer instructions, on the other hand, transfer control to some predefined address or the address somehow specified in the instruction, after their execution*. For example, INT, CALL, RET and JUMP instructions fall under this category.

The addressing modes for sequential and control transfer instructions are explained as follows:

1. Immediate In this type of addressing, immediate data is a part of instruction, and appears in the form of successive byte or bytes.

Example 2.1

```
MOV AX, 0005H
MOV BL, 06H
```

In the above examples 0005H and 06H are the immediate data. The immediate data may be 8-bit or 16-bit in size.

2. Direct In the direct addressing mode, a 16-bit memory address (offset) or an IO address is directly specified in the instruction as a part of it.

Example 2.2

```
MOV AX, [5000H]
IN 80H
```

Here, data resides in a memory location in the data segment, whose effective address may be computed using 5000H as the offset address and content of DS as segment address. The effective address, here, is 10H*DS+5000H. In the second instruction 80H is IO address.

3. Register In the register addressing mode, the data is stored in a register and it is referred using the particular register. All the registers, except IP, may be used in this mode.

Example 2.3

```
MOV BX, AX.
ADC AL, BL
```

The operands in these instructions are provided in registers BX, AX and AL, BL respectively.

4. Register Indirect Sometimes, the address of the memory location which contains data or operand is determined in an indirect way, using the offset registers. This mode of addressing is known as register indirect mode. In this addressing mode, the offset address of data is in either BX or SI or DI register. The default segment is either DS or ES. The data is supposed to be available at the address pointed to by the content of any of the above registers in the default data segment.

Example 2.4

```
MOV AX, [BX]
```

Here, data is present in a memory location in DS whose offset address is in BX. The effective address of the data is given as 10H*DS+[BX].

5. Indexed In this addressing mode, offset of the operand is stored in one of the index registers. DS is the default segment for index registers SI and DI. In case of string instructions DS and ES are default segments for SI and DI respectively. This mode is a special case of the above discussed register indirect addressing mode.

Example 2.5

```
MOV AX, [SI]
MOV CX, [DI]
```

Here, data is available at an offset address stored in SI in DS. The effective address, in this case, is computed as 10H*DS+[SI]. The content of address 10H*DS+[SI] will be transferred into register CX.

6. Register Relative In this addressing mode, the data is available at an effective address formed by adding an 8-bit or 16-bit displacement with the content of any one of the registers BX, BP, SI and DI in the default (either DS or ES) segment. The example given below explains this mode.

Example 2.6

```
MOV AX, 50H[BX]
MOV 10H[SI], DX
```

Here, the effective address is given as 10H*DS+50H+[BX] and 10H*DS+10H+[SI] respectively.

7. Based Indexed The effective address of data is formed, in this addressing mode, by adding content of a base register (any one of BX or BP) to the content of an index register (any one of SI or DI). The default segment register may be ES or DS.

Example 2.7

```
MOV AX, [BX] [SI]
MOV [BX] [DI], AX
```

Here, BX is the base register and SI is the index register. The effective address is computed as 10H*DS+[BX]+[SI].

8. Relative Based Indexed The effective address is formed by adding an 8 or 16-bit displacement with the sum of contents of any one of the base registers (BX or BP) and any one of the index registers, in a default segment.

Example 2.8

```
MOV AX,50H [BX][SI]
ADD 50H [BX] [SI], BP
```

Here, 50H is an immediate displacement, BX is a base register and SI is an index register. The effective address of data is computed as 10H*DS+[BX]+[SI]+50H. The second instruction adds content of B with memory location of which offset is given by adding 50H of content of BX and SI. The result is stered in the memory location.

For the control transfer instructions, the addressing modes depend upon whether the destination location is within the same segment or in a different one. It also depends upon the method of passing the destination address to the processor. Basically, there are two addressing modes for the control transfer instructions, viz. intersegment and intrasegment addressing modes.

If the location to which the control is to be transferred lies in a different segment other than the current one, the mode is called intersegment mode. If the destination location lies in the same segment, the mode is called intrasegment mode.

Figure 2.1 shows the modes for control transfer instructions.

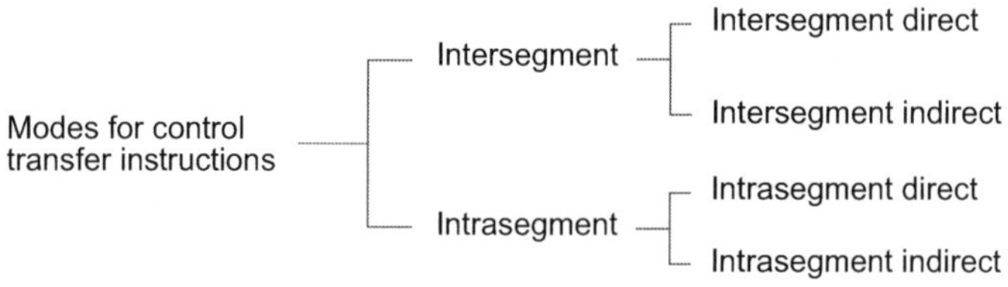

Fig. 2.1 *Addressing Modes for Control Transfer Instructions*

9. Intrasegment Direct Mode In this mode, the address to which the control is to be transferred lies in the same segment in which the control transfer instruction lies and appears directly in the instruction as an immediate displacement value. In this addressing mode, the displacement is computed relative to the content of the instruction pointer IP.

The effective address to which the control will be transferred is given by the sum of 8 or 16 bit displacement and current content of IP. In case of jump instruction, if the signed displacement (d) is of 8 bits (i.e. $-128 < d < +127$), we term it as *short jump* and if it is of 16 bits (i.e. $-32768 < d < +32767$), it is termed as *long jump*.

Example 2.9

```
JMP SHORT LABEL; LABEL lies within -128 TO +127 from the current IP
content.
```

Thus SHORT LABEL is 8-bit signed displacement.

A 16-bit target address of a label indicates that it lies within − 32768 to + 32767. But a problem arises when one requires a forward jump at a relative address greater than 32767 or backward jump at relative address − 32768; in the same segment. Suppose current contents of IP are 5000H then a forward jump may be allowed at all the displacement DISP so that IP + DISP = FFFFH or DISP = FFFF − 5000 = AFFFH. Thus forward jumps may be allowed for all 16-bit displacement values from 0000H to AFFFH. If displacement exceeds AFFFH i.e. from B000H to FFFFH, then all such jumps will be treated as backward jumps. All such jumps are called NEAR PTR jumps and coded as below.

```
JMP NEAR PTR LABEL
```

10. Intrasegment Indirect Mode In this mode, the displacement to which the control is to be transferred, is in the same segment in which the control transfer instruction lies, but it is passed to the instruction indirectly. Here, the branch address is found as the content of a register or a memory location. This addressing mode may be used in unconditional branch instructions.

Example 2.10

```
JMP [BX]; Jump to effective address stored in BX.
                         JMP [ BX + 5000H ]
```

11. Intersegment Direct In this mode, the address to which the control is to be transferred is in a different segment. This addressing mode provides a means of branching from one code segment to another code segment. Here, the CS and IP of the destination address are specified directly in the instruction.

Example 2.11

```
JPM 5000H : 2000H;
Jump to effective address 2000H in segment 5000H.
```

12. Intersegment Indirect In this mode, the address to which the control is to be transferred lies in a different segment and it is passed to the instruction indirectly, i.e. contents of a memory block containing four bytes, i.e. IP(LSB), IP(MSB), CS(LSB) and CS(MSB) sequentially. The starting address of the memory block may be referred using any of the addressing modes, except immediate mode.

Example 2.12

```
JMP [2000H];
```

Jump to an address in the other segment specified at effective address 2000H in DS, that points to the memory block as said above.

Forming the Effective Addresses The following examples explain forming of the effective addresses in the different modes.

Example 2.13

The contents of different registers are given below. Form effective addresses for different addressing modes.
Offset (displacement) = 5000H
[AX]-1000H, [BX]-2000H, [SI]-3000H, [DI]-4000H, [BP]-5000H,
[SP]-6000H, [CS]-0000H, [DS]-1000H, [SS]-2000H, [IP]-7000H.
Shifting a number four times is equivalent to multiplying it by 16_D or 10_H.

(i) Direct addressing mode

```
MOV AX, [5000H]
```

DS:OFFSET ⇔ 1000H: 5000H
10H* DS ⇔ 10000
Offset ⇔ + 5000

15000H - Effective address

(ii) Register indirect

```
MOV AX, [BX]
```

DS:BX ⇔ 1000H:2000H
10H*DS ⇔ 10000
[BX] ⇔ + 2000

12000H - Effective address

(iii) Register relative

```
MOV AX, 5000 [BX]
```

DS: [5000 + BX]
10H*DS ⇔ 10000
Offset ⇔ + 5000
[BX] ⇔ + 2000

17000H - Effective address

(iv) Based indexed

```
MOV AX, [BX] [SI]
```

DS:[BX + SI]
10H*DS ⇔ 10000
[BX] ⇔ + 2000
[SI] ⇔ + 3000

15000H - Effective address

(v) Relative based indexed

```
MOV AX, 5000 [BX] [SI]
```

DS: [BX + SI + 5000]
10H*DS ⇔ 10000
[BX] ⇔ + 2000
[SI] ⇔ + 3000
Offset ⇔ + 5000

1A000 - effective address

Below, we present examples of address formation in control transfer instructions.

Example 2.14

Suppose our main program resides in the code segment where CS = 1000H. The main program calls a subroutine which resides in the same code segment. The base register contains offset of the subroutine, i.e. BX = 0050H. Since the offset is specified indirectly, as the content of BX, this is indirect addressing. The instruction CALL [BX] calls the subroutine located at an address 10H*CS + [BX] = 10050H, i.e. in the same code segment. Since the control goes to the subroutine which resides in the same segment, this is an example of intrasegment indirect addressing mode.

Example 2.15

Let us now assume that the subroutine resides in another code segment, where CS = 2000H. Now CALL 2000H:0050H is an example of intersegment direct addressing mode, since the control now goes to different segment and the address is directly specified in the instruction. In this case, the address of the subroutine is 20050H.

2.3 INSTRUCTION SET OF 8086/8088

The 8086/8088 instructions are categorised into the following main types. This section explains the function of each of the instructions with suitable examples wherever necessary.

(i) **Data Copy/Transfer Instructions** These types of instructions are used to transfer data from source operand to destination operand. All the store, move, load, exchange, input and output instructions belong to this category.

(ii) **Arithmetic and Logical Instructions** All the instructions performing arithmetic, logical, increment, decrement, compare and scan instructions belong to this category.

(iii) **Branch Instructions** These instructions transfer control of execution to the specified address. All the call, jump, interrupt and return instructions belong to this class.

(iv) **Loop Instructions** If these instructions have REP prefix with CX used as count register, they can be used to implement unconditional and conditional loops. The LOOP, LOOPNZ and LOOPZ instructions belong to this category. These are useful to implement different loop structures.

(v) **Machine Control Instructions** These instructions control the machine status. NOP, HLT, WAIT and LOCK instructions belong to this class.

(vi) **Flag Manipulation Instructions** All the instructions which directly affect the flag register, come under this group of instructions. Instructions like CLD,STD,CLI,STI, etc. belong to this category of instructions.

(vii) **Shift and Rotate Instructions** These instructions involve the bitwise shifting or rotation in either direction with or without a count in CX.

(viii) **String Instructions** These instructions involve various string manipulation operations like load, move, scan, compare, store, etc. These instructions are only to be operated upon the strings.

2.3.1 Data Copy/Transfer Instructions

MOV: Move This data transfer instruction transfers data from one register/memory location to another register/memory location. The source may be any one of the segment registers or other general or special purpose registers or a memory location and, another register or memory location may act as destination.

However, in case of immediate addressing mode, a segment register cannot be a destination register. In other words, direct loading of the segment registers with immediate data is not permitted. To load the segment registers with immediate data, one will have to load any general purpose register with the data and then it will have to be moved to that particular segment register. The following example instructions explain the fact.

Example 2.16

Load DS with 5000H.

1. MOV DS, 5000H; Not permitted (invalid)
   Thus to transfer an immediate data into the segment register, the correct procedure is given below.
2. MOV AX, 5000H
   MOV DS, AX
   It may be noted here that both the source and destination operands cannot be memory locations (except for string instructions). Other MOV instruction examples are given below with the corresponding addressing modes.
3. MOV AX, 5000H; Immediate
4. MOV AX, BX; Register
5. MOV AX, [SI]; Indirect
6. MOV AX, [2000H]; Direct
7. MOV AX, 50H[BX]; Based relative, 50H Displacement

PUSH: Push to Stack This instruction pushes the contents of the specified register/memory location on to the stack. The stack pointer is decremented by 2, after each execution of the instruction. The actual current stack-top is always occupied by the previously pushed data. Hence, the push operation decrements SP by two and then stores the two byte contents of the operand onto the stack. The higher byte is pushed first and then the lower byte. Thus out of the two decremented stack addresses the higher byte occupies the higher address and the lower byte occupies the lower address.

The actual operation takes place as given below SS : SP points to the stack top of 8086 system as shown in Fig. 2.2 and AH, AL contains data to be pushed.

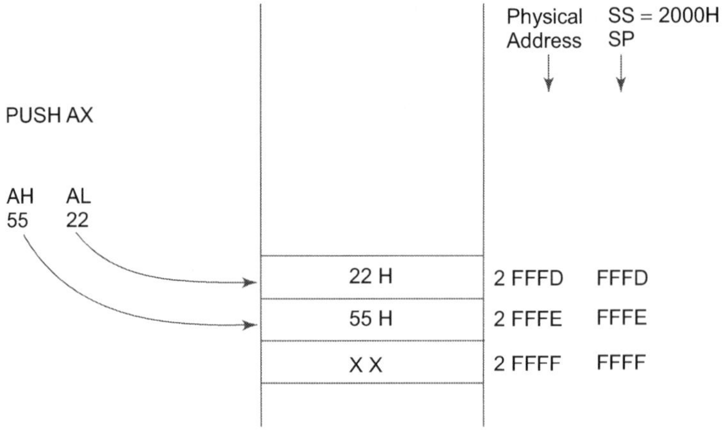

Fig. 2.2 *Pushing Data to Stack Memory*

The sequence of operation as below:

1. Current stack top is already occupied so decrement SP by one then store AH into the address pointed to by SP.
2. Further decrement SP by one and store AL into the location pointed to by SP.

Thus SP is decremented by 2 and AH–AL contents are stored in stack memory as shown in Fig. 2.2. Contents of SP points to a new stack top.

The examples of these instructions are as follows:

Example 2.17

1. PUSH AX
2. PUSH DS
3. PUSH [5000H]; Content of location 5000H and 5001H in DS are pushed onto the stack

POP: Pop from Stack This instruction when executed, loads the specified register/memory location with the contents of the memory location of which the address is formed using the current stack segment and stack pointer as usual. The stack pointer is incremented by 2. The POP instruction serves exactly opposite to the PUSH instruction.

16-bit contents of current stack top are poped into the specified operand as follows.

The sequence of operation is as below.

1. Contents of stack top memory location is stored in AL and SP is incremented by one
2. Further contents of memory location pointed to by SP are copied to AH and SP is again incremented by 1

Effectively SP is incremented by 2 and points to next stack top.

The examples of these instructions are shown as follows:

Example 2.18

```
1.POP    AX
2.POP    DS
3.POP    [5000H]
```

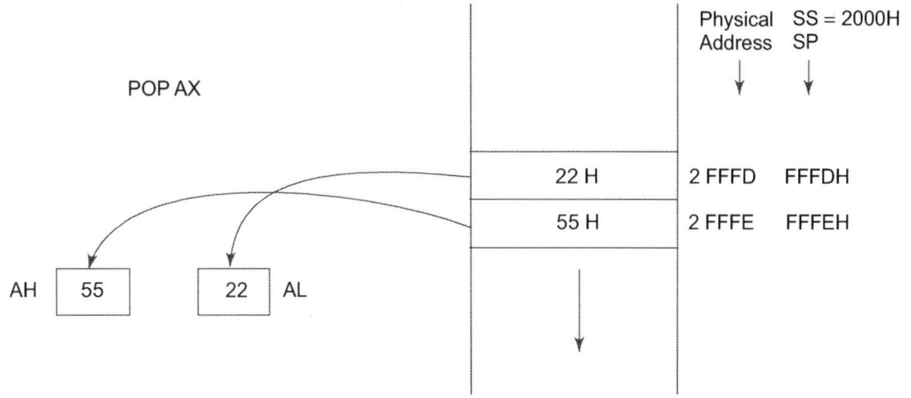

Fig. 2.3 *Popping Register Contents from Stack Memory*

XCHG: Exchange This instruction exchanges the contents of the specified source and destination operands, which may be registers or one of them may be a memory location. However, exchange of contents of two memory locations is not permitted. Immediate data is also not allowed in these instructions. The examples are as follows:

Example 2.19

```
1. XCHG  [5000H], AX    ;This instruction exchanges data between AX and a
                        ; memory location [5000H] in the data segment.
2. XCHG  BX, AX         ;This instruction exchanges data between AX and BX.
```

IN: Input the Port This instruction is used for reading an input port. The address of the input port may be specified in the instruction directly or indirectly. AL and AX are the allowed destinations for 8 and 16-bit input operations. DX is the only register (implicit) which is allowed to carry the port address. If the port address is of 16 bits it must be in DX. The examples are given as shown:

Example 2.20

```
1. IN AL,03H        ;This instruction reads data from an 8-bit port whose address
                    ; is 03H and stores it in AL.
2. IN AX, DX        ;This instruction reads data from a 16-bit port whose
                    ; address is in DX (implicit) and stores it in AX.
3. MOV DX,0800H     ;The 16-bit address is taken in DX.
   IN AX, DX        ; Read the content of the port in AX.
```

OUT: Output to the Port This instruction is used for writing to an output port. The address of the output port may be specified in the instruction directly or implicitly in DX. Contents of AX or AL are transferred to a directly or indirectly addressed port after execution of this instruction. The data to an odd addressed port is transferred on D_8-D_{15} while that to an even addressed port is transferred on D_0-D_7. The registers AL and AX are the allowed source operands for 8-bit and 16-bit operations respectively. If the port address is of 16 bits it must be in DX. The examples are given as shown:

Example 2.21

```
1. OUT    03H,AL     ;This sends data available in AL to a port whose
                     ; address is 03H.
2. OUT    DX, AX     ;This sends data available in AX to a port whose
                     ; address is specified implicitly in DX.
3. MOV DX, 0300H     ;The 16-bit port address is taken in DX.
   OUT DX, AX        ;Write the content of AX to a port of which address is in DX.
```

XLAT: Translate The translate instruction is used for finding out the codes in case of code conversion problems, using look up table technique. We will explain this instruction with the aid of the following example.

Suppose, a hexadecimal key pad having 16 keys from 0 to F is interfaced with 8086 using 8255. Whenever a key is pressed, the code of that key (0 to F) is returned in AL. For displaying the number corresponding to the pressed key on the 7-segment display device, it is required that the 7-segment code corresponding to the key pressed is found out and sent to the display port. This translation from the code of the key pressed to the corresponding 7-segment code is performed using XLAT instruction.

For this purpose, one is required to prepare a look up table of codes, starting from an offset say 2000H, and store the 7-segment codes for 0 to F at the locations 2000H to 200FH sequentially. For executing the

XLAT instruction, the code of the pressed key obtained from the keyboard (i.e. the code to be translated) is moved in AL and the base address of the look up table containing the 7-segment codes is kept in BX. After the execution of the XLAT instruction, the 7-segment code corresponding to the pressed key is returned in AL, replacing the key code which was in AL prior to the execution of the XLAT instruction. To find out the exact address of the 7-segment code from the base address of look up table, the content of AL is added to BX internally, and the contents of the address pointed to by this new content of BX in DS are transferred to AL. The following sequence of instructions perform the task.

Example 2.22

```
MOV AX, SEG TABLE    ; Address of the segment containing look-up-table
MOV DS,AX            ; is transferred in DS
MOV AL, CODE         ; Code of the pressed key is transferred in AL
MOV BX, OFFSET TABLE; Offset of the code look-up-table in BX
XLAT                 ; Find the equivalent code and store in AL
```

Mnemonics & Description	*Instruction Code*			
Data Transfer				
MOV = Move	76543210	76543210	76543210	76543210
Register/Memory to/from Register	100010 dw	mod reg r/m		
Immediate to Register/Memory	1100011 w	mod 000 r/m	data	data if w = 1
Immediate to Register	1011 w reg	data	data if w = 1	
Memory to Accumulator	1010000 w	addr-low	addr-high	
Accumulator to Memory	1010001 w	addr-low	addr-high	
Register/Memory to Segment Register	10001110	mod 0 reg r/m		
Segment Register to Register/Memory	10001100	mod 0 reg r/m		
PUSH = Push:				
Register/Memory	11111111	mod 110 r/m		
Register	01010 reg			
Segment Register	000 reg 110			
POP = Pop:				
Register/Memory	10001111	mod 000 r/m		
Register	01011 reg			
Segment Register	000 reg 111			
XCHG = Exchange				
Register/Memory with Register	1000011 w	mod reg r/m		
Register with Accumulator	10010 reg			
IN = Input from:				
Fixed Port	1110010 w	port		
Variable Port	1110110 w			
OUT = Output to				
Fixed Port	1110011 w	port		
Variable Port	1110111 w			
XLAT = Translate Byte to AL	11010111			
LEA = Load EA to Register	10001101	mod reg r/m		
LDS = Load Pointer to DS	11000101	mod reg r/m		
LES = Load Pointer to ES	11000100	mod reg r/m		
LAHF = Load AH with Flags	10011111			
SAHF = Store AH into Flags	10011110			
PUSHF = Push Flags	10011100			
POPF = Pop Flags	10011101			
ARITHMETIC	**76543210**	**76543210**	**76543210**	**76543210**
ADD = Add:				
Reg/Memory with Register to Either	000000 dw	mod reg r/m		
Immediate to Register/Memory	100000 sw	mod 000 r/m	data	data if s w = 01

Mnemonics & Description	*Instruction Code*			
Immediate to Accumulator	0000010 w	data	data if w = 1	
ADC = Add with Carry:				
Reg/Memory with Register to Either	000100 dw	mod reg r/m		
Immediate to Register/Memory	100000 sw	mod 010 r/m	data	data if s w = 01
Immediate to Accumulator	0001010 w	data	data if w = 1	
INC = Increment:				
Register/Memory	1111111 w	mod 000 r/m		
Register	01000 reg			
AAA = ASCII Adjust for Addition	00110111			
DAA = Decimal Adjust for Addition	00100111			
SUB = Subtract				
Reg/Memory and Register to Either	001010 dw	mod reg r/m		
Immediate from Register/Memory	100000 sw	mod 101 r/m	data	data if s w = 01
Immediate from Accumulator	0010110 w	data	data if w = 1	
SBB = Subtract with Borrow				
Reg/Memory and Register to Either	000110 dw	mod reg r/m		
Immediate from Register/Memory	100000 sw	mod 011 r/m	data	data if s w = 01
Immediate from accumulator	0001110 w	data	data if w = 1	
DEC = Decrement:				
Register/Memory	1111111 w	mod 001 r/m		
Register	01001 reg			
NEG = Change sign	1111011 w	mod 011 r/m		
CMP = Compare:				
Register/Memory and Register	001110 dw	mod reg r/m		
Immediate with Register/Memory	100000 sw	mod 111 r/m	data	data if s w = 01
Immediate with Accumulator	0011110 w	data	data if w = 1	
AAS = ASCII Adjust for Subtract	00111111			
DAS = Decimal Adjust for Subtract	00101111			
MUL = Multiply (Unsigned)	1111011 w	mod 100 r/m		
IMUL = Integer Multiply (Signed)	1111011 w	mod 101 r/m		
AAM = ASCII Adjust Multiply	11010100	00001010		
DIV = Divide (Unsigned)	1111011 w	mod 110 r/m		
IDIV = Integer Divide (Signed)	1111011 w	mod 111 r/m		
AAD = ASCII Adjust for Divide	11010101	00001010		
CBW = Convert Byte to Word	10011000			
CWD = Convert Word to Double Word	10011001			
LOGICAL	76543210	76543210	76543210	76543210
NOT = Invert	1111011 w	mod 010 r/m		
SHL/SAL = Shift Logical/Arithmetic Left	110100 v w	mod 100 r/m		
SHR = Shift Logical Right	110100 v w	mod 101 r/m		
SAR = Shift Arithemtic Right	110100 v w	mod 111 r/m		
ROL = Rotate Left	110100 v w	mod 000 r/m		
ROR = Rotate Right	110100 v w	mod 001 r/m		
RCL = Rotate Through Carry Flag Left	110100 v w	mod 010 r/m		
RCR = Rotate Through Carry Right	110100 v w	mod 011 r/m		
AND = And:				
Reg/Memory and Register to Either	001000 dw	mod reg r/m		
Immediate to Register/Memory	1000000 w	mod 100 r/m	data	data if w = 1
Immediate to Accumulator	0010010 w	data	data if w = 1	
TEST = And Function to Flags, No Result:				
Register/Memory and Register	1000010 w	mod reg r/m		
Immediate Data and Register/Memory	1111011 w	mod 000 r/m	data	data if w = 1
Immediate Data and Accumulator	1010100 w	data	data if w = 1	
OR = Or:				
Reg/Memory and Register to Either	000010 dw	mod reg r/m		
Immediate to Register/Memory	1000000 w	mod 001 r/m	data	data if w = 1
Immediate to Accumulator	0000110 w	data	data if w = 1	

Mnemonics & Description	Instruction Code			
XOR = Exclusive or:				
Reg/Memory and Register to Either	001100 dw	mod reg r/m		
Immediate to Register/Memory	1000000 w	mod 110 r/m	data	data if w = 1
Immediate to Accumulator	0011010 w	data	data if w = 1	
STRING MANIPULATIONS				
REP = Repeat	1111001 z			
MOVS = Move Byte/Word	1010010 w			
CMPS = Compare Byte/Word	1010011 w			
SCAS = Scan Byte/Word	1010111 w			
LODS = Load byte/Wd to AL/AX	1010110 w			
STOS = Stor Byte/Wd from AL/A	1010101 w			
CONTROL TRANSFER				
CALL = Call:				
Direct Within Segment	11101000	disp-low	disp-high	
Indirect Within Segment	11111111	mod 010 r/m		
Direct Intersegment	10011010	offset-low	offset-high	
		seg-low	seg-high	
	76543210	76543210	76543210	
Indirect Intersegment	11111111	mod 011 r/m		
JMP = Unconditional Jump:				
Direct Within Segment	11101001	disp-low	disp-high	
Direct Within Segment-short	11101011	disp		
Indirect Within Segment	11111111	mod 100 r/m		
Direct Intersegment	11101010	offset-low	offset-high	
		seg-low	seg-high	
Indirect Intersegment	11111111	mod 101 r/m		
RET = Return from CALL:				
Within Segment	11000011			
Within Seg Adding Immediate to SP	11000010	data-low	data-high	
Intersegment	11001011			
Intersegment Adding Immediate to SP	11001010	data-low	data-high	
JE/JZ = Jump on Equal/Zero	01110100	disp		
JL/JNGE = Jump on Less/Not Greater or Equal	011111100	disp		
JLE/JNG = Jump on Less or Equal/Not Greater	01111110	disp		
JB/JNAE = Jump on Below/Not Above or Equal	01110010	disp		
JBE/JNA = Jump on Below or Equal/Not Above	01110110	disp		
JP/JPE = Jump on Parity/Parity Even	01111010	disp		
JO = Jump on Overflow	01110000	disp		
JS = Jump on Sign	01111000	disp		
JNE/JNZ = Jump on Not Equal/Not Zero	01110101	disp		
JNL/JGE = Jump on Not Less/Greater or Equal	01111101	disp		
JNLE/JG = Jump on Not Less or Equal/Greater	01111111	disp		
JNB/JAE = Jump on Not Below/Above or Equal	01110011	disp		
JNBE/JA = Jump on Not Below or Equal/Above	01110111	disp		
JNP/JPO = Jump on Not Par/Par Odd	01111011	disp		
JNO = Jump on Not Overflow	01110001	disp		
JNS = Jump on Not Sign	01111001	disp		
LOOP = Loop CX Times	11100010	disp		
LOOPZ/LOOPE = Loop While Zero/	11100001	disp		

Mnemonics & Description	Instruction Code		
Equal			
LOOPNZ/LOOPNE = Loop While Not Zero/Equal	11100000	disp	
JCXZ = Jump on CX Zero	11100011	disp	
INT = Interrupt			
Type Specified	11001101	type	
Type 3	11001100		
INTO = Interrupt on Overflow	11001110		
IRET = Interrupt Return	11001111		
	76543210	76543210	
PROCESSOR CONTROL			
CLC = Clear Carry	11111000		
CMC = Complement Carry	11110101		
STC = Set Carry	11111001		
CLD = Clear Direction	11111100		
STD = Set Direction	11111101		
CLI = Clear Interrupt	11111010		
STI = Set Interrupt	11111011		
HLT = Halt	11110100		
WAIT = Wait	10011011		
ESC = Escape (to External Device)	11011xxx	mod xxx r/m	
LOCK = Bus Lock Prefix	11110000		

*The v, w, d, s and z bits and the mod, reg, r/m fields are discussed in the addressing modes' section.

Fig. 2.4 *8086/8088 Instruction Set Summary*

LEA: Load Effective Address The load effective address instruction loads the effective address formed by destination operand into the specified source register. This instruction is more useful for assembly language rather than for machine language. The examples are given below.

Example 2.23

```
LEA BX,ADR      ; Effective address of Label ADR i.e. offset of ADR will be
                  transferred to Reg : BX.
LEA SI, ADR[Bx]; offsetofLabelADRwillbeaddedtocontentofBxtoformeffective
                ; address and it will be loaded in SI
```

LDS/LES: Load Pointer to DS/ES This instruction loads the DS or ES register and the specified destination register in the instruction with the content of memory location specified as source in the instruction. The example in Fig. 2.5 explains the operation.

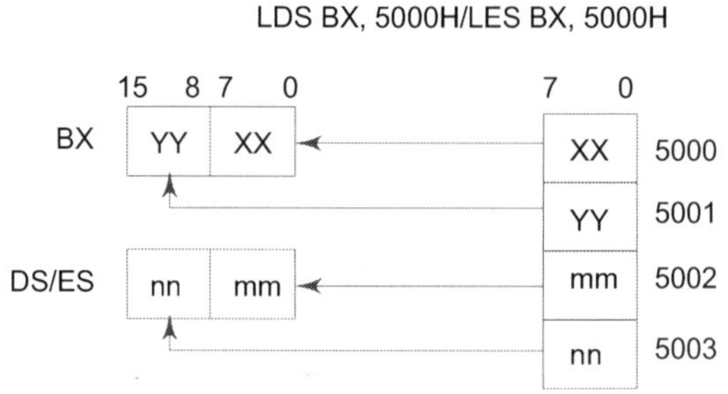

Fig. 2.5 *LDS/LES Instruction Execution*

LAHF : Load AH from Lower Byte of Flag This instruction loads the AH register with the lower byte of the flag register. This command may be used to observe the status of all the condition code flags (except over flow) at a time.

SAHF: Store AH to Lower Byte of Flag Register This instruction sets or resets the condition code flags (except overflow) in the lower byte of the flag register depending upon the corresponding bit positions in AH. If a bit in AH is 1, the flag corresponding to the bit position is set, else it is reset.

PUSHF: Push Flags to Stack The push flag instruction pushes the flag register on to the stack; first the upper byte and then the lower byte is pushed on to it. The SP is decremented by 2, for each push operation. The general operation of this instruction is similar to the PUSH operation.

POPF: Pop Flags from Stack The pop flags instruction loads the flag register completely (both bytes) from the word contents of the memory location currently addressed by SP and SS. The SP is incremented by 2 for each pop operation.

Figure 2.4 shows the data sheet for the hand coding of all the 8086 instructions. The MOD and R/M fields are to be decided as already described in this chapter. This type of instructions do not affect any flags.

2.3.2 Arithmetic Instructions

These instructions perform the arithmetic operations, like addition, subtraction, multiplication and division along with the respective ASCII and decimal adjust instructions. The increment and decrement operations also belong to this type of instructions. The 8086/8088 instructions falling under this category are discussed below in significant details. The arithmetic instructions affect all the condition code flags. The operands are either the registers or memory locations or immediate data depending upon the addressing mode.

ADD: Add This instruction adds an immediate data or contents of a memory location specified in the instruction or a register (source) to the contents of another register (destination) or memory location. The result is in the destination operand. However, both the source and destination operands cannot be memory operands. That means memory to memory addition is not possible. Also the contents of the segment registers cannot be added using this instruction. All the condition code flags are affected, depending upon the result. The examples of this instruction are given along with the corresponding modes.

Example 2.24

```
1.ADD AX, 0100H          Immediate
2.ADD AX, BX             Register
3.ADD AX, [SI]           Register indirect
4.ADD AX, [5000H]        Direct
5.ADD [5000H], 0100H     Immediate
6.ADD 0100H              Destination AX (implicit)
```

ADC: Add with Carry This instruction performs the same operation as ADD instruction, but adds the carry flag bit (which may be set as a result of the previous calculations) to the result. All the condition code flags are affected by this instruction. The examples of this instruction along with the modes are as follows:

Example 2.25

```
1.ADC 0100H               Immediate (AX implicit)
2.ADC AX, BX              Register
3.ADC AX, [SI]            Register indirect
4.ADC AX, [5000H]         Direct
5.ADC [5000H], 0100H      Immediate
```

INC: Increment This instruction increases the contents of the specified register or memory location by 1. All the condition code flags are affected except the carry flag CF. This instruction adds 1 to the contents of the operand. Immediate data cannot be operand of this instruction. The examples of this instruction are as follows:

Example 2.26

```
1. INC    AX       Register
2. INC    [BX]     Register indirect
3. INC    [5000H]  Direct
```

DEC: Decrement The decrement instruction subtracts 1 from the contents of the specified register or memory location. All the condition code flags, except the carry flag, are affected depending upon the result. Immediate data cannot be operand of the instruction. The examples of this instruction are as follows:

Example 2.27

```
1.DEC     AX        Register
2.DEC     [5000H]   Direct
```

SUB: Subtract The subtract instruction subtracts the source operand from the destination operand and the result is left in the destination operand. Source operand may be a register, memory location or immediate data and the destination operand may be a register or a memory location, but source and destination operands both must not be memory operands. Destination operand can not be an immediate data. All the condition code flags are affected by this instruction. The examples of this instruction along with the addressing modes are as follows:

Example 2.28

```
1.SUB     AX, 0100H       Immediate [destination AX]
2.SUB     AX, BX          Register
3.SUB     AX, [5000H]     Direct
4.SUB     [5000H], 0100   Immediate
```

SBB: Subtract with Borrow The subtract with borrow instruction subtracts the source operand and the borrow flag (CF) which may reflect the result of the previous calculations, from the destination operand. Subtraction with borrow, here means subtracting 1 from the subtraction obtained by SUB, if carry (borrow) flag is set.

The result is stored in the destination operand. All the flags are affected (Condition code) by this instruction. The examples of this instruction are as follows:

Example 2.29

```
1.SBB    AX, 0100H       Immediate [destination AX]
2.SBB    AX, BX          Register
3.SBB    AX, [5000H]     Direct
4.SBB    [5000H], 0100   Immediate
```

CMP: Compare This instruction compares the source operand, which may be a register or an immediate data or a memory location, with a destination operand that may be a register or a memory location.

For comparison, it subtracts the source operand from the destination operand but does not store the result anywhere. The flags are affected depending upon the result of the subtraction. If both of the operands are equal, zero flag is set. If the source operand is greater than the destination operand, carry flag is set or else, carry flag is reset. The examples of this instruction are as follows:

Example 2.30

```
1.CMP BX, 0100H            Immediate
2.CMP AX, 0100H            Immediate
3.CMP [5000H], 0100H       Direct
4.CMP BX, [SI]             Register indirect
5.CMP BX, CX               Register
```

AAA: ASCII Adjust After Addition The AAA instruction is executed after an ADD instruction that adds two ASCII coded operands to give a byte of result in AL. The AAA instruction converts the resulting contents of AL to unpacked decimal digits. After the addition, the AAA instruction examines the lower 4 bits of AL to check whether it contains a valid BCD number in the range 0 to 9. If it is between 0 to 9 and AF is zero, AAA sets the 4 high order bits of AL to 0. The AH must be cleared before addition. If the lower digit of AL is between 0 to 9 and AF is set, 06 is added to AL.The upper 4 bits of AL are cleared and AH is incremented by one. If the value in the lower nibble of AL is greater than 9 then the AL is incremented by 06, AH is incremented by 1, the AF and CF flags are set to 1, and the higher 4 bits of AL are cleared to 0. The remaining flags are unaffected. The AH is modified as sum of previous contents (usually 00) and the carry from the adjustment, as shown in Fig. 2.6. This instruction does not give exact ASCII codes of the sum, but they can be obtained by adding 3030H to AX.

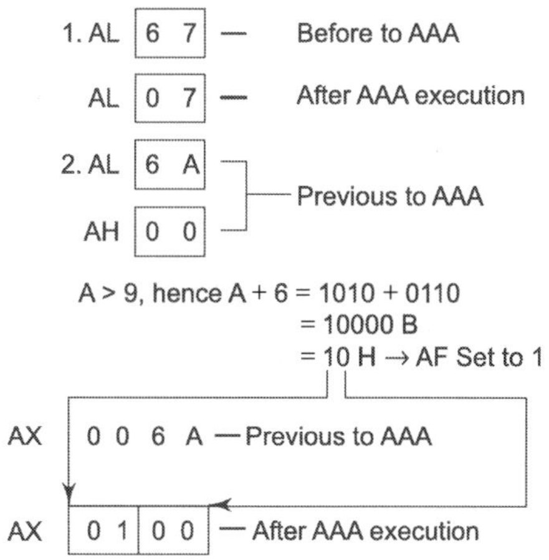

Fig. 2.6 *ASCII Adjust after Addition Instruction*

AAS: ASCII Adjust AL after Subtraction AAS instruction corrects the result in AL register after subtracting two unpacked ASCII operands. The result is in unpacked decimal format. If the lower 4 bits of AL register are greater than 9 or if the AF flag is 1, the AL is decremented by 6 and AH register is decremented by 1, the CF and AF are set to 1. Otherwise, the CF and AF are set to 0, the result needs no correction. As a result, the upper nibble of AL is 00 and the lower nibble may be any number from 0 to 9. The procedure is similar to the AAA instruction except for the subtraction of 06 from AL. AH is modified as difference of the previous contents (usually zero) of AH and the borrow for adjustment.

AAM : ASCII Adjust after Multiplication This instruction, after execution, converts the product available in AL into unpacked BCD format. The AAM—ASCII Adjust After Multiplication—instruction follows a multiplication instruction that multiplies two unpacked BCD operands, i.e. higher nibbles of the multiplication operands should be O. The multiplication of such operands is carried out using MUl instruction. Obviously the result of multiplication is available in AX. The following AAM instruction replaces content of AH by tens of the decimal multiplication and AL by singles of the decimal multiplication.

Example 2.31

```
MOV AL, 04  ;  AL ← 04
MOV BL, 09  ;  BL ← 09
MUL BL      ;  AH-AL ← 24H (9×4)
AAM         ;  AH ← 03
            ;  AL ← 06
```

AAD: ASCII Adjust before Division Though the names of these two instructions (AAM and AAD) appear to be similar, there is a lot of difference between their functions. The AAD instruction converts two unpacked BCD digits in AH and AL to the equivalent binary number in AL. This adjustment must be made before dividing the two unpacked BCD digits in AX by an unpacked BCD byte. PF, SF, ZF are modified while AF, CF, OF are undefined, after the execution of the instruction AAD. The example explains the execution of the instruction. In the instruction sequence, this instruction appears before DIV instruction unlike AAM appears after MUL. Let AX contains 0508 unpacked BCD for 58 decimal, and DH contains 02H.

Example 2.32

```
AX |05|08|
AAD result in AL |00 | 3A|    58D = 3A H in AL
```

The result of AAD execution will give the hexadecimal number 3A in AL and 00 in AH. Note that 3A is the hexadecimal equivalent of 58 (decimal). Now, instruction DIV DH may be executed. So rather than ASCII adjust for division, it is ASCII adjust before division. All the ASCII adjust instructions are also called as unpacked BCD arithmetic instructions. Now, we will consider the two instructions related to packed BCD arithmetic.

DAA: Decimal Adjust Accumulator This instruction is used to convert the result of the addition of two packed BCD numbers to a valid BCD number. The result has to be only in AL. If the lower nibble is greater than 9, after addition or if AF is set, it will add 06 to the lower nibble in AL. After adding 06 in the lower nibble of AL, if the upper nibble of AL is greater than 9 or if carry flag is set, DAA instruction adds 60H to AL. The examples given below explain the instruction.

Example 2.33

```
(i) AL = 53        CL = 29
    ADD AL, CL     ; AL ← (AL) + (CL)
                   ; AL ← 53 + 29
                   ; AL ← 7C
    DAA            ; AL ← 7C + 06 (as C>9)
                   ; AL ← 82
```

```
(ii) AL = 73        CL = 29
     ADD AL, CL     ; AL ← AL + CL
                    ; AL ← 73 + 29
                    ; AL ← 9C
     DAA            ; AL ← 02 and CF = 1
                      AL = 7 3
                         +
                    CL = 2 9
                    ---------
                         9 C
                       + 6
                    ---------
                         A 2
                       + 6 0
                    ---------
                     CF = 1  0 2  in AL
```

The instruction DAA affects AF, CF, PF, and ZF flags. The OF is undefined.

DAS: Decimal Adjust after Subtraction This instruction converts the result of subtraction of two packed BCD numbers to a valid BCD number. The subtraction has to be in AL only. If the lower nibble of AL is greater than 9, this instruction will subtract 06 from lower nibble of AL. If the result of subtraction sets the carry flag or if upper nibble is greater than 9, it subtracts 60H from AL. This instruction modifies the AF, CF, SF, PF and ZF flags. The OF is undefined after DAS instruction. The examples are as follows:

Example 2.34

```
(i) AL = 75         BH = 46
    SUB AL, BH      ; AL ← 2 F = (AL) - (BH)
                    ; AF = 1
    DAS             ; AL ← 2 9 (as F > 9, F - 6 = 9)
(ii) AL = 38        CH = 6 1
    SUB AL, CH      ; AL ← D 7  CF = 1 (borrow)
    DAS             ; AL ← 7 7  (as D > 9, D - 6 = 7)
                    ; CF = 1 (borrow)
```

DAA and DAS instructions are also called packed BCD arithmetic instructions.

NEG: Negate The negate instruction forms 2's complement of the specified destination in the instruction. For obtaining 2's complement, it subtracts the contents of destination from zero. The result is stored back in the destination operand which may be a register or a memory location. If OF is set, it indicates that the operation could not be completed successfully. This instruction affects all the condition code flags.

MUL: Unsigned Multiplication Byte or Word This instruction multiplies an unsigned byte or word by the contents of AL. The unsigned byte or word may be in any one of the general purpose registers or memory locations. The most significant word of the result is stored in DX, while the least significant word of the result is stored in AX. All the flags are modified depending upon the result. The example instructions are as shown. Immediate operand is not allowed in this instruction. If the most significant byte or word of the result is '0' CF and OF both will be set.

Example 2.35

```
1. MUL BH               ; (AX) ← (AL) × (BH)
2. MUL CX               ; (DX) (AX) ← (AX) × (CX)
3. MUL WORD PTR [SI]    ; (DX) (AX) ← (AX) × ([SI])
```

IMUL: Signed Multiplication This instruction multiplies a signed byte in source operand by a signed byte in AL or a signed word in source operand by a signed word in AX. The source can be a general purpose register, memory operand, index register or base register, but it cannot be an immediate data. In case of 32-bit results, the higher order word (MSW) is stored in DX and the lower order word is stored in AX. The AF, PF, SF, and ZF flags are undefined after IMUL. If AH and DX contain parts of 16 and 32-bit result respectively, CF and OF both will be set. The AL and AX are the implicit operands in case of 8 bits and 16 bits multiplications respectively. The unused higher bits of the result are filled by sign bit and CF, AF are cleared. The example instructions are given as follows:

Example 2.36

```
1.IMUL    BH
2.IMUL    CX
3.IMUL    [SI]
```

CBW: Convert Signed Byte to Word This instruction converts a signed byte to a signed word. In other words, it copies the sign bit of a byte to be converted to all the bits in the higher byte of the result word. The byte to be converted must be in AL. The result will be in AX. It does not affect any flag.

CWD: Convert Signed Word to Double Word This instruction copies the sign bit of AX to all the bits of the DX register. This operation is to be done before signed division. It does not affect any flag.

DIV: Unsigned Division This instruction performs unsigned division. It divides an unsigned word or double word by a 16-bit or 8-bit operand. The dividend must be in AX for 16-bit operation and divisor may be specified using any one of the addressing modes except immediate. The result will be in AL (quotient) while AH will contain the remainder. If the result is too big to fit in AL, type 0 (divide by zero) and an interrupt is generated. In case of a double word dividend (32-bit), the higher word should be in DX and lower word should be in AX. The divisor may be specified as already explained. The quotient and the remainder, in this case, will be in AX and DX respectively. This instruction does not affect any flag.

IDIV: Signed Division This instruction performs the same operation as the DIV instruction, but with signed operands. The results are stored similarly as in case of DIV instruction in both cases of word and double word divisions. The results will also be signed numbers. The operands are also specified in the same way as DIV instruction. Divide by 0 interrupt is generated, if the result is too big to fit in AX (16-bit dividend operation) or AX and DX (32-bit dividend operation). All the flags are undefined after IDIV instruction.

2.3.3 Logical Instructions

These type of instructions are used for carrying out the bit by bit shift, rotate, or basic logical operations. All the condition code flags are affected depending upon the result. Basic logical operations available with 8086 instruction set are AND, OR, NOT, and XOR. The instruction for each of these operations are discussed as follows.

AND: Logical AND This instruction bit by bit ANDs the source operand that may be an immediate, a register or a memory location to the destination operand that may be a register or a memory location. The result is stored in the destination operand. At least one of the operands should be a register or a memory operand. Both the operands cannot be memory locations or immediate operands. An immediate operand cannot be a destination operand. The examples of this instruction are as follows:

Example 2.37

```
1.AND AX, 0008H
2.AND AX, BX
3.AND AX, [5000H]
4.AND [5000H], DX
```

If the content of AX is 3F0FH, the first example instruction will carry out the operation as given below. The result 3F9FH will be stored in the AX register.

```
 0 0 1 1    1 1 1 1    0 0 0 0    1 1 1 1   = 3F0F H [AX]
 ↓ ↓ ↓ ↓    ↓ ↓ ↓ ↓    ↓ ↓ ↓ ↓    ↓ ↓ ↓ ↓     AND
 0 0 0 0    0 0 0 0    0 0 0 0    1 0 0 0   = 0008 H
--------------------------------------------------------
 0 0 0 0    0 0 0 0    0 0 0 0    1 0 0 0   = 0008 H [AX]
```

The result 0008H will be in AX.

OR: Logical OR The OR instruction carries out the OR operation in the same way as described in case of the AND operation. The limitations on source and destination operands are also the same as in case of AND operation. The examples are as follows:

Example 2.38

```
1.OR AX, 0098H
2.OR AX, BX
3.OR AX, [5000H]
4.OR [5000H], 0008H
```

The contents of AX are say 3F0FH, then the first example instruction will be carried out as given below.

```
 0 0 1 1    1 1 1 1    0 0 0 0    1 1 1 1   = 3F0F H
 ↓ ↓ ↓ ↓    ↓ ↓ ↓ ↓    ↓ ↓ ↓ ↓    ↓ ↓ ↓ ↓     OR
 0 0 0 0    0 0 0 0    1 0 0 1    1 0 0 0   = 0098 H
--------------------------------------------------------
 0 0 1 1    1 1 1 1    1 0 0 1    1 1 1 1   = 3F9F H
```

Thus the result 3F9FH will be stored in the AX register.

NOT: Logical Invert The NOT instruction complements (inverts) the contents of an operand register or a memory location, bit by bit. The examples are as follows:

Example 2.39

```
NOT AX
NOT [5000H]
```

If the content of AX is 200FH, the first example instruction will be executed as shown.

```
   AX    = 0 0 1 0    0 0 0 0    0 0 0 0    1 1 1 1
 invert    ↓ ↓ ↓ ↓    ↓ ↓ ↓ ↓    ↓ ↓ ↓ ↓    ↓ ↓ ↓ ↓
           1 1 0 1    1 1 1 1    1 1 1 1    0 0 0 0
```

```
Result
in AX =        D              F              F              0
```

The result DFF0H will be stored in the destination register AX.

XOR: Logical Exclusive OR The XOR operation is again carried out in a similar way to the AND and OR operation. The constraints on the operands are also similar. The XOR operation gives a high output, when the 2 input bits are dissimilar. Otherwise, the output is zero. The example instructions are as follows:

Example 2.40

```
1.XOR    AX, 0098H
2.XOR    AX, BX
3.XOR    AX, [5000H]
```

If the content of AX is 3F0FH, then the first example instruction will be executed as explained. The result 3F97H will be stored in AX.

```
 AX = 3F0FH =      0 0 1 1     1 1 1 1     0 0 0 0     1 1 1 1
         XOR       ↓ ↓ ↓ ↓     ↓ ↓ ↓ ↓     ↓ ↓ ↓ ↓     ↓ ↓ ↓ ↓
       0098H =     0 0 0 0     0 0 0 0     1 0 0 1     1 0 0 0
AX = Result =      0 0 1 1     1 1 1 1     1 0 0 1     0 1 1 1
             = 3F97H
```

TEST: Logical Compare Instruction The TEST instruction performs a bit by bit logical AND operation on the two operands. Each bit of the result is then set to 1, if the corresponding bits of both operands are 1, else the result bit is reset to 0. The result of this ANDing operation is not available for further use, but flags are affected. The affected flags are OF, CF, SF, ZF and PF. The operands may be registers, memory or immediate data. The examples of this instruction are as follows:

Example 2.41

```
1.TEST    AX, BX
2.TEST    [0500], 06H
3.TEST    [BX] [DI], CX
```

SHL/SAL: Shift Logical/Arithmetic Left These instructions shift the operand word or byte bit by bit to the left and insert zeros in the newly introduced least significant bits. In case of all the SHIFT and ROTATE instructions, the count is either 1 or specified by register CL. The operand may reside in a register or a memory location but cannot be an immediate data. All flags are affected depending upon the result. Figure 2.7 explains the execution of this instruction. It is to be noted here that the shift operation is through carry flag.

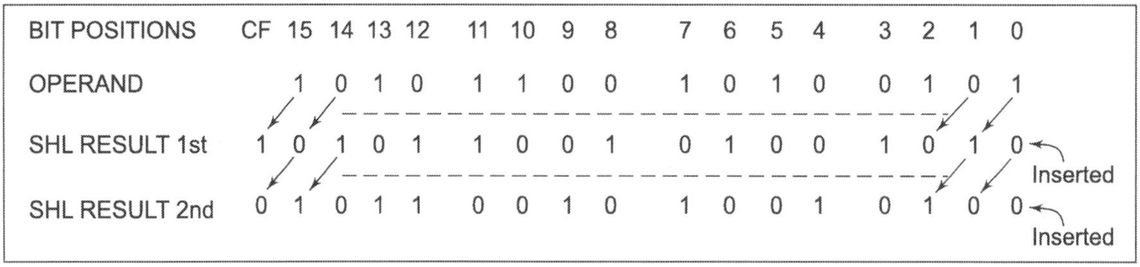

Fig. 2.7 *Execution of SHL/SAL Instruction*

SHR: Shift Logical Right This instruction performs bit-wise right shifts on the operand word or byte that may reside in a register or a memory location, by the specified count in the instruction and inserts zeros in the shifted positions. The result is stored in the destination operand. Figure 2.8 explains execution of this instruction. This instruction shifts the operand through the carry flag.

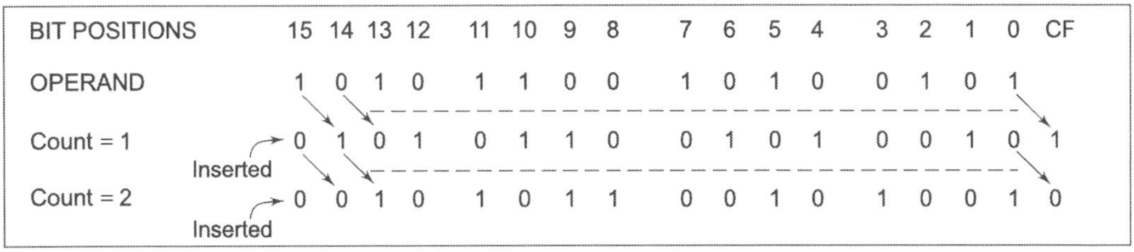

Fig. 2.8 *Execution of SHR Instruction*

SAR: Shift Arithmetic Right This instruction performs right shifts on the operand word or byte, that may be a register or a memory location by the specified count in the instruction. It inserts the most significant bit of the operand in the newly inserted positions. The result is stored in the destination operand. Figure 2.9 explains execution of the instruction. All the condition code flags are affected. This shift operation shifts the operand through the carry flag.

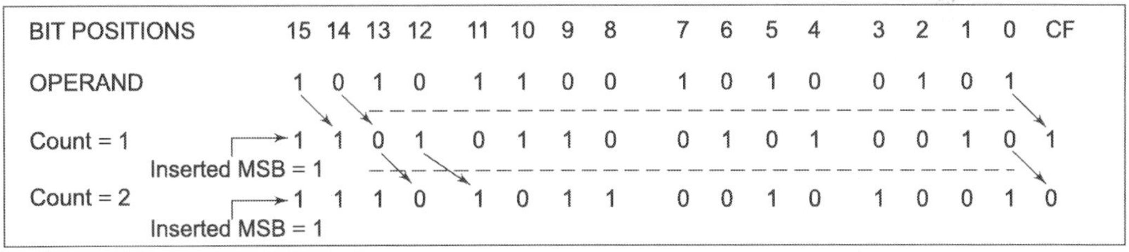

Fig. 2.9 *Execution of SAR Instruction*

Immediate operand is not allowed in any of the shift instructions.

ROR: Rotate Right without Carry This instruction rotates the contents of the destination operand to the right (bit-wise) either by one or by the count specified in CL, excluding carry. The least significant bit is pushed into the carry flag and simultaneously it is transferred into the most significant bit position at each operation. The remaining bits are shifted right by the specified positions. The PF, SF, and ZF flags are left unchanged by the rotate operation. The operand may be a register or a memory location but it cannot be an immediate operand. Figure 2.10 explains the operation. The destination operand may be a register (except a segment register) or a memory location.

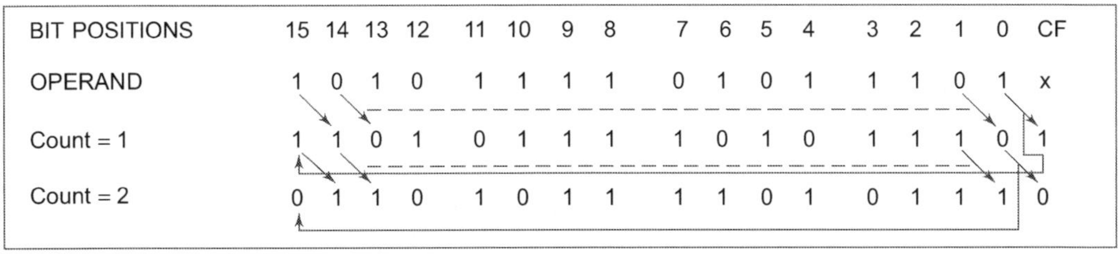

Fig. 2.10 *Execution of ROR Instruction*

ROL: Rotate Left without Carry This instruction rotates the content of the destination operand to the left by the specified count (bit-wise) excluding carry. The most significant bit is pushed into the carry flag as well as the least significant bit position at each operation. The remaining bits are shifted left subsequently by the specified count positions. The PF, SF, and ZF flags are left unchanged in this rotate operation. The operand may be a register or a memory location. Figure 2.11 explains the operation.

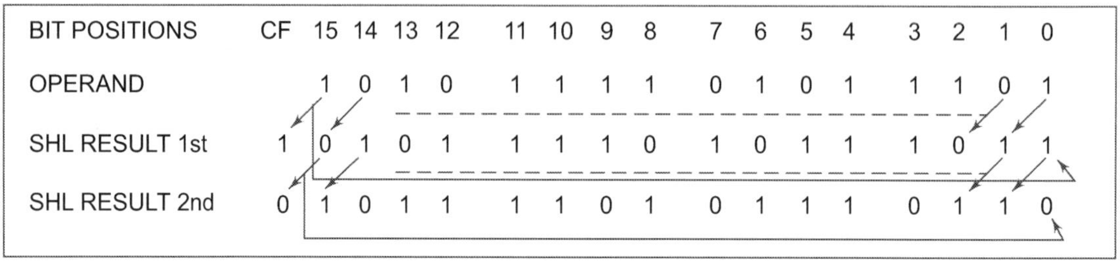

Fig. 2.11 *Execution of ROL Instruction*

RCR: Rotate Right through Carry This instruction rotates the contents (bit-wise) of the destination operand right by the specified count through carry flag (CF). For each operation, the carry flag is pushed into the MSB of the operand, and the LSB is pushed into carry flag. The remaining bits are shifted right by the specified count positions. The SF, PF, ZF are left unchanged. The operand may be a register or a memory location. Figure 2.12 explains the operation.

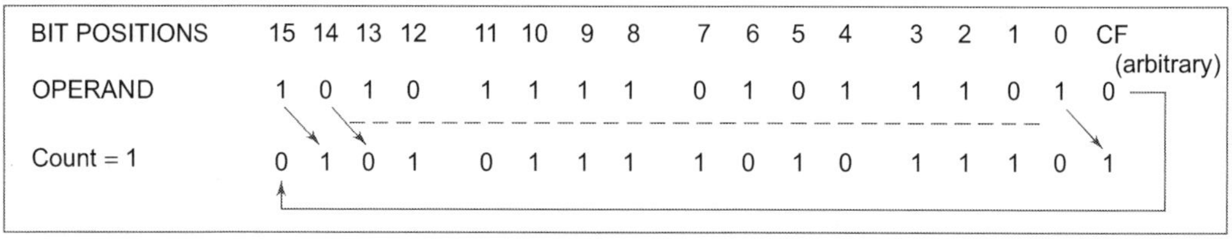

Fig. 2.12 *Execution of RCR Instruction*

RCL: Rotate Left through Carry This instruction rotates (bit-wise) the contents of the destination operand left by the specified count through the carry flag (CF). For each operation, the carry flag is pushed into LSB and the MSB of the operand is pushed into carry flag. The remaining bits are shifted left by the specified positions. The SF, PF, ZF are left unchanged. The operand may be a register or a memory location. Figure 2.13 explains the operation.

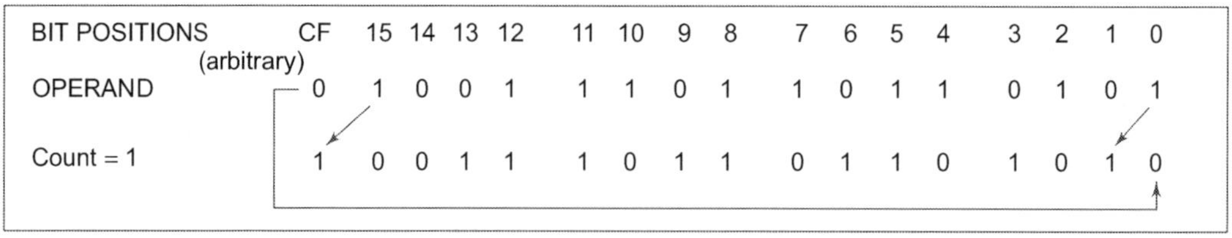

Fig. 2.13 *Execution of RCL Instruction*

The count for rotation or shifting is either 1 or is specified using register CL, in case of all the shift and rotate instructions.

2.3.4 String Manipulation Instructions

A series of data bytes or words available in memory at consecutive locations, to be referred to collectively or individually, are called as *byte strings* or *word strings*. For example, a string of characters may be located in consecutive memory locations, where each character may be represented by its ASCII equivalent. For referring to a string, two parameters are required, (a) starting or end address of the string and (b) length of the string. The length of a string is usually stored as count in the CX register. In case of 8085, similar structures can be set up by the pointer and counter arrangements which may be modified at each iteration, till the required condition for proceeding further is satisfied. On the other hand, the 8086 supports a set of more powerful instructions for string manipulations. The incrementing or decrementing of the pointer, in case of 8086 string instructions, depends upon the Direction Flag (DF) status. If it is a byte string operation, the index registers are updated by one. On the other hand, if it is a word string operation, the index registers are updated by two. The counter in both the cases, is decremented by one.

REP: Repeat Instruction Prefix This instruction is used as a prefix to other instructions. The instruction to which the REP prefix is provided, is executed repeatedly until the CX register becomes zero (at each iteration CX is automatically decremented by one). When CX becomes zero, the execution proceeds to the next instruction in sequence. There are two more options of the REP instruction. The first is REPE/REPZ, i.e. repeat operation while equal/zero. The second is REPNE/REPNZ allows for repeating the operation while not equal/not zero. These options are used for CMPS, SCAS instructions only, as instruction prefixes.

MOVSB/MOVSW: Move String Byte or String Word Suppose a string of bytes stored in a set of consecutive memory locations is to be moved to another set of destination locations. The starting byte of the source string is located in the memory location whose address may be computed using SI (Source Index) and DS (Data Segment) contents. The starting address of the destination locations where this string has to be relocated is given by DI (Destination Index) and ES (Extra Segment) contents. The starting address of the source string is 10H*DS+[SI], while the starting address of the destination string is 10H*ES+[DI]. The MOVSB/MOVSW instruction thus, moves a string of bytes/words pointed to by DS: SI pair (source) to the memory location pointed to by ES: DI pair (destination). The REP instruction prefix is used with MOVS instruction to repeat it by a value given in the counter (CX). The length of the byte string or word string must be stored in CX register. No flags are affected by this instruction.

After the MOVS instruction is executed once, the index registers are automatically updated and CX is decremented. The incrementing or decrementing of the pointers, i.e. SI and DI depend upon the direction flag DF. If DF is 0, the index registers are incremented, otherwise, they are decremented, in case of all the string manipulation instructions. The following string of instructions explain the execution of the MOVS instruction.

Example 2.42

```
MOV AX, 5000H    ; Source segment address is 5000h
MOV DS, AX       ; Load it to DS
MOV AX, 6000H    ; Destination segment address is 6000h
MOV ES, AX       ; Load it to ES
MOV CX, 0FFH     ; Move length of the string to counter register CX
MOV SI, 1000H    ; Source index address 1000H is moved to SI
MOV DI, 2000H    ; Destination index address 2000H is moved to DI
CLD              ; Clear DF, i.e. set autoincrement mode
REP MOVSB        ; Move 0FFH string bytes from source address to destination
```

CMPS: Compare String Byte or String Word The CMPS instruction can be used to compare two strings of bytes or words. The length of the string must be stored in the register CX. If both the byte or word strings are equal, zero flag is set. The flags are affected in the same way as CMP instruction. The DS:SI and ES:DI point to the two strings.The REP instruction prefix is used to repeat the operation till CX(counter) becomes zero or the condition specified by the REP prefix is false.

The following string of instructions explain the instruction. The comparison of the string starts from initial byte or word of the string, after each comparison the index registers are updated depending upon the direction flag and the counter is decremented. This byte by byte or word by word comparison continues till a mismatch is found. When, a mismatch is found, the carry and zero flags are modified appropriately and the execution proceeds further.

Example 2.43

```
MOV AX, SEG1              ; Segment address of STRING1, i.e. SEG1 is moved
                            to AX
MOV DS, AX                ; Load it to DS
MOV AX, SEG2              ; Segment address of STRING2, i.e. SEG2 is moved
                            to AX
MOV ES, AX                ; Load it to ES
MOV SI, OFFSET STRING1    ; Offset of STRING1 is moved to SI
MOV DI, OFFSET STRING2    ; Offset of STRING2 is moved to DI
MOV CX, 010H              ; Length of the string is moved to CX
CLD                       ; Clear DF, i.e. set autoincrement mode
REPE CMPSW                ; Compare 010H words of STRING1 and
                          ; STRING2, while they are equal, If a mismatch is found,
                          ; modify the flags and proceed with further execution
```

If both strings are completely equal, i.e. CX becomes zero, the ZF is set, otherwise, ZF is reset.

SCAS: Scan String Byte or String Word This instruction scans a string of bytes or words for an operand byte or word specified in the register AL or AX. The string is pointed to by ES:DI register pair. The length of the string is stored in CX. The DF controls the mode for scanning of the string, as stated in case of MOVSB instruction. Whenever a match to the specified operand, is found in the string, execution stops and the zero flag is set. If no match is found, the zero flag is reset. The REPNE prefix is used with the SCAS instruction. The pointers and counters are updated automatically, till a match is found. The following string of instructions elaborates the use of SCAS instruction.

Example 2.44

```
  MOV AX,SEG     ; Segment address of the string, i.e. SEG is moved to AX
  MOV ES,AX      ; Load it to ES
  MOV DI,OFFSET  ; String offset, i.e. OFFSET is moved to DI
  MOV CX,010H    ; Length of the string is moved to CX
  MOV AX,WORD    ; The word to be scanned for, i.e. WORD is in AL
  CLD            ; Clear DF
REPNE SCASW      ; Scan the 010H bytes of the string, till a match to
                 ; WORD is found
```

This string of instructions finds out, if it contains WORD. If the WORD is found in the word string, before CX becomes zero, the ZF is set, otherwise the ZF is reset. The scanning will continue till a match is found. Once a match is found the execution of the programme proceeds further.

LODS: Load String Byte or String Word The LODS instruction loads the AL/AX register by the content of a string pointed to by DS:SI register pair. The SI is modified automatically depending upon DF. The DF plays exactly the same role as in case of MOVSB/MOVSW instruction. If it is a byte transfer(LODSB), the SI is modified by one and if it is a word transfer(LODSW), the SI is modified by two. No other flags are affected by this instruction.

STOS: Store String Byte or String Word The STOS instruction stores the AL/AX register contents to a location in the string pointed by ES: DI register pair. The DI is modified accordingly. No flags are affected by this instruction.

The direction flag controls the string instruction execution. The source index SI and destination index DI are modified after each iteration automatically. If DF = 1, then the execution follows autodecrement mode. In this mode, SI and DI are decremented automatically after each iteration (by 1 or 2 depending upon byte or word operations). Hence, in autodecrementing mode, the strings are referred to by their ending addresses. If DF = 0, then the execution follows autoincrement mode. In this mode, SI and DI are incremented automatically (by 1 or 2 depending upon byte or word operation) after each iteration, hence the strings, in this case, are referred to by their starting addresses. Chapter 3 on assembly language programming explains the use of some of these instructions in assembly language programs.

2.3.5 Control Transfer or Branching Instructions

The control transfer instructions transfer the flow of execution of the program to a new address specified in the instruction directly or indirectly. When this type of instruction is executed, the CS and IP registers get loaded with new values of CS and IP corresponding to the location where the flow of execution is going to be transferred. Depending upon the addressing modes specified in Chapter 1, the CS may or may not be modified. This type of instructions are classified in two types:

Unconditional Control Transfer (Branch) Instructions In case of unconditional control transfer instructions, the execution control is transferred to the specified location independent of any status or condition. The CS and IP are unconditionally modified to the new CS and IP.

Conditional Control Transfer (Branch) Instructions In the conditional control transfer instructions, the control is transferred to the specified location provided the result of the previous operation satisfies a particular condition, otherwise, the execution continues in normal flow sequence. The results of the previous operations are replicated by condition code flags. In other words, using this type of instruction the control will be transferred to a particular specified location, if a particular flag satisfies the condition.

2.3.6 Unconditional Branch Instructions

CALL: Unconditional Call This instruction is used to call a subroutine from a main program. In case of assembly language programming, the term procedure is used interchangeably with subroutine. The address of the procedure may be specified directly or indirectly depending upon the addressing mode. There are again two types of procedures depending upon whether it is available in the same segment (Near CALL, i.e. ±32K displacement) or in another segment (FAR CALL, i.e. anywhere outside the segment). The modes for them are called as intrasegment and intersegment addressing modes respectively. This instruction comes under unconditional branch instructions and can be described as shown with the coding formats. On execution, this instruction stores the incremented IP (i.e. address of the next instruction) and CS onto the stack and loads the CS and IP registers, respectively, with the segment and offset addresses of the procedure to be called. In case of NEAR CALL it pushes only IP register and in case of FAR CALL it pushes IP and CS both onto the stack. The NEAR and FAR CALLS are discriminated using opcode.

Direct Near

D_7 … D_0	D_7 … D_0	D_7 D_1 D_0
OPCODE	DISP.LB	DISP.HB

Indirect Near

D_7 … D_0	D_7 … D_0		D_7 D_6	D_5	D_4	D_3	D_2 D_1 D_0
OPCODE	OPCODE	→	MOD	0	1	0	r/m

Direct Far

D_7 … D_0	D_7 D_0	D_7 D_0	D_7 D_0	D_7 D_0
OPCODE	LB	HB	LB	HB
	OFFSET		SEGMENT	

Indirect Far

D_7 … D_0	D_7 … D_0		D_7 D_6	D_5	D_4	D_3	D_2 D_1 D_0
OPCODE	OPCODE	→	MOD	0	1	0	r/m

RET: Return from the Procedure At each CALL instruction, the IP and CS of the next instruction is pushed onto stack, before the control is transferred to the procedure. At the end of the procedure, the RET instruction must be executed. When it is executed, the previously stored content of IP and CS along with flags are retrieved into the CS, IP and flag registers from the stack and the execution of the main program continues further. The procedure may be a near or a far procedure. In case of a FAR procedure, the current contents of SP points to IP and CS at the time of return. While in case of a NEAR procedure, it points to only IP. Depending upon the type of procedure and the SP contents, the RET instruction is of four types.

1. Return within segment
2. Return within segment adding 16-bit immediate displacement to the SP contents.
3. Return intersegment
4. Return intersegment adding 16-bit immediate displacement to the SP contents.

INT N: Interrupt Type N In the interrupt structure of 8086/8088, 256 interrupts are defined corresponding to the types from 00H to FFH. When an INT N instruction is executed, the TYPE byte N is multiplied by 4 and the contents of IP and CS of the interrupt service routine will be taken from the hexadecimal multiplication (N´4) as offset address and 0000 as segment address. In other words, the multiplication of type N by 4 (offset) points to a memory block in 0000 segment, which contains the IP and CS values of the interrupt service routine. For the execution of this instruction, the IF must be enabled.

Example 2.45

Thus the instruction INT 20H will find out the address of the interrupt service routine as follows:

```
INT     20H
Type* 4 = 20 * 4 = 80H
```

Pointer to IP and CS of the ISR is 0000 : 0080 H

Figure 2.14 shows the arrangement of CS and IP addresses of the ISR in the interrupt vector table.

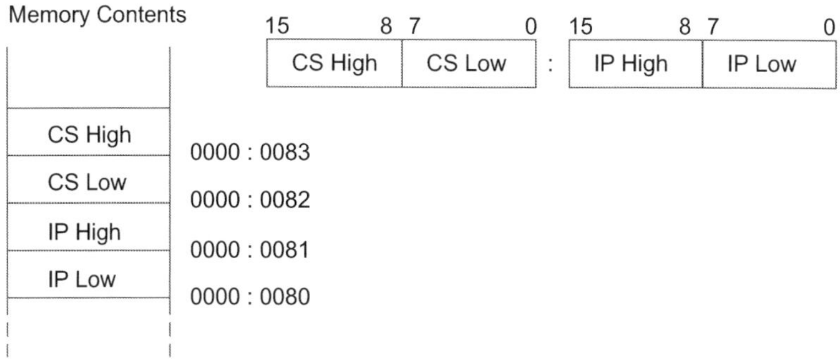

Fig. 2.14 *Contents of IVT*

INTO: Interrupt on Overflow This command is executed, when the overflow flag OF is set. The new contents of IP and CS are taken from the address 0000:0010 as explained in INT type instruction. This is equivalent to a Type 4 interrupt instruction.

JMP: Unconditional Jump This instruction unconditionally transfers the control of execution to the specified address using an 8-bit or 16-bit displacement (intrasegment relative, short or long) or CS: IP (intersegment direct far). No flags are affected by this instruction. Corresponding to the methods of specifying jump addresses, the JUMP instruction may have the following three formats. For other JMP types the reader may refer to the following datasheet.

JUMP DISP 8-bit	Intrasegment, relative, short jump
JUMP | DISP.16-bit (LB) | DISP.16-bit (HB) |	Intrasegment, relative, short jump
JUMP | IP (LB) | IP (HB) | CS (LB) | S (HB) |	Intrasegment, direct, far jump

IRET: Return from ISR When an interrupt service routine is to be called, before transferring control to it, the IP, CS and flag register are stored on to the stack to indicate the location from where the execution is to be continued, after the ISR is executed. So, at the end of each ISR, when IRET is executed, the values of IP, CS and flags are retrieved from the stack to continue the execution of the main program. The stack is modified accordingly.

LOOP: Loop Unconditionally This instruction executes the part of the program from the label or address specified in the instruction up to the loop instruction, CX number of times. The following sequence explains the execution. At each iteration, CX is decremented automatically. In other words, this instruction implements DECREMENT COUNTER and JUMP IF NOT ZERO structure.

Example 2.46

```
        MOV  CX, 0005  ; Number of times in CX
        MOV  BX, OFF7H ; Data to BX
Label : MOV  AX, CODE1
        OR   BX, AX
        AND  DX, AX
        Loop Label
```

The execution proceeds in sequence, after the loop is executed, CX number of times. If CX is already 00H, the execution continues sequentially. No flags are affected by this instruction.

2.3.7 Conditional Branch Instructions

When these instructions are executed, execution control is transferred to the address specified relatively in the instruction, provided the condition implicit in the opcode is satisfied. If not the execution continues sequentially. The conditions, here, means the status of condition code flags. These type of instructions do not affect any flag. The address has to be specified in the instruction relatively in terms of displacement which must lie within –80H to 7FH (or – 128 to 127) bytes from the address of the branch instruction. In other words, only short jumps can be implemented using conditional branch instructions. A label may represent the displacement, if it lies within the above specified range. The different 8086/8088 conditional branch instructions and their operations are listed in Table 2.3.

Table 2.3 *Conditional Branch Instructions*

	Mnemonic	*Displacement*	*Operation*
1.	JZ/JE	Label	Transfer execution control to address 'Label', if ZF=1.
2.	JNZ/JNE	Label	Transfer execution control to address 'Label', if ZF=0.
3.	JS	Label	Transfer execution control to address 'Label', if SF=1.
4.	JNS	Label	Transfer execution control to address 'Label', if SF=0.
5.	JO	Label	Transfer execution control to address 'Label', if OF=1.
6.	JNO	Label	Transfer execution control to address 'Label', if OF=0.
7.	JP/JPE	Label	Transfer execution control to address 'Label', if PF=1.
8.	JNP	Label	Transfer execution control to address 'Label', if PF=0.
9.	JB/JNAE/JC	Label	Transfer execution control to address 'Label', if CF=1.
10.	JNB/JAE/JNC	Label	Transfer execution control to address 'Label', if CF=0.
11.	JBE/JNA	Label	Transfer execution control to address 'Label', if CF=1 or ZF=1.
12.	JNBE/JA	Label	Transfer execution control to address 'Label', if CF=0 or ZF=0.
13.	JL/JNGE	Label	Transfer execution control to address 'Label', if neither SF=1 nor OF=1.
14.	JNL/JGE	Label	Transfer execution control to address 'Label', if neither SF=0 nor OF=0.
15.	JLE/JNC	Label	Transfer execution control to address 'Label', if ZF=1 or neither SF nor OF is 1.
16.	JNLE/JE	Label	Transfer execution control to address 'Label', if ZF=0 or at least any one of SF and OF is 1(Both SF and OF are not 0).

While the remaining instructions can be used for unsigned binary operations, the last four instructions are used in case of decisions based on signed binary number operations. The terms above and below are generally used for unsigned numbers, while the terms less and greater are used for signed numbers. A conditional jump instruction, that does not check status flags for condition testing, is given as follows:

```
JCXZ    'Label'   Transfer execution control
                  to address 'Label', if CX=0.
```

The conditional LOOP instructions are given in Table 2.4 with their meanings. These instructions may be used for implementing structures like DO_WHILE, REPEAT_UNTIL, etc.

Table 2.4 *Conditional Loop Instructions*

Mnemonic	*Displacement*	*Operation*
LOOPZ/LOOPE (Loop while ZF = 1; equal)	Label	Loop through a sequence of instructions from 'Label' while ZF=1 and CX ^{1} 0.
LOOPNZ/LOOPENE (Loop while ZF = 0; not equal)	Label	Loop through a sequence of instructions from 'Label' while ZF=0 and CX ^{1} 0.

These instructions will be clear with programming practice. This topic aims at introducing them to the readers. Of course, examples are quoted wherever possible, but the JUMP and the LOOP instructions require a sequence of instructions for explanations and they will be emphasized more in Chapter 3.

2.3.8 Flag Manipulation and Processor Control Instructions

These instructions control the functioning of the available hardware inside the processor chip. These are categorized into two types; (a) flag manipulation instructions and (b) machine control instructions. *The flag manipulation instructions directly modify some of the flags of 8086. The machine control instructions control the bus usage and execution*. The flag manipulation instructions and their functions are listed in Table 2.5.

Table 2.5 *Flag Manipulation Instructions*

CLC	-	Clear carry flag
CMC	-	Complement carry flag
STC	-	Set carry flag
CLD	-	Clear direction flag
STD	-	Set direction flag
CLI	-	Clear interrupt flag
STI	-	Set interrupt flag

These instructions modify the Carry (CF), Direction (DF) and Interrupt (IF) flags directly. The DF and IF, which may be modified using the flag manipulation instructions, further control the processor operation; like interrupt responses and autoincrement or autodecrement modes. Thus, the respective instructions may also be called machine or processor control instructions. The other flags can be modified using POPF and SAHF instructions, which are termed as data transfer instructions, in this text. No direct instructions, are available for modifying the status flags except carry flag.

The machine control instructions supported by 8086 and 8088 are listed in Table 2.6 along with their functions. They do not require any operand.

Table 2.6 *Machine Control Instructions*

WAIT	-	Wait for Test input pin to go low
HLT	-	Halt the processor
NOP	-	No operation
ESC	-	Escape to external device like NDP (numeric co-processor)
LOCK	-	Bus lock instruction prefix.

As explained in Chapter 1, after executing the HLT instruction, the processor enters the halt state. The two ways to pull it out of the halt state are to reset the processor or to interrupt it. When NOP instruction is executed, the processor does not perform any operation till 4 clock cycles, except for incrementing the IP by one. It then continues with further execution after 4 clock cycles. ESC instruction when executed, frees the bus for an external master like a coprocessor or peripheral devices. The LOCK prefix may appear with another instruction. When it is executed, the bus access is not allowed for another master till the lock prefixed instruction is executed completely. This instruction is used in case of programming for multiprocessor systems. The WAIT instruction when executed, holds the operation of processor with the current status till the logic level on the $\overline{\text{TEST}}$ pin goes low. The processor goes on inserting WAIT states in the instruction cycle, till the $\overline{\text{TEST}}$ pin goes low. Once the $\overline{\text{TEST}}$ pin goes low, it continues further execution.

2.4 ASSEMBLER DIRECTIVES AND OPERATORS

The main advantage of machine language programming is that the memory control is directly in the hands of the programmer enabling him to manage the memory of the system more efficiently. However, there are more disadvantages. The programming, coding and resource management techniques are tedious. As the programmer has to consider all these functions, the chances of human errors are more. To understand the programs one has to have a thorough technical knowledge of the processor architecture and instruction set.

The assembly language programming is simpler as compared to the machine language programming. The instruction mnemonics are directly written in the assembly language programs. The programs are now more readable than that of machine language programs. The advantage that assembly language has over machine language is that now the address values and the constants can be identified by labels. If the labels are clear then certainly the program will become more understandable, and each time the programmer will not have to remember the different constants and the addresses at which they are stored, throughout the programs. Due to this facility, the tedious byte handling and manipulations are got rid of. Similarly, now different logical segments and routines may be assigned with the labels rather than the different addresses. The memory control feature of machine language programming is left unchanged by providing storage define facilities in assembly language programming. The documentation facility which was not possible with machine language programming is now available in assembly language. Readers will get a better glimpse of the different features of assembly language, when we discuss assembly language programming in the next chapter.

An assembler is a program used to convert an assembly language program into the equivalent machine code modules which may further be converted to executable codes. It decides the address of each label and substitutes the values for each of the constants and variables. It then forms the machine code for the mnemonics and data in the assembly language program. While doing these things, the assembler may find out syntax errors.The logical errors or other programming errors are not found out by the assembler. For completing all these tasks, an assembler needs some hints from the programmer, i.e. the required storage for a particular constant or a variable, logical names of the segments, types of the different routines and modules, end of file, etc. These types of hints are given to the assembler using some predefined alphabetical strings called *assembler directives*, which help the assembler to correctly understand the assembly language programs to prepare the codes.

Another type of hint which helps the assembler to assign a particular constant with a label or initialise particular memory locations or labels with constants is an *operator*. In fact, the operators perform the arithmetic and logical tasks unlike directives that just direct the assembler to correctly interpret the program to code it appropriately. The following directives are commonly used in the assembly language programming practice using Microsoft Macro Assembler or Turbo Assembler. The directives and operators are discussed here but their meanings and uses will be more clear in Chapter 3 on assembly language programming techniques.

DB: Define Byte The DB directive is used to reserve byte or bytes of memory locations in the available memory. While preparing the EXE file, this directive directs the assembler to allocate the specified number of memory bytes to the said data type that may be a constant, variable, string, etc. Another option of this directive also initialises the reserved memory bytes with the ASCII codes of the characters specified as a string. The following examples show how the DB directive is used for different purposes.

Example 2.47

```
RANKS   DB 01H, 02H, 03H, 04H
```

This statement directs the assembler to reserve four memory locations for a list named RANKS and initialise them with the above specified four values.

```
MESSAGE DB 'GOOD MORNING'
```

This makes the assembler reserve the number of bytes of memory equal to the number of characters in the string named MESSAGE and initialise those locations by the ASCII equivalent of these characters.

```
VALUE   DB  50H
```

This statement directs the assembler to reserve 50H memory bytes and leave them uninitialised for the variable named VALUE.

DW: Define Word The DW directive serves the same purposes as the DB directive, but it now makes the assembler reserve the number of memory words (16-bit) instead of bytes. Some examples are given to explain this directive.

Example 2.48

```
WORDS   DW  1234H, 4567H, 78ABH, 045CH,
```

This makes the assembler reserve four words in memory (8 bytes), and initialize the words with the specified values in the statements. During initialisation, the lower bytes are stored at the lower memory addresses, while the upper bytes are stored at the higher addresses. Another option of the DW directive is explained with the DUP operator.

```
   WDATA   DW 5 DUP (6666H)
```

This statement reserves five words, i.e. 10-bytes of memory for a word lable WDATA and initialises all the word locations with 6666H.

DQ: Define Quadword This directive is used to direct the assembler to reserve 4 words (8 bytes) of memory for the specified variable and may initialise it with the specified values.

DT: Define Ten Bytes The DT directive directs the assembler to define the specified variable requiring 10-bytes for its storage and initialise the 10-bytes with the specified values. The directive may be used in case of variables facing heavy numerical calculations, generally processed by numerical processors.

ASSUME: Assume Logical Segment Name The ASSUME directive is used to inform the assemble, the names of the logicals segments to be assumed for different segments used in the program. In the assembly language program, each segment is given a name. For example, the code segment may be given the name CODE, data segment may be given the name DATA etc. The statement ASSUME CS : CODE directs the assembler that the machine codes are available in a segment named CODE, and hence the CS register is to be loaded with the address (segment) allotted by the operating system for the label CODE, while loading. Similary, ASSUME DS : DATA indicates to the assembler that the data items related to the program, are available in a logical segment named DATA, and the DS register is to be initialised by the segment address value decided by the operating system for the data segment, while loading. It then considers the segment DATA as a default data segment for each memory operation, related to the data and the segment CODE as a source segment for the machine codes of the program. The ASSUME statement is a must at the starting of each assembly language program, without which a message 'CODE/DATA EMITTED WITHOUT SEGMENT' may be issued by an assembler.

END: END of Program The END directive marks the end of an assembly language program. When the assembler comes across this END directive, it ignores the source lines available later on. Hence, it should be ensured that the END statement should be the last statement in the file and should not appear in between. Also, no useful program statement should lie in the file, after the END statement.

ENDP: END of Procedure In assembly language programming, the subroutines are called procedures. They may be independent program modules which return particular results or values to the calling programs. The ENDP directive is used to indicate the end of a procedure. A procedure is usually assigned a name, i.e. label. To mark the end of a particular procedure, the name of the procedure, i.e. label may appear as a prefix with the directive ENDP. The statements, appearing in the same module but after the ENDP directive, are neglected from that procedure. The structure given below explains the use of ENDP.

```
PROCEDURE STAR
      :
   STAR ENDP
```

ENDS: END of Segment This directive marks the end of a logical segment. The logical segments are assigned with the names using the ASSUME directive. The names appear with the ENDS directive as prefixes to mark the end of those particular segments. Whatever are the contents of the segments, they should appear in the program before ENDS. Any statement appearing after ENDS will be neglected from the segment. The structure shown below explains the fact more clearly.

```
DATA        SEGMENT
               :
DATA        ENDS
ASSUME      CS : CODE, DS : DATA
CODE        SEGMENT
               :
CODE        ENDS
END
```

The above structure represents a simple program containing two segments named DATA and CODE. The data related to the program must lie between the DATA SEGMENT and DATA ENDS statements. Similary, all the executable instructions must lie between CODE SEGMENT and CODE ENDS statements.

EVEN: Align on Even Memory Address The assembler, while starting the assembling procedure of any program, initialises a location counter and goes on updating it, as the assembly proceeds. It goes on assigning the available addresses, i.e. the contents of the location counter, sequentially to the program variables, constants and modules as per their requirements, in the sequence in which they appear in the program. The EVEN directive updates the location counter to the next even address, if the current location counter contents are not even, and assigns the following routine or variable or constant to that address. The structure given below explains the directive.

```
          EVEN
PROCEDURE        ROOT
                  :
          ROOT   ENDP
```

The above structure shows a procedure ROOT that is to be aligned at an even address. The assembler will start assembling the main program calling ROOT. When the assembler comes across the directive EVEN, it checks the contents of the location counter. If it is odd, it is updated to the next even value and then the ROOT procedure is assigned to that address, i.e. the updated contents of the location counter. If the content of the location counter is already even, then the ROOT procedure will be assigned with the same address.

EQU: Equate The directive EQU is used to assign a label with a value or a symbol. The use of this directive is just to reduce the recurrence of the numerical values or constants in a program code. The recurring value is assigned with a label, and that label is used in place of that numerical value, throughout the program. While assembling, whenever the assembler comes across the label, it substitutes the numerical value for that label and finds out the equivalent code. Using the EQU directive, even an instruction mnemonic can be assigned with a label, which can then be used in the program in place of that mnemonic. Suppose, a numerical constant which appears in a program ten times. If that constant is to be changed at a later time, one will have to make the correction 10 times. This may lead to human errors, because it is possible that a human programmer may miss one of those corrections. This will result in the generation of wrong codes. If the EQU directive is used to assign the value with a label that can be used in place of each recurrence of that constant, only one change in the EQU statement will give the correct and modified code. The examples given below show the syntax.

Example 2.49

```
LABEL       EQU    0500H
ADDITION    EQU    ADD
```

The first statement assigns the constant 500H with the label LABEL, while the second statement assigns another label ADDITION with mnemonic ADD.

EXTRN: External and PUBLIC: Public The directive EXTRN informs the assembler that the names, procedures and labels declared after this directive have already been defined in some other assembly language modules. While in the other module, where the names, procedures and labels actually appear, they must be declared public, using the PUBLIC directive. If one wants to call a procedure FACTORIAL appearing in MODULE1 from MODULE 2; in MODULE1, it must be declared PUBLIC using the statement PUBLIC FACTORIAL and in module 2, it must be declared external using the declaration EXTRN FACTORIAL. The statement of declaration EXTRN must be accompained by the SEGMENT and ENDS directives of the MODULE 1, before it is called in MOBULE 2. Thus the MODULE1 and MODULE 2 must have the following declarations.

```
MODULE1     SEGMENT
PUBLIC      FACTORIAL FAR
MODULE1     ENDS
MODULE2     SEGMENT
EXTRN       FACTORIAL FAR
MODULE2     ENDS
```

GROUP: Group the Related Segments This directive is used to form logical groups of segments with similar purpose or type. This directive is used to inform the assembler to form a logical group of the following segment names. The assembler passes an information to the linker/loader to form the code such that the group declared segments or operands must lie within a 64Kbyte memory segment. Thus all such segments and labels can be addressed using the same segment base.

```
PROGRAM GROUP CODE, DATA, STACK
```

The above statement directs the loader/linker to prepare an EXE file such that CODE, DATA and STACK segment must lie within a 64kbyte memory segment that is named as PROGRAM. Now, for the ASSUME statement, one can use the label PROGRAM rather than CODE, DATA and STACK as shown.

```
ASSUME CS: PROGRAM, DS: PROGRAM, SS: PROGRAM
```

LABEL: Label The Label directive is used to assign a name to the current content of the location counter. When the assembly process starts, the assembler initialises a location counter to keep track of memory locations assigned to the program. As the program assembly proceeds, the contents of the location counter are updated. During the assembly process, whenever the assembler comes across the LABEL directive, it assigns the declared label with the current contents of the location counter. The type of the label must be specified, i.e. whether it is a NEAR or a FAR label, BYTE or WORD label, etc.

A LABEL directive may be used to make a FAR jump as shown below. A FAR jump cannot be made at a normal label with a colon. The label CONTINUE can be used for a FAR jump, if the program contains the following statement.

```
CONTINUE  LABEL FAR
```

The LABEL directive can be used to refer to the data segment along with the data type, byte or word as shown.

```
DATA          SEGMENT
DATAS DB 50H DUP (?)
DATA-LAST LABEL BYTE FAR
DATA ENDS
```

After reserving 50H locations for DATAS, the next location will be assigned a label DATA-LAST and its type will be byte and far.

LENGTH: Byte Length of a Label This directive is not available in MASM. This is used to refer to the length of a data array or a string.

```
MOV CX, LENGTH ARRAY
```

This statement, when assembled, will substitute the length of the array ARRAY in bytes, in the instruction.

LOCAL The lables, variables, constants or procedures declared LOCAL in a module are to be used only by that particular module. After some time, some other module may declare a particular data type LOCAL, which was previously declared LOCAL by an other module or modules. Thus the same label may serve different purposes for different modules of a program. With a single declaration statement, a number of variables can be declared local, as shown.

```
LOCAL a, b, DATA, ARRAY, ROUTINE
```

NAME: Logical Name of a Module The NAME directive is used to assign a name to an assembly language program module. The module, may now be referred to by its declared name. The names, if selected to be suggestive, may point out the functions of the different modules and hence may help in the documentation.

OFFSET: Offset of a Label When the assembler comes across the OFFSET operator along with a label, it first computes the 16-bit displacement (also called as offset interchangebly) of the particular label, and replaces the string 'OFFSET LABEL' by the computed displacement. This operator is used with arrays, strings, lables and procedures to decide their offsets in their default segments. The segment may also be decided by another operator of similar type, viz, SEG. Its most common use is in the case of the indirect, indexed, based indexed or other addressing techniques of similar types, used to refer to the memory indirectly. The examples of this operator are as follows:

Example 2.50

```
CODE SEGMENT
MOV SI, OFFSET LIST
CODE ENDS
DATA SEGMENT
LIST DB 10H
DATA ENDS
```

ORG : Origin The ORG directive directs the assembler to start the memory allotment for the particular segment, block or code from the declared address in the ORG statement. While starting the assembly process for a module, the assembler initialises a location counter to keep track of the allotted addresses for the module. If the ORG statement is not written in the program, the location counter is initialised to 0000. If an ORG 200H statement is present at the starting of the code segment of that module, then the code will start from 200H address in code segment. In other words, the location counter will get initialised to the address 0200H instead of 0000H. Thus, the code for different modules and segments can be located in the available memory as required by the programmer. The ORG directive can even be used with data segments similarly.

PROC: Procedure The PROC directive marks the start of a named procedure in the statement. Also, the types NEAR or FAR specify the type of the procedure, i.e whether it is to be called by the main program located within 64K of physical memory or not. For example, the statement RESULT PROC NEAR marks the start of a routine RESULT, which is to be called by a program located in the same segment of memory. The FAR directive is used for the procedures to be called by the programs located in different segments of memory. The example statements are as follows:

Example 2.51

```
RESULT    PROC  NEAR
ROUTINE   PROC  FAR
```

PTR: Pointer The POINTER operator is used to declare the type of a label, variable or memory operand. The operator PTR is prefixed by either BYTE or WORD. If the prefix is BYTE, then the particular label, variable or memory operand is treated as an 8-bit quantity, while if WORD is the prefix, then it is treated as a 16-bit quantity. In other words, the PTR operator is used to specify the data type—byte or word. The examples of the PTR operator are as follows:

Example 2.52

```
MOV AL, BYTE PTR [SI] -      Moves content of memory location
                             addressed by SI (8-bit) to AL
INC BYTE PTR [BX]-           Increments byte contents of memory
                             location addressed by BX
MOV BX, WORD PTR [2000H]-    Moves 16-bit content of memory
                             location 2000H to BX, i.e. [2000H] to BL
                             [2001H] to BH
INC WORD PTR [3000H] -       Increments word contents of memory
                             location 3000H considering contents
                             of 3000H (lower byte) and 3001H
                             (higher byte) as a 16-bit number
```

In case of JMP instructions, the PTR operator is used to specify the type of the jump, i.e. near or far, as explained in the examples given below.

```
JMP NEAR PTR [BX]-NEAR Jump
JMP FAR PTR [BX]-FAR Jump.
```

PUBLIC As already discussed, the PUBLIC directive is used along with the EXTRN directive. This informs the assembler that the labels, variables, constants, or procedures declared PUBLIC may be accessed by other assembly modules to form their codes, but while using the PUBLIC declared lables, variables, constants or procedures the user must declare them externals using the EXTRN directive. On the other hand, the data types declared EXTRN in a module of the program, may be declared PUBLIC in at least any one of the other modules of the same program. (Refer to the explanation on EXTRN directive to get the clear idea of PUBLIC.)

SEG: Segment of a Label The SEG operator is used to decide the segment address of the label, variable, or procedure and substitutes the segment base address in place of ''SEG'' label. The example given below explains the use of SEG operator.

Example 2.53

```
MOV AX, SEG ARRAY  ; This statement moves the segment address of ARRAY in
MOV DS, AX         ; which it is appearing, to register AX and then to DS.
```

SEGMENT: Logical Segment The SEGMENT directive marks the starting of a logical segment. The started segment is also assigned a name, i.e. label, by this statement. The SEGMENT and ENDS directive must bracket each logical segment of a program. In some cases, the segment may be assigned a type like PUBLIC (i.e. can be used by other modules of the program while linking) or GLOBAL (can be accessed by any other modules). The program structure given below explains the use of the SEGMENT directive.

```
EXE.CODE SEGMENT GLOBAL; Start of Segment named EXE.CODE,
                       ; that can be accessed by any other module.
EXE.CODE ENDS          ; END of EXE.CODE logical segment.
```

SHORT The SHORT operator indicates to the assembler that only one byte is required to code the displacement for a jump (i.e. displacement is within –128 to +127 bytes from the address of the byte next to the jump opcode). This method of specifying the jump address saves the memory. Otherwise, the assembler may reserve two bytes for the displacement. The syntax of the statement is as given below.

```
JMP SHORT LABEL
```

TYPE The TYPE operator directs the assembler to decide the data type of the specified label and replaces the 'TYPE' label by the decided data type. For the word type variable, the data type is 2, for double word type, it is 4, and for byte type, it is 1. Suppose, the STRING is a word array. The instruction MOV AX, TYPE STRING moves the value 0002H in AX.

GLOBAL The labels, variables, constants or procedures declared GLOBAL may be used by other modules of the program. Once a variable is declared GLOBAL, it can be used by any module in the program. The following statement declares the procedure ROUTINE as a global label.

```
ROUTINE PROC      GLOBAL
```

'+ & –' Operators These operators represent arithmetic addition and subtraction respectively and are typically used to add or subtract displacements (8 or 16 bit) to base or index registers or stack or base pointers as given in the example:

Example 2.54

```
MOV AL, [ SI +2 ]
MOV DX, [ BX – 5 ]
MOV BX, [ OFFSET LABEL + 10 H ]
MOV AX, [ BX + 9I ]
```

FAR PTR This directive indicates the assembler that the label following FAR PTR is not available within the same segment and the address of the label is of 32-bits i.e. 2 bytes offset followed by 2 bytes segment address.

Example 2.55

```
JMP FAR PTR LABEL
CALL FAR PTR ROUTINE
```

Both the above instructions indicate to the assembles that the target address is going to require four bytes; Lower byte of offset, higher byte of offset, lower byte of segment and higher byte of segment; indicating intersegment addressing mode.

NEAR PTR This directive indicates that the label following NEAR PTR is in the same segment and needs only 16 bit i.e. 2 byte offset to address it.

Example 2.56

```
JMP NEAR PTR LABEL
CALL NEAR PTR ROUTINE
```

If a label is not preceded by NEAR PTR or FAR PTR, then it is by default considered a NEAR PTR label and two bytes are reserved by the assembler for its address during the process of assembling.

2.5 Dos and Don'ts While Using Instructions

1) The logic required for implementing a program must be visualized very clearly. There may be many methods or alternative logics to implement a program. A simple-to-implement method must be selected.
2) Express the selected logic in terms of a flowchart or algorithm.
3) Identify the most appropriate instructions to implement the algorithmic steps of the logic.
4) Arrange them in logical sequence to solve the problem.
5) Use more efficient instructions in terms of length in bytes and execution time for implementing the logic. For example, one can use INC AL instead of ADD AL, O1H.
6) Simulate the program on paper assuming a few possible sets of inputs.
7) Provide comments with each instruction regarding its role in the overall implementation of the logic.
8) Remove unnecessary or redundant instructions from the program.
9) If the simulation in 6) goes wrong, repeat from Step 3.

Don'ts While Using Instructions

1) Don't use any instruction, till its operation is very clear to you. You must be convinced about its role in implementing the logic.
2) Don't use unnecessarily complex addressing modes and instructions, until there is no simpler alternative. Indirect addressing modes must be used conservatively.
3) Don't use mismatching size operands in any instruction until it is demanded by the operation.

```
MOV AX, DL          ; Not allowed.
DIV BL              ; Divide DX-AX (32 bit)
                    ; by BL (8 bit) is allowed.
```

4) Don't use both the operands in an instruction as memory operands. Only one memory operand can be specified in one instruction.

```
MOV [SI], [DI]      ; Not allowed.
MOV AX, [SI]              ; Allowed.
```

5) Don't use immediate 8-bit or 16-bit operand as a destination operand. Destination operand must be a storage element like a register or a memory location. The immediate operand can only be a source operand.

```
MOV 55H, AL         ; Not allowed.
ADD 5779H, AX       ; Not allowed.
ADD AX, 5779H       ; Allowed.
```

6) Both the operands of an instruction can't be immediate operands.
7) Don't use stack operations unnecessarily. Stack operations must be used very carefully.
8) Don't write very big continuous single program for an application. Rather divide the big task in small modules and write modular programmes using subroutines or interrupt service routines if required.
9) Don't use segment registers as operands for arithmatic or logical instructions. It is not allowed.

SUMMARY

This chapter is aimed at introducing the readers with the instruction set of 8086/88 and the most commonly used assembler directives and operators. To start with, the available instruction formats in 8086/88 instruction set are explained in details. Further, the addressing modes available in 8086/88 are discussed in significant details with necessary examples. The 8086/88 instructions can be broadly categorized in six types depending upon their functions, namely data transfer instructions, arithmetic instructions and logical instructions, shift and rotate instructions, string manipulation instructions, control transfer instructions and processor control instructions. All these instruction types have been discussed before proceeding with the assembler directives and operators. The coding information details of all these instructions may be obtained from the Intel data sheets. The necessary assembler directives have been discussed later with their possible syntax, functions and examples. Most of these directives are available in Microsoft MASM. The detailed discussion on every assembler directive and operator is out of the scope of this book. The readers may refer to MASM Programmer's Guide and Technical reference for further details of the directives and operators, discussed in this chapter. Chapter 3 elaborates on how to use the instructions, assembler directives and operators to write assembly language programs.

EXERCISES

2.1 State and explain the different instruction formats of 8086/8088.
2.2 What do you mean by addressing modes? What are the different addressing modes supported by 8086? Explain each of them with suitable examples.
2.3 Explain the physical address formation in different addressing modes.
2.4 Explain the addressing modes for control transfer instructions.
2.5 What are the different instruction types of 8086?
2.6 'A single instruction may use more than one addressing mode or some instructions may not require any addressing mode'. Explain.
2.7 Bring out the developments in 8086 instruction set over 8085 instruction set, in details.
2.8 Explain the execution of all the instructions of 8086 with suitable examples.
2.9 What are the assembler directives and pseudo-ops?
2.10 Explain all the assembler directives, pseudo-ops and operators presented in this chapter with suitable examples.
2.11 How does the CPU identify between 8-bit and 16-bit operations?
2.12 How is the addressing mode of an instruction communicated to the CPU?
2.13 What is the difference between the jump and loop instructions.
2.14 Which instruction of 8086 can be used for look up table manipulations?
2.15 What is the difference between the respective shift and rotate instructions?
2.16 How will you enter the single step mode of 8086?
2.17 What is LOCK prefix? What is its use?
2.18 What is REP prefix? What is its use?

3 The Art of Assembly Language Programming with 8086/8088

INTRODUCTION

In the previous chapter, the 8086/8088 instruction set and assembler directives were discussed in significant detail. This chapter aims at making the reader more familiar with the instructions and assembler directives and their use in implementing the different structures required for the implementation of algorithms. In this chapter, the different structures are implemented by using the instruction set of 8086. A number of example programs are discussed to explain the use of these structures. While in the second chapter, a qualitative study of all the addressing modes has been presented, in this chapter, the ideas about the addressing modes and their typical uses will be presented more clearly through example programs. After studying this chapter, one will be in a position to use the instructions and directives properly to translate an algorithm into a program. While emphasizing on different programming techniques, we have stressed more on managing the processor resources and capabilities because while solving a particular problem, the programmer may find a number of solutions (instruction sequences). A skilled programmer selects an optimum solution out of them for that specific application. For example, the instruction INC AL and ADD AL,01H may serve the same purpose but the first one requires less memory and execution time than the second one. Hence, the INC instruction will be preferred over ADD. Also the improper use of general purpose and special purpose registers may lead to the requirement of more instructions for a particular algorithm resulting in more execution time and memory requirement. While implementing an algorithm, the processor capabilities should be optimally utilized. For example, while writing a simple program to move a string of data from the source to destination location, a programmer may initialize a pointer to memory source, another pointer to destination and a counter to count the number of data elements to be moved. Each data element is then fetched from the source location and transferred to the destination location. This process should continue till all the data elements are transferred. He may use the INR, DCR, JNZ instructions to update pointers, counters, and check the counter for zero. All these instructions are available in the instruction set of 8085 as well as 8086. They can be used to implement the same algorithm in a similar fashion but by using the MOVS instruction of 8086, the same algorithm can be implemented with less number of instructions and memory requirement. When all these elements come into picture, the assembly language programming becomes a skill rather than a technique.

In the following section, we will consider some program examples. Starting from simple arithmetic operation programs, the discussion concludes with some example programs based on DOS function calls. Before starting to write a program, the task must be put in a clear form so that the simplest required algorithm may be put forward in terms of a flow chart. The implementation of the flow chart may then require the different structures like IF-THEN-ELSE, DO WHILE, REPEAT (NUMBER OF TIMES), REPEAT UNTIL, etc. The implementation of these structures by using the instruction set completely depends upon the skill of the programmer.

3.1 A FEW MACHINE LEVEL PROGRAMS

In this section, a few machine level programming examples, rather, instruction sequences are presented for comparing the 8086 programming with that of 8085. These programs are in the form of instruction sequences just like 8085 programs. These may even be hand-coded, entered byte by byte and executed on an 8086 based system but due to the complex instruction set of 8086 and its tedious opcode conversion procedure, most of the programmers prefer to use assemblers. However, we will briefly discuss the hand-coding (opcode conversion) technique in the next section.

Example 3.1

Write a program to add a data byte located at offset 0500H in 2000H segment to another data byte available at 0600H in the same segment and store the result at 0700H in the same segment.

Solution The flow chart for this problem may be drawn as shown in Fig. 3.1.

```
MOV   AX, 2000H    ; Initialising DS with value
MOV   DS, AX       ; 2000H
MOV   AX, [500H]   ; Get first data byte from 0500H
                     offset
ADD   AX, [600H]   ; Add this to the second byte
                     from 0600H
MOV   [700H], AX   ; Store AX in 0700H (result).
HLT                ; Stop
```

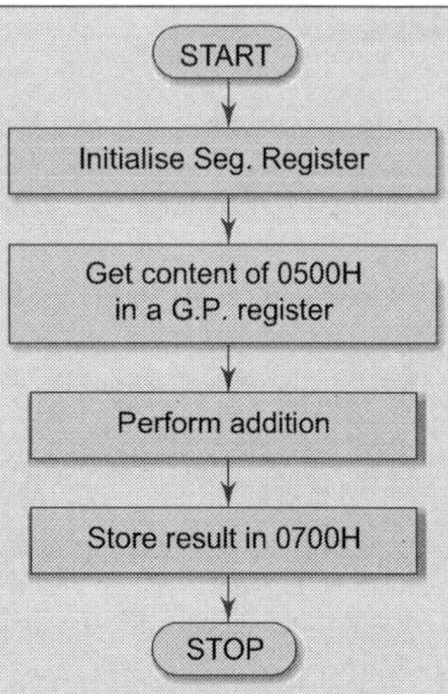

Fig. 3.1 *Flow Chart for Example 3.1*

The above instruction sequence is quite straightforward. As the immediate data cannot be loaded into a segment register, the data is transferred to one of the general purpose registers, say AX, and then the register content is moved to the segment register DS. Thus the data segment register DS contains 2000H. The instruction MOV AX, [500H] signifies that the contents of the particular location, whose offset is specified in the brackets with the segment pointed to by DS as segment register, is to be moved to AX. The MOV [0700H], AX instruction moves the contents of the register AX to an offset 0700H in DS (DS = 2000H). Note that the code segment register CS gets automatically loaded by the code segment address of the program whenever it is executed. Actually it is the monitor program that accepts the CS:IP address of the program and passes it to the corresponding registers at the time of execution. Hence no instructions like DS or SS are required for loading the CS register.

Example 3.2

Write a program to move the contents of the memory location 0500H to register BX and to CX. Add immediate byte 05H to the data residing in memory location, whose address is computed using DS = 2000H and offset = 0600H. Store the result of the addition in 0700H. Assume that the data is located in the segment specified by the data segment register DS which contain 2000H.

Solution The flow chart for the program is shown in Fig. 3.2.

```
MOV   AX, 2000H
MOV   DS, AX       ; Initialize data segment register
MOV   BX, [0500H]  ; Get contents of 0500H in BX
```

```
MOV   CX, BX          ; Copy the same contents in
                        CX
ADD   [0600H], 05H; Add byte 05H to contents
                        of 0600H
MOV   DX, [0600H] ; Store the result in DX
MOV   [0700H], DX ; Store the result in 0700H
HLT               ; Stop
```

After initialising the data segment register, the content of location 0500H are moved to the BX register using MOV instruction. The same data is moved also to the CX register. For this data transfer, there may be two options as shown.

```
(a) MOV CX, BX      ; As the contents of BX will be
                    ; same as 0500H after execution
                    ; of MOV BX,[0500H].
(b) MOV CX, [0500H]; Move directly from 0500H
                     to register CX
```

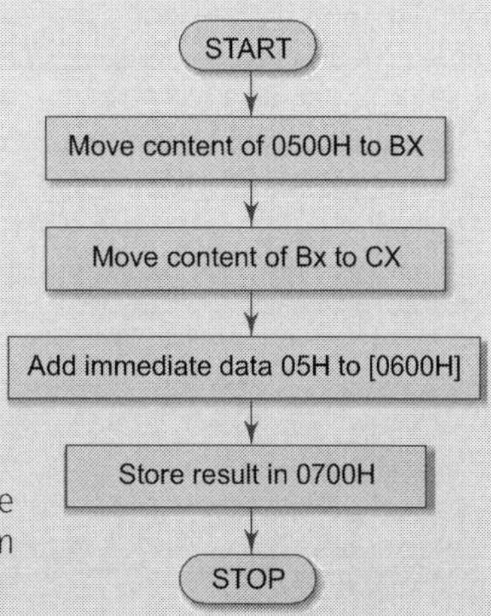

Fig. 3.2 *Flow Chart for Example 3.2*

Example 3.3

Add the contents of the memory location 2000H:0500H to contents of 3000H:0600H and store the result in 5000H:0700H.

Solution Unlike the previous example programs, this program refers to the memory locations in different segments, hence, while referring to each location, the data segment will have to be newly initialised with the required value. Figure 3.3 shows the flow chart.

The instruction sequence for the above flow chart is given along with the comments.

```
MOV   CX, 2000H     ; Initialize DS at 2000H
MOV   DS, CX
MOV   AX, [500H]    ; Get first operand in AX
MOV   CX, 3000H     ; Initialize DS at 3000H
MOV   DS, CX
MOV   BX, [0600H]   ; Get second operand in BX.
ADD   AX, BX        ; Perform addition
MOV   CX, 5000H     ; Initialize DS at 5000H
MOV   DS, CX
MOV   [0700H],AX    ; Store the result of
                      addition in
HLT                 ;  0700H and stop
```

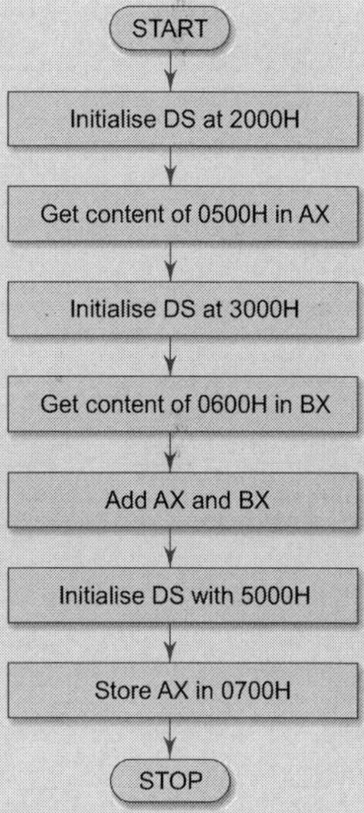

Fig. 3.3 *Flow Chart for Example 3.2*

The *opcode* in the first option is only of 2 bytes, while the second option will have 4 bytes of *opcode*. Thus the second option will require more memory and execution time. Due to these reasons, the first option is preferable.

The immediate data byte 05H is added to the content of 0600H using the ADD instruction. The result will be in the destination operand 0600H. This is next stored at the location 0700H. In case of the 8086/8088 instruction set, there is no instruction for the direct transfer of data from the memory source operand to the memory destination operand except, the string instructions. Hence the result of addition which is present at 0600H, should be moved to any one of the general purpose registers, except BX and CX, otherwise the contents of CX and BX will be changed. We have selected DX (we could have selected AX also, because once DS is initialised to 2000H the contents of AX are no longer useful) for this purpose. Thus the transfer of result from 0600H to 0700H is accomplished in two stages using successive MOV instructions, i.e. at first, the content of 0600H is moved to DX and then the content of DX is moved to 0700H. The program ends with the HLT instruction.

Actually, the program simply performs the addition of two operands which are located in different memory segments. The program has become lengthy only due to data segment register initialization instructions.

Example 3.4

Move a byte string, 16-bytes long, from the offset 0200H to 0300H in the segment 7000H.

Solution According to the program statement, a string that is 16-bytes long is available at the offset address 0200H in the segment 7000H. The required program should move this complete string at offset 0300H, in the same segment. Let us emphasize this program in the light of comparison between 8085 and 8086 programming techniques.

An 8085 program to perform this task, is given neglecting the segment addresses.

```
        MVI   C, 010H ; Count for the length of string
        LXIH  0200H   ; Initialization of HL pair for source string
        LXID  0300H   ; Initialization of DE pair for destination
BACK :  MOV   A, M    ; Take a byte from source in A
        STAX D        ; Store contents of A to address pointed to by DE
                        pair
        INX   H       ; Increment source pointer
        INX   D       ; Increment destination pointer
        DCRC          ; Decrement counter
        JNZ BACK      ; Continue if counter is not zero
        HLT           ; Stop if counter is zero
```

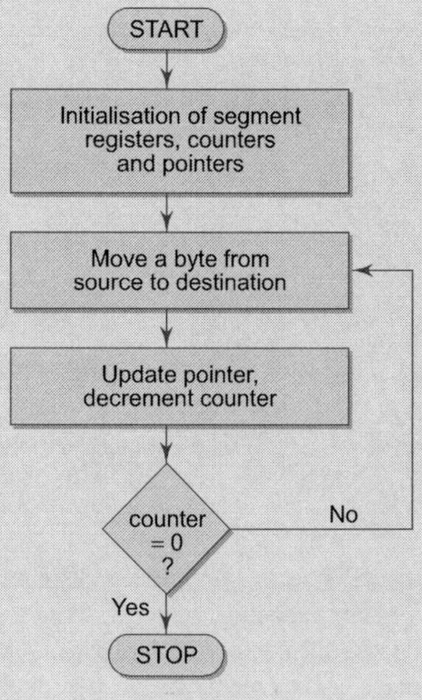

Fig. 3.4 *Flow Chart for Example 3.4*

The programmers, fluent with 8085 assembly language programming but starting with 8086, may translate the above 8085 assembly language program listings to 8086 assembly language programs using the analogous or comparable instructions. Of course, this method of programming is not efficient, however, it may help those who are familiar to 8085 programming and wish to start writing programs in 8086 assembly language. The reason for the inefficiency of this method is that the special features and capabilities of 8086 have not been taken into account while preparing the 8086 assembly language program.

Now, let us think about how the above program may be transferred to 8086 assembly language using analogous instructions. Note that the segment initialization is to be added. Let us consider that the code and data segment address is 7000H. Consider that the code starts at offset 0000H.

```
       MOV   AX, 7000H
       MOV   DS, AX      ;  Data segment initialization
       MOV   SI, 0200H   ;  Pointer to source string
       MOV   DI, 0300H   ;  Pointer to destination string
       MOV   CX, 0010H   ;  Count for length of string
BACK : MOV   AL, [SI]    ;  Take a source byte in AL
       MOV   [DI], AL    ;  Move it to destination
       INC   SI          ;  Increment source pointer
       INC   DI          ;  Increment destination pointer
       DEC   CX          ;  Decrement count by 1
       JNZ   BACK        ;  Continue if count is not 0
       HLT               ;  Stop if the count is 0
```

The above list has been prepared using the program written in 8085 ALP. Indexed addressing mode is used for string byte accesses and transfer in this case. The functions of all the 8086 instructions and the 8086 addressing modes have already been explained in Chapter 2. In this program, all the instructions used are more or less analogous to the 8085 program, and the special software capabilities of 8086 like string instructions and loop instructions have not been considered. The 8086 programs based on 8085 codes are inefficient due to the reason that the full capability of the rich 8086 instruction set and the enhanced architecture of 8086 cannot be fully exploited.

The above program uses the decrement and jump-if-not-zero instructions for checking whether the transfer is complete or not. The 8086 instruction set provides LOOP instructions for this purpose. Using these instructions, the program is modified as shown:

```
        MOV   AX, 7000H
        MOV   DS, AX          ; Data segment initialization
        MOV   SI, 0200H       ; Source pointer initialization
        MOV   DI, 0300H       ; Destination pointer initialization
        MOV   CX, 0010H       ; Counter initialization
BACK :  MOV   AL, [SI]        ; Take a byte of string from source
        MOV   [DI], AL        ; and then move it to destination
        INC   SI              ; Update source pointer
        INC   DI              ; Update destination pointer continue
        LOOP BACK             ; till CX =0,[DEC CX and JNZ BACK]
        HLT                   ; Stop if CX =0
```

Thus the two instructions bracketed in the comment field are replaced by a single loop instruction which results in the saving of memory and execution time. The loop instruction needs the additional instructions for updating the pointers (for example, INC SI, INC DI). It does not need counter decrement and check-if-zero instruction.

One more feature of the 8086 instruction set is the string instruction, i.e MOVSB and MOVSW. Using these instructions one can move a string byte/word from source to destination. The length of the string is specified by the CX register. The SI and DI point to the source and destination locations. The DS and ES registers should be initialised to source and destination segment addresses respectively. Before the use of string instructions, the program should initialise all these registers properly. Using the string byte instruction the same program may be written as shown:

```
        MOV AX, 7000H
        MOV DS, AX          ;  Source segment initialisation
        MOV ES, AX          ;  Destination segment initialisation
        MOV CX, 0010H       ;  Counter initialisation
        MOV SI, 0200H       ;  Source pointer initialisation
        MOV DI, 0300H       ;  Destination pointer initialisation
        CLD                 ;  Clear DF
   REP  MOVSB               ;  Move the complete string
        HLT                 ;  Stop
```

The MOVSB instruction needs neither counter decrement and jump back nor pointer update instructions. All these functions are done automatically. An experienced programmer will thus directly use the string instructions instead of using other options. The flow chart of the final program is presented in Fig. 3.4.

Example 3.5

Find out the largest number from an unordered array of sixteen 8-bit numbers stored sequentially in the memory locations starting at offset 0500H in the segment 2000H.

Solution The logic for this procedure can be described as follows. The first number of the array is taken in a register, say AL. The second number of the array is then compared with the first one. If the first one is greater than the second one, it is left unchanged. However, if the second one is greater than the first, the second number replaces the first one in the AL register. The procedure is repeated for every number in the array and thus it requires 15 iterations. At the end of 15th iteration the largest number will reside in the register AL. This may be represented in terms of the flow chart as shown in Fig. 3.5. The listing is given below:

```
         MOV  CX, OF H    ; Initialize counter for number of iterations
         MOV  AX, 2000H   ; Initialize data segment
         MOV  DS, AX      ;
         MOV  SI, 0500H   ; Initialize source pointer
         MOV  AL, [SI]    ; Take first number in AL
BACK :   INC  SI          ; Increment source pointer
         CMP  AL, [SI]    ; Compare next number with the previous
         JNC  NEXT        ; If the next number is larger
         MOV  AL, [SI]    ; replace the previous one with the next
NEXT :   LOOPBACK         ; Repeat the procedure 15 times
         HLT
```

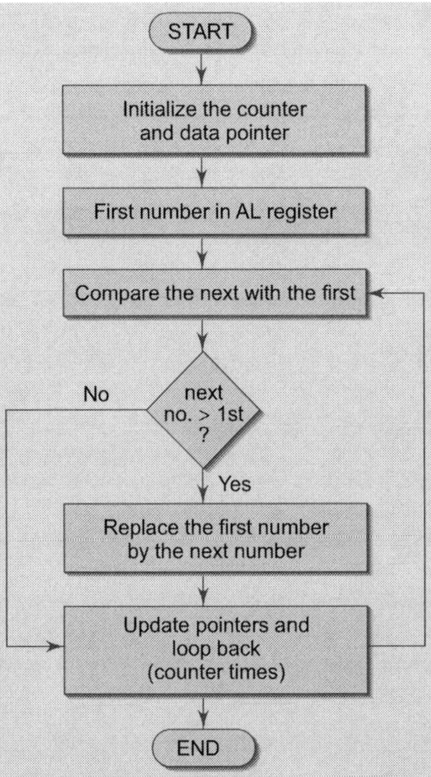

Fig. 3.5 *Flow Chart for Example 3.5*

3.2 MACHINE CODING THE PROGRAMS

So far we have discussed five programs which were written for handcoding by a programmer. In this section, we will have a brief look at how these programs can be translated to machine codes. In Chapter 2, the instruction set along with the data sheet are presented. This data sheet is self-explanatory to handcode most of the instructions. The S,V,W,D,MOD,REG and R/M fields are suitably decided depending upon the data types, addressing mode and the registers used. The data sheet Fig. 2.4 shows the details about how to select these fields.

Most of the instructions either have specific opcodes or they can be decided only by setting the S,V,W,D,REG,MOD and R/M fields suitably but the critical point is the calculation of jump addresses for intrasegment branch instructions. Before starting the coding of jump or call instructions, we will see some easier coding examples.

Example 3.6

```
MOV BL, CL
```

For handcoding this instruction, we will have to first note down the following features:

(i) It fits in the register/memory to/from register format.
(ii) It is an 8-bit operation.
(iii) BL is the destination register and CL is the source register.

Now from the feature (i) using the Fig. 2.4 data sheet, the opcode format is given as shown.

D_7	D_6	D_5	D_4	D_3	D_2	D_1	D_0	D_7D_6	$D_5D_4D_3$	$D_2D_1D_0$
1	0	0	0	1	0	d	w	(MOD)	(REG)	(R/M)

If d =1, then transfer of data is to the register shown by the REG field, i.e the destination is a register (REG). If d = 0, the source is a register shown by the REG field.

It is an 8-bit operation, hence *w* bit is 0. If it had been a 16-bit operation, the *w* bit would have been 1.

Refer to Table 2.2 to search the REG to REG addressing in it, i.e the last column with MOD 11. According to the data sheet when MOD is 11, the R/M field is treated as a REG field. The REG field is used for source register and the R/M field is used for the destination register, if d is 0. If d =1, the REG field is used for destination and the R/M field is used to indicate source.

Now the complete machine code of this instruction comes out to be

	D_7 code	d	w D_0	D_7 MOD	REG	R/M D_0	
MOV BL, CL	1 0 0 0 1 0	0	0	1 1	0 0 1	0 1 1	= 88 CB

Note that the register codes are to be found out from the Table 2.1.

Example 3.7

MOV BX, 5000H

From data sheet Fig. 2.4, the coding format is as shown:

$D_7D_6D_5D_4$	D_3	$D_2D_1D_0$	D_7	D_0	D_7	D_0
1 0 1 1	W	REG	DATA LOW BYTE		DATA HIGH BYTE	

Following the procedure as in Example 3.6, the code comes out to be (BB 00 50) as shown.

CODE	W	REG	Data LB	Data HB
1 0 1 1	1	0 1 1	00000000	01010000
B		B	0 0	5 0

Example 3.8

MOV [SI], DL

This instruction belongs to the register to memory format. Hence from the data sheet Fig. 2.4 and using the already explained procedure, the machine code can be found as shown.

OPCODE	D	W	MOD	REG	R/M
1 0 0 0 1 0	0	1	0 0	0 1 0	1 0 0
8	9		1		4

The machine code is 89 14.

Example 3.9

MOV BP[SI], 0005H

OPCODE	W	MOD	OPCODE	R/M
1 1 0 0 0 1 1	1	0 0	0 0 0	0 1 0
C 7		0		2

LOWER BYTE	HIGHER BYTE
0 0 0 0 0 1 0 1	0 0 0 0 0 0 0 0
0 5	0 0

The machine code of this instruction is C7 02 05 00.

Example 3.10

MOV BP [SI+ 500H], 7293H

OPCODE	W	MOD	OPCODE	R/M
1 1 0 0 0 1 1	1	1 0	0 0 0	0 1 0
C	7	8		2

LOWER BYTE DISP.	HIGHER BYTE DISP.
0 0 0 0 0 0 0 0	0 0 0 0 0 1 0 1
0 0	0 5

Displacement 500H

LOWER BYTE DATA	HIGHER BYTE DATA
1 0 0 1 0 0 1 1	0 1 1 1 0 0 1 0
9 3	7 2

Data 7293 H

The complete machine code comes out to be C7 82 00 05 93 72.

Example 3.11

ADD AX, BX

The machine code is formed as shown by referring to data sheet Fig. 2.4 and using the Tables 2.1 and 2.2 as has been already described.

OPCODE	D	W	MOD	REG	R/M
0 0 0 0 0 0	1	1	11	0 0 0	0 1 1

The machine code is 03 C3.

Example 3.12

ADD AX, 5000H

The code formation is explained as follows:

OPCODE	S	W	MOD	OPCODE	R/M
1 0 0 0 0 0	0	1	0 0	0 0 0	0 0 0
8	1			0	0

LOWER BYTE DATA	HIGHER BYTE DATA
0 0 0 0 0 0 0 0	0 1 0 1 0 0 0 0
0 0	5 0

The machine code is 81 00 00 50.

If S bit is 0, the 16-bit immediate data is available in the instruction.

If S bit is 1, the 16-bit immediate data is the sign extended form of 8-bit immediate data.

For example, if the eight bit data is 11010001, then its sign extended 16-bit version will be 11111111 11010001.

Example 3.13

SHR AX

OPCODE	V	W	MOD	REG	R/M
1 1 0 1 0 0	0	1	1 1	1 0 1	0 0 0
D	1		E		8

The instruction code is D1 E8.

Finding out Machine Code for Conditional JUMP (Intrasegment) Instructions The data sheet Fig. 2.4 shows that, corresponding to each of the conditional jump instructions, the first byte of the opcode is fixed and the jump displacement must be less than or equal to 127(D) bytes and greater than or equal to –128(D). This type of jump is called as short jump. The following conditional forward jump example explains how to find the displacement. The displacement is an 8-bit signed number. If it is positive, it indicates a forward jump, otherwise it indicates a backward jump. The following example is a sequence of instructions rather than a single instruction to elaborate the procedure of the calculation of positive displacement for a forward jump.

Example 3.14

```
2000, 01                    XOR AX, BX
2002, 03                    JNZ OK
2004                        NOP
2005                        NOP
2006, 7, 8, 9               ADD BX, 05H
200A                   OK : HLT
```

The above sequence shows that the programmer wants a conditional jump to label OK, if the zero flag is not set. For finding out the displacement corresponding to the label OK, subtract the address of the jump instruction (2002H), from the address of label (200AH). The required displacement is 200AH - 2002H = 08H. The 08H is the displacement for the forward jump.

Let us find out the displacement for a backward jump. Consider the following sequence of instructions.

Example 3.15

```
2000, 01, 02                      MOV CL, 05H
2003          Repeat :      INC    AX
2004                        DEC  CL
2005, 2006                  JNZ    Repeat
```

For finding out the backward displacement, subtract the address of the label (repeat) from the address of the jump instruction. Complement the subtraction. The lower byte gives the displacement. In this example, the signed displacement for the JNZ instruction comes out to be (2005H-2003H = 02, complement-FDH) The magnitude of the displacement must be less than or equal to 127(D). The MSB of the displacement decides whether it is a forward or backward jump. If it is 1, it is a backward jump or else it is a forward jump.

A similar procedure is used to find the displacement for intrasegment short calls.

Finding out Machine Code for Unconditional JUMP Intrasegment For this instruction there are again two types of jump, i.e short jump and long jump. The displacement calculation procedures are again the same as given in case of the conditional jump. The only new thing here is that, the displacement may be beyond ±127(D). This type of jump is called the long jump. The method of calculation of the displacement is again similar to that for short jump.

Finding out Machine Code for Intersegment Direct Jump This type of instruction is used to make a jump directly to the address lying in another segment. The opcode itself specifies the new offset and the segment of jump address, directly.

Example 3.16

```
JUMP 2000 : 5000
```

This instruction implies a jump to a memory location in another code segment with CS = 2000H and Offset = 5000H. The code formation is as shown.

Code formation	1110 1010	0000 0000	0101 0000	0000 0000	0010 0000
	Opcode	Offset LB	Offset HB	Seg. LB	Seg. HB

The opcode forms the first byte of this instruction and the successive bytes are formed from the segment and the offset of the jump destination.While specifying the segment and offset, the lower byte (LB) is specified first and then the higher byte (HB) is specified. Finally, the opcode comes out to be EA 00 50 00 20. The procedure of coding the CALL instructions is similar.

Hand-Coding a Complete Program After studying the hand-coding procedures of different instructions, let us now try to code a complete program. We will consider Example 3.17 for complete hand-coding. The program and the code corresponding to it is given. These codes, found using hand-coding, may be entered byte-by-byte into an 8086 based system and executed, provided it supports the memory requirements of the program.

Example 3.17

A Hand-coding Program Example

Addresses	Opcodes	Labels	Mnemonics
2000, 01, 02	B9 0F 00		MOV CX, 0F H
2003, 04, 05	B8 00 02		MOV AX, 2000H
2006, 07	8E D8		MOV DS, AX
2008, 09, 0A	BE 00 05		MOV SI, 0500H
200B, 0C	89 04		MOV AX, [SI]
200D	46	BACK :	INC SI
200E, 0F	3B 04		CMP AX, [SI]
2010, 11	77 04		JNC NEXT
2012, 13	89 04		MOV AX, [SI]
2014, 15	E2 F7	NEXT :	LOOP BACK
2016	F4		HLT

3.3 PROGRAMMING WITH AN ASSEMBLER

The procedure of hand-coding 8086 programs is somewhat tedious, hence in general a programmer may find it difficult to get a correct listing of the machine codes. Moreover, the procedure of handcoding is time consuming. This programming procedure is called as machine level programming. The obvious disadvantages of machine level programming are as given:

1. The process is complicated and time consuming.
2. The chances of error being committed are more at the machine level in hand-coding and entering the program byte-by-byte into the system.
3. Debugging a program at the machine level is more difficult.
4. The programs are not understood by everyone and the results are not stored in a user-friendly form.

A program called 'assembler' is used to convert the mnemonics of instructions alongwith the data into their equivalent object code modules. These object code modules may further be converted in executable code using the linker and loader programs. This type of programming is called assembly level programming. In assembly language programming, the mnemonics are directly used in the user programs. The assembler performs the task of coding. The advantages of assembly language over machine language are as given:

1. The programming in assembly language is not so complicated as in machine language because the function of coding is performed by an assembler.
2. The chances of error being committed are less because the mnemonics are used instead of numerical opcodes. It is easier to enter an assembly language program.
3. As the mnemonics are purpose-suggestive the debugging is easier.
4. The constants and address locations can be labeled with suggestive labels hence imparting a more friendly interface to user. Advanced assemblers provide facilities like macros, lists, etc. making the task of programming much easier.
5. The memory control is in the hands of users as in machine language.
6. The results may be stored in a more user-friendly form.
7. The flexibility of programming is more in assembly language programming as compared to machine language because of advanced facilities available with the modern assemblers.

Basically, the assembler is a program that converts an assembly input file also called as source file to an object file that can further be converted into machine codes or an executable file using a linker. The recent versions of the assembler are designed with many facilities like macroassemblers, numerical processor assemblers, procedures, functions and so on. A discussion on the principles of assembler design and its working is presented in Chapter 12.

As far as this book is concerned, we will consider the assembly language programming using MASM (Microsoft Macro Assembler). There are a number of assemblers available like MASM, TASM and DOS assembler. MASM is one of the popular assemblers used along with a LINK program to structure the codes generated by MASM in the form of an executable file. MASM reads the source program as its input and provides an object file. The LINK accepts the object file produced by MASM as input and produces an EXE file.

While writing a program for an assembler, your first step will be to use a text editor and type the program listing prepared by you. Then check the listing typed by you for any typing mistake and syntax error. Before you quit the editor program, do not forget to save it. Once you save the text file with any name (permissible on operating system), you are free to start the assembly process. A number of text editors are available in the market, e.g. Norton's Editor [NE], Turbo C [TC], EDLIN, etc. Throughout this book, the NE is used. Any other free form editor may be used for a better user-friendly environment. Thus for writing a program in assembly language, one will need NE editor, MASM assembler, linker and DEBUG utility of DOS. In the following section, the procedures of opening a file for a program, assembling it, executing it and checking its result are described for beginners.

3.3.1 Entering a Program

In this section, we will explain the procedure for entering a small program on IBM PC with DOS operating system. Consider a program of addition of two bytes, as already discussed in the Section 3.1 for handcoding. The same program is written along with some syntax modifications in it for MASM. The directives and pseudo-ops used have been discussed in Chapter 2, Section 2.4.

Before starting the process, ensure that all the files namely NE.COM (Norton's Editor), MASM.EXE (Assembler), LINK.EXE (linker), DEBUG.EXE (debugger) are available in the same directory in which you are working. Start the procedure with the following command after you boot the terminal and enter the directory containing all the files mentioned.

```
C> NE
```

You will get display on the screen as in Fig. 3.6.

Now type the file name. It will be displayed on the screen. Suppose one types KMB.ASM as file name, the screen display will be as shown in Fig. 3.7.

```
Enter Filename :

Norton's Editor
press any key
to continue
```

Fig. 3.6 *Norton's Editor's Opening Screen*

```
Enter Filename:KMB.ASM

Norton's Editor
press any key
to continue
```

Fig. 3.7 *Norton's Editor Alternative*

Press any of the keys, you will get Fig. 3.8 as the screen display.

Note that, for every assembly language program, the extension .ASM must be there. Though every time the assembler dose not use the complete name KMB.ASM and uses just KMB to handle the file, the extension shows that it is an assembly language program file. Even if you enter a file name without the .ASM extension, the assembler searches for the file and if it is not available, issues the message 'File not found'. Once you get the display as in Fig. 3.8 you are free to type the program. One may use another type of command line.

```
C> NE KMB.ASM
```

```
KMB.ASM
```

Fig. 3.8 *Norton's Editor Opens a New File KMB.ASM*

Which will directly give the display as shown in Fig. 3.8, if KMB.ASM is a newly opened file. Otherwise, if KMB.ASM is already existing in the directory, then it will be opened and the program in it will be displayed. *You may modify it and save (command F3-E) it again, if you want the changes to be permanent.* Otherwise, simply quit (command F3-Q) it to abandon the changes and exit NE. The entered program in NE looks like in Fig. 3.9. We have to just consider that it is an assembly language program to be assembled. Store it with command F3-E. This will generate a new copy of the program in the secondary storage. *Then quit the NE with command F3-Q.*

Once the above procedure is completed, you may now focus on assembling the program. Note that all the commands and displays shown in this section are for Norton's Editor. Other editors may require some other commands and their display style may be some what different but the overall procedure is the same.

```
ASSUME      CS:CODE, DS:DATA
DATA        SEGMENT
            OPR1 DW 1234 H
            OPR2 DW 0002 H
            RESULT DW 01 H DUP(?)

DATA        ENDS
CODE        SEGMENT
START       MOV AX, DATA
            MOV DS, AX
            MOV AX, OPR 1
            MOV BX, OPR 2
            CLC
            ADD AX, BX
            MOV DI, OFFSET RESULT
            MOV [DI], AX
            MOV AH, 4CH
            INT 21 H
CODE        ENDS
            END START
---------------------------------
            KBM.ASM
```

Fig. 3.9 *A Program KMB.ASM in Norton's Editor*

Note that before quitting the editor program the newly entered or modified file must be saved, otherwise it will be lost and will not be available for further assembling process.

3.3.2 Assembling a Program

Microsoft Assembler MASM is an easy to use and popular assemblers. This section deals with the MASM. As already discussed, the main task of any assembler program is to accept the text_assembly language program file as an input and prepare an object file. The text_assembly language program file is prepared by using any of the editor programs as discussed in Section 3.3.1. The MASM accepts the file names only with the extension. ASM. Even if a filename without any extension is given as input, it provides an .ASM extension to it. For example, to assemble the program in Fig. 3.9, one may enter the following command options:

```
C> MASM KMB
        or
C> MASM KMB.ASM
```

If any of the command option is entered as above, the screen displays, as shown in Fig. 3.10.

```
C>MASM KMB
Microsoft @ Macro Assembler Version 5.10
Copyright (c) Microsoft Corp.1981, 1989.
All Rights Reserved




Object filename [.OBJ]:
List filename[NUL.LST]:
Cross Reference[NUL.CRF]:
```

Fig. 3.10 *MASM Screen Display*

Another command option, available in MASM, that does not need any filename in the command line, is given along with the corresponding result display in Fig. 3.11.

```
C>MASM
Microsoft @ Macro Assembler Version 5.10
Copyright (c) Microsoft Corp.1981, 1989.
All Rights Reserved




Source filename [.ASM]:
Object filename [FILE.OBJ]:
List filename[NUL.LST]:
List filename[NUL.CRF]:
```

Fig. 3.11 *MASM Alternative Screen Display*

If you do not enter the filename to be assembled at the command line as shown in Fig. 3.10, then you may enter it as a source filename as shown in Fig. 3.11. The source filename is to be typed in the source filename line with or without the extension .ASM. The valid filename entry is accepted with a pressure of enter key. On the next line, the expected. OBJ filename is to be entered which creates the object file of the assembly language program. The .OBJ file is created with the entered name and the .OBJ extension. If no filename is entered for it before pressing enter key, the new .OBJ file is created with the same name as source file and extension .OBJ.

The .OBJ file contains the coded object modules of the program to be assembled. On the next line, a filename is entered for the expected listing file of the source file, in the same way as the object filename was entered. The listing file is automatically generated in the assembly process. The listing file is identified by the entered or source filename and an extension .LST. This file contains the total offset map of the source file including labels, offset addresses, opcodes, memory allotment for different labels and directives and relocation information. The cross reference filename is also entered in the same way as discussed for the listing file. This file is used for debugging the source program. It contains the statistical information size of the file in bytes, number of labels, list of labels, routines to be called, etc. about the source program.

After the cross-reference file name is entered, the assembly process starts. If the program contains syntax errors, they are displayed using error code number and the corresponding line number at which they appear. Once these syntax errors and warnings are taken care of by the programmer, the assembly process is completed successfully. The successful assembly process may generate the .OBJ, .LST and .CRF files, which may further be used by the linker programmer to link the object modules and generate an executable (.EXE) file from a .OBJ file. All the above said files may not be generated during the assembling of every program. The generation of some of them may be suppressed using the specific command line options of MASM. The discussions regarding the different command line options of MASM are out of the scope of this book. Here we intend to highlight just a routine assembling procedure. The files generated by the MASM are further used by the program LINK.EXE to generate an executable file of the source program.

3.3.3 Linking a Program

The DOS linking program LINK.EXE links the different object modules of a source program and function library routines to generate an integrated executable code of the source program. The main input to the linker is the .OBJ file that contains the object modules of the source programs. Other supporting information may be obtained from the files generated by MASM. The linker program is invoked using the following options.

```
    C> LINK
       or
C> LINK KMB.OBJ
```

The .OBJ extension is a must for a file to be accepted by the LINK as a valid object file. The first option may generate a display asking for the object file, list file and libraries as inputs and an expected name of the .EXE file to be generated. The other option also generates the similar display, but will not ask for the .OBJ filename, as it is already specified at the command line. If no filenames are entered for these files, by default, the source filename is considered with different extensions. The procedure of entering the filenames in LINK is also similar to that in MASM. The LINK command display is as shown in Fig. 3.12.

```
C>LINK

Microsoft @ Overlay Linker Version. 3.64
Copyright(c)Microsoft Corp. 1983-88. All Rights Reserved.


Object Module[.OBJ]:
Run file[.EXE]:
List filename[NUL.MAP]:
Libraries[LIB]:
```

Fig. 3.12 *Link Command Screen Display*

The option input 'Libraries' in the display of Fig. 3.12 expects any special library name of which the functions were used by the source program. The output of the LINK program is an executable file with the entered filename and .EXE extension. This executable filename can further be entered at the DOS prompt to execute the file.

In the advanced versions of MASM, the complete procedure of assembling and linking is combined under a single menu invokable compile function. The recent versions of MASM have much more sophisticated and user-friendly facilities and options that cannot be detailed here for the obvious reasons. For further details users may refer to "Technical reference and Users' Manual-MASM, Version 5".

3.3.4 Using DEBUG

DEBUG.COM is a DOS utility that facilitates the debugging and trouble-shooting of assembly language programs. In case of personal computers, all the processor resources and memory resource management functions are carried out by the operating systems. Hence, users have very little control over the computer hardware at lower levels. The DEBUG utility enables you to have the control of these resources up to some extent. In short, the DEBUG enables you to use the personal computer as a low level microprocessor kit.

The DEBUG command at DOS prompt invokes this facility. A '_' (dash) display signals the successful invoke operation of DEBUG, that is further used as DEBUG prompt for debugging commands. The following command line, DEBUG prompt and the DEBUG command character display explain the DEBUG command entry procedure, as in Fig. 3.13.

```
C>DEBUG ↵

- ↵

-R ↵



    ↵-Symbol of <ENTER>key
```

Fig. 3.13 *DEBUG Command Line and Prompt*

A valid command is accepted using the enter key. The list of generally used valid commands of DEBUG is given in Table 3.1 along with their respective syntax.

The program DEBUG may be used either to debug a source program or to observe the results of execution of an .EXE file with the help of the .LST file and the above commands. The .LST file shows the offset address allotments for result variables of a program in the particular segment. After execution of the program, the offset address of the result variables may be observed using the D command. The results available in the registers may be observed using the R command. Thus the DEBUG offers a reasonably good platform for trouble shooting, executing and observing the results of the assembly language programs. Here one should note that the DEBUG is able to troubleshoot only .EXE files.

Table 3.1 *DEBUG Commands*

COMMAND CHARACTER	*Format/Formats*	*Functions*
-R	<ENTER>	Display all Registers and flags
-R	reg<ENTER> old contents:New contents	Display specified register contents and modify with the entered new contents.
-D	<ENTER>	Display 128 memory locations of RAM starting from the current display pointer.
-D	SEG:OFFSET1 OFFSET2<ENTER>	Display memory contents in SEG from OFFSET1 to OFFSET2.
-E	<ENTER>	Enter Hex data at current display pointer SEG:OFFSET.
-E	SEG:OFFSET1 <ENTER>	Enter data at SEG:OFFSET1 byte by byte. The memory pointer is to be incremented by space key, data entry is to be completed by pressing the <ENTER> key.
-f	SEG:OFFSET1 OFFSET2 BYTE <ENTER>	Fill the memory area starting from SEG:OFFSET1 to OFFSET2 by the byte BYTE.
-f	SEG:OFFSET1 OFFSET2BYTE1,BYTE2,BYTE3<ENTER>	Fill the memory area as above with the sequence BYTE1, BYTE2, BYTE3, etc.
-a	<ENTER>	Assemble from the current CS:IP.
-a	SEG:OFFSET <ENTER>	Assemble the entered instruction from SEG:OFFSET address.
-u	<ENTER>	Unassemble from the current CS:IP.
-u	SEG:OFFSET <ENTER>	Unassemble from the address SEG:OFFSET.
-g	<ENTER>	Execute from current CS:IP. By modifying CS and IP using R command this can be used for any address.
-g	=OFFSET <ENTER>	Execute from OFFSET in the current CS.

(Contd.)

Table 3.1 *(Contd.)*

COMMAND CHARACTER	*Format/Formats*	*Functions*
-s	SEG:OFFSET1 to OFFSET2 BYTE/BYTES <ENTER>	Searches a BYTE or string of BYTES separated by ',' in the memory block SEG:OFFSET1 to OFFSET2, and displays all the offsets at which the byte or string of bytes is found.
-q	<ENTER>	Quit the DEBUG and return to DOS
-T	SEG:OFFSET <ENTER>	Trace the program execution by single stepping starting from the address SEG:OFFSET.
-m	SEG:OFFSET1 OFFSET2 NB <ENTER>	Move NB bytes from OFFSET1 to OFF-SET2 in segment SEG
-c	SEG:OFFSET OFFSET2 NB <ENTER>	Copy NB bytes from OFFSET1 to OFF-SET2 in segment SEG.
-n	FILENAME.EXE <ENTER>	Set filename pointer to FILENAME
-l	<ENTER>	Load the file FILENAME.EXE as set by the -n command in the RAM and set the CS:IP at the address at which the file is loaded.

- Note that, changing the case of the command letters does not change the command option.
- The entered numbers are considered as hexadecimal.

3.4 ASSEMBLY LANGUAGE EXAMPLE PROGRAMS

In the previous chapter, we studied the complete instruction set of 8086/88, the assembler directives and pseudo-ops. In the previous sections, the procedure of entering an assembly language program into a computer and coding it, i.e. preparing an EXE file from the source code were described. In this section, we will study some programs which elucidate the use of instructions, directives and some other facilities that are available in assembly language programming.

After studying these programs, it is expected that the reader would have got a clear idea about the use of different directives, pseudo-ops and their syntaxes, besides understanding the logic of each program. If one writes an assembly language program and tries to code it, the chances of error are high in the first attempt. Error free programming depends upon the skill of the programmer, which can be developed by writing and executing a number of assembly programs, besides studying the example programs given in this text.

Before explaining the written programs, we have to explain an important point about the DOS function calls available under INT 21H instruction. DOS is an operating system, which is a program that stands between a bare computer system hardware and a user. It acts as a user interface with the available computer hardware resources. It also manages the hardware resources of the computer system. In the Disk Operating System, the hardware resources of the computer system like memory, keyboard, CRT display, hard disk, and floppy disk drives can be handled with the help of the instruction INT 21H. The routines required to refer to these resources are written as interrupt service routines for 21H interrupt. Under this interrupt, the specific resource is selected depending upon the value in AH register. For example, if AH contains 09H, then CRT display is to be used for displaying a message or if, AH contain 0AH, then the keyboard is to be accessed. These interrupts are called 'function calls' and the value in AH is called 'function value'. In short, the purpose of 'function calls' under INT 21 H is to be decided by the 'function value' that is in AH. Some function values also control the software operations of the machine. The list of the function values available under INT 21 H, their corresponding functions, the required parameters and the returns are given in tabulated form in the Appendix-B. Note that there are a number of interrupt functions in DOS, but INT 21H is used more frequently. The readers may find other interrupts of DOS and BIOS from the respective technical references.

In this chapter, a few example programs are presented. Starting from very simple programs, the chapter concludes with more complex programs.

Program 3.1

Write a program for addition of two numbers.

Solution The following program adds two 16-bit operands. There are various methods of specifying operands depending upon the addressing modes that the programmer wants to use. Accordingly, there may be different program listings to achieve a single programming goal. A skilled programmer uses a simple logic and implements it by using a minimum number of instructions. Let us now try to explain the following program:

```
ASSUME CS:CODE, DS:DATA
DATA SEGMENT
OPR1 DW 1234H                      ; 1st operand
OPR2    DW 0002H                   ; 2nd operand
RESULT  DW 01 DUP(?)               ; A word of memory reserved for re-
                                     sult
DATA    ENDS
CODE    SEGMENT
START:  MOV AX, DATA               ; Initialize data segment
        MOV DS, AX                 ;
        MOV AX, OPR1               ; Take 1st operand in AX
        MOV BX, OPR2               ; Take 2nd operand in BX
        CLC                        ; Clear previous carry if any
        ADD AX, BX                 ; Add BX to AX
        MOV DI, OFFSET RESULT      ; Take offset of RESULT in DI
        MOV [DI], AX               ; Store the result at memory address in DI
        MOV AH, 4CH                ; Return to DOS prompt
        INT 21H
CODE    ENDS                       ; CODE segment ends
        END START                  ; Program ends
```

Program 3.1(a) *Listings*

3.4.1 How to Write an Assembly Language Program

The first step in writing an assembly language program is to define and study the problem. Then, decide the logical modules required for the program. From the statement of the program one may guess that some data may be required for the program or the result of the program that is to be stored in memory. Hence the program will need a logical space called DATA segment. Invariably the CODE segment is a part of a program containing the actual instruction sequence to be executed. If the stack facility is to be used in the program, it will require the STACK segment. The EXTRA segment may be used as an additional destination data segment. Note that the use of all these logical segments is not compulsory except for the CODE segment. Some programs may require DATA and CODE segments, while the others may also contain STACK and EXTRA. For example, Program 3.1 (a) requires only DATA and CODE segment.

The first line of the program containing the 'ASSUME' directive declares that the label CODE is to be used as a logical name for CODE segment and the label DATA is to be used for DATA segment. These labels CODE and DATA are reserved by MASM for these purposes only. They should not be used as general labels. Once this statement is written in the program, CODE refers to the code segment and DATA refers to data segment throughout the program. If you want to change it in a program you will have to write another ASSUME statement in the program.

The second statement, DATA SEGMENT marks the starting of a logical data space DATA. Inside the DATA segment, OPR1 is the first operand. The directive DW defines OPR1 as a word operand of value 1234H and OPR2 as a word operand of value 0002H. The third DW directive reserves 01H words of memory for storing the result of the program and leaves it undefined due to the directive DUP(?). The statement DATA ENDS marks the end of the DATA segment. Thus the logical space DATA contains OPR1, OPR2 and RESULT, which will be allotted physical memory locations whenever the logical SEGMENT DATA is allocated memory or loaded in the memory of a computer as explained in the previous topic of relocation. The assembler calculates that the above data segment requires 6 bytes, i.e. 2 bytes each for OPR1, OPR2 and RESULT.

The code segment in the above program starts with the statement CODE SEGMENT. The code segment, as already explained, is a logical segment space containing the instructions. The label STARTS marks the starting point of the execution sequence. The ASSUME statement just informs the assembler that the label CODE is used for the code segment and the label DATA is used for the DATA segment. It does not actually put the address corresponding to CODE in Code Segment (CS) register and address corresponding to DATA in the Data Segment (DS) register. This procedure of putting the actual segment address values into the corresponding segment registers is known as segment register initialisation. A programmer has to carry out these initializations for DS, SS and ES using instructions, while the CS is automatically initialised by the loader at the time of loading the EXE file into the memory for actual execution. The first two instructions in the program are for data segment initialization.

Note that, no segment register in 8086 can be loaded with immediate segment address value, instead the address value should be first loaded into any one of the general purpose registers which can then be transferred to any of the segment registers DS, ES and SS. Also one should note that CS cannot be loaded at all. Its contents can be changed by using a long jump instruction, a call instruction or an interrupt instruction. For each of the segments DS, ES and SS, the programmer will have to carry out initialization if they are used in the program, while CS is automatically initialized by the loader program at the time of loading and execution. Then the two instructions move the two operands OPR1 and OPR2 in AX and BX respectively. Carry is cleared before addition operation (optional in this program). The ADD instruction will add BX into AX and store the result in AX. The instruction used to store the result in RESULT uses a different addressing mode than that used for taking OPR1 into AX. The indexed addressing mode is used to store the result of addition in memory locations labeled RESULT.

The instruction MOV DI, OFFSET RESULT stores the offset of the label RESULT into DI register. The next instruction stores the result available in AX into the address pointed to by DI, i.e. address of the RESULT. A lot has been already discussed about the function calls under INT 21H. The function value 4CH is for returning to the DOS prompt. If instead of these one writes HLT instruction there will not be any difference in program execution except that the computer will hang as the processor goes to HLT state, and the user will not be able to examine the result. In that case, for further operation, one will have to reset the computer and boot it again. To avoid this resetting of the computer every time you run the program and enable it to check the result, it is better to use the function call 4CH at the end of each program so that after executing the program, the computer returns back to DOS prompt. The statement CODE ENDS marks the end of the CODE segment. The statement END START marks the end of the procedure that started with the label START. At the end of each file, the END statement is a must.

Until now, we have discussed Program 3.1(a) in significant detail. As we have already said, the program contains two logical segments CODE and DATA, but it is not at all necessary that all the programs must contain the two segments. A programmer may use a single segment to cover up data as well as instructions. Program 3.1(b) explains the fact.

```
ASSUME CS:CODE
        CODE        SEGMENT
        OPR1        DW      1234H
        OPR2        DW      0002H
        RESULT      DW      01 DUP(?)
START :  MOV AX, CODE
        MOV DS, AX
        MOV AX, OPR1
        MOV BX, OPR2
        CLC
        ADD AX, BX
        MOV DI, OFFSET RESULT
        MOV [DI], AX
        MOV AH,4CH
        INT 21H
CODE    ENDS
        END START
```

Program 3.1(b) *Alternative listing for Program 3.1*

We have discussed all the properties of this program in detail. For all the following programs, we will not explain the common things like forming segments using directives and operators, etc. Instead, just the logic of the program will be explained. The use of proper syntax of the 8086/8088 assembler MASM is self explanatory. The comments may help the reader in getting the ideas regarding the logic of the program.

Assemble the above written program using MASM after entering it into the computer using the procedure explained in Section 3.3.1. Once you get the EXE file as the output of the LINK program, Your listing is ready for execution. The Program 3.1 is prepared in the form of EXE file with the name KMB.EXE in the directory. Next, it can be executed with the command line as given below.

```
C> KMB
```

This method of execution will store the result of the program in memory but will not display it on the screen. To display the result on the screen the programmer will have to use DOS function calls, which will make the programs too lengthy. Hence, another method to check the results is to run the program under the control of DEBUG. To run the program under the control of debug and to observe the results one must prepare the LST file, that gives information about memory allotment to different labels and variables of the program while assembling it. The LST file can be displayed on the screen using NE-Norton's Editor.

Program 3.2

Write a program for the addition of a series of 8-bit numbers. The series contains 100(numbers).

Solution In the first program, we have implemented the addition of two numbers. In this program, we show the addition of 100 (D) numbers. Initially, the resulting sum of the first two numbers will be stored. To this sum, the third number will be added. This procedure will be repeated till all the numbers in the series are added. A conditional jump instruction will be used to implement the counter checking logic. The comments explain the purpose of each instruction.

```
ASSUME CS:CODE, DS:DATA
DATA SEGMENT                         ; Data segment starts
NUMLIST DB 52H, 23H,-                ; List of byte numbers
COUNT EQU 100D                       ; Number of bytes to be added
RESULT DW 01H DUP(?)                 ; One word is reserved for result
DATA ENDS                            ; Data segment ends
CODE SEGMENT                         ; Code segment starts at relative
ORG 200H                             ; address 0200h in code segment
START:      MOV AX, DATA             ; Initialize data segment
            MOV DS, AX
            MOV CX, COUNT            ; Number of bytes to be added in CX
            XOR AX, AX               ; Clear AX and CF
            XOR BX, BX               ; Clear BH for converting the byte to
                                       word
            MOV SI,OFFSET NUMLIST    ; Point to the first number in the
                                       list
AGAIN:      MOV BL, [SI]             ; Take the first number in BL,BH is zero
            ADD AX, BX               ; Add AX with BX
            INC SI                   ; Increment pointer to the byte list
            DEC CX                   ; Decrement counter
            JNZ AGAIN                ; If all numbers are added,point to re-
                                       sult
            MOV DI, OFFSET RESULT    ; destination and store it
            MOV [DI], AX
            MOV AH, 4CH              ; Return to DOS
            INT 21H
            CODE ENDS
END         START
```

Program 3.2 *Listings*

The use of statement ORG 200H in this program is not compulsory. We have used this statement here just to explain the way to use it. It will not affect the result at all. Whenever the program is loaded into the memory whatever is the address assigned for CODE, the executable code starts at the offset address 0200H due to the above statement. Similar to DW, the directive DB reserves space for the list of 8-bit numbers in the series. The procedure for entering the program, coding and execution has already been explained. The result of addition will be stored in the memory locations allotted to the label RESULT.

Program 3.3

A program to find out the largest number from a given unordered array of 8-bit numbers, stored in the locations starting from a known address.

Solution Compare the *i*th number of the series with the (*i*+1)th number using CMP instruction. It will set the flags appropriately, depending upon whether the ith number or the (*i*+1)th number is greater. If the *i*th number is greater than (*i*+1)th, leave it in AX (any register may be used). Otherwise, load the (*i*+1)th number in AX, replacing the *i*th number in AX. The procedure is repeated till all the members in the array have been compared.

```
ASSUME CS:CODE, DS:DATA
DATA SEGMENT                          ; Data segment starts
LIST DB 52H, 23H, 56H, 45H, --        ; List of byte numbers
COUNT EQU OF                          ; Number of bytes in the list
LARGEST DB 01H DUP(?)                 ; One byte is reserved for the largest
                                        number.
DATA ENDS                             ; Data segment ends
CODE SEGMENT                          ; Code segment starts.
START:      MOV AX, DATA              ; Initialize data segment.
            MOV DS, AX
            MOV SI, OFFSET LIST
            MOV CL, COUNT             ; Number of bytes in CL.
            MOV AL, [SI]              ; Take the first number in AL
AGAIN:      CMP AL, [SI+1]            ; and compare it with the next number.
            JNL NEXT
            MOV AL, [SI+1]
NEXT:       INC SI                    ; Increment pointer to the byte list.
            DEC CL                    ; Decrement counter.
            JNZ AGAIN                 ; If all numbers are compared, point to
                                        result
            MOV SI, OFFSET LARGEST ; destination and store it.
            MOV [SI], AL
            MOV AH, 4CH               ; Return to DOS.
            INT 21H
            CODE ENDS
END         START
```

Program 3.3 *Listings*

Program 3.4

Modify the Program 3.3 for a series of words.

Solution The logic is similar to the previous program written for a series of byte numbers. The program is directly written as follows without any comment leaving it to the reader to find out the use of each instruction and directive used.

```
ASSUME CS:CODE, DS:DATA
DATA SEGMENT
LIST DW 1234H, 2354H, 0056H, 045AH, -
COUNT EQU OF
LARGEST DW 01H DUP(?)
DATA ENDS
CODE SEGMENT
START:      MOV AX, DATA
            MOV DS, AX
            MOV SI, OFFSET LIST
```

```
            MOV CL, COUNT
            MOV AX, [SI]
AGAIN:      CMP AX, [SI+2]
            JNL NEXT
            MOV AX, [SI+2]
NEXT:       INC SI
            INC SI
            DEC CL
            JNZ AGAIN
            MOV SI, OFFSET LARGEST
            MOV [SI], AX
            MOV AH, 4CH
            INT 21H
CODE        ENDS
            END     START
```

Program 3.4 *Listings*

Program 3.5

A program to find out the number of even and odd numbers from a given series of 16-bit hexadecimal numbers.

Solution The simplest logic to decide whether a binary number is even or odd, is to check the least significant bit of the number. If the bit is zero, the number is even, otherwise it is odd. Check the LSB by rotating the number through carry flag, and increment even or odd number counter.

```
ASSUME CS:CODE, DS:DATA
DATA SEGMENT
LIST DW 2357H, 0A579H, 0C322H, 0C91EH, 0C000H, 0957H
COUNT EQU 006H
DATA ENDS
CODE SEGMENT
START:      XOR BX, BX
            XOR DX, DX
            MOV AX, DATA
            MOV DS, AX
            MOV CL, COUNT
            MOV SI, OFFSET LIST
AGAIN:      MOV AX, [SI]
            ROR AX, 01
            JC ODD
            INC BX
            JMP NEXT
ODD:        INC DX
NEXT:       ADD SI, 02
            DEC CL
            JNZ AGAIN
            MOV AH, 4CH
            INT 21H
            CODE ENDS
            END START
```

Program 3.5 *Listings*

Program 3.6

Write a program to find out the number of positive numbers and negative numbers from a given series of signed numbers.

Solution Take the *i*th number in any of the registers. Rotate it left through carry. The status of carry flag, i.e. the most significant bit of the number will give the information about the sign of the number. If CF is 1, the number is negative; otherwise, it is positive.

```
ASSUME CS:CODE, DS:DATA
DATA SEGMENT
LIST DW 2579H, 0A500H, 0C009H, 0159H, 0B900H
COUNT EQU 05H
DATA ENDS
CODE SEGMENT
START:          XOR BX, BX
                XOR DX, DX
                MOV AX, DATA
                MOV DS, AX
                MOV CL, COUNT
                MOV SI, OFFSET LIST
AGAIN:          MOV AX, [SI]
                SHL AX, 01
                JC NEG
                INC BX
                JMP NEXT
NEG:            INC DX
NEXT:           ADD SI, 02
                DEC CL
                JNZ AGAIN
                MOV AH, 4CH
                INT 21H
                CODE ENDS
                END START
```

Program 3.6 *Listings*

The logic of Program 3.6 is similar to that of Program 3.5, hence comments are not given in Program 3.6 except for a few important ones.

Program 3.7

Write a program to move a string of data words from offset 2000H to offset 3000H the length of the string is 0FH.

Solution To write this program, we will use an important facility, available in the 8086 instruction set, i.e. move string byte/word instruction. We will also study the flexibility imparted by this instructions to the 8086 assembly language program. Let us first write the Program 3.7 for 8085, assuming that the string is available at location 2000H and is to be moved at 3000H.

```
                LXI H , 2000H
                LXI D , 3000H
                MVI C , 0FH
AGAIN :                 MOV A , M
```

```
        STAX   D
        INX    H
        INX    D
        DCR    C
        JNZ    AGAIN
        HLT
```

An 8085 Program for Program 3.7

Now assuming DS is suitably set, let us write the sequence for 8086. At first using the index registers, the program can be written as given:

```
            MOV    SI , 2000H
            MOV    DI , 3000H
            MOV    CX , 0FH
    AGAIN : MOV    AX , [SI]
            MOV    [DI], AX
            ADD    SI, 02H
            ADD    DI, 02H
            DEC    CX
            JNZ    AGAIN
            HLT
```

An 8086 Program for Program 3.7

Comparing the above listings for 8085 and 8086, we may infer that every instruction in 8085 listing is replaced by an equivalent instruction of 8086. The above 8086 listing is absolutely correct but it is not efficient. Let us try to write the listings for the same purpose using the string instruction. Due to the assembler directives and the syntax, one may feel that the program is lengthy, though it eliminates four instructions for a MOVSW instruction.

```
ASSUME CS:CODE, DS:DATA
DATA SEGMENT
SOURCESTRT EQU 2000H
DESTSTRT EQU 3000H
COUNT EQU 0FH
DATA ENDS
CODE SEGMENT
START:       MOV AX, DATA
             MOV DS, AX
             MOV ES, AX
             MOV SI, SOURCESTRT
             MOV DI, DESTSTRT
             MOV CX, COUNT
             CLD
REP          MOVSW
             MOV AH, 4CH
             INT 21H
CODE ENDS
END START
```

Program 3.7 *An 8086 Program listing for Program 3.7 using String instruction*

Compare the above two 8086 listings. Both contain ten instructions. However, in case of the second program, the instruction for the initialisation of segment register and DOS interrupt are additional while the first one neither contains initialisation of any segment registers nor does it contain the DOS interrupt instruction. We can say that the first program uses 9 instructions, while the second one uses only 5 for implementing the same algorithm.

This program and the related discussions are aimed at explaining the importance of the string instructions and the method to use them.

Program 3.8

Write an assembly language program to arrange a given series of hexadecimal bytes in ascending order.

Solution There exist a large number of sorting algorithms. The algorithm used here is called *bubble sorting.* The method of sorting is explained as follows. To start with, the first number of the series is compared with the second one. If the first number is greater than second, exchange their positions in the series otherwise leave the positions unchanged. Then, compare the second number in the recent form of the series with third and repeat the exchange part that you have carried out for the first and the second number, and for all the remaining numbers of the series. Repeat this procedure for the complete series ($n-1$) times. After ($n-1$) iterations, you will get the largest number at the end of the series, where n is the length of the series. Again start from the first address of the series. Repeat the same procedure right from the first element to the last element. After ($n-2$) iterations you will get the second highest number at the last but one place in the series. Continue this till the complete series is arranged in ascending order. Let the series be as given:

```
53 , 25 , 19, 02                 n = 4
25 , 53 , 19, 02                 1st operation
25 , 19 , 53 , 02                2nd operation
25 , 19 , 02 , 53                3rd operation
largest no.            ⇒         4 - 1 = 3 operations
19 , 25 , 02 , 53                1st operation
19 , 02 , 25 , 53                2nd operation
2nd largest number     ⇒         4 - 2 = 2 operations
02 , 19 , 25 , 53                1st operation
3rd largest number     ⇒         4 - 3 = 1 operations
```

Instead of taking a variable count for the external loop in the program like (n – 1), (n – 2), (n–3), ..., etc. It is better to take the count (n – 1) all the time for simplicity. The resulting program is given as shown.

```
ASSUME CS:CODE, DS:DATA
DATA SEGMENT
LIST DW 53H, 25H, 19H, 02H
COUNT EQU 04
DATA ENDS
CODE SEGMENT
START:      MOV AX, DATA
            MOV DS, AX
            MOV DX, COUNT-1
AGAIN0:     MOV CX, DX
            MOV SI, OFFSET LIST
AGAIN1:     MOV AX, [SI]
```

```
                CMP AX, [SI+2]
                JL  PR1
                XCHG [SI+2], AX
                XCHG [SI], AX
      PR1:      ADD SI, 02
                LOOP AGAIN1
                DEC DX
                JNZ AGAIN0
                MOV AH, 4CH
                INT 21H
      CODE      ENDS
                END START
```

Program 3.8 *Listings*

With a similar approach, the reader may write a program to arrange the string in descending order. For this, instead of the JL instruction in the above program, one will have to use a JG instruction.

Program 3.9

Write a program to perform a one byte BCD addition.

Solution It is assumed that the operands are in BCD form, but the CPU considers it hexadecimal and accordingly performs addition. Consider the following example for addition. Carry is set to be zero.

```
         92
       + 59
       -----
         EB      Actual result after addition considering hex.
                 operands

         1011
       + 0110       As 0BH (LSD of addition) > 09, add 06 to it.
       --------
        10001       Least significant nibble of result (neglect the
                    auxiliary carry) → AF is set to 1
  0110 is added to most significant nibble of the result if it is greater
than 9 or AF is set.
                       1     Carry from previous digit (AF)
         E     →    1110
               +    0110
               ---------
 CF is set to 1     0101     next significant nibble of result

Result CF    Most significantLeast significant digit
    1               5                  1

      ASSUME CS:CODE, DS:DATA
      DATA SEGMENT
                OPR1 EQU 92H
                OPR2 EQU 52H
      RESULT DB 02 DUP(00)
      DATA ENDS
```

```
CODE SEGMENT
START:          MOV AX, DATA
                MOV DS, AX
                MOV BL, OPR1
                XOR AL, AL
                MOV AL, OPR2
                ADD AL, BL
                DAA
                MOV RESULT, AL
                JNC MSBO
                INC [RESULT+1]
MSBO:           MOV AH, 4CH
                INT 21H
CODE ENDS
END START
```

Program 3.9 *Listings*

In this program, the instruction DAA is used after ADD. Similarly, DAS can be used after SUB instruction. The reader may try to write a program for BCD subtraction for practice.

Program 3.10

Write a program that performs addition, subtraction, multiplication and division of the given operands. Perform BCD operation for addition and subtraction.

Solution Here we have directly given the routine for Program 3.10.

```
ASSUME CS:CODE, DS:DATA
DATA SEGMENT
                OPR1 EQU 98H
                OPR2 EQU 49H
                SUM DW 01 DUP(00)
                SUBT DW 01 DUP(00)
                PROD DW 01 DUP(00)
                DIVS DW 01 DUP(00)
DATA            ENDS
CODE            SEGMENT
START:          MOV AX, DATA
                MOV DS, AX
                MOV BL, OPR2
                XOR AL, AL
                MOV AL, OPR1
                ADD AL, BL
                DAA
                MOV BYTE PTR SUM, AL
                JNC MSBO
                INC [SUM+1]
MSBO:           XOR AL, AL
                MOV AL, OPR1
                SUB AL, BL
                DAS
```

```
                MOV BYTE PTR SUBT, AL
                JNB MSB1
                INC [SUBT+1]
MSB1:           XOR AL, AL
                MOV AL, OPR1
                MUL BL
                MOV WORD PTR PROD, AX
                XOR AH, AH
                MOV AL, OPR1
                DIV BL
                MOV WORD PTR DIVS, AX
                MOV AH, 4CH
                INT 21H
CODE            ENDS
                END START
```

Program 3.10 *Listings*

Program 3.11

Write a program to find out whether a given byte is in the string or not. If it is in the string, find out the relative address of the byte from the starting location of the string.

Solution The given string is scanned for the given byte. If it is found in the string, the zero flag is set; else, it is reset. Use of the SCASB instruction is quite obvious here. A count should be maintained to find out the relative address of the byte found out. Note that, in this program, the code segment is written before the data segment.

```
ASSUME CS:CODE, DS:DATA
CODE SEGMENT
START:          MOV AX, DATA
                MOV DS, AX
                MOV ES, AX
                MOV CX, COUNT
                MOV DI, OFFSET STRING
                MOV BL, 00H
                MOV AL, BYTE1
SCAN1:          NOP
                SCASB
                JZ XXX
                INC BL
                LOOP SCAN1
XXX:            MOV AH, 4CH
                INT 21H
                CODE ENDS
DATA SEGMENT
BYTE1 EQU 25H
COUNT EQU 06H
STRING DB 12H, 13H, 20H, 20H, 25H, 21H
DATA ENDS
                END START
```

Program 3.11 *Listings*

Program 3.12

Write a program to convert the BCD numbers 0 to 9 to their equivalent seven segment codes using the look-up table technique. Assume the codes [7-seg] are stored sequentially in CODELIST at the relative addresses from 0 to 9. The BCD number (CHAR) is taken in AL.

Solution Refer to the explanation of the XLAT instruction. The statement of the program itself gives the explanation about the logic of the program.

```
ASSUME CS:CODE, DS:DATA
DATA SEGMENT
                CODELIST DB 34, 45, 56, 45, 23, 12, 19, 24, 21, 00
                CHAR EQU 05
                CODEC    DB 01H DUP(?)
DATA ENDS
CODE SEGMENT
START:          MOV AX, DATA
                MOV DS, AX
                MOV BX, OFFSET CODELIST
                MOV AL, CHAR
                XLAT
                MOV BYTE PTR CODEC,AL
                MOV AH, 4CH
                INT 21H
CODE            ENDS
                END START
```

Program 3.12 *Listings*

Program 3.13

Decide whether the parity of a given number is even or odd. If parity is even set DL to 00; else, set DL to 01. The given number may be a multibyte number.

Solution The simplest algorithm to check the parity of a multibyte number is to go on adding the parity byte by byte with 00H. The result of the addition reflects the parity of that byte of the multibyte number. Adding the parities of all the bytes of the number, one will obtain the over all parity of the number:

```
ASSUME CS:CODE, DS:DATA
DATA SEGMENT
                NUM DD 335A379BH
                BYTE_COUNT EQU 04
DATA ENDS
CODE SEGMENT
START:          MOV AX, DATA
                MOV DS, AX
                MOV DH, BYTE_COUNT
                XOR AL, AL
                MOV CL, 00
                MOV SI, OFFSET NUM
NEXT_BYTE:      ADD AL, [SI]
                JP EVENP
```

```
                INC CL
EVENP:          INC SI
                MOV AL, 00
                DEC DH
                JNZ NEXT_BYTE
                MOV DL, 00
                RCR CL, 1
                JNC CLEAR
                INC DL
CLEAR:          MOV AH, 4CH
                INT 21H
CODE            ENDS
                END START
```

Program 3.13 *Listings*

The contents of CL are incremented depending upon either the parity for that byte is even or odd. If LSB of CL is 1, after testing for all bytes, it means the parity of the multibyte number is odd otherwise it is even and DL is modified correspondingly.

Program 3.14

Write a program for the addition of two 3 × 3 matrices. The matrices are stored in the form of lists (row wise). Store the result of addition in the third list.

Solution In the addition of two matrices, the corresponding elements are added to form the corresponding elements of the result matrix as shown:

$$\begin{bmatrix} a_{11} & a_{12} & a_{13} \\ a_{21} & a_{22} & a_{23} \\ a_{31} & a_{32} & a_{33} \end{bmatrix} + \begin{bmatrix} b_{11} & b_{12} & b_{13} \\ b_{21} & b_{22} & b_{23} \\ b_{31} & b_{32} & b_{33} \end{bmatrix} = \begin{bmatrix} a_{11} + b_{11} + a_{12} + b_{12} + a_{13} + b_{13} \\ a_{21} + b_{21} + a_{22} + b_{22} + a_{23} + b_{23} \\ a_{31} + b_{31} + a_{32} + b_{32} + a_{33} + b_{33} \end{bmatrix}$$

$$[A] \quad + \quad [B] \quad = \quad [A + B]$$

The matrix *A* is stored in the memory at an offset MAT1, as given:

a_{11}, a_{12}, a_{13}, a_{21}, a_{22}, a_{23}, a_{31}, a_{32}, a_{33}, etc.

A total of 3 × 3 = 9 additions are to be done. The assembly language program is written as shown:

```
ASSUME CS:CODE,DS:DATA
DATA SEGMENT
                DIM EQU 09H
                MAT1 DB 01, 02, 03, 04, 05, 06, 07, 08, 09
                MAT2 DB 01, 02, 03, 04, 05, 06, 07, 08, 09
                RMAT3 DW 09H DUP(?)
DATA ENDS
CODE SEGMENT
START:          MOV AX, DATA
                MOV DS, AX
                MOV CX, DIM
                MOV SI, OFFSET MAT1
                MOV DI, OFFSET MAT2
                MOV BX, OFFSET RMAT3
```

```
NEXT:        XOR AX, AX
             MOV AL, [SI]
             ADD AL, [DI]
             MOV WORD PTR [BX], AX
             INC SI
             INC DI
             ADD BX, 02
             LOOP NEXT
             MOV AH, 4CH
             INT 21H
CODE         ENDS
             END START
```

Program 3.14 *Listings*

Program 3.15

Write a program to find out the product of two matrices. Store the result in the third matrix. The matrices are specified as in the Program 3.14.

Solution The multiplication of matrices is carried out as shown:

$$\begin{bmatrix} a_{11} & a_{12} & a_{13} \\ a_{21} & a_{22} & a_{23} \\ a_{31} & a_{32} & a_{33} \end{bmatrix} \times \begin{bmatrix} b_{11} & b_{12} & b_{13} \\ b_{21} & b_{22} & b_{23} \\ b_{31} & b_{32} & b_{33} \end{bmatrix}$$

$$= \begin{bmatrix} a_{11}\,b_{11} + a_{12}\,b_{21} + a_{13}\,b_{31} & a_{12}\,b_{12} + a_{22}\,b_{12} + a_{13}\,b_{32} & a_{13}\,b_{13} + a_{12}\,b_{23} + a_{13}\,b_{23} \\ a_{21}\,b_{11} + a_{22}\,b_{21} + a_{23}\,b_{31} & a_{21}\,b_{12} + a_{22}\,b_{22} + a_{23}\,b_{32} & a_{21}\,b_{13} + a_{22}\,b_{23} + a_{23}\,b_{23} \\ a_{31}\,b_{11} + a_{32}\,b_{21} + a_{33}\,b_{31} & a_{31}\,b_{12} + a_{32}\,b_{22} + a_{33}\,b_{32} & a_{31}\,b_{13} + a_{32}\,b_{23} + a_{33}\,b_{23} \end{bmatrix}$$

The listings to carry out the above operation is given as shown:

```
ASSUME CS:CODE,DS:DATA
DATA SEGMENT
ROCOL EQU 03H
MAT1 DB 05H, 09H, 0AH, 03H, 02H, 07H, 03H, 00H, 09H
MAT2 DB 09H, 07H, 02H, 01H, 0H, 0DH, 7H, 06H, 02H
PMAT3 DW 09H DUP(?)
DATA ENDS
CODE SEGMENT
START:       MOV AX, DATA
             MOV DS, AX
             MOV CH, ROCOL
             MOV BX, OFFSET PMAT3
             MOV SI, OFFSET MAT1
NEXTROW:     MOV DI, OFFSET MAT2
             MOV CL, ROCOL
NEXTCOL:     MOV DL, ROCOL
             MOV BP, 0000H
             MOV AX, 0000H
             SAHF
NEXT_ELE:    MOV AL, [SI]
```

```
                MUL BYTE PTR[DI]
                ADD BP, AX
                INC SI
                ADD DI, 03
                DEC DL
                JNZ NEXT_ELE
                SUB DI, 08
                SUB SI, 03
                MOV [BX], BP
                ADD BX, 02
                DEC CL
                JNZ NEXTCOL
                ADD SI, 03
                DEC CH
                JNZ NEXTROW
                MOV AH, 4CH
                INT 21H
CODE ENDS
END START
```

Program 3.15 *Listings*

Program 3.16

Write a program to add two multibyte numbers and store the result as a third number. The numbers are stored in the form of the byte lists stored with the lowest byte first.

Solution This program is similar to the program written for the addition of two matrices except for the addition instruction.

```
ASSUME CS:CODE,DS:DATA
DATA SEGMENT
BYTES EQU 08H
NUM1 DB 05, 5AH, 6CH, 55H, 66H, 77H, 34H, 12H
NUM2 DB 04, 56H, 04H, 57H, 32H, 12H, 19H, 13H
NUM3 DB 0AH DUP(00)
DATA ENDS
CODE SEGMENT
START:          MOV AX, DATA
                MOV DS, AX
                MOV CX, BYTES
                MOV SI, OFFSET NUM1
                MOV DI, OFFSET NUM2
                MOV BX, OFFSET NUM3
                XOR AX, AX
NEXTBYTE:       MOV AL, [SI]
                ADC AL, [DI]
                MOV BYTE PTR[BX], AL
                INC SI
                INC DI
                INC BX
```

```
                DEC CX
                JNZ NEXTBYTE
                JNC NCARRY
                MOV BYTE PTR[BX], 01
NCARRY:         MOV AH, 4CH
                INT 21H
CODE ENDS
                END START
```

Program 3.16 *Listings*

Program 3.17

Write a program to add more than two multibyte numbers. The numbers are specified in a single list byte-wise one after another.

Solution In this program, all the numbers are stored in a single list byte-wise. The least significant byte of the first number is stored first, then the next significant byte and so on. After the most significant byte of the first number, the least significant byte of the second number will be stored. The series thus will end with the most significant byte of the last number. Let each number be of 8 bytes and 10 numbers are to be added. The list will contain $8 \times 10 = 80$ bytes. The result may have more than 8 bytes. Let us assume that the result requires 9 bytes to be stored. A separate string of 9 bytes is reserved for the result. The result is also stored in the same form as the numbers. The assembly language program for this problem is given as shown.

```
ASSUME CS:CODE, DS:DATA
DATA SEGMENT
BYTES EQU 04
NUMBERS EQU 02
NUMBERLIST DB 55H, 22H, 0BCH, 0FFH, 76H, 56H, 0FFH, 0F0H
RESULT DB BYTES+1 DUP(?)
DATA ENDS
CODE SEGMENT
START:          MOV AX, DATA
                MOV DS, AX
                XOR AX, AX
                MOV BL, BYTES
                MOV SI, OFFSET NUMBERLIST
                MOV DI, OFFSET RESULT
                MOV CL, BYTES
NEXTBYTE:       MOV CH, NUMBERS
NEXTNUM:        MOV AL, [SI]
                ADD SI, BYTES
                ADD [DI], AL
                JNC NOCARY
                INC BYTE PTR[DI+1]
NOCARY:         DEC CH
                JNZ NEXTNUM
                SUB SI, BYTES
                SUB SI, BYTES
                INC DI
                INC SI
```

```
                    DEC BL
                    JNZ NEXTBYTE
                    MOV AH,4CH
                    INT 21H
          CODE ENDS
                    END START
```

Program 3.17 *Listings*

Program 3.18

Write a program to convert a 16 bit binary number into equivalent BCD number.

Solution The program to convert the binary number into equivalent BCD number is developed below :

```
ASSUME CS:CODE,DS:DATA
DATA SEGMENT
BIN EQU
RESULT DW (?)
DATA ENDS
CODE SEGMENT
START :    MOV AX, DATA    ;  INITIALIZE DATA SEGMENT
           MOV DS, AX
           MOV BX, BIN
           MOV AX, 0       ;  INITIALIZE TO 0
           MOV CX, 0       ;  INITIALIZE TO 0
CONTINUE : CMP BX, 0       ;  COMPARISION FOR ZERO BINARY NUMBER.
           JZ ENDPROG      ;  IF ZERO END THE PROGRAM
           DEC BX          ;   DECREMENT BX BY 1
           MOV AL, CL
           ADD AL, 1       ;   ADD 1 TO AL
           DAA             ;  DECIMAL ADJUST AFTER ADDITION
           MOV CL, AL      ;  STORING RESULT IN CL REGISTER
           MOV AL, CH
           ADC AL, 00H     ;  ADD WITH CARRY
           DAA
           MOV CH, AL      ;  STORING RESULT IN CH REGISTER
           JMP CONTINUE
ENDPROG :  MOV RESULT, CX  ;  STORING RESULT IN DATA SEGMENT
           MOV AH, 4CH
           INT 21H
           CODE ENDS
           END START
```

Program 3.18 *Listings*

Program 3.19

Write a program to convert a BCD number into an equivalent binary number.

Solution A program to convert a BCD number into binary equivalent number is developed below.

```
ASSUME CS:CODE,DS:DATA
DATA SEGMENT
BCD_NUM EQU 4576H
BIN_NUM DW (?)
DATA ENDS
CODE SEGMENT
START :         MOV AX, DATA     ; INITIALIZE DATA SEGMENT
                MOV DS, AX
                MOV BX, BCD_NUM  ; BX IS NOW HAVING BCD NUMBER
                MOV CX, 0        ; INITIALIZATION
CONTINUE :      CMP BX, 0        ; COMPARISON TO CHECK BCD NUM IS ZERO
                J2 ENDPROG       ; IF ZERO END THE PROGRAM
                MOV AL, BL       ; 8 LSBs OF NUMBER IS TRANSFERRED TO
                                   AL
                SUM AL, 1        ; SUBTRACT ONE FROM AL
                DAS              ; DECIMAL ADJUST AFTER SUBTRACTION
                MOV BL, AL       ; RESULT IS STORED IN BL
                MOV AL, BH       ; 8 MSB IS TRANSFERRED TO AL
                SBB AL, 00H      ; SUBTRACTION WITH BORROW
                DAS              ; DECIMAL ADJUST AFTER SUBTRACTION
                MOV BH, AL       ; RESULT BACK IN BH REGISTER
                INC CX           ; INCREMENT CX BY 1
                JMP CONTINUE
ENDPROG :       MOV BIN_NUM, CX  ; RESULT IS STORED IN DATA SEGMENT
                MOV AH, 4CH      ; TERMINATION OF PROGRAM
                INT 21H          ; TERMINATION OF PROGRAM
                CODE ENDS
                END START
```

Program 3.19 *Listings*

Program 3.20

Write a program to convert an 8 bit binary number into equivalent gray code.

Solution A program to convert an 8 bit binary number into equivalent gray code is written below.

Binary → B_7 B_6 B_5 B_4 B_3 B_2 B_1 B_0

Gray → G_7 G_6 G_5 G_4 G_3 G_2 G_1 G_0

$$G_7 = B_7$$

$$G_i = B_i \oplus B_{i+1}$$

Where i = 0 to 6

```
ASSUME CS:CODE,DS:DATA
DATA SEGMENT
NUM EQU 34H
RESULT DB (?)
```

```
DATA ENDS
START :     MOV AX, DATA      ;  INITIALIZE DATA SEGMENT
            MOV DS, AX
            MOV AL, NUM       ;  NUMBER IS TRANSFERRED TO AL
            MOV BL, AL
            CLC               ;  CLEAR CARRY FLAG
            RCR AL, 1         ;  ROTATE THROUGH CARRY THE CONTENT
                                    OF AL
            XOR BL, .AL       ;  XORING BL AND AL TO GET GRAY CODE
            MOV RESULT, BL    ;  STORING RESULT IN DMS
            MOV AH,4CH
            INT 21H
            CODE ENDS
            END START
```

Program 3.20 *Listings*

Program 3.21

Find square root of a two digit number. Assume that the number is a perfect square.

Solution The 2 digit number of which the square root is to be found out is considered as a perfect square. The program for this problem is presented below:

```
ASSUME CS:CODE,DS:DATA
DATA SEGMENT
NUM EQU 36
RESULT DB (?)
DATA ENDS
CODE SEGEMENT
START :     MOV AX, DATA      ;  INITIALIZE DATA SEGMENT
            MOV DS, AX
            MOV CL, NUM       ;  NUMBER IS TRANSFERRED TO CL
            MOV BL, 1         ;  BL IS INITIALISE TO 1
            MOV AL, 0         ;  AL INITIALISE TO 0
UP :        CMP CL, 0         ;  CHECK FOR ZERO NUMBER
            JZ ZRESULT        ;  IF ZERO THEN GO TO ZRESULT LABEL
            SUB CL, BL        ;  IF NOT ZERO SUBSTRACT BL FROM CL
            INC AL            ;  INCREMENT THE CONTENT OF AL
            ADD BL, 02        ;  ADD TWO TO REGISTER BL
            JMP UP            ;  GO BACK TO LABEL UP
ZRESULT :   MOV RESULT, AL    ;  RESULT IS SAVED IN DATA SEGMENT
            MOV AH, 4CH
            INT 21H
            CODE ENDS
            END START
```

Program 3.21 *Listings*

3.4.2 Programs to Utilize the Resources of an IBM Microcomputer Using DOS Function Calls

In this section, we will study the method of utilizing the hardware resources of an IBM microcomputer system working under DOS, using assembly language. In a computer system, each peripheral is assigned an address. The data can be written to or read from the peripheral using the write or read instructions, e.g. MOV, IN, OUT, etc. along with the address of the particular peripheral. The disk operating system has a unique way of accessing the hardware resources through the interrupt INT 21H.

For example, suppose we want to display a message on the CRT, then we will have to prepare a string of the message, then execute the instruction INT 21H with the function value 09H in AH and DS : DX set as a pointer to the start of the string.

Appendix-B tabulates the different function values and their purposes under the INT 21 H interrupt. With the help of the information in Appendix-B and the instruction set of 8086, we are able to access the hardware resources of the system like CRT, keyboard, hard disk, floppy disk, memory, etc. Also, the software resources like directory structure, file allocation table, can be referred by using the information in Appendix-B. With the help of a few simple programs, we now explain, how to use the particular resource. It is assumed that the computer system is working under DOS.

Program 3.22

Display the message "The study of microprocessors is interesting." on the CRT screen of a microcomputer.

Solution A program to display the string is given as follows:

```
ASSUME     CS :CODE, DS :DATA
DATA       SEGMENT
MESSAGE    DB ODH, OAH,"   STUDY OF MICROPROCESSORS IS INTERESTING",
                           ODH, OAH, "$"
                           ;PREPARING STRING OF THE MESSAGE
DATA       ENDS
CODE       SEGMENT
START:     MOV AX, DATA    ;INITIALIZE DS
           MOV DS, AX
           MOV AH, 09H     ;SET FUNCTION VALUE  FOR DISPLAY
           MOV DX, OFFSET MESSAGE
           INT 21H         ;POINT TO MESSAGE AND RUN
           MOV AH, 4CH     ;THE INTERRUPT
           INT 21H         ;RETURN TO DOS
CODE       ENDS            ;STOP
           END START
```

Program 3.22 *Listings*

The above listing starts with the usual statement ASSUME. In the data segment, the message is written in the form of a string of the message characters and cursor control characters. The characters 0AH and 0DH are the line feed and carriage feed characters. The "$" is the string termination character. At the end of every message to be displayed the "$" must be there. Otherwise, the computer loses the control, as it is unable to find the end of the string. The character 0DH brings the cursor to next line. The character 0AH brings cursor to the next position (column wise). In case of DB operator, the characters written in the statement in inverted double commas are built in the form of their respective ASCII codes in the allotted memory bytes for the string.

Then the data segment that contains the message string is initialised. The register AH is loaded with the function value 09H for displaying the message on the CRT screen. The instruction INT 21H after execution, causes the message to be displayed. The register DX points to the message in the data segment. After the message is displayed the control is returned to DOS prompt.

Program 3.23

Write a program to open a new file KMB.DAT in the current directory and drive. If it is successfully opened, write 200H bytes of data into it from a data block named BLOCK. Display a message, if the file is not opened successfully.

Solution This type of programs, written for the utilization of resources of a computer system does not require much of logic. These programs contain the specific function calls along with some instructions to load the registers to prepare the environment (required data) for the interrupt call. A flow chart for Program 3.23 is shown in Fig. 3.14. It is up to the application designer to combine these programs with the actual application programs.

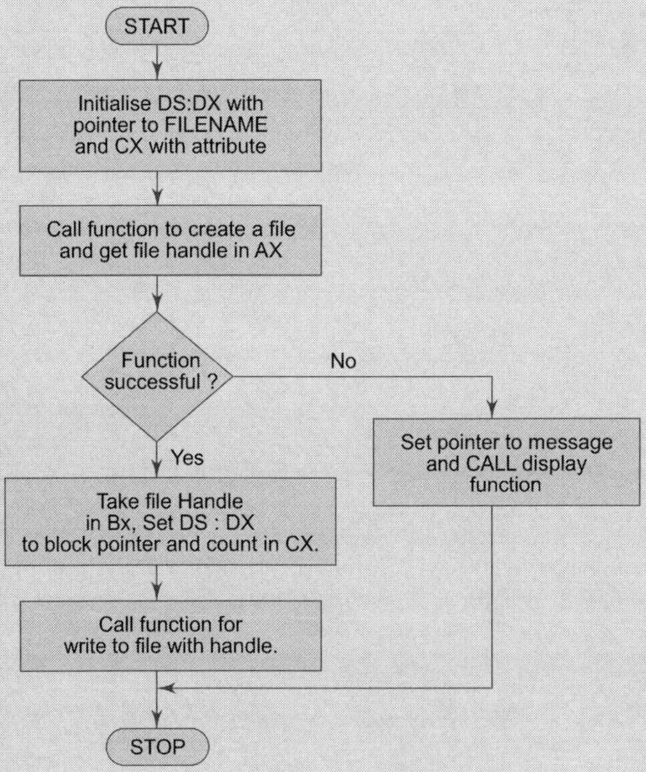

Fig. 3.14 *Flow Chart for Program 3.23*

```
ASSUME CS:CODE,DS:DATA
DATA SEGMENT
        DATABLOCK DB 200H DUP (?)
        FILENAME DB "KMB.DAT", "$"
        MESSAGE DB 0AH, 0DH, "FILE NOT CREATED
        SUCCESSFULLY", 0AH, 0DH, "$"
```

```
DATA    ENDS
CODE    SEGMENT
START:  MOV AX, DATA                ;INTIALIZE DS
        MOV DS, AX
        MOV DX, OFFSET FILENAME     ;OFFSET OF FILE NAME
        MOV CX, 00H                 ;FILE ATTRIBUTE IN CX,REFER TO
        MOV AH, 3CH                 ;APPENDIX B FUNCTION 3CH
        INT 21H                     ;T0 CREATE A FILE, FOR more DE-
                                    ;TAILS.
        JNC WRITE                   ;IF FILE IS CREATED SUCCESSFULLY
                                    ;WRITE DATA IN TO IT
        MOV AX, DATA
        MOV DS, AX
        MOV DX, OFFSET MESSAGE      ;ELSE DISPLAY THE
        MOV AH, 09H                 ;MESSAGE AND RETURN TO
        INT 21H                     ;DOS PROMPT WITHOUT WRITING
        JMP STOP                    ;DATA IN FILE
WRITE:  MOV BX, AX                  ;FILE HANDLE IN BX
        MOV CX, 0200H               ;LENGTH OF THE DATA BYTES TO BE
                                     WRITTEN
        MOV DX, OFFSET DATABLOCK    ;OFFSET OF THE SOURCE BLOCK
        MOV AH, 40H                 ;IN DX AND USE 40H FUNCTION
        INT 21H
STOP:   MOV AH, 4CH
        INT 21H
CODE    ENDS
        END START
```

Program 3.23 *Listings*

Program 3.24

Write a program to load a file KMB.EXE in the memory at the CS value of 5000H with zero relocation factor. The file is just to be observed and not to be executed (overlay loading).

Solution This type of loading of a file is called as overlay loading. The function value 4BH in AH and 03 in AL serves the purpose. The program is given as shown. The reader may refer to Appendix-B for details of the function calls.

```
ASSUME          CS:CODE;DS:DATA
DATA            SEGMENT
LODPTR  DB 00, 50H, 00, 00
MESSAGE DB 0AH,0DH, "LOADING FAILURE", 0AH,0DH, "$"
FILENAME DB "PROG3-5.EXE","$"
DATA            ENDS
CODE            SEGMENT
START:          MOV AX, DATA
                MOV DS, AX              ;SET DS:DX TO STRING CONTAINING
                MOV DX, OFFSET FILENAME;FILE NAME
                MOV BX, OFFSET LODPTR   ;SET ES&BX TO POINT
```

```
                MOV AX, SEG LODPTR      ;A BLOCK CONTAINING
                MOV ES, AX              ;CS & RELOCATION FACTOR
                MOV AX, 4B03H           ;LOAD FUNCTION VALUE AND
                INT 21H
                JNC OKAY                ;IF LOADING IS NOT SUCCESSFULL,
                MOV AX, DATA
                MOV DS, AX
                MOV DX, OFFSET MESSAGE  ;DISPLAY THE FAILURE
                MOV AH, 09H             ;MESSAGE.
                INT 21H
OKAY:           MOV AH, 4CH             ;RETURN TO DOS PROMPT.
                INT 21H
CODE            ENDS
                END START
```

Program 3.24 *Listings*

Refer to **MS DOS Encyclopedia by Ray Duncan** for more information on the function calls.

Program 3.25

Write a program using the AUTOEXEC.BAT file that hangs the computer and waits for the entry of the string 'ROY BHURCHANDI' from the key board and then returns to the DOS prompt, if the string is entered. The key board entries are not echoed (not displayed on the screen).

Solution The file AUTOEXEC.BAT is automatically run whenever the computer is reset. The listings for this program may be written in any assembly language file. This file should then be assembled, i.e.. EXE file should be prepared as already discussed in this chapter. The name of this .EXE file should be written in the AUTOEXEC.BAT file with the complete path of this .EXE file. The AUTOEXEC.BAT file must be available in the main (root) directory and default drive.

```
ASSUME CS:CODE, DS:DATA
DATA SEGMENT
STRING DB "ROY BHURCHANDI"
LENGTH DW 0EH
BUFFER DB 0FH DUP(?)
MESSAGE DB 0AH, 0DH, "SORRY!", 0AH, 0DH, "$"
DATA ENDS
CODE SEGMENT
START:     MOV AX, DATA             ; Initialize DS
           MOV DS, AX
WAIT:      MOV CX, LENGTH           ; String length in CX
           MOV DI, OFFSET BUFFER    ; DI points to buffer for keyboard
NXTCHAR:   MOV AH, 08H              ; entries under function 21H
           INT 21H
           CMP AL, 0DH              ; If entries are over proceed for
           JE STOP                  ; string comparison else store the
                                      character
           MOV [DI], AL             ; in the buffer and
           INC DI                   ; increment DI,
           DEC CX                   ; decrement CX for next entry
           JNZ NXTCHAR              ; Go for entering next character
```

```
STOP:      MOV CX, LENGTH             ; Set CX to length again.
           MOV SI, OFFSET STRING      ; Set SI and DI for string
           MOV DI, OFFSET BUFFER      ; comparison.
           MOV AX, SEG BUFFER         ; Set ES as segment pointer
           MOV ES, AX                 ; to the string.
REP        CMPSB                      ; Compare the string with the buffer
           JNZ SORRY                  ; If string does not match with buffer
                                      ; display 'Sorry!', otherwise return
           MOV AH, 4CH                ; to DOS prompt.
           INT 21H
SORRY:     MOV DX, OFFSET MESSAGE     ; Set offset pointer to display
                                        'Sorry!'.
           MOV AH, 09H                ; Set function value to 09H under
           INT 21H                    ; DOS interrupt 21h.
           JMP WAIT                   ; Wait for the next entries.
CODE       ENDS
           END START
```

Program 3.25 *Listings*

In these programs, setting the supporting parameters and the function values is of prime importance. One may go through Appendix-B and try to write more and more programs for different functions available under INT 21H of DOS.

SUMMARY

This chapter starts with simple programs written for hand-coding. Further, hand-coding procedures of a few example instructions are studied. Advantages of the assembly language over machine language are then presented in brief. With an overview of the assembler operation, we have initiated the discussion of assembly language programming. The procedures of writing, entering and coding the assembly language programs are then discussed in brief. Further, DOS debugging program - DEBUG, a basic tool for trouble-shooting the assembly language programs, is discussed briefly with an emphasis on the most useful commands. Then we have presented various examples of 8086/8088 programs those highlight the actual use and the syntax of the instructions and directives. Finally, a few programs that enable the programmer to access the computer system resources using DOS function calls are discussed. We do not claim that each program presented here is the most efficient one, rather it just suggests a way to implement the algorithm asked in the problem. There may be a number of alternate algorithms and program listings to implement a logic but amongst them a programmer should choose one which requires minimum storage, execution time and complexity.

EXERCISES

3.1 Find out the machine code for following instructions.

(i) ADC AX,BX	(ii) OR AX,[0500H]	(iii) AND CX,[SI]
(iv) TEST AX,5555H	(v) MUL [SI+5]	(vi) NEG 50[BP]
(vii) OUT DX,AX	(viii) LES DI,[0700H]	(ix) LEA SI,[BX+500H]

(x) SHL [BX+2000],CL (xi) RET 0200H (xii) CALL 7000H
(xiii) JMP 3000H:2000H (xiv) CALL [5000H] (xv) DIV [5000H]

3.2 Describe the procedure for coding the intersegment and intrasegment jump and call instructions.
3.3 Enlist the advantages of assembly language programming over machine language.
3.4 What is an assembler?
3.5 What is a linker?
3.6 Explain various DEBUG commands for troubleshooting executable programs. (Refer to MSDOS Encyclopedia by Ray Duncan.)
3.7 What are the DOS fuction calls?
3.8 Write an ALP to convert a four digit hexadecimal number to decimal number.
3.9 Write an ALP to convert a four digit octal number to decimal number.
3.10 Write an ALP to find out ASCII codes of alphanumeric characters from a look up table.
3.11 Write an ALP to change an already available ascending order byte string to descending order.
3.12 Write an ALP to perform a 16-bit increment operation using 8-bit instructions.
3.13 Write an ALP to find out average of a given string of data bytes neglecting fractions.
3.14 Write an ALP to find out decimal addition of sixteen four digit decimal numbers.
3.15 Write an ALP to convert a four digit decimal number to its binary equivalent.
3.16 Write an ALP to convert a given sixteen bit binary number to its GRAY equivalent.
3.17 Write an ALP to find out transpose of a 3x3 matrix.
3.18 Write an ALP to find out cube of an 8-bit hexadecimal number.
3.19 Write an ALP to display message 'Happy Birthday!' on the screen after a key 'A' is pressed.
3.20 Write an ALP to open a file in the drive C of your hard disk , accept 256 byte entries each separated by comma and then store all these 256 bytes into the opened file. Issue suitable messages where-ever necessary.
3.21 Write an ALP to print a message 'The Printer Is Busy' on to a dot matrix printer.
3.22 Write an ALP to load a file from hard disk of your system into RAM system at segment address 5000H with zero relocation factor.
3.23 Write an ALP that goes on accepting the keyboard entries and displays them on line on the CRT display. The control escapes to DOS prompt if enter key is pressed.
3.24 Write an ALP to set interrupt vector of type 50H to an address of a routine ISR in segment CODE1.
3.25 Write an ALP to set and get the system time. Assume arbitary time for setting the system time.
3.26 What is the function 4CH under INT 21H?

Excercises 3.8 to 3.25 may be executed using a Windows based PC and any version of MASM as a part of Lab exercise.

4 Special Architectural Features and Related Programming

INTRODUCTION

This chapter elaborates some of the special features of the 8086/8088 architecture and their supporting programming techniques. The other advanced microprocessors also have these features with little or no modifications. Their programming techniques are also similar to that of 8086/8088. In general, the programming techniques of the advanced microprocessors are upward compatible with that of 8086/8088, with some added features. In other words, the programs written for an 8086/8088 machine, can be executed on the machines based on the other advanced microprocessors, with no modifications, but the reverse may not be true. All the techniques discussed in this chapter are also applicable to the advanced microprocessors.

4.1 INTRODUCTION TO STACK

In the third chapter on '*Assembly Language Programming on 8086/88*', we have studied a few example programs. Most of the example programs we have presented there has a sequential flow and they are essentially meant for some calculation or simple database manipulation. We have also presented some programs which require the access of the hardware facilities of a computer system working under DOS.

Most of the application software are however, not straightforward. For example think of a PID temperature controller using 8086; to control the temperature of a furnace. The software for implementing the above system should perform the following tasks typically.

1. Sample the output of a signal conditioning block.
2. Send start of conversion signal to ADC.
3. Wait for delay time (conversion time) and sense end of conversion signal.
4. After the conversion is over read the ADC output.
5. Take number of samples using steps 1 to 4.
6. Find proportional, differential and integral error signals.
7. Derive control signal from result of step 6.
8. Apply the control signal to control the flow of energy to the heater.

The above procedure contains eight steps. Steps 1 to 4 are to be repeated for each sample. Suppose, for finding out the proportional, integral and differential error signal one decides to take say ten samples, then steps 6 to 8 shall be repeated after each group of ten samples.

The above program needs to control the operation of ADC. Also, it computes the proportional, integral and differential control laws and then serves digital control signal to the control element to decide the appropriate action. This program needs a number of general purpose registers as there may be a number of intermediate results which should be temporarily stored. The 8086 has only four 16-bit general purpose registers. Here, the stack provides a sequential mechanism to store the partial results.

Thus instead of writing a single big program for such application, one should split it into number of subtasks that constitute the complete application and then write separate routines for each subtask. After that, prepare a main program that calls the specific routines for the specific tasks. Suppose the processor is executing a main program that calls a subroutine. After executing the main program up to the CALL instruction, the control will be transferred to the subroutine address. Now, the microprocessor must know where the control is to be returned after the execution of the subroutine. A similar problem may arise while handling interrupts. This address of re-entry into the main program may be stored onto the stack. Also, the stack is useful for storing the register status of the processor at the time of calling a subroutine and getting it back at the time of returning, so that the registers or memory locations already used during the main program can be reused by the subroutine without any loss of data. The stack mechanism provides a temporary storage of data in these cases.

The stack is a block of memory that may be used for temporarily storing the contents of the registers inside the CPU. The stack is a block of memory locations which is accessed using the SP and SS registers. In other words, it is a top-down data structure whose elements are accessed using a pointer that is implemented using the SP and SS registers. As we go on storing the data words onto the stack, the pointer goes on decrementing and on the other hand, the pointer goes on incrementing as we go on retrieving the word data. For each such access, the stack pointer is decremented or incremented by two. The stack is required in case of CALL instructions. The data in the stack, may again be transferred back from stack to register, whenever required by the CPU. The process of storing the data in the stack is called 'pushing into' the stack and the reverse process of transferring the data back from the stack to the CPU register is known as 'popping off' the stack. The stack is essentially *Last-In-First-Out* (LIFO) data segment. This means that the data which is pushed into the stack last will be on top of stack and will be popped off the stack first. For example, let us consider a stack of, say, five books lying randomly on the table which one wants to arrange in a stack. He will place one book out of the five in a position and mark it with 1, then the second book is placed above it and marked 2 and so on. Thus all the five books can be placed one above the other and marked with respective numbers. If one wants to refer to them at some later time, the upper most book on top of the stack marked 5, will be accessed first. If one wants to access book 3, he will have to first take out book 5, then book 4, out of the stack, and then only book 3 can be accessed. Thus to access book 1, one will have to take out all the upper books from the stack.

4.2 STACK STRUCTURE OF 8086/88

As has been mentioned, the stack contains a set of sequentially arranged data bytes , with the last item appearing on top of the stack. This item will be popped off the stack first for use by the CPU. The stack pointer (SP) register is a 16-bit register that contains the offset of the address that lies in the stack segment. The stack segment, like any other segment, may have a memory block of a maximum of 64 Kbyte locations, and thus may overlap with any other segments. The Stack Segment register (SS) contains the base address of the stack segment in the memory. The Stack Segment register (SS) and Stack Pointer register (SP) together address the stack-top as explained in the following lines.

Let the content of SS be 5000 H and the content of the stack pointer register be 2050 H. To find out the current stack-top address, the stack segment register content is shifted left by four bit positions (multiplied by 10 H) and the resulting 20-bit content is added with the 16-bit offset value, stored in the stack pointer register. In the above case, the stack top address can be calculated as shown:

SS ⇒ 5000 H					
SP ⇒ 2050 H					
SS ⇒	0101	0000	0000	0000	
10H * SS ⇒	0101	0000	0000	0000	0000
+					
SP ⇒		0010	0000	0101	0000
Stack-top	0101	0010	0000	0101	0000
address	5	2	0	5	0

Thus the stack top address is 52050 H. Figure 4.1 makes the concept more clear.

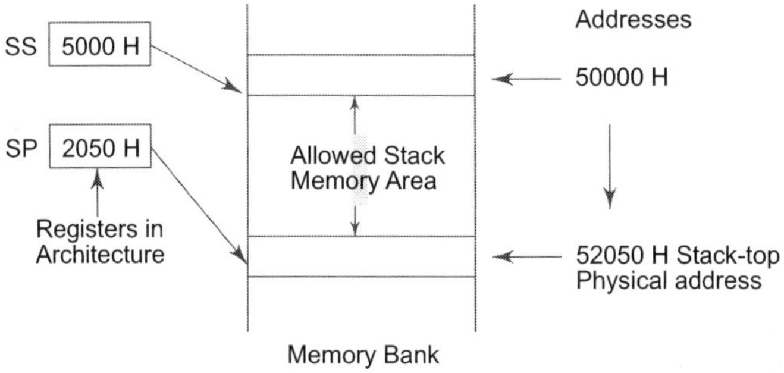

Fig. 4.1 *Stack-top Address Calculation*

If the stack top points to a memory location 52050 H, it means that the location 52050 H is already occupied, i.e. previously pushed data is available at 52050 H. The next 16-bit push operation will decrement the stack pointer by two, so that it will point to the new stack-top 5204EH, and the decremented contents of SP will be 204E H. This location will now be occupied by the recently pushed data. Thus, if a 16-bit data is pushed onto the stack, the push operation will decrement the SP by two because two locations will be required for a 2-byte (16-bit) data. Thus it may be noted here that the stack grows down.

Thus for a selected value of SS, the maximum value of SP = FFFF H and the segment can have maximum of 64K locations. Thus after starting with an initial value of FFFFH, the Stack Pointer (SP) is decremented by two, whenever a 16-bit data is pushed onto the stack. After successive push operations, when the Stack Pointer contains 0000 H, any attempt to further push the data to the stack will result in stack overflow.

Each PUSH operation decrements the SP as explained above, while each POP operation increments the SP. The POP operation is used to retrieve the data stored on to the stack. Figure 4.2 shows the stack overflow conditions, while Fig. 4.3 shows the effect of PUSH and POP operations on the stack memory block.

Suppose, a main program is being executed by the processor. At some stage during the execution of the program, all the registers in the CPU may contain useful data. In case there is a subroutine CALL instruction at this stage, there is a possibility that all or some of the registers of the main program may be modified due to the execution of the subroutine. This may result in loss of useful data, which may be avoided by using the stack. At the start of the subroutine, all the registers' contents of the main program may be pushed onto the stack one by one. After each PUSH operation SP will be modified as already explained before. Thus all the registers can be copied to the stack. Now these registers may be used by the subroutine, since their original contents are saved onto the stack. At the end of the execution of the subroutine, all the registers can get back their original contents by popping the data from the stack. The sequence of popping is exactly the reverse of the pushing sequence. In other words, the register or memory location that is pushed into the stack at the end should be popped off first.

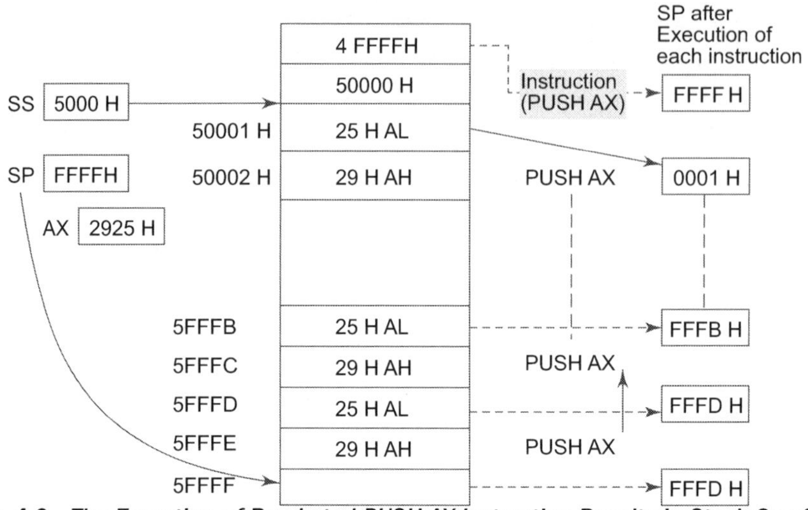

Fig. 4.2 *The Execution of Bracketed PUSH AX Instruction Results in Stack Overflow*

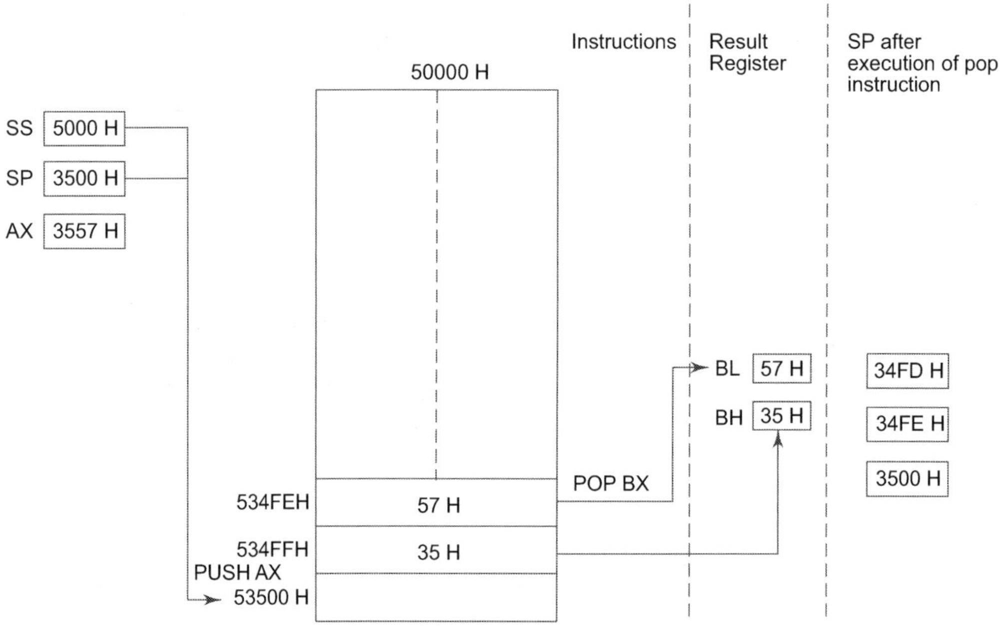

Fig. 4.3 *Effect of PUSH and POP on SP*

4.2.1 Programming for Stack

As it has been discussed in Chapter 1, the memory bank of 8086/88 is organised according to segments. The 8086/8088 has four segment registers, namely, CS,DS,SS and ES. Out of these segment registers, SS, i.e. 'stack segment register' contains the segment value for stack while SP contains the offset for the stack-top. In a program the stack segment can be defined in a similar way as the data segment. The ASSUME directive directs the name of the stack segment to the assembler. The SS register and the SP register must be initialised in the program suitably. Program 4.1 explains the use of the stack segment.

Program 4.1

Write a program to calculate squares of BCD numbers 0 to 9 and store them sequentially from 2000H offset onwards in the current data segment. The numbers and their squares are in the BCD format. Write a subroutine for the calculation of the square of a number.

The procedure of computing the square of a number is to be repeated for all the numbers. A subroutine for calculating the square is written which is called repetitively from the main program. The 8086/88 does not have single instruction for calculation of the square of a number. Thus you may calculate the square of a number using ADD and DAA instructions. The result of the ADD instruction is in hexadecimal format and it should be converted to decimal form, before it is stored into the memory. Here, one may ask: why not to use the MUL instruction for calculating the squares of the number? A point to be noted here is that, the MUL instruction does not calculate the square of a decimal number and moreover, the DAA instruction is to be used only after the ADD or ADC instructions.

One of the advantages of the subroutine is that, a recurring sequence of instructions can be assigned with a procedure name, which may be called again and again whenever required, resulting in a comparatively smaller sequence of instructions.

After a subroutine is called using the CALL instruction, the IP is incremented to the next instruction. Then the contents of IP, CS and flag register are pushed automatically to the stack. The control is then transferred to the specified address in the CALL instruction, i.e the starting address of the subroutine. Then the subroutine is executed. It may be noted that there should be an equal number of PUSH and POP instructions in the subroutine that has to be executed so that the SP contents at the time of calling the subroutine must be equal to the contents of SP at the time of executing the RET instruction, at the end of the subroutine. Otherwise, the control that should be returned to the next instruction after the CALL instruction will not be returned back properly.

The assembly language listing for the above procedure is given as shown. Note that 8086 does not support any instruction available for direct BCD packed multiplication to calculate the square of numbers. Hence to calculate the squares, the multiplication is implemented as successive addition, and the DAA instruction is used after each addition operation to convert the result in decimal format.

```
ASSUME CS : CODE, DS : DATA, SS : STACK
DATA      SEGMENT
          ORG 2000H
SQUARES DB OFH DUP (?)
DATA      ENDS
STACK     SEGMENT
STAKDATA DB 100H DUP (?)           ; Reserve 256 bytes for stack
STACK     ENDS
CODE      SEGMENT
START:  MOV AX, DATA               ; Initialise data segment
        MOV DS, AX
        MOV AX, STACK              ; Initialise stack segment
        MOV SS, AX
        MOV SP, OFFSET STAKDATA    ; Initialise stack pointer
        MOV CL, OAH                ; Initialise counter for numbers
        MOV SI, OFFSET SQUARES     ; Set pointer to array of squares
```

```
        MOV AL, 00                          ; Start from 00
NEXTNUM : CALL SQUARE                       ; Calculate square
        MOV BYTE PTR [SI],AH                ; Store square in the array
        INC AL                              ; Go for the next number
        INC SI                              ; Increment the array pointer
        DCR CL                              ; Decrement count
        JNZ NEXTNUM                         ; Stop, if CL = 0, else, continue
        MOV AH, 4CH                         ; Return to DOS prompt
        INT 21H                             ;
PROCEDURE SQUARE NEAR                       ; SQUARE is a local procedure
                                            ; called only by this segment
        MOV BH,AL                           ;
        MOV CH,AL                           ; Duplicate AL to CH and BH
        XOR AL,AL                           ; Clear flags and AL
AGAIN : ADD AL,CH                           ; Successively add CH to AH
        DAA                                 ; Get BCD equivalent
        DCR CH                              ; Decrement successive addition
        JNZ AGAIN                           ; counter till it becomes
        MOV AH,AL                           ; Zero, store the square and
        MOV AL,BH                           ; get back the original number
        RET                                 ; Return
SQUARE        ENDP
CODE  ENDS
    END START
```

Program 4.1 *Listings*

Program 4.2

Write a program to change a sequence of sixteen 2-byte numbers from ascending to descending order. The numbers are stored in the data segment. Store the new series at addresses starting from 6000 H. Use the LIFO property of the stack.

```
ASSUME      CS : CODE, DS : DATA, SS : DATA
DATA            SEGMENT
LIST        DW 10H
STACKDATA   DB FFH DUP (?)
                ORG6000H
                RESULT DW 10H
DATA        ENDSCOUNT EQU 10H
CODE        SEGMENT
START: MOV AX, DATA                         ; Initialize data segment and
       MOV DS, AX                           ; stack segment
       MOV SS, AX
       MOV SP, OFFSET LIST                  ; Initialize stack pointer
       MOV CL, COUNT                        ; Initialize counter for word
                                                number
       MOV BX, OFFSET RESULT + COUNT        ; Initialize BX at last
                                              address
```

```
                            ; (stack) for destination series
NEXT: POP AX                ; Get the first word from series
     MOV DX, SP             ; Save source stack pointer
     MOV SP, BX             ; Get destination stack pointer
     PUSH AX                ; Save AX to stack
     MOV BX, SP             ; Save destination stack pointer
     MOV SP, DX             ; Get source stack pointer for
                            ; the next number
     DCR CL                 ; Decrement count
     JNZ NEXT               ; If count is not zero, go to the next num
     MOV AH, 4CH            ; Else, return to DOS
     INT 21H                ; prompt
CODE ENDS
     END    START
```

Program 4.2 *Listing*

The above program may also be written using just simple data transfer instructions. Here we have used the stack to change the order of data words.

It is a common practice to push all the registers to the stack at the start of a subroutine and pop it at the end of the subroutine so that the original contents are retrieved. Thus during the subroutine execution, all the registers except SP and SS are free for use.

The stack mechanism is also used in case of interrupt service routines to store the instruction pointer and code segment of the return address. The maximum size of stack segment like a general segment is 64 K. The stack size for a particular program may be set using DB or DW directive as per the requirements, as shown in the above program.

4.3 INTERRUPTS AND INTERRUPT SERVICE ROUTINES

The dictionary meaning of the word 'interrupt' is to break the sequence of operation. While the CPU is executing a program, an 'interrupt' breaks the normal sequence of execution of instructions, diverts its execution to some other program called *Interrupt Service Routine* (ISR). After executing ISR, the control is transferred back again to the main program which was being executed at the time of interruption.

Suppose you are reading a novel and have completed up to page 100. At this instant, your younger brother distracts you. You will somehow mark the line and the page you are reading, so that you may be able to continue after you attend to him. Say you have marked page number 101. You will now go to his room to solve his problem. While you are helping him a friend of yours comes and asks you for a textbook. Now, there are two options in front of you. The first is to make the friend wait till you complete serving your brother, and thereafter you serve his request. In this, you are giving less priority to your friend. The second option is to ask your brother to wait; remember the solution of his problem at the intermediate state; serve the friend; and after the friend is served, continue with the solution that was in the intermediate state. In this case, it may be said that you have given higher priority to your friend. After serving both of them, again you may continue reading from page 101 of the novel. Here, first you are interrupted by your brother. While you are serving your brother, you are again interrupted by a friend. This type of sequence of appearance of interrupts is called nested interrupt, i.e. interrupt within interrupt.

Whenever a number of devices interrupt a CPU at a time, and if the processor is able to handle them properly, it is said to have *multiple interrupt processing capability*. For example, 8085 has five hardware interrupt pins and it is able to handle the interrupts simultaneously under the control of software. In case of 8086, there are two interrupt pins, viz. NMI and INTR. The NMI is a *nonmaskable* interrupt input pin which means that any interrupt request at NMI input cannot be masked or disabled by any means.The INTR interrupt, however, may be masked using the Interrupt Flag (IF). The INTR, further, is of 256 types. The INTR types may be from 00 to FFH (or 00 to 255). If more than one type of INTR interrupt occurs at a time, then an external chip called programmable interrupt controller is required to handle them. The same is the case for INTR interrupt input of 8085. Interrupt Service Routines (ISRs) are the programs to be executed by interrupting the main program execution of the CPU, after an interrupt request appears. After the execution of ISR, the main program continues its execution further from the point at which it was interrupted.

4.4 INTERRUPT CYCLE OF 8086/8088

Broadly, there are two types of interrupts. The first out of them is *external interrupt* and the second is *internal interrupt*. In external interrupt, an external device or a signal interrupts the processor from outside or, in other words, the interrupt is generated outside the processor, for example, a keyboard interrupt. The internal interrupt, on the other hand, is generated internally by the processor circuit, or by the execution of an interrupt instruction. The examples of this type are divide by zero interrupt, overflow interrupt, interrupts due to INT instructions, etc.

Suppose an external device interrupts the CPU at the interrupt pin, either NMI or INTR of the 8086, while the CPU is executing an instruction of a program. The CPU first completes the execution of the current instruction. The IP is then incremented to point to the next instruction. The CPU then acknowledges the requesting device on its $\overline{\text{INTA}}$ pin immediately if it is a NMI, TRAP or Divide by Zero interrupt. If it is an INT request, the CPU checks the IF flag. If the IF is set , the interrupt request is acknowledged using the $\overline{\text{INTA}}$ pin. If the IF is not set, the interrupt requests are ignored. Note that the responses to the NMI, TRAP and Divide by Zero interrupt requests are independent of the IF flag. After an interrupt is acknowledged , the CPU

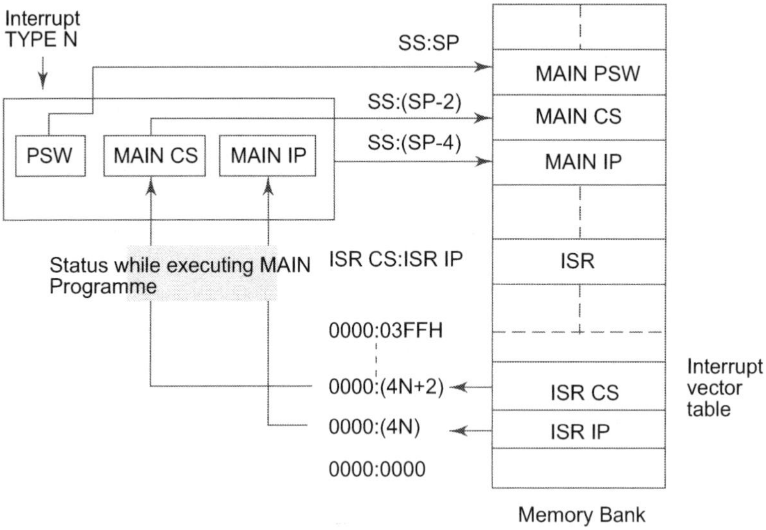

Fig. 4.4 *Interrupt Response Sequence*

computes the vector address from the type of the interrupt that may be passed to the interrupt structure of the CPU internally (in case of software interrupts, NMI, TRAP and Divide by Zero interrupts) or externally, i.e. from an interrupt controller in case of external interrupts. (The contents of IP and CS are next pushed to the stack. The contents of IP and CS now point to the address of the next instruction of the main program from which the execution is to be continued after executing the ISR. The PSW is also pushed to the stack.) The Interrupt Flag (IF) is cleared. The TF is also cleared, after every response to the single step interrupt. The control is then transferred to the interrupt service routine for serving the interrupting device. The new address of ISR is found out from the interrupt vector table. The execution of the ISR starts. If further interrupts are to be responded to during the time the first interrupt is being serviced, the IF should again be set to 1 by the ISR of the first interrupt. If the interrupt flag is not set, the subsequent interrupt signals will not be acknowledged by the processor, till the current one is completed. The programmable interrupt controller is used for managing such multiple interrupts based on their priorities. At the end of ISR the last instruction should be IRET. When the CPU executes IRET , the contents of flags, IP and CS which were saved at the start by the CALL instruction are now retrieved to the respective registers. The execution continues onwards from this address, received by IP and CS.

We now discuss how the 8086/88 finds out the address of an ISR. Every external and internal interrupt is assigned with a type (N), that is either implicit (in case of NMI, TRAP and divide by zero) or specified in the instruction INT N (in case of internal interrupts). In case of external interrupts, the type is passed to the processor by an external hardware like programmable interrupt controller. In the zeroth segment of physical

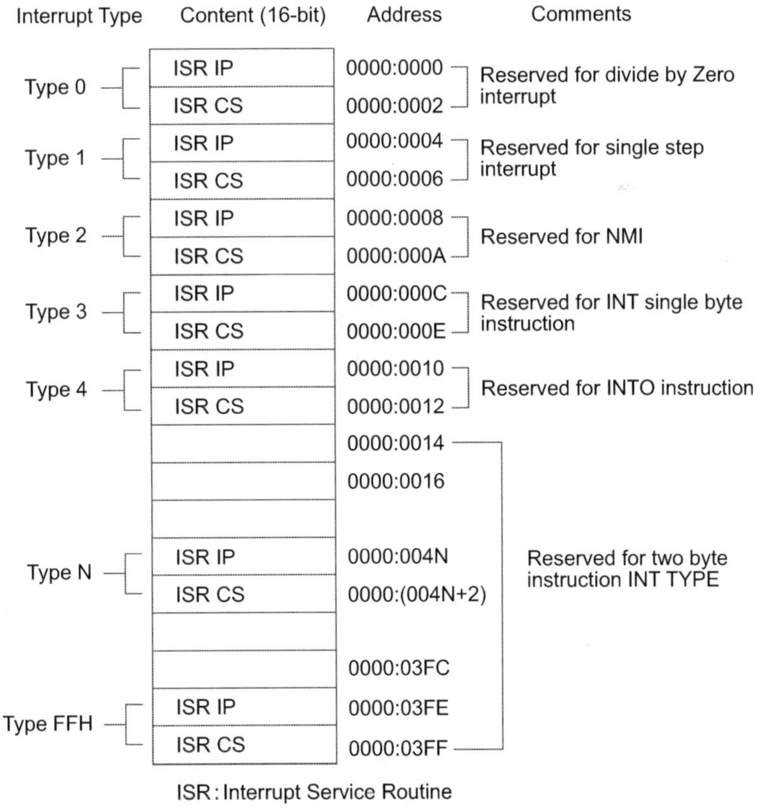

Fig. 4.5 *Structure of Interrupt Vector Table of 8086/88*

address space, i.e. CS = 0000, Intel has reserved 1,024 locations for storing the interrupt vector table. The 8086 supports a total of 256 types of the interrupts, i.e. from 00 to FFH. Each interrupt requires 4 bytes, i.e. two bytes each for IP and CS of its ISR. Thus a total of 1,024 bytes are required for 256 interrupt types, hence the interrupt vector table starts at location 0000:0000 and ends at 0000:03FFH. The interrupt vector table contains the IP and CS of all the interrupt types stored sequentially from address 0000:0000 to 0000:03FF H. The interrupt type N is multiplied by 4 and the hexadecimal multiplication obtained gives the offset address in the zeroeth code segment at which the IP and CS addresses of the interrupt service routine (ISR) are stored. The execution automatically starts from the new CS:IP.

Figure 4.4 shows the interrupt sequence of 8086/88 and Fig. 4.5 shows the structure of interrupt vector table.

4.5 NON MASKABLE INTERRUPT

The processor 8086/88 has a Non-Masksable Interrupt input pin (NMI), that has the highest priority among the external interrupts. TRAP(Single Step-Type 1) is an internal interrupt having the highest priority amongst all the interrupts except the Divide By Zero (Type0) exception. The NMI is activated on a positive transition (low to high voltage). The assertion of the NMI interrupt is equivalent to an execution of instruction INT 02, i.e. Type 2 INTR interrupt.

The NMI pin should remain high for at least two clock cycles and need not synchronized with the clock for being sensed. When the NMI is activated, the current instruction being executed is completed and then the NMI is served. In case of string type instructions, this interrupt will be served only after the complete string has been manipulated. Another high going edge on the NMI pin of 8086, during the period in which the first NMI is served, triggers another response. The signal on the NMI pin must be free of logical bounces to avoid erratic NMI responses.

4.6 MASKABLE INTERRUPT (INTR)

The processor 8086/88 also provides a pin INTR, that has lower priority as compared to NMI. Further the priorities within the INTR types are decided by the type of the INTR signal that is to be passed to the processor via data bus by some external device like the programmable interrupt controller. The INTR signal is level triggered and can be masked by resetting the interrupt flag. It is internally synchronized with the high transition of the CLK. For the INTR signal, to be responded to in the next instruction cycle, it must go high in

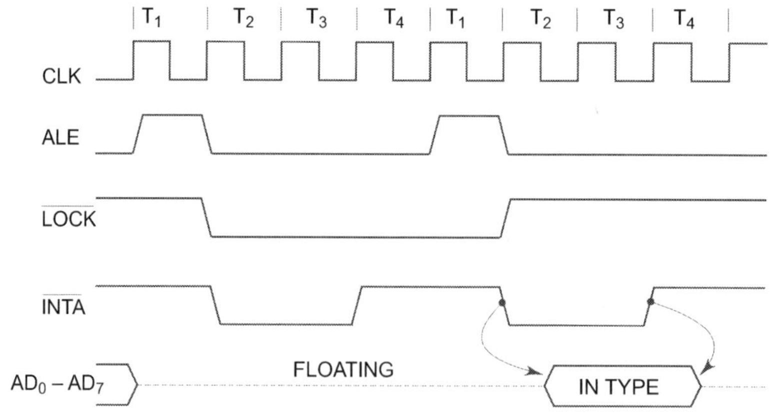

Fig. 4.6 *Interrupt Acknowledge Sequence of 8086*

the last clock cycle of the current instruction or before that. The INTR requests appearing after the last clock cycle of the current instruction will be responded to after the execution of the next instruction. The status of the pending interrupts is checked at the end of each instruction cycle.

If the IF is set, the processor is ready to respond to any INTR interrupt if the IF is reset, the processor will not serve any interrupt appearing at this pin. However, once the processor responds to an INTR signal, the IF is automatically reset. If one wants the processor to further respond to any type of INTR signal, the IF should again be set. The interrupt acknowledge sequence is as shown in Fig. 4.6.

Suppose an external signal interrupts the processor and the pin $\overline{\text{LOCK}}$ goes low at the trailing edge of the first ALE pulse that appears after the interrupt signal preventing the use of bus for any other purpose.

The pin $\overline{\text{LOCK}}$ remains low till the start of the next machine cycle.

With the trailing edge of $\overline{\text{LOCK}}$, the $\overline{\text{INTA}}$ goes low and remains low for two clock states before returning back to the high state.

It remains high till the start of the next machine cycle, i.e. next trailing edge of ALE.

Then $\overline{\text{INTA}}$ again goes low, remains low for two states before returning to the high state.The first trailing edge of ALE floats the bus AD_0-AD_7 , while the second trailing edge prepares the bus to accept the type of the interrupt. The type of the interrupt remains on the bus for a period of two cycles.

4.7 INTERRUPT PROGRAMMING

While programming for any type of interrupt, the programmer must, either externally or through the program, set the interrupt vector table for that type preferrably with the CS and IP addresses of the interrupt service routine. The method of defining the interrupt service routine for software as well as hardware interrupt is the same. Figure 4.7 shows the execution sequence in case of a software interrupt. It is assumed that the interrupt vector table is initialised suitably to point to the interrupt service routine. Figure 4.8 shows the transfer of control for the nested interrupts.

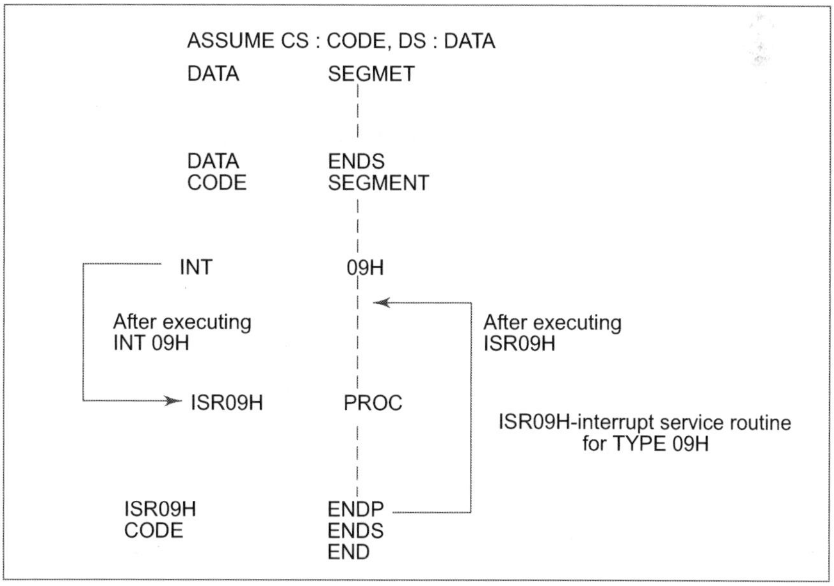

Fig. 4.7 *Transfer of Control during Execution of an Interrupt Service Routine*

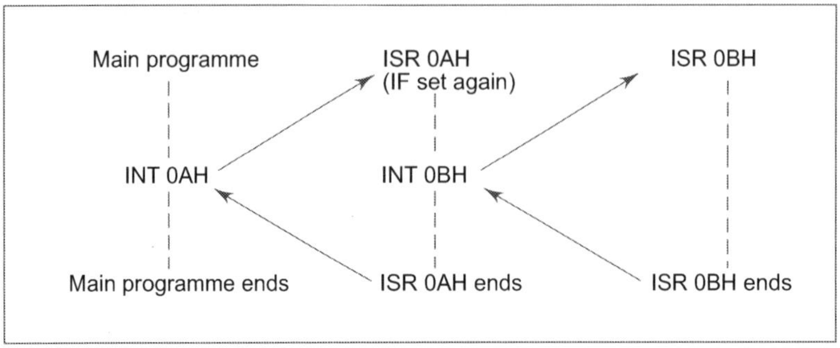

Fig. 4.8 *Transfer of Control for Nested Interrupts*

Program 4.3

Write a program to create a file RESULT and store in it 500H bytes from the memory block starting at 1000:1000, if either an interrupt appears at INTR pin with Type 0AH or an instruction equivalent to the above interrupt is executed.

Note: Pin IRQ_2 available at IO channel of PC is equivalent to Type 0AH interrupt.

```
ASSSUME CS : CODE, DS : DATA
DATA        SEGMENT
    FILENAME     DB "RESULT", "$"
    MESSAGE DB "FILE WASN'T CREATED SUCCESSFULLY",0AH,0DH,"$"
DATA        ENDS
CODE        SEGMENT
START:      MOV AX, CODE
            MOV DS, AX                  ; Set DS at CODE for setting IVT.
            MOV DX, OFFSET ISR0A        ; Set DX at the offset of ISR0A.
            MOV AX,250AH                ; Set IVT using function value 250AH
                                                     in AX
            INT 21H                     ; under INT21H.
            MOV DX, OFFSET FILENAME     ; Set pointer to Filename.
            MOV AX, DATA                ; Set the DS at DATA for Filename
            MOV DS, AX
            MOV CX, 00H
            MOV AH, 3CH                 ; Create file with the File name
                                                     'RESULT'.
            INT 21H
            JNC FURTHER                 ; If no carry, create operation is
            MOV DX,OFFSET MESSAGE       ; successful else
            MOV AH,09H                  ; display the MESSAGE.
            INT 21H
            JMP STOP
FURTHER :        INT 0AH                ; If the file is created
successfully,
STOP :           MOV AH,4CH             ; write into it and return
                 INT 21H                ; to DOS prompt.
                                        ; This interrupt service routine
                                              writes 500 bytes into the
```

```
                                        ; file RESULT and returns to the main
                                              program.
ISROA PROC NEAR
    MOV BX, AX                          ; Take file handle in BX,
    MOV CX, 500H                        ; byte count in CX,
    MOV DX, 1000H                       ; offset of block in DX,
    MOV AX, 1000H                       ; Segment value of block
    MOV DS, AX                          ; in DS.
    MOV AH, 40 H                        ; Write in the file and
    INT 21 H                            ; return.
    IRET                                ;
ISROA      ENDP
CODE       ENDS
    END START
```

Program 4.3 *Listing*

To execute the above program, first assemble it using MASM.EXE, link it using LINK.EXE. Then execute the above program at a DOS prompt. After execution, you will find a new file RESULT in the directory. Then apply an external pulse to IRQ2 pin of the IBM PC IO channel. This will again cause the execution of ISR that writes 500 H bytes into the file. For further details of the DOS function calls under INT 21H, refer the MSDOS Encyclopedia or MS-DOS Technical Reference.

Program 4.4

Write a program that gives display 'IRT2 is OK' if a hardware signal appears on IRQ_2 pin and 'IRT3 is OK' if it appears on IRQ_3 pin of PC IO Channel.

```
ASSUME     CS:CODE, DS:DATA
DATA          SEGMENT
MSG1          DB "IRT2 IS OK" ,OAH, ODH, "$"
MSG2          DB "IRT3 IS OK",OAH,ODH, "$"
DATA          ENDS
CODE          ES

START:     MOV AX, CODE
           MOV DS, AX                   ; Set IVT for Type OAH
           MOV DX, OFFSET ISR1
           MOV AX,250AH                 ; IRQ2 is equivalent to Type OAH
           INT 21H
           MOV DX, OFFSET ISR2          ; Set IVT for Type OBH
           MOV AX, 250BH                ; IRQ3 is equivalent to TYPE OBH
           INT 21H
HERE :     JUMP HERE
                                        ; ISR1 and ISR2 dispaly the message
ISR1       PROC  LOCAL
           MOV AX, DATA
           MOV DS, AX
```

```
            MOV DX, OFFSET MSG1              ; Display message MSG1
            MOV AH, 09H
            INT 21 H
            IRET
ISR1        ENDP
ISR2        PROC LOCAL
            MOV AX, DATA
            MOV DS, AX
            MOV DX, OFFSET MSG2              ; Display message MSG2
            MOV AH,09H
            INT 21H
            IRET
ISR2        ENDP
CODE        ENDS
    END     START
```

Program 4.4 *Listings*

Prepare the EXE file of the above program as usual. Execute it at DOS prompt that will hang the system. Now apply a pulse to IRQ_2 pin. The message 'IRT_2 is OK' is displayed on the screen. Then apply a pulse to IRQ_3 pin of IO channel. The message 'IRT3 is OK' is displayed on screen.

4.8 PASSING PARAMETERS TO PROCEDURES

Procedures or subroutines may require input data or constants for their execution. Their data or constants may be passed to the subroutine by the main program (host or calling program) or some subroutine may access readily available data of constants available in memory.

Generally, the following techinques are used to pass input data/parameter to procedures in assembly language programs.

(i) Using global declared variable
(ii) Using registers of CPU architecutre
(iii) Using memory locations (reserved)
(iv) Using stack
(v) Using PUBLIC & EXTRN.

Besides these methods if a procedure is interactive it may directly accept inputs from input devices.

As discussed in Chapter 2, a variable or a parameter label may be declared global in the main program and the same variable or parameter label can be used by all the routines or procedures of the application. Examples of passing parameters.

Example 4.1

```
ASSUME CS:CODE1,DS:DATA
DATA SEGMENT
NUMBER EQU 77H GLOBAL
DATA ENDS
CODE1 SEGMENT
    START :             MOV AX,DATA
```

```
                MOV DS,AX
                    •
                    •
                MOV AX,NUMBER
                    •
                CODE1 ENDS
ASSUME CS:CODE2
CODE2 SEGMENT
          MOV AX,DATA
          MOV DS,AX
          MOV BX,NUMBER

    CODE2 ENDS
          END START
```

The CPU general purpose registers may be used to pass parameters to the procedures. The main program may store the parameters to be passed to the procedure in the available CPU registers and the procedure may use the same register contents for execution. The original contents of the used CPU register may change during execution of the procedure. This may be avoided by pushing all the register content to be used to the stack sequentially at the start of the procedure and by poping all the register contents at the end of the procedure in opposite sequence.

Example 4.2

```
ASSUME CS:CODE
CODE SEGMENT
    START :      MOV AX,5555H
                 MOV BX,7272H
                     •
                     •
                 CALL PROCEDURE1
                     •
                     •
                     •
    PROCEDURE    PROCEDURE1 NEAR
                     •
                     •
                 ADD AX,BX
                     •
                     •
                 RET
    PROCEDURE1   ENDP
    CODE ENDS
                 END START
```

Memory locations may also be used to pass parameters to a procedure in the same way as registers. A main program may store the parameter to be passed to a procedure at a known memory address location and the procedure may use the same location for accessing the parameter.

Example 4.3

```
ASSUME CS:CODE, DS:DATA
DATA SEGMENT
NUM DB (55H)
COUNT EQU 10H
DATA ENDS
CODE SEGMENT
    START :        MOV AX,DATA
                   MOV DS,AX
                       •
                       •
                   CALL ROUTINE
                       •
                       •
                       •
    PROCEDURE      ROUTINE NEAR
                   MOV BX,NUM
                   MOV CX,COUTN
                       •
    ROUTINE        ENDP
    CODE           ENDS
                   END START
```

Stack memory can also be used to pass parameters to a procedure. A main program may store the parameters to be passed to a procedure in its CPU registers. The registers will further be pushed on to the stack. The procedure during its execution pops back the appropriate parameters as and when required. This procedure of poping back the parameters must be implemented carefully because besides the parameters to be passed to the procedure the stack contains other important information like contents of other pushed registers, return addresses from the current procedure and other procedure or interrupt service routines.

Example 4.4

```
ASSUME CS:CODE, SS:STACK
CODE SEGMENT
    START :        MOV AX,STACK
                   MOV SS,AX
                   MOV AX,5577H
                   MOV BX,2929H
                       •
                   PUSH AX
                   PUSH BX
                   CALL ROUTINE ; Decrements SP by 2 (by 4 far routine)
                       •
                       •
```

```
    PROCEDURE   ROUTINE NEAR
                      •
         •
         MOV DX,SP
         ADD SP,02    ;      Leave initial two stack bytes of
                             return offset and
                             segment address after executing
                             subroutine
                             POP BX             ;      The data is
                             POP AX             ;      Passes in BX,AX
                             MOV SP,DX
                                  •
                                  •
                                  •
STACK SEGMENT
STACKDATA DB 200H DUP (?)
STACK ENDS
```

For passing the parameters to procedures using the PUBLIC & EXTRN directives, must be declared PUBLIC (for all routines) in the main routine and the same should be declared EXT RN in the procedure. Thus the main program can pass the PUBLIC parameter to a procedure in which it is declared EXTRN (external)

Example 4.5

```
ASSUME CS:CODE, DS:DATA
DATA SEGMENT
PUBLIC NUMBER EQU 200H
         DATA ENDS
         CODE SEGMENT
    START :   MOV AX,DATA
              MOV DS,AX
                 •
                 •
                 •
              CALL ROUTINE
                 •
                 •
                 •
              PROCEDURE ROUTINE NEAR
          EXTRN NUMBER
              MOV AX,NUMBER
                 •
                 •
                 •
          ROUTINE   ENDP
```

4.9 HANDLING PROGRAMS OF SIZE MORE THAN 64K

As already discussed in Chapter 1, the maximum size of an 8086 segment is 64 KB. The same limitation is applicable to a code segment that contains executable program code. This obviously puts limitation on the maximum size of a program and thus how to write programs of size more than 64 K is going to be an interesting question, which is addressed in this section.

Unfortunately there is no techinque to estimate the size of an executable program before it is assembled and linked. Thus one cannot come to know the physical byte size of a memory segment program while it is being developed. However, premeditating the assembly language program for a particular application may be too big a modular programming approach must be accepted to develop it. The big programming task should be divided into independent modules, which may be developed and tested individual functions of the module to implement the complete tasks.

As far as the programming methodology is concerned there are two approaches to solve this problem.

(i) Writing programs with more than one segment for Data, Code or Stack .
(ii) Writing programs with FAR subroutines each of which can be of size up to 64 K.

A program example with more than one segment is shown below.

Example 4.6

```
ASSUME CS:CODE1, DS:DATA1
CODE1 SEGMENT
    START :      MOV AX,DATA1
                 MOV DS,AX
                      •
                      •
    CODE1              ENDS
ASSUME CS:CODE2, DS:DATA2
CODE2 SEGMENT
                 MOV AX,DATA2
                 MOV DS,AX
                     •
                     •
  CODE2          ENDS
    DATA1              SEGMENT
          •
          •
    DATA1              ENDS

    DATA2              SEGMENT
                       •
                       •
    DATA2              ENDS
                       END START
```

Example 4.7 is the program example with more than one intersegment routine.

Example 4.7

```
ASSUME CS:cODE1, DS:DATA1
DATA SEGMENT
    •
    •
DATA ENDS
CODE1 SEGMENT
START :                  MOV AX,DATA
                         MOV DS,AX
                         •
                         •
                         CALL FAR_PTR ROUTINE1
                         •
                         •
                         CALL FAR_PTR ROUTINE2
                         •
                         •
CODE1                    ENDS
PROCEDURE                ROUNTINE1 FAR
                         •
                         •
                         •
ROUTINE1                 ENDP
PROCEDURE                ROUTINE2 FAR
                         •
                         •
ROUTINE2                 ENDP
    END                  START
```

4.10 MACROS

Till now, we have studied the stack, subroutines, interrupts and interrupt service routines. It is a notable point that the control is transferred to a subroutine or an interrupt service routine whenever it is called or an interrupt signal appears at the interrupt pin of the processor. After executing these routines the control is again transferred back to the main calling program. Hence rather than writing a complete routine again and again, one may call it as many times as required. This imparts flexibility in programming as well as ease of troubleshooting. The concept of subroutine as well as interrupt service routine can be compared with an office where the main (calling) program acts as a head while the subroutines and interrupt service routines act as subordinates. The head may ask his subordinates to work out a particular task and be ready with the results. Here the main program calls subroutines and interrupt service routines and may refer the results of their execution for further processing. The subroutines and interrupt service routines are assigned labels for references.

The macro is also a similar concept. Suppose, a number of instructions are repeating through in the main program, the listings becomes lengthy. So a macro definition, i.e. a label, is assigned with the repeatedly appearing string of instructions. The process of assigning a label or macroname to the string is called defining a macro. A macro within a macro is called a nested macro. The macroname or macro definition is then used throughout the main program to refer to that string of instructions.

The difference between a macro and a subroutine is that in the macro the complete code of the instructions string is inserted at each place where the macro-name appears. Hence the EXE file becomes lengthy. Macro does not utilise the service of stack. There is no question of transfer of control as the program using the macro inserts the complete code of the macro at every reference of the macroname. On the other hand, subroutine is called whenever necessary, i.e. the control of execution is transferred to the subroutine, every time it is called. The executable code in case of the subroutines becomes smaller as the subroutine appears only once in the complete code. Thus, the EXE file is smaller as compared to the program using macro. The control is transferred to a subroutine whenever it is called, and this utilizes the stack service. The program using subroutine requires less memory space for execution than that using macro. Macro requires less time for execution, as it does not contain CALL and RET instructions as the subroutines do.

4.10.1 Defining a MACRO

A MACRO can be defined anywhere in a program using the directives MACRO and ENDM. The label prior to MACRO is the macro name which should be used in the actual program. The ENDM directive marks the end of the instructions or statements sequence assigned with the macro name. The following macro DISPLAY displays the message MSG on the CRT. The syntax is as given:

```
DISPLAY MACRO
        MOV AX, SEG MSG
        MOV DS, AX
        MOV DX, OFFSET MSG
        MOV AH, 09 H
        INT 21 H
ENDM
```

The above definition of a macro assigns the name DISPLAY to the instruction sequence between the directives MACRO and ENDM. While assembling, the above sequence of instructions will replace the label 'DISPLAY', whenever it appears in the program.

A macro may also be used in a data segment. In other words, a macro may also be used to represent statements and directives. The concept of macro remains the same independent of its contents. The following example shows a macro containing statements. The macro defines the strings to be displayed.

```
STRINGS MACRO
      MSG1 DB 0AH,0DH, "Program terminated normally",0AH,0DH, "$"
      MSG2 DB 0AH,0DH, "Retry , Abort, Fail",0AH,0DH, "$"
ENDM
```

A macro may be called by quoting its name, along with any values to be passed to the macro. Calling a macro means inserting the statements and instructions represented by the macro directly at the place of the macroname in the program.

4.10.2 Passing Parameters to a MACRO

Using parameters in a definition, the programmer specifies the parameters of the macro those are likely to be changed each time the macro is called. For example, the DISPLAY macro written in Section 4.10.1 can be made to display two different messages MSG1 and MSG2, as shown.

```
DISPLAY MACRO MSG
        MOV AX, SEG MSG
        MOV DS, AX
```

```
                    MOV DX, OFFSET MSG
                    MOV AH, 09 H
                    INT 21 H
               ENDM
```

This parameter MSG can be replaced by MSG1 or MSG2 while calling the macro as shown.

```
                       :
                       :
                DISPLAY MSG1
                       :
                       :
                DISPLAY MSG2
                       :
                       :
MSG1 DB 0AH,0DH, "Program Terminated Normally",0AH,0DH, "$"
MSG2 DB 0AH,0DH, "Retry, Abort, Fail",0AH,0DH, "$"
```

There may be more than one parameter appearing in the macro definition, meaning thereby that there may be more than one parameters to be passed to the macro, and each of them is liable to be changed. All the parameters are specified in the definition sequentially and also in the call with the same sequence.

A macro may be defined in another macro or in other words a macro may be called from inside a macro. This type of macro is called a nested macro. All the directives available in MASM can also be used in a macro and carry the same significance.

4.11 TIMINGS AND DELAYS

It is obvious from the studies of the timing diagrams that every instruction requires a definite number of clock cycles for its execution. Thus every instruction requires a fixed amount of time, i.e. multiplication of the number of clock cycles required for the execution of the instruction and the period of the clock at which the microprocessor is running. The duration required for the execution of an instruction can be used to derive the required delays. A sequence of instructions, if executed by a microprocessor, will require a time duration that is the sum of all the individual time durations required for execution of each instruction. Note that in a loop program, the number of instructions in the program may be less but the number of instructions actually executed by the microprocessor depend on the loop count. Also in case of subroutines and interrupt service routines the actual number of instructions executed by the microprocessor depends on the procedure or interrupt service routine length along with the main calling program. The required number of clock states for execution of each instruction of 8086/88 are given in Appendix A.

The procedure of generating delays using a microprocessor based system can be stepwise described as follows.

1. Determine the exact required delay.
2. Select the instructions for delay loop. While selecting the instructions, care should be taken that the execution of these instructions does not interfere with the main program execution. In other words, any memory location or register used by the main program must not be modified by the delay routine. The instructions executed for the delay loop are dummy instructions in the sense that the result of those instructions is useless but the time required for their execution is an elemental part of the required delay.

3. Find out the number of clock states required for execution of each of the selected delay loop instructions. Further find out the number of clock states required (n) to execute the loop once by adding all the clock states required to execute the instructions individually.
4. Find out the period of the clock frequency at which microprocessor is running, i.e. duration of a clock state (T).
5. Find out the time required for the execution of the loop once by multiplying the period T with the number of clock states required (n) to execute the delay loop once.
6. Find out the count (N) by dividing the required time delay T_d by the duration for execution of the loop once ($n*T$).

$$\text{Count } N = \frac{\text{Required Delay } (T_d)}{n * T}$$

Note that it may not be possible to generate the exact time delays using this method but the delays obtained using this method are sufficiently accurate to be used in most of the practical problems. When more accurate delays are required a programmable timer/counter chip 8253 or 8254 may be used. The timer 8253 is discussed in details in Chapter 5. Program 4.5 explains the generation of a delay using some instructions of 8086.

Program 4.5

Write a program to generate a delay of 100 ms using an 8086 system that runs on 10 MHz frequency.

Solution The required delay T_d = 100 ms

Instructions selected	States for execution
MOV CX, Count	4
DEC CX	2
NOP	3
JNZ label	16

Number of clock cycles for execution of the loop once = 2 + 3 + 16 = 21
The instruction MOV CX, COUNT is not in the delay generation loop.
Time required for execution of the loop once = nT = 21 ¥ 0.1 = 2.1 ms

$$\text{Count } N = \frac{\text{Required Delay } (T_d)}{n * T}$$

$$\text{Required count} = \frac{T_d}{n * T} = \frac{100 * 10^{-3}}{10^{-6}} = 47.619 * 10^{3}$$

$$= 47619 = \text{BA03H}$$

The ALP to generate this delay is given in Program 4.5.

```
PROC            DELAY LOCAL
ASSUME CS : CODEP
CODEP           SEGMENT
                MOV CX, BA03 H       ; Load count Register
WAIT:           DEC CX               ; Decrement
                NOP                  ; Wait till
                JNZ WAIT             ; Count register
                RET                  ; becomes zero and
                DELAY ENDP           ; return to main
                                     ; program
```

Program 4.5 *ALP to Generate 100 ms Delay*

The exact delay obtained using the above routine can be calculated as shown:

$$\begin{aligned} T_d\,(\text{exact}) &= 0.1 * 4 + (2 + 3) * 47619 * 0.1 + 16 * 47618 * 0.1 + 4 * 0.1 + 8 * 0.1 \\ &= 0.4 + 23809.5 + 76188.8 + 0.4 + .8 \\ &= 99999.998\ \mu\text{s} = 99.9999\ \text{ms} \\ &\approx 100\ \text{ms} \end{aligned}$$

Note that if the zero condition is satisfied, the JNZ instruction takes only 4 clock states, otherwise, the instruction takes 16 clock states for execution. Also the instructions MOV CX, BA03 H and RET are executed only once during the execution of the delay loop.

It may be observed that in the above delay there is an error of 0.1 ms. The error is only of one clock state, and it cannot be corrected by adding further instructions to the ALP, after the JNZ instruction because the smallest execution time of an 8086 instruction is 2 states, i.e. 0.2 μs for this system.

In case of a 16-bit count register, the maximum count value can be FFFFH. This may put a limitation on the maximum delay that can be generated using these instructions. Whenever large delays are required, more than one count register may be used to serve the purpose. Program 4.6 explains the use of another count register BX to obtain the required large delay.

Program 4.6

Using the ALP of Program 4.5 design a delay of ten minutes.

Solution Required delay T_d = 10 minutes = 600 sec

INSTRUCTIONS SELECTED	CLOCK STATES
MOV BX, COUNT 1	4
MOV CX, COUNT 2	4
DEC CX	2
DEC BX	2
JNZ Lable	16
NOP	3
RET	8

Clock frequency = 10 MHZ

T = 0.1 μSEC

There will be two nested counter loops for decrementing the two counting registers. Let the first loop has a count FFFF.

count2 = FFFFH

```
PROC DELAY LOCAL
      ASSUME CS : CODE
      CODE   SEGMENT
             MOV BX, Count1          ; Load count1.
      BBB :  MOV CX, Count2                  ; Load count2, i.e. FFFFH.
      CCC :  NOP                             ;
             DEC CX                          ; Decrement the count 2,
             JNZ CCC                         ; till it becomes zero.
             DEC BX                          ; Decrement the count 1
             JNZ BBB                         ; till it becomes zero.
             RET                             ; Return to main routine.
DELAY        ENDP
CODE         ENDS
      END
```

Program 4.6 *ALP to Generate 10 Minutes Delay*

Inner loop requires $T_1 = 0.1 * 4 + (2 + 3 + 16) * 65535 * 0.1$

seconds for complete execution $= 0.137605$ sec

Outer loop requires $T_2 = 0.137605 + (16 + 2) * 10^{-6} * 0.1$

seconds for one interation $= 0.1376068$ sec

Required delay $T_d = 10 * 60 \text{ sec} = 600 \text{ sec}$

$$\text{Count } 1 = \frac{T_d}{T_2} = \frac{600}{0.1376068} = 4359.58$$

$$\approx 4360$$

$$= 1107 \text{ H}$$

Program 4.6 also generates an approximate time delay of ten minutes. The exact error may be calculated by using the procedure adopted for Program 4.5.

SUMMARY

In this chapter, initially, we have studied the stack structure of 8086/88. As an application of stack, we have also described how to write subroutines. Then the interrupt structure related details and the programming techniques have been presented. Further the concept of macro has been discussed along with an example. Finally, we have presented the procedure to write programs for generating delays. For the detailed information about the number of clock cycles required for execution of each instruction, readers may refer to the 8086 instruction set Appendix-A. Note that, intention of this chapter is not to give the details of all the syntaxes, facilities and the advanced programming techniques related to the above points but to introduce general methods and concepts for utilising these facilities. For more details the programmer may refer to the 'MASM Users Manual and Technical Reference'.

EXERCISES

4.1 Explain the stack structure of 8086 in details.

4.2 What is the role of stack in calling a subroutine and returning from the routine?

4.3 Describe execution of a CALL instruction.

4.4 Write an ALP to calculate the hexadecimal factorial of a one digit hexadecimal number.

4.5 Write an ALP to convert a 4-digit decimal number to its binary equivalent, using a procedure for dividing a number by two.

4.6 What is the difference between a NEAR and a FAR procedure?

4.7 Draw and discuss interrupt structure of 8086 in details.
4.8 What is interrupt vector table of 8086? Explain its structure.
4.9 Explain the interrupt responce sequence of 8086.
4.10 How do you set or clear the interrupt flag IF? What is its importance in the interrupt structure of 8086?
4.11 What are the interrupt vector addresses of the following interrupts in the 8086 IV T?
(i) INTO (ii) NMI (iii) INT 20H (iv) INT 55H
4.12 What is the difference between hardware and software interrupt?
4.13 Explain the term 'nested interrupt'.
4.14 How will you differentiate between the two procedures, the first of which is a subroutine and the second is an interrupt service routine?
4.15 What do you mean by a macro? What are the differences between a macro and a subroutine?
4.16 How do you pass parameters to macro?
4.17 Define a macro 'SQUARE' that calculates square of a number.
4.18 What is a nested macro?
4.19 How do you generate delays in software? What are the limitations of this method of generating delays? How will you synchronize one such delay with an external process?
4.20 Write ALPs to generate the following delays, using a microprocessor system that runs at 5 MHz.
(i) 1 sec (ii) 100 ms (iii) 5 sec

Exercises 4.4, 4.5, 4.10, 4.20 should be implemented as laboratory exercies.

5 Basic Peripherals and Their Interfacing with 8086/88

INTRODUCTION

In the previous chapters, we have presented the architecture, instruction set and the art of programming with 8086/88. In this chapter, the general peripheral devices and their interfacing techniques with the microprocessor 8086/88 are discussed. In the minimal working system configuration of a general microprocessor, we consider a keyboard, display system, memory system and I/O ports along with the CPU. In general, all these devices are called peripheral devices. There are also some additional dedicated peripheral devices like PIC [Programmable Interrupt Controller], DMA [Direct Memory Access] controller, CRT controller, etc. All these dedicated peripherals are studied in the next chapter. The microprocessor may be seen as the heart of the system while all the peripheral circuits including memory system are built around the microprocessor. Since a processor without memory is not meaningful, memory (primary) may also be considered as an integral part of a microprocessor system.

Most of the peripheral devices are designed and interfaced with a CPU either to enable it to communicate with the user or an external process and to ease the circuit operations so that the microprocessor works more efficiently and effectively. The use of a special purpose peripheral integrated device simplifies both—the hardware circuits and the software, considerably. Each of these special purpose devices need a typical sequence of instructions to make it work. This instruction sequence appropriately initialises the peripheral and makes it work under the control of the microprocessor. Thus each dedicated peripheral device needs suitable initialisation. However memory, unlike the peripheral devices, does not need any initialisation and does not directly participate in the process of communication between CPU and the user. Rather, it acts as a media for the communication between a peripheral with the microprocessor. While memory may be treated as a peripheral, on the other hand, peripheral devices are often treated as memory locations. Thus as far as the CPU is concerned, there is no special difference in the method of handling memory or peripherals, except for the use of respective control signals. In this chapter, we will present interfacing techniques of semiconductor memories, I/O ports and a few other peripherals with 8086/8088.

5.1 SEMICONDUCTOR MEMORY INTERFACING

Semiconductor memories are of two types, viz. RAM (Random Access Memory) and ROM (Read Only Memory).

5.1.1 Static RAM Interfacing

The semiconductor RAMs are of broadly two types–static RAM and dynamic RAM. In this section, we will consider the interfacing of static RAM and ROM with 8086/8088. The semiconductor memories are organised as two dimensional arrays of memory locations. For example, 4K × 8 or 4K byte memory contains 4096 locations, where each location contains 8-bit data and only one of the 4096 locations can be selected at a time. Once a location is selected all the bits in it are accessible using a group of conductors called 'data bus'. Obviously, for addressing 4K bytes of memory, twelve address lines are required. In general, to address a memory location out of N memory locations , we will require at least n bits of address, i.e. n address lines where $n = \text{Log}_2 N$. Thus if the microprocessor has n address lines, then it is able to address at the most N locations of memory, where $2^n = N$. However, if out of N locations only P memory locations are to be interfaced, then the least significant p address lines out of the available n lines can be directly connected from the microprocessor to the memory chip while the remaining $(n–p)$ higher order address lines may be used for address decoding (as inputs to the chip selection logic). The memory address depends upon the hardware circuit used for decoding the chip select ($\overline{CS}$). The output of the decoding circuit is connected with the $\overline{CS}$ pin of the memory chip.

The general procedure of static memory interfacing with 8086 is briefly described as follows:

1. Arrange the available memory chips so as to obtain 16-bit data bus width. The upper 8-bit bank is called 'odd address memory bank' and the lower 8-bit bank is called 'even address memory bank', as described in memory organisation in Chapter 1.
2. Connect available memory address lines of memory chips with those of the microprocessor and also connect the memory $\overline{RD}$ and $\overline{WR}$ inputs to the corresponding processor control signals. Connect the 16-bit data bus of the memory bank with that of the microprocessor 8086.
3. The remaining address lines of the microprocessor, $\overline{BHE}$ and A_0 are used for decoding the required chip select signals for the odd and even memory banks. The $\overline{CS}$ of memory is derived from the O/P of the decoding circuit.

The procedure will be clearer while solving problems on memory interfacing with 8086/88.

As a good and efficient interfacing practice, the address map of the system should be continuous as far as possible, i.e. there should be no windows in the map and no fold back space should be allowed. A memory location should have a single address corresponding to it, i.e. absolute decoding should be preferred, and minimum hardware should be used for decoding. In a number of cases, linear decoding may be used to minimise the required hardware.

Let us now consider a few example problems on memory interfacing with 8086.

Program 5.1

Interface two 4K × 8 EPROMS and two 4K × 8 RAM chips with 8086. Select suitable maps.

Solution We know that, after reset, the IP and CS are initialised to form address FFFF0H. Hence, this address must lie in the EPROM. The address of RAM may be selected any where in the 1MB address space of 8086, but we will select the RAM address such that the address map of the system is continuous, as shown in Table 5.1.

Table 5.1 *Memory Map for Problem 5.1*

Address	A_{19}	A_{18}	A_{17}	A_{16}	A_{15}	A_{14}	A_{13}	A_{12}	A_{11}	A_{10}	A_{09}	A_{08}	A_{07}	A_{06}	A_{05}	A_{04}	A_{03}	A_{02}	A_{01}	A_{00}
FFFFFH	1	1	1	1	1	1	1	1	1	1	1	1	1	1	1	1	1	1	1	1
							EPROM						8K × 8							

(*Contd.*)

Table 5.1 *(Contd.)*

Address	A_{19}	A_{18}	A_{17}	A_{16}	A_{15}	A_{14}	A_{13}	A_{12}	A_{11}	A_{10}	A_{09}	A_{08}	A_{07}	A_{06}	A_{05}	A_{04}	A_{03}	A_{02}	A_{01}	A_{00}
FE000H	1	1	1	1	1	1	1	0	0	0	0	0	0	0	0	0	0	0	0	0
FDFFFH	1	1	1	1	1	1	0	1	1	1	1	1	1	1	1	1	1	1	1	1
							RAM					8K × 8								
FC000H	1	1	1	1	1	1	0	0	0	0	0	0	0	0	0	0	0	0	0	0

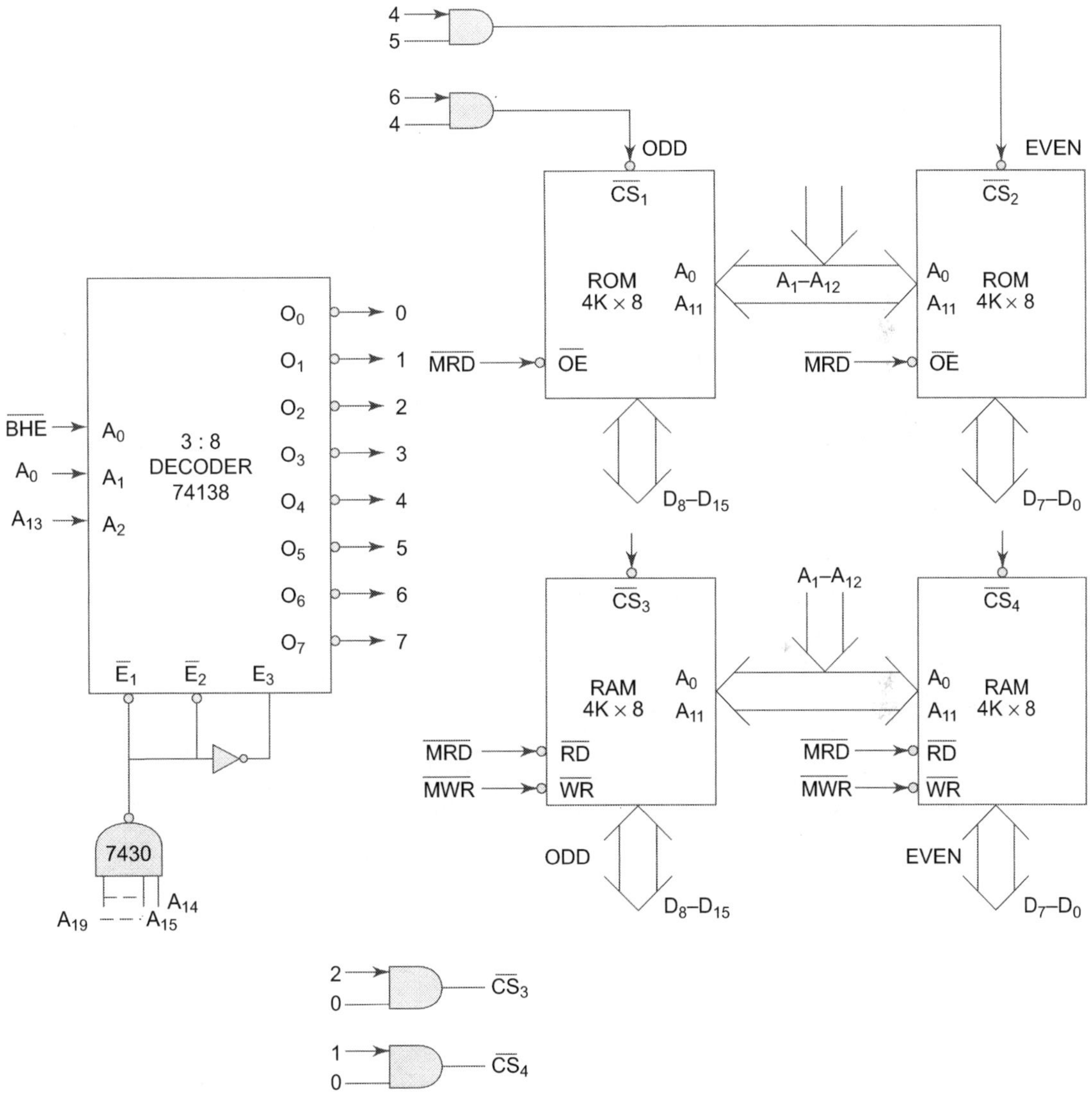

Fig. 5.1 *Interfacing Problem 5.1*

Total 8K bytes of EPROM need 13 address lines A_0–A_{12} (since $2^{13} = 8K$). Address lines A_{13}–A_{19} are used for decoding to generate the chip select. The $\overline{BHE}$ signal goes low when a transfer is at odd address or higher byte of data is to be accessed. Let us assume that the latched address, $\overline{BHE}$ and demultiplexed data lines are readily available for interfacing. Figure 5.1 shows the interfacing diagram for the memory system.

The memory system in this example contains in total four 4K × 8 memory chips.

The two 4K × 8 chips of RAM and ROM are arranged in parallel to obtain 16-bit data bus width. If A_0 is 0, i.e. the address is even and is in RAM, then the lower RAM chip is selected indicating 8-bit transfer at an even address. If A_0 is 1, i.e. the address is odd and is in RAM, the $\overline{BHE}$ goes low, the upper RAM chip is selected, further indicating that the 8-bit transfer is at an odd address. If the selected addresses are in ROM, the respective ROM chips are selected. If at a time A_0 and $\overline{BHE}$ both are 0, both the RAM or ROM chips are selected, i.e. the data transfer is of 16 bits. The selection of chips here takes place as shown in Table 5.2.

Table 5.2 *Memory Chip Selection for Problem 5.1*

Decoder I/P → Address/ $\overline{BHE}$ →	A_2 A_{13}	A_1 A_0	A_0 $\overline{BHE}$	Selection/ Comment
Word transfer on $D_0 - D_{15}$	0	0	0	Even and odd addresses in RAM
Byte transfer on $D_7 - D_0$	0	0	1	Only even address in RAM
Byte transfer on $D_8 - D_{15}$	0	1	0	Only odd address in RAM
Word transfer on $D_0 - D_{15}$	1	0	0	Even and odd addresses in ROM
Byte transfer on $D_0 - D_7$	1	0	1	Only even address in ROM
Byte transfer on $D_8 - D_{15}$	1	1	0	Only odd address in ROM

Program 5.2

Design an interface between 8086 CPU and two chips of 16K × 8 EPROM and two chips of 32K × 8 RAM. Select the starting address of EPROM suitably. The RAM address must start at 00000H.

Solution The last address in the map of 8086 is FFFFFH. After resetting, the processor starts from FFFF0H. Hence this address must lie in the address range of EPROM. Figure 5.2 shows the interfacing diagram, and Table 5.3 shows complete map of the system.

Table 5.3 *Address Map for Problem 5.2*

Addresses	A_{19}	A_{18}	A_{17}	A_{16}	A_{15}	A_{14}	A_{13}	A_{12}	A_{11}	A_{10}	A_{09}	A_{08}	A_{07}	A_{06}	A_{05}	A_{04}	A_{03}	A_{02}	A_{01}	A_{00}
FFFFFH	1	1	1	1	1	1	1	1	1	1	1	1	1	1	1	1	1	1	1	1
								32KB		EPROM										
F8000H	1	1	1	1	1	0	0	0	0	0	0	0	0	0	0	0	0	0	0	0
0FFFFH	0	0	0	0	1	1	1	1	1	1	1	1	1	1	1	1	1	1	1	1
							64KB RAM													
00000H	0	0	0	0	0	0	0	0	0	0	0	0	0	0	0	0	0	0	0	0

It is better not to use a decoder to implement the above map because it is not continuous, i.e. there is some unused address space between the last RAM address (0FFFFH) and the first EPROM address (F8000H). Hence the logic is implemented using logic gates, as shown in Fig. 5.2.

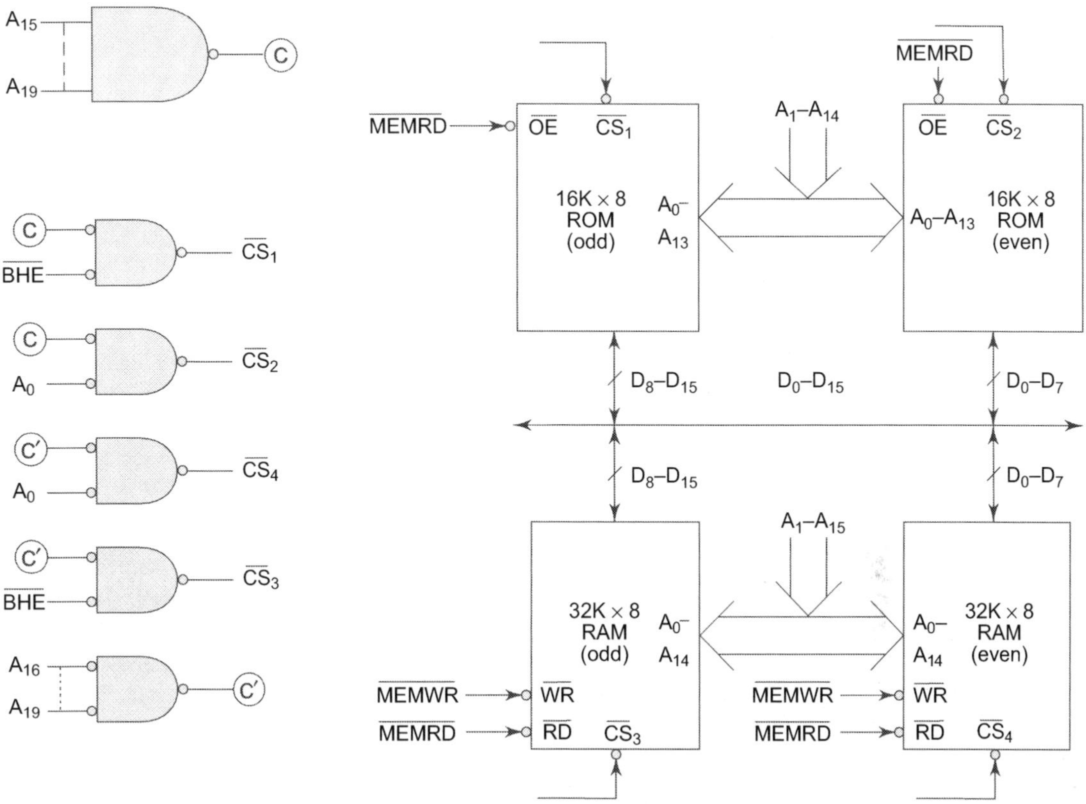

Fig. 5.2 *Interfacing Problem 5.2*

Let us select a variable C for memory address pulse, i.e. output of 6-input NAND gate. $\overline{BHE}$ is abbreviated as B. The chip selection logic can be designed as shown in Table 5.4.

Table 5.4

I/P		*O/P*	
A_0	$B(\overline{BHE})$	C_1	C_2
0	0	0	0
0	1	1	0
1	0	0	1
1	1	1	1

$$C_2 = A_0$$
$$C_1 = \overline{BHE}$$

To find out $\overline{CS_1}$ and $\overline{CS_2}$ we will have to combine C_1 and C_2 with C.

Table 5.5

I/P			*O/P*	
C_1	C_2	C	$\overline{CS_1}$	$\overline{CS_2}$
0	0	0	0	0
1	0	0	1	0
1	1	0	1	1
0	1	0	0	1

Table 5.5 shows that

$$\overline{CS_1} = C + C_1 = C + \overline{BHE} \text{ and } \overline{CS_2} = C + C_2 = C + A_0$$

Similarly we can find out CS_3 and CS_4.

Problem 5.3

It is required to interface two chips of 32K × 8 ROM and four chips of 32K × 8 RAM with 8086, according to the following map.

ROM 1 and 2 F0000H - FFFFFH, RAM 1 and 2 D0000H - DFFFFH

RAM 3 and 4 E0000H - EFFFFH

Show the implementation of this memory system.

Solution Let us write the memory map of the system as shown in Table 5.6.

The implementation of the above map is shown in Fig. 5.3 using the same technique as in Problem 5.1 and Problem 5.2. All the address, data and control signals are assumed to be readily available.

Table 5.6 *Address Map for Problem 5.3*

Address	A_{19}	A_{18}	A_{17}	A_{16}	A_{15}	A_{14}	A_{13}	A_{12}	A_{11}	A_{10}	A_{09}	A_{08}	A_{07}	A_{06}	A_{05}	A_{04}	A_{03}	A_{02}	A_{01}	A_0
F0000H	1	1	1	1	0	0	0	0	0	0	0	0	0	0	0	0	0	0	0	0
ROM 1and2										64K										
FFFFFH	1	1	1	1	1	1	1	1	1	1	1	1	1	1	1	1	1	1	1	1
D0000H	1	1	0	1	0	0	0	0	0	0	0	0	0	0	0	0	0	0	0	0
RAM 1and2										64K										
DFFFFH	1	1	0	1	1	1	1	1	1	1	1	1	1	1	1	1	1	1	1	1
E0000H	1	1	1	0	0	0	0	0	0	0	0	0	0	0	0	0	0	0	0	0
RAM 3and4										64K										
EFFFFH	1	1	1	0	0	0	0	0	0	0	0	0	0	0	0	0	0	0	0	0

5.1.2 Interfacing Memories with 8088

The techniques of interfacing semiconductor memory with 8088 is exactly like that of 8085. The processor 8088 externally has 8-bit data bus just like 8085. Also the 8088 memory system is not divided into even or odd memory banks. Unlike 8086, the memory in an 8088 system can be seen as a continuous block of memory locations. The control bus of 8088 is similar to 8085. Rather, 8088 was designed to be software compatible with 8086 but to work in the circuits which were designed around 8085.The following problems explain the memory interfacing techniques with 8088.

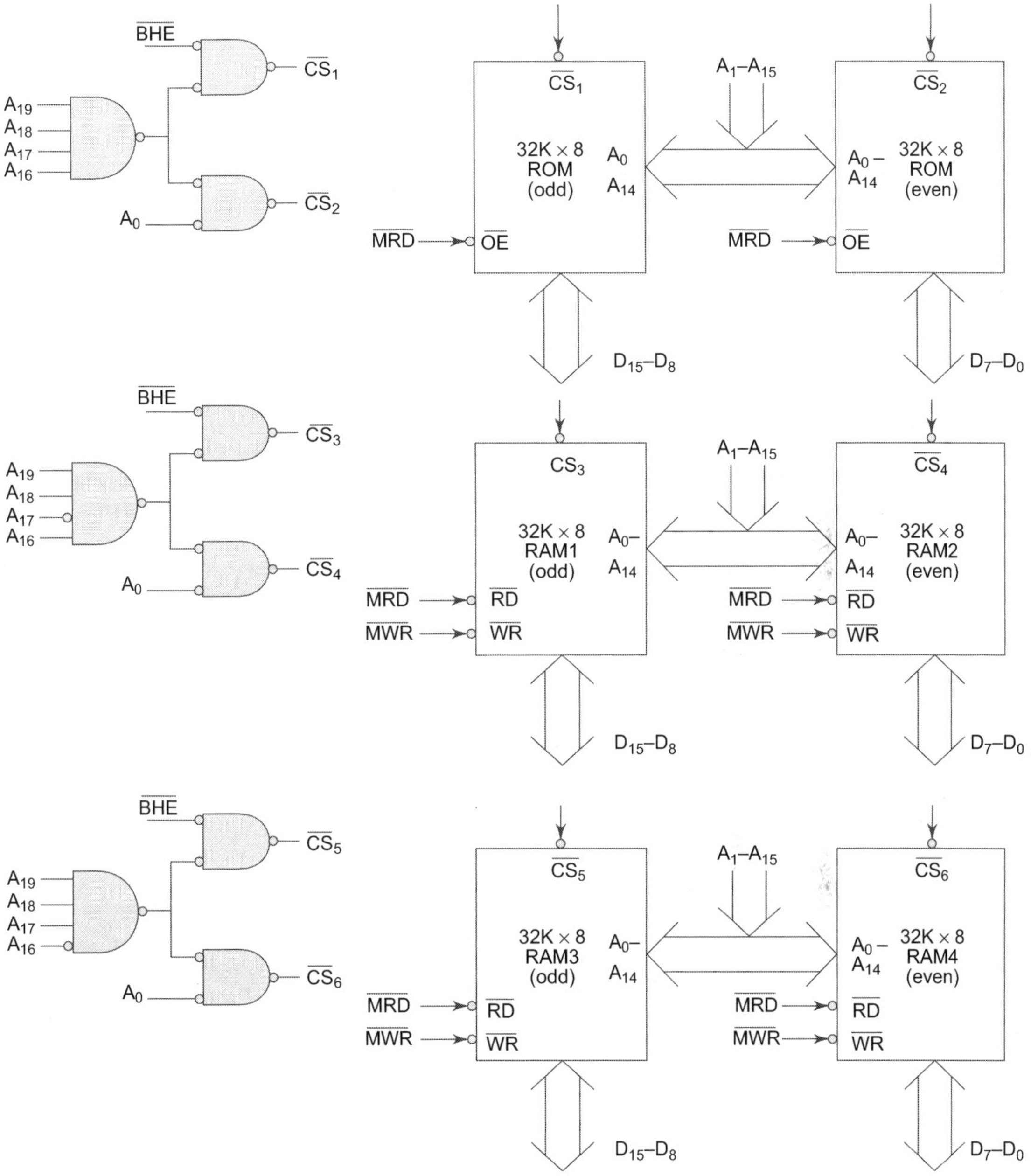

Fig. 5.3 *Interfacing Problem 5.3*

Problem 5.4

Design a memory system around 8088, that has total 16K × 8 EPROM and 32K × 8 RAM. The EPROM chips are available in modules of 8K × 8 and the RAM chips are available in modules of 8K × 8. The memory map should be specified below:

EPROM 1 - F0000H - F1FFFH

EPROM 2 - Decide suitably for a practical system.

RAM 1 - Contains Interrupt vector table

RAM 2 - 30000H - 31FFFH

RAM 3 - 40000H - 41FFFH

RAM 4 - 50000H - 51FFFH

Solution Like 8086, the processor 8088 also starts execution from the address FFFF0H, after reset. Hence EPROM 2 should be allotted the address space so as to accommodate the locations FFFF0H to FFFFFH, in it. Thus the starting address of EPROM 2 should be FE000H so that the last address is FFFFFH for an 8K × 8 EPROM chip.

The interrupt vector table of 8086/88 lies in the zeroth segment of memory system, i.e. RAM 1 must start at 00000H so that the last address is 01FFFH so as to accommodate interrupt vector table in it. Let us write the map of the system as shown in Table 5.7.

Table 5.7 *Address Map for Problem 5.4*

Address	A_{19}	A_{18}	A_{17}	A_{16}	A_{15}	A_{14}	A_{13}	A_{12}	A_{11}	A_{10}	A_{09}	A_{08}	A_{07}	A_{06}	A_{05}	A_{04}	A_{03}	A_{02}	A_{01}	A_0
00000H	0	0	0	0	0	0	0	0	0	0	0	0	0	0	0	0	0	0	0	0
(RAM 1)																				
01FFFH	0	0	0	0	0	0	0	1	1	1	1	1	1	1	1	1	1	1	1	1
30000H	0	0	1	1	0	0	0	0	0	0	0	0	0	0	0	0	0	0	0	0
										(RAM 2)										
31FFFH	0	0	1	1	0	0	0	1	1	1	1	1	1	1	1	1	1	1	1	1
40000H	0	1	0	0	0	0	0	0	0	0	0	0	0	0	0	0	0	0	0	0
										(RAM 3)										
41FFFH	0	1	0	0	0	0	0	1	1	1	1	1	1	1	1	1	1	1	1	1
50000H	0	1	0	1	0	0	0	0	0	0	0	0	0	0	0	0	0	0	0	0
										(RAM 4)										
51FFFH	0	1	0	1	0	0	0	1	1	1	1	1	1	1	1	1	1	1	1	1
F0000H	1	1	1	1	0	0	0	0	0	0	0	0	0	0	0	0	0	0	0	0
										(EPROM 1)										
F1FFFH	1	1	1	1	0	0	0	1	1	1	1	1	1	1	1	1	1	1	1	1
FE000H	1	1	1	1	1	1	1	0	0	0	0	0	0	0	0	0	0	0	0	0
										(EPROM 2)										
FFFFFH	1	1	1	1	1	1	1	1	1	1	1	1	1	1	1	1	1	1	1	1

The available 8K memory chips has [213 = 8192(8K)] 13 address lines. Total 20 address lines (A_{19}–A_0) are available from the processor. The A_0–A_{12} of the available lines are directly connected to the pins A_0–A_{12} of the memory chips. The higher order address lines (A_{13}–A_{19}) are used for deriving chip selects as shown in Fig. 5.4. In this case, as the addresses accommodated by the RAM and ROM are quite distant in the overall system map, separate decoding circuits are used for deriving the chip selects of RAM and ROM.

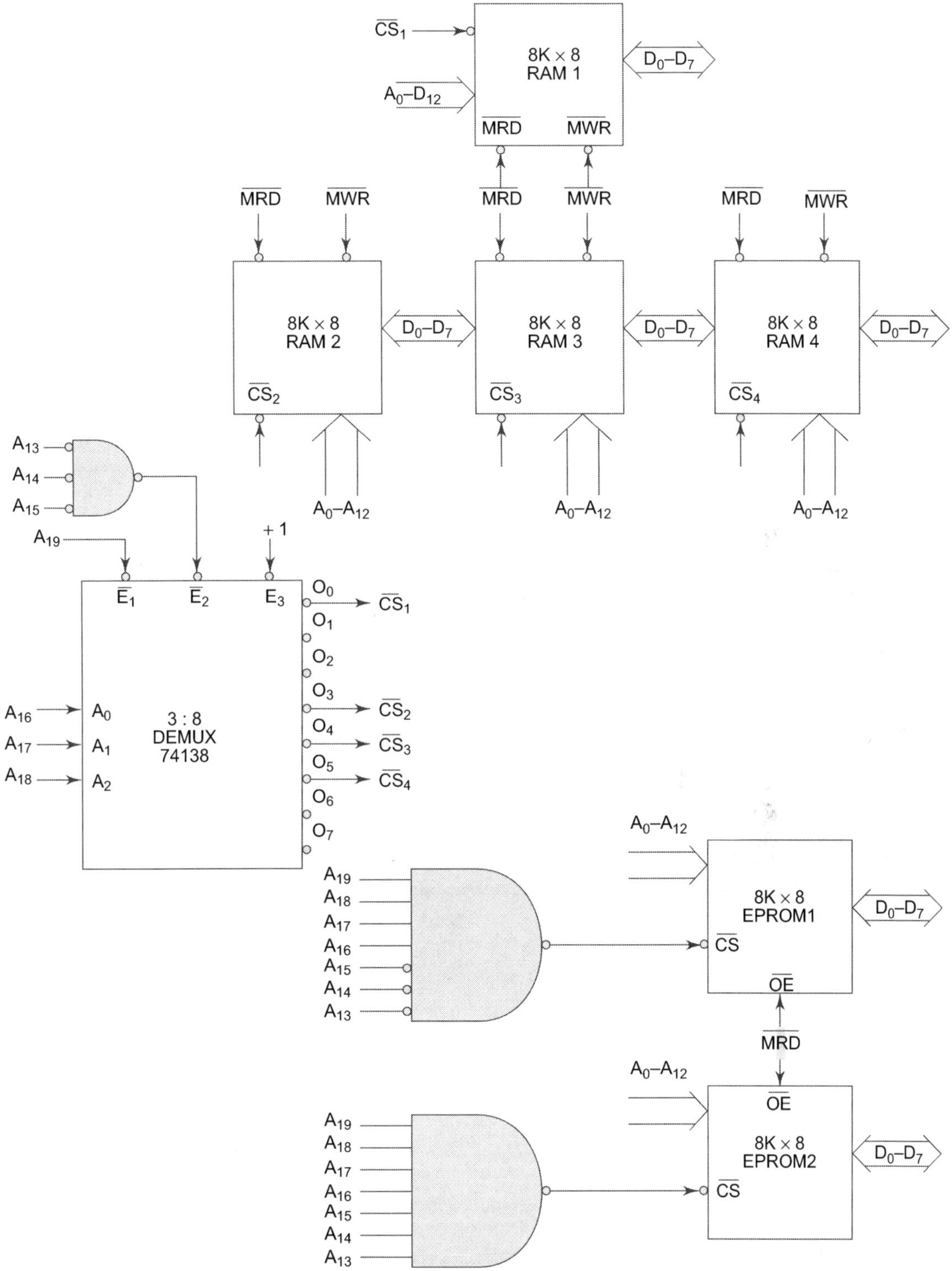

Fig. 5.4 *Interfacing Problem 5.4*

Problem 5.5

Interface a 4K × 8 EPROM, one chip of 8K × 8 RAM, two chips of 8K × 4 RAM with 8088. The map should be as given in Table 5.8.

EPROM - FF000H - FFFFFH

One 8K × 8 RAM - 00000H - 01FFFH

Two 8K × 4 RAM - 05000H - 06FFFH

Solution Let us write the complete map of the interfacing scheme.

Table 5.8 *Memory Map for Problem 5.5.*

Address	A_{19}	A_{18}	A_{17}	A_{16}	A_{15}	A_{14}	A_{13}	A_{12}	A_{11}	A_{10}	A_{09}	A_{08}	A_{07}	A_{06}	A_{05}	A_{04}	A_{03}	A_{02}	A_{01}	A_0
FF000H	1	1	1	1	1	1	1	1	0	0	0	0	0	0	0	0	0	0	0	0
(EPROM - 4K ↔ 8)																				
FFFFFH	1	1	1	1	1	1	1	1	1	1	1	1	1	1	1	1	1	1	1	1
00000H	0	0	0	0	0	0	0	0	0	0	0	0	0	0	0	0	0	0	0	0
(8K ↔ 8 RAM)																				
01FFFH	0	0	0	0	0	0	0	1	1	1	1	1	1	1	1	1	1	1	1	1
05000H	0	0	0	0	0	1	0	1	0	0	0	0	0	0	0	0	0	0	0	0
(8K ↔ 4 + 8K ↔ 4 RAM)																				
06FFFH	0	0	0	0	0	1	1	0	1	1	1	1	1	1	1	1	1	1	1	1

The above map can be implemented as shown in Fig. 5.5. 4K × 8 EPROM needs 12 address lines while 8K × 4 RAM need 13 address lines. Observe line A_{12} in the address map it needs to be inverted.

Note that A_{13} is abandoned here while interfacing 8K × 4 RAMs, because as it is varying, it cannot be used as input to the NAND gate for selecting the 8K × 4 RAMs. This is not a good interfacing practice. This problem can be avoided by using 3 to 8 demultiplexer for decoding the chip selects of the RAM chips as shown in Fig. 5.6.

In the maximum mode, the 8086 is prepared to operate in multiprocessor mode. All the control signals in this mode are derived by a chip called bus controller (8288). While interfacing memory or I/O devices in maximum mode, the control signals derived by the bus controller (8288) are used. Instead of $\overline{RD}$, for memory operations $\overline{MRDC}$ (Memory Read Command) output of 8288 is used and instead of $\overline{WR}$, $\overline{AMWC}$ (advanced memory write command) output of 8288 is used. The rest of the procedure in minimum and maximum mode is similar while interfacing the memories as well as peripherals.

Along with these $\overline{MRDC}$, $\overline{IOWC}$, $\overline{AIOWC}$, $\overline{AMWC}$ two more signals, namely $\overline{IOWC}$ and $\overline{MWTC}$, are provided by 8288. These signals are similar to $\overline{AIOWC}$ and $\overline{AMWC}$ in significance and operation but there activation is delayed by a clock cycle as compared to $\overline{AIOWC}$ and $\overline{MWTC}$.

5.2 DYNAMIC RAM INTERFACING

Whenever a large memory is required in a microcomputer system, the memory subsystem is generally designed using dynamic RAM as it has various advantages e.g. higher packaging density, lower cost and less power consumption.

A typical static RAM cell may require six transistors while the dynamic RAM cell requires only a transistor along with a capacitor. Hence it is possible to obtain higher packaging density and hence low cost units are available. On the other side, there are some serious drawbacks of dynamic RAMs. The basic dynamic RAM cell uses a capacitor to store the charge as a representation of data. This capacitor is manufactured as a diode that is reverse-biased so that the storage capacitance comes into the picture. This storage capacitance is utilized for storing the charge representation of data but the reverse-biased diode has a leakage current that

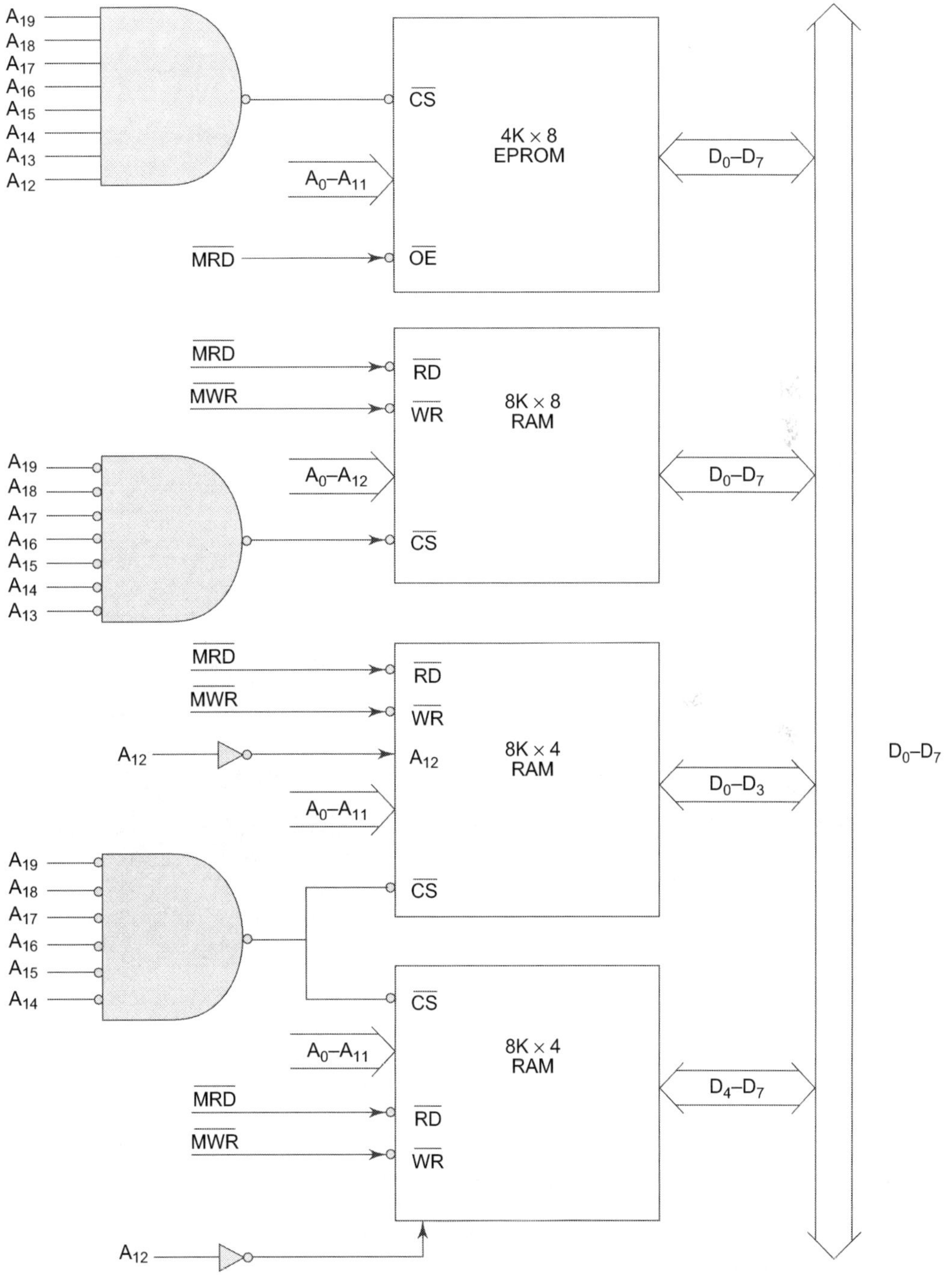

Fig. 5.5 *Interfacing Problem 5.5*

tends to discharge the capacitor giving rise to the possibility of data loss. To avoid this possible data loss, the data stored in a dynamic RAM cell must be refreshed after a fixed time interval regularly. The process of refreshing the data in the RAM is known as *refresh cycle*. This activity is similar to reading the data from each cell of the memory, independent of the requirement of microprocessor, regularly. During this refresh period all other operations (accesses) related to the memory subsystem are suspended. Hence the refresh activity

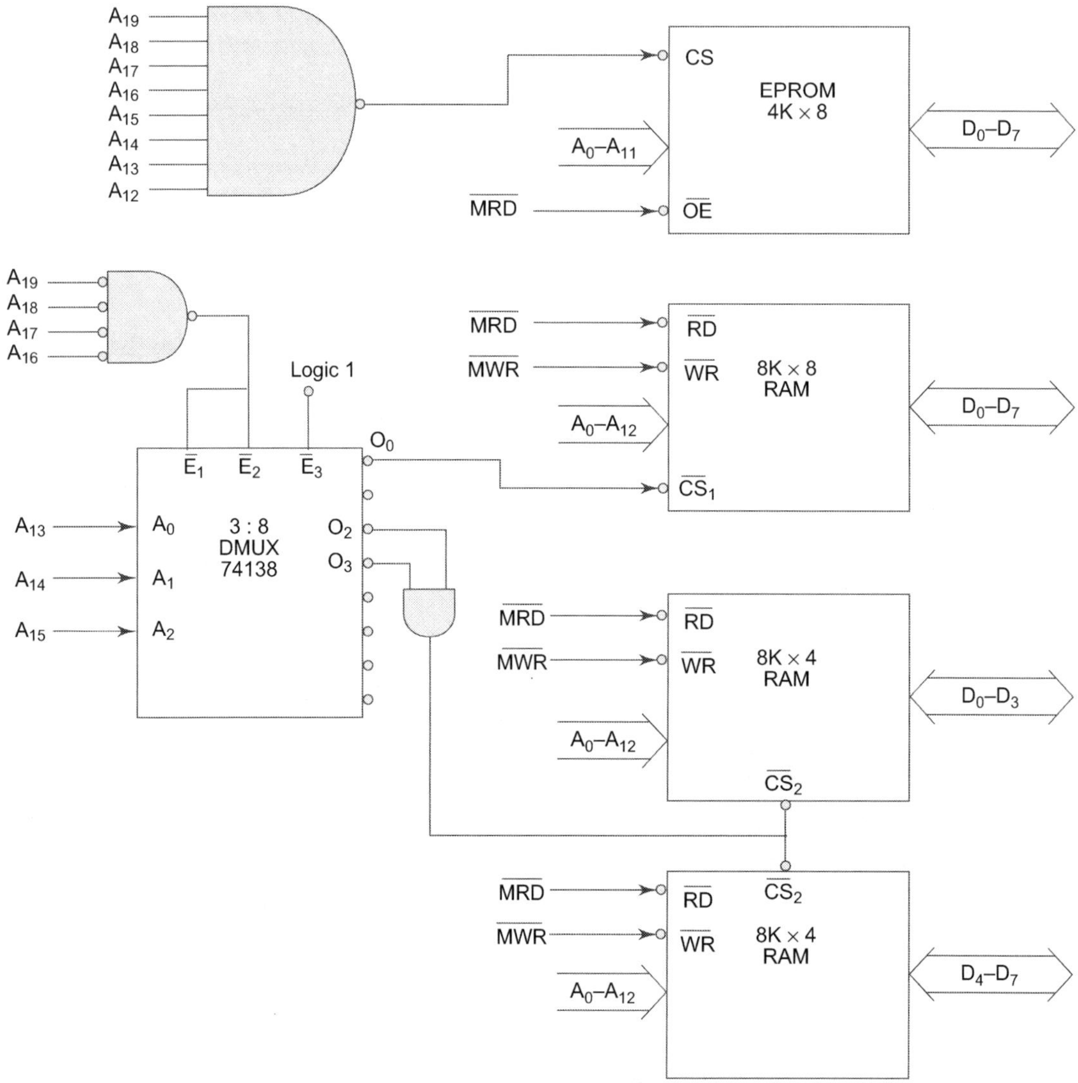

Fig. 5.6 *Alternative Implementation for Problem 5.5*

causes loss of time, resulting in reduced system performance. However, keeping in view the advantages of dynamic RAM, like low power consumption, higher packaging density and low cost, most of the advanced computer systems are designed using dynamic RAMs, of course, at the cost of operating speed. Also, the refresh mechanism and the additional hardware required makes the interfacing hardware, in case of dynamic RAM, more complicated, as compared to static RAM interfacing circuit. A dedicated hardware chip called as dynamic RAM controller is the most important part of the interfacing circuit.

The refresh cycle is different from the memory read cycle in the following aspects.

1. The memory address is not provided by the CPU address bus, rather, it is generated by a refresh mechanism counter known as refresh counter.
2. Unlike memory read cycle, more than one memory chip may be enabled at a time so as to reduce the number of total memory refresh cycles.
3. The data enable control of the selected memory chip is deactivated, and data is not allowed to appear on the system data bus during refresh, as more than one memory units are refreshed simultaneously. This is to avoid the data from the different chips to appear on the bus simultaneously.
4. Memory read is either a processor initiated or an external bus master initiated operation while memory refresh is an independent regular activity, initiated and carried out by the refresh mechanism.

Generally, dynamic RAM is available in units of several kilobits to even megabits of memory (note that it is not in terms of bytes or nibbles as in a static RAM). This memory is arranged internally in a two dimensional matrix array so that it will have *n* rows and *m* columns. The row address *n* and column address *m* are important for the refreshing operation. For example, a typical 4K bit dynamic RAM chip has an internally arranged bit array of dimension 64 × 64, i.e. 64 rows and 64 columns. Thus the row address and column address will require 6 bits each. These 6 bits for each row address and column address will be generated by the refresh counter, during the refresh cycles. A complete row of 64 cells is refreshed at a time to minimize the refreshing time. Thus the refresh counter needs to generate only row addresses. The row addresses are multiplexed, over lower order address lines. The refresh signals act to control the multiplexer, i.e. when refresh cycle is in process the refresh counter puts the row address over the address bus for refreshing. Otherwise, the address bus of the processor is connected to the address bus of DRAM, during normal processor initiated activities. A timer, called *refresh timer*, derives a pulse for refreshing action after each refresh interval, which can be qualitatively defined as the time for which a dynamic RAM cell can hold data charge level practically constant, i.e. no data loss takes place. Suppose the typical dynamic RAM chip has 64 rows, then each row should be refreshed after each refresh interval, or in other words, all the 64 rows are to be refreshed in a single refresh interval. This refresh interval depends upon the manufacturing technology of the dynamic RAM cell. It may range anywhere from 1 ms to 3 ms. Let us consider 2 ms as a typical refresh time interval. Hence, the frequency of the refresh pulses will be calculated as shown:

$$\text{Refresh Time (per row) } t_r = \frac{2\times10^{-3}}{64}$$

$$\text{Refresh Frequency} \qquad f_r = \frac{64}{2\times10^{-3}} = 32\times10^{3}\text{ Hz}$$

The block diagram in Fig. 5.7 explains the refreshing logic and 8086 interfacing with dynamic RAM. Each of the used chips is a16K × 1-bit dynamic RAM cell array. The system contains two 16K byte dynamic RAM units. All the address and data lines are assumed to be available from an 8086 microcomputer system. The $\overline{OE}$ pin controls output data buffers of the memory chips. The CE pins are active high chip selects of memory chips. The refresh cycle starts, if the refresh output of the refresh timer goes high, $\overline{OE}$ and CE also tend to go high. The high CE enables the memory chip for refreshing, while high $\overline{OE}$ prevents the data from appearing on the data bus, as said in the description of the memory refresh cycle. The 16K × 1-bit dynamic RAM has an internal array of 128 × 128 cells, requiring 7 bits for row addresses. The lower order seven lines A_0–A_6 are multiplexed with the refresh counter output $A_{10} - A_{16}$. The logic is shown in Fig. 5.7.

The pin assignments for 2164 dynamic RAM is shown in Fig. 5.8 (a). The $\overline{RAS}$ and $\overline{CAS}$ are row and column address strobes and are driven by the dynamic RAM controller outputs. $A_0 - A_7$ lines are the row or column address lines, driven by $OUT_0 - OUT_7$ outputs of the controller. The $\overline{WE}$ pin indicates memory write cycles. The D_{IN} and D_{OUT} pins are data pins for write and read operations, respectively. In practical circuits, the refreshing logic is integrated inside dynamic RAM controller chips like 8203, 8202 and 8207, etc.

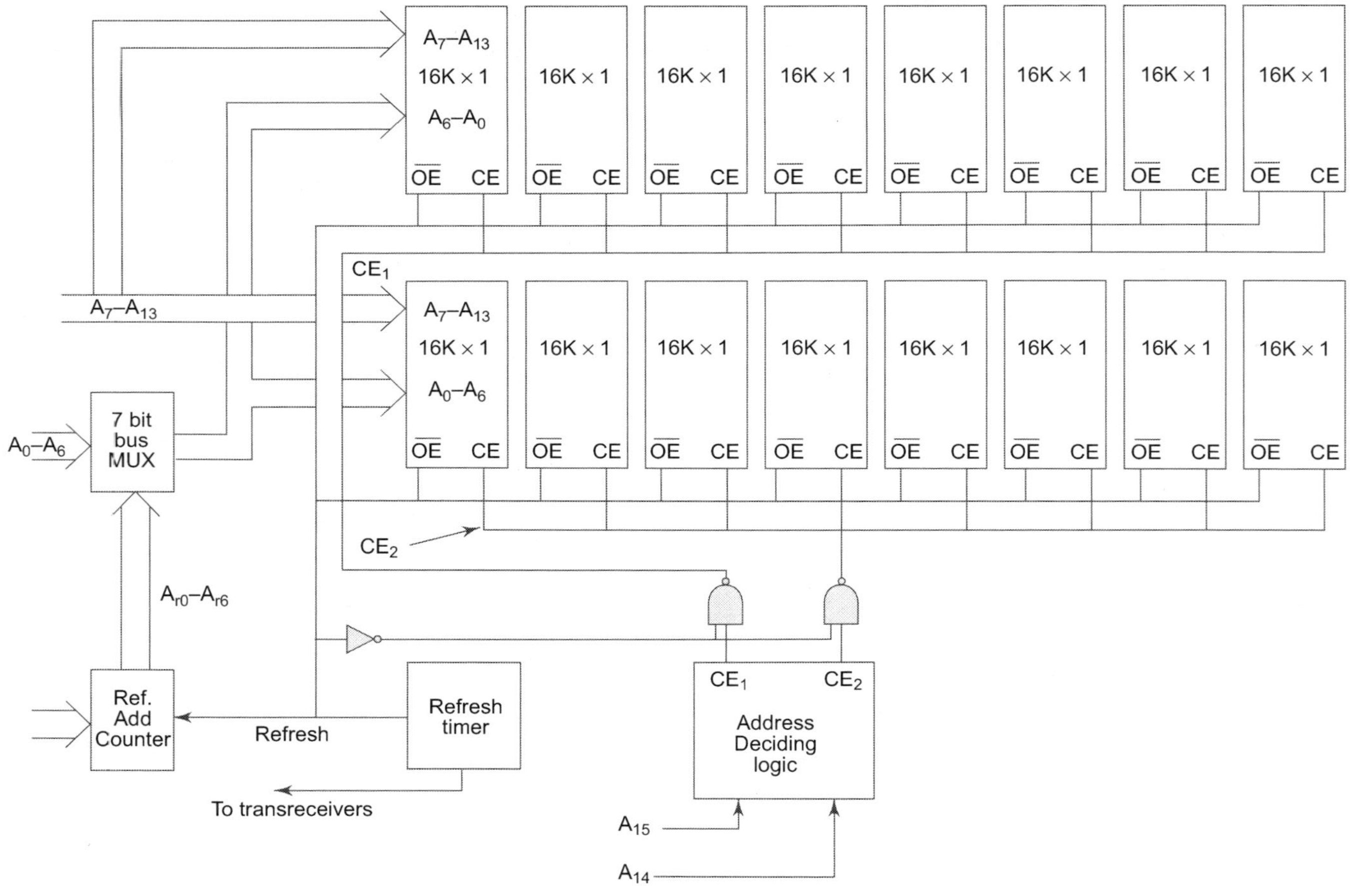

Fig. 5.7 *Dynamic RAM Refreshing Logic*

Intel's 8203 is a dynamic RAM controller (Fig. 5.8(b)) that supports 16K or 64K dynamic RAM chips. This selection is done using pin 16K/64K. If it is high, the 8203 is configured to control 16K dynamic RAM, else it controls 64K dynamic RAM. The address inputs of 8203 controller accept address lines A_1 to A_{16} on lines AL_0–AL_7 and AH_0–AH_7. The A_0 line is used to select the even or odd bank. The $\overline{RD}$ and $\overline{WR}$ signals decode whether the cycle is a memory read or memory write cycle and are accepted as inputs to 8203 from the microprocessor. The $\overline{WE}$ signal specifies the memory write cycle and is an output from 8203 that drives the $\overline{WE}$ input of dynamic RAM memory chip. The $\overline{OUT_0} - \overline{OUT_7}$ set of eight pins is an 8-bit output bus that carries multiplexed row and column addresses of a bit location in a dynamic RAM chip. The $\overline{CAS}$ signal strobes the column address on $\overline{OUT_0} - \overline{OUT_7}$. The $\overline{RAS_1} - \overline{RAS_0}$ pins strobes row address on $\overline{OUT_0} - \overline{OUT_7}$ for at the most two banks of 2164 dynamic RAM chips. Actually the row and column addresses are derived from the address lines $A_1 - A_{16}$ accepted by the controller on its inputs AL_0–AL_7 and AH_0–AH_7. An external crystal may be applied between X_0 and X_1 pins, otherwise, with the OP_2 pin at +12V, a clock signal may be applied at the pin CLK. The $\overline{PCS}$ pin accepts the chip select signal derived by an address decoder.

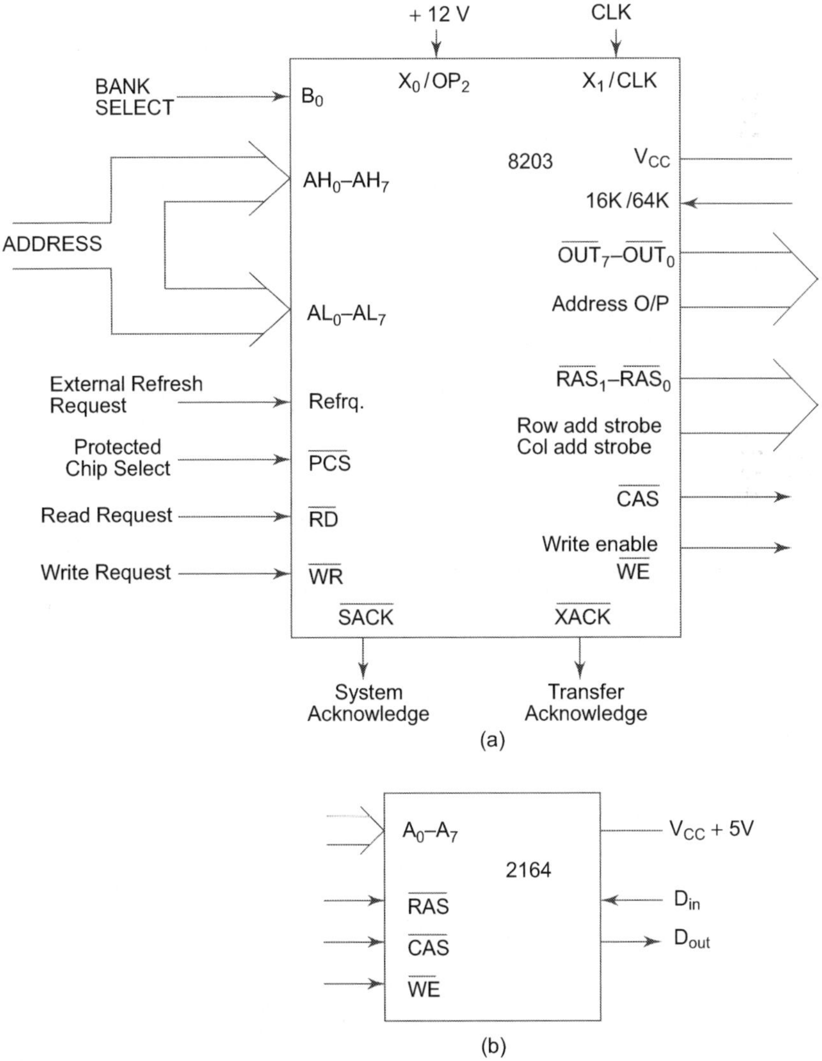

Fig. 5.8 *(a) Dynamic RAM controller (b) 1-bit Dynamic RAM*

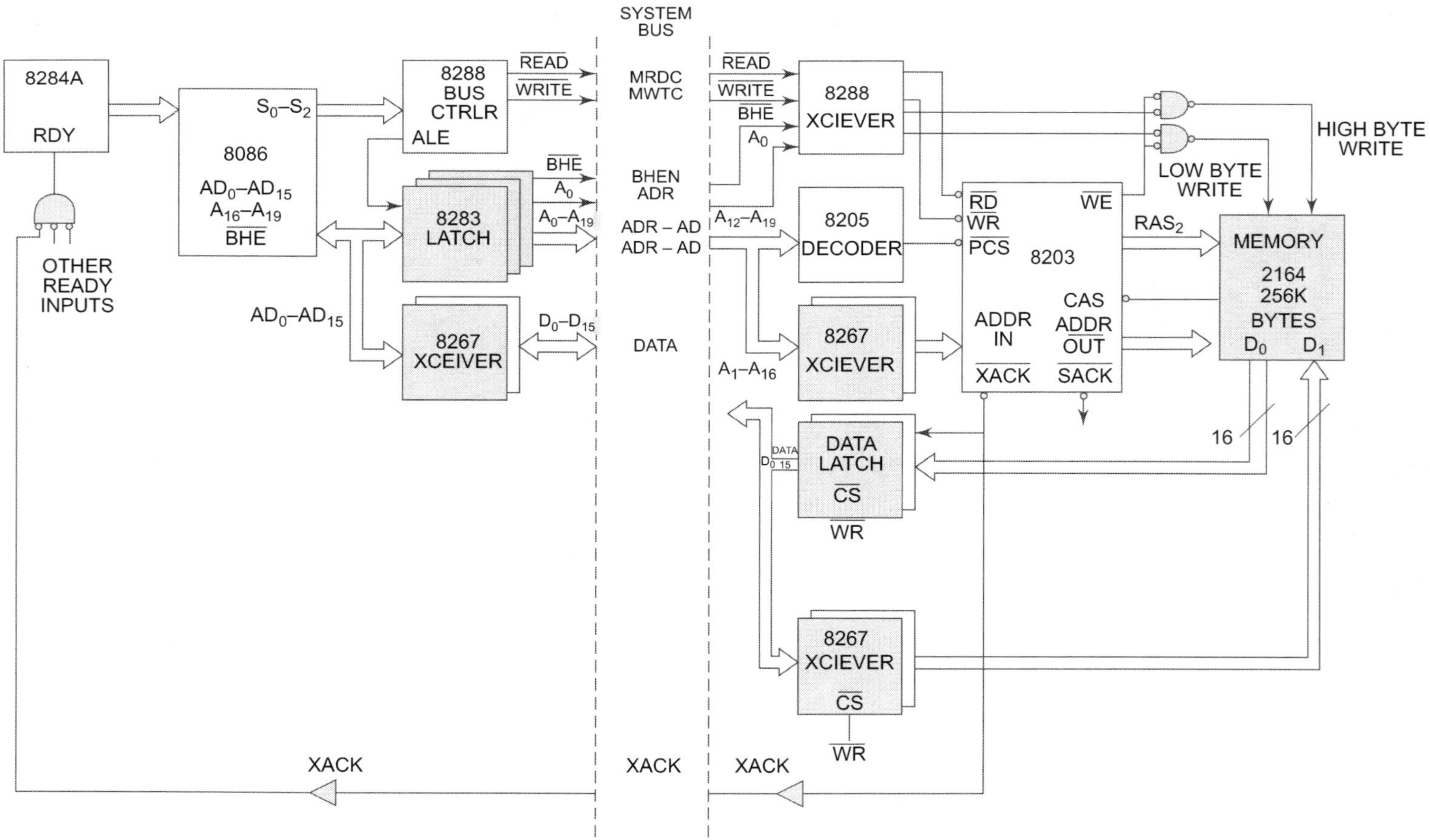

Fig. 5.9 *Interfacing 2164 Using 8203*

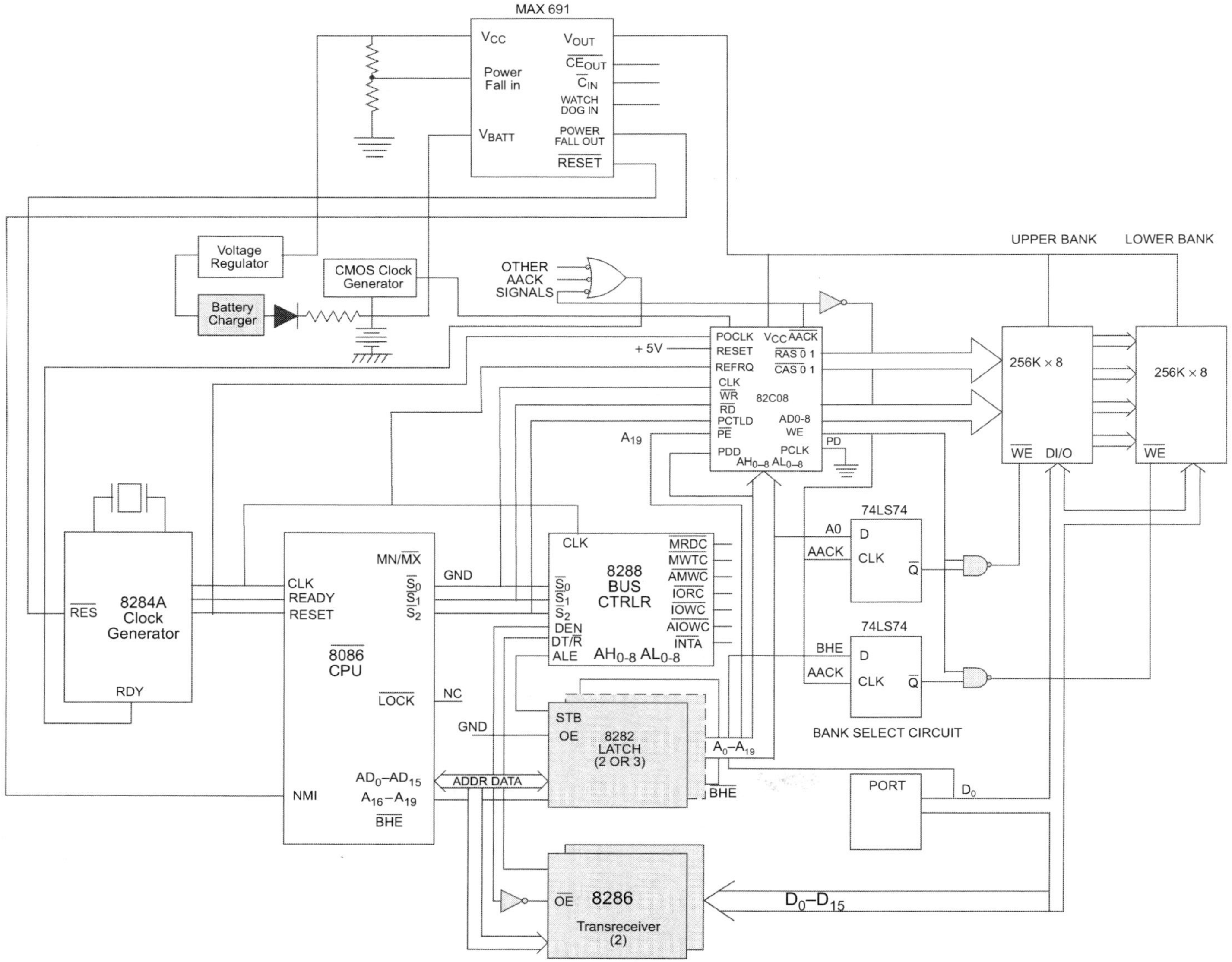

Fig. 5.10 *Interfacing 512 Kbyte of Dynamic RAM with 8086*

The REFREQ pin is used whenever the memory refresh cycle is to be initiated by an external signal. The $\overline{XACK}$ signal indicates that data is available during a read cycle or it has been written if it is a write cycle. It can be used as a strobe for data latches or as a ready signal to the processor. The $\overline{SACK}$ output signal marks the beginning of a memory access cycle. If a memory request is made during a memory refresh cycle, the $\overline{SACK}$ signal is delayed till the starting of memory read or write cycle. Figure 5.9 shows how the 8203 can be used to control a 256K bytes memory subsystem for a maximum mode 8086 microprocessor system. This design assumes that data and address busses are inverted and latched, hence the inverting buffers and inverting latches are used (8283-inverting buffer and 8287-inverting latch).

Figure 5.10 shows the interfacing of 512K byte dynamic RAM with 8086 using an advanced dynamic RAM controller 8208. Most of the functions of 8208 and 8203 are similar but 8208 can be used to refresh the dynamic RAM using DMA approach. The memory system is divided into even and odd banks of 256Kbyte each, as required for an 8086 system. The inverted $\overline{AACK}$ output of 8208 latches the A_0 and $\overline{BHE}$ signals required for selecting the banks. If the latched bank select signal and the $\overline{WE}$/PCLK output of 8208 both go low it indicates a write operation to the respective bank.

5.3 INTERFACING I/O PORTS

I/O ports or Input/Output ports are the devices through which the microprocessor communicates with other devices or external data sources/destinations. Input activity, as one may expect, is the activity that enables the microprocessor to read data from external devices , for example keyboards, joysticks, mouse, etc. These devices are known as input devices as they feed data into a microprocessor system.

Output activity transfers data from the microprocessor to the external devices, for example CRT display, 7-segment displays, printers, etc. The devices which accept the data from a microprocessor system are called output devices. Thus for a microprocessor the input activity is similar to read operation, while the output activity is similar to write operation. Note that an input device can only be read and an output device can only be written.

Hence $\overline{IORD}$ operation is related with reading data from an input device and not an output device and $\overline{IOWR}$ operation means writing data to an output device and not an input device. The control word and status word may be written and read respectively in both, input or output, devices, in case of programmable devices.

After executing an OUT operation, the data appears on the data bus and simultaneously a device select signal is generated from the address and control signals. Now, if the data is to be there, at the output of the

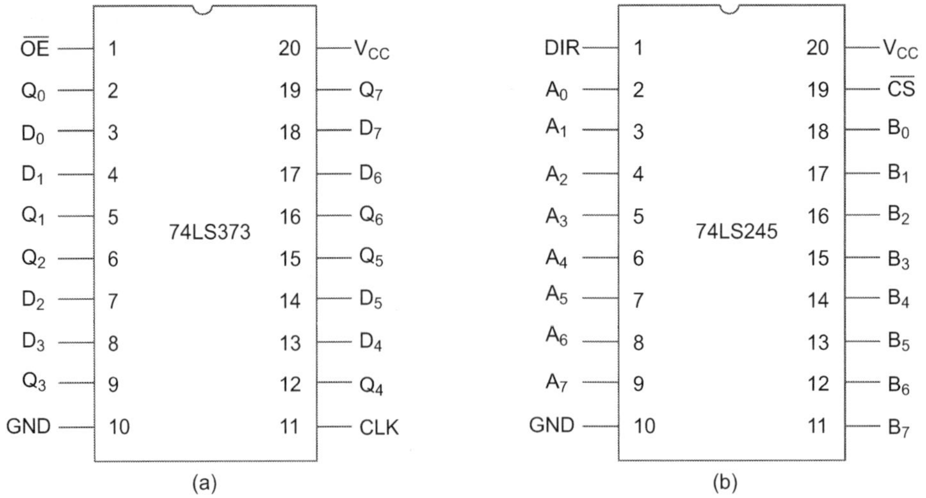

Fig. 5.11 *(a) Latch (O/P port) (b) Buffer (I/P port)*

device till the next change, it must be latched. Also if the output port is to source large currents the port lines must be bufferred. Hence the latch acts as a good output port. The chip 74LS373, contains eight bufferred latches and can be used as an 8-bit output port. While reading, an input device one must take care that much current should not be sourced or sunk from the data lines to avoid loading. To overcome this problem, one may use a tristate buffer as an input device. An input port may not be a latch as it reads the status of a signal at a particular instant. The chip 74LS245 contains eight buffers and may be used as an 8-bit input port. Actually, 74LS245 is a bidirectional buffer, but while using it as an input device, only one direction is useful. This direction of data transfer in 74LS245 is selected using its DIR pin. The pin diagrams of 74LS373 and 74LS 245 are shown in Figs 5.11 (a) and (b). The $\overline{OE}$ and $\overline{CS}$ are the chip selects of 74LS373 and 74LS245 respectively. Ds and Qs are corresponding latch inputs and outputs respectively.

The CLK pin is clock input for D flip-flops. If DIR is 1, then the direction is from A(I/Ps) to B(O/Ps), otherwise the data direction is from B(I/Ps) to A(O/Ps).

Steps in Interfacing an I/O Device The following steps are performed to interface a general I/O device with a CPU:

(i) Connect the data bus of the microprocessor system with the data bus of the I/O port.
(ii) Derive a device address pulse by decoding the required address of the device and use it as the chip select of the device.
(iii) Use a suitable control signal, i.e. $\overline{IORD}$ and/or $\overline{IOWR}$ to carry out device operations, i.e. connect $\overline{IORD}$ to $\overline{RD}$ input of the device if it is an input device, otherwise connect $\overline{IOWR}$ to $\overline{WR}$ input of the device. In some cases the $\overline{RD}$ or $\overline{WR}$ control signals are combined with the device address pulse to generate the device select pulse.

Methods of Interfacing I/O Devices There are two methods of interfacing general I/O devices.

(i) I/O mapped
(ii) Memory-mapped

The principal distinction in the two approaches is that in I/O mapped interfacings the devices are viewed as distinct I/O devices and are addressed accordingly. While *in memory-mapped scheme,* the devices are viewed as memory locations and are addressed likewise. In I/O mapped interfacing, all the available address lines of a microprocessor may not be used for interfacing the devices. The processor 8086 has 20 address lines. The I/O mapped scheme may use at the most 16 address lines $A_0 - A_{15}$ or even 8 address lines for address decoding. The unused higher order address lines are logic zero, while addressing the device. An I/O mapped device requires the use of IN and OUT instructions for accessing them. The I/O mapped method requires less hardware for decoding, as less number of address lines are used. In case of 8086, a maximum of 64K input and 64K byte output devices or 32K input and 32K word output devices can be interfaced. In addition to address and data busses, to address an input device, we require the $\overline{IORD}$ signal and to address an output device, we use $\overline{IOWR}$ signal for the respective operations. The $\overline{IOWR}$ and $\overline{IORD}$ signals are used for I/O mapped interfacing.

In memory-mapped interfacing, all the available address lines are used for address decoding. Thus each memory-mapped I/O device with 8086 has a 20-bit address, i.e. 8086 can have as many as 1M memory-mapped input and as many byte output devices. Practically this is impossible, as memory-mapped I/O devices consume the addresses in the memory map of the CPU. 1M byte devices will require the complete 1Mbyte of the memory map and nothing will be left as program memory. Also the memory locations and the memory-mapped devices cannot have common addresses. The $\overline{MRDC}$ and $\overline{MRTC}$ signals are used for interfacing in memory-mapped I/O scheme. All the applicable data transfer instructions (e.g. MOV, LEA) can be used to communicate with memory-mapped I/O devices. However, I/O operations are much more sluggish compared to the memory operations which are faster. Moreover, complex decoding hardware is required in this case since all the address lines are used for decoding.

In case of the 8086 systems, the memory-mapped method is seldom used. Hence all the peripheral devices in most of the practical systems are essentialy I/O mapped devices. In this book, only the I/O mapped method of interfacing is elaborated. 8086 has a 16-bit data bus, hence interfacing of 8-bit devices with 8086 need special consideration. Usually, 8-bit I/O devices are interfaced with lower order data bus of 8086, i.e. D_0–D_7. The 16-bit devices are interfaced directly with the 16-bit data bus, using A_0 and $\overline{BHE}$ pins of 8086. The following problems explain the actual method of interfacing I/O devices with 8086. The interfacing hardware always need supporting application programs to carry out the desired operations. Hence each interfacing example is accompanied with a supporting 8086 ALP.

Problem 5.6

Interface an input port 74LS245 to read the status of switches SW_1 to SW_8. The switches, when shorted, input a '1' else input a '0' to the microprocessor system. Store the status in register BL. The address of the port is 0740H.

Solution The hardware interface circuit is shown in Fig. 5.12. The address, control and data lines are assumed to be readily available at the microprocessor system.

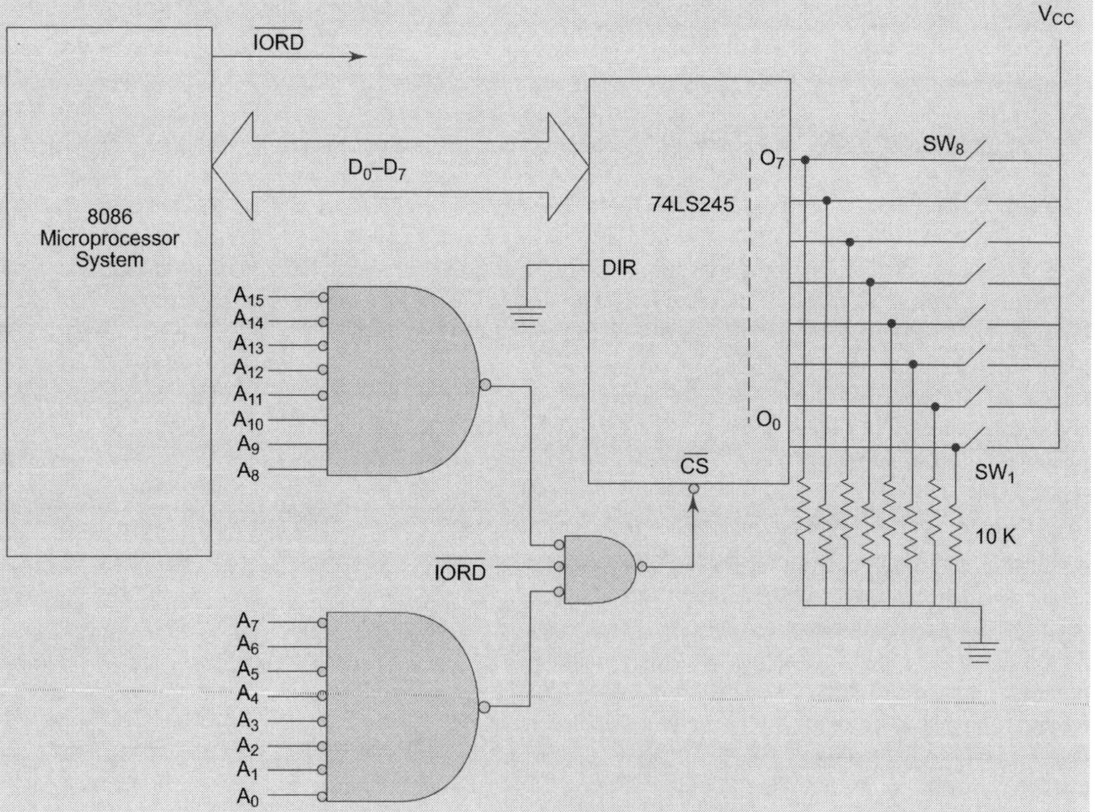

Fig. 5.12 *Interfacing Input Port 74LS245*

```
THE ALP IS GIVEN AS FOLLOWS:
MOV BL, 00H      ; Clear BL for status
MOV DX, 0740H    ; 16-bit port addrenss in DX
IN AL, DX        ; Read port 0740H for switch positions
MOV BL, AL       ; Store status of switches from AL into BL
HLT              ; Stop
```

Program 5.1 *ALP for Problem 5.6.*

Here LSB bit of BL corresponds to the status of SW_1 and likewise the MSB of BL corresponds to the status of SW_8. The '1' indicates 'on' or shorted switch and the '0' indicates an 'off' or opened switch. The pull-up registers in Fig. 5.12 are necessary because the open switches should input a '0' to the system but the TTL port 74LS245 will read the free input as '1'. (Free TTL inputs are always read as logic '1'.)

Problem 5.7

Design an interface of an input port 74LS245 to read the status of switches SW_1 to SW_8 (as in the previous problem), and an output port 74LS373 with 8086. Display the number of a key that is pressed, i.e. from 1 to 8 on a 7-seg display with help of the output port. Write an ALP for this task, assume that only one key is pressed at a time. Draw the schematic of the required hardware. The input port address is 0008H and the output port address is 000AH.

Solution In the previous problem, one might have noted that a lot of hardware is required to decode the port address absolutely. Thus instead of decoding the address completely, only a part of it may be decoded. For example, instead of using 16 address lines A_{15}–A_0, one may use only A_3–A_0. In this problem, the address 0008H may then be converted to xxx8H, where x denotes a don't care condition. Thus the port may have more than one address, for example 2358H, 1728H etc. Only the least significant nibble of the address needs to be 8H. The disadvantage of the scheme is that there are a number of addresses of the same port. Hence, the system must have only one port that has the lowest nibble address 8H, otherwise, the system may malfunction. Thus for smaller systems containing a few I/O ports, this scheme is suitable and advantageous as it requires less hardware.

The status of the switches is first read into the register AL. For displaying the shorted switch number in the 7-seg display, the bit corresponding to the switch is checked by rotating AL through carry and then checking the carry flag. If the carry flag is '1', after one left rotation, it means SW_1 is on. If the carry flag sets after two rotations, SW_2 is on and so on. Register CL is incremented after each rotation so that it contains the pressed switch number. The 8-bit contents of register CL are converted to 7-segment codes by a BCD to 7-seg decoder. The complete hardware (Fig. 5.13) and the ALP is given as shown. Note that both the ports are interfaced at even addresses, i.e. with lower order data bus $D_0 - D_7$.

Common cathode displays are used along with corresponding BCD to 7-seg decoder.

```
MOV BL, 00    ; Clear BL for switch status
MOV CL, 00    ; Clear CL for switch number
XOR AX, AX    ; Clear accumulators and flag
IN AL,08H     ; Read switch status
```

```
       INC CL      ; Increment CL for 1st switch
YY:    RCR AL      ; Rotate switch status
       JC XX       ; If carry, halt,
       INC CL      ; else increment CL for next switch
       JMP YY      ; number till carry is 1
XX:    MOV AL,CL   ; Take switch number into AL
       OUT 0AH,AL  ; Out BCD switch number for display
       HLT         ; Stop
```

Program 5.2 *ALP for Problem 5.7*

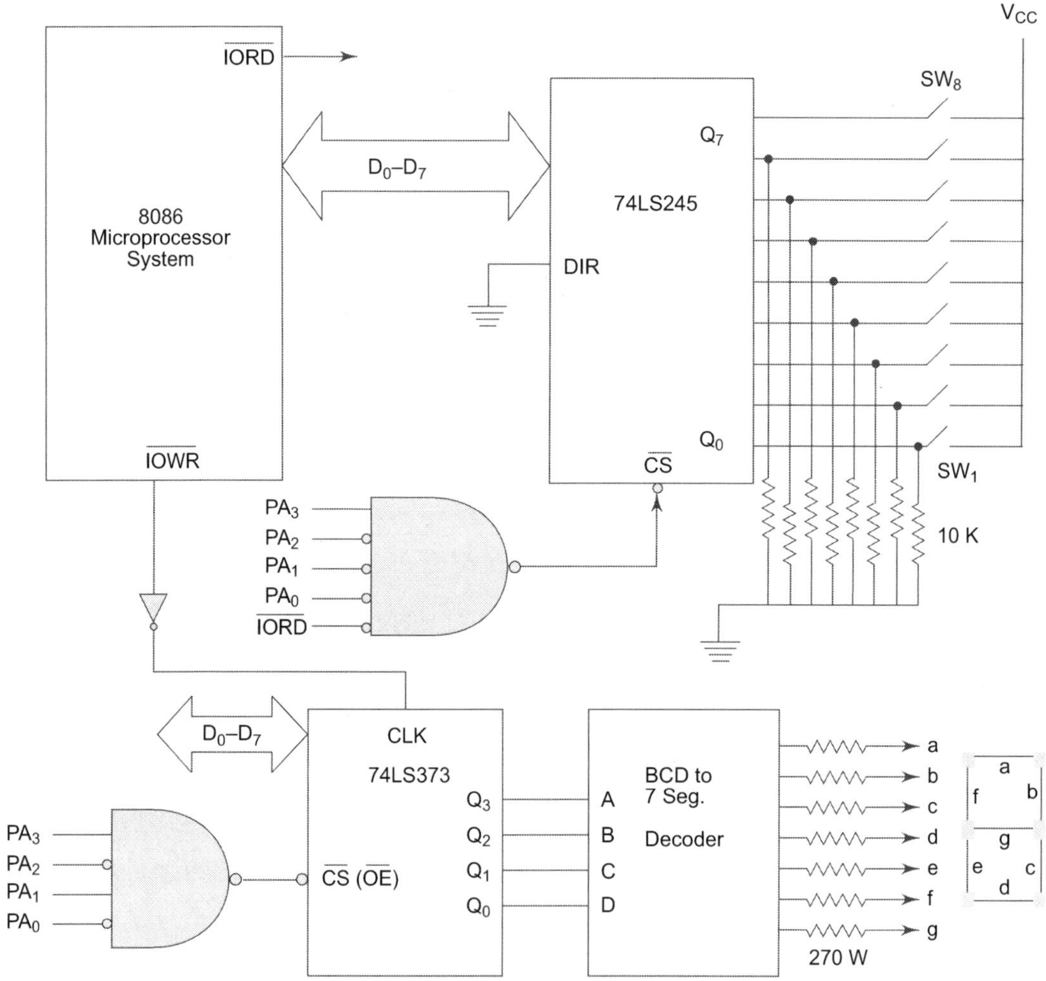

Fig. 5.13 *Interfacing Switches and Displays for Problem 5.7*

Problem 5.8

Using 74LS373 output ports and 7-segment displays, design a seconds counter that counts from 0 to 9. Draw the suitable hardware schematic and write an ALP for this problem. Assume that a delay of 1sec is available as a subroutine. Select the port address suitably.

Solution The counter hardware is shown in Fig. 5.14. Common cathode displays are used along with a suitable BCD to 7-segment decoder. The ALP calls the subroutine 'DELAY' that generates a delay program of 1sec. After counting from 0 to 9, it again starts from 0. The output port is interfaced at address 0008H.

The ALP for generating the seconds count is given below.

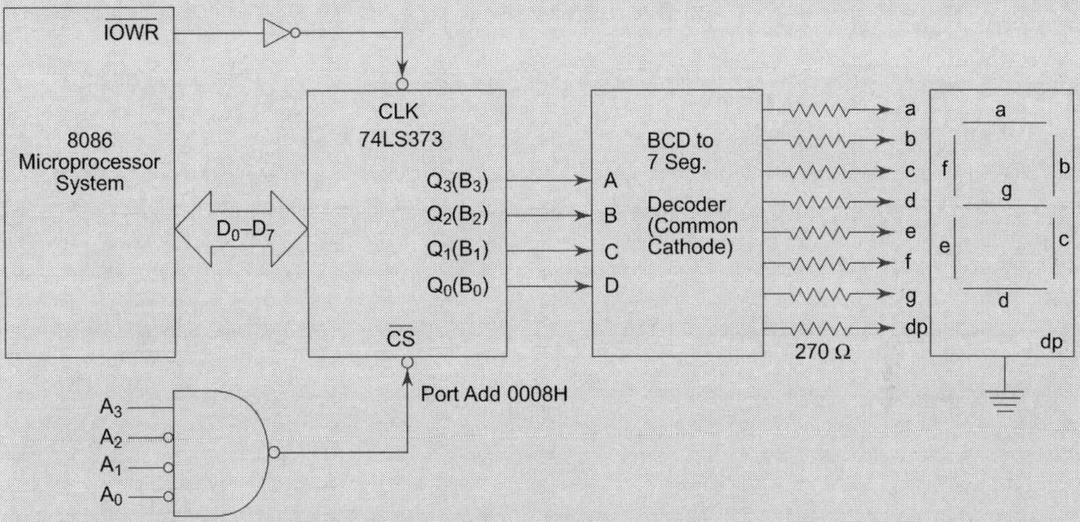

Fig. 5.14 *Interfacing Circuit Diagram for Problem 5.8*

```
XX : MOV AL,00H        ; Start from 00
YY : XOR AL,AL         ; Clear AL and flags
     OUT 08H,AL        ; Display 0H
     CALL DELAY        ; Wait for one second
     INC AL            ; Increment count for next
     CMP AL,0A H       ; display. Is it above 9H?
     JZ XX             ; If yes, start from 00,
     JMP YY            ; else continue.
```

Program 5.3 *ALP for Problem 5.8*

Multiplexed 7-seg Displays To display a single digit, at least one output port is required. Suppose one wants a 5-digit display for some practical application, Five such ports will be required, i.e. the hardware will be very complex and costly. To minimize the complexity and cost of hardware one may implement an almost visually identical display using only two ports. Suppose there are four 7-seg displays, numbered 1, 2, 3 and 4. One of the two ports, say port1 selects one of these displays, say display 1 at a time, while port 2 sends the data to be displayed (i.e. a,b,c,d,e,f,g and dp) to the first display for a fixed short duration. Port 1 next, selects the display 2 and port 2 sends the appropriate display data to it. Each of the display unit remains active for a short duration and the process continues in a loop. This is repeated at a high frequency so that the complete display containing more than one7-seg display appears to be stationary due to the persistence of vision. Instead of BCD to 7-seg decoder circuit, look up table technique may be used for converting BCD numbers to equivalent 7-seg codes.

Problem 5.9

Draw a schematic hardware circuit for interfacing five, 7-seg displays (common cathode) with 8086 using output ports. Display numbers 1 to 5 on them continuously. The 7-seg codes are stored in a look-up table serially at the address 2000:0000 H onwards starting from code for 1.

Solution Let us select the two port addresses 0004H and 0008H for the output ports. The first port 0004H outputs 7-seg code while the second output port 0008H selects the display by grounding the common cathode. The hardware is given in Fig. 5.15.

The 7-seg codes for C.C. displays can be decided as given. For a LED to be 'on', that particular anode should be 1 and the common cathode line should be grounded, using a port line that drives a transistor. Thus for the numbers to be displayed the code is calculated as shown.

Decimal no.	*a* A_7	*b* A_6	*c* A_5	*d* A_4	*e* A_3	*f* A_2	*g* A_1	*dp* A_0	
1—	1	1	0	0	0	0	0	0	= C0
2—	1	1	0	1	1	0	1	0	= DA
3—	1	1	1	1	0	0	1	0	= F2
4—	0	1	1	0	0	1	1	0	= 66
5—	1	0	1	1	0	1	1	0	= B6

These codes are stored in a look up table starting from 2000H:0000, as shown below.

2000 : 0000 → C0 H
2000 : 0001 → DA H
2000 : 0002 → F2 H
2000 : 0003 → 66 H
2000 : 0004 → B6 H

Only one display should be selected at a time, i.e. only the corresponding bit of port 2 should be high for selecting a common cathode display. All the other bits should be low to keep the other displays disabled. Thus to enable the least significant display, the LSB of the 8-bit selected port should remain '1'. Hence AL should have 01 or E1H in it to select the least significant display. The codes for the selection of displays and 7-segment codes directly depend upon the hardwared connections between them.

```
        MOV AX, 2000H          ; Initialize pointer to
        MOV DS, AX             ; Code table DS:BX
        MOV BX, 0000H
NEXT :  MOV AL, 00H            ; Get 1st number from the table.
        MOV DH,AL
        MOV CL, 05H            ; Count for display
        MOV DL, E1H            ; Selection code for 1st display
AGAIN : XLAT                   ;
        OUT 04H, AL            ; Out the code for the first
                               ; number to port 04H.
        MOV AL,DL              ; Get to be enabled display code.
        OUT 08H,AL             ; Select 1st display.
        ROL DL                 ; decide code for selecting next
        INC DH                 ; display for next number
        MOV AL,DH              ; get next num. to be displayed.
        LOOP AGAIN             ; Repeat five times
        JMP NEXT               ; Continue the procedure
```

Program 5.4 *ALP for Problem 5.9*

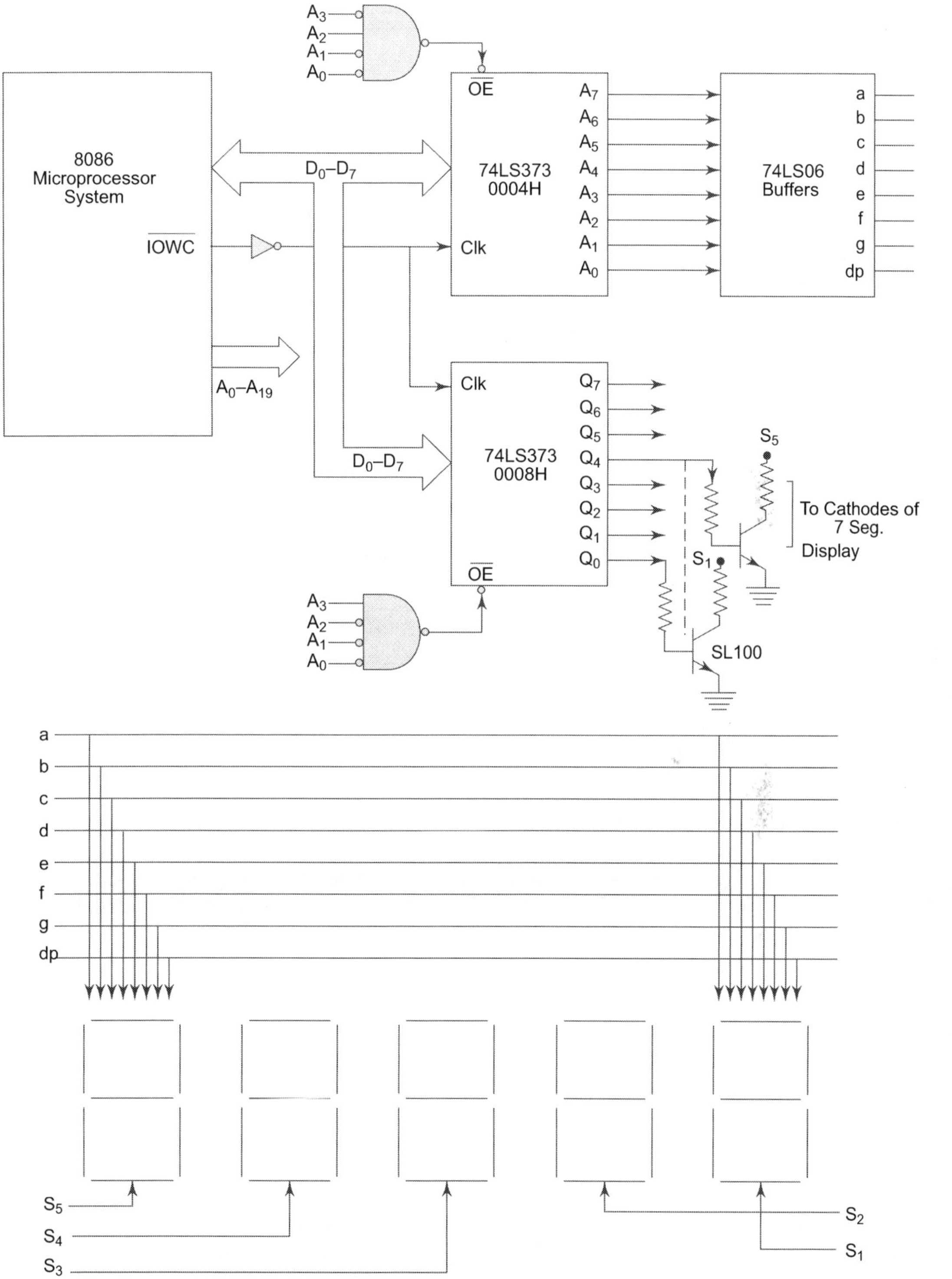

Fig. 5.15 *Interfacing Circuit Diagram of Problem 5.9*

For interfacing a 16-bit output port with 8086, we may use two 8-bit output ports to form a 16-bit port, with a single address, as shown in Fig. 5.16. Both the 8-bit ports are in this case addressed as a single 16-bit port with a single address.

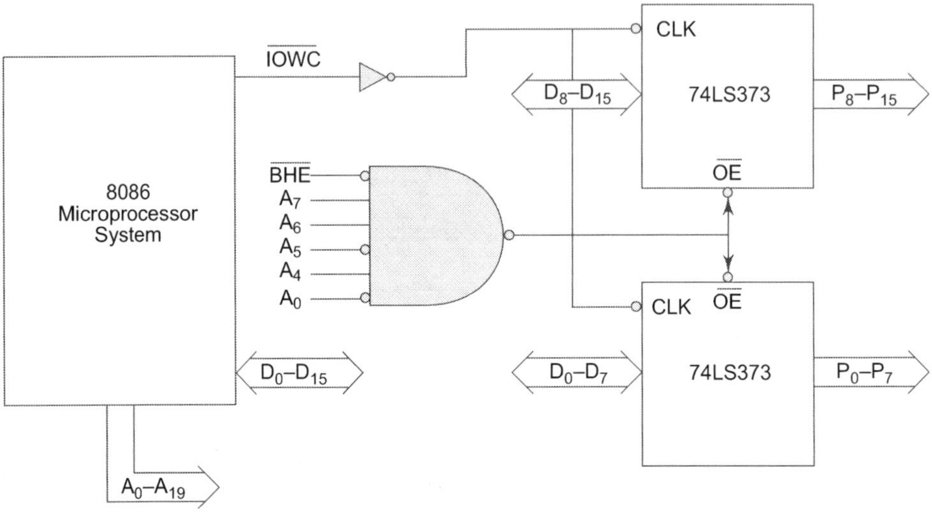

Fig. 5.16 *Interfacing a Circuit of 16 bit output port*

The OUT instruction of 8086 is able to output 16-bit data directly in a single cycle, and the programming technique is identical to that of the 8-bit port. The instruction uses 16-bit register AX as source operand as shown:

```
OUT Port_Add, AX
OUT [DX], AX
```

A 16-bit input port may also be interfaced similarly. Note the use of A0 and BHE signals in interfacing the 16-bit ports. One may find out address of the output port in Fig. 5.16.

Till now we have studied some common interfacing methods for I/O ports and have also solved some problems based on I/O ports. A few more problems will be discussed while studying the Programmable Peripheral Input/Output port chip 8255. The ports in this section were either input or output, but in 8255 the same port may be programmed either to work as input port or as output port. Hence the chip is called Programmable Input-Output (PIO) device.

5.4 PIO 8255 [PROGRAMMABLE INPUT-OUTPUT PORT]

The parallel input-output port chip 8255 is also known as programmable peripheral input-output port. The Intel's 8255 is designed for use with Intel's 8-bit, 16-bit and higher capability microprocessors. It has 24 input/output lines which may be individually programmed in two groups of twelve lines each, or three groups of eight lines. The two groups of I/O pins are named as Group A and Group B. Each of these two groups contain a subgroup of eight I/O lines called as 8-bit port and another subgroup of four I/O lines or a 4-bit port. Thus Group A contains an 8-bit port A along with a 4-bit port, C upper. The port A lines are identified by symbols PA_0–PA_7 while the port C lines are identified as PC_4–PC_7. Similarly, Group B contains an 8-bit port B, containing lines PB_0 – PB_7 and a 4-bit port C with lower bits PC_0–PC_3. The port C upper and port C lower can be used in combination as an 8-bit port C. Both the port Cs are assigned the same address. Thus one may have either three 8-bit I/O ports or two 8-bit and two 4-bit I/O ports from 8255. All of these ports can function independently either as input or as output ports. This can be achieved by programming the bits of an internal register of 8255 called as Control Word Register (CWR). The internal block diagram and the pin configuration of 8255 are shown in Figs 5.17 (a) and (b).

The 8-bit data bus buffer is controlled by the read/write control logic. The read/write control logic manages all of the internal and external transfers of both data and control words. $\overline{RD}$, $\overline{WR}$, A_1, A_0 and RESET are the inputs, provided by the microprocessor to the READ/WRITE control logic of 8255. The 8-bit, 3-state bidirectional buffer is used to interface the 8255 internal data bus with the external system data bus. This buffer receives or transmits data upon the execution of input or output instructions by the microprocessor. The control words or status information is also transferred through the buffer.

The signal descriptions of 8255 are briefly presented as follows:

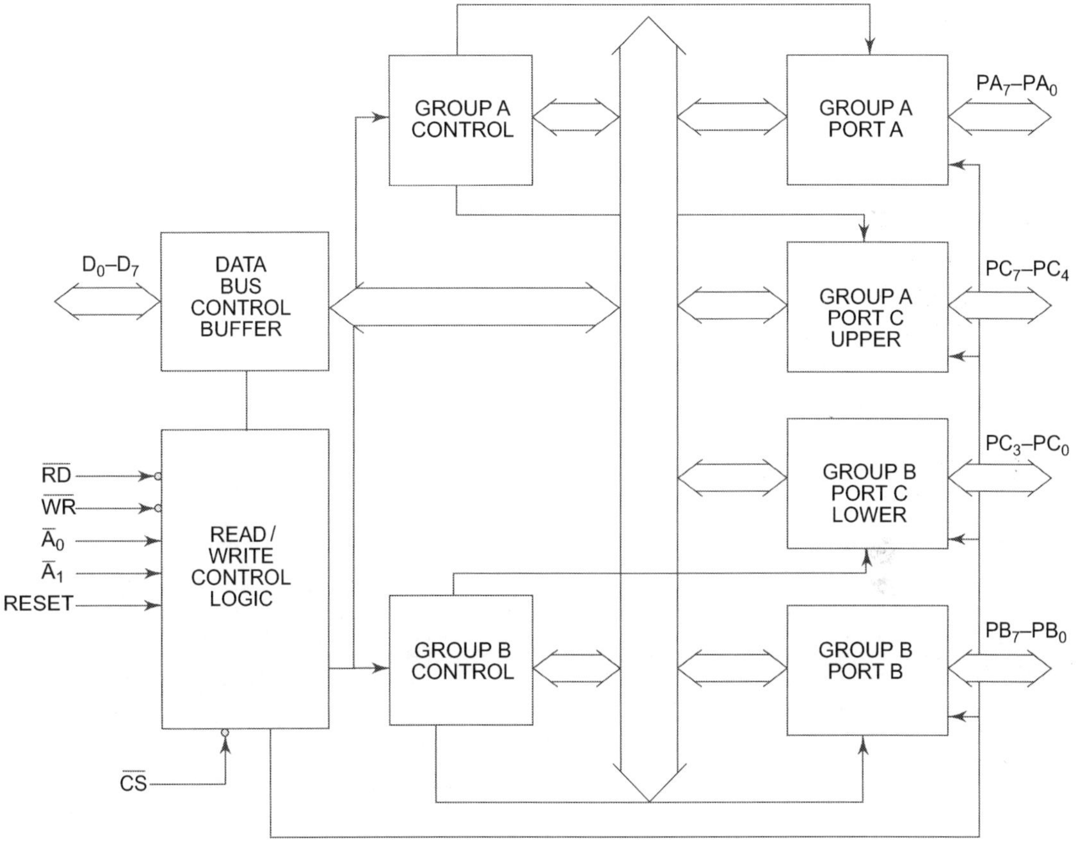

Fig. 5.17(a) *8255 Internal Architecture*

PA_7–PA_0 These are eight port A lines that act as either latched output or buffered input lines depending upon the control word loaded into the control word register.

PC_7–PC_4 Upper nibble of port C lines. They may act as either output latches or input buffers lines. This port also can be used for generation of handshake lines in mode1 or mode 2.

PC_3–PC_0 These are the lower port C lines, other details are the same as PC_7–PC_4 lines.

PB_0–PB_7 These are the eight port B lines which are used as latched output lines or buffered input lines in the same way as port A.

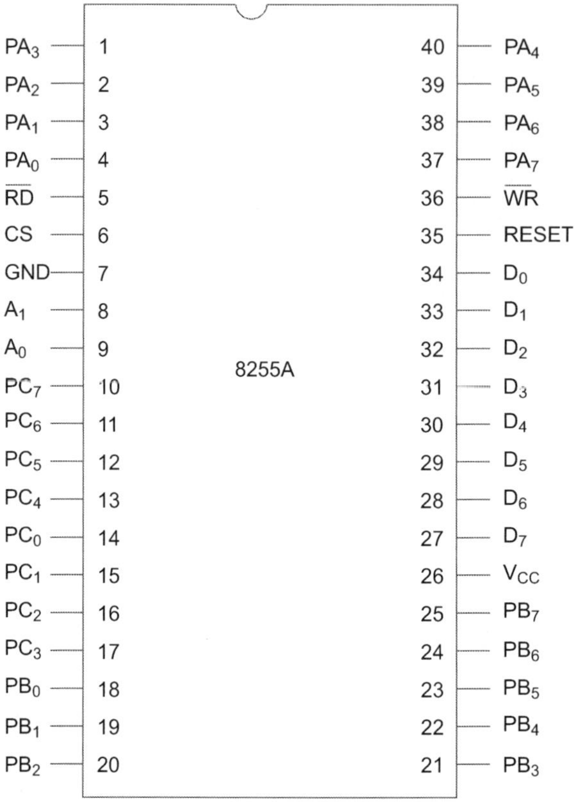

Fig. 5.17(b) *8255A Pin Configuration*

$\overline{RD}$ This is the input line driven by the microprocessor and should be low to indicate read operation to 8255.

$\overline{WR}$ This is an input line driven by the microprocessor. A low on this line indicates write operation.

$\overline{CS}$ This is a chip select line. If this line goes low, it enables the 8255 to respond to $\overline{RD}$ and $\overline{WR}$ signals, otherwise $\overline{RD}$ and $\overline{WR}$ signals are neglected.

A_1–A_0 These are the address input lines and are driven by the microprocessor. These lines ($A_1 - A_0$) with $\overline{RD}$, $\overline{WR}$ and $\overline{CS}$ form the following operations for 8255. These address lines are used for addressing any one of the four registers, i.e. three ports and a control word register as given in Tables 5.9 (a), (b) and (c).

In case of 8086 systems, if the 8255 is to be interfaced with lower order data bus, the A_0 and A_1 pins of 8255 are connected with A_1 and A_2 respectively.

Table 5.9(a)

$\overline{RD}$	$\overline{WR}$	$\overline{CS}$	A_1	A_0	*Input (Read) cycle*
0	1	0	0	0	Port A to data bus
0	1	0	0	1	Port B to data bus
0	1	0	1	0	Port C to data bus
0	1	0	1	1	CWR to data bus

Table 5.9 (b)

$\overline{RD}$	$\overline{WR}$	$\overline{CS}$	A_1	A_0	*Output (Write) cycle*
1	0	0	0	0	Data bus to Port A
1	0	0	0	1	Data bus to Port B
1	0	0	1	0	Data bus to Port C
1	0	0	1	1	Data bus to CWR

Table 5.9 (c)

$\overline{RD}$	$\overline{WR}$	$\overline{CS}$	A_1	A_0	*Function*
X	X	1	X	X	Data bus tristated
1	1	0	X	X	Data bus tristated

D_0–D_7 These are the data bus lines those carry data or control word to/from the micro-processor.
RESET A logic high on this line clears the control word register of 8255. All ports are set as input ports by default after reset.

5.5 MODES OF OPERATION OF 8255

There are two basic modes of operation of 8255–I/O mode and Bit Set-Reset mode (BSR). In the I/O mode, the 8255 ports work as programmable I/O ports, while in BSR mode only port C(PC_0–PC_7) can be used to set or reset its individual port bits. Under the IO mode of operation, further there are three modes of operation of 8255, so as to support different types of applications, viz. *mode 0* , *mode 1* and *mode 2*. These modes of operation are discussed in significant details along with application problems in this section, so as to present a clear idea about 8255 operation and interfacing in different modes with 8086.

5.5.1 BSR Mode

In this mode, any of the 8-bits of port C can be set or reset depending on B_0 of the control word. The bit to be set or reset is selected by bit select flags B_3, B_2 and B_1 of the CWR as given in Table 5.10. The CWR format is shown in Fig. 5.18(a).

Table 5.10

B_3	B_2	B_1	*Selected Bits of port C*
0	0	0	B_0
0	0	1	B_1
0	1	0	B_2
0	1	1	B_3
1	0	0	B_4
1	0	1	B_5
1	1	0	B_6
1	1	1	B_7

5.5.2 I/O MODES

MODE 0 (Basic I/O mode) This mode is also known as *basic input/output mode*. This mode provides simple input and output capability using each of the three ports. Data can be simply read from and written to the input and output ports respectively, after appropriate initialisation.

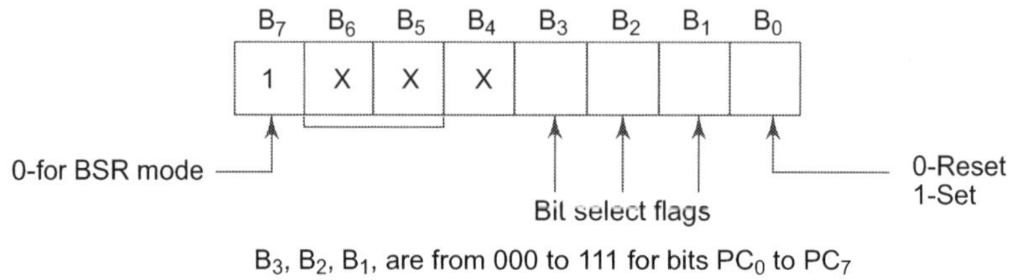

Fig. 5.18(a) *BSR Mode Control Word Register Format*

The salient features of this mode are as listed below:

(i) Two 8-bit ports (port A and port B) and two 4-bit ports (port C upper and lower) are available. The two 4-bit ports can be combinedly used as a third 8-bit port.
(ii) Any port can be used as an input or output port.
(iii) Output ports are latched. Input ports are not latched.
(iv) A maximum of four ports are available so that overall 16 I/O configurations are possible.

All these modes can be selected by programming a register internal to 8255, known as Control Word Register (CWR) which has two formats. The first format is valid for I/O modes of operation, i.e. modes 0, mode 1 and mode 2 while the second format is valid for bit set/reset (BSR) mode of operation. This format is shown in Fig. 5.18(b).

Now let us consider some interfacing problems so as to elaborate the hardware interfacing and I/O programming ideas using 8255 in mode 0.

Problem 5.10

Interface an 8255 with 8086 to work as an I/O port. Initialize port A as output port, port B as input port and port C as output port. Port A address should be 0740H. Write a program to sense switch positions SW_0–SW_7 connected at port B. The sensed pattern is to be displayed on port A, to which 8 LEDs are connected, while the port C lower displays number of on switches out of the total eight switches.

Solution The control word is decided upon as follows:

B7	B_6	B_5	B_4	B_3	B_2	B_1	B_0	Control word
1	0	0	0	0	0	1	0	= 82H
I/O mode	Port A in mode 0		Port A,o/p	Port C,o/p	Port B,mode 0	Port B,i/p	Port C,o/p	

Thus 82H is the control word for the requirements in the problem. The port address decoding can be done as given below. The 8255 is to be interfaced with lower order data bus, i.e. D_0–D_7. The A_0 and A_1 pins of 8255 are connected to A_{01} and A_{02} pins of the microprocessor respectively. The A_{00} pin of the microprocessor is used for selecting the transfer on the lower byte of the data bus. Hence any change in the status of A_{00} does not affect the port to be selected, rather A_{01} and A_{02} of the microprocessor decide the port to be selected as they are connected to A_0 and A_1 of 8255. The 8255 port addresses are tabulated as shown below.

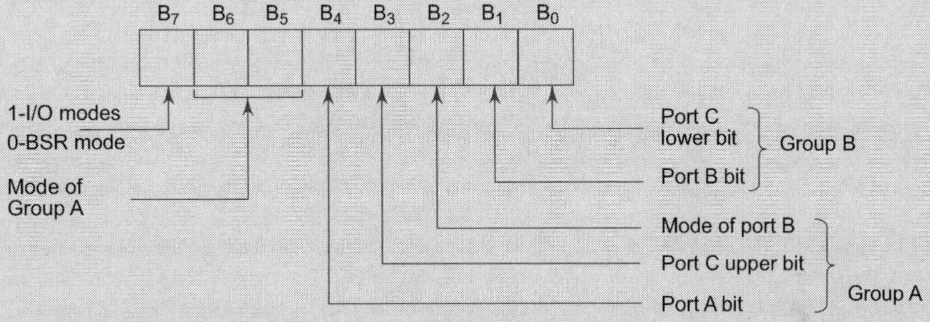

Group A modes

B_6	B_5	Mode
0	0	mode 0
0	1	mode 1
1	0	mode 2
1	1	x

(i) Port B mode is either 0 or 1 depending upon B2 bit.

(ii) A port is an output port if the port bit is 0 else it is input port

Fig. 5.18(b) *I/O Mode Control Word Register Format*

8255 Ports	*I/O Address lines* A_{15}	A_{14}	A_{13}	A_{12}	A_{11}	A_{10}	A_{09}	A_{08}	A_{07}	A_{06}	A_{05}	A_{04}	A_{03}	A_{02}	A_{01}	A_{00}	*Hex. Port Addresses*
PortA	0	0	0	0	0	1	1	1	0	1	0	0	0	0	0	0	0740H
Port B	0	0	0	0	0	1	1	1	0	1	0	0	0	0	1	0	0742H
Port C	0	0	0	0	0	1	1	1	0	1	0	0	0	1	0	0	0744H
CWR	0	0	0	0	0	1	1	1	0	1	0	0	0	1	1	0	0746H

Let us use absolute decoding scheme that uses all the 16 address lines for deriving the device address pulse. Out of $A_0 - A_{15}$ lines, two address lines A_{02} and A_{01} are directly required by 8255 for the three port and CWR address decoding. Hence only A_3 to A_{15} are used for decoding addresses. The complete hardware scheme is shown in Fig. 5.19. In the diagram, the 8086 is assumed to be in the maximum mode so that $\overline{IORD}$ and $\overline{IOWR}$ are readily available. If the 8086 is in minimum mode, $\overline{RD}$ and $\overline{WR}$ of 8086 are to be connected accordingly to 8255 and M/ $\overline{IO}$ pin is combined with the chip select of above hardware suitably so as to select the 8255 when M/$\overline{IO}$ is low.

The ALP for the problem is developed as follows:

```
     MOV DX, 0746 H          ; Initialise CWR with
     MOV AL, 82 H            ; control word 82H
     OUT DX, AL              ;
     SUB DX,04               ; Get address of port B in DX
     IN AL, DX               ; Read port B for switch
     SUB DX,02               ; positions in to AL and get port A address
                             ; in DX.
     OUT DX, AL              ; Display switch positions on port A
     MOV BL, 00 H            ; Initialise BL for switch count
     MOV CH, 08H             ; Initialise CH for total switch number
YY:  ROL AL                  ; Rotate AL through carry to check,
     JNC XX                  ; whether the switches are on or
     INC BL                  ; off, i.e. either 1 or 0
XX  :DEC CH                  ; Check for next switch. If
     JNZ YY                  ; all switch are checked, the
     MOV AL, BL              ; number of on switches are
     ADD DX, 04              ; in BL.Display it on port C
     OUT DX,AL               ; lower.
     HLT                     ; Stop
```

Program 5.5 *ALP for Problem 5.10*

Problem 5.11

Interface a 4*4 Keyboard with 8086 using 8255. and write an ALP for detecting a key closure and return the key code in AL. The debouncing period for a key is 10 ms. Use software key debouncing technique. DEBOUNCE is an available 10 ms delay routine.

Solution Port A is used as output port for selecting a row of keys while port B is used as an input port for sensing a closed key. Thus the keyboard lines are selected one by one through port A and the port B lines are polled continuously till a key closure is sensed. Then routine DEBOUNCE is called for key debouncing. The key code is decided depending upon the selected row and a low sensed column. The hardware circuit diagram is shown in Fig. 5.21.

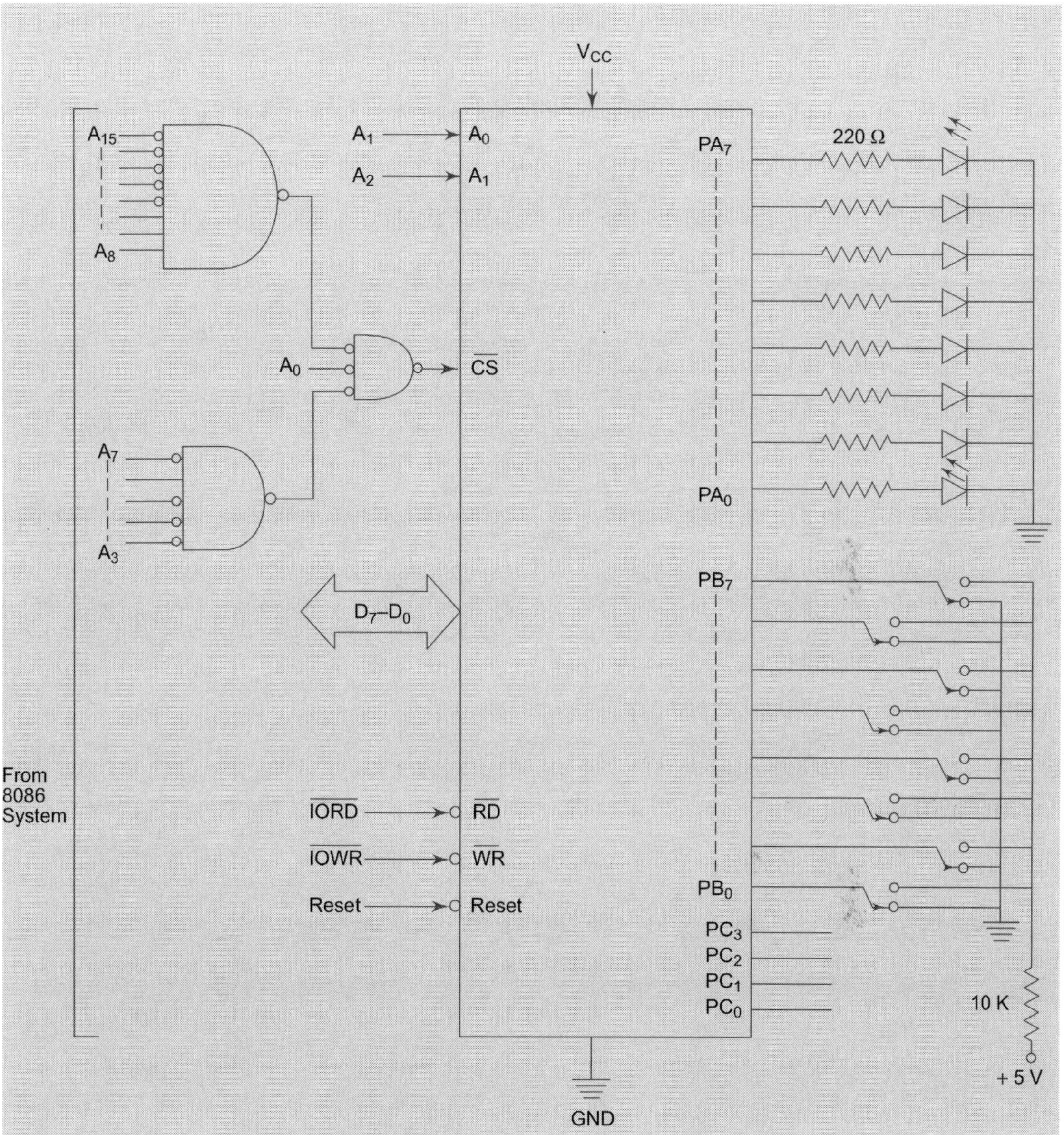

Fig. 5.19 *8255 Interfacing with 8086 for Problem 5.10*

The higher order lines of port A and port B are left unused. The addresses of port A and port B will be respectively 8000 H and 8002 H while the address of CWR will be 8006 H. The flow chart of the complete program is given in Fig. 5.22.

The ALP for the problem is given along with comments. The control word for this problem will be 82 H. Let us write this program using assembler directives. In this problem no major data is required hence only

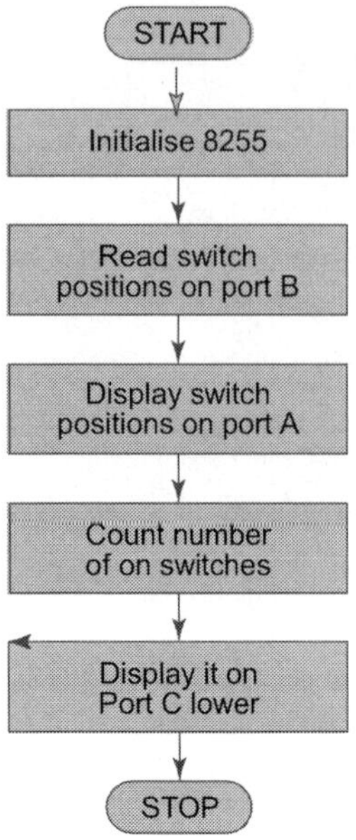

Fig. 5.20 *Flow chart for the ALP of Problem 5.10*

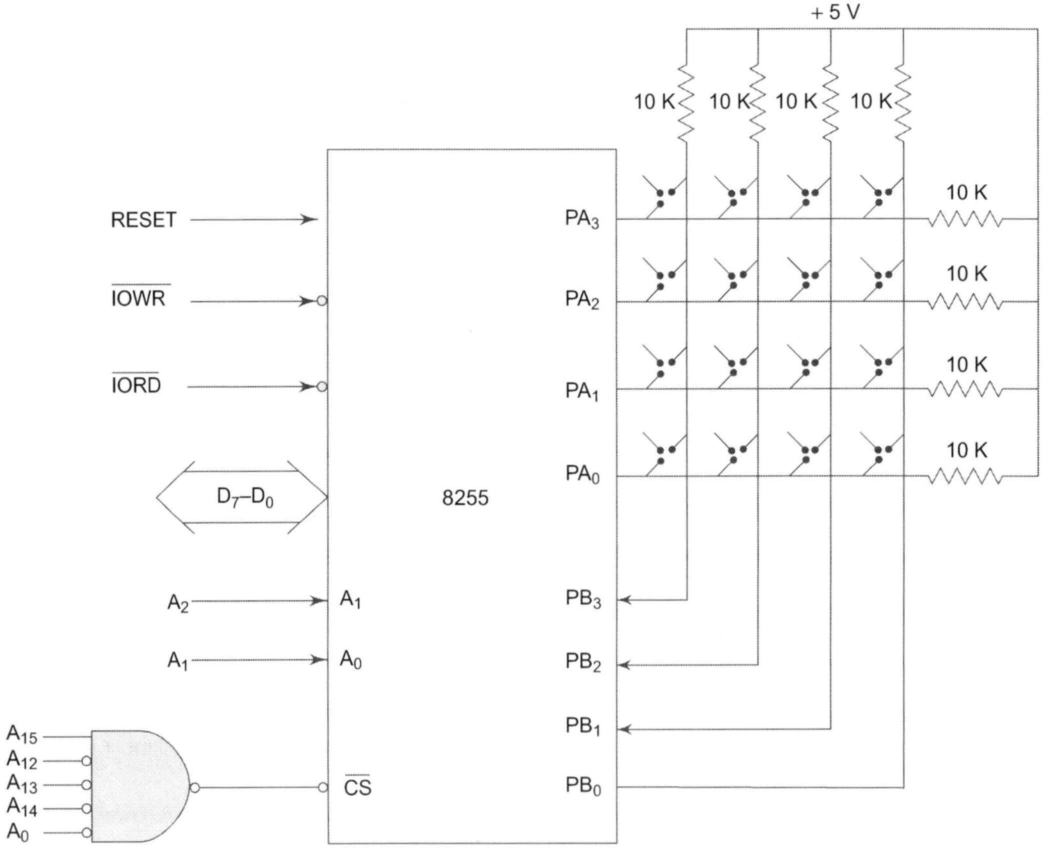

Fig. 5.21 *Interfacing 4 × 4 Keyboard for Problem 5.11*

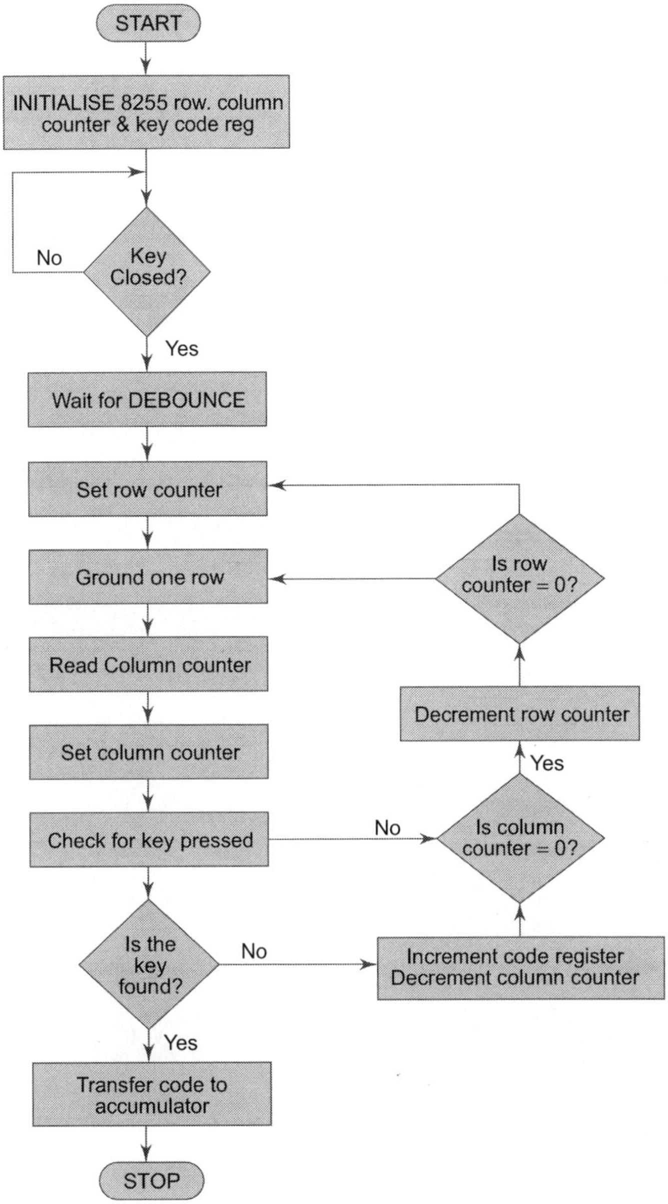

Fig. 5.22 *Flow chart for ALP of Problem 5.11*

one segment is used for storing the program code, i.e. code segment (CS). This program is written in MASM syntax. The 8255 is again interfaced to the lower byte of the 8086 data bus. Absolute decoding scheme is not used here to implement the circuit using minimum hardware.

```
CODE        SEGMENT
ASSUME      CS : CODE
START:      MOV AL, 82H         ; Load CWR with
```

```
          MOV DX, 8006H      ; control word
          OUT DX, AL         ; required
          MOV BL, 00H        ; Initialize BL for key code
          XOR AX, AX         ; Clear all flags
          MOV DX, 8000H      ; Port Address in AX.
          OUT DX, AL         ; Ground all rows.
          ADD DX,02          ; Port B address in DX.
WAIT :    IN AL, DX          ; Read all columns.
          AND AL, 0F H       ; Mask data lines D7-D4.
          CMP AL, 0F H       ; Any key closed?
          JZ WAIT            ; If not, wait till key
          CALL DEBOUNCE      ; closure else wait for 10 ms
          MOV AL, 7FH        ; Load data byte to ground
          MOV BH, 04H        ; a row and set row counter.
NXTROW :  ROL AL, 01         ; Rotate AL to ground next row.
          MOV CH, AL         ; Save data byte to ground next row.
          SUB DX,02          ; Output port address is in DX.
          OUT DX, AL         ; Ground one of the rows.
          ADD DX,02          ; Input port address is in DX.
          IN AL, DX          ; Read input port for key closure.
          AND AL, 0FH        ; Mask D4-D7.
          MOV CL, 04H        ; Set column counter.
NXTCOL :  ROR  AL, 01        ; Move D0 in CF.
          JNC CODEKY         ; Key closure is found, if CF=0.
          INC BL             ; Increment BL for next binary
                             ; key code.
          DEC CL             ; Decrement column counter,
                             ; if no key closure found.
          JNZ NXTCOL         ; Check for key closure in next column
          MOV AL,CH          ; Load data byte to ground next row.
          DEC BH             ; if no key closer found in column
                             ; get ready to ground next row.
          JNZ NXTROW         ; Go back to ground next row.
          JMP WAIT           ; Jump back to check for key.
                             ; closure again.
CODEKY :  MOV AL, BL         ; Key code is transferred to AL.
          MOV AH, 4CH        ; Return to DOS prompt.
          INT 21 H
```

This procedure generates 10 ms delay at 5 MHz operating frequency.

```
DEBOUNCE PROC NEAR
          MOV CL, 0E2H
BACK:     NOP
          DEC CL
          JNZ BACK
          RET
DEBOUNCE  ENDP
CODE      ENDS
          END START
```

Program 5.6 *ALP for Problem 5.11*

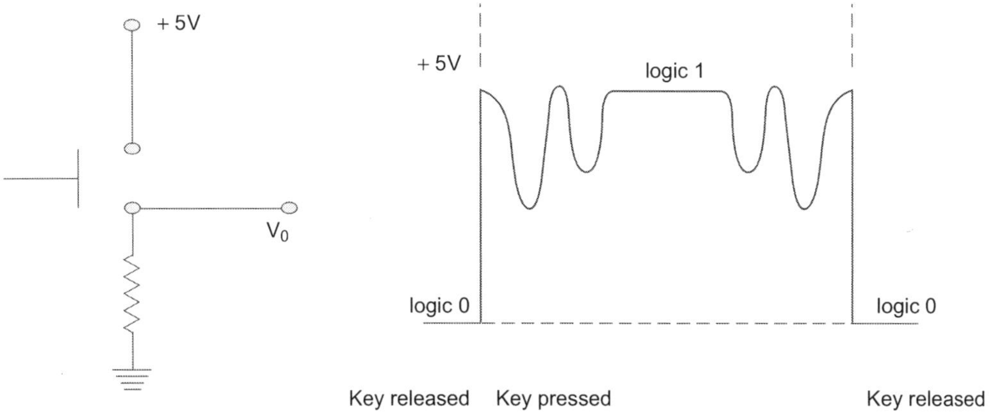

Fig. 5.23 *A Mechanical Key and Its Response*

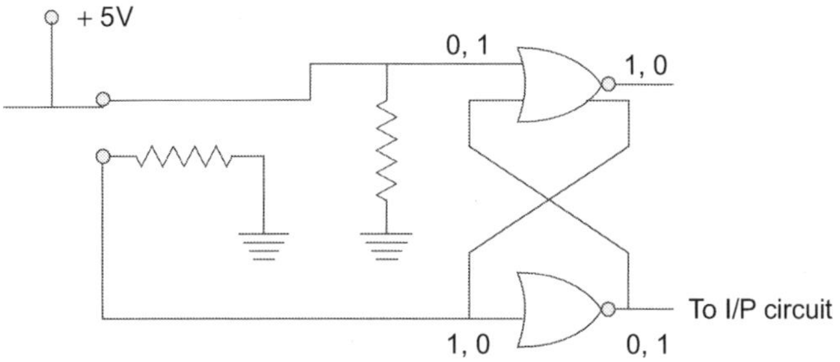

Fig. 5.24 *Hardware Debouncing Circuit*

Key Debounce Whenever a mechanical push-button is pressed or released once, the mechanical components of the key do not change the position smoothly, rather, it generates a transient response as shown in Fig. 5.23. These transient variations may be interpreted as the multiple key pressures and responded accordingly by the microprocessor system. To avoid this problem, two schemes are suggested: the first one utilizes a bistable multivibrator at the output of the key to debounce it as shown in Fig. 5.24. The other scheme suggests that the microprocessor should be made to wait for the transient period (usually 10 msec), so that the transient response settles down and reaches a steady state. A logic '0' will be read by the microprocessor when the key is pressed.

In a number of high precision applications, a designer may need to read or write more than 8-bits of data. In these cases, a system designer may have two options—the first is to have more than one 8-bit port, read(write) the ports one by one and then form the multibyte data; the second option allows forming 16-bit ports using two 8-bit ports and use 16-bit read or write operations. The following example elaborates interfacing of a 16-bit port using two 8-bit ports.

Problem 5.12

Interface 16-bit 8255 ports with 8086. The address of port A is F0H.

Solution To implement a 16-bit port two 8255s are required. One will act as the lower 8-bit port, i.e. D_0–D_7, while the other will act as the upper 8-bit port D_8–D_{15}. The overall scheme is as shown in Fig. 5.25. While initialising AL and AH (AX) both should be loaded with a suitable (common) control word. In this system, port A, port B and port C all may work as 16-bit ports.

Problem 5.13

Interface an 8255 with 8086 at 80H as an I/O address of port A. Interface five 7 segment displays with the 8255. Write a sequence of instructions to display 1, 2, 3, 4 and 5 over the five displays continuously as per their positions starting with 1 at the least significant position.

Solution The hardware scheme for the above problem is shown in Fig. 5.26. In this scheme, I/O port A is multiplexed to carry data for all the 7-segment displays. The port B selects (grounds) one of the displays at a time.

The displays used in the above hardware scheme are common cathod type. To glow a segment, logic 1 is applied on the corresponding line and the corresponding 7-segment display is selected by applying logic 1 on the port line that drives a transistor to ground the common cathode pin of the display. Thus the codes are decided as shown. For a common cathode display, a '1', applied to a segment glows it and a '0' blanks it.

Table 5.11

Number to be displayed	PA_7 *dp*	PA_6 *a*	PA_5 *b*	PA_4 *c*	PA_3 *d*	PA_2 *e*	PA_1 *f*	PA_0 *g*	*Code*
1	1	1	0	0	1	1	1	1	CF
2	1	0	0	1	0	0	1	0	92
3	1	0	0	0	0	1	1	0	86
4	1	1	0	0	1	1	0	0	CC
5	1	0	1	0	0	1	0	0	A4

All these codes, decided as above, are stored in a look up table starting at 2000:0001. The ALP along with comments is given as follows:

```
AGAIN:   MOV CL, 05H          ; Count for displays
         MOV BX, 2000H        ; Initialise data segment
         MOV DS, BX           ; for look up table
         MOV CH, 01H          ; 1st number to be displayed
         MOV AL, 80H          ; Load control word in the
         OUT 86H,AL           ; CWR
         MOV DL,01H           ; Enable code for Least significant
                              ; 7-seg display
NXTDGT : MOV BX, 0000H        ; Set pointer to look up table
         MOV AL, CH           ; First no to display
                              ; Store number to be displayed in AL.
         XLAT                 ; Find code from look up table
         OUT 80H,AL           ; Display the code
         MOV AL, DL           ; Enable the display
         OUT 81H,AL           ;
         ROL DL               ; Go for selecting the next display
```

```
INC CH                    ; Next number to display
DEC CL                    ; Decrement count.
JNZ NXTDGT                ; Go for next digit display
JMP AGAIN                 ; Repeat the procedure
```

Program 5.7 *ALP for Problem 5.13*

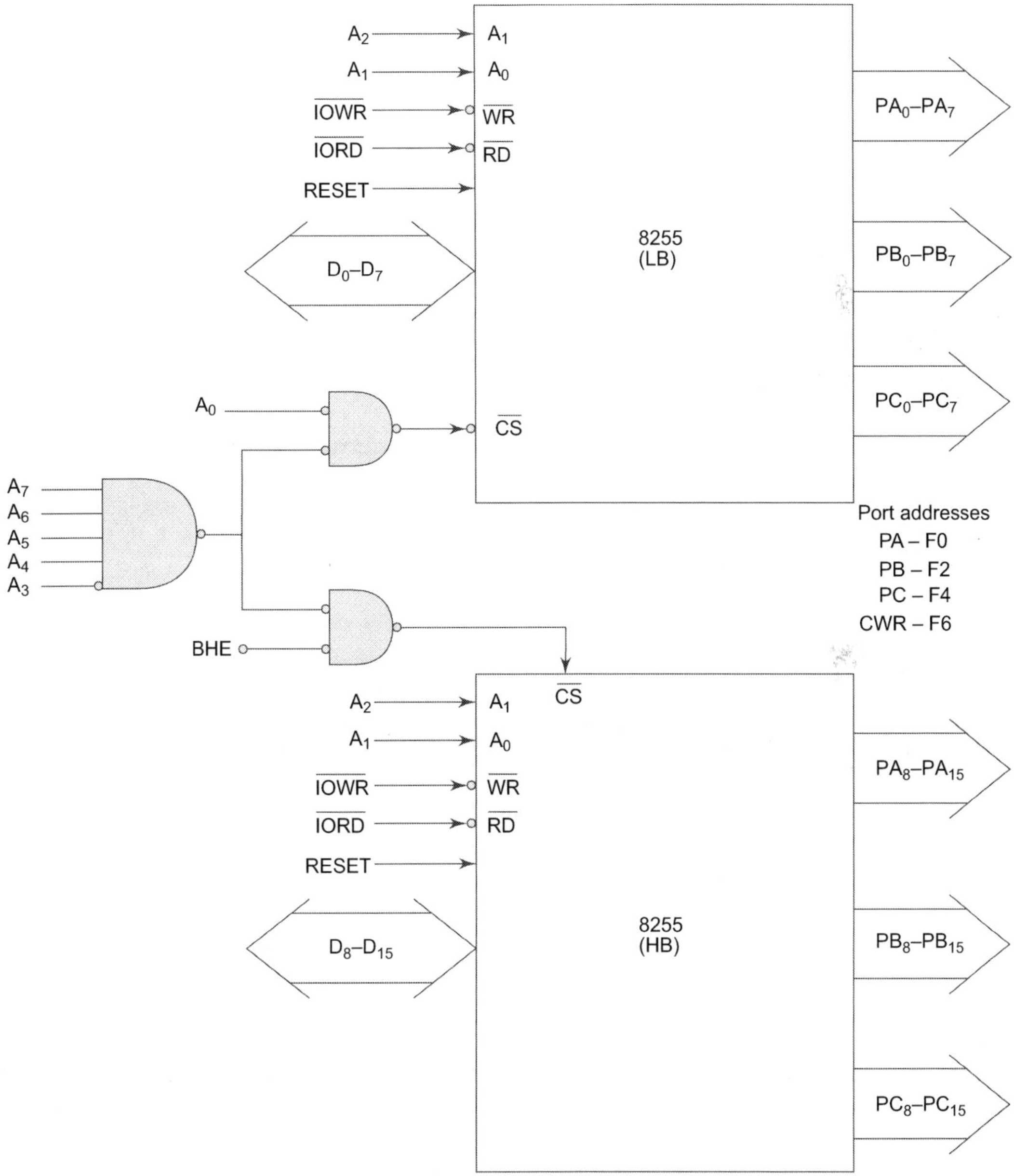

Fig. 5.25 *Interfacing 16-bit 8255 ports with 8086*

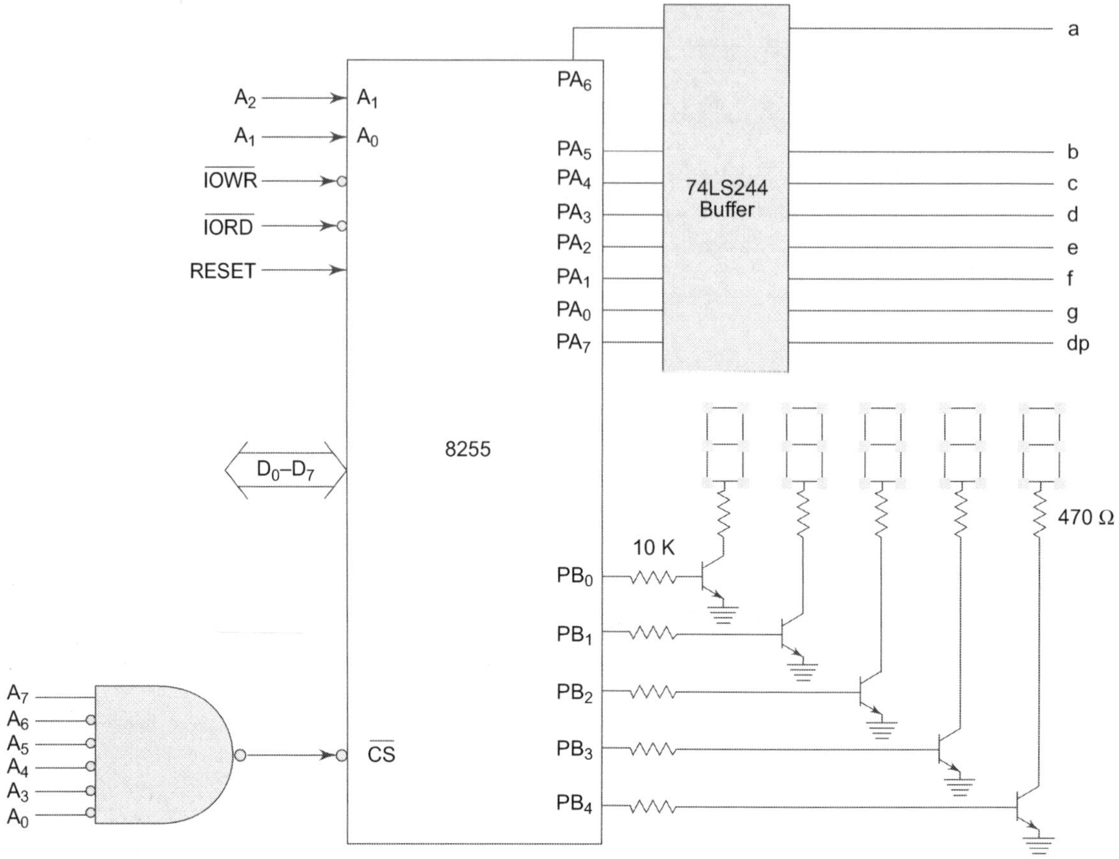

Fig. 5.26 *Interfacing Multiplexed 7-Segment Display*

MODE I (Strobed I/O mode) This mode is also called as strobed input/output mode. In this mode the handshaking signals control the input or output action of the specified port. Port C lines PC_0–PC_2, provide strobe or handshake lines for port B. This group which includes port B and PC_0–PC_2 is called as group B for strobed data input/output. Port C lines PC_3–PC_5 provide strobe lines for port A. This group including port A and PC_3–PC_5 forms group A. Thus port C is utilized for generating handshake signals. The salient features of mode 1 are listed as follows:

(i) Two groups—group A and group B are available for strobed data transfer.
(ii) Each group contains one 8-bit data I/O port and one 4-bit control/data port.
(iii) The 8-bit data port can be either used as input or an output port. Both the inputs and outputs are latched.
(iv) Out of 8-bit port C, P C_0–PC_2 are used to generate control signals for port B and PC_3–PC_5 are used to generate control signals for port A. The lines PC_6, PC_7 may be used as independent data lines.

The control signals for both the groups in input and output modes are explained as follows:

Input control signal definitions (mode 1)

$\overline{\text{STB}}$ (Strobe input)—If this line falls to logic low level, the data available at 8-bit input port is loaded into input latches.

IBF(Input buffer full)—If this signal rises to logic 1, it indicates that data has been loaded into the latches, i.e. it works as an acknowledgement. IBF is set by a low on **$\overline{\text{STB}}$** and is reset by the rising edge of **$\overline{\text{RD}}$** input.

INTR (Interrupt request) This active high output signal can be used to interrupt the CPU whenever an input device requests the service. INTR is set by a high at $\overline{\textbf{STB}}$ pin and a high at IBF pin. INTE is an internal flag that can be controlled by the bit set/reset mode of either PC_4 ($INTE_A$) or PC_2 ($INTE_B$) as shown in Figs 5.27(a) and (b). INTR is reset by a falling edge on $\overline{\textbf{RD}}$ input. Thus an external input device can request the service of the processor by putting the data on the bus and sending the strobe signal. Figure 5.27 explains the signal definitions clearly.

The strobed data input cycle waveforms are shown in Fig. 5.28(a).

Output control signal definitions (mode 1)

OBF (Output buffer full)—This status signal, whenever falls to logic low, indicates that the CPU has written data to the specified output port. The OBF flip-flop will be set by a rising edge of $\overline{\textbf{WR}}$ signal and reset by a low going edge at the $\overline{\textbf{ACK}}$ input.

$\overline{\textbf{ACK}}$ **(Acknowledge input)**— $\overline{\textbf{ACK}}$ signal acts as an acknowledgement to be given by an output device. $\overline{\textbf{ACK}}$ signal, whenever low, informs the CPU that the data transferred by the CPU to the output device through the port is received by the output device.

INTR (Interrupt request)—Thus an output signal that can be used to interrupt the CPU when an output device acknowledges the data received from the CPU. INTR is set when $\overline{\textbf{ACK}}$, $\overline{\textbf{OBF}}$ and INTE are '1'. It is reset by a falling edge on $\overline{\textbf{WR}}$ input. The INTEA and INTEB flags are controlled by the bit set-reset mode of PC_6 and PC_2, respectively.

The waveforms in Fig. 5.28 may help in understanding the handshake data transfers. The following Figs 5.29 (a) and (b) explains the signal definitions of mode1 in output mode clearly.

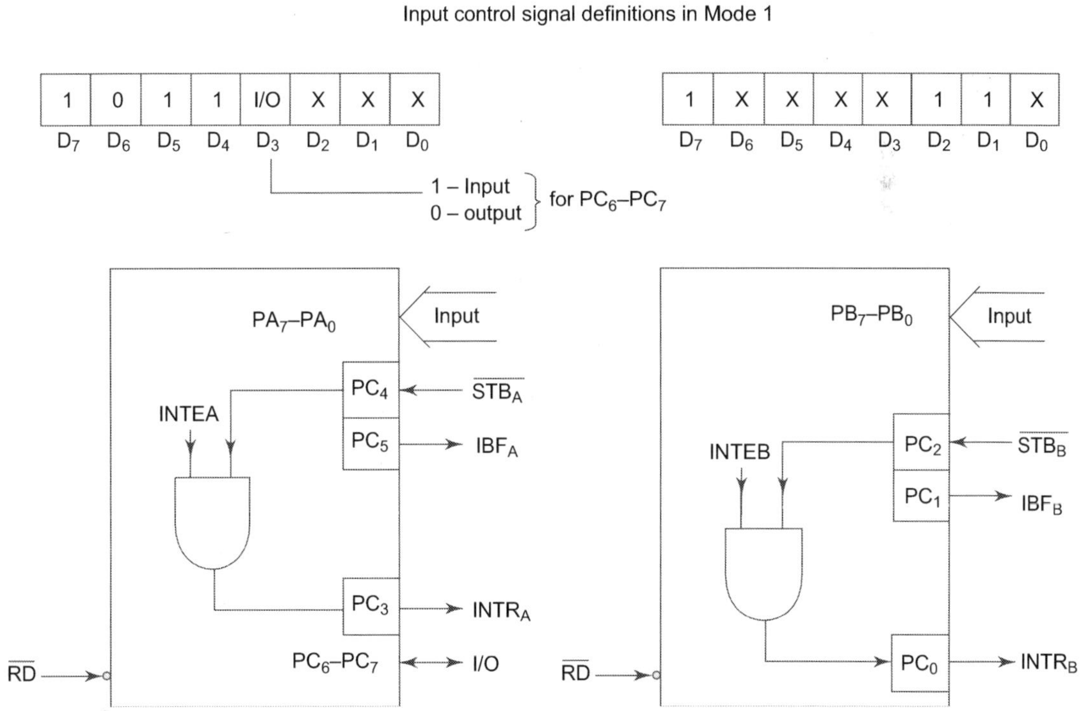

Fig. 5.27 *(a) Mode1 Control Word Group A I/P (b) Mode 1 Control Word Group B I/P*

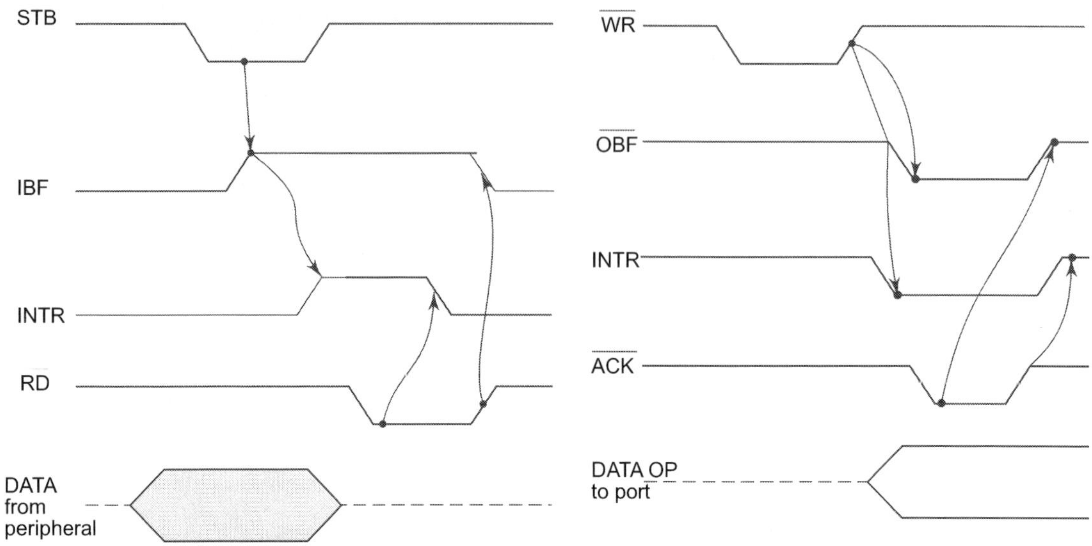

Fig. 5.28 *(a) Mode1 Strobed Input Data Transfer (b) Mode1 Strobed Data Output*

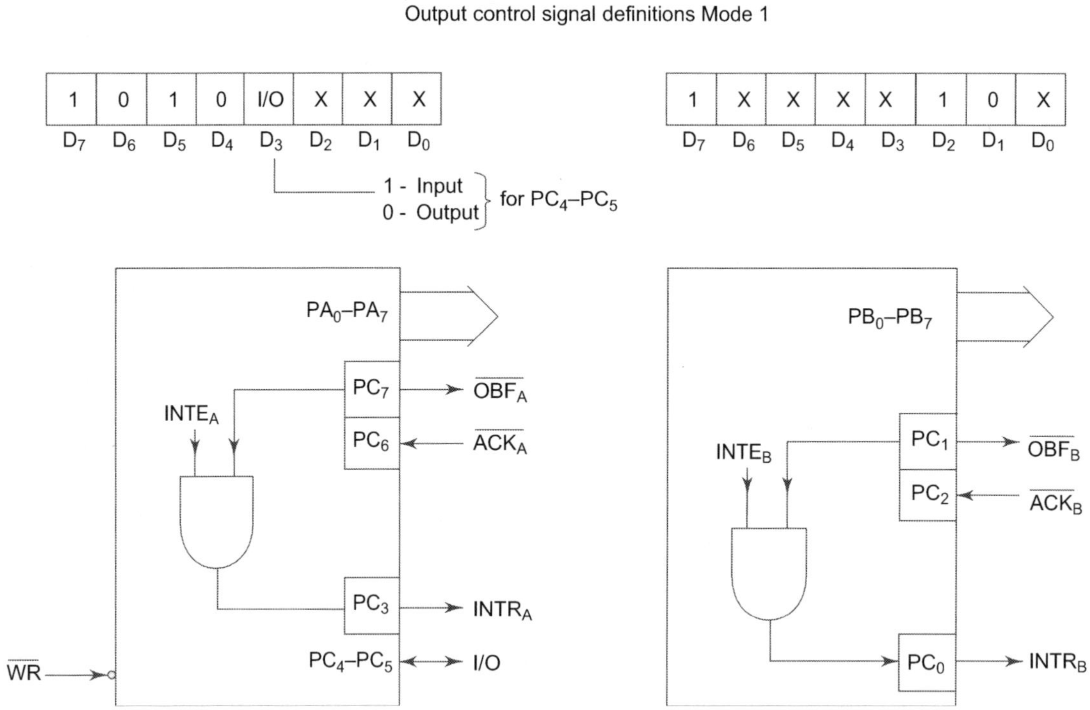

Fig. 5.29 *(a) Mode 1 Control Word Group A o/p (b) Mode 1 Control Word Group B o/p*

After discussing mode 1 in necessary details, let us now consider some hardware interfacing examples that utilize this mode of operation of 8255.

Problem 5.14

Interface a standard IEEE-488 parallel bus printer with 8086. Draw the necessary hardware scheme required for the same and write an ALP to print a character whose ASCII code is available in AL.

Solution Before going through this solution, one should refer to the standard Centronix, INB or EPSON printer pin configuration, given in Table 5.12. There are two types of parallel cables used to connect a microcomputer with a printer, viz. 25 pin cables and 36 pin cables. Basically the 25 pin and the 36 pin cables are similar except for the 11 extra pins for ground (GND) used as 'RETURN' lines for different signals.

The group A is used in mode 1 for handshake data transfer so that port A is used for data transfer and port C lines PC_3–PC_5 are used as handshake lines. Port B lines are used for checking the printer status, hence port B is used as input port in mode 0. Port C lower is used as output port for enabling the printer. The control words are shown in Fig. 5.30.

Table 5.12 *Pin Connections and Descriptions for Centronix-type Parallel Interface to IBM PC and EPSON FX-100 Printers*

Printer Controller Signal Pin No.	*Return Pin No.*	*Signal*	*Direction*	*Description*
1	19	$\overline{\text{STROBE}}$	IN	STROBE pulse to read data in. Pulse width must be more than 0.5 μs at receiving terminal. The signal level is normally "high"; read-in of data is performed at the "low" level of this signal.
2	20	DATA 1	IN	These signals represent information of the 1st to 8th bits of parallel data respectively. Each signal is at "high" level when data is logical "1" and "low" when logical "0".
3	21	DATA 2	IN	
4	22	DATA 3	IN	
5	23	DATA 4	IN	
6	24	DATA 5	IN	
7	25	DATA 6	IN	
8	26	DATA 7	IN	
9	27	DATA 8	IN	
10	28	$\overline{\text{ACKNLG}}$	OUT	Approximately 5 μs pulse; "low" indicates the data has been received and the printer is ready to accept other data.
11	29	BUSY	OUT	A "high" signal indicates that the printer cannot receive data. The signal becomes "high" in the following cases. 1. During data entry. 2. During printing operation. 3. In "outline" state. 4. During printer error status.
12	30	PE	OUT	A "high" signal indicates that the printer is out of paper.

(Contd.)

Table 5.12 *(Contd.)*

Signal Pin No.	*Return Pin No.*	*Signal*	*Direction*	*Description*
13	—	SLCT	OUT	This signal indicates that the printer is in the selected
14	—	$\overline{\text{AUTO}}$ $\overline{\text{FEED XT}}$	IN	With this signal being at "low" level, the paper is automatically fed one line after printing. (The signal level can be fixed to "low" with DIPSW Pin 2-3 provided on the control circuit board.)
15	—	NC		Not used.
16	—	0V		Logic GND Level.
17	—		CHASIS GND	Printer chasis GND. In the printer, the chasis GND and the logic GND are isolated from each other.
18	—	NC	—	Not used.
19–30	—	GND	—	"Twisted-Pair Return" signal; GND level.
31	—	$\overline{\text{INIT}}$	IN	When the level of this signal becomes "low" the printer controller is reset to its initial state and the print buffer is cleared. This signal is normally at "high" level, and its pulse width must be more than 50 μs at the receiving terminal.
32		$\overline{\text{ERROR}}$	OUT	The level of this signal becomes "low" when the printer is in "Paper End "state, "Offline" state and "Error" state.
33	—	GND	—	Same as with pin numbers 19 to 30.
34	—	NC	—	Not used.
35				Pulled up to + 5 Vdc through 4.7 k-ohms resistance.
36	—	$\overline{\text{SLCT IN}}$	IN	Data entry to the printer is possible only when the level of this signal is "low". (Internal fixing can be carried out with DIP SW 1-8. The condition at the time of shipment is set "low" for this signal.)

Note:
1. "Direction" refers to the direction of signal flow as viewed from the printer.
2. "Return" denotes "Twised-Pair Return" and is to be connected at signal-ground level. When wiring the interface, be sure to use a twisted-pair cable for each signal and never fail to complete connection on the return side. To prevent noise effectively, these cables should be shielded and connected to the chassis of the system unit.
3. All interface conditions are based on TTL, level. Both the rise and fall times of each signal must be less than 0.2 μs.
4. Data transfer must not be carried out by ignoring the $\overline{\text{ACKNLG}}$ or BUSY signal. (Data transfer to this printer can be carried out only after interfacing the $\overline{\text{ACKNLG}}$ signal or when the level of the BUSY signal is "low".)
5. Remaining pins on the connector are no connection pins.
6. x-not available in 25 pins connector.

Printer Operation The printer interface connections with 8255 and the printer connector shown in Fig. 5.31 and Fig. 5.32 respectively. First of all the printer should be initialised by sending a 50 μs (minimum) pulse on the $\overline{\text{INIT}}$ pin of the printer. Then the BUSY pin is to be checked to confirm if the printer is ready. If this signal is low, it indicates that the printer is ready to accept a character from the CPU. Port pins of 8255 may not have sufficient drive capacity to drive the printer input signals so that the open collector buffers 74LSOY are used to enhance the drive capacity. When this happens the ASCII code of the character to be printed is sent on the eight parallel port lines. Once the data is sent on eight parallel lines, the $\overline{\text{STROBE}}$ signal is activated after at least 0.5 μs, to indicate that the data is available on the eight data lines. The falling edge of the $\overline{\text{STROBE}}$ signal causes the printer to make its BUSY pin high, indicating that the printer is busy. After a minimum period of 0.5 μs, the $\overline{\text{STROBE}}$ signal can be sent high. The data must be valid on the data lines for at least 0.5 μs after the $\overline{\text{STROBE}}$ signal goes high. After receiving the appropriate $\overline{\text{STROBE}}$ pulse, the printer starts the necessary electromechanical action to print the character and when it is ready to receive the next character, it asserts its $\overline{\text{ACKNLG}}$ signal low approximately for 5 ms. The rising edge of the $\overline{\text{ACKNLG}}$ signal indicates to the computer that it is ready to receive the next character. The rising edge of the $\overline{\text{ACKNLG}}$ signal also resets the BUSY signal from the printer. A low on the BUSY pin further indicates that the printer is ready to accept the next character. The $\overline{\text{ACKNLG}}$ and BUSY signals can be used interchangeably for handshaking purposes. The waveforms for the above printer operation are shown in Fig. 5.33.

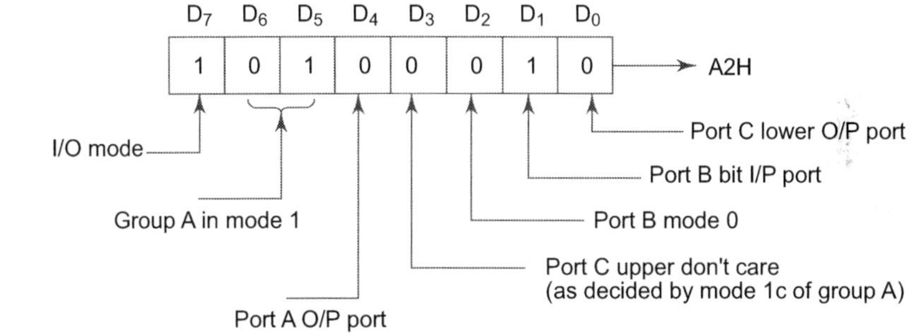

Strobed I/O mode control word

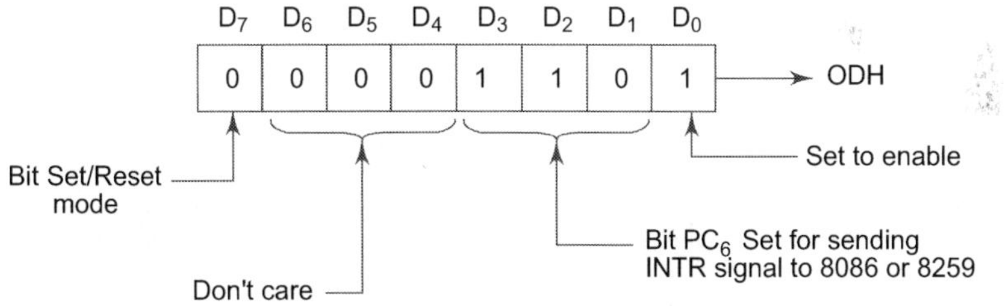

Fig. 5.30 *Bit Set/Reset Control Word*

```
        MOV BL,AL        ; Get the ASCII code in BL.
        MOV AL,0A2H      ; Control word for 8255
        OUT 0F6H,AL      ; Load CWR with the control word.
BUSY:   IN AL,0F2H       ; Read printer status from the BUSY pin.
        AND AL,08H       ; Mask all bits except PB3
        JNZ BUSY         ; If AL#0, printer is busy. Wait till
                         ; it becomes free.
        MOV AL, BL       ; Get the character for printer in AL
        OUT 0F0H,AL      ; Send it to the port for the printer
        NOP              ; Wait for some time
        MOV AL,08 H      ; Pull STROBE low
```

```
OUT 0F6H          ; Reset PC4
NOP               ; Wait
MOV AL,09 H       ; Raise STROBE high
OUT 0F6H          ; SET PC4
HLT
```

Program 5.8 *ALP for Printing a Character for Problem 5.14*

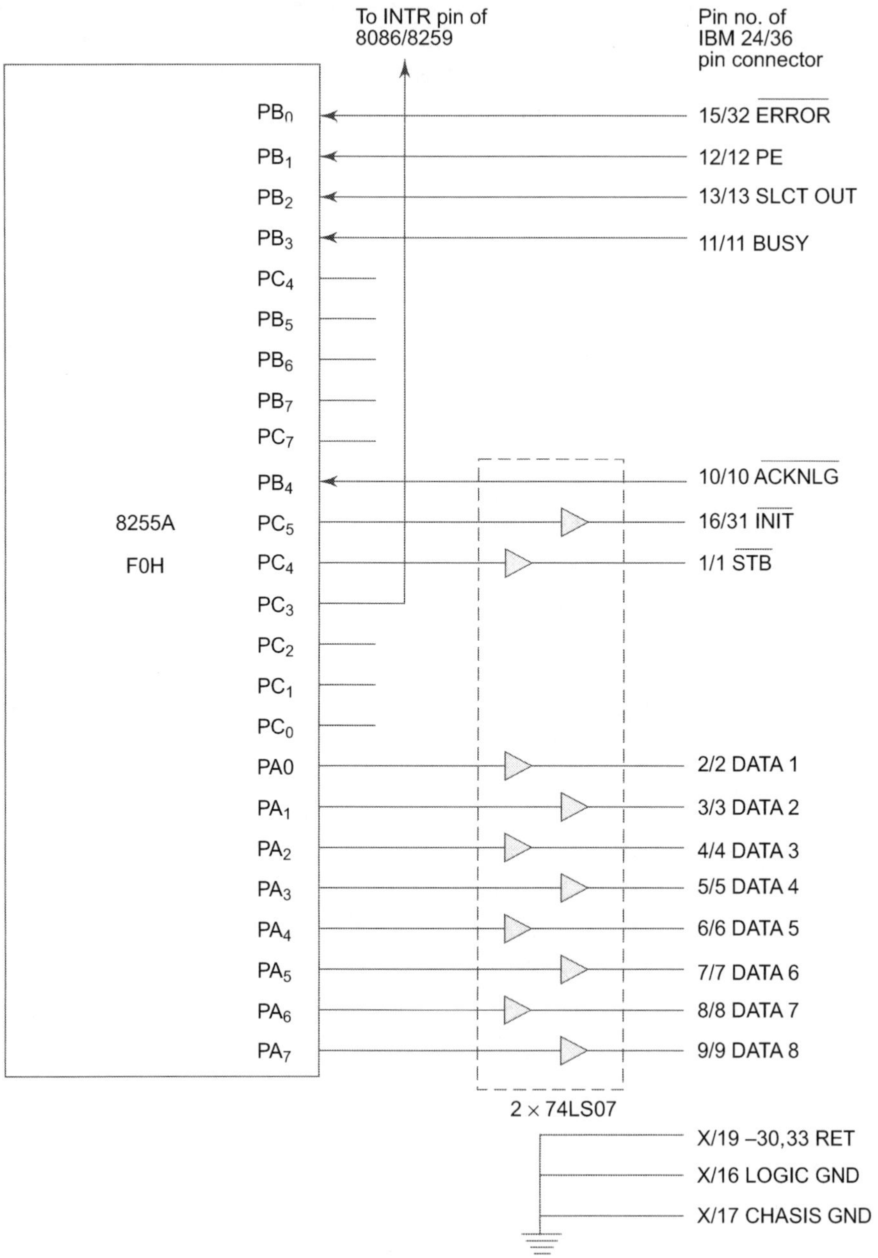

Fig. 5.31 *Printer Interface with 8255*

MODE 2 (Strobed bidirectional I/O) This mode of operation of 8255 is also known as *strobed bidirectional I/O*. This mode of operation provides 8255 with an additional feature for communicating with a peripheral device on an 8-bit data bus. Handshaking signals are provided to maintain proper data flow and synchronization between the data transmitter and receiver. The interrupt generation and other functions are similar to mode 1. Thus in this mode, 8255 is a bidirectional 8-bit port with handshake signals. The $\overline{RD}$ and $\overline{WR}$ signals decide whether the 8255 is going to operate as an input port or output port.

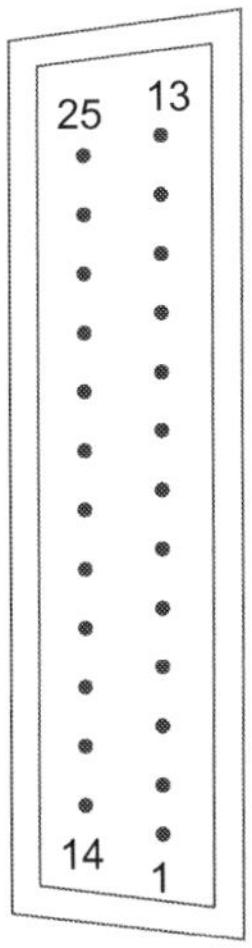

Fig. 5.32 *Centronics Printer Connector*

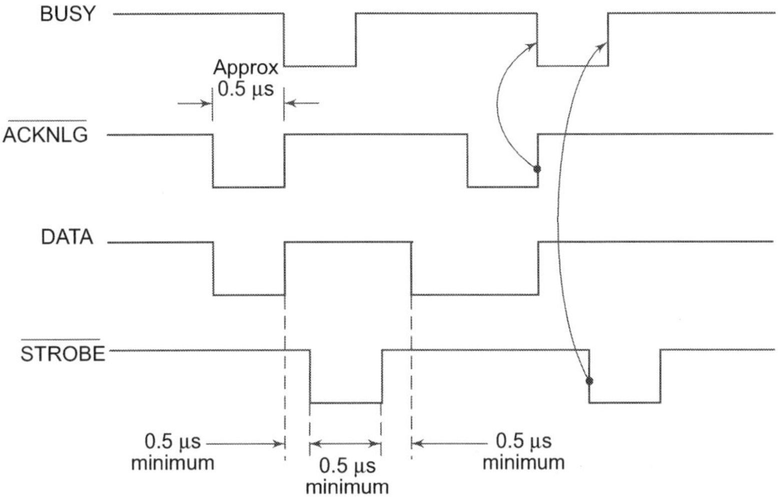

Fig. 5.33 *Timing Waveforms of Data Transfer to a Centronix Compatible Parallel Printer*

The salient features of mode 2 of 8255 are listed as follows:

1. The single 8-bit port in group A is available.
2. The 8-bit port is bidirectional and additionally a 5-bit control port is available.
3. Three I/O lines are available at port C,viz. PC_2–PC_0.
4. Inputs and outputs are both latched.
5. The 5-bit control port C (PC_3–PC_7) is used for generating/accepting handshake signals for the 8-bit data transfer on port A.

Control signal definitions in mode 2

INTR (Interrupt request) As in mode 1, this control signal is active high and is used to interrupt the microprocessor to ask for transfer of the next data byte to/from it. This signal is used for input (read) as well as output (write) operations.

Control signals for output operations

$\overline{OBF}$ (Output buffer full) This signal, when falls to logic low level, indicates that the CPU has written data to port A.

$\overline{ACK}$ (Acknowledge) This control input, when falls to logic low level, acknowledges that the previous data byte is received by the destination and the next byte may be sent by the processor. This signal enables the internal tristate buffers to send out the next data byte on port A.

INTE1 (A flag associated with $\overline{OBF}$) This can be controlled by bit set/reset mode with PC_6.

Control signals for input operations

$\overline{STB}$ (Strobe input) A low on this line is used to strobe in the data into the input latches of 8255.

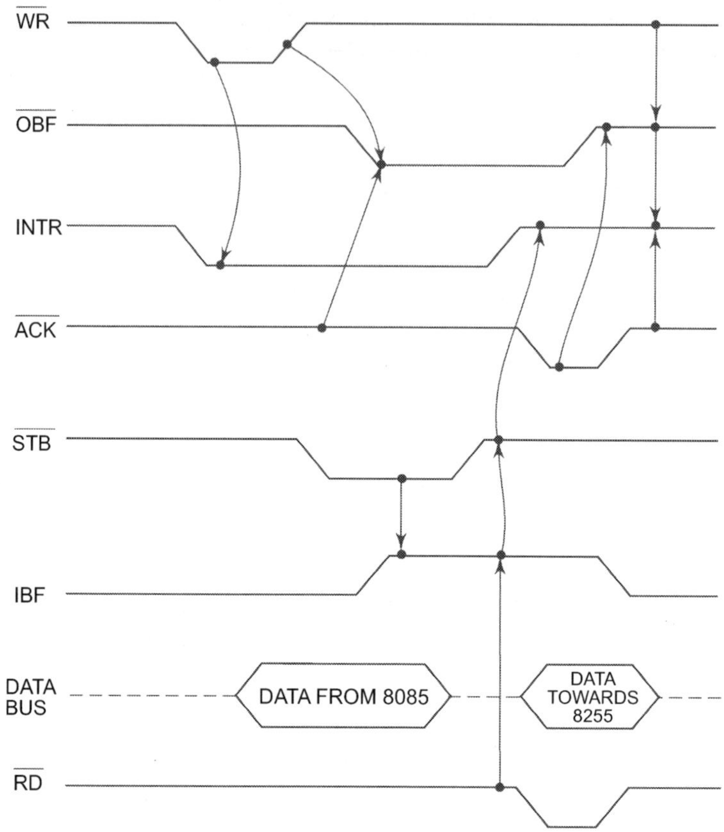

Fig. 5.34 *Mode 2 Bidirectional Data Transfer*

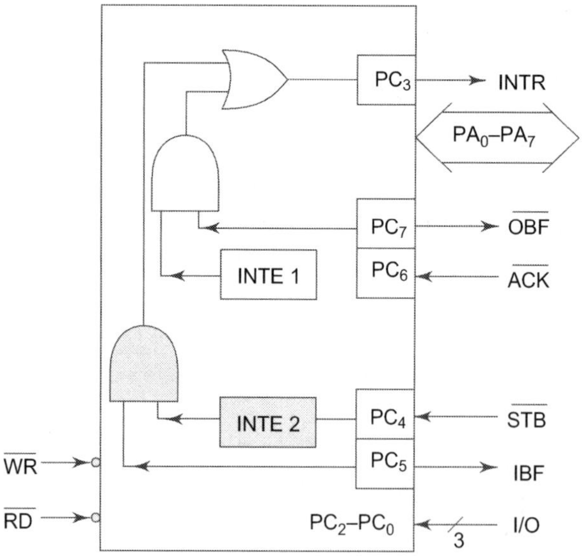

(a)

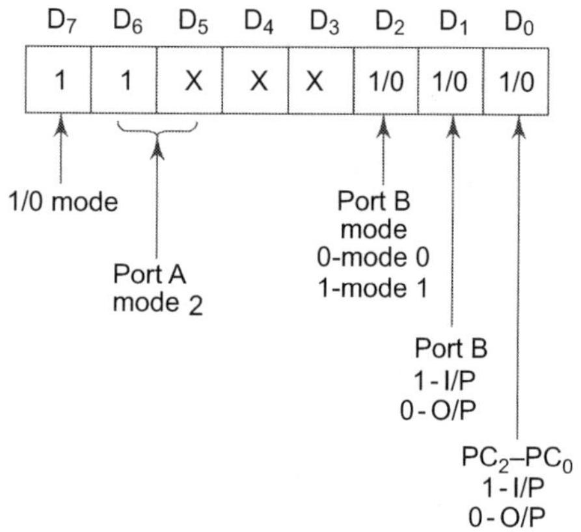

(b)

Fig. 5.35 *(a) Mode 2 pins (b) Mode 2 control word*

IBF (Input buffer full) When the data is loaded into the input buffer, this signal rises to logic '1'. This can be used as an acknowledgement that the data has been received by the receiver.

The waveforms in Fig. 5.34 show the operation in mode 2 for output as well as input port.

Note: $\overline{WR}$ must occur before $\overline{ACK}$ and $\overline{STB}$ must be activated before $\overline{RD}$.

Figure 5.35 (a) shows a schematic diagram containing an 8-bit bidirectional port, 5-bit control port and the relation of INTR with the control pins. Port B can either be set to mode 0 or mode 1 while port A (Group A) is in mode 2. Mode 2 is not available for port B. Figure 5.35 (b) shows the necessary control word.

The INTR goes high only if either IBF, INTE2, $\overline{STB}$ and $\overline{RD}$ go high or $\overline{OBF}$, INTE1, $\overline{ACK}$ and $\overline{WR}$ go high. The port C can be read to know the status of the peripheral device, in terms of the control signals, using the normal I/O instructions.

The following problem emphasizes the use of 8255 in mode 2.

The programming in assembly language is divided into two parts. The first is the transmitter or sender part and the second being the receiver part. The transmitter program sends data to the receiver 8086 system while the receiver program accepts the data from the transmitting 8086 system. To interchange the blocks of data between the two systems, each one will require the transmitter as well as the receiver program.

The interrupt vector address for NMI is 0000 : 0008H. At this location the IP and CS values of the transmitter program addresses are stored. The execution of the transmitter program on one system causes execution of the receiver program on the other system through NMI interrupt. Rather, the receiver is executed as the NMI interrupt service routine as a response to the execution of the transmitter program.

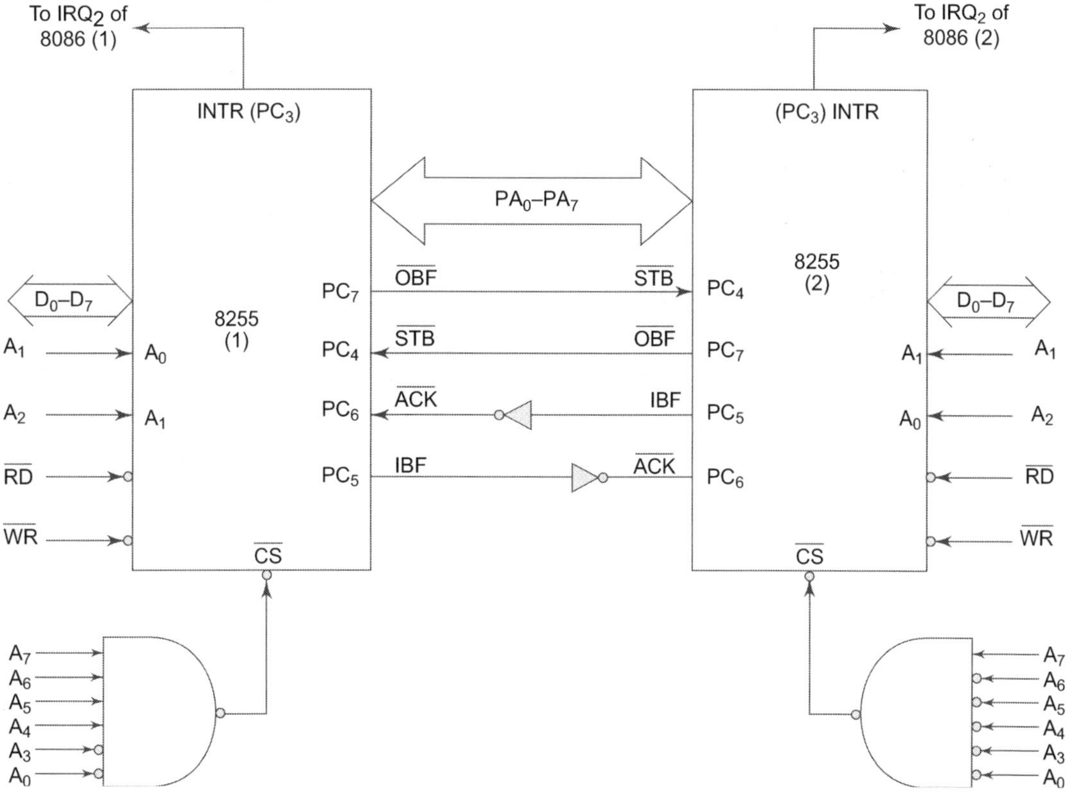

Fig. 5.36 *Interconnections between the two 8255s in Mode 2 for Problem 5.16*

Problem 5.15

An 8086 system with a 8255 interfaced at port A address F0H, has a block of 100 data bytes stored in it. Another 8086 system with another 8255 interfaced at port A address 80H has another block of 100 data bytes stored in it. Interchange these blocks of data bytes between the two 8086 systems. Draw the necessary hardware scheme and write the necessary sequence of instructions. Both systems run on the same CLK rate.

Solution The complete hardware schematic is shown in Fig. 5.36. The INTR pin of 8255 in mode 2 is applied to the respective 8086 processor at NMI pin. The inverted IBF signal of the first 8255 is connected to $\overline{\text{ACK}}$ of the second and the inverted IBF signal of the second 8255 is connected to $\overline{\text{ACK}}$ of the first 8255, so that input buffer full signal of one 8255 acknowledges the receipt of data byte sent by the other. The $\overline{\text{OBF}}$ signal of one 8255 is connected to $\overline{\text{STB}}$ signal of the other 8255 and vice versa, so that the output buffer full signal of an 8255 informs the other 8255 that the data is ready on the data bus for it. The 8-bit data bus, i.e. PA_0–PA_7 of the two 8255s are connected with each other.

```
          ; This program transmits parallel data byte by byte to another
            system through
          ; 8255 IN MODE 2.
DATA      SEGMENT
CW1       EQU COH
BLOCK1 DB 100D DUP (?)
DATA      ENDS
ASSUME    CS : CODE,DS : DATA
CODE      SEGMENT
          MOV AX, 0000H             ; Initialise interrupt
          MOV DS, AX                ; vector table of
          MOV AX, OFFSET TRANS      ; 8086 at table
          MOV [0008H],AX ; TRANS.
          MOV [000AH],SEG TRANS
          MOV CL,101D               ; count CL (one additional)
          MOV AX, DATA              ; Initialise data segment
          MOV DS,AX
          MOV AL, CW1               ; Initialise 8255 in
          MOV DS, AX                ; mode 2
          OUT F6H, AL               ;
          STI                       ;
          MOV [SI], OFFSET BLOCK1-1
TRANS :   INT 2
          CALL FAR PTR SYNCHRO      ; Wait for synchronization
          INC SI                    ; Pointer to block in SI
          DEC CL                    ; Decrement count
```

```
        JZ STOP                    ; If = 0, then stop else
        MOV AL,[SI]                ; Go for transfer of the next
        OUT F0H,AL                 ; byte and out it to port A
WAIT :  JMP WAIT                   ; Wait for acknowledgement
STOP :  HLT                        ; Stop if the complete block
CODE    ENDS                       ; is transferred
        END
```

Program 5.9(a) *Transmitter ALP for Problem 5.15*

```
        ; The receiver program receives data bytes
        ; transmitted by the other system and stores
        ; them in the array as asked in the program.
STACK       SEGMENT
        STACKD DB   500H
STACK       ENDS
DATA        SEGMENT
        CW2 EQU C0H
        BLOCK2 DB 100D DUP (?)
DATA        ENDS
CODE        SEGMENT
ASSUME CS : CODE, DS : DATA ,SS: STACK
          MOV AX, STACK
          MOV SS, AX
          MOV AX, 0000H            ; Initialise interrupt
          MOV DS, AX               ; vector table
          MOV [0008H],OFFSET NEXT
          MOV [000AH],SEG NEXT
          MOV CL,101 D             ; count for bytes
          MOV AX,DATA              ; Initialise data segment
          MOV DS,AX
          MOV AL,CW2               ; Initialise 8255 in mode 2
          OUT 86H,AL               ; to receive data
          MOV SI,OFFSET BLOCK2-1   ; Point to block 2
WAIT :    JMP WAIT                 ; to store received data and wait
NEXT :    INC SI                   ; Increment SI, point to start
          DEC CL                   ; of block 2 and decrement
                                   ; COUNTER
          JZ STOP
          IN 80H
          MOV [SI],AL
          JMP WAIT
STOP :    HLT
CODE      ENDS
     END
```

Program 5.9(b) *Receiver ALP for Problem 5.15*

After the transmitter transmits the data bytes, the receiver receives it and stores it in the array BLOCK 2 but acknowledge $\overline{ACK}$ is sent to the transmitter immediately. Hence the transmitter should wait before sending the next data byte to the receiver so as to give it the sufficient time to read, store and upgrade count for the received data. Transmitter runs its delay procedure SYNCHRO to solve this problem.

```
SYNCHRO    PROC   FAR
     INC DI                    ; All the instructions in this routine are dummy
     DEC CH                    ; instructions, just to cause the same delay as the
     JZ OK                     ; requires takes, to be prepared for accepting
                                     the next data
                               ; byte after getting interrupted by the
                                            transmitter.
OK :IN AL,0F3H
     MOV [DI] AL               ; These are comparable with the
     IRET                      ; corresponding receiver program
SYNCHRO    ENDP                ; instructions.
```

Program 5.10 *ALP for Synchronization Delay*

It may be noted that for the execution of this program, procedure SYNCHRO must be entered with the transmitter program before the END statement.

These programs should be entered in both the 8086 systems. The procedure SYNCHRO is to be entered with the transmitter program as it is called by it. Thus after entering the complete set of these programs into the two 8086 systems, run the receiver program on the receiver 8086 kit. It will initialise the receiver 8086 IVT, its 8255 in receiver mode and wait for the interrupt from the transmitting terminal. Now run the program on the transmitter 8086 kit. This program initialises the transmitter 8086 IVT. Its 8255, in transmitter mode, goes on transmitting data byte by byte and waits for the delay caused by the SYNCHRO before each byte is transmitted so as to give sufficient time to the receiver 8086 to read data, store it in array and upgrade counters and pointers.

Note that the procedure SYNCHRO contains all the dummy instructions. They do not serve any purpose for the algorithm, but just provide their execution delay.The instructions in the procedure are the same as the instructions in the receiving program, from label NEXT to the JMP WAIT instruction. This is not merely a coincidence but an accurate way of providing the required delay for the receiver. As both the 8086 CPUs run at the same clock speed, each of the instructions, which from the procedure and correspondingly those from the receiver program will take the same time for execution. Thus the transmitter will provide the exact delay as required by the receiver.

5.6 INTERFACING ANALOG TO DIGITAL DATA CONVERTERS

This topic is aimed at the study of 8-bit and 12-bit analog to digital converters and their interfacing with 8086. In most of the cases, the PIO 8255 is used for interfacing the analog to digital converters with a microprocessor. We have already studied 8255 interfacing with 8086 as an I/O port, in the previous section. This section will only emphasize the interfacing techniques of analog to digital converters with 8255.

The analog to digital converter is treated as an input device by the microprocessor, that sends an initialising signal to the ADC to start the analog to digital data conversion process. The start of conversion signal is a pulse of a specific duration . The process of analog to digital conversion is a slow process, and the microprocessor has to wait for the digital data till the conversion is over. After the conversion is over, the ADC sends end of conversion (EOC) signal to inform the microprocessor about it and the result is ready at the output buffer of the ADC. These tasks of issuing an SOC pulse to ADC, reading EOC signal from the ADC and reading the digital output of the ADC are carried out by the CPU using 8255 I/O ports.

The time taken by the ADC from the active edge of SOC pulse (the edge at which the conversion process actually starts) till the active edge of EOC signal is called as the *conversion delay* of the ADC. Or broadly speaking, the time taken by the converter to calculate the equivalent digital data output from the moment of the start of conversion is called conversion delay. It may range anywhere from a few microseconds, in case of fast ADCs, to even a few hundred milliseconds in case of slow ADCs. A number of ADCs are available in the market. The selection of ADC for a particular application is done, keeping in mind the required speed, resolution and the cost factor. The available ADCs in the market use different conversion techniques for the conversion of analog signals to digital signals. Successive approximation and dual slope integration techniques are the most popular techniques used in the integrated ADC chips. Whatever may be the technique used for conversion, a general algorithm for ADC interfacing contains the following steps.

1. Ensure the stability of analog input, applied to the ADC
2. Issue start of conversion (SOC) pulse to ADC
3. Read end of conversion (EOC) signal to mark the end of conversion process
4. Read digital data output of the ADC as equivalent digital output

It may be noted that the analog input voltage must be a constant at the input of the ADC right from the beginning to the end of the conversion to get correct results. This may be ensured by a sample and hold circuit which samples the analog signal and holds it constant for a specified time duration. The microprocessor may issue a hold signal to the sample and hold circuit. If the applied input changes before the complete conversion process is over, the digital equivalent of the analog input calculated by the ADC may not be correct.

In this section, we are going to study a few ADC chips and their interfacing techniques with 8086. The first is the ADC0808 an 8-bit ADC and the second is ICL7109, Intersil's 12-bit dual slope ADC. Before proceeding with the interfacing part each of the chip is discussed in significant details so that the interfacing circuits and the algorithms can clearly be understood.

5.6.1 ADC 0808/0809

The analog to digital converter chips 0808 and 0809 are 8-bit CMOS, *successive approximation converters*. Successive approximation technique is one of the fastest technique used for the process of analog to digital conversion. The conversion delay is 100 μs at a clock frequency of 640 kHz, which is quite low as compared to other converters. These converters do not need any external zero or full scale adjustments as they are already taken care of by internal circuits. These converters internally have a 3:8 analog multiplexer so that at a time eight different analog inputs can be connected to the chips. Out of these eight inputs only one can be selected for conversion by using address lines ADD A, ADD B and ADD C, as shown. Using these address inputs, multichannel data acquisition systems can be designed using a single ADC. The CPU may drive these lines using output port lines in case of multichannel applications. In case of single input applications, these may be hardwared to select the proper input.

Table 5.13

Analog I/P selected	*Address lines*		
	C	*B*	*A*
I/P 0	0	0	0
I/P 1	0	0	1
I/P 2	0	1	0
I/P 3	0	1	1

(Contd.)

Table 5.13 (*Contd.*)

Analog I/P selected	*Address lines*		
	C	*B*	*A*
I/P 4	1	0	0
I/P 5	1	0	1
I/P 6	1	1	0
I/P 7	1	1	1

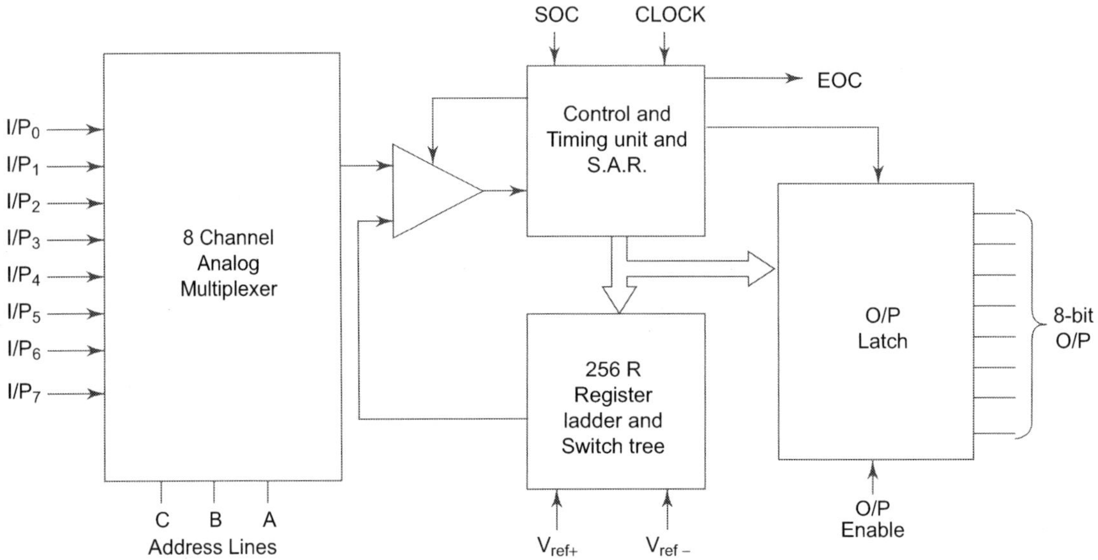

Fig. 5.37(a) *Block Diagram of ADC 0808/0809*

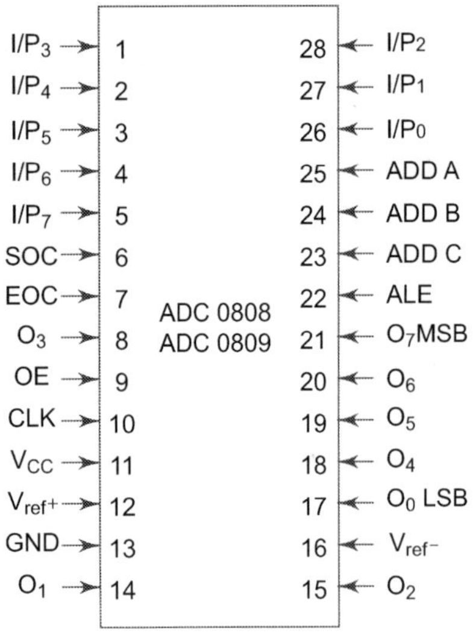

I/P_0–I/P_7	Analog inputs
ADD A, B, C	Address lines for selecting analog inputs
O_7–O_0	Digital 8-bit output with O_7 MSB and O_0 LSB
SOC	Start of conversion signal pin
EOC	End of conversion signal pin
OE	Output latch enable pin, if high enable output
CLK	Clock input for ADC
V_{CC}, GND	Supply pins +5V and GND
V_{ref+} and V_{ref-}	Reference voltage positive (+5 Volts maximum) and Reference voltage negative (0V minimum)

Fig. 5.37(b) *Pin Diagram of ADC 0808/0809*

These are unipolar analog to digital converters, i.e. they are able to convert only positive analog input voltages to their digital equivalents. These chips do not contain any internal sample and hold circuit. If one needs a sample and hold circuit for the conversion of fast signals into equivalent digital quantities, it has to be externally connected at each of the analog inputs. Figures 5.37(a) and (b) show the block diagrams and pin diagrams for ADC 0808/0809. Some electrical specifications of the ADC 0808/0809 are given in Table 5.14.

Table 5.14

Minimum SOC pulse width	100 ns
Minimum ALE pulse width	100 ns
Clock frequency	10 to 1280 kHz
Conversion time	100 ms at 640 kHz
Resolution	8-bit
Error	+/–1 LSB
V_{ref^+}	Not more than +5V
V_{ref^-}	Not less than GND
+ V_{cc} supply	+ 5 V DC
Logical 1 i/p voltage	minimum V_{cc} –1.5 V
Logical 0 i/p voltage	maximum 1.5 V
Logical 1 o/p voltage	minimum V_{cc}–0.4 V
Logical 0 o/p voltage	maximum 0.45 V

Till now we have studied the necessary details of the analog to digital converter chips 0808/0809. Now we consider some interfacing examples of these chips with 8086 so that the working of these ADCs will be absolutely clear along with the required algorithms for interfacing.

Problem 5.16

Interface ADC 0808 with 8086 using 8255 ports. Use Port A of 8255 for transferring digital data output of ADC to the CPU and Port C for control signals. Assume that an analog input is present at I/P_2 of the ADC and a clock input of suitable frequency is available for ADC. Draw the schematic and write required ALP.

The timing diagram of different signals of ADC0808 is shown in Fig. 5.38.

Fig. 5.38 *Timing Diagram of ADC 0808*

Solution Figure 5.39 shows the interfacing connections of ADC0808 with 8086 using 8255. The analog input I/P_2 is used and therefore address pins A,B,C should be 0,1,0 respectively to select I/P_2. The OE and ALE pins are already kept at +5V to select the ADC and enable the outputs. Port C upper acts as the input port to receive the EOC signal while port C lower acts as the output port to send SOC to the ADC. Port A acts as a 8-bit input data port to receive the digital data output from the ADC. The 8255 control word is written as follows:

D_7	D_6	D_5	D_4	D_3	D_2	D_1	D_0	Control word
1	0	0	1	1	0	0	0	= 98 H

The required ALP is given as follows:

```
        MOV AL,98 H        ; Initialise 8255 as
        OUT CWR,AL         ; discussed above
        MOV AL,02H         ; Select I/P2 as analog
        OUT PORT B,AL      ; input
        MOV AL,00H         ; Give start of conversion
        OUT PORT C,AL      ; pulse to the ADC.
        MOV AL,01 H        ;
        OUT PORT C,AL      ;
        MOV AL,00H         ;
        OUT PORT C,AL      ;
WAIT :  IN AL,PORTC        ; Check for EOC by
        RCL                ; reading port C upper and
        JNC WAIT           ; rotating through carry.
        IN AL,PORTA        ; If EOC, read digital equivalent in
                                AL
        HLT                ; Stop
```

Program 5.11 *ALP for Problem 5.16*

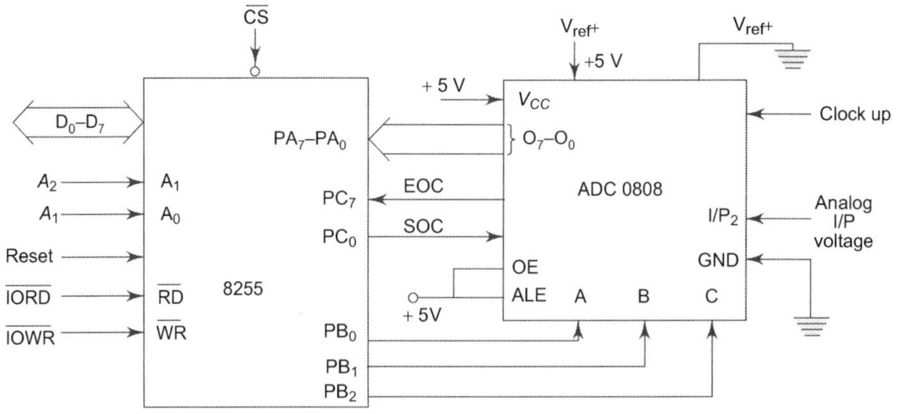

Fig. 5.39 *Interfacing 0808 with 8086*

5.6.2 ADC 7109—A Dual Slope 12-bit ADC

Intersil's ICL 7109 is a dual slope integrating analog to digital converter. This 12-bit ADC is designed to work with 8-bit and 16-bit or higher order microprocessors with great ease. As compared to other 12-bit ADCs, it is a very low cost option, useful for slow practical applications, as the method used for analog to digital conversion is dual slope integration.

The 12-bit data output, polarity and overrange signals can be directly accessed under the software control of two byte enable inputs $\overline{\text{LBEN}}$ and $\overline{\text{HBEN}}$. The RUN/$\overline{\text{HOLD}}$ and STATUS outputs allow monitoring and control of the conversion process. The salient features of the ADC 7109 are as given as follows:

1. 12-bit data output equivalent to analog input along with polarity, over range and under range outputs
2. It can be operated in parallel or serial output mode
3. Differential input and differential reference
4. Low noise (Typical 15 mV p-p)
5. Low input current (Typical 1pA)
6. Can operate up to 30 conversions per second, with an external crystal or RC circuit used to decide the operating clock frequency.

The pin diagram of the ADC is given here followed by brief signal descriptions, in Fig. 5.40 and Table 5.15 respectively.

Table 5.15 *Pin Assignment and Function Description*

Pin	*Symbol*	*Description*		
1.	GND	Digital Ground return for all digital logic		
2.	STATUS	Output High during integrate and deintegrate until data is latched Output Low when analog section is in Auto-Zero configuration		
3.	POL	Polarity-High for Positive input		
4.	OR	Over range-High if Overranged		
5.	B12	Bit 12	(Most Significant Bit)	
6.	B11	Bit 11		
7.	B10	Bit 10		All
8.	B9	Bit 9		three
9.	B8	Bit 8		state
10.	B7	Bit 7	High = true	output
11.	B6	Bit 6		data
12.	B5	Bit 5		bits
13.		B4		
14.		B3		
15.		B2		
16.		B1 (Least Significant Bit)		
17.	TEST	Input High—Normal Operation. Input Low—Forces all bit outputs high Note: This input is used for test purposes only. Tie high if not used.		

(*Contd.*)

Table 5.15 *(Contd.)*

Pin	*Symbol*	*Description*
18.	$\overline{\text{LBEN}}$	Low Byte Enable—With Mode (Pin 21) low, and $\overline{\text{CE / LOAD}}$ (Pin 20) low, taking this pin low activities low order byte outputs B1–B8. — With Mode (Pin 21) high, this pin serves as a low byte flag output used in handshake mode.
19.	$\overline{\text{HBEN}}$	High Byte Enable—With Mode (Pin 21) low, and $\overline{\text{CE / LOAD}}$ (Pin 20) low, taking this pin low activates high order byte outputs B9–B12. POL OR — With Mode (Pin 21) high. This pin serves as a high byte flag output used in handshake mode.
20.	$\overline{\text{CE / LOAD}}$	Chip Enable Load—With Mode (Pin 21) low. $\overline{\text{CE / LOAD}}$ serves as a master output enable. When high, B1–B12, POL OR outputs are disabled. —With Mode (Pin 21) high, this pin serves as a load strobe used in handshake mode.
21.	Mode	Input Low—Direct output mode where $\overline{\text{CE / LOAD}}$ (Pin 20). $\overline{\text{HBEN}}$ (Pin 19) and $\overline{\text{LBEN}}$ (Pin 18) act as inputs directly controlling byte outputs. Input Pulsed High—Causes Immediate entry into handshake mode and outputs data are available accordingly. Input High—Enables $\overline{\text{CE / LOAD}}$ (Pin 20). $\overline{\text{HBEN}}$ (Pin 19), and $\overline{\text{LBEN}}$ (Pin 18) as outputs, handshake mode will be entered and data output is available after conversion completion.
22.	OSC IN	Oscillator Input
23.	OSC OUT	Oscillator Output
24.	OSC SEL	Oscillatory Select—Input high configures OSC IN, OSC OUT, BUF OSC OUT as RC oscillator—clock will be of same phase and duty cycle as BUF OSC OUT. —Input low configures OSC IN, OSC OUT for crystal oscillator—clock frequency will be 1/58 of frequency at BUF OSC OUT.
25.	BUF OSC OUT	Buffered Oscillator Output
26.	RUN/ $\overline{\text{HOLD}}$	Input High—Conversion continuously performed every 8 192 clocks pulses. Input Low—converter will stop in Auto-Zero 7 counts before integrate.
27.	SEND	Input—Used in handshake mode to indicate ability of an external device to accept data. Connect to + 5V if not used.
28.	V^-	Analog Negative Supply—Nominally –5V with respect to GND (Pin 1).

(Contd.)

Table 5.15 *(Contd.)*

Pin	*Symbol*	*Description*
29.	REF OUT	Reference Voltage Output—Nominally 2.88 V down from V^- (Pin 40)
30.	BUFFER	Buffer Amplifier Output
31.	AUTO-ZERO	Auto-Zero Node—Inside foil of CAZ
32.	INTEGRATOR	Integrator Output—Outside foil of C_{INT}
33.	COMMON	Analog Common—System is Auto-Zeroed to COMMON
34.	INPUT LO	Differential Input Low Side
35.	INPUT HI	Differential Input High Side
36.	REF IN +	Differential Reference Input Positive
37.	REF CAP +	Reference Capacitor Positive
38.	REF CAP –	Reference Capacitor Negative
39.	REF IN	Differential Reference Input Negative
40.	V^-	Positive Supply Voltage—Nominally + 5V with respect to GND (Pin 1).

Note: All digital levels are positive true.

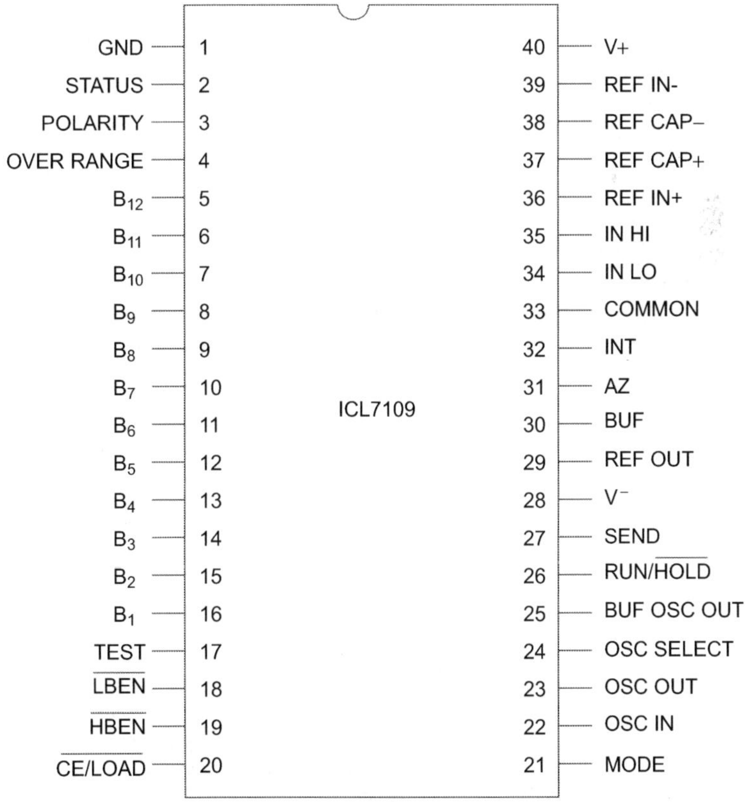

Fig. 5.40 *Pin Configuration of ICL 7109ADC*

The internal circuit of ICL 7109 is slightly complicated. Hence it is divided in two parts namely—analog section and digital section for better understanding. The following text explains the internal operation in terms of the separate sections.

Analog Section The block diagram of the internal analog section of ICL 7109 is shown in Fig. 5.41. If RUN/$\overline{\text{HOLD}}$ is either left open or connected to $+V_{cc}$, the ADC starts conversion at the rate determined by the clock frequency, to be decided either by a crystal or by an RC circuit. The total conversion cycle is divided into three phases namely *autozero phase, signal integrate phase* and *deintegrate phase.*

Autozero phase During autozero phase, input high (IN HI) and input low (IN LO) are disconnected from the external input signal and shorted to analog common. Then the reference capacitor is charged to reference voltage. A feedback loop is closed around the system to charge the autozero capacitor CAZ to compensate for the offset voltages in the buffer amplifier, integrator and comparator.

Signal integrate phase In this phase the autozero capacitor CAZ is opened out. The external input signal is connected with the internal circuit. The differential input voltage between IN LO and IN HI pins is then integrated by the internal integrator for a fixed period of 2048 clock cycles.

De-integrate phase This is the final phase of the analog to digital conversion. The input low is internally connected to analog common, and input high is connected across the previously charged reference capacitor. The capacitor then discharges through the internal circuit of the chip. Hence integrator output returns to zero crossing with a fixed slope. This time taken by the integrator output to return to zero is proportional to the input signal.

Digital Section The digital section includes the clock oscillator, 12-bit binary counter, output latches, TTL compatible output drivers, polarity, overrange and their control logics and UART handshake logic as organised in Fig. 5.42.

The digital section uses a positive logic system wherein logical 'low' corresponds to a low voltage and logical 'high' corresponds to a high voltage. The actual ranges for logical 'low' and 'high' can be obtained from the data sheets.

Intersil's 'Component Data Catalogue may be referred for the detailed information about the chip and its functioning. This text is only aimed at giving some brief introduction of the chip before we proceed for its interfacing with 8086.

Typical component value selection For the proper working of ICL 7109, it is necessary that the component values of the practical circuit are properly chosen. All the component values are recommended in the data manual but, the three components, viz. Rint, Cint and CAz should be selected suitably as all of them directly determine the required input voltage range and the operating clock frequency. The full scale input voltage range is double the voltage between REF IN- and REF IN+. The clock frequency should be integral multiple of the power supply frequency (50Hz) to achieve the optimum power supply frequency rejection. The formulae for component values selection are given as follows:

$$\text{Rint} = \frac{\text{Full scale i / p voltage}}{20\mu\text{A}}$$

$$\text{Cint} = \frac{2048 * (\text{Clockperiod}) * 20\mu\text{A}}{\text{Integrator o / p voltage swing}}$$

The ADC 7109 can either be driven with a clock frequency, derived from a crystal or from an RC circuit. If the clock frequency is derived from the crystal then the actual operating frequency is given by *f*.

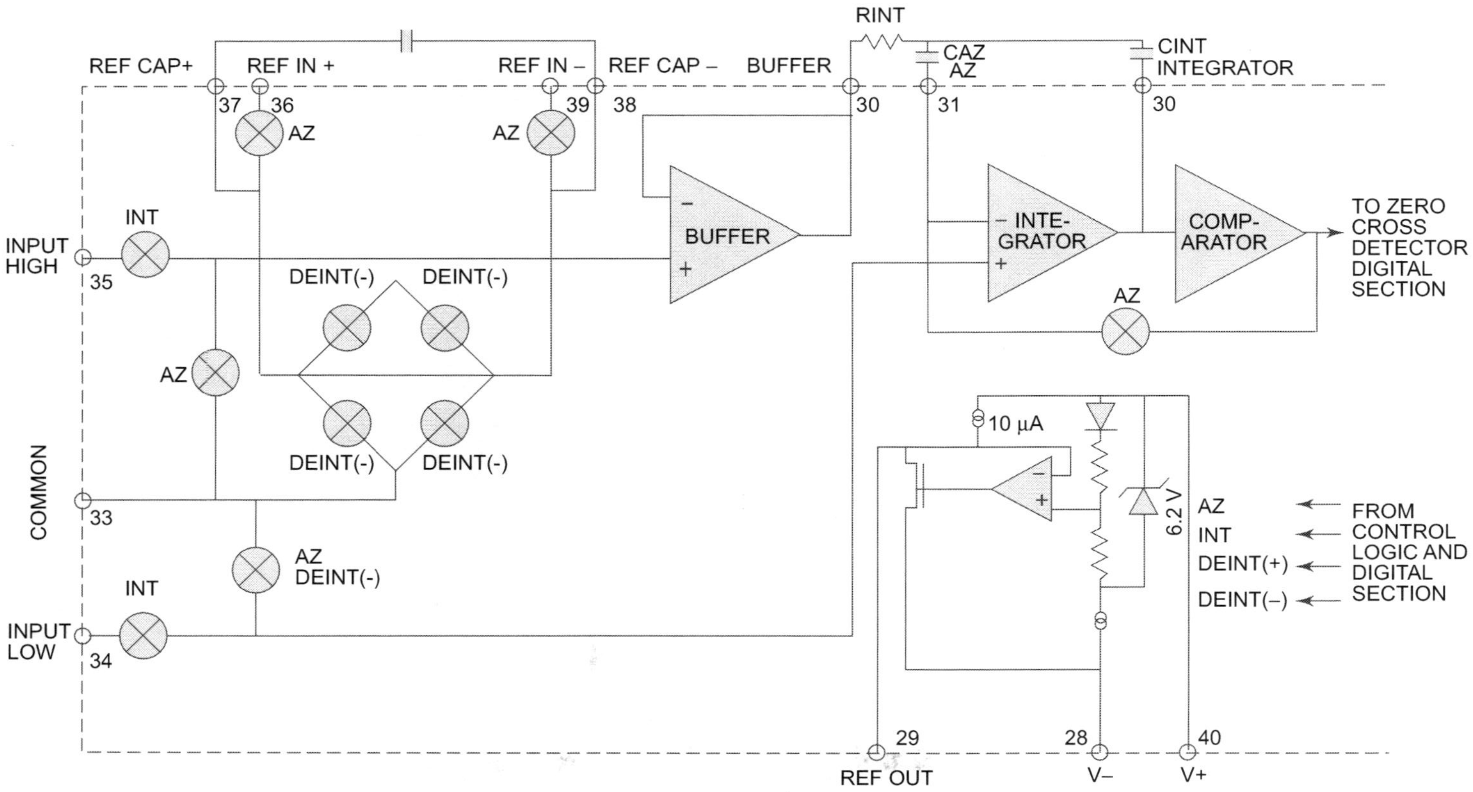

Fig. 5.41 *Analog Section of 7109*

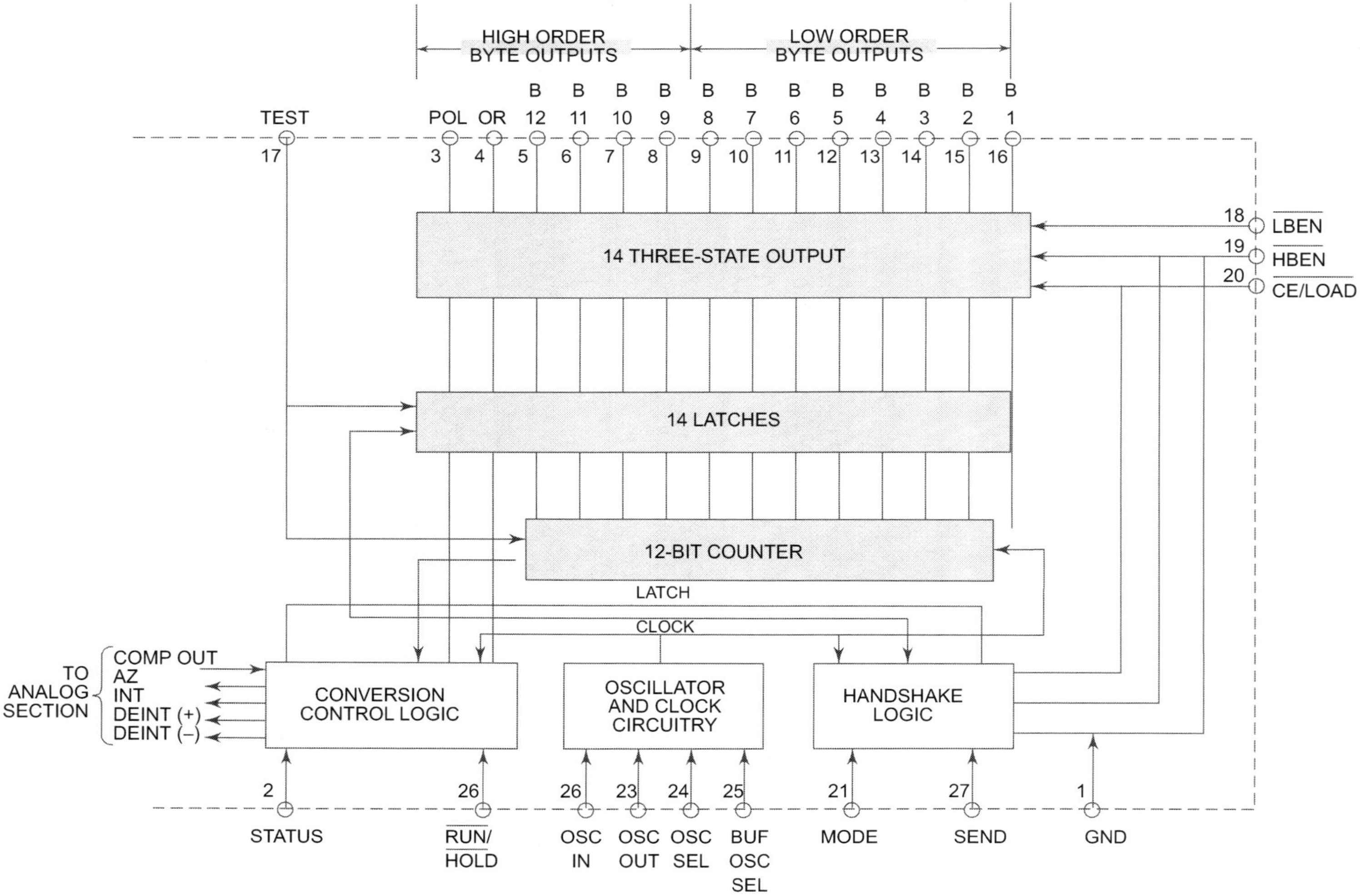

Fig. 5.42 *Digital Section of ICL 7109*

$$f = \frac{\text{Crystal freq}}{58}$$

Otherwise, if the ADC is driven by a clock frequency derived from an RC circuit it is given by the formula.

$$f = \frac{0.45}{RC}$$

5.6.3 Interfacing with 8086

Figure 5.43 shows the interfacing of ICL 7109 with 8086 using 8255. The assembly language program reads the digital equivalent output from ADC 7109 and stores it in the register CX. Note that the ADC gives only 12-bit output, hence the most significant nibble of CX must be masked.

The parallel I/O port chip 8255 is used to interface ICL 7109 with 8086. Being a 12-bit ADC, it will require 12 I/O lines for data outputs. Port A and Port C lower are used as input ports to read digital data output from the ADC. The pins $\overline{\text{LBEN}}$ and $\overline{\text{HBEN}}$ are permanently grounded to enable all the data lines from

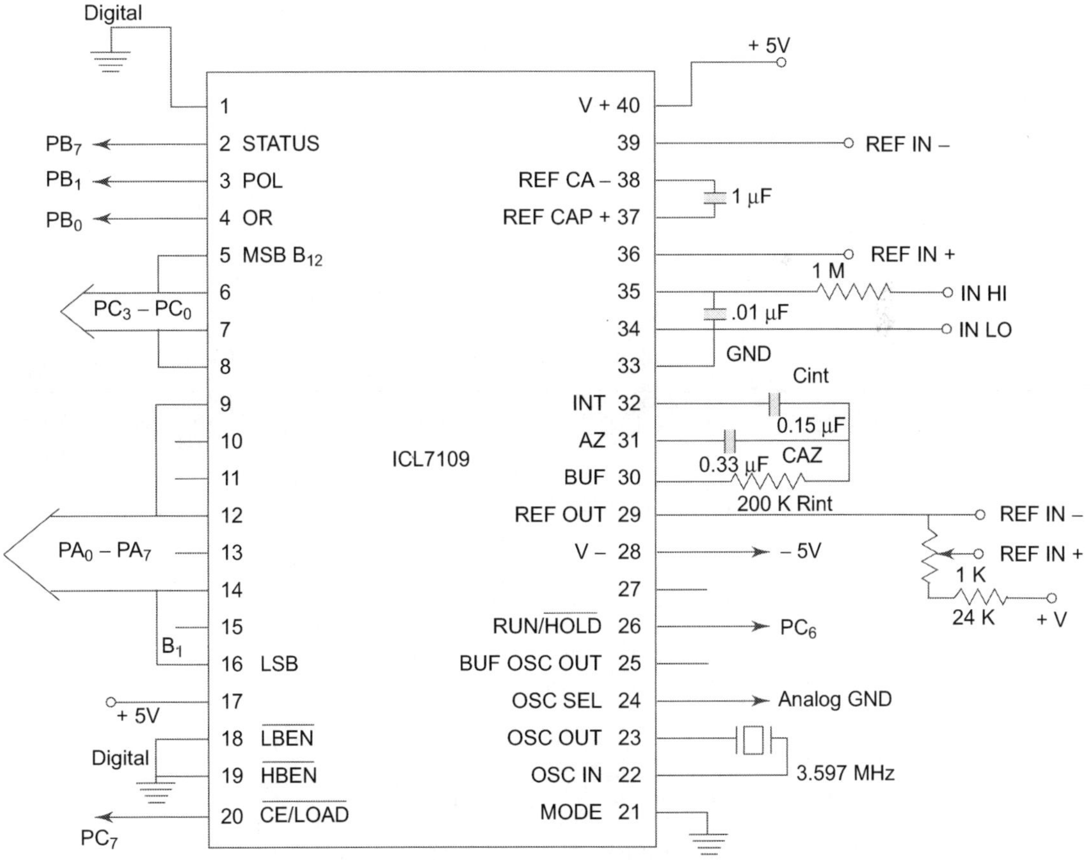

Fig. 5.43 *Interfacing 7109 with 8086 through 8255*

B_1 to B_{12} at a time. The lines $\overline{CE/LOAD}$ and RUN/$\overline{HOLD}$ are controlled using port C upper of 8255, that is used as an output port and finally port B is used to read the STATUS, POL and OR signals and hence is used as an input port. The polarity (POL) and overrange data (OR) will be available in DL register with D_0 corresponding to OR and D_1 corresponding to POL. The digital data is read from the ports if STATUS goes low, i.e. conversion if the over. Figure 5.44 shows the algorithm for the analog to digital conversion with ADC 7109. After the execution of the program the digital equivalent of the analog input is in register CX, while the overrange and polarity information is in DL. From the above description 8255 control word comes out to be 93H.

The above circuit components are designed for 4096 mV full scale analog input range. As specified in the manual the Rint for this range is 200 K. The reference input voltage between REF IN- and REF IN+ will be half of full scale analog input voltage.

```
              ; This program issues a RUN signal to ICL7109,checks for
              ; STATUS(EOC) and reads digital output with POL and OR
                     outputs.
ASSUME        CS : CODE
CODE          SEGMENT
START:        MOV AL, 93H                   ; Initialization of
              OUT CWR, AL                   ; 8255
              MOV AL, 40 H                  ; RUN (PC6) to go high and
              OUT PORT C, AL                ; CE(PC7) to go low, for start of
                                                 conversion.
              WAIT : IN AL, PORTB           ; Read STATUS signal.
              RCL AL, 01                    ; Check STATUS using carry flag.
              JC WAIT                       ; Wait till carry (STATUS) goes
              IN AL, PORTA                  ; low i.e. conversion is over.
              MOV CL, AL
              IN AL, PORTC                  ; Read digital data output and store
                                                 the
              AND AL, OFH                   ; lower byte in CL and higher byte
                                                 in CH. Mask
              MOV CH, AL                    ; higher bits of CH as of only 12
                                                 bits are of interest.
              IN AL,PORTB                   ; Store OR and POL in D0 and D1 in
              MOV DL,AL                     ; DL register.
              MOV AH,4CH                    ; Return to DOS.
              INT 21H
 CODE         ENDS
              END START
```

Program 5.12 *ALP for Interfacing ICL 7109 with 8086*

Readers may find a number of other 8-bit and 12-bit ADCs, their details and interfacing techniques from the respective data manuals or other textbooks. The discussion here is mainly aimed at explaining the general interfacing techniques of ADCs though the specific ADCs are discussed in detail.

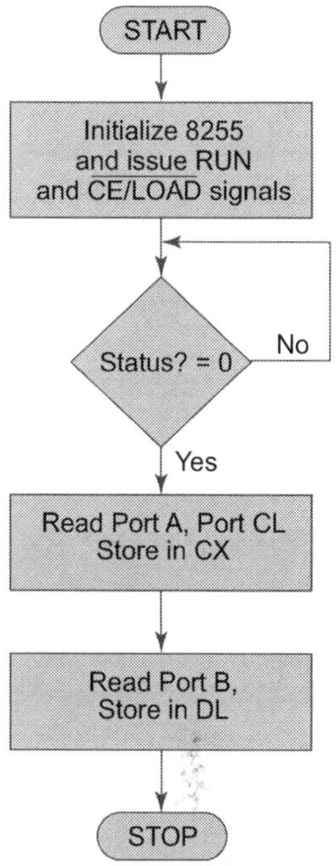

Fig. 5.44 *Algorithm for reading O/P of 7109*

5.7 INTERFACING DIGITAL TO ANALOG CONVERTERS

The digital to analog converters convert binary numbers into their analog equivalent voltages. The DAC find applications in areas like digitally controlled gains, motor speed controls, programmable gain amplifiers, etc. This text explains the generally available DAC integrated circuits and their interfacing techniques with the microprocessor.

5.7.1 AD 7523 8-bit Multiplying DAC

Intersil's AD 7523 is a 16 pin DIP, multiplying digital to analog converter, containing R-2R ladder (R = 10 K) for digital to analog conversion along with single pole double throw NMOS switches to connect the digital inputs to the ladder.

Pin diagram of AD7523 is shown in Fig. 5.45.

The supply range extends from +5V to +15V, while V_{ref} may be any where between –10V to +10V. The maximum analog output voltage will be +10V, when all the digital inputs are at logic high state. Usually a Zener is connected between OUT1 and OUT2 to save the DAC from negative transients. An operational amplifier is used as a current-to-voltage converter at the output of AD 7523 to convert the current output of AD7523 to a proportional output voltage. It also offers additional drive capability to the DAC output. An external feedback resistor acts to control the gain. One may not connect any external feedback resistor, if no gain control is required. The following example explains the interfacing of AD 7523 with 8086.

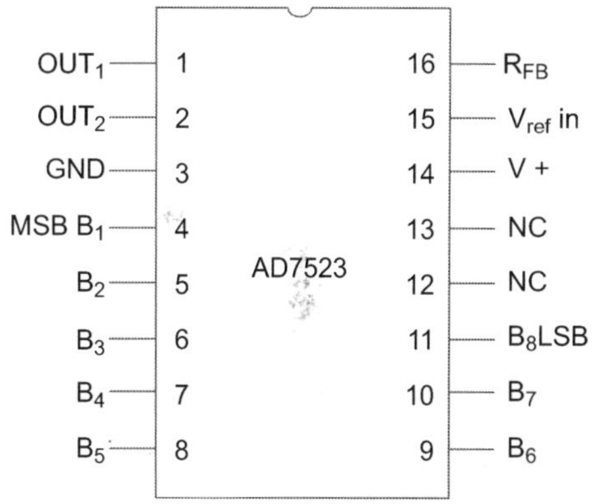

Fig. 5.45 *Pin Diagram of AD7523*

Problem 5.17

Interface DAC AD7523 with an 8086 CPU running at 8 MHz and write an assembly language program to generate a sawtooth waveform of period 1 ms with V_{max} 5V.

Solution Figure 5.46 shows the interfacing circuit of AD 7523 with 8086 using 8255. Program 5.13 gives an ALP to generate a sawtooth waveform using this circuit.

```
ASSUME      CS : CODE
```

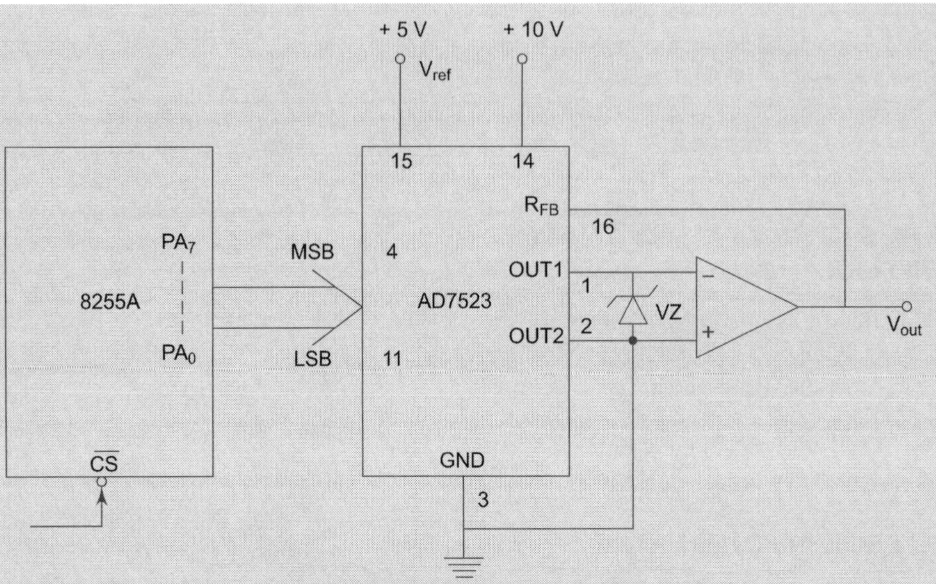

Fig. 5.46 *Interfacing of AD7523*

```
CODE      SEGMENT
START:    MOV AL,80 H        ; Initialise port A as output
          OUT CWR,AL         ; port
AGAIN:    MOV AL,00H         ; Start the ramp from 0V
BACK :    OUT PORTA,AL       ; Input 00H to DAC
          INC AL             ; Increment AL to increase ramp output
          CMP AL,0F2H        ; Is upper limit reached?
          JB BACK            ; If not, then increment the ramp
          JMP AGAIN          ; Else start again from 00H
CODE      ENDS
          END START
```

Program 5.13 *ALP for Generating Sawtooth Waveform Using AD 7523*

In the above program, port A is initialized as the output port for sending the digital data as input to DAC. The ramp starts from the 0V (analog), hence AL starts with 00H. To increment the ramp, the content of AL is incremented during each execution of the loop till it reaches F2H. After that the saw tooth wave again starts from 00H, i.e. 0V(analog), and the procedure is repeated. Note that the ramp period given by this program is precisely 1.000625 ms. Here the count F2H has been calculated by dividing the required delay of 1ms by the time required for the execution of the loop once. The ramp slope can be controlled (reduced) by calling a controllable delay after the OUT instruction. It may be noted here that meeting the frequency, i.e. time and amplitude requirement exactly is slightly difficult in such applications.

5.7.2 DAC0800 8-bit Digital to Analog Converter

The DAC 0800 is a monolithic 8-bit DAC manufactured by National Semiconductor. It has settling time around 100 ms and can operate on a range of power supply voltages, i.e. from 4.5 V to + 18 V. usually the supply V+ is 5 V or +12 V. The V-pin can be kept at a minimum of –12 V. The pin diagram of DAC 0800 is shown in Fig. 5.47. The pin definitions are self explanatory. Figure 5.48 shows interfacing of 0800 DAC with 8086.

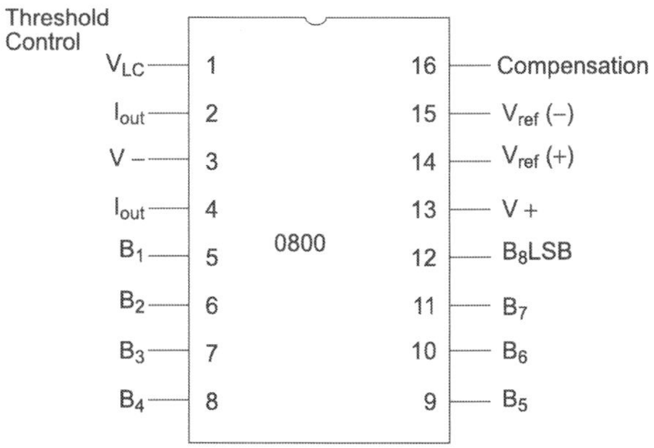

Fig. 5.47 *Pin Diagram of DAC 0800*

Problem 5.18

Write an assembly language program to generate a triangular wave of frequency 500 Hz using the interfacing circuit given in Fig. 5.48. The 8086 system operates at 8 MHz. The amplitude of the triangular wave should be +5 V.

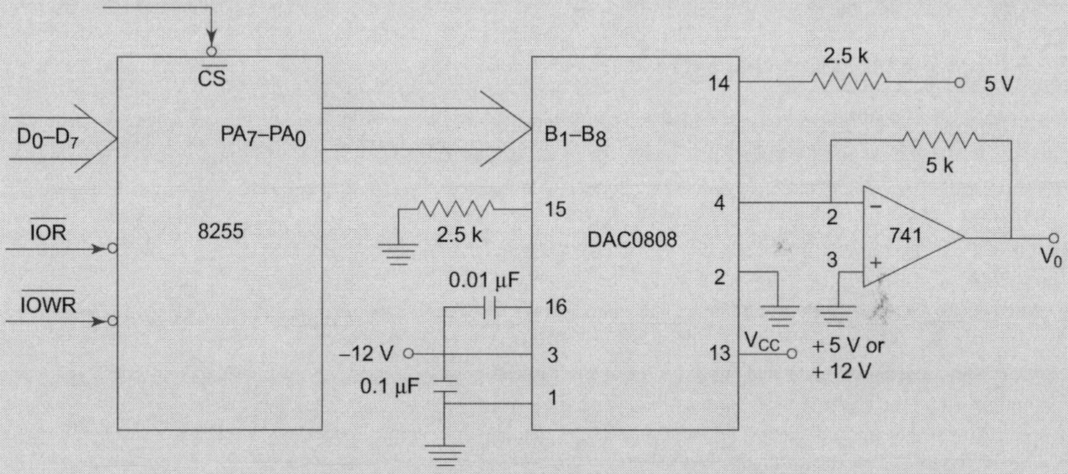

Fig. 5.48 *Interfacing DAC0800 with 8086*

Solution The V_{ref+} should be tied to +5 V to generate a wave of +5V amplitude. The required frequency of the output is 500 Hz, i.e. the period is 2 ms. Assuming the wave to be generated is symmetric, the waveform will rise for 1 ms and fall for 1 ms. This will be repeated continuously. In the previous program, we have already written an instruction sequence for period 1 ms. Using the same instruction sequence one can derive this triangular waveform. The ALP is given as follows:

```
ASSUME    CS : CODE
CODE      SEGMENT
START :   MOV AL,80 H          ; Initialise 8255 ports
          OUT CWR,AL           ; suitably.
          MOV AL,00H           ; Start rising ramp from
```

```
BACK :    OUT PORT A,AL      ; 0V by sending 00H to DAC.
          INC AL             ; Increment ramp till 5V
          CMP AL,FFH         ; i.e. FFH.
          JB BACK            ; If it is FFH then,
BACK1 :   OUT PORT A,AL      ; Output it and start the falling
          DEC AL             ; ramp by decrementing the
          CMP AL,00          ; counter till it reaches
          JA BACK1           ; zero. Then start again
          JMP BACK           ; for the next cycle.
CODE      ENDS
          END START
```

Program 5.14 *ALP for Generating a Triangular Wave Using DAC 0800*

The technique of interfacing 12-bit DACs with 8086 is also similar. If 8-bit ports are used for interfacing a 12-bit DAC, two successive 8-bit OUT instructions are required to apply input to the DAC. If a 16-bit port is used for interfacing a 12-bit DAC, a single OUT instruction is sufficient to apply the 12-bit input to the DAC. 12-bit DACs generate more precise analog voltages ($2^{12} = 4096$ steps in full output range) as compared to 8-bit DACs ($2^8 = 256$ steps in full output range).

5.8 STEPPER MOTOR INTERFACING

A stepper motor is a device used to obtain an accurate position control of rotating shafts. It employs rotation of its shaft in terms of steps, rather than continuous rotation as in case of AC or DC motors. To rotate the shaft of the stepper motor, a sequence of pulses is needed to be applied to the windings of the stepper motor, in a proper sequence. The number of pulses required for one complete rotation of the shaft of the stepper motor are equal to its number of internal teeth on its rotor. The stator teeth and the rotor teeth lock with each other to fix a position of the shaft. With a pulse applied to the winding input, the rotor rotates by one teeth position or an angle x. The angle x may be calculated as:

$$x = 360°/\text{no. of rotor teeth}$$

After the rotation of the shaft through angle x, the rotor locks itself with the next tooth in the sequence on the internal surface of stator. The internal schematic of a typical stepper motor with four windings is shown in Fig. 5.49(a). The stepper motors have been designed to work with digital circuits. Binary level pulses of 0–5V are required at its winding inputs to obtain the rotation of shafts. The sequence of the pulses can be decided, depending upon the required motion of the shaft. Figure 5.49(b) shows a typical winding arrangement of the stepper motor. Figure 5.49(c) shows conceptual positioning of the rotor teeth on the surface of rotor, for a six teeth rotor.

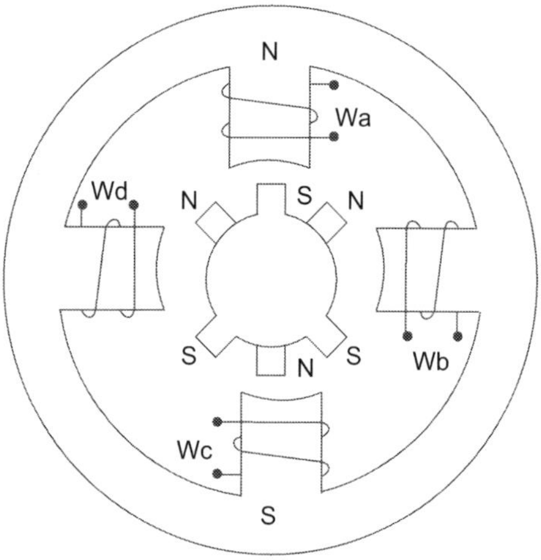

Fig. 5.49(a) *Internal Schematic of a Four Winding Stepper Motor*

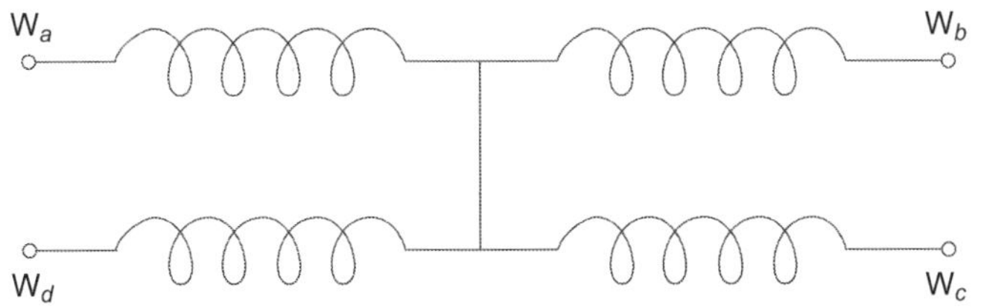

Fig. 5.49(b) *Winding Arrangement of a Stepper Motor*

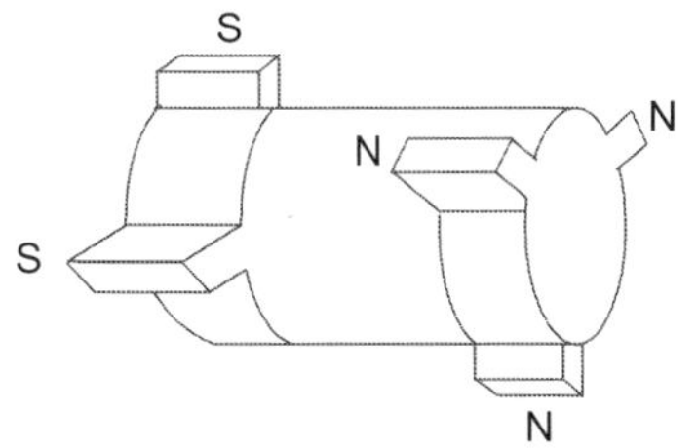

Fig. 5.49(c) *A Stepper Motor Rotor*

The circuit for interfacing a winding W_n with an I/O port is given in Fig. 5.50. Each of the windings of a stepper motor need this circuit for its interfacing with the output port. A typical stepper motor may have parameters like torque 3 kg-cm, operating voltage 12 V, current rating 0.2 A and a step angle 1.8°, i.e. 200 steps/revolution (number of rotor teeth).

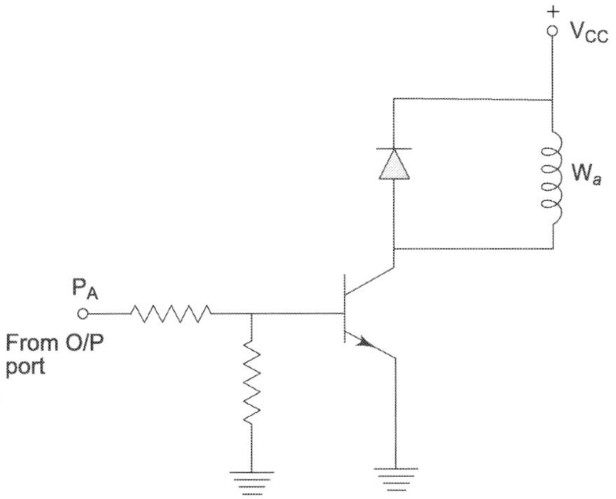

Fig. 5.50 *Interfacing Stepper Motor Winding W_a*

A simple scheme for rotating the shaft of a stepper motor is called a wave scheme. In this scheme, the windings W_a, W_b, W_c and W_d are applied with the required voltage pulses, in a cyclic fashion. By reversing the sequence of excitation, the direction of rotation of the stepper motor shaft may be reversed. Table 5.16(a) shows the excitation sequences for clockwise and anticlockwise rotations. Another popular scheme for rotation of a stepper motor shaft applies pulses to two successive windings at a time but these are shifted only by one position at a time. This scheme for rotation of stepper motor shaft is shown in Table 5.16(b).

Table 5.16(a) *Excitation Sequences of a Stepper Motor Using Wave Switching Scheme*

Motion	*Step*	*A*	*B*	*C*	*D*
Clockwise	1	1	0	0	0
	2	0	1	0	0
	3	0	0	1	0
	4	0	0	0	1
	5	1	0	0	0

(Contd.)

Table 5.16(a) *(Contd.)*

Motion	*Step*	*A*	*B*	*C*	*D*
Anticlockwise	1	1	0	0	0
	2	0	0	0	1
	3	0	0	1	0
	4	0	1	0	0
	5	1	0	0	0

The following problem elaborates stepper motor interfacing circuit and the required programming. A number of schemes are available for rotating shaft of a stepper motor. The above two schemes are generally used in practical applications.

Problem 5.19

Design a stepper motor controller and write an ALP to rotate shaft of a 4-phase stepper motor:

(i) in clockwise 5 rotations

(ii) in anticlockwise 5 rotations

Table 5.15(b) *An Alternative Scheme for Rotating Stepper Motor Shaft*

Motion	*Step*	*A*	*B*	*C*	*D*
Clockwise	1	0	0	1	1
	2	0	1	1	0
	3	1	1	0	0
	4	1	0	0	1
	5	0	0	1	1
Anticlockwise	1	0	0	1	1
	2	1	0	0	1
	3	1	1	0	0
	4	0	1	1	0
	5	0	0	0	0

The 8255 port A address is 0740H. The stepper motor has 200 rotor teeth. The port A bit PA_0 drives winding W_a, PA1 drives W_b and so on. The stepper motor has an inertial delay of 10 m sec. Assume that the routine for this delay is already available.

Solution The stepper motor connections for all the four windings are shown in Fig. 5.51. The ALP for rotating the shaft of the stepper motor is shown in Program 5.15.

```
ASSUME CS : CODE
CODE SEGMENT
START:     MOV AL, 80H
```

```
          OUT CWR, AL
          MOV AL, 88H          ; Bit pattern 10001000 to start
          MOV CX, 1000         ; the sequence of excitation
AGAIN1:   OUT PORT A,AL        ; from WA. Excite WA, WB,
          CALL DELAY           ; WC and WD in sequence with delay. For 5
                                    clockwise
          ROL AL, 01           ; rotations the count is 200*5 = 1000.
          DEC CX               ; Excite till count = 0.
          JNZ AGAIN1
          MOV AH, 88H          ; Bit pattern to excite WA.
          MOV CX, 1000         ; Count for 5 rotations
```

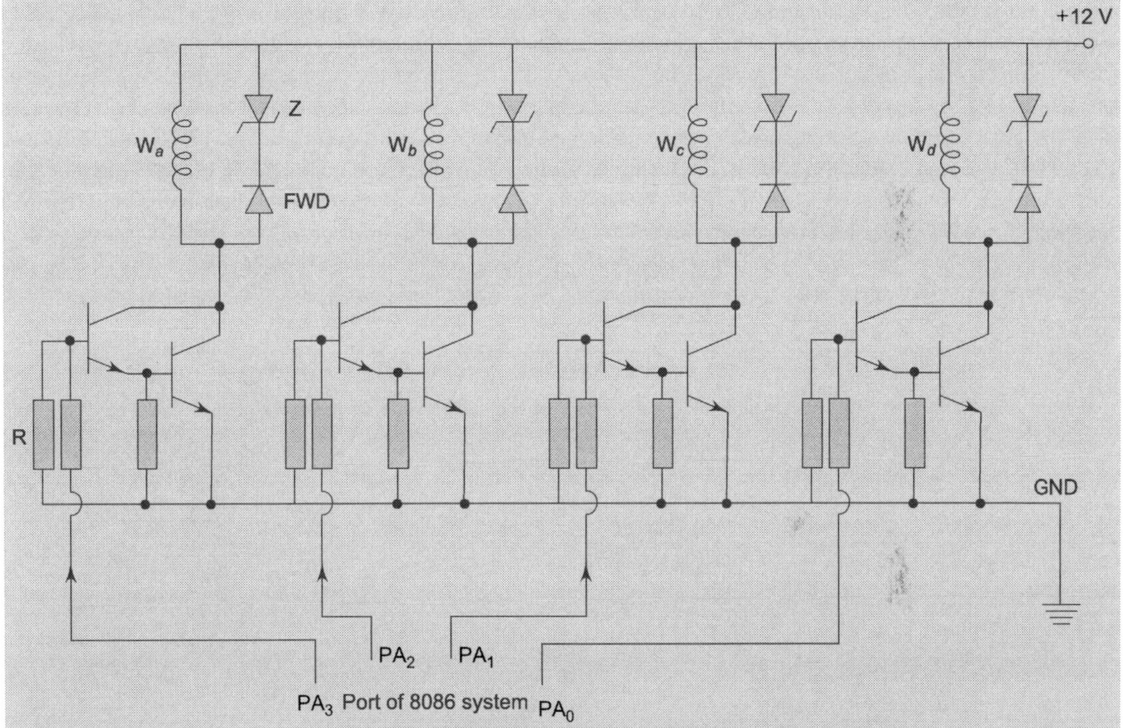

Fig. 5.51 *Stepper Motor Windings Connections*

```
AGAIN2:   OUT PORTA,AL         ; Excite WA, WB, WC, and WD.
          CALL DELAY           ; Wait.
          ROR AL, 01           ; Rotate bit pattern right to obtain
                                    anticlockwise
          DEC CX               ; motion of shaft. Decrement count.
          JNZ AGAIN2           ; If 5 rotations are completed
          MOV AH, 4CH          ; return to DOS else
          INT 21H              ; Continue
CODE      ENDS
          END START
```

Program 5.15 *ALP for Problem 5.19*

The count for rotating the shaft of the stepper motor through a specified angle may be calculated from the number of rotor teeth. The number of rotor teeth is equal to the count for one rotation, i.e. 360°. Hence for any specified angle $\theta°$ the count is calculated as:

$$C = \frac{\text{Number of rotor teeth}}{350} \times \theta°$$

5.9 CONTROL OF HIGH POWER DEVICES USING 8255

High power devices like motors, heating furnaces, temperature baths and other process equipments may be controlled using I/O ports of a microcomputer system. These are controlled using power electronics devices like SCRs, triacs, etc. These devices control the flow of energy to the processes to be controlled. This is obtained by controlling the firing angle of SCRs or Triacs. In the early days, the firing angles of thyristors were controlled using pulse generating circuits like relaxation oscillators but with the advancement in the field of microprocessors, it was observed that SCRs or triacs can be more accurately fired using a microprocessor. The main problem in this method lies in isolation between low power and high power circuits. A microprocessor circuit is a low power circuit, while an electrical circuit of a furnace is a high power circuit. Even any switching component of a high power circuit may be sufficient to damage the microprocessor system. Hence to protect this low power circuit, isolation is necessary. Isolation transformers are generally used for this purpose. Optoisolators also provide excellent isolation between high power and low power sides. Moreover, they are compact in size and cost effective as compared to the pulse transformers. The I/O signals generated by the microprocessor for these high power devices are applied through these isolating circuits as shown in Figs 5.52 (a) and (b).

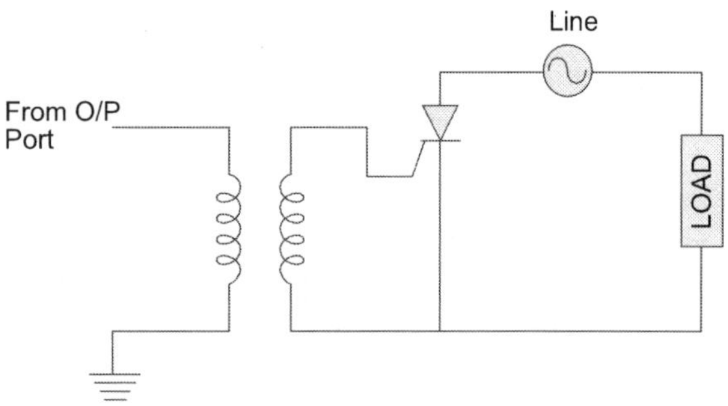

Fig. 5.52(a) *Isolation Using Transformers*

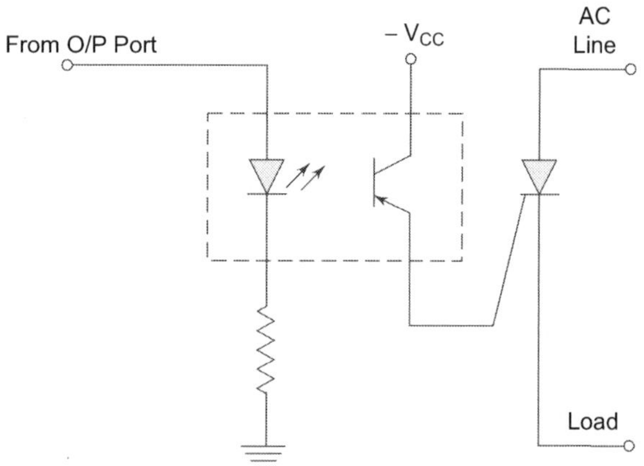

Fig. 5.52(b) *Isolation Using Opto-Isolators*

SUMMARY

In this chapter, we have presented some of the peripheral devices and their interfacing circuits. To start with, the interfacing of static and dynamic memories have been discussed with examples. Then general concepts of I/O devices and their interfacing with 8086 are briefly explained. The parallel programmable peripheral interface

8255 has been presented in significant details along with the interfacing examples and programs for each of its operating modes. Further, a few important devices like ADCs, DACs and stepper motor have been discussed with an emphasis on their interfacing with 8086. The discussion concludes with a brief note on control of power (control) electronics devices. A number of advanced I/O devices are available which can be interfaced with the CPU using I/O ports, and the interfacing techniques of all these devices to be interfaced using I/O ports are similar in principle. Besides this, a large family of special purpose programmable peripheral devices is also available. This contributes considerably to the development of the recently available advanced computer, communication and automatic control systems. Some of these peripherals are explained in the next chapter.

EXERCISES

5.1 Interface four 8K chips of static RAM and four 4K chips of EPROM with 8086. Interface two of the RAM chips in the zeroth segment so as to accommodate IVT in them. The remaining two RAM chips are to be interfaced at the end of the fifth segment. Two EPROM chips should be interfaced so that the system is restartable as usual, and the remaining two EPROM chips should be interfaced at the starting of A000th segment. Use absolute decoding scheme.

5.2 Interface eight 8K chips of RAM and four 8K chips of EPROM with 8086. Interface the RAM bank at a segment address 0B00H and the EPROM bank at a physical address F8000H. Do not allow any fold back space.

5.3 Interface eight 8K chips of RAM and four 8K $\times$ 4 chips of EPROM with 8086 at the further specified address map. You may use linear decoding scheme for minimising the required hardware.

Chips	Segment Address	Starting Offset Address
RAM1 and RAM2	0000H	0000H
RAM3 and RAM4	0500H	5000H
RAM5 and RAM6	7000H	2000H
RAM7 and RAM8	E000H	A000H
EPROM1 and EPROM2	F000H	0000H
EPROM3 and EPROM4	D000H	7000H

Will this system be practically useful? Explain. If not then what minimum change do you suggest in this address map?

5.4 Interface two 8K RAM chips and two 4K EPROM chips with 8088 so as to form a completely working system configuration.

5.5 Describe the procedure of interfacing static memories with a CPU? Bring out the differences between interfacing the memories with 8086 and 8088.

5.6 Bring out the differences between static and dynamic RAM.

5.7 Design a 2-digit seconds counter using 74373 output ports.

5.8 Design a 3-digit pulse counter using 74373 output ports to count TTL compatible pulses using an input line of a 74245 input port.

5.9 Generate a square wave of period 1sec using 74373 output ports.

5.10 Design a multiplexed display scheme to display seconds, minutes and hours counter using 8255 ports. Assume that a standard delay of 1 second is available.

5.11 Design a one unit 14-segment alphanumeric display and write a program to display an alphanumeric character of which the code is in AX.

5.12 Interface an 8255 with 8086 so as to have port A address 00, port B address 02, port C address 01 and CWR address 03.

5.13 Explain the different modes of operation of 8255.

5.14 Explain the control word format of 8255 in I/O and BSR mode.

5.15 Write a program to print message—'This is a printer test routine.' to a printer using 8255 port initialised in mode1.

5.16 Interface an 8´8 keyboard using two 8255 ports and write a program to read the code of a pressed key.

5.17 Interface a typical 12-bit DAC with 8255 and write a program to generate a triangular waveform of period 10 ms. The CPU runs at 5 MHz clock frequency.

5.18 Using a typical 12-bit DAC generate a step waveform of duration 1sec, maximum voltage 3 volts and determine duration of each step suitably.

5.19 Draw and discuss analog and digital section of 7109 in brief.

5.20 Design a 7109 circuit to convert the analog voltage to digital equivalent at a rate of 30 samples per second.

5.21 Draw a typical stepper motor interface with 8255.

5.22 Write ALPs to rotate a 200 teeth, 4 phase stepper motor as specified below.
   (i) Five rotations clockwise and then five rotations anticlockwise.
   (ii) Rotate through angle 135° in 2 sec.
   (iii) Rotate the shaft at a speed of 10 rotations per minute.

5.23 Write ALPs to trigger a triac with a +5 V pulse of 200 msec as specified below.
   (i) At an angle 45° in each positive and negative half cycle.
   (ii) At an angle 30° in each positive half cycle.
   (iii) At an angle 20° in each negative half.

   Assume that after each zero crossing of a 50 Hz line signal an external zero crossing circuit generates an interrupt to the CPU which runs at a frequency of 5 MHz.

6 Special Purpose Programmable Peripheral Devices and Their Interfacing

INTRODUCTION

In the previous chapter, we discussed a few general purpose peripheral devices along with their interfacing techniques and example programs. More or less all the peripheral devices provide interface between the CPU and slow electromechanical processes or devices. Previously, all these interfaces were taken care of by the CPU using interrupt mechanism or polling techniques. However, due to the low speed of the processes a considerable amount of CPU time gets consumed in the interface and communication activities, resulting in reduced overall efficiency and low processing speed. To minimize the slow speed I/O communication overhead, a set of dedicated programmable peripheral devices have been introduced. Once initiated by the CPU, these programmable peripheral devices take care of all the interface activities for which they have been designed. Thus the CPU becomes free from the interface activities and can execute its main task more efficiently. In this chapter, we present several integrated programmable peripherals and their interfacing techniques. More advanced peripherals based on DMA controlled data transfer will be discussed in the next chapter.

6.1 PROGRAMMABLE INTERVAL TIMER 8254

In Chapter 4, we have shown that it is not possible to generate an arbitrary time delay precisely using delay routines. Intel's programmable counter/timer device (8254) facilitates the generation of accurate time delays. When 8254 is used as a timing and delay generation peripheral, the microprocessor becomes free from the tasks related to the counting process and can execute the programs in memory, while the timer device may perform the counting tasks. This minimizes the software overhead on the microprocessor.

6.1.1 Architecture and Signal Descriptions

The programmable timer device 8254 contains three independent 16-bit counters, each with a maximum count rate of 10 MHz. It is thus possible to generate three totally independent delays or maintain three independent counters simultaneously. All the three counters may be independently controlled by programming the three internal command word registers.

The 8-bit, bidirectional data buffer interfaces internal circuit of 8254 to microprocessor systems bus. Data is transmitted or received by the buffer upon the execution of IN or OUT instruction. The read/write logic controls the direction of the data buffer depending upon whether it is a read or a write operation. It may be noted that IN instruction reads data while OUT instruction writes data to a peripheral. The internal block diagram and pin diagram of 8254 are shown in Figs 6.1(a) and 6.1(b), respectively.

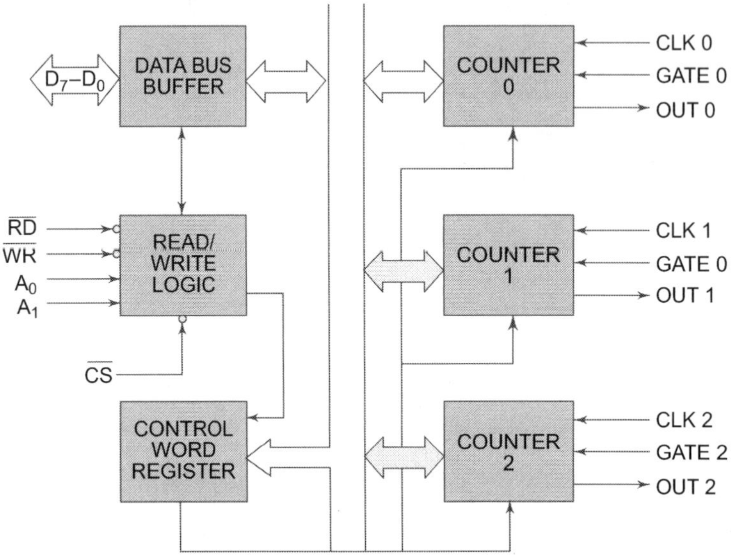

Fig. 6.1(a) *Internal Block Diagram of 8254*

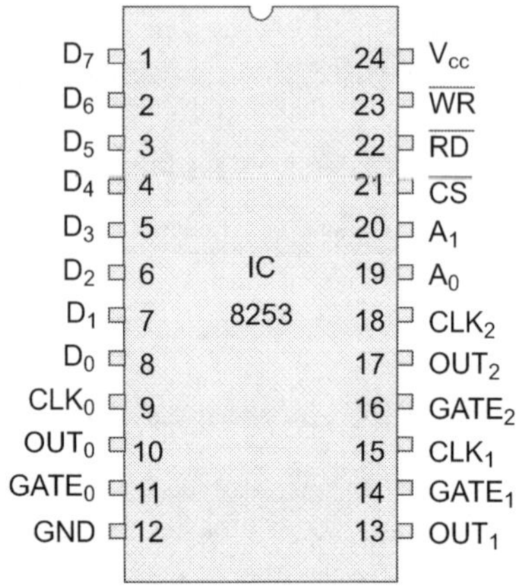

Fig. 6.1(b) *Pin Configuration of 8254*

The three counters available in 8254 are independent of each other in operation, but they are identical to each other in organization. These are all 16-bit presettable, down counters, able to operate either in BCD or in hexadecimal mode. The mode control word register contains the information that can be used for writing or reading the count value into or from the respective count register using the OUT and IN instructions. The speciality of the 8254 counters is that they can be easily read on line without disturbing the clock input to the counter. This facility is called as "on the fly" reading of counters, and is invoked using a mode control word.

A_0, A_1 pins are the address input pins and are required internally for addressing the mode control word registers and the three counter registers. A low on '$\overline{CS}$' line enables the 8254. No operation will be performed by 8254 till it is enabled. Table 6.1 shows the selected operations for various control inputs.

Table 6.1 *Selected Operations for Various Control Inputs of 8254*

$\overline{CS}$	$\overline{RD}$	$\overline{WR}$	A_1	A_0	*Selected Operation*
0	1	0	0	0	Write Counter 0
0	1	0	0	1	Write Counter 1
0	1	0	1	0	Write Counter 2
0	1	0	1	1	Write Control Word
0	0	1	0	0	Read Counter 0
0	0	1	0	1	Read Counter 1
0	0	1	1	0	Read Counter 2
0	0	1	1	1	No Operation (tristated)
0	1	1	×	×	No Operation (tristated)
1	×	×	×	×	Disabled (tristated)

A control word register accepts the 8-bit control word written by the microprocessor and stores it for controlling the complete operation of the specific counter. It may be noted that, the control word register can only be written and cannot be read as it is obvious from Table 6.1. The CLK, GATE and OUT pins are available for each of the three timer channels. Their functions will be clear when we study the different operating modes of 8254.

6.1.2 Control Word Register

The 8254 can operate in any one of the six different modes. A control word must be written in the respective control word register by the microprocessor to initialize each of the counters of 8254 to decide its operating mode. Each of the counter works independently depending upon the control word decided by the programmer as per the needs. In other words, all the counters can operate in any one of the modes or they may be even in different modes of operation, at a time. The control word format is presented, along with the definition of each bit, in Fig. 6.2.

While writing a count in the counter, it should be noted that, the count is written in the counter only after the data is put on the data bus and a falling edge appears at the clock pin of the peripheral thereafter. Any reading operation of the counter, before the falling edge appears may result in garbage data.

With this much information, on the general functioning of 8254, one may proceed further for the details of the operating modes of 8254. However, the concepts shall be clearer after one goes through the interfacing examples and the related assembly language programs.

D_7	D_6	D_5	D_4	D_3	D_2	D_1	D_0
SC1	SC0	RL1	RL0	M2	M1	M0	BCD

Control Word Format

SC_1	SC_0	OPERATION
0	0	Select Counter 0
0	1	Select Counter 1
1	0	Select Counter 2
1	1	Illegal

SC-Select Counter Bit Definitions

RL_1	RL_0	OPERATION
0	0	Latch Counter for 'ON THE FLY' reading
0	1	Read/Load Least Significant Byte only
1	0	Read/Load MSB only
1	1	Read/Load LSB first then MSB

RL-Read/Load Bit Definitions

M_2	M_1	M_0	Selected Mode
0	0	0	Mode 0
0	0	1	Mode 1
x	1	0	Mode 2
x	1	1	Mode 3
1	0	0	Mode 4
1	0	1	Mode 5

$M_2M_1M_0$ Mode Select Bit Definitions

BCD	Operation
0	Hexadecimal Count
1	BCD Count

HEX/BCD Bit Definition

Fig. 6.2 *Control Word Format and Bit Definitions*

6.1.3 Operating Modes of 8254

Each of the three counters of 8254 can be operated in one of the following six modes of operation:

1. Mode 0 (Interrupt on terminal count)
2. Mode 1(Programmable monoshot)
3. Mode 2 (Rate generator)
4. Mode 3 (Square wave generator)
5. Mode 4 (Software triggered strobe)
6. Mode 5 (Hardware triggered strobe)

In this section, we will discuss all these modes of operation of 8254 in brief.

MODE 0 This mode of operation is generally called as *interrupt on terminal* count. In this mode, the output is initially low after the mode is set. The output remains low even after the count value(5) is loaded in the counter. The counter starts decrementing the count value after the falling edge of the clock, if the GATE input is high. The process of decrementing the counter continues at each falling edge of the clock till the terminal count is reached, i.e. the count becomes zero. When the terminal count is reached, the output goes high and remains high till the selected control word register or the corresponding count register is reloaded with a new mode of operation or a new count, respectively. This high output may be used to interrupt the processor whenever required, by setting a suitable terminal count. Writing a count register while the previous counting is in process, generates the following sequence of response.

The first byte of the new count when loaded in the count register, stops the previous count. The second byte when written, starts the new count, terminating the previous count then and there.

The GATE signal is active high and should be high for normal counting. When GATE goes low counting is terminated and the current count is latched till the GATE again goes high. Figure 6.3 shows the operational waveforms in mode 0.

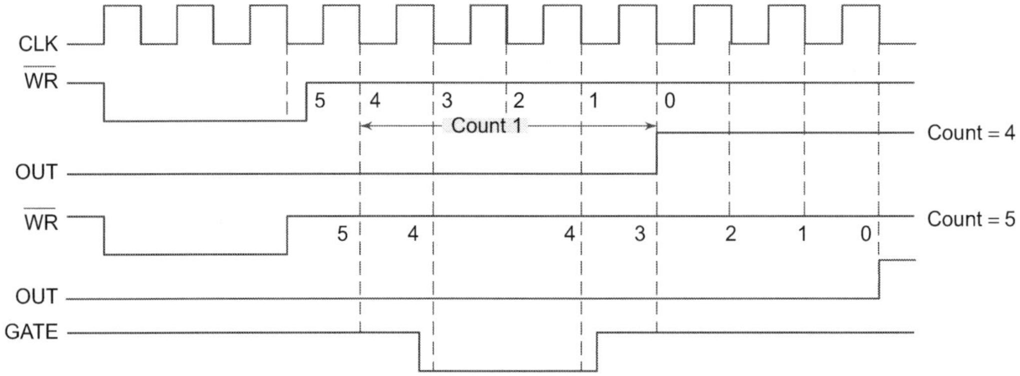

Fig. 6.3 *Waveforms of $\overline{WR}$, OUT and GATE in Mode 0*

MODE 1 This mode of operation of 8254 is called as *programmable one-shot mode*. As the name implies, in this mode, the 8254 can be used as a *monostable multivibrator*. The duration of the quasistable state of the monstable multivibrator is decided by the count loaded in the count register. The gate input is used as trigger input in this mode of operation. Normally the output remains high till the suitable count is loaded in the count register and a trigger is applied. After the application of a trigger (on the positive edge), the output goes low and remains low till the count becomes zero. If another count is loaded when the output is already low, it does not disturb the previous count till a new trigger pulse is applied at the GATE input. The new counting starts after the new trigger pulse. Figure 6.4 shows the related waveforms for mode 1.

MODE 2 This mode is called either *rate generator* or *divide by N counter*. In this mode, if *N* is loaded as the count value, then, after (*N*–1) cycles, the output becomes low only for one clock cycle. The count *N* is reloaded and again the output becomes high and remains so for (*N*–1) clock pulses. The output is normally high after initialisation or even a low signal on GATE input can force the output to go high. If GATE goes high, the counter starts counting down from the initial value. The counter generates an active low pulse at the

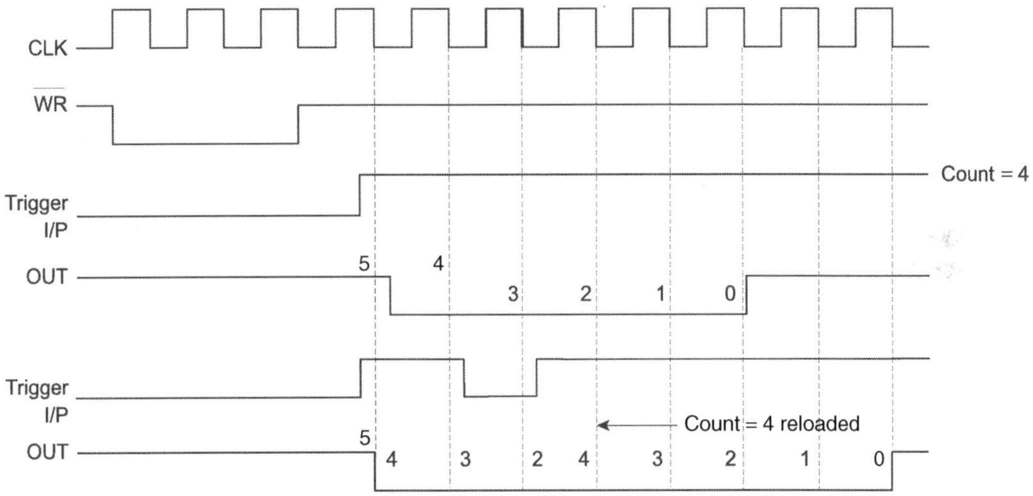

Fig. 6.4 *$\overline{WR}$, GATE and OUT Waveforms for Mode 1*

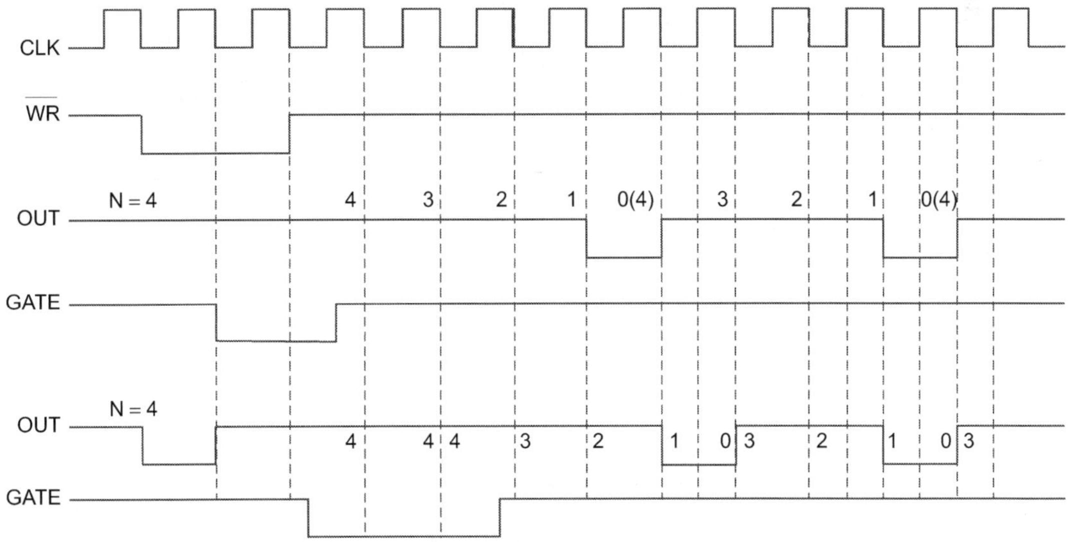

Fig. 6.5 *Waveforms at Pin $\overline{WR}$ and OUT In Mode 2*

output initially, after the count register is loaded with a count value. Then count down starts and whenever the count becomes zero another active low pulse is generated at the output. The duration of these active low pulses are equal to one clock cycle. The number of input clock pulses between the two low pulses at the output is equal to the count loaded. Figure 6.5 shows the related wave- forms for mode 2. Interestingly, the counting is inhibited when GATE becomes low.

MODE 3 In this mode, the 8254 can be used as a *square wave rate generator*. In terms of operation this mode is somewhat similar to mode 2. When, the count *N* loaded is even, then for half of the count, the output remains high and for the remaining half it remains low . If the count loaded is odd, the first clock pulse decrements it by 1 resulting in an even count value (holding the output high). Then the output remains high for half of the new count and goes low for the remaining half. This procedure is repeated continuously resulting in the generation of a square wave. In case of odd count , the output is high for longer duration and low for shorter duration. The difference of one clock cycle duration between the two periods is due to

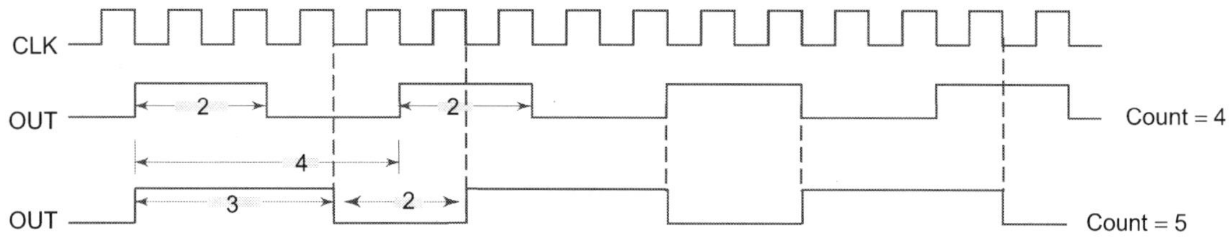

Fig. 6.6 *Waveforms for Mode 3*

the initial decrementing of the odd count. The waveforms for mode 3 are shown in Fig. 6.6. In general, if the loaded count value '*N*' is odd, then for $(N+1)/2$ pulses the output remains high and for $(N-1)/2$ pulses it remains low.

MODE 4 This mode of operation of 8254 is named as *software triggerred strobe*. After the mode is set, the output goes high. When a count is loaded, counting down starts. On terminal count, the output goes low for one clock cycle,and then it again goes high. This low pulse can be used as a strobe, while interfacing the microprocessor with other peripherals. The count is inhibited and the count value is latched, when the GATE signal goes low. If a new count is loaded in the count register while the previous counting is in progress, it is accepted from the next clock cycle. The counting then proceeds according to the new count. The related waveforms are shown in Fig. 6.7.

MODE 5 This mode of operation also generates a strobe in response to the rising edge at the trigger input. This mode may be used to *generate a delayed strobe* in response to an externally generated signal. Once this mode is programmed and the counter is loaded, the output goes high. The counter starts counting after the rising edge of the trigger input (GATE). The output goes low for one clock period, when the terminal count is reached. The output will not go low until the counter content becomes zero after the rising edge of any trigger. The GATE input in this mode is used as trigger input. The related waveforms are shown in Fig. 6.8.

6.1.4 Programming and Interfacing 8254

As it is evident from the previous discussion, there may be two types of write operations in 8254, viz. (i) writing a control word into a control word register and (ii) writing a count value into a count register. The control word

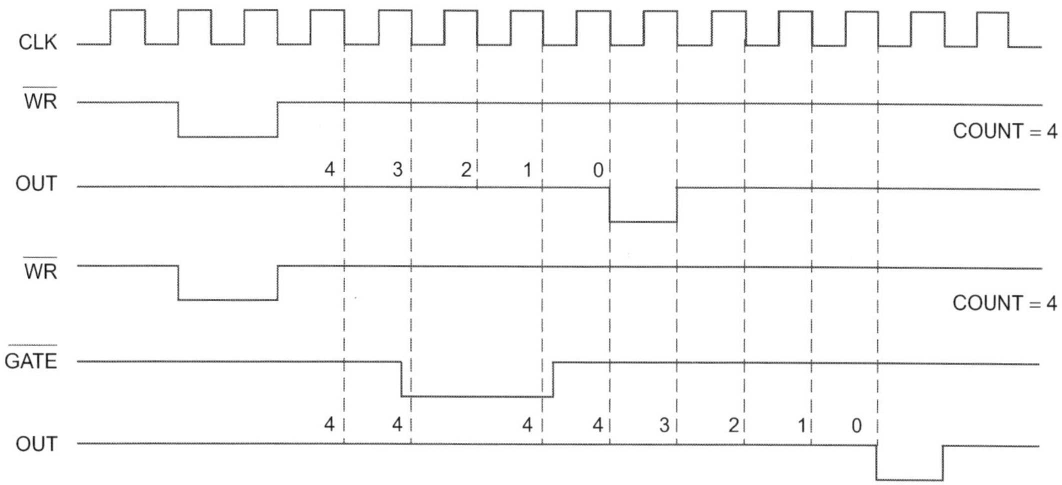

Fig. 6.7 *$\overline{WR}$, GATE and OUT Waveforms for Mode 4*

register, accepts data from the data buffer and initialises the counters, as required. The control word register contents are used for (a) initialising the operating modes (mode0–mode4) (b) selection of counters (counter0–counter2) (c) choosing binary/BCD counters (d) loading of the counter registers. The mode control register is a write only register and the CPU cannot read its contents.

One can directly write the mode control word for counter 2 or counter 1 prior to writing the control word for counter 0. Mode control word register has a separate address, so that it can be written independently. A count register must be loaded with the count value, in the same byte sequence that was

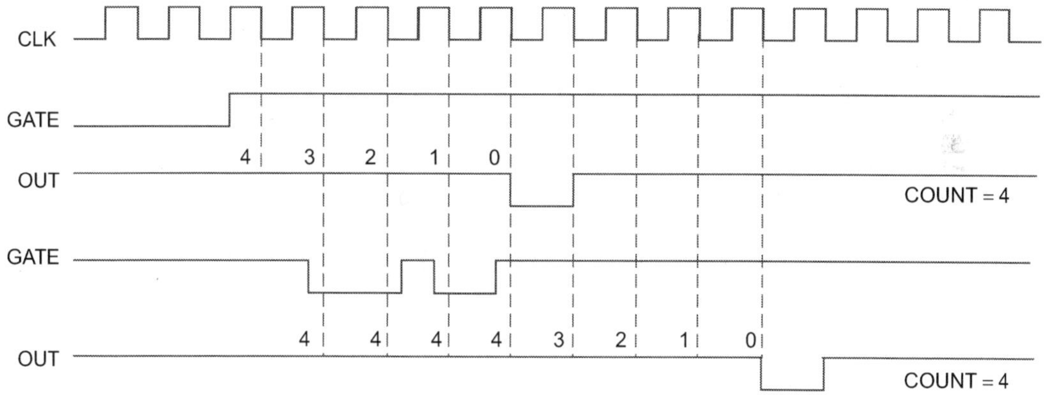

Fig. 6.8 *Waveforms in Mode 5*

programmed in the mode control word of that counter, using the bits RL_0 and RL_1. The loading of the count registers of different counters is again sequence independent. One can directly write the16-bit count register for count 2 before writing count 0 and count 1, but the two bytes in a count must be written in the byte sequence programmed using RL_0 and RL_1 bits of the mode control word of the counter. All the counters in 8254 are down counters, hence their count values go on decrementing if the CLK input pin is applied with a valid clock signal. A maximum count is obtained by loading all zeros into a count register, i.e. 2^{16} for binary counting and 10^4 for BCD counting. The 8254 responds to the negative clock edge of the clock input. The maximum operating clock frequency of 8254 is 2.6 MHz. For higher frequencies one can use timer 8254, which operates up to 10 MHz, maintaining pin compatibility with 8254. The following Table 6.2 shows the selection of different mode control words and counter register bytes depending upon address lines A_0 and A_1.

Table 6.2 *Selection of Count Registers and Control Word Register with A_1 and A_0*

Selected Register	A_1	A_0
Mode Control Word Counter 0	1	1
Mode Control Word Counter 1	1	1
Mode Control Word Counter 2	1	1
Counter Register Byte Counter 2 LSB	1	0
Counter Register Byte Counter 2 MSB	1	0
Counter Register Byte Counter 1 LSB	0	1
Counter Register Byte Counter 1 MSB	0	1
Counter Register Byte Counter 0 LSB	0	0
Counter Register Byte Counter 0 MSB	0	0

In most of the practical applications, the counter is to be read and depending on the contents of the counter a decision is to be taken. In case of 8254, the 16-bit contents of the counter can simply be read using successive 8-bit IN operations. As stated earlier, the mode control register cannot be read for any of the counters. There are two methods for reading 8254 counter registers. In the first method, either the clock or the counting procedure (using GATE) is inhibited to ensure a stable count. Then the contents are read by selecting the suitable counter using A_0, A_1 and executing using IN instructions. The first IN instruction reads the least significant byte and the second IN instruction reads the most significant byte. Internal logic of 8254 is designed in such a way that the programmer has to complete the reading operation as programmed by him, using RL_0 and RL_1 bits of control word.

In the second method of reading a counter, the counter can be read while counting is in progress. This method, as already mentioned is called as *reading on fly*. In this method, neither clock nor the counting needs to be inhibited to read the counter. The content of a counter can be read 'on fly' using a newly defined control word register format for on-line reading of the count register. Writing a suitable control word, in the mode control register internally latches the contents of the counter. The control word format for 'read on fly' mode is given in Fig. 6.9 along with its bit definitions. After latching the content of a counter using this method, the programmer can read it using IN instructions, as discussed before.

D_7	D_6	D_5	D_4	D_3	D_2	D_1	D_0
SC1	SC0	0	0	X	X	X	X

D_7–D_6 = SC1, SC0—Specify the counter to be selected as in Fig. 6.2

D_5–D_4 = 00—Designate counter latching operation

X = Don't Care—All other bits are neglected

Fig. 6.9 *Mode Control Word for Latching Count*

Problem 6.1

Design a programmable timer using 8254 and 8086. Interface 8254 at an address 0040H for counter 0 and write the following ALPs. The 8086 and 8254 run at 6 MHz and 1.5 MHz respectively.

(i) To generate a square wave of period 1 ms.

(ii) To interrupt the processor after 10 ms.

(iii) To derive a monoshot pulse with quasistable state duration 5 ms.

Solution

Neglecting the higher order address lines (A_{16}–A_8), the interfacing circuit diagram is shown in Fig. 6.10. The 8254 is interfaced with lower order data bus (D_0–D_7), hence A_0 is used for selecting the even bank. The A_0 and A_1 of the 8254 are connected with A_1 and A_2 of the processor. The counter addresses can be decoded as given below. If A_0 is 1, the 8254 will not be selected at all.

A_7	A_6	A_5	A_4	A_3	A_2	A_1	A_0	
0	1	0	0	0	0	0	0	= 40H Counter 0
					0	1	0	= 42H Counter 1
					1	0	0	= 44H Counter 2
					1	1	0	= 46H Control word Reg.

(i) For generating a square wave, 8254 should be used in mode 3.

Let us select counter 0 for this purpose, that will be operated in BCD mode (may even be operated in HEX mode). Now suitable count is to be calculated for generating 1 ms time period.

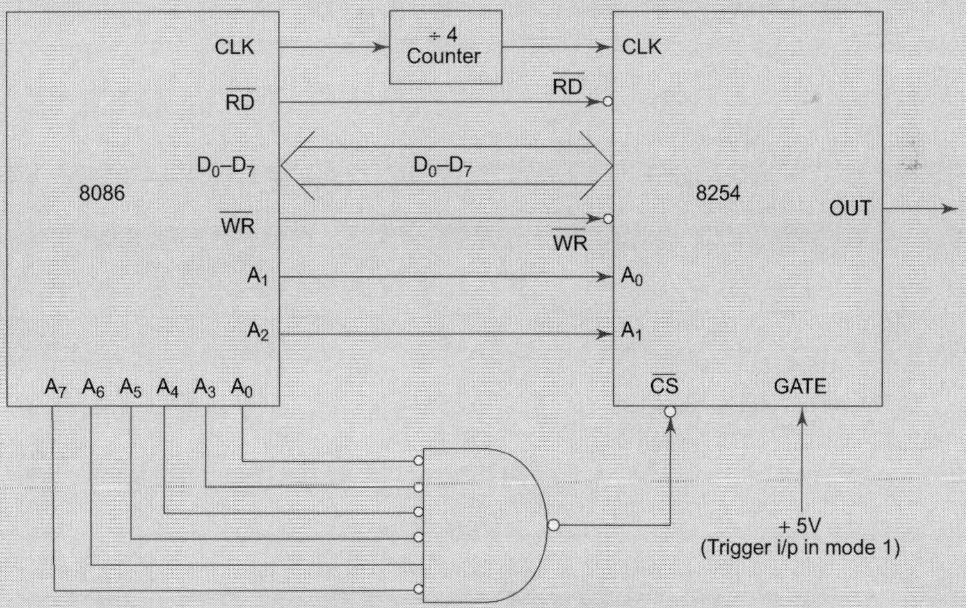

Fig. 6.10 *Interfacing 8254 with 8086 for Problem 6.1*

$f = 1.5$ MHz,

$$\Rightarrow \qquad T = \frac{1}{1.5 \times 10^{-6}} = 0.66\,\mu s$$

If N is the number of T states required for 1ms,

$$N = \frac{1 \times 10^{-3}}{0.66 \times 10^{-6}} = 1.5 \times 10^{3}$$
$$= 1500 \text{ states}$$

The control word is decided as below:

SC1	SC0	RL1	RL0	M2	M1	M0	BCD
0	0	1	1	0	1	1	1

= 37 H

The ALP is given in Program 6.1.

```
CODE        SEGMENT
ASSUME      CS : CODE
START:      MOV AL,37H          ; Initialize 8254,
            OUT 46H,AL          ; counter 0 in mode3.
            MOV AL, 00          ; Write 00 decimal
            OUT 40H, AL         ; in LSB of count reg. and
            MOV AL, 15          ; 15 decimal in MSB as a
            OUT 40 H, AL        ; count.
            MOV AH,4CH
            INT 21H
 CODE       ENDS
            END START
```

Program 6.1 *ALP For Problem 6.1(a)*

(ii) For generating interrupt to the processor after 10 ms, the 8254 is to be used in mode 0. The OUT1 pin of 8254 is connected to interrupt input of the processor. Let us use counter 1 for this purpose, and operate the 8254 in HEX count mode.

No. of T states required for 10 ms delay $= \dfrac{10 \times 10^{-3}}{0.66 \times 10^{-6}} = 15 \times 10^{3}$

$= 15000$

$= 3A98$ H

The Control word is written below:

SC1	SC0	RL1	RL0	M2	M1	M0	BCD
0	1	1	1	0	0	0	0

= 70 H

The ALP is written in Program 6.2.

```
CODE        SEGMENT
ASSUME      CS : CODE
START:      MOV AL, 70 H        ; Initialize 8254 with
            OUT 46H, AL         ; Counter1 in mode 0.
            MOV AL, 98H         ; Load 98H as LSB of count
            OUT 42H, AL         ; in count reg of counter1
            MOV AL, 3AH         ; then load 3AH in MSB
```

```
            OUT 42H, AL         ; of counter1
            MOV AH,4CH          ; RETURN TO DOS
            INT 21H             ;
CODE        ENDS
            END START
```

Program 6.2 *ALP for Problem 6.1(b)*

(iii) For generating a 5 ms quasistable state duration, the count required is calculated first. The counter 2 of 8254 is used in mode 1, to count in binary. The OUT2 signal normally remains high after the count is loaded, till the trigger is applied. After the application of a trigger signal, the output goes low in the next cycle, count down starts and whenever the count goes zero the output again goes high.

Number of T states required for 05 ms $= \dfrac{5\times10^{-3}}{0.66\times10^{-6}} = 7500$ states

$= 1\text{ D4C H}$

The Control word is written below:

SC1	SC0	RL1	RL0	M2	M1	M0	BCD
1	0	1	1	0	0	1	0

= B2 H

The ALP for the above purpose is written in Program 6.3.

```
CODE        SEGMENT
ASSUME      CS : CODE
START:      MOV AL, B2 H        ; Initialize 8254 with
            OUT 46H, AL         ; Counter 2 in mode 1
            MOV AL, 4CH         ; Load 4CH (LSB of count)
            OUT 44H, AL         ; into count register
            MOV AL, 1D          ; Load 1 DH (MSB of count)
            OUT 44H, AL         ; into count register
            MOV AH, 4CH         ; Stop
            INT2IH
CODE        ENDS
            END START
```

Program 6.3 *ALP for Problem 6.1 (c)*

Problem 6.2

Interface 8254 with 8086 at counter 0 address 7430 H and write a program to call subroutine after 100 ms. Assume that the system clock available is 2 MHz.

Solution

Address Decoding table for 8254 PIT.

Port	*HEX. address*				*Binary address*			
		A_{15} ------------			A_3	A_2	A_1	A_0
Counter 0	7430 H	0111	0100	0011	0	0	0	0
Counter 1	7432 H	0111	0100	0011	0	0	1	0
Counter 2	7434 H	0111	0100	0011	0	1	0	0
CWR	7436 H	0111	0100	0011	0	1	1	0

Description:

1. Input circuit signal to counter 0 is 2 MHz, Counter 0 is utilized in mode 3 to generate a square wave of 1 kHz.
2. Output square wave of counter 0 is given as circuit signal to counter 1, counter 1 is utilized in mode 0, t_d i.e. interrupt on terminal count.

Counter 1: For generating hardware delay of 100 ms counter 1 is used in mode 0 (i.e. interrupt on terminal count).

$$t_d = n \times t_c$$

where t_d = delay time

n = no. of count loaded in counter 1

t_c = time period of applied circuit

$$\therefore \quad t_c = \frac{1}{1\text{kHz}} = 1\text{ms}$$

Given $t_d = 100$ ms.

$$\therefore \quad n = \frac{t_d}{t_c} = \frac{100\text{ms}}{1\text{ms}} = 00$$

$$n = (100)_{\text{Decimal}}$$

Counter 0: For generating a square wave of 1 kHz counter 0 is used in mode 3 (i.e. square wave generation mode).

In mode 3 $$n = \frac{\text{input frequencey}}{\text{output frequency}} = \frac{2\text{MHz}}{1\text{kHz}} = \frac{2000\text{kHz}}{1\text{kHz}}$$

$$\therefore \quad n = (2000)_{\text{Decimal}}$$

2. Output square wave of counter 0 is given as Clk signal to Counter 1, Counter 1 is utilized in mode 0, i.e. interrupt on terminal count.

   Counter 1: For generating hardware delay of 100 msec Counter 1 is used in mode 0 (i.e. interrupt on terminal count).

$$t_d = n \times t_c$$

Where t_d = delay time

n = count loaded in Counter 1

t_c = time period of applied circuit.

$$\therefore \quad t_c = \frac{1}{1\text{kHz}} = 1\text{ms}$$

Given $t_d = 100$ ms

$$\therefore \quad n = \frac{t_d}{t_c} = \frac{100\text{ms}}{1\text{ms}} = 100$$

$$\therefore \quad n = (100)\ \text{Decimal}$$

CWR:

SC 1 SC 0 RL 1 RL 0 M 2 M 1 M 0 BCD

For Counter 0:

0	0	1	0	0	1	1	1	→ 27 H
Counter 0		Loading Only MSB		Mode 3			Counter as a BCD,	

∴ $n = (2000)_{\text{Decimal}}$

We have to load only MSB, i.e. $(20)_D$, whereas Counter is automatically initialized to $(00)_D$

For Counter 1:

0	1	1	0	0	0	0	1	→ 61 H
Counter 1		Loading only MSB			Mode 0		BCD Counter.	

$n = (0100)_D$

∴ We have to load only MSB, i.e. $(01)_D$

```
ASSUME CS : CODE, SS : STACK
STACK SEGMENT
TOP DW 100 DUP (?)
STACK ENDS
CODE SEGMENT
START  :  MOV AX, STACK
            MOV      SS, AX
            LEA        SP, TOP + 200
    MOV    DX, 7436 H          ; CWR address is transferred to DX
register.
    MOV    AL, 27H             ; Initialization of  counter 0.
    OUT    DX, AL.
    MOV    AL, 61H             ; Initialization of counter 1
    OUT    DX, AL
    MOV    AL, 20H
    MOV    DX, 7430H           ; Count 20 loaded in BCD counter 0 MSBs.
    OUT    DX, AL
    MOV    AL, 01H
    MOV    DX, 7432 H          ; Count 01 is loaded in MSBs of  counter 1
    OUT    DX, AL
    STI                        ; Set IF Flag.
    MOV    AH, 4 CH
    INT    21H
    CODE   ENDS
    END    START
```

Program 6.4 *ALP for Problem 6.2*

The circuit arrangment for this interfacing problem is as shown below:

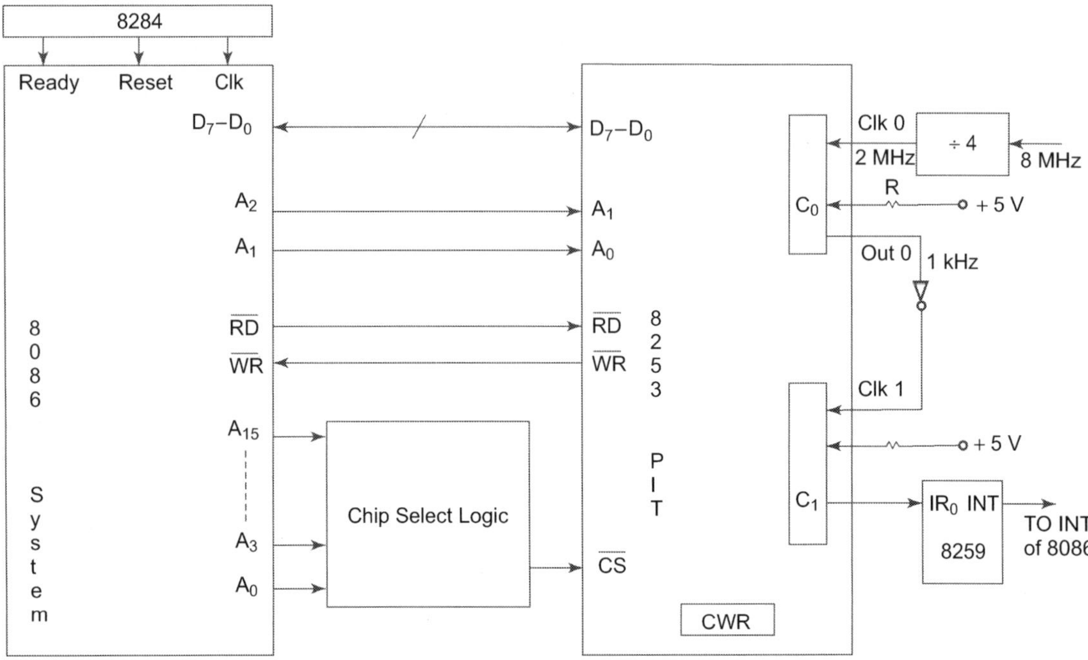

Fig. 6.11 *Interfacing 8254 with 8086 for Problem 6.2*

In all the above programs, the counting down starts as soon as the writing operation to the count register is over, and the $\overline{WR}$ pin goes high after writing. In case of 'read on fly' operation, the READ ON FLY control word for the specific counter is to be loaded in the control word register followed by the successive read operations. The 8254 and 8254 are the most widely used peripherals to generate accurate delays for industrial or laboratory purposes. The 8254 is similar to 8254 in architecture, programming and operation, hence 8254 is not discussed in this text.

6.2 PROGRAMMABLE INTERRUPT CONTROLLER 8259A

The processor 8085 had five hardware interrupt pins. Out of these five interrupt pins, four pins were allotted fixed vector addresses but the pin INTR was not allotted any vector address, rather an external device was supposed to hand over the type of the interrupt, i.e. (Type 0 to 7 for RST0 to RST7), to the microprocessor. The microprocessor then gets this type and derives the interrupt vector address from that. Consider an application, where a number of I/O devices connected with a CPU desire to transfer data using interrupt driven data transfer mode. In these types of applications, more number of interrupt pins are required than available in a typical microprocessor. Moreover, in these multiple interrupt systems, the processor will have to take care of the priorities for the interrupts, simultaneously occurring at the interrupt request pins.

To overcome all these difficulties, we require a programmable interrupt controller which is able to handle a number of interrupts at a time. This controller takes care of a number of simultaneously appearing interrupt requests along with their types and priorities. This relieves the processor from all these tasks. The programmable interrupt controller 8259A from Intel is one such device. Its predecessor 8259 was designed to operate only with 8-bit processors like 8085. A modified version, 8259A was later introduced that is compatible with 8-bit as well as 16-bit processors.

6.2.1 Architecture and Signal Descriptions of 8259A

The architectural block diagram of 8259A is shown in Fig. 6.12. The functional explanation of each block is given in the following text in brief:

Interrupt Request Register (IRR) The interrupts at IRQ input lines are handled by Interrupt Request Register internally. IRR stores all the interrupt requests in it in order to serve them one by one on the priority basis.

In-Service Register (ISR) This stores all the interrupt requests those are being served, i.e. ISR keeps a track of the requests being served.

Priority Resolver This unit determines the priorities of the interrupt requests appearing simultaneously. The highest priority is selected and stored into the corresponding bit of ISR during $\overline{\text{INTA}}$ pulse. The IR_0 has the highest priority while the IR_7 has the lowest one, normally in fixed priority mode. The priorities however may be altered by programming the 8259A in rotating priority mode.

Interrupt Mask Register (IMR) This register stores the bits required to mask the interrupt inputs. IMR operates on IRR at the direction of the Priority Resolver.

Interrupt Control Logic This block manages the interrupt and the interrupt acknowledge signals to be sent to the CPU for serving one of the eight interrupt requests. This also accepts the interrupt acknowledge (INTA) signal from CPU that causes the 8259A to release vector address on to the data bus.

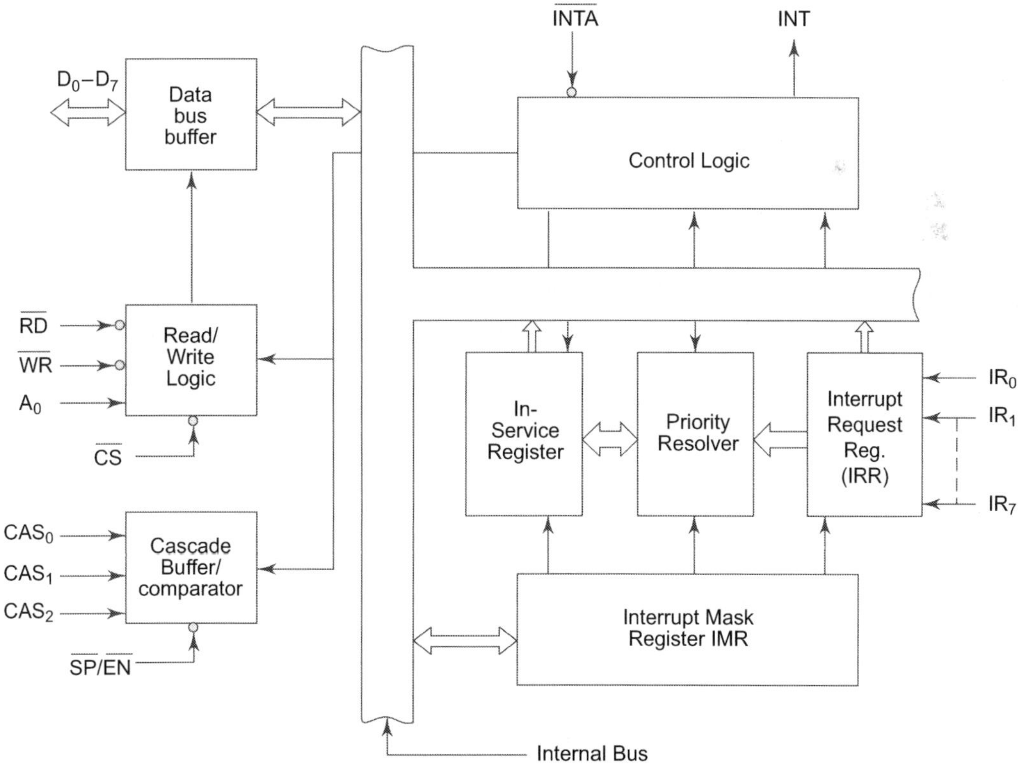

Fig. 6.12 *8259A Block Diagram*

Data Bus Buffer This tristate bidirectional buffer interfaces internal 8259A bus to the microprocessor system data bus. Control words, status and vector information pass through data buffer during read or write operations.

Read/Write Control Logic This circuit accepts and decodes commands from the CPU. This block also allows the status of the 8259A to be transferred on to the data bus.

Cascade Buffer/Comparator This block stores and compares the IDs of all the 8259As used in the system. The three I/O pins CAS0-2 are outputs when the 8259A is used as a master. The same pins act as inputs when the 8259A is in the slave mode. The 8259A in the master mode, sends the ID of the interrupting slave device on these lines. The slave thus selected, will send its pre-programmed vector address on the data bus during the next $\overline{INTA}$ pulse.

Figure 6.13 shows the pin configuration of 8259A, followed by their functional description of each of the signals in brief.

CS This is an active-low chip select signal for enabling $\overline{RD}$ and $\overline{WR}$ operations of 8259A. $\overline{INTA}$ function is independent of $\overline{CS}$.

$\overline{WR}$ This pin is an active-low write enable input to 8259A. This enables it to accept command words from CPU.

$\overline{RD}$ This is an active-low read enable input to 8259A. A low on this line enables 8259A to release status onto the data bus of CPU.

D_7–D_0 These pins form a bidirectional data bus that carries 8-bit data either to control word or from status word registers. This also carries interrupt vector information.

CAS_0–CAS_2 Cascade Lines A single 8259A provides eight vectored interrupts. If more interrupts are required, the 8259A is used in the cascade mode in which a master 8259A along with eight slaves 8259A can provide up to 64 vectored interrupt lines. These three lines act as select lines for addressing the slaves 8259A.

$\overline{PS}/\overline{EN}$ This pin is a dual purpose pin. When the chip is used in buffered mode, it can be used as a buffer enable to control buffer transreceivers. If this is not used in buffered mode then the pin is used as input to designate whether the chip is used as a master ($\overline{SP}$ = 1) or a slave ($\overline{EN}$ = 0).

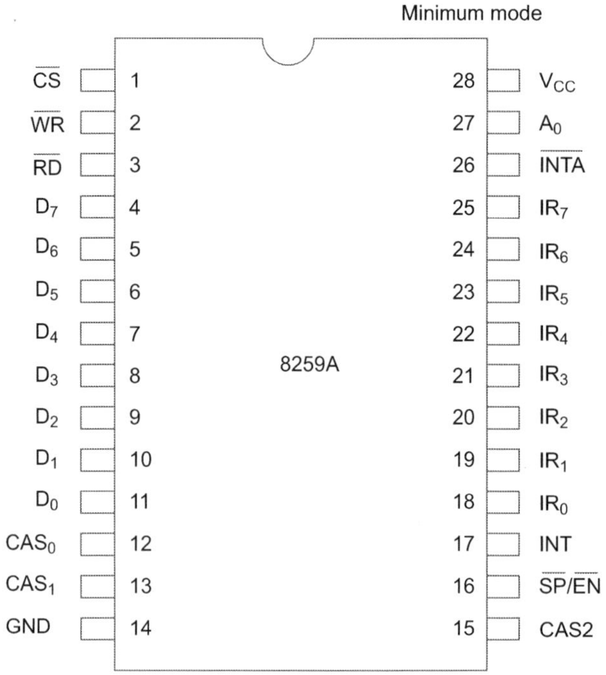

Fig. 6.13 *8259 Pin Diagram*

INT This pin goes high whenever a valid interrupt request is asserted. This is used to interrupt the CPU and is connected to the interrupt input of CPU.

IR_0–IR_7(Interrupt requests) These pins act as inputs to accept interrupt requests to the CPU. In the edge triggered mode, an interrupt service is requested by raising an IR pin from a low to a high state. It is held high until it is acknowledged, and just by latching it to high level, if used in the level triggered mode.

$\overline{INTA}$ (Interrupt acknowledge) This pin is an input used to strobe-in 8259A interrupt vector data on to the data bus. In conjunction with $\overline{CS}$, $\overline{WR}$, and $\overline{RD}$ pins, this selects the different operations like, writing command words, reading status word, etc.

The device 8259A can be interfaced with any CPU using either polling or interrupt. In polling, the CPU keeps on checking each peripheral device in sequence to ascertain if it requires any service from the CPU. If any such service request is noticed, the CPU serves the request and then goes on to the next device in sequence. After all the peripheral devices are scanned as above the CPU again starts from the first device. This type of system operation results in the reduction of processing speed because most of the CPU time is consumed in polling the peripheral devices.

In the interrupt driven method, the CPU performs the main processing task till it is interrupted by a service requesting peripheral device. The net processing speed of these type of systems is high because the CPU serves the peripheral only if it receives the interrupt request. If more than one interrupt requests are received at a time, all the requesting peripherals are served one by one on priority basis. This method of interfacing may require additional hardware if number of peripherals to be interfaced is more than the interrupt pins available with the CPU.

6.2.2 Interrupt Sequence in an 8086 System

The interrupt sequence in an 8086-8259A system is described as follows:

1. One or more IR lines are raised high that set corresponding IRR bits.
2. 8259A resolves priority and sends an INT signal to CPU.
3. The CPU acknowledges with $\overline{INTA}$ pulse.
4. Upon receiving an $\overline{INTA}$ signal from the CPU, the highest priority ISR bit is set and the corresponding IRR bit is reset. The 8259A does not drive data bus during this period.
5. The 8086 will initiate a second $\overline{INTA}$ pulse. During this period 8259A releases an 8-bit pointer on to data bus from where it is read by the CPU.
6. This completes the interrupt cycle. The ISR bit is reset at the end of the second $\overline{INTA}$ pulse if automatic end of interrupt (AEOI) mode is programmed. Otherwise ISR bit remains set until an appropriate EOI command is issued at the end of interrupt subroutine.

6.2.3 Command Words of 8259A

The command words of 8259A are classified in two groups, viz. Initialization Command Words (ICWs) and Operation Command Words (OCWs).

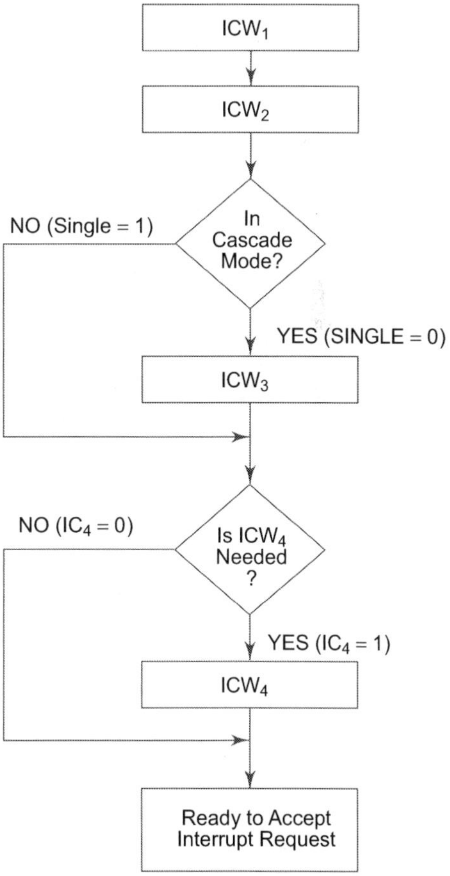

Fig. 6.14 *Initialization Sequence of 8259A*

Initialization Command Words (ICWs) Before it starts functioning, the 8259A must be initialized by writing two to four command words into the respective command word registers. These are called as Initialization Command Words (ICWs). If $A_0 = 0$ and $D_4 = 1$, the control word is recognized as ICW_1. It contains the control bits for edge/level triggered mode, single/cascade mode, call address interval and whether ICW_4 is required or not, etc. If $A_0 = 1$, the control word is recognized as ICW_2. The ICW_2 stores details regarding interrupt vector addresses. The initialisation sequence of 8259A is described in from of a flow chart in Fig. 6.14. The bit functions of the ICW_1 and ICW_2 are self explanatory as shown in Fig. 6.15.

Once ICW_1 is loaded, the following initialization procedure is carried out internally.

(a) The edge sense circuit is reset, i.e. by default 8259A interrupts are edge sensitive
(b) IMR is cleared
(c) IR7 input is assigned the lowest priority
(d) Slave mode address is set to 7
(e) Special mask mode is cleared and the status read is set to IRR
(f) If $IC_4 = 0$, all the functions of ICW_4 are set to zero. Master/slave bit in ICW_4 is used in the buffered mode only.

In an 8085 based system, $A_{15} - A_8$ of the interrupt vector address are the respective bits of ICW_2. In 8086/88 based system, five most significant bits of the interrupt type byte are inserted in place of $T_7 - T_3$ respectively and the remaining three bits (A_8, A_9 and A_{10}) are inserted internally as 000 (as if they are pointing

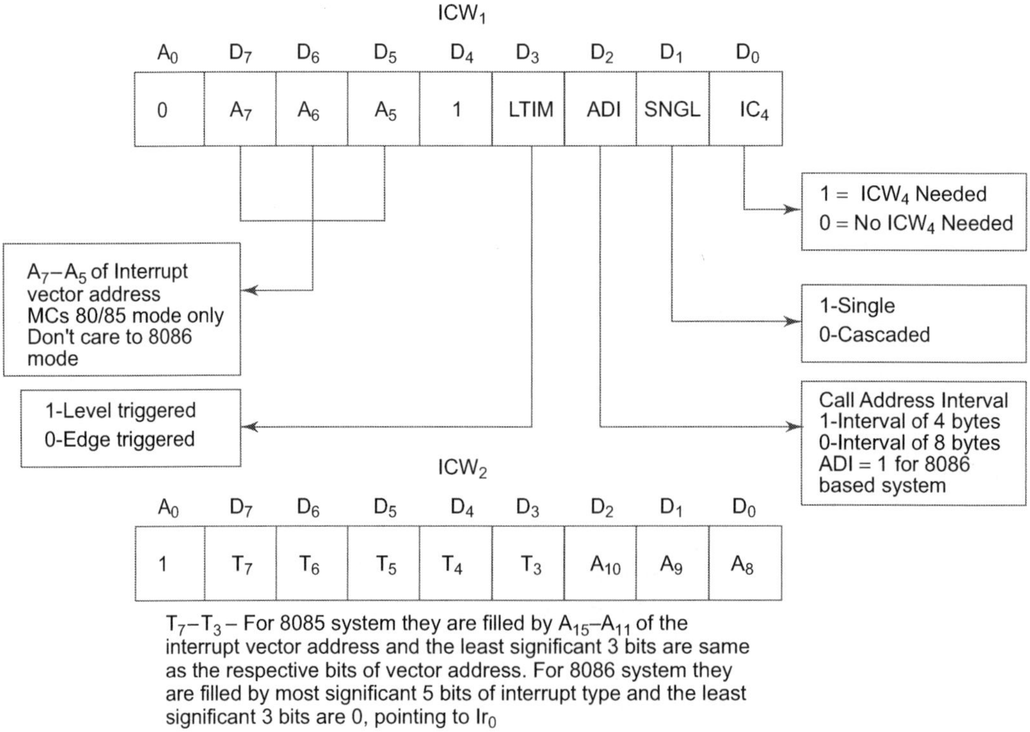

Fig. 6.15 *Initialization Command Words ICW_1 and ICW_2*

to IR_0). Other seven interrupt levels' vector addresses are internally generated automatically by 8259 using IR_0vector. Address interval is always four in an 8086 based system.

ICW_1 and ICW_2 are compulsory command words in initialization sequence of 8259A as is evident from Fig. 6.14, while ICW_3 and ICW_4 are optional. The ICW_3 is read only when there are more than one 8259As in the system, i.e. cascading is used (SNGL = 0). The SNGL bit in ICW_1 indicates whether the 8259A is in the cascade mode or not. The ICW_3 loads an 8-bit slave register. Its detailed functions are as follows:

In the master mode (i.e. $\overline{SP}$ = 1 or in buffer mode M/S = 1 in ICW_4), the 8-bit slave register will be set bit-wise to '1' for each slave in the system, as shown in Fig. 6.16. The requesting slave will then release the second byte of a CALL sequence.

In slave mode (i.e. $\overline{SP}$ = 0 or if BUF = 1 and M/S = 0 in ICW_4) bits D_2 to D_0 identify the slave, i.e. 000 to 111 for slave1 to slave8. The slave compares the cascade inputs with these bits and if they are equal, the second byte of the CALL sequence is released by it on the data bus.

ICW_4 The use of this command word depends on the IC_4 bit of ICW_1. If IC_4 = 1, ICW_4 is used, otherwise it is neglected. The bit functions of ICW_4 are described as follows:

SFNM Special fully nested mode is selected, if SFNM = 1.

BUF If BUF = 1, the buffered mode is selected. In the buffered mode, SP/EN acts as enable output and the master/slave is determined using the M/S bit of ICW_4.

M/S If M/S = 1, 8259A is a master. If M/S = 0, 8259A is a slave. If BUF = 0, M/S is to be neglected.

Master mode ICW_3

A_0	D_7	D_6	D_5	D_4	D_3	D_2	D_1	D_0
1	S_7	S_6	S_5	S_4	S_3	S_2	S_1	S_0

Sn = 1-IRn Input has a slave
= 0-IRn Input does not have a slave

Slave mode ICW_3

A_0	D_7	D_6	D_5	D_4	D_3	D_2	D_1	D_0
1	0	0	0	0	0	ID_2	ID_1	ID_0

$D_2D_1D_0$ - 000 to 111 for IR_0 to IR_7 or slave 1 to slave 8

Fig. 6.16 *ICW_3 in Master and Slave Mode*

AEOI If AEOI = 1, the automatic end of interrupt mode is selected.

mPM If the mPM bit is 0, the Mcs-85 system operation is selected and if mPM =1, 8086/88 operation is selected.

Figure 6.17 shows the ICW_4 bit positions:

ICW_4

A_0	D_7	D_6	D_5	D_4	D_3	D_2	D_1	D_0
1	0	0	0	SFNM	BUF	M/$\overline{S}$	AEOI	mPM

Fig. 6.17 *ICW_4 Bit Functions*

Operation Command Words Once 8259A is initialized using the previously discussed command words for initialisation, it is ready for its normal function, i.e. for accepting the interrupts but 8259A has its own ways of handling the received interrupts called as modes of operation. These modes of operations

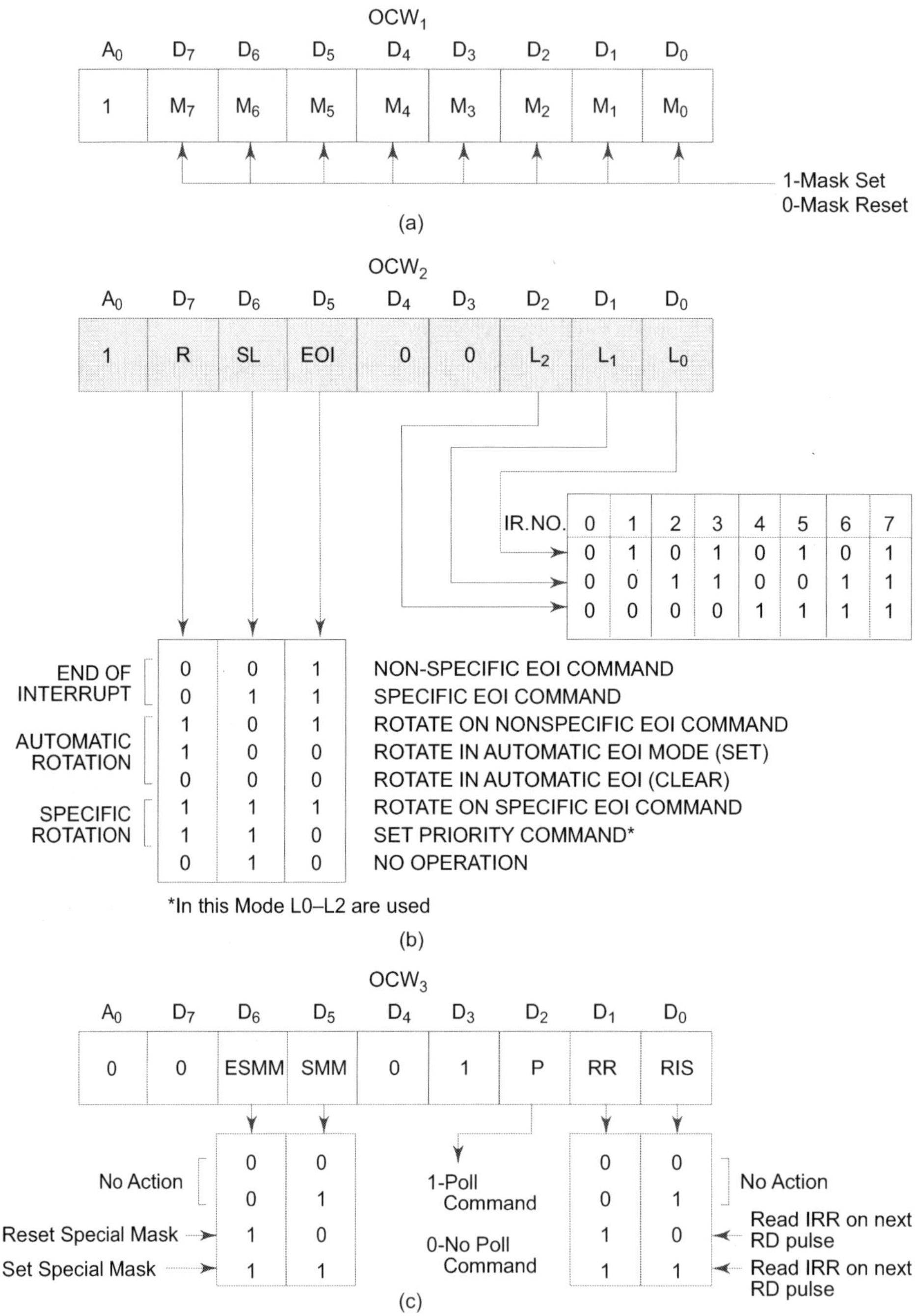

Fig. 6.18 *Operation Command Words*

can be selected by programming, i.e. writing three internal registers called as *operation command word registers*. The data written into them (bit pattern) is called as *operation command words*. In the three operation command words OCW_1, OCW_2 and OCW_3, every bit corresponds to some operational feature of the mode selected, except for a few bits those are either '1' or '0'. The three operation command words are shown in Fig. 6.18 (a), (b) and (c) with the bit selection details. OCW_1 is used to mask the unwanted interrupt requests. If the mask bit is '1', the corresponding interrupt request is masked, and if it is '0', the request is enabled. In OCW_2 the three bits, viz. R,SL and EOI control the end of interrupt, the rotate mode and their combinations as shown in Fig. 6.18 (b). The three bits L_2, L_1 and L_0 in OCW_2 determine the interrupt level to be selected for operation , if the SL bit is active, i.e. '1'. The details of OCW_2 are shown in Fig. 6.18(b).

In operation command word 3 (OCW3), if the ESMM bit, i.e. *Enable Special Mask Mode* bit is set to '1', the SMM bit is enabled to select or mask the *Special Mask Mode*. When ESMM bit is '0', the SMM bit is neglected. If the SMM bit, i.e. *Special Mask Mode* bit is '1', the 8259A will enter special mask mode provided ESMM = 1.

If ESMM = 1 and SMM = 0, the 8259A will return to the normal mask mode. The details of bits of OCW_3 are given in Fig. 6.18 (c) along with their bit definitions.

6.2.4 Operating Modes of 8259

The different modes of operation of 8259A can be programmed by setting or resting the appropriate bits of the ICWs or OCWs as discussed previously. The different modes of operation of 8259A are explained in the following text:

Fully Nested Mode This is the default mode of operation of 8259A. IR_0 has the highest priority and IR_7 has the lowest one. When interrupt requests are noticed, the highest priority request amongst them is determined and the vector is placed on the data bus. The corresponding bit of ISR is set and remains set till the microprocessor issues an EOI command just before returning from the service routine or the AEOI bit is set. If the ISR (In Service) bit is set, all the same or lower priority interrupts are inhibited but higher levels will generate an interrupt, that will be acknowledged only if the microprocessor's Interrupt enable Flag (IF) is set. The priorities can afterwards be changed by programming the rotating priority modes.

End of Interrupt (EOI) The ISR bit can be reset either with AEOI bit of ICW_1 or by EOI command, issued before returning from the interrupt service routine. There are two types of EOI commands specific and non-specific. When 8259A is operated in the modes that preserve fully nested structure, it can determine which ISR bit is to be reset on EOI. When non-specific EOI command is issued to 8259A it will automatically reset the highest ISR bit out of those already set.

When a mode that may disturb the fully nested structure is used, the 8259A is no longer able to determine the last level acknowledged. In this case a specific EOI command is issued to reset a particular ISR bit. An ISR bit that is masked by the corresponding IMR bit, will not be cleared by a non-specific EOI of 8259A, if it is in special mask mode.

Automatic Rotation This is used in the applications where all the interrupting devices are of equal priority. In this mode, an Interrupt Request (IR) level receives lowest priority after it is served while the next device to be served gets the highest priority in sequence. Once all the devices are served like this, the first device again receives highest priority.

Automatic EOI Mode Till AEOI = 1 in ICW_4, the 8259A operates in AEOI mode. In this mode, the 8259A performs a non-specific EOI operation at the trailing edge of the last $\overline{INTA}$ pulse automatically. This mode should be used only when a nested multilevel interrupt structure is not required with a single 8259A.

Specific Rotation In this mode a bottom priority level can be selected, using L_2, L_1 and L_0 in OCW_2 and R = 1, SL = 1, EOI = 0. The selected bottom priority fixes other priorities. If IR_5 is selected as a bottom priority, then IR_5 will have least priority and IR_4 will have a next higher priority. Thus IR_6 will have the highest priority. These priorities can be changed during an EOI command by programming the rotate on specific EOI command in OCW_2.

Special Mask Mode In the special mask mode, when a mask bit is set in OCW_1, it inhibits further interrupts at that level and enables interrupt from other levels, which are not masked.

Edge and Level Triggered Mode This mode decides whether the interrupt should be edge triggered or level triggered. If bit LTIM of ICW_1 = 0, they are edge triggered, otherwise the interrupts are level triggered.

Reading 8259 Status The status of the internal registers of 8259A can be read using this mode. The OCW_3 is used to read IRR and ISR while OCW_1 is used to read IMR. Reading is possible only in no polled mode.

Poll Command In the polled mode of operation, the INT output of 8259A is neglected, though it functions normally, by not connecting INT output or by masking INT input of the microprocessor. The poll mode is entered by setting P = 1 in OCW_3. The 8259A is polled by using software execution by microprocessor instead of the requests on INT input. The 8259A treats the next $\overline{RD}$ pulse to the 8259A as an interrupt acknowledge. An appropriate ISR bit is set, if there is a request. The priority level is read and a data word is placed on to data bus, after $\overline{RD}$ is activated. The data word is shown in Fig. 6.19.

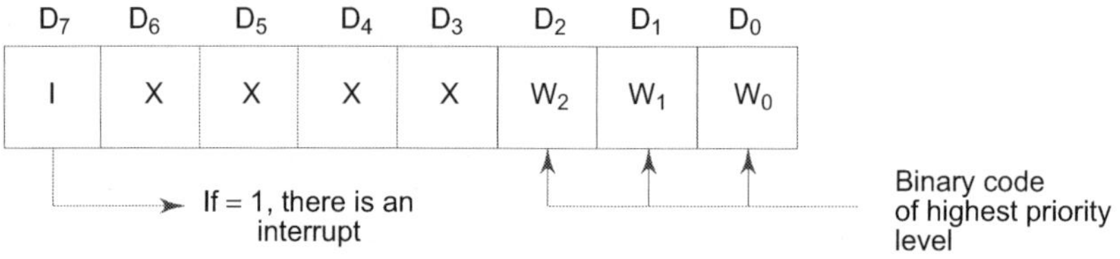

Fig. 6.19 *Data Word of 8259*

A poll command may give you more than 64 priority levels. Note that this has nothing to do with the 8086 interrupt structure and the interrupt priorities.

Special Fully Nested Mode This mode is used in more complicated systems, where cascading is used and the priority has to be programmed in the master using ICW_4. This is somewhat similar to the normal nested mode. In this mode, when an interrupt request from a certain slave is in service, this slave can further send requests to the master, if the requesting device connected to the slave has higher priority than the one being currently served. In this mode, the master interrupts the CPU only when the interrupting device has a higher or the same priority than the one currently being served. In normal mode, other requests than the one being served are masked out.

When entering the interrupt service routine the software has to check whether this is the only request from the slave. This is done by sending a non-specific EOI command to the slave and then reading its ISR and checking for zero. If its zero, a non-specific EOI can be sent to the master, otherwise no EOI should be sent. This mode is important, since in the absence of this mode, the slave would interrupt the master only once and hence the priorities of the slave inputs would have been disturbed.

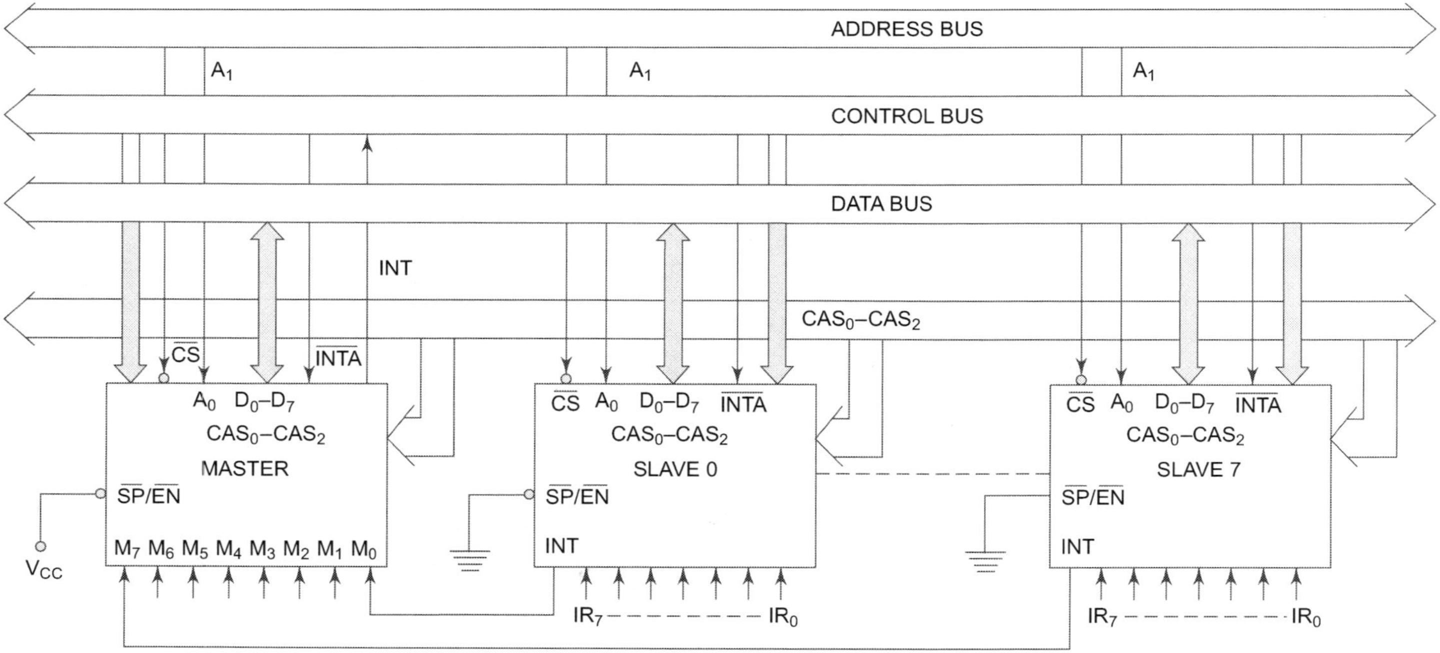

Fig. 6.20 *8259A in Cascaded Mode*

Buffered Mode When the 8259A is used in the systems in which bus driving buffers are used on data buses (e.g. cascade systems), the problem of enabling the buffers arises. The 8259A sends a buffer enable signal on $\overline{SP}/\overline{EN}$ pin, whenever data is placed on the bus.

Cascade Mode The 8259A can be connected in a system containing one master and eight slaves (maximum) to handle upto 64 priority levels. The master controls the slaves using CAS_0–CAS_2 which act as chip select inputs (encoded) for slaves. In this mode, the slave INT outputs are connected with master IR inputs. When a slave request line is activated and acknowledged, the master will enable the slave to release the vector address during the second pulse of $\overline{INTA}$ sequence. The cascade lines are normally low and contain slave address codes from the trailing edge of the first $\overline{INTA}$ pulse to the trailing edge of the second $\overline{INTA}$ pulse. Each 8259A in the system must be separately initialized and programmed to work in different modes. The EOI command must be issued twice, one for master and the other for the slave. A separate address decoder is used to activate the chip select line of each 8259A. Figure 6.20 shows the details of the circuit connections of 8259As in cascade scheme.

6.2.5 Interfacing and Programming 8259

The following example elucidates the interfacing and programming of 8259 in an 8086 based system.

Problem 6.3

Show 8259A interfacing connections with 8086 at the address 074x. Write an ALP to initialize the 8259A in single level triggered mode, with call address interval of 4, non-buffered, no special fully nested mode. Then set the 8259A to operate with IR6 masked, IR4 as bottom priority level, with special EOI mode. Set special mask mode of 8259A. Read IRR and ISR into registers BH and BL respectively. IR_0 of 8259 will have type 80H.

Solution

Let the starting vector address is 0000:0200H (80H X 4 in segment 0000H). The interconnections of 8259A with 8086 are shown in Fig. 6.21. The 8259 is interfaced with lower byte of the 8086 data bus, hence A_0 line of the microprocessor system is abandoned and A_1 of the microprocessor system is connected with A_0 of the 8259A. Before going for an ALP, all the initialization command words (ICWs) and Operation Command Words (OCWs) must be decided. ICW_1 decides single level triggered, address interval of 4 as given below.

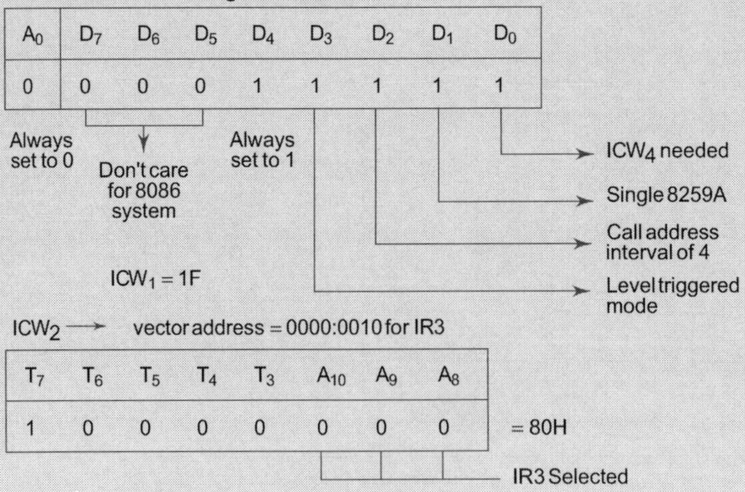

There is no slave hence the ICW_3 is as given below:

A_0	D_7	D_6	D_5	D_4	D_3	D_2	D_1	D_0
11	0	1	0	0	0	0	0	0

$ICW_3 = 0\,0$ H

Actually ICW_3 is not at all needed, because in ICW_1 the 8259 A is set for single mode.

The ICW_4 should be set as shown below:

A_0	D_7	D_6	D_5	D_4	D_3	D_2	D_1	D_0
1	0	0	0	0	0	0	0	1

$ICW_4 = 0\,1$ H

For special fully nested mode masking

Non buffered mode

For 8086 system

Normal EOI

The OCW_1 sets the mask of IR6 as below:

A_0	D_7	D_6	D_5	D_4	D_3	D_2	D_1	D_0
1	0	1	0	0	0	0	0	0

IR6 masked

OCW1 = 40 H

The OCW_2 sets the modes and rotating priority as shown below:

A_0	D_7	D_6	D_5	D_4	D_3	D_2	D_1	D_0
0	1	1	1	0	0	1	0	0

Specific EOI command with rotating priority

Bottom priority level set at IR4

OCW_2 = E4H

The OCW_3 sets the special mask mode and reads ISR and IRR using the following control commands:

For reading IRR -

For reading IRR

A_0	D_7	D_6	D_5	D_4	D_3	D_2	D_1	D_0
0	0	1	1	0	1	0	1	0

Special mask mode

No poll command

Read IRR

OCW_3 = 6AH

For reading IRR

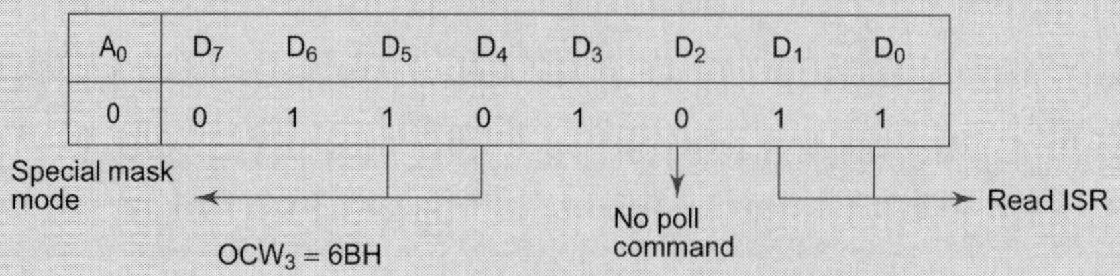

The following ALP writes these commands to initialize the operation of the 8259A as required in the problem. Program 6.5 gives an ALP for the required initialization of 8259A.

```
CODE      SEGMENT
ASSUME    CS : CODE
START:    MOV AL, 1FH          ; Set the 8259A in single, level
          MOV DX, 0740H
          OUT DX, AL           ; triggered mode with call address of
                                          interval of 4
          MOV DX, 0742H
          MOV AL, 80H          ; Select vector address 0000:0200H
          OUT DX, AL           ; for IR3 (ICW2)
          MOV AL, 01H          ; ICW4 for 8086 system, normal
          OUT DX, AL           ; EOI, non-buffered, special fully nested
                                          mode masked
          MOV AL, 40H          ;
          OUT DX, AL           ; OCW1 for IR6 masked,
          MOV AL, 0E4H         ; Specific EOI with rotating
          MOV DX, 0740H
          OUT DX, AL           ; Priority and bottom level of IR4 with
                                     OCW2
          MOV AL, 6AH          ; Write OCW3 for reading
          OUT DX, AL           ; IRR and store in BH
          IN AL, DX            ;
          MOV BH, AL
          MOV AL, 6BH          ; Write OCW3 to read
          OUT DX, AL           ; ISR and store in
          IN AL, DX            ; BL
          MOV BL, AL
          MOV AH, 4CH          ; Return to DOS
          INT 21H
    CODE  ENDS
          END START
```

Program 6.5 *ALP to Initialize 8259A for Problem 6.3*

The interfacing circuit for Problem 6.3 has been shown below in Fig. 6.21.

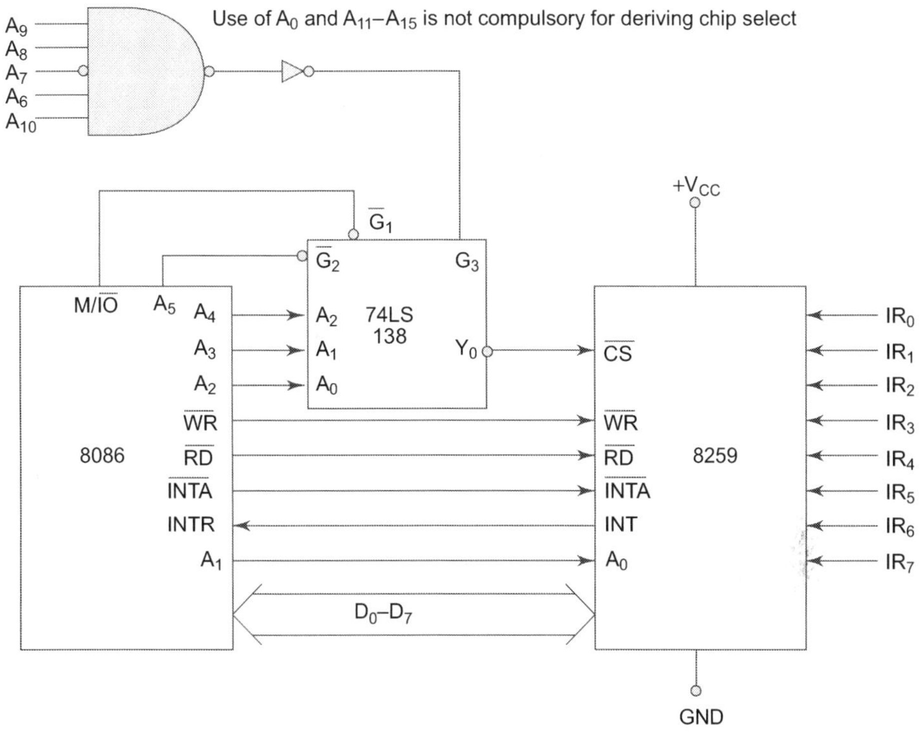

Fig. 6.21 *Interfacing 8259A with 8086*

Problem 6.4

Interface 3 ICS of 8259 PIC with 8086 system in such a way that one is master and rest two are slaves connected at IR_3 and IR_6 interrupt request level of the master. The 8259s are having vector address 60H, 70H and 80H. Write a program to initialize 8259 PIC so that IR_2 and IR_7 levels of master are masked. Initialize master in AEOI mode and automatic rotation mode in minimum mode of operation.

Solution

Address Decoding table for 8259 interfaced at even addresses.

Table 6.3

	Port	*Hex. Address*	A_{15}	A_{14}	A_1		A_0
Master	Port 0	C000H	1100	0000	0000	000	0
8259	Port 1	C002H	1100	0000	0000	001	0
Slave$_3$	Port 0	0004H	1100	0000	0000	010	0
	Port 1	C006H	1100	0000	0000	011	0
Slave$_6$	Port 0	C008H	1100	0000	0000	100	0
	Port 1	C00AH	1100	0000	0000	101	0

* A_1 Pin of 8086 system is connected with A_0 pin of 8259 PIC master as well as slave.
* A_3, A_2 are used to generate chip select for three 8259 PIC.
* $A_{15} - A_4$ used as shown in the decoder diagram
* A_0 is used to generate chip select for even bank

Control Words

ICW_1:

	X	X	X	1	LTM	X	SNGL	ICW_4	
Master	X	X	X	1	1	X	0	1	
					Or				
	0	0	0	1	1	1	1	1	19 H
Slave 3	0	0	0	1	1	0	0	1	19 H
Slave 6	0	0	0	1	1	0	0	1	19 H

ICW_2:

	T_7	T_6	T_5	T_4	T_3	0	0	0	
	0	1	1	0	0	0	0	0	60 H for Masks
	0	1	1	1	0	0	0	0	70 H for Slave 3
	1	0	0	0	0	0	0	0	80 H for Slave 6

ICW_3:

For Master

SL_7	SL_6	SL_5	SL_4	SL_3	SL_2	SL_1	SL_0	
0	1	0	0	1	0	0	0	48 H for Master

For Slave

	0	0	0	0	0	ID_2	ID_1	ID_0	
Slave 3	0	0	0	0	0	0	1	1	03 H
Slave 6	0	0	0	0	0	1	1	0	06 H

ICW_4:

	0	0	0	SFNM	BUF	M/S	AEOI	UPM	
Master	0	0	0	1	0	0	1	1	13 H
Slave 3	0	0	0	0	0	0	0	1	01 H
Slave 6	0	0	0	0	0	0	0	1	01 H

Master is initialized in SFNM in Cascade mode

OCW_1:

	M_7	M_6	M_5	M_4	M_3	M_2	M_1	M_0	
Master	1	0	0	0	0	1	0	0	84 H

OCW_2:

	R	SL	EOI	0	0	L_2	L_1	L_0	
Master	1	0	0	0	0	0	0	0	80 H

For rotating priority in AEOI mode.

Program for this problem is presented below.

```
        ASSUME CS : CODE, DS : DATA
        STACK SEGMENT
        TOP DW 100 DUP (?)      Stack segment of 200 by ks
        STACK ENDS              are reserved
        CODE SEGMENT
START : MOV AX, STACK
        MOV SS, AX              Initialization of SS 3 SP
        LEA SP, TOP+200
        CLI
        MOV DX, 0C000H          Port 0 address of Master in DX
        MOV AL, 19H             ICWI of Master
        OUT DX, AL              Out to Port 0 of Master
        ADD DX, 02H             Port 1 address in Dx
        MOV AL, 60H             Vector address of Master for IR0
                                      (ICW2)
        OUT DX, AL              ICW2 is out to Port 1
        MOV AL, 48H             ICW3 for Master
        OUT DX, AL              ICW3 is out to Port 1
        MOV AL, 13H             ICW4  is out to Port 1
        OUT DX, AL              OCWI for Master
        MOV AL, 84H             OCWI is Out to Port 1
        OUT DX, AL
        MOV AL, 80H             OCW2 for Master
        OUT DX, AL.             OCW2 is out to Port 1
                                Now initialization of Slave 3.
        MOV DX, 0C004H          Port address of Slave 3 in DX
        MOV AL, 19H             ICWI
        OUT DX, AL
        ADD DX, 02H             Port 1 address of Slave 3 in Dx
        MOV AL, 70H             ICW2 for Slave 3
        OUT DX, AL
        MOV AL, 03H             ICW3 for Slave 3
        OUT DX, AL
        MOV AL, 01H             ICW4 for Slave 3
        OUT DX, AL              Now initialization of Slave 6
        MOV DX, 0C008H          Port 0 address of Slave 6 in Dx
        MOV AL, 19H             ICW1 for Slave 6
        OUT DX, AL
```

```
ADD DX, 02H          Port 1 address of Slave 6 in Dx
MOV AL, 80H          ICW2 for Slave 6
OUT DX, AL
MOV AL, 06H          ICW3 for Slave 6
OUT DX, AL
MOV AH, 01H          ICW4 FOR SLAVE 6
OUT DX, AL
MOV AH, 4CH
INT 21H
CODE ENDS
END START
```

Program 6.6 *ALP to Initialize Cascaded 8259A for Problem 6.4*

Interfacing circuit for this problem is presented below in Fig. 6.22.

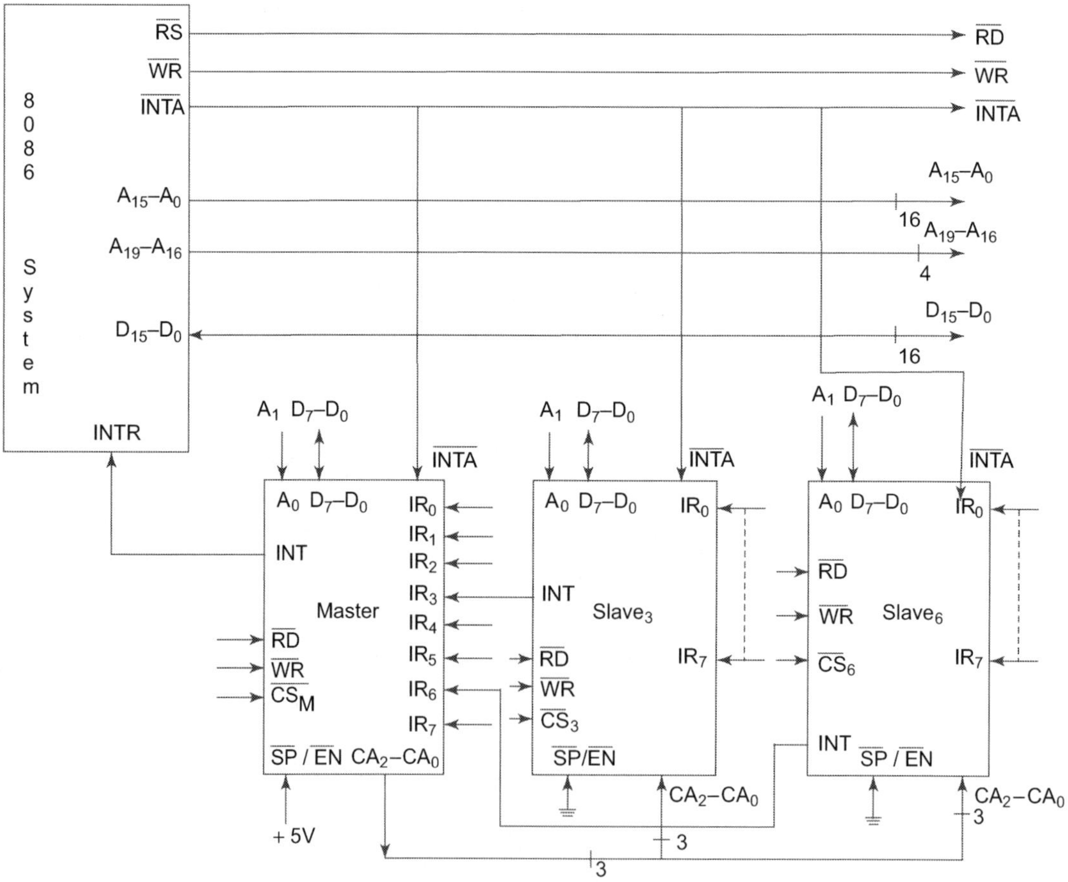

Fig. 6.22 *Cascaded 8259 Interfacing for Problem 6.4*

6.3 THE KEYBOARD/DISPLAY CONTROLLER 8279

In Chapter 5, while studying 8255, we have explained the use of 8255 in interfacing keyboards and displays with 8086. The disadvantage of this method is that the processor has to refresh the display and check the status of the keyboard periodically using polling technique. Thus a considerable amount of CPU time is wasted, reducing the system operating speed and hence the throughput.

Intel's 8279 is a general purpose keyboard display controller that simultaneously drives the display of a system and interfaces a keyboard with the CPU, leaving it free for its routine task. The keyboard-display interface scans the keyboard to identify if any key has been pressed and sends the code of the pressed key to the CPU. It also transmits the data received from the CPU, to the display device. Both of these functions are performed by the controller in repetitive fashion without involving the CPU. The keyboard is interfaced either in the interrupt or the polled mode. In the interrupt mode, the processor is requested service only if any key is pressed, otherwise the CPU can proceed with its main task. In the polled mode, the CPU periodically reads an internal flag of 8279 to check for a key pressure. The keyboard section can interface an array of a maximum of 64 keys with the CPU. The keyboard entries (key codes) are debounced and stored in an 8-byte FIFO RAM, that is further accessed by the CPU to read the key codes. If more than eight characters are entered in the FIFO (i.e. more than eight keys are pressed), before any FIFO read operation, the overrun status is set. If a FIFO contains a valid key entry, the CPU is interrupted (in interrupt mode) or the CPU checks the status (in polling) to read the entry. Once the CPU reads a key entry, the FIFO is updated, i.e. the key entry is pushed out of the FIFO to generate space for new entries. The 8279 normally provides a maximum of sixteen 7-seg display interface with CPU. It contains a 16-byte display RAM that can be used either as an integrated block of 16×8-bits or two 16×4-bit blocks of RAM. The data entry to RAM block is controlled by CPU using the command words of the 8279.

6.3.1 Architecture and Signal Descriptions of 8279

The keyboard display controller chip 8279 provides (a) a set of four scan lines and eight return lines for interfacing keyboards (b) a set of eight output lines for interfacing display. Figure 6.23 shows the functional block diagram of 8279 followed by its brief description.

I/O Control and Data Buffers The I/O control section controls the flow of data to/from the 8279. The data buffers interface the external bus of the system with internal bus of 8279. The I/O section is enabled only if $\overline{D}$ is low. The pins A_0, $\overline{RD}$ and $\overline{WR}$ select the command, status or data read/write operations carried out by the CPU with 8279.

Control and Timing Register and Timing Control These registers store the keyboard and display modes and other operating conditions programmed by CPU. The registers are written with $A_0 = 1$ and $\overline{WR} = 0$. The timing and control unit controls the basic timings for the operation of the circuit. Scan counter divide down the operating frequency of 8279 to derive scan keyboard and scan display frequencies.

Scan Counter The scan counter has two modes to scan the key matrix and refresh the display. In the encoded mode, the counter provides a binary count that is to be externally decoded to provide the scan lines for keyboard and display (four externally decoded scan lines may drive up to 16 displays). In the decoded scan mode, the counter internally decodes the least significant 2 bits and provides a decoded 1 out of 4 scan on SL_0–SL_3 (four internally decoded scan lines may drive up to 4 displays). The keyboard and display both are in the same mode at a time.

Return Buffers and Keyboard Debounce and Control This section scans for a key closure row-wise. If it is detected, the keyboard debounce unit debounces the key entry (i.e. wait for 10 ms). After the

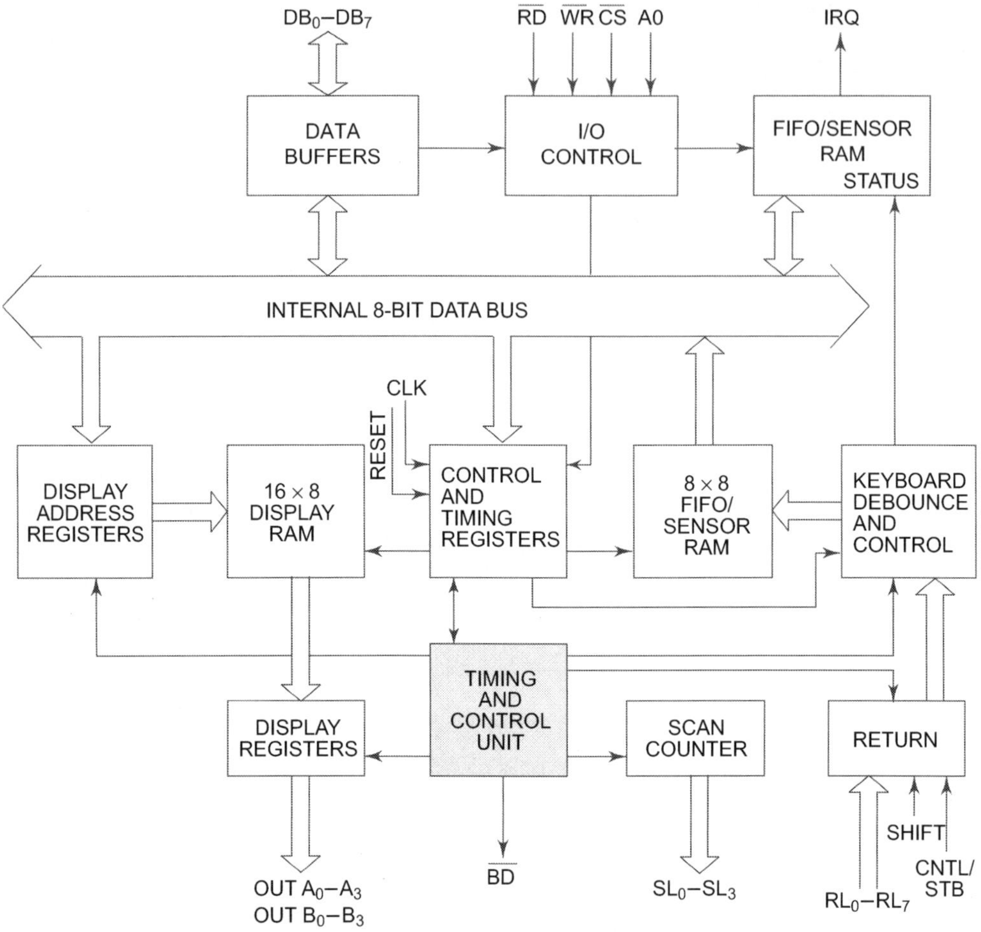

Fig. 6.23 *8279 Internal Architecture*

debounce period, if the key continues to be detected. The code of the key is directly transferred to the sensor RAM along with SHIFT and CONTROL key status.

FIFO/Sensor RAM and Status Logic In keyboard or strobed input mode, this block acts as 8-byte first-in-first-out (FIFO) RAM. Each key code of the pressed key is entered in the order of the entry, and in the meantime, read by the CPU, till the RAM becomes empty. The status logic generates an interrupt request after each FIFO read operation till the FIFO is empty. In scanned sensor matrix mode, this unit acts as sensor RAM. Each row of the sensor RAM is loaded with the status of the corresponding row of sensors in the matrix. If a sensor changes its state, the IRQ line goes high to interrupt the CPU.

Display Address Registers and Display RAM The display address registers hold the address of the word currently being written or read by the CPU to or from the display RAM. The contents of the registers are automatically updated by 8279 to accept the next data entry by CPU. The 16-byte display RAM contains the 16-bytes of data to be displayed on the sixteen 7-seg displays in the encoded scan mode.

Pin diagram of 8279 is shown below in Fig. 6.24.

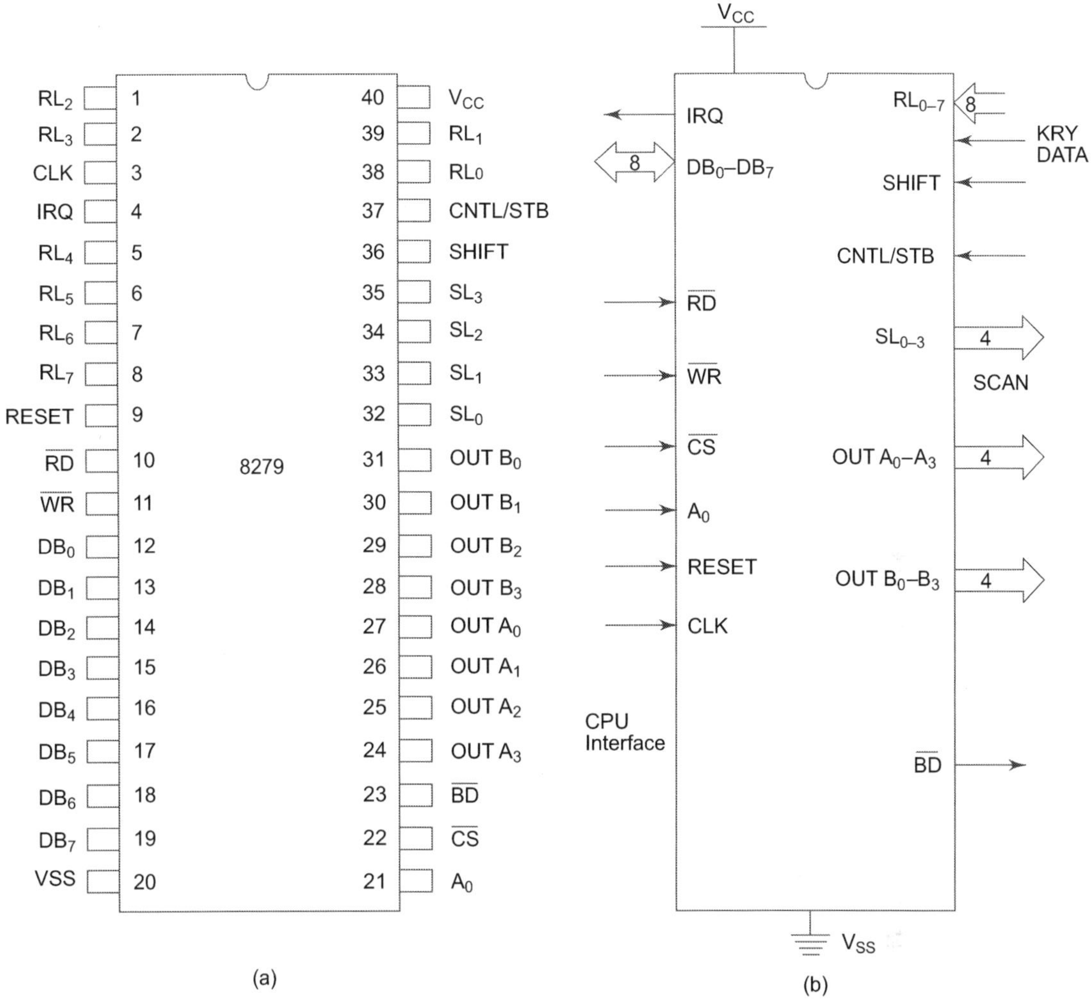

Fig. 6.24 *8279 Pin Configuration and Logic Diagram*

The signal discription of each of the pins of 8279 is presented below in brief:

DB_0–DB_7 These are bidirectional data bus lines. The data and command words to and from the CPU are transferred on these lines.

CLK This is a clock input used to generate internal timings required by 8279.

RESET This pin is used to reset 8279. A high on this line resets 8279. After resetting 8279, its in sixteen 8-bit display, left entry encoded scan, 2-key lock out mode. The clock prescaler is set to 31.

$\overline{CS}$ Chip Select: A low on this line enables 8279 for normal read or write operations. Otherwise, this pin should remain high.

A_0 A high on the A_0 line indicates the transfer of a command or status information. A low on this line indicates the transfer of data. This is used to select one of the internal registers of 8279.

$\overline{RD}$, $\overline{WR}$ (Input/Output) READ/WRITE input pins enable the data buffers to receive or send data over the data bus.

IRQ This interrupt output line goes high when there is data in the FIFO sensor RAM. The interrupt line goes low with each FIFO RAM read operation. However, if the FIFO RAM further contains any key-code entry to be read by the CPU, this pin again goes high to generate an interrupt to the CPU.

V_{ss}, V_{cc} These are the ground and power supply lines for the circuit.

SL_0–SL_3-Scan Lines These lines are used to scan the keyboard matrix and display digits. These lines can be programmed as encoded or decoded, using the mode control register.

RL_0–RL_7-Return Lines These are the input lines which are connected to one terminal of keys, while the other terminal of the keys are connected to the decoded scan lines. These are normally high, but pulled low when a key is pressed.

SHIFT The status of the shift input line is stored along with each key code in FIFO in the scanned keyboard mode. Till it is pulled low with a key closure it is pulled up internally to keep it high.

CNTL/STB-CONTROL/STROBED I/P Mode In the keyboard mode, this line is used as a control input and stored in FIFO on a key closure. The line is a strobe line that enters the data into FIFO RAM, in the strobed input mode. It has an internal pull up. The line is pulled down with a key closure.

$\overline{BD}$ -Blank Display This output pin is used to blank the display during digit switching or by a blanking command.

$OUTA_0$–$OUTA_3$ and $OUTB_0$–$OUTB_3$ These are the output ports for two 16×4 (or one 16×8) internal display refresh registers. The data from these lines is synchronized with the scan lines to scan the display and keyboard. The two 4-bit ports may also be used as one 8-bit port.

6.3.2 Modes of Operation of 8279

The modes of operation of 8279 are next discussed briefly:

(i) Input (Keyboard) modes
(ii) Output (Display) modes

Input (Keyboard) Modes 8279 provides three input modes which are discussed below in brief:

1. Scanned Keyboard Mode This mode allows a key matrix to be interfaced using either encoded or decoded scans. In the encoded scan, an 8×8 keyboard or in decoded scan, a 4×8 keyboard can be interfaced. The code of key pressed with SHIFT and CONTROL status is stored into the FIFO RAM.

2. Scanned Sensor Matrix In this mode, a sensor array can be interfaced with 8279 using either encoded or decoded scans. With encoded scan 8×8 sensor matrix or with decoded scan 4×8 sensor matrix can be interfaced. The sensor codes are stored in the CPU addressable sensor RAM.

3. Strobed input In this mode, if the control line goes low, the data on return lines, is stored in the FIFO byte by byte.

Output (Display) Modes 8279 provides two output modes for selecting the display options. These are discussed briefly:

1. Display Scan In this mode, 8279 provides 8 or 16 character multiplexed displays those can be organized as dual 4-bit or single 8-bit display units.

2. Display Entry (right entry or left entry mode) 8279 allows options for data entry on the displays. The display data is entered for display either from the right side or from the left side. The concepts regarding these modes will be more clear when the commands are discussed later in this chapter.

All these modes may be selected by programming the 8279 suitably. Further, these modes are discussed in significant details.

6.3.3 Details of Modes of Operation

Keyboard Modes

(i) Scanned Keyboard Mode with 2 Key Lockout In this mode of operation, when a key is pressed, a debounce logic comes into operation. During the next two scans, other keys are checked for closure and if no other key is pressed the first pressed key is identified. The key code of the identified key is entered into the FIFO with SHIFT and CNTL status, provided the FIFO is not full, i.e. it has at least one byte free. If the FIFO does not have any free byte, naturally the key data will not be entered and the error flag is set. If FIFO has at least one byte free, the above code is entered into it and the 8279 generates an interrupt (on IRQ line) to the CPU to inform about the previous key closures. If another key is found closed during the subsequent two scans, no entry to FIFO is made. If all the other keys are released before the first key, the keycode is entered into FIFO. If the first pressed key is released before the others, the first will be ignored. A keycode is entered to FIFO only once for each valid depression, independent of other keys pressed along with it, or released before it. If two keys are pressed within a debounce cycle (simultaneously), no key is recognized till one of them remains closed, and the other is released. The last key, that remains depressed is considered as single valid key depression.

(ii) Scanned Keyboard with N-Key Rollover In this mode, each key depression is treated independently. When a key is pressed, the debounce circuit waits for 2 keyboard scans and then checks whether the key is still depressed. If it is still depressed, the code is entered in FIFO RAM. Any number of keys can be pressed simultaneously and recognized in the order, the keyboard scan recorded them. All the codes of such keys are entered into FIFO. Note that, in this mode, the first pressed key need not be released before the second is pressed. All the keys are sensed in the order of their depression, rather in the order the keyboard scan senses them, and independent of the order of their release.

(iii) Scanned Keyboard Special Error Mode This mode is valid only under the N-Key rollover mode. This mode is programmed using *end interrupt/error mode set* command. If during a single debounce period (two keyboard scans) two keys are found pressed, this is considered a simultaneous depression and an error flag is set. This flag, if set, prevents further writing in FIFO but allows generation of further interrupts to the CPU for FIFO read. The error flag can be read by reading the FIFO status word. The error flag is set by sending normal clear command with CF = 1.

(iv) Sensor Matrix Mode In the Sensor Matrix mode, the debounce logic is inhibited. The 8-byte FIFO RAM now acts as 8×8-bit memory matrix. The status of the sensor switch matrix is fed directly to sensor RAM matrix. Thus the sensor RAM bits contains the row-wise and column-wise status of the sensors in the sensor matrix. The IRQ line goes high, if any change in sensor value is detected at the end of a sensor matrix scan or the sensor RAM has a previous entry to be read by the CPU. The IRQ line is reset by the first data read operation, if AI = 0, otherwise, by issuing the end interrupt command. AI is a bit in read sensor RAM word.

Display Modes There are various options of data display. For example, the command number of characters can be 8 or 16, with each character organised as single 8-bit or dual 4-bit codes. Similarly there are two display formats. The first one is known as left entry mode or type writer mode, since in a type writer the first character typed appears at the left-most position, while the subsequent characters appear successively to the right of the first one. The other display format is known as right entry mode, or calculator mode, since in a calculator the first character entered appears at the rightmost position and this character is shifted one position left when the next character is entered. Thus all the previously entered characters are shifted left by one position when a new character is entered.

(i) Left Entry Mode In the left entry mode, the data is entered from the left side of the display unit. Address 0 of the display RAM contains the leftmost display character and address 15 of the RAM contains the right most display character. It is just like writing in our note books, i.e. from left to write. If the 8279 is in autoincrement mode, the display RAM address is automatically updated with successive reads or writes. The first entry is displayed on the leftmost display and the sixteenth entry on the rightmost display. The seventeenth entry is again displayed at the leftmost display position.

(ii) Right Entry Mode In the right entry mode, the first entry to be displayed is entered on the rightmost display. The next entry is also placed in the right most display but after the previous display is shifted left by one display position. The leftmost character is shifted out of that display at the seventeenth entry and is lost, i.e. it is pushed out of the display RAM.

6.3.4 Command Words of 8279

All the command words or status words are written or read with $A_0 = 1$ and $\overline{CS} = 0$ to or from 8279. This section describes the various commands available in 8279.

(a) Keyboard Display Mode Set The format of the command word to select different modes of operation of 8279 is given below with its bit definitions.

D_7	D_6	D_5	D_4	D_3	D_2	D_1	D_0	A_0
0	0	0	D	D	K	K	K	1

D	*D*	*Display modes*
0	0	Eight 8-bit character Left entry
0	1	Sixteen 8-bit character Left entry (Default after reset)
1	0	Eight 8-bit character Right entry
1	1	Sixteen 8-bit character Right entry

K	*K*	*K*	*Keyboard modes*
0	0	0	Encoded scan, 2 key lockout (Default after reset)
0	0	1	Decoded scan, 2 key lockout
0	1	0	Encoded scan N-Key roll over
0	1	1	Decoded scan N-Key roll over
1	0	0	Encoded scan sensor matrix
1	0	1	Decoded scan sensor matrix
1	1	0	Strobed Input Encoded scan
1	1	1	Strobed Input Decoded scan

(b) Programmable Clock The clock for operation of 8279 is obtained by dividing the external clock input signal by a programmable constant called prescaler.

D_7	D_6	D_5	D_4	D_3	D_2	D_1	D_0	A_0
0	0	1	P	P	P	P	P	1

PPPPP is a 5-bit binary constant. The input frequency is divided by a decimal constant ranging from 2 to 31, decided by the bits of an internal prescaler, PPPPP.

(c) Read FIFO/Sensor RAM The format of this command is given as shown below:

D_7	D_6	D_5	D_4	D_3	D_2	D_1	D_0	A_0
0	1	0	AI	X	A	A	A	1

X — don't care
AI — Auto Increment flag
AAA — Address pointer to 8 bit FIFO RAM

This word is written to set up 8279 for reading FIFO/sensor RAM. In scanned keyboard mode, AI and AAA bits are of no use. The 8279 will automatically drive data bus for each subsequent read, in the same sequence, in which the data was entered. In sensor matrix mode, the bits AAA select one of the 8 rows of RAM. If AI flag is set, each successive read will be from the subsequent RAM location.

(d) Read Display RAM This command enables a programmer to read the display RAM data.

D_7	D_6	D_5	D_4	D_3	D_2	D_1	D_0	A_0
0	1	1	AI	A	A	A	A	1

The CPU writes this command word to 8279 to prepare it for display RAM read operation. AI is auto increment flag and AAAA, the 4-bit address, points to the 16-byte display RAM that is to be read. If AI = 1, the address will be automatically, incremented after each read or write to the display RAM. The same address counter is used for reading and writing.

(e) Write Display RAM

D_7	D_6	D_5	D_4	D_3	D_2	D_1	D_0	A_0
1	0	0	AI	A	A	A	A	1

AI — Auto Increment flag
AAAA — 4-bit address for 16-bit display RAM to be written
Other details of this command are similar to the 'Read Display RAM Command'.

(f) Display Write Inhibit/Blanking

	D_7	D_6	D_5	D_4	D_3	D_2	D_1	D_0	A_0
	1	0	1	X	IW	IW	BL	BL	1
Output nibbles			→		A	B	A	B	

The IW (Inhibit Write flag) bits are used to mask the individual nibble as shown in the above command. The output lines are divided into two nibbles ($OUTA_0$–$OUTA_3$ and $OUTB_0$–$OUTB_3$), those can be masked by setting the corresponding IW bit to 1. Once a nibble is masked by setting the corresponding IW bit to 1, the entry to display RAM does not affect the nibble even though it may change the unmasked nibble. The blank display bit flags (BL) are used for blanking A and B nibbles. Here D_0 and D_2 corresponds to $OUTB_0$–$OUTB_3$ while D_1 and D_3 corresponds to $OUTA_0$–$OUTA_3$ for blanking and masking respectively.

If the user wants to clear the display, blank (BL) bits are available for each nibble as shown in the format. Both BL bits will have to be cleared for blanking both the nibbles.

(g) Clear Display RAM

D_7	D_6	D_5	D_4	D_3	D_2	D_1	D_0	A_0
1	1	0	CD_2	CD_1	CD_0	CF	CA	1

The CD_2, CD_1, CD_0 is a selectable blanking code to clear all the rows of the display RAM as given below. The characters A and B represent the output nibbles.

CD_2	CD_1	CD_0	
1	0	x	All zeros (x don't care) AB = 00
1	1	0	A_3–A_0 = 2 (0010) and B_3–B_0 = 00 (0000)
1	1	1	All ones (AB = FF), i.e. clear RAM

CD_2 must be 1 for enabling the clear display command. If $CD_2 = 0$, the clear display command is invoked by setting CA = 1 and maintaining CD_1, CD_0 bits exactly same as above. If CF = 1, FIFO status is cleared and IRQ line is pulled down. Also the sensor RAM pointer is set to row 0. If CA = 1, this combines the effect of CD and CF bits. Here, CA represents Clear All and CF represents Clear FIFO RAM.

End Interrupt/Error Mode Set

D_7	D_6	D_5	D_4	D_3	D_2	D_1	D_0	A_0
1	1	1	E	x	x	x	x	1

x—do not care

For the sensor matrix mode, this command lowers the IRQ line and enables further writing into the RAM. Otherwise, if a change in sensor value is detected, IRQ goes high that inhibits writing in the sensor RAM.

For N-key roll over mode, if the E bit is programmed to be '1', the 8279 operates in Special Error mode. Details of this mode are described in scanned keyboard special error mode.

6.3.5 Key-code and Status Data Formats

This section briefly describes the formats of the key-code/sensor data in their respective modes of operation and the FIFO Status Word formats of 8279.

Key-code Data Formats After a valid key closure, the key code is entered as a byte code into the FIFO RAM, in the following format, in scanned keyboard mode. The data format of the keycode in scanned

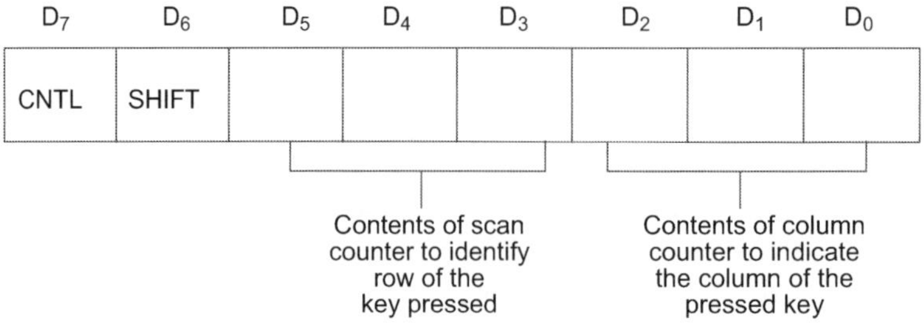

keyboard mode is given below. The keycode format contains 3-bit contents of the internal row counter, 3-bit contents of the column counter and status of the SHIFT and CNTL keys.

In the sensor matrix mode, the data from the return lines is directly entered into an appropriate row of sensor RAM, that identifies the row of the sensor that changed its status. The SHIFT and CNTL keys are ignored in this mode. RL bits represent the return lines. Rn represents the sensor RAM row number that is equal to the row number of the sensor array in which the status change was detected.

	D_7	D_6	D_5	D_4	D_3	D_2	D_1	D_0
Rn	RL_7	RL_6	RL_5	RL_4	RL_3	RL_2	RL_1	RL_0

Data Format of the Sensor Code in sensor matrix mode is given above.

In strobed input mode, data is entered to the FIFO RAM at the rising edges of CNTL/STB line, in the same format as in the sensor matrix mode.

FIFO Status Word The FIFO status word is used in keyboard and strobed input mode to indicate the error. Overrun error occurs, when an already full FIFO is attempted an entry. Underrun error occurs when an empty FIFO read is attempted. FIFO status word also has a bit to show the unavailability of FIFO RAM because of the ongoing clearing operation. In sensor matrix mode, a bit is reserved to show that at least one sensor closure indication is stored in the RAM. The S/E bit shows the simultaneous multiple closure error in special error mode.

The status word contains FIFO status, error and display unavailable signals. This is read, when $A_0 = 1$, $\overline{RD} = 0$ and $\overline{CS} = 0$. Data is read when A_0, $\overline{CS}$, $\overline{RD}$ are low. The source of data is specified by the read FIFO or read display command. The address of RAM being read is automatically incremented, if AI = 1. FIFO read always increments the address independent of AI. Data is written to the display RAM, with A_0, $\overline{WR}$ and $\overline{CS}$ tied low. The address is specified by the previous read display or write display command. The address is auto-incremented for subsequent write operations, if AI is set to. The FIFO status word format is as shown below:

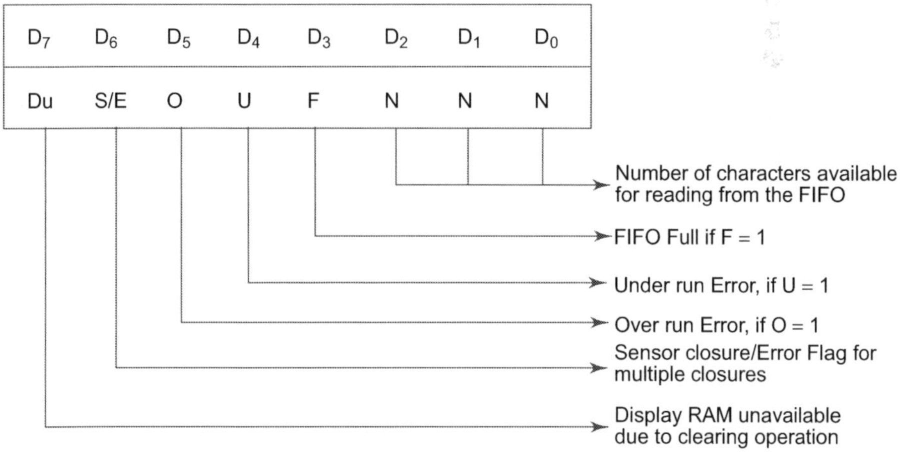

6.3.6 Interfacing and Programming 8279

The following problem on 8279 interfacing and programming explains the interfacing and programming of 8279 with an 8086 microprocessor system.

Problem 6.5

Interface keyboard and display controller 8279 with 8086 at address 0080H. Write an ALP to set up 8279 in scanned keyboard mode with encoded scan, N-key rollover mode. Use a 16-character display in right entry display format. Then clear the display RAM with zeros. Read the FIFO for key closure. If any key is closed, store it's code to register CL. Then write the byte 55 to all the displays, and return to DOS. The clock input to 8279 is 2 MHz, operate it at 100 kHz.

Solution

The 8279 is interfaced with lower byte of the data bus, i.e. D_0–D_7. Hence the A_0 input of 8279 is connected with address line A_1. The data register of 8279 is to be addressed as 0080H, i.e. $A_0 = 0$. As already discussed, the data is either read from or written to this address ($A_0 = 0$). For addressing the command or status word A_0 input of 8279 should be 1 (the address line A_1 of 8086 should be 1), i.e. the address of the command word should be 0082H. Figure 6.25 shows the interfacing schematic.

The next step is to write all the required command words for this problem.

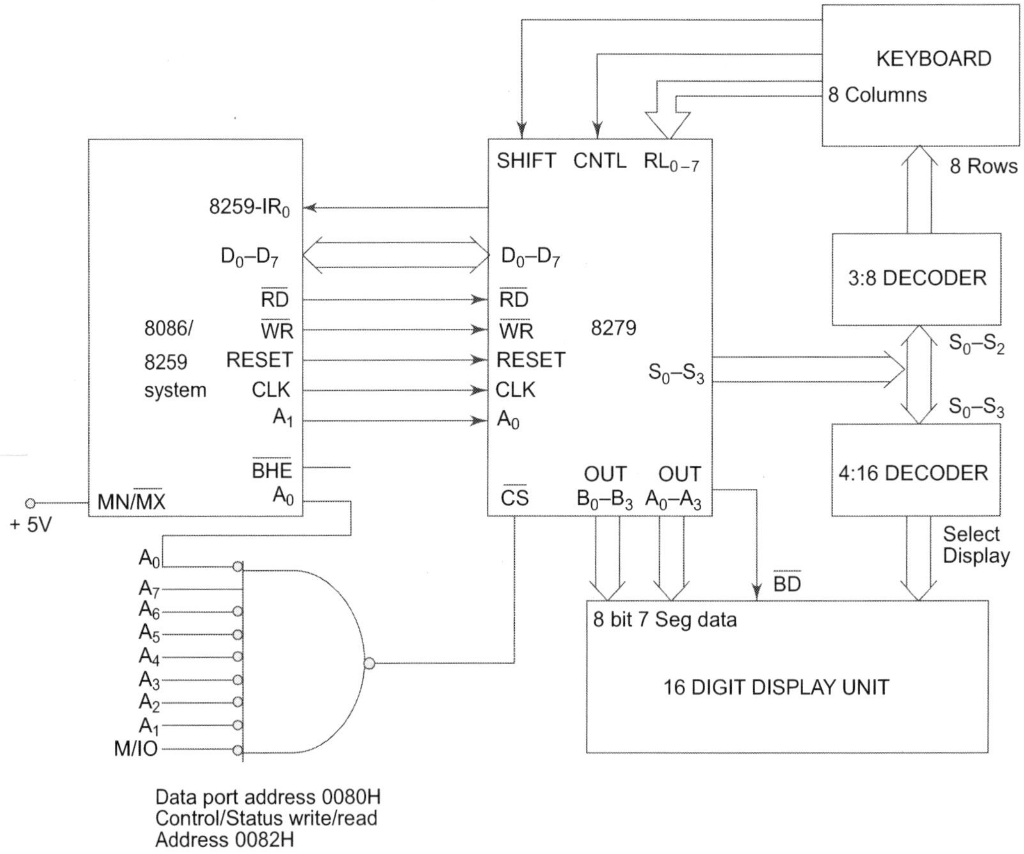

Fig. 6.25 *8279 Interfacing with 8086*

Keyboard/Display Mode Set CW This command byte sets the 8279 in 16-character right entry and encoded scan N-key rollover mode.

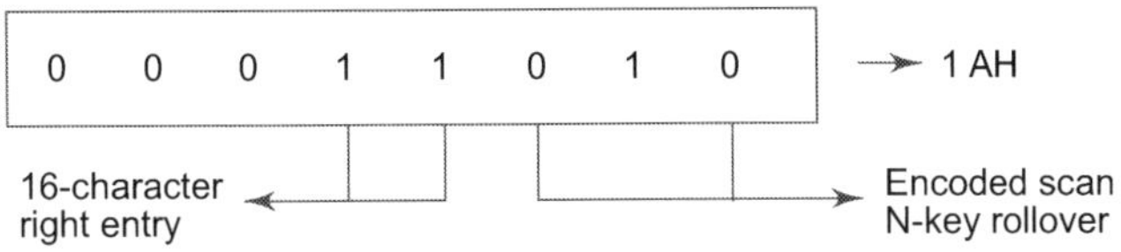

Program Clock Selection The clock input to 8279 is 2 MHz, but the operating frequency is to be 100 kHz, i.e. the clock input is to be divided by 20 (10100). Thus the prescalar value is 10100 and the command byte is set as given.

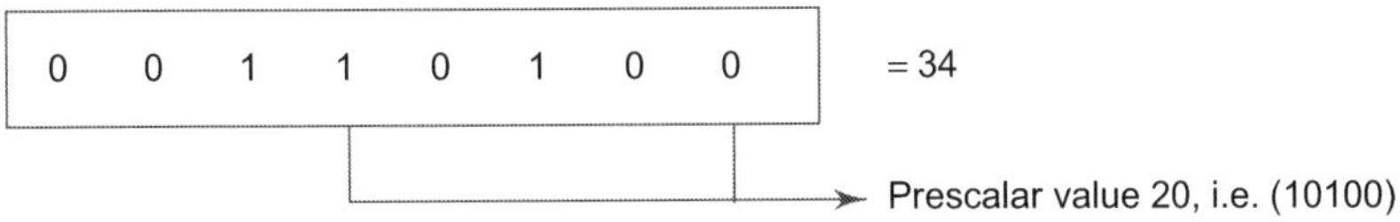

Clear Display RAM This command clears the display RAM with the programmed blanking code.

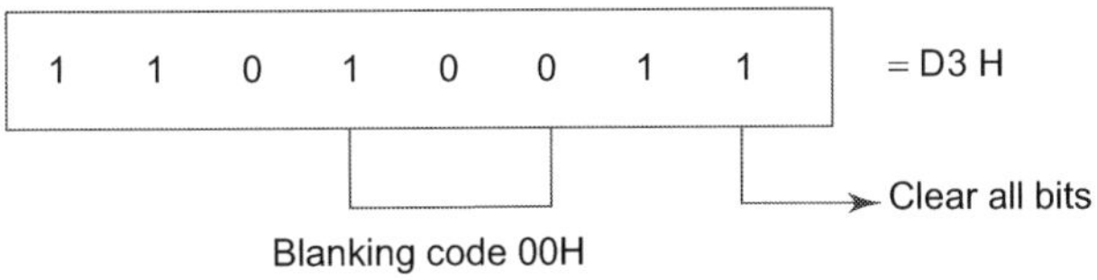

Read FIFO This command byte enables the programmer to read a key code from the FIFO RAM.

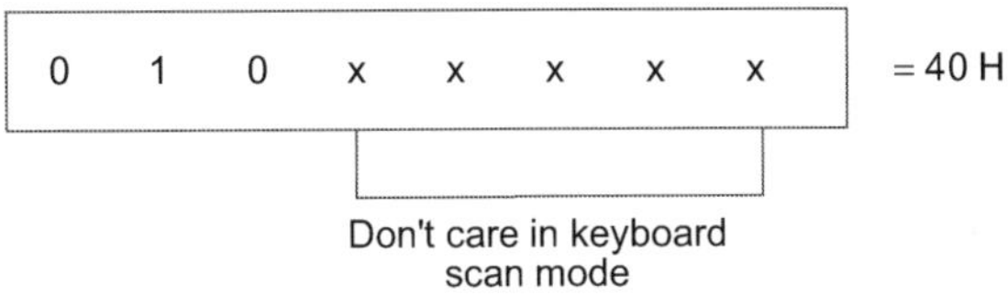

Write Display RAM This command enables the programmer to write the addressed display locations of the RAM as presented below.

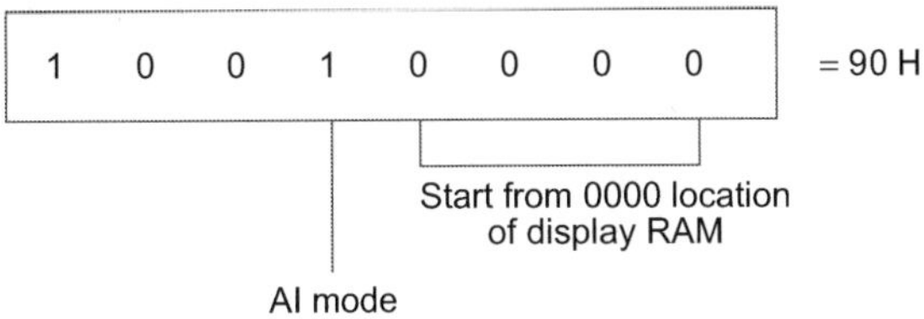

Program 6.6 gives the ALP required to initialise the 8279 as required.

```
ASSUME    CS : CODE
CODE      SEGMENT
START:    MOV AL, 1AH    ; SEt 8279 in Encoded scan,
          OUT 82H, AL    ; N key rollover, 16 display, Right entry mode.
          MOV AL, 34H    ; Set clock prescalar to
```

```
            OUT 82H, AL          ; 100 kHz
            MOV AL, 0D3H         ; Clear display ram
            OUT 82H, AL          ; command
WAIT:       MOV AL, 40H          ; Read FIFO command
            OUT 82H, AL          ; for checking display RAM
            IN AL, 82H           ; Wait for clearing of
            AND AL, 80H          ; Display RAM by reading
            CMP AL, 80H          ; FIFO Du bit of the status word i.e.
            JNZ WAIT             ; If DU bit is not set wait, else proceed
            IN AL, 82H           ; Read FIFO status
            AND AL, 07H          ; Mask all bits except the
            CMP AL, 00           ; number of characters bits
            JNZ KEYCODE          ; If any key is pressed, take
WRAM:       MOV AL, 90H          ; required action, otherwise
            OUT 82H, AL          ; proceed to write display
            MOV AL, 55H          ; RAM by using write display
            MOV CH, 10H          ; command.Write the byte
NEXT:       OUT 80H, AL          ; 55H TO ALL DISPLAY RAM
            DEC CH               ; locations
            JNZ NEXT             ;
            JMP STOP             ;
KEYCODE:    CALL READCODE        ; Call routine to read the key
            MOV CL, AL           ; store the keycode in CL.
            JMP WRAM             ; code of the pressed key is assumed available
READCODE:   MOV AL, 40H
            OUT 82H, AL
            IN AL, 80H
            RET
STOP:       MOV AH, 4CH          ; stop
            INT21H
CODE        ENDS
            END START
```

Program 6.7 *Initialisation of 8279 using an 8086 ALP for Problem 6.6*

6.4 PROGRAMMABLE COMMUNICATION INTERFACE 8251 USART

Intel's 8251A is a *universal synchronous asynchronous receiver and transmitter* compatible with Intel's Processors. This may be programmed to operate in any of the serial communication modes built into it. This chip converts the parallel data into a serial stream of bits suitable for serial transmission. It is also able to receive a serial stream of bits and convert it into parallel data bytes to be read by a microprocessor.

Before presenting the detailed account of 8251, a brief look into data communication methods will be useful to the readers.

6.4.1 Methods of Data Communication

The data transmission between two points involves unidirectional or bidirectional transmission of meaningful digital data through a medium. There are basically three modes of data transmission:

(a) Simplex
(b) Duplex
(c) Half Duplex

In simplex mode, data is transmitted only in one direction over a single communication channel. For example, a computer (CPU) may transmit data for a CRT display unit in this mode. In duplex mode, data may be transferred between two transreceivers in both directions simultaneously. In the half duplex mode, on the other hand, data transmission may take place in either direction, but at a time data may be transmitted only in one direction. For example, a computer may communicate with a terminal in this mode. When the terminal sends data (i.e. terminal is sender), the message is received by the computer (i.e. the computer is receiver). However, it is not possible to transmit data from the computer to the terminal and from terminal to the computer simultaneously.

6.4.2 Architecture and Signal Descriptions of 8251

The architectural block diagram of 8251A is shown in Fig. 6.26, followed by the functional description of each block.

The data buffer interfaces the internal bus of the circuit with the system bus. The read write control logic controls the operation of the peripheral depending upon the operations initiated by the CPU. This unit also selects one of the two internal addresses those are control address and data address at the behest of the $C/\overline{D}$ signal. The modem control unit handles the modem handshake signals to coordinate the communication between the modem and the USART. The transmit control unit transmits the data byte received by the data buffer from the CPU for further serial communication. This decides the transmission rate which is controlled by the $\overline{TXC}$ input frequency. This unit also derives two transmitter status signals namely

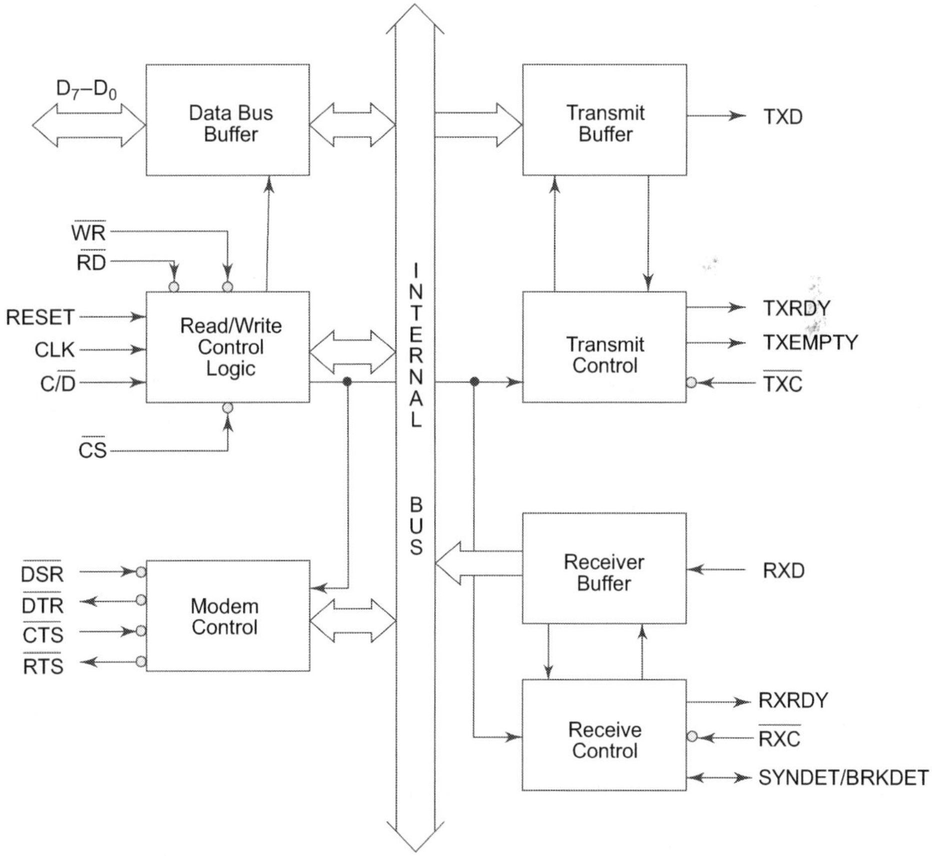

Fig. 6.26 *8251A Internal Architecture*

TXRDY and TXEMPTY. These may be used by the CPU for handshaking. The transmit buffer is a parallel to serial converter that receives a parallel byte for conversion into a serial signal and further transmission onto the communication channel. The receive control unit decides the receiver frequency as controlled by the $\overline{RXC}$ input frequency. This unit generates a receiver ready (RXRDY) signal that may be used by the CPU for handshaking. This unit also detects a break in the data string while the 8251 is in asynchronous mode. In synchronous mode, the 8251 detects SYNC characters using SYNDET/BD pin.

The pin configuration of 8251A is shown in Fig. 6.27. The following text describes the signal descriptions of 8251A:

D_0–D_7 This is an 8-bit data bus used to read or write status, command word or data from or to the 8251A.

C/$\overline{D}$ –Control Word/Data This input pin, together with $\overline{RD}$ and $\overline{WR}$ inputs, informs the 8251A that the word on the data bus is either a data or control word/status information. If this pin is 1, control/status is on the bus, otherwise data is on the bus.

$\overline{RD}$ This active-low input to 8251A is used to inform it that the CPU is reading either data or status information from its internal registers.

$\overline{WR}$ This active-low input to 8251A is used to inform it that the CPU is writing data or control word to 8251A.

$\overline{CS}$ This is an active-low chip select input of 8251A. If it is high, no read or write operation can be carried out on 8251. The data bus is tristated if this pin is high.

CLK This input is used to generate internal device timings and is normally connected to clock generator output. This input frequency should be at least 30 times greater than the receiver or transmitter data bit transfer rate.

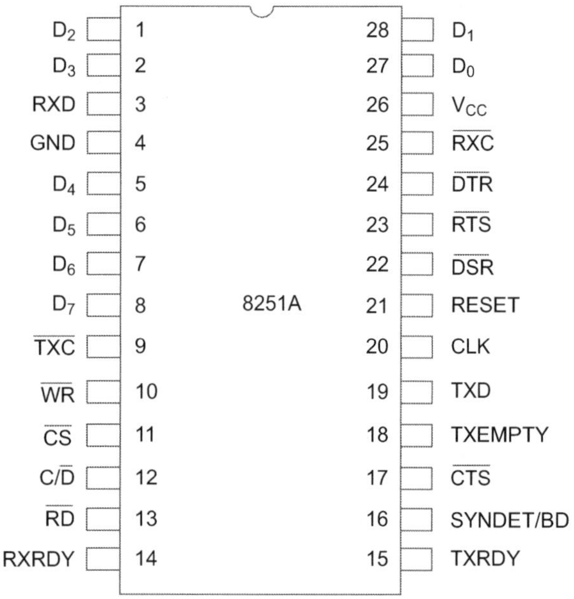

Fig. 6.27 *8251A Pin Configuration*

RESET A high on this input forces the 8251A into an idle state. The device will remain idle till this input signal again goes low and a new set of control word is written into it. The minimum required reset pulse width is 6 clock states, for the proper reset operation.

$\overline{TXC}$ Transmitter Clock Input This transmitter clock input controls the rate at which the character is to be transmitted. The baud rate (1x) is equal to the $\overline{TXC}$. frequency in synchronous transmission mode. In asynchronous mode, the baud rate is one of the three fractions, i.e. 1, 1/16 or 1/64 of the $\overline{TXC}$. The serial data is shifted out on the successive negative edge of the $\overline{TXC}$.

TXD Transmitted Data Output This output pin carries serial stream of the transmitted data bits along with other information like start bit, stop bits and parity bit, etc.

$\overline{RXC}$ Receiver Clock Input This receiver clock input pin controls the rate at which the character is to be received. In synchronous mode, the baud rate is equal to the $\overline{RXC}$ frequency. In asynchronous mode, the baud rate is one of the three fractions, i.e. 1, 1/16 and 1/64th of the $\overline{RXC}$ frequency. The received data is read into the 8251 on rising edge of $\overline{RXC}$. In most of the systems, the $\overline{RXC}$ and $\overline{RXC}$ frequencies are equal.

RXD-Receive Data Input This input pin of 8251A receives a composite stream of the data to be received by 8251A.

RXRDY-Receiver Ready Output This output indicates that the 8251A contains a character to be read by the CPU. The RXRDY signal may be used either to interrupt the CPU or may be polled by the CPU. To set the RXRDY signal in asynchronous mode, the receiver must be enabled to sense a start bit and a complete character must be assembled and then transferred to the data output register. In synchronous mode, to set the RXRDY signal, the receiver must be enabled and a character must finish assembly and then be transferred to the data output register. If the data is not successfully read from the receiver data output register before assembly of the next data byte, the overrun condition error flag is set and the previous byte is over written by the next byte of the incoming data and hence it is lost.

TXRDY-Transmitter Ready This output signal indicates to the CPU that the internal circuit of the transmitter is ready to accept a new character for transmission from the CPU. The TXRDY signal is set by a leading edge of write signal if a data character is loaded into it from the CPU. In the polled operation, the TXRDY status bit will indicate the empty or full status of the transmitter data input register.

$\overline{DSR}$-Data Set Ready This input may be used as a general purpose one bit inverting input port. Its status can be checked by the CPU using a status read operation. This is normally used to check if the data set is ready when communicating with a modem.

$\overline{DTR}$-Data Terminal Ready This output may be used as a general purpose one bit inverting output port. This can be programmed low using the command word. This is used to indicate that the device is ready to accept data when the 8251 is communicating with a modem.

$\overline{RTS}$-Request to Send Data This output also may be used as a general purpose one bit inverting output port that can be programmed low to indicate the modem that the receiver is ready to receive a data byte from the modem. This signal is used to communicate with a modem.

$\overline{CTS}$-Clear to Send If the clear to send the input line is low, the 8251A is enabled to transmit the serial data, provided the enable bit in the command byte is set to '1'. If a Tx disable or $\overline{CTS}$ divsable command occurs, while the 8251A is transmitting data, the transmitter transmits all the data written to the USART prior to disabling the $\overline{CTS}$ or Tx. If the $\overline{CTS}$ disable or Tx disable command occurs just before the last character appears in the serial bit string, the character will be retransmitted again whenever the $\overline{CTS}$ is enabled or the Tx enable occurs.

TXE-Transmitter Empty If the 8251A, while transmitting, has no characters to transmit, the TXE output goes high and it automatically goes low when a character is received from the CPU, for further transmission. In synchronous mode, a 'high' on this output line indicates that a character has not been loaded and the SYNC character or characters are about to be or are being transmitted automatically as 'fillers'. The TXE signal can be used to indicate the end of a transmission mode.

SYNDET/BD-Synch Detect/Break Detect This pin is used in the synchronous mode for detecting SYNC characters (SYNDET) and may be used as either input or output. This can be programmed using the control word. After resetting, it is in the output mode. When used as an output, the SYNDET pin will go high to indicate that the 8251A has located a SYNC character in the receive mode. The SYNDET signal is automatically reset upon a following status read operation. When this is used as input, a positive going signal will cause the 8251A to start assembling a data character on the rising edge of the next RXC.

In the asynchronous mode, the pin acts as a break detect output. This goes high whenever the RXD pin remains low through two consecutive stop bit sequences. A stop bit sequence contains a stop bit, a start bit, data bits and parity bits. This is reset only with master chip reset or the RXD returning high. If the RXD returns to '1', during the last bit of the next character after the break, the break detect is latched up. The 8251A can now be cleared only with chip reset.

6.4.3 Description of 8251A Operating Modes

The 8251A can be programmed to operate in its various modes using its mode control words. A set of control words is written into the internal registers of 8251A to make it operate in the desired mode.

Once the 8251A is programmed as required, the TXRDY output is raised 'high' to signal the CPU that the 8251A is ready to receive a data byte from it that is to be further converted to serial format and transmitted. This automatically goes low when CPU writes a data byte into 8251A. In receiver mode, the 8251A receives a serial data byte from a modem or an I/O device. After receiving the entire data byte, the RXRDY signal is raised high to inform the CPU that the 8251A has a character ready for it. The RXRDY signal is automatically reset after the CPU reads the received byte from the 8251A . The 8251A cannot initiate transmission until the TX enable bit in the command word is set and a $\overline{\text{CTS}}$ signal is received from the modem or receiving I/O device.

The control words of 8251A are divided into two functional types:

1. Mode Instruction control word
2. Command Instruction control word

Asynchronous Mode

Mode Instruction Control Word This defines the general operational characteristics of 8251A. After internal (reset command) or external (reset input pin) reset, this must be written to configure the 8251A as per the required operation. Once this has been written into 8251A, SYNC characters or command instructions may be programmed further as per the requirements. To change the mode of operation from synchronous to asynchronous or vice-a-versa, the 8251A has to be reset using master chip reset.

Figure 6.28 shows asynchronous mode instruction control word format.

Asynchronous Mode (Transmission) When a data character is sent to 8251A by the CPU, it adds start bits prior to the serial data bits, followed by optional parity bit and stop bits using the asynchronous mode instruction control word format. This sequence is then transmitted using TXD output pin on the falling edge of $\overline{\text{TXC}}$. When no data characters are sent by the CPU to 8251A the TXD output remains 'high', if a 'break' has not been detected.

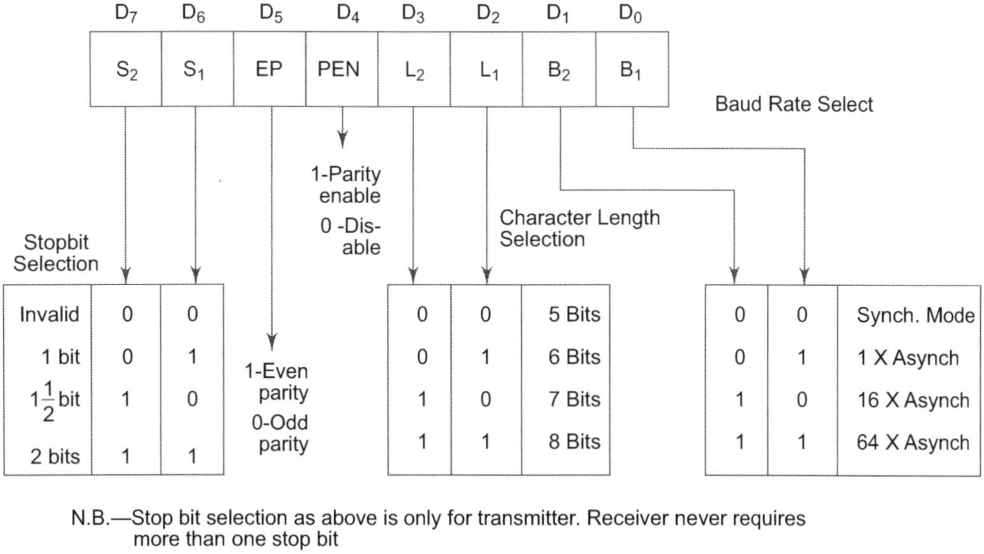

Fig. 6.28 *Mode Instruction Format Asynchronous Mode*

Asynchronous Mode (Receive) A falling edge on RXD input line marks a start bit. At baud rates of 16x and 64x, this start bit is again checked at the center of start bit pulse and if detected low, it is a valid start bit which starts counting. The bit counter locates the data bits, parity bit and stop bit. If a parity error occurs, the parity error flag is set. If a low level is detected as the stop bit, the framing error flag is set. The receiver requires only one stop bit to mark end of the data bit string, regardless of the stop bit programmed at the transmitting end. This 8-bit character is then loaded into parallel I/O buffer of 8251A. RXRDY pin is then raised high to indicate to the CPU that a character is ready for it. If the previous character has not been read by the CPU, the new character replaces it, and the overrun flag is set indicating that the previous character is lost. These error flags can be cleared using an error reset instruction. Figure 6.29 shows asynchronous mode transmission and receiver data formats. If character length is 5 to 7 bits then the remaining bits are set to zero.

Synchronous Mode Figure 6.30 shows the synchronous mode instruction format with its bit definitions.

Synchronous Mode (Transmission) The TXD output is high until the CPU sends a character to 8251A which usually is a SYNC character. When $\overline{\text{CTS}}$ line goes low, the first character is serially transmitted out. All the characters are shifted out on the falling edges of $\overline{\text{TXC}}$. Data is shifted out at the same rate as $\overline{\text{TXC}}$, over TXD output line. If the CPU buffer becomes empty, the SYNC character or characters are inserted in the data stream over TXD output. The TXEMPTY pin is raised high to indicate that the 8251A is empty (i.e. it does not have any byte to transmit) and is transmitting SYNC characters. The TXEMPTY pin is reset, automatically when a data character is written to 8251A by the CPU. Figure 6.31 shows the relation between TXEMPTY and SYNC character insertion.

Synchronous Mode (Receiver) In this mode, the character synchronization can be achieved internally or externally. If this mode is programmed, then 'ENTER HUNT' command should be included in the first command instruction word written into the 8251A. The data on RXD pin is sampled on rising edge of the $\overline{\text{RXC}}$.

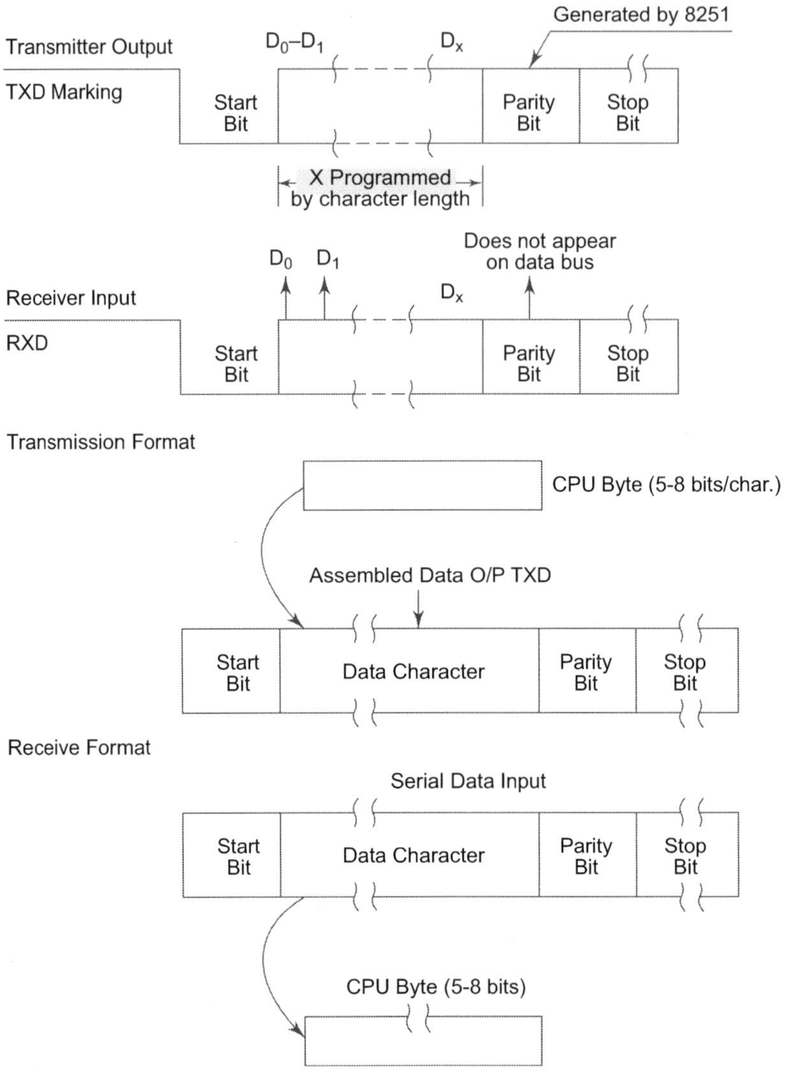

Fig. 6.29 *Asynchronous Mode Transmit and Receive Formats*

The content of the receiver buffer is compared with the first SYNC character at every edge until it matches. If 8251A is programmed for two SYNC characters, the subsequent received character is also checked. When both the characters match, the hunting stops. The SYNDET pin is set high and is reset automatically by a status read operation. If a parity bit is programmed, the SYNDET signal will not go as high as the middle of parity bit, or till the middle of the last data bit.

In the external SYNC mode, synchronization is achieved by applying a high level on the SYNDET input pin, that forces 8251A out of HUNT mode. The high level can be removed after one $\overline{RXC}$ cycle. An ENTER HUNT command has no meaning in asynchronous mode. The parity and overrun error both are checked in the same way as in asynchronous mode. Figure 6.32 shows synchronous mode transmit and receive data formats.

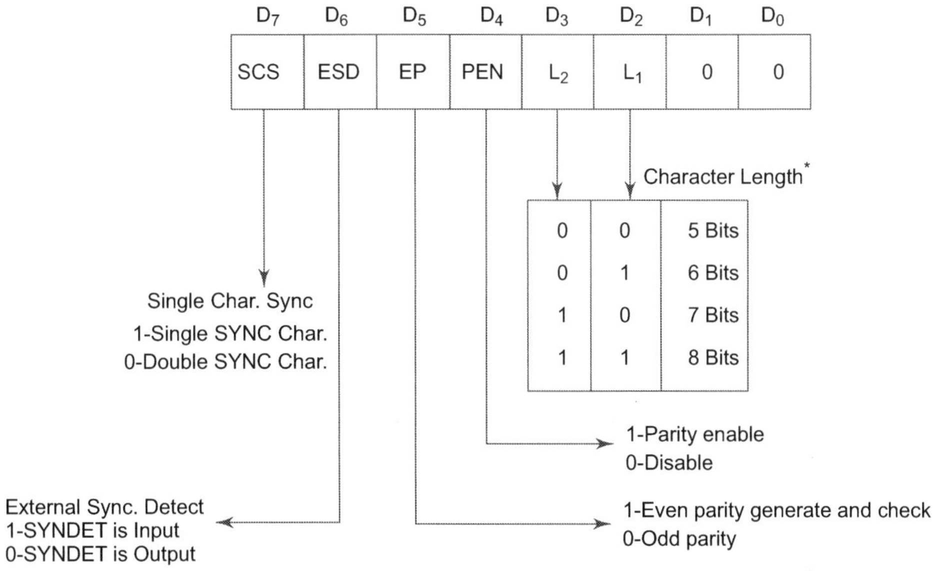

* If the character size less than 8-bits, the remaining bits are set to 'O'.

Fig. 6.30 *Synchronous Mode Instruction Format*

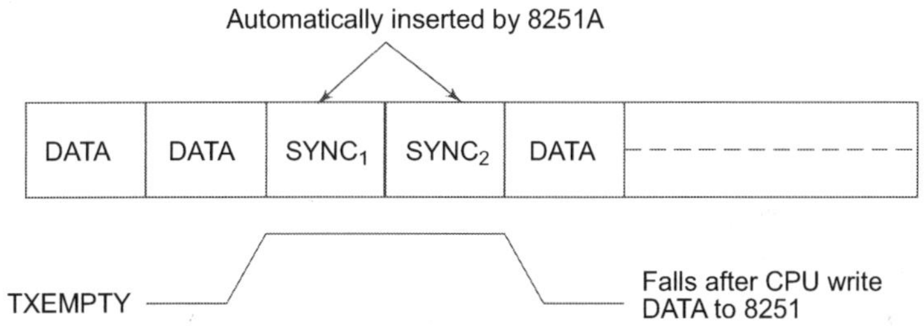

Fig. 6.31 *TXEMPTY Signal and SYNC Characters*

Command Instruction Definition The command instruction controls the actual operations of the selected format like enable transmit/receive, error reset and modem control. Once the mode instruction has been written into 8251A and the SYNC characters are inserted internally by 8251A, all further control words written with $C/\overline{D} = 1$ will load a command instruction. A reset operation returns 8251A back to mode instruction format. The command instruction format is shown in Fig. 6.33, with its bit definitions.

Status Read Definition This definition is used by the CPU to read the status of the active 8251A to confirm if any error condition or other conditions like the requirement of processor service has been detected, during the operation.

A read command is issued by processor with $C/\overline{D} = 1$ to accomplish this function. Some of the bits in the definition have the same significances as those of the pins of 8251A. These are used to interface the 8251A in a polled configuration, besides the interrupt controlled mode. The pin TXRDY is an exception. The status 'read format' is shown in Fig. 6.34, with its bit definitions.

* N.B.—If the character size is less than 8-bits, the remaining bits are set to '0'.

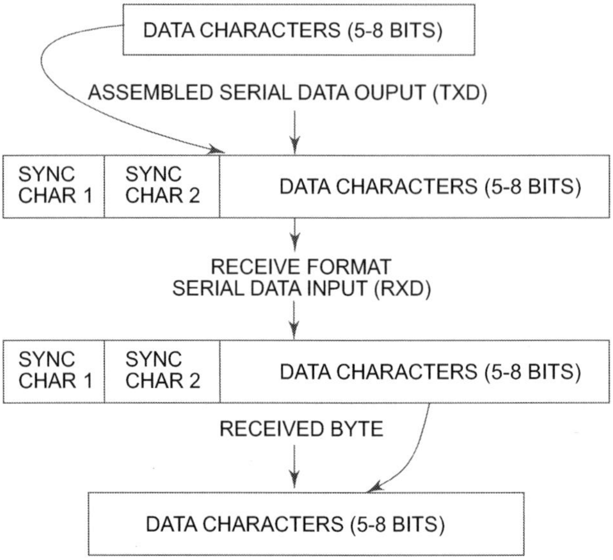

Fig. 6.32 *Data Formats of Synchronous Mode*

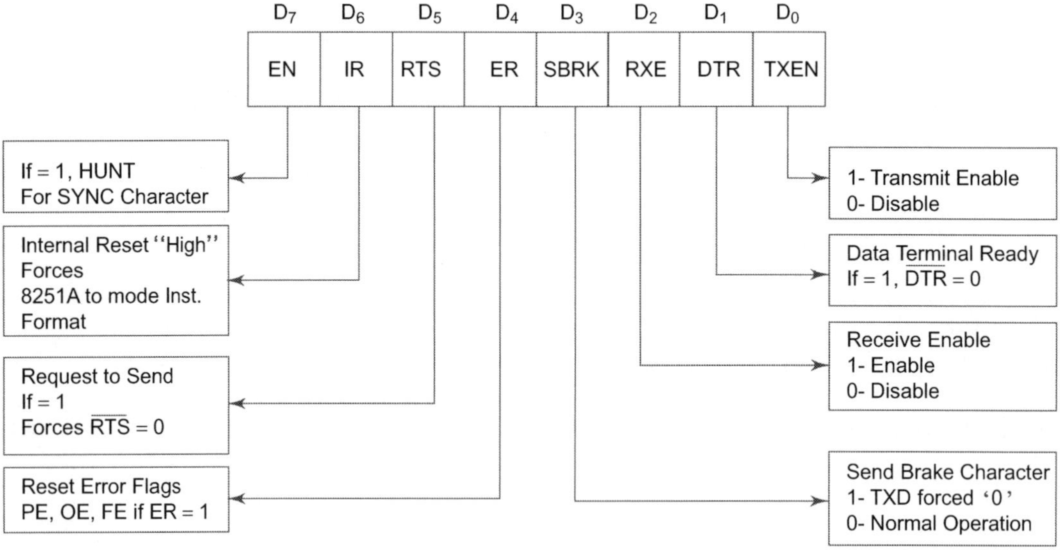

Fig. 6.33 *Command Instruction Format*

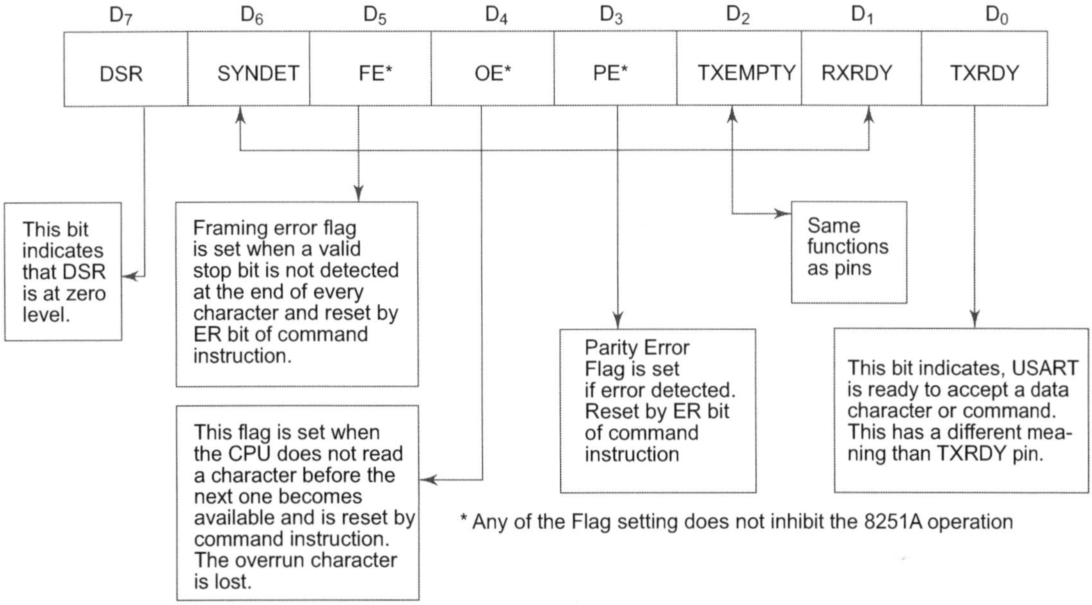

Fig. 6.34 *Status Read Instruction Format*

6.4.4 Interfacing and Programming 8251 with 8086

The following problem explains the interfacing and programming of 8251A in an 8086 system.

Problem 6.7

Design the hardware interface circuit for interfacing 8251 with 8086. Set the 8251A in asynchronous mode as a transmitter and receiver with even parity enabled, 2 stop bits, 8-bit character length, frequency 160 kHz and baud rate 10 K.

(a) Write an ALP to transmit 100 bytes of data string starting at location 2000:5000H.

(b) Write an ALP receive 100 bytes of data string and store it at 3000:4000H.

Solution

The interfacing connections of 8251A with 8086 are shown in Fig. 6.35.

Asynchronous mode control word for Problem 6.6 (a)

D_7	D_6	D_5	D_4	D_3	D_2	D_1	D_0	
1	1	1	1	1	1	1	0	= 0FE H
2 stop bits		Even parity enabled		8-bit format		CLK scaled by 16		

(a) ALP to initialize 8251 and transmit 100 bytes of data

```
ASSUME    CS : CODE
CODE      SEGMENT
START:    MOV AX, 2000H      ;
          MOV DS, AX         ; DS points to byte string segment
          MOV SI, 5000H      ; SI points to byte string
          MOV CL, 64H        ; length of the string in CL(hex)
          MOV AL, 0FEH       ; Mode control word out to
          OUT 0FEH, AL       ; D0-D7.
          MOV AX, 11H        ; Load command word
          OUT 0FEH, AL       ; to transmit enable and error reset
WAIT:     IN AL, 0FEH        ; Read status,
          AND AL, 01H        ; check transmitter enable
          JZ WAIT            ; bit,if zero wait for the transmitter to
                               be ready
          MOV AL, [SI]       ; If ready, first byte of string data
          OUT 0FCH, AL       ; is transmitted.
          INC SI             ; Point to next byte.
          DEC CL             ; Decrement counter.
          JNZ WAIT           ; If CL is not zero, go for next byte.
          MOV AH, 4CH        ; If CX is zero, return to DOS
          INT 21H
CODE      ENDS
          END START
```

Program 6.8 *ALP to Transmit 100 Bytes of Data*

For Problem 6.6 (b), the command instruction word can be calculated as 14H.

(b) An ALP to initialize 8251 and receive 100 bytes of data.

```
ASSUME    CS : CODE
CODE      SEGMENT
START:    MOV AX, 3000H      ;
          MOV DS, AX         ; Data segment set to 3000H
          MOV SI, 4000H      ; Pointer to destination offset
          MOV CL, 64H        ; Byte count in CL
          MOV AL, 7EH        ; Only one stop bit for
          OUT 0FEH, AL       ; receiver is set
          MOV AL, 14H        ; Load command word to enable
          OUT 0FEH, AL       ; the receiver and disable
                               transmitter
NXTBT:    IN AL, 0FEH        ; Read status
          AND 38H            ; Check FE, OE and PE,
          JZ READY           ; If zero, jump to READY
          MOV AL, 14H        ; If not zero, clear them
          OUT 0FEH, AL       ;
READY:    IN AL, 0FEH        ; Check RXRDY.If the
          AND 02H            ; receiver is not ready,
          JZ READY           ; wait
          IN AL, 0FCH        ; If it is ready,
          MOV [SI], AL       ; receive the character
          INC SI             ; Increment pointer to next byte
```

```
        DEC CL              ; Decrement counter
        JNZ NXTBT           ; Repeat,if CL is not zero
        MOV AH,4CH          ; If CL is 0, return to DOS
        INT 21H
CODE    ENDS
        END START
```

Program 6.9 *ALP to Receive 100 Bytes*

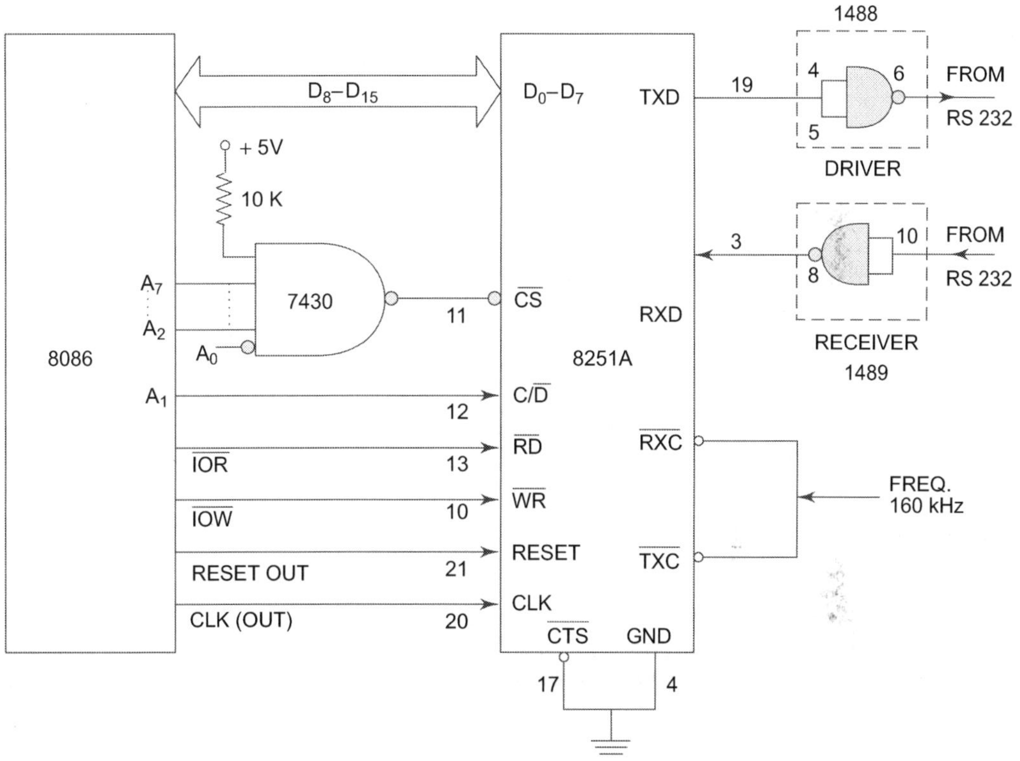

Fig. 6.35 *Interfacing of 8251A with 8086*

6.4.5 High-Speed Communication Standard; Universal Serial Bus (USB) Functional Description

Universal serial bus is the most popular serial communication standard introduced by USB Implementers Forum (USB-IF). RS-232c had been used for long and has a few serous disadvantages like limited speed of communication, high-voltage level signaling and big-size communication adapters. The USB standards are available with speeds from a few hundred kilobytes per second (USB1.x) to around 5 GB per second (USB3.x). The logic levels used for representing the bits use voltages less than 5 volts and currents less than 500 mA. A USB uses comparatively small size of connectors for establishing connection with compatible devices. In fact, in addition to the standard USB connector available with PCs, many small-size versions are introduced specially for embedded products. Recent USB ports are used for many other activities like battery charging, communication with PC and even device-to-device communications.

USB implements an asynchronous serial communication. Initially, it used to be half-duplex. However, the new USB standard supports full-duplex communication at the cost of additional two conductors. The data is transmitted in the form of packets containing start, data, parity and stop bits. The attached devices are detected and configured automatically, provided they are USB compatible. USB standards provide automatic detection and correction of errors. Design and implementation of a USB compatible system requires design certification and licensing from the USB-IF.

In its original form, USB provides a serial bus standard for connecting peripherals such as mouse, keyboard, gamepads and joysticks, scanners, cameras, printers, external memory devices and other networking components. USB 1.0 was introduced in 1995 and 1996 followed by its advanced version, USB1.1, in 1998 for communication up to the speed of 1.5 MB/second. USB 2.0 was introduced in 2000 and supported data transfers up to 12 MB/second. USB 2.0 was revised in 2002 to provide three different speeds of communications up to 480 MB/second to support a wide variety of peripherals.

A USB communication system consists of three basic units: 1) Host, 2) Cable, and 3) Device. The host detects a connected device, and manages flow of control information and actual data between the system and the device. USB cable is a metallic medium of communication. It consists of four conductors.

- The VBUS conductor is a power supply pin and carries voltage from 4.2 V to 5.25 V.
- The Gnd connector extends the system ground to the device.
- There are two data pins D+ and D- for differential signaling of the logic levels.

A USB device monitors device address in each communication and prepares itself for communication if selected. It responds to all the requests from the host. It adds bits to the packets being set to the host for detecting errors. It detects and corrects errors in the data received from the host.

USB transfers are of four types.

- The interrupt USB transfer is meant for low-volume data transfer like keyboards, mouse and touch pads. Bulk data transfers are implemented in terms of block data transfers and are intended for devices requiring bigger data volumes like printers and scanners.
- Isochronous mode of transfers are meant for devices like speakers and microphones that require real-time synchronization for reproducing the original signal. These transfers do not require error detection and correction.
- The control transfers are used to configure and control the connected devices. The control transfers are handled as highest priority, automatic error protection and high data rate transfers.
- The USB asynchronous communication transfers four types of bit packets over the cable.
    - The first type of packet is called 'Handshake Packet'. The handshake packet consists of a packet identification, i.e., PID byte, and are used for reliable communication of data packets.
    - The second type of packet is called 'Token Packet'. The token packets are always sent by the host and contain 2 bytes including 11-bit address and 5 bits of cyclic redundancy code. The token packet commands the device either to receive data or transmit data in response to specific demands from the host.
    - Data packets contain actual bytes of data up to 1024 bytes. It also includes a 16-bit CRC code.

- A fourth type of packets called PRE packets are only of importance to low-speed USB devices. They contain a special PID value allotted to low-speed devices. High-speed devices neglect the PRE packets. However, the PRE values are used by network hubs while communicating with USB devices over a network. Over networks, the hubs control the data flow rate even to the high-speed devices subject to the instantaneous network traffic.

Signaling in USB Systems Available USB standards support four signaling rates.

- Low-speed USB 1.0 rate of 1.5 Mbps is suitable for human interface devices.
- Full-speed USB 1.0 rate of 12 Mbps is suitable for communication with network hubs using networks like LAN.
- High-speed USD 2.0 rate of 480 Mbps is suitable for higher speed devices but it is also compatible with full-speed devices with USB 1.0 standard.
- Super-speed USB 3.0 rates of up to 5.0 Gbps or 596 Mbps support full-duplex operation. However, it is backward compatible with the earlier USB standards though they require an additional pair of D+ and D– connectors for full-duplex communication.

USB signaling is implemented in differential for using 0 to 0.3 volts for logic 0 and 2.6 to 3.6 volts for logic 1 in low- and full-speed options. In higher speed modes, it uses –10 mV to +10 mV for logic 1 and 360 mV to 400 mV for logic 1. The host pulls down the D+ and D– lines using a 15 K resistor indicating no device is connected with the port. If a device is connected, it pulls one of the data lines high with a pull up of 1.5 K indicating that a device is connected with the port.

It must be noted that the D+ and D– conductors carry a valid bit only when their state is different and thus the name 'differential coding'. If both have zero state, it indicates end of the packet. To mark the next start of the packet, the D+ line must go high while D– remains low. Serial bus states are described in terms of a 'J' and a 'K' state. Duration of each state for full-speed communication in 1/12 MHz = 83 ns, i.e., bit-clock rate duration. In the 'J' state , the D+ line is high (2.6 to 3.6 V)and D– line is low (0 to 0.3 V) as shown in Fig. 6.36(a). In the 'K' state , the D+ line is low (0 to 0.3 V) and D– line is high (2.6 to 3.6 V) as shown in Fig. 6.36(b). A toggling between the two states represents a logical 0 bit. A repetition of either 'J' or 'K' states represents a logical 1 bit. The successive 'J' and 'K' states are shown in Figs 6.36 (c) and (d). A bit stream '0100100' is shown coded in Fig. 6.36(e). In the idle state, both lines are low. A starting of a data packet is marked by the D+ line going high while the D– line remains low. In the next bit period, the lines enter the 'K' state. The states toggle six times to mark a valid start of packet and then the 'K' state continues for one bit duration to mark start of a data bit stream as shown in Fig. 6.36(e). The next state is now 'J', i.e., there is a toggling, so the bit in the 'J' state is '0'. Further, there is again a 'J' state, i.e., a state continues, it represents a '1' bit. Thus, if there is a toggling between J to K or K to J, it represents a '0' bit and if there is a continuation of states, either J to J or K to K, it represents a '1' bit. A data packet may contain up to 1024 bits followed by a 16-bit CRC code. The end of the packet is marked by both the lines D+ and D– being pulled low for more than one-bit duration. If there are more than six successive '1' bits in the stream, a zero is inserted by the host or a USB compatible device after the sixth '1'. This is called bit stuffing. Thus, received seven consecutive '1' are considered an error. In case of an error, the same data packet may be requested again by the device using a special type of the handshake packet.

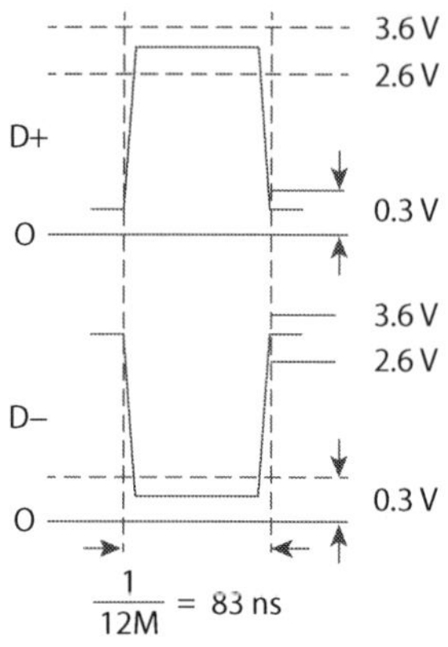

Fig. 6.36(a) *J State*

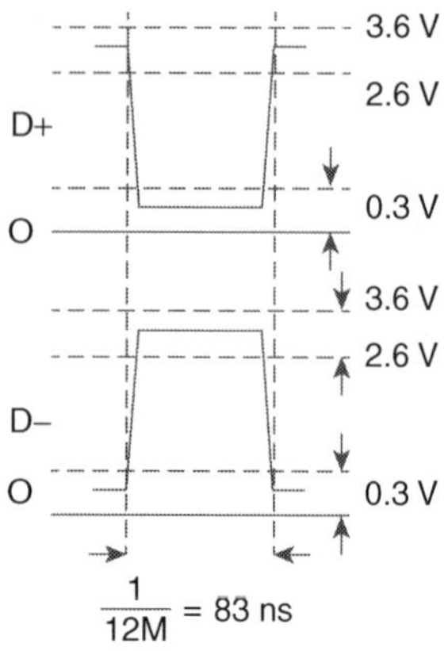

Fig. 6.36(b) *K State*

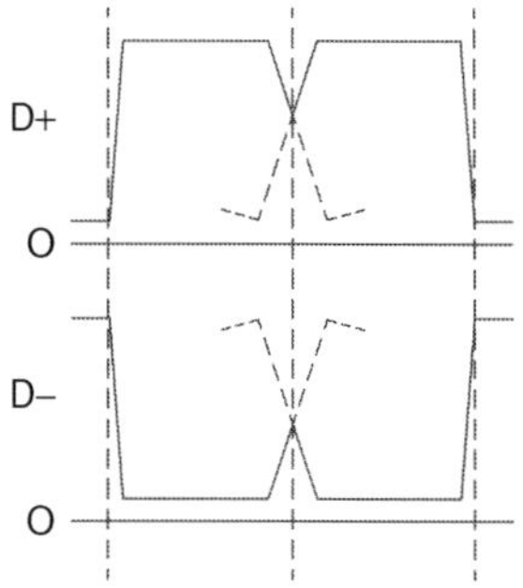

Fig. 6.36(c) *Successive J States*

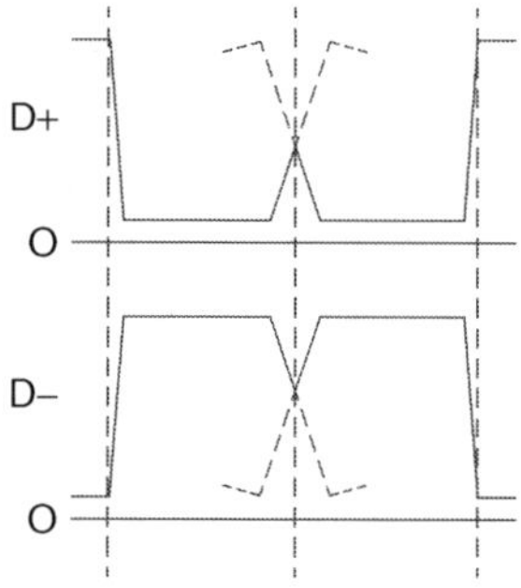

Fig. 6.36 (d) *Successive K States*

- Toggling between J & K states indicates a logics
- Successive states either J or K indicate logic 1

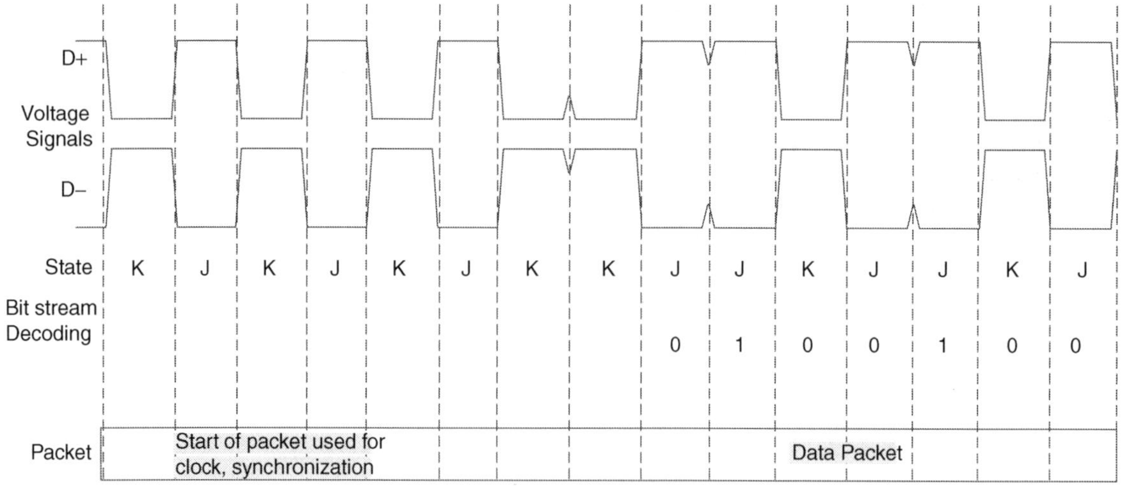

Fig. 6.36(e) *Coding of a Bit Stream Using the USB Signalling Scheme.*

SUMMARY

In this chapter, we have presented a detailed account of the functioning of some of the important Intel peripherals. With the recent advances in the field, the Intel family of the peripherals, has been continuously increasing. Those, which are frequently used in the industrial and general systems are discussed in this chapter, in significant details. This chapter has been started with the discussion on the programmable timer 8254. The necessary functional details of 8254 have been discussed along with an interfacing example and supporting programs. Further, the peripherals like programmable interrupt controller 8259A, programmable keyboard display controller 8279A, programmable communication interface 8251A have been discussed along with their architectures, signal descriptions, interfacing and programming examples.

Thus this chapter has provided an insight into the operations, programming and interfacing of the dedicated peripherals.

EXERCISES

6.1 Draw and discuss the internal architecture of 8254.

6.2 Draw and discuss the different modes of operation of 8254.

6.3 Explain the significances of different bits of the control word register format of 8254.

6.4 Design a real time clock using 8254 interfaced with 8086. The CLK input to the 8254 is of 1.5 MHz frequency. Assume suitable addresses for 8254. Further, display the time using a 6-digit 7-segment multiplexed display unit which is interfaced with the 8086 using 8255. The 7-segment data port address of 8255 is 00 and the digit select port address of 8255 is 01. Draw the hardware schematic and write a program.

6.5 Design an 8086 microprocessor based stop-watch using 8254 and 8255. The stop-watch counts up to 100 seconds in the steps of 10 ms and displays the time on a four-digit 7-segment multiplexed display. The CLK input frequency to 8254 is 2.4 MHz. Draw the required hardware scheme and write the required ALP. Select suitable addresses for 8254 and 8255.

6.6 A flow transducer, which generates number of TTL compatible pulses proportional to the volume of the liquid passed through it, is available. It generates a pulse, if 5 ml volume of the liquid passes through it. Design an 8086 based system using 8254 for measuring up to 1000 litres of the liquid at a precision of 10 ml. Assume the required addresses suitably.

6.7 Draw and discuss the internal architecture of 8259A.

6.8 Explain the functions of the following pins of 8259A.
(i) CAS_0–CAS_2 (ii) $\overline{SP/EN}$

6.9 Describe an interrupt request response of an 8086 system.

6.10 What is the difference between 8259 and 8259A?

6.11 Explain the initialisation sequence of 8259A.

6.12 How will you provide more than eight interrupt input lines to an 8086 based system?
Design an interrupt system which provides twenty nine interrupt inputs to the 8086 system.

6.13 Explain the following terms in relation to 8259A.
(i) EOI (ii) Automatic rotation

(iii) Automatic EOI
(iv) Specific rotation
(v) Special mask mode
(vi) Edge and level triggered mode
(vii) Cascading
(viii) Special fully nested mode
(ix) Buffered mode
(x) Polling

6.14 Show interfacing schematic for connecting 13 interrupting devices to 8086 using 8259. Connect the slave 8259 at IR4 of the master 8259. The master should use the vectors 10H to 17H and the slave should use the vectors 30H to 34H. The master and slave PICs are selected at addresses 90H and 94H respectively. Write an ALP to initialise the 8259s in fixed priority, level triggered, normal EOI and special mask mode.

6.15 How does 8259A differentiates between an 8-bit and 16-bit processors?

6.16 How do you interface 8259A with 8086 in maximum mode? Draw the schematic.

6.17 Elaborate the need of a dedicated keyboard display controller.

6.18 Draw and discuss architecture of 8279.

6.19 Explain the functions of the following signals of 8279.
(i) IRQ
(ii) SL_0–SL_3
(iii) RL_0-RL_7
(iv) SHIFT
(v) CNTL/STB
(vi) $\overline{BD}$
(vii) $OUTA_0$–$OUTA_3$ and $OUTB_0$–$OUTB_3$

6.20 Will it be possible to interface more than sixteen 7-segment display units using 8279? If yes, explain how.

6.21 What is the sensor matrix mode of 8279? Explain the function of the 8 × 8-bit RAM in this mode.

6.22 Explain the following terms in relation to 8279.
(i) Two key lock out
(ii) N-key roll-over
(iii) Right entry
(iv) Left entry
(v) FIFO
(vi) Display RAM

6.23 Explain the different commands of 8279 in brief.

6.24 Explain the key-code format of 8279.

6.25 Explain the FIFO status word of 8279.

6.26 Explain the mode set register of 8279.

6.27 Draw the schematic of an 8279 keyboard controller interfaced to 8086. An 11 key keyboard and an 8-digit 7-segment display is to be driven by the system so that by reading the FIFO we should directly get the number of the key pressed (the number corresponding to the key, i.e. 0 to 9 must be same as the keycode formed by 8279). The first 10 keys are allotted to the numbers 0 to 9 and the eleventh key is a 'CLEAR', which should clear the contents of the display RAM. Program the 8279 in left entry, 2-key lock out mode.

6.28 Design an 8086 and 8279 based system to interface sixteen 7-segment display units using any four port lines of 8279 $OUTA_0$–$OUTA_3$. You may use any additional hardware if required. Write a program to display the hex numbers 0 to FH on these sixteen displays using right entry mode. For example, 0 will be displayed at the LSB position of the display for half second , then 0 will be shifted to the next left display and 1 will be displayed at the LSB position for half second and so on. After all the numbers up to FH are displayed, the display should be blanked by glowing all the segments of all the 7-segment units for half second and then the same procedure should be repeated continuously.

6.29 Interface a 26-keys keyboard with 8279. The keys represent the alphabets 'a' to 'z'. Write an 8086 ALP to find out the ASCII equivalent of the alphabet corresponding to the pressed key. The 8086 system runs at 6 MHz while the 8279 should work at 200 kHz. Will the internal prescalar reduce 6 MHz to 200 kHz? If any external prescalar is required, design it with minimum hardware.

6.30 Draw and discuss internal architecture of USART 8251.

6.31 Explain the following signal descriptions of 8251.

(i) $C/\overline{D}$	(ii) $\overline{TXC}$	(iii) TXD
(iv) $\overline{RXC}$	(v) RXD	(vi) RXRDY
(vii) TXRDY	(viii) $\overline{DSR}$	(ix) $\overline{DTR}$
(x) $\overline{RTS}$	(xi) $\overline{CTS}$	(xii) TXEMPTY
(xiii) SYNDET/BD		

6.32 Explain the mode instruction control word format of 8251.

6.33 Draw and discuss the asynchronous mode transmitter and receiver data formats of 8251.

6.34 Draw and discuss the status word format of 8251.

6.35 Draw and discuss the synchronous mode transmit and receive data formats of 8251.

6.36 Interface 8251 with 8086 at an address 80H. Initialise it in asynchronous transmit mode, with 7-bits character size, baud factor 16, one start bit, one stop bit, even parity enabled. Further transmit a message 'HAPPY NEW YEAR' in ASCII coded form to a modem.

6.37 Write a program to initialise 8251 in synchronous mode with even parity, single SYNCH character, 7-bit data character. Then receive FFH bytes of data from a remote terminal and store it in the memory at address 5000H:2000H.

7 DMA, and High Storage Capacity Memory Devices

INTRODUCTION

In the previous chapter, we studied some of the dedicated peripherals and their interfacing techniques with 8086. In this chapter, we will further discuss a few advanced peripherals and their interfacing techniques with 8086. In the applications where the CPU is to transfer bulk data, it may be a waste of time to transfer the data from source to destination using program controlled data transfer or interrupt driven data transfer. The alternate way of transferring the bulk data is the Direct Memory Access (DMA) technique in which the data is transferred under the control of a DMA controller, after it is properly initialised by the CPU. A DMA controller is designed to complete the bulk data transfer task much faster than the CPU. One such application which involves bulk data transfer is the storage of programs or data into secondary memories. At the end we have presented a brief overview of high capacity memory devices like old days floppy, Compact disk, Digital video disk and Hard disk drive.

7.1 DMA CONTROLLER 8257

The *Direct Memory Access* or DMA mode of data transfer is the fastest amongst all the modes of data transfer. In this mode, the device may transfer data directly to/from memory without any interference from the CPU. The device requests the CPU (through a DMA controller) to hold its data, address and control bus, so that the device may transfer data directly to/from memory. The DMA data transfer is initiated only after receiving HLDA signal from the CPU. For facilitating DMA type of data transfer between several devices, a DMA controller may be used.

Intel's 8257 is a four channel DMA controller designed to be interfaced with their family of microprocessors. The 8257, on behalf of the devices, requests the CPU for bus access using local bus request input i.e. HOLD in minimum mode. In maximum mode of the microprocessor $\overline{RQ}/\overline{GT}$ pin is used as bus request input. On receiving the HLDA signal (in minimum mode) or $\overline{RQ}/\overline{GT}$ signal (in maximum mode) from the CPU, the requesting device gets the access of the bus, and it completes the required number of DMA cycles for the data transfer and then hands over the control of the bus back to the CPU.

7.1.1 Internal Architecture of 8257

The internal architecture of 8257 is depicted in Fig. 7.1. The chip supports four DMA channels, i.e. four peripheral devices can independently request for DMA data transfer through these channels at a time. The DMA controller has 8-bit internal data buffer, a read/write unit, a control unit, a priority resolving unit along with a set of registers. We will discuss each one of them in the following sections. Next, we describe the register organisation of 8257.

Register Organisation of 8257 The 8257 performs the DMA operation over four independent DMA channels. Each of the four channels of 8257 has a pair of two 16-bit registers, viz. DMA *address register* and *terminal count register*. Also, there are two common registers for all the channels, namely, *mode set register* and *status register*. Thus there are a total of ten registers. The CPU selects one of these ten registers using address lines A_0–A_3. Table 7.1 shows how the A_0–A_3 bits may be used for selecting one of these registers. We will now describe each register as follows:

DMA Address Registers Each DMA channel has one DMA address register. The function of this register is to store the address of the starting memory location, which will be accessed by the DMA channel. Thus the starting address of the memory block which will be accessed by the device is first loaded in the DMA address register of the channel. Naturally, the device that wants to transfer data over a DMA channel, will access the block of memory with the starting address stored in the DMA Address Register.

Terminal Count Register As in the previous case, each of the four DMA channels of 8257 has one terminal count register (TC). This 16-bit register is used for ascertaining that the data transfer through a DMA channel ceases or stops after the required number of DMA cycles. Thus this register should be appropriately written before the actual DMA operation starts. The low order 14-bits of the terminal count register are initialised with the binary equivalent of the number of required DMA cycles minus one. After each DMA cycle, the terminal count register content will be decremented by one and finally it becomes zero after the required number of DMA cycles are over.

The bits 14 and 15 of this register indicate the type of the DMA operation (transfer). If the device wants to write data into the memory, the DMA operation is called DMA write operation. Bit 14 of the register in this case will be set to one and bit 15 will be set to zero. Table 7.2 gives details of DMA operation selection and the corresponding bit configuration of the bits 14 and 15 of the TC register.

Mode Set Register The mode set register is used for programming the 8257 as per the requirements of the system. The function of the mode set register is to enable the DMA channels individually and also to set the various modes of operation. A DMA channel should not be enabled till the DMA address register and the terminal count register contain valid information, otherwise, an unwanted DMA request may initiate a DMA cycle, probably destroying the valid memory data.

Table 7.1 *8257 Register Selection*

Register	*Byte*	*Address Inputs*				*F/L*	*BI-Directional Data Bus*							
		A_3	A_2	A_1	A_0		D_7	D_6	D_5	D_4	D_3	D_2	D_1	D_0
CH-0 DMA Address	LSB	0	0	0	0	0	A_7	A_6	A_5	A_4	A_3	A_2	A_1	A_0
	MSB	0	0	0	0	1	A_{15}	A_{14}	A_{13}	A_{12}	A_{11}	A_{10}	A_9	A_8
CH-0 Terminal Count	LSB	0	0	0	1	0	C_7	C_6	C_5	C_4	C_3	C_2	C_1	C_0

(*Contd.*)

Table 7.1 *(Contd.)*

Register	*Byte*	*Address Inputs*				*F/L*	*BI-Directional Data Bus*							
		A_3	A_2	A_1	A_0		D_7	D_6	D_5	D_4	D_3	D_2	D_1	D_0
	MSB	0	0	0	1	1	Rd	Wr	C_{13}	C_{12}	C_{11}	C_{10}	C_9	C_8
CH-1 DMA Address	LSB	0	0	1	0	0	A_7	A_6	A_5	A_4	A_3	A_2	A_1	A_0
	MSB	0	0	1	0	1	A_{15}	A_{14}	A_{13}	A_{12}	A_{11}	A_{10}	A_9	A_8
CH-1 Terminal Count	LSB	0	0	1	1	0	C_7	C_6	C_5	C_4	C_3	C_2	C_1	C_0
	MSB	0	0	1	1	1	Rd	Wr	C_{13}	C_{12}	C_{11}	C_{10}	C_9	C_8
CH-2 DMA Address	LSB	0	1	0	0	0	A_7	A_6	A_5	A_4	A_3	A_2	A_1	A_0
	MSB	0	1	0	0	1	A_{15}	A_{14}	A_{13}	A_{12}	A_{11}	A_{10}	A_9	A_8
CH-2 Terminal Count	LSB	0	1	0	1	0	C_7	C_6	C_5	C_4	C_3	C_2	C_1	C_0
	MSB	0	1	0	1	1	Rd	Wr	C_{13}	C_{12}	C_{11}	C_{10}	C_9	C_8
CH-3 DMA Address	LSB	0	1	1	0	0	A_7	A_6	A_5	A_4	A_3	A_2	A_1	A_0
	MSB	0	1	1	0	1	A_{15}	A_{14}	A_{13}	A_{12}	A_{11}	A_{10}	A_9	A_8
CH-3 Terminal Count	LSB	0	1	1	1	0	C_7	C_6	C_5	C_4	C_3	C_2	C_1	C_0
	MSB	0	1	1	1	1	Rd	Wr	C_{13}	C_{12}	C_{11}	C_{10}	C_9	C_8
MODE SET	—	1	0	0	0	0	AL	TCS	EW	RP	EN3	EN2	EN1	EN0
(Programme only)														
STATUS (Read only)	—	1	0	0	0	0	0	0	0	UP	TC3	TC2	TC1	TC0

A_{10}–A_{15} DMA Starting Address, C_0–C_{13} Terminal Count Value (N-1), Rd & Wr-DMA verify (00), Write (01) or Read (10) cycle selection. AL Auto Load, TCS-TC STOP, EW-Extended Write, RP-Rotating Priority, EN3-EN0-Channel Mask Enable, UP-Update Flag, TC3-TC0-Terminal Count Status Bits.

The mode set register format is shown in Fig. 7.2. It is thus extremely important that the mode set register should be programmed by the CPU for enabling the DMA channels only after initializing the DMA address register and terminal count register appropriately.

Table 7.2 *DMA Operation Selection Using A_{15}/RD and A_{14}/WR*

Bit 15	*Bit 14*	*Type of DMA Operation*
0	0	Verify DMA Cycle
0	1	Write DMA Cycle
1	0	Read DMA Cycle
1	1	(Illegal)

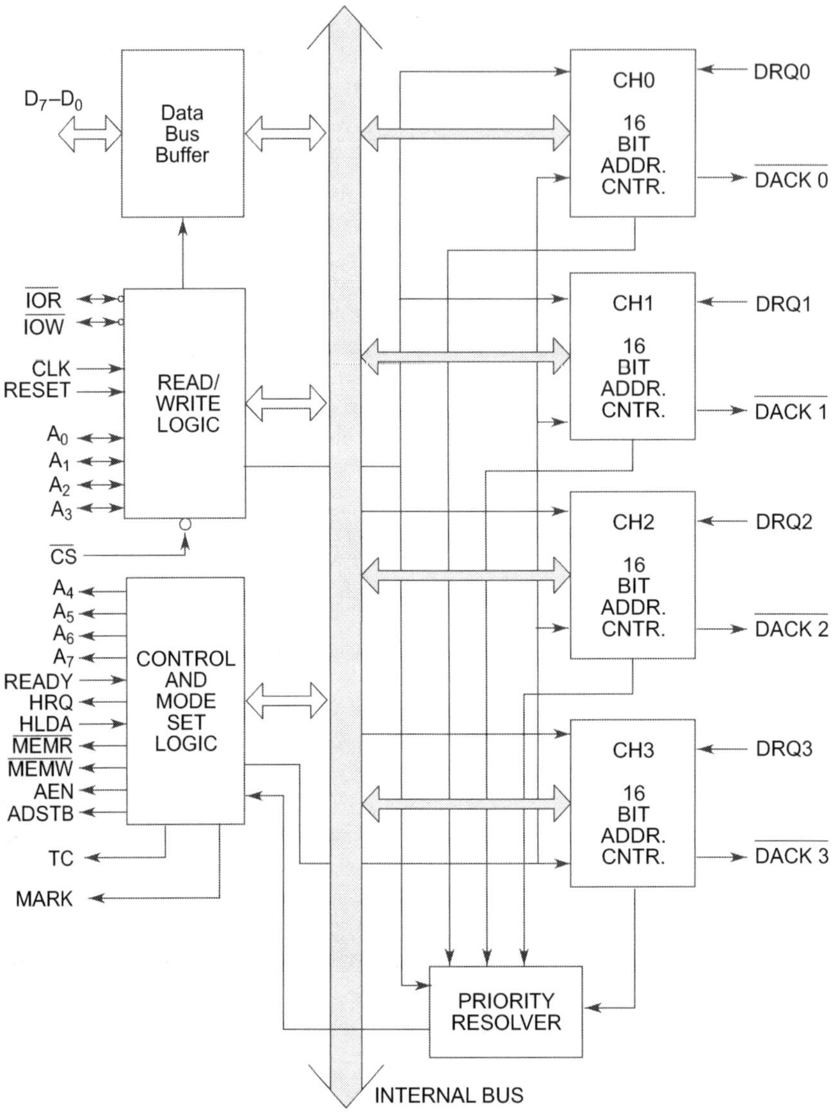

Fig. 7.1 *Internal Architecture of 8257*

The bits D_0–D_3 enable one of the four DMA channels of 8257. For example, if D_0 is '1', channel 0 is enabled. If bit D_4 is set, rotating priority is enabled, otherwise, the normal, i.e. fixed priority is enabled. The normal and rotating priorities will be explained later in this text.

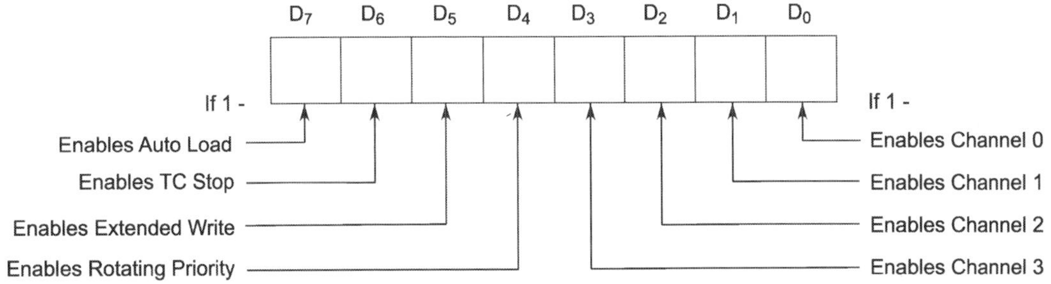

Fig. 7.2 *Bit Definitions of the Mode Set Register*

If the TC STOP bit is set, the selected channel is disabled after the *terminal count* condition is reached, and it further prevents any DMA cycle on the channel. To enable the channel again, this bit must be reprogrammed. If the TC STOP bit is programmed to be zero, the channel is not disabled, even after the count reaches zero and further requests are allowed on the same channel.

The auto load bit, if set, enables channel 2 for the repeat block chaining operations, without immediate sofware intervention between the two successive blocks. The channel 2 registers are used as usual, while the channel 3 registers are used to store the block reinitialisation parameters, i.e. the DMA starting address and the terminal count. After the first block is transferred using DMA, the channel 2 registers are reloaded with the corresponding channel 3 registers for the next block transfer, if the *Update* flag is set.

The extended write bit, if set to '1', extends the duration of $\overline{\text{MEMW}}$ and $\overline{\text{IOW}}$ signals by activating them earlier. This is useful in interfacing the peripherals with different access times. If the peripheral is not accessed within the stipulated time, it is expected to give the 'NOT READY' indication to 8257, to request it to add one or more wait states in the DMA cycle. The mode set register can only be written into.

Status Register The status register of 8257 is shown in Fig. 7.3. The lower order 4-bits of this register contain the terminal count status for the four individual channels. If any of these bits is set, it indicates that the specific channel has reached the terminal count condition. These bits remain set till either the status is read by the CPU or the 8257 is reset. The update flag is not affected by the read operation. This flag can only be cleared by resetting 8257 or by resetting the auto load bit of the mode set register. If the update flag is set, the contents of the channel 3 registers are reloaded to the corresponding registers of

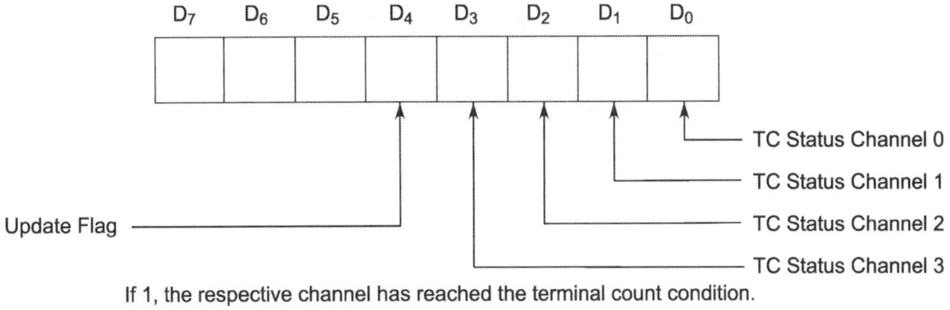

Fig. 7.3 *Bit Definitions of Status Register of 8257*

channel 2, whenever the channel 2 reaches a terminal count condition, after transferring one block and the next block is to be transferred using the autoload feature of 8257. The update flag is set every time, the channel 2 registers are loaded with contents of the channel 3 registers. It is cleared by the completion of the first DMA cycle of the new block. This register can only be read.

7.1.2 Data Bus Buffer, Read/Write Logic, Control Unit and Priority Resolver

The 8-bit, tristate, bidirectional buffer interfaces the internal bus of 8257 with the external system bus under the control of various control signals. In the slave mode, the read/write logic accepts the I/O Read or I/O Write signals, decodes the A_0–A_3 lines and either writes the contents of the data bus to the addressed internal register or reads the contents of the selected register depending upon whether $\overline{IOW}$ or $\overline{IOR}$ signal is activated. In master mode, the read/write logic generates the $\overline{IOR}$ and $\overline{IOW}$ signals to control the data flow to or from the selected peripheral. The control logic controls the sequences of operations and generates the required control signals like AEN, ADSTB, $\overline{MEMR}$, $\overline{MEMW}$, TC and MARK along with the address lines A_4–A_7, in master mode. The priority resolver resolves the priority of the four DMA channels depending upon whether normal priority or rotating priority is programmed.

7.1.3 Signal Descriptions of 8257

Figure 7.4 shows pin configuration of 8257, followed by the functional description of each signal.

DRQ_0–DRQ_3 These are the four individual channel DMA request inputs, used by the peripheral devices for requesting DMA services. The DRQ_0 has the highest priority while DRQ_3 has the lowest one, if the fixed priority mode is selected.

$\overline{DACK_0}$ – $\overline{DACK_3}$ These are the active-low DMA acknowledge output lines which inform the requesting peripheral that the request has been honoured and the bus is relinquished by the CPU. These lines may act as strobe lines for the requesting devices.

D_0–D_7 These are bidirectional, data lines used to interface the system bus with the internal data bus of 8257. These lines carry command words to 8257 and status word from 8257, in slave mode, i.e. under the control of CPU. The data over these lines may be transferred in both the directions. When the 8257 is the bus master (master mode, i.e. not under CPU control), it uses D_0–D_7 lines to send higher byte of the generated address to the latch. This address is further latched using ADSTB signal. The address is transferred over D_0–D_7 during the first clock cycle of the DMA cycle. During the rest of the period, data is available on the data bus.

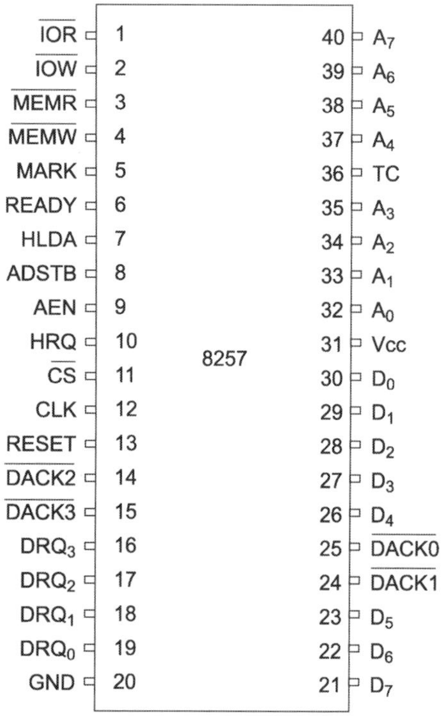

Fig. 7.4 *Pin Diagram of 8257*

$\overline{IOR}$ This is an active-low bidirectional tristate input line that acts as an input in the slave mode. In slave mode, this input signal is used by the CPU to read internal registers of 8257. This line acts as output in master mode. In master mode, this signal is used to read data from a peripheral during a memory write cycle.

$\overline{IOW}$ This is an active-low, bidirectional tristate line that acts as input in slave mode to load the contents of the data bus to the 8-bit mode register or upper/lower byte of a 16-bit DMA address register or terminal count register. In the master mode, it is a control output that loads the data to a peripheral during DMA memory read cycle (write to peripheral).

CLK This is a clock frequency input required to derive basic system timings for the internal operation of 8257.

RESET This active-high asynchronous input disables all the DMA channels by clearing the mode register and tristates all the control lines.

A_0–A_3 These are the four least significant address lines. In slave mode, they act as input which select one of the registers to be read or written. In the master mode, they are the four least significant memory address output lines generated by 8257.

$\overline{CS}$ This is an active-low chip select line that enables the read/write operations from/to 8257, in slave mode. In the master mode, it is automatically disabled to prevent the chip from getting selected (by CPU) while performing the DMA operation.

A_4–A_7 This is the higher nibble of the lower byte address generated by 8257 during the master mode of DMA operation.

READY This is an active-high asynchronous input used to stretch memory read and write cycles of 8257 by inserting wait states. This is used while interfacing slower peripherals.

HRQ The hold request output requests the access of the system bus. In the non-cascaded 8257 systems, this is connected with HOLD pin of CPU. In the cascade mode, this pin of a slave is connected with a DRQ input line of the master 8257, while that of the master is connected with HOLD input of the CPU.

HLDA The CPU drives this input to the DMA controller high, while granting the bus to the device. This pin is connected to the HLDA output of the CPU. This input, if high, indicates to the DMA controller that the bus has been granted to the requesting peripheral by the CPU.

$\overline{MEMR}$ This active-low memory read output is used to read data from the addressed memory locations during DMA read cycles.

$\overline{MEMW}$ This active-low three state output is used to write data to the addressed memory location during DMA write operation.

ADSTB This output from 8257 strobes the higher byte of the memory address generated by the DMA controller into the latches.

AEN This output is used to disable the system data bus and the control the bus driven by the CPU. This may be used to disable the system address and data bus by using the enable input of the bus drivers to inhibit the non-DMA devices from responding during DMA operations. This also may be used to transfer the higher byte of the generated address over the data bus. If the 8257 is I/O mapped, this should be used to disable the other I/O devices, when the DMA controller address is on the address bus.

TC Terminal count output indicates to the currently selected peripheral that the present DMA cycle is the last for the previously programmed data block. If the TC STOP bit in the mode set register is set, the selected channel will be disabled at the end of the DMA cycle. The TC pin is activated when the 14-bit content of the terminal count register of the selected channel becomes equal to zero. The lower order 14 bits of the terminal count register are to be programmed with a 14-bit equivalent of (n-1), if n is the desired number of DMA cycles.

MARK The modulo 128 mark output indicates to the selected peripheral that the current DMA cycle is the 128th cycle since the previous MARK output. The mark will be activated after each 128 cycles or integral multiples of it from the beginning of the data block (the first DMA cycle), if the total number of the required DMA cycles (n) is completely divisible by 128.

V_{cc} This is a +5V supply pin required for operation of the circuit.

GND This is a return line for the supply (ground pin of the IC).

7.2 DMA TRANSFERS AND OPERATIONS

The 8257 is able to accomplish three types of operations, viz. verify DMA operation, write operation and read operation. The complete operational sequence of 8257 is described using a state diagram in Fig. 7.5 for a single channel.

A single byte transfer using 8257 may be requested by an I/O device using any one of the 8257 DRQ inputs. In response, the 8257 sends HRQ signal to the CPU at its HLD input and waits for acknowledgement at the HLDA input. If the HLDA signal is received by the DMA controller, it indicates that the bus is available for the transfer. The $\overline{\text{DACK}}$ line of the used channel is pulled down by the DMA controller to indicate the I/O device that its request for the DMA transfer has been honoured by the CPU. The DMA controller generates the read and write commands to transfer the byte from/to the I/O device. The $\overline{\text{DACK}}$ line is pulled transfer is over, to indicate the DMA controller that the transfer, as requested by the device, is over. The HRQ line is lowered by the DMA controller to indicate the CPU that it may regain the control of the bus. The DRQ must be high until acknowledged and must go low before S_4 state of the DMA operation state diagram to avoid another unwanted transfer.

If more than one channel requests service simultaneously, the transfer will occur as a *burst transfer*. This will be discussed further in case of 8237. No overhead is required in switching from one channel to another. In each S_4, the DRQ lines are sampled and the highest priority request is recognized during the next transfer. Once the higher priority transfer is over; the lower priority transfer requests may be served, provided their DRQ lines are still active. The HRQ line is maintained active till all the DRQ lines go low.

The burst or continuous transfer, described above may be interrupted by an external device by pulling down the HLDA line. After each transfer, the 8257 checks the HLDA line. If it is found active, it completes the current transfer and releases the HRQ line (i.e. sends it low) and returns to its idle state. If the DRQ line is still active, the 8257 will again activate HRQ and proceed as already described. The 8257 uses four clock cycles to complete a transfer. The 8257 has a READY input to interface it with low speed devices. The READY pin status is checked in S_3 of the state diagram. If it is low, the 8257 enters a wait state. The status is sampled in every state till it goes high. Once the READY pin goes high, the 8257 continues from state S_4 to complete the transfer. The 8257 can be interfaced as a memory mapped device or an I/O mapped device. If it is connected as memory mapped device, proper care must be taken while programming Rd/A_{15} and Wr/A_{14} bits in the terminal count register.

7.2.1 Priorities of the DMA Requests

The 8257 can be programmed to select any of the two priority schemes using the command register. The first is the *fixed priority scheme*, while the second is the *rotating priority scheme*. In the fixed priority scheme, each device connected to a channel is assigned a fixed priority. In this scheme, the $DREQ_3$ has the lowest priority followed by DRQ_2 and DRQ_1. DRQ_0 has the highest priority. In the rotating priority mode, the priorities assigned to the channels are not fixed. At any point of time, suppose DRQ_0 has highest priority and DRQ_3 the lowest, then after the device at channel 0 gets the service, its priority goes down and the channel 0 becomes the lowest priority channel. Channel1 now becomes the highest priority channel, and remains the highest priority channel till it gets the service. Once channel 1 is served, it becomes the lowest priority channel and the channel 2 now becomes the highest priority channel. If you select the rotating priority, in a single chip DMA system any device requesting the service is guaranteed to be recognized after no more than three higher priority requests, thus avoiding dominance of any one channel. The priority allotment in the rotating priority mode is as shown in Fig. 7.6.

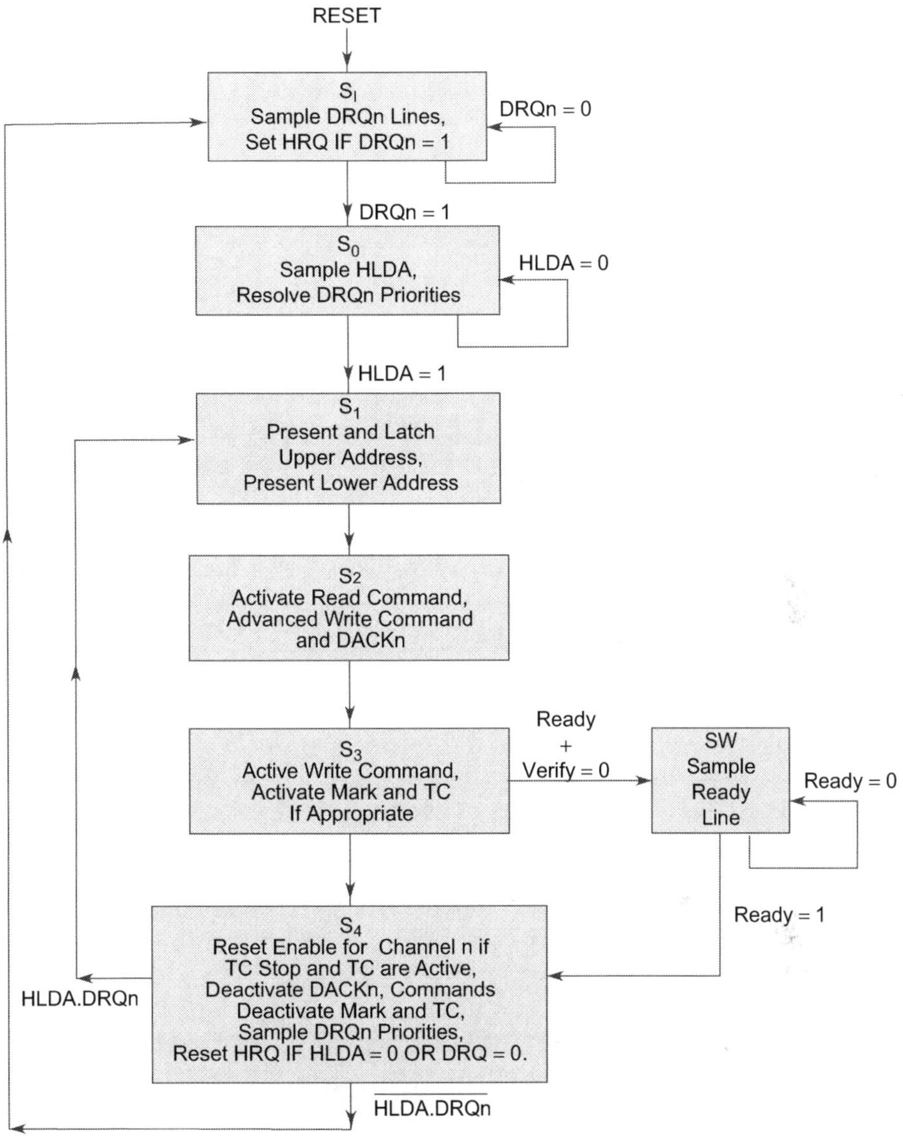

DRQn refers to anv DRQ line of an enabled DMA channel

Fig. 7.5 *DMA Operation State Diagram*

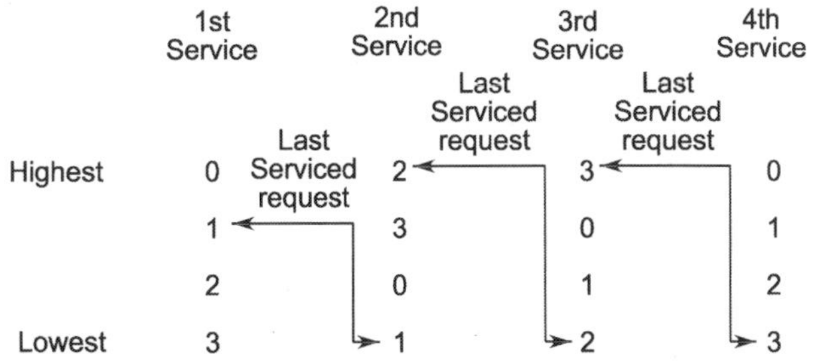

Fig. 7.6 *Priority Allotment in Rotating Priority Mode*

7.2.2 Programming and Reading the 8257 Registers

The selected register may be read or written depending upon the instruction executed by the CPU but the mode set register can only be written in, while the status register can only be read. The 16-bit register pair of each channel is read or written in two successive read or write operations. The Least Significant Byte (LSB) and the Most Significant Byte (MSB) of each register for a specific channel has the same address, but they are differentiated by an internal First/Last (F/L) flip-flop. If the F/L flip-flop is 0, it indicates the first operation, i.e. the LSB is to be read or written, otherwise, it is the last operation, i.e. the MSB is to be read or written. The F/L flip-flop can be cleared by resetting 8257. Thus the first operation after RESET will always be a LSB operation and the successive one for the same register address will be a MSB operation. The least significant three address bits A_0–A_2 indicate the specific register for a specific channel. The A_3 address line is used to differentiate between all the channel registers and the common registers, i.e. mode set and status registers. The higher order address lines A_4–A_{15} may be used to derive the chip select signal $\overline{CS}$ of 8257. All the accesses to any of the terminal count registers and DMA address registers must be in pairs, i.e. the LSB accesses must be followed by the MSB accesses. In verify transfer mode, no actual data transfer takes place. In this mode, the 8257 acts in the same way as read or write transfer to generate addresses, but no control lines are activated.

7.2.3 Interfacing 8257 with 8086

Once a DMA controller is initialised by a CPU properly, it is ready to take control of the system bus on a DMA request, either from a peripheral or itself (in case of memory-to-memory transfers). The DMA controller sends a HOLD request to the CPU and waits for the CPU to assert the HLDA signal. The CPU relinquishes the control of the bus before asserting the HLDA signal. Once the HLDA signal goes high, the DMA controller activates the $\overline{DACK}$ signal to the requesting peripheral and gains the control of the system bus. The DMA controller is the sole master of the bus, till the DMA operation is over. The CPU remains in the HOLD status (all of its signals are tristated except HOLD and HLDA), till the DMA controller is the master of the bus. In other words, the DMA controller interfacing circuit implements a switching arrangement for the address, data and control busses of the memory and peripheral subsystem from/to the CPU to/from the DMA controller. A conceptual implementation of the system is shown in Fig. 7.7(a).

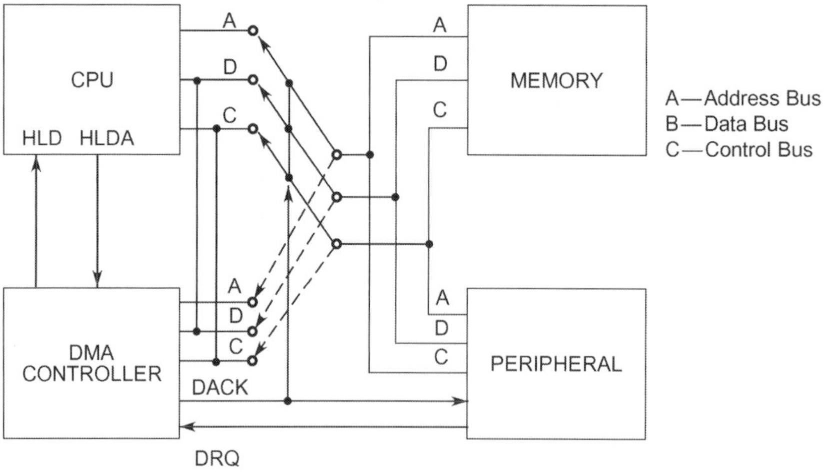

Fig. 7.7(a) *Interfacing a Typical DMA Controller with a System*

To explain the interfacing of 8257 with 8086 let us consider an interfacing example.

Problem 7.1

Interface DMA controller 8257 with 8086 so that the channel 0 DMA address register has an I/O address 80H and the mode set register has an address 88H. Initialize the 8257 with normal priority, TC stop and non-extended write. Autoload is not required. The transfer is to take place using channel 0. Write an ALP to move 2KB of data from a peripheral device to memory address 2000:5000H, with the above initialisation.

Solution Figure 7.7(b) shows interfacing connections of DMA controller 8257 with 8086. As the DMA controller can generate only 16-bit address, while the CPU generates 20-bit address, the four upper address bits are generated and latched on the bus externally using a latch 8212. The 8086 uses three more 8212 latches and two 74245 buffers to demultiplex the address and data buses. These latches are controlled using the AEN signal of the DMA controller. If the DMA controller is in master mode, these will be automatically disabled and if the DMA controller is in slave mode, i.e. the buses are in the control of the CPU, these latches are enabled, using the $\overline{DS_1}$ signal. The data bus D_0–D_{15} is the general system data bus while the bus DD_0–DD_7 is a data bus to be used by an 8-bit peripheral that works under the control of the DMA controller. The 8-bit data bus DD_0–DD_7 is generated from the system data bus D_0–D_{15} using two additional data buffers which enable the 8-bit peripheral to access the even as well as odd addressed memory locations over the 8-bit data bus DD_0–DD_7. The $\overline{MEMRD}$ and $\overline{MEMWD}$ signals decide the direction of data flow under the control of the DMA controller. The A_0 and $\overline{DACK_0}$ signals enable the two buffers only for the DMA controlled data transfer on channel 0. The DMA controller requires an additional latch to demultiplex the address bus A_8–A_{15} from the data bus D_0–D_7, generated by it. This latch is enabled by the ADSTB signal generated by the DMA controller. An additional 74245 is used to read and write the DMA controller registers under the control of the CPU. The inverted clock delays the DMA controller operation as compared to the CPU. Note that the upper data bus D_8–D_{15} is used for initialising the DMA controller in the slave mode. Also note the corresponding 16-bit instructions used to initialise the 8-bit peripheral using the upper 8-bit data bus D_8–D_{15}. Note the circuit arrangements made for accessing the even as well as odd addresses using D_0–D_7. All the initialisation command words should be derived before writing the program.

Mode Set Register As per the problem specification, we need the following: enable TC stop, enable channel 0, disable auto-load, Disable extended-write, disable rotating priority, disable all other channels. As already discussed, the individual bits of the mode set register are set or reset as shown below.

D_7	D_6	D_5	D_4	D_3	D_2	D_1	D_0	
0	1	0	0	0	0	0	1	= 41 H

DMA Address Register The DMA address register contains the starting address of the memory block which is to be accessed using DMA, i.e. 5000H.

Terminal Count Register As has been mentioned in Section 7.1.1, the last significant 14-bits of this register will contain the binary equivalent of the required number of the DMA cycles, i.e. number of bytes to be transferred minus one. As per the requirement, 2Kbytes of data have to be transferred from the device to memory. Therefore, the low order 14-bits of TC register will contain 7FFH. Moreover, the DMA operation in this case is going to be a memory write operation, hence A_{15} and A_{14} of this register should be 0 and 1. The TC register contents for these specifications are shown below.

A_{15}	A_{14}	A_{13}	A_{12}	A_{11}	A_{10}	A_9	A_8	A_7	A_6	A_5	A_4	A_3	A_2	A_1	A_0	
0	1	0	0	0	1	1	1	1	1	1	1	1	1	1	1	= 47FFH

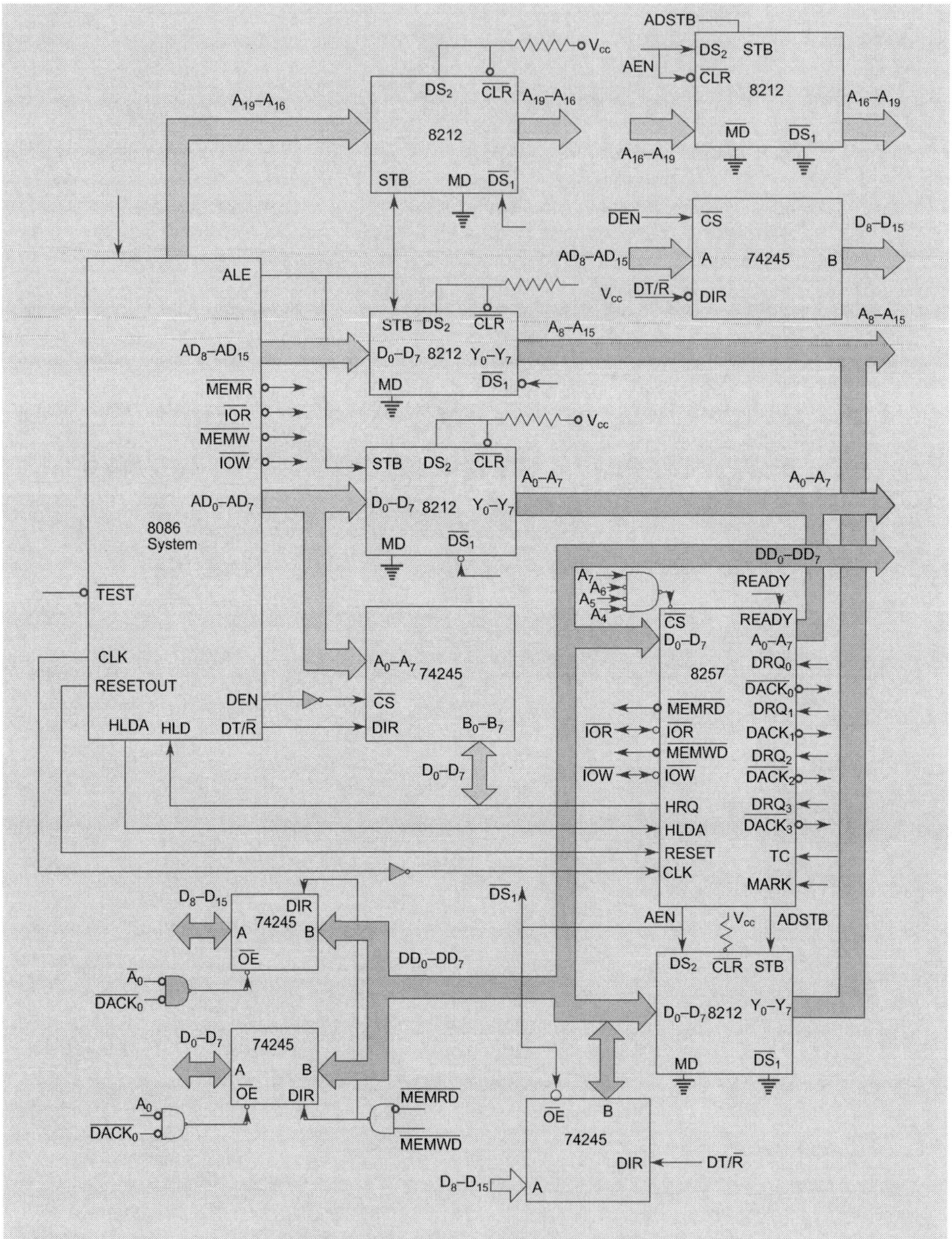

Fig. 7.7(b) *Interfacing 8257 with 8086*

The ALP for Problem 7.1 is given as follows.

```
ASSUME      CS:CODE,DS:DATA
CODE        SEGMENT
START:      MOV AX, DATA        ; Initialize Data Segment
            MOV DS, AX          ;
            MOV AX, DMAL        ; Load DMA address register with
            OUT 80H, AX         ; lower byte of DMA address
            MOV AX, DMAH        ; Load higher byte of DMA address
            OUT 80H, AX         ; register of Channel 0
            MOV AX, TCL         ; Load lower byte TC register of
            OUT 81H, AX         ; channel 0
            MOV AX, TCH         ; Load higher byte of TC register
            OUT 81H, AX         ;
            MOV AX, MSR         ; MODE SET Register
                                ; Initialization, The F/L flip-flop
            OUT 88H, AX         ; is assumed to be cleared
            MOV AH, 4CH         ; Latch segment address on A16-A19
            INT 21H             ; externally, i.e. 0010(2H) and wait
                                  for the
                                ; DMA request
    CODE ENDS                   ; After the request is served, the
                                ; CPU may continue the execution
    DATA SEGMENT
    MSR EQU 4141H               ; Mode Set Register content
    DMAL EQU 0000H              ; DMA Address lower byte
    DMAH EQU 5050H              ; DMA Address higher byte
    TCL EQU FFFFH               ; Terminal count lower byte
    TCH EQU 4747H               ; Terminal count higher byte
    DATA        ENDS
                END START
```

Program 7.1 *ALP for Problem 7.1*

7.3 PROGRAMMABLE DMA INTERFACE 8237

We have described the DMA controller 8257 in the previous section. Now, we will discuss an advanced Programmable DMA Controller 8237, which provides a better performance, compared to 8257. This is capable of transferring a byte or a bulk of data between system memory and peripherals in either direction. Memory to memory data transfer facility is also available in this peripheral. As in the case of 8257, the 8237 also supports four independent DMA channels which may be expanded to any number by cascading more number of 8237. But the distinctive feature of this chip is that it provides, many programmable control and dynamic reconfigurability features which enhance the data transfer rate of the system remarkably. Since, there are architectural differences between 8257 and 8237, we will describe this chip also with adequate details.

7.3.1 Internal Architecture of 8237

The internal block diagram of 8237 is shown in Fig. 7.8. The 8237 contains three basic blocks of its operational logic. The timing and control block generates the internal timings and external control signals. The program command control block decodes the various commands given to the 8237 by the CPU before servicing a DMA request. It also decodes the mode control word used to select the type of the programmed DMA transfer. The Priority Encoder block resolves priority between the DMA channels requesting the services simultaneously. The timing and control block derives necessary timings from the CLK input.

7.3.2 Register Organisation of 8237

8237 houses a set of twelve types of registers. Some of these registers are present in each of the four channels while the remaining are common for all the channels. Considering the multiple existence of the registers, there are 25 registers in 8237 which are described in detail as follows:

Current Address Register Each of the four DMA channels of 8237 has a 16-bit current address register that holds the current memory address, being accessed during the DMA transfer. The address is automatically incremented or decremented after each transfer and the resulting address value is again stored in the current address register. This can be byte-wise programmed by the CPU, i.e. lower byte first and the higher byte later. This may be reinitialized by an auto-initialization command to its original value after EOP.

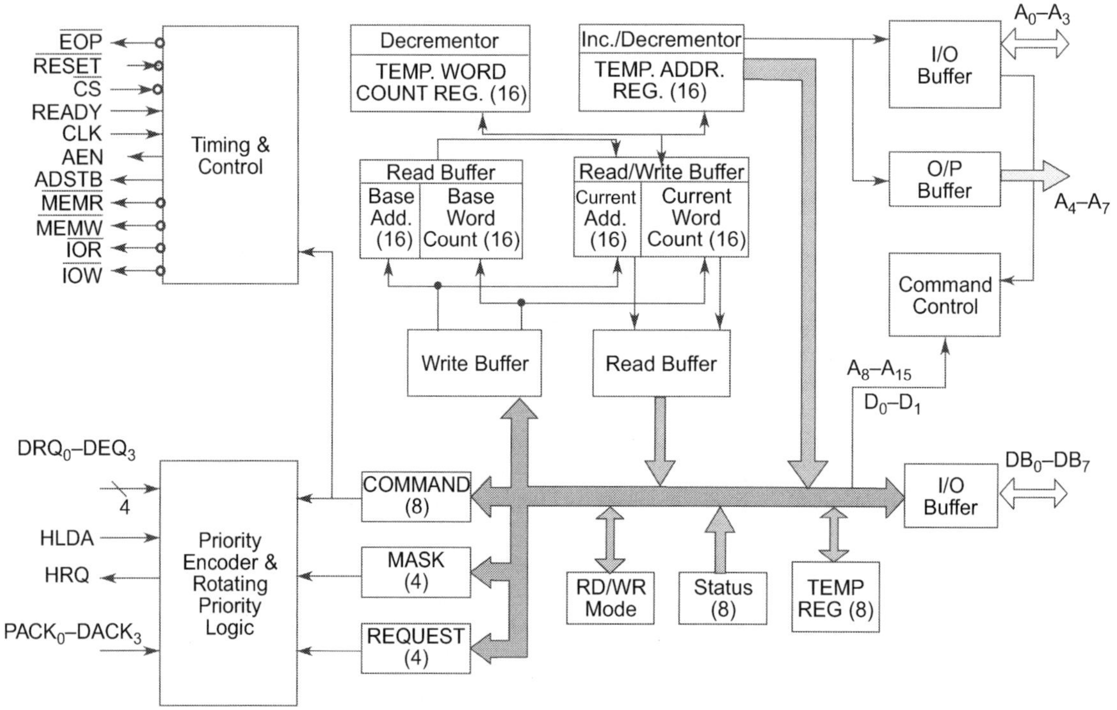

Fig. 7.8 *Block Diagram of 8237*

Current Word Register Each channel has a 16-bit current word register that holds the number of (counts) data byte transfers to be carried out. The word count is decremented after each transfer and the new value is again stored back to the current word register. When the count becomes zero an EOP (end of process) signal will be generated. This can be written in successive bytes by the CPU, in program mode. After the EOP, this may be reinitialized using autoinitialize command.

Base Address and Base Word Count Registers Each channel has a pair of these registers. These maintain an original copy of the respective initial current address register and current word register (before incrementing or decrementing), respectively. These are automatically written along with the current registers. These cannot be read by the CPU. The contents of these registers are used internally for auto-initialization.

Command Register This 8-bit register controls the complete operation of 8237. This can be programmed by the CPU and cleared by a reset operation. Figure 7.9 shows the definition of the command register.

Mode Register Each of the DMA channel has an 8-bit mode register. This is written by the CPU in program mode. Bits 0 and 1 of the mode register determine which of the four channel mode registers is to be written. The bits 2 and 3 indicate the type of DMA transfer. As we have discussed earlier, there are three types of DMA transfer, viz. memory read, memory write and verify transfer. Bit 4 of the mode register indicates whether auto-initialization is selected or not, while bit 5 indicates whether address increment or address decrement mode is selected. The definition of the mode register is presented in Fig. 7.10.

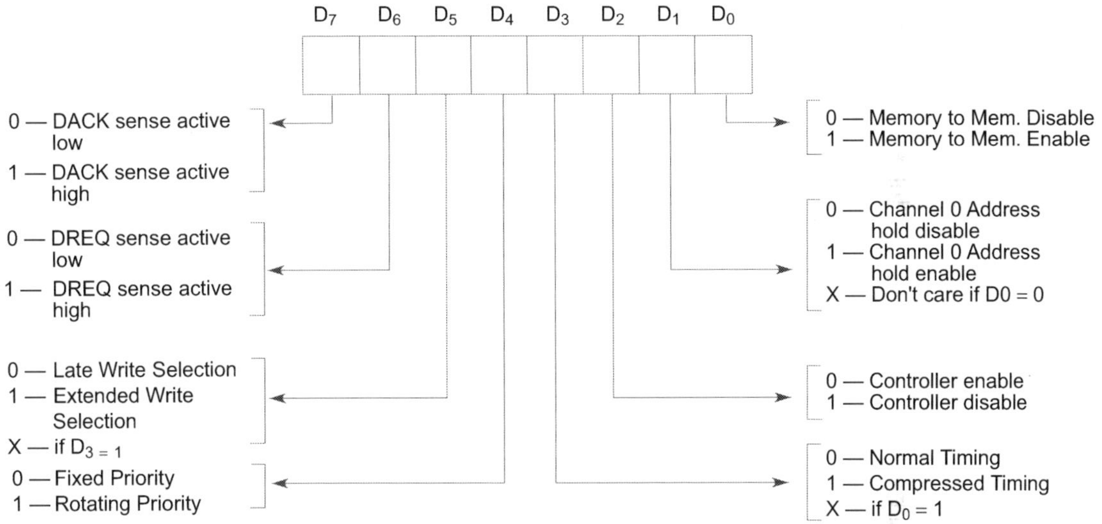

Fig. 7.9 *Command Register Definition*

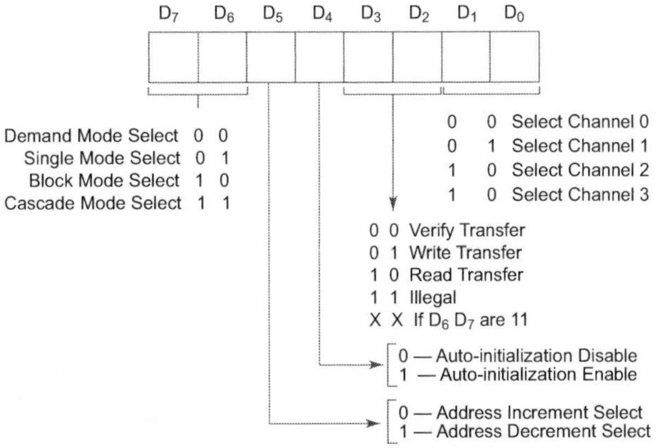

Fig. 7.10 *Mode Register Definition*

Request Register Each channel has a request bit associated with it, in the request register. These are nonmaskable and subject to prioritization by the priority resolving network of 8237. Each bit is set or reset under program control or is cleared upon generation of a TC or an external EOP. This register is cleared by a reset. The bit definitions of the request register are shown in Fig. 7.11.

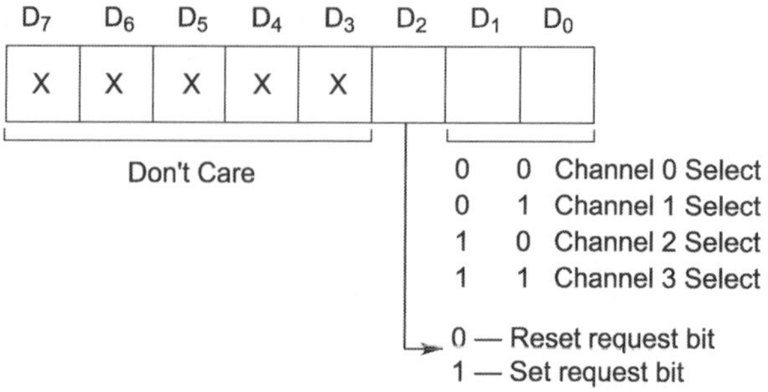

Fig. 7.11 *Request Register Definition*

Mask Register Sometimes it may be required to disable a DMA request of a certain channel. Each of the four channels has a mask bit which can be set under program control to disable the incoming DREQ requests at the specific channel. This bit is set when the corresponding channel produces an EOP signal, if the channel is not programmed for auto-initialization. The register is set to FFH after a reset operation. This disables all the DMA requests till the mask register is cleared. The bit definitions of the mask register are shown in Figs 7.12(a) and (b) respectively. Interestingly, all these mask bits may be cleared using a software command to enable the devices at the respective channels to proceed further for DMA access.

Temporary Register The temporary register holds data during memory-to-memory data transfers. After the completion of the transfer operation, the last word transferred remains in the temporary register till it is cleared by a reset operation.

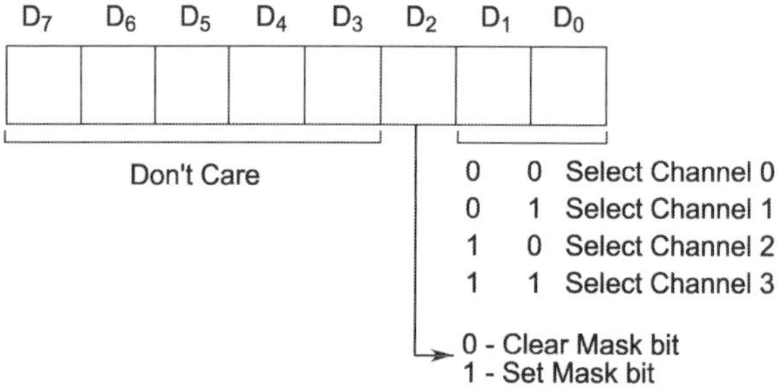

Fig. 7.12(a) *Mask Register Definition to Program the Mask Bits Individually*

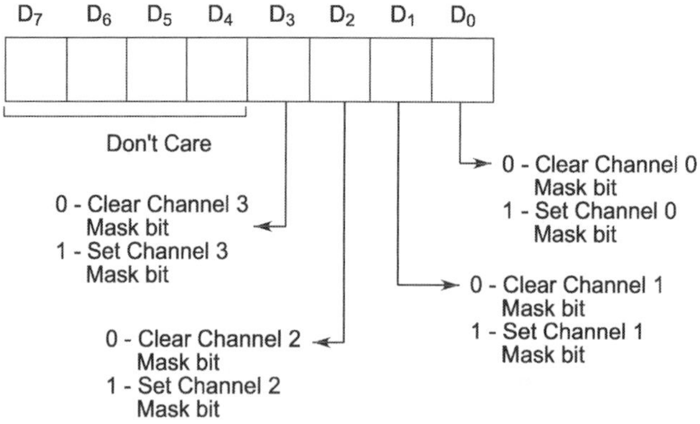

Fig. 7.12(b) *Mask Register Definition to Program all the Mask Bits Simultaneously*

Status Register The status register keeps the track of all the DMA channel pending requests and the status of their terminal counts. The bits D_0-D_3 are updated (set) every time, the corresponding channel reaches TC or an external $\overline{EOP}$ occurs. These are cleared upon reset and also on each status read operation. Bits D_4-D_7 are set, if the corresponding channels request services. Figure 7.13 shows the definition of the status register.

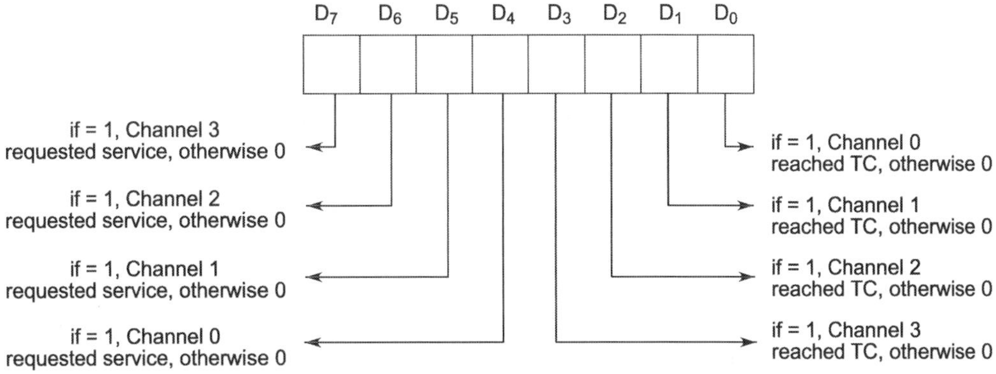

Fig. 7.13 *Status Register Definition*

7.3.3 Signal Descriptions of 8237

Figure 7.14 shows the pin diagram of 8237. The functional signal description of each pin is discussed in brief as follows:

V_{cc} This is a +5V supply pin required for operation of the circuit.

GND This is a return line for the supply (ground pin of the IC).

CLK This is the internally required CLK signal for deriving the internal timings required for the circuit operation.

$\overline{CS}$ This is an active-low chip select input of the IC.

RESET A high on this input line clears the command, status, request and temporary registers. It also clears the internal first/last flip-flop and sets the mask register. The 8237 remains stuck to reset till the RESET pin is high.

READY This active-high input is used to match the read or write speed of 8237 with slow memories or I/O devices.

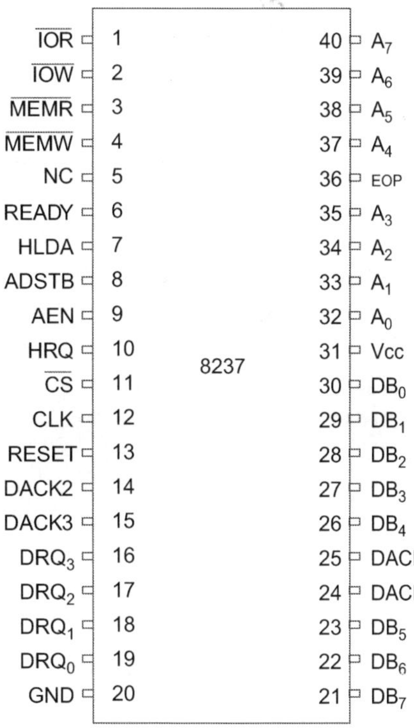

* Pin 5 should be always at logic high. An inter nal pull-up pulls it up when floating else it should be tied to V_{CC}.

Fig. 7.14 *Pin Diagram of 8237*

HLDA(Hold Acknowledge) This active-high input signal is to be connected with HLDA pin of the CPU, to indicate to the 8237 that the CPU has relinquished the control of the bus, as a response to a bus request.

$DREQ_0$–$DREQ_3$(DMA Request Inputs) These active-high input lines are the individual channel request inputs driven by peripheral devices to request a DMA service. $DREQ_0$ has the highest priority while $DREQ_3$ has the lowest one. The priorities of the DREQ lines is programmable. After reset, these lines become active-high. The active level of these lines is also programmable. The DREQ must be maintained high until the corresponding DACK pin goes high.

DB_0–DB_7-(Data Bus) These are bidirectional lines used to transfer data to/from I/O or memory. During I/O read, the contents of address register, status register, temporary register or word count register are sent to the CPU over these lines. During I/O write, the CPU sends the data to any of the above registers. In memory to memory operation, the 8237 fetches data from memory using these lines during read-memory transfer cycle. Also the data is transferred to the memory on these eight lines during write-memory transfer cycle.

$\overline{IOR}$ I/O read is a bidirectional active-low line. In idle cycle or slave mode, this is an input control signal used by the CPU to read its registers. In the active cycle or master mode, it is an output control signal used by 8237 to access data from a peripheral.

$\overline{IOW}$ I/O write is a bidirectional active-low line. In an idle cycle, it is an input control signal used by CPU to load information into the 8237. In the active cycle, it is an output control signal used by 8237 to transfer data to peripherals.

A_0–A_3 These four least significant address lines are bidirectional three state signals. In idle cycle, they are inputs and are used by C.P.U. to address the control registers to be read or written. In an active cycle, they provide the lowest 4 bits of the output addresses generated by 8237.

A_4–A_7 These are the four most significant address lines activated only during DMA services to generate the respective address bits.

HRQ (Hold Request) The HRQ is an output pin used to request the control of the system bus from CPU. If the corresponding mask bit is not set, every valid DREQ to 8237 will issue a HRQ signal to the CPU. This is connected either to HLD (minimum mode) or to $\overline{RQ}/\overline{GT}$ (maximum mode) pin of the CPU.

$DACK_0$–$DACK_3$-(DMA acknowledge) These DMA acknowledge output pins are used to indicate the individual peripheral that it has been granted a DMA cycle by the CPU, in coordination with 8237. After reset, these are active-low, but may be programmed as required.

AEN (Address Enable) This active-high output enables the 8-bit latch that drives the upper 8 bit address bus. The AEN pin is used to disable other bus drivers during DMA transfers.

ADSTB (Address Strobe) This output line is used to strobe the upper address byte generated by 8237, in master mode into, an external latch.

$\overline{MEMR}$ This active-low output is used to access data from the selected memory location, during DMA read or a memory to memory transfer.

$\overline{MEMW}$ This active-low output signal is used to write data to the selected memory location during DMA write or a memory to memory transfer.

$\overline{EOP}$ (End of Process) This is an active low-bidirectional (input or output) pin, used to indicate the completion of a DMA operation. Also, an external signal can terminate a DMA operation by driving this pin low. The 8237 generates a pulse when terminal count is reached, i.e. the transfer byte count reaches zero. This generates EOP signal at this pin. The reception of EOP, either internal or external, will cause 8237 to terminate the service, reset the request and to copy the base registers into the current registers, if auto-initialize is enabled. During memory to memory transfers, EOP signal will be generated, when the terminal count for channel 1 occurs. The $\overline{EOP}$ pin should be pulled high, if it is not in use, to avoid erratic end of process.

7.3.4 DMA Operations with 8237

The 8237 operates in two cycles, viz. idle or *passive cycle* and *active cycle*. Each cycle contains a fixed number of states. The 8237 can assume six states, when it is in active cycle. During idle cycle, it is in state SI (Idle State).

The 8237 is initially in a state SI, i.e. an idle state where the 8237 does not have any valid pending DMA request. During this time, although the 8237 may be idle, the CPU may program it in this state. Once there is a DMA request, the 8237 enters state S_0, which is the first state of the DMA operation. When the 8237 requests the CPU for a DMA operation, and the CPU has not acknowledged the request, the 8237 waits in S_0 state. The acknowledge signal from the CPU indicates that the data transfer may now begin. The S_1, S_2, S_3 and S_4 are the working states of DMA operation, in which the actual data transfer is carried out. If more time is required to complete a transfer (by the peripheral) than that is allowed (by the controller), wait states (S_W) may be inserted between S_2 and S_3 or S_3 and S_4 using the READY pin of 8237. From the above discussion, it is clear that a memory read or a memory write DMA operation actually requires four states, i.e. S_1 to S_4.

A memory-to-memory transfer is a two cycle operation, and requires a read-from and a write-to memory cycle to complete each DMA transfer. Each of these two types of cycles, require four states for its completion. Thus eight states may be required for a single memory-to-memory DMA transfer. Each of these four states use two digit numbers for its identification. For example, for a memory read DMA cycle, the four states required may be represented as S_{11}, S_{12}, S_{13} and S_{14}. The first four states (S_{11}, S_{12}, S_{13} and S_{14}) are used for read-from-memory cycle and the next four states (S_{21}, S_{22}, S_{23} and S_{24}) are used for write-to-memory cycle. A memory to memory transfer cycle is explained in more details later in this section.

7.3.5 Transfer Modes of 8237

The 8237 is in the idle cycle if there is no pending request or the 8237 is waiting for a request from one of the DMA channels. Once a channel requests a DMA service, the 8237 sends the HOLD request to the CPU using its HRQ pin. If the CPU acknowledges the hold request on HLDA, the 8237 enters an active cycle. In the active cycle, the actual data transfer takes place in one of the following transfer modes, as is programmed.

Single Transfer Mode In this mode, the device transfers only one byte per request. The word count is decremented and the address is decremented or incremented (depending on programming) after each such transfer. The Terminal Count (TC) state is reached, when the count becomes zero. For each transfer, the DREQ must be active until the DACK is activated, in order to get recognized. After TC, the bus will be relinquished for the CPU. For a new DREQ to 8237, it will again activate the HRQ signal to the CPU and the HLDA signal from the CPU will push the 8237 again into the single transfer mode. This mode is also called as 'cycle stealing'.

Block Transfer Mode In this mode, the 8237 is activated by DREQ to continue the transfer until a TC is reached, i.e. a block of data is transferred. The transfer cycle may be terminated due to $\overline{\text{EOP}}$ (either internal or external) which forces Terminal Count (TC). The DREQ needs to be activated only till the DACK signal is activated by the DMA controller. Auto-initialization may be programmed in this mode.

Demand Transfer Mode In this mode, the device continues transfers until a TC is reached or an external $\overline{\text{EOP}}$ is detected or the DREQ signal goes inactive. Thus a transfer may exhaust the capacity of data transfer of an I/O device. After the I/O device is able to catch up, the service may be re-established activating the DREQ signal again. Only the EOP generated by TC or external EOP can cause the auto-initialization, and only if it is programmed for.

Cascade Mode In this mode, more than one 8237 can be connected together to provide more than four DMA channels. The HRQ and HLDA signals from additional 8237s are connected with DREQ and DACK pins of a channel of the host 8237 respectively. The priorities of the DMA requests may be preserved at each level. The first device is only used for prioritizing the additional devices (slave 8237s), and it does not generate any address or control signal of its own. The host 8237 responds to DREQ generated by slaves and generates the DACK and the HRQ signals to coordinate all the slaves. All other outputs of the host 8237 are disabled.

Memory to Memory Transfer To perform the transfer of a block of data from one set of memory address to another one, this transfer mode is used. Programming the corresponding mode bit in the command word, sets the channel 0 and 1 to operate as source and destination channels, respectively. The transfer is initialized by setting the $DREQ_0$ using software commands. The 8237 sends HRQ (Hold Request) signal to the CPU as usual and when the HLDA signal is activated by the CPU, the device starts operating in block transfer mode to read the data from memory. The channel 0 current address register acts as a source pointer. The byte read from the memory is stored in an internal temporary register of 8237. The channel 1 current address register acts as a destination pointer to write the data from the temporary register to the destination memory location. The pointers are automatically incremented or decremented, depending upon the programming. The channel 1 word count register is used as a counter and is decremented after each transfer. When it reaches zero, a TC is generated, causing EOP to terminate the service.

The 8237 also responds to external EOP signals to terminate the service. This feature may be used to scan a block of data for a byte. When a match is found the process may be terminated using the external EOP.

Under all these transfer modes, the 8237 carries out three basic transfers namely, write transfer, read transfer and verify transfer. In write transfer, the 8237 reads from an I/O device and writes to memory under the control of $\overline{IOR}$ and $\overline{MEMW}$ signals. In read transfer, the 8237 reads from memory and writes to an I/O device by activating the $\overline{MEMR}$ and $\overline{IOW}$ signals. In verify transfers, the 8237 works in the same way as the read or write transfer but does not generate any control signal.

7.3.6 Address Generation in DMA

The 8237 multiplexes the eight higher order address bits (A_8–A_{15}) on the data lines. The state S_1(idle) is used to transfer the higher order address bits to a latch from which they are to be placed on the address bus. The falling edge of the Address Strobe (ADSTB) signal is used to load these higher address bits from data lines to the latch while that of AEN is used to place the same to the system address bus through a tristate buffer. The lower order address A_0–A_7 is directly generated by 8237 on its A_0–A_7 pins.

7.3.7 8237 Commands and Programming

There are several commands which can be executed by 8237 when it is in program condition. Some of these commands are discussed as follows:

Clear First/Last Flip-Flop As we have discussed in case of 8257, there exists an internal flip-flop in 8237 also which is called First/Last flip-flop (F/L ff). This flip-flop output decides whether the lower byte or the upper byte of the selected 16-bit register will be read or written. Here, the selected register means the current address register or the current word count register. Thus by clearing the first/last flip-flop by this command, the CPU will address the higher or lower byte in an appropriate sequence.

Clear Mask Register As has been described earlier, a mask set register when set, may disable the DMA channels, so that the DMA requests are not entertained. A clear mask register command will clear the bits of the mask register individually or collectively, so that the DMA channels are enabled for accepting DMA requests.

Master Clear Command Using this command, all the internal registers of 8237 are cleared, while all the bits of the mask register are set. This means after executing this command , the DMA controller disables all the DMA channels and enters an idle cycle.

Along with these commands, a few others have been tabulated in Fig. 7.15(a), while Fig. 7.15(b) tabulates the command codes for manipulating the current address registers and the current word count registers. These commands may be executed while the 8237 is under the control of the CPU. If $\overline{CS}$ is low and the HLDA is inactive, the 8237 enters the program condition. The lines A_0 to A_3, $\overline{IORD}$ and $\overline{IOWD}$ are used to select and program the registers of 8237. Note that the address lines A_1 and A_2 select one of the four DMA channels, while the line A_0 selects one of the two registers for a channel.

Problem 7.2

Design an interface between the programmable DMA controller 8237 and 8086. The command register address of the 8237 is F8H. Select the corresponding addresses for all the other registers of 8237.

Solution The interface between 8086 and 8237 is shown in Fig. 7.16. The interesting part of the circuit lies in the transfer of data to/from the odd addresses on the 8-bit data bus. Being an 8-bit device, the 8237 is able to transfer data on D_0–D_7 but for an odd address, the 8086 memory system transfers data on D_8–D_{15}. Hence, the higher byte of the data bus is imposed on the lower byte, using two 74LS245 buffers, if the 8237 is in master mode. Note that the data transfer at an even address is carried out necessarily on D_0–D_7, while the transfer at an odd address is carried out on D_8–D_{15} data lines of the memory system. The transfers at odd addresses will receive/send data from/to AX (the unused AL will be don't care), during initialization of 8237.

Signals						Operations
A_3	A_2	A_1	A_0			
1	0	0	0	0	1	Read Status Register
1	0	0	0	1	0	Write Command Register
1	0	0	1	0	1	Illegal
1	0	0	1	1	0	Write Request Register
1	0	1	0	0	1	Illegal
1	0	1	0	1	0	Write Single Mask Register Bit
1	0	1	1	0	1	Illegal
1	0	1	1	1	0	Write Mode Register
1	1	0	0	0	1	Illegal
1	1	0	0	1	0	Clear Byte Pointer Flipflop
1	1	0	1	0	1	Read Temporary Register
1	1	0	1	1	0	Master Clear
1	1	1	0	0	1	Illegal
1	1	1	0	1	0	Clear Mask Register
1	1	1	1	0	1	Illegal
1	1	1	1	1	0	Write All Mask Register Bit

Fig. 7.15(a) *Software Command Codes*

Channel	Register	Operation	Signals							Internal Flip-Flop	Data Bus DB_0-DB_7
			$\overline{CS}$	$\overline{IOR}$	$\overline{IOW}$	A_3	A_2	A_1	A_0		
0.	Bass and Current Address	Write	0	1	0	0	0	0	0	0	A_0–A_7
			0	1	0	0	0	0	0	1	A_8–A_{15}
	Current Address	Read	0	0	1	0	0	0	0	0	A_0–A_7
			0	0	1	0	0	0	0	1	A_8–A_{15}
	Base and Current Word Count	Write	0	1	0	0	0	0	1	0	W_0–W_7
			0	1	0	0	0	0	1	1	W_8–W_{15}
	Current Word Count	Read	0	0	1	0	0	0	1	0	W_0–W_7
			0	0	1	0	0	0	1	1	W_8–W_{15}
1.	Base and Current Address	Write	0	1	0	0	0	1	0	0	A_0–A_7
			0	1	0	0	0	1	0	1	A_8–A_{15}
	Current Address	Read	0	0	1	0	0	1	0	0	A_0–A_7
			0	0	1	0	0	1	0	1	A_8–A_{15}
	Base and Current Word Count	Write	0	1	0	0	0	1	1	0	W_0–W_7
			0	1	0	0	0	1	1	1	W_8–W_{15}
	Current Word Count	Read	0	0	1	0	0	1	1	0	W_0–W_7
			0	0	1	0	0	1	1	1	W_8–W_{15}
2.	Bass and Current Address	Write	0	1	0	0	1	0	0	0	A_0–A_7
			0	1	0	0	1	0	0	1	A_8–A_{15}
	Current Address	Read	0	0	1	0	1	0	0	0	A_0–A_7
			0	0	1	0	1	0	0	1	A_8–A_{15}
	Base and Current Word Count	Write	0	1	0	0	1	0	1	0	W_0–W_7
			0	1	0	0	1	0	1	1	W_8–W_{15}
	Current Word Count	Read	0	0	1	0	1	0	1	0	W_0–W_7
			0	0	1	0	1	0	1	1	W_8–W_{15}
3.	Base and Current Address	Write	0	1	0	0	1	1	0	0	A_0–A_7
			0	1	0	0	1	1	0	1	A_8–A_{15}
	Current Address	Read	0	0	1	0	1	1	0	0	A_0–A_7
			0	0	1	0	1	1	0	1	A_8–A_{15}
	Base and Current Word Count	Write	0	1	0	0	1	1	1	0	W_0–W_7
			0	1	0	0	1	1	1	1	W_8–W_{15}
	Current Word Count	Read	0	0	1	0	1	1	1	0	W_0–W_7
			0	0	1	0	1	1	1	1	W_8–W_{15}

Fig. 7.15(b) *Word Count and Address Register Commands*

The addresses of the internal registers of the 8237 are listed as follows:

Command Register	FEH
Mode Register	FBH
Request Register	F9H
Mask Register	FA/FFH Individual/ Common Mask
Status Register	F8H
Temporary Register	FDH
Byte Pointer Flip-Flop	FCH
Base and Current Address Registers	
Channel 0	F0H
Channel 1	F2H
Channel 2	F4H
Channel 3	F6H
Base and Current Word Count Register	
Channel 0	F1H
Channel 1	F3H
Channel 2	F5H
Channel 3	F7H

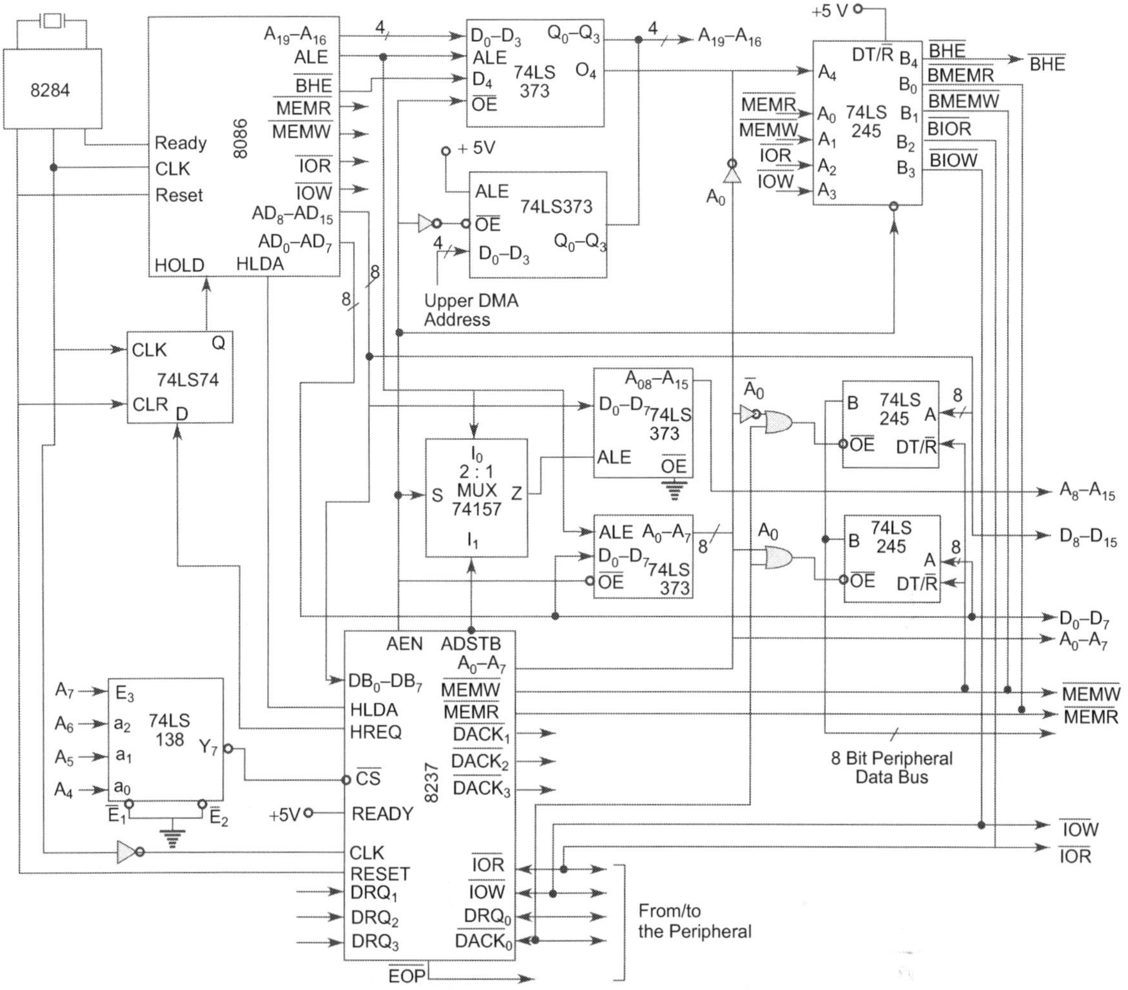

Fig. 7.16 *Interfacing 8237 with 8086*

Problem 7.3

With the above hardware system of Problem 7.2, initialize the 8237 for memory-to-memory DMA transfer mode using channel 0, masking all other channels. Initialize the 8237 for normal timings, fixed priority, extended write with DREQ active high and DACK active-high. The 8237 should work in auto-initialization mode with address increment, block mode select with read transfer on channel 0. Further, write a program to transfer a data block of size 4KB available at 5000:0000H to 5000:1000H.

Solution Different programmable register contents for the initialization as per the problem specifications are given. Note that the upper data bus D_8-D_{15} drives the data lines of the DMA controller. The reader may refer to the bit patterns for each register presented in the register organisation section.

Command Word Register

D_7	D_6	D_5	D_4	D_3	D_2	D_1	D_0	
1	0	1	0	0	0	0	1	= A1 H

Mode Register Word

D_7	D_6	D_5	D_4	D_3	D_2	D_1	D_0	
1	0	0	1	1	0	0	0	= 98 H

Request Register

D_7	D_6	D_5	D_4	D_3	D_2	D_1	D_0	
0	0	0	0	0	1	0	0	= 04 H

Mask Register

D_7	D_6	D_5	D_4	D_3	D_2	D_1	D_0	
0	0	0	0	1	1	1	0	= 0E H

In memory to memory transfer, channel 0 acts as source, i.e. the channel 0 current address register contains source address and the channel 1 current address register contains destination address. The channel 1 current word count register contains the block length count. Program 7.2 gives the ALP for this problem.

```
ASSUME      CS : CODE
CODE        SEGMENT
START:      MOV AX,0A100H          ; Out command word A1
            OUT 0F8H,AX            ; to port F8 for initialization
            MOV AX, 9800H          ; Out mode word to port FB
            OUT 0FBH,AX            ; for mode programming
            MOV AX,0E00H           ; Mask all requests
            OUT 0FFH,AX            ; except channel 0 (DREQ0).
            MOV AX, 00H            ; Clear byte pointer
            MOV 0FCH,AX            ; flip-flop
            MOV AX, 00H            ; Write base and current address
            OUT 0F0H,AX            ; Register of channel 0 in
            OUT 0F0H,AX            ; successive byte transfers
            MOV AX, 00H            ; Clear byte pointer flip-flop
            OUT 0FCH,AX            ;
            MOV AX, 00H            ; Write base and current address
            OUT 0F2H,AX            ; register of channel 1 in
            MOV AX, 1000H          ; successive byte transfers
            OUT 0F2H, AX           ;
            MOV AX, 00H            ; Clear byte pointer flip-flop
            OUT 0FCH,AX            ;
            MOV AX,0FF00H          ; Load word count 0FFFH
            OUT 0F3H,AX            ; in channel 1 word count
            MOV AX,0F00H           ; register in successive bytes
            OUT 0F3H,AX            ;
            MOV AX,0400H           ; Initialize the transfer
            OUT 0F9H,AX            ; by setting DREQ request
            NOP                    ; Wait for transfer to start
            MOV AH,4CH             ; Return to DOS
            INT 21H
CODE        ENDS
            END START
```

Program 7.2 ALP for Problem 7.3

Note that the segment addresses cannot be handled by 8237. Hence in a single DMA operation only 64K bytes of data can be transferred, in block transfer mode.

7.4 HIGH STORAGE CAPACITY MEMORY DEVICES

7.4.1 Floppy Disks

Floppies are the most commonly used secondary memory devices, which store data by the virtue of the magnetic material coated on their surface. The floppies are available in three sizes, viz. standard 8", $5^{1/4}$" mini-floppy and $3^{1/2}$" microfloppy. Previously, the 8" standard size was mostly in use, but its large size, low memory capacity and low mechanical strength made it obsolete. Whatever their physical sizes and storage formats, all the floppies incorporate the basic principles of magnetic data recording and reading.

The data is stored on a set of concentric rings known tracks, on their surfaces, which is further divided into sectors. A sector is supposed to contain either 512 or 1024 bytes of data at maximum. However, the sector size may vary from 128 bytes to the entire size of the track. The concentric tracks are subdivided into sectors using radial logical separations, as shown in Fig. 7.17(a).

The circular disk type flexible media, coated with the magnetic material is enclosed in a plastic jacket for its protection. The jacket has a small circular hole near the central circular (big) hole that is used to drive (rotate) the circular disk inside the jacket. This rotation of the disk enables a drive head to scan a complete circular track. The small hole is called the index hole. This enables the drive to identify the beginning of a track and its first sector. The track 00 is the outermost track on the disk surface and the sector 00 is the first sector on the track. The track number and sector number go on increasing till the numbering reaches the innermost track, and its last sector. The head slot allows the drive head to move radially over the disk surface to refer to the different tracks. The write protect notch is to be covered by a sticker to inhibit writing to the disk. Figure 7.17(b) shows a typical $5^{1/4}$" floppy with its details.

The floppy media is rotated at the speed of 300 RPM (Revolution per minute) inside its jacket. A recent development has been the recording of data on both sides of the disk. These types of disks are called double sided disks. The two tracks on the two surfaces beneath each other are collectively referred to as cylinders. Thus a cylinder contains two tracks. The cylinders are numbered in the same way as tracks. The Double Density Double Sided (DSDD) disks are organised with 40 tracks on each side of the disk. A Double Density (DD) disk track is divided into nine sectors each containing 512 bytes of data. Thus the disk contains 40 (tracks) $\times$ 2 (surfaces) $\times$ 9 (sectors) $\times$ 512 (bytes per sector), i.e. 360 Kbytes of data.

The high density diskettes have 80 tracks per side with 8 sectors per track and 1024 bytes per sector. Thus these diskettes can store up to $80 \times 2 \times 8 \times 1024$, i.e. 1.2M bytes. The magnetic recording technique used for storing data onto the disks is called as Non-Return to Zero (NRZ) recording. In this technique, the magnetic flux on the disk surface never returns to zero, i.e. no erase operation is carried out.

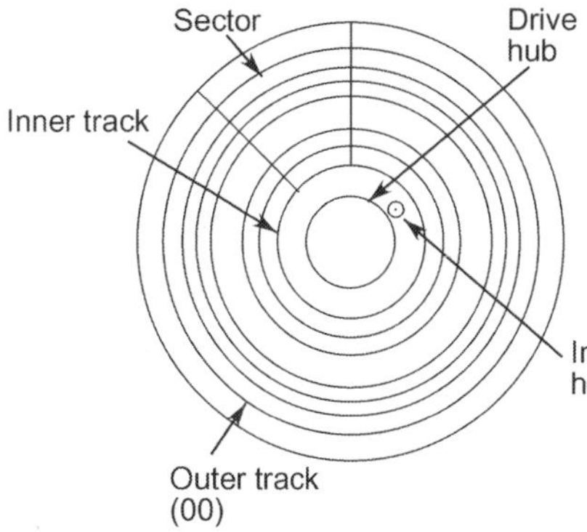

Fig. 7.17(a) *Format of a $5^{1/4}$" Floppy*

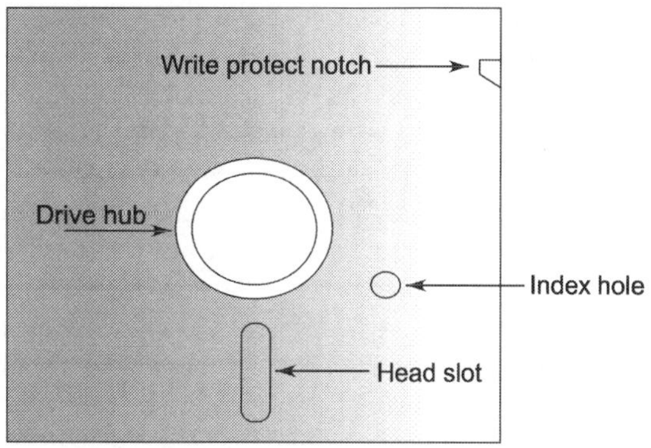

Fig. 7.17(b) *$5^{1/4}$" Mini Floppy*

The most recent form of a floppy disk is its $3^{1/2}$" microfloppy format. This is a much improved version of the $5^{1/4}$" floppy disk. This is small in size and packed in a strong plastic jacket that does not bend easily. Thus a microfloppy is easy to handle and is more durable. The other problem with $5^{1/4}$" floppy was its permanently open head slot that exposed the media to other contaminants and dust, reducing the media life due to wear problems. The microfloppy has a head slot covered with a spring controlled door that only opens at the time of media access. The write protect window is located at the corner of the jacket. The sticker or the tape used for write protection in $5^{1/4}$" disk is now replaced by an unremoveable sliding plastic square disk, that is only to be slided for write protecting the disk. Previously, the sticker or tapes used for write protections used to get dislodged inside the floppy drives, causing problems.

The index hole is replaced by a slightly different drive mechanism. The $3^{1/2}$" floppy has a drive mechanism that fits the drive hub only in a unique position inside the floppy drive. Thus, the $3^{1/2}$" floppy has gotten rid of the index hole, that used to create problems due to dirt or dust.

The DSDD $3^{1/2}$" floppy is organized in 80 tracks per side, containing nine sectors each. Each of the sectors can store 512 bytes of data. Thus the disk can store $80 \times 2 \times 9 \times 512$, i.e. 720 KB of data. The $3^{1/2}$" DSHD floppy is organized in 80 tracks per side, each containing 18 sectors. Each of the sectors can store upto 512 bytes. Thus the disk can store $80 \times 2 \times 18 \times 512$, i.e. 1.44MB of the data. Figure 7.17(c) shows the $3^{1/2}$" floppy diskette.

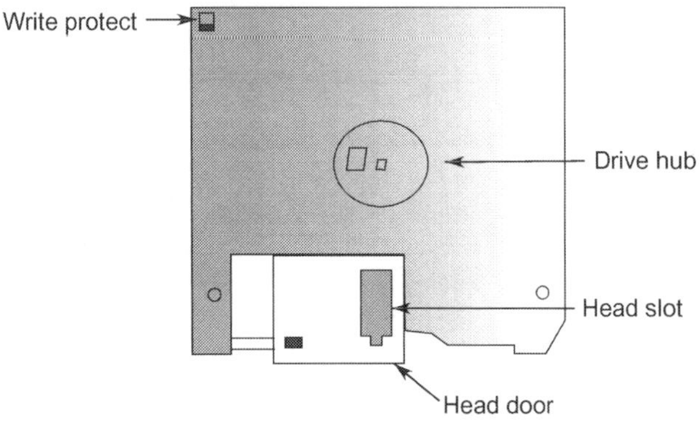

Fig. 7.17(c) *$3^{1/2}$" Micro Floppy*

7.4.2 Compact Disc (CD)

The Compact Disc (CD) is an optical disk used to store digital data. It was originally developed to store and playback sound recordings exclusively, but the format was later adapted for storage of data (CD-ROM), write-once audio and data storage (CD-R), rewritable media (CD-RW), Video Compact Discs (VCD), etc. Standard CDs have a diameter of 120 millimeters (4.7 in) and can hold up to 80 minutes of uncompressed audio or 700 MB (700×2^{20} bytes) of data. Mini CDs have various diameters ranging from 60 to 80 millimeters (2.4 to 3.1 in). They are sometimes used for CD delivering device drivers. CDs in various forms are widely used in computer industry.

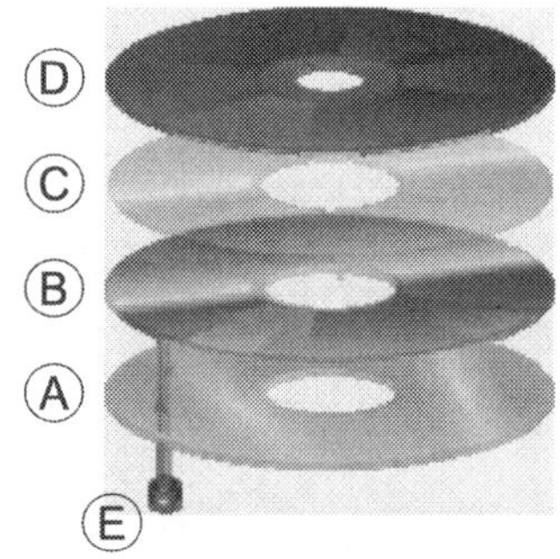

Fig. 7.18 *A Typical CD Structure*

The CD technology is an advanced form of the Laser Disc technology. A typical CD is a circular disk with a holding ring at the center. The Drive arrangement holds the CD tightly at the central ring and can rotate it. A movable laser beam can scan the disk radially due to its own movement as well as along the circular concentric tracks similar to those on a floppy disk due to rotation. While recording digital data on the polycarbonate disk, the laser beam creates pits for logical '1' and no pits for logical '0' using a non-return to zero type of coding scheme. While reading the data, a laser beam scans the pits or no-pits tracks generated by the recording beam and interprets the pits or no-pits track in terms of the recorded sequences of '1's and '0's using the reflected optical laser beam from the tracks. A typical CD structure is shown in Fig.7.18.

A polycarbonate disk layer has the recorded data using pits or no-pits. A shining layer below the data layer reflects the layer for reading. A lacquer layer below the shining protects the shining layer. A label or artwork graphics is screen printed on the top of the lacquer layer of the disk. A laser beam scans the CD along the tracks and reflects it back to a sensor, which is further converted into a bit sequence waveform and interpreted in terms of '1's and '0's. Different standards and formats have been used for storing different types of data like audio, video, or computer files on the CDs. Though CDs were initially introduced as read only (CD-ROM)disks, very soon they were advanced to Read/Write CD(RD/WR). CDs have typical data transfer rates of a few MB per second. The writing however is very slow.

7.4.3 Digital Video Disk

A DVD represents a family of CD type of disks for digital video signal storage. Amongst other similar video storages, **DVDR** is for recordable DVD and **DVDRW** for rewriteable DVD. Using recent DVDs, it is also possible to have up to 4.6 GB ordinary data on a recordable DVD. Due to its high storage capacity and density, DVDs have also become popular as portable computer data storage devices. DVD data transfer rates of up to 30 Mbps have been achieved so far.

A DVD is also basically an optical disk that uses a red laser for reading the disks. DVDs offer higher storage capacity than compact disks while having the same dimensions. Pre-recorded DVDs are produced in large quantities using molds that physically impress data onto the DVDs. Such disks are called DVD ROM. DVD ROMs are not re-recordable. Blank one-time recordable DVDs (DVD-R and DVD+R) can be recorded using a DVD recorder. Rewritable DVDs (DVD-RW or DVD-RAM) can be erased and then written many times. Standard formats are available to write video data onto the disks. DVDs containing other data may follow other recording standards for storing non-video data. Unlike CDs, DVDs can store data in multiple layers. Some DVD specifications (e.g. for DVD-Video) are openly available and have to be purchased from the DVD Format/Logo Licensing Corporation by paying the license fees.

The disk is held by a centrally located hub with rotating mechanism. A very fine laser beam (635 nm) and an optical system can scan the underside of the disk by rotating it and moving the reading laser beam radially. In fact, the CD and DVD driving mechanisms are very complex and are not the topic of discussion here.

A dual-layer disk incorporates a second physical layer within the disk itself. The dual-layer disk accesses the second layer by penetrating the laser beam through the first semitransparent layer. The dual-layer disks are costlier than single-layer disks. There are two modes for dual-layer orientation. Dual-layer disk data transfer rates are slow especially when a change of layer is required.

7.4.4 Blue Ray Disk

Blue ray Disk (**BD**) is also an optical medium that outperforms the DVDs. Physically, it is similar to a CD or DVD, but it can store data up to 25 GB per layer and is being popularly used for storing long-duration videos like movies. BDs are different compared to CDs and DVDs in terms of hardware specifications and multimedia storage formats. They can provide better resolution compared to DVDs. The Blue-ray Disk uses a high-frequency blue laser with a very small wavelength to read the disk. Thus, BDs can store data at much greater density than DVDs. In course of time, they have been named 'Blu-ray' disks. With advancements in BD technology, BDs have outperformed DVDs and have become more popular in movie markets. Due to huge storage capacities, BDs also require high-speed motors (around 10000 rpm) to access them. However, writing of disks at this high speed causes improper writing due to wobbling. Many formats for storing data and multimedia on to BDs are available. A few formats store data at high speed but at low resolution, and the remaining formats store data at low speed but at higher resolution. BD standards like BDXL are able to store up to 128 GB data on the disks. Re-recordable BDs are also available. Audio, video, and other synchronization streams are multiplexed and stored on the disks in a container format like data packets. Different BD formats are available for audio, video and other data-storage applications. BDs can support reading rates of 24 frames per second for a resolution of 1920 x 1080 pixels. The data-transfer rates achieved till date are around 54 Mbits/second.

7.4.5 Hard Disk Drives

A Hard Disk Drive (HDD) is the main and largest secondary data storage in a computer. The operating system, device drivers, system software, user application programs and most other files are stored in the hard disk drives. The HDD is an electromechanical arrangement to handle and access the magnetic storage media available in the form of single or multiple coaxial thick cylindrical disks. The cylindrical disk surfaces are coated with magnetic media and the bits are stored on the circular tracks similar to floppy disks. A single head or multiple heads can access the surface areas of the disks. A read/write head can radially scan the surface while rapid rotation of the disks facilitates complete surface access in terms of concentric rings called tracks. Tracks are further divided into sectors. Thus, each cylinder has tracks and sectors on its upper and lower circular surface. The common axis of the cylinders is driven by an electric motor to obtain the rotations. However, all the cylinders rotate even if the data is being accessed on only one cylinder surface due to the common axis. An electronic drive mechanism precisely controls the position of the head, disks and other electrical and mechanical parts of the drive. The data bit stream reading and writing is basically an electromagnetic phenomenon. The digital data bits are stored in the form of orientations of electromagnetic dipoles along the tracks and sectors on the surface of cylindrical disks. Thus, the data is permanently available even in the absence of power supply. The HDD is also called hard drive, hard disk, fixed drive, fixed disk or fixed disk drive. The currently available HDDs have huge data storing capacities like 1000 to 1200 GB. The physical dimensions of HDDS have reduced from several feet to a few inches and the weight has reduced from several hundred kilograms to a few hundred grams in the last fifty years. On the other hand, their data-storage capacity has been increased millions of times. Currently available HDDs have data-transfer rates of up to 1 Gbps with a disk rotation system of 7200 rpm. A typical hard disk drive component are shown in Fig. 7.19. The top left part of the image shows the first part of HHD chassis that mounts the electronic control mechanism. The top right part shows the second part of the metal chassis that holds the coaxial cylindrical disks. The bottom left image shows the read/write head carrying the lever and the electronic control card. The bottom right part of the image shows the magnetic storage media disks and the disk holding bay.

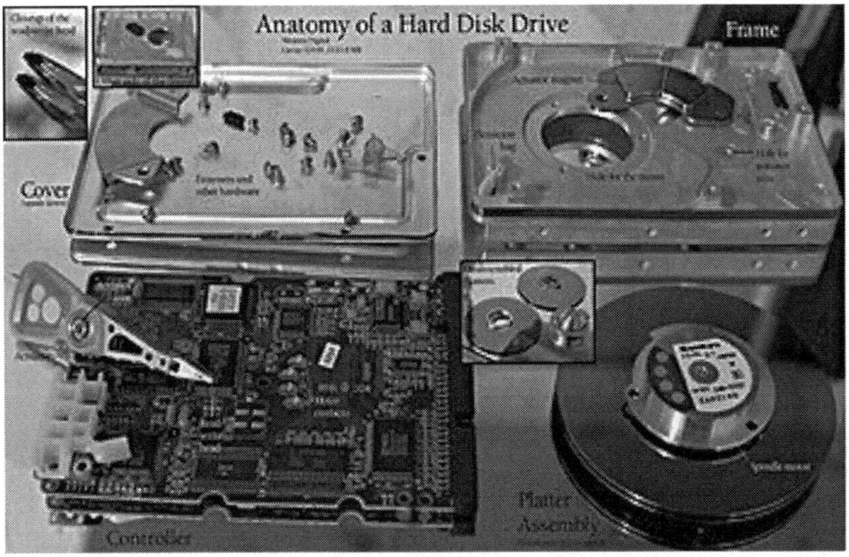

Fig. 7.19 *Internal Components of an HDD Drive*

Before actually using a hard disk drive, it must be formatted using an appropriate operating system. A HDD can, however, have multiple partitions to store more than one operating system. The hard disk drive can be logically partitioned into many drives that can virtually act as physically separate drives. Hard disk drives spare some of their memory capacity for defect management and error correction. Resident programs like operation systems and device drivers also consume some portion of the memory capacity. The remaining memory capacity is used for storing user data. Access time of an HDD is the time duration from the instant of issuing a read or write command to the instant at which the byte becomes available or the write operation is complete. *Seek time* is a measure of how long it takes the head assembly to travel to the track of the disk radially that contains data. Rotational latency causes some duration to pass before the desired disk sector comes under the head when data transfer is requested. These two delays are of the order of a few milliseconds each. Once the head reaches the appropriate position, the bit rate causes a delay depending upon the read-write speed of the media and the size of the block to be read. Additional delay may also be introduced if the drive disks are stopped in between for some reason.

SUMMARY

This chapter presents a detailed account of the operation of some of the DMA based advanced peripherals. With the recent advances in the field, the Intel family of the peripherals, has been continuously enhanced with a number of new peripherals. Of course, all of them cannot be discussed here, but a few of them, which are frequently used in the industrial and general systems are discussed in this chapter, in significant details. Some of the advanced peripherals like the floppy disk controllers and the CRT controllers are covered here in details, since they are the unavoidable parts of the advanced microprocessor based systems.

This chapter starts with the discussion on a DMA controller 8257. The necessary functional details of 8257 have been discussed along with an interfacing example and the supporting program. Then, the advanced DMA controller 8237 has been studied in significant details. At the end, a brief introduction to high capacity memory devices has been presented.

EXERCISES

7.1 What is the advantage of DMA controlled data transfer over interrupt driven or program controlled data transfer? Why are DMA controlled data transfers faster?

7.2 Draw and discuss the architecture of 8257.

7.3 Draw and discuss the mode set register of 8257.

7.4 Explain the functions of the following signals of 8257.

(i) $\overline{IOR}$ (ii) $\overline{IOW}$ (iii) HRQ (iv) HLDA

(v) $\overline{MEMR}$ (vi) $\overline{MEMW}$ (vii) TC (viii) AEN

(ix) ADSTB (x) MARK

7.5 Draw and discuss the status register of 8257.

7.6 What are the registers available in 8257? What are their functions?

7.7 Discuss the priorities of DMA request inputs of 8257.

7.8 An 8086 system has a DMA controller 8257 interfaced such that address of its mode set register is F8H and address of its DMA address register of channel 0 is F0H. Write an ALP to read 2K bytes of data from location 5000H : 2000H in the system memory to a peripheral on channel of the DMA controller. Disable all other channels, program TC stop, no autoload is required, normal priority.

7.9 Bring out the advances in 8237 over 8257.

7.10 Discuss the functions of different registers of 8237.

7.11 Discuss the formats of the following registers of 8237.

(i) Command Register (ii) Mode Register

(iii) Request Register (iv) Mask Register

(v) Status Register

7.12 Discuss the function of EOP signal of 8237.
7.13 Discuss different states of operation of 8237 during different types of transfers.
7.14 Discuss the following modes of DMA transfer.
(i) Signal transfer mode (ii) Block transfer mode
(iii) Demand transfer mode (iv) Memory to memory transfer
7.15 What do you mean by the cascade operation of 8237? Why is it required?
7.16 Discuss the address generation by 8237 during DMA operation.
7.17 Discuss the different commands supported by 8237.
7.18 What do you mean by cycle stealing?
7.19 Write a program to initialise 8237 for all channels enabled, rotating priority, non-extended write, DREQ active low and cycle stealing. The 8237 need not be in autoinitialization mode. The DACK output should be active high. The DMA controller should wait for a DMA request on any of the channels and transfer 32 Kbytes of data to the first requesting channel.
7.20 Write short notes on.
(i) CD (ii) BD (iii) DVD (iv) HDD

8 Multimicroprocessor Systems

INTRODUCTION

With the developments in semiconductor technology and the advances in machine architecture, the processing speed of the computing systems has appreciably increased in recent times. The speed of any system depends, along with other factors, upon the clock frequency at which it is operating. The maximum clock frequency at which a system operates may be considered as one of the measures of the processing capability of the system. Whatever may be the advancement in the architecture or semiconductor technology, a single processor system has an upper limit of its processing capability. For further enhancement of the speed of operation, an appropriate system involving several connected microprocessors, using a certain topology may provide the answer. The study of such a system, known as multimicroprocessor architecture thus assumes paramount importance.

The choice of this option for achieving higher processing speed is obvious. If a system having a single microprocessor takes a fixed time duration to complete a specific task, a system having two microprocessors may require lesser time than the former. A few simple multimicroprocessor based system design concepts have been discussed in this chapter to introduce the readers to multimicro-processor systems.

The simplest type of multimicroprocessor systems is one containing a CPU and a numeric data processor (NDP) or/and an Input/Output Processor (IOP). The Numeric Data Processor is an independent processing unit that is capable of performing complicated numeric calculations in comparatively less time which, otherwise, would have consumed more time of the main processor. The NDP works in coherence with the main processor and adds to its numeric processing capabilities.

It is a well known fact that most of the input/output operations are sluggish due to the low operating speeds of I/O devices. An I/O processor takes care of the I/O activities of a system and thus saves the time of the main processor. These processors (NDP and IOP) work in tune with the main processor to complete the specific tasks and are known as coprocessors. Coprocessors are unable to work independently as they are unable to fetch the code from memory and thus they work under the control of the main processor. Additional hardware elements like bus controllers, bus arbiters may be used to coordinate the activities of the number of processors working at a time in the system. In short, more than one microprocessor synchronis with each other to complete a specific task, in a multimicroprocessor system.

Before designing a Multimicroprocessor System, one should study the commonly used supporting chips and coprocessors. It is also important to study how microprocessors may be connected with each other to form a suitable multimicroprocessor system for a typical application. The methods of interconnections amongst the microprocessors are called interconnection topologies. The selection of a topology is an application specific task and requires a detailed knowledge of the different topologies and the application for the actual system design.

8.1 INTERCONNECTION TOPOLOGIES

A microprocessor with its external bus connections is an incomplete device and needs memory to form a minimum workable processing system configuration. While studying a multimicroprocessor system, the first concept is to visualize a number of microprocessors connected with each other using a single bus.The bus may further address a shared single I/O port or a multiport memory. The former requires resolution of bus control and connections when more than one microprocessor are linked to a single bus. The other option, i.e. multiport memory is simpler but costlier. In both the cases, the memory serves the following three purposes.

1. It acts as a storage for individual (local) instructions and data for each processor.
2. It acts as a temporary storage for the instructions, data and other parameters during data transfers (communications) between the processors.
3. It stores the common (global) instructions or data for all the processors.

Based on the modes of communication, amongst the microprocessors, we now discuss some of the interconnection topologies.

Figure 8.1 shows a *shared bus* architecture that uses a common memory which may be partitioned into local memory banks for different processors. At a time, only one processor performs a bus cycle to fetch instructions or data from the memory. Once the bus cycle is complete, it may internally start the execution allowing the other processors to use the bus. Additional hardware is required for controlling the access of the bus by different processors. All the processors in Fig. 8.1 share a common memory but they all can have a local memory unit individually to store the local data or instructions.

Figure 8.2 shows a *multiport* memory configuration. The processors P1 and P2 address a multiport memory which can be accessed at a time by both the processors. In addition to the multiport memory, both the processors have local memories which are used by them to store the individual instructions and data. Each of the processors uses its local memory for the execution of its individual task. The multiport memory may be used for storing the instructions, data and the results to be shared by more than one processor.

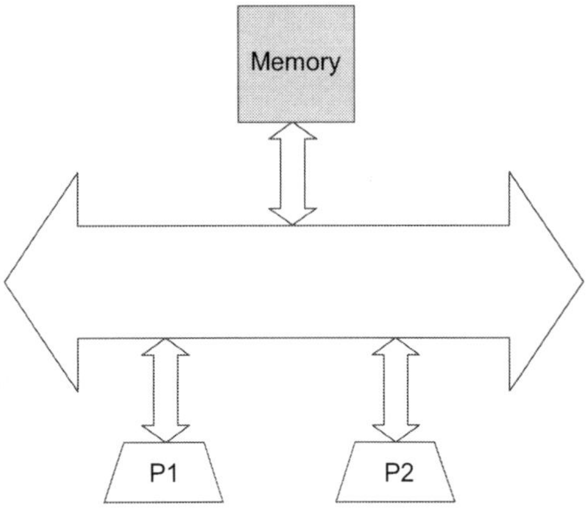

Fig. 8.1 *Shared Bus*

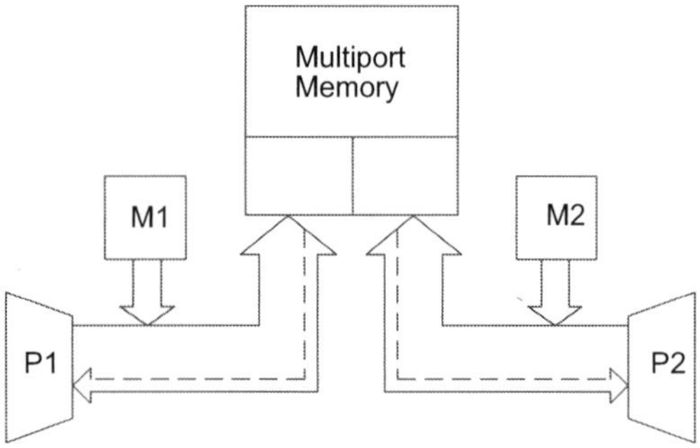

Fig. 8.2 *Multiport Memory*

The third type of interconnection method is shown in Fig. 8.3. This utilizes input/output capabilities of a system to communicate with other systems. For example, parallel input/output or serial input/output may be used to establish communications with other processors. In fact, the input/output links connect two separate computers. The direct access of common data and instructions which are already available in a local system memory is not possible in this case.

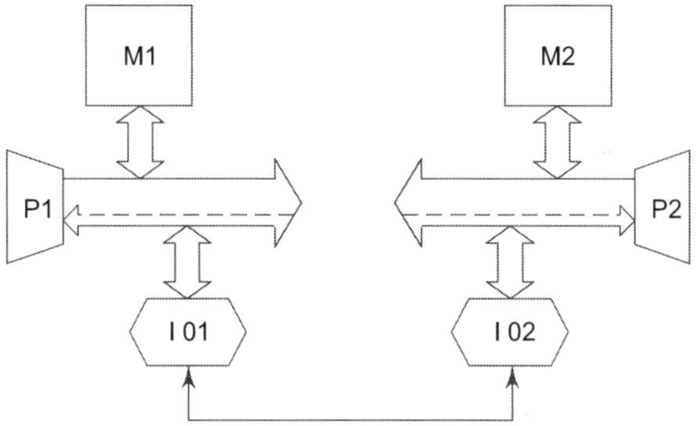

Fig. 8.3 *Linked Input/Output*

The fourth method of interconnection between the processors is known as *bus window* technique. Figure 8.4 shows this interconnection topology. The bus window is a memory space of a processor that is mapped to other processor/processors and vice versa. The bus window is used to conceptually connect two individual buses of the independent microprocessors which are required to communicate with each other. The bus window is a portion of memory that both the microprocessors can address. For a given prespecified address zone, the bus requests of one microprocessor are treated as the bus requests of the other microprocessor. Thus, for this address space, the devices of the first bus are ignored and the second bus acts as if it is connected to the first microprocessor. This then avails the first microprocessor with the access of the memory of the second microprocessor, for the specific address zone of the memory used as bus window. Thus by using a bus window, any of the microprocessors can read or write the memory of the other one. DMA may be used to access the bus window by both the processors. The disadvantages of the bus window technique is that both the processors must know implicitly about the existence of the bus window, its size and the address map. Moreover, as the bus window is used only for communication, it results in a loss of effective local memory space.

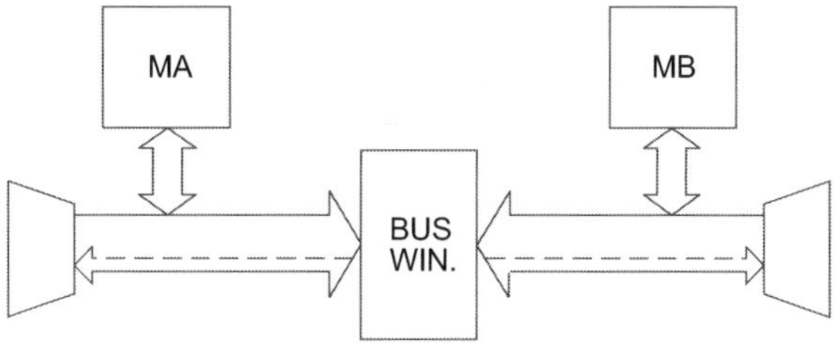

Fig. 8.4 *Bus Window*

The fifth interconnection topology is an extension of the concept of shared memory for a number of processors as shown in Fig. 8.5. In this topology, more than one processor can have simultaneous accesses to the different memory modules to be shared individually as long as there is no conflict. The total memory is divided into modules. While one processor is accessing a memory module, the other processor will be denied an access of the same module till it is relinquished by the former processor. The crossbar switch provides the interconnection paths between the memory modules and the processors. In such structures, several parallel data paths are possible. Each node of the crossbar represent a bus switch. All these nodes may be controlled by one of these processors or by a separate one.

The configurations discussed so far are based purely on the method of communication between the microprocessors of a multimicroprocessor system. Besides these, there are few configurations, based on the physical interconnections between the processors, listed as follows:

1. Star configuration
2. Loop configuration
3. Complete interconnection
4. Regular topologies
5. Irregular topologies

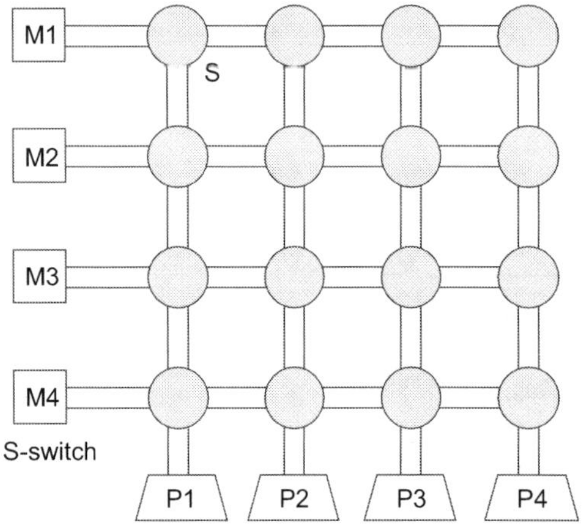

Fig. 8.5 *Crossbar Switching*

Star Configuration In this configuration, all the processing elements are connected to a central switching element that may be an independent processor via dedicated paths, as shown in Fig. 8.6. The switching element controls the interconnections between the processing elements. All communication between the processing elements are done via the switching elements. Each switching element may be an independent computer with a memory bank divided into different blocks. Each of the processing elements is allotted with one of these memory blocks for communication with the central computer.

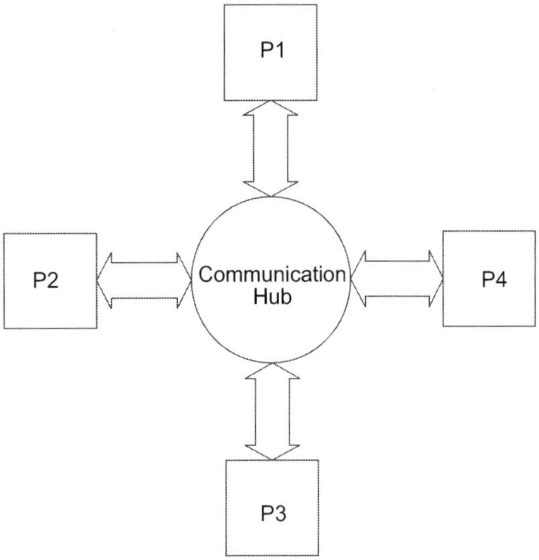

Fig. 8.6 *Star Configuration*

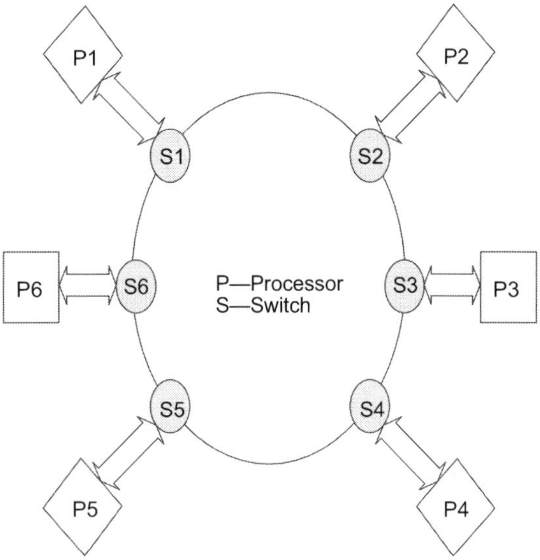

Fig. 8.7 *Loop Configuration*

Loop or Ring Configuration The loop or ring configuration is shown in Fig. 8.7. The processing elements are arranged in a loop, i.e. each processing element can communicate with the other one through intermediate processing elements in the path. The number of intermediate processing elements depends upon the position of sender and receiver in the loop. Note that the direction of data transfer along the loop may be unidirectional or bidirectional. A message is passed from, the source processor to the destination processor, via a series of neighbouring nodes till it reaches the destination processor.

Completely Connected Configuration In the complete interconnection scheme shown in Fig. 8.8, every processing element can directly communicate with another processor at a time. The main problem with this type of configuration is that, the required number of dedicated interconnection paths is $\sum_{n=1}^{N-1} n$ where N is the total number of processors, which is very high as compared to those in other schemes. For a large number of processors, this type of configuration is impractical due to the large number of interconnection paths.

Regular Topology In this configuration, the processing elements are arranged in a regular fashion. The array processor architecture is an example of the regular topology. The processing elements in this scheme may be arranged in any of the regular structures like linear array, hexagonal, square configurations. Even a set of processors may be configured in a regular 3-dimensional array like cubic, pyramidal, etc. Each of the nodes (processors) has a local memory to be accessed only by that processing element. Each of the processing elements can communicate with a fixed number of neighbours in the specific regular structure. For example, in the square structure, a node may communicate with eight neighbouring nodes. One of the regular topologies is shown in Fig. 8.9.

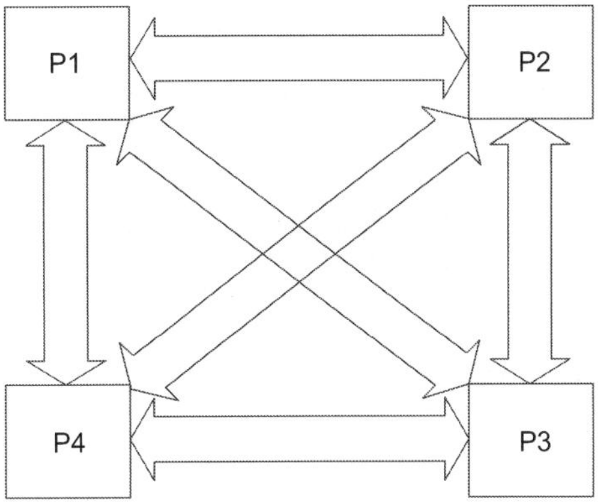

Fig. 8.8 *Complete Interconnection*

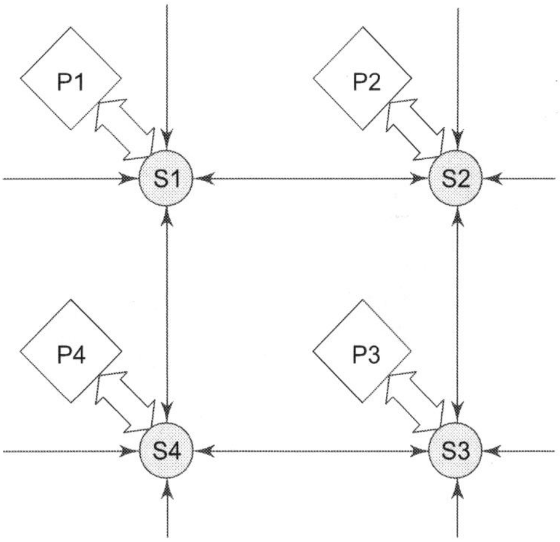

Fig. 8.9 *Regular Topology*

Irregular Topology The processing elements in this scheme do not follow any uniform or regular connection pattern. The number of neighbouring processors, with which a processing element can communicate is not fixed and may even be programmable. This topology is application specific and thus cannot be generalized. One such irregular topology is shown in Fig. 8.10.

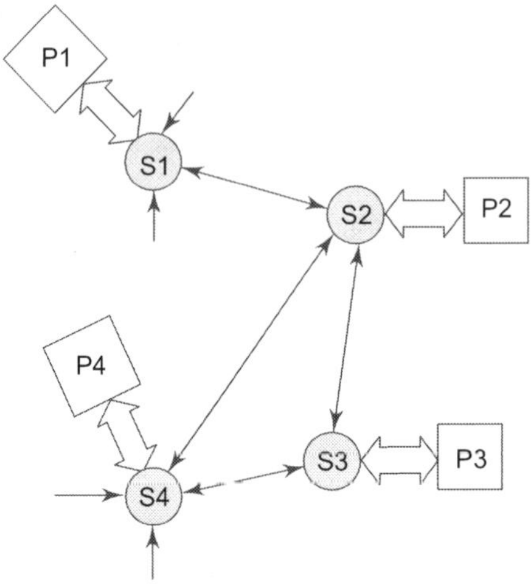

Fig. 8.10 *Irregular Topology*

8.2 SOFTWARE ASPECTS OF MULTIMICROPROCESSOR SYSTEMS

All these interconnection topologies are implemented using a microprocessor or a processing unit as a node. The microprocessors or processing units, used as nodes, may also work as stand-alone processors or subprocessing units under the control of other microprocessors or processing units. Once the processing elements are arranged in a topology, an appropriate operating system and system software which will be able to handle or work in coordination with the new system resources, are required.

Obviously, an operating system and the system software should have the flexibility and ability to work with or under the control of more than one processor at a time. There has been a lot of research work in the field of distributed operating systems and the related system software. In general, however, most of the available softwares have been developed for single processor systems. The initial efforts of using these available softwares and methodologies over the multiprocessor systems most of the times failed due to the fact that the softwares written for the single processor systems could not be appropriately tuned to the multiprocessor environment.

The multiprocessor architectures could not as yet be fully standardised and there are many variations in the multiprocessor architectures, which stood in the way of the software developments for multiprocessor systems. The other feature of multimicroprocessor architectures is that they have always been task dependent. In other words, a multimicroprocessor architecture designed for a specific task may not be that useful or may even be useless for another set of tasks. A multimicroprocessor system, which can fully exploit parallelism in a specific task, may not be able to exploit the parallelism in another task.

Greater throughput and enhanced fault tolerance may be the main objectives in building a multimicroprocessor system. These systems incorporate multiplicity of hardware and software, for the purpose. The distributed software methodology is required to provide appropriate software for implementing the varying architecture systems for different applications. As the distributed systems are expected to undergo architectural changes, the distributed software is also supposed to be modular and tolerant to adapt to these architectural changes.

A lot of work has already been done in the field of structured programming to modularise the programs written for single processor systems. These programs clearly define the interactions between the modules and possibly support the multimicroprocessor architectures. The objective of this discussion is only to introduce the users with the requirements of the appropriate softwares to be tuned with multimicro-processor systems.

Distributed Operating Systems An *operating system* is an important program that resides in the computer memory and *acts as an interface between the user or an application program and the system resources*. As discussed further in Chapter 12, an operating system provides a means of hardware and software resource management, including input/output and memory management. It also enables the user to communicate with the hardware using relatively simple commands. In fact, a monitor program resident on an EPROM in a microprocessor kit is a rudimentary form of an operating system. While running a program under the control of the operating system, considerable time is spent in the operating system program execution that slows down the overall execution speed. This reduction in execution speed is the price paid for the improved user interface and resource management capabilities of the computer systems.

Just like single processor systems, the success of a multimicroprocessor system relies on a suitable operating system. As already discussed, uniprocessor operating system concepts can not be applied to multiprocessor environments due to the inherent architectural differences. Distributed systems are designed to run *parallel processes*. Hence, it is essential that a proper environment exists for *concurrent processes* to communicate and cooperate in order to complete the allotted task. Thus all the functions which are implemented for a uniprocessor operating system are to be re-implemented keeping these things in view. A multiprocessor operating system should be capable of handling the *structural or architectural changes* in the system due to expected or unexpected reasons like faults or deliberate modifications. A distributed operating system should provide a mechanism for *interprocess and interprocessor communication*. A multiprocessor operating system should also take care of the *unauthorised data accesses* and *data protection*, as the data sets in these systems may be referred by more than one processes or processors. These operating systems should be able to analyze and exploit parallelism in a task and accordingly reconfigure the hardware so as to *optimize the system performance*. The operating system must have a mechanism to split the given task into concurrent subtasks which can be executed in parallel on different processors. Further, the operating system must have a mechanism to collect the results of the subtasks and further process these to obtain the final result. These operating systems must also have process-processor allocation strategies implemented in them. The operating systems should also extract accurate knowledge about the dependency of a task on the other tasks and on the hardware and link it with the available hardware and software to improve the overall performance of the system. Figure 8.11 shows the relation between a typical multiprocessor system and a distributed operating system.

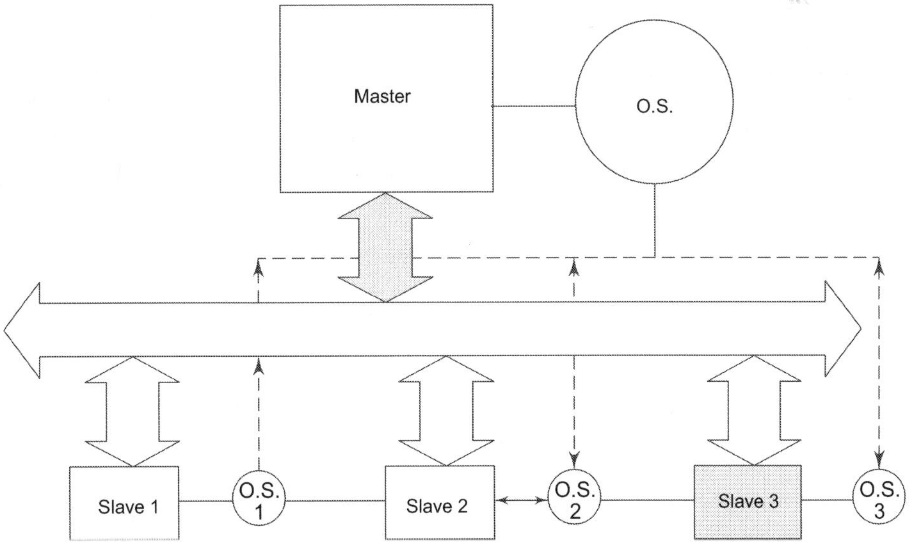

Fig. 8.11 *A Distributed Processing System and Distributed Operating System*

8.3 NUMERIC PROCESSOR 8087

As already discussed, a most preliminary form of a multiprocessor system is a system containing a CPU and coprocessors. The numeric processor 8087 is a coprocessor which has been designed to work under the control of the processor 8086 and offer it additional numeric processing capabilities. Packaged in a 40 pin ceramic DIP package, it is available in 5 MHz, 8 MHz and 10 MHz versions compatible with 8086, 8088, 80186 and 80188 processors.

The 8086 is supposed to perform the opcode fetch cycles and identify the instructions for 8087. Once the instruction for 8087 is identified by 8086, it is allotted to 8087 for further execution. Thus 8086-8087 couplet implements instruction level master-slave configuration. After the completion of the 8087 execution cycle, the results may be referred back to the CPU. Thus the operation of the processor 8087 is transparent to the programmer. The 8087 instructions may lie interleaved in the 8086 program as if they belong to the 8086 instruction set. It is the task of 8086 to identify the 8087 instructions from the program, send it to 8087 for execution and get back the results. The operation of 8087 does not need any software support from the system software or operating system. The 8087 adds 68 new instructions to the instruction set of 8086.

8.3.1 Architecture of 8087

The internal architecture of 8087 is shown in Fig. 8.12(a).

The 8087 is divided into two sections internally. The *Control Unit* (CU) and the *Numeric Extension Unit* (NEU). The numeric extension unit executes all the numeric processor instructions while the Control Unit (CU) receives, decodes instructions, reads and writes memory operands and executes the 8087 control instructions. These two units may work asynchronously with each other. The control unit is mainly responsible for establishing communication between the CPU and memory and also for coordinating the internal coprocessor execution. The CPU, while fetching the instructions from memory, monitors the data bus to check for the 8087 instructions. Meanwhile, the 8087 CU internally maintains a parallel queue, identical to the status queue of the main CPU. The CU automatically monitors the $\overline{BHE}$ /S7 line to detect the CPU type, i.e. 8086 or 8088 and accordingly adjusts the queue length. The 8087 further uses the QS_0 and QS_1 pins to obtain and identify the instructions fetched by the host CPU, which identifies the coprocessor instructions using the ESCAPE code bits in them. Once the CPU recognises the ESCAPE code, it triggers the execution of the numeric processor instruction in 8087.

While executing, the ESCAPE code identifies the coprocessor instruction that requires memory operand and also one that does not require any memory operands. If the instruction requires a memory operand to be fetched from memory, then the physical address of the operand is calculated using any one of the addressing modes allowed in 8086 and a dummy read cycle is initiated by the CPU. However, the CPU does not read the operand, rather the 8087 reads it and proceeds for execution. If the coprocessor instruction does not require any memory operand, then it is directly executed. Whenever the 8087 is ready with the execution results, the CU gets the control of the bus from 8086 and executes a write cycle to write the results in the memory at the prespecified address.

The Numeric Extension Unit (NEU) executes all the instructions including arithmetic, logical, transcendental, and data transfer instructions. The internal data bus is 84 bits wide including 68-bit fraction, 15-bit exponent and a sign bit. When the NEU begins the execution, it pulls up the BUSY signal. This BUSY signal is connected to the $\overline{TEST}$ input of 8086. If the BUSY signal of 8087, is asserted by it, the CPU recognizes that the instruction execution is not yet complete. This makes 8086 wait till the BUSY pin of 8087, i.e. the $\overline{TEST}$ input pin of 8086 goes low or, in other words, till the coprocessor executes the instruction completely. The microcode control unit generates the control signals required for execution of the instructions. 8087 contains a programmable shifter which is responsible for shifting the operands during the execution of instructions like FMUL and FDIV. The data bus interface connects the internal data bus of 8087 with the CPU system data bus.

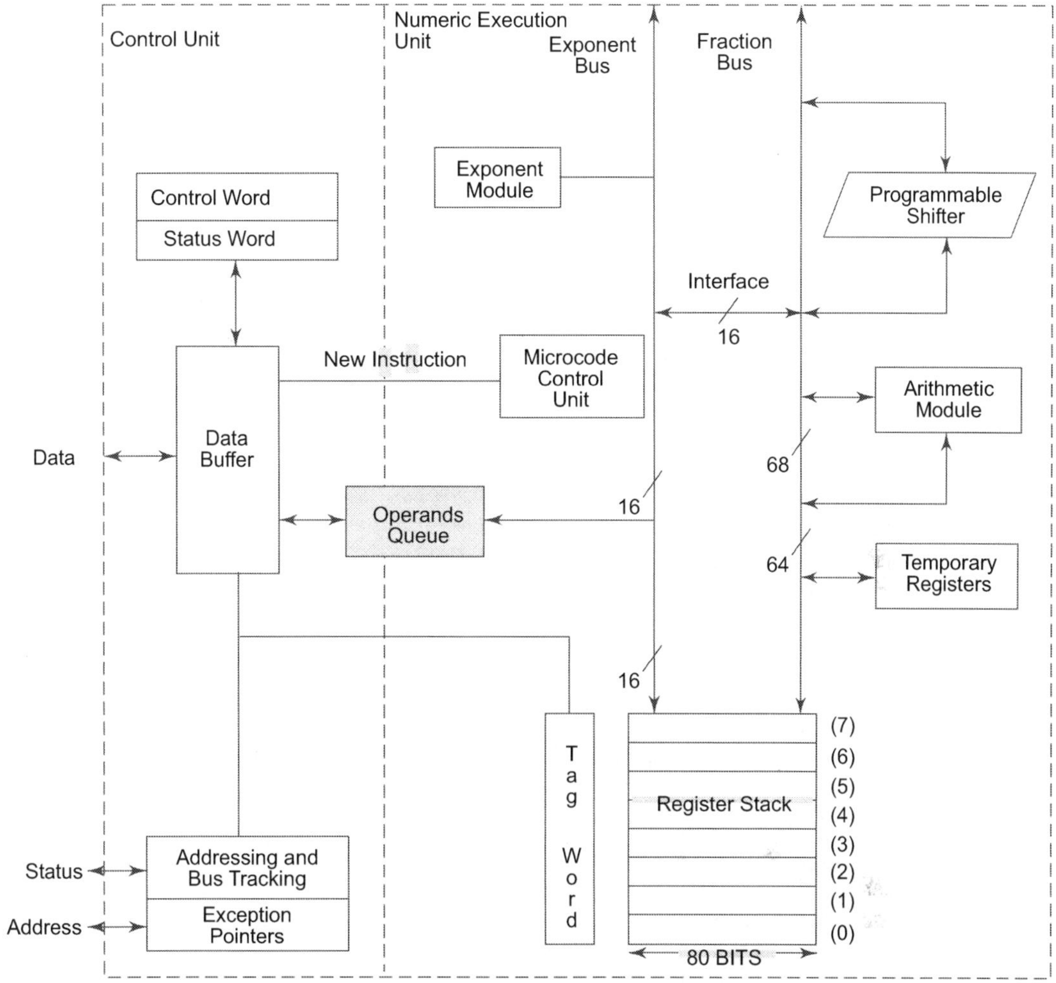

Fig. 8.12(a) *8087 Architecture*

8.3.2 Signal Descriptions of 8087

The pin diagram of 8087 is shown in Fig. 8.12(b). This section deals with the different signals of 8087.

AD_0–AD_{15} These are the time multiplexed address/data lines. These lines carry addresses during T_1 and data during T_2, T_3, T_W and T_4 states. A_0 is used, whenever the transfer is on lower byte (D_0–D_7) of data bus, to derive the chip select. These act as input lines for CPU driven bus cycles, and become input/output lines for the NDP initiated cycles.

A_{19}/S_6–A_{16}/S_3 These lines are the time multiplexed address/status lines. These function in a similar way to the corresponding pins of 8086. The S_6, S_4 and S_3 are permanently high, while the S_5 is permanently low.

$\overline{BHE}$ /S7 During T_1 the $\overline{BHE}$ /S_7 pin is used to enable data on to the higher byte of the 8086 data bus. During T_2, T_3, T_W and T_4 this is a status line S_7. This does not carry any significance in 8088 based systems. Ti, here, denotes the ith clock state of an instruction cycle.

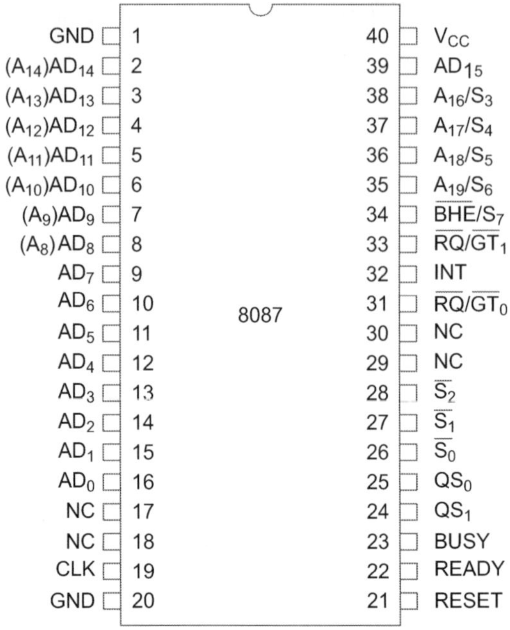

Fig. 8.12(b) *8087 Pin Diagram*

QS_1, QS_0 The queue status input signals QS_1 and QS_0 enable 8087 to keep track of the instruction prefetch queue status of the CPU, to maintain synchronism with it. The status of these lines can be decoded as given in Table 8.1. These lines of 8087 are connected with the respective lines of 8086/8088. From these signals, 8087 comes to know about the status of the internal instruction prefetch queue of 8086.

Table 8.1 ***QS_1, QS_0 Status***

QS_1	QS_0	*Queue Status*
0	0	No operation
0	1	First byte of opcode from queue.
1	0	Empty queue
1	1	Subsequent byte from queue.

INT The interrupt output is used by 8087 to indicate that an unmasked exception has been received during execution. This is usually handled by 8259A.

BUSY This output signal, when high, indicates to the CPU that it is busy with the execution of an allotted instruction. This is usually connected to the $\overline{\text{TEST}}$ pin of 8086 or 8088.

READY This input signal may be used to inform the coprocessor that the addressed device will complete the data transfer from its side and the bus is likely to be free for the next bus cycle. Usually this is synchronized by the clock generator 8284.

RESET This input signal is used to abandon the internal activities of the coprocessor and prepare it for further execution whenever asked by the main CPU.

CLK The CLK input provides the basic timings for the processor operation.

V_{CC} A +5V supply line required for operation of the circuit.

GND A return line for the power supply.

$\overline{S}_2$, $\overline{S}_1$ and $\overline{S}_0$ These can either be 8087 driven (output) or externally driven (input) by the CPU. If these are driven by 8087, they can be decoded as given in Table 8.2.

Table 8.2

$\overline{S}_2$	$\overline{S}_1$	$\overline{S}_0$	*Queue Status*
0	X	X	Unused
1	0	0	Unused
1	0	1	Memory read
1	1	0	Memory write
1	1	1	Passive

These lines become active during T_4 (previous), i.e. prior to actual starting of the bus cycle and remain active till T_1 or T_2 (current). They are suspended during T_3 for the next bus cycle. These are used by bus controllers to derive the read and write signals. These signals act as input signals if the CPU is executing a task.

$\overline{RQ}/\overline{GT}_0$ The Request/Grant pin is used by the 8087 to gain control of the bus from the host 8086/8088 for operand transfers. It must be connected to one of the request/grant pins of the host. The request/grant sequence is described as follows:

An active-low pulse of one clock duration is generated by 8087 for the host to inform it that it wants to gain control of the local bus either for itself or for other coprocessor connected to $\overline{RQ}/\overline{GT}$ pin of the 8087. The 8087 waits for the grant pulse from the host. When it is received, it either initiates a bus cycle if the request is for itself or else, it passes the grant pulse to $\overline{RQ}/\overline{GT}_1$ if the request is for the other coprocessor. The 8087 will release the bus by sending one more pulse on RQ/GT_0 line to the host either after completion of the last bus cycle initiated by it or as a response to a release pulse on the $\overline{RQ}/\overline{GT}$ line issued by the other coprocessor.

$\overline{RQ}/\overline{GT}_1$ This bidirectional pin is used by the other bus masters to convey their need of the local bus access to 8087. This request is further conveyed to the host CPU. At the time of the request, if the 8087 does not have control of the bus, the request is passed on to the host CPU using $\overline{RQ}/\overline{GT}_0$ pin. If however, the 8087 has control over the bus when it receives a valid request on $\overline{RQ}/\overline{GT}_1$ pin, the 8087 sends a grant pulse during the following T_4 or T_1 clock cycle, to the requesting master indicating that it has floated the bus. The requesting master gains the control of the bus till it needs. At the end, the requesting master issues an active low, one clock state wide pulse for 8087, to indicate that the task is over and 8087 may regain the control of the bus. The request grant pins may be used by the other bus masters like DMA controllers.

8.3.3 Register Set of 8087

The 8087 has a set of eight 80-bit registers, that can be used either as a stack or a set of general registers. When operating as a stack, it operates from the top on one or two registers. While operating as a register set, they may be used only with the instructions designed for them. These registers are divided into three fields, viz-sign (1-bit), exponent (15-bits) and significand (64 bits). Corresponding to each of these eight registers, there is a two bit TAG field to indicate the status of contents as shown in Fig. 8.13. The TAG word register presents all the TAG fields to the CPU. The instructions may address data registers either implicitly or explicitly. An internal status register field, 'TOP' is used to address any one of the eight registers implicitly. While explicitly addressing the registers, they may be addressed relative to 'TOP'.

The status word of 8087 is shown in Fig. 8.14. The bit definitions are explained as follows:

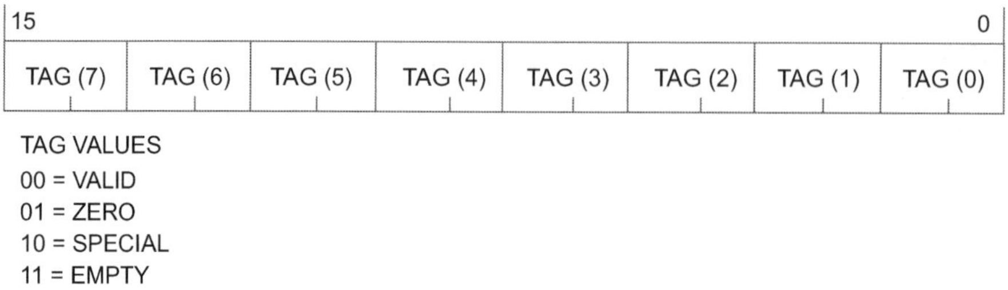

Fig. 8.13 *Tag Word of 8087*

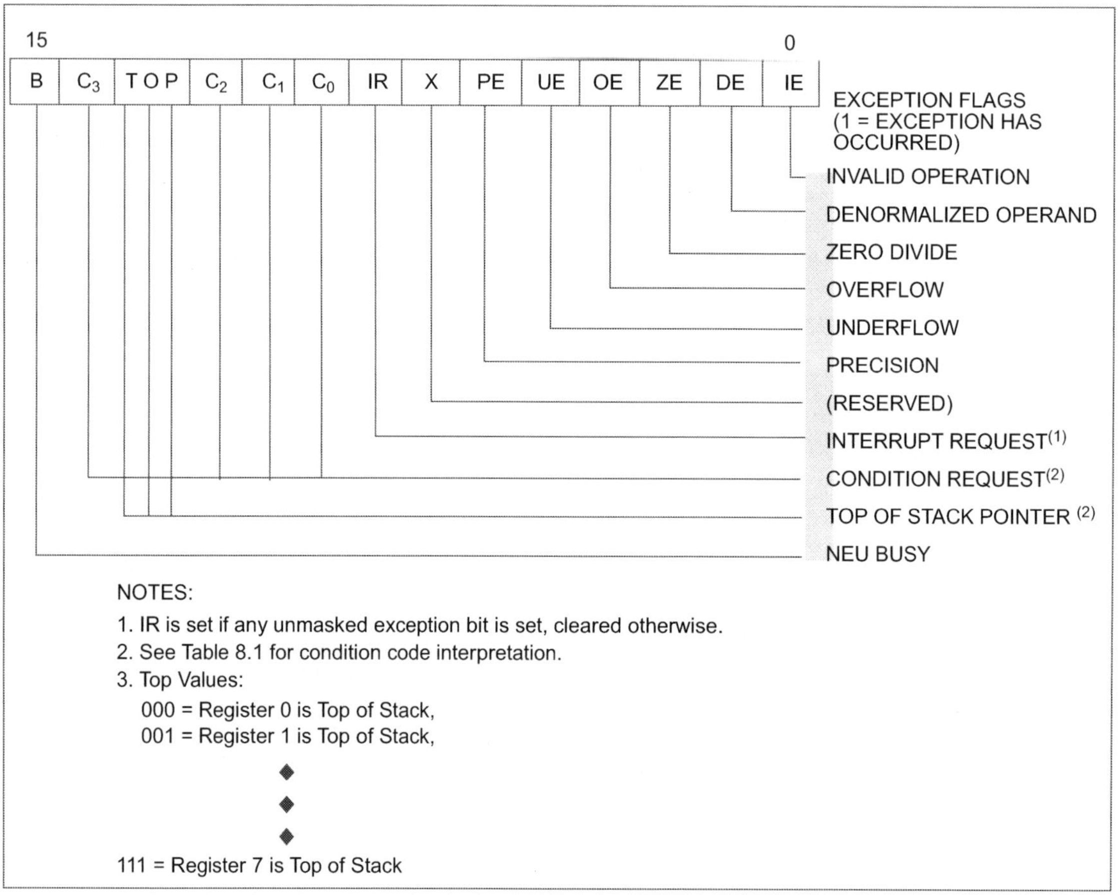

Fig. 8.14 *Status Word of 8087*

B_0–B_5 These bits indicate that an exception has been detected. These 6 bits are used to indicate the six types of previously generated exceptions.

B_7 This bit is set if any unmasked exception has been detected (the corresponding exception bit is set); otherwise, this is cleared.

B_{12}–B_{14} These 3 bits are used as the current top of the stack pointer to any of the eight registers.

B_8–B_{10} and B_{14} These four condition code bits reflect the status of the results calculated by the 8087 as shown in Table 8.3.

B_{15} The BUSY bit shows the status of NEU, i.e. if $B_{15} = 1$ the NEU is busy with execution; otherwise, it is free.

Table 8.3 *Condition Code Bits Definitions*

Instruction Type	*C3*	*C2*	*C1*	*C0*	*Interpretation*
Compare, Test	0	0	X	0	ST > Source or 0 (FTST)
	0	0	X	1	ST < Source or 0 (FTST)
	1	0	X	0	ST = Source or 0 (FTST)
	1	1	X	1	ST is not comparable
Remainder	Q1	0	Q0	Q2	Complete reduction with three low bits of quotient
	U	1	U	U	Incomplete Reduction
Examine	0	0	0	0	Valid, positive unnormalized
	0	0	0	1	Invalid, positive, exponent = 0
	0	0	1	0	Valid, negative, unnormalized
	0	0	1	1	Invalid, negative, exponent = 0
	0	1	0	0	Valid, positive, normalized
	0	1	0	1	Infinity, positive
	0	1	1	0	Valid, negative, normalized
	0	1	1	1	Infinity, negative
	1	0	0	0	Zero, positive
	1	0	0	1	Empty
	1	0	1	0	Zero, negative
	1	0	1	1	Empty
	1	1	0	0	Invalid, positive, exponent = 0
	1	1	0	1	Empty
	1	1	1	0	Invalid, negative, exponent = 0
	1	1	1	1	Empty

Notes:

1. ST = Top of stack
2. X = Value is not affected by instruction
3. U = Value is undefined following instruction
4. Qn = Quotient bit n

Instruction and Data Pointers The instruction and data pointers are used to enable the programmers to write their own exception handling subroutines. Before executing a mathematical instruction, the 8087 forms a table in memory containing the instruction address in the fields of the instruction pointer, the opcode of the instruction, operand (data) address in the field of data pointer, TAG word, status word, control word in their respective fields in the table. In short, the instruction pointer and the data pointer contain the current address of the instruction and the corresponding data. Figure 8.15 shows a map of the table in memory.

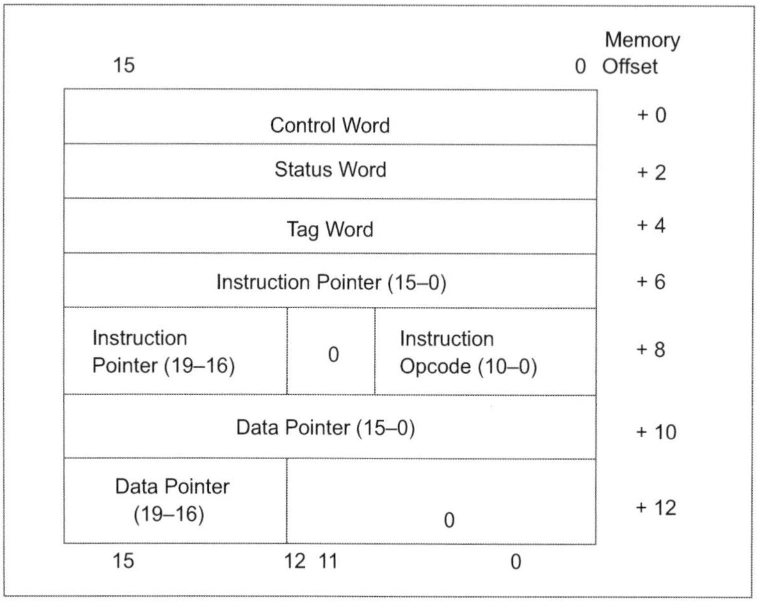

Fig. 8.15 *Table Containing Instruction and Data Pointers in Memory*

Control Word Register The control word register of 8087 allows the programmer to select the required processing options out of available ones. In other words, the 16-bit control word register is used to control the operation of the 8087.

The bits B_0– B_5 are used for masking the different exceptions. An exception may be masked by setting the respective bit in the control word register. The M bit is a common interrupt mask for all the interrupts. If it is set, all the exceptions generated will be masked and the execution may continue. The precision control and rounding control bits control the precision option and rounding option as shown in Fig. 8.16. The infinity result control bit IC provides control over the number size on both sides, i.e. either $+\infty$ (affine closure) or $-\infty$ (protective closure). Figure 8.16 shows the format and bit definitions of the control word register.

8.3.4 Exception Handling

The 8087, while executing an instruction, may generate six different exceptions. These are already listed in the status register format. This section presents a brief discussion on these exceptions. Any of these exceptions, if generated, causes an interrupt to the CPU provided it is not masked. The CPU will respond if the interrupt flag of the CPU is set. If the exceptions are masked the 8087 continues the execution, independent of the responses from the CPU (after clearing the exception). If any of the six exceptions is masked and it is detected, the 8087 modifies the corresponding bit in the status register, and executes an on-chip exception handler that allows it to continue with the execution.

Invalid Operation These are the exceptions generated due to stack overflow, or, stack underflow, indeterminate form as result, or, non-number (NAN) as operand.

Overflow A too big result to fit in the format generates this exception. The condition code bits indicate that the result is prohibitively large (infinity).

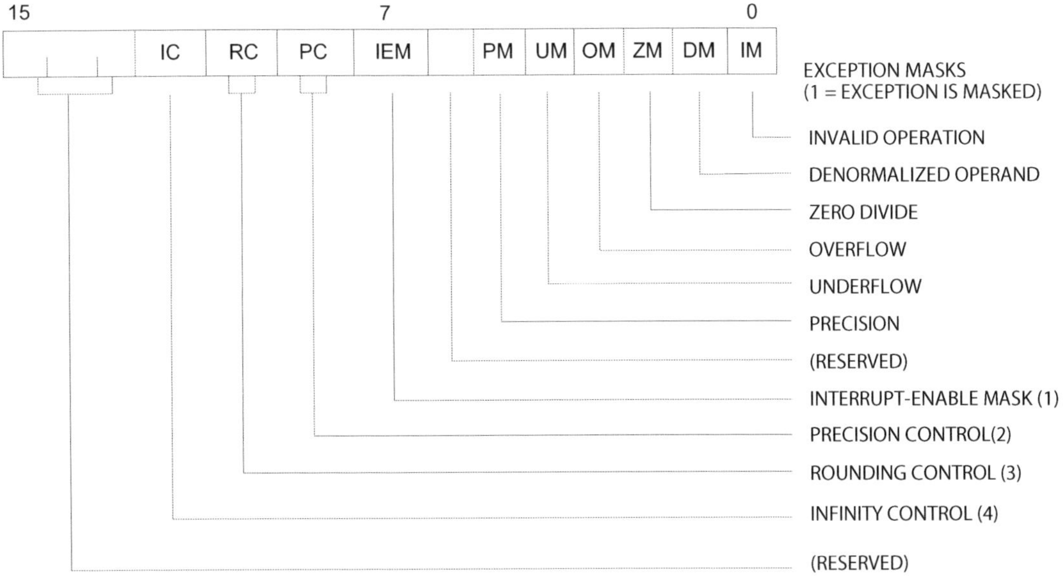

(1) Interrupt - Enable Mask:
  0 = Interrupts Enabled
  1 = Interrupts Disabled (Masked)

(2) Precision Control:
  00 = 24 bits
  01 = (reserved)
  10 = 53 bits
  11 = 64 bits

(3) Rounding Control:
  00 = Round to Nearest or Even
  01 = Round Down (toward – ¥)
  10 = Round Up (toward + ¥)
  11 = Chop(Truncate Toward Zero)

(4) Infinity Control:
  0 = Projective
  1 = Affine

Fig. 8.16 *Control Word Register and the bit definitions*

Underflow If a small (in magnitude) result is generated, to fit in the specified format, 8087 generates this exception. If this exception is masked, the 8087 denormalizes the fraction until the exponent fits in the specified destination format.

Zero Divide If any non-zero finite operand is divided by zero, this exception is generated. The resulting condition code bits indicate that the result is infinity, even if the exception is masked.

Denormalized Operand This exception is generated, if at least one of the operands is denormalized. This may also be generated, if the result is denormalized. If this is masked, 8087 continues the execution normally.

Inexact Result If it is impossible to fit the actual result in the specified format, the result is rounded according to the rounding control bits and an exception is generated. This sets the precision exception flag.

8.3.5 Interconnections of 8087 with the CPU

The communication between 8087 and the host CPU has already been discussed in Section 8.3.1. In this section, we study the physical interconnections of 8087 with 8086/8088 and 80186/80188. 8087 can be connected with any of these CPUs only in their maximum mode of operation, i.e. only when the

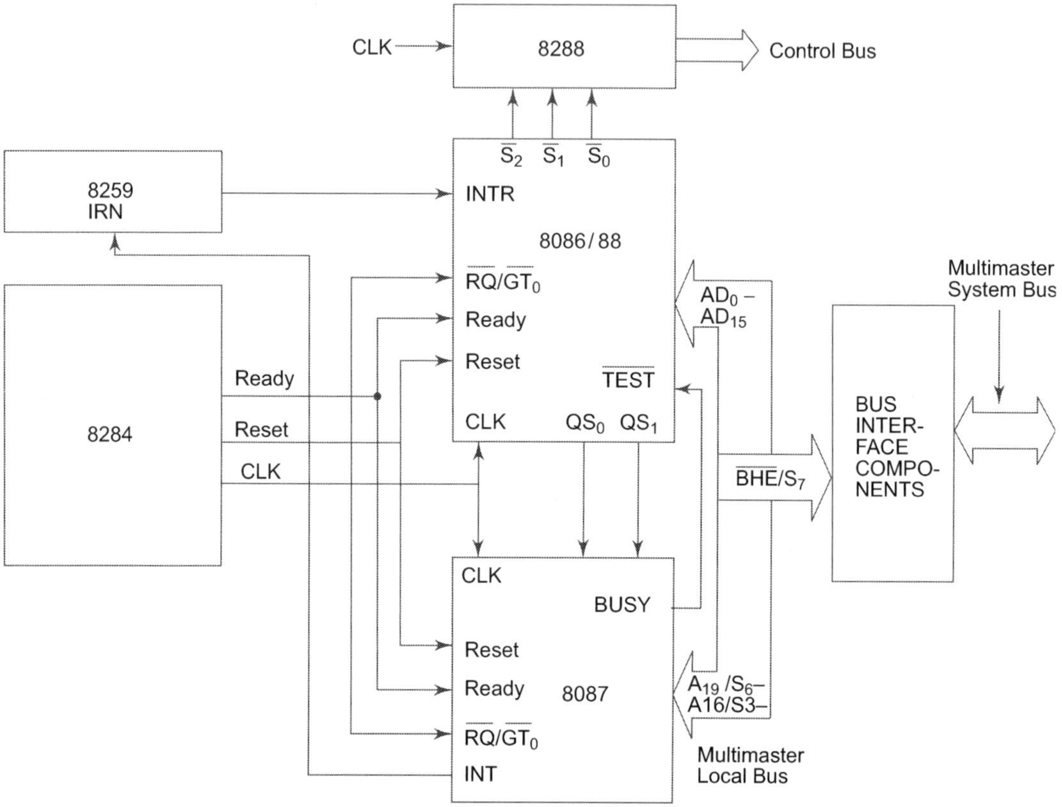

Fig. 8.17 *Interconnections of 8087 with 8086/8088*

MN/ $\overline{MX}$ pin of the CPU is grounded. In maximum mode, all the control signals are derived using a separate chip known as a bus controller. The 8288 is 8086/88 compatible bus controller while 82188 is 80186/80188 compatible bus controller.

The BUSY pin of 8087 is connected with the $\overline{TEST}$ pin of the used CPU. The QS_0 and QS_1 lines may be directly connected to the corresponding pins in case of 8086/8088 based systems. However, in case of 80186/80188 systems these QS_0 and QS_1 lines are passed to the CPU through the bus controller. In case of 8086/8088 based systems the $\overline{RQ}/\overline{GT_0}$ of 8087 may be connected to $\overline{RQ}/\overline{GT_1}$ of the 8086/8088. The clock pin of 8087 may be connected with the CPU 8086/8088 clock input. The interrupt output of 8087 is routed to 8086/8088 via a programmable interrupt controller. The pins AD_0– AD_{15}, $\overline{BHE}/S_7$, RESET, A_{19}/S_6–A_{16}/S_3 are connected to the corresponding pins of 8086/8088. In case of 80186/80188 systems the RQ/GT lines of 8087 are connected with the corresponding $\overline{RQ}/\overline{GT}$ lines of 82188. The interconnections of 8087 with 8086/8088 and 80186/80188 are shown in Fig. 8.17 and Fig. 8.18 respectively.

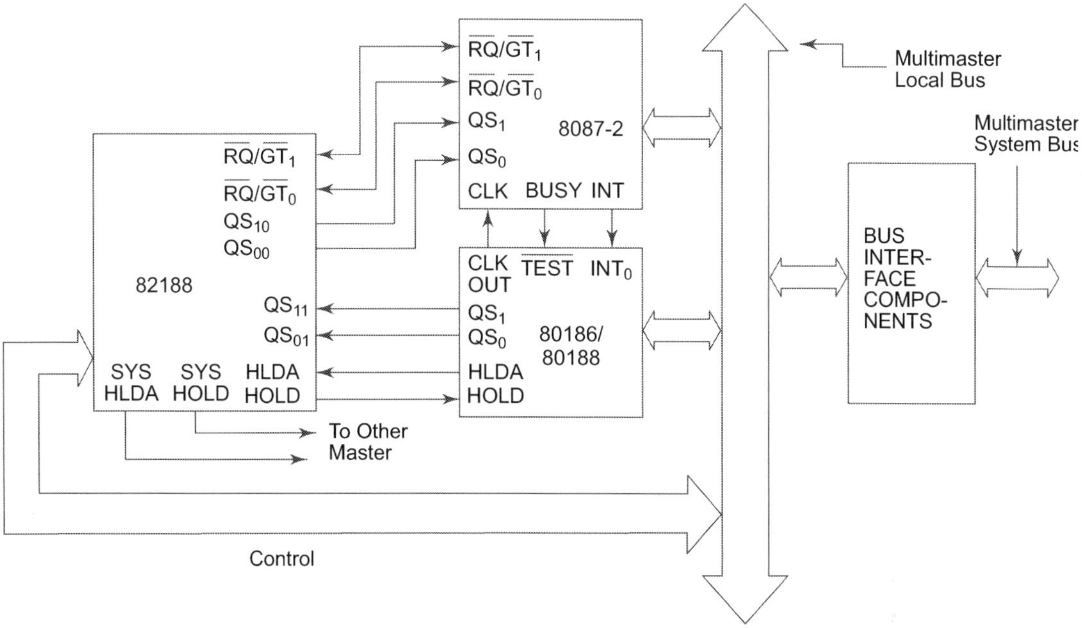

Fig. 8.18 *Interface of 8087 with 80186/80188*

8.3.6 Instruction Set of 8087

The NDP 8087 adds 68 new instructions to the instruction set of 8086, all of which may lie interleaved in an 8086 ALP, as if they were its instructions. The execution of 8087 instructions is transparent to the programmer. These instructions are fetched by 8086 but are executed by 8087. Whenever the 8086 comes across 8087 instruction, it executes the ESCAPE instruction code to pass over the instruction opcode and control of the local bus to 8087. The additional instructions supported by 8087 can be categorized into the following types.

1. Data Transfer Instructions.
2. Arithmetic Instructions.
3. Comparison Instructions.
4. Transcendental Operations.
5. Constant Operations.
6. Coprocessor Control Operations.

All these instructions are briefly discussed in this section. One may refer to Intel data book for details of 8087 instruction set.

Data Transfer Instructions Depending upon the data types handled, these are further grouped into three types.

- Floating Point Data Transfer
- Integer Data Transfer
- BCD Data Transfer

Floating Point Data Transfer Instructions The instructions explained below belong to this group of 8087 instructions.

FLD (Load Real to Top of Stack) This instruction loads a real operand to the top of stack of the 80-bit registers, as shown:

```
FLD ST(7)    ; Stack Top ← [Reg 7]
FLD MEM      ; Stack Top ← [MEM]
```

FST (Store Top of Stack to the Operand) This instruction stores current content of the top of stack register to the specified operand, as shown:

```
FST ST (7)   ; Stack Top → [ST(7)]
FST MEM      ; Stack Top → [MEM]
```

FSTP (Store Floating Point Number and Pop) This instruction stores a copy of top of stack into memory or any coprocessor register and then pops the top of stack, as shown:

```
FSTP MEM     ; Stack Top → [MEM]
FSTP ST(2)   ; Stack Top → ST(2)
```

FXCH (Exchange with Top of Stack) This instruction exchanges the contents of the top of stack with the specified operand register. For example:

```
FXCH ST(6)   ; Stack Top ↔ ST(6)
FXCH ST(1)   ; Stack Top ↔ ST(1)
```

Integer Data Transfer Instructions The instruction set of 8087 contains three instructions of this type. These are explained as follows:

FILD (Load Integer to Stack Top) This instruction loads the specified integer data operand to the top of stack. For example,

```
FILD MEM     ; Stack Top ← MEM i
FILD ST(5)   ; Stack Top ← ST(5)
```

The character I in the mnemonic specifies the integer operand.

FIST/FISTP Both the instructions work in an exactly similar manner as FST/FSTP except the fact that the operands are integer operands.

BCD Data Transfer Instructions The 8087 instruction set has two instructions of this type, namely, FBLD and FBSTP. Both the instructions work in an exactly similar manner as FLD and FSTP except for the operand type BCD.

Arithmetic Instructions The 8087 instruction set contains 11 instructions that can either be directly used to perform arithmetic operations or supporting operations like scaling, rounding, negation, absolute value, etc. These instructions are discussed as follows:

FADD The instruction FADD performs real or integer addition of the specified operand with the stack top. The results are stored in destination operand controlled by the D-bit. The operand may be any of the stack registers or a memory location.

FSUB The instruction FSUB performs real or integer subtraction of the specified operand from the stack top. The operand may be any of the stack register or memory. The result of the operation is stored in the destination operand, controlled by the D-bit.

FMUL This instruction performs real or integer multiplication of the specified operand with stack top. The specified operand may be a register or a memory location. The result is stored in the destination operand controlled by the D-bit.

FDIV The instruction performs real or integer division. If the destination is not specified, the ST (Stack Top) is the destination and source (SRC) must be a memory operand of short real or long real type. If both are specifed [ST and ST(i)], then any one of the two may act as source, while the other acts as the destination (as decided by the D-bit). When neither is specified then ST(i) and ST are assumed as destination and source respectively and after the operation, the stack is popped and the result is stored at the new stack top. The same limitations on operands are also followed by all the above arithmetic instructions.

FSQRT This instruction finds out the square root of the content of the stack top and stores the result on the stack top again.

FSCAL This instruction multiplies the content of the stack top (ST) by 2n, where n is the integer part of ST(1) and stores the result in ST.

FPREM This instruction divides the stack top (ST) by ST(1) and then stores the remainder to the stack top (ST).

FRNDINT This instruction rounds the content of ST(0) to its integer value. The rounding is controlled by the RC field of the control word.

FXTRACT This instruction extracts the exponent and fraction of the stack top and stores them in the stack of registers. The exponent of the current ST is stored in temporary register 2. The content of temporary register 1 (exponent) is stored in the current ST and the content of temporary register 2 (fraction) is stored by decrementing the stack top address.

FABS This instruction replaces the content of the stack top by its absolute value (magnitude). The sign is neglected in operation.

FCSH This instruction changes the sign of the content of the stack top.

The instructions FADD, FSUB, FMUL and FDIV are available with their different options decided by the opcode bits D, P and R. The D-bit decides the source and destination operands as in the case of 8086. The P-bit indicates whether an execution is followed by a pop operation. The R-bit indicates the reverse mode. This is valid only in case of FSUB and FDIV instructions. If R is 0, the destination operand is either subtracted from or divided by the source operand. If R is 1, the source operand is either subtracted from or divided by the destination operand. The result is stored in the destination operand. This definition of R is exactly opposite if D = 1, because if D = 1, it interchanges the source and destination operands.

Transcendental Instructions The 8087 provides five instructions for transcendental calculations described as follows. The operands usually are ST(0) and ST(1) or only ST(0).

FPTAN This instruction calculates the partial tangent of an angle θ, where θ must be in the range from $0 \leq \theta < 90°$. The value of θ must be stored at the stack top (stack top is the implicit operand). The result is given in the form of a ratio of ST/ST(1). If the result is out of capacity of the destination operand, an invalid error occurs.

FPATAN This instruction calculates the arc tangent (inverse tangent) of a ratio ST/ST(1). The stack is popped at the end of the execution and the result (θ) is stored on the top of stack. The contents of ST and ST(1) should follow the inequality,

$$0 \leq ST(1) < ST < 00$$

F2XMI This instruction calculates the expression (2x – 1). The value of x is stored at the top of the stack. The result is stored back at the top of the stack.

FLY2X This instruction calculates the expression 'ST(1)*$\log_2$ ST'. A pop operation is carried out on the top of stack, and the result is stored at the top of stack. The ST must be in the range 0 to $+\infty$, while the ST(1) must be in the range $-\infty$ to $+\infty$.

FLY2XP1 This instruction is used to calculate the expression 'ST(1)*$\log_2$ [(ST)+1]'. The result is stored back on the stack top after a pop operation. The value of |ST| must lie between 0 and ($1\text{-}2^{1/2}/2$) and the value of ST(1) must be between $-\infty$ to $+\infty$.

Comparison Instructions All the comparison instructions compare the operands and modify the condition code flags, as shown in Tables 8.4 (a) and (b). The instructions available in 8087 for comparison are discussed as follows:

Table 8.4(a) ***Condition Code Bits Definition***

Comparison	C_3	C_0
Stack Top > Source	0	0
Stack Top < Source	0	1
Stack Top = Source	1	0
Not Comparable	1	1

Table 8.4(b)

Exam. Result	C_3	C_2	4	C_0
+ Unnormal	0	0	0	0
+ NAN	0	0	0	1
– Unnormal	0	0	1	0
– NAN	0	0	1	1
Normal	0	1	0	0
+ ∞	0	1	0	1
– Normal	0	1	1	0
– ∞	0	1	1	1
+ 0	1	0	0	0
Empty	1	0	0	1
– 0	1	0	1	0
Empty	1	0	1	1
+ Denormal	1	1	0	0
Empty	1	1	0	1
– Denormal	1	1	1	0
Empty	1	1	1	1

FCOM This instruction compares real or integer operands specified by stack registers or memory. This instruction has the top of stack as an implicit operand. The content of the top of stack is compared either with the contents of a memory location or with the contents of another stack register. The MF bit in the opcode format decides whether the comparison is between floating point or integer operands. The condition code flag bits are accordingly modified as shown in Table 8.4(a).

FCOMP and FCOMPP These instructions also work in an exactly similar manner as FCOM does. But the FCOMP instruction carries out one pop operation after the execution of the FCOM instruction, and FCOMPP carries out two pop operations after the execution of the FCOM instruction. The condition code flag bits are modified as indicated in Table 8.4(a). The FCOMP and FCOMPP instructions have the top of stack as an implicit operand. In case of FCOMP instruction the other operand may be a register operand (ST(0) – ST(7)) or a memory operand. However, in case of the FCOMPP instruction the other operand must only be any of the stack register contents (a memory operand is not allowed).

FIST This instruction tests if the contents of the stack top is zero, i.e. the content of the stack top is compared with zero and the condition code flags are accordingly modified as shown in Table 8.4(a). The zero (0.0) is considered as the source operand.

FXAM This instruction examines the contents of the stack top and modifies the contents of the condition code flags as shown in Table 8.4(b).

Constant Returning Instructions These instructions load the specific constants to the top of the register stack. The 8087 has seven such instructions. The stack top is an implicit operand in all these instructions. The constants to be loaded to the stack top are internally stored in the coprocessor. These instructions are listed with their descriptions.

FLDZ	Load +0.0 to stack top.
FLD1	Load +1.0 to stack top.
FLDPI	Load π to stack top.
FLD2T	Load the constant $\log_2 10$ to stack top
FLDL2E	Load the constant $\log_2 e$ to stack top
FLDLG2	Load the constant $\log_{10} 2$ to stack top
FLDLN2	Load the constant $\log_e 2$ to stack top.

Coprocessor Control Instructions The coprocessor control instructions are either used to program the numeric processor or to handle the internal housekeeping functions like exception handling, flags manipulations, processor environment maintenance and preparation, etc. The 8087 instruction set has sixteen such instructions. All these instructions are listed below with their functions in brief.

FINIT This instruction prepares the 8087 for further execution. In other words, this just performs the same function as the hardware reset. The control word is set to 03FF and the TAG status is set empty. All the flags are cleared and the stack top is initialized at ST (0).

FENI This instruction enables the interrupt structure and response mechanism of 8087. In other words, the interrupt mask flag is cleared.

FDISI This instruction sets the interrupt mask flag to disable the interrupt response mechanism of 8087.

FLDCW This instruction loads the control word of 8087 from the specified source operand. The only memory source operand is an allowed operand. Any addressing mode, allowed in 8086, may be used to refer the memory operand.

FSTCW This instruction may be used to store the contents of the 8087 control word register to a memory location, addressed using any of the 8086 addressing modes.

FSTSW This instruction stores the current content of the status word register to a memory location, addressed using any of the 8086 addressing modes.

FCLEX This instruction clears all the previously set exception flags in the status register. This also clears the BUSY and IR flags of the status word. The other bits of the status word are left unaffected.

FINCSTP This instruction modifies the TOP bits of the status register so as to point to the next stack register. For example, if TOP = 000 the stack top is ST(0). Then after the FINCSTP instruction is executed, the TOP bits will be updated to 001 and the corresponding stack top is ST(1).

FDECSTP This instruction updates the TOP bits of the stack register so as to point to the previous register in stack. For example, if the TOP bits are 100, the current stack top will be ST(4). If the FDECSTP instruction is executed, the TOP bits will be modified to 011 and the stack top will be ST(3).

FFREE This instruction marks the TAG field of the operand stack register to be empty.

FNOP This is a NOP instruction of the coprocessor. No internal status or control flag bits change. This requires up to 16 clock cycles for execution.

FWAIT This instruction is used by 8087 to make 8086 wait till it completes the current operation. The BUSY pin of 8087 is tied high by 8087 to inform the host CPU that the allotted task is still under execution.

FSTENV This instruction is used to store the environment of the coprocessor to a destination memory location specified in the instruction using any of the 8086 addressing modes. To store the complete environment of the processor, 8087 needs a 14-byte memory space. The destination operand points to the address of the lowest byte. The environment of the processor 8087 consists of the contents of the following registers: control register (2-bytes), status register (2-bytes), tag register (2-bytes), instruction pointer (4-bytes) and data pointer (4-bytes), i.e. total 14 bytes. The store-in-memory operation starts with the control register which is stored at the specified destination operand. The store operation proceeds in the same sequence as stated above, and the destination memory pointer is incremented as per the size of the register or pointer to be stored. The storage format is shown in Fig. 8.19.

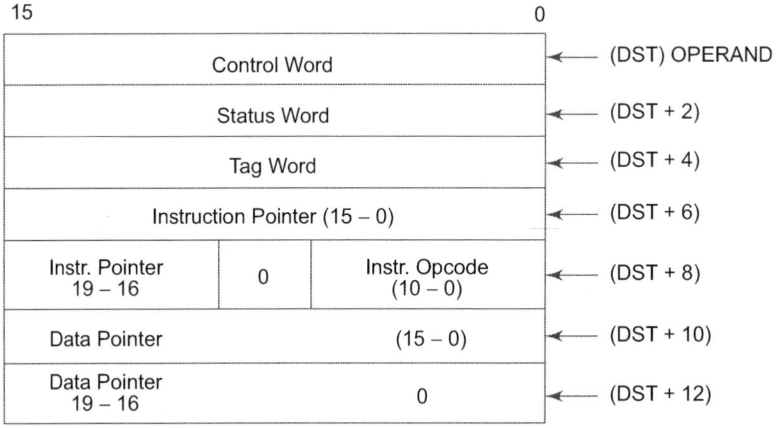

The 0 marked fields are reserved by Intel.

Fig. 8.19 *Storage Format for FSTENV Instruction*

FLDENV This instruction loads the environment (that may be previously stored in the memory using FSTENV instruction) of the coprocessor into it. This instruction reads the environment content in the same format in which the FSTENV instruction stores the same in the memory. The format is shown in Fig. 8.19.

FSAVE This instruction saves the complete processor status into the memory, at the address specified by the destination operand. The complete status of the processor requires 94 bytes of memory. The status of the processor consists of all the parameters saved by the FSTENV instructions (14 bytes as shown in Fig. 8.19) along with the complete contents of all the stack registers (ST_0– ST_7). The eight stack registers require 80 bytes, i.e. 10 bytes per stack register (note that each one is an 80-bit register). The complete storage format is shown in Fig. 8.20.

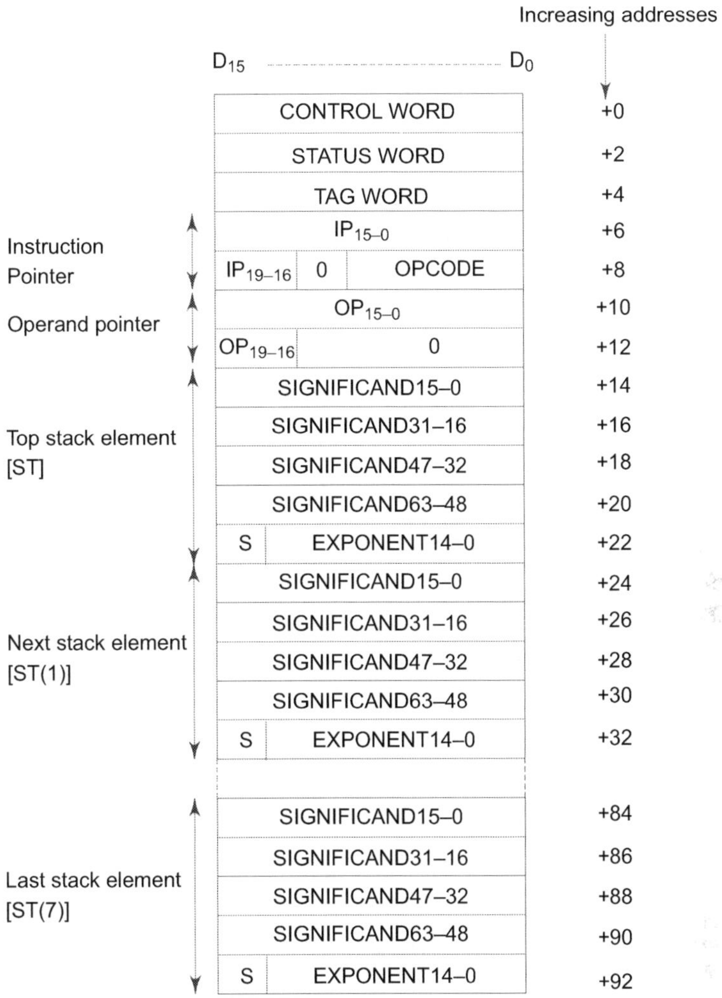

*S is a sign bit for the respective stack element.
*Bit 0 of each field is the rightmost least significant bit.
*Bit 63 of significand is the integer bit (assumed binary point is immediately to the right of this bit).
*Each row in the above diagram represents two bytes (16-bits).

Fig. 8.20 *Storage Format for FSAVE Instruction*

FRSTOR Using this instruction it is possible to restore the previous status of the coprocessor (previously stored into the memory using FSAVE instruction) from a source memory operand that may be addressed using any of the 8086 addressing modes. The status parameters must be stored in the memory in the format shown in Fig. 8.20, before execution of this instruction.

8.3.7 Addressing Modes and Data Types

8087 supports all the addressing modes supported by 8086. The data types supported by 8087 are shown in Table 8.3.

Table 8.5 *8087 Data Type*

Data Formats	*Range*	*Precision*	*Most Significant Byte*
			7 0 | 7 0 | 7 0 | 7 0 | 7 0 | 7 0 | 7 0 | 7 0 | 7 0 | 7 0
Word Integer	10^4	16 Bits	I_{15} … I_0 Two's Complement
Short Integer	10^4	32 Bits	I_{31} … I_0 Two's Complement
Long Integer	10^{18}	64 Bits	I_{63} … I_0 Two's Complement
Packed BCD	10^{18}	18 Digits	S | $D_{17}D_{16}$ | … D_1D_0
Short Real	10 + 38	24 Bits	S | E_7 … E_0 | F_1 … F_{23} F_0 Implicit
Long Real	10 + 308	53 Bits	S | E_{10} … E_0 | F_1 … F_{52} Implicit F_0
Temporary Real	10 +4932	64 Bits	S | E_{14} … E_0 | F_0 … F_{63}

Integer: 1
Packed BCD: $(-1)^S (D_{17} \ldots D_0)$
Real: $(-1)^S (2^{E\text{-}Bias}) (F_0 . F_1 ..)$
bias = 127 for short Real
1023 for long Real
16383 for Temp. Real

8.3.8 Programming Using 8087

As already explained, the 8087 instructions may lie interleaved in an 8086 assembly language program. It is the task of the 8086 to identify and hand them over to 8087 for execution. If the programming is done using MASM the directives .8087, .287 and .387 inform the assembler about the coprocessor programming model to be used for coding of the program. This section illustrates a few programming examples using 8087. The same programs may be executed using other advanced coprocessors like 80287, 80387 and 80487.

Program 8.1

Write a procedure to calculate the volume of a sphere using MASM syntax.

Solution: This procedure utilizes services of the register stack of 8087 to store the data temporarily. The procedure is given as follows:

```
      ;This procedure calculates volume of a sphere. The radius of the sphere is specified
      ; in the program. The result is stored in the memory location VOLUME.
      ;Volume of a sphere is given by 4/3*(pi)*(r**3).
        .8087
        DATA SEGMENT
        RADIUS DD 5.0233
        CONST EQU 1.333
        VOLUME DD 01 DUP(?)
DATA ENDS
ASSUME CS:CODE, DS:DATA
```

```
VOL PROC FAR
CODE SEGMENT
START      MOV AX,DATA          ; Initialize data segment
           MOV DS,AX
           FINIT                ; Initialize 8087
           FLD RADIUS           ; Read radius in to stack top
           FST ST(4)            ; Store stack top.
           FMUL ST(4)           ; ST(0) ¬ ST(0)*ST(4)
                                ; I.E.{ [ST(4)]^2}
           FMUL ST(4)           ; ST(0) ¬ {[ST(0)]^2}*ST(4)
                                ; = {[ST(0)]^3}
           FLD CONST            ; Get constant 1.333
           FMUL                 ; Multiply with (r^3)
           FLDPI                ; Get PI(p)
           FMUL                 ; Multiply with PI
           FST VOLUME           ; Store volume in VOLUME
           RETP
VOL ENDP
CODE ENDS
END START
```

Program 8.1 *A Procedure to Calculate Volume of a Sphere*

Program 8.2

Write a program to convert a fractional binary number to its decimal equivalent.

Solution: The procedure of converting a fractional binary number is explained as follows:
Let us choose a fractional binary number x = 0101 0001 1001.1101

$$= 0^* (2^{11}) + 1^* (2^{10}) + 0^* (2^9) + 1^* (2^8) + 0^* (2^7) + 0^* (2^6) +$$
$$0^* (2^5) + 1^* (2^4) + 1^* (2^0) + 0^* (2^2) + 0^* (2^1) + 1^* (2^0) +$$
$$1^* (2^{-1}) + 1^* (2^{-2}) + 0^* (2^{-3}) + 1^* (2^{-4})$$
$$= 1305.9375$$

For simplicity, let us assume that the integer part is represented using 12-bits and the fraction is represented using 4 bits. The listing is given in Program 8.2.

```
  ASSUME CS:CODE,DS:DATA
  DATA SEGMENT
     INIT DW 0000010100011001B      ; Integer part
     FRACT DW 1101B                 ; Fraction part (4-bit)
     COUNTI EQU 0CH                 ; Integer bit count
     COUNTF EQU 04H
     EXP EQU 0CH
     POWER EQU ?
DATA ENDS
.8087
CODE SEGMENT
START: MOV AX,DATA
```

```
        MOV DS,AX
        MOV CH,COUNTI
        MOV CL,COUNTF
        FINIT                          ; Initialize 8087
        NXTBIT : MOV AX,INTG
        ROR AX
        JNC YY
        MOV BL,COUNTI
        MOV BH,EXP
        SUB BL,BH
        MOV POWER,BL                   ; Get 2n, where n=COUNTI-EXP
        FLD POWER
        F2AMI
        FLDI
        FADDP
        FADD
YY:     DEC EXP
        JNZ NXTBIT
MOV     BL,COUNTF
        FLD COUNTF
        F2AMI
        FLDI
        FADDP
        FLDI
        FDIVP
        FADD
ZZ:     DEC BL
        JNZ NXTBIT1
        FST DECI
        MOV AH,4CH
        INT 21H
CODE ENDS
END START
```

Program 8.2 *ALP for Program 10.2*

8087 uses the internal stack of registers for storing intermediate results. After the execution of some of the instructions, the stack automatically gets modified. Hence, the programmer must have a thorough idea of the stack changes after execution of each instruction to appropriately access the partial or intermediate results, stored on the stack.

8.4 I/O PROCESSOR 8089

8.4.1 Introduction

A practical microprocessor system may have a number of peripheral devices connected with it. Each of the peripheral devices, interfaced with the CPU, may offer it a specific additional capability. As already discussed in Chapter 6, all such peripherals can be interfaced with the CPU using the dedicated peripheral interface chips. However, the CPU still has to initialize the peripheral controllers and keep track of their operations, to ensure proper functioning of the system. Also after the completion of the IO task, the CPU has to maintain the post-operation status and records. Thus the maintenance of these peripheral devices consumes considerable CPU time, thereby reducing the throughput.

An IO processor is supposed to take care of all the system IO activities. Once initiated by the host CPU, the IO processor receives requests from the system peripherals, it issues commands to the system peripherals and also keeps track of the operations of the peripherals. The IO processor may establish communication with the host, using its interrupt services.

8089 is an I/O processor, designed to work with Intels xx86 family of processors. It communicates with the host processors using a memory table, which contains the details of the task to be executed. These tables are prepared by the host CPU to allot a task to the IOP. The host interrupts the IOP after allotting a task to it. Once interrupted, the IOP reads the memory tables prepared by the host CPU to get the details of the allotted task. This memory table has an address of a program, written in 8089 instructions, known as a *channel program*. The 8089 executes the channel program. Unlike 8087, the 8089 can fetch and execute its

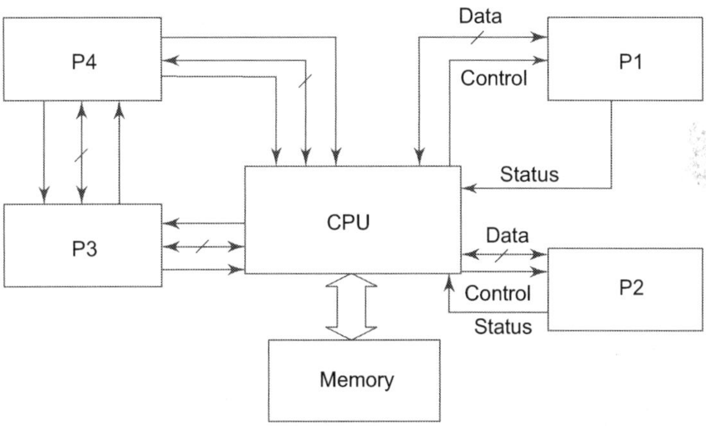

Fig. 8.21(a) *I/O handled by a CPU*

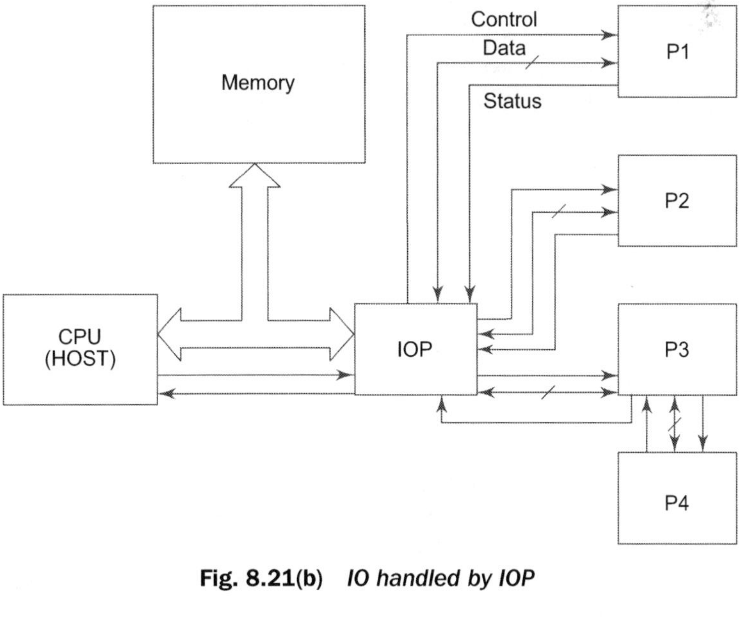

Fig. 8.21(b) *IO handled by IOP*

instructions on its own. When it completes the task, it either interrupts the CPU or maintains a busy flag in the memory based table, which is periodically checked by the host CPU. The 8089 may be operated in *tightly coupled* or *loosely coupled* configurations. In a tightly coupled configuration, the 8089 shares the system bus and memory with the host CPU using its $\overline{RQ}/\overline{GT}$ pins, in the same way as 8087 does. In a loosely coupled system, 8089 has its own local bus and communicates with the host using bus arbiter and controller. In a loosely coupled configuration, IOP even has its own set of latches and buffers for driving its system bus, that can further be shared by other masters.

In a loosely coupled system, the $\overline{RQ}/\overline{GT}$ pin of 8089 may be used to communicate with other 8089, that will be treated as a slave by the former 8089. The conceptual respresentation of IO handled by the main CPU and I/O handled by the I/O processor are shown in Figs 8.21 (a) and (b).

The 8089 I/O processor use only 16 address lines and thus it can address only 64Kbytes of IO space. The 8089 handled IO devices need not have the same data bus width as that of 8089. This enables even 8-bit IO devices to be interfaced easily with 8089.

8.4.2 8089 Architecture

In this section, the base architecture of 8089 is discussed briefly along with its signal descriptions. The base architecture of 8089 is shown in Fig. 8.22.

The 8089 has two internal IO channels which can be programmed independently, to handle two separate IO tasks for the host CPU. The common ALU is shared by both the channels. The control unit derives the control signals required for the operation of the IOP channels. The IOP channels also share the common control unit. The bus interface and control unit handles all the bus activities, under the control of the control unit. The CCP, i.e. channel control pointer, available for programmers, automatically gets loaded with the 20-bit address of a memory table for the channel. This table is prepared by the host CPU to allot a task to the IOP. The address of the memory table for channel 2 is calculated by adding 8 to the contents of CCP, i.e. the memory table address for channel 1. For allotting a task to the IOP, the CPU first prepares the memory table in the memory that contains the details of the task. It then, asserts the Channel Attention signal (CA) and simultaneously selects one of the two channels using the SEL line. The SEL line is usually connected to the A_0 line of the host CPU, so that two consecutive addresses are assigned to the two channels.

The two channels are identical in their organization and may be used interchangeably for each other. Each of the channels has two sets of registers, viz. pointers and registers. The pointers are 20-bit registers normally used to address memory, while the registers are 16-bit general purpose data registers. Each of the pointers, except PP, has a tag bit assigned with each of them. This bit indicates whether the 20-bit register content is to be used (i.e. for addressing 1Mbyte system memory) or the lower 16-bit register content is to be used as the pointer (i.e. for addressing within 64 Kbyte local memory).

The pointer pp is a 20-bit pointer. The registers GA,GB,GC, BC, IX and MC can also be used as general purpose registers in the channel programs, if they are not used as pointers or for any special function. The memory operands can only be accessed using one of the pointer, viz., GA,GB,GC or PP as a base pointer. GA and GB can be used for source and destination pointers respectively for DMA operations. The DRQ and EXT pins are used for data transfer control and operation termination signals during DMA operations. The SINTR pins are used by the channels either to inform the CPU that the previous operation is over or to ask for its attention or interference if required, before the completion of the task. The internal 8-bit program status word contains the current channel status, which contains source and destination address widths, channel activity, interrupt control and servicing, bus load limit and priority information. The PSW is not user accessible directly, but can be modified using channel commands.

The most important feature of the IOP 8089 is its ability to perform DMA operations with a great flexibility and number of options. The direct transfer between an 8-bit peripheral and a 16-bit destination or source is possible with 8089. These options are programmed using the channel control register, that contains flags

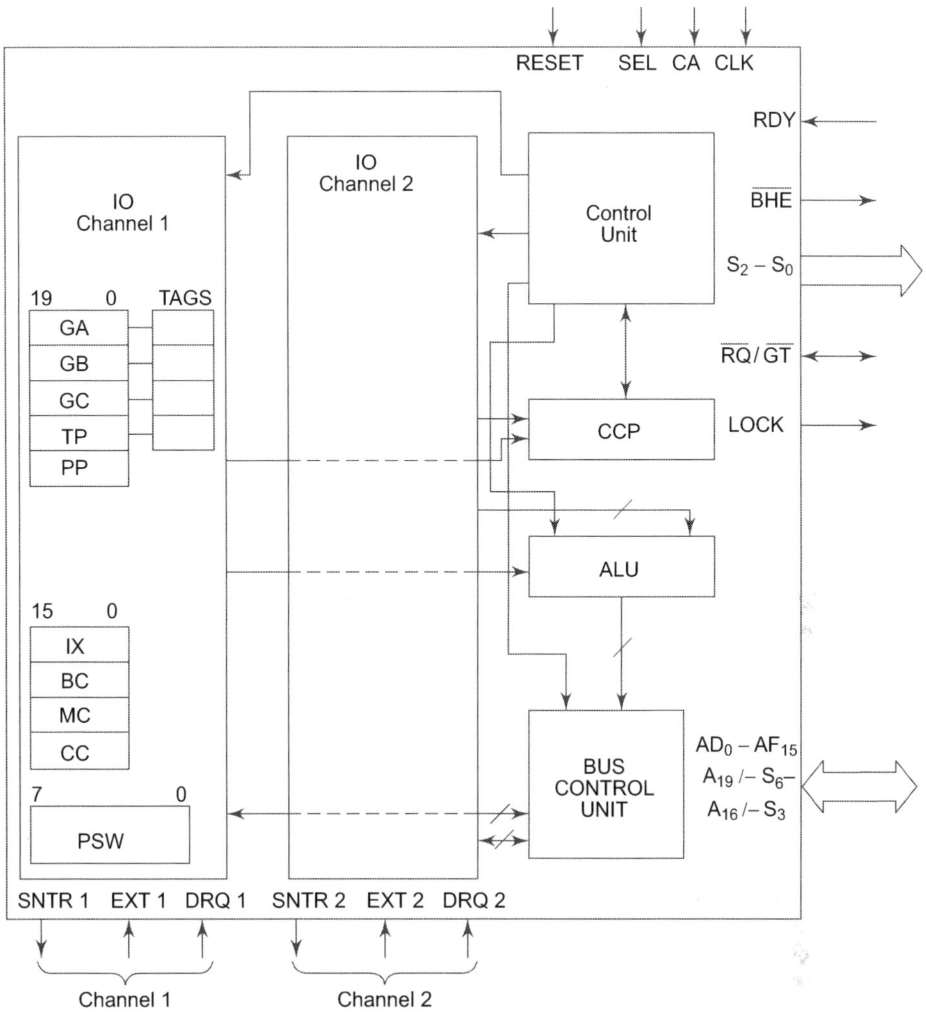

Fig. 8.22 *Base Architecture of 8089*

for the transfer type, translation mode, synchronization control, source/destination indicator, lock control, chaining control, single transfer mode and termination control.

With the advanced developments in the computing field, and launching of very high speed processors, the utility of this I/O processor is on decline. A more detailed discussion on this I/O processor has thus been avoided here. Figure 8.23 presents a general idea of interfacing connections between 8086 and 8089 in a loosely coupled system.

8.5 BUS ARBITRATION AND CONTROL

The shared bus multimicroprocessor configuration was introduced to enhance the processing speed limits of a single processor system. Many multimicroprocessor systems have been designed using this configuration. With the increased demand for more and more processing power, the number of microprocessors sharing the bus may be increased, giving rise to various schemes of bus contention and interprocessor communication problems. To resolve these problems, different hardware strategies and algorithms have been worked out.

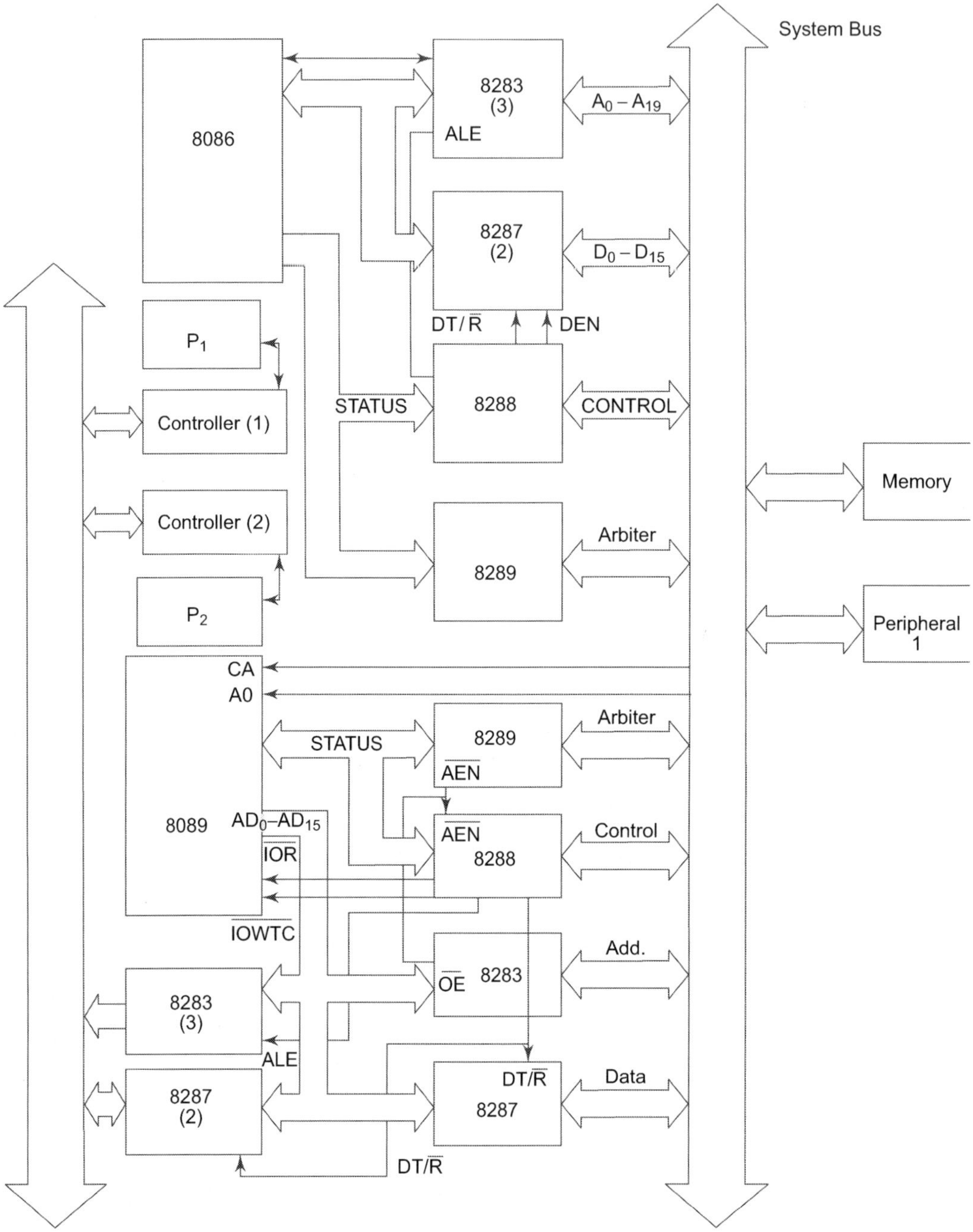

Fig. 8.23 *General Interfacing Connections between 8086 and 8089 (Loosely Coupled)*

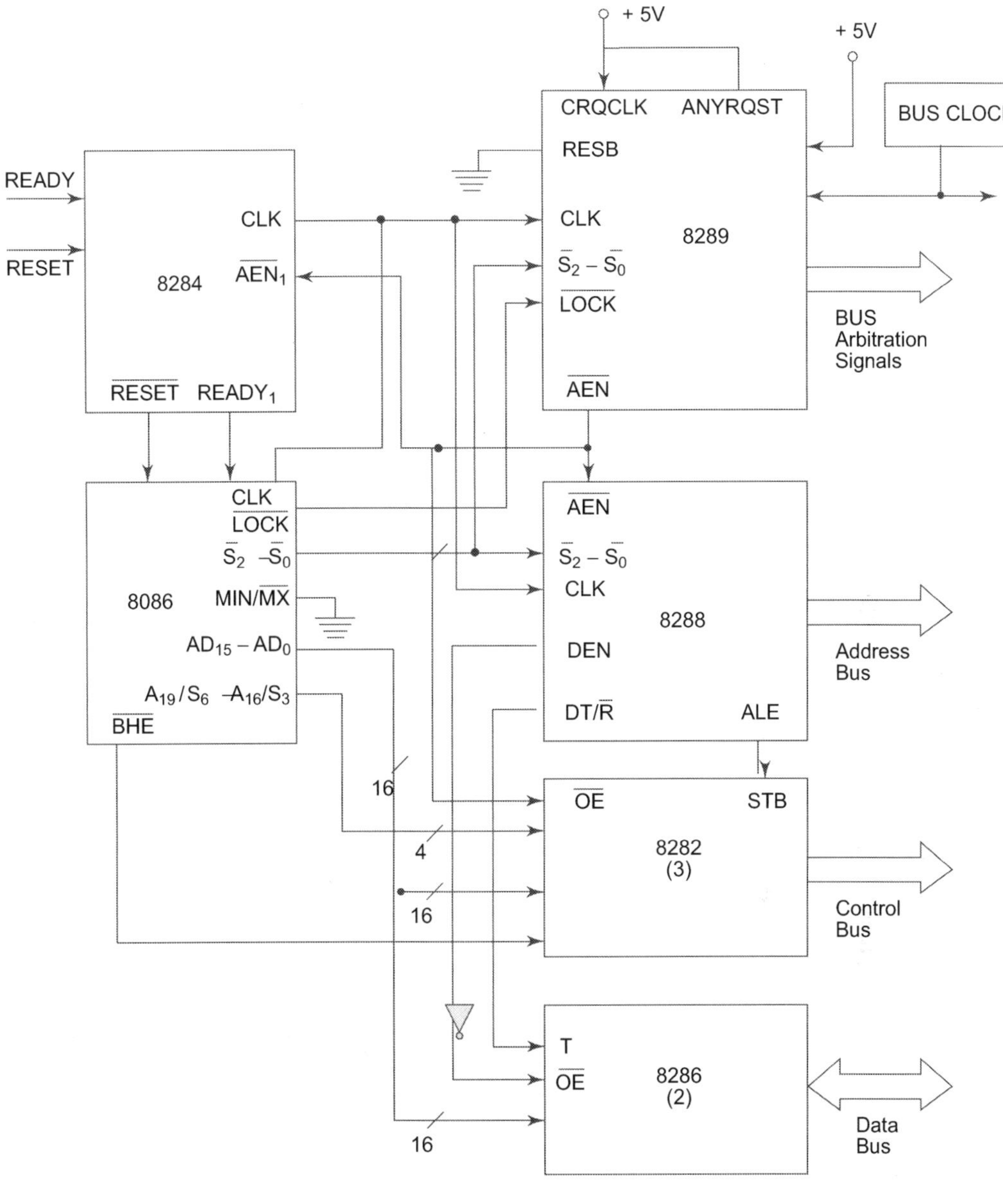

Fig. 8.24 *8089 Interconnections with 8086 and 8288*

These incorporated functions like bus allotment and control, bus arbitration and priority resolving, into them. In this section, we will briefly study the different bus sharing algorithms and their implementations using the available hardware. Before starting the discussion, we will introduce an integrated circuit IC 8289 used for the arbitration of the shared system bus. The 8289 to offers to the CPU, a capability to request for a bus access and it recognizes the bus allotted to itself and also to the other processors in the system. The 8289, popularly called Bus Arbiter, takes care of all the bus access control functions and bus handshake activities. While operating hand-in-hand with the bus controller 8288, the 8289 controls the access of the bus for its host CPU and maintains status about the current access of the bus. To allow the bus access to its master CPU, it uses either daisy chaining or independent request strategies for resolving the contention. These strategies are discussed later in this chapter. Figure 8.24 shows a single processor system, ready to hook up on a shared bus system.

The 8289 accepts status lines $\overline{S}_2 - \overline{S}_1$ as inputs and decodes the processor status from them, which is further used to control the access of the system bus. The bus controller also monitors the status simultaneously to derive different control signals. When the CPU initiates a bus cycle, the ALE pulse latches the address DEN and DT/$\overline{R}$ lines from the 8288 bus controller to present the address and data to the system bus. However, if the system bus is not free, the 8289 raises its $\overline{AEN}$ output, that tristates the address, data outputs of the latches and buffers. The $\overline{AEN}$ output also drives the $\overline{AEN}$ input of the clock generator. If $\overline{AEN}$ is high, the clock generator delays the READY signal till the $\overline{AEN}$ goes low. Once the $\overline{AEN}$ goes low the bus arbiter activates its BUSY output to indicate to the other masters that the bus is busy. Thus till the $\overline{AEN}$ goes low, the CPU is in wait state. After the 8289 gets the bus access, it pulls down $\overline{AEN}$. The CPU comes out of the wait state (as the READY is activated by the clock generator) and continues execution till any other master requests the bus access. The $\overline{LOCK}$ output of the CPU is connected to the bus arbiter input. The bus controller does not relinquish the bus, till the $\overline{LOCK}$ input is low. The RESB (Resident Bus Mode) and IOB (I/O Bus) inputs determine the respective bus modes, i.e. resident memory or I/O mode.

The independent request method of bus arbitration uses four signals to accomplish the bus access control, viz. Bus Request $(\overline{BREQ})$, Bus Priority in $(\overline{BPRN})$, Common Bus Request $\overline{(CBRQ)}$ and Bus Priority Out $(\overline{BPRO})$. These are the handshake signals to transfer the access of the bus from one CPU to the another. The $\overline{BREQ}$ line usually drives a priority resolving network that actually accepts the bus request inputs from all the masters and derives the priority outputs which further drive the $\overline{BPRN}$ inputs of all the masters. The Bus Priority input $(\overline{BPRN})$, if activated, indicates to the bus master that it has the highest priority at that time and may gain the bus control.

The Common Bus Request $(\overline{CBRQ})$ and $\overline{BUSY}$ lines of all the masters may be pulled-up to +5V. These lines are the bidirectional lines, used by all the masters to indicate their status to the system. After a bus master completes its task it releases the bus and deactivates the $\overline{BUSY}$ signal. The next requesting master accepts the $\overline{BPRN}$ signal and activates its busy output. A bus master of lower priority may use the $\overline{(CBRQ)}$ line to acquire the bus from a higher priority master. If the $\overline{(CBRQ)}$ goes low, the current master relinquishes the bus, if it is in idle state. Otherwise, it will complete the bus cycle and then relinquish the bus. The next requesting master will gain the bus access, if the priority resolver allows it. The two input pins ANYRQST (Any Request) and $\overline{CRQLCK}$ (Common Request Lock) are used, when the lower priority masters are allowed to gain bus access from the higher priority masters. If the ANYRQST pin is high, the $\overline{(CBRQ)}$ pin may be pulled high to release the bus at the end of the current bus cycle. If $\overline{CRQLCK}$ input is high, the $\overline{(CBRQ)}$ input is neglected. If $\overline{CRQLCK}$ pin is low, it prevents the 8289 from relinquishing the bus for the lower priority bus masters.

In case of the daisy chain method, the $\overline{BPRO}$ pin of one master is connected with the $\overline{BPRN}$ pin of the next lower priority master, in sequence. A low input on any of the $\overline{BPRN}$ pins indicates to the corresponding master that it has the highest priority at that instant and may complete its bus cycle. The $\overline{BPRN}$ pin of the top priority master is grounded, to allow it all-time bus access. The bus accesses for lower priority masters will be at the behest of higher priority masters. The $\overline{BCLK}$ input of 8289 allots afixed time slice to its master to complete its bus cycle.

8.5.1 Arbitration Schemes

There are three basic bus access control and arbitration schemes.

1. Daisy Chaining
2. Independent Request
3. Polling

Daisy Chaining The Daisy Chain method of bus arbitration is the simplest and cheapest scheme. It does not require any priority resolving network, rather the priorities of all the devices are essentially assumed to be in sequence.

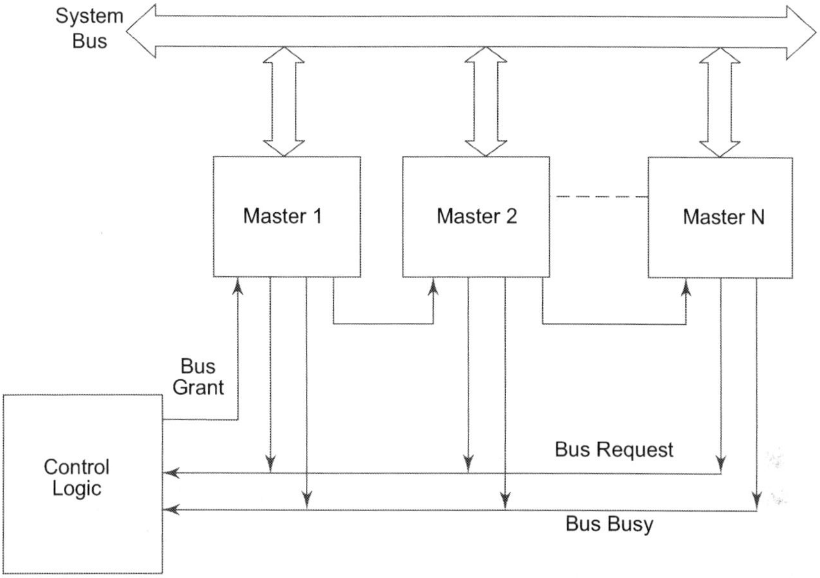

Fig. 8.25(a) *Daisy Chaining*

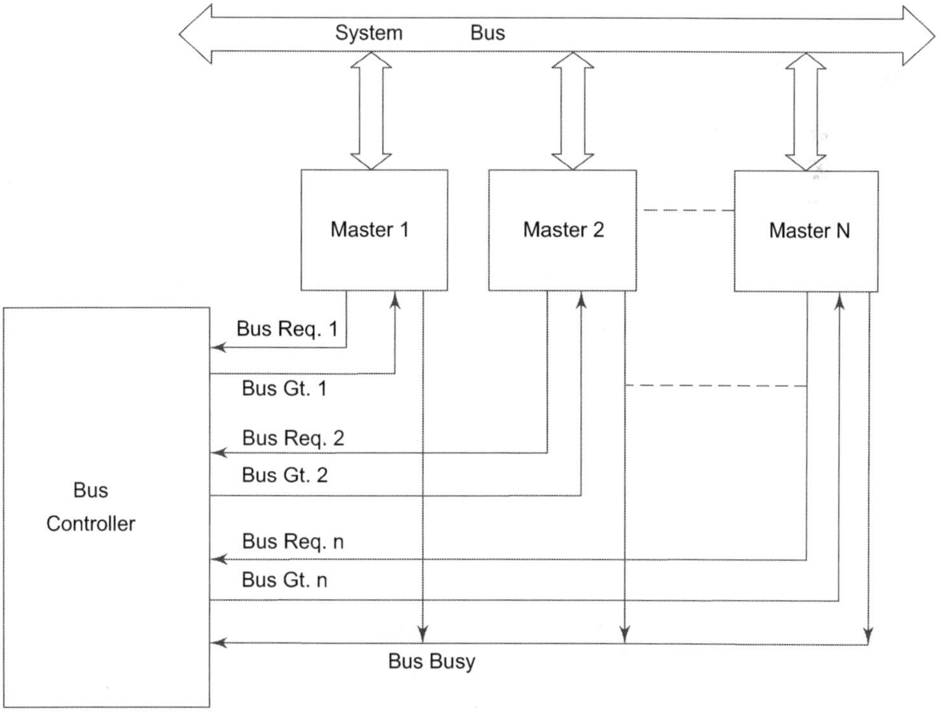

Fig. 8.25(b) *Independent Request*

All the masters use a single bus-request line for requesting the bus access. The controller sends a bus-grant signal, in response to the request, if the BUSY signal is inactive, i.e. when the bus is free. The bus grant pulse goes to each of the masters in the sequence till it reaches a requesting master. The master then receives the grant signal, activates the busy line and gains control of the bus. The priority is decided by the position of the requesting master in the sequence. The Daisy Chain scheme is shown in Fig. 8.25(a).

This scheme requires less hardware, but the response time is high due to the propagation of the bus grant signal through the chain.

2. Independent Bus Request Scheme The Independent Bus Request Scheme is the most complicated due to the hardware required. Each of the masters requires a pair of request and grant pins which are connected to the controlling logic. The BUSY line is common for all the masters. If the controlling logic receives a request on a bus request line, it immediately grants the bus access using the corresponding Bus grant signal, provided the BUSY line is not active. If it is already active, the controller waits for the BUSY line to go inactive, and then grants the request. The scheme is shown in Fig. 8.25(b). As compared to other schemes, this is quite fast, because each of the masters can independently communicate with the controller.

3. Polling In the Polling scheme, a set of address lines is driven by the controller to address each of the masters in sequence. When a bus request is received from a device by the controller, it generates the addresses on the address lines. If the generated address matches with that of the requesting master, the controller activates the BUSY line. Once the BUSY line is activated, the controller stops generating further addresses. This scheme is shown in Fig. 8.25(c).

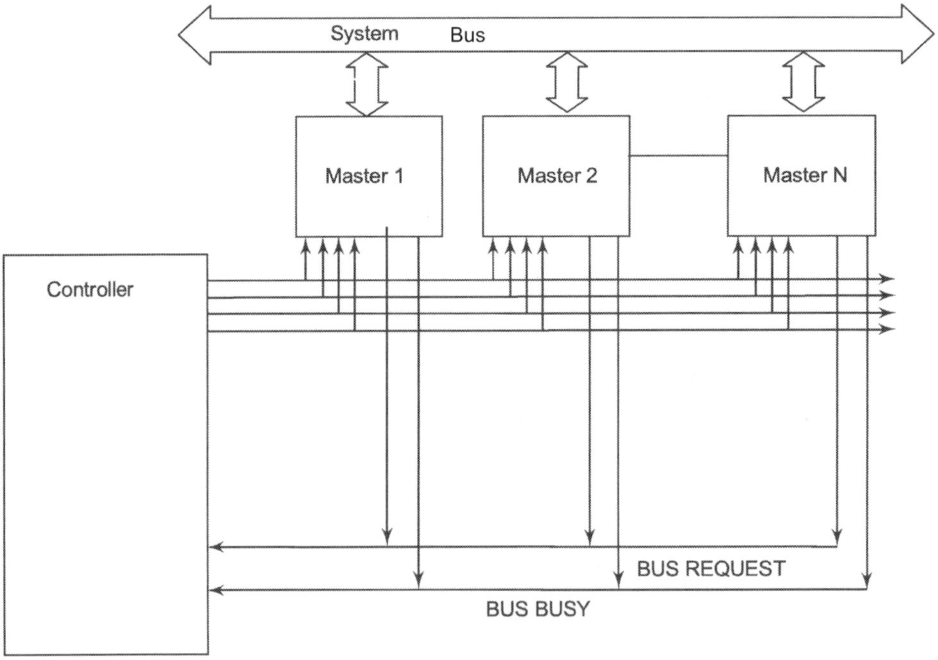

Fig. 8.25(c) *Polling Scheme*

8.6 TIGHTLY COUPLED AND LOOSELY COUPLED SYSTEMS

The multimicroprocessor systems are also classified as tightly (closely) coupled or loosely coupled systems, depending upon whether the microprocessors share a common memory and a common system bus or not.

The processors used in multimicroprocessor systems are either coprocessors or independent processors. A coprocessor executes the instructions fetched for it by the host processor. An independent processor may ask for a bus access, may itself fetch the instructions and execute them independently.

In a tightly coupled system, the microprocessors (either coprocessors or independent processors) may share a common clock and bus control logic. The two processors in a closely coupled system may communicate using a common system bus or common memory. The microprocessor in a closely coupled system either uses a status bit in memory or interrupts the host to inform it about the completion of the task allotted to it. A typical closely coupled configuration is shown in Fig. 8.26. A coprocessor that cannot fetch the instructions from memory on its own is always interconnected with the host in the tightly coupled configuration. The independent processors request bus accesses using the $\overline{RQ}/\overline{GT}$ inputs of the host. When a processor is using the bus, all other processors maintain their local buses in high impedance state, and wait for the currently executing processor to complete its task. After it is completed, one of the processors may get the bus access, if the priority resolver allows it.

In a loosely coupled multiprocessor system, on the other hand, each CPU may have its own bus control logic. The bus arbitration is handled by an external circuit, common to all the processors. The loosely coupled system configurations like LAN (Local Area Network) and WAN (Wide Area

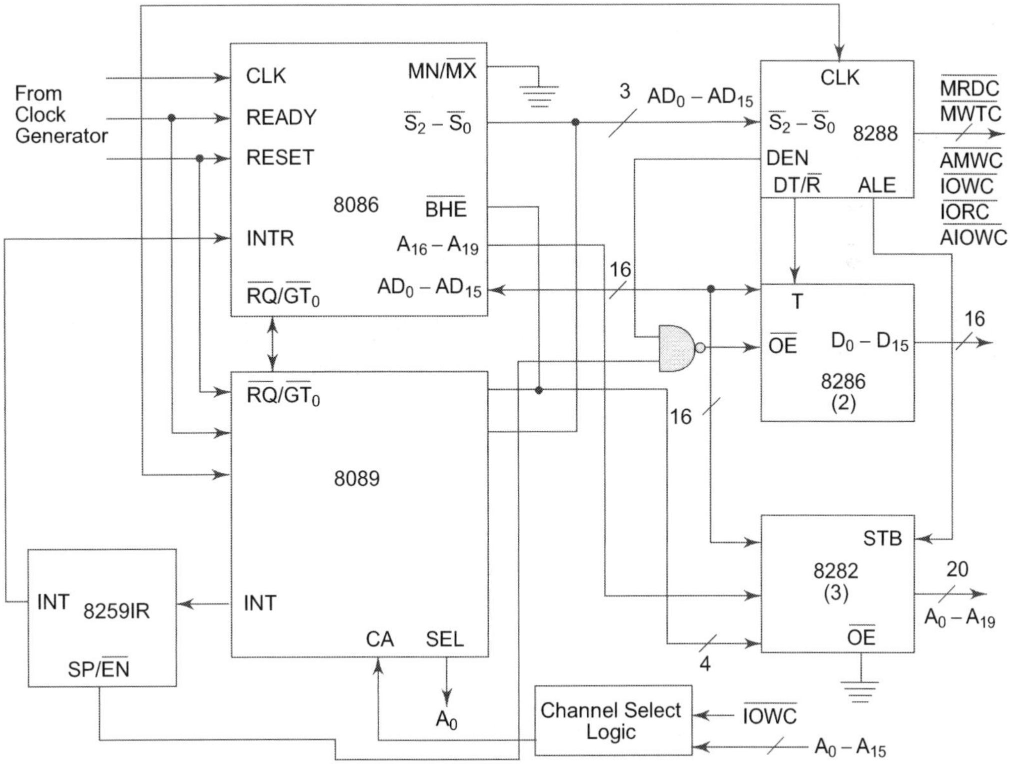

Fig. 8.26 *8086/8089 Closely Coupled Configuration*

Network) can be spreaded over a large area. The tightly coupled systems are usually designed in the form of physically small computing systems. The recent supercomputing systems are suitable combinations of both these configurations. The loosely coupled systems have the following advantages over the tightly coupled systems:

1. More number of CPUs can be added in a loosely coupled system to improve the system performance.
2. The system structure is modular and hence easy to maintain and troubleshoot.
3. A fault in a single module does not lead to a complete system breakdown.
4. Due to the independent processing modules used in the system, it is more fault- tolerant.
5. More suitable to parallel applications due to its modular organization.

In spite of all these advantages, the loosely coupled systems are more complicated due to the required additional communication hardware. They are less portable and more expensive due to the additional hardware and the communication media requirement. Figure 8.27 shows a block diagramatic sketch of a loosely coupled system. The bus arbitration schemes discussed in Section 8.5 are important in case of the loosely coupled systems.

With this information on multimicroprocessor systems, we now present a case study of an 8088 based multiprocessor system. This system along with its control program was developed by us and is discussed here with minimal necessary details of the hardware and software.

8.7 DESIGN OF A PC BASED MULTIMICROPROCESSOR SYSTEM

8.7.1 Introduction

This section presents an overview of a PC based multimicroprocessor system. Two subprocessing cards with an 8088 based system and 64K memory on each, were designed and developed. These IBM PC compatible cards having one 8088 minimal system on each along with the required switching logic can be inserted in a PC simultaneously. Thus the overall system contains three 8088 processors with one CPU operating as a master processor while the other two operating in the slave mode. Here the master CPU means the main CPU in the PC and we will use both these terms interchangeably. Also the slave CPUs will sometimes be referred to as subprocessors. The job is communicated with the system using the master processor of PC, in the form of a sequence of file-names. These EXE files are residing in the current drive and directory of the hard-disk. The master processor checks if there is any invalid filename in the sequence of .EXE filenames. If any invalid file-name is found, it accepts the next file in the sequence for execution, after displaying the invalid filename. Then the master processor distributes the tasks in the form of .EXE filenames to the subprocessors according to the sequence, in which they appear in the command line. Both the slave processors start executing the programs one by one. Each slave processor interrupts the main processor to ask for a new job, when the current one is over. After the execution of each program is over, the slave processors store the result in their respective result memory buffers and the master processor stores the result buffers on to the harddisk with the same filename as input .EXE file but with extension .RES. When all the programs are executed, the system returns to the DOS prompt. The overall system architecture is thus a tree structure with two slave 8088 CPUs connected to the parent root node which is a master CPU in the form of a PC. The system gives program level parallel operation.

The hardware design section describes the design procedure of the modules in the proposed architecture. The hardware design section describes the details of the design of the subprocessing cards rather than the 8088 minimal system. The software unit describes the monitoring algorithms which have been designed for the expected operation of the circuit. The result, conclusion and future expansion section presents

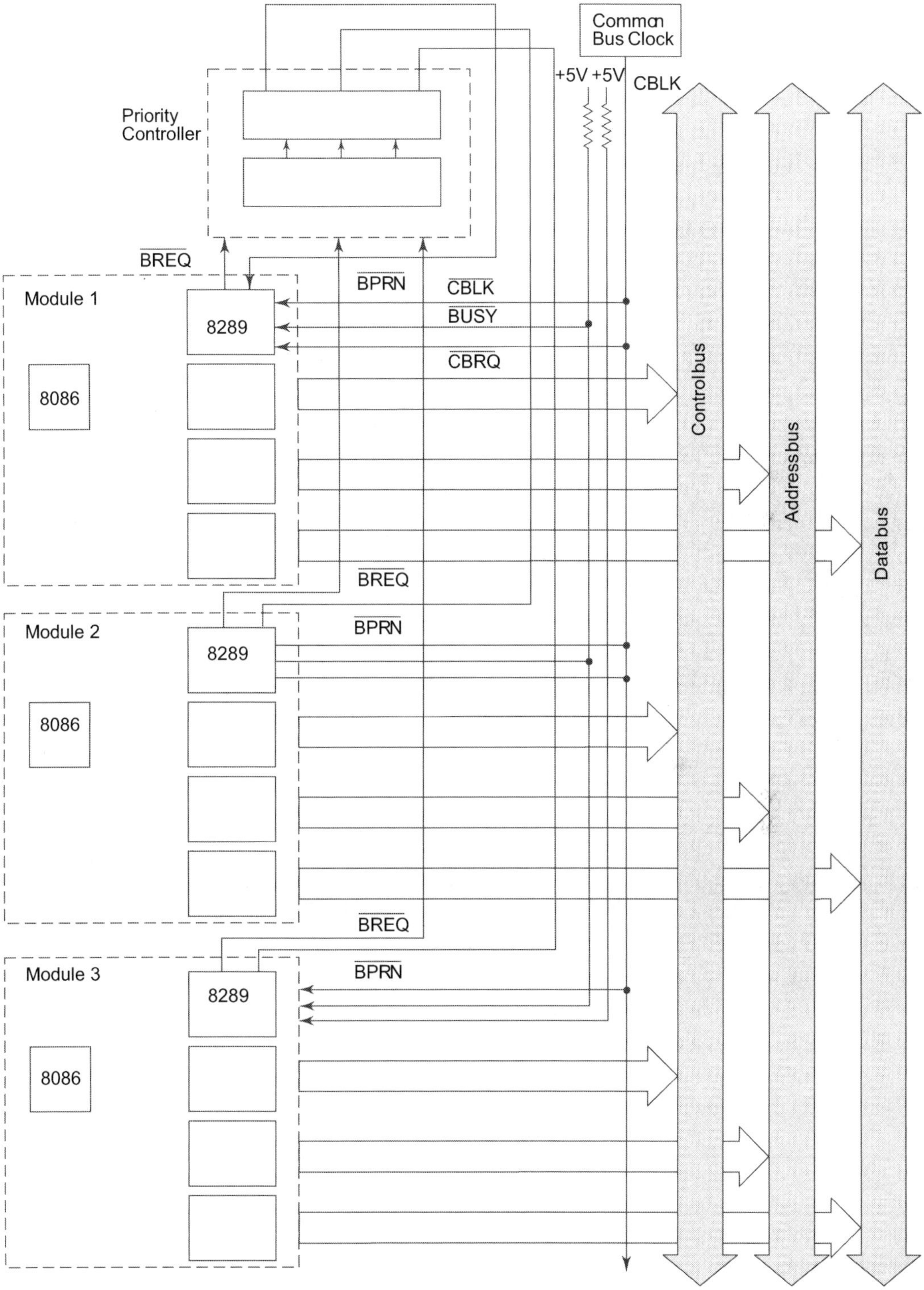

Fig. 8.27 *8086 Loosely Coupled Configuration*

a comparative time requirement of the multimicroprocessor system for execution of a typical job with respect to a uniprocessor based system and highlights a comparison between a multimicroprocessor system and a uniprocessor system.

8.7.2 Design of the Subprocessing Units

Design of the Address/Data Separating Circuit The system is built around a PC that has the main processor 8088 which acts as a root node or a master in our multimicroprocessor based system. The main processor and both the slave processors address a memory externally interfaced to PC. Both the slave processors have been chosen to be of the same type, because, from the sequence of input file names, it is not confirmed which input program goes to which slave processor. The 8088 CPUs are used in maximum mode so as to allow the occasional use of a numerical coprocessor 8087. The data and address buses of 8088 are multiplexed, so latches have been used for separating the address lines from the data lines. To derive the data lines from the multiplexed address/data bus, the transreceivers are required. The latches are enabled by the ALE signal and the data will be enabled by the DEN signal. The DEN signal, in combination with the DT/$\bar{R}$ signal, decides the direction of data flow. All these signals ALE, DEN and DT/$\bar{R}$ are derived by a separate 8288 bus controller chip. Since the 8088 is used in maximum mode, all the control signals are derived by 8288. In our system, the subprocessors will be able to run only .EXE files. Each subprocessor supports 64 Kbyte memory. There is thus another constraint on the system, i.e. the EXE files should not be more than 60 Kbytes in size. The remaining 4K is reserved for the result buffer of the subprocessor. The same 64 K memory supported by a slave is also interfaced with the CPU of the PC. For each of the slave processors, a separate by driven clock generator may be chosen. The clock

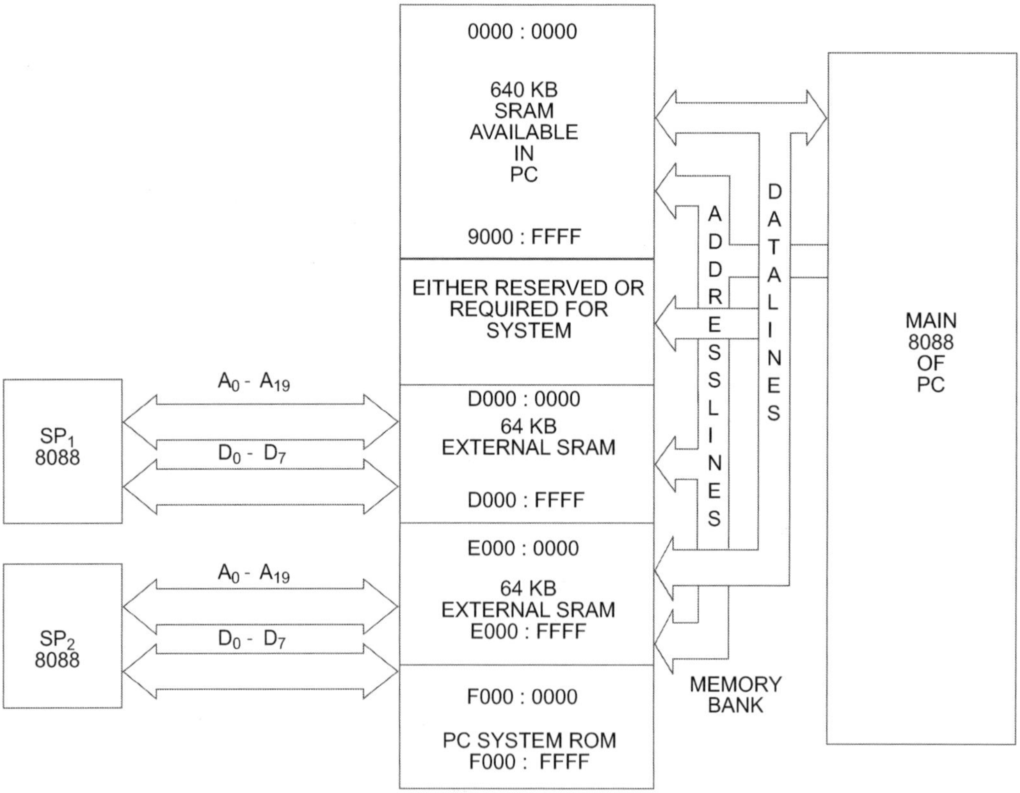

Fig. 8.28 *Complete Memory Map of the Developed System*

available at the IO channel of the PC may be used for driving the slave CPUs. Then there will be the constraint on the slave processors that the maximum speed of their operation can never be more than that of the main CPU. A separate clock generator will add some flexibility of operation and development without interfering with the operation of the main processor. The next part of the circuit is the interfacing logic. The 64 Kbyte local memory of a subprocessor is to be interfaced with it, such that the subprocessor and the main processor identify a particular location by the same physical address. This may be required to avoid any change, required in the EXE file for relocation, when the EXE file is loaded from the hard disk to the local 64 Kbyte memory module.

Design of the Bus Window According to the definition of bus window, it is a part of memory which can be addressed by more than one processor for communication. There are two slave processors, and thus there will be two bus windows, one for each. Both the windows are addressable by the master processor of PC which is the main processor, but each slave processor can address only one of them. Conceptually, the map of the complete system is as shown in Fig. 8.28.

The main processor has 640 Kbyte personal memory under the map 00000 to 9FFFF. The two slots, each of 64 K, starting from D0000H to DFFFFH and E0000H to EFFFFH are free, as specified in the technical reference of PC. These 64 K memory slots can be used as the bus windows as well as the local memories for the individual slave CPUs. To avoid relocation and the related calculations, it will be better to identify the memory locations in the bus window by the same physical addresses for both the processors. This suggests that the memory interfacing logic should be identical for both, i.e. the main and the subprocessors, so that they will be able to identify a particular location by a single physical address. Diagrammatically it can be represented as shown in Fig. 8.29.

Control Signals for Bus Windows After deciding the common decoding logic for a bus window, the next step is to derive the read and write signals for them. As a bus window is to be written or read by both the processors, the $\overline{\text{MEMR}}$ and $\overline{\text{MEMWR}}$ signals of both processors are to be connected to $\overline{\text{WR}}$ and $\overline{\text{RD}}$ pins of memory. An appropriate buffer should be used for isolating the read/write operations of the CPUs as shown in Fig. 8.30.

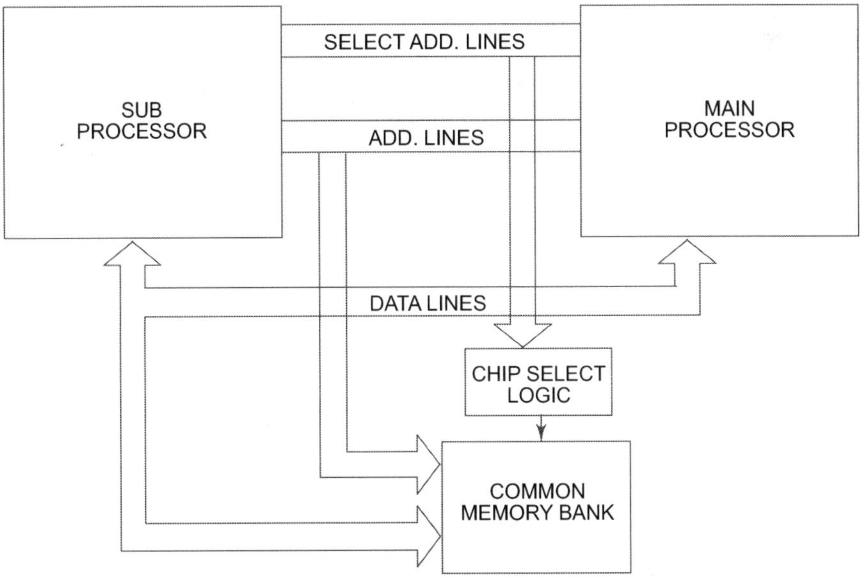

Fig. 8.29 *Common Chip Selection Logic*

Design of Isolation between the Processors When both the processors, i.e. a slave and a master, address a common memory, all of their data lines and some of their address lines may be required to be connected with each other. When both the CPUs desire to access the common memory concurrently, a conflict may arise because of bus contention amongst the CPUs. To resolve this conflict, additional hardware is needed which will prevent one processor from referring to the bus window when another processor is using it. When one processor is using the bus window, the other one should not be allowed to access the bus, i.e. the other processor should not place the address or data on the bus.

The operation described above suggests the use of solid state switches in the address and data lines as well as control lines, which can be controlled by the main processor using the control program. To drive these switches, external hardware like address decoders and 8255 I/O cards will be required. The address, data and control lines should be buffered. IC 74245 which is a tristate buffer that provides both the functions described above. Figure 8.31 shows the conceptual implementation of the isolation between the processors.

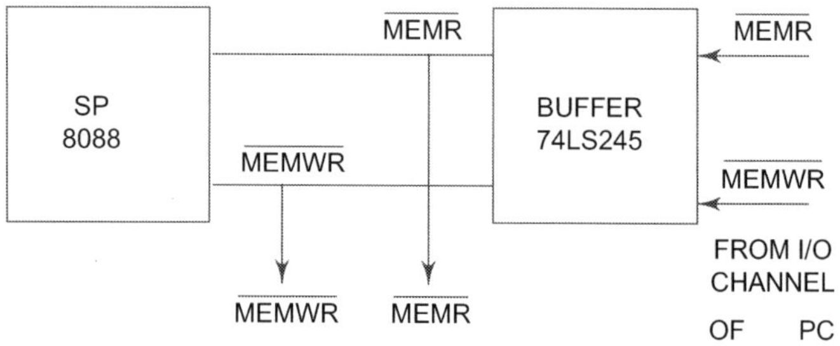

Fig. 8.30 *Deriving Control Signals for a Bus Window*

Isolation Controllers (Switch Controllers) An 8255 IO card has been used to control the tristate buffers that provide isolation. When a subprocessor wants to communicate with the bus window, it informs the main processor to disable the tristate buffers. The master CPU outputs a '1' bit on the particular pin of the port which is used to drive the chip enable lines of the 74245s which are used for the isolation. Then a reset pulse is generated on another pin of 8255 to reset the slave processor, using one more OUT instruction to start the execution. While changing the status of isolation, care should be taken that the change of isolation status for one processor should not interfere with the working of the other subprocessor. For implementing this, each change in the status should be saved and while making any further changes only the relevant bits related to a particular subprocessor should be modified.

Interrupt Mechanism As has been said earlier, the job is transferred to a bus window of a subprocessor for execution. Then a reset pulse is issued to the subprocessor using the OUT operation. The subprocessor starts execution and when it completes the execution, it shows the halt status on the status lines. From these status lines, a signal is derived which interrupts the main processor. The results of execution are next transferred to the master and the slave asks for the next task.

After entering the halt state, the status at $\overline{S}_2, \overline{S}_1, \overline{S}_0$ becomes 011. A signal which is low for all other status and high for the above status is to be generated. A simple 3-input logic will serve the purpose as shown in Fig. 8.32. For any other operation of the processor, the status will be different than that for halt. The output of the above given logic will be high for the above said halt status. Thus a transition from low to high logic level is achieved on the interrupt line of PC. The subprocessor will remain in the halt state, till the main processor allocates it a new task and resets it. After that, it will run the next allocated program and again enter the halt state after the execution is over. However, it is to be noted that, to write a HLT instruction at the end of the user's program to be run by a subprocessor is a must.

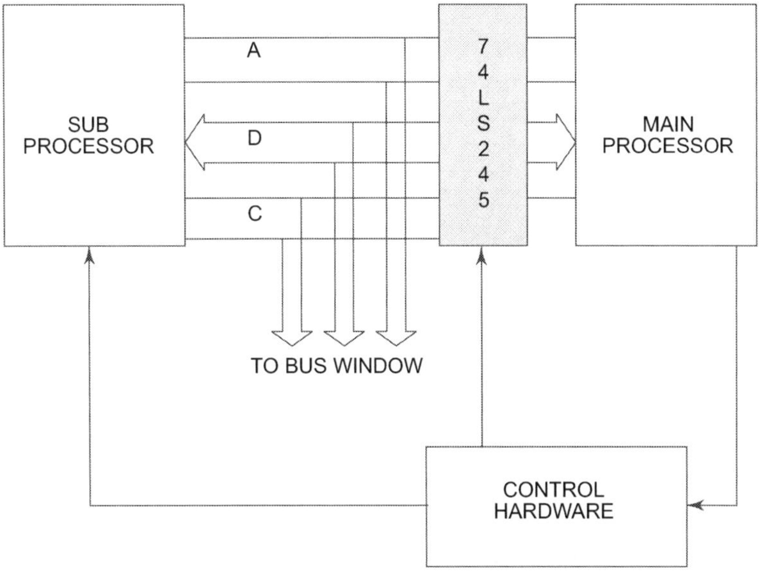

Fig. 8.31 *Isolation between Two Processors*

Deriving the Required Control Signals As discussed above, 74245 chips are selected for isolation. If the main processor wants to communicate with the bus window, all the 74245s should be enabled. The signal flow through the 74245 used for isolating the address bus is unidirectional and it only transmits the address information. The enabling or disabling of isolation chips is controlled by the isolation driver. Another control line is the $\overline{\text{RESETIN}}$ pin of each 8284A clock generator. When a LOGIC '0' is applied on this pin, it resets and the subprocessor remains in that state till a logic '1' is applied to it. When a processor is stuck to reset, it tristates its address, data and control bus. The design of the control signal used to drive the isolation chip to isolate the data bus is slightly different, since the data flow through them is bidirectional. The DT/$\overline{\text{R}}$ of PC is not available on the IO channel, hence it is to be derived from $\overline{\text{MEMR}}$ and $\overline{\text{MEMWR}}$ signals. That signal will drive the DIR pin of data bus isolation. For $\overline{\text{MEMR}}$ operation, the data flows from memory to the CPU, hence the isolation buffer should be in receiver mode and the data flows from the CPU to memory in case of the $\overline{\text{MEMWR}}$ operation, so the isolation buffer should be in the transmit mode. The circuit in Fig. 8.33 shows the circuit for the data bus isolation. If the DIR pin of the isolation chip is high, it enters the transmit mode; if it is 0, it enters into the receive mode. Enabling the data isolation buffer is not as straight forward as enabling the address isolation buffers. If the data buffers are enabled at the wrong moment then all the irrelevant, erratic or random data, present on the data bus of the subprocessing unit, will be placed over the data bus of the PC and causing a malfunction. So the data buffers should be enabled, only if any bus window chip is selected and the main processor sends the isolation control signal through the isolation drivers. The circuit in Fig. 8.34 shows the data isolation control signal.

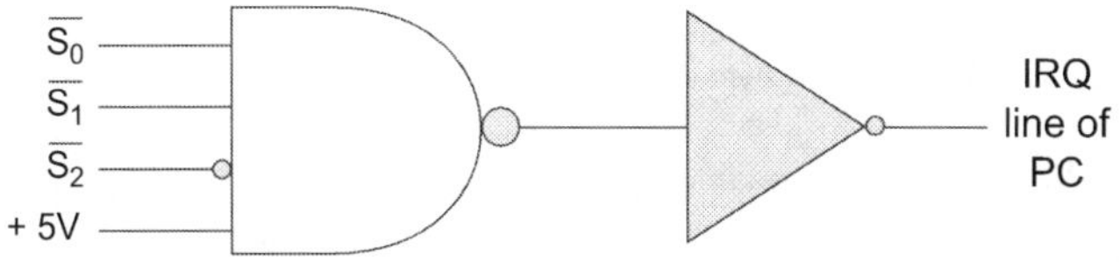

Fig. 8.32 *Deriving Hardware Interrupt Signal*

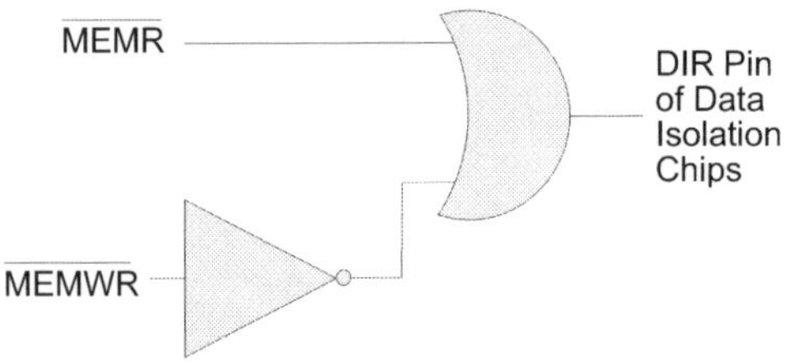

Fig. 8.33 *Deriving Data Direction*

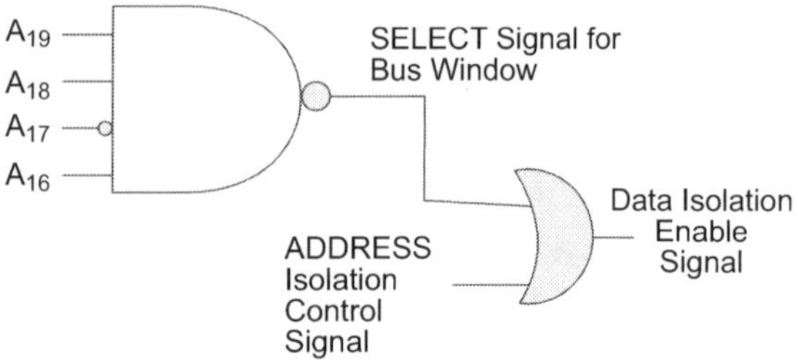

Fig. 8.34 *Data Isolation Control Signal*

8.7.3 System Software Design

System software of the complete system consists of three parts. The first part is the main control program that controls the total operation of the system, and the remaining two parts are the small local initialisation programs for each of the subprocessors.

MAIN Program Design While designing software for a multimicroprocessor system, it should be designed as modular as possible. Moreover, the software modules to be used only by a particular processor should be placed in its local memory. The total system is interrupt driven, hence the complete software may be divided into three parts as described:

1. MAIN program
2. Interrupt routine IRT2 for first subprocessing the unit
3. Interrupt routine IRT3 for second subprocessing unit

The MAIN program accepts the file name inputs at its prompt. It then looks for invalid file names. To discards and accepts the next filename in the sequence for execution by a slave processor. Once a subprocessor starts execution, the MAIN program makes the master processor wait for the completion of the execution. The two slave processors use two interrupt inputs of the master (available at IO channel of the PC) to inform it that the previously allotted task is over and the master may read the results and allot them the next tasks. Accordingly, the main program consists of two interrupt service routines for the two slaves. Each of these interrupt service routines will have to perform the following functions:

1. Store the results of the previous program run by the subprocessor
2. Select the next program from the EXE filename sequence
3. Load it to the bus window of that particular subprocessor
4. Issue run message to the subprocessor

For each of these functions from (1) to (4) a separate routine is written. All of the routines are to be linked together to form a complete program. Each program is checked independently for the passed input parameters. Then the list of the required inputs to each routine is prepared and it is checked whether a particular routine prepares the expected output parameters which are to be passed as inputs to the next module. This is checked till the complete program runs successfully. The last step is now to run the complete program and search for bugs if any and to remove them. The program is then optimized by making use of the alternative better instructions and studying their effect on the required execution time and memory. Also, the program was optimized reducing the number of independent subroutines. The flow charts of the main program and the interrupt service routines are presented in Figs 8.35 and 8.36.

Local Monitors These local monitor programs contain initialisation routines which initialise the internal registers of the slave processors suitably for the execution of the allotted task, in the local memory. These programs are available in the local memory and are not accessible to the master.

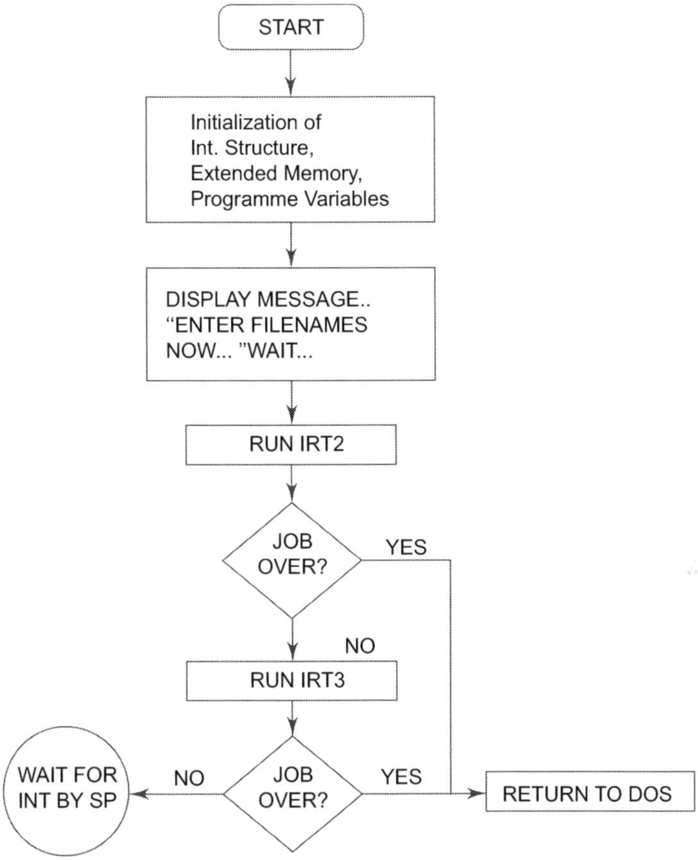

Fig. 8.35 *Main Program*

Initialization Routine Once a program is loaded in the bus window of a particular slave processor, the segment registers of that processor should be initialised according to the available local memory, after reset so that it will be able to run the allotted program. This routine just contains the initialisation of all the segment registers and stack pointer. The total relocation is taken care of at the time of the loading itself. After the initialisation of the processor, the execution starts from 0200H, which is fixed by the local monitor as the program entry point. Hence, the user's program must contain the ORG 200H statement at the start of the code segment. The local monitor initialization program is given below for subprocessor 1 (for the local memory address range D0000H to DFFFFH)

```
Mov AX, 0D000H
Mov DS, AX
Mov SS, AX
Mov ES, AX
Mov SP, 0F7FFH
JMP 0D000:0200H
```

For the other subprocessor, the same program is used but the segment address of the code and the data segment is 0E000H intead of 0D000H.

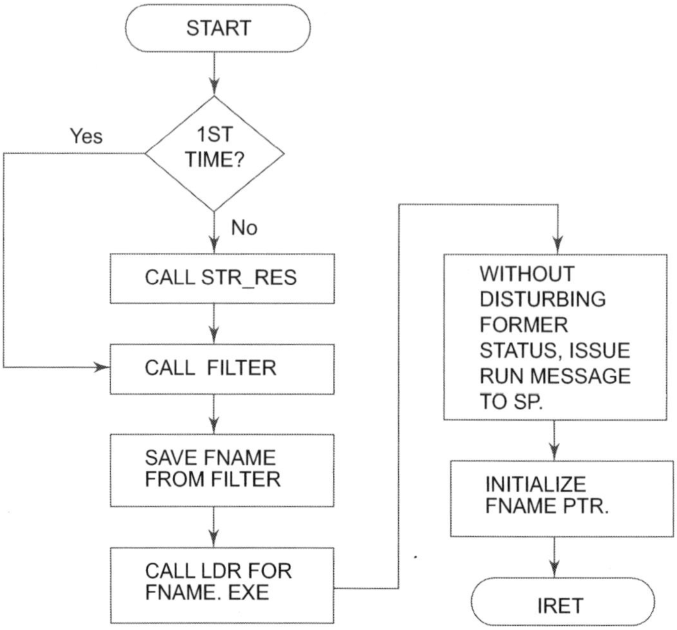

Fig. 8.36 *IRT Interrupt Service Routine*

8.7.4 DOS Functions Interface (Virtual) to the Multi-microprocessor System

In this section, a method of interfacing DOS functions with the subprocessors is proposed. Here we are proposing a communication protocol between the main processor and a subprocessor using the bus window. The interface will be totally virtual as far as the subprocessor is concerned. In other words, actually all the DOS functions are going to be executed by the main processor but on request from one of the subprocessors. The other point is that along with the available hardware, the written software may not be able to provide all the DOS features. However, some general facilities like secondary memory, display, printer, etc. may be referred to or used by the subprocessors at the behest of the main processor.

Design of Communication Protocols The communication protocols required for the communication between the main processor and the subprocessors are divided in two modules. The first is the subprocessor communication protocol and the second is the main processor communication protocol.

Design of Subprocessor Communication Protocols As already explained, the interface of the subprocessor with the DOS facilities is virtual. Any request by the subprocessor to use the DOS resources will be transferred to the main processor along with all the environment details. The main processor will accept the request of the subprocessor through the bus window. Before going to serve the request of the subprocessor, the main processor will save its complete status in its main memory and then gets the request details from the bus window to serve the subprocessor. When the main processor is serving the request of the subprocessor, the subprocessor will wait for the completion of the master's service by holding its contents unchanged, during the wait period. The hardware features like interrupt structure, TEST-facility can be used for implementing the concept described. It can also be represented as shown in Fig. 8.37.

Whenever the subprocessor needs to execute a DOS function call, it accepts the details about the function call from the subprocessor program under execution. The subprocessor saves the details, i.e. the contents of

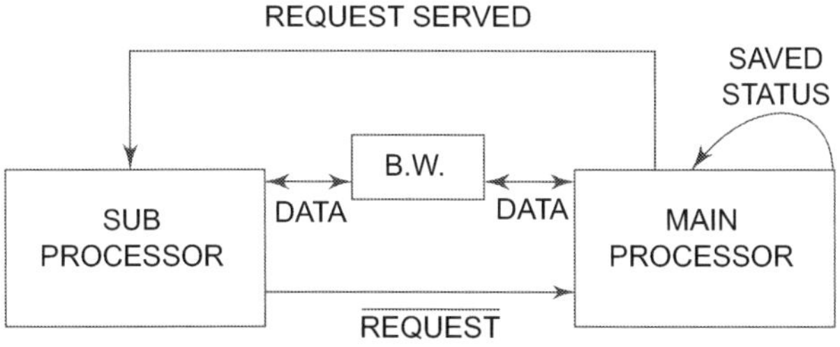

Fig. 8.37 *DOS Functions Interface with the Multiprocessor System*

all the registers in memory (bus window) and generates an interrupt request to the main processor. The main processor may be currently executing a task. After receiving the request from the subprocessor, the main processor saves all of its register contents in its local memory (640 K), and gets the request details from the bus window. The part of the communication protocol, that saves the contents of all the registers of a subprocessor in the memory (bus window) and generates an interrupt to the main processor, is the subprocessor communication protocol. The flow chart of the subprocessor communication protocol is shown in Fig. 8.38.

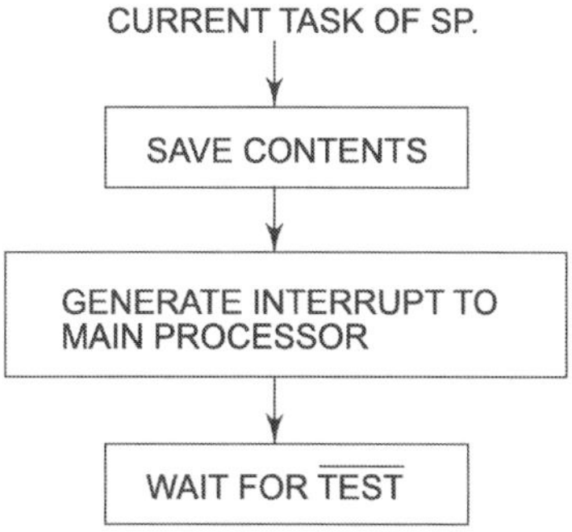

Fig. 8.38 *Subprocessor Communication Protocol*

Design of Main Processor Communication Protocol The design of the main processor communication protocol faces a critical problem, i.e. saving the status of all the registers right from CS, IP, general purpose registers to the pointers to its memory and also getting them back completely when the service is over. The 8086/8088 instruction set has the following limitations in this regard:

1. It cannot push/pop the CS or IP registers directly
2. It cannot load the code segment register directly
3. Pushing or popping the SP and SS will loose the original system SS and SP and hence the system stack data.

The above problems can be overcome by using the following alternatives.

(a) The CS, IP can be saved on to the stack using a dummy call or by using a dummy interrupt. The RET or IRET instructions retrieve the previously saved status of CS and IP.

(b) The stack area of both the processors can be considered simply as a data memory segment and the data transaction can be carried out with it using the data transfer instructions. The last-in first-out structure of the stack should be carefully handled to carry out the appropriate data transactions.

The flow chart of the protocol is shown in Fig. 8.39.

For saving the status of the main processor, the SP should be initialized newly for providing security to the user's stack data that may be useful in continuing the current task after completion of the request.

The $\overline{TEST}$ pin of the subprocessor should be set high to make the subprocessor wait till the request is served. The main processor should now enable the bus window memory (referred as BW in the Fig. 8.39) without affecting the status of the other subprocessor to get the details of the request. Depending on the contents of the registers which provide the details of the request, the main processor serves the specific request. The service may return result messages from DOS to the main processor, which are to be sent back to the subprocessor. For this purpose, the main processor carries out the save operation. It then disables the memory after storing the return messages to the bus window. The subprocessor will now be able to get the return message directly from the bus window and continue further execution. The overall circuit diagram is shown in Fig. 8.40.

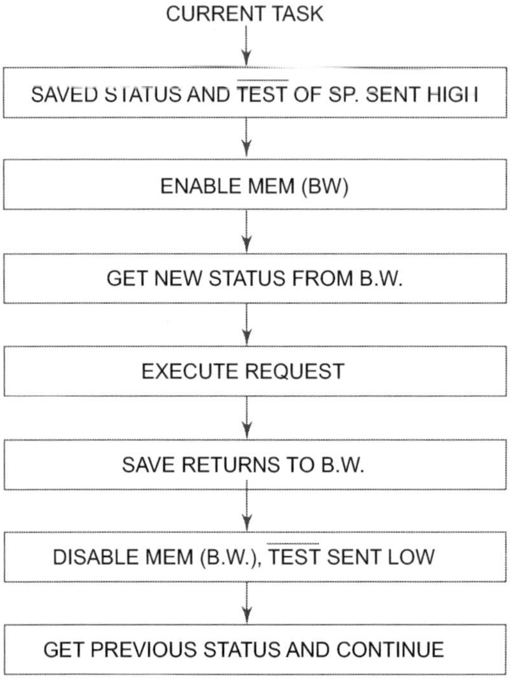

Fig. 8.39 *Main Processor Communication Protocol*

The interrupt to the main processor may be generated using an output port line. The $\overline{TEST}$ pin of the subprocessor may be driven suitably using an output port by the interrupt service routine. The circuit contains a memory chip 6132 used for storing the interrupt vector table of the subprocessor; a latch chip used as an output port and the combinational logic for selecting the output port.

8.7.5 Result and Conclusion

The main program has a provision to measure the time required for execution of the sequence of input programs on the multimicroprocessor system. The DOS function calls are used for the time measurement. The same sequence of the programs have been run using the AUTOEXEC.BAT file on the PC. The time required to execute the task on a single processor system is approximately 4.72 seconds while the same task takes 2.14 seconds on the multimicroprocessor system. This results in a speed up, which may be given as:

% improvement = (4.72-2.14) * 100 / 4.72 %
= 2.58 * 100 / 4.72 %
= 54.66 %

It should be noted that the user's program considered above, processed a large number of instructions as compared to the control program and the result storage program. The ratio of the user's program bytes to the overhead program bytes is nearly 10. As this ratio goes on increasing the improvement tends to 66%, but it will never be exactly 66%, because in any case one of the three processors will have to process the overhead programs. The developed cards may be used as independent processing channels for distributed processing and control.

The supporting programs have been developed to load the specified program to the RAM of each card and to issue the run message and store the results of the programs back to the drive. If a continuous loop program is loaded to the memory of the card and a run message is issued, the subprocessor starts the execution of the program and the main processor becomes free. The operation of the subprocessors can be interrupted by the main processor whenever required, by resetting it.

SUMMARY

This chapter has been devoted to the study of coprocessors and multimicroprocessor based systems. Starting with the need of multimicroprocessor systems, we have discussed different interconnection topologies and configurations. Further the software aspects of the multimicroprocessor systems are discussed briefly. A detailed account of the numeric coprocessor 8087 has been presented, starting from its architecture, pin diagram, instruction set, to the interfacing of 8087 with 8086 and programming examples. The architectural details of an I/O processor 8089 has been included to introduce the readers with the I/O processor concepts. Different bus arbitration and allotment schemes are then elaborated to highlight the bus sharing schemes used by the multimicroprocessor systems to avoid the resource contention problems. Multimicroprocessor systems based on their physical interconnections and the geographical placement of the processing nodes, viz. tightly coupled systems and loosely coupled systems have been briefly presented with circuit examples. The chapter concludes with a case study of 8088 based multimicroprocessor architecture designed by us.

EXERCISES

8.1 Write short notes on the following multiprocessor configurations:
   (i) Shared bus configuration (ii) Multiport memory configuration
   (iii) Linked I/O (iv) Bus window
   (v) Crossbar switching

8.2 Write short notes on the following interconnection topologies:
   (i) Star interconnection (ii) Loop interconnection
   (iii) Complete interconnection (iv) Regular Topology
   (v) Irregular Topology

8.3 Discuss the software design of multimicroprocessor systems.

8.4 Draw and discuss the architecture of 8087.

8.5 Discuss the functions of following signals of 8087.
   (i) BUSY (ii) $\overline{RQ}/\overline{GT_0}$ (iii) $\overline{RQ}/\overline{GT_1}$

(iv) QS_0 and QS_1 (v) INT

8.6 Discuss the register organisation of 8087.

8.7 Discuss bit definitions of TAG word and status word of 8087.

8.8 Discuss bit definitions of control word register of 8087.

8.9 What are the different types of instructions available in the instruction set of 8087?

8.10 Write a program to calculate the nth power of an 8-bit hexadecimal number, where n is less than eight, using 8087 instructions.

8.11 How does the CPU differentiate the 8087 instructions from its own instructions?

8.12 Draw and discuss the interface between 8086 and 8087.

8.13 Discuss the communication between 8086 and 8087.

8.14 Draw and discuss the architecture of 8089 I/O processor.

8.15 Discuss the communication between IOP 8089 and the CPU 8086.

8.16 What is the difference between a closely coupled and a loosely coupled system? What are the relative advantages and disadvantages?

8.17 Discuss the following bus arbitration strategies.

(i) Polling (ii) Daisy chain

(iii) Independent bus request scheme.

8.18 What are the different types of exceptions which may be generated by 8087?

8.19 What are the different data types supported by 8087?

9 80286-80287—A Microprocessor with Memory Management and Protection

INTRODUCTION

The microprocessor 8086 was the first 16-bit microprocessor designed by Intel. In due course of time, a number of peripheral chips and circuits were designed around the 8086. The processor 80186 was designed with more or less the same architecture with a few more instructions and additional on-chip circuits like clock generator, timers, DMA controller, and interrupt controller. 80186 was thus described as a microprocessor with integrated peripherals. Both the processors 8086 and 80186 were able to address 1Mbyte of memory. With the growing requirement of large memory for advanced applications, the need was felt to design microprocessors which could address large memory. However, the main problem with the conventional design was the limitation on the number of physical address lines. As the addressing capability of a microprocessor increases, the number of address lines also increase. At this point, the concepts of memory management, and specially virtual memory management techniques drew the attention of the designers. The 80286 is the first member of the family of advanced microprocessors with memory management and protection abilities. In this chapter, we will present the architecture along with some special features like, memory management and other functional details of 80286 and its math coprocessor 80287.

9.1 SALIENT FEATURES OF 80286

In this section, we present some of the important features of 80286. The concepts related to many of these features have been further explained in the rest of the chapter.

The 80286 CPU, with its 24-bit address bus is able to address 16 Mbyte of physical memory. Various versions of 80286 are available that run on 12.5 MHz, 10 MHz and 8 MHz clock frequencies. 80286 is upwardly compatible with 8086 in terms of instruction set.

We will now briefly explain the need of memory management and introduce the concepts of virtual memory. It may be noted here that the physical memory of 16 Mbyte, addressed by the 80286 CPU may not be large enough to store the operating system along with the set of application program required to be executed by the CPU. Moreover, the part of the main memory in which the operating system (and other systems program) is stored, is not accessible to the users. In view of this, an appropriate management of the memory system is required to ensure the smooth execution of the running processes and also to ensure their protection. The memory management which is an important task of the operating system is now supported by a hardware unit called memory management unit. Intel's 80286 is the first CPU to incorporate the *integrated memory management unit.*

Let us now consider that one or more application program have to be executed using an 80286 system. The program may be divided into a set of segments. At any instant, a segment portion of the actual program, required for execution at that instant, exists in the physical memory at the time of execution. These segments portions of the program which have been already executed or are not required for execution at that instant, are available in the secondary memory. Whenever the portion of a program is required for execution by the CPU, it is fetched from the secondary memory and placed in the physical memory. This is called *swapping in* of the program. A portion of the program or important partial results required for further execution, may be saved back on secondary storage to make the physical memory free for further execution of another required portion of the program. This is called *swapping out* of the executable program. Thus from a programmer's view point, there exists a large memory space which is not actually present in the system memory. Although the system may only have 16 Mbytes of physical memory, large application program, requiring much more than the physically available 16 Mbytes memory, may be executed using the available memory by dividing it into smaller segments. Thus to the user, there exists a very large logical memory space which is actually not available. As the name suggests, *virtual memory* thus does not exist physically in a system. It is, however, possible to map a large virtual memory space onto the real physical memory.

This complete process of virtual memory management is taken care of by the 80286 CPU and the supporting operating system. Recently, more advanced memory management techniques and concepts have been developed for advanced microprocessors.

Another important aspect of memory management is *data protection* or *unauthorised access prevention*. These concepts came with the concept of *segmented memory* that was able to isolate different types of information available in the physical memory of a system at an instant. For example, the data lies in data segment, executable code lies in code segment and stack information lies in the stack segment. In case the stack data overlaps the executable code or the code segment overlaps the stack data, the complete program execution will lead to random results. Thus separation of these data types into different logical segments is the first step towards data protection.

The 80286 works in two operating modes, viz. *real address mode* and protected *virtual address mode*. In real address mode, the 80286 just acts as a fast 8086. All the memory management and protection mechanisms are disabled in this mode. In the protected virtual address mode, the 80286 works with all of its memory management and protection capabilities with the advanced instruction set. In both the modes, 80286 is an upward object code compatible with 8086/8088.

9.2 INTERNAL ARCHITECTURE OF 80286

9.2.1 Register Organisation of 80286

The 80286 CPU contains almost the same set of registers, as in 8086, viz.

(a) Eight 16-bit general purpose registers
(b) Four 16-bit segment registers
(c) Status and control register
(d) Instruction pointer.

The register set of 80286 is shown in Fig. 9.1.

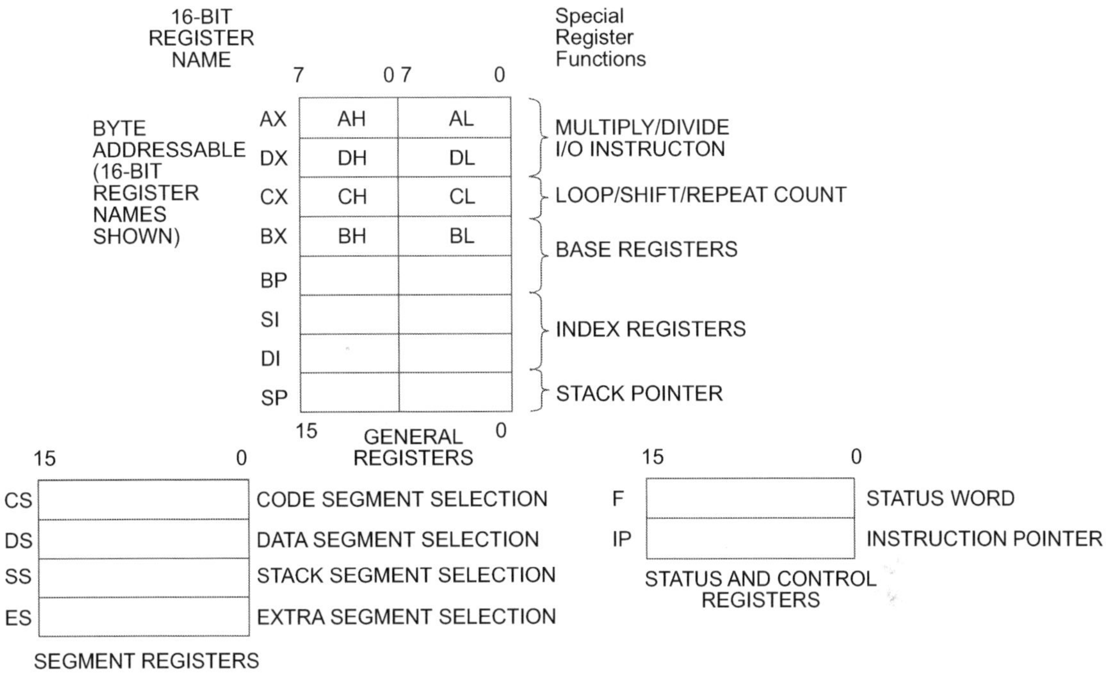

Fig. 9.1 *Register Set of 80286 (Intel Corp.)*

The flag register reflects the results of logical and arithmetic instructions. The flag register bits D_0, D_2, D_4, D_6, D_7 and D_{11} are modified according to the result of the execution of logical and arithmetic instructions. These are called as status flag bits. The bits D_8 and D_9 namely, Trap Flag (TF) and Interrupt Flag (IF) bits, are used for controlling machine operation and thus they are called control flags. All the above discussed flags are also available in 8086. Figure 9.2 shows the flag register of 80286 with the bit definitions, and the additional field definitions.

The additional fields available in 80286 flag register are, IOPL-I/O *Privilege Field* (bits D_{12} and D_{13}), NT-*Nested Task flag* (bit D_{14}), PE-*Protection Enable* (bit D_{16}), MP-*Monitor Processor Extension* (bit D_{17}), *Processor Extension Emulator* (bit D_{18}) and TS-*Task Switch* (bit D_{19}). All these fields are described briefly in Table 9.1.

Table 9.1 *Description of MSW*

FLAG	*Description*
PE	Protection enable flag places the 80286 in protected mode, if set. This can only be cleared by reseting the CPU.
MP	If set, Monitor Processor extension flag allows WAIT instruction to generate a processor extension not present exception, i.e. exception number 7.
EM	Emulate Processor extension flag, if set, causes a processor extension absent exception and permits the emulation of processor extension by CPU.
TS	If set, this flag indicates the next instruction using extension will generate exception 7, permitting the CPU to test whether the current processor extension is for the current task.

Machine Status Word (MSW) The machine status word consists of four flags. These are—PE, MP, EM and TS of the four lower order bits D_{19} to D_{16} of the upper word of the flag register. The LMSW and SMSW instructions are available in the instruction set of 80286 to write and read the MSW in real address mode.

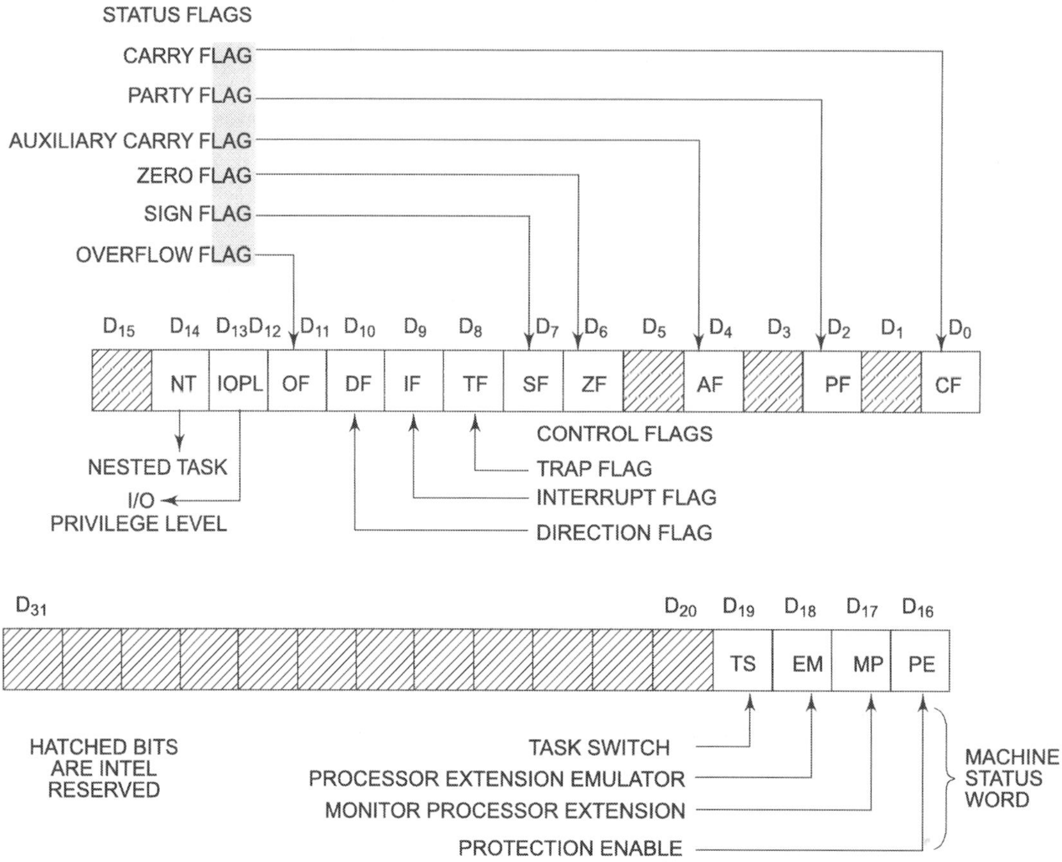

Fig. 9.2 *80286 Flag Register (Intel Corp.)*

9.2.2 Internal Block Diagram of 80286

The internal block diagram showing the overall architecture of 80286 is presented in Fig. 9.3. The CPU may be viewed to contain four functional parts, viz.

(i) Address Unit (AU)
(ii) Bus Unit (BU)
(iii) Instruction Unit (IU)
(iv) Execution Unit (EU).

The address unit is responsible for calculating the physical addresses of instructions and data that the CPU wants to access. Also the address lines derived by this unit may be used to address different peripherals.

This physical address computed by the address unit is handed over to the Bus Unit (BU) of the CPU. The address latches and drivers in the bus unit transmit the physical address thus formed over the address bus A_0-A_{23}. One major function of the bus unit is to fetch instruction bytes from the memory. In fact, the instructions are fetched in advance and stored in a queue to enable faster execution of the instructions. This concept is known as *instruction pipelining.* Thus for fetching the next instruction, the CPU need not wait till the completion of execution of the previous instruction. Rather, when one instruction is getting executed, the subsequent instruction is being prefetched, decoded and kept ready for execution. The prefetcher module in the bus unit performs this task of prefetching. The bus unit also contains a bus control module that controls the prefetcher module. These fetched instructions are arranged in a 6 byte prefetch queue. Thus usually the

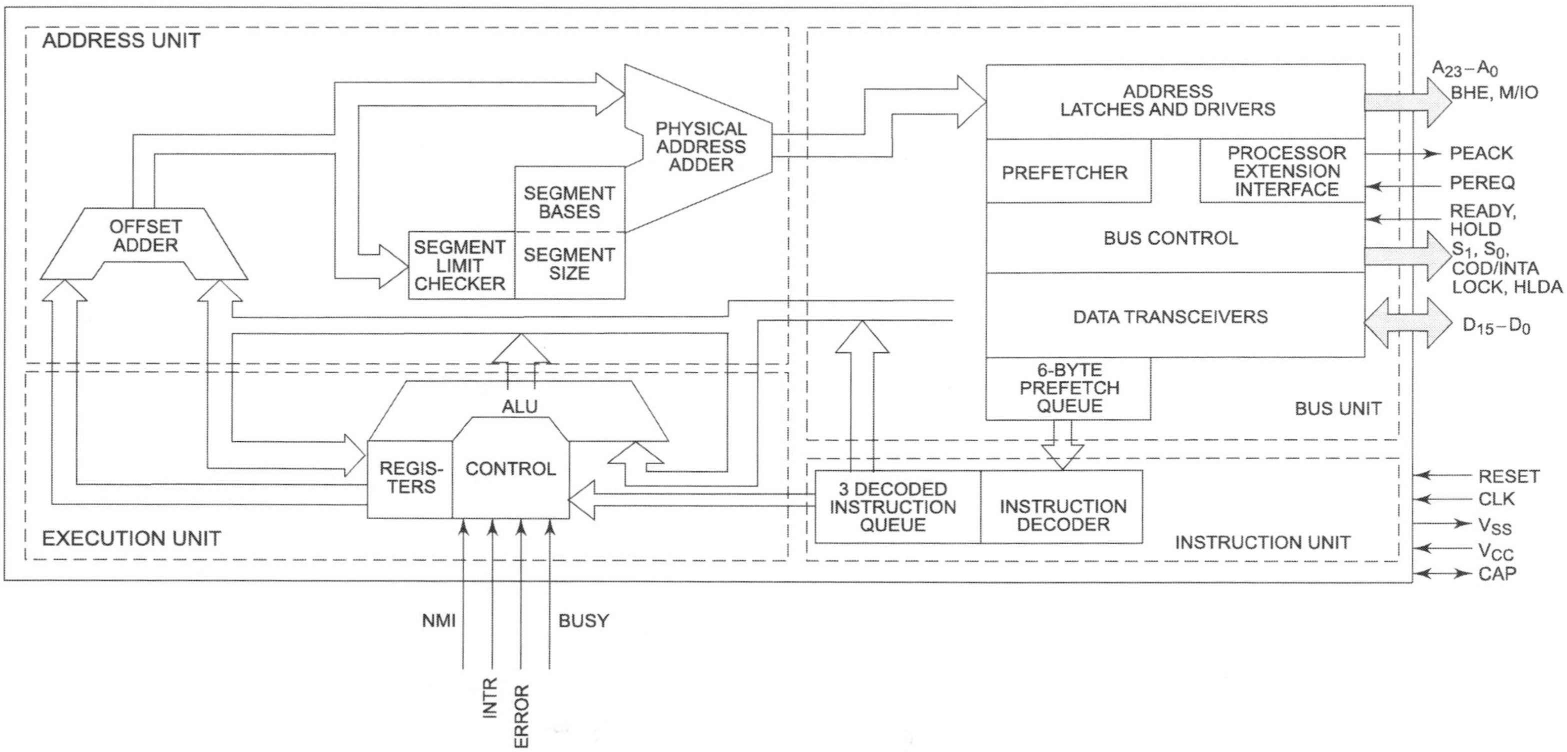

Fig. 9.3 *Internal Block Diagram of 80286 (Intel Corp.)*

CPU prefetches the instructions, to enhance the speed of execution. However, one interesting situation very often arises, when there are branch instructions. In case of an unconditional branch, the CPU will have to flush out the prefetched instructions immediately following the branch instruction, since the control will be transferred to the branch destination address. In case of a conditional branch, depending upon the success of the condition, the prefetched instructions will be flushed out of the queue and further prefetching may be carried out, if required. Another major module in the bus unit is the processor extension interface module which takes care of communication between the CPU and a coprocessor.

The 6-byte prefetch queue forwards the instructions arranged in it to the *Instruction Unit* (IU). The instruction unit accepts instructions from the prefetch queue and an instruction decoder decodes them one by one. The decoded instructions are latched onto a decoded instruction queue. The *data transreceivers* interface and control the internal data bus with the system bus.

The output of the decoding circuit drives a control circuit in the *Execution Unit* (EU), which is responsible for executing the instructions received from the decoded instruction queue, which sends the data part of the instruction over the data bus. The EU contains the register bank, used for storing the data as scratch pad, or used as special purpose registers. The ALU, the heart of the EU, carries out all the arithmetic and logical operations and sends the results either over the data bus or back to the register bank.

9.2.3 Interrupts of 80286

The interrupts of 80286 may be divided into three categories, viz. (a) External or Hardware interrrupts, (b) INT instruction or software interrupts and (c) Interrupts generated internally by exceptions. While executing an instruction, the CPU may sometimes be confronted with a special situation because of which further execution is not permitted. For example, while trying to execute a divide by zero instruction, the CPU detects a major error and stops further execution. In this case, we say that an exception has been generated. In other words, an instruction exception is an unusual situation encountered during execution of an instruction that stops further execution. The return address from an exception, in most of the cases, points to the instruction that caused the exception.

As in the case of 8086, the interrupt vector table of 80286 requires 1 Kbytes of space for storing 256, four-byte pointers to point to the corresponding 256 interrupt service routines (ISR). Each pointer contains a 16-bit offset followed by a 16-bit segment selector to point to a particular ISR. The calculation of vector pointer address in the interrupt vector table from the (8-bit) INT type is exactly similar to 8086. Like 8086, the 80286 supports the software interrupts of type 0 (INT 00) to type FFH (INT FFH). However, out of these types, some of the interrupt types are reserved for specific functions by Intel. Table 9.2 shows the interrupt vector assignments of 80286.

Table 9.2 *Interrupt Vector Assignments (Intel Corp.)*

Function	*Interrupt Number*	*Related Instruction*	*Does Return Address Point to Instruction Causing Exception?*
Divide error exception	0	DIV, IDIV	Yes
Single step interrupt	1	All	
NMI interrupt	2	INT 2 or NMI pin	
Breakpoint interrupt	3	INT 3	
INTO detected overflow exception	4	INT 0	No
BOUND range exceeded exception	5	BOUND	Yes
Invalid opcode exception	6	Any undefined opcode	Yes

(*Contd.*)

Table 9.2 *(Contd.)*

Function	*Interrupt Number*	*Related Instruction*	*Does Return Address Point to Instruction Causing Exception?*
Processor extension not available exception	7	ESC or WAIT	Yes
Intel reserved, do not use	8-15		
Processor extension error interrupt	16	ESC or WAIT	
Intel reserved, do not use	17-31		
User defined	32-255		

Maskable Interrupt INTR This is a maskable interrupt input pin of which the INT type is to be provided by an external circuit like an interrupt controller. The other functional details of this interrupt pin are exactly similar to the INTR input of 8086.

Non-maskable Interrupt NMI has higher priority than the INTR interrupt. Whenever this interrupt is received, a vector value of 02 is supplied internally to calculate the pointer to the interrupt vector table. Once the CPU responds to a NMI request, it does not serve any other interrupt request (including NMI). Further it does not serve the processor extension (coprocessor) segment overrun interrupt, till it either executes IRET or is reset. To start with, this clears the IF flag which is set again with the execution of IRET, i.e. return from interrupt.

Single Step Interrupt As in 8086, this is an internal interrupt that comes into action, if the trap flag (TF) of 80286 is set. The CPU stops the execution after each instruction cycle so that the register contents (including flag register), the program status word and memory, etc. may be examined at the end of each instruction execution. This interrupt is useful for troubleshooting the software. An interrupt vector type 01 is reserved for this interrupt.

Interrupt Priorities If more than one interrupt signals occur simultaneously, they are processed according to their priorities as shown in Table 9.3.

Table 9.3 *Interrupt Processing Priority (Intel Corp.)*

Order	*Interrupt*
1	Instruction exception
2	Single step
3	NMI
4	Processor extension segment overrun
5	INTR
6	INT instruction

9.3 SIGNAL DESCRIPTIONS OF 80286

The 80286 is available in 68-pin PLCC (Plastic Leaded Chip Carrier), 68-pin LCC (Lead Less Chip Carrier) and 68-pin PGA(Pin Grid Array) packages. There is no difference in pin allotments of PLCC and LCC packages only except in PLCC, conducting leads are provided for external connections while in LCC only conducting pads are provided in place of each pin. The pin diagram of 80286 are shown in Fig. 9.4(a) and (b) for PLCC/LCC and PGA packages. The signal descriptions of 80286 are briefly discussed below.

CLK This is the system clock input pin. The clock frequency applied at this pin is divided by two internally and is used for deriving fundamental timings for basic operations of the circuit. The clock is generated using 82284 clock generator.

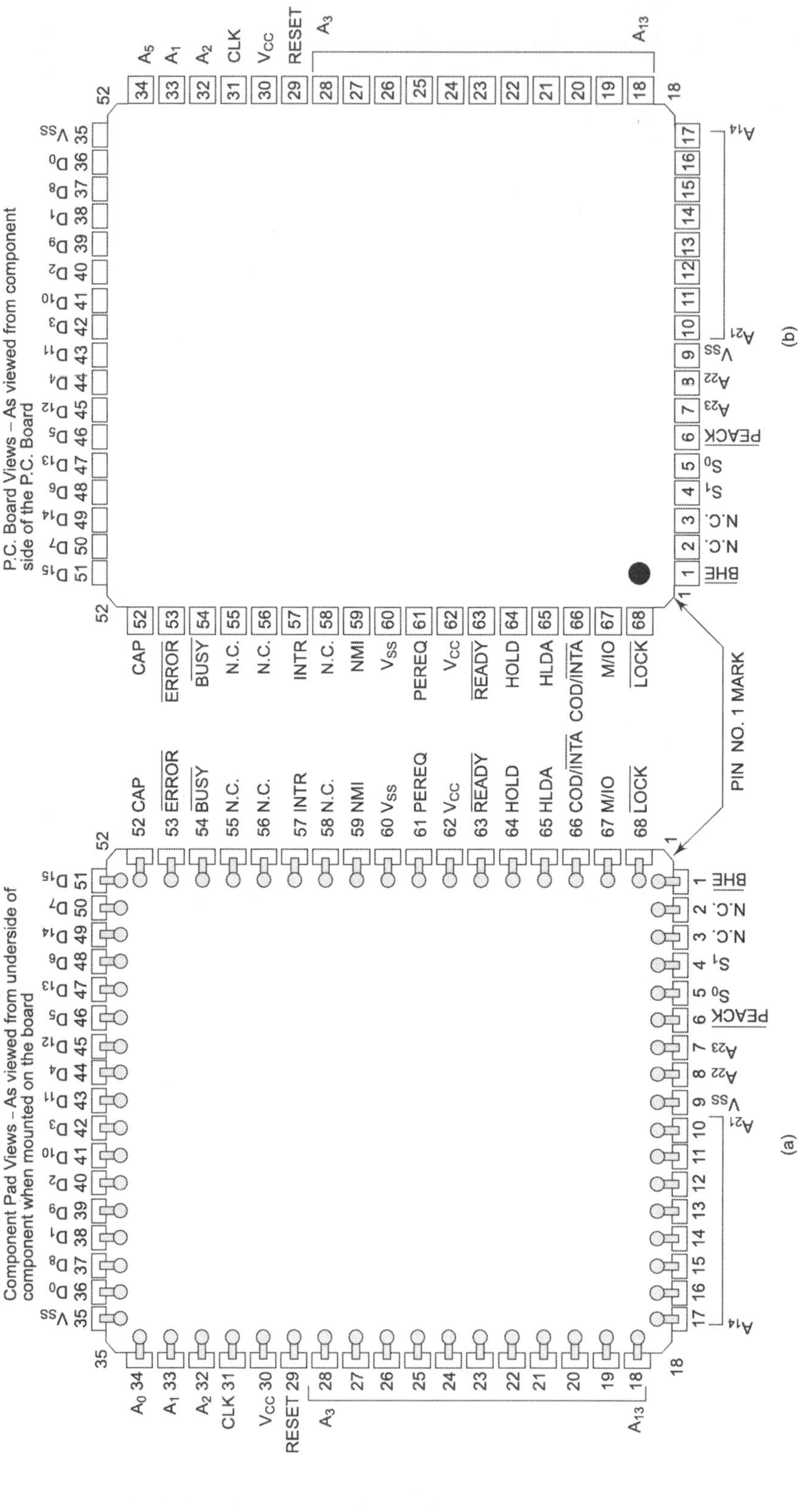

Fig. 9.4 *Pin Configuration of 80286 (Intel Corp.)*

D15-D0 These are sixteen bidirectional data bus lines.

A_{23}-A_0 These are the physical address output lines used to address memory or I/O devices. The address lines $A_{23} - A_{16}$ are zero during I/O transfers.

$\overline{BHE}$ This output signal, as in 8086, indicates that there is a transfer on the higher byte of the data bus ($D_{15} - D_8$).

$\overline{S_1}$, $\overline{S_0}$ These are the active-low status output signals which indicate initiation of a bus cycle and with M/$\overline{IO}$ and COD/$\overline{INTA}$, they define the type of the bus cycle as shown in Table 9.4.

M/$\overline{IO}$ This output line differentiates memory operations from I/O operations. If this signal is "0", it indicates that an I/O cycle or INTA cycle is in process and if it is "1" , it indicates that a memory or a HALT cycle is in progress.

COD/$\overline{INTA}$ This output signal, in combination with M/$\overline{IO}$ signal and $\overline{S_1} - \overline{S_0}$ distinguishes different memory, I/O and INTA cycles.

Table 9.4 *80C286 Cycle Status Definition (Intel Corp.)*

80C286 Bus Cycle Status Definition				
COD/$\overline{INTA}$	*M/$\overline{IO}$*	*$\overline{S_1}$*	*$\overline{S_0}$*	*Bus Cycle*
0 (LOW)	0	0	0	Interrupt acknowledge
0	0	0	1	Will not occur
0	0	1	0	Will not occur
0	0	1	1	None; not a status cycle
0	1	0	0	IF $A_1 = 1$ then halt; else shutdown
0	1	0	1	Memory data read
0	1	1	0	Memory data write
0	1	1	1	None; not a status cycle
1 (HIGH)	0	0	0	Will not occur
1	0	0	1	I/O read
1	0	1	0	I/O write
1	0	1	1	None; not a status cycle
1	1	0	0	Will not occur
1	1	0	1	Memory instruction read
1	1	1	0	Will not occur
1	1	1	1	None; not a status cycle

$\overline{LOCK}$ This active-low output pin is used to prevent the other masters from gaining the control of the bus for the current and the following bus cycles. This pin is activated by a "LOCK" instruction prefix, or automatically by hardware during XCHG, interrupt acknowledge or descriptor table access.

$\overline{READY}$ This active-low input pin is used to insert wait states in a bus cycle, for interfacing low speed peripherals. This signal is neglected during HLDA cycle.

HOLD and HLDA This pair of pins is used by external bus masters to request for the control of the system bus (HOLD) and to check whether the main processor has granted the control (HLDA) or not, in the same way as it was in 8086.
INTR Through this active high input, an external device requests 80286 to suspend the current instruction execution and serve the interrupt request. Its function is like that of INTR pin of 8086.
NMI The Non-Maskable Interrupt request is an active-high, edge-triggered input that is equivalent to an INTR signal of type 2. No acknowledge cycles are needed to be carried out.

PEREQ and $\overline{\text{PEACK}}$ (Processor Extension Request and Acknowledgement) As has been mentioned earlier, processor extension refers to coprocessor (80287 in case of 80286 CPU). This pair of pins extend the memory management and protection capabilities of 80286 to the processor extension 80287. The PEREQ input requests the 80286 to perform a data operand transfer for a processor extension. The $\overline{\text{PEACK}}$ active-low output indicates to the processor extension that the requested operand is being transferred.

$\overline{\text{BUSY}}$ and $\overline{\text{ERROR}}$ Processor extension BUSY and ERROR active-low input signals indicate the operating conditions of a processor extension to 80286. The $\overline{\text{BUSY}}$ goes low, indicating 80286 to suspend the execution and wait until the $\overline{\text{BUSY}}$ becomes inactive. In this duration, the processor extension is busy with its allotted job. Once the job is completed the processor extension drives the $\overline{\text{BUSY}}$ input high indicating 80286 to continue with the program execution. An active $\overline{\text{ERROR}}$ signal causes the 80286 to perform the processor extension interrupt while executing the WAIT and ESC instructions. The active $\overline{\text{ERROR}}$ signal indicates to 80286 that the processor extension has committed a mistake and hence it is reactivating the processor extension interrupt.
CAP A 0.047 µf, 12V capacitor must be connected between this input pin and ground to filter the output of the internal substrate bias generator. For correct operation of 80286 the capacitor must be charged to its operating voltage. Till this capacitor charges to its full capacity, the 80286 may be kept stuck to reset to avoid any spurious activity.
V_{ss} This pin is a system ground pin of 80286.
V_{cc} This pin is used to apply +5V power supply voltage to the internal circuit of 80286.
RESET The active-high RESET input clears the internal logic of 80286, and reinitializes it. The active-high reset input pulse width should be at least 16 clock cycles. The 80286 requires at least 38 clock cycles after the trailing edge of the RESET input signal, before it makes the first opcode fetch cycle.

9.4 REAL ADDRESSING MODE

As we have mentioned earlier, the 80286 CPU operates in two modes: (a) Real address mode and (b) Protected virtual address mode.

In the real addressing mode of operation of 80286, it just acts as a fast 8086. The instruction set is upwardly compatible with that of 8086. The 80286 addresses only 1 Mbytes of physical memory using A_0–A_{19}. The lines A_{20}–A_{23} are not used by the internal circuit of 80286 in this mode. The registers and addressing modes will be discussed later in this chapter.

In real address mode, while addressing the physical memory, the 80286 uses $\overline{\text{BHE}}$ along with A_0–A_{19}. The 20-bit physical address is again formed in the same way as that in 8086. The contents of segment registers are used as segment base addresses. The other registers, depending upon the addressing mode, contain the offset addresses. The address formation in real address mode is shown in Fig. 9.5. An interesting question may be raised at this point: In the real address mode, are the speeds of 8086 and 80286 identical? Because of extra pipelining and other circuit level improvements, in real address mode also, the 80286 operates at a much faster rate than 8086, although functionally they work in an identical fashion.

As in 8086, the physical memory is organised in terms of segments of 64 Kbyte maximum size. An exception is generated, if the segment size limit is exceeded by the instruction or the data. The overlapping of physical memory segments is allowed to minimize the memory requirements for a task.

The 80286 reserves two fixed areas of physical memory for system initialization and interrupt vector table. In the real mode the first 1 Kbyte of memory starting from address 00000H to 003FFH is reserved for interrupt vector table. Also the addresses from FFFF0H to FFFFFH are reserved for system initialization. The program execution starts from FFFF0H after reset and initialization. The interrupt vector table of 80286 is organised in the same way as that of 8086. Some of the interrupt types are reserved for exceptions, single-stepping and processor extension segment overrun, etc. When the 80286 is reset, it always starts its execution in real address mode, wherein it performs the following functions: it initialises the IP and other registers of 80286, initializes the peripheral, enables interrupts, sets up discreptor tables and then it prepares for entering the protected virtual address mode.

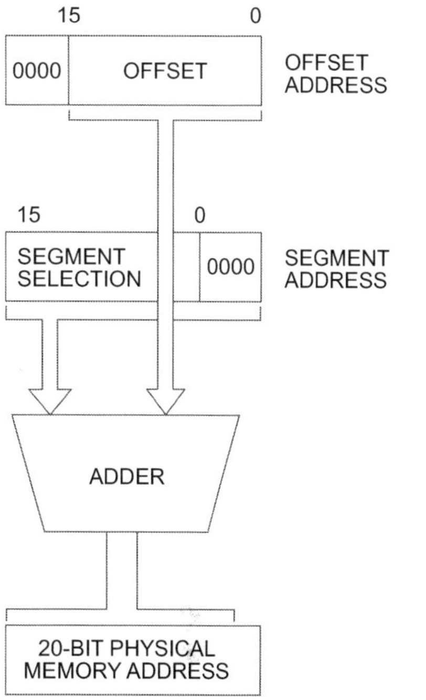

Fig. 9.5 *Real Address Mode Address Calculation (Intel Corp.)*

9.5 PROTECTED VIRTUAL ADDRESS MODE (PVAM)

9.5.1 Introduction

The 80286 is the first processor to support the concepts of virtual memory and memory management. Though the virtual memory does not exist physically it still appears to be available within the system. The concept of virtual memory is implemented using physical memory that the CPU can directly access and secondary memory that is used as a storage for data and program, which are stored in secondary memory initially. The segment of the program or data, required for actual execution at that instant, is fetched from the secondary memory into physical memory. After the execution of this fetched segment, the next segment required for further execution is again fetched from the secondary memory, while the results of the executed segment are stored back into the secondary memory for further references. This continues till the complete program is executed. During the execution, the partial results of the previously executed portions are again fetched into the physical memory, if required for further execution. The procedure of fetching the chosen program segments or data from the secondary storage into the physical memory is called *swapping*.

The procedure of storing back the partial results or data back on to the secondary storage is called *unswapping*. The virtual memory is alloted per task. The 80286 is able to address 1Gbyte (2^{30} bytes) of virtual memory per task. As discussed above, the complete virtual memory is mapped on to the 16Mbyte physical memory. In other words, if a program larger than 16Mbyte is stored on the hard disk and is to be executed, it is fetched in terms of data or program segments of less than 16Mbyte in size into the physical memory by swapping sequentially as per sequence of execution. The handling of branch instructions like, JUMP and CALL is taken care of by the swapping and unswapping mechanism and the operating system. Besides the memory management, the concepts of protection were introduced in 80286. All these topics are discussed in the following section.

In case of huge programs (in general greater than physical memory in size), they are divided in either smaller segments or pages which are arranged in appropriate sequence and are swaped in or out of primary memory as per the requirements, for execution of the complete program. These segments or pages have been associated with a data structure called as a descriptor. The descriptor contains information of the program segment or page. For example a school teacher may stack all the answer sheets solved by the students in a bundle and attached a small slip of paper with it containing information like name, subject, class, date and year of examination, his own name, number of students, present and absent, roll numbers of absent students etc. From this information return on the small slip of paper a third person can easily know the details of the particular bundle of papers. This information may further be used by anybody for preparing a detailed analysis of results of all subjects. The data structure *descriptor* is essentially one such identifier of a particular program segment or page. A set of such descriptors arranged in a proper sequence describes the complete program. This set of the decriptors may also be called the descriptor table. In case of multiprogramming environment many of such sets of decriptors may be available in the system at an instant of time. All this sets of descriptors (descriptors table) are prepared and managed by the operating system. Thus corresponding to different types of program segments there may be different type of descriptors. For example for data segment there may be a data segment descriptors for code segments there may be code segment descriptors. For system programs there are system segments descriptors, for subroutines and interrupt service routines there are gate descriptors etc.

9.5.2 Physical Address Calculation in PVAM

In PVAM, the 80286 uses the 16-bit content of a segment register as a selector to address a descriptor stored in physical memory. The descriptor is a block of contiguous memory locations containing information of a segment, like segment base address, segment limit, segment type, privilege level, segment availability in physical memory, descriptor type and segment use by another task. The base address, i.e. the starting location of a segment is an important descriptor information. The segment limit indicates the maximum size of a segment. Thus using the base address of a segment and the segment limit, one can determine the last location in the segment. Similarly, each segment has a type and its privilege level, which indicate the importance of the segment. The privilege level indicates the privilege measure of a segment. A segment with lower privilege level will not be allowed to access another segment having higher privilege, thus offering protection to the segment from the unauthorised accesses. Moreover, a certain segment may or may not be present in the physical memory at a given time instant. This information is also stored in a descriptor. Finally, an important information, i.e. whether the segment has been accessed by another task in the past, is also stored in the segment descriptor. This information helps in deciding, whether the segment should be unswapped from the physical memory or not. A segment which has not been accessed in the recent past may probably be unswapped from the main memory. The segment base address is a 24-bit pointer that addresses the first location in that segment. This 24-bit segment base address is added with 16-bit offset to calculate a 24-bit physical address. The maximum segment size will be of 64 Kbyte, since the offset is only of 16 bits. Figure 9.6 shows the calculation of physical address in PVAM. The descriptors are automatically referred to by the CPU when a segment register is loaded with a selector.

9.5.3 Descriptors and Their Types

In general, descriptors carry all the relevant information regarding a segment and its access rights. Besides this information, special types of descriptors which are used to carry out additional functions like *transfer of control* and *task switching*, may have additional information. The 80286 has *segment descriptors* for code, stack and data segments as basic descriptors. In addition to this, it has *system control descriptors* for special system data segments and control transfer operations. Figure 9.7 shows the structure of a code or data segment descriptor. Each descriptor is 8-bytes long. The information stored in the 8-bytes of a descriptor can be used

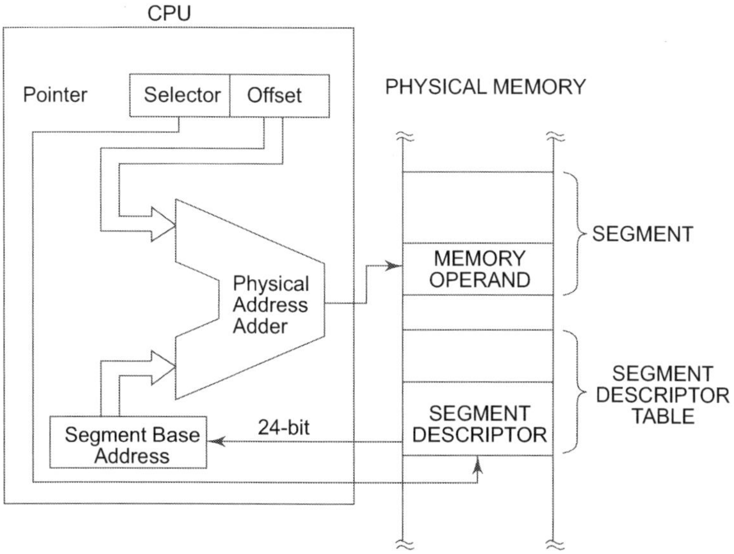

Fig. 9.6 *Physical Address Calculation in PVAM (Intel Corp.)*

by the operating system to support the implementation of memory management and protection schemes. The definition of access rights byte of code or data segment descriptor is given in Table 9.5.

For accessing any program segment or page its descriptor is first accessed and its access rights byte contents are verified with those of the requesting program. If the contents of accesses rights byte allow only then can the requesting program access the program segment corresponding to the descriptor. The base and limit fields of the descriptor contain information which is used for finding out physical address of the program segment corresponding to the descriptor at which the program segment is placed for the execution of the program. The Intel reserved bytes are reserved by Intel for future use and compatibility with future processors.

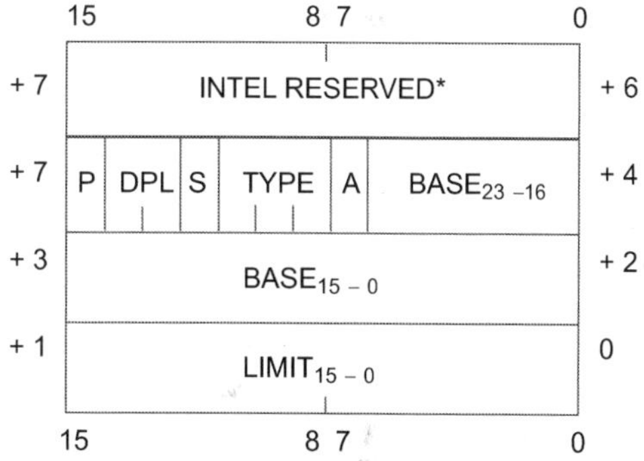

*Must be set to 0 for compatibility with 80386

Fig. 9.7 *Data or Code Segment Descriptor (Intel Corp.)*

Table 9.5 *Access Rights Byte Definition (Intel Corp.)*

Bit Position	*Name*		*Function*
7	Present (P)	P = 1	Segment is mapped into physical memory.
		P = 0	No mapping to physical memory exits, base and limit are not used.
6-5	Descriptor Privilege Level (DPL)		Segment privilege attribute used in privilege tests.
4	Segment Descriptor (S)	S = 1	Code or Data (includes stacks) segment descriptor
		S = 0	System Segment Descriptor or Gate Descriptor

(*Contd.*)

Table 9.5 *(Contd.)*

Bit Position	*Name*		*Function*	
3	Executable (E)	E = 0	Data segment descriptor type is:	If
2	Expansion Direction	ED = 0	Expand up segment, offsets must be < limit.	Data
	(ED)	ED = 1	Expand down segment, offsets must be > limit.	Segment
1	Writable (W)	W = 0	Data segment may not be written into.	(S = 1,
		W = 1	Data segment may be written into.	E = 0)
3	Executable (E)	E = 1	Code Segment Descriptor type is:	If
2	Conforming (C)	C = 1	Code segment may only be executed when CPL > DPL and CPL remains unchanged.	Code Segment
1	Readable (R)	R = 0	Code segment may not be read	(S = 1,
		R = 1	Code segment may be read.	E = 1)
0	Accessed (A)	A = 0	Segment has not been accessed.	
		A = 1	Segment selector has been loaded into segment register or used by selector test instructions.	

A code or data segment descriptor contains 16-bit segment limit, 24-bit segment base address, 8-bit access rights byte and the remaining 16-bits are reserved by Intel for upward compatibility. Any segment access, violating the specified access rights in the descriptor, prevents memory cycle and generates an exception interrupt. *Code segment descriptors* are used to refer code segments and *data segment descriptors* are used to refer data segments. The descriptor is either a code segment descriptor or a data segment descriptor if the S bit in the access rights byte is '1'. The system segment descriptors are selected by clearing the S bit, i.e. S = 0. The code segments are distinguished from data segments by the E bit. Thus E = 1 indicates code segment while E = 0 indicates data segment. The present (P) bit indicates use of DPL field in such descriptors. The limit field determines the size of the code/data segment.

Thus descriptor is a tag of a segment. The actual memory address at which the segment or page will be loaded and executed is not fixed. It is decided by the operating system at the time of loading into primary memory from the secondary for execution. This is done to facilitate the relocation of segments and pages. This starting address is decided based on the available memory addresses in the primary memory using a memory allocation table which maintains a record of the allocated memory and available memory out of the total primary memory. Once a starting address is allocated to a segment, it is considered the base address. In 80286, the base address is of 24 bits i.e. the same as size of the address bus and thus it can address 16 MB of physical memory. With the given base address, the last address of the segment is decided by the limit field. The limit field i.e. the maximum allowed offset address is of 16 bits. Thus a segment in 80286 can be of 64KB size at the maximum. The limit field thus puts an upper limit on the offset address value and the segment size. If the limit is exceeded, an internal exception interrupt is generated. However every segment may not be of 64KB. Thus the limit field, unlike 8086 where the segment size was fixed with non overlapped segmentation, offers the flexibility of defining variable size segments within the limit without overlapping them. In other words, the base address and the offset address that may be available in one of the pointer registers, jointly point to the physical memory address. All the available descriptors are maintained in a descriptor table which is maintained in a fast cache memory. As soon as a descriptor is loaded into descriptor registers, the corresponding descriptor is automatically loaded into primary memory at a location decided by the operating system and the base address is loaded into the base field of the descriptor. Thus in 80286, there can be total 8K global and 8K local descriptors due to the 13 bit selector address size and 1 bit for descriptor type to select a global and a local descriptor. Thus there can be total 16 K descriptors for the segments to address a virtual memory of 16K × 64K = 1GB size. This virtual memory size is for each task. The operating system can allot different virtual addresses for each task. Thus in the protected virtual address mode 80286 can address a huge memory.

The total memory it can address depends upon the number of tasks it can handle simultaneously. For accessing each segment or page the descriptor is first selected out of the descriptor table and then the corresponding segment is loaded into the primary memory for execution. If the segment is already available in the memory as indicated by the P bit, it need not be loaded again. After the segment is executed or accessed, it is marked with A bit high for future actions. The other descriptor bits are already explained in table 9.5 in significant details.

System Segment Descriptors In addition to code and data segment descriptors, the other types of descriptors with S = 0 are used by 80286 to store system data and execution state of a task (for multitasking systems). These are called as system segment descriptors. The system segment descriptors are of seven types. The types 1 to 3 are called *system descriptors* and the types 4 to 7 are called *gate descriptors* as they are used to control the access of entry points within the code to be executed.

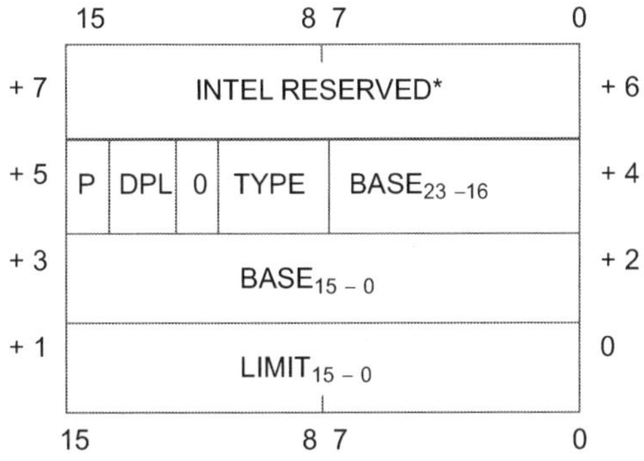

*Must be set to 0 for compatibility with 80386

Name	Value	Description
TYPE	1 2 3	Available Task State Segment (TSS) Local Descriptor Table Busy Task State Segment (TSS)
P	0 1	Descriptor Contents are not Valid Descriptor Contents are Valid
DPL	0-3	Descriptor Privilege Level
BASE	24-bit number	Base Address of special system data segment in real memory
LIMIT	24-bit number	Offset of last byte in segment

Fig. 9.8 (a) *System Segment Descriptor (b) System Segment Descriptor bit Definitions (Intel Corp.)*

Type 1-3 System Segment Descriptors Figures 9.8 (a) and (b) show the *type 1-3 system segment descriptor* format and the corresponding bit definitions respectively.

This descriptor contains 16-bit segment limit, 24-bit segment base address, and an access rights byte that contains P-bit, a 2-bit DPL field, S-bit (0) and a 4-bit type field.The fourth word of the descriptor is reserved by Intel for compatibility with future processors.

Type 4-7 Gate Descriptors The gate descriptors control the access to entry points of the code to be executed. There are four types of gate descriptors, viz. *call gate, task gate*, *interrupt gate* and *trap gate*. The gate descriptors contain information regarding the destination of control transfer, required stack manipulations, whether it is present in memory or not, privilege level and its type. Gate descriptors provide a mechanism to keep track of source and destination of control transfer. Hence, the CPU can perform protection checks and control the entry points of destination codes.

Call gates are used to alter the privilege levels. Task gates are used to switch from one task to another. Interrupt and trap gates are used to specify corresponding service routines. Figures 9.9 (a) and (b) show the gate descriptor format and the corresponding bit definitions respectively. If a destination selector does not refer to a correct descriptor type, exception 13 is generated. The task gate does not use the destination offset field. The task gate may only refer to a task state segment. The word count field is only used by a call gate descriptor to indicate the number of bytes to be transferred from the stack of the calling routine to the stack of the called routine, when a control transfer changes the privilege levels. The access rights byte format and its bit definitions are the same as code or data segment descriptor.

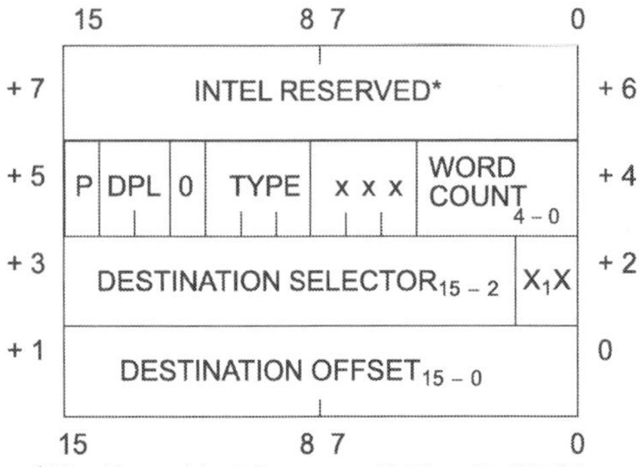

*Must be set to 0 for compatibility with 80386
(X is don't care)

Name	Value	Description
TYPE	4	- Call Gate
	5	- Task Gate
	6	- Interrupt Gate
	7	- Trap Gate
P	0	Descriptor Contents are not Valid
	1	Descriptor Contents are Valid
DPL	0-3	Descriptor Privilege Level
WORD COUNT	0-31	Number of words to copy from callers stack to called procedures stack. Only used with call gate.
DESTINATION SELECTOR	16-bit selector	Selector to the target code segment (Call, Interrupt of Trap Gate) Selector to the target task state segment (Task Gate)
DESTINATION OFFSET	16-bit offset	Entry point within the target code segment

Fig. 9.9 (a) *Gate Descriptor Format (b) Bit Definition of Gate Descriptor Format (Intel Corp.)*

9.5.4 Segment Descriptor Cache Registers

A concept of caching was introduced in 80286 to minimise the time required for fetching the frequently required descriptor information from the main memory. The caching is nothing but maintaining the most

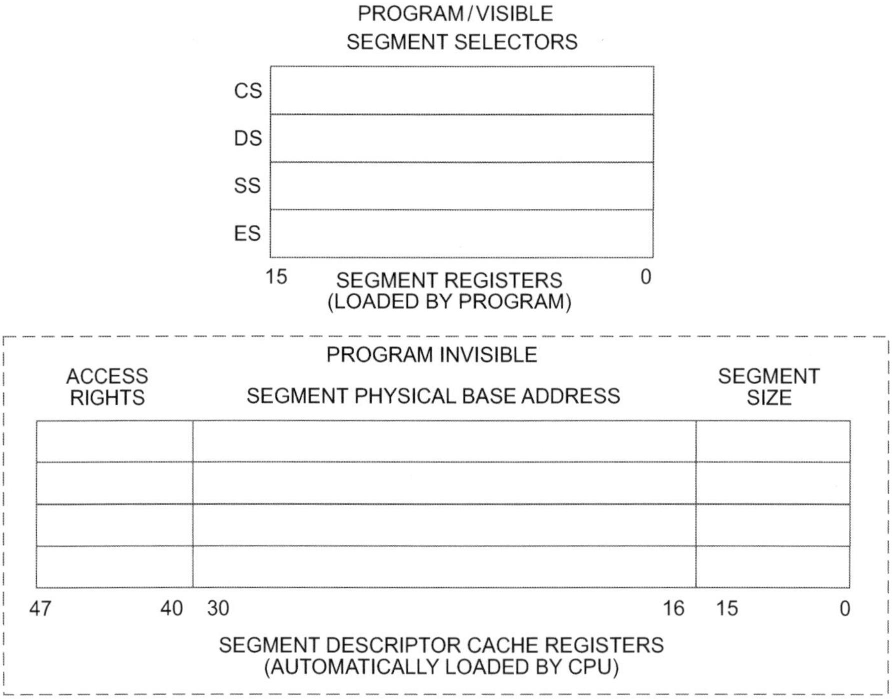

Fig. 9.10 *Descriptor Cache Register and their Formats (Intel Corp.)*

frequently required data for execution in a high speed memory called *cache memory*. A 6-byte segment descriptor cache register is assigned to each of the four segments, i.e. CS, DS, SS and ES. A segment descriptor is automatically loaded in a segment descriptor cache register, whenever the associated segment register is loaded with a selector. Once a cache register is loaded, all the information regarding the segment is obtained from the cache register, instead of referring to the main memory for the descriptor again and again. These cache registers are not available for programming. They automatically change when a segment register is reloaded. Figure 9.10 shows the 6-byte format of the cache registers and the corresponding segment registers.

Selector Fields In the protected mode, the contents of the segment registers are known as selectors. The selector contains three fields in its 16-bit format. The 2-bit field D_0-D_1 is called as RPL field, i.e. *requested privilege level*, that describes the desired privilege of the segment. The D_2 bit indicates the descriptor table type, i.e. local descriptor table, if it is 1 and global descriptor table, if it is 0. The index field D_3-D_{15} points to the required descriptor base in the descriptor table. Figure 9.11 shows the selector field format.

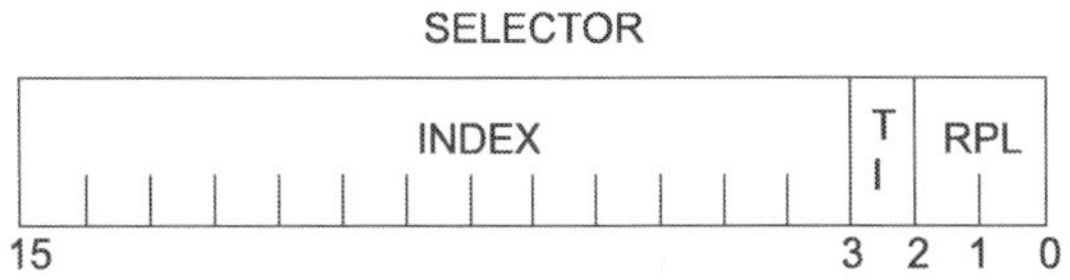

BITS	NAME	FUNCTION
1-0	REQUESTED PRIVILEGE LEVEL (RPL)	INDICATES SELECTOR PRIVILEGE LEVEL DESIRED
2	TABLE INDICATOR (TI)	TI = 0 USE GLOBAL DESCRIPTOR TABLE (GDT) TI = 1 USE LOCAL DESCRIPTOR TABLE (LDT)
15-3	INDEX	SELECT DESCRIPTOR ENTRY IN TABLE

Fig. 9.11 *Selector Field and Definitions (Intel Corp.)*

Local and Global Descriptor Table Every descriptor required by a task is either in a *Local Descriptor Table* (LDT) or a *Global Descriptor Table* (GDT). A descriptor table is an array of 8K descriptors. The upper 13 bits of a selector field (i.e. index) point to a particular entry in a descriptor table. This means that there may be 8K descriptors in a descriptor table. Each descriptor is an 8-byte entry in the table. Thus a descriptor table, either global or local, requires 8K*8 = 64 Kbyte of memory. Obviously, to point to 8K descriptors, a 13-bit address (2^{13} = 8 Kbyte) is required. Each selector can address a segment of size 64 Kbytes. There can be at most, 8K local and 8K global descriptors per task, i.e. a total of 16K (2^{14}). Thus the total virtual memory that can be addressed per task is 64 Kbyte*16K = 1 Gbyte (2^{30}). Exception 13 will be generated, if any attempt is made to refer a descriptor outside any of the descriptor tables. A Global Descriptor Table (GDT) contains Global Descriptors common to all the tasks. A Local Descriptor Table (LDT) contains descriptors specific to a particular task. All the tasks may have their private LDTs. The GDT may contain all the descriptor types except interrupt and trap descriptors. The LDT contains segment, task gate and call gate descriptors. A segment cannot be accessed, if its descriptor does not exist in either LDT or GDT at that instant.

The LGDT (Load Global Descriptor Table) and LLDT (Load Local Descriptor Table) instructions load the base and limit fields of GDT and LDT respectively. The LGDT and LLDT instructions are privileged and may be executed only at privilege level 0. The LLDT instruction loads a selector which refers to a local descriptor table containing the base address and limit for an LDT as shown in Figs. 9.8(a) and (b). Figure 9.12 elaborates global and local descriptor table definitions. Figure 9.13 shows a global descriptor data type.

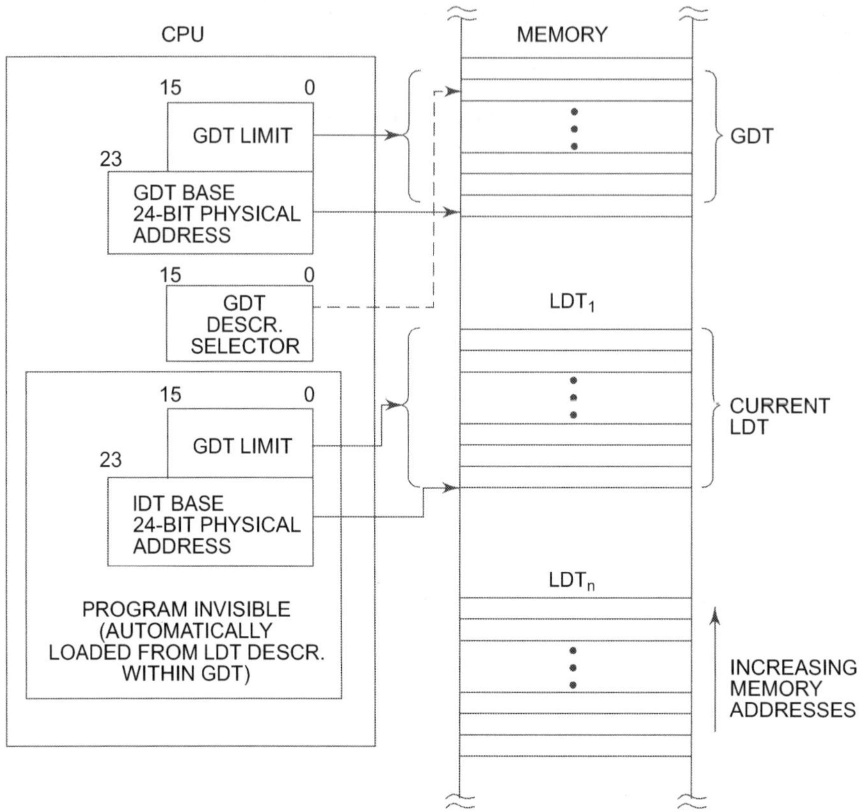

Fig. 9.12 *Local and Global Descriptor Table Definition (Intel Corp.)*

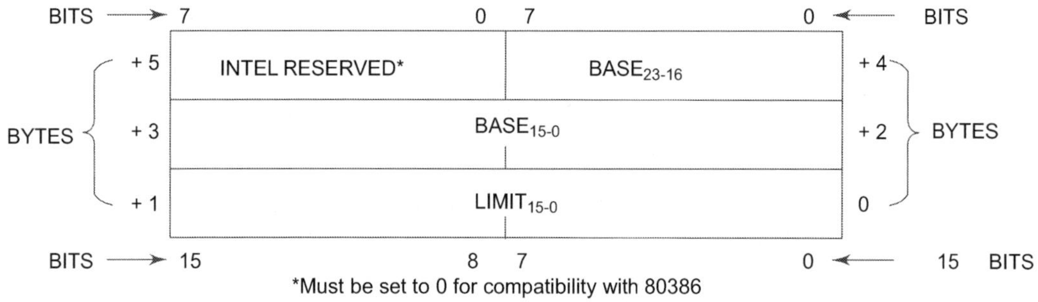

Fig. 9.13 *Global and Interrupt Descriptor Data Type*

Interrupt Descriptor Table Besides the local and global descriptor tables, the 80286 has a third type of descriptor table known as *Interrupt Descriptor Table* (IDT). These are used to store task gates, interrupt gates and trap gates. The IDT has a 24-bit base address and a 16-bit limit register in the CPU. Load Interrupt Descriptor Table register or LIDT the instruction loads these internal registers with a 6-byte value in the same way as the LGDT instruction. The IDT data format is shown in Figure 9.13. The IDT of 80286 is able to handle up to 256 interrupt descriptors. Figure 9.14 shows the arrangements of interrupt gates for different interrupts in physical memory. The IDT entries can be referred to by using INT instructions or external interrupts or exceptions. Six bytes are required for each interrupt in an interrupt descriptor table.

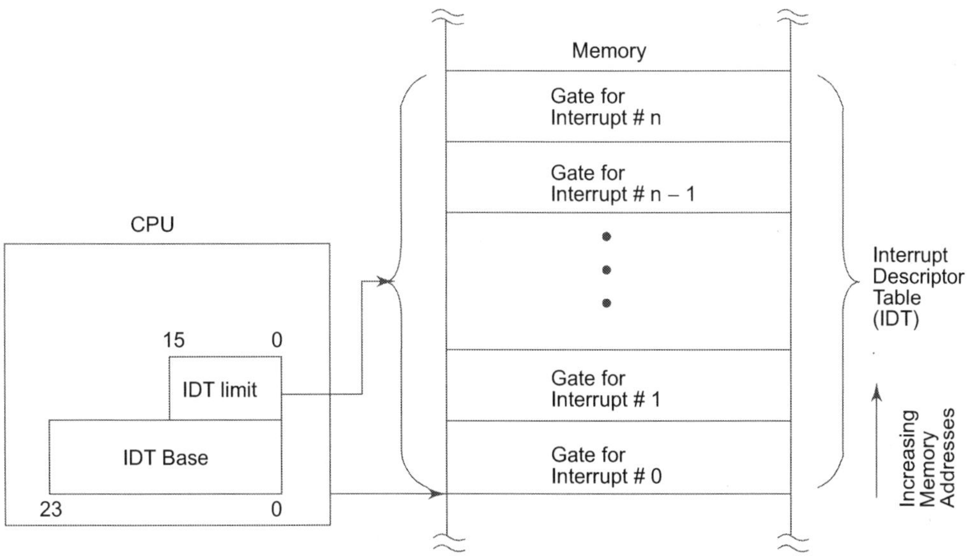

Fig. 9.14 *Interrupt Descriptor Table Organisation*

9.6 PRIVILEGE

The 80286 supports a four level hierarchical privilege mechanism to control the access to descriptors and hence to the corresponding segments of the task. The control of the access to descriptors results in the prevention of unwanted or undue access to any of the code or data segments or unintentional interference in the higher priviledge level tasks. Level 0 is the most privilege level while level 4 is the least. The privilege levels provide protection within a task. The operating system, interrupt handlers and other system softwares can be protected from unauthorised accesses in virtual address space of each task using the privilege mechanism. Each task in the system has a separate stack for each of privilege levels. The privilege mechanism

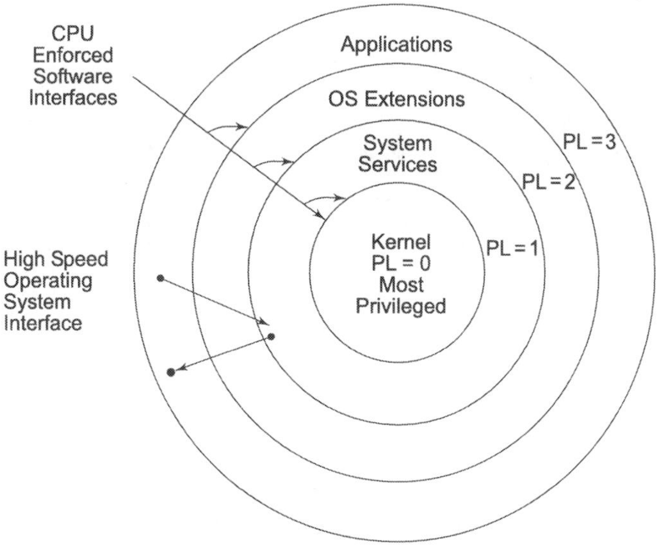

Note: PL Becomes Numerically Lower as Privilege Level Increases

Fig. 9.15 *Four Level Privilege Mechanism*

offers or denies access to a segment at the behest of the privilege bits of the corresponding descriptor. The task privilege controls the use of instructions and descriptors. Figure. 9.15 shows the four level privilege mechanism. The capabilities of the privilege mechanism are explored using the privileged instructions.

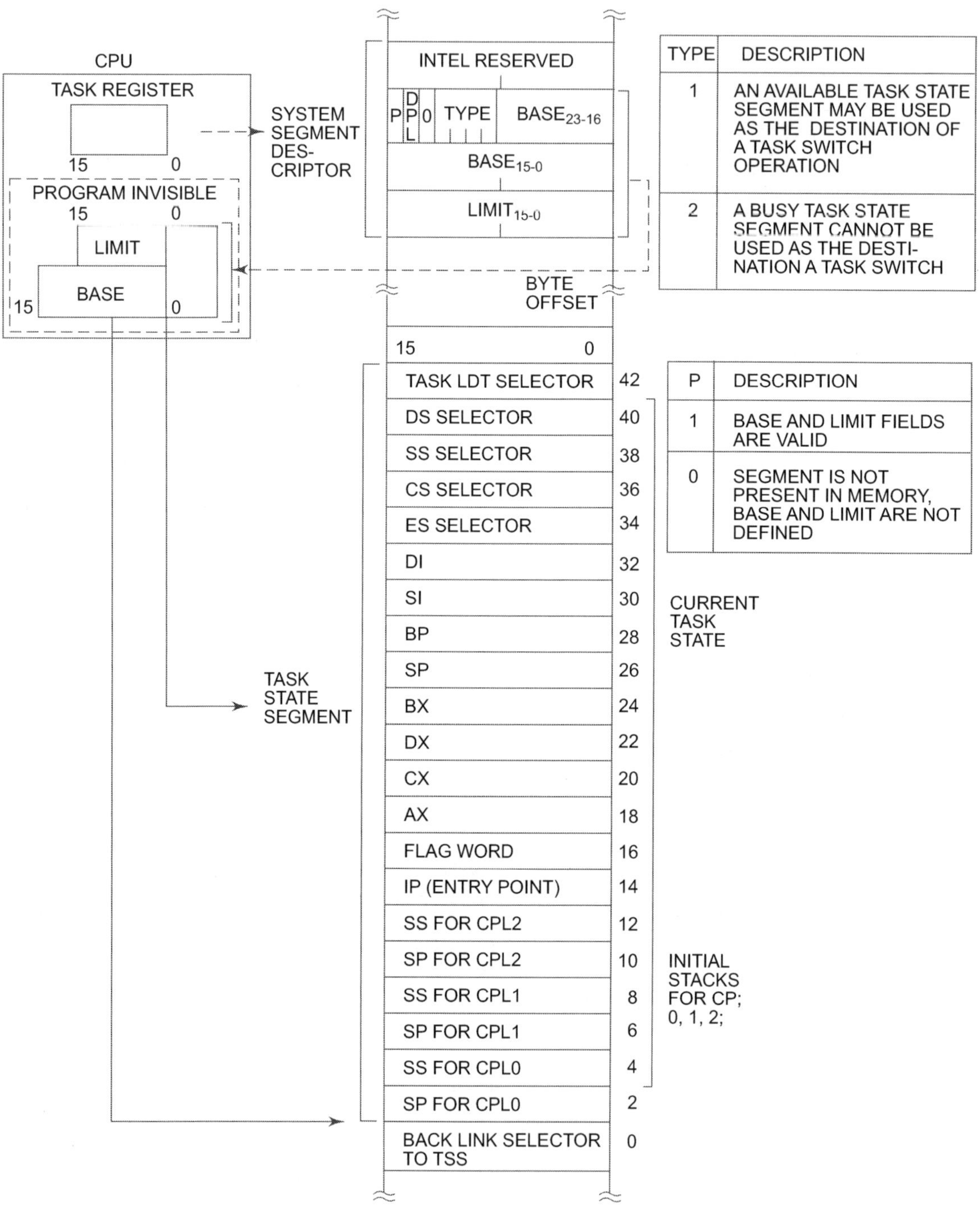

Fig. 9.16 *Task State Segment and TSS Registers*

9.6.1 Task Privilege

Each task is assigned a privilege level, which indicates the priority or privilege of that task. Any one of the four privilege levels may be used to execute a task. The task privilege level at that instant is called the *Current Privilege Level* (CPL). The CPL is defined by the lower order two bits of the CS register for an executable segment. Once the CPL is selected, it cannot be changed during the execution normally in a single code segment. It can only be changed by transferring the control, using gate descriptors, to a new segment. The task begins execution at the selected CPL values specified by the CS within TSS, if it is initiated via a task switch operation. A task executing at level 0, the most privileged level, can access all the data segments defined in GDT and the LDT of the task. Obviously, a task executing at level 3, the least privileged level, will have the most limited accesses to data and other descriptors. Figure 9.16 shows Task State Segment (TSS) and TSS registers used by a task privilege.

9.6.2 Descriptor Privilege

The descriptor privilege is specified by the DPL field of the access rights byte. The DPL specifies the least task privilege level (CPL) that may be used to refer to the descriptor. Hence the task with privilege level 0, can refer to all the lower level privilege descriptors. However, the task with privilege level 3 can refer to only level 3 descriptors. This rule applies to all the descriptors except the LDT descriptors.

9.6.3 Selector Privilege

This privilege is specified by the RPL field of a segment register (selector). A selector RPL may use a less trusted privilege than the current privilege level for further use. This is known as the *Effective Privilege Level* (EPL) of the task. The effective privilege level is thus the maximum of RPL and CPL (i.e. numeric maximum and privilege minimum). The RPL is used to ensure that the pointer parameters passed to a more privileged procedure are not given the access of data at the privilege higher than the caller routine. The pointer testing instructions are used for this purpose.

9.6.4 Descriptor Access and Privilege Check

The task requesting an access to a descriptor is allowed access to it and to the corresponding segment, only after checking (a) Type of the descriptor (b) Privilege level (CPL, RPL, DPL). The basic types of segment accesses are control transfers (in which selectors are loaded into CS) and data accesses (in which the new selectors are loaded either in ES or DS or SS). These two types of accesses are discussed in short in the following text:

Control Transfer Accesses A selector is loaded into CS by a control transfer instruction using one of the four control transfer options, if an appropriate type of descriptor is referenced. If the descriptor usage rules are not followed, an exception 13 is generated. A CALL or JUMP instruction can reference only a code segment descriptor with DPL equal to CPL of the task or a segment with a DPL of equal or greater privilege than CPL.The RPL of a selector that referred to the code descriptor must have the same privilege as CPL. The RET or IRET instructions are to refer to only code segment descriptors with DPL equal to or less than the task CPL. After return, the selector RPL is the new CPL of the task. If the CPL changes, the old SP is popped after the return address. When a JMP or CALL instruction references a TASK STATE SEGMENT (TSS) descriptor, the DPL must be less or equally privileged than the CPL of the task. If this condition is satisfied, a task switch operation takes place. If a TSS descriptor is referred to at a higher privilege level than the CPL of the task, an exception 13 is generated. When a gate descriptor is referred to by an interrupt or an instruction, the gate DPL must have equal or less privilege than CPL of the task, otherwise an exception 13 is generated. If the destination selector of a gate descriptor refers to a code segment descriptor, the CS DPL must be more or equally priviledged than the task CPL, otherwise, an exception 13 is generated. After the control transfer, the CPL of the task is replaced by new code segment DPL. If a task state segment is referred to by the destination selector in the gate, the task switch is said to occur. The control transfer follows the following privilege rules:

1. JMP or CALL can only be confirmed to the segment, if the segment DPL is of equal or greater privilege than the task CPL or a non-confirming segment at the same privilege level.
2. Interrupts within the task or the calls that may change privilege levels, are only able to transfer the control through a gate to a CS at the same or higher privilege level than CPL.
3. Return instructions that do not switch tasks can return control to a CS at the same or less privileged level.
4. Task switch is performed by a call, jump or interrupt that refers to either a task gate or to a TSS at the same or less privileged level. Table 9.6 shows the different control transfer types, the referenced descriptors, used tables and operations in a tabular form.

Table 9.6 *Control Transfer Descriptor Types (Intel Corp.)*

Control Transfer Types	*Operation Types*	*Descriptor Referenced*	*Descriptor Table*
Intersegment within the same privilege level	JMP, CALL, RET, IRET*	Code Segment	GDT/LDT
Intersegment to the same or higher privilege level interrupt within task may change CPL.	CALL	Call Gate	GDT/LDT
	Interrupt Instruction, Exception, External interrupt	Trap or interrupt Gate	IDT
Intersegment to a lower privilege level (changes task CPL)	RET, IRET*	Code Segment	GDT/LDT
	CALL, JMP	Task State Segment	GDT
Task Switch	CALL, JMP	Task Gate	GDT/LDT
	IRET**		
	Interrupt Instruction Exception, external Interrupt	Task Gate	IDT

* NT (Nested Task bit of flag word) = 0
** NT (Nested Task bit of flag word) = 1

Data Segment Accesses Loading DS, ES or SS for referring to a new descriptor comes under the *data segment accesses*. Loading DS or ES necessarily means a data segment or a readable code segment descriptor is to be referred to. The CPL of the task and RPL of the selector must have a higher or at least equal privilege as DPL, if the descriptor is to be referenced. A task can access data from equally or less privileged data segments as compared to CPL or RPL, whichever is at lowest privilege to prevent a lower privileged program from accessing a higher privileged data. However, a readable confirming code segment can be read from any privilege level. If the privilege test is negative or an improper segment is referenced, an exception 13 is generated. If the referenced segment is not present in physical memory, an exception 11 is generated.

Loading of SS register always refers to data segment descriptors (stack data) that are writable. The DPL and RPL must be equal to CPL to prevent unwanted cross referencing of stack data. The negative privilege tests and improper descriptor references generate exception 13. If the stack data segment to be referred to is not present in physical memory, an exception 12 is generated.

9.6.5 Privilege Level Alteration

If a task needs to change its privilege level during the control transfers within it, the stack must be manipulated correspondingly. The current SS:SP for task privilege levels 0, 1 and 2 are stored in the task state segment. If the control is to be transferred using JMP and CALL, the new SS:SP contents are loaded and the previous stack pointer is pushed to the new stack. While returning to the original privilege level, the stack is restored as a part of control transfer operation after execution of RET or IRET instructions. For subroutine calls which use stack for passing parameters to subroutines and then cross the priviledge levels, a fixed number of words are copied from the previous stack to the current stack (Refer to word count field of the gate descriptors.). The corresponding RET instruction with a stack adjustment value will correctly retain the previous stack pointer.

9.7 PROTECTION

As it is obvious from the foregoing discussion, the 80286 can utilize its privilege mechanism for protecting its data or code from the unwanted accesses. The 80286 has instructions designed to exploit its protection capabilities. The 80286 supports the following three basic mechanisms to provide protection.

1. **Restricted use of segments (segment load check)** This is accomplished with the help of read/write privileges. The segment usages are restricted by classifying the corresponding descriptors under LDT (Local Descriptor Table) and GDT (Global Descriptor Table).
2. **Restricted Accesses to Segment (operation reference check)** This is accomplished using descriptor usages limitations and the rules of privilege check, i.e. DPL, TPL and CPL.
3. **Privileged Instructions or Operations (privileged instruction check)** These are to be executed or carried out at certain privilege levels determined by CPL and I/O privilege level (IOPL) as defined by the flag register.

The three types of checks discussed above, if the result is negative, generate exceptions as shown in Table 9.7, Table 9.8 and Table 9.9 respectively. The IRET and POPF instructions do not perform any of their functions, if CPL is not of the required privilege level. For example, IF remains unaffected, if CPL is greater than 0. No exception is generated for this condition.

Table 9.7 *Segment Register Load Check Exceptions*

Error Description	*Exception Number*
Descriptor table limit exceeded	13
Segment descriptor not-present	11 or 12
Invalid descriptor/segment type segment register load:	
— Read only data segment load to SS	
— Special Control descriptor load to DS, ES, SS	13
— Execute only segment load to DS, ES, SS	
— Data segment load to CS	
— Read/Execute code segment load to SS	

Table 9.8 *Operand References Check Exceptions*

Error Description	*Exception Number*
Write into code segment	13
Read from execute-only code segment	13
Write to read-only data segment	13
Segment limit exceeded	12 or 13

Exceptions in Protected Mode In the protected mode, 80286 specially generates some exceptions and interrupts as a result of the violation of the corresponding conditions. These are listed in Table 9.10. Some of these exceptions are restartable, i.e. execution can further be continued, if the cause of its generation is eliminated. The interrupt service routines for them can read an error code and return address from the stack. The return address identifies the selector and points to the failing instruction. For a processor extension segment overrun exception, the return address does not point at the ESC instruction at which the exception was generated but the processor extension registers contain the address of the failing instruction. Though some of the exceptions are restartable, their generation indicates fatal error somewhere and hence the restart is not advisable. These checks are performed for all the instructions and operations. A 'Not Present' exception generates interrupt 11 or 12 and is restartable.

Table 9.9 *Privilege Instruction Check*

Error Description	*Exception Number*
CPL $\neq$ 0 when executing the following instructions:	
LIDT, LLDT, LGDT, LTR, LMSW, CTS, HLT	13
CPL > IOPL when executing the following instructions:	
INS, IN, OUTS, OUT, STI, CLI, LOCK	13

Table 9.10 *Protected Mode Exceptions*

Interrupt Vector	*Function*	*Return Address at Falling Instruction*	*Always Restart-able?*	*Error Code on Stack*
8	Double exception detected	Yes	No	Yes
9	Processor extension segment overrun	No	No	No
10	Invalid task state segment	Yes	Yes	Yes
11	Segment not present	Yes	Yes	Yes
12	Stack segment overrun or stack segment not present	Yes	Yes	Yes
13	Great Protection	Yes	No	Yes

9.8 SPECIAL OPERATIONS

The 80286 carries out five operations, which should be studied in details before we start with the bus cycles and instruction set. These are:

1. Processor reset and initialization
2. Task switch operation
3. Pointer testing instructions
4. Protected mode initialization
5. How to enter protected mode?
6. Halt

9.8.1 Processor Reset and Initialization

The processor is reset by applying a high on RESET input that terminates all the execution and internal bus activities till RESET remains high. At the trailing edge of RESET, the 80286 starts internal initialization (that requires 34 clock states) and then starts executing instructions from the physical address FFFFF0(H). The other registers are initialized after RESET as shown in Table 9.11. The HOLD must not be active during the time from the leading edge of RESET signal to at least 34 clock cycles after the trailing edge of the RESET signal. After reset, 80286 is always in the real address mode.

Table 9.11 *Register Initialization after RESET*

FLAG	0002 H
MSW	FFF0 H
IP	FFF0 H
CS	F000 H
DS, ES, SS	0000 H

9.8.2 Task Switch Operation

The 80286 supports multitasking, i.e. more than one task may be ready for execution at a time. A job may be divided into a number of tasks. These tasks are to be executed one by one using 80286, for completion of the job. A number of task allocation strategies like first come first serve, shortest task first, time sharing, etc. have been experimented by the operating system designers. In case of the time sharing technique, the CPU's time is divided into equal duration slices. Each of the task in the queue is then allotted a fixed time slice serially for the execution on the CPU. If the task is completed within the allotted time slice, then it is removed from the queue of the tasks to be executed. Otherwise, whatever is its state at the end of the allotted time slice, it is saved back with all the required details and is made to wait for its next turn. The CPU is allotted to the next task in the queue for an identical time slice. Thus each task will receive the attention of the CPU sequentially, after a fixed duration time slice. After the first cycle is over, the first task will again be scheduled for the next cycle and the process continues. The previous task that was incomplete, may be completed during its coming turns of the allotted CPU time slice. This switch-over operation from one task to another is called as *task switch operation*.

The 80286 internal architecture provides a task switch operation to save the execution state of a task (that includes registers, address space, and link to the previous task) and to load a new task to be executed. The execution of the new task commences after its execution state is loaded. The task switch operation is carried out using a JMP or CALL to a new segment of the new task that refers to the corresponding Task State Segment (TSS) or Task Gate Descriptor in the GDT or LDT. A software interrupt instruction, exception or external interrupt (hardwired setting of the time slice externally) can also be used to carry out task switch operation. However, a corresponding task gate descriptor must be selected in the associated IDT to use any type of interrupt or exception for this purpose. A task gate descriptor contains a TSS selector. The TSS descriptor specifies a segment containing the new task execution state.

Each task has a TSS for it. The TSS currently under execution is pointed to by a special function register known as the task register TR. The selector in TR refers to a TSS descriptor that defines current TSS. An internal hidden base and limit registers are loaded automatically when the TR is loaded with a new selector. The IRET instruction is internally executed to return the control to the main task that called the current task or was itself interrupted. The NT (nested task flag) bit of the flag register controls the function of IRET instruction. If NT is 1, the IRET instruction gets back the execution state of the previous task. Otherwise the IRET instruction lets the current task continue after popping the required values from stack.

If a CALL, JMP or INT instruction is used to start the task switching operation, the new TSS is marked busy and the back link field of the new TSS is set to the selector of old TSS. The NT flag is set by CALL or INT initiated task switch operations. An interrupt does not clear NT. NT is either set or cleared by POPF or IRET instructions. The task segment can be marked busy by changing the descriptor type 1 to type 3. Any attempt to refer a busy task state segment generates an exception 13. Figure 9.16 shows the TSS and the corresponding registers.

9.8.3 Pointer Testing Instructions

The pointer testing instructions of 80286 use the memory management hardware to verify whether the loaded selector value refers to a valid segment without generating any exception. The ZF indicates that the selector loaded or the referred segment may or may not generate an exception. Table 9.12 shows the pointer testing instructions and their details.

Table 9.12 *Pointer Testing Instructions of 80286 (Intel Corp.)*

Instruction	*Operands*	*Functions*
APRL	Selector, Register	Adjust Requested Privilege Level: adjust the RPL of the selector to the numeric maximum of current selector RPL value and the RPL value in the register. Set zero flag if selector RPL was changed by ARPL.
VERR	Selector	VERify for Read: sets the zero flag if the segment referred to by the selector can be read.
VERW	Selector	VERify for write sets the zero flag if the segment referred to by the selector can be written.
LSL	Register, Selector	Load Segment Limit: reads the segment limit into the register if privilege rules and descriptor type allow. Set zero flag if successful.
LAR	Register, Selector	Load Access Rights: reads the descriptor access rights byte into the register if privilege rules allow. Set zero flag if successful.

9.8.4 Protected Mode Initialization

After 80286 is reset, it starts the execution in real address mode. The address lines A_{20}-A_{23} are pulled down to zero level for addressing peripherals and memory. Initially the CS:IP value is set at F000H:FFF0H to allot a segment of 64Kbytes for initialization. The initialization of protected mode is carried out in real mode by setting the internal registers of 80286 suitably. The GDT and IDT base registers must point to a valid GDT and IDT, before 80286 enters the protected mode.To enter into protected mode, 80286 executes LMSW instruction that sets PE flag. The 80286 then clears the instruction queue that may contain opcodes fetched in real mode. The operating system assumes the initial state in protected mode and accordingly initialises the internal registers of 80286. After entering the protected mode, the 80286 executes a jump instruction that directs the control to a selector that refers to the initial TSS. This jump instruction initialises the task register, LDT register and segment registers.

9.8.5 How to Enter PVAM

After the reset, 80286 enters in real address mode. The execution of instruction LIDT (Load Interrupt Descriptor Table base) prepares the 80286 for protected virtual address mode. This instruction loads the 24-bit interrupt table base and 16-bit limit from memory into the interrupt descriptor table register. This instruction also can set the base and limit of interrupt vector table in real mode. Then the PE flag of MSW is set to enter the protected virtual address mode, using the LMSW (Load Machine Status Word) instruction.

9.8.6 HALT

This instruction stops program execution and prevents the CPU from restarting, till it is interrupted or RESET is asserted. If the CPU is interrupted in the HALT state, the execution starts from the next instruction after HLT. On the other hand, if the CPU is RESET, the execution starts from the physical address FFFFF0H. The CPU status lines reflect the halt status.

9.9 80286 BUS INTERFACE

The 80286 provides a set of signals to interface the memory and I/O devices with it. This set contains 24 address lines to address 16Mbytes of physical memory, 16 data lines to enable 16-bit data transfer at a time and 8 control signals to coordinate the transfers. The supporting chip 82284 provides synchronized RESET and $\overline{\text{READY}}$ signals, along with the system clock. The 82288 derives various control signals from the signals provided by 80286 to encode the bus cycles.

The 80286 is able to address 16 Mbytes (2^{24}) of memory, that is addressed in the same way as 8086, i.e. in the terms of even address bank and odd address bank, using the signals A_0 and $\overline{\text{BHE}}$. The 80286 is able to address 64K 8-bit output and 64K 8-bit input devices or 32K 16-bit input and 32K 16-bit output devices. The I/O devices are also addressed using even address and odd address banks technique, using A_0 and $\overline{\text{BHE}}$. The upper byte of the 16-bit data that is to be transferred to/from an I/O device is transferred on D_8-D_{15} to an odd address, while the lower byte of the 16-bit data is transferred on D_0–D_7 to an even address, in the same way as in 8086. The interrupt controller 8259A is interfaced at an even address.

The 80286 divides the input clock frequency applied at input CLK pin by two to derive the actual operating clock frequency PCLK, that determines the bus timings. According to the type of bus operation, the 80286 bus cycles are of six types, viz. memory read, memory write, I/O read, I/O write, interrupt acknowledge and halt. The readers are already familiar with these type of bus cycles.

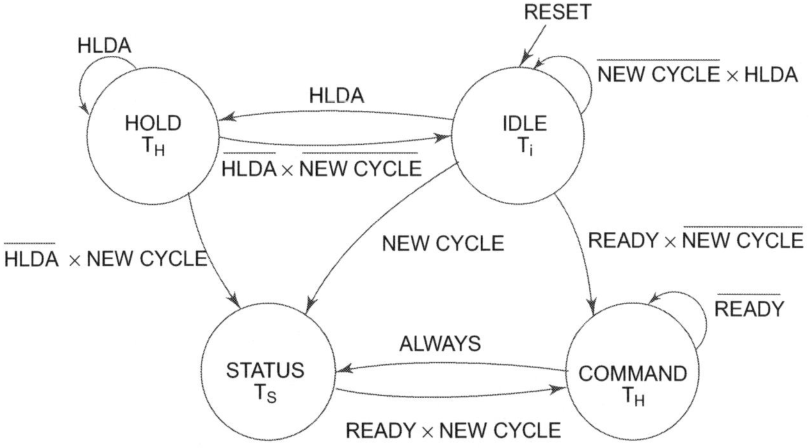

Fig. 9.17 *80286 Bus States and their Correlation (Intel Corp.)*

The 80286 bus at a particular instant may be in either of these four states: (i) Idle state (T_i) (ii) Perform command state (T_c) (iii) Send status state (T_s) and (iv) Hold state (T_H). In the idle state, the local bus remains idle, while in perform command state and sent status state, it performs memory/IO read/write operations. When a device desires to have a DMA data transfer, the hold state indicates that the local bus is being relinquished for another bus master. These bus states are shown in Fig. 9.17.

The 80286 uses pipelining technique to speed up the data access procedure. Each individual bus operation is three cycles long. Suppose the CPU, at an instant has initiated a memory read bus operation. This operation will continue for three cycles. Suppose also that the next operation is a memory write operation. Then the address of the next memory location to be written, as a part of the next bus cycle will be available during the current bus operation. Thus the next bus cycle will be initiated after two clock cycles of the current bus cycle. This is pipelining operation, i.e. the first clock of the second bus operation, which is a memory write operation overlaps with last clock of the previous operation, which is a memory read operation. The address of the current bus operation remains valid only for the first processor clock cycle.

9.10 BASIC BUS OPERATIONS

The bus controller 82288 derives ALE, $\overline{RD}$ and $\overline{WR}$ commands, DT/$\overline{R}$ and DEN signals to control the data transfer to/from the 80286. The bus controller uses the CPU output signals $\overline{S_1}, \overline{S_0}$ and M/$\overline{IO}$ as inputs. The basic bus operation, here, is studied only in terms of the signals derived by 80286. The basic bus cycle is shown in Fig. 9.18, that elaborates two successive read cycles by 80286. These basic timings of 80286 can be controlled, using two command control options, namely, command extension (input $\overline{READY}$) and command delay (CMDL input) of 82C288.

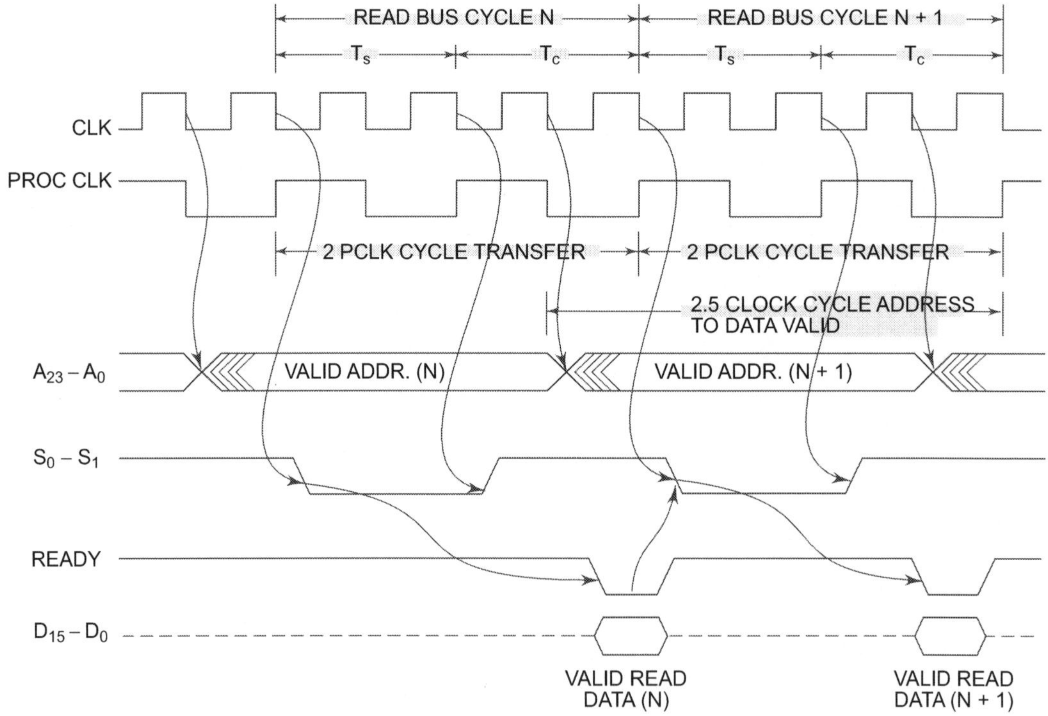

Fig. 9.18 *Basic Bus cycle of 80286 (Read-Read cycles) (Intel Corp.)*

The command extension option inserts the wait states in the basic bus cycle using external hardware to interface 80286 with low speed peripherals. The command delay option stretches the interval between read/write data setup to system bus command active interval for any of the bus operations. The 82C288 checks the CMDLY input at each trailing edge of CLK. If it is high, the 82C288 will not activate the command signal. Once the command is activated the CMDLY is not sampled. If a command is delayed, the duration between the command active read data or write data is reduced. Figure 9.19 shows the effect of CMDLY over the basic 80286 bus cycle. The CMDLY signal does not affect ALE, DEN or DT/$\overline{R}$. Figures 9.20, 9.21 and 9.22 show the different sequences of the basic operations and the behaviour of data control signals for each operation.

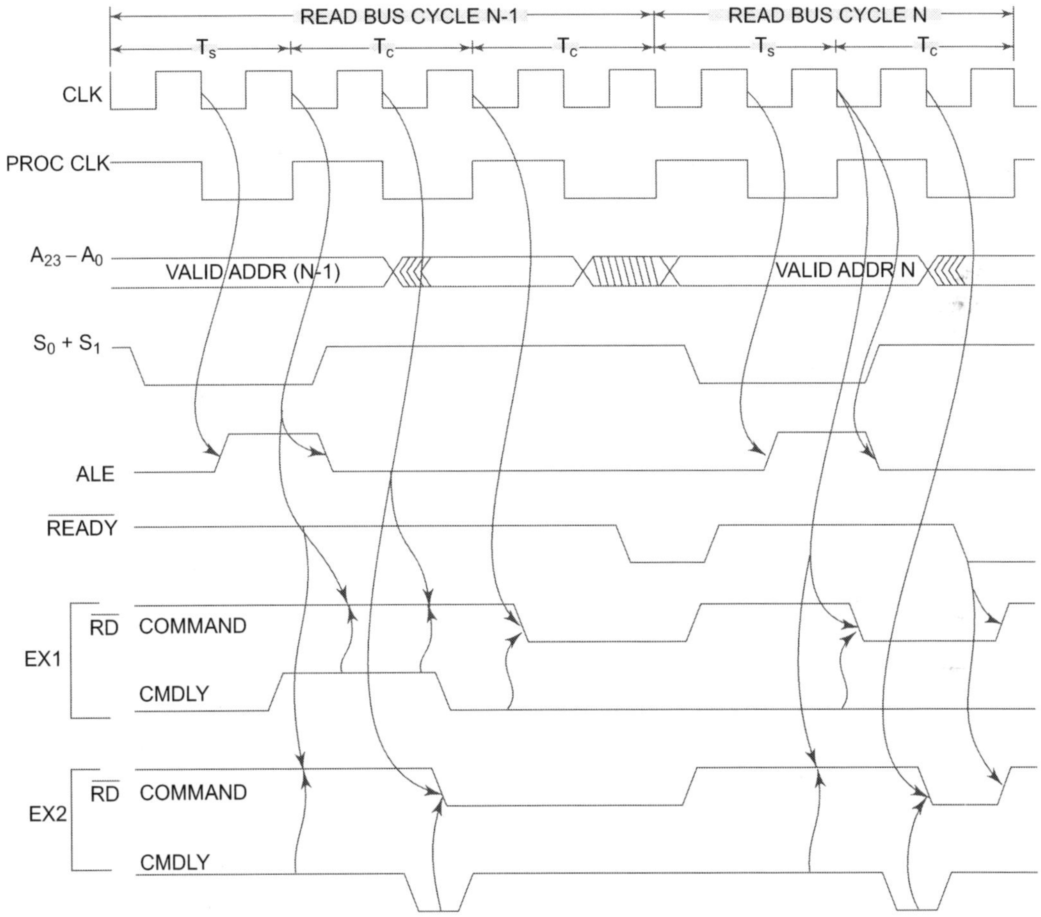

Fig. 9.19 *Use of CMDLY to Control Command Signal (Intel Corp.)*

9.11 FETCH CYCLES OF 80286

The 80286 architecture implements pipelined fetching of instructions. In other words, the 80286 prefetches the initial bytes of the next instruction, while executing the current instruction. These prefetched instruction bytes are arranged in a 6 byte prefetch queue, from where they are accepted further for decoding and execution, as has been discussed in Section 9.2.2. This fetch operation is carried out only if at least two bytes of the queue are empty. It usually fetches two bytes of the program code at a time, sequentially, independent of byte-wise instruction alignment, in the physical memory. The prefetcher fetches only one byte at

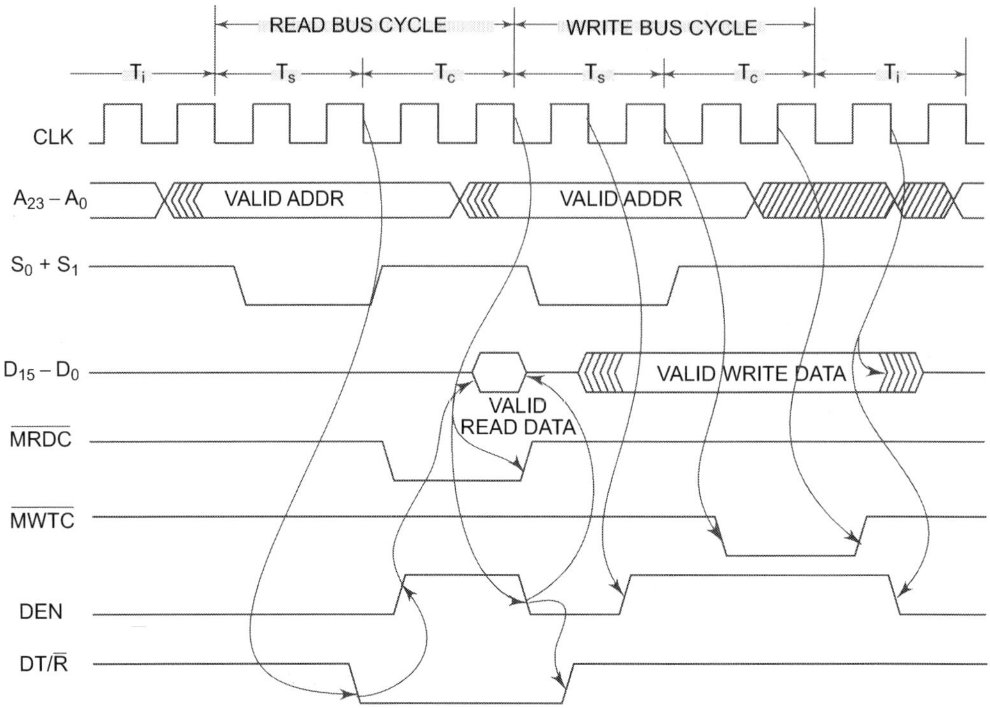

Fig. 9.20 *Successive Read and Write Cycles (Intel Corp.)*

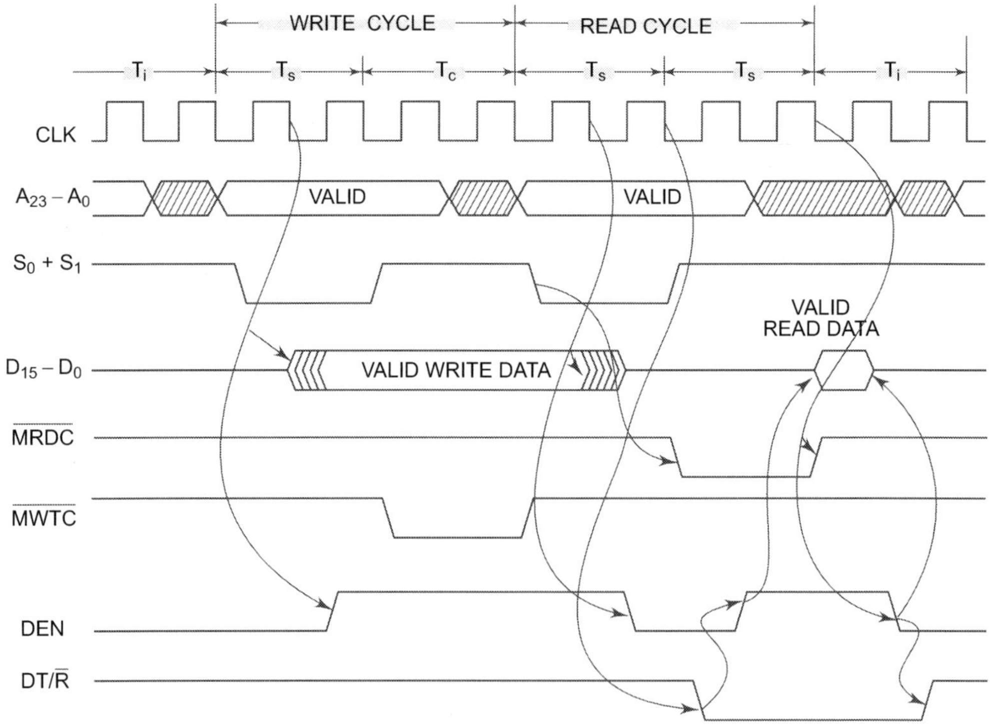

Fig. 9.21 *Successive Write and Read Cycles (Intel Corp.)*

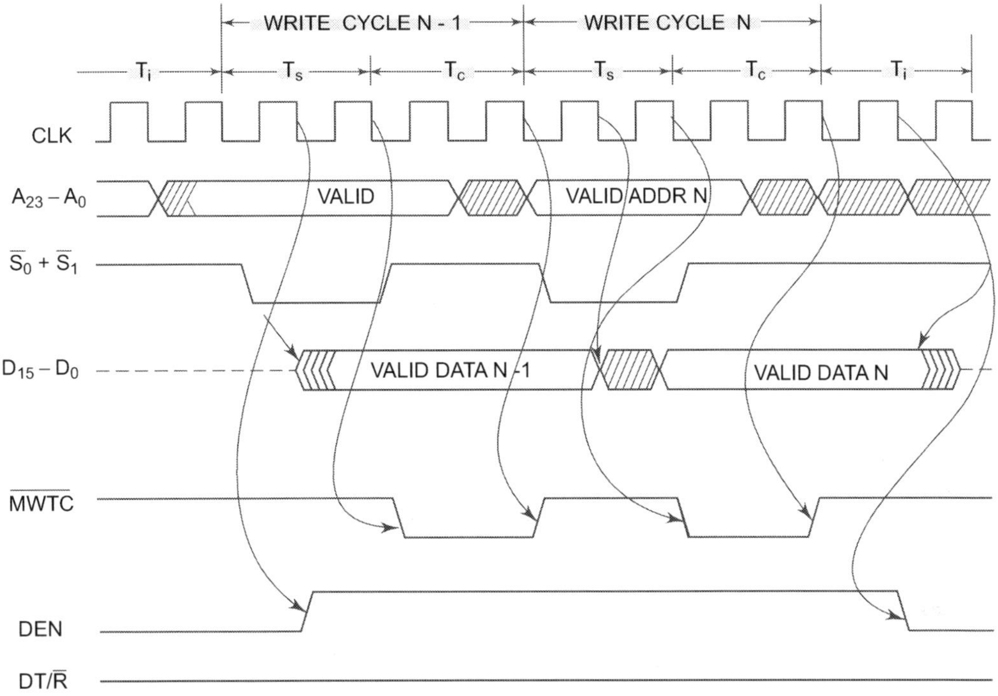

Fig. 9.22 *Successive Write-Write Cycles (Intel Corp.)*

a time if and only if the word fetch operation begins at an odd address. In case of a branch type instruction, where the sequential instruction execution may be hampered, the prefetching operation stops and the already prefetched queue is flushed. The 80286 continues the prefetching till HLT instruction is executed. Thus the 80286 may blindly prefetch 6 bytes even after the HLT instruction has been fetched. In the protected mode, the 80286 prefetcher cannot cross the segment limit, i.e. the segment overrun exception cannot be generated. The prefetcher stops at the last word in the segment, otherwise exception 13 is generated.

9.12 80286 MINIMUM SYSTEM CONFIGURATION

Unlike 8086 system, the Numeric Data Processor (Processor Extension) 80287 is an integral (but optional) part of the system, i.e. 80286 is always in maximum mode. Also, the interrupt controller 8259A, clock generator 82C284 and bus controller 82C288 are the unavoidable members of the family of supporting chips of 80286. All these components along with a processor extension 80287 form an integrated processing system. All the data transfers to/from memory or I/O are carried out by 80286. The 80286 also controls the data transfer and instruction execution of 80287. The 80287 adds its instruction set to the instruction set of 80286, as if the 80286-80287 couplet is an integrated processor. The execution by 80287 is transparent to the users, but has all the protection features of 80286 at its service.

As already discussed, the addresses available on the local bus of 80286 are for the next, i.e. (N+1)th fetch operation. The chip select, decoding and address transmission for data transfer of Nth cycle may overlap with fetch operation for the (N+1)th cycle. The decode logic in an 80286 system is usually designed using PROM or PLA. The decode logic uses the overlap between address and data of the 80286 bus cycles to generate the advanced memory and I/O select signals. The COD/$\overline{\text{INTA}}$ and M/$\overline{\text{IO}}$ signals are applied to the decoding logic to differentiate between interrupt, I/O, code fetch and data bus cycles. Figure 9.23 shows a minimum 80286 system configuration.

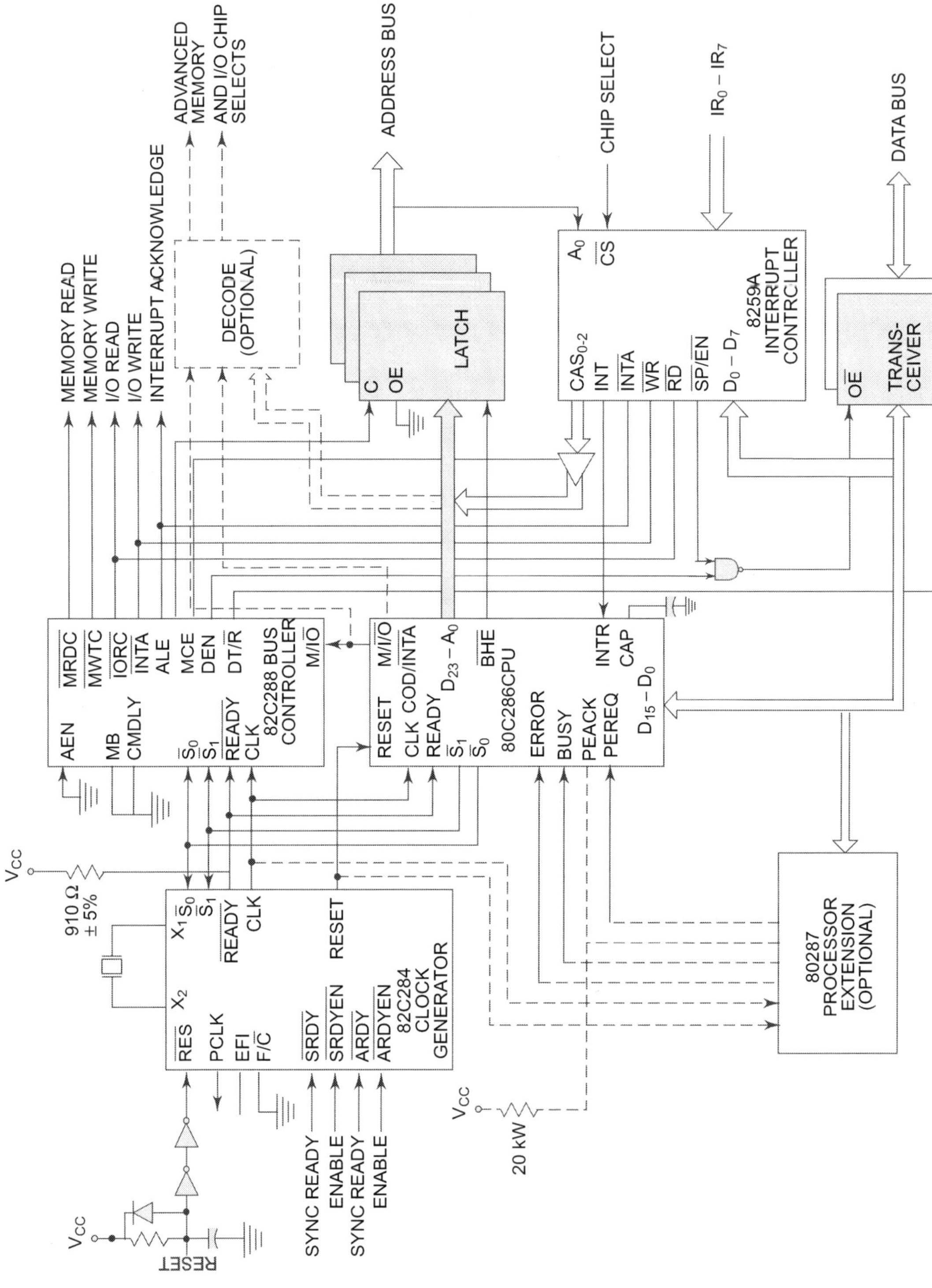

Fig. 9.23 *80286 Minimum System Configuration (Intel Corp.)*

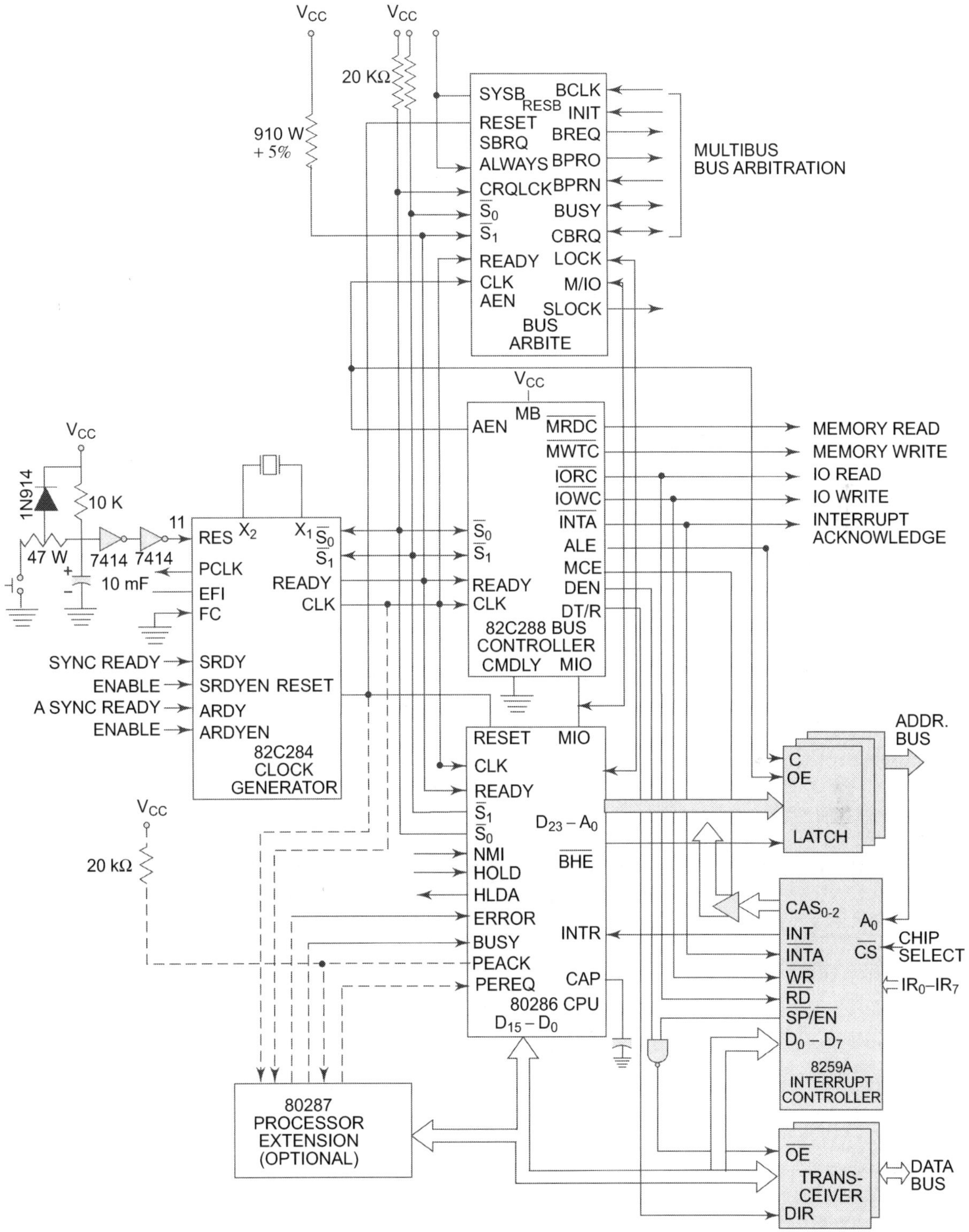

Fig. 9.24 *80286 Multibus System Interface (Intel Corp.)*

The addition of just a single chip 82C289 known as bus arbiter, to the configuration of Fig. 9.23, gives the multibus structure of Fig. 9.24. The ALE signal of 82C288 in Fig. 9.26 is connected to the CMDLY input, to add at least one extra T_c state to each bus operation of the multibus system.

The addition of one or more bus controllers, additional latches and transreceivers to the circuit in Fig. 9.24 generates a bus for local memory and peripheral interfacing besides the multibus.

9.13 INTERFACING MEMORY AND I/O DEVICES WITH 80286

The memory interfacing technique with 80286 is similar to that of 8086 in the maximum mode. The maximum mode 8086 system has 8288 and 8289 as bus controller and bus arbiter respectively, which derive and control the system bus. In 80286 systems, compatible bus controller 82288 and bus arbiter 82289 are used for the same purpose. The 80286 may use its local bus address, its local memory, I/O devices and a system bus to share with other masters, as shown in Fig. 9.25. This configuration uses two 82288 bus controllers one each for local and system bus. The bus arbiter is required for arbitration of system bus only. The ARDYEN and $\overline{\text{SRDYEN}}$ inputs are the enable pins for ARDY and SRDY which generate ready input to 80286. The ARDYEN pin is to be activated, if the 80286 is to use system bus. The SRDYEN pin is to be grounded, if the local bus is to be kept dedicated to 80286. If the pin MBYTES (Multibus Mode Select) of 82288 is tied high, it places the bus controller in multibus mode, else the bus controller is in single bus mode. As the commands are not to be delayed, the CMDLY pin is grounded. The MBYTES input selects the function of CEN/AEN pin. If MBYTES is high, the pin serves as AEN else it serves as CEN. The CENL pin is used for selecting one of the available 82288s. The SYS/$\overline{\text{RESB}}$ input of 82289 enables it whenever the system bus is to be used.

With this much information regarding the buses, one may go for interfacing the memory with 80286. As already said, the 80286 also addresses the memory in terms of even and odd banks. Figure 9.26 shows a bank of memory interfaced with 80286 in the same way as in case of 8086. The address and the data lines of 80286 are not multiplexed hence no latches are required in an 80286 system. Rather the addresses of the next bus cycle are displayed in advance, hence latches are required for latching the address and decode the select signals. For this, the ALE derived by 82288 is used. The problem with this method is that it does not allow insertion of wait states for interfacing low speed devices. Figure 9.27 shows an interfacing scheme to interface slower memory devices without compromising for the data transfer rate.

For interfacing I/O devices with 80286, a separate set of latches may be used that may be strobed using $\overline{\text{IORD}}$ and $\overline{\text{IOWR}}$ signals. Generally, the ALE is not used for latching the I/O addresses. The strobed data transfer allows various slow devices to be interfaced with 80286. The 80286 can address at the most 64K, 8-bit input and 64K, 8-bit output ports or 32K 16-bit input and 32K 16-bit output ports. The port addresses are either 8-bit (usually specified in the instructions) or 16-bit (stored in DX register). The 8-bit port addresses are zero extended or, in other words, unused higher order addressing lines which are pulled low by 80286 while addressing an I/O device. The I/O port addresses 00F8H to 00FFH are reserved by Intel, hence these should not be used while designing practical systems around 80286.

9.14 PRIORITY OF BUS USE BY 80286

The 80286 uses its local bus for different purposes during its operation. Rather, the internal units of 80286 ask for the access of the local bus whenever they require it. If at any instant of time, only one of the units of 80286 ask for the access of the bus, there is no problem. However, if there is more than one request for the access of the bus, contention may arise. To avoid this problem, the internal architecture of 80286 has allotted priorities to different usages of the bus. The higher priority usage may supercede the lower priority usage and the units may accordingly gain the control of the bus. The relative priorities of the usages are as listed below, starting from the highest one to the lowest one:

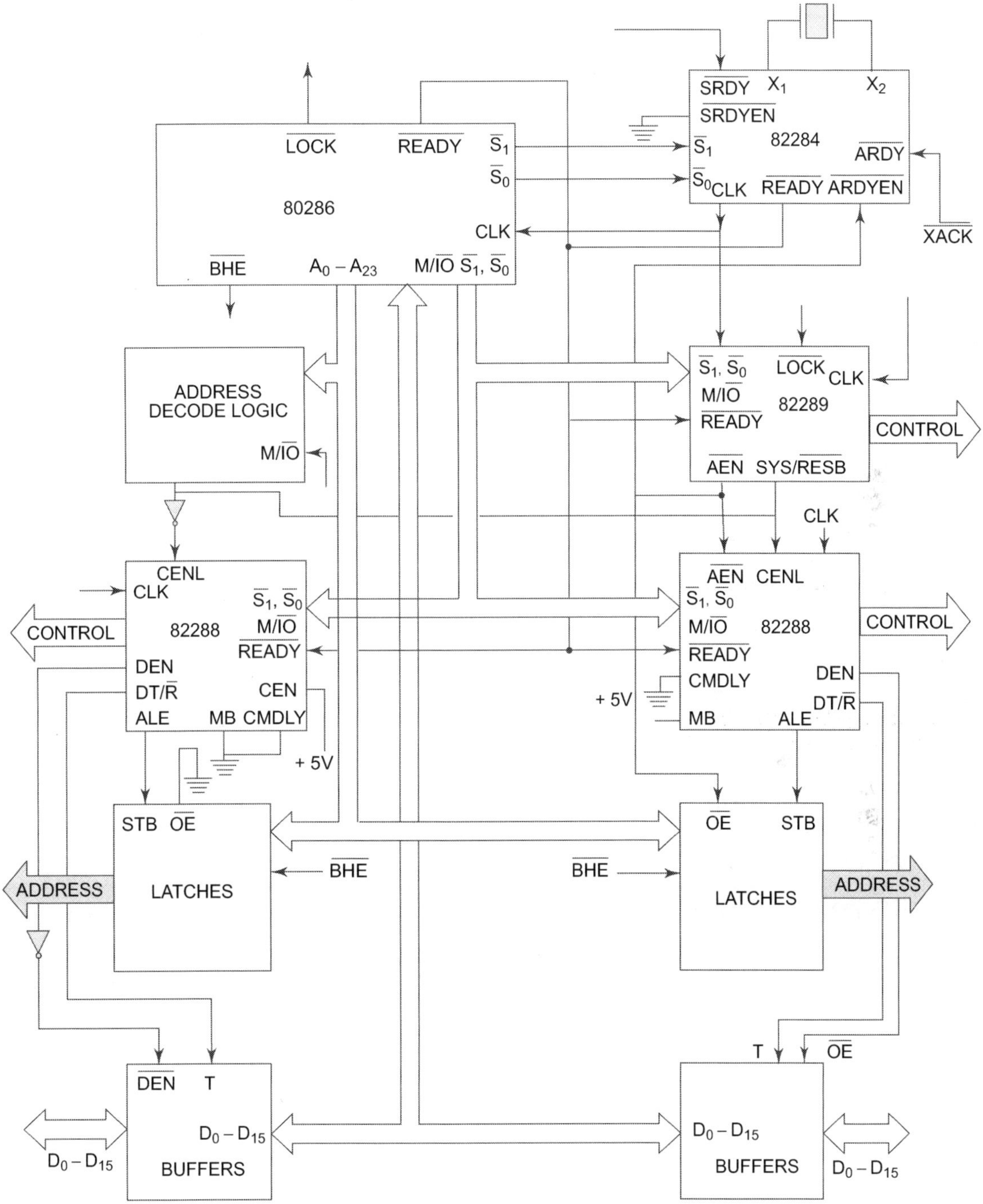

Fig. 9.25 *Deriving System Bus and Local Bus (Intel Corp.)*

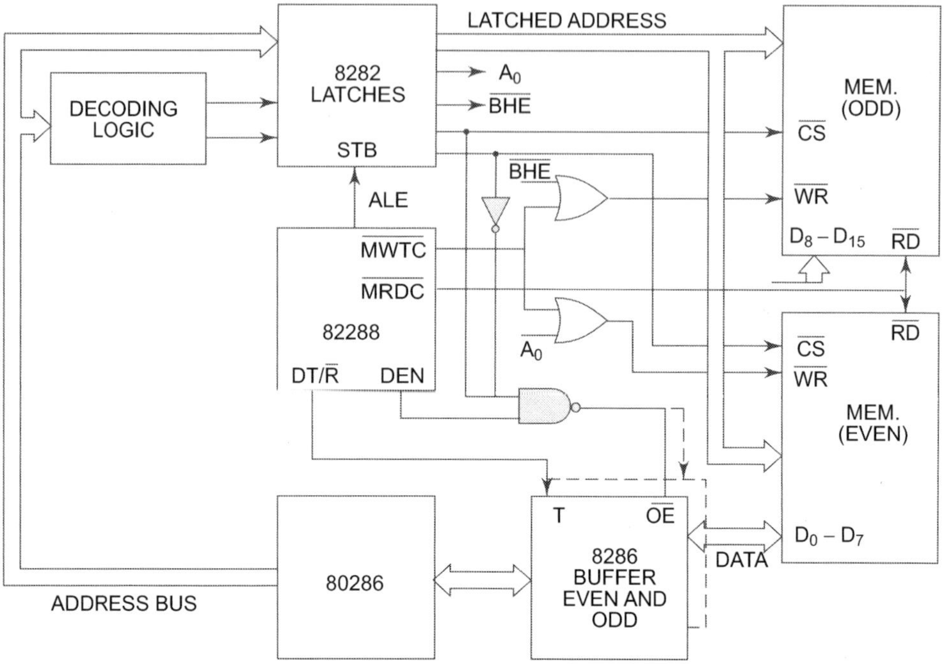

Fig. 9.26 *Memory Interfacing Using ALE Signal (Intel Corp.)*

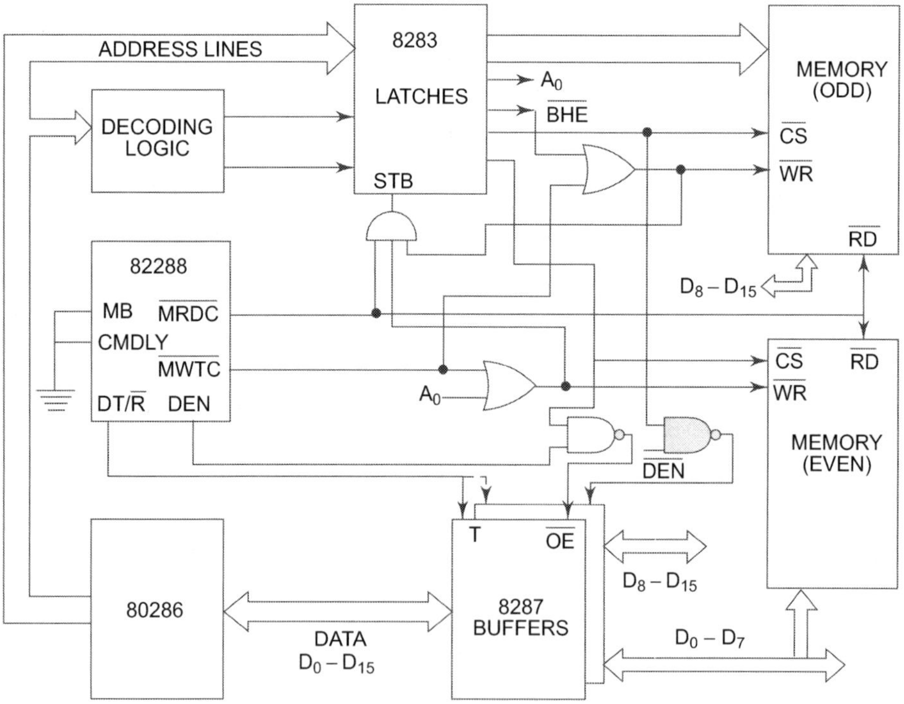

Fig. 9.27 *Memory Interfacing Using Strobe Logic (Intel Corp.)*

Highest Priority

1. Transfer with $\overline{LOCK}$ activated.
2. The second byte transfer of the 2-byte transfer at an odd address.
3. The second or third transfer cycle of a processor extension data transfer.
4. HOLD request.
5. Processor extension data transfer using PEREQ.
6. Data transfer performed by EU for instruction execution.

Lowest Priority

7. A prefetch operation to fetch and arrange the next instruction bytes in queue.

Once the processor halts or enters a shut down state, the local bus goes into tristate condition. Only RESET or NMI may pull 80286 out of these states, unconditionaly. If IF is set, the INTR or coprocessor segment overrun exception will pull the 80286 out of halt or shut down. Processor enters the halt state as a result of execution of a HLT instruction. It enters shut down due to multiple violations of the protection norms.

9.15 BUS HOLD AND HLDA SEQUENCE

The 80286 local bus is relinquished for another bus master if a valid bus hold request is received at the HOLD input pin. As a response to a valid bus hold request, the bus is pushed into the T_H state. The status lines are relinquished by 80286 during T_H, but are pulled up internally by 82C284. The address, M/$\overline{IO}$ and

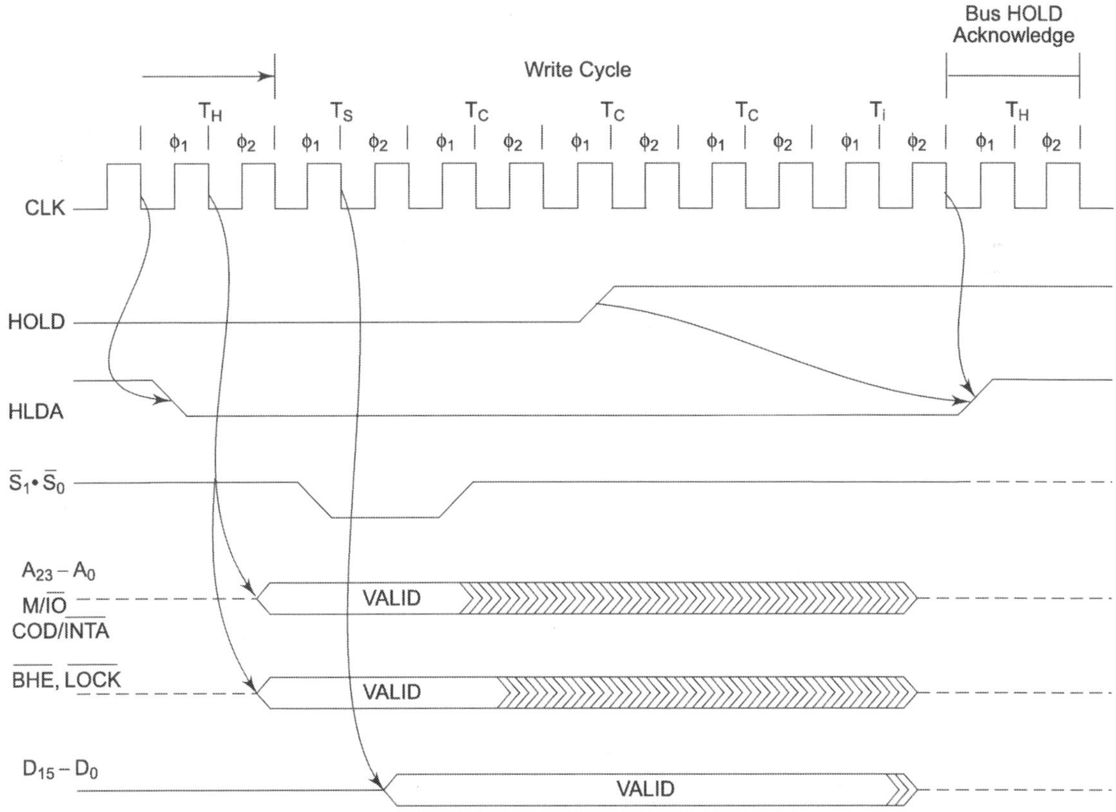

Fig. 9.28 *HOLD and HLDA Sequence of 80286 (Intel Corp.)*

COD/$\overline{\text{INTA}}$ are also relinquished by the bus arbiter. The sequence of control transfer from 80286 to another master is shown in Fig. 9.28. If during any operation, another local bus master requests the local bus from the 80286 using a HOLD signal, the 80286 completes the current operation, remains idle for one PCLK (2 CLK states to allow the current operation to be completed in all respects) and then enters T_H, sending HLDA high. As has been already discussed, only after 34 clock cycles, after the 80286 is reset(trailing edge of RESET), a valid HOLD request should be ascertained.

9.16 INTERRUPT ACKNOWLEDGE SEQUENCE

This is carried out in response to a valid INTR request. The interrupt acknowledge sequence consists of two $\overline{\text{INTA}}$ pulses. In response to the first $\overline{\text{INTA}}$ pulse from 80286, the master PIC 8259A (master) decides which of its slave interrupt controllers (8259A) is to return the vector address. After the second pulse, the selected slave sends the vector on D_0–D_7 and the 80286 reads it. The MCE (Master Cascade Enable) signal of the 82C288 enables the cascade address drivers during INTA cycles, to select the slave using the local address bus. The $\overline{\text{LOCK}}$ signal is activated during T_s of the first INTA cycle. Thus any bus request using HOLD is not responded till the end of the second INTA cycle. The 80286 allows three T_i between the two INTA cycles to meet the 8259A speed and cascade address output delay. The second INTA cycle always contains an additional T_c added by the controlling logic of $\overline{\text{READY}}$ to meet the 8259A $\overline{\text{INTA}}$ pulse width. The interrupt acknowledge sequence is shown in Fig. 9.29:

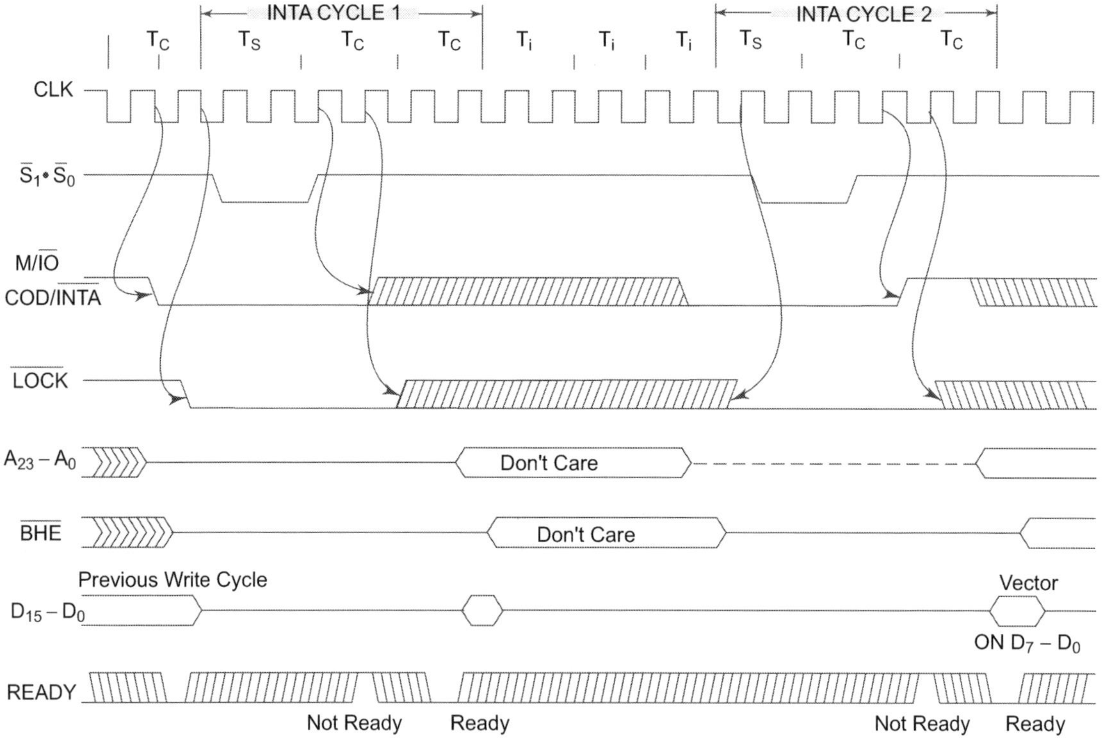

Fig. 9.29 *Interrupt Acknowledge Sequence of 80286 (Intel Corp.)*

9.17 INSTRUCTION SET FEATURES

In this section, we will discuss features of 80286 instruction set, like addressing modes, supported data types and the additional instructions of 80286.

9.17.1 Addressing Modes

The 80286 supports eight addressing modes to access the operands stored in memory. These are briefly discussed as follows:

Register Operand Mode The operand, in this mode, is located in one of the 8-bit or 16-bit general purpose registers.

Immediate Operand Mode In this mode, the immediate operand is included in the instruction itself. In the remaining six addressing modes, the operand is located in a memory segment. A memory operand address, in these modes may be computed using two 16-bit components: segment selector and offset. The different combinations of immediate displacement, base register, pointers and index registers result in the following six operating modes.

Direct Mode The offset is a part of instruction either as 8-bit or 16-bit immediate operand (displacement).

Register Mode The operand is stored either in any of the general purpose registers or in SI, DI, BX or BP.

Based Mode The offset is obtained by adding a displacement and the contents of one of the base registers, either BX or BP.

Indexed Mode The offset is obtained by adding a displacement with the contents of an index register, either SI or DI.

Based Indexed Mode The operand is stored at a location whose address is calculated by adding the contents of any of the base registers with the contents of any of the index registers.

Based Indexed Mode with Displacement In this mode, the offset of the operand is calculated by adding an 8-bit or16-bit immediate displacement with contents of a base register and an index register.

Besides these, a few instructions handle implicit data operands, for example LAHF. A few others may not need any data at all, for example, machine control instructions like HLT, WAIT, LOCK, etc. The 80286 supports all the 8086 supported addressing modes for branching instructions.

9.17.2 80286 Supported Data Types

The 80286 supports the following seven data types:

(i) **Integer** 8-bit or 16-bit signed binary operands using 2's complement representation.
(ii) **Ordinal (unsigned)** 8-bit or 16-bit unsigned numeric value in binary.
(iii) **Pointer** 32-bit pointers consisting of two 16-bit parts for segment selector and offset.
(iv) **String** A data string of maximum 64 Kbytes or 32 K words
(v) **ASCII** Different characters in ASCII standard.
(vi) **BCD** BCD representations and operations on decimal digits 0-9.
(vii) **Packed BCD** Two digit decimal number represented by using BCD symbols.

The 80286 supported data types are shown in Fig. 9.30.

9.17.3 Additional Instructions in 80286

The 80286 instruction set is upwardly compatible with that of 8086. Most of the instructions of 80286 are the same as the corresponding instructions of 8086. Hence, in this section, we will consider only these instructions which are not available with 8086.

PUSH Imd This instruction pushes a 16-bit immediate data to the stack after decrementing SP by 2. If the new value of SP is outside the stack segment limit, a stack fault exception is generated. If the new segment reference is illegal (protected or privileged segment), a general protection exception is generated for a push operation on such addresses. None of the flags are affected.

PUSH*A This instruction pushes AX, CX, DX, BX, and also SP, BP, SI, DI onto the stack. The stack pointer is hence decremented by 16 (eight 2-byte registers). All these registers are pushed in the same order

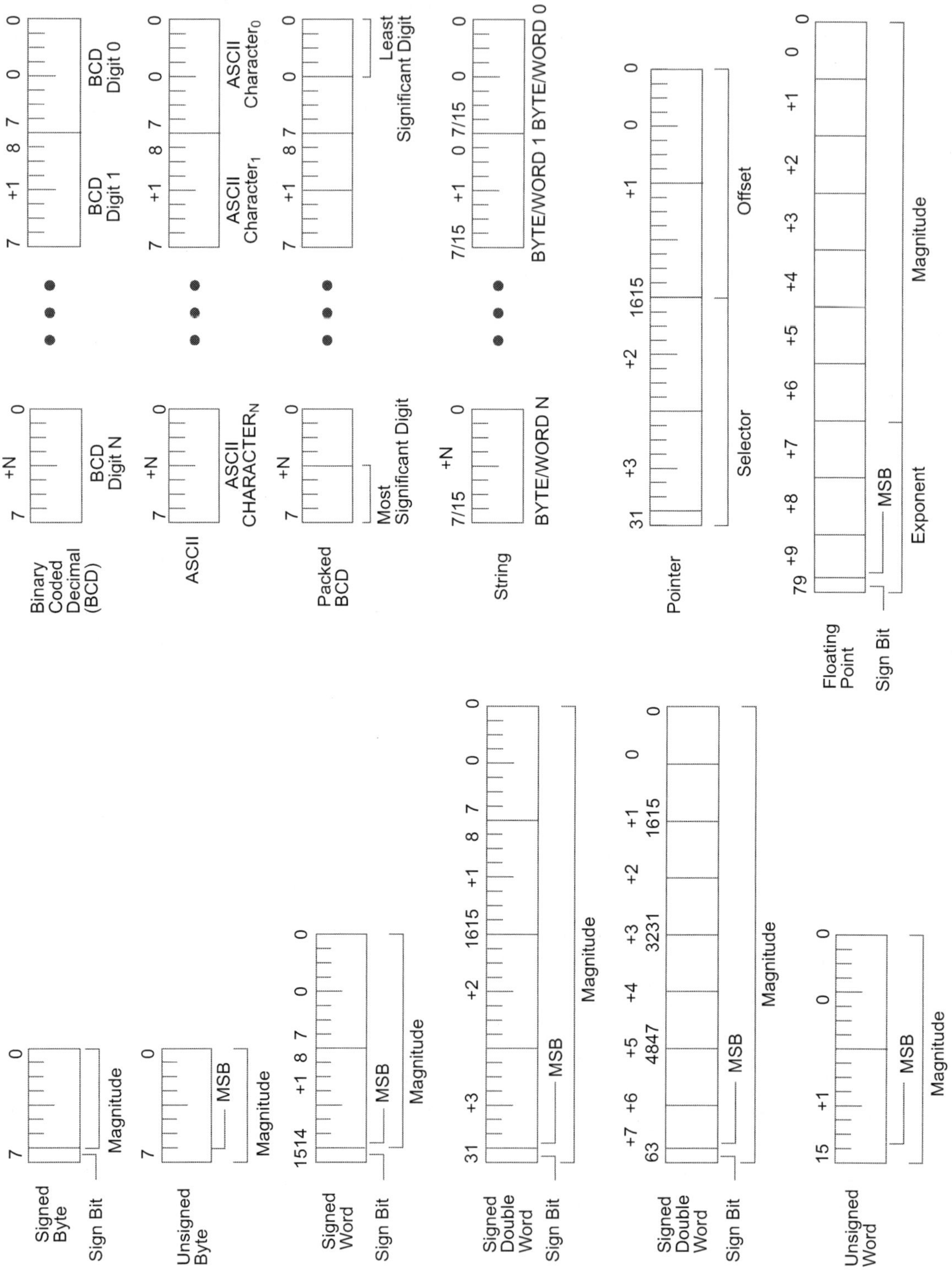

Fig. 9.30 *Data Types Supported by 80286 (Intel Corp.)*

as stated previously. Due to the LIFO structure of the stack, the last pushed register contents appear first, in the stack memory segment. This does not require any operand. A stack fault exception is generated, if the stack segment limit is overrun. This does not affect any flag. When the memory operand overruns the segment limit, exception 13 is generated.

POP*A The POPA, i.e. pop all instruction, pops all the contents of the registers DI, SI, BP, SP, BX, DX, CX and AX from the stack in this sequence that is exactly opposite to that of pushing. No operands are required for this instruction. No flags are affected. Exceptions, possibly generated during the execution of this instruction, are exactly the same as PUSH A instruction.

IMUL Imd-Oper The IMUL instruction multiplies the content of AL with a signed immediate operand and the signed 16-bit result is stored in AX. The CF and OF are cleared, if the AH is a sign extension of AL, else CF and OF are set. If the Imd-oper is a signed 16-bit data, then it is multiplied by signed contents of AX and the signed result is stored in DX: AX combination, with DX as MSB. CF and OF are cleared, if DX is the sign extension of AX, else they are set. All the other flags are undefined. An invalid reference to a memory operand may generate a general protection exception. If a word operand is at the last segment address, exception 13 is generated.

Rotate Source, Count Actually, this is a group of four instructions containing RCL, RCR, ROL, ROR. Though these instructions work exactly the same way as in 8086, an additional mode of count is allowed. In 8086, it used to be either 1 or CL but in 80286 it can be an immediate count upto 31 (decimal). Even if it is above 31, only the lower order five bits are used as the count. Only the OF and CF flags are affected. If the CF is equal to MSB of the operand (source), the overflow flag is cleared, otherwise, it is set to 1. If the result is to be written in a write protected segment, a general protection error exception is generated. The same is generated, if an illegal memory reference is tried. If SS contains an illegal address, a stack fault exception is generated. In the real mode, the exception 13 is generated for the other usual reasons.

INS (INSB, INSW) This instruction reads a string of byte data or word from a variable port address specified only in DX. The fixed port address can be of 16-bits. No flags are affected by this instruction. The data string read by this instruction is automatically stored in memory at the address pointed by ES:DI, in the same sequence (at the behest of DF) in which they were read in from the addressed port. After execution, the DI is automatically advanced depending upon the direction flag DF, in the same way as the other string instructions. When the value of CPL is greater than that of IOPL, a general protection exception is generated. Also, if the ES:DI is in a write protected segment, the general protection exception is generated. Any reference to stack segment generates a stack fault exception.

Example 9.1

```
INSB ES[DI], DX.
```

OUTS (OUTSB/OUTSW) This instruction writes a byte or a word string from the memory location pointed to by DS:SI to a port pointed to by DX. All other parameters (including significance of DF) of this instruction are similar to the INS instruction. The SI is automatically incremented by 1 for byte and 2 for word operations.

Example 9.2

```
OUTS DX, DS:SI
OUT SB DX, DS:SI
OUT SW DX, OFFSET STRING
```

ENTER (Enter Procedure) This instruction prepares a stack structure for parameters of a procedure to be executed further. This instruction which is used by most of the structured high level languages requires two operands. The first operand specifies how many bytes of dynamic stack will be required for the procedure to be executed. The second operand specifies the nesting level of the routine within the program. The format of this instruction is given as follows.

```
ENTER Operand 1, Operand 2
```

No flags are affected by this instruction. The ENTER instruction determines the number of bytes to be copied into the new stack frame from the previous stack. If the operand 2 is zero, ENTER pushes BP, sets BP to SP and then subtracts the operand 1 from SP. A stack fault exception is generated, if stack segment limit overrun occurs. operand 1 may be a 16-bit data, while operand 2 may be upto 8-bits depending upon the nesting level.

LEAVE (Leave the Procedure) This instruction is generally used with high level languages to exit a procedure. This performs exactly the opposite operation to that of ENTER. This liberates all the procedure variables and sets BP to SP, returning all the registers to their original values before calling the procedure. The stack memory area used by the procedure is released. The old stack frame is popped back into BP, thus retrieving the original calling program stack. The RET instruction executed after LEAVE, returns the control to the calling program. This does not require any operand. If BP points to a location within the current stack segment, a stack fault exception arises.

BOUND (Check Index Against Bound) This instruction is used to check whether a signed array offset is within the limit defined for it by the starting and ending index. The operand 1 must be greater than or equal to the first operand (starting index) and less than or equal to the second operand (ending index). If these conditions are not met, an exception 5 is generated. The stack fault exception and general protection failure exception are generated for the obvious reasons. In the real address mode, if the second operand is a register, INT 6 is generated. If the second operand is at offset 0FFFDH or higher, INT13 is generated.

Example 9.3

```
BOUND BX, BLOCK
```

BLOCK is a memory block starting address containing four bytes, two bytes for the starting index and the other two for ending index.

CLTS (Clear Task Switch Flag) This instruction clears the task switched flag of the status flag word. This instruction is a privileged instruction to be executed at the level 0 by the operating system software. This instruction records every execution of WAIT and ESC and is trapped, if the MP flag and task switched flag are set. If the privilege level check fails, a general protection error exception is generated, in protected mode.

9.17.4 Instructions for Protection Control

LGDT/LIDT-(Load Global Descriptor/Interrupt Descriptor Table Register) These instructions respectively load 6 bytes from a memory block pointed to by the effective address of the operand into the global or interrupt descriptor table register. The first word is loaded into the LIMIT field of the descriptor table register. The next three bytes are loaded into the BASE field of the register and the remaining byte is ignored. These instructions are used by operating systems, to prepare the 80286 for protected mode.

Example 9.4

```
LGDT OPERAND
```

The general protection exception is generated, if the privilege level is not equal to 0. If operand is a register, invalid opcode exception is generated. Any invalid reference to the operand generates general protection error. Also stack fault exception may be generated for the usual reason.

LLDT (Load Local Descriptor Table Register) The LLDT instruction loads a local descriptor table register from a word operand that contains a selector (14-bit) pointing to a valid global descriptor table. If the global descriptor table has this local descriptor entry, the LDTR is loaded from the entry. This instruction is used by operating systems. No flags are affected. If the privilege level is not 0, a general protection error exception occurs. Also, if the GDT entry is not pointed to by the selector or if the GDT entry does not point to a valid LDT, a general protection error exception is generated. If the LDT descriptor is not present, a descriptor not present exception is generated. The general protection exception and stack fault exceptions are also generated for the usual reasons.

Example 9.5

```
LLDT BP
```

LMSW/SMSW (Load/Store Machine Status Word) This loads/stores the MSW from to the effective address of the operand. If the operand points to a write protected segment or if invalid memory reference is tried, a general protection error exception is generated. The stack fault exception is generated for unauthorised stack data accesses or stack segment limit overrun.

Example 9.6

```
LMSW BP; LOAD MSW FROM ADDRESS DS:BP
SMSW BP; STORE MSW TO ADDRESS ES:BP
```

SGDT/SIDT (Store Global/Interrut Descriptor Table Register) The instructions store either global interrupt descriptor table register contents to a 6 byte memory block pointed to by the effective address of the operand, in the same sequence as LGTD/ LIDT instructions do. No flags are affected. The exceptions generated are also the same as that for LGDT/LIDT instructions. If the operand is a register, undefined opcode exception is generated. If the word operand is at 0FFFFH, exception 13 is generated.

Example 9.7

```
SGDT Operand 1
SIDT Operand 2
```

LTR/STR (Load/Store Task Register from/to Memory or Register) These instructions load/store the contents of the task register from/to a 16-bit register or memory pointed to by the operand.

A general protection exception is generated, if there is an attempt of a write operation in a write protected segment or if an invalid memory reference is tried. A stack fault exception is generated for usual reasons.

Example 9.8

```
STR [5000H]
LTR [3000H]
```

VERR/VERW (Verify Read/Write Accesses) The VERR/VERW instructions determine whether the segment pointed to by a 16-bit register or a memory operand can be accessed from the current privilege level. This also determines whether the segment can be read or written to. If the segment is accessible, ZF is set to 1, else it is set to zero. The general protection error exception is generated for an invalid memory reference while the stack fault exception is generated for an invalid stack reference.

Example 9.9

```
VERR BP
VERW MEMORY
```

LSL (Load Segment Limit) This instruction loads the destination 'operand 2' that must be a register with a word that specifies the limit of the descriptor pointed to by the selector, i.e. operand 2, if it is accessible. The ZF is set to 1, if the operation is carried out successfully, else, ZF is cleared. A general protection exception and stack fault exceptions are generated for the usual reasons. If tried in the real mode, this instruction generates INT6.

Example 9.10

```
LSL   Reg, selector
LSL   Ax, Selector
```

LAR (Load Access Rights Byte) With this instruction, the access rights byte of the descriptor associated with the operand 2 as a selector is loaded into the higher byte of the operand 1 and the lower byte of the operand1 is set to 00. All the exceptions generated for this instruction, are similar to those for LSL instruction.

Example 9.11

```
LAR   Operand1, Operand2
LAR   Ax, 5000
```

ZF is set to 1, if the operation is successful, otherwise it is cleared. The loading takes place only if the current priviledge level and the requested privilege level of the selector support to access the descriptor.

ARPL (Adjust Requested Privilege Level of the Selector) The ARPL instruction enables the lower privileged routines to access higher privileged routines or data. Operand1 of ARPL is a 16-bit memory variable or register that contains a selector value. The operand 2 is a 16-bit register. If the RPL of operand 1 is less than the RPL field of operand 2, the ZF is set to 1 and the RPL of operand 1 is updated to match that of operand 2. Otherwise, ZF is reset to 0 without making any change to RPL of operand 1.

If a write protected segment is tried with a write operation or if an invalid memory reference is tried, a general protection exception is generated. Any invalid reference to stack generates a stack fault exception. INT 6 is generated in real address mode, if the execution is tried.

Example 9.12

```
ARPL    Operand1, Operand2
ARPL    BP, WORD
```

All the instructions of 80286, which were not available in 8086, were discussed in this section in significant details. With this, we conclude the topic on 80286. We proceed further with a discussion on 80287 that is a 80286 compatible math coprocessor.

9.18 80287 MATH COPROCESSOR

The 80287 is a numeric data coprocessor specially designed to operate with the processor 80286. The 80287 adds nearly 70 more instructions to the basic instruction set of 80286. These instructions mainly offer numeric processing capabilities to 80286 and are executed coherently by 80287 under the control of 80286. The 80287 may also be considered as an extension of 8087 that supports memory management. The 80287 offers an instruction set that supports integer, floating point, BCD, trigonometric and logarithmic calculations.

9.18.1 Architecture of 80287

The internal architecture of 80287 is shown in Fig. 9.31. The register set of 80287 is exactly the same as 8087, hence a detailed description of the register set has not been covered in this chapter.

The architecture of 80287 is divided into three sections, (a) bus control logic, (b) data interface and control unit and (c) floating point unit. The control logic provides and controls the interface between the internal 80287 bus and the 80286 bus via a data buffer. The data interface and control unit contains status and control words, TAG words and error pointers. The status word reflects the current status of 80287. The control word selects one of the processing options provided by it and is to be programmed by the CPU. The TAG word optimizes the NDP performance by maintaining a record of empty and non-empty register locations. It helps the exception handler to identify special values in the contents of the stack locations. The error pointer points to the source of exception (address of the instruction that generated the exception) generated. The instruction decoder and sequencer decodes and forwards the instructions for further execution by the floating point unit. The floating point unit is an actual processing section of the NDP. The data bus interface and data alignment and operand checking section checks the alignment and validity of the data. If any error is found, a suitable error exception is generated by the 80287. The eight 80-bit registers are used for storing operand data and are arranged as a stack. The data bus in floating point unit is of 84-bits, out of which the lower 68 bits are significant (mantissa) data bit, the next 16 bits are used for exponent. The exponential operand registers are used to store the operands in exponential form during the operation. The 80-bit registers maintain 80-bit operands required for 80287 operations. The barrel shifter arranges and presents the data to be shifted successively whenever required for the execution.

9.18.2 Status and Control Words

(a) Status Word This is a set of 16 flags which are modified depending upon the current status of 80287. The different flag definitions for the various flags are discussed as follows:

B Flag (D_{15}) The BUSY flag has the same status as ES flag. This is just for maintaining the compatibility with 8087. This is not at all related with the BUSY output of 80287.

TOP(D_{13}–D_{11}) These bits point to one of the eight stack registers as a stack top.

C_3, C_2, C_1 and C_0 (D_{14} and D_{10}–D_8) These condition code bits are similar to the flags of a CPU. These are modified depending upon the result of the execution of arithmetic instructions.

ES(D_7) Error summary bit is set, if an unmasked exception is generated. If this is set, the ERROR signal is activated.

SF (D_6) The stack flag is set, if the operation goes invalid due to stack overflow or underflow. If this is set, and $C_1 = 1$, the stack has overflown and if this is set and $C_1 = 0$, stack has underflown.

Exception Flags (D_5–D_0) These exception flags are described in the Fig. 9.31. These are used to show the generation of an exception while 80287 is executing.

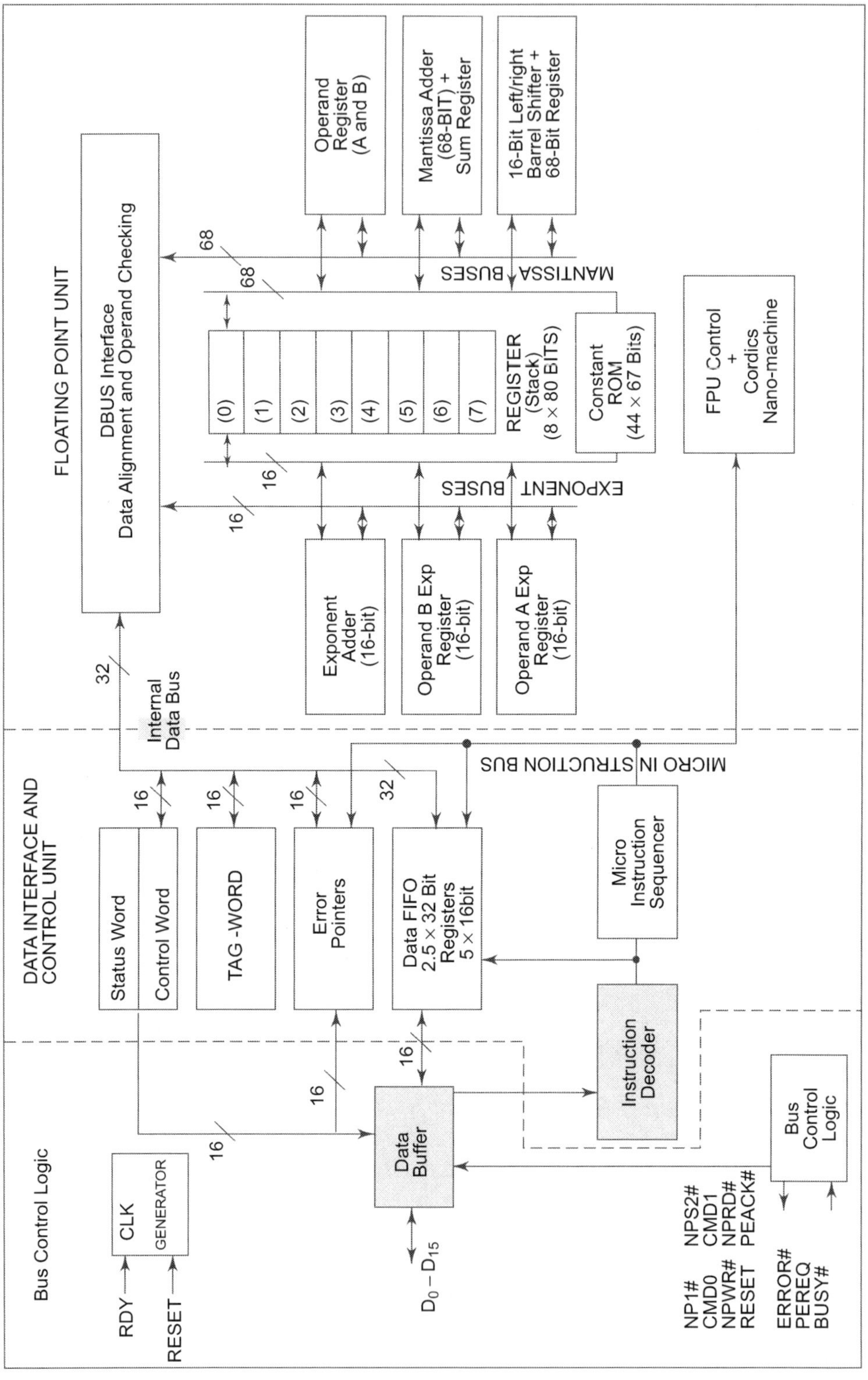

Fig. 9.31 *Internal Architecture of 80287 (Intel Corp.)*

The status word of 80287 is shown in the Fig. 9.32. This can also be written by using FLDENV or FRSTOR instructions.

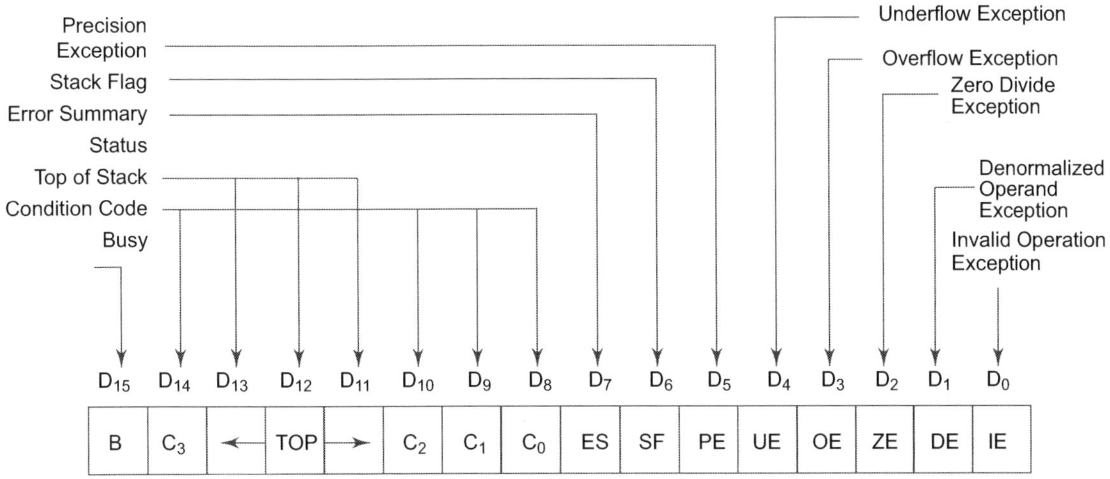

Notes:

1. ES is set if any unmasked exception bit is set, cleared otherwise.
2. See Table 8.1 for condition code interpretation.
3. TOP Values
   000 = Register 0 is Top of Stack
   001 = Register 1 is Top of Stack
   •
   •
   •
   111 = Register 7 is Top of Stack

Fig. 9.32 *Status Word of 80287 (Intel Corp.)*

(b) Control Word The control word is used to select one of the processing options amongst the ones provided by 80287. The various bits of the control word are discussed as follows:

Masking Bits (D_0–D_5) These are the six masking bits used to mask the six exceptions shown in the status register. If this is '1', the respective exception is masked.

Precision Control bits (D_8–D_9) These are used to set the internal precision of 80287.

These bits affect ADD, SUB, DIV, MUL and SQRT results. For other instructions the precision is decided by the opcode or the extended precision format.

Rounding Control Bits (D_{10}–D_{11}) These bits are used to set rounding or chopping, as specified in IEEE standard. Rounding control bits affect only the instructions which perform rounding after the operation, for example, in arithmetic and transcendental instructions.

Infinity Control Bit (D_{12}) Infinity control bit is meaningless in case of 80287 TMXL but can be programmed for compatibility with 80287. This is initialized to zero after reset.

The control word is shown in Fig. 9.33 with the definitions in short.

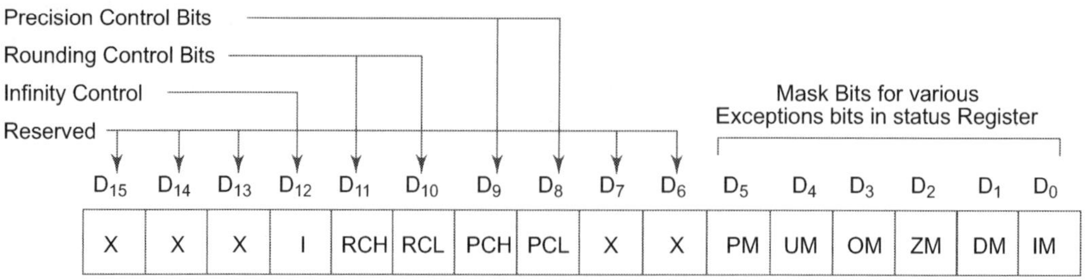

RCHRCL			PCH	PCL		
0	0	-Round to nearest even	0	0	24-bit (Single)
0	1	-Round Down (to – ¥)	0	1	Reserved
1	0	-Round Up (to + ¥)	1	0	53-bit (Double)
1	1	-Truncate towards zero (Chop)	1	1	64-bit (Extended)

Fig. 9.33 *Control Word of 80287 (Intel Corp.)*

9.18.3 Signal Descriptions of 80287

Figure 9.34 shows the pin configuration of 80287, followed by its pin descriptions:

D_0–D_{15} This is a 16-bit data bus to be connected with the 80286 data bus.

CLK This is an input pin that accepts the clock required for deriving the basic system timings.

RESET This is a reset input pin. A high on this pin resets 80287.

$\overline{NPWR}$ Numeric Processsor Write active-low input pin, if activated, enables a data transfer from 80286 to 80287.

$\overline{NPRD}$ Numeric Processor Read active-low input pin, if activated, enables a data transfer from 80287 to 80286.

$\overline{NPS_1}$ and NPS_2 Numeric Processor Select input lines indicate that the CPU is performing an escape operation and enables 80287 to execute the next instruction. The NPS_1 and NPS_2 pins are active-low and active-high respectively.

CMD_0 and CMD_1 The CPU uses this active-high input pins along with select pins to control the operations of 80287.

ERROR The error status active-high output pin represents the ES bit of the internal status register. If this is active, it indicates that an exception has occurred.

This is to be connected with the ERROR pin of 80286.

BUSY This active-low output pin indicates to the CPU that it is busy with the execution of an instruction. This is connected to the $\overline{TEST}$ pin of 80286.

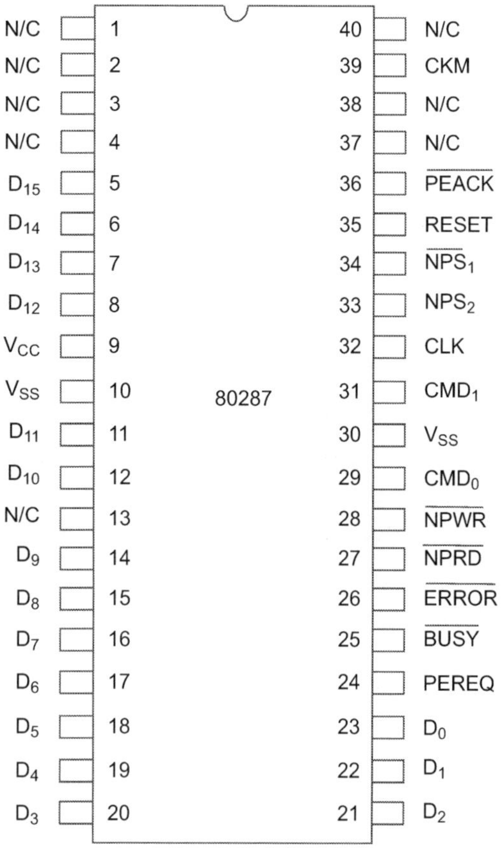

Fig. 9.34 *Pin Configuration of 80287 (Intel Corp.)*

PEREQ (Processor Extension Request) This active-high output pin indicates to the 80286 that the NDP is ready for data transfer.

$\overline{\text{PEACK}}$ **(Processor Extension Acknowledge)** This active-low input pin is used by the CPU to acknowledge a receipt of a valid PEREQ signal.

CKM (Clock Mode) If clock mode input pin is held high, the CLK input is directly used for deriving the internal timings. Else, it is divided by two. This must be stable at reset to decide the mode of operation properly.

Note that, as the NDP is not supposed to perform any fetch operation, it does not have any address line.

9.18.4 Interface with 80286

The 80287 establishes its interface with an 80286 system using a set of 10 pins, namely PEREQ, PEACK#, BUSY#, ERROR#, $\overline{\text{NPRD}}$#, $\overline{\text{NPWR}}$#, NPS1#, NPS0#, CMD0 and CMD1. The functions of all these pins have already been explained, while describing the signal description section of this chapter. A typical interface of 80287 with 80286 system is shown in Fig. 9.35.

The 80287 synchronises its operation with 80286. The 80286 activates $\overline{\text{NSP1}}$# and NSP2# signals to start the bus cycle of 80287. In the same clock period in which the $\overline{\text{NSP1}}$# and NPS2# are activated, the NDP checks $\overline{\text{NPRD}}$# and $\overline{\text{NPWR}}$# signals to check whether it is a read or write cycle. Also it checks CMD_0 and CMD_1 to decide whether it is an opcode, operand or control/status register transfer. The NDP activates its BUSY output after it receives a valid read or write command. The PEREQ (Processor Extension Request) signal is used by 80287 to inform the CPU that it is ready for a data transfer. Here the processor or extension refers to the coprocessor 80287. When the data transfer is over, the CPU activates $\overline{\text{PEACK}}$#(Processor Extension Acknowledge) pin, which results in deactivating the PEREQ# pin by 80287.

9.18.5 Data Types Supported by 80287

The 80287 supports, in all, seven data types. The data operands are stored in memory with the least significant byte at the lowest memory address and so on. The operands are referred to by this lowest address. Instructions which read data from memory automatically convert them in the standard formats acceptable to 80287. The standard data formats of 80287 are shown in Table 9.13.

9.18.6 Instruction Set Summary

The instructions of 80287 fit in one of the five formats shown below. All these instructions are 2-byte instructions. The CPU, after its fetch operation, identifies these instructions from the five most significant bits (ESCAPE code) of the first byte. The same addressing modes as that of 80286 can be used to specify the memory operands.

The definitions and significances of the MOD and R/M fields are similar to that of 8086. The DISP field is optional and depends on the values of MOD and R/M in the same way as 8086. The instruction formats available in 80287 are listed as follows. OP represents the opcode bit field. MF field represents the memory format of the operands. The displacement is optional in the first two formats.

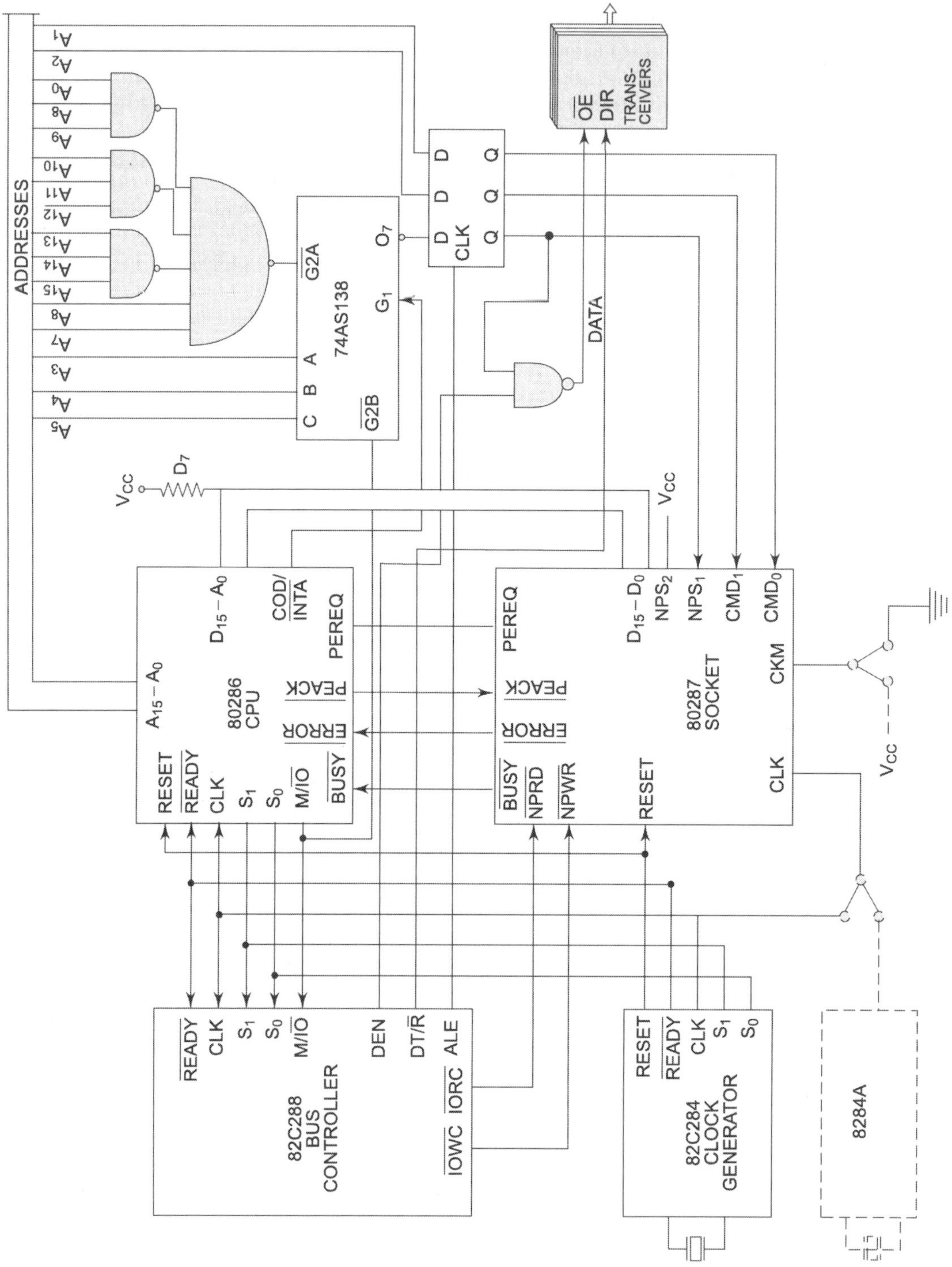

Fig. 9.35 *Interface between 80286 and 80287 (Intel Corp.)*

Table 9.13 *Data Formats of 80287 (Intel Corp.)*

S.NO.	Format	Range	Size	Definition	1st byte	Last byte
1.	Word Integer	$\pm 10^4$	16 bits		D_{15} ———— D_0 2's complement form	
2.	Short Integer	$\pm 10^9$	32 bits		D_{31} ———— D_0 2's complement form	
3.	Long Integer	$\pm 10^{18}$	64 bits		D_{63} ———— D_0 2's complement form	
4.	Single Precision	$\pm 10^{\pm 38}$	24 bits	D_{31} Sign	D_{30} — D_{24} Biased Exponent	D_{23} — D_0 significand
5.	Double Precision	$\pm 10^{\pm 308}$	53 bits	D_{63} Sign	D_{62} — D_{53} Biased Exponent	D_{52} — D_0 significand
6.	Extended Precision	$\pm 10^{\pm 4932}$	64 bits	D_{79} Sign	D_{78} — D_{64} Biased Exponent	D_{71} — D_0 significand
7.	Packed BCD	$\pm 10^{18}$	18 Digits	D_{79} Sign	D_{78} — D_{72} (x)	D_{71} — D_0 (18 digits) four bits per digit

1.

D_{15}——D_{11}	$D_{10}D_9$	D_8	D_7D_6	D_5	D_4D_3	$D_2D_1D_0$	Optional Displace
11011	OPA	1	MOD	1	OPB	R/M	

2.

D_{15}——D_{11}	$D_{10}D_9$	D_8	D_7D_6	$D_5D_4D_3$	$D_2D_1D_0$	Optional Displace
11011	MF	OPA	MOD	OPB	R/M	

MF(memory format)
00–32 bit real
01–32 bit integer
10–64 bit real
11–64 bit integer

OPA and OPB are two parts of the opcode.

3.

D_{15}——D_{11}	D_{10}	D_9	D_8	D_7	D_6	$D_5D_4D_3$	$D_2D_1D_0$
11011	d	P	OPA	1	1	OPB	ST(i)

d-destination
if d = 0, destination is ST (0) (0th stack register).
if d = 1, destination is ST (i) (ith stack register).
Here D_3 is the reserved bit R.
if R XOR d = 0, the format is—Destination Opcode Source
if R XOR d = 1, the format is—Source Opcode Destination
P—Pop stack
if P = 0, Don't pop stack.

if P = 1, Pop stack.
ST (i) - 000 to 111 for stack top ST(0) to ST(7)

4.

D_{15}—D_{11}	D_{10}	D_9	D_8	D_7	D_6	D_5	D_4—D_0
11011	0	0	1	1	1	1	OPCODE

5.

D_{15}—D_{11}	D_{10}	D_9	D_8	D_7	D_6	D_5	D_4—D_0
11011	0	1	1	1	1	1	OPCODE

In all the above formats, the code 11011 corresponding to bits D_{15}-D_{11} informs the CPU to execute an ESCAPE sequence and initiate a NDP bus cycle.

The complete instruction set summary of 80287TMXL is given in Table 9.14.

Table 9.14 *80287 XM TL Instruction Set Summary*

Intel 287^{TM} XL MCP Extension to the CPU's Instruction Set

Instruction	*Encoding*			*Clock Count Range*			
	Byte 0	*Byte 1*	*Optional Bytes 2-3*	*32-Bit Real*	*32-Bit Integer*	*64-Bit Real*	*16-Bit Integer*
DATA TRANSFER							
FLD-Load							
Integer/real memory to ST(0)	ESC MP 1	MOD 000 R/M	SIB/DISP	36	61-68	45	61-65
Long Integer memory to ST(0)	ESC 111	MOD 101 R/M	SIB/DISP			76-87	
Extended real memory to ST(0)	ESC 011	MOD 101 R/M	SIB/DISP			48	
BCD memory to ST(0)	ESC 111	MOD 100 R/M	SIB/DISP			270-279	
ST(i) memory to ST(0)	ESC 001	11000 ST(i)				21	
FST-Store							
ST(0) to Integer/real memory	ESC MF 1	MOD 010 R/M	SIB/DISP	51	86-100	56	88-101
ST(0) to ST(i)	ESC MF1	MOD 010 R/M				18	
FSTP-Store and Pop							
ST(0) to Integer/real memory	ESC MF 1	MOD 011 R/M	SIB/DISP	51	86-100	56	88-101
ST(0) to Long Integer memory	ESC 111	MOD 111 R/M	SIB/DISP			91-108	
ST(0) to extend real	ESC 011	MOD 111 R/M	SIB/DISP			61	
ST(0) to BCD memory	ESC 111	MOD 110 R/M	SIB/DISP			520-542	
ST(0) to ST(i)	ESC 101	11001 ST(i)				19	
FXCH-Exchange							
ST(i) to ST(0)	ESC 001	11001 ST(i)				25	
COMPARISON							
FCOM-Compare							
Integer/real memory to ST(0)	ESC MF 0	MOD 010 R/M	SIB/DISP	42	72-79	51	71-75
ST(i) to ST(0)	ESC 000	11010 ST(i)				31	

(*Contd.*)

Table 9.14 (*Contd.*)

Instruction	*Encoding*			*Clock Count Range*			
	Byte 0	*Byte 1*	*Optional Bytes 2-3*	*32-Bit Real*	*32-Bit Integer*	*64-Bit Real*	*16-Bit Integer*
FCOMP-Compare and pop							
Integer/real memory to ST	ESC MF 0	MOD 011 R/M	SIB/DISP	42	72-79	51	71-77
ST(i) to ST(0)	ESC 000	11011 ST(i)			33		
FCOMPP-Compare and pop twice							
ST(i) to ST(0)	ESC 110	1101 1001			33		
FTST-Test ST(0)	ESC 001	1110 0100			35		
FUCOM-Unordered Compare	ESC 101	11100 ST(i)			31		
FUCOMP-Unordered Compare							
and pop	ESC 101	11101 ST(i)			33		
FUCOMPP-Unordered Compare							
and pop twice	ESC 010	0110 1001			33		
FXAM-Examine ST(0)	ESC 001	11100101			37-45		
CONTANTS							
FLDZ-Load + 0.0 into ST(0)	ESC 001	1110 1110			27		
FLD1-Load + 1.0 into ST(0)	ESC 001	1110 1000			31		
FLDP1-Load pi into ST(0)	ESC 001	1110 1001			47		
FLDL2T-Load $Log_2(10)$ into ST(0)	ESC001	11101001			47		
CONSTANTS (Compared)							
FLDL2E-Load $Log_2(e)$ into ST(0)		ESC 001	1110 1010		47		
FLDLG2-Load $Log_{10}(2)$ into ST(0)		ESC 001	1110 1100		48		
FLDLG2-Load $Log_e(2)$ into ST(0)		ESC 001	1110 1101		48		
ARITHMETIC							
FADD-Add							
Integer/real memory with ST(0)	ESC MF 0	MOD 000 R/M	SIB/DISP	40-48	73-789	49-79	71-85
ST(i) and ST(0)	ESCdP 0	11000 ST(i)			30-38		
FSUB-Subtract							
Integral/real memory to ST(0)	ESC MF 0	MOD 10 R R/M	SIB/DISP	40-48	73-96	49-77	71-83
ST(i) and ST(0)	ESC d P0	1110 R R/M			33-41		
FMUL-Multiply							
ST(0) to Integer/real memory	ESC MF 0	MOD 001 R/M	SIB/DISP	43-51	77-88	52-77	76-87
ST(i) and ST(0)	ESC d P0	1100 1 R/M			25-53		
FDIV-Divided							
ST(0) to integer/real memory	ESC MF 0	MOD 11R R/M	SIB/DISP	105	135-143	114	136-140
ST(i) and ST(0)	ESC d P0	1111R R/M			95		

(*Contd.*)

Table 9.14 *(Contd.)*

Instruction	*Encoding*			*Clock Count Range*			
	Byte 0	*Byte 1*	*Optional Bytes 2-3*	*32-Bit Real*	*32-Bit Integer*	*64-Bit Real*	*16-Bit Integer*
FSQRTI-Square root	ESC 001	1111 1010				129-136	
FSCALE-Scale ST(0) by ST(1)	ESC 001	1111 1101				74-95	
FPREM-Partial remainder of ST(0) + ST(1)	ESC 001	1111 1000				81-162	
FPREM1-Partial remainder of (IEEE)	ESC 001	1111 010				102-198	
FRNDINT-Round ST(0) to integer	ESC 001	1111 1100				73-87	
FXTRACT-Extract components of ST(0)	ESC 001	1111 0100				75-83	
FABS-Absolute value of ST(0)	ESC 001	1110 0001				29	
FCHS-Change sign of ST(0)	ESC 001	1110 0000				31-37	
TRANSCENDENTAL							
FCCS-cosine of ST(0)	ESC 001	1111 1111				130-779	
FPTAN-Partial tangent of ST(0)	ESC 001	1111 0010				198-504	
FPATAN-Partial arctangent	ESC 001	1111 0011				321-494	
FSIN-sine of ST(0)	ESC 001	1111 1110				124-678	
FSINCOS-sine and cosine of ST(0)	ESC 001	1111 1011				201-815	
F2XM1-2ST(0) - 1	ESC 001	1111 0000				215-483	
FYL2X-ST(1) * $\log_2$(ST(0))	ESC 001	1111 0001				127-545	
FYL2XP1-ST(1)*$\log_2$(ST(0) + 1.0)	ESC 001	1111 1001				264-554	
PROCESSOR CONTROL							
FINIT-Initialize MCP	ESC 001	1110 0011				25	
FSETPM-Set protected mode	ESC 001	1110 0100				12	
FRSETPM-Reset protected mode	ESC 001	1111 0100				12	
FSTSW AX-Stone status word	ESC 111	1110 0000				18	
FLDCW-Load control word	ESC 001	MOD 101 R/M	SIB/DISP			33	
FSTCW-Store control word	ESC 101	MOD 111 R/M	SIB/DISP			18	
FSTSW-Store status word	ESC 101	MOD 111 R/M	SIB/DISP			18	
FCLEX-Clear exception	ESC 011	1110 0010				8	
FSTENV-Store environment	ESC 001	MOD 110 R/M	SIB/DISP			192-193	
FLDENV-Load environment	ESC 001	MOD 100 R/M	SIB/DISP			85	
FSAVE-Save state	ESC 101	MOD 110 R/M	SIB/DISP			521-522	
FRSTOR-Restore state	ESC 101	MOD 100 R/M	SIB/DISP			396	

(Contd.)

Table 9.14 *(Contd.)*

Instruction	*Encoding*			*Clock Count Range*			
	Byte 0	*Byte 1*	*Optional Bytes 2-3*	*32-Bit Real*	*32-Bit Integer*	*64-Bit Real*	*16-Bit Integer*
FINSCTP-Increment stack pointer	ESC 001	1111 0111				28	
FDECSTP-Decrement stack	ESC 001	1111 0110)				29	
FFREE-Free ST(i)	ESC 101	1100 0ST(i)				25	
FNOP-No operations	ESC 001	1101 0000				19	

SUMMARY

This chapter starts with an introduction of 80286 as a processor with memory management capabilities. The signal description and architecture of 80286 have been discussed along with the functional description of the architecture in necessary details. Several architectural features of 80286 like register set, addressing modes and interrupt structure are elaborated further. The two operating modes of 80286, viz. real address mode and protected virtual address mode have been discussed in the light of their special features like effective address formation and memory management. The memory management feature that offers the capability of addressing a large amount of virtual memory to the advanced processors have been studied further in significant depth. The concepts of privilege and protection are explained in details so as to introduce the readers with these ideas. To conclude the topic on 80286, the interfacing technique, basic bus operations, HOLD and interrupt acknowledge cycles have been discussed along with the additional instructions available with 80286.

Finally, the 80286 compatible math coprocessor, 80287 has been introduced with its architecture, status and control word, data types and the instruction set summary. This chapter provides a complete insight on the principles, architecture and operations of an 80286-287 based system.

EXERCISES

9.1 Explain the concept of virtual memory.
9.2 Explain swapping in and swapping out.
9.3 Draw and discuss the internal block diagram of 80286.
9.4 Draw and discuss the flag register of 80286.
9.5 Draw and discuss the machine control word of 80286.
9.6 Draw and discuss register organisation of 80286.
9.7 What are the different interrupts available in 80286?
9.8 Discuss the following signals available in 80286.

(i) PEREQ (ii) $\overline{\text{PEACK}}$ (iii) CODE/$\overline{\text{INTA}}$ (iv) CAP
(v) $\overline{\text{BUSY}}$ (vi) $\overline{\text{ERROR}}$

9.9 What are the salient features of 80286 in real address mode?
9.10 Explain the physical address formation in real address mode.
9.11 What are the salient features of protected virtual address mode?
9.12 Explain physical address formation in protected virtual address mode.

9.13 What do you mean by a descriptor? Draw and discuss the structure of a general 80286 descriptor.
9.14 Discuss different types of descriptors supported by 80286 and their typical functions.
9.15 What are the different exceptions which may be generated in 80286?
9.16 How many descriptors can be accessed at the most by 80286? How much memory can be addressed by a descriptor? Justify the virtual memory addressing capability of 80286.
9.17 Explain the following terms.
  (i) Task Privilege (ii) Descriptor Privilege
  (iii) Selector Privilege
9.18 What is the use of privilege types and the privilege check mechanism?
9.19 What do you mean by boundary testing instructions? What is their use?
9.20 What do you mean by a task switch operation? Explain in details.
9.21 How do you prepare the 80286 for entering into PVAM? How do you enter PVAM?
9.22 What are the different data types supported by 80286?
9.23 What are the different addressing modes supported by 80286?
9.24 Draw and discuss a minimum system of 80286.
9.25 Draw and discuss basic read, write and fetch cycles of 80286.
9.26 Explain execution of all the additional instructions of 80286 over 8086 with one example each.
9.27 Enlist the priority of bus usage in 80286.
9.28 Draw and discuss the architecture of 80287.
9.29 Enlist the different data types supported by 80287.
9.30 Enlist different instruction formats of 80287.
9.31 Draw and discuss the control and status words of 80287.
9.32 Draw and discuss the interface between 80286 and 80287.
9.33 Explain the function of the following signals of 80287.
  (i) CKM (ii) CMD0 and CMD1
  (iii) NPWR (iv) NPRD
  (v) NPS_1 and NPS_2

10 80386–80387 and 80486—The 32-Bit Processors

INTRODUCTION

In the previous chapter, we presented the concepts of memory management, privilege and protection around 80286, which was the first processor to incorporate these ideas into it. The 16-bit word length of 80286 put limitations on its operating speed. However, the development of advanced applications and technology demanded high speed machines, with a more powerful instruction set and all the above features of 80286. Also as we have noted in Chapter 9, although 80286 can be operated in both real and protected virtual mode, the procedure of switching from real to protected mode involves a lot of overheads. In the due course of time, the semiconductor technology could support the fabrication of a CPU with a 32-bit word size and higher operating frequency, resulting in a higher speed of operation. Thus the 32-bit processor 80386 was born. In the first 32-bit processor 80386, designers have tried to overcome the limitations of 80286.

The 80387, an 80386 compatible math coprocessor, supports higher precision numerical operations with its extended word size of 32-bits. The 80387 executes the allotted task hand in hand with 80386 to support its memory management and protection capabilities, as if it is an integral part of the host 80386. Thus the couplet 80386–80387 provides a high speed processing environment with a number of advanced features and capabilities.

Further, the 80486DX, launched by Intel, combines all the features of 80386 along with the numerical processing capabilities of 80387. It does not need any external mathematical data processor to support complicated mathematical calculations. In fact, the mathematical data processor is already built into it.

This chapter presents an overview of the new architectural and operational features of 80386–80387 and 80486.

10.1 SALIENT FEATURES OF 80386DX

The 80386DX is a 32-bit processor that supports, 8-bit/16-bit/32-bit data operands. The 80386 instruction set is upward compatible with all its predecessors. The 80386 can run 8086 applications under protected mode in its virtual 8086 mode of operation. With its 32-bit address bus, the 80386 can address up to 4 Gbytes of physical memory. The physical memory is organised in terms of segments of 4 Gbytes size at maximum. The 80386 CPU supports 16K(16384) number of segments and thus the total virtual memory space is 4 Gbytes × 16K = 64 terrabytes. The memory management section of 80386 supports the virtual memory, paging and four levels of protection, maintaining full compatibility with 80286. The concept of paging which is introduced in 80386, enables it to organise the available physical memory into pages of size 4 Kbytes each, under the segmented memory. The 80386 can be supported by 80387 for mathematical data processing. It also offers a set of total eight debug registers DR_0–DR_7 for hardware debugging and control. The 80386 has an on-chip address translation cache. The 80386 is available in another version—80386SX—which has identical architecture as 80386DX with the difference that it has only a 16-bit data bus and 24-bit address bus. This low cost, low power version of 80386 may be used in a number of applications. 80386DX is available in a 132-pin grid array package and has 20 MHz and 33 MHz versions.

10.2 ARCHITECTURE AND SIGNAL DESCRIPTIONS OF 80386

The architecture of 80386 is shown in Fig. 10.1(a) along with all the internal details.

The internal architecture of 80386 is divided into three sections viz., *central processing unit, memory management unit* and *bus interface unit*. The central processing unit is further divided into *execution unit* and *instruction unit*. The execution unit has eight general purpose and eight special purpose registers which are either used for handling data or calculating offset addresses. The instruction unit decodes the opcode bytes received from the 16-byte instruction code queue and arranges them into a 3-instruction decoded-instruction queue, after decoding them so as to pass it to the control section for deriving the necessary control signals. The barrel shifter increases the speed of all shift and rotate operations. The multiply/divide logic implements the bit-shift-rotate algorithms to complete the operations in minimum time. Even 32-bit multiplications can be executed within one microsecond by the multiply/divide logic.

The Memory Management Unit (MMU) consists of a *segmentation unit* and a *paging unit*. The segmentation unit allows the use of two address components, viz. segment and offset for relocability and sharing of code and data. The segmentation unit allows a maximum size of 4 Gbytes segments. The paging unit organizes the physical memory in terms of pages of 4 Kbytes size each. The paging unit works under the control of the segmentation unit, i.e. each segment is further divided into pages. The virtual memory is also organized in terms of segments and pages by the memory management unit.

The segmentation unit provides a four level protection mechanism for protecting and isolating the system's code and data from those of the application program. The paging unit converts linear addresses into physical addresses. The control and attribute PLA checks the privileges at the page level. Each of the pages maintains the paging information of the task. The limit and attribute PLA checks segment limits and attributes at segment level to avoid invalid accesses to code and data in the memory segments.

The *bus control unit* has a prioritizer to resolve the priority of the various bus requests. This controls the access of the bus. The *address driver* drives the bus enable and address signals A_0–A_{31}. The *pipeline* and *dynamic bus sizing units* handle the related control signals. The *data buffers* interface the internal data bus with the system bus.

Pin diagram of 80386, as seen from the pin side, is shown in Fig. 10.1(b).

The signal descriptions of 80386 are briefly presented in the following text.

CLK This input pin provides the basic system clock timing for the operation of 80386.

D_0–D_{31} These 32 lines act as bidirectional data bus during different access cycles.

A_{31}–A_2 These are the upper 30 bits of the 32-bit address bus.

BE_0# to BE_3# The 32-bit data bus supported by 80386 and the memory system of 80386 can be viewed as a 4-byte wide memory access mechanism. The four byte enable lines, BE_0# to BE_3#, may be used for enabling

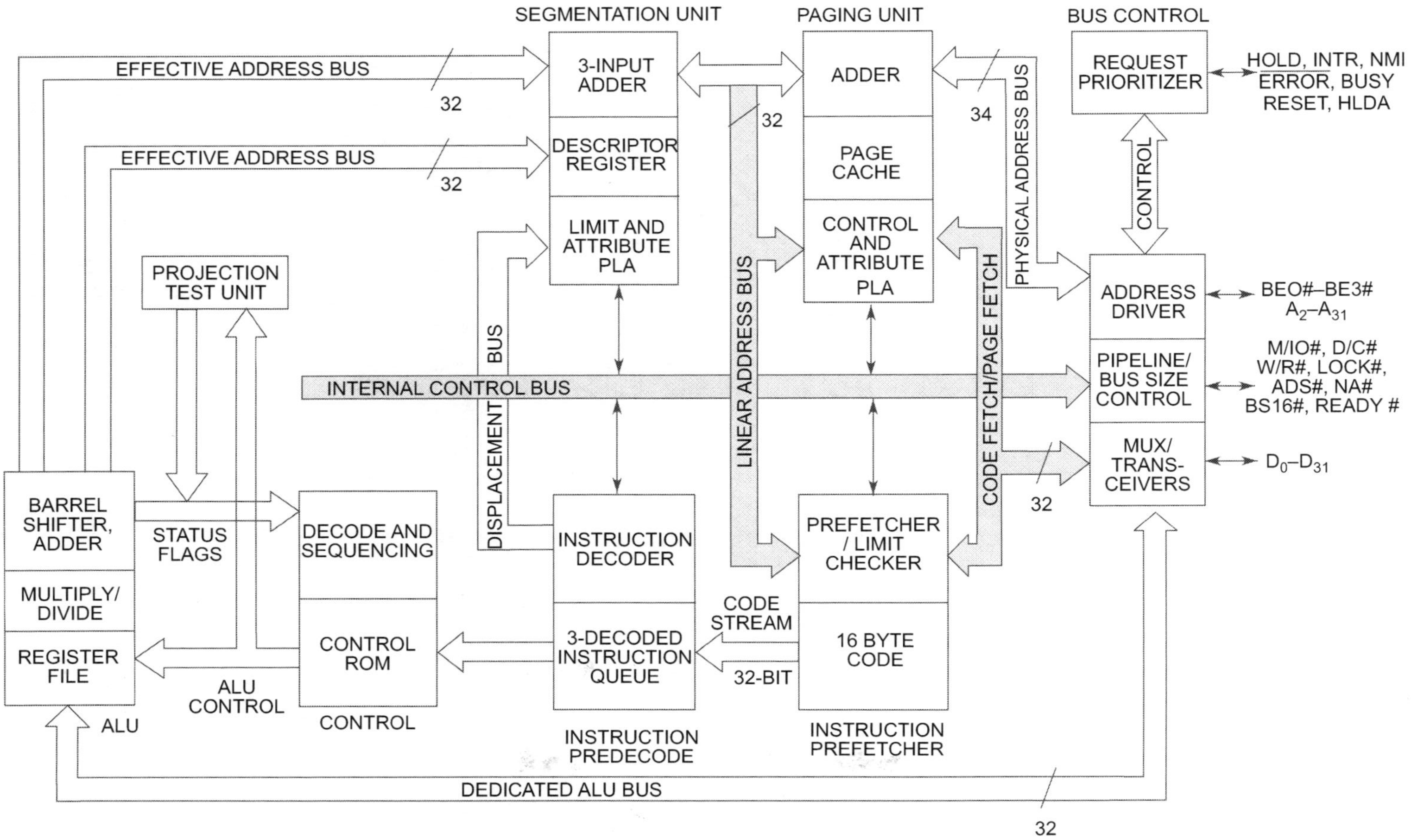

Fig. 10.1(a) *80386 Architecture*

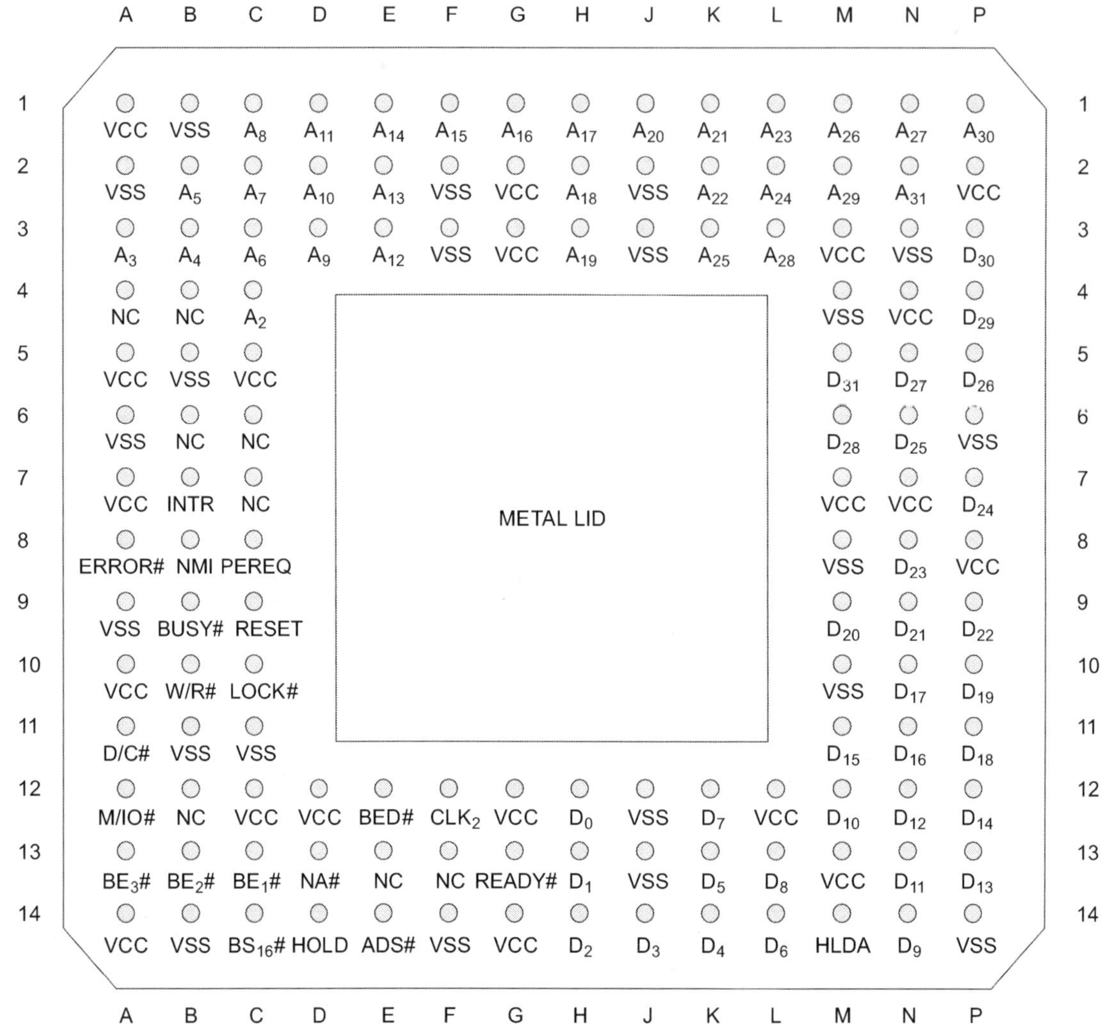

Fig. 10.1(b) *Pin Diagram of 80386 (Intel Corp.)*

these four banks. Using these four enable signal lines, the CPU may transfer 1byte/2bytes/3bytes or 4bytes of data simultaneously.

W/R# The write/read output distinguishes the write and read cycles from one another.

D/C# This data/control output pin distinguishes between a data transfer cycle from a machine control cycle like interrupt acknowledge.

M/IO# This output pin differentiates between the memory and I/O cycles.

LOCK# The LOCK# output pin enables the CPU to prevent the other bus masters (like coprocessors) from gaining the control of the system bus.

ADS# The address status output pin indicates that the address bus and bus cycle definition pins (W/R#, D/C#, M/IO#, BE_0#–BE_3) are carrying the respective valid signals. The 80386 does not have any ALE signal and so this signal may be used for latching the address to external latches.

NA# The next address input pin, if activated, allows address pipelining, during 80386 bus cycles.

READY# The ready signal indicates to the CPU that the previous bus cycle has been terminated and the bus is ready for the next cycle. This signal is used to insert WAIT states in a bus cycle and is useful for interfacing of slow devices with the CPU.

BS_{16}# The bus size-16 input pin allows the interfacing of 16-bit devices with the 32-bit wide 80386 data bus. Successive 16-bit bus cycles may be executed to read a 32-bit data from a peripheral.

HOLD The bus hold input pin enables the other bus masters to gain control of the system bus if it is asserted.

HLDA The bus hold acknowledge output indicates that a valid bus hold request has been received and the bus has been relinquished by the CPU.

BUSY# The busy input signal indicates to the CPU that the coprocessor is busy with the allotted task.

ERROR# The error input pin indicates to the CPU that the coprocessor has encountered an error while executing its instruction.

PEREQ The processor extension request output signal indicates to the CPU to fetch a data word for the coprocessor.

INTR INTR interrupt pin is a maskable interrupt input, that can be masked using the IF of the flag register.

NMI A valid request signal at the non-maskable interrupt request input pin internally generates a non-maskable interrupt of type 2.

RESET A high at this input pin suspends the current operation and restarts the execution from the starting location.

N/C No connection pins are expected to be left open while connecting the 80386 in the circuit.

V_{cc} These are system power supply lines.

V_{ss} These are return lines for the power suply.

10.3 REGISTER ORGANISATION OF 80386

The 80386 has eight 32-bit general purpose registers which may even be used either as 8-bit or 16-bit registers. A 32-bit register, known as an extended register, is represented by the register name with prefix E. For example, a 32-bit register corresponding to AX is EAX, similarly that corresponding to BX is EBX etc. The AX now represents the lower of the 32-bit register EAX. While AH and AL have the same meaning as in the case of 8086. Similarly, the registers BX, CX and DX have their 8-bit, 16-bit and 32-bit representations.

The 16-bit registers BP, SP, SI and DI in the architecture of 8086, are now available with their extended size of 32 bits and are named as EBP, ESP, ESI and EDI. However, the names BP, SP, SI and DI represent the lower 16-bits of their 32-bit counterparts, and can be used as independent 16-bit registers.

The six segment registers available in 80386 are CS, SS, DS, ES, FS and GS. The CS and SS are the code and the stack segment registers respectively, while DS, ES, FS and GS are the four data segment registers. The use of these segment registers will be clear when we study the physical address formation in different modes. A 16-bit Instruction Pointer IP, is available along with its 32-bit counterpart EIP, and both serve their conventional functions as per requirement. The 16-bit or lower size registers are used by 16-bit addressing, but the 32-bit addressing modes may use all the register widths, i.e. 8, 16 or 32 bits.

Flag Register of 80386 The flag register of 80386 is a 32-bit register. Out of the 32 bits, Intel has reserved bits D_{18} to D_{31}, D_{15}, D_5 and D_3, while D_1 is always set at 1. The lower 15 bits (D_0–D_{14}) of this flag register are exactly the same as the 80286 flag registers, right from their position to the corresponding functions. Only two extra new flags are added to the 80286 flag register to derive the flag register of 80386. These are the VM and RF flags.

VM-Virtual Mode Flag If this flag is set, the 80386 enters the virtual 8086 mode within the protected mode. This is to be set only when the 80386 is in protected mode. In this mode, if any privileged instruction is executed an exception 13 is generated. This bit can be set using the IRET instruction or any task switch operation only in the protected mode.

RF-Resume Flag This flag is used with the debug register breakpoints. It is checked at the starting of every instruction cycle and if it is set, any debug fault is ignored during the instruction cycle. The RF is automatically reset after successful execution of every instruction, except for the IRET and POPF instructions. Also, it is not cleared automatically after the successful execution of JMP, CALL and INT instructions causing a task switch. These instructions are used to set the RF to the value specified by the memory data available at the stack.

IOPL Flag bits indicate the privilege level of the current IO operations.

Figure 10.2(a) shows the general and special purpose registers of 80386. Figure 10.2(b) shows the flag register of 80386.

Segment Descriptor Registers The segment descriptor registers of 80386 are not available for programmers, rather, they are internally used to store the descriptor information, like attributes, limit and base addresses of segments. The six segment registers have corresponding six 73-bit descriptor registers. Each of them contains 32-bit base address, 32-bit base limit and 9-bit attributes as shown in Table 10.1. These are automatically loaded when the corresponding segment registers are loaded with selectors.

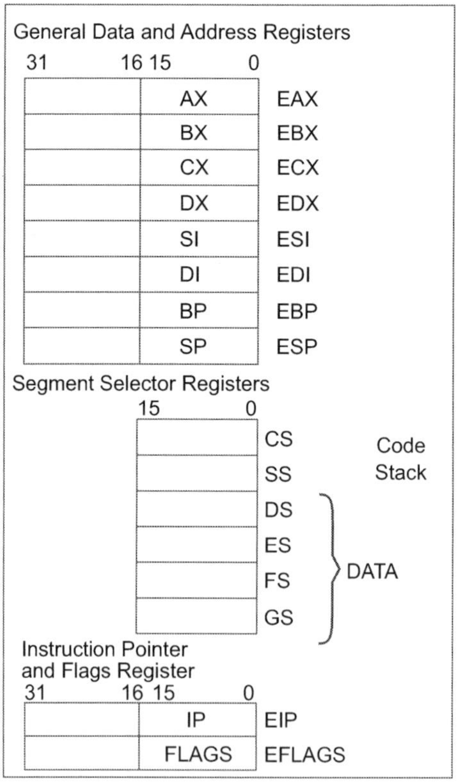

Fig. 10.2(a) *Registers Bank of 80386 (Intel Corp.)*

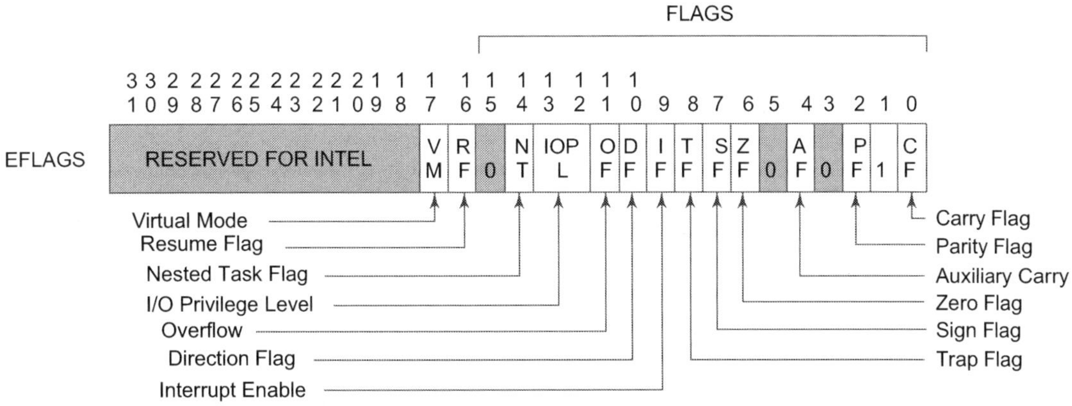

Note: 0 indicates Intel reserved

Fig. 10.2(b) *Flag Register of 80386 (Intel Corp.)*

Table 10.1 *80386 Segment and the Corresponding Descriptor Registers (Intel Corp.)*

Segment Registers 15 0		*Descriptor Registers (Loaded Automatically)* Physical Base Address	Segment Limit	Other Segment Attributes from Descriptor		
Selector	CS-				—	
Selector	SS-			—		—
Selector	DS-			—	—	—
Selector	ES-			—	—	—
Selector	FS-			—	—	—
Selector	GS-			—	—	—

Control Registers The 80386 has three 32-bit control registers CR_0, CR_2 and CR_3 to hold global machine status independant of the executed task. The load and store instructions are available to access these registers. The control register CR_1 is reserved for use in future Intel processors.

System Address Registers Four special registers are defined to refer to the descriptor tables supported by 80386. The 80386 supports four types of descriptor tables, viz. Global Descriptor Table (GDT), Interrupt Descriptor Table (IDT), Local Descriptor Table (LDT) and Task State Segment Descriptor (TSS). The system address registers and system segment registers hold the addresses of these descriptor tables and the corresponding segments. These registers are known as GDTR, IDTR, LDTR and TR respectively. The GDTR and IDTR are called as system address and LDTR and TR are called as system segment registers.

Debug and Test Registers Intel has provided a set of eight debug registers for hardware debugging. Out of these eight registers-DR_0 to DR_7, two registers DR_4 and DR_5 are Intel reserved. The initial four registers DR_0

to DR_3 store four program controllable breakpoint addresses, while DR_6 and DR_7 respectively hold breakpoint status and breakpoint control information. Two more test registers are provided by 80386 for page cacheing, namely test control and test status registers. The debug and test registers are shown in Fig. 10.3.

10.4 ADDRESSING MODES

The 80386 supports eleven addressing modes to facilitate efficient execution of higher level language programs. The 80386 has all the addressing modes which were available with 80286. In case of all those modes, the 80386 can now have 32-bit immediate or 32-bit register operands or displacements. Besides these, the 80386 has a family of scaled modes. In case of the scaled the modes, any of the index register values can be multiplied by a valid scale factor to obtain the displacement. The valid scale factors are 1, 2, 4 and 8. The different scaled modes are discussed as follows:

Scaled Indexed Mode Contents of an index register are multiplied by a scale factor that may be added further to get the operand offset.

Example 10.1

```
MOV EBX, LIST [ESI*2] List displacement
MUL ECX, LIST [EBP*4]
```

Based Scaled Indexed Mode Contents of an index register are multiplied by a scale factor and then added to base register to obtain the offset.

DEBUG REGISTERS

31 0	
Linear Breakpoint Address 0	DR_0
Linear Breakpoint Address 1	DR_1
Linear Breakpoint Address 2	DR_2
Linear Breakpoint Address 3	DR_3
Intel Reserved.	DR_4
Intel Reserved.	DR_5
Breakpoint Status	DR_6
Breakpoint Control	DR_7

Test Register (for Page Cache)

31 0	
Test Control	TR_6
Test Status	TR_7

Fig. 10.3 *Debug and Test Registers of 80386 (Intel Corp.)*

Example 10.2

```
MOV EBX, [EDX*4] [ECX]
MOV EAX, [EBX*2] [ECX]
```

Based Scaled Indexed Mode with Diplacement The contents of an index register are multiplied by a scaling factor and the result is added to a base register and a displacement to get the offset of an operand.

Example 10.3

```
MOV EAX, LIST [ESI*2] [EBX + 0800]
MUL EBX, LIST [EDI*8] [ECX + 0100]
```

The displacement may be any 8-bit, 16-bit or 32-bit immediate number. The base and index register may be any general purpose register except ESP.

10.5 DATA TYPES OF 80386

The 80386 supports the following 17 data types, each of which is discussed here in brief. Some of them have already been discussed in the previous chapter.

1. Bit
2. Bit Field—A group of at the most 32 bits (4 bytes)
3. Bit String—A string of contiguous bits of maximum 4 Gbytes in length.
4. Signed Byte—Signed byte data
5. Unsigned Byte—Unsigned byte data.
6. Integer word—Signed 16-bit data.
7. Long Integer—32-bit signed data represented in 2's complement form.
8. Unsigned Integer Word—Unsigned 16-bit data
9. Unsigned Long Integer—Unsigned 32-bit data
10. Signed Quad Word—A signed 64-bit data or four word data.
11. Unsigned Quad Word—An unsigned 64-bit data.
12. Offset—A 16 or 32-bit displacement that references a memory location using any of the addressing modes.
13. Pointer—This consists of a pair of 16-bit selector and 16/32-bit offset.
14. Character—An ASCII equivalent to any of the alphanumeric or control characters.
15. Strings—These are the sequences of bytes, words or double words. A string may contain minimum one byte and maximum 4 Gigabytes.
16. BCD—Decimal digits from 0-9 represented by unpacked bytes.
17. Packed BCD—This represents two packed BCD digits using a byte, i.e. from 00 to 99.

10.6 REAL ADDRESS MODE OF 80386

After reset, the 80386 starts from the memory location FFFFFFF0H under the real address mode. In the real mode, 80386 works as a fast 8086 with 32-bit registers and data types. The addressing techniques, memory size, interrupt handling in this mode of 80386 are similar to the real address mode of 80286. All the instructions of 80386 are available in this mode except for those designed to work with or for protected address mode. In the real mode, the default operand size is 16-bit but 32-bit operands and addressing modes may be used with the help of override prefixes. The segment size in real mode is 64K, hence the 32-bit effective addresses must be less than 0000FFFFFH. The real mode initializes the 80386 and prepares it for protected mode.

10.6.1 Memory Addressing in Real Mode

In the real mode, the 80386 can address at the most 1Mbytes of physical memory using address lines A_0–A_{19}. Paging unit is disabled in the real address mode, and hence the real addresses are the same as the physical addresses. To form a physical memory address, appropriate segment register contents (16-bits) are shifted left by four positions and then added to the 16-bit offset address formed using one of the addressing modes, in the same way as in the 80386 real address mode. The segments in 80386 real mode can be read, written or executed, i.e. no protection is available. Any fetch or access past the end of the segment limit generate exception 13 in real address mode. The segments in 80386 real mode may be overlapped or non-overlapped. The interrupt vector table of 80386 has been allocated 1Kbyte space starting from 00000H to 003FFH. Figure 10.4 shows the physical address formation in real mode of 80386.

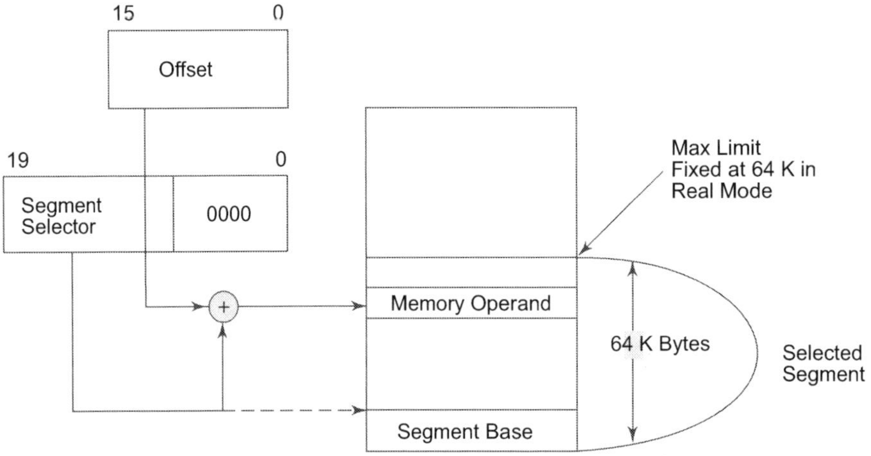

Fig.10.4 *Physical Address Formation in Real Mode of 80386 (Intel Corp.)*

10.7 PROTECTED MODE OF 80386

All the capabilities of 80386 are available for utilization in its protected mode of operation. In this mode, the 80386 can address 4 Gigabytes of physical memory and 64 terrabytes of virtual memory per task. The 80386 in the protected mode supports all softwares written for 80286 and 8086 to be executed under the control of memory management and protection abilities of 80386. The protected mode allows the use of additional instructions, addressing modes and capabilities of 80386.

10.7.1 Addressing in Protected Mode

In this mode, the contents of segment registers are used as selectors to address descriptors which contain the segment limit, base address and access rights byte of the segment. The effective address (offset) is added with segment base address to calculate linear address. This linear address is further used as physical address, if the paging unit is disabled. Otherwise, the paging unit converts the linear address into physical address.

The paging unit is a memory management unit enabled only in the protected mode. The paging mechanism allows handling of large segments of memory in terms of pages of 4 Kbyte size. The paging unit operates under the control of segmentation unit. The paging unit if enabled converts linear addresses into physical addresses, in protected mode. Figures 10.5(a) and (b) show addressing in protected mode without and with paging unit enabled respectively.

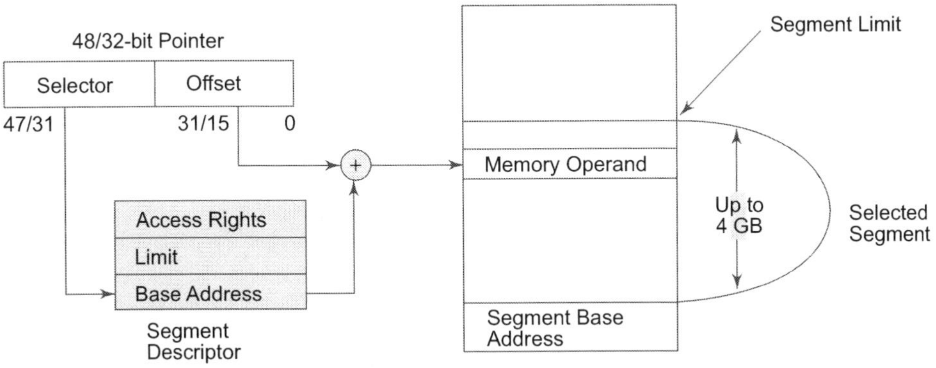

Fig. 10.5(a) *Protected Mode Addressing without Paging Unit* (*Intel Crop.*)

10.8 SEGMENTATION

10.8.1 Descriptor Tables

A lot has already been said about segmentation while dealing with 8086 and 80286. In short, the segmentation scheme is a way of offering protection to different types of data and code. The 80386 also utilizes the three types of segment descriptor tables as the 80286 does. However, there are slight differences between the 80386 and the 80286 descriptor structures. Again, associated with each descriptor, there are the corresponding descriptor table registers, which are manipulated by the operating system to ensure the correct operation of the processor, and hence the correct execution of the program.

The three types of the 80386 descriptor tables are listed as follows:

1. Global Descriptor Table (GDT)
2. Local Descriptor Table (LDT)
3. Interrupt Descriptor Table (IDT)

Their respective significances are also similar to the corresponding descriptor table significances in 80286.

10.8.2 Descriptors

Unlike 80286 descriptors, the 80386 descriptors have a 20-bit segment limit and 32-bit segment address. The descriptors of 80386 are 8-byte quantities containing access right or attribute bits along with the base and limit of the segments.

Descriptor Attribute Bits The A (accessed) attribute bit indicates whether the segment has been accessed by the CPU or not. The TYPE field decides the descriptor type and hence the segment type. The S-bit decides whether it is a system descriptor (S = 0) or code/data segment descriptor (S = 1). The DPL field specifies the descriptor privilege level. The D-bit specifies code segment operation size. If D-1, the segment is a 32-bit operand segment, else, it is a 16-bit operand segment. The P-bit (Present) signifies whether the segment is present in the physical memory or not. If P = 1, the segment is present in the physical memory. The G-(granularity) bit indicates whether the segment is page addressable. The zero bit must remain zero for compatibility with future processors. The AVL (Available) field specifies whether the descriptor is available to the user or to the operating system. Figure 10.6 shows the general structure of a segment descriptor of 80386.

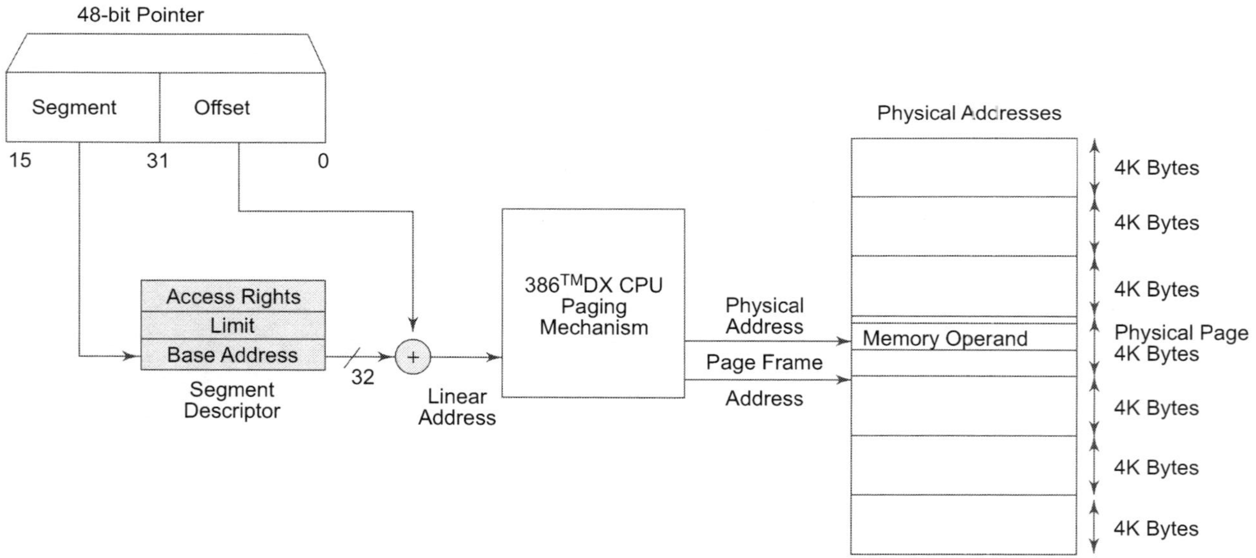

Fig. 10.5(b) *Paging Unit Enabled in Protected Mode Addressing (Intel Corp.)*

The five types of descriptors that the 80386 has are as follows:

1. Code or data Segment Descriptors
2. System Descriptors
3. Local descriptors
4. TSS (Task State segment) Descriptors
5. GATE Descriptors

All these descriptors have similar definitions as in the case of 80286. Their respective structures may be slightly different as compared to the general segment descriptor structure of 80286, but they have similar functions as in 80286. The 80386 provides a four level protection mechanism, exactly in the same way as the 80286 does.

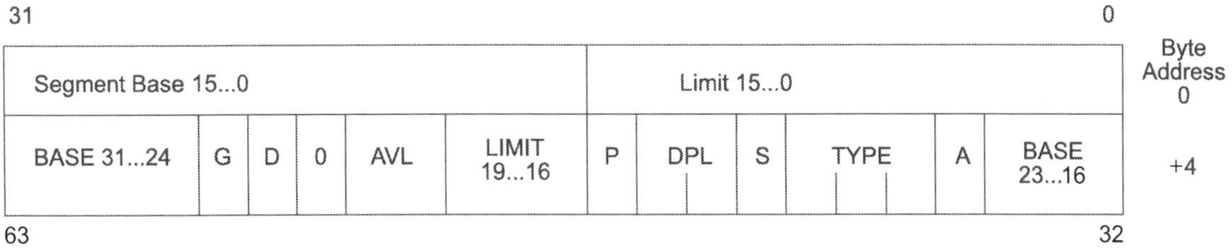

BASE	Base Address of the segment
LIMIT	The length of the segment
P	Present Bit-1 = Present, 0 = Not Present
DPL	Descriptor Privilege Level 0–3
S	Segment Descriptor-0 = System Descriptor, 1 = Code or Data Segment Descriptor
TYPE	Type of Segment
A	Accessed Bit
G	Granularity Bit-1 = Segment length is page granular, 0 = Segment length is byte granular
D	Default Operation Size (recognized in code segment descriptors only)-1 = 32-bit segment, 0 = 16-bit segment
0	Bit must be zero (0) for compatibility with future processors
AVL	Available field for user or OS

Fig. 10.6 *Structure of an 80386 Descriptor (Intel Corp.)*

As explained in section 9.5.3, the segment base addresses and a memory pointer jointly address the available physical memory. The base address that marks the starting address of the segment in physical memory is decided by the operating system and is of 32 bits. The physical address bus is also of 32 bits. The limit field of the descriptor is of 20 bits. Thus starting with a 32 bit base address and an offset of 20 bits, the maximum segment size can be 1MB. 80386 can also handle total 16 K descriptors and hence segments. Thus it appears that, on the lines of 80286, 80386 may be able to address a virtual memory of 16K × 1MB = 16GB per task if operated with segmentation scheme. However in case of operation under paging scheme, the memory is managed in terms of segments of 4GB size which are further organized in terms of pages of fixed 4KB size each. Thus instead of bigger size segments, pages are now fetched into primary memory one by one for execution. A structure called page table contains entries for a particular page. The page table can store such 1024 entries. Another structure called page table directory or simply page directory contains the entries of page tables. It also can accommodate 1024 such entries. Thus at an instant, the page management structure can have 1024 × 1024 = 1M such page entries under each segment. Each page is of 4KB size. Thus 1M × 4KB = 4GB can be the maximum size of each segment. The necessary support for organizing this operation is provided by the operating system and the processor hardware both. The 80386 can thus address maximum 16K × 4GB = 64TB of virtual memory per task. 80386 has the flexibility to operate with 16 bit data size or 32 bit data size only for code segments for downward compatibility as controlled by the D bit. All other bit functions of the 80386 segment descriptors are similar to the respective bits of 80286 descriptors and have also been discussed in significant details in Chapter 9.

10.9 PAGING

10.9.1 Paging Operation

Paging is one of the memory management techniques used for virtual memory multitasking operating systems. The segmentation scheme may divide the physical memory into variable size segments but the paging divides the memory into fixed size pages. The segments are supposed to be the logical segments of the program, but the pages do not have any logical relation with the program. The pages are just the fixed size portions of the program module or data. The advantage of the paging scheme is that the complete segment of a task need not be in the physical memory at any time. Only a few pages of the segments, which are required currently for the execution need to be available in the physical memory. Thus the memory requirement of the task is substantially reduced, relinquishing the available memory for other tasks. Whenever the other pages of the task are required for execution, they may be fetched from the secondary storage. The previous pages which are executed, need not be available in the memory, and hence the space occupied by them may be relinquished for other tasks. Thus the paging mechanism provides an effective technique to manage the physical memory for multitasking systems.

Paging Unit The paging unit of 80386 uses a two level table mechanism to convert the linear addresses provided by segmentation unit into physical addresses. The paging unit converts the complete map of a task into pages, each of size 4K. The task is then handled in terms of its pages, rather than segments. The paging unit handles every task in terms of three components namely page directory, page tables and the page itself.

Page Descriptor Base Register The control register CR_2 is used to store the 32-bit linear address at which the previous page fault was detected. The CR_3 is used as page directory physical base address register, to store the physical starting address of the page directory. The lower 12 bits of CR_3 are always zero (page size $2^{12} = 4$ K) to ensure the page size aligned with the directory. A move operation to CR_3 automatically loads the page table entry caches and a task switch operation, to load CR_0 suitably.

Page Directory This is at the most 4 Kbytes in size. Each directory entry is of four bytes, thus a total of 1024 entries are allowed in a directory. The following Fig. 10.7(a) shows a typical directory entry. The upper 10 bits of the linear address are used as an index to the corresponding page directory entry. The page directory entries, point to the page tables.

Page Tables Each page table is of 4 Kbytes in size and may contain a maximum of 1024 entries. The page table entries contain the starting address of the page and the statistical information about the page as

31 … 12	11 10 9	8	7	6	5	4	3	2	1	0
Page Frame Address 31..12	OS RESERVED	0	0	D	A	0	0	U/S	R/W	P

Fig. 10.7(a) *Page Directory Entry (Intel Corp.)*

31 … 12	11 10 9	8	7	6	5	4	3	2	1	0
Page Frame Address 31..12	OS RESERVED	0	0	D	A	0	0	U/S	R/W	P

Fig. 10.7(b) *Page Table Entry (Intel Corp.)*

shown in Fig. 10.7(b). The upper 20-bit page frame address is combined with the lower 12 bits of the linear address. The address bits A_{12}–A_{21} are used to select the 1024 page table entries. The page tables can be shared between the tasks.

The P-bit of the above entries indicate, if the entry can be used in address translation. If P = 1, the entry can be used in address translation, otherwise, it cannot be used. The P-bit of the currently executed page is always high. The accessed bit A is set by 80386 before any access to the page. If A = 1, the page is accessed, otherwise, it is unaccessed. The D-bit (Dirty bit) is set before a write operation to the page is carried out. The D-bit is undefined for page directory entries. The OS reserved bits are defined by the operating system software.

The User/Supervisor (U/S) bit and Read/Write (R/W) bit are used to provide protection. These bits can be decoded as shown in Table 10.2 to provide protection under the four level protection model. The level 0 is supposed to have the highest privilege, while the level 3 is supposed to have the least privilege.

Table 10.2

U/S	*R/W*	*Permitted level 3 for*	*Permitted for levels 2,1 or 0*
0	0	None	Read/Write
0	1	None	Read/Write
1	0	Read only	Read/Write
1	1	Read-Write	Read/Write

This protection provided by the paging unit is transparent to the segmentation unit. Figure 10.8 shows the block digrammatic representation of the complete paging mechanism of 80386.

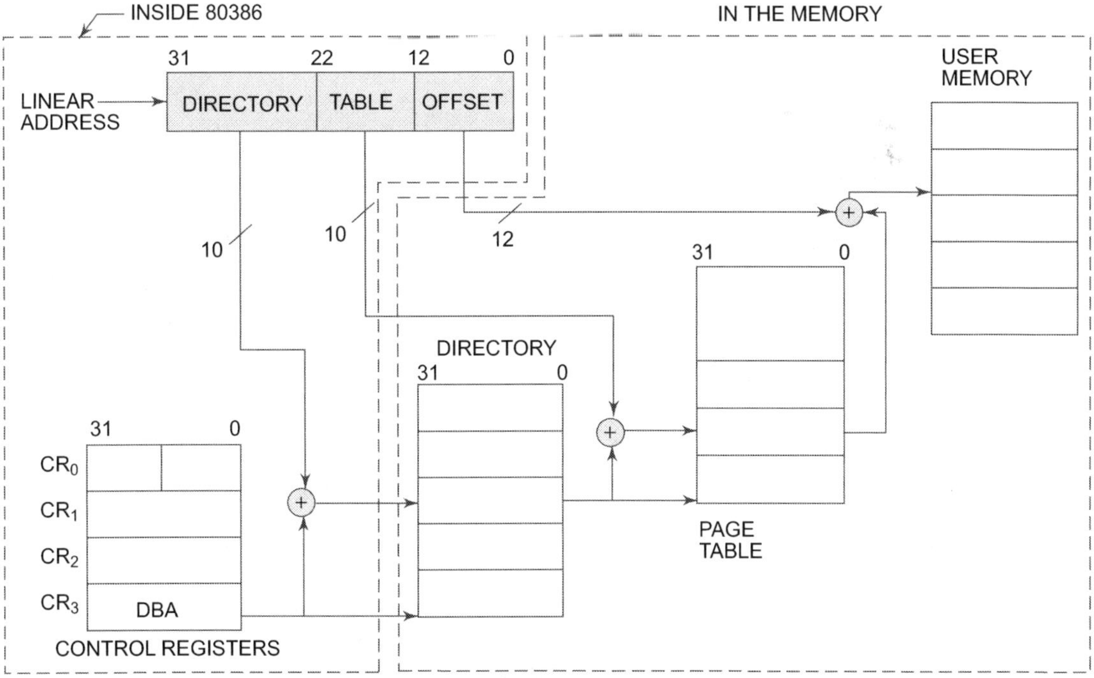

DBA-Physical Directory Base Address

Fig. 10.8 *Paging Mechanism of 80386 (Intel Corp.)*

10.9.2 Conversion of a Linear Address to a Physical Address

The paging unit receives a 32-bit linear address from the segmentation unit. The upper 20 linear address bits (A_{12}–A_{31}) are compared with all the 32 entries in the translation look aside buffer to check if it matches with any of the entries. If it matches, the 32-bit physical address is calculated from the matching TLB entry and placed on the address bus.

For converting all the linear addresses to physical addresses, if the conversion process uses the two level paging for every conversion, a considerable time will be wasted in the process. Hence, to optimize this, a 32-entry (32 × 4bytes) page table cache is provided which stores the 32 recently accessed page table entries. Whenever a linear address is to be converted to physical address, it is first checked to see, whether it corresponds to any of the page table cache entries. This page table cache is also knows Translation Look-aside Buffer (TLB).

If the page table entry is not in TLB, the 80386 reads the appropriate page directory entry. It then checks the P-bit of the directory entry. If P = 1, it indicates that the page table is in the memory. Then 80386 refers to the appropriate page table entry and sets the accessed bit A. If P = 1, in the page table entry, the page is available in the memory. Then the processor updates the A and D bits and accesses the page. The upper 20 bits of the linear address, read from the page table are stored in TLB for future possible access. If P = 0, the processor generates a page fault exception number 14. This exception is also generated, if page protection rules are violated. Every time a page fault exception is generated, the CR_2 is loaded with the page fault address. Figure 10.9 shows the overall paging operation with TLB.

10.10 VIRTUAL 8086 MODE

In its protected mode of operation, 80386DX provides a virtual 8086 operating environment to execute the 8086 programs. The real mode also can be used to execute the 8086 programs along with the capabilities of 80386, like protection and a few additional instructions. However, once the 80386 enters the protected mode from the real mode, it cannot return back to the real mode without a reset operation. Thus, the virtual 8086 mode of operation of 80386, offers an advantage of executing 8086 programs while in protected mode.

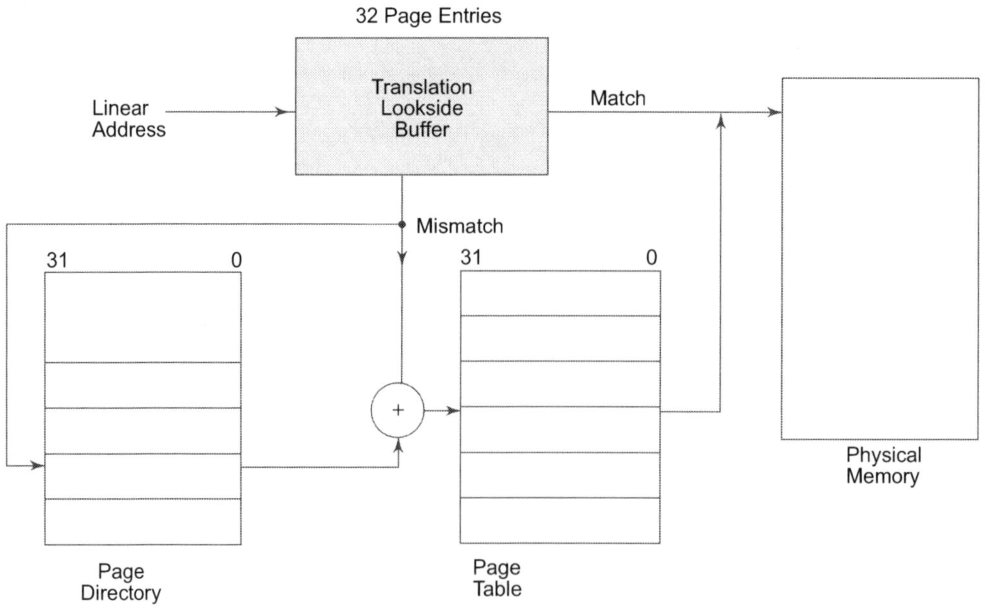

Fig. 10.9 *Paging Operation with TLB (Intel Corp.)*

The address forming mechanism in virtual 8086 mode is exactly identical with that of 8086 real mode. In virtual mode, 8086 can address 1 Mbytes of physical memory that may be anywhere in the 4 Gbytes address space of the protected mode of 80386. Like 80386 real mode, the addresses in virtual 8086 mode lie within 1 Mbytes of memory. In the virtual mode, the paging mechanism and protection capabilities are available at the service of the programmers (note that the 80386 supports multiprogramming, hence more than one programmer may use the CPU at a time). Paging unit may not be necessarily enabled in the virtual mode, but may be needed to run the 8086 programs which require more than 1 Mbyte of memory for memory management functions.

In the virtual mode, the paging unit allows only 256 pages, each of 4 Kbytes size. Each of the pages may be located anywhere within the maximum 4 Gbytes physical memory. The virtual mode allows the multiprogramming of 8086 applications. Figure 10.10 shows how the memory is managed in multitasking virtual 8086 environment.

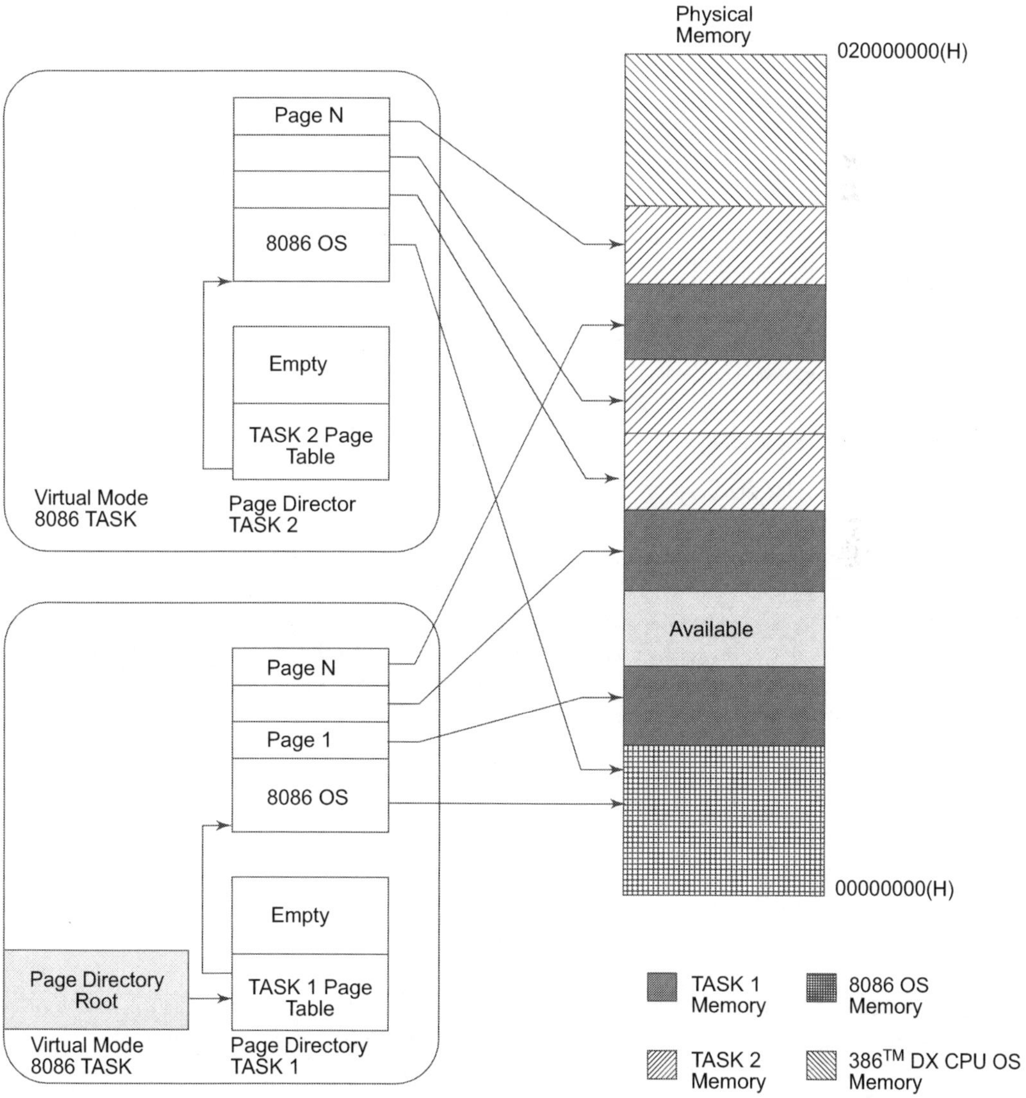

Fig. 10.10 *Memory Management in Virtual 8086 Mode (Multitasking) (Intel Corp.)*

The virtual 8086 mode executes all the programs at the privilege level 3. Any of the other programmes may deny access to the virtual mode programs or data. However, the real mode programs are executed at the highest privilege level, i.e. level 0. Note that the instructions to prepare the processor for protected mode can only be executed at level 0.

The virtual mode may be entered using an IRET instruction at CPL = 0 or a task switch at any CPL, while executing any task whose TSS is having a flag image with VM flag set to 1. The IRET instruction may be used to set the VM flag and consequently enter the virtual mode. The PUSHF and POPF instructions are unable to read or set the VM bit, as they do not access it. Even in the virtual mode, all the interrupts and exceptions are handled by the protected mode interrupt handler. To return to the protected mode from the virtual mode, any interrupt or exception may be used. As a part of interrupt service routine, the VM bit may be reset to zero to pull back the 80386 into the protected mode.

10.11 ENHANCED INSTRUCTION SET OF 80386

The instruction set of 80386 contains all the instructions supported by 80286. The 80286 instructions are designed to operate with 8-bit or 16-bit data, while the same mnemonics for 80386 instruction set may be executed over the 32-bit operands, besides 8-bit and 16-bit operands. Moreover, because of the enhanced architecture of 80386 over 80286, with additional general purpose registers, segment registers and flag register, a number of additional instructions were introduced in the instruction set of 80286, to form the instruction set of 80386. An additional addressing mode, viz. *scaled mode*, also contributes considerably to the enhancement of the 80386 instruction set. These newly added instructions may be categorized into the following functional groups:

1. Bit scan instructions
2. Bit test instructions
3. Conditional set byte instructions
4. Shift double instructions
5. Control transfer via gates instructions

Various instructions under these groups are explained briefly in the following text:

1. Bit Scan Instructions 80386 instruction set has two bit scan mnemonics, viz. BSF (Bit Scan Forward) and BSR (Bit Scan Reverse). Both of these instructions scan the operand for a '1' bit, without actually rotating it. The BSF instruction scans the operand from right to left. If a '1' is encountered during the scan, zero flag is set and the bit position of '1' is stored into the destination operand. If no '1' is encountered, zero flag is reset. The BSR instruction also performs the same function but scans the source operand from the left most bit towards right.

2. Bit Test Instructions 80386 has four bit test instructions, viz. BT (Test a Bit), BTC (Test a Bit and Complement), BTR (Test and Reset a Bit) and BTS (Test and Set a bit). All these instructions test a bit position in the destination operand, specified by the source operand.

If the bit position of the destination operand specified by the source operand satisfies the condition specified in the mnemonic, the carry flag is affected appropriately. For example, in the case of BT instruction, if the bit position in the destination operand, specified by the source operand, is '1', the carry flag is set, otherwise, it is cleared.

3. Conditional Set Byte Instruction This instruction sets all the operand bits, if the condition specified by the mnemonic is true. This instruction group has 16 mnemonics corresponding to 16 conditions as shown in Table 10.3.

For example, SETO EAX; This instruction sets all the bits of EAX, if the overflow flag is set.

Table 10.3

Sr.No.	*Mnemonic*	*Instruction*
1.	SETO	Set on overflow
2.	SETNO	Set on no overflow
3.	SETB/SETNAE	Set on below/not above or equal
4.	SETNB/SETAE	Set on not below/above or equal
5.	SETE/SETZ	Set on equal/zero
6.	SETNE/SETNZ	Set on not equal/not zero
7.	SETBE/SETNA	Set on below or equal/not above
8.	SETNBE/SETA	Set on not below or equal/above
9.	SETS	Set on sign
10.	SETNS	Set on not sign
11.	SETP/SETPE	Set on parity/parity even
12.	SETNP	Set on not parity/parity odd.
13.	SETL/SETNGE	Set on less/not greater or equal
14.	SETNL/SET GE	Set on not less/greater or equal
15.	SETLE/SETNG	Set on less or equal/not greater
16.	SETNLE/SETG	Set on not less or equal/greater

4. Shift Double Instructions These instructions shift the specified number of bits from the source operand into the destination operand. The 80386 instruction set has two mnemonics under this category, viz. SHLD (Shift Left Double) and SHRD (Shift Right Double). The SHLD instruction shifts the specified number of bits (in the instruction) from the upper side, i.e. MSB of the source operand into the lower side, i.e. LSB of the destination operand. The SHRD instruction shifts the number of bits specified in the instruction from the lower side, i.e. LSB of the source operand into the upper side, i.e. MSB of the destination operand.

Example 10.4

1. SHLD EAX,ECX,5
   This instruction shifts 5 MSB bits of ECX into the LSB positions of EAX one by one starting from the MSB of ECX.
2. SHRD EAX, ECX, 8
   This instruction shifts 8 LSB bits of ECX into the MSB positions of EAX one by one starting from the LSB of ECX.

5. Control Transfer Instructions The 80386 instruction set does not have any additional instructions for the intrasegment jump. However, for intersegment jumps, it has got a set of new instructions which are variations of the previous CALL and JUMP instructions, and are to be executed only in the protected mode. These instructions are used by 80386 to transfer the control either at the same privilege or at a different privilege level. Also, different versions of control transfer instructions are available to switch between the different task types and TSS (Task State Segment). The corresponding RET instructions are also available to switch back from the new task initiated via CALL, JMP or INT instructions to the parent task.

10.12 THE COPROCESSOR 80387

The 80387 math coprocessor was designed to operate coherently with 80386. The instruction execution of the 80387 is completely transparent to the programmers. The 80387 is code compatible with its predecessors, 80287 and 8087. A lot has already been said regarding 80287 in Chapter 9. Here, we discuss only the improvements and additions in 80387 over 80287 along with the architecture of 80387.

10.12.1 Architecture of 80387

The 80387 has an 80-bit internal architecture that offers six to eleven times improvement in performance as compared to 80287. The architecture of 80387 is shown in Fig. 10.11.

The architecture and functional operation of 80387 is like that of 80287, except for the data bus size. The data bus of 80387 has 32 data lines D_0–D_{31}. The 80387 has two clock inputs to allow the possible asynchronous or synchronous operations with 80386. These operations are selected using the CKM pin of 80387. If the CKM is high, the 80387 operates in synchronous mode, otherwise, it operates in the asynchronous mode. The bus control unit of 80387 always operates synchronously with 80386, independent of the mode of operation of the floating point unit. In conjunction with READY input, the ADS input pin can be used to delay the bus cycles in reference to $CPUCLK_2$ pin. The status enable pin acts as a chip select for the MCP 80387. The other pins of 80387 have similar functions as the corresponding pins of 80287. The data interface and control unit handle the data and direct it to either FIFO or instruction decoder depending upon the bus control logic directive. The decoder decodes the instruction and derives the control signals to control the data flow inside the 80387. This unit generates the synchronization signals for 80386. The FPU is responsible for carrying out all the floating point calculations allotted to the coprocessor by 80386. Figure 10.12 shows the pin diagram of 80387.

Register set of 80387 Intel's 80387 has eight 80-bit floating point data registers, which are used to store signed 80-bit data in the form of exponent and significand as shown in Fig. 10.13. Each of these registers has a corresponding 2-bit tag field. The 80387 has a 16-bit control, status and tag word registers. The 80387 has two more 48-bit registers known as instruction and data pointers. The instruction and data pointer registers respectively point to the failing math coprocessor instruction and the corresponding numeric data, which is referred by the CPU. Two bits are alloted for each of the registers R_0–R_7 in the tag word. These are used to optimize the performance of the coprocessor by identifying between the empty and non-empty of the R_0–R_7 registers. Also the tag bits can be used by the exception handlers to check the contents of a stack location without any manipulation. The status word represents the overall status of the coprocessor.

The tag word register and the MCP status registers have exactly similar formats as those of 80287 respectively. The 80387 can be configured by loading a control word from memory to its control word register. The control word register has exactly similar format as that of 80287. The data types of 80387 are also like the data types of 80287.

10.12.2 Interconnections with 80386

Figure 10.14 shows the interfacing of 80387 with 80386. The pins BUSY #, ERROR #, PEREQ ADS #, W/R # and D_0–D_{31} of 80387 can be directly connected with the corresponding pins of 80386. A separate clock generator may be added to the circuit , if 80387 is required to be run at a different frequency than the 80386. Otherwise, the 80387 may be driven by the same frequency generator that drives 80386. An optional wait state generator combines the ready signal from 80387 and ready signals given by the other peripherals to push the 80386 into wait state till 80387 execution is over. The NPS_1 and NPS_2 (Numeric Processor Select) lines are directly connected with M/IO and A_{31} respectively to inform the 80387 that the CPU wants to communicate with it (NPS_1) and it is using one of the reserved I/O addresses for 80387 (NPS_2), i.e. 800000F8

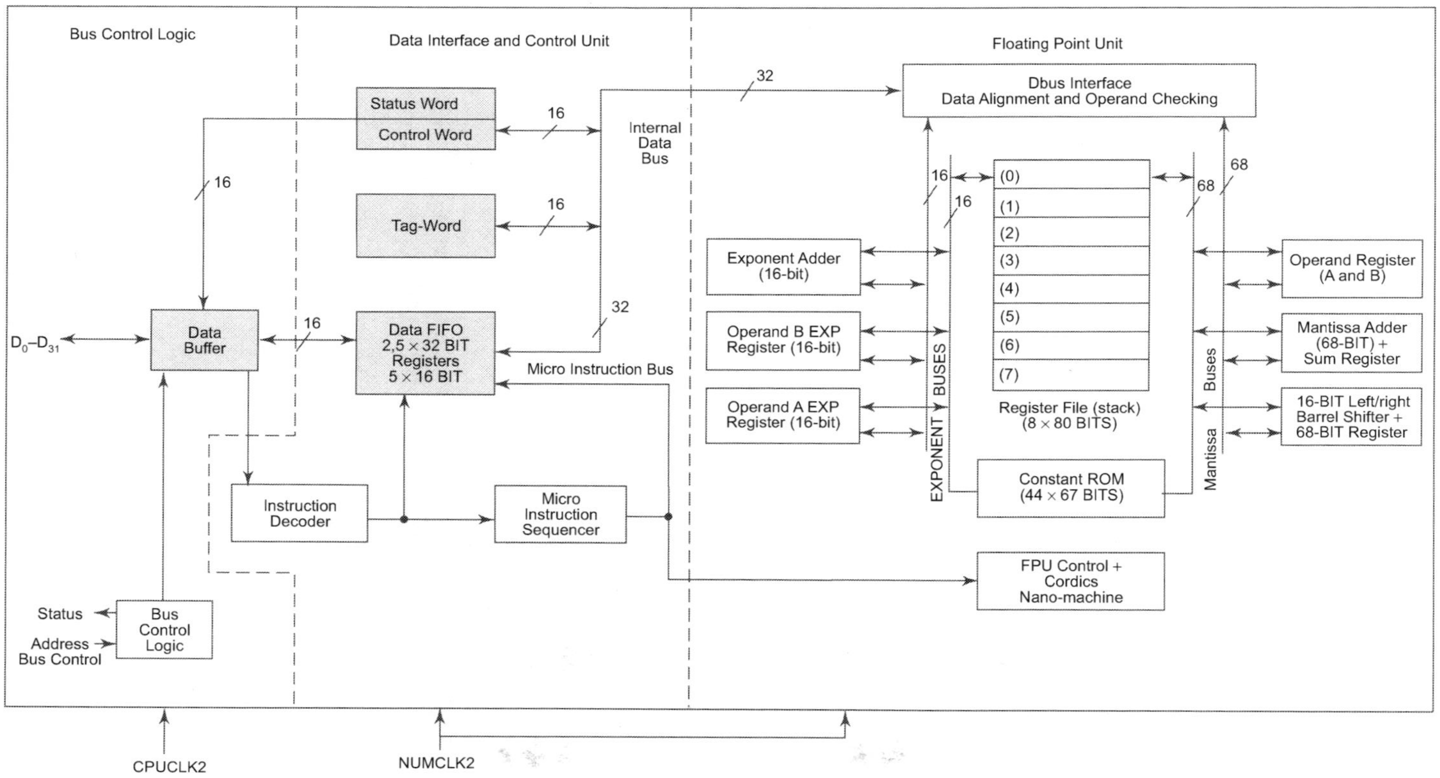

Fig. 10.11 *Internal Architecture of 80387*

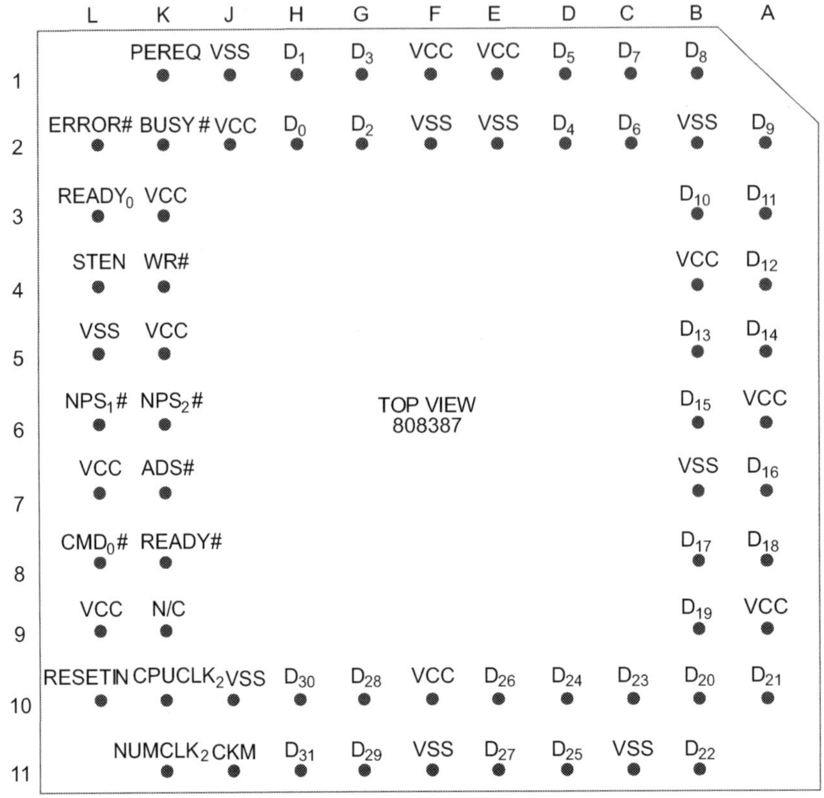

Fig. 10.12 *Pin Diagram of 80387*

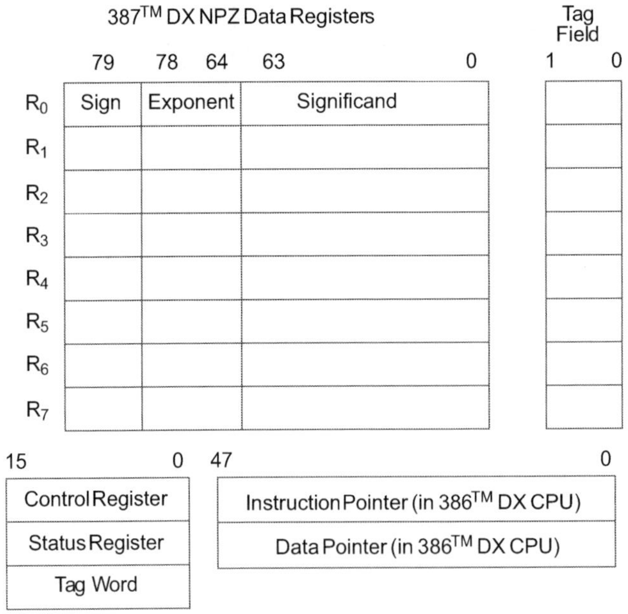

Fig. 10.13 *Register Format of 80387*

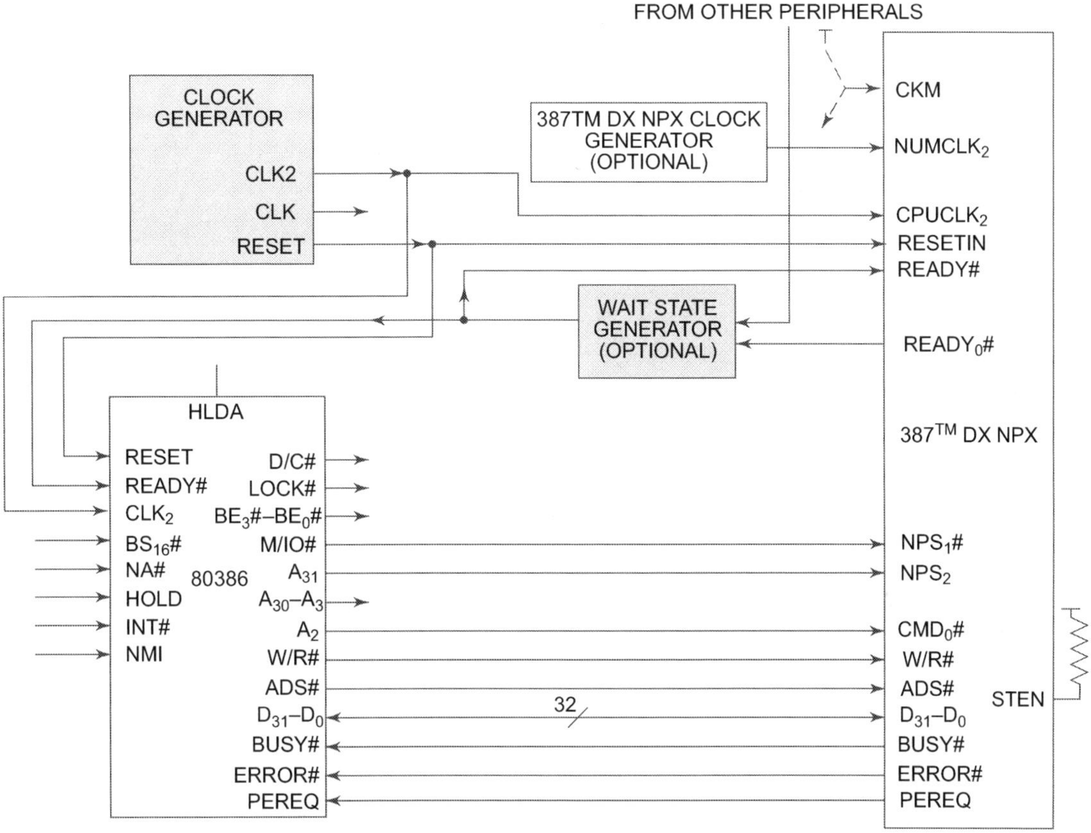

Fig. 10.14 *Interconnections of 80387 with 80386*

or 800000FC. The CMD_0# input of 80387 is driven by the address line A_2, and indicates to 80387 that an opcode or data is being sent to it, during a write cycle. During a read cycle, it indicates, that either the control or status or data register of 80387 is to be read by 80386. The STEN, NPS_1, NPS_2, CMD_0 and W/R inputs of 80387 decode the bus cycle operation of 80387.

10.13 THE CPU WITH A NUMERIC COPROCESSOR—80486DX

The 80386–80387 couplet, when it was introduced, was seen as the most powerful processing unit, wherein the use of 80387 was optional. However, with the increasing demand for more and more processing capability for advanced applications, the use of 80387 became more often compulsory than optional. Also, the designers thought of integrating the floating-point unit inside the CPU itself. The 32-bit CPU 80486 from Intel is the first processor with an *inbuilt floating-point unit.* It retained the complex instruction set of 80386, but introduced *more pipelining* for speed enhancement.

The 80486 is packaged in a 168-pin grid array package. The 25 MHz, 33 MHz, 50 MHz and100 MHz (DX-4) versions of 80486 are available in the market. The 80486 is also available as 80486SX that does not have the numeric coprocessor integrated into it. The 80486DX is the most popular version of 80486. All the discussions in this text are thus related to 80486DX.

10.13.1 Salient Features of 80486

As mentioned in the introductory note, 80486DX is the first CPU with an on chip floating-point unit. For fast execution of complex instructions of the xxx86 family, the 80486 has introduced a five stage pipeline. Two

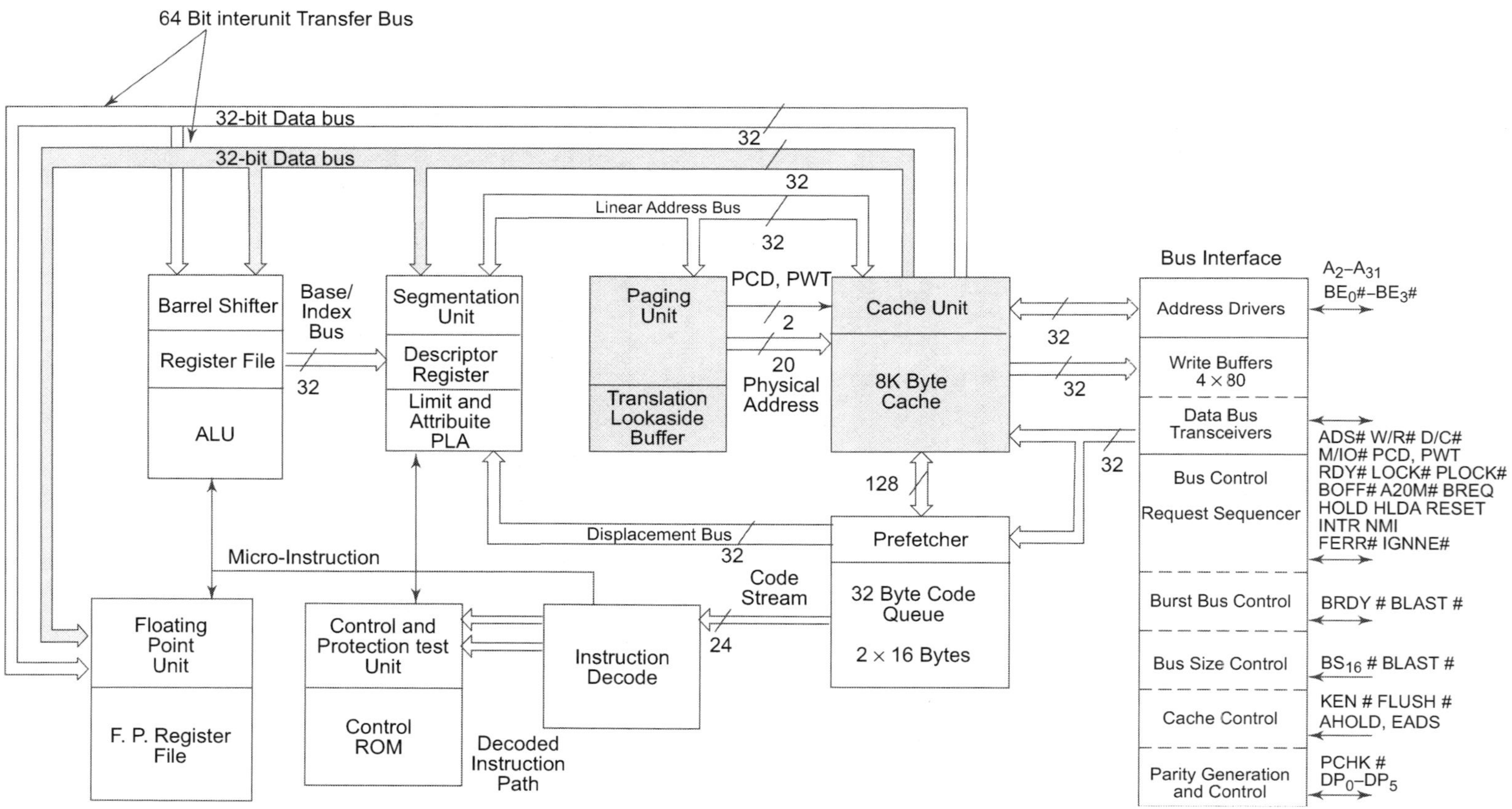

Fig. 10.15 *Architecture of 80486*

out of the five stages are used for decoding the complex instructions of the xxx86 architecture. This feature which has been used widely in RISC architectures results in a very fast instruction execution which will be explained later. The 80486 is also the first amongst the xxx86 processors to have an *on-chip cache*. This 8Kbytes cache is a unified data and code cache and acts on physical addresses. The details of the cache and cache controller operations are discussed later in this chapter. Further, features like boundary scan test and on-line parity check were introduced in 80486 to make it more susceptible to fault tolerant architectures. The memory and I/O capabilities of 80486 are similar to 80386DX. There are certain signals and architectural features, not available in 80386, which enhance the overall performance of 80486.

10.13.2 Architecture of 80486

The 32-bit pipelined architecture of Intel's 80486 is shown in Fig. 10.15. The internal architecture of 80486 can be broadly divided into three sections, namely bus interface unit, execution and control unit and floating-point unit.

The *bus interface unit* is mainly responsible for coordinating all the bus activities. The address driver interfaces the internal 32-bit address output of cache unit with the system bus. The data bus transreceivers interface the internal 32-bit data bus with the system bus. The 4 × 80 write data buffer is a queue of four 80-bit registers which hold the 80-bit data to be written to the memory (available in advance due to pipelined execution of write operation). The bus control and request sequencer handles the signals like ADS#, W/R#, D/C#, M/IO#, PCD, PWT, RDY#, LOCK#, PLOCK#, BOFF#, A20M#, BREQ, HOLD, HLDA, RESET, INTR, NMI, FERR# and IGNNE# which basically control the bus access and operations.

The *burst control signal* BRDY# informs the processor that the burst is ready (i.e. it acts as ready signal in burst cycle). The BLAST# output indicates to the external system that the previous burst cycle is over. The bus size control signals BS_{16}# and BS_8# are used for dynamic bus sizing. The cache control signals KEN#, FLUSH, AHOLD and EADS# control and maintain the cache in coordination with the cache control unit. The *parity generation* and *control unit* maintain the parity and carry out the related checks during the processor operation. The *boundary scan control unit*, that is built in 50 MHz and advanced versions only, subject the processor operation to boundary scan tests to ensure the correct operation of various components of the circuit on the mother board, provided the TCK input is not tied high. The *prefetcher unit* fetches the codes from the memory ahead of execution time and arranges them in a 32-byte code queue.

The *instruction decoder* gets the code from the code queue and then decodes it sequentially. The output of the decoder drives the control unit to derive the control signals required for the execution of the decoded instructions. But prior to execution, the *protection unit* checks, if there is any violation of protection norms. In case of violation, an appropriate exception is generated. The control ROM stores a microprogram for deriving control signals for execution of different instructions. The register bank and ALU are used for their conventional usages. The barrel shifter helps in implementing the shift and rotate algorithms. The *segmentation unit, descriptor registers, paging unit, translation look aside buffer* and *limit and attribute PLA* work together to manage the virtual memory of the system and provide adequate protection to the codes or data in the physical memory. The *floating-point unit* with its register bank communicates with the *bus interface unit* under the control of *memory management unit*, via its 64-bit internal data bus. The floating-point unit is responsible for carrying out mathematical data processing at a higher speed as compared to the ALU, with its built in floating-point algorithms.

Register Organisation of 80486 The register set of 80486 is similar to that of the 80386. Only a flag called as *alignment check flag* is added to the flag register of 80386 at position D_{18} as shown in Fig. 10.16. If the AC flag bit is set to '1', whenever there is an access to a misaligned address, a fault (exception) is generated. The misaligned address means a word access to an odd address or a double word access to an address that is not on a double word boundary and so on. The alignment faults are generated only at privilege level 3.

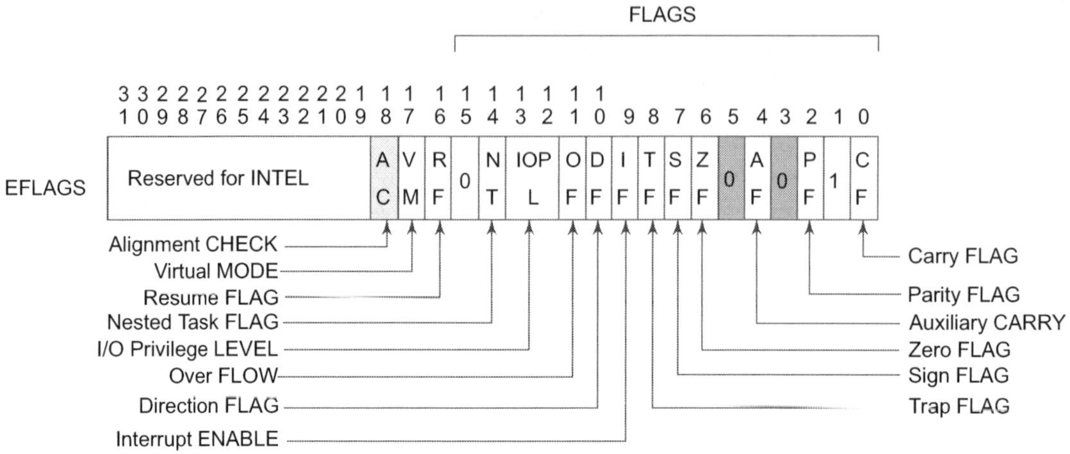

Fig. 10.16 *Flag Register of 80486*

10.13.3 Signal Descriptions of 80486

The 80486 pin grid array package and the pin positions are shown in Fig. 10.17, followed by the signal descriptions of 80486 in brief. The signals are grouped according to their functions as follows. The important groups of the signals which are not present in 80386 are highlighted appropriately, so that the readers can concentrate on those signals. The detailed explanation of these signals have been provided, wherever necessary.

Timing Signal CLK This input provides the basic system timing for the operation of 80486.

Address Bus

A_{31}–A_2 These are the address lines of the microprocessor, and are used for selecting memory/IO devices. However, for memory/IO addressing we also need another set of signals known as byte enable signals BE_0–BE_3. These active-low byte enable signals(BE_0#–BE_3#) indicate which byte of the 32-bit data bus is active during the read or write cycle. For example, BE_0# = '0' indicates that the least significant byte is active. Similarly, BE3# = '0', implies that the most significant byte in 32-bit data is accessed.

Data Bus

D_0-D_{31} This is a bidirectional data bus with D_0 as the least and D_{31} as the most significant data bit.
Data Parity Group The pins of this group of signals are extremely important, because they are used to detect the parity during the memory read and write operations.
DP_0-DP_3 These four data parity input/output pins are used for representing the individual parity of 4bytes (32 bits) of the data bus.

For example, during a memory write operation, the CPU sends a 32-bit data to the memory. The CPU also generates an even parity bit for each byte of the 32-bit data. The even parity bit for the least significant byte is sent to the DP_0 pin while the even parity bit for the most significant byte is sent to DP_3 pin. Thus the CPU outputs four parity bits (DP_0–DP_3) corresponding to the four bytes. Interestingly, the CPU also stores these parity bits in a separate parity data memory bank. During the future memory read operation for the same data, the even parities of each of the data bytes are checked and then compared with the corresponding

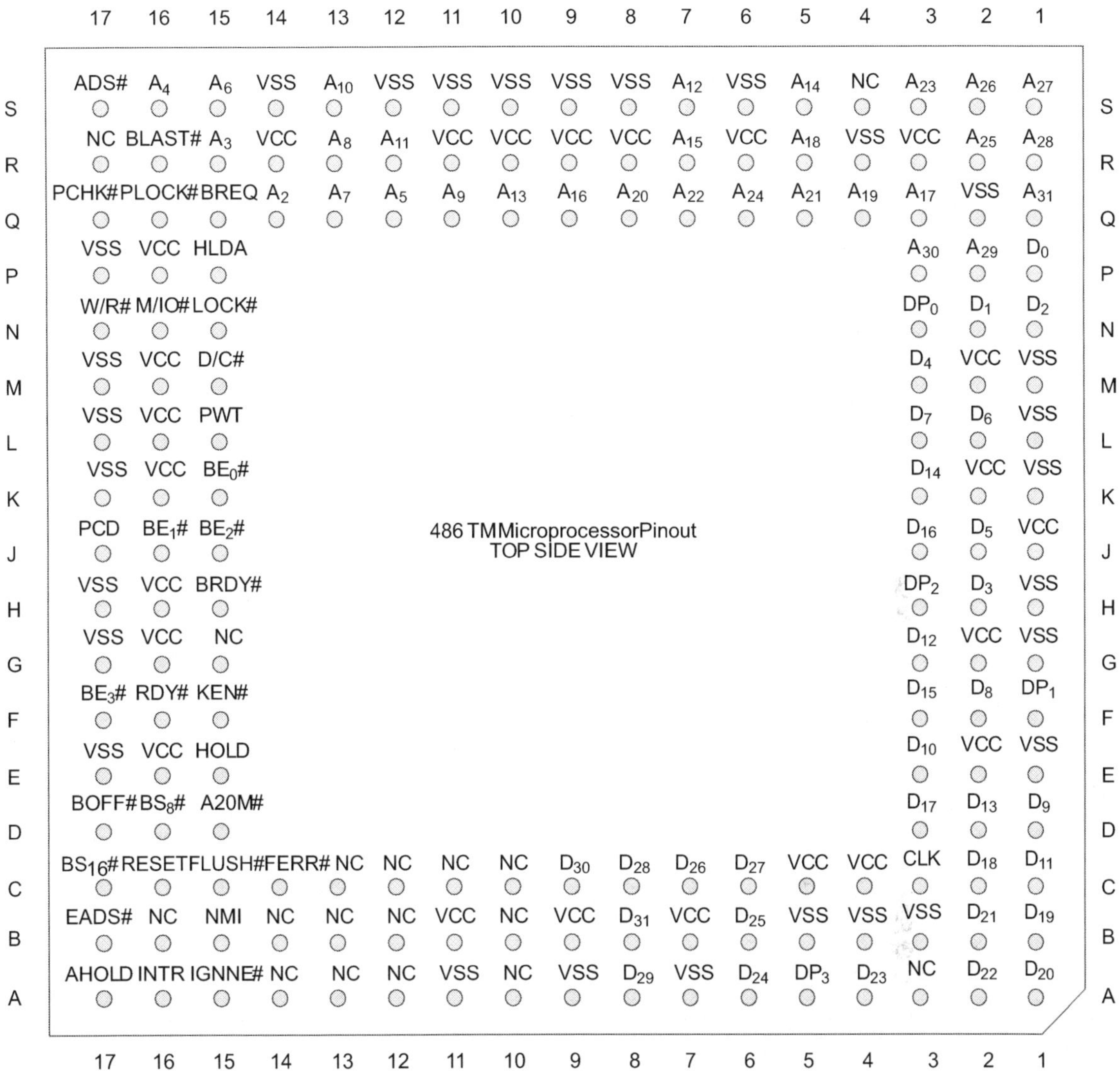

Fig. 10.17 *Pin Diagram of 80486 (Pin Side)*

stored parity bits in the parity memory bank. If there is any mismatch, the CPU sends an active-low signal to the PCHK pin.

Bus Cycle Definition Group

M/IO# This output pin differentiates between memory and I/O operations.
D/C# This output pin differentiates between data/control operations.
W/R# This output pin differentiates between read and write bus cycles.
LOCK# This output pin indicates that the current bus cycle is locked.
PLOCK# This pseudo lock pin indicates that the current operation may require more than one bus cycle for its completion. The bus is to be locked until then.

Bus Control Group

ADS# The address status output pin indicates that a valid bus cycle definition and addresses are currently available on the corresponding pins.
RDY# This input pin acts as a ready signal for the current non-burst cycle.

Burst Control Group

BRDY# The burst mode of memory read or memory operation is undertaken when a number of read or write operations are attempted or to from successive memory locations one after another. In the burst mode, the speed of memory access may even be doubled compared to normal memory read/write operations. The BRDY# and BLAST# signals are used for facilitating burst mode of memory read and write operations. The burst ready input pin acts as ready input for the current burst cycle. The DRAM controller asserts the BRDY# signal when it is ready with the data word.
BLAST# When the 80486 CPU initiates the burst mode of memory access, it asserts the BLAST# signal high. Thereafter, the BRDY# signal is next asserted for starting the memory access operation. When the requisite number of memory read or write operations have been performed, the CPU asserts BLAST# low. This indicates the end of the burst data transfer operation.

Interrupts

RESET This input pin resets the processor, if it goes high.
INTR This is a maskable interrupt input that is controlled by the IF in the flag register.
NMI This is a non-maskable interrupt input, of type 2.

Bus Arbitration Group

BREQ This active-high output indicates that the 80486 has generated (internally) a bus request. When a number of 80486 processors share a common bus, the CPU that intends to get the access of the common bus asserts this bus request BREQ line.
HOLD This pin acts as a local bus hold input, to be activated by another bus master like DMA controller, to enable it to gain the control of the system bus. This pin is functionally similar to the BREQ pin.
HLDA This is an output that acknowledges the receipt of a valid HOLD request.
BOFF# When a CPU requests access to the bus, and if the bus is granted to it, then the current bus master which is currently in charge of the bus will be asked to back off or release the bus . This active-high BACK OFF input signal thus forces the current bus master (80486) to release the bus in the next clock cycle.

Cache Invalidation Group

AHOLD The address hold request input pin enables other bus masters to use the 80486 system bus during a cache invalidation cycle.
EADS# The external address input signal indicates that a valid address for external bus cycle is available on the address bus.

Cache control Group

KEN# The cache enable input pin is used to determine whether the current cycle is cacheable or not.

FLUSH# The cache flush input, if activated, clears the cache contents and validity bits.

Page Cachebility Group

PCD, PWT The page cache disable and page write-through output pins reflect the status of the corresponding bits in page table or page directory entry.

FPU Error Group

FERR The FERR output pin is activated if the floating point unit reports any error.
IGNNE If ignore numeric processor extension input pin is activated, the 80486 ignores the numeric processor (FPU) errors and continues executing non-control floating-point instructions. The FERR pin is still kept asserted by the CPU.

Bus Size Control Group

BS8# and BS16# The bus size-8 and bus size-16 inputs are used for the dynamic bus sizing feature of 80486. These two pins enable 80486 to be interfaced with 8-bit or 16-bit devices though the CPU has a bus width of 32 bits. The 32-bit data (possibly) presented by external device may be read in successive 8-bit or 16-bit read cycles.

Address Mask

$A_{20}M_3$ If this input pin is activated, the 80486 masks the physical address line A_{20} before carrying out any memory or cache cycle. This is useful to wrap the complete physical address space around the 1Mbyte memory size, i.e. physical memory space of 8086 in virtual 8086 mode.
Test Access Port Group (Available in 50MHz version only) This is a unique facility available in 80486 which enables it to check the fault conditions of the other on-board components. This is invoked using the JTAG instruction.

TCK The test clock input provides the basic clock required by the boundary scan (test) feature.
TDI The test data input is the serial input pin used to shift the JTAG instructions and data into the component.
TDO The test data output is the serial output pin used to shift the JTAG instruction and data out of the component under test. The TDI and TDO are sampled or driven during the SHIFT-IR and SHIFT-DR TAP controller states.
TMS The test mode select input is decoded by the JTAG TAP (tap access port) to select the operation of this test logic.

Supply Lines

V_{cc} In all 24 pins are allotted for the power supply (+5V).

Ground Lines

V_{ss} These act as return lines for the power supply. In all 28 pins are allotted for the power supply return lines.

No Connection Lines

N/C No connection pins are expected to be left open while connecting the 80486 in the circuit.

10.13.4 General Features of 80486

Floating Point Unit One of the major limitations in 80386–387 system is that the 80386 sends the instruction or data to 80387 using an I/O handshake technique. To perform this handshaking and to carry out the additional housekeeping task, the 80386 requires about 15 clockcycles or more. Thus it was felt that even if the coprocessor architecture is enhanced to achieve a higher speed, the major bottleneck of the communication overhead remains. Hence designers concluded that having an on-chip floating-point unit was imperative and not optional. With this idea, Intel's 80486 CPU integrated an on-chip floating-point unit. Due to the space limitation, however, 80486 implements the FPU based on a partial multiplier array. The FPU contains a shift and add data path which is controlled by microcode.The FPU registers of 80486 are similar to those in 80387. The FPU TAG word, control word and status words are also the same as those of 80387. The FPU can work either under the control of the Memory Management Unit MMU (protected mode) or without any control of MMU (read mode). The FPU supports all the data types supported by 80387. The floating-point unit instruction set of 80486 is upwardly compatible with that of 80387. A large number of instructions supporting floating-point arithmetic are supported by 80486. Some of the important ones include FSQRT (Floating-point Square Root), floating-point transcendental like FSIN and floating-point arithmetic instructions like FMUL. The detailed discussion of the instruction set of 80486 is out of the scope of this book and hence avoided.

Addressing Modes The addressing modes supported by 80486 are exactly the same as those of 80386. The physical address calculation methods of 80486 are also similar to those of 80386 in real as well as protected virtual address mode. The memory organisation and addressing techniques are the same as those of 80386. The memory and I/O addressing capability of 80486 is the same as that of 80386.

Interrupts of 80486 Like other 8086 family processors, the 80486 can also handle 256 (00 to FFH) hardware interrupts on its INTR pin. The interrupt type N(00 to FF) is to be passed to the CPU by an external hardware like interrupt controller. In the real mode, the structure of the Interrupt Vector Table (IVT) is exactly the same as that of 8086. However in protected mode, the interrupt vectors are 8-byte quantities and are handled by an interrupt descriptor table, containing 256 possible interrupt vectors ($256 \times 8 = 2$ Kbytes). Out of the total of the 256 interrupts, 32 are reserved by Intel while the remaining 224 are free for use by the users. The interrupt priorities and other details are same as the other 8086 family processors.

Data Types of 80486

The 80486 CPU supports a wide range of data types including the floating-point data types, as listed briefly. Please note that the FPU does not support any unsigned data type.

(i) Signed/unsigned Data Type 8-bit, 16-bit, 32-bit signed and unsigned integers are supported by 80486 while the FPU supports 16-bit, 32-bit and 64-bit signed data.

(ii) Floating Point Data Types Single precision, double precision, extended precision real data are supported only by the FPU.

(iii) BCD Data Types Packed and unpacked BCD data types. The CPU supports 8-bit packed and unpacked data types. The FPU supports 80-bit packed BCD data types.

(iv) String Data Types Strings of bits, bytes, words and double words are supported by the CPU. Each of the strings may contain up to 4 Gbytes.

(v) ASCII Data Types The ASCII representation of the characters are supported by 80486.

(vi) Pointer Data Types 48-bit pointers containing 32-bit offset at the least significant bits and 16-bit selector at the most significant bits are supported by the CPU. Also 32-bit pointers containing 32-bit offsets are supported by the CPU.

(vii) Little Endian and Big Endian Data Types Normally, the 8086 family uses the Little Endian data format. This means for a data of size bigger than one byte, the least significant byte is stored at the lowest memory address while the most significant byte is stored at the highest memory address. The complete data is referred to by the lowest memory address, i.e. the address of the least significant byte.

The Big Endian format allows the storage of data in the exactly opposite manner, i.e. the MSB is stored at the lowest memory address, while the LSB is stored at highest memory address. The 80486 has two special instructions to convert a data from Little to Big Endian or vice versa. The pointers and Big Endian data types were not supported by 80386.

Modes of Operation of 80486 After reset, the 80486, just like 80286 and 80386, starts execution in the real address mode. The real address mode operation of 80486 is exactly similar to 80386. While executing in real address mode, the 80486 initializes registers, peripherals, IVT sets up descriptor tables and prepares itself for the protected mode. The protected mode operation of 80486 is also similar to that of 80386, right from the address formation to descriptor types and structures. In the protected virtual address mode, the 80486 also supports a virtual 8086 mode for execution of 8086 applications. The protection schemes and privilege levels allowed by 80486 are similar to those of 80386. The other operations like task switching, paging and exception handling of 80486 are also similar to the corresponding operations in 80386.

10.13.5 On Chip Cache and Cache Control Unit

This is a unique feature of 80486 that is not available in 80386. The on-chip cache is used for storing the opcodes as well as data. For this new enhancement, to the architecture of 80386, the two bits, PWT (Page Write Through) and PCD (Page Cache Disable) are defined in the page directory entry and page table entry of 80486 as shown in Figs 10.18(a) and (b).

The Page Write Through (PWT) bit controls the write policy for the current page. If PWT = 1, then the current page is write through otherwise, it is write back. The PCD bit controls the cachebility of the corresponding page. If PCD = 0, the caching is enabled for on-chip cache subject to the favourable status of KEN# (cache enable) input, the status of CD (cache disabled) and NW (No Write-Through) bits in the control register 0 (CR_0). If PCD = 1, independent of all other pins or bit status, the cacheing is disabled. The 80486 maintains a write through cache, hence the PWT bit is ignored internally, still it can be used to control the write policy of the second level cache (external). The PWT and PCD bits' status is displayed on the PWT and PCD pins of 80486 during a memory access.

To accelerate the speed of operation, the 80486 is provided with an 8 Kbytes on-chip cache. However, even with this added feature, the 80486 is fully software compatible with 80386. The physical organization of the cache is shown in Fig. 10.19. The 8 Kbytes of on-chip cache is divided into four 2Kbytes associative memory blocks. Each 2Kbytes memory block is arranged in 16 byte (columns) and 128 rows, i.e. each of 128 rows, contain 16 bytes. Each of the 128 rows is associated with a 21-bit tag register. The cache is referred to by the row number (address) and block number. A 16-byte row is divided into 4-byte lines. Any of the four lines cannot be accessed partially. If a write operation is attempted to an address of which the segment descriptor is available in cache, along with the cache, the data is written to the external memory, otherwise, it is only written to external memory.

31 … 12	11 10 9	8	7	6	5	4	3	2	1	0
Page Table Address 31..12	OS Reserved	0	0	D	A	PCD	PWT	U/S	R/W	P

Fig. 10.18(a) *Page Directory Entry (Point to Page Table)*

31 … 12	11 10 9	8	7	6	5	4	3	2	1	0
Page Frame Address 31..12	OS Reserved	0	0	D	A	PCD	PWT	U/S	R/W	P

Fig. 10.18(b) *Page Table Entry (Point to Page)*

Cache Maintenance The on-chip cache is controlled using the Cache Disable (CD) and No Write-through (NW) bits of control register CR_0 as shown in Table 10.3. To completely disable the cache, the CD and NW bits must be set to 11 and the cache must be flushed. Otherwise, every cache hit to the previous contents will unnecessarily generate a cache read cycle internally. Any memory block can be defined as cacheable or noncacheable by using external hardware or system software. The external hardware informs the microprocessor, by deactivating the KEN# pin, that the referenced area is noncacheable.

Table 10.3 *Control of Cache using CD and NW Bits of CR_0*

Mode of Operation	*NW*	*CD*
Cache fill enabled, Write-through and invalidates enabled	0	0
INVALID, If CR_0 loaded with this, a General protection fault with error code 0 is generated	0	1
Cache fill disabled, Write-through and invalidates enabled	1	0
Cache fill disabled, Write-through and invalidates disabled	1	1

The system software uses PCD page table entry to avoid the cacheing of the memory pages. The data is supplied from the cache, if a cache hit occurs during a read operation, otherwise, a read cycle is generated using an external system bus. If a read operation is carried out over a cacheable portion of memory, the CPU starts a cache line fill operation. The cache lines are filled only during the cache miss that occurred for a read operation. A write operation does not start any cache line fill even on cache misses. However, a cache line is updated during a write operation, only on cache hits. The cache line fill operation is carried out using the dynamic bus sizing feature of 80486DX. In other words, though the data bus size of 80486 is 32-bit, a cache line fill may use only 8-bit or 16-bit data bus as per requirement.

The cache memory is expected to keep track of the recently used external memory area. Obviously, as the microprocessor goes on executing, the cache contents need to be upgraded. That is, the least recently used cache line should be invalidated, while the recently used memory block should be allotted a cache line. The 80486 offers a software as well as hardware mechanism to carry out the invalidation operations.

An external memory read operation, on cache-miss generates an external read cycle. If this reference is to be cacheable, the block of cache memory must be updated with this new reference. If the cache is already full, the microprocessor checks, if there is any invalid line that can be replaced to create space for the new reference. If any invalid line (out of the four) is found out, that is replaced with the newly

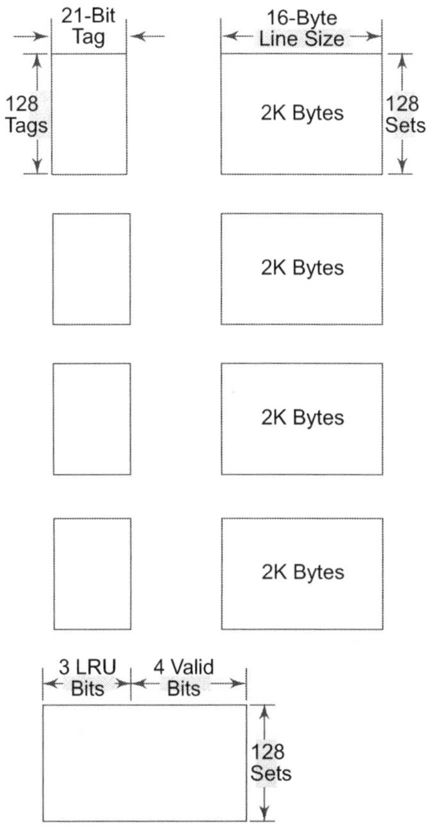

Fig. 10.19 *Physical Organisation of on-chip Cache*

referred data. If all the four lines in the set are valid, a Least Recently Used (LRU) line is replaced by the new one. A block of cache mechanism, containing 128 sets of 7-bits each, maintain the record of recent uses and valid lines. A 16-byte row contains four 4-bytes lines named as I_0, I_1, I_2 and I_3. Each of the lines has a valid bit associated with it. Thus the four lines have four valid bits. The LRU mechanism refers to the three LRU bits - B_0, B_1 and B_2 and decides the line to be replaced by the new one as shown in Fig. 10.20.

The address hold input pin and external address valid input pins are used during cache line invalidate cycles.

The on-chip cache can be flushed using external hardware via pin FLUSH#, or using software. The flushing operation clears all the valid bits for all the cache lines. The flush pin is to be asserted for flushing the cache and is to be deasserted again for further execution. If it is not done so, the execution stops as the CPU is busy with the flushing of the cache again and again. The INVD and WBINVD instructions are also used for flushing the internal as well as external cache.

The 80486 processor has a paging unit with a Translation Look-aside Buffer (TLB) containing 32 most recently used page table entries. The paging unit of 80486 also uses the least recently used mechanism to update the Translation Look-aside Buffer. The page directory and page table entries may be stored into the on-chip cache by setting the PCD bits in CR_3 to 0. If the PCD bits are set to 1, the page cacheing is not allowed, i.e. storing the page table entry and page directory entry into the cache is not allowed.

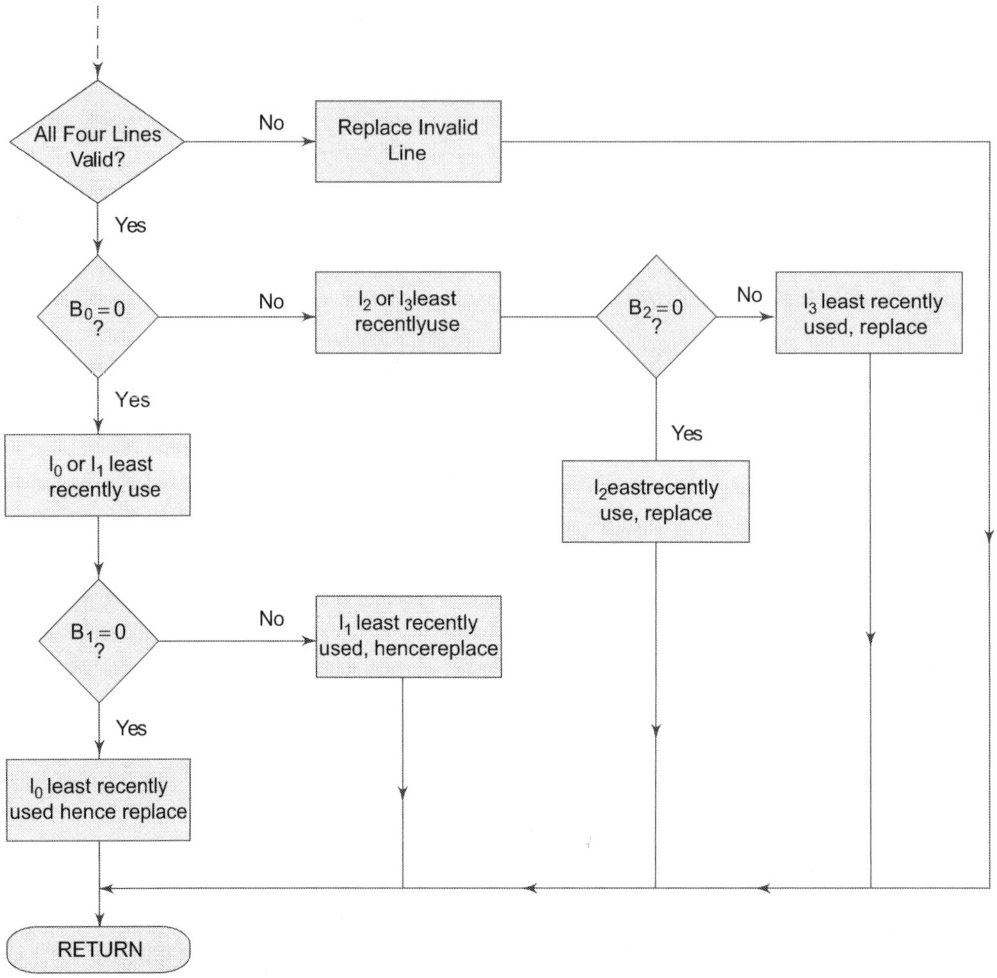

Fig. 10.20 *LRU Replacement Algorithm*

SUMMARY

This chapter introduces two elegant CPUs- the first, 32-bit processor 80386 followed by 80486. Some of the functional concepts of 80386 are similar to 80286, and those have not been repeated again in this chapter. Further architectural developments, addressing modes, data formats and register set of 80386 have been discussed in comparison with 80286. The real address mode of operation and protected virtual address mode of operation have been discussed in significant details and compared with 80286. The paging unit, a new feature in 80386, is discussed in details along with the virtual 8086 mode of operation of 80386. This mode enables the 80386 to execute the 8086 applications even in the protected mode. Then the numeric coprocessor 80387 has been discussed highlighting its architecture, pin diagram, register set and interconnections with 80386. To end with, salient features of 80486 have been briefly discussed here.

EXERCISES

10.1 Enlist the salient features of 80386.
10.2 Draw and discuss internal architecture of 80386 in detail.
10.3 Explain the following signal functions of 80386.
(i) BE_0#–BE_3# (ii) W/R# (iii) D/C
(iv) ADS# (v) NA# (vi) BS_{16}
10.4 Draw and discuss the register set of 80386 and explain a typical function of each of the registers in brief.
10.5 Draw and discuss the flag register of 80386 in detail.
10.6 Explain the use of each of the following registers of 80386.
(i) Segment Descriptor Registers (ii) Control Registers
(iii) Debug and Test Registers (iv) System Address Registers
10.7 Explain the different additional addressing modes supported by 80386 over 80286.
10.8 Enlist the different data types supported by 80386.
10.9 Explain the physical address formation in real address mode of 80386.
10.10 Explain the physical address formation in PVAM of 80386.
10.11 Draw and discuss the structures of the different descriptors supported by 80386.
10.12 What do you mean by a descriptor table?
10.13 How many maximum descriptors can be accessed by 80386 for a single task? What is the memory addressing capability of a single descriptor? Justify the virtual memory addressing capability of 80386 per task.
10.14 Discuss the different descriptor types supported by 80386.
10.15 What are the different exceptions generated by 80386?
10.16 What do you mean by paging? What are its advantages and disadvantages?
10.17 Draw and discuss the paging mechanism of 80386 in details.
10.18 What are the differences between the logical addresses, linear addresses and physical addresses?
10.19 Explain the procedure of converting a linear address into a physical address.
10.20 What is translation look aside buffer? How does it speed up the execution of the programs?
10.21 Write a short note on virtual 8086 mode of 80386.
10.22 Draw and discuss the architecture of 80387.
10.23 Enlist the different data types supported by 80387.
10.24 Discuss the register set of 80387.
10.25 Draw and discuss the interface of 80387 with 80386.
10.26 Enlist the salient features of 80486.
10.27 Draw and discuss the flag register of 80486.
10.28 Enlist four major architectural advancement in 80486 over 80386.
10.29 What is the use of TEST and DEBUG facility in 80486?
10.30 What do you mean by cache memory? How does it speed up the program execution?
10.31 Explain the cache management unit of 80486.
10.32 Write short notes on the following.
(i) Cache Maintenance Operations (ii) Paging Unit
10.33 Enlist the data types supported by 80486.
10.34 Enlist the different functional groups of signals provided by 80486.

11

Recent Advances in Microprocessor Architectures—A Journey from Pentium Onwards

INTRODUCTION

In the course of man's journey towards building more powerful PCs, the introduction of Pentium CPU from Intel is an important landmark. The high performance level of this processor is owing to its superscalar architecture with massive integer pipelining and a powerful on-chip floating-point unit.

We start our discussions with a look at the scenario of PC and workstation world when Pentium was first introduced. This discussion will help one to understand the course of development of the advanced microprocessors from Intel Pentium onwards.

When 80386/486 was ruling the PC world, a number of RISC based workstations with much better performance in terms of speed and graphic resolution, viz. 50 MHz microSPARC processor from SUN, or DEC's 100 MHz Alpha AXP family, etc., were already in the workstation market. Thus workstations based on RISC architecture had an edge over the PCs developed around 386 or 486 CPUs.

The essential elegance of RISC architecture lies in adopting a simple set of instructions with less complex addressing modes and obviously an associated simple instruction decoder. The power of a RISC architecture also lies in the massive pipelining (parallelism) that it employs along with other architectural features, e.g. register windowing, etc. While comparing the CISC based PC architecture with RISC based system, a number of important observations could be made. Apart from the complexity in the addressing modes and also in the instruction set of the conventional CISC CPUs like 386 or 486, there was not much parallelism (pipelining) in these processors, which resulted in a comparatively slower speed compared to the RISC based CPUs. One of the major bottlenecks in case of the earlier CPUs was possibly the inclusion of a separate math coprocessor. The 8087, math coprocessor which is a companion of 8086 executes a floating-point instruction, whenever it comes across such an instruction. The architecture of these math coprocessors have continuously evolved from 8087 to 80387, the companion processor of 80386 CPU.

Interestingly, the instruction and data transfer between 80386 and 80387 takes place through an I/O handshaking mode. The 80386 requires around 15 clock cycles to perform the I/O handshaking with 80387 and to take care of some internal housekeeping operations. Thus, as we can see that even if the operating speed of these math co-processors are increased, the overall floating-point speed performance does not increase appreciably.

This was the reason, why an on-chip coprocessor was included while designing the 80486 CPU. One may note that 80486 requires only about four clock cycles for floating-point transactions, resulting in a better floating-point performance. Another limitation of this coprocessor architecture is that the total number of internal registers is less, i.e. only eight in case of 8087/387 or even 80487 CPU. These are essentially stack oriented, rather than register oriented processors, which restrict their speed. There are however other floating-point processors from other vendors (say Weitek math coprocessor) which can perform single-precision floating-point operations in a single cycle or double-precision in two cycles, etc. These math coprocessors have more number of internal registers, and are essentially based on register oriented architecture. All that we wanted to convey is the fact that floating-point operation was really a major bottleneck in the CPUs like 286, 386, or 486.

Keeping in view the above scenario, we will now present the architecture of Pentium which was an extremely challenging attempt to bridge the gap between CISC based low-end PCs and RISC based high-end workstations.

11.1 SALIENT FEATURES OF 80586 (PENTIUM)

In the introductory note we have hinted that the designers of Pentium had basically two clear points in mind:

(a) To design a CPU with enhanced complex instruction sets, which should remain code compatible with earlier X86 CPUs—from 8086 to 486 and,
(b) To achieve performance so as to match the third generation RISC performances.

Both these objectives were, to a large extent met while designing the Pentium CPU. Thus Pentium designers introduced a lot of RISC features while retaining the complex instruction sets supported by the earlier X86 CPUs.

A salient feature of Pentium is its *superscalar*, *superpipelined* architecture. It has two integer pipelines U and V, where each one is a 4-stage pipeline. This enhances the speed of integer arithmetic of Pentium to a large extent. Moreover, it has an on-chip floating-point unit, which has increased the floating-point performance manifold compared to the floating-point performances of 80386/486 processors.

Another feature of Pentium is that it contains two separate caches, viz. data cache and instruction cache. One may recall that in 80486 there was a single unified data/instruction cache. All these features will be explained in detail later in this section.

Before presenting the Pentium architecture, a few advanced architectural concepts will be explained first. This will help the reader to understand the superscalar pipelined architectures of advanced CPUs like Pentium.

11.2 A FEW RELEVANT CONCEPTS OF COMPUTER ARCHITECTURE

One of the key issues in the design of modern computer architecture may be stated like this: 'How to ensure maximum throughput from a system?'. There are various advanced architectural techniques which have been employed to achieve maximum throughput. We will discuss only a few of them.

So far while discussing the Intel CPU architectures up to 80486, we have seen that only one instruction is issued to the execution unit per cycle. This obviously leads to a comparatively slow process of decoding and execution. For enhancement of processor performance, beyond one instruction per cycle, the computer architects employ the technique of *Multiple Instruction Issue* (MII). Thus a microprocessor which is capable of issuing more than one instruction per single processor cycle will be termed as MII microprocessor. Obviously, for executing more than one instruction in a cycle, the microprocessor must have more than one execution channels. Thus there are two problems, viz. (a) How to issue multiple instructions and (b) How to execute them concurrently. Keeping in view these two issues, MII architectures may again be redivided in two classes of architectures—(i) Very Long Instruction Word (VLIW) architecture and (ii) Superscalar architecture.

In VLIW processors, the compiler reorders the sequential stream of code that is coming from memory into a fixed size instruction group and issues them in parallel for execution. On the other hand, in superscalar architecture the hardware decides which instructions are to be issued concurrently at run time.

The Pentium CPU is based on superscalar architecture. The hardware, in case of a superscalar architecture like Pentium, becomes enormously complex because in such a processor multiple instructions have to be issued in each cycle to the execution unit.

Another important concept involved here is that of pipelining. We have already explained pipelined architecture for computing integer arithmetic in an 80486 CPU. As a matter of fact, pipelining has been implemented in all the processors from 8086 onwards, in a limited sense when instructions have been prefetched and stored in a queue. With these few remarks, we now present the architecture of Pentium.

11.3 SYSTEM ARCHITECTURE

The block diagram showing the overall organisation of the Pentium processor is presented in Fig. 11.1. The important features are detailed next.

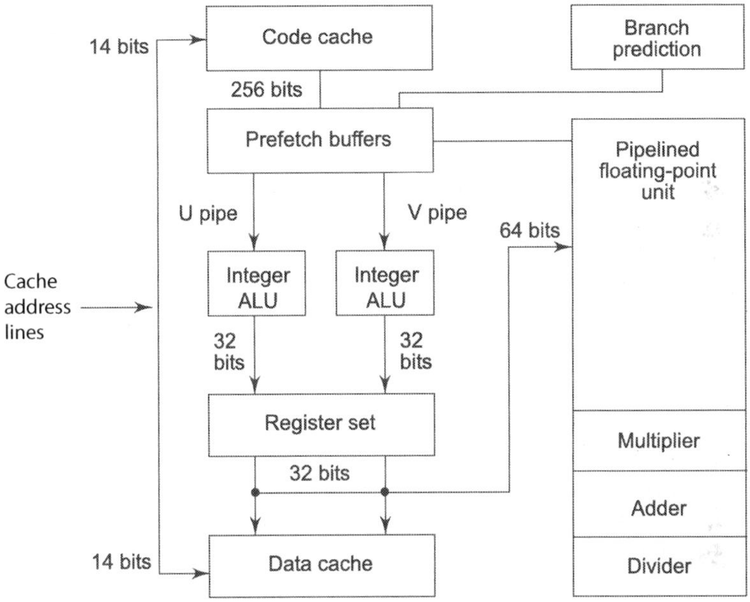

Fig. 11.1 *Pentium CPU Architecture*

11.3.1 Superscalar Execution

A salient feature of Pentium is that it supports superscalar architecture which has been explained in the previous section. For execution of multiple instructions concurrently, Pentium microprocessor issues two instructions in parallel to the two independent integer pipelines known as U and V pipelines. Each of these two pipelines has 5 stages, as shown in Fig. 11.2. These pipeline stages are similar to the one in 80486 CPU. Functions of these pipelines have been presented in brief:

1. In the prefetch stage of the pipeline, the CPU fetches the instructions from the instruction cache, which stores the instructions to be executed. In this stage, the CPU also aligns the codes appropriately. This is required since the instructions are of variable length and the initial opcode bytes of each instruction should be appropriately aligned. After the prefetch stage, there are two decode stages D_1 and D_2.
2. In the D_1 stage, the CPU decodes the instruction and generates a control word. For simple RISC like instructions involving register data transfer or arithmetic and logical operations, only a single control word might be sufficient enough for starting the execution. However, as we know X86 architecture supports complex CISC instructions and require microcoded control sequencing.

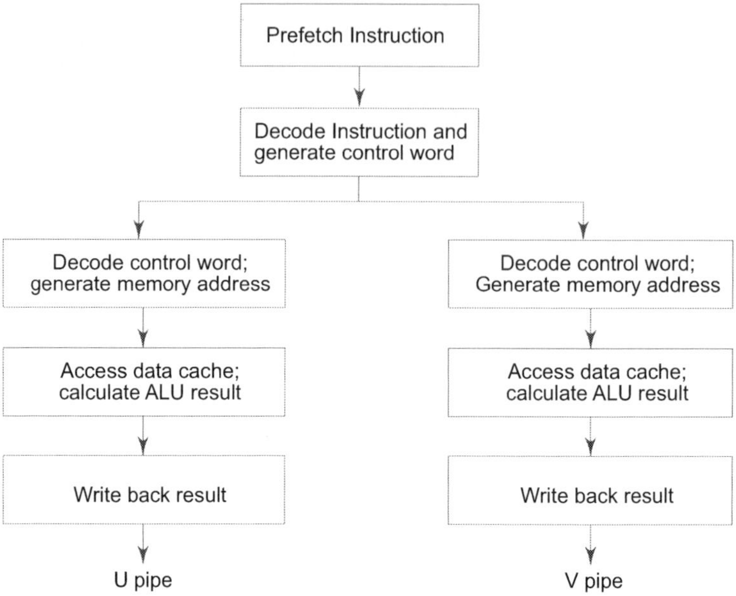

Fig. 11.2 *Superscalar Organisation*

3. Thus a second decode stage D_2 is required where the control word from D_1 stage is again decoded for final execution. Also the CPU generates addresses for data memory references in this stage.
4. In the execution stage, known as E stage, the CPU either accesses the data cache for data operands or executes the arithmetic/logic computations or floating-point operations in the execution unit.
5. In the final stage of the five-stage pipeline, which is the WB (writeback) stage, the CPU updates the registers' contents or the status in the flag register depending upon the execution result.

Although, as we mentioned Pentium pipeline structure is somewhat similar to the 80486 pipeline structure, Pentium achieves a lot of speed-up by integrating additional hardware in each pipeline stages. Thus while 80486 may take two clock cycles to decode some instructions, Pentium takes only one.

11.3.2 Separate Code and Data Cache

Unlike 80486 microprocessors' unified code/data cache of 8 Kbyte size, Pentium has introduced two separate 8 Kbyte caches for code and data. From the fundamental principles of cache operation, one may observe that a unified cache, as in 80486 will always have a higher hit ratio than two separate caches. Why then Pentium has gone in for separate caches? The answer probably lies in the fact that to support the superscalar organisation, it demanded more bandwidth that a unified cache could not provide. Moreover to efficiently execute the branch prediction (explained later in the section), separate caches are more meaningfully employed.

11.3.3 Floating-point Unit

We have already mentioned in the introductory note in this chapter that to reduce the communication overhead, there is a need to eliminate the coprocessor which has been actually implemented in 80486 CPU. The 80486 CPU contains a floating-point unit which is not pipelined. The FPU of Pentium has introduced massive pipelining with an eight stage pipeline. The first five stages of the pipeline are identical to the U and V integer pipelines as discussed earlier. In the operand fetch stage, the FPU fetches the operands either from the floating-point register file or from the data cache. There are eight general purpose floating point registers in the FPU. There are, however, two execution stages in Pentium, unlike in 80486, viz. the first execution stage (X1 stage) and second execution stage (X2 stage). In these two stages, the floating point unit reads the data from data cache and executes the floating-point computation. In the write back stage of the pipeline, the FPU writes the results to the floating-point register file. There is an additional error reporting stage where the FPU reports the internal status (including error) which may necessitate additional processing for completion of the floating-point execution.

The block diagram of the floating-point unit is shown in Fig. 11.3. The unit broadly contains five segments, capable of performing five different floating-point computations. These are briefly explained as follows:

Floating-point Adder Segment (FADD) This segment is responsible for addition of floating-point numbers and executes many floating-point instructions like addition, subtraction and comparison. This segment is active during X_1 and X_2 stages of the pipeline and executes on single-precision, double-precision and extended precision data.

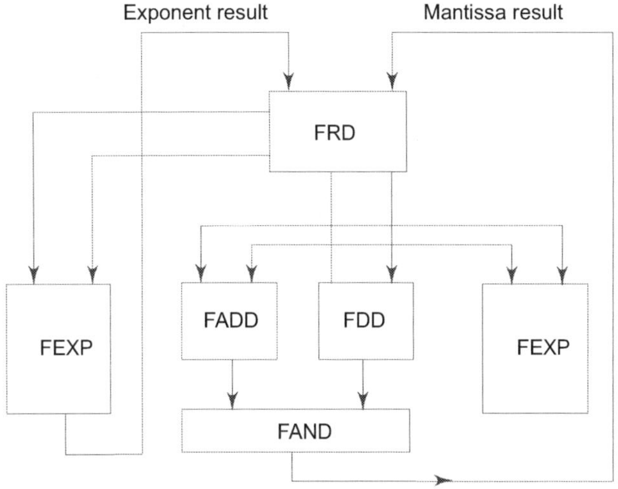

Fig. 11.3 *Organisation of Floating-point Unit Block*

Floating-point Multiplier Segment (FAND) This segment performs floating-point multip-lication in single-precision, double-precision and extended precision modes.

Floating-point Divider Segment (FDD) This segment executes floating-point division and square root instructions. It calculates 2 bits of quotient every cycle and operates during both X_1 and X_2 pipeline stages.

Floating-point Exponent Segment (FEXP) This segment calculates the floating-point exponent. This is an important segment which interacts with all other floating-point segments for necessary adjustment of mantissa and exponent fields in the final stage of a floating-point computation.

Floating-point Rounder Segment (FRD) The results of floating-point addition or division process may be required to be rounded off before write back to the floating-point registers. This segment performs rounding off operation before write back stage.

11.3.4 Floating-point Exceptions

As in the case of integer arithemetic, there are six possible floating-point exceptions in Pentium. These are: 1. Divide by zero 2. Overflow 3. Underflow 4. Denormal operand and 5. Invalid operation. These exceptions carry their usual meanings. The divide by zero exception, invalid operation exception and denormal operand exception can be easily detected even before the actual floating-point calculation.

A mechanism known as *Safe Instruction Recognition* (SIR) had been employed in Pentium. This mechanism determines whether a floating-point operation will be executed without creating any exception. In case an instruction can safely be executed without any exception, the instruction is allowed to proceed for final execution. If a floating-point instruction is not safe, then the pipeline stalls the instruction for three cycles and after that the exception is generated.

11.4 BRANCH PREDICTION

Amongst all the instructions in the X86 instruction set, branch instructions occur moderately frequently, (on the average 15% to 25%). These instructions change the normal sequential control flow of the program and may stall the pipelined execution in the Pentium system. Branches again may be of two types—conditional branch and unconditional branch. In case of a conditional branch, the CPU has to wait till the execution stage to determine whether the condition is met or not. When the condition satisfies, a branch is to be taken.

Pentium designers implemented a branch prediction algorithm for speed up of the instruction execution. A 256 entry branch target buffer in Pentium CPU holds branch target addresses for previously executed branches. The branch target buffer is a four-way set-associative memory. Whenever a branch is taken, the CPU enters the branch instruction address and also the destination address in the branch target buffer. When an instruction is decoded, the CPU searches the branch target buffer to determine whether there exists any entry for a corresponding branch instruction. If there is a hit, i.e. if there exist such entries, then the CPU uses the history to decide whether the branch will be taken or not. If the CPU, based upon its previous history decides to take the branch, it fetches the instructions from the target address and decodes them. However, the issue of whether the branch is correctly taken or not will be resolved only during the early 'write back' stage of the pipeline. If the prediction is correct, the process continues. If the prediction is incorrect, the CPU flushes the pipeline and fetches from the correct target address.

A correctly predicted branch will thus never cause any pipeline bubble. Simulations show that the performance increases by 25 per cent using the BTB.

11.5 ENHANCED INSTRUCTION SET OF PENTIUM

Besides the instructions of X86 family, Pentium also supports computation of several trigonometric and exponential functions through a set of transcendental instructions as shown:

(a) FSIN — to compute sin(θ)
(b) FCOS — to compute cos(θ)
(c) FSINCOS — to compute sine and cosine
(d) FPTAN — to compute tan(θ)
(e) FPATAN — to compute arctan(X)
(f) F2XMI — to compute (2X–1)
(g) FYL2X — to compute Y*log2X
(h) FYL2XP — to compute Y*log2(X+1)

Where θ is an operand angle and X and Y are the operands stored in appropriate floating-point registers.

The above functions have been implemented using polynomial approximation technique, instead of using cordic algorithms for trigonometric function computation. The approximation tables for computation of the above functions are stored in a ROM table which also contains other constants which are required for computation of other floating-point operations.

11.6 WHAT IS MMX?

Intel introduced the MMX(multimedia extension) technology at a time when there was a tremendous need to improve the 2-D and 3-D imaging for multimedia applications.

Most of the algorithms in multimedia applications involve operations on several pixels (picture cell) simultaneously. For example, in a colour image, a pixel comprises three components, red, green and blue, where each component of the pixel is an 8-bit integer. Thus the intensity of the pixel varies from 0 to 255 in each component—red, green and blue. A pixel of an image thus may be represented by a 24-bit quantity. Similarly, in case of a black and white image, a pixel may be represented by an 8-bit number. Most of the image processing algorithms and image compression techniques required for multimedia applications involve matrix multiplication and matrix convolution type of operations and involve operations on multiple number of pixels simultaneously. Thus most of the multimedia applications require SIMD (*Single Instruction Stream Multiple Data Stream*) kind of architecture. This is precisely what Intel provides through a set of the 57 MMX instructions. These instructions help the programmer to write efficient programs for image filtering, image enhancement, coding and other algorithms. Using conventional CPUs, we can operate on two pixels at the most, concurrently. Using MMX instruction set, on the other hand, we can load eight pixels simultaneously and perform concurrent operations on them. Here lies the elegance of the MMX technology.

11.7 INTEL MMX ARCHITECTURE

While explaining Intel Pentium architecture, we have stated that there are eight general purpose floating-point registers in the floating-point unit. Each of these eight registers are 80-bits wide. For floating-point operations, 64 bits are used for the mantissa and the rest 16 bits for exponent. Intel MMX instructions use these floating-point registers as MMX registers and use only the 64-bit mantissa portion of these registers to store MMX operands. Thus the MMX programmers virtually get eight new MMX registers, each of 64 bits. The question, however, is whether a programmer can use these registers both as floating-point registers for storing floating-point data and as MMX registers for storing MMX operands, in the same program. Although it is possible to use the same set of registers as floating-point registers and MMX register in the same program, it is preferable not to use them concurrently. Rather, after a sequence of MMX instructions is executed, these registers should be cleared by an instruction 'EMMS', which implies empty the MMX stack. Similarly, the floating-point users should use the same instruction after executing the floating-point instructions. Although context switching between multimedia program execution and floating-point execution is permissible, it is not recommended. Generally, it is advisable that the multimedia program developers should partition the MMX instructions into a separate library routine.

As may be pointed out here that the MMX instructions are essentially integer type instructions, the integer pipelined architecture of Pentium is ideally suited for implementation of MMX instructions. Since the MMX registers are all 64 bits long, one can pack a total of 8 pixel values (each 8-bit) in a single register.

Thus while any X86 CPU can manipulate only one pixel at a time, using MMX architecture, we can manipulate eight such pixels, packed in a single 64-bit register, concurrently. This is a great achievement so far as the multimedia applications are concerned.

11.8 MMX DATA TYPES

The MMX technology supports the following four data types.

1. Packed bytes—In this data type, eight bytes can be packed into one 64-bit quantity.
2. Packed word—Here four words can be packed into 64-bit.
3. Packed double word—Here two double words can be packed into 64-bit.
4. One quadword—One single 64-bit quantity.

The MMX instructions have been so designed that they can perform parallel operations on multiple data elements. More specifically they can operate on packed data, i.e. group of eight packed bytes or four packed words etc. For example, to add two groups of eight packed bytes we can use the instruction PADDB, i.e. add packed bytes. Similarly PADDW denotes 'add two groups of four packed words'.

11.9 WRAPAROUND AND SATURATION ARITHMETIC

While computing fixed point arithmetic, if there is any overflow or underflow, the most significant bit is lost. For example, while adding two unsigned 16-bit numbers in 8086 we may get an unsigned 17-bit result. This 17-bit result cannot be represented in a 16-bit register of the CPU resulting in a truncation of the result and only the lower 16-bits of the result are stored in the register. This is known as wrap-around effect. This overflow/underflow condition is, however, reflected in status flag. In saturation arithmetic, instead of losing the 17th bit, the result is clamped to the largest possible unsigned number that can be represented in a 16-bit register, i.e. FFFF (16-bit).

11.10 MMX INSTRUCTION SET

The MMX technology adds 57 new instructions to the instruction set of X86 processors. These instructions are known as enhanced MMX instructions and are designed specifically for performing multimedia tasks. Before we explain the instructions, the following discussion may be useful:

1. All the MMX instructions operate on two operands, (a) the source operand and (b) the destination operand. Usually, in an instruction, the right operand is the source operand while the left one is the destination operand. After the execution of the instruction, the result is kept in the destination operand. Please note that EMMS instruction does not have any operand.
2. In all the MMX instructions, the source operand may be found either in an MMX register or in memory. The destination operand, however, resides in an MMX register only. In case of data transfer group of instructions, however, both the source and destination data may reside in memory location or an internal MMX register.
3. All the MMX instructions may operate on any of the data type mentioned earlier: packed byte, word or doubleword. Thus each instruction may have several variations. If the operands are in packed mode, the prefix P is used to indicate packed data. For example, PADDB implies addition of two data in packed byte (B) format. Similarly W, D and Q denote word, double word and quadword respectively.
4. Suffix S of an instruction indicates signed Saturation and US indicates Unsigned Saturation, while executing arithmetic computation in saturation mode as has been discussed already.
5. The ordering of the bytes in the multibyte format is little endian. This means that the less significant byte is always in the lower addresses.
6. None of the MMX instruction will affect the flag register.

The major instructions supported by MMX architecture are briefly discussed as follows.

PADD (B, W, D) These instructions perform addition of two sets of packed 8-byte data/packed four word data/ packed two double-word data in parallel using wraparound, unsigned saturation and signed saturation arithmetic, as discussed earlier. The parallel addition takes place in a single cycle. The upper and lower saturation limits for unsigned byte addition are FFH(FFFFH for 16-bit) and 00(0000 for 16-bit) respectively. For signed byte addition they are 7FH and 80H respectively.

PSUB (B, W, D) These instructions perform subtraction in packed byte, word and doubleword format.

PCMPEQ (B, W, D) These instructions compare the respective data elements of two packed data types in parallel. If the result of comparison is a success, i.e. 'true', then a mask of 1s is generated; otherwise, a mask of 0s is generated, in destination operand. We have already mentioned that these instructions do not affect the flag bits.

PCMPGT (B, W, D) These are similar instructions as in 3 which compares to check the greater than condition. The results of the mask generation is shown below:

51	38	23	FF

42	20	35	0A

1..1	1..1	00..0	11..1

PMULLW (Packed multiply high) This instruction multiplies two operands; each of four signed packed words in parallel using 16-bit precision multiplication. This means that four 16 X 16 bit multiplications are performed and the lower order 16 bits of the 32-bit products are stored in destination.

PMULHW (Packed multiply low) This is similar to PMULLW. The higher order 16-bits of the 32-bit products are stored in the destination here.

PMADDWD (Packed multiply and add) This is an extremely important multimedia instruction which multiplies four signed words of destination operand with four signed words of source operand which results in two 32-bit double words. The two higher order words are added and the result is stored in the higher double word of the destination operand. Similarly, two low order words are added and stored in the lower doubleword of the destination operand.

PAND; POR; PXOR These instructions perform bit-wise logical AND/OR/EX-OR operations on the 64-bits of source and destination operands stored in packed format and the result is stored in the destination operand.

MOV (D, Q) This is a data transfer instruction which transfers 32-bit doubleword or 64-bit quadword between memory and MMX registers. This instruction, however cannot transfer data form one memory location to another.

PSRA (W, B); PSLL (W, D, Q) These instructions perform arithmetic shift right or logical shift left/right in a single cycle. It supports only the shifting of packed word and doubleword data types.

EMMS This instruction empties the floating-point register tag bits and is an extremely important instruction, which should be compulsorily used during switching form multimedia to floating-point routines and vice versa. This has also been explained earlier in this chapter.

11.11 SALIENT POINTS ABOUT MULTIMEDIA APPLICATION PROGRAMMING

The following salient points should be remembered while programming using MMX instruction set. In a multitasking operating system environment, each task should return its own state which should be saved when the task switching occurs. The processor state here means the contents of the registers—both integer and floating-point/MMX register. In a preemptive multitasking O.S., the application does not know when it is preemptied. It is the job of the O.S. to save and restore the FP and MMX states when performing a context switch. Thus the user need not save or restore the state.

MMX instruction set generates the same type of memory access exception as the X86 instructions namely; page fault, segment not present, limit violation, etc.

When an MMX instruction is getting executed, the floating-point tag word is marked valid, i.e. '00'. If we do not use EMMS at the end of MMX routine, subsequent floating-point instructions will produce erratic results. EMMS instruction is an imperative when a floating-point routine calls an MMX routine or vice-versa.

11.12 JOURNEY TO PENTIUM-PRO AND PENTIUM-II

A number of small, yet significant changes over the basic architecture of Pentium resulted in a number of most advanced processors running at higher speed. Pentium-Pro has incorporated some of these advancements in Pentium architecture.

One of the constraints of the Pentium architecture is that it obeys a linear instruction sequencing, i.e. the instructions pass through the fetch, decode and execution stages sequentially. Now, suppose the first instruction needs to transfer data from cache to a CPU register and the next instruction adds this register content with some other register content. Naturally until the first instruction is executed, the next one cannot be executed. Now if there is a cache miss, then execution of the next instruction will be stalled. Only after the bus interface unit of the CPU reads this data from the main memory and returns it to the register, the next instruction execution will commence. This problem arises because of speed mismatch between the CPU and the memory device. Increasing the size of the L2 cache will reduce the probability of cache miss. However, this may not be the best solution. The problem, however, may be tackled by adopting the alternate strategy, where the conventional linear instruction sequencing may be changed. An optimised scheduling algorithm may be used where the CPU may look ahead for other instructions and speculatively execute them.

One such optimum and intelligent dynamic execution strategy has been adopted in Pentium-Pro microprocessor. Pentium's superscalar architecture employs five stage pipeline with U and V pipes. Thus it can execute two instructions per clock. Pentium-Pro has used twelve stages of pipeline, thus enhancing the speed of Pentium to a large extent. We will next discuss the optimised scheduling strategy adopted in Pentium-Pro.

11.12.1 Dynamic Execution of Instructions

There exist three important concepts which have been incorporated in Pentium-Pro architecture. These are:

Speculative Execution Which means that the CPU should speculate which of the next instructions can be executed earlier. As in our example just now cited, the CPU will not be able to execute the second instruction before the first instruction is excuted, since the second instruction requires the value of the register, which is loaded from memory after the first instruction is executed. However, some of the next instructions may be executed earlier since they are independent of the previous instructions. The CPU may speculate this and may execute these next instructions earlier.

Out of Turn Execution Naturally the consecutive instruction execution in a sequential flow will be hampered and the CPU should be able to execute out of turn instructions.

Dual Independent Bus Pentium-Pro incorporates a *dual independent bus* architecture to get an enhanced system bandwith. Pentium-Pro uses two separate and independent buses- one between the CPU and the main memory and the other between the CPU and the cache memory. The CPU can thus access both, the main memory and the cache simultaneously. This obviously yields a high throughput.

Multiple Branch Prediction The concept of branch prediction in Pentium has been extended to achieve multiple branch prediction in Pentium-Pro. Based on the past history of the branches taken, multiple branch prediction logic enhances the performance of Pentium. The processor uses an associative memory called *branch target buffer* for implementing this algorithm.

11.12.2 Implementation of the Dynamic Instruction Execution Scheme

To implement the speculative instruction execution, the processer looks ahead of a pool of instructions and executes some of these next instructions ahead of time. Typically Pentium-Pro looks 20-30 instructions ahead. Out of these instructions about 20 per cent instructions may be branch instructions. So if the CPU

executes the next instructions ahead of time, there exists a probability that these speculative instruction execution results may be wrong. The results of these speculative instruction excecution should not be stored in visible CPU registers and are temporarily stored, since they may have to be discarded, in case there is a branch instruction before these speculative instruction execution.

Pentium-Pro incorporates three independent engines, viz. (a) Fetch-decode unit (b) Dispatch-execute unit (c) Retire unit.

The fetch-decode unit accepts the sequence of instructions from the instruction cache as input and then decodes them. Here the prefetching of the instructions is performed in a speculative manner. A set of three parallel decoders accepts this stream of fetched instructions and decodes them. The decoder unit converts these instructions into microoperations. Each microoperation contains two logical sources and one logical destination. Some complex instructions are microcoded into a set of microoperations. These microoperations are then sent to the *Register Alias Table* (RAT). The RAT translates the logical register references to the physical register set actually available in the CPU. The pool of instructions which are fetched is stored as an array of content addressable memory, called reorder buffer.

The dispatch-execute unit actually does the scheduling of instructions by determining the data dependencies after which the microoperations of the scheduled instruction are executed in the execution unit. It may be noted here that the scheduling algorithm is based on speculation. The results of the speculative instruction execution are temporarily stored.

The retire unit first reads the instruction pool containing the instructions and removes the microoperations which have been executed from the instruction pool.

All the above features incorporated in Pentium-Pro enhance its speed to twice that of Pentium.

Pentium II, the next version of Pentium incorporates all these features of Pentium-Pro. Moreover, it has a larger cache and it can operate at 2.8 volts, thereby reducing the power consumption. One of the most important changes in Pentium-II lies in the fact that it can support INTEL's MMX instructions which has been discussed in detail in the previous sections. Note that while the high ended Pentium-Pro does not support the MMX instruction set, the Pentium-II does.

11.13 PENTIUM III (P-III)—THE CPU OF THE NEXT MILLENNIUM

Pentium III is the most recent and advanced CPU from Intel. It has a number of architectural features which make it the best option for use in computers—from high performance desktop to workstations and servers, running on advanced operating systems like Windows NT, Windows 98 and UNIX.

While designing an advanced microprocessor at the fag end of this millennium, what should the designers aim at? The architecture of the CPU must support features which should make the CPU suitable for applications like imaging, image processing, speech processing, multimedia and of course internet applications. It must have more processing power at less space and must be able to work at lower power requirements. The P-III architecture provides all these and possibly many more features.

We now discuss the salient points of some of its architectural features:

1. P-III CPU has been developed using 0.25 micron technology and includes over 9.5 million transistors. It has three versions operating at 450 MHz, 500 MHz and 550 MHz which are commercially available.
2. P-III incorporates multiple branch prediction algorithm
3. Seventy new instructions have been added to Pentium III. These instructions are useful in advanced imaging, speech processing and multimedia applications.
4. Dual independent bus architecture increases bandwith.
5. P-III employs dynamic execution technology, which has already been discussed.
6. A 512 Kbyte unified, non-blocking level 2 cache has been used.
7. Eight 64-bit wide Intel MMX registers along with a set of 57 instructions for multimedia applications are available

SUMMARY

In this chapter we have undertaken a journey to the wonderful realm of the advanced architecture of Pentium processors. Starting with a discussion on limitations of CISC architectures, we have shown how the RISC features could be introduced to make a better architecture as has been implemented in Pentium. The introduction of MMX technology in X86 family of microprocessors is an interesting step in the world of advanced architectures. Finally, the more recent advances in Pentium-Pro and Pentium-II have been highlighted. This chapter concludes with a note on Pentium III the most recent and advanced microprocessor architecture and its features

EXERCISES

11.1 Bring out the architectural differences between 80486 and Pentium.
11.2 Enlist the salient features of Pentium.
11.3 Explain the following terms.
(i) MII (ii) VLIW
(iii) Superscalar architecture.
11.4 What do you mean by superscalar execution?
11.5 Draw and discuss the architecture of Pentium.
11.6 Explain the advantage of having separate code and data cache in Pentium.
11.7 Write a short note on 'FPU of Pentium'.
11.8 What do you mean by branch prediction? How does it enhance the speed of execution? Explain the use of branch target buffer in branch prediction.
11.9 Explain the different floating-point instructions newly available in Pentium.
11.10 What do you mean by MMX?
11.11 Explain the different MMX instructions.
11.12 Write a short note on Multimedia programming.
11.13 How advanced is Pentium-Pro over Pentium?
11.14 Explain the difference between Pentium-Pro and Pentium II.
11.15 Explain dynamic execution in Pentium-Pro.
11.16 Explain the following terms.
(i) Speculative execution (ii) Out of term execution
(iii) Dual independent bus (iv) Multiple branch prediction
11.17 Does Pentium-Pro support Multimedia applications? Why? Which is the first processor to support Multimedia?
11.18 Explain the features of Pentium-Pro architecture which support dynamic execution of instructions.
11.19 Enlist the salient features of Pentium III.

12 Pentium 4—Processor of the New Millennium

INTRODUCTION

In Chapter 11, we have presented some of the salient features of the Pentium architecture. We have reviewed Pentium II and Pentium-Pro processors in moderate detail.One of the interesting features which has been introduced is the MMX instruction set, which is indeed a big step in advanced architecture. However, with passage of time designers found that this is not enough. The recent applications in three dimensional graphics, video processing, surveillance, gaming and multimedia technology demand faster performances from the processors. For example, some of the present day applications, like two and three dimensional static and moving image analysis, video surveillance, Internet audio streaming video, speech recognition and analysis etc. require speech, image and video encoding and processing in real time. The processors of 21st century should be able to perform encoding, such as JPEG or MPEG 4 in real time. Also it is important that the system should support more storage, i.e., RAM and cache (usually L1 (Level 1) cache is integrated in the chip while L2 (Level 2) cache is external to the chip). Thus at the end of the last century, there was a requirement to look for a high performance processor with novel architecture, which supported such high speed computations. This chapter provides glimpses of the features of such advanced processor like Pentium 4.

12.1 GENESIS OF BIRTH OF PENTIUM 4

For increasing the system performances in several such applications, duplicating or multiplying the number of processors or the number of execution units in a processor does not necessarily enhance the system performance proportionately. The reasons are manifold. Quite often the limited parallelism in the instruction flow reduces the rate of instruction flow. Similarly doubling the clock speed does not double the performance. This is because a number of processor cycles may be lost due to several factors, such as the branch misprediction. Thus as the applications grew, a necessity to change the traditional approaches for processor design was felt.

In view of the above discussions, it is important that newer concepts like super pipelining, branch prediction, super scalar execution, out of order execution, caches are needed to be introduced in the micro architecture. Traditionally we have always looked for higher clock speeds and instruction level parallelism. By incorporating these features the performances of the processor could be enhanced substantially.

But that was not enough to meet the challenges of newer applications.

This was the genesis of the birth of Pentium 4 processor which implemented Intel Netburst architecture. Pentium 4 is a processor with novel IA-32 microarchitecture which supports along with the above features, a host of other features like dynamic execution, advanced transfer cache, execution trace cache, rapid execution engine, enhanced set of SIMD instructions, like Streaming SIMD Extension and so on. We will briefly discuss some of these ideas in moderate detail in this chapter.

12.2 SALIENT FEATURES OF PENTIUM 4

Pentium 4 microprocessor arrived in the scene in June, 2000. After Pentium PRO processor, designed using P6 micro-architecture, which was released in 1995, Pentium-4 is the next x86 processor from Intel. This new processor with Pentium-4 Net Burst architecture utilizes all the features of earlier P6 architecture of Pentium 3 and includes many more. Some of the features of Pentium 4 are as follows:

(i) It is based on NetBurst microarchitecture
(ii) It has 42 million transistors, fabricated using 0.18 micron CMOS process.
(iii) Its die size is 217 sq. mm, and power consumption is 50W
(iv) Clock speed varies from 1.4 GHz to 1.7 GHz. At 1.5 GHz the microprocessor delivers 535 SPECint2000 and 558 SPECfp 2000 of performance.
(v) It has hyper-pipelined technology—Its pipeline depth extends to 20 stages.
(vi) In addition to the L1 8 KB data cache, it also includes an Execution Trace Cache that stores up to 12 K decoded micro-ops in the order of program execution.
(vii) The on-die 256KB L2-cache is non-blocking, 8-way set associative. It employs 256-bit interface that delivers data transfer rates of 48 GB/s at 1.5 GHz.
(viii) Pentium-4 NetBurst microarchitecture introduces Internet Streaming SIMD Extensions 2 (SSF2) instructions. This extends the SIMD capabilities that MMX technology and SSF techonology delivered by adding 144 new instructions. These instructions includes 128-bit SIMD integer arithmetic and 128-bit SIMD double-precision floating-point operations.
(ix) It supports 400 MHz system bus, which provides up to 3.2 GB/s of bandwidth. The bus is fed by dual PC800 Rambus channel. This compares to the 1.06 GB/s delivered on the Pentium-III processor's 133-MHz system bus.
(x) Two Arithmetic Logic Units (ALUs) on the Pentium 4 processor are clocked at twice the core processor frequency. This allows basic integer instructions such as Add, Subtract, Logical AND, Logical OR, etc. to execute in a half clock cycle.
(xi) Advanced dynamic execution.

In the next section we will briefly review Pentium 4 microarchitecture.

12.3 NETBURST MICROARCHITECTURE FOR PENTIUM 4

The pentium 4 architecture may be viewed as having four basic modules, (A) Front end module (B) Out of order execution engine (C) Execution module and (D) Memory subsystem module. This has been shown in Fig. 12.1(a).We will now describe each of these modules briefly.

12.3.1 Front-End Module

The front-end module of Pentium 4 processor contains (i) IA 32 Instruction decoder, (ii) Trace Cache, (iii) Microcode ROM and (iv) Front End branch Predictor.

12.3.2 IA 32 Instruction Decoder

The instructions supported by Pentium 4 are of variable length and are supported by many different addressing modes.The role of Instruction decoder is to decode these instructions concurrently and translate them into micro-operations known as μops. A single instruction decoder decodes one instruction per clock cycle. Some instructions are translated into single μop while others are translated into multiple number of μops.

In case of a complex instruction, when the instruction needs to be translated into more than four μops, the decoder usually does not decode such instructions. Rather it transfers the task to a Microcode ROM. The problem assumes more complexity when several instructions need to be decoded in a single clock cycle. The only solution is to use several stages of the pipeline to decode the instructions. This will be explained later.

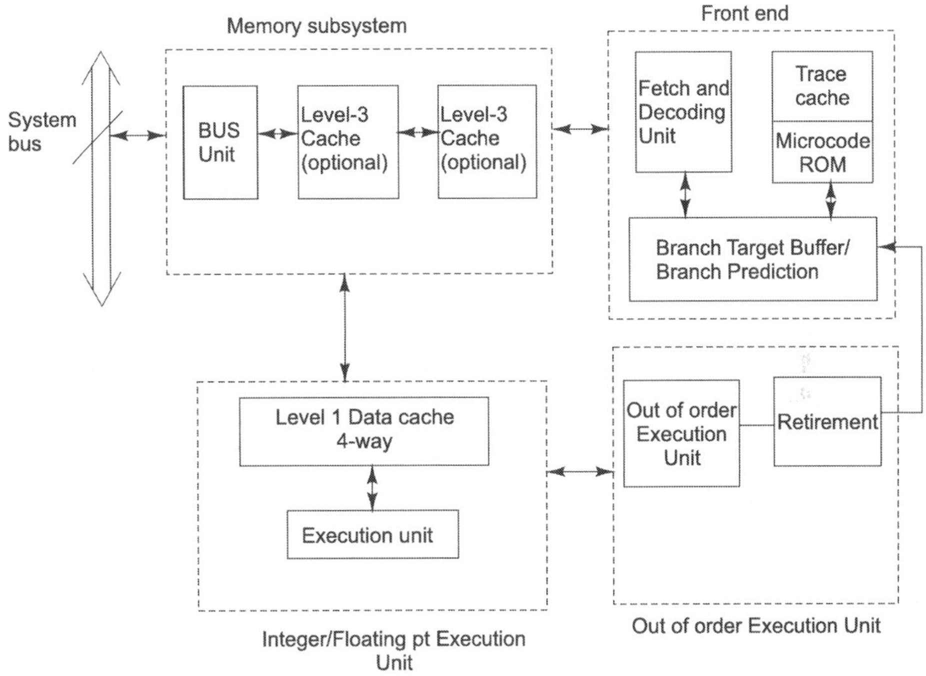

Figure 12.1 (a)*Block diagram of Pentium 4 Microarchitecture*

Figure 12.1(b) presents in detail architechture of Pentium IV.

12.3.3 Trace Cache (TC)

The basic function of the front end module is to fetch the instructions to be executed, decode them and feed decoded instructions to the next module, which is the out of order execution module. The instructions are first decoded into basic micro operations known as μops, and the stream of decoded instructions are fed to a level-1 (L1) instruction cache. This special instruction cache is known as Trace Cache, which is a special feature of Pentium 4 microarchitecture. It is special because it does not store the instructions but the decoded stream of instructions, i.e., micro-operations or μops, thus enhancing the execution speed considerably. The Trace cache can store up to12 K μops. The cache assembles the decoded μops into ordered sequence of μops called Traces. A single trace has many Trace lines and each Trace line has six μops.

Usually the instructions are fetched and executed through Trace Cache (also known as Execution Trace Cache) only. In case there is a Trace Cache miss the microarchitecture allows the instructions to be fetched from Level 2 cache.

Two sets of next-instruction-pointers independently track the progress of the two software threads executing. We will discuss about threads later in the chapter. There are two logical processors in the CPU and when both want to access the Trace Cache every clock cycle simultaneously, then only of them is granted the access, while the other is granted access in the alternating clock cycle. For example, if one cycle is used to fetch a line for one logical processor, the next cycle would be used to fetch a line for the other logical

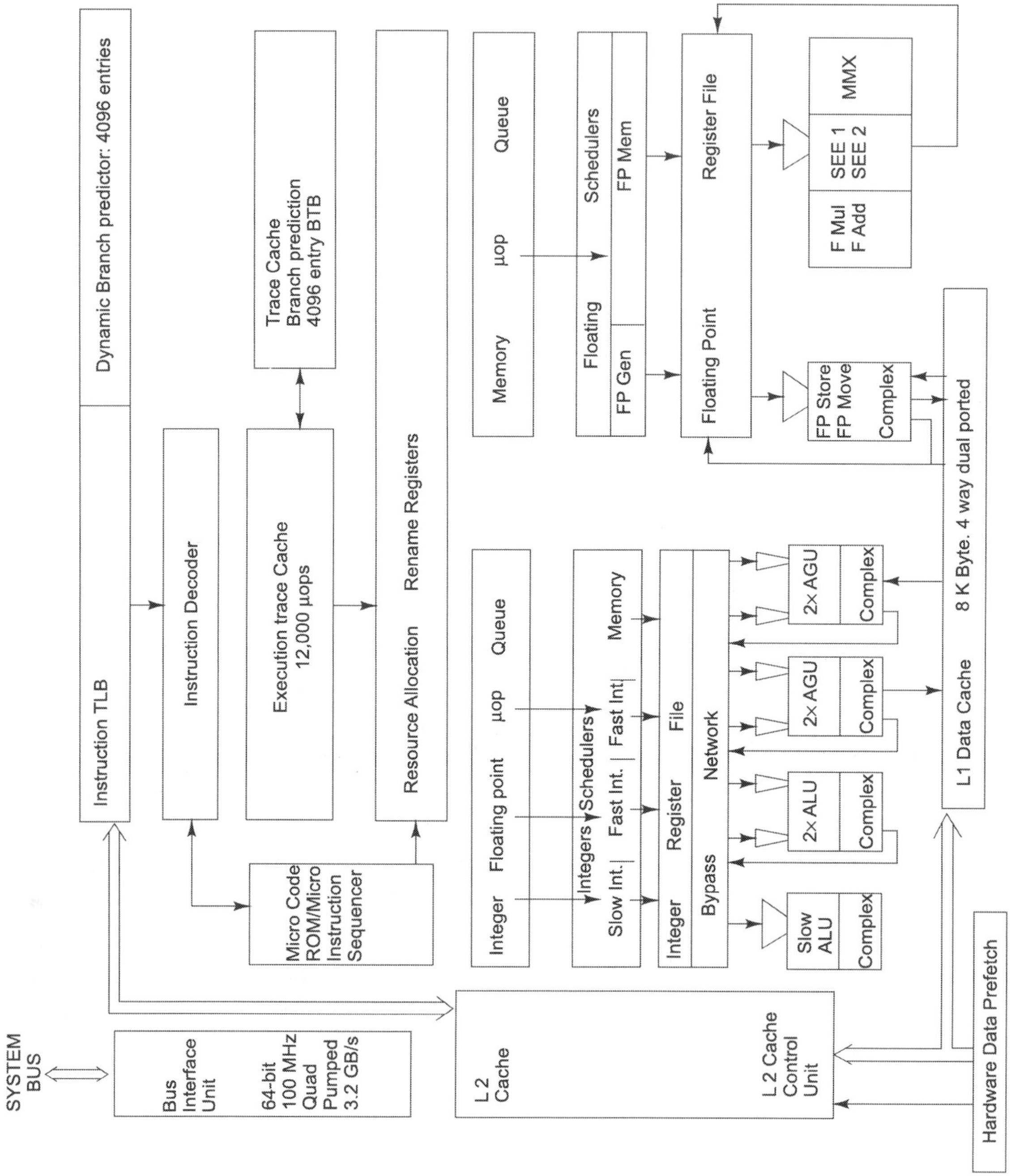

Fig. 12.1 (b) *Detail Architecture of Pentium processor*

processor, provided that both logical processors requested access to the trace cache. If one logical processor is stalled or is unable to use the Trace Cache, the other logical processor is free to use the full bandwidth of the trace cache in every cycle.

12.3.4 Microcode ROM

When some complex instructions like interrupt handling or string manipulation etc. appear, the Trace Cache transfers the control to a Micro code ROM, which stores the μops corresponding to these complex instructions. When the control is passed to the Microcode ROM, the corresponding μops are issued. After the μops are issued by the Microcode ROM, the control goes to the Trace Cache once again. The μops delivered by the Trace cache and the Microcode ROM are buffered in a queue in an orderly fashion. The resultant flow of μops is next fed to the execution engine.

As we have observed earlier, if both the logical processors want to execute complex IA-32 instructions simultaneously, then we need two microcode instruction pointers, which will access the microcode ROM. This is required for independent flow of control. In that case both the logical processors will be able to share the Microcode ROM entries. However, both the processors will not get the access concurrently. The access to the Microcode ROM will be alternately assigned to the two logical processors.

12.3.5 Front-End Branch Predictor in Pentium 4

The other important unit in the front end is the Branch Prediction Logic unit.

This unit predicts the locations from where the next instruction bytes are fetched. The predictions are made based on past history of the program execution.

The earlier generation processors follow simple branching strategy. When the processor comes across a branch instruction, it evaluates the branch condition.The condition evaluation may involve a complex calculation, which may consume time and the processor has to wait till the condition is computed and thereafter it decides whether to take the branch or not. Let us look at the problem in more detail.

12.3.6 Branch Prediction

The modern day fast processors cannot wait till the branch condition is evaluated to decide whether to take a branch, since this will unnecessarily slow down the speed of execution. These processors take the strategy of speculating whether the branch condition will be satisfied. Pentium, for example, makes a guess about the branching using a strategy called "speculative execution". This strategy involves making a guess at which direction the branch is going to be taken and then branching at the new branch target even before the branching condition is actually evaluated. Many strategies have been suggested for speculative prediction and the guess is made used one of these branch prediction strategies.

If, however, the processor incorrectly predicts a branch, it may lead to a severe problem. In case of an incorrect prediction, the instructions are fetched from wrong branch locations and may be executed incorrectly for a wrong speculation. In such a case, the pipeline has to be flushed of the erroneous, speculative instructions and results. After flushing out the wrong instructions, the instructions from the correct branch target address are fetched, and executed. Flushing the pipeline of instructions and results is expensive and produces a delay of several cycles. The delay depends on the level of pipelining in the processor. Also there is a delay associated with loading the new instruction stream. The resulting delay invariably degrades the system performance significantly, if such erroneous predictions take place often.

As the length of pipeline in a processor increases, the degradation also increases proportionately. In case of a wrong prediction, Pentium-4 with 20-stages will have to wait for considerable number of cycles, while new instructions are loaded from the cache. The P4 has a minimum loss of 19 clock cycles due to each erroneous prediction. This is the loss incurred when the code resides in the L1 cache.The loss will be still higher if the correct branch is not found in the L1 cache, since in that case the data has to be fetched from L2 cache.

In view of the above discussion, it may be noted that the advanced processors of today, like Pentium 4, which has massive pipelining embedded in them, suffers performance degradation, if there is an erroneous branch prediction. It is thus extremely important that the processor uses a robust strategy which should ensure correct branch prediction.

There are two main types of branch prediction: static prediction and dynamic prediction. Static branch prediction is based on a statistical assumption that the majority of backward branches occur in the context of repetitive loops. In a repetitive loop, a branch instruction determines whether or not to repeat the loop again. Most of the times the condition to be evaluated to ascertain whether the loop will be "taken", is affirmative. In static prediction this the processor is instructed to repeat the code inside the loop one more time, The static branch prediction always assumes that all backward branches are "taken". For a branch that points forward to a block of code that comes later in the program, the static predictor assumes that the branch is "not taken".

Static prediction is usually fast and simple, since it does not require any table lookups or calculations. As is evident from the above, in case program contains a number of loops, static prediction performs without much degradation. Otherwise, if it contains lot of forward branches, the static prediction performs quite poorly.

The "dynamic branch prediction" algorithms, on the contrary, involve the use of two types of tables, the Branch History Table (BHT) and the Branch Target Buffer (BTB), to record information about outcomes of branches that have already been executed.The BHT preserves the history of each conditional branch that the speculative branch prediction unit encounters during last several cycles. It also keeps a record that indicates the likelihood that the branch will be taken based on its past history. The branches may be grouped as "strongly taken", "taken", "not taken", and "strongly not taken". For creating this record we need only two bit branch history. When the front end encounters a branch instruction that has an entry in its BHT, the branch predictor uses branch history information to decide whether or not to speculatively execute the branch.

Once such a speculative branch prediction scheme is decided, and the branch prediction logic decides to speculatively execute the branch, the next important thing is to know exactly the location in the L1 cache at which the branch is pointing. This implies that a branch target buffer is needed. The Branch Target Buffer (BTB) stores the branch targets of previously executed branches. Thus when a branch is taken the branch prediction unit speculates the branch target address, collects it from the BTB and finally the front end starts fetching instructions from that address. In case the BTB contains an entry, which is incorrect, this may lead to an erroneous branching. Pentium 4 uses both static and dynamic branch prediction techniques to prevent such wrong predictions and the resulting delays.

If a branch instruction does not have an entry in the BHT, both processors will use static prediction to decide which path to take. If the instruction does have a BHT entry, dynamic prediction is used. The Pentium 4 BHT has 4K entries—large enough to store information on most of the branches in a code of moderate complexity. The probability of error in correctly predicting the branches is less than 10 percent in case of Pentium III and is much less in case of Pentium 4. The BTB and BHT are often conbined under the lebel "the front-end BTB".

12.4 INSTRUCTION TRANSLATION LOOKASIDE BUFFER (ITLB) AND BRANCH PREDICTION

If there is a Trace Cache miss, then instruction bytes are required to be fetched from the L2 cache.These are next decoded into μops to be placed in the Trace Cache (TC). The Instruction Translation Lookaside Buffer (ITLB) receives the request from the TC to deliver new instruction, and it translates the next-instruction pointer address to a physical address. A request is sent to the L2 cache, and instruction bytes are returned. These bytes are placed into streaming buffers, which hold the bytes until they are decoded.

Since there are two logical processors there are two ITLBs. Thus each logical processor has its own ITLB and its own instruction pointer to track the progress of instruction fetch for each of them. Now suppose both the logical processors request the access of L2 cache, the instruction fetch logic performs arbitration based on which processor request has arrived first. Accordingly, it sends requests to the L2 cache and grants the request of the first processor. It, however, reserves at least one request slot for each logical processor. In this way, both logical processors can access and fetch data from L2 cache without any conflict.

Before the instructions are decoded, they are stored in streaming buffers.Thus each logical processor has its own set of two 64-byte streaming buffers, which store the instruction bytes and subsequently they are dispatched to the instruction decode stage.

12.5 WHY OUT-OF-ORDER EXECUTION

One of the major features of micro architecture is super pipelining. We have discussed about super pipelining in the Chapter 11. A super scalar processor has multiple parallel execution units, which can process the instructions simultaneously.

Quite often, the instructions are sequentially dependant on each other. That means if one instruction depends on the result of its previous instruction, then the processor will not be able to execute them concurrently.

To solve this problem, the concept of out of order execution was developed.

In this method, we may choose a large window of instructions and select those instructions from this window which are not dependent on their previous instructions. After scheduling this set of independent instructions, which can be executed concurrently, we move over to the next set of instructions which are dependent on the previous set. The out of order execution solves the problem of parallel execution of instructions by identifying the dependencies amongst the set of instructions.

12.5.1 Out-of-Order Execution Engine

The out-of-order execution engine consists of the allocation, register renaming, scheduling, and execution functions. This part of the machine re-orders instructions and executes them as quickly as their inputs are ready, without regard to the original program order.

The allocator logic takes μops from the μop queue and allocates many of the key machine buffers needed to execute each uop, including the 126 re-order buffer entries, 128 integer and 128 floating-point physical registers, 48 load and 24 store buffer entries. Some of these key buffers are partitioned such that each logical processor can use at most half the entries. Specifically, each logical processor can use up to maximum of 63 re-order buffer entries, 24 buffers, and 12 store buffer entries.

If there are μops for both logical processor in the μop queue, the allocator will alternate selecting uops from the logical processors every clock cycle to assign resources. If a logical processor has used its limit of needed resources, such as store buffer entries, the allocator will signal "stall" for that logical processor and continue to assign resources for the other logical processor. In addition, if the μop queue only contains μops for one logical processor, the allocator will try to assign resources for that logical processor every cycle to optimize allocation bandwidth, though the resource limits would still be enforced.

By limiting the maximum resource usage of key buffers, the machine helps to enforce fairness and prevents deadlocks.

12.5.2 Register Rename

The function of the register rename logic is to rename the IA-32 registers onto the machine's physical registers. This allows the 8 general-use IA-32 integer registers to be dynamically expanded to use the available 128 physical registers. The renaming logic uses a Register Alias Table (RAT) to track the latest version of each architectural register to tell the next instruction(s) where to get its input operands.

Since each logical processor must maintain and track its own complete architecture state, there are two RAT's one for each logical processor. The register renaming process is done in parallel to the allocator logic described above, so the register rename logic works on the same μops to which the allocator is assigning resources.

Once μops have completed the allocation and register rename processes, they are placed into two sets of queues, one for memory operations (loads and stores) and another for all other operations. The two sets of queues are called the memory instruction queue and the general instruction queue, respectively. They are also partitioned such that μops from each logical processor can use at most half the entries.

12.5.3 Instruction Scheduling

The function of a scheduler is to schedule different micro-operations (μops) to an appropriate execution engine. There are five schedulers which are used for scheduling different types of μops for the various execution units. The implies that multiple number of μops can be dispatched in each clock cycle. A micro operation can be executed only when the operands residing in the registers are available. Also the specific execution unit should be available for execution of each microoperation.Thus the scheduling strategy dispatches an μop when the register operands are ready and the execution units are available.

The memory instruction queue and general instruction queues send μops to the five scheduler queues, alternating between μops for the two logical processors every clock cycle, as needed.

Each scheduler has its own scheduler queue of eight to twelve entries from which it selects μops to send to the execution units. The schedulers choose μops regardless of whether they belong to one logical processor or the other. The schedulers are effectively oblivious to logical processor distinctions. The μops are simply evaluated based on dependent inputs and availability of execution resources. For example, the schedulers could dispatch two μops from one logical processor and two μops from the other logical processor in the same clock cycle. To avoid deadlock and ensure fairness, there is a limit on the number of active entries that a logical processor can have in each scheduler's queue. This limit is dependent on the size of the scheduler queue.

12.6 RAPID EXECUTION MODULE

Pentium 4 has two ALUs (Arithmetic Logic Unit) and two AGUs (Address Generation Unit), which run at twice the processor speed. This implies that the ALUs in a 1.4 Ghz processor works at 2.8 Ghz. The doubled speed of these units means twice the number of instructions being executed per clock cycle.

Arithmetic and Logic unit is responsible for carrying out all integer calculations (add, subtract, multiplication, division) and logical operations. AGUs are primarily used to resolve indirect mode of memory addressing. As can be comprehended, these units are quite important for high-speed processing which includes frequent fetching of instructions and arithmetic calculations.

12.7 MEMORY SUBSYSTEM

The memory subsystem involving virtual memory and paging is briefly described below.

12.7.1 Paging and Virtual Memory

With the flat or the segmented memory model, linear address space is mapped into the processors physical address space either directly or through paging when using direct mapping (paging disabled), each linear address has a one-to-one correspondence with a physical address. Linear address bits are sent out on the processor's address lines without translation.

When using IA-32 architecture's paging mechanism (paging enabled) linear address space is divided into pages which are mapped to virtual memory. The pages of virtual memory are then mapped as needed into physical memory when an operating system or execution uses paging. The paging mechanism is transparent to an application program. All that the application sees is linear address space.

In addition, IA-32 architecture's paging mechanism includes extension that support:

- Page Address Extensions (PAE) to address physical address space greater than 4G Bytes.
- Page Size Extension (PSE) to map linear address to physical address in 4 M bytes page.

12.7.2 Cache

The access to DRAM main memory is often very slow. To enhance the speed of data access fast SRAM caches are used to reduce this latency. The instructions or the data which are more frequently accessed are stored in the caches. Present day processors now employ cache hierarchy, in which fast yet small caches are located very close to the processor core. The progressively less frequently accessed data or instructions are stored in caches with longer access latencies.

12.8 HYPERTHREADING TECHNOLOGY

Before discussing the Hyperthreading technology, let us look into the concept of threading and multithreading. As we have observed earlier, each process has a "context" that reflects all the information which completely describes the current state of execution of the process. For example, a process may use as its context the contents of the CPU registers, the program counter, the flags, etc. Each process, in turn, contains at least one thread and sometimes more than one thread. In case a process has multiple threads, each of these threads has its own local context. Also the process, as such, has a context, which is shared by all the threads in that process.

The features of the thread are (i) the threads may be bunched together into a process, (ii) the threads may be independent, (iii) the threads are usually simple in structure and are lightweight in the sense that they may enhance the speed of operation of the overall process. In a multiprocessor environment, different processes may run on different processors. Also different threads from the same process can also run on different processors. Thus compared to the use of single thread, multiple threads enhance the performance in a multiprocessor system.

12.8.1 Thread Level Parallelism (TLP)

In many applications it is important to have multiple number of processes or threads to be executed in parallel. For example, in multiple object tracking in on line video surveillance, it is advantageous to execute several threads concurrently. These threads, may correspond to the tracking of each individual object. This kind of parallelism, known as thread level parallelism, yields better performance in many on line applications. Also most of the server applications today require multiple threads or processes that can be executed in parallel.

When the time slice assigned to the currently executing process is over, its context is saved to the memory. When the process begins executing again, the context of this process is again restored to the exactly same state that it was in when its execuction was halted. This whole process of (i) saving the context of the currently executing process, when the time slice is over, (ii) flushing the CPU of the same process and (iii) loading the context of the new next process is called a context switch. Now if a process contains M number of threads, then the total time for this context switching will obviously be M times that of a single thread context switching time. Thus context switching consumes a number of CPU cycles. Thus we infer two things here: (i) Multiple number of threads yields better performance, (ii) More number of threads consumes more time in context switching.

From the above discussion it is clear that to enhance the performances, we have to (i) reduce the number of context switches and (ii) provide more CPU execution time to each process. The solution is to execute more than one process at the same time. This again can be done by increasing the number of CPUs. In a system with multiple number of processors, the scheduler in the OS can schedule two processes to two different CPUs simultaneously for execution at the exact same time. Thus with two or more number of CPUs in the system, the process will not have to wait for a long duration to get executed.

12.8.2 Strategies of Implementation

There are several strategies to implement hyperthreading.

As has been mentioned earlier, a single processor can execute multiple threads by switching between them. The scheme of context switching may again be of several types.

They are:

(i) *Time-slice multithreading* In this scheme the processor switches between different process threads after a fixed time slice. Since there is only one processor, Time-slice multithreading can result in loss of execution cycles. However, each thread is guaranteed to get attention of the processor when its turn comes. In case there is a cache miss, which is a long latency event, automatically the processor will switch to another thread.

(ii) *On chip multiprocessing* (CMP) This scheme involves the use of two processors on a single die. The two processors each have a full set of execution and architectural resources. The processors may or may not share a large on-chip cache. CMP is largely orthogonal to conventional multiprocessor systems, as you can have multiple CMP processors in a multiprocessor configuration. CMP chip is significantly larger than the size of single core-chip and therefore more expensive to manufacture (i) the die size is obviously more and (ii) power consumption is also higher.

(iii) *Hyperthreading* Finally, there is simultaneous multi-threading, where multiple threads can be executed on a single processor without switching. The threads execute simultaneously and make much better use of the resources. This approach makes the most effective use of processor resources. How can it be done ?

12.9 HYPERTHREADING IN PENTIUM

This new technology which was first introduced on the Intel Xeon processor in early 2002 was subsequently employed in Pentium 4 in November 2002 at clock frequencies of 3.06 GHz and higher.

In Pentium architecture a single physical processor appears as two logical processors. All the physical resources of the system are shared between these two logical processors. This means that the user programs can schedule the processes or threads to the two logical processors as if there are indeed two different physical processors. The instructions from both the logical processors can be executed simultaneously on shared execution resources.

Hyperthreading used the concept of simultaneous multithreading and shows an improvement in the Intel microarchitecture development. At the expense of an added cost of less than only 5 percent in added die area, the performance increases by about 25 percent.

The major elegance of this architecture lies in devising appropriate resource sharing policy for each shared resource. Several resource sharing strategies have been investigated by the developers. Some of these are (a) partitioned resources, (b) threshold sharing, and (c) full sharing. The choice of sharing strategy to be adopted depends on several factors, such as, the traffic pattern, size of the resource, potential deadlock probabilities and other considerations.

To do this, there is one copy of the architecture state for each logical processor, and the logical processors share a single set of physical execution resources. From a software or architecture perspective, this means operating systems and user programs can schedule processes or threads to logical processors as they would on conventioal physical processors in a multi-processor system. From a microarchitecture perspective, this means that instructions from logical processors will persist and execute simultaneously on shared execution resouces.

Figure 12.2 shows a multiprocessor system with two processors which does not incorporate Hyper-threading Technology.

12.9.1 Architecture State (AS)

Hyperthreading Technology was first implemented on the Intel® Xeon TM processor family. There are two logical processors per physical processor in this processor. Each logical processor maintains a complete set of the architecture state.

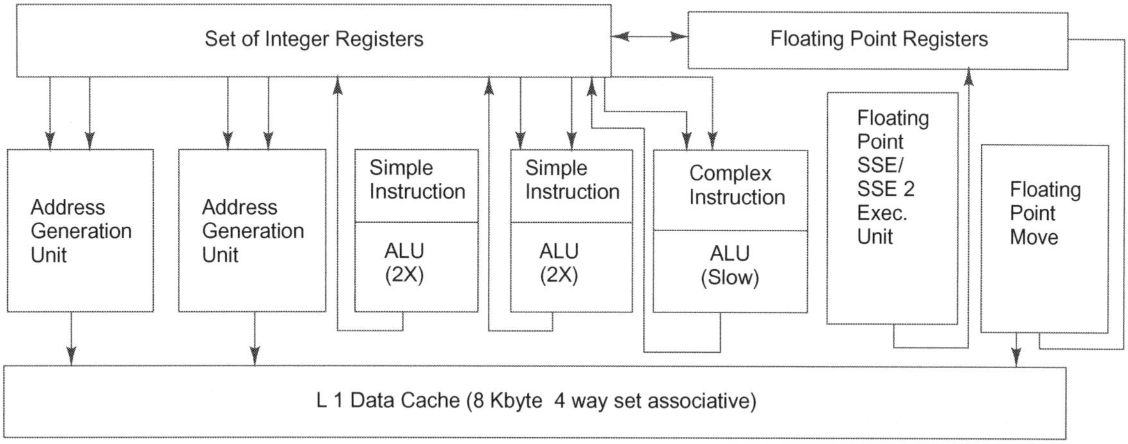

Fig.12.2 *A Multiprocessor System Without Hyperthreading Technology*

The architecture state consists of (i) registers including the general-purpose registers, (ii) the control register, (iii) advanced programmable interrupt controller (APIC) registers, and (iv) machine state registers. From a software perspective, once the architecure state is duplicated, the processor appears to be two processors.

Logical processors share nearly all other resources on the physical processor, such as caches, execution units, branch predictors, control logic, and buses.

Each logical processor has its own interrupt controller or APIC. Interrupts sent to a specific logical processor are handled only by that logical processor.

12.9.2 Design Issues in Hyperthreading Technology

There are several issues which need to be considered while implementing Hyperthreading Technology.

(i) Hyperthreading technology automatically involves increase of the die area. One of the objectives is to minimize the die area while implementing Hyperthreading Technology. This can be achieved by replicating only few Components. The logical processors share most of the resources in the architecture and thus there is little necessity to replicate the resources.

(ii) A second goal was to ensure that when one logical processor is stalled the other logical processor should continue to make forward progress. A logical processor may be temporarily stalled for a variety of reasons, including servicing cache misses, handling branch mispredictions, or waiting for the results of previous instructions. Independent forward progress was ensured by managing buffering queues such that no logical processor can use all the entries when two active software threads were executing.This is accomplished by either partitioning or limiting the number of active entries each thread can have.

(iii) A third goal was to allow a processor running only one active software thread to run at the same speed on a processor with Hyperthreading Technology as on a processor without this capability. This means that partitioned resources should be recombined when only one software thread is active. As shown, buffering queues separate major pipeline logic blocks. The buffering queues are either partitioned or duplicated to ensure independent forward progress through each logic block.

12.9.3 Operating System

The operating system views a single processor system using hyperthreading technique as if it has two physical processors. This is because each processor is viewed as having two logical processors. Operating system manages each logical processor like a physical processor. They schedule the tasks or threads to each of the logical processor. An efficient OS, however, should optimize management of both the logical processors. For example, sometimes only one logical processor may be active while the other one is idle. The OS may continue to use this idle logical processor, which may result in deterioration of performance, since the resources are still allocated to the idle logical processor by the OS. An optimization in this regard may require the use of HALT instruction, when either of the two logical processors is idle. HALT allows the processor to transition to either ST0 or ST1 mode. Before we proceed further, let us discuss about Single Task (ST mode) and Multi task modes (MT mode).

When there is only one software thread to execute, there are two modes—Single Task and Multi Task modes. In multi task mode, we assume that there are two active logical processors and resources are partitioned amongst these two processors.

In single task mode, on the other hand, only one of the two logical processors is active. All the resources in this case are assigned to the single active logical processor, ST0 or ST 1. In this case, we may have Single Task Logical Processor 0 (ST0) or Single Task Logical processor 1 (ST1) modes.

The operating system should use the HALT instruction, which stops the Processor execution. The HALT instruction is a privileged instruction and can be used only by the OS.

When the operating system uses HALT instruction on a processor which supports multithreading, the operation moves from multitasking (MT) mode to single tasking mode, i.e., ST0 or ST1 mode, depending on which logical processor is active. Let us assume a situation when logical processor 0 goes into idle mode and executes HALT instruction. That means the physical processor now has only logical processor 1 active and all the resources now go to this logical processor. If this active logical processor, i.e., ST1 also executes HALT, then the physical processor goes to a low power mode. A comparison between IA-32 supporting hyperthreading and traditional processor is shown in Fig. 12.3.

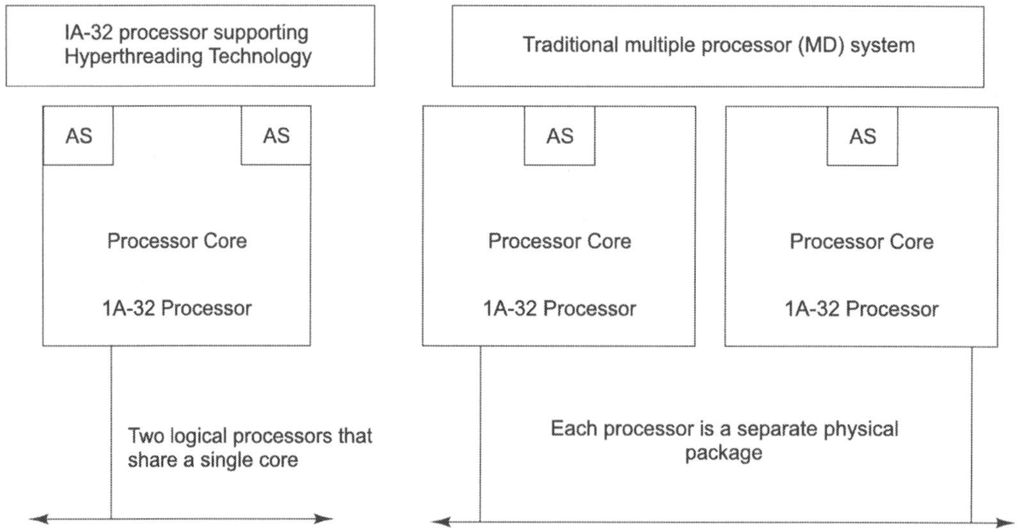

Fig. 12.3 *Comparison of an IA-32 Processor Supporting Hyperthreading Technology and a Traditional Data Processor System*

12.10 EXTENDED INSTRUCTION SET IN ADVANCED PENTIUM PROCESSORS

In the previous chapter, we have presented the details of MMX instructions, which find applications in imaging and multimedia applications. Most of these advanced applications require parallel computation and thus new enhancements in the instruction set are needed. The most important enhancement, known as SIMD (Single Instruction Multiple Data Stream) instructions have been incorporated in MMX and later in SSE instructions.

In this chapter, we will discuss about new extensions for the new generation of Pentium processors, Pentium III and Pentium 4. We will not attempt to present extended instruction set, but will discuss their features and advantages. First, let us see the features and limitations of the MMX instructions,we discussed in Chapter 12.

(i) The MMX instructions are for SIMD architectures and they support only integer data type.
(ii) The eight MMX registers are named mm0, ..., mm7.
(iii) For executing MMX instructions, the designers have not allocated any specific set of registers.
(iv) These instructions are executed using the eight floating point registers in the floating point unit in the CPU. They use 64 bits mantissa portion of these 80 bit registers.
(v) As a consequence, it is not possible to execute an MMX instruction and a floating point execution simultaneously.
(vi) Since many multimedia operations, such as in video processing, require operations involving floating-point numbers, the use of MMX instructions are disadvantageous.
(vii) Since MMX instructions are executed using only the floating point registers, a large number of processor clock cycles are unnecessarily consumed for switching from the state of executing MMX instructions to the state of executing floating-point operations and vice versa.

12.10.1 Streaming SIMD Extension

In view of the above discussion, there was a necessity to extend the MMX instructions to include floating point instructions. These extended instructions called Streaming SIMD Extensions or SSE instruction, have been used in Pentium III and SSE instruction set has further been enhanced in Pentium 4.

We will now present some of the features of SSE and indicate how SSE has come over the limitations of MMX instructions:

(i) SSE instructions are SIMD instructions for single-precision floating-point numbers.
(ii) These instructions operate on four 32-bit floating points concurrently.
(iii) For executing these instructions, a set of eight new registers have been specifically defined for SSE. SSE registers are named xmm0 through xmm7.
(iv) Each of the registers for SSE is 128 bits long. Each of them can hold four 32 bit single-precision floating-point numbers.
(v) Since different registers have been allocated, it is possible to execute both fixed point and floating point operations simultaneously.
(vi) There is thus no necessity to switch from one mode to the other in case we use SSE instructions. In case of MMX instructions, such switching consumes lot of cycles unnecessarily.
(vii) These instructions can also execute non-SIMD floating-point and SIMD floating-point instructions simultaneously.

(viii) In memory streaming instruction extensions, the data is prefetched into a specified level of the cache hierarchy. Most multimedia applications use the streaming data access pattern; that is, data are accessed sequentially and seldom reused. Therefore, prefetching this type of data into the L2 cache is an effective way to improve the memory system performance.

12.10.2 Features of Pentium III SSE Instructions

The pentium III SSE instructions allow for SIMD operations on four single-precision floating-point numbers in one instruction.

(i) The applications of speaker and speech recognition require extensive use of floating point operations. While there are a large set of image processing operations which use fixed point operations, there are many applications in object segmentation, pattern recognition, tracking and surveillance where extensive use of floating point operations are required.

(ii) In graphics, both two- and three-dimensional, to specify the position of a point in two- or three-dimensional space, we need extensive floating point computations.
(iii) With the help of SSE instructions, the matrix and vector operations are executed quite fast resulting in the increase in performance.

A set of seventy new instructions have been added in SSE and out of these seventy new instructions, fifty are SIMD for floating point operations, twelve instructions are for SIMD integer operations, and the remaining eight are cacheability instructions. Also a new status/control word has been added. SSE requires support from the operting system, which can save and restore processor state as required.
SSE defines new instructions, new data types and instruction categories.

12.10.3 Types of SSE Instructions

The SSE insructions can operate on packed data or on scalar data.

Accordingly those instructions using packed data are termed as packed instructions (with ps suffix) and others as scalar instructions (with ss suffix).

The packed instructions in SSE have their scalar equivalents.

As we have stated earlier, the128 bit floating point registers for executing the SSE instructions can store four 32 bit single precision floating point numbers. SSE instructions support a data type that allows the storage and execution of the four single-precision floating-point numbers.

There are instructions in SSE which operate on the entire 128 bit packed data (four data elements each of 32 bits) and these instruction are referred as packed data. Scalar instructions are those which operate only on the least significant element (least significant 32 bits), i.e., a scalar data. These instructions do not operate on the vector form of full four element data.

The SSE instructions can grouped as

(i) Data transfer instructions
(ii) Data type conversion instructions
(iii) Arithmetic, logic and comparison group of instruction
(iv) Jump or Branch group of instruction
(v) Shuffle instructions
(vi) Data management and ordering
(vii) Cacheability instructions
(viii) State management instructions

The SSE instructions, which are essentially single instruction multiple data stream instructions reduce the computational complexity in a significant way. For example, in a program requiring 'm' number of floating point operations, say in matrix multiplication, the same number of multiplications may be executed in m/4 cycles, instead of m cycles. This is because four floating point multiplications can be done in a single cycle. However, the rearrangment of data in a format which is acceptable for SIMD computation is required. This consumes few clock cycles.

12.10.4 Streaming SIMD Extensions 2 (SSE2) and Extensions 3 (SSE3) Instructions

The Streaming SIMD (Single Instruction Multiple Data) Extensions or SSE in short is a set of new instructions in the Pentium III and Pentium 4. This new instruction set increases the accuracy of the double-precision floating point operations, supports new formats of packed data and increase the speed of manipulation of 128-bit SIMD integer operations. These additions have been made, keeping in view the new capabilities and the architectural changes introduced within the Pentium 4.

The new set of Pentium-4 SSE2 instructions, which are extension of SSE contain 144 new instructions. They support new data types, such as double-precision floating points. With the introduction of SSE2, the

Intel Net Burst microarchitecture extended the SIMD capabilities that Intel MMX technology and SSE technology delivered by adding 144 instructions.

The next generation 90 nm process-based Pentium 4 processor introduces the Streaming SIMD Extensions 3 (SSE3). This version was introduced by Intel in 2004, when they released their latest version of Pentium 4, the Prescot. The SSE 2 instruction set has been extended in SSE3, which includes 13 additional SIMD instructions over SSE2. These instructions comprise five different types:

(i) floating-point-to-integer conversion.
(ii) complex arithmetic operations
(iii) video encoding
(iv) SIMD floating-point operations using array-of-structures format and
(v) thread synchronization

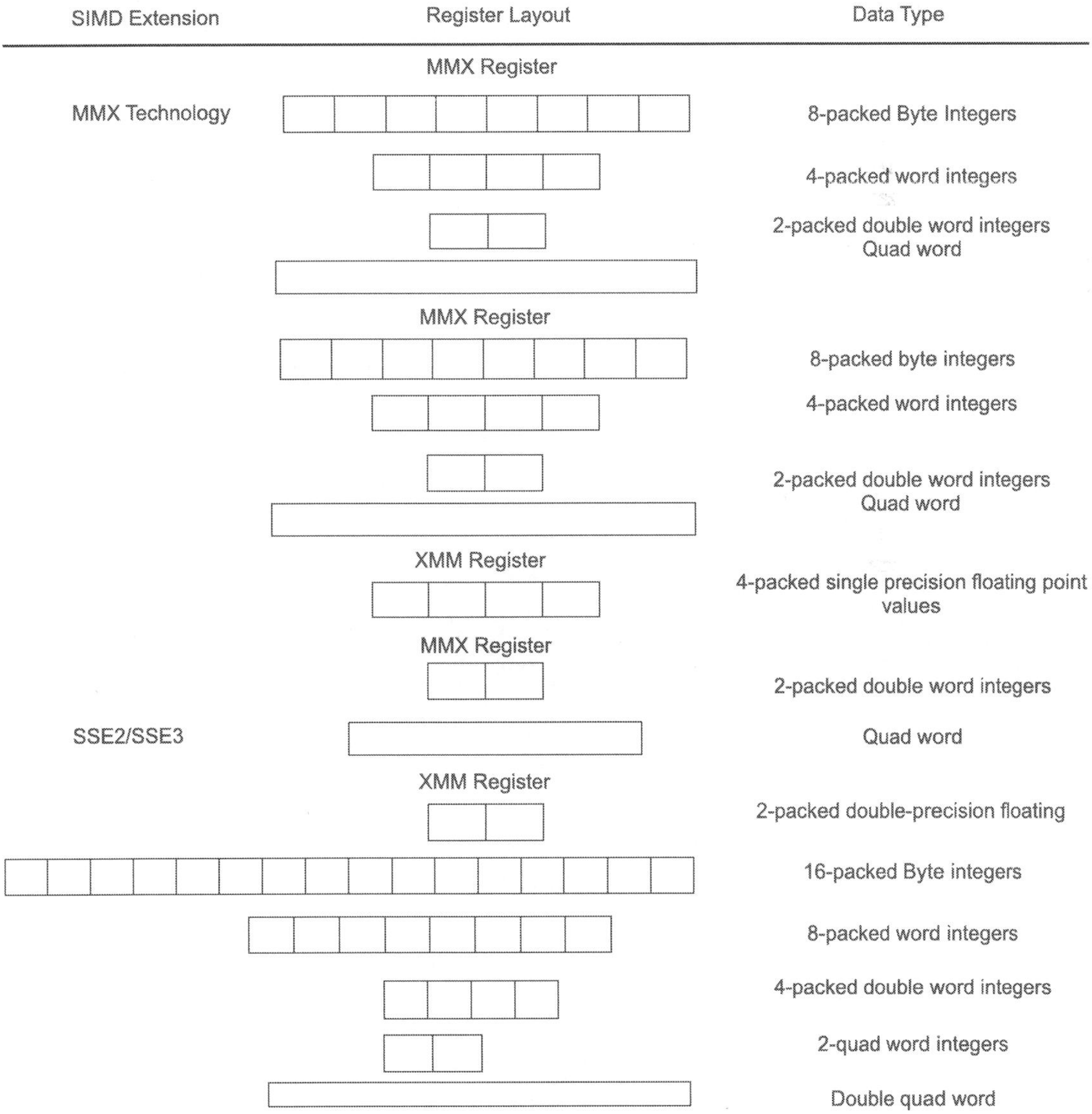

Fig. 12.4 *Streaming SIM Extension*

As may be observed, these new set of extended instructions in SSE3 are mainly targeted towards enhancing three dimensional graphics, video and multimedia applications. Some of them will be useful for improving thread synchronization. In short they increase processor's ability to handle faster floating point computations in parallel, which are essential in applications in three dimensional graphics, multimedia and gaming. The register layouts and data types for streaming SIMD extension is given in Fig. 12.4.

12.10.5 IA-32 Instruction Decode

IA-32 instructions are cumbersome to decode because the instructions have a variable number of bytes and have many different options. A significant amount of logic and intermediate state are needed to decode these instructions. Fortunately, the TC provides most of the μops, and decoding is only needed for instructions that miss the TC.

The decoder logic takes instruction bytes from the streaming buffers and decodes them into μops. Assume a process having two threads, both the threads active simultaneously; in such cases, the streaming buffers alternate between threads so that both the threads share the same decoder logic. The decoder logic preserves two copies of all the states needed to decode IA-32 instructions for the two logical processors, even though it only decodes instructions for one logical processor at a time. In fact several instructions are decoded for one logical processor one after other, before the control switches to the other logical processor. The decoded instructions are written into the TC and forwarded to the μop queue.

12.10.6 Queue for Microcodes

After μops are fetched from the trace cache or the Microcode ROM (in case of complex instructions) or forwarded from the instruction decode logic, they are placed in a "μop queue". The μop queue may be viewed as the interface between the Front End and the Out-of-order Execution Engine in the pipeline flow. The μop queue is partitioned such that each of the two logical processor has half the entries. This partitioning allows both logical processors to make independent forward progress regardless of front-end stalls (e.g. TC miss) or execution stalls.

12.11 INSTRUCTION SET SUMMARY

In this section we present the set of instructions supported by Pentium 4 processor. The various groups of instructions and the IA-32 processor support are presented in Table 12.1.

Table 12.1 *Instruction Groups and IA-32 Processors Supporting them*

Instruction set Architecture	*IA-32 Processor Support*
• General Purpose	All IA-32 processors
• X87 FPU	Intel 486, Pentium, Pentium with MMX Technology, Celeron, Pentium Pro. Pentium II, Pentium II Xeon, Pentium III, Pentium II, Pentium II Xeon. Pentium III, Pentium III Xeon, Pentium 4, Intel Xeon processor.
• X87 FPU and SIMD state Management	Pentium II, Pentium II Xeon, Pentium III, Pentium III Xeon, Pentium 4, Intel xeon processors
• MMX Technology	Pentium with MMX Technology, celeron, Pentium II, Pentium II xeon, Pentium III, Pentium III xeon, Pentium 4, Intel xeon processors.

(Contd.)

Table 12.1 *(Contd.)*

Instruction set Architecture	*IA-32 Processor Support*
• SSE extensions	Pentium III, Pentium III xeon, Pentium 4, Intel xeon processors.
• SSE2 Extensions	Pentium 4, Intel xeon processors
• SSE3 Extensions	Pentium 4 supporting HT Technology (build on 90 nm process technology)
• IA-32 e: 64-bit Mae	Pentium 4, Intel xeon processors
• System Instructions	All IA-32 processors.

12.11.1 General Purpose Instructions for Pentium 4 Processor

The general purpose instructions perform basic data operations, such as data movement, arithmetic, logical, shift, control and string operations that programmes commonly use. They operate on data contained in memory, in the general purpose registers , such as EAX, EBX, ECX, EDX, EDI, ESJ, EBP, and ESP or even the EFLAG register. They also operate on address information maintained in memory, the general purpose registers and the segment registers (CS, DS, SS, ES, FS and GS).

The set of instructions have been grouped under (i) data transfer, (ii) binary integer arithmetic, (iii) decimal arithmetic, (iv) logic, (v) shift and rotate, (vi) bit and byte operations, (vii) program control instructions, (viii) string, (ix) input output (x) flag control (xi) Segment register and (xii) miscellaneous subgroups. The instructions under each group are briefly described below.

(i) DATA TRANSFER GROUP

MOV	:	MOVE data between general purpose register, memory and general purpose or segment registers: move immediate to general purpose registers
CMDVE/CMOVZ	:	Conditional move if equal/Conditional move if zero.
CMDVNE/CMOVNZ	:	Conditional move if not equal/Conditional move if not zero.
CMDVA/CMOVNBE	:	Conditional move if above/Conditional move if not below or equal.
CMOVB/CMDVNAE	:	Conditional move if below/Conditional move if not below or equal.
CMOVBE/CMDVNA	:	Conditional move if below or equal/Conditional move if not be above.
CMOVG/CMOVNLE	:	Conditional move if greater/Conditional move if not less or equal
CMOVGE/CMOVNL	:	Conditional move if greater or equal/Conditional move if not less
CMOVL/CMOVNGE	:	Conditional move if less/Conditional move if not greater or equal
CMDVLE/CMOVNG	:	Conditional move if less or equal/Conditional move if not greater.
CMOVC	:	Conditional move if carry.
CMOVNC	:	Conditional move if not carry.
CMOVO	:	Conditional move if overflow.
CMOVNO	:	Conditional move if not overflow
CMOVS	:	Conditional move if sign (negative)
CMOVNS	:	Conditional move if not sign (non-negative)
CMOVP/CMOVPE	:	Conditional move if parity/Conditional move if parity even
CMOVNP/CMOVPO	:	Conditional move if not parity/Conditonal move if parity data
XCHG	:	Exchange
BSWAP	:	Byte swap
XADD	:	Exchange and add
CMPXCHG	:	Compare and exchange
CMPXCHG8B	:	Compare and exchange 8 bytes
PUSH	:	Push onto stack

POP	:	PUP off of stack
PUSHA/PUSHAD	:	Push general purpose registers onto stack
POPA/POPAD	:	Pop general purpose registers from stack.
CWD/CDQ	:	Current word to double word/current double word to equal word.
CBW/CWDE	:	Current byte to word/current word to equal in EAX register.
MOVSX	:	Move and sign extend.
MOVZX	:	Move and zero extend.

(ii) BINARY ARITHMETIC INSTRUCTIONS

ADD	:	Integer add
ADC	:	Add with carry
SUB	:	Subtract
SBB	:	Subtract with borrow
IMUL	:	Signed multiply
MUL	:	Unsigned multiply
IDIV	:	Signed divide
DIV	:	Unsigned divide
INC	:	Increment
DEC	:	Decrement
NEG	:	Negate
CMP	:	Compare

(iii) DECIMAL ARITHMETIC INSTRUCTIONS

DAA	:	Decimal adjust after addition
DAS	:	Decimal adjust after subtraction
AAA	:	ASCII adjust after addition
AAS	:	ASCII adjust after subtraction
AAM	:	ASCII adjust after multiplication
AAD	:	ASCII adjust after subtraction

(iv) LOGIC INSTRUCTIONS

AND	:	Perform bit wise logical AND
OR	:	Perform bit wise logical OR
XOR	:	Perform bit wise logical exclusive OR
NOT	:	Perform bit wise logical NOT

(v) SHIFT AND ROTATE INSTRUCTIONS

SAR	:	Shift arithmetic right
SHR	:	Shift logical right
SAL/SHL	:	Shift arithmetic left/shift logical left
SHRD	:	Shift right double
SHLD	:	Shift left double
ROR	:	Rotate right
ROL	:	Rotate right
RCR	:	Rotate through carry right
RCL	:	Rotate through carry left.

(vi) BIT AND BYTE INSTRUCTIONS

BT	:	Bit test
BTS	:	Bit test and set

BTR	:	Bit test and reset
BTC	:	Bit test and complement
BSF	:	Bit scan and forward
BSR	:	Bit scan and reverse
SETE/SETZ	:	Set byte if equal/set byte if zero
SETNE/SETNZ	:	Set byte if not equal/set byte if not zero
SETA/SETNBE	:	Set byte if above/set byte if note below or equal
SETAE/SETNB/SETNC	:	Set byte if above equal/set byte if note below/set if not carry.
SETB/SETNAE/SETC	:	Set byte if below/set byte if not above or equal/set byte if carry.
SETBE/SETNA	:	Set byte if below or equal/set byte if not above
SETG/SETNLE	:	Set byte if greater/set byte if not less or equal
SETGE/SETNLE	:	Set byte if greater or equal/set byte if not less.
SETL/SETGE	:	Set byte if less or equal/set byte if not greater.
SETLE/SETNG	:	Set byte if less or equal/set byte if not greater.
SETS	:	Set byte if sign (negative)
SETNS	:	Set byte if not sign (non-negative)
SETO	:	Set byte if overflow
SETNO	:	Set byte if note overflow
SETPE/SETP	:	Set byte if parity even/set byte if parity
SETPO/SETNP	:	Set byte if parity odd/set byte if not parity.
TEST	:	Logical compare

(vii) CONTROL TRANSFER INSTRUCTIONS

JMP	:	Jump
JE/JNZ	:	Jump equal/Jump if zero
JNE/JZ	:	Jump if not equal/Jump if zero
JA/JNBE	:	Jump if above/Jump if not below or equal
JAE/JVB	:	Jump if above or equal/Jump if not below
JB/JNAE	:	Jump if below/Jump if not above or above
JG/JNLE	:	Jump if greater/Jump if not less or equal
JGE/JNL	:	Jump if greater or equal/Jump if not less
JL/JNGE	:	Jump of less/Jump if not greater or equal
JLE/JNG	:	Jump if less or equal/Jump if not greater.
JC	:	Jump if carry
JNC	:	Jump if not carry.
JO	:	Jump if overflow
JNO	:	Jump if not overflow
JS	:	Jump if sign (negative)
JNS	:	Jump if not sign (non-negative)
JPO/JNP	:	Jump if parity odd/Jump if not parity
JPE/JP	:	Jump if parity even/Jump if parity
JCXZ/JECXZ	:	Jump register CX zero/Jump register ECX zero
LOOP	:	Loop with ECX counter
LOOPZ/LOOPE	:	Loop with ECX and zero/Loop with ECX and equal
LOOPZ/LOOPNE	:	Loop with ECX and not zero/Loop with ECX and not equal
CALL	:	Call procedure
RET	:	Return

IRET	:	Return from interrupt
INT	:	Software interrupt
INTO	:	Interrupt on overflow
BOUND	:	Detect value out of range
ENTER	:	High level procedure entry
LEAVE	:	High level procedure exit

(viii) STRING INSTRUCTIONS

MOVS/MOVSB	:	Move string/move byte string
MOVS/MOVSW	:	Move string/move word string
MOVES/MOVSD	:	Move string/move double word string
CMPS/CMPSW	:	Compare string/compare word string
CMPS/CMPSD	:	Compare string/compare double word string
CMPS/CMPSB	:	Compare string compare byte string
SCAS/SCASB	:	Scan string/scan byte string
SCAS/SCASW	:	Scan string/scan word string
SCAS/SCASD	:	Scan string/scan double word string
LODS/LODSB	:	Load string/load byte string
LODS/LODSW	:	Load string/load word string
LODS/CODSD	:	Load string/Load double word string
STOS/STOSB	:	Store string/store byte string
STOS/STOSW	:	Store string/store word string
STOS/STOSD	:	Store string/store double word string
REP	:	Repeat while ECX not zero
REPE/REPZ	:	Repeat while equal/Repeat while zero
REPNE/REPNZ	:	Repeat while not equal/Repeat while not zero.

(ix) I/O INSTRUCTIONS

IN	:	Read from a port
OUT	:	Write to a port
INS/INSB	:	Input string from port/Input byte string from port
INS/INSW	:	Input string from port/Input word string from port
INS/INSD	:	Input string from port/Input double word from port
OUTS/OUTSB	:	Output string to port/Output byte string to port
OUTS/OUTSW	:	Output string to port/Output word to port
OUTS/OUTSD	:	Output string to port/Output double word string to port.

(x) FLAG CONTROL INSTRUCTIONS

STC	:	Set carry flag
CLC	:	Clear carry flag
CMC	:	Complement carry flag
CLD	:	Clean the direction flag
STD	:	Set direction flag
LAHF	:	Loads flags into AH register
SAHF	:	Store AH register into flags
PUSH/PUSHFD	:	Push EFLAGS onto stack
POPE/POPED	:	Pop EFLAGS from stack
SII	:	Set interrupt flag
CLI	:	Clean the interrupt flag

(xi) SEGMENT REGISTER INSTRUCTIONS

LDS	:	Load for pointer using DS
LES	:	Load for pointer using ES
LFS	:	Load for pointer using FS
LGS	:	Load for pointer using GS
LSS	:	Load for pointer using SS

(xii) MISCELLANEOUS INSTRUCTIONS

LEA	:	Load effective address
NOP	:	No operation
UDZ	:	Undefined Instruction
XLAJ / ZLAJB	:	Table look up translation
CPUID	:	Processor Identification

12.11.2 SSE SIMD Single-Precision Floating Point Instruction Set

In this section we present the Precision Floating Point instruction set in SSE under several groups.

(i) SSE Data Transfer Instruction

MOVAPS	:	Move four aligned packed single precision floating point values between XMM registers or between XMM register and memory.
MOVUPS	:	Move few unaligned packed single precision floating point values between XMM registers or between XMM register and memory.
MOVHPS	:	Move two packed single precision floating point values to and from the high quad word of XMM register and memory.
MOVHLPS	:	Move two packed single precision floating point values from the high quad word of an XMM register to the low quad word of another XMM register.
MOVLPS	:	Move two packed single precision floating point values to and from the low quad word of an XMM register and memory.
MOVLHPS	:	Move two packed single precision floating point values from the low quad word of an XMM register to the high quad word of another XMM register.
MOVMSKPS	:	Extract sign task from four packed single precision floating point values.
MOVSS	:	Move scalar single precision floating point value between XMM register or between an XMM register and memory.

(ii) SSE Packed Arithmetic Instruction

ADDPS	:	Add packed single precision floating point values
ADDSS	:	Add scalar single precision floating point values
SUBPS	:	Subtract packed single precision floating point values
SUBSS	:	Subtract scalar single precision floating point values
MULPS	:	Multiply packed single precision floating point values
MULSS	:	Multiply scalar single precision floating point values
DIVPS	:	Divide packed single precision floating point values
DIVSS	:	Divide scalar single precision floating point values
RCPPS	:	Compute reciprocals of packed single precision floating point values

RCPSS	:	Compute reciprocals of scalar single precision floating point values
SQRTPS	:	Computer square roots of packed single precision floating point values
SQRTSS	:	Computer square root of scalar single precision floating point values
MAXPS	:	Return maximum packed single precision floating point values
MINPS	:	Return minimum packed single precision floating point values
MINSS	:	Return minimum scalar single precision floating point values

(iii) SSE Comparison Instructions

CMPPS	:	Compare packed single-precision floating point values
CMPES	:	Compare scalar single-precision floating point values
COMISS	:	Perform ordered comparison of scalar single precision floating point values and set flags in EFLAGS register
UCOMISS	:	Perform unordered comparison of scalar single-precision floating point values and set flags in EFLAGS register

(iv) SSE Logical Instruction

ANDPS	:	Perform bit wise AND of packed single precision floating point values
ANDNPS	:	Perform bit wise AND NOT packed single precision floating point values
ORPS	:	Perform bit wise OR of packed single precision floating point values
XORPS	:	Perform bit wise OR of packed single precision floating point values

(v) SSE Shuffle and Unpack Instructions

SHUFPS	:	Shuffles values in packed single precision floating point operands
UNPCKHPS	:	Unpacks and interleaves the two high order values from two single precision floating point operands
UNPCKLPS	:	Unpacks and interleaves the two low order values from two single precision floating point operands

(vi) SSE MXCSR State Management Instructions

LDMXCSR	:	Load MXCSR register
ST MXCSR	:	Save MXCSR register state

(vii) SSE Cache Ability Control, Prefetch and Instruction Ordering Instructions

MASKMOVQ	:	Non-temporal store of selected bytes from an MMX register into memory.
MOVNTQ	:	Non-temporal store of quad word from an MMX register into memory.
MOVNTPS	:	Non-temporal store of few packed single precision floating point values from an XMM register into memory.
PREFETCH	:	Load 32 or more of bytes from memory to a selected level of the processors cache hierarchy.
SFENCE	:	Serializes store operations.

12.11.3 SSE2 Packed and Scalar Double Precision Floating Point Instructions

The following instructions are included in SSE2 and are used for Double Precision Floating Point operations.

(i) SSE2 Data Movement Instructions

MOVAPD	:	Move two aligned packed double precision floating point values between XMM or between XMM register and memory
MOVUPD	:	Move two unaligned packed double precision floating point values between XMM register or between XMM register and memory
MOVHPD	:	Move high packed double precision floating point values to and from the high quad word of an XMM register and memory.
MOVLPD	:	Move low packed double precision floating point value to and from the low quad word of an XMM register and memory.
MOVMSKPD	:	Extract sign mask from two packed double precision floating point values
MOVSD	:	Move scalar double precision floating point value between XMM registers or between register and memory.

(ii) SSE2 Packed Arithmetic Instructions

ADDPD	:	Add packed double precision floating point values
ADDSD	:	Add scalar double precision floating point values
SUBPD	:	Subtract packed double precision floating point values
SUBSD	:	Subtract scalar double precision floating point values
MULPD	:	Multiply packed double precision floating point values
MULSD	:	Multiply scalar double precision floating point values
DIVPD	:	Divide packed double precision floating point values
DIVSD	:	Divide scalar double precision floating point values
SQRTPD	:	Compute square roots of packed double precision floating point values
SQRTSD	:	Compute square roots of scalar double precision floating point values
MAXPD	:	Return maximum packed double precision floating point values
MINPD	:	Return maximum scalar double precision floating point values
MAXSD	:	Return maximum scalar double precision floating point values
MINSD	:	Return minimum scalar double precision floating point values

(iii) SSE2 Logical Instructions

ANDPD	:	Perform bit wise logical AND of packed double precision floating point
ANDNPD	:	Perform bit wise logical AND NOT of packed double precision floating point
ORPD	:	Perform bit wise logical OR of packed double precision floating point
XORPD	:	Perform bit wise logical XOR of packed double precision floating point

(iv) SSE2 Compare Instructions

CMPPD	:	Compare packed double precision floating point values
CMPSD	:	Compare scalar double precision floating point values
COMISD	:	Perform ordered comparison of scales double precision floating point values and set flags in EFLAGS register.
VCOMISD	:	Perform unordered comparison of scalar double precision floating point values and set flags in EFLAGS register.

(v) SSE2 Shuffle and Unpack Instructions

SHUFPD	:	Shuffles values in packed double precision floating point operands
UNPCKHPD	:	Unpacks and interleaves the high values from two packed double precision floating point operands.
UNPCKLPD	:	Unpacks and interleaves the two values from two packed double precision floating point operands.

(vi) SSE2 Cache Ability Control and Ordering Instructions

CLFLUSH	:	Flushes and invalidates a memory operand and its associated cache line from all levels of processors cache hierarchy.
LFENCE	:	Serializes load operations
MFENCE	:	Serializes load and store operations.
PAUSE	:	Improves the performance of "spin-wait loops"
MASK MOVDQU	:	Non-temporal store of selected bytes from an XMM register into memory.
MOVNTPD	:	Non-temporal store of two packed double precision floating point values from an XMM register into memory.
MOVNTDQ	:	Non-temporal store of double quadword from an XMM register into memory.
MOVNTI	:	Non-temporal store of double word from a general purpose register into memory.

12.11.4 SSE3 Instructions

SSE3 Extension offers 13 instructions that accelerate performance of streaming SIMD extension technology.

(i) SSE3 X 87-FP Integer Conversion Instruction

FISTTP	:	Behaves like the FISTP instruction byte uses truncation, irrespective of the Floating point Control Word (FCW).

(ii) SSE3 Specialised 128-bit Unaligned Data Load Instruction

LDDQU	:	Special 128-bit unaligned load designed to avoid cache line splits.

(iii) SSE3 SIMD Floating Point Packed ADD/SUB Instructions

ADDSUBPS	:	Performs signal precision addition on the second and fourth pairs of 32-bit data elements within the operands, single precision subtraction in the first and third pairs.
ADDSUBPD	:	Performs doubled precision addition on the second pair of quad words, and double-precision subtraction on the first pair.

(iv) SSE3 SIMD Floating-point LOAD/MOVE/DUPLICATE Instructions

MOVSHDUP	:	Loads/moves 128 bits; duplicating the second and fourth 32-bit data elements.

MOVSLDUP	:	Loads/Moves 128 bits, duplicating the first and third 32-bit data elements.
MOVDDUP	:	Load/Moves 64 bits and returns the same 64 bits in both the lower and upper halves of the 128-bit result register, duplicates the 64 bits from the source.

(v) SSE3 Agent Synchronisation Instructions

STD	:	Set direction flag
MONITOR	:	Sets up an address range used to monitor write back stores
MWAIT	:	Enables a logic processor to enter into an optimized stack while waiting for a write-back store to the address range set up by the MONITOR instruction

(vi) SSE3 SIMD Floating Point Horizontal ADD/SUB Instructions

HADDPS	:	Performs a single precision addition on contiguous data elements. The first data element of the result is obtained by adding the first and second elements of the first operand; the second element by adding the third and fourth elements of the first operand; the third by adding the first and second elements of the second operands, and the fourth by adding the third and fourth elements of the second operand.
HSUBPS	:	Performs a single precision subtraction on contiguous data elements. The first data element of the result is obtained by subtracting the second element of the first operand from the first element of the first operand; the second element by subtracting the fourth element of first operand from the third element of the first operand; the third by subtracting the second element of the second operand from the first element of the second operand; and the fourth by subtracting the fourth element of the second operand from the third element of the second operand.
HADDPD	:	Performs a double precision addition on contiguous data elements. The first data element of the result is obtained by adding the first and second elements of the first operand; the second element by adding the first and second elements of the second operand.
HSUBPD	:	Performs a double precision subtraction on contiguous data elements. The first data of the result is obtained by subtracting the second element of the first operand from the first element of the first operand: the second element by subtracting the second operand from the first element of second operand.

12.12 NEED FOR FORMAL VERIFICATION

It is extremely important that a microprocessor as complex as Pentium 4 with a novel IA-32 microarchitecture and a host of features like dynamic execution, advanced transfer cache, execution trace cache, rapid execution engine, Streaming SIMD Extension 2, needs logical correctness of the design. A formal design verification team at Intel has done significant work in the area of formal verification of the floating point execution module and also the instruction decoder logic. By the term formal verification, we mean the verification of the logic using formal mathematical tools. It is important to develop the tools and methodologies to handle a large number of proofs using which it will be possible to detect the bugs in the design. By using such formal techniques they could detect more than 100 logical bugs, which without validation would have gone undetected as it happened in the first version of Pentium when it was released. The modern day processors are all designed to operate at a very high speed and even with the lower operating voltages, the power consumption is high enough to require expensive cooling technology.

SUMMARY

The Intel Net Burst IA-32 micro architecture of Pentium 4 supports a host of interesting features like dynamic execution, execution trace cache, rapid execution engine, coupled with an enhanced set of SIMD insturctions, like Streaming SIMD Extension and so on. We have attempted to describe some of these ideas in moderate detail in this chapter. The concept of multithreading and hyperthreading are extremely important in today's architecture. We have reviewed how this feature has been integrated in Pentium 4 in this chapter.

EXERCISES

12.1 Enlist salient features of P4 Architecture.

12.2 Write short notes on:

(i) Trace cache
(ii) Branch prediction
(iii) Out of order execution
(iv) Hyperthreading in P4
(v) SSE instructions.

12.3 Draw and discuss: (i) Block diagram of P4 (ii) Detail Architecture of P4.

12.4 Explain instruction decoding in IA-32 Architectures.

12.5 Explain the function of ITLB.

12.6 Discuss paging and virtual memory in brief with reference to P4.

12.7 Explain: (i) Register rename (ii) Instruction celluling (iii) Architecture state

12.8 Write a case study on 'Instruction set of Pentium 4.

13 RISC Architecture—An Overview

INTRODUCTION

As we have observed in the previous chapters, the complexities of the instructions supported by a CISC processor went on increasing, as more and more sophisticated processors were designed and marketed. This resulted in an increase of processor die size to accommodate the large microcode required by the complex instructions. The larger die size in turn meant more cost, since it consumes more silicon. Also as the chip size increases, the power consumption increases, resulting in more heating of the chip. This in turn requires more cooling arrangement.

If we use processors, which support a set of simpler instructions, which do not require complex decoding, then the design of the processor becomes simple, with an associated reduction in cost and power consumption. Also the execution of these instructions becomes very fast.

As the name implies, the Reduced Instruction Set Computer or RISC as it is popularly known is a type of architecture that utilises a small, highly optimized set of instructions, rather than a more specialised set of instructions often found in other types of architectures. Typically every instruction is executed in a single clock after it is fetched and decoded. These instructions are executed very fast. Lot of disc space is consumed by micro codes in a CISC design which could be otherwise used for enhanced features. It is thus possible to produce more RISC processors per silicon wafer. This makes RISC processors smaller, with lesser energy consumption.

13.1 A SHORT HISTORY OF RISC PROCESSORS

It was possibly John Cocke of IBM Research in Yorktown, New York, who had first originated the RISC concept in 1974 by stressing upon the fact that about 20% of the instructions in a computer perform about 80% of the tasks in an application in his project on IBM 801. Subsequently IBM's RISC System/6000, made use of the idea. The term RISC was however, first used by David Patterson of University of California in Berkeley, in the early 1980's, while investigating the design of RISC-1 architecture. About the same time in 1981 another project at Stanford investigated by Hennessy led to the development of the MIPS (Microprocessor without Interlocked Pipeline Stages) processors. The first RISC processors were thus initiated by IBM, Stanford, and UC-Berkeley in the late 70s and early 80s. The IBM 801, Stanford MIPS, and Berkeley RISC-1 and 2 were all designed with a similar philosophy which has become known as RISC. The RISC based processors in the subsequent days were basically modeled after one of these early designs.

With the recent advances in electronic gadget technologies and specially mobile communication. ARM processors developed by ACORN company have become most popular. The ARM product tree that started with ARM1 has now reached ARM11. In this chapter a brief overview of a few of these RISC processors has been presented with emphasis on ARM7 architecture. IBM RISC processors starting with R 6000 series were designed based on the concepts of IBM 801. This evolution finally led to the development of IBM Power PCs. The development of MIPs series continued from early Stanford MIPS. The concept was used in Sun Microsystems' SPARC microprocessors and led to the founding of what is now MIPS Technologies, part of Silicon Graphics. DEC's Alpha microchip also uses RISC technology.

13.2 HYBRID ARCHITECTURE—RISC AND CISC CONVERGENCE

Till the mid 1990s, processor designers were split into two opposing camps. Some used CISC designs due to its low burden on compiler developers and wide availability of existing software. Others used RISC designs because of its simplicity and efficiency.

However, today, most CISC processors are based on hybrid CISC-RISC architecture. Such a hybrid architecture uses a decoder to convert CISC instructions into RISC instructions before execution. These are then processed by a RISC core, which performs a few basic instructions very quickly. Also a RISC core allows performance enhancing features, such as branch prediction and pipelining. Traditionally, these have only been possible in RISC designs, since fixed length instructions are required for such features to work.

Some of the popular examples of hybrid architectures include the Pentium and Athlon family of processors. These processors are compatible with the software developed for their CISC predecessors, yet they perform competitively against processors based on RISC designs. However, CISC-RISC hybrids continue to consume a lot of power and are not the best candidates for mobile and embedded applications.

Apart from having a RISC core, the number of general pupose registers in CISC processors has also grown. This follows RISC ideals and allows more instructions to be processed simultaneously. The Intel Pentium III with its SSE technology has an additional set of eight 128-bit vector registers for running SIMD [Single Instruction Multiple Data] instructions. AMD's new x86-64 chips also have an additional eight general purpose registers and eight SSE registers. The future successor to the Pentium series, Intel Itanium IA-64, will even raise the bar further by implementing 128 general purpose registers.

RISC processors, on the other hand, have also become more CISC-like by supporting more functions. Many modern RISC processors support more instructions than old CISC designs. Example includes the Motorola G4 processor used in power Macs and eMacs. Its Alti Vac unit adds 162 new instructions to the existing RISC architecture. By adding more instructions, some applications can be run much faster. These include multimedia applications, such as telecommunications encoding/decoding, image conversions and video processing.

13.3 THE ADVANTAGES OF RISC

There are several advantages of a RISC processor over its CISC counterpart. Implementing a processor with a simplified instruction set design provides several advantages over implementing a comparable CISC design. Some of the advantages are as below.

(i) RISC instructions, being simple, can be hard-wired, while CISC architectures may have to use micro-programming in order to implement complex instructions.
(ii) A set of simple instructions results in reduced complexity of the control unit and the data-path; as a consequence, the processor can work at a high clock frequency and thus yields higher speed.
(iii) As a result several extra functionalities, such as memory management units or floating point arithmetic units, can also be placed on the same chip.

(iv) Smaller chips allow a semiconductor manufacturer to place more parts on a single silicon wafer, which can lower the per-chip cost dramatically.

(v) High-level language compilers produce more efficient codes in a RISC processor than its counterpart CISC processor, because they tend use the smaller set of instructions in a RISC computer.

(vi) Shorter design cycle—A new RISC processor can be designed, developed and tested more quickly since RISC processors are simpler than corresponding CISC processors.

(vii) The application programmers who use the microprocessor's instructions will find it easier to develop code with a smaller and optimized instruction set.

(viii) Another advantage is that the loading and decoding of instructions in a RISC processor is simple and fast, as it is not needed to wait until the length of an instruction is known in order to start decoding the following one. Decoding is simplified as opcode and address fields are located in the same position for all instructions.

13.4 BASIC FEATURES OF RISC PROCESSORS

(i) Simple instruction set: In a RISC machine, the instruction set contains simple, basic instructions, from which more complex instructions can be composed. Thus instructions with less latency are preferred.

(ii) Same length instruction: Each instruction is of the same length, so that it may be fetched in a single operation. The traditional microprocessors from Intel or Motorola supports variable length instructions.

(iii) Single machine-cycle instructions: Most instructions complete in one machine cycle, which allows the processor to handle several instructions at the same time. RISC processors have unity CPI (clock per instruction), which is due to the optimization of each instruction on the CPU and massive pipelining embedded in a RISC processor.

(iv) Pipelining: Usually massive pipelining is embedded in a RISC processor. The pipelining is key to speed up RISC machines.

(v) Very few addressing modes and formats: Unlike the CISC processors, where the number of addressing modes are very high, in RISC processors, the addressing modes are much less and it supports few formats.

(vi) Large number of registers: The RISC design philosophy generally incorporates a larger number of registers to prevent in large amounts of interactions with memory.

(vii) Microcoding not required: Unlike in a CISC machine, in RISC architecture, instruction microcoding is not required. This is because of the availability of a set of simple instructions, and simple instructions may be easily built into the hardware.

(viii) Load and Store architecture: The RISC architecture is primarily a Load and Store architecture, implying that all the memory accesses take place using Load or Store type operations.

In the next section we will investigate some of the critical issues involved in the design of RISC Architecture.

13.5 DESIGN ISSUES OF RISC PROCESSORS

In this section we will briefly discuss some of the important issues involved in the design of RISC based processors.

13.5.1 Register Windowing

The concept of register windowing involves a mechanism where the chips expose 32 registers to the programmer at any one time, but these registers are just a "window" into a larger set of physical registers. The additional registers are hidden from view until you call a subroutine. For example other processor would push parameters on a stack for the called routine to pop off, SPARC processors just "rotate" the register window to give the called routine a fresh set of registers. The old window and the new window overlap, so that some registers are shared. As long as you're careful about placing parameters in the right registers, the windows are a slick way to pass operands without using the stack at all.

Slick as it seems, registers windows have their drawback. The concept has been around for decades, yet SPARC is almost the only CPU architecture to use it. First, register windows only help up to a point—the number of physical registers is finite and eventually SPARC runs out of space for more windows. When that happens, you're back to pushing and popping operands on and off the stack. It's next to impossible to predict when the register file will overflow or underflow, so performance can be unpredictable. Finally, the processor doesn't handle the overflow/underflow automatically in hardware. It generates a software fault, which the operating system has to handle, consuming more cycles.

Many hardware engineers aren't particular fans of register windowing. It puts enormous demands on multiplexers and register ports to make any physical register appear to be any logical register. In the 1990's when there were nearly a dozen different vendors designing and marketing SPARC-compatible processor, their designers complained bitterly about the headaches in routing interconnect over, around, and through the register file in the middle of every SPARC processor.

That register windowing, which is an inherent and permanent feature of every SPARC, has so far made it impossible to add multithreading, and difficult to keep clock speeds up. The 900-MHz and new 1.05-GHz UltraSPARC-III chips both use TI's 0.15-micron copper process for their 29 million transistors. Fortunately, most SPARC processors are buried inside Sun workstations, where the value of Sun's software base and systems-level expertise outshine the relative shortcomings of its processors.

13.5.2 Massive Pipelining

A RISC processor pipeline operates in much the same way, although the stages in the pipeline are different. While different processors have different number of steps, they are basically variations of the five steps as follows.

(a) fetch instructions from memory
(b) read registers and decode the instruction
(c) execute the instruction or calculate an address
(d) access an operand in data memory
(e) write the result into a register.

There are, however, problems relating to pipelining. In practice, RISC processors operate at more than one cycle per instruction. The processor might occasionally stall a result due to data dependencies and branch instructions.

A data dependency occurs when an instruction depends on the results of the previous instructions. A particular instruction might need data in a register, which has not yet been stored since that is the job of a preceeding instruction, which has not yet reached that step in the pipeline.

Branch instructions are those which instruct the processor to make a decision about the next instruction to be executed, depending upon whether the condition is satisfied or not. Branch instructions can be troublesome in a pipeline if it is conditional, and may be taken, which has not yet finished its path through the pipeline.

13.5.3 Single Cycle Instruction Execution

In a typical pipelined RISC design, each instruction takes one clock cycle for each stage, so the processor can accept one new instruction per clock. Pipelining doesn't improve the latency of instructions (each instruction still requires the same amount of time to complete), but it does improve the overall throughput.

As with CISC computers, the ideal is not always achieved. Sometimes pipelined instructions take more than one clock to complete a stage. When that happens, the processors has to stall and not accept new instructions until the slow instruction has moved on to the next stage.

Idling of RISC Processor—Since the processor remains idle when stalled, the designers of RISC systems employ several techniques, to avoid the idling of the CPU, as shown in the following sections.

The RISC concept has led to a more thoughtful design of the microprocessor. Among design considerations are how well an instruction can be mapped to the clock speed of the microprocessor (ideally, an instruction can be performed in one clock cycle); how "simple" an architecture is required; and how much work can be done by the microchip itself without resorting to software help.

13.6 PERFORMANCE ISSUES IN PIPELINED SYSTEMS

A pipelined processor can stall for a variety of reasons, including delays in reading information from memory, a poor instruction set design, or dependencies between instructions. The question is how to address these problems.

Memory speed issues are commonly solved using caches. A cache is a section of fast memory placed between the processor and slower memory. When the processor wants to read location in main memory, that location is also copied into the cache. Subsequent reference to that location can come from the cache, which will return a result much more quickly than the main memory.

Caches present one major problem to system designers and programmers, and that is the problem of coherency. When the processor writes a value to memory, the result goes into the cache instead of going directly to main memory. Therefore, special hardware (usually implemented as part of the processor) needs to write the information out to main memory before something else tries to read that location or before re-using that part of the cache for some different information.

13.6.1 Instruction Latency

A poorly designed instruction set can cause a pipelined processor to stall frequently. Some of the more typical CISC instructions, which have more instruction latency should be avoided.

These are:

(i) Highly encoded instructions, such as those used on CISC machines need complex decoders. These should be avoided.

(ii) Variable-length instructions which require multiple references to memory to fetch the entire instruction should not be considered for inclusion.

(iii) Instructions which access main memory, instead of registers, are slow in execution, since main memory is comparatively slow.

(iv) Complex instructions, which require multiple clocks for their execution, such as floating point multiplication should be avoided.

13.6.2 Dependency Issues

Dependence on single-point resources such as a condition code register. If one instruction sets the conditions in the condition code register and the following instruction tries to read those bits, the second instruction may have to stall until the first instruction's write completes.

One problem that RISC designers confront is that, because of improper choice of instructions, the processor performances can really get degraded to a large extent. Since each instruction takes some amount of time to store its result, and several instruction are being handled at the same time, later instructions may have to wait for the results of earlier instructions to be stored. However, a simple rearrangement of the instructions in a program (called Instruction Scheduling) can remove these performance limitation from RISC programs.

One common optimization involves "common subexpression elimination." A complier which encounters the statements

$$f_1 = a + b * c / d \text{ and}$$
$$f_2 = a / (a + b + b * c / d) .$$

calculates (b * c/d) first, put that result into a temporary variable, and then use the temporary variable in computing f_1 and f_2.

Another optimization involves "loop unrolling." Instead of executing a sequence of instruction inside a loop, the complier may replicate the instructions multiple times. This eliminates the overhead of calculating and testing the loop control variable.

Compilers also perform function inlining, where a call to a small subroutine is replaced by the code of the subroutine itself. This gets rid of the overhead of a call/return sequence.

This is only a small sample of the optimizations which are available. A good textbook on compilers may be referred for other ideas on how compiled code may be optimized.

13.6.3 Cautions on the Use of RISC

The transition from a CISC to RISC design strategy is, however, not without its problems. The following points need to be considered while using a RISC based system. And the software engineers should be aware of the key issues which arise when moving code from a CISC processor to a RISC processor.

(i) Code Quality: The performance of a RISC processor depends greatly on the code that it executes. If the programmer (or compiler) does a poor job of instruction scheduling, the processor can spend quite a bit of time stalling: waiting for the result of one instruction before it can proceed with a subsequent instruction.

(ii) Scheduling: Since the scheduling rules can be complicated, most programmers use a high level language (such as C or C+ +) and leave the instruction scheduling to the compiler. This makes the performance of RISC application depend critically on the quality of the code generated by the compiler. Therefore, developers (and development tool suppliers such as Apple) have to choose the compiler carefully based on the quality of the generated code.

(iii) Debugging: Unfortunately, instruction scheduling can make debugging difficult. If scheduling (and other optimizations) are turned off, the machine-language instructions show a clear connection with their corresponding lines of source. However, once the instruction scheduling is turned on, the machine language instructions for one line of source may appear in the middle of the instructions for another line of source code.

Such an intermingling of machine language instructions not only makes the code hard to read, it can also defeat the purpose of using a source-level complier, since single lines of code can no longer be executed by themselves.

Therefore, many RISC programmers debug their code in an un-optimized, un-scheduled form and then turn on the scheduler (and other optimizations) and hope that the program continues to work in the same way.

(iv) Code expansion: Since CISC machines perform complex actions using a single instruction, whereas RISC machines may require multiple instructions for the same action, code expansion can be a problem. Code expansion refers to the increase in size which results from a program that had been compiled for a CISC machine.

Fortunately for us, the code expansion between a 68K processor used in the non-PowerPC Mac and the PowerPC seems to be only 30–50% on the average, although size-optimized PowerPC code can be of the same size (or smaller) than corresponding 68K code.

(v) On chip cache: RISC machines require very fast memory systems to feed them instructions. RISC-based systems typically contain large caches, usually on the chip itself.

13.7 ARCHITECTURE OF SOME RISC PROCESSORS

In this section we will have overview of some of the popular RISC processors. We will discuss about ARM and MIPS, followed by SUN UltraSpark.

13.7.1 ARM7 Architecture—A Brief Overview

Advanced RISC Machine (ARM) architectures were developed by Acorn Company. The series started with ARM1 and has till now reached ARM11. In this section, a brief introduction to ARM 7 architecture and its general features is presented. ARM 7 is intended for applications, which require power efficient processors, such as wireless telecommunications, data communication (protocol converter), portable instruments, portable computers and smart cards.

Introduction The principle feature of the ARM 7 microcontroller is that it is a register oriented load-and-store architecture. Unlike other processors it can operate in a number of operating modes. While the ARM7 is a 32 bit microcontroller, it is also capable of running a 16-bit instruction set, known as "THUMB" i.e. earlier ARM instruction set. This helps it achieve a greater code density and enhanced power saving. To increase the performance of these instructions, the ARM 7 has a three-stage pipeline. Due to the inherent simplicity of the design and low gate count, ARM 7 is the industry leader in low-power processing on a watts per MIP basis. Finally, to assist the developer, the ARM core has a built-in JTAG debug port and on-chip "embedded ICE" that allows programs to be downloaded and fully debugged in-system. Thus using the JTAG port and embedded ice one can trace the execution of a program during debugging.

While all of the register-to-register data processing instructions are single-cycle, other instructions such as data transfer instructions, are multi-cycle. In order to keep the ARM 7 both simple and cost-effective, the code and data regions are accessed via a single data bus. Thus while the ARM 7 is capable of single-cycle execution of all data processing instructions, data transfer instructions may take several cycles since they will require at least two bus cycles; one for the instruction code and another for the data. In order to improve performance, a three stage pipeline is used that allows up to three instructions to be processed simultaneously.

The pipeline has three stages; FETCH, DECODE and EXECUTE. The hardware of each stage is designed to be independent so up to three instructions can be processed simultaneously. As we shall see later the ARM 7 designers had some clever ideas to solve this problem. Fig 13.1 shows the concept of a 3 stage pipelined execution.

Actions	**Fetch**		Decode	Execute	Execution complete		
Instru. 1							
Actions			Fetch	Decode	Execute		
Instru. 2							
Actions				Fetch	Decode	Waiting to Execute	
Instru. 3							
Instructions being executed at a time	1	1	2	3	2	2	

Fig. 13.1 *3 Stage Pipelined execution of Instructions in ARM7*

The pipeline is most effective in speeding up sequential code. However a branch instruction will cause the pipeline to be flushed marring its performance due to jump at unexpected address.

ARM7 Programming Model (Register set) The programmer's model of the ARM 7 consists of 15 user registers, as shown in Fig. 13.2, with R15 being used as the Program Counter (PC). Since the ARM 7 is a load-and-store architecture, a user program must load data from memory into the CPU registers, process this data and then store the result back into memory. Unlike other processors no memory to memory instructions are available.

As stated above R15 is the Program Counter. R13 and R14 also have special functions; R13 is used as the stack pointer, though this has only been defined as a programming convention. Unusually the ARM instruction set does not have PUSH and POP instructions so stack handling is done via a set of instructions that allow loading and storing of multiple registers in a single operation. Thus it is possible to PUSH or POP the entire register set onto the stack in a single instruction. R14 has special significance and is called the "link register". When a call is made to a procedure, the return address is automatically placed into R14, rather than onto a stack, as might be expected. A return can then be implemented by moving the contents of R14 into R15, the PC. For nested subroutines, the contents of R14 (the link register) must be placed onto the stack.

In addition to the 16 CPU registers, there is a current program status register (CPSR). This contains a set of condition code flags in the upper four bits that record the result of a previous instruction, as shown in Fig 13.3. In addition to the condition code flags, the CPSR contains a number of user-configurable bits that can be used to change the processor mode, enter Thumb processing and enable/disable interrupts.

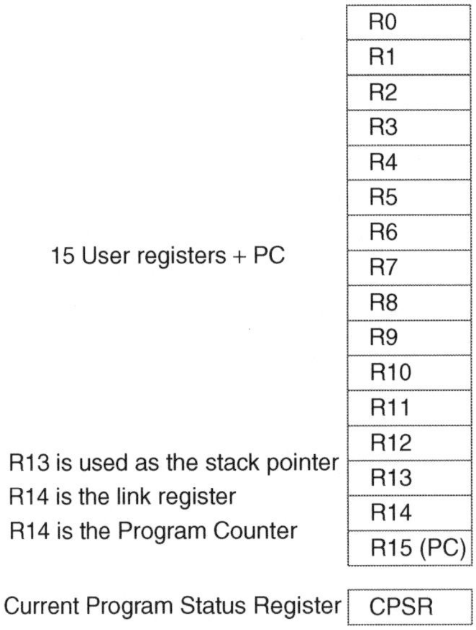

Fig. 13.2 *Register Model of ARM7*

Instruction Decoder and Logic Control: The function of instruction decoder and logic control is to fetch, decode instructions and generate control signals to other parts of processor and external circuits for execution of instructions.

Address Register: To hold a 32-bit address for sending to address bus.

Address Incrementer: It is used to increment an address by four and place it in address register.

Register Bank: Register bank contains thirty one 32-bit registers and six status registers.

Barrel Shifter: It is used for fast shift operation with large number of shifts with single instruction.

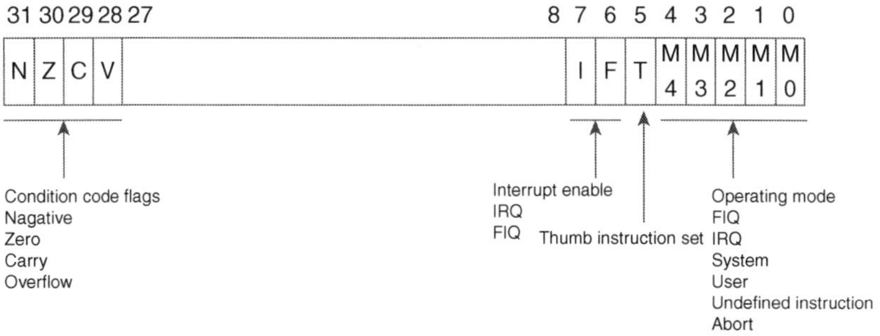

Fig. 13.3 *Current Program Status Register and Flags*

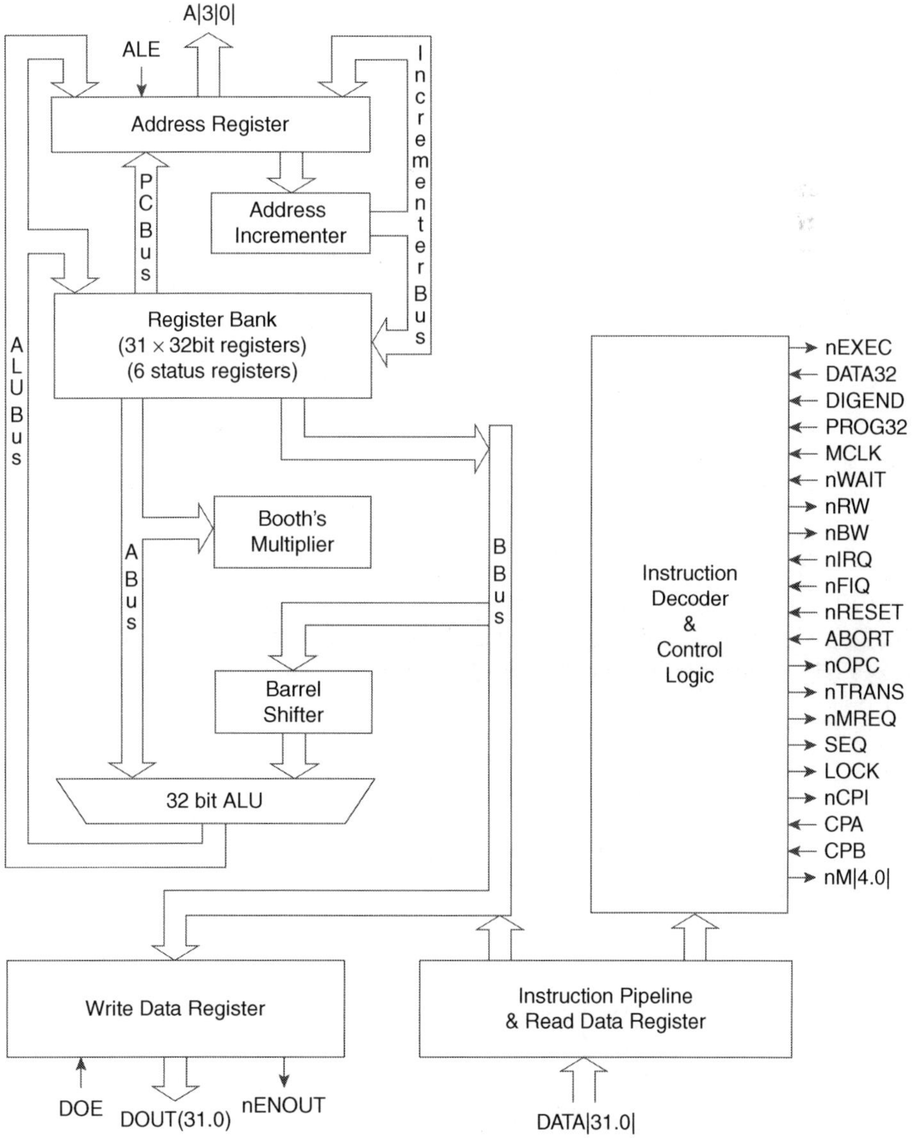

Fig. 13.4 *Load and Store Architecture of ARM 7*

ALU: 32-bit ALU is used for Arithmetic and Logic Operation.
Write/Read Data Register: The processor stores the data in Write Data Register (DR) for write operation. When processor reads from memory or IO, it places the data in the Read Dataregister. The schematic archtecture of the processor ARM7 is presented in fig. 13.4.
It is quiet obvious that the large number of busses in the architecture enhance the parallelism in the architecture. The non-multiplexed addresses and data bus and separate read and write data bus will also enhance speed of execution. The separate busses A and B for the ALU operands eliminate the use of temporary registers. The separate ALU output bus and the A and B operand busses achieve overlap of writing of the results of the current operation into the register bank and fetching operands of the next operation from the register bank. The Booths multiplier and Barrel shifter circuits speed up the computationally expensive operations of multiplication and shifting by large number of bits. A separate address incrementer circuit increments the addresses by 4 as word size of the machine is 4 bytes. The instruction pipeline achieves overlap between the execution of the current instruction and fetching and/or decoding of the next instruction. The architecture houses total 31 registers in all the modes of operations excluding the respective program status registers. The Current status and flag register that uses only 12 bits out of 32 bits of the ARM7 register is presented in fig.13.3.
N (negative): N=1 means result of an operation is negative and N=0 means result of an operation is positive.
Z (zero): Z=1 means result of an operation is zero and Z=0 result of an operation is not zero.
C (carry): C=1 means result of an operation generated a carry, and C=0 means result of an operation did not produce a carry.
V (overflow): V=1 means result of an operation generated an overflow and V=0 means result of an operation did not generate an overflow.

Control Bits **I** (interrupt bit): When this bit set to one, it will disable the interrupt and this means the processor does not accept any software interrupt.

F bit is used to disable and enable fast interrupt request mode (FIQ) mode.
M4, M3, M2, M1 and M0 are mode status bits and they are equal to 10000 for user mode.
T (State bit): T=1 Processor executing thumb instructions, T=0 processor executing ARM instructions.

Exception and Interrupt Modes The ARM 7 architecture has a total of six different operating modes, as shown below. These modes are protected or exception modes which have associated interrupt sources and their own register sets.
User: This mode is used to run the application code. Once in user mode the CPSR cannot be written to and modes can only be changed when an exception is generated.
FIQ: (Fast Interrupt reQuest) This supports high speed interrupt handling. Generally it is used for a single critical interrupt source in a system.
IRQ: (Interrupt ReQuest) This supports all other interrupt sources in a system.
Supervisor: A "protected" mode for running system level code to access hardware or run OS calls. The ARM 7 enters this mode after reset.
Abort: If an instruction or data is fetched from an invalid memory region, an abort exception will be generated.
Undefined Instruction: If a FETCHED opcode is not an ARM instruction, an undefined instruction exception will be generated.
Register Set: The User registers R0-R7 are common to all operating modes. However FIQ mode has its own R7 –R14 that replace the user registers when FIQ is entered. Similarly, each of the other modes have their

own R13 and R14 so that each operating mode has its own unique Stack pointer and Link register. The CPSR is also common to all modes. However in each of the exception modes, an additional register - the saved program status register (SPSR), is added. When the processor changes the current value of the CPSR stored in the SPSR, this can be restored on exiting the exception mode.

System & User	FIQ	Supervisor	Abort	IRQ	Undefined
R0	R0	R0	R0	R0	R0
R1	R1	R1	R1	R1	R1
R2	R2	R2	R2	R2	R2
R3	R3	R3	R3	R3	R3
R4	R4	R4	R4	R4	R4
R5	R5	R5	R5	R5	R5
R6	R6	R6	R6	R6	R6
R7	R7_fiq	R7	R7	R7	R7
R8	R8_fiq	R8	R8	R8	R8
R9	R9_fiq	R9	R9	R9	R9
R10	R10_fiq	R10	R10	R10	R10
R11	R11_fiq	R11	R11	R11	R11
R12	R12_fiq	R12	R12	R12	R12
R13	R13_fiq	R13_svc	R13_abt	R13_irq	R13_und
R14	R14_fiq	R14_svc	R14_abt	R14_irq	R14_und
R15 (PC)	R15 (PC)	R15 (PC)	R15 (PC)	R15 (PC)	R15 (PC)
CPSR	CPSR	CPSR	CPSR	CPSR	CPSR
	SPSR_fiq	SPSR_svc	SPSR_abt	SPSR_irq	SPSR_und

Fig. 13.5 *Full Register Set For ARM7*

Entry to the Exception modes is through the interrupt vector table. Exceptions in the ARM processor can be split into three distinct types.

(i) Exceptions caused by executing an instruction, these include software interrupts, undefined instruction exceptions and memory abort exceptions

(ii) Exceptions caused as a side effect of an instruction such as a abort caused by trying to fetch data from an invalid memory region.

(iii) Exceptions unrelated to instruction execution, this includes reset, FIQ and IRQ interrupts.

In each case entry into the exception mode uses the same mechanism. On generation of the exception, the processor switches to the privileged mode, the current value of the PC+4 is saved into the Link register (R14) of the privileged mode and the current value of CPSR is saved into the privileged mode's SPSR. The IRQ interrupts are also disabled and if the FIQ mode is entered, the FIQ interrupts are also disabled. Finally the Program Counter is forced to the exception vector address and processing of the exception can start. Usually the first action of the exception routine will be to push some or all of the user registers onto the stack.

Only two external interrupts are available in ARM7. Fig. 13.5 presents the register set of ARM7 in all the modes of operation.

Data Types in ARM7: The ARM7 architecture supports 1 byte signed and unsigned, 2bytes signed and unsigned and 4bytes signed and unsigned register and immediate data. This supports little and big endian formats of data.

Instruction Set Features of ARM7:

- Most of the instructions have three operands:
- A few with two operands or one operand or none.
- The destination operand follows the mnemonic, the remaining are source operands.
- The default operand sequence can be reversed using R as prefix to instructions.
  ADD R0,R1,R2 ; does not affect flag.
- Adding S to the mnemonic affects status flags. Fror eg ADDS
- A few instructions only affect flags, results are not stored. TST(AND), TEQ(test if equal)
- Conditional instructions and unconditional instructions- A condition prefix will execute the instruction only if the condition is satisfied. For Eg. EQ (most significant four bits of the opcode. Sixteen conditions are there. EQ suffixes the mnemonic in asm program.
- All registers can be used as pointers [Rn]. Relative address can be added to a pointer content [Rn,#4]!, Autoincrement by 4 after the operation is allowed.pointer is modified.
- PC relative mode is available.
- Data Processing Instructions (arithmetic, logical, shift and rotate applied to only second operand)
- Multiply Instructions; multiply between registers
- Single data Swap ; source Reg moves to destination Reg/mem
- Single data Transfer
- Block Data Transfer is available
- Branch conditional and unconditional
- PUSH and POP for complete register set is available.

13.7.2 MIPS

MIPS or "Microprocessor without Interlocked Pipeline Stages" is a RISC architecture without (ideally) any hardware interlocks, a design goal that MIPS has very nearly kept for all these years.

One of the earliest RISC processors was initiated in early 80's at Stanford by Hennessy who subsequently formed in 1984 MIPS Computer systems which brought out 32 bit R2000 in 1985, followed by R3000 in 1988 and 64 bit R4000 in 1991. Subsequently in 1999, 32 bit MIPS 2 and 64 bits MIPS 64 were released.

The MIPS processor used 32 registers, each 32 bits wide. The instruction set consisted of 111 instructions. The MIPS multistage pipeline architecture is conceptually presented in fig. 13.6. The instruction set consisted of a variety of basic instructions enlisted as as follows:

- 21 arithmetic instructions (+, -, *, /, %)
- 8 logic instructions (&, \, ~)
- 8 bit manipulation instructions
- 12 comparison instructions (>, <, =, >=, <=, ¬)
- 25 branch/jump instructions
- 15 load instructions
- 10 store instructions
- 8 move instructions
- 4 miscellaneous instructions

The instructions are simpler and much less in number compared to the CISC microprocessors. Even the addressing modes are simpler and much less in number compared to, say, the Intel microprocessors.

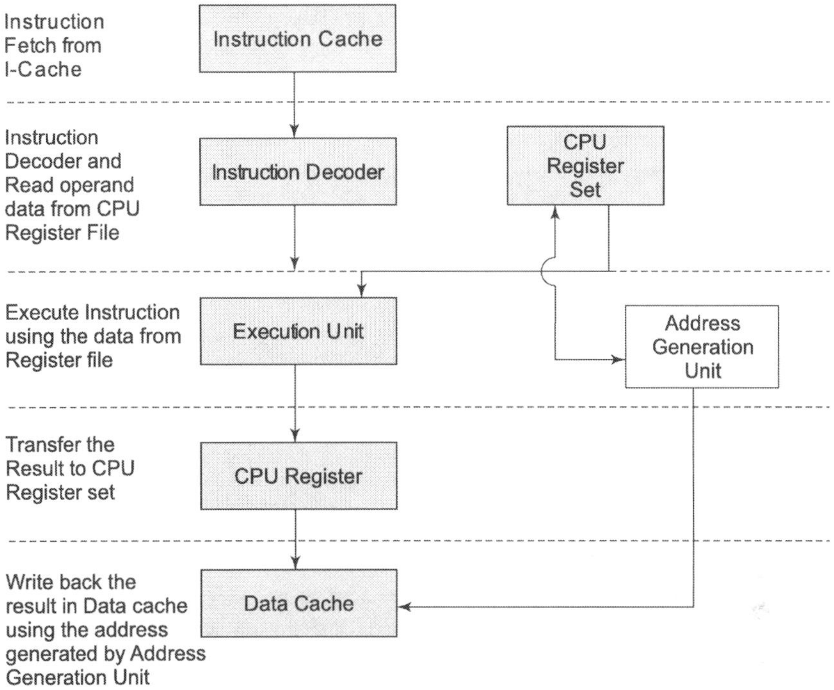

Fig. 13.6 *Multistage Pipeline for MIPS 2000/3000 System*

MIPS R2000 CPU, all the arithmetic and logical instructions are of register mode of addressing, where the operands reside in the set of 32 bit registers. The load and store instructions are data transfer instructions from the register to the memory and vice versa. For such data transfer, Base Displacement addressing mode is used, where the effective address is computed by adding the content of register (base) with a displacement provided immediately in the instruction. Many instructions supported by this processor are three address instructions. For example in arithmetic instructions, two of the operands may reside in the two registers while the result is stored in the third register. Some of the floating point registers are of 64 bits, for floating point operations.

Today, MIPS powers many consumer electronic and other devices. It is a licensed architecture, used by over a dozen chip-making companies around the world for their consumer devices (like handheld PCs), video games (Nintendo 64 and PlayStation), and countless network boxes. Many networking companies use MIPS cores (some officially licensed, some not) in their chips, but not because MIPS is particularly good at network processing. It is not. MIPS is just a convenient, clean, and easily scaled architecture around which special-purpose network processors or protocol engines can be added. Indeed, MIPS is one of the cleanest and most generic processor designs around.

13.7.3 Sun Ultra SPARC

This contains an integer unit, a FPU, and an optional coprocessor. Concepts borrowed from Berkeley RISC chips, TMS 9900.

SPARC architecture-

The 64 bit UltraSPARC architecture has the following features:

(i) 14 stage non-stalling pipeline

(ii) Six execution units including two for integer, two for floating point, one for Load/Store and one for address generation unit.

(iii) It has a large number of buffers, but only one Load/Store unit, it dispatches them one instruction at a time from the instruction stream.

(iv) It contains 32 KB L1 instruction cache, 64 KB L1 data cache, 2 KB prefetch cache and 2 KB write cache. It also has 1 MB on chip L2 cache. [Based on UltraSPARC 3.]

(v) Like Pentium MMX, UltraSPARC also contains instructions to support multimedia. These instructions are helpful for the implementation of image processing codes.

(vi) One of the major limitations of SPARC system is its low speed compared to most of the modern day processors.

(vii) SPARC stores multibyte numbers using BIG endian format, i.e., the most significant byte will be stored at the lowest address of memory.

(viii) UltraSPARC supports a pipelined floating point processor: The FPU again has five separate functional units for performing floating point operations. The floating point instructions can be issued per cycle and executed by the FPU unit. The source and data results are stored in 32 register files. Majority of the floating point instructions have a throughput of one cycle and a latency of three cycles. Although the single precision (32 bit) or double precision floating point computations can be performed by hardware, quad precision, i.e., 128 bit operation can be performed only in software.

Register Organisation and Windowed Registers The SPARC architecture is a unique case of RISC architecture. A window of 32 number of registers is accessible to the programmer at any point of time. A set of thirty two number of 32 bit registers is accessible to a program in each register window. Out of these 32 registers, eight are global registers and the rest 24 are local registers. Out of these 24 registers again the first eight registers are called IN registers while the other set of 8 registers are OUT registers. The rest 8 registers are like standard scratch pad registers as used by any program. When a function is called, the arguments may be stored in the IN register. Actually when a program calls another function, the caller program saves its parameters in the OUT registers. The caller's OUT register actually becomes the called functions IN register. SPARC processor supports seven such overlapping windows with actual number of 119 registers. The actual number of physical registers are hidden from the view of the programmmer.

The elegance of SPARC processor lies in the fact that SPARC uses the register windows and provides these register windows to the called routine, instead of pushing the parameters on to a stack. Thus the parameters may be stored in the register window, without using stacks at all. Also in case of interrupts including TRAP, these register windows are used for saving the context of the processor. In other words the register windows may act as stacks. These register windows may sometimes overlap. This means that there may be some registers which are common to both windows. SPARC processor uses a rotation scheme to ensure the effective allotment of the register windows. Fig. 13. 7 (a) & (b) present the register bank and the overlapped windows technique used in SPARC processors.

There is, however, a major drawback of using windows, since the number of physical registers is finite there may be situations when it does not have enough register windows to allocate. Under such circumstances there is no option other than pushing the parameters on the stack and then popping them off. It is thus important to predict when the register file will overflow or even underflow. In addition SPARC has a set of 32 bit floating point register in its floating point unit. These registers are non-windowed registers.

Another drawback of register windowing is that it is not possible to use multithreading, as is extensively used by Pentium 4 as discussed in the previous chapter.

Instruction Set of SPARC SPARC is a 32 bit word machine, supporting 16 bit halfword and 64 bit double word and signed and unsigned integer data tyes. It also supports floating point numbers of 32 bits, 64 bits (double word) and 128 bits (quad words). SPARC supports 74 instructions including floating point operations.

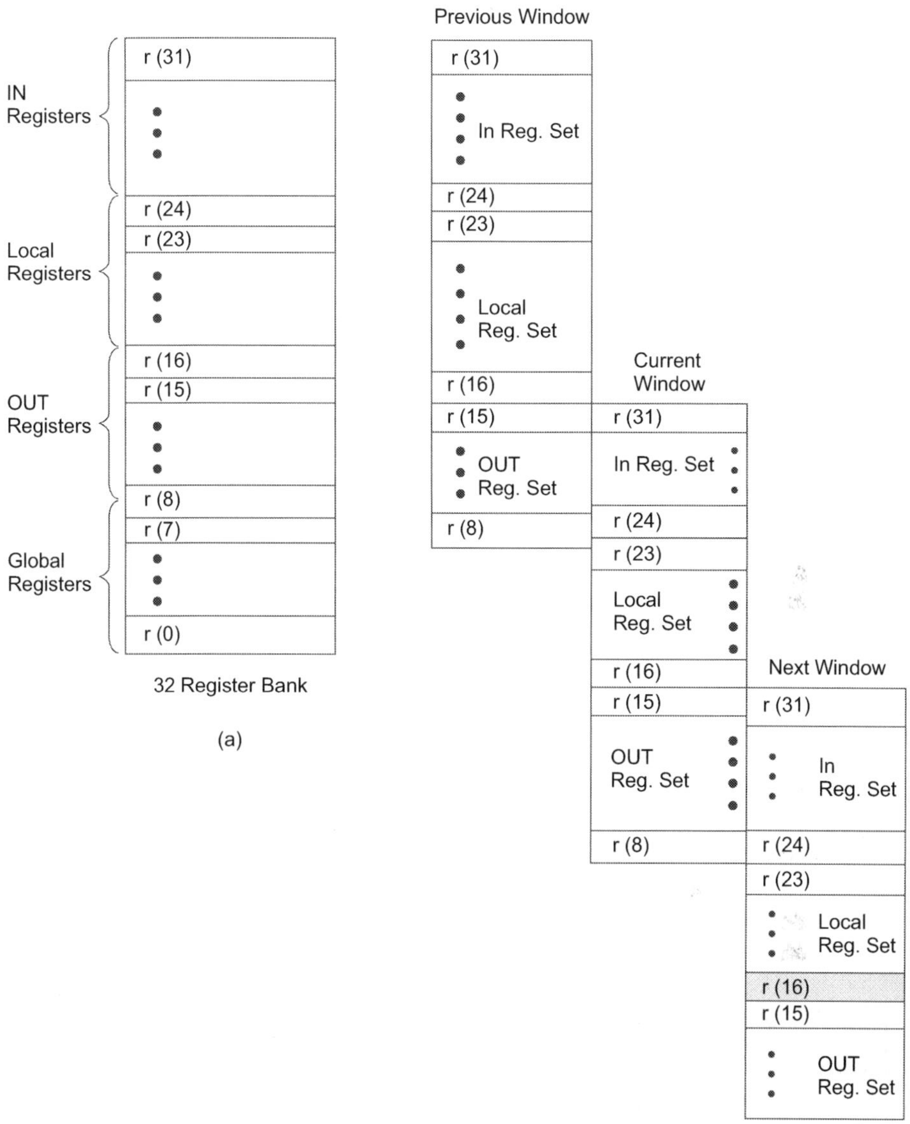

Fig. 13.7 (a) *Bank of 32 Registers and their Classification (b) Three Overlapping Register Windows in SPARC Architecture*

Memory Management Unit The memory management unit implements virtual memory and translates virtual addresses of each process to the corresponding physical addresses in the memory.

The virtual address space is partitioned into pages which are mapped into physical memory. The operating system translates the 64 bit address to a 44 bit address, supported by the processor. The memory managemnet unit in turn translates this 44 bit address space into 64 bits physical address. A Translation Lookaside buffer is used by the MMU to perform this translation.

The second important function of MMU is to provide protection to the memory so that a running process is prohibited from reading or writing the address space of another, if it is not authorized to access the same.

The MMU also has an important function of performing arbitration amongst the instruction cache, data cache and TLB references to memory. This arbitration may be necessary when the I/O device along with the Instruction and Data cache competes for accessing the main memory.

Interesting Programming Issues (i) Most of the RISC instructions are of three register formats, as below.

In a CISC processor we use two register format instructions like ADD AX, BX, which implies that the contents of AX and BX are added and the result is stored in BX. The corresponding three register format RISC instruction will be ADD AX, BX, CX which implies that add the contents of AX with BX and store the results in CX. To write the same instruction in a CISC processor, we need two instructions:

```
ADD AX, BX
MOV BX, CX
```

Delayed load

We want:

```
ADD R1, R3
LOAD 500, R4
Add R3, R4
```

Note the ADD R1, R3 instruction between two instructions using R4. If successive instruction uses R4 it may create problem in pipeline execution.

We can't access R4 on that third line (it's an operand as well as the target) could insert a NOP better yet, rewrite :

```
LOAD 500, R4
ADD R1, R3
ADD R3, R4
```

13.8 DISCUSSION ON SOME RISC ARCHITECTURES

Conceptually some of the older concepts are bouncing back. For example, the floating point processors supporting floating point data types are now being introduced. The TX9956CXBG is the first standard 64 bit microprocessor to employ the high-performance TX99/H4 CPU core and industry-leading 90 nm process technology. The TX49xx 64bit, MIPS-based processor family has been created for high-end, performance-demanding applications in the consumer electronics market, such as portable audio and wireless systems. A new 64 bit RISC microprocessor from Toshiba offers a combination of improved performance with space, power and cost savings in applications where Ethernet connectivity and high-speed, high-capacity data and program storage are required. ARM family with 3 stage pipeline has gained tremendous popularity as far as embedded and mobile communication applications are concerned.

Ultra SPARC-III has a 14-stage pipeline, six execution units: two for integer, two for floating-point, one load/store unit and one address-generation unit. With only one load/store unit, Ultra SPARC-III can't process multiple memory transactions. Ultra SPARC III supports 1MB, 4way set associative and physical indexed, physical tagged L2 caches.

The story of the evolution is continuing and the future is simply going to be breathtaking.

SUMMARY

In this chapter, initially , a short history of RISC Architecture has been presented. Further various advantages of RISC have been presented in comparison with CISC. Basic features of RISC processors have been enlisted followed by different design issues of RISC Architectures. Performance issues in case of pipeline architecture, such as instruction latency and dependency have also been elaborated. While selecting a RISC Architecture for a particular application one must be cautious about the limitations of RISC Architectures. Finally three popular RISC Architectures have been discussed in brief along with glimpses of their features.

EXERCISES

13.1 Enlist the advantages and features of RISC Architecture.

13.2 Write short notes on
 (i) Register windowing
 (ii) Massive pipelining
 (iii) Single cycle instruction execution.

13.3 Define instruction latency.

13.4 Discuss disadvantages of RISC Processors.

13.5 Compare and contrast between RISC and CISC Architecture.

13.6 Discuss the following to RISC Architectures.
 (i) MIPS
 (ii) SUN UltraSPARC
 (iii) ARM7

13.7 Discuss register bank of SUN UltraSPARC.

13.8 Discuss register bank of ARM7 in detail.

13.9 Discuss architecture of ARM7.

13.10 Enlist instruction set features of ARM7.

13.11 Discuss programming model of ARM7.

14 Microprocessor-Based Aluminium Smelter Control

14.1 GENERAL PROCESS DESCRIPTION OF AN ALUMINIUM SMELTER

The process of extracting aluminium in a smelter involves electrolysis of Al_2O_3 (alumina) in fused cryolite. The electrolysis process takes place in an electrolytic cell, popularly known as a 'Pot'. The electrolytic cell is an iron box internally coated with refractory material. A layer of carbon on this lining acts as cathode of the electrolytic chamber. The anode is made up of an array of carbon rods which can be moved in the vertical direction. Aluminium is produced by electrolytic reduction of alumina (Al_2O_3) in the electrolytic chamber where the carbon anode and carbon cathode reacts with O_2 to yield CO_2 and CO. The configuration of a single electrolytic cell is shown in Fig. 14.1. After aluminium is deposited at the bottom of a bath, it is tapped out from time to time. Only one such electrolytic cell produces very little aluminium and hence a large number of such cells are connected in series, so as to be fed from a single supply, as shown in Fig. 14.2. Each electrolytic cell is connected in such a way that the cathode of the ith cell is connected to the anode of the (i+1) th cell. The carbon anodes, in the form of carbon rods are dipped inside the electrolyte so that the current needed for electrolysis flows through these anodes in a distributed fashion as shown in Fig. 14.1. Gradually, as the process of electrolysis continues, the carbon gets corroded, and anodes are lowered more and more so that the carbon anodes get dipped into the electrolyte.

In case of a healthy electrolytic cell, the anode to cathode voltage may remain within 4 V to 6 V while the line current may vary between 30 KA to 70 KA. In the next section, we describe the normal control of the electrolytic cell.

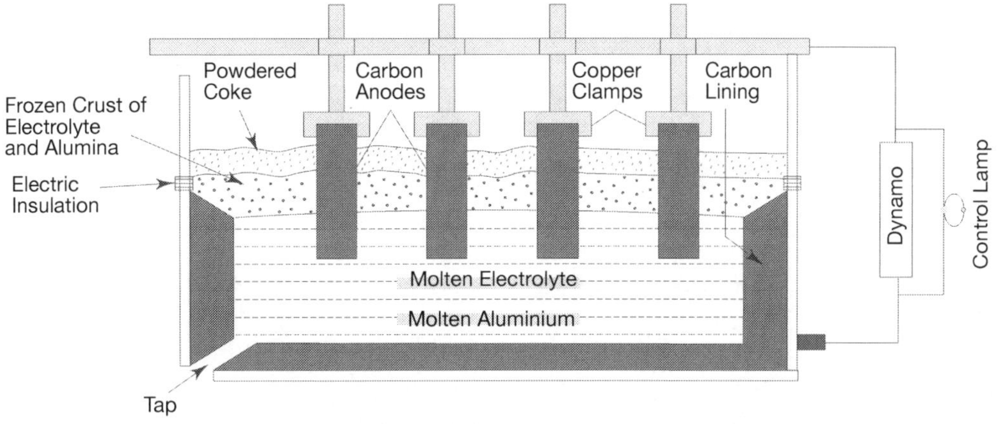

Fig. 14.1 *Electrolytic Cell in Aluminium Smelter*

14.2 NORMAL CONTROL OF ELECTROLYSIS CELL

Assume that there are eight cells connected in series as shown in Fig. 14.2.

The resistance of any cell may be computed from the voltage V_m between the anode and cathode and I_m the measured series current. Assume E_b to be the back-emf of a cell. Then the measured resistance of a cell R_m is given by Eq. (14.1).

$$R_m = \frac{V_m - E_b}{I_m} \tag{14.1}$$

The back-emf of a cell usually does not vary and is a constant. Now for the proper operation of a cell, there is a target value of line current I_t and a target value of the anode-cathode voltage V_t, and using Eq. (14.2) we get a target value of resistance.

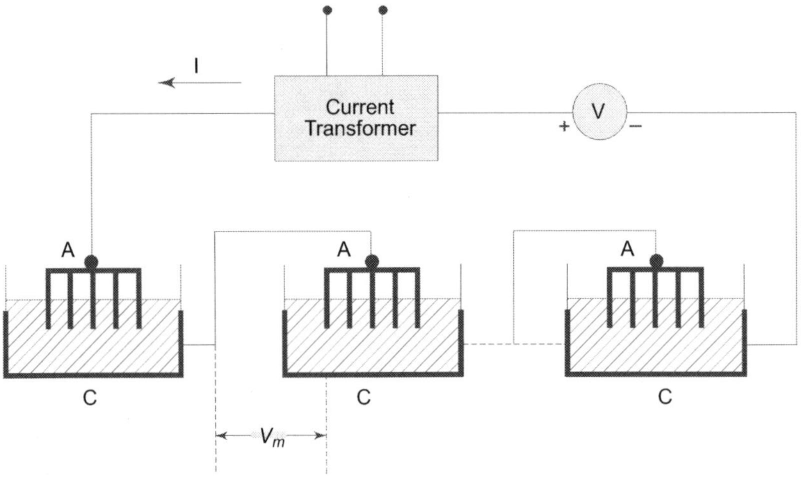

C : Cathode A : Anode

Fig. 14.2 *Connection of Cells*

$$R_t = \frac{V_t - E_b}{I_t} \tag{14.2}$$

For the ideal operation of the smelter, each cell should possess this target resistance value R_t.

However, as electrolysis of alumina takes place, the carbon anode gets corroded, and thus the effective distance between the anode and cathode increases, resulting in an increase in the cell resistance. The cell resistance may be decreased by lowering the anode, to maintain it at the target value.

Our aim is to keep the cell resistance almost constant and equal to the target resistance R_t. Thus we have to control the anode position by raising or lowering the anode, so that the measured cell resistance can be kept constant. This forms the normal anode position control action, which is continuously performed so as to maintain good condition of each cell, thereby enhancing the aluminium production.

Thus for regular process control, our control law is as follows:

Step 1—Measure I_m, V_m and compute R_m.

Step 2—Compare R_m with R_t and do the following:

(a) If $R_m > R_t$, then lower the anode
(b) If $R_m < R_t$, then raise the anode
(c) If $R_m = R_t$, then no action

14.3 CELL ABNORMALITIES IN AN ALUMINIUM SMELTER

The above discussion pertains to the cells which are healthy and normal and the regular control implies raising and lowering the anode in a particular cell.

However, several abnormalities are often manifested during the process of electrolysis. Some of these abnormal conditions are briefly discussed below:

(a) Sometimes it is observed that the voltage between anode and cathode of a particular cell is fluctuating. This unsteady behaviour is known as shakiness of a cell. Usually, the normal anode to cathode voltage varies within 4 V – 6 V. To take care of shakiness, a separate control law is used.
(b) After the process of electrolysis, when molten aluminium which settles at the bottom of the cell, is tapped out of the cell, the cell is known as a tapped cell. A separate control law takes care of the tapped status of a cell.
(c) As has been mentioned in Section 14.1, when the carbon is consumed because of electrolytic reaction, the carbon rods have to be pushed more inside the electrolytic cells by lowering these rods. Under these circumstances, the concerned cells are called as 'rodded' and a separate control law is needed for these cells.
(d) The most pronounced effect of abnormality is sometimes observed in a cell when the voltage between anode and cathode becomes extremely high. This means that the cell resistance of the affected cell has increased to a large extent. This is known as anode effect. The anode effect takes place in a smelter because of the fact that the carbon anode electrodes may not be in direct contact with the electrolyte, due to a coating of oxide (gases) or solid crust formation creating an insulating effect between the carbon anode and the electrolyte.

To remove the anode effect, it is important to break the insulating crust by lowering the anode in steps and then raising it in identical steps. This is done to perform the cleaning operation of the pot. The process of quenching the anode effect continues for a long period and a separate anode effect quenching program is needed for this purpose.

14.4 BRIEF DESCRIPTION OF THE CONTROL LAWS FOR ABNORMAL CELLS

This process controller continuously monitors the system variables like the line current, anode to cathode voltage of each cell, then detects any kind of abnormality in a cell and finally controls the anode position according to the status of the cell.

The control action is initiated for each type of abnormality and continues for a specified period of time depending upon the intensity and type of cell abnormality till the cell becomes normal.

For example, a cell is detected as shaky after monitoring a set of say, 8 or 16 sampled values of anode to cathode voltage and the line current. A cell is considered shaky only if there exists a variation of the measured anode to cathode voltage in the consecutive sampled voltage values for that cell and if this variation goes beyond a threshold voltage, say 1V.

For removing of shakiness, the target voltage V_t is chosen as:

$$V_t = V_{t\text{ basic}} + V_{t\text{ shaky}} \tag{14.3}$$

Where $V_{t\text{ basic}}$ is the basic target anode to cathode voltage for a cell and is to be specified by the control operator and $V_{t\text{ shaky}}$ is the extra target voltage to be considered only for a shaky cell.

The anode raising and lowering control continues considering V_t as the total target voltage and the process is continued for hours until the cell behaves in a normal way.

In case of a shaky cell, the extra target voltage $V_{t\text{ shaky}}$ which is provided for computing V_t, should be continued in steps for a specified time duration, say, T_{shaky} (in hours) and the excess target voltage should also be withdrawn in steps of T_{shaky} (in hours) time.

As in the case of a shaky cell, the rodded and tapped cells also receive extra target voltage $V_{t\ rod}$ and $V_{t\ tap}$ which is increased in steps of T_{rod} and T_{tap} time duration. Also the excess target voltage applied is reduced in steps of T_{rod} and T_{tap} time duration, till the cell comes back to the normal condition. The most important type of control is, however, the anode effect quenching program which is explained next.

Anode Effect Quenching A cell is considered to be in the anode effect, if the anode to cathode voltage V_m is found to exceed a certain threshold limit, say 10V to 15V, depending upon the nature of the cell. During anode effect, sometimes the measured voltage, V_m, may shoot up to a large value, and thus the line current, I_m, may be reduced. Moreover, if a number of cells are affected with the anode effect, there may be a considerable drop in the line current. Thus this drop in the measured line current may be indicative of the anode effect in one or more cells in the smelter. A quick scan of the anode to cathode voltage of all the cells in the smelter network may reveal the status of the cell, i.e. whether it has been affected by anode effect or not.

In case, anode effect is detected in a cell, the cell is immediately isolated and anode effect quenching program is executed. This involves lowering of the anode in steps till the anode moves very close to the cathode, resulting in a spark which breaks the crust and cleans the cell. There is a pause between every lowering operation resulting in a pattern—lower (T_1), pause (T_2), lower (T_1), pause (T_2) ... for specified durations, T_1 and T_2 respectively. Likewise, the anode is next raised in steps with a pause between every raise operation. This full cycle of lowering and raising of the anodes stepwise is continued for a large number of cycles, till the cell becomes normal.

14.5 SALIENT ISSUES IN DESIGN

While designing a microprocessor based process control system of such complexity, we have to take into consideration a set of important issues.

From the previous discussions, it must be clear now that the overall control involves three basic steps. These are:

(a) Acquiring voltage and current data for each cell.
(b) Based on the measured quantities and pre-specified parameter values, supplied by the process experts, compute the output signal using the control laws.
(c) Apply the control signal to the anode of the concerned electrolytic cell. The process should be repeated for all the cells in a sequential fashion.

Keeping in view the low frequency process operation, one may decide on the following two options:

1. Scan the ith cell for T secs: Acquire a set of sampled digital values of the measurable quantities like line current, anode to cathode voltage etc. say for T_1 seconds, complete the control laws for T_2 seconds and initiate the control action for ith cell for T_3 seconds, thus

$$T = T_1 + T_2 + T_3 \tag{14.4}$$

Alternately, the other option is as follows:

2. Initiate the control action for (i-1)th cell; scan the ith cell for T seconds; complete the data acquisition and control computation for ith cell. In the second option, the process of data acquisition and controller computations for ith cell are performed within T seconds, while the control action for (i-1)th cell is initiated at the same time instant, thus ensuring an overlapping of two tasks for two consecutive cells at the same instant.

Another important issue concerns the choice of ADC. For example, if we assume that the dynamic range of the input analog signal is say, 16 volts and the process engineer desires to have 10 mV resolution, then we need a 11-bit ADC. Thus we may choose a 12-bit ADC with a moderately low conversion time.

14.6 SMELTER CONTROLLER HARDWARE

The overall block diagram of the 8086 based system for current and voltage data monitoring, anode control, status display is shown in Fig. 14.3.

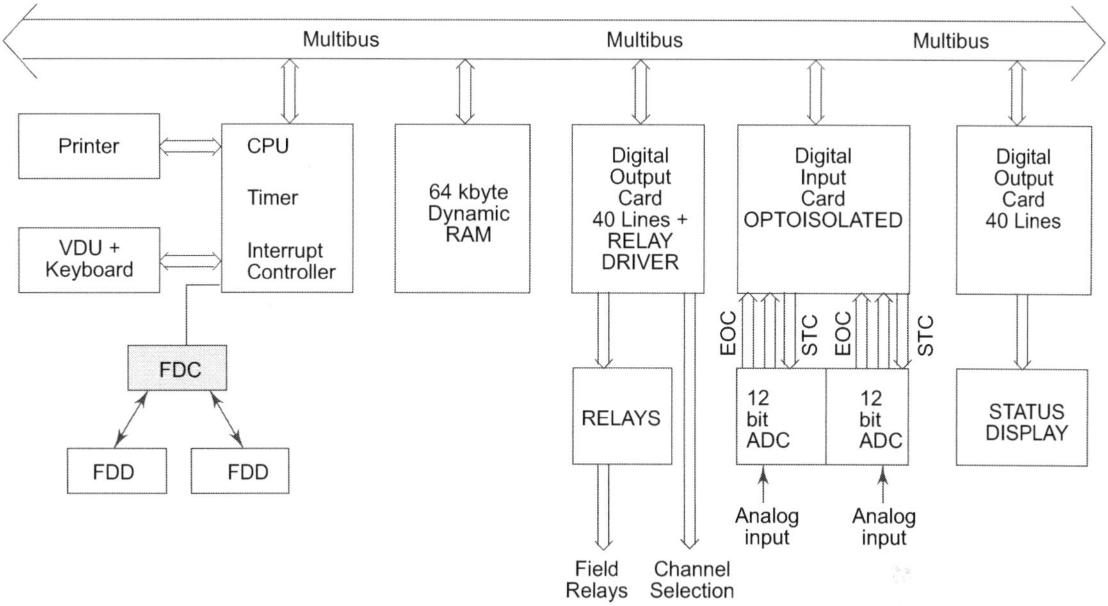

Fig. 14.3 *Block Diagram of the Process Controller*

As has been mentioned earlier, the same line current flows through all the electrolytic cells and sensing of this current is absolutely essential for cell resistance computation and also for the final anode position control.

The line current is fed to an isolator circuit followed by its digitization using an appropriately chosen analog to digital convertor. The digitised line current is fed to the CPU through the line current measuring port, programmed in the input mode.

The anode to cathode voltage between each cell is also an important quantity to be measured continuously. Special type of Reed relays are usually employed for switching between one channel to the next one. If we assume a group of 16 channels, i.e. cells to be controlled, a cell selection logic is needed to monitor the anode to cathode voltage of a particular cell. This may be realised by a demultiplexer, controlled by the CPU, where the selected cell number may be fed to the relay.

The anode to cathode voltage is fed to an ADC and the digitised signal is logged into the microprocessor system through a cell voltage measuring port.

14.7 CONTROL ALGORITHM

The whole control action can be divided into two categories. The first is normal control action and the second is abnormal situation control action. In normal control action, the anode of a particular cell has to be raised or lowered for a time duration proportional to the difference of the measured and the target voltages. The abnormal situations consists of the shaky, tapped, rodded and anode effect situations. In the first three abnormal situation cases, the control actions are akin to the normal action through the modification of the target voltage. Shakiness of a cell is detected by a program, and extra target voltage is applied in steps accordingly. Rodded and tapped conditions are detected by operators and the extra target voltage is given by them. All these cases, discussed for a particular cell, are to be considered for all the cells. In case of anode effect, the control action is completely different and all other actions are to be stopped, so long as the anode effect quenching continues. All these situations are to be considered while deciding the overall control algorithm. Figure 14.4 displays the complete control algorithm.

Stepwise description of all modules of the control algorithm is presented in the next section.

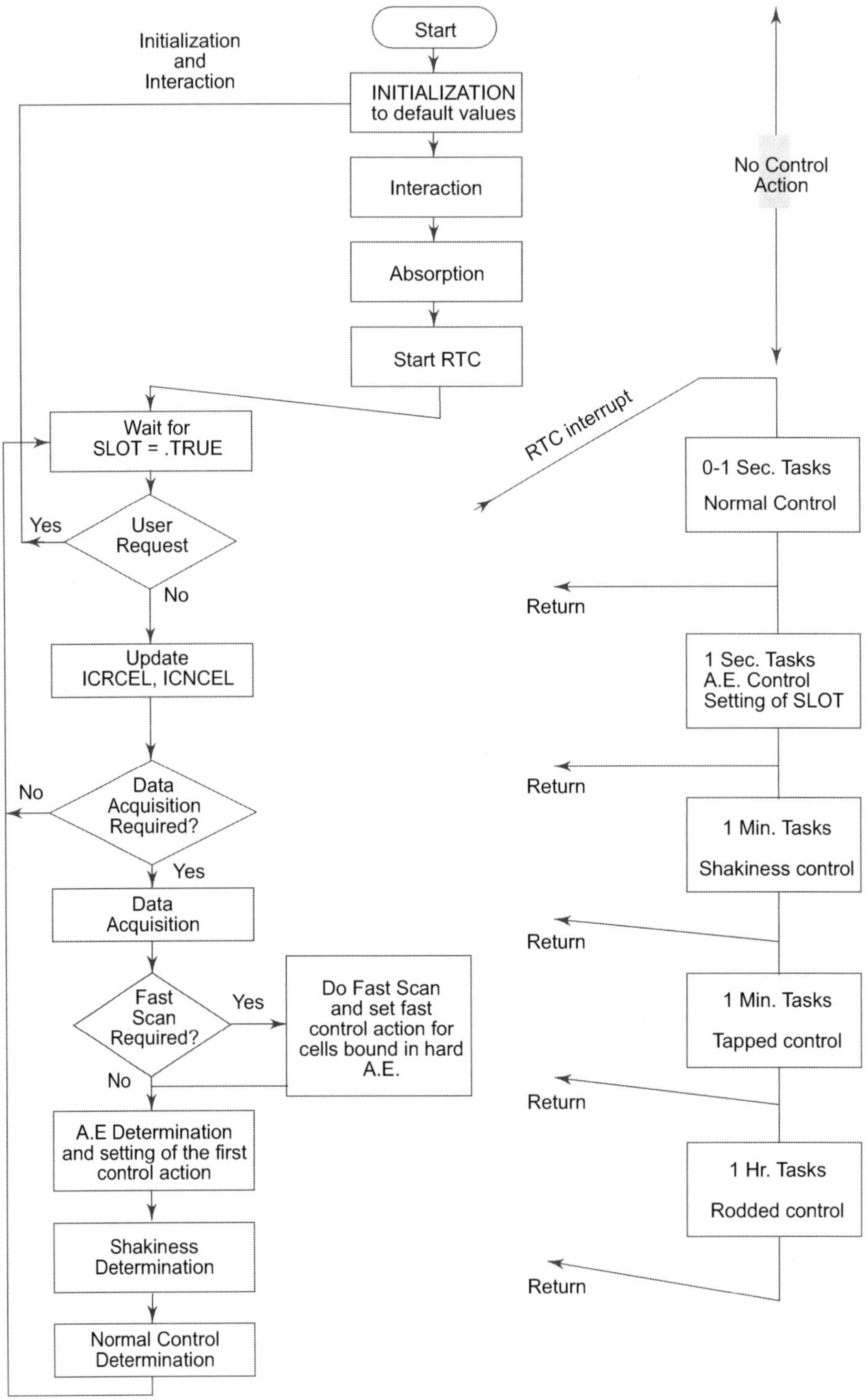

Fig. 14.4 *Control Action*

14.7.1 Data/Parameter Description

The software maintains two data tables. One of them, used for storing the addresses of the status tables for the cells, is known as an address table. While the other, used for storing the status values of a cell is known as a status table. These data structures handle all the data and status parameters for all the cells. Besides these parameters, the control algorithm requires the following parameters to be set either by the control engineer or by the process itself.

NOCEL	:	Number of cells in the process
CURCEL	:	Current cell number being scanned
CNTWRD	:	Count word for timer
VMAX	:	Maximum value of voltage for one scan
VMIN	:	Minimum value of voltage for one scan
VOAV	:	Average value of voltage for one scan
LOLMT	:	Lower limit of input voltage
HILMT	:	Higher limit of input voltage
ILOLT	:	Lower limit of line current converted to voltage
IHILT	:	Higher limit of line current converted to voltage
VTI	:	Line shift target voltage correction
DELVT	:	Extra target voltage
TIME	:	Timer value for control action
IOLOC	:	Location for target current

All these values can be given by the operator. This part of the program is accessible to him and the values here are programmable. Next, we will very briefly explain only a few modules of the control software.

14.7.2 Initialisation

1. Initialize stack pointer
2. For J = 0 to 7 (for eight cells), Do

    begin

        clear status reg for *J*th cell for normal status

        clear control reg for *J*th cell for null action

    end
3. Call system parameter initialization routine
4. Call interval timer interrupt service routine

After switching on the system, first, the system initialization task has to be performed. This initializes the stack pointer. Initially, it clears all status values and control register values for the cells as we do not yet know these parameters. The status of each cell has to be displayed in the display panel for easy interaction of the operator. Control register contains the raise/lower flag for proper control action. Control actions will be initiated based on the measured voltage depending upon whether it is less than, equal to or greater than the target voltage.

The operator has to set many parameters in the system after initialization. These are already described in the data area description. This routine should be of interactive type, so that the operator can easily understand and set the asked parameter accordingly.

An 8253 programmable interval timer has been used for generating precise time intervals for anode control.

Interval-timer Routine

$i = i+1$; $(i+1) \leq 8$

INT. TIMER = "T" ; T = 3 sec

RETURN

On receiving the time-out interrupt from the timer, after the alloted time period of 3 secs for each cell, this routine will be executed by the processor. This routine will select the (i+1)th cell and set the interval timer again for 3 seconds.

14.7.3 Module 1

Here, the number of cells in the process line is obtained from the data area. Also, the current cell number is obtained and updated. This is done by the interval timer interrupt. Here, the cell number is incremented. If we reach the end of the process line, we start from the 0th cell. Next, this cell is selected by the multiplexer. The control action of the previous cell is initiated. The algorithm is given as follows:

1. Load count for number of cells (N_C-1) ; N_C is the number of cells in operation.
2. Load current cell number N_i.
3. If $N_C = N_i$, then start from zero
   else $N_i = N_i + 1$; this is updating of current cell
4. Call MUXCEL ; multiplexer selects the cell
5. Get the control time ; this is prespecified
6. Start the counter for previous cell, which is decremented to zero for control action
7. Get the control word and feed it to normal control port

14.7.4 Module 2

Next, we check the status of the cell. This can also be displayed in the display panel. By observing this display, the operator can interact with the process and give different values accordingly. If the cell is in the manual or absent mode, you may go to the NO SCAN routine which detaches the cell from the line and waits for another status. Otherwise, if there is anode effect, A.E. control routine is performed.

1. Get the status of the cell from status table via address table
2. If Manual or Absent then Go to 'No SCAN'
   else
3. If under Anode Effect, then Goto the A.E. control routine
   else
4. Save status table pointer

14.7.5 Module 3

The start conversion signals are sent to the two ADCs, used for digitising the line current and cell voltage. The value of E_b is obtained from the status table and complemented. The sample counter is initialized with a value of 8.

Next, the digitised value of the cell voltage between anode and cathode is obtained from the ADC through I/O ports. The processor waits for the 'end of conversion' signal from the ADC, and on receiving the signal, the cell voltage is stored in two bytes (12-bits) at two successive locations.

14.7.6 Module 4

The average value of the cell voltage is initialized to zero. The average value of the eight measured voltages in a single scan is next calculated for a particular cell. The target voltage for the cell is obtained from the status table and may be updated according to the cell condition. For detecting if a cell is shaky, the difference $V_{max} - V_{min}$ between the maximum and minimum values of the voltage samples of each cell is calculated. If this difference exceeds some predefined value twice in four consecutive scans, then the cell may be termed shaky.

SUMMARY

This chapter presents a case study of a microprocessor based process control system to control the position of the electrodes in an aluminium smelter. A brief overview of the process has been presented along with a few relevent details of the electrolysis process of alumina in an aluminium smelter. Further, the various abnormal conditions of the aluminium smelter cells have been described and the control laws for quenching these abnormalities have been presented. Thus this chapter highlights an interesting application of microprocessors in process control.

15 Design of a Microprocessor-Based Pattern Scanner System

INTRODUCTION

One of the major problems in on line pattern recognition and image processing systems is the development of an interface between the real-world image data and the processor. A scanner is a category of such interfaces which provides a computer-compatible form of pictorial patterns for subsequent processing and classification.

A picture is a distribution of light intensity on a two-dimensional plane. It may be viewed as a two-dimensional matrix F, where each element f (i, j) in the matrix F represents the optical intensity at (i, j)th point. This optical intensity at a point is the brightness value at that point in the image and this value may vary from absolute white, to absolute dark in case of monochrome images. Assuming 256 such gray levels between absolute dark (corresponding to zero gray value) to absolute white (corresponding to 255 gray value), we may represent an image by a matrix F of say 64×64 size where each element f (i, j) may assume values between 0 and 255. There are certain applications, where we may not need a digitised gray value matrix to represent a picture. For example, in alphabetic and numerical character reading machines only a binary matrix having '0' (dark) and '1' (light) elements are sufficient to represent the picture for further pattern recognition. Such an image is known as a binary image. A number of optical scanning systems have been designed for obtaining a digitised image of an object, using CCD camera, photosensor array, etc.

In mechanical drum scanners, the picture is wound on a drum with an optical system mounted along it, the horizontal scan being provided by the rotation of the drum, while the movement of the optical system on the lead screw results in the vertical line feeding of the picture.

The flying spot oscillating mirror scanners utilize the principle of an oscillating light spot moving across the pattern and the amount of light transmitted through the pattern is subsequently measured by a photomultiplier tube.

The IBM 1975 optical page reader involves a CRT scanner with raster-type motion of its flying spot which is used to transform the optical image of the pattern into analog signals. These signals, in turn, are converted into bits representing the dark and white areas of the document.

The Rabinow Engineering Division of the Control Data Corporation has developed a scanner with matrices of photocells where characters are scanned on the fly as the document moves past the cells.

Solid-state scanners using a silicon photodiode array of linear and two-dimensional configuration are being widely used in high-speed on-line data acquisition systems. The latest systems have combined the advantages of charge-coupled devices simplifying low-level signal extraction with the advantages of semiconductor array technology having nearly ideal sensor characteristics to derive charge-coupled integrated image sensors.

In this chapter, we will present the design and development of a microprocessor-based optical scanner system. The different modes of storage options for on line and off line usage are described. Finally, it is concluded that, although the speed of the scanning process reduces for an on-line microprocessor controlled acquisition system, the flexibility, reliability and accuracy of the system may be enhanced at the cost of speed.

15.1 ORGANISATION OF THE SCANNER SYSTEM

The overall organization of the scanner (digitizer) system developed using a high resolution integrated photodiode array is described here. These integrated photosensor arrays are available as linear or 2-dimensional array of photodiodes or phototransistors. The linear arrays contain 64, 128, 256, 512 or 1024 phototransistors with inter-element spacing of about 1 micron or less. The picture to be digitised is focussed over the linear array of phototransistors in such a way that the first row of the picture is first scanned by the linear array. The array is next moved incrementally by a stepper motor so that it scans the second line of the picture and the process continues till the whole picture is scanned and the digitised values are stored in the memory.

The two dimensional arrays contain photosensors of various matrix sizes, say from 64 × 64 element to 1024 × 1024 elements of phototransistors with inter-element spacing along the rows and columns within a range from 0.5-1 microns or even less. The pattern to be processed is focussed over this phototransistor array with the aid of an optical system using a number of clear lenses, and the scanned data output is stored in memory. A flow chart of the whole scheme is shown in Fig. 15.1. The digitized data may be stored in memory in the following modes of operation:

1. The data is stored into a local RAM which may subsequently be used for off-line processing. The scanned data is written here at a relatively high speed by manual initialization, and the data may be read from the RAM.
2. The data may be transferred into microprocessor system memory from the local RAM This option may be useful when the recognition of a number of patterns are under study.
3. *Microprocessor-controlled on-line storage* at a relatively low speed. In this mode, the clock generation, initialization, etc. are achieved completely under program control. Data in this mode is stored in 8-bit form, i.e. 256 levels may be taken care of.

Ideally, a photosensor saturates for a certain amount of incident light from the optical system and it goes into cut-off in dark condition. For a typical pattern projected over the array, the boundary is not sharply defined and the video output lies at some intermediate level between saturation and cut-off. Thus a threshold level is chosen such that a binary-valued output signal is stored in the memory, depending on the threshold level. In the following sections, the on line scanning mode will be described.

15.2 DESCRIPTION OF THE SCANNING SYSTEM

Assume that we have an array of 14 × 40 photosensors in our scanner card from Reticon Corpn. The video output signal from the photodiode array, for example, may lie between 0V (saturation) and – 2V (dark). This means that when the photodiode is fully lighted, its output voltage becomes 0 Volts and under fully dark condition, the voltage remains – 2 Volts. A level translation is required to translate these values to TTL level.

Usually you receive a 'SYNC' control signal from the scanner card. This SYNC signal signifies the completion of a row scan and may be used for initialization before the next row is scanned. Suppose, the level of the SYNC signal output from the scanner card is non-standard, i.e., not TTL compatible, say the 'SYNC' signal output lies between –15 V and –7V. This signal level should be translated

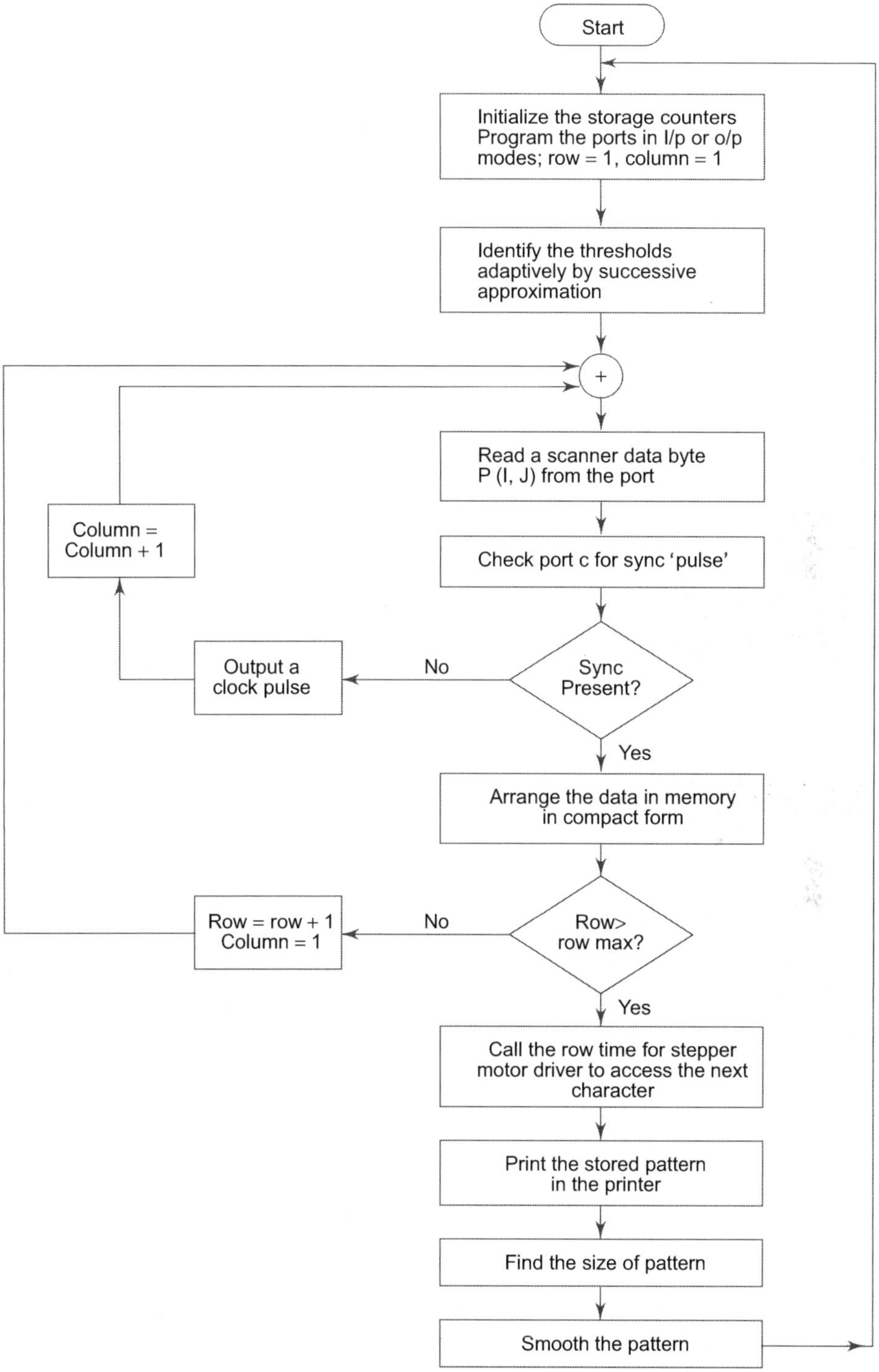

Fig. 15.1 *Overall Flow Diagram of the Scanner System*

to the TTL level by using an appropriately biased transistor which is normally saturated as shown in Fig. 15.2. The TTL SYNC output is fed to the CPU via a non-inverting buffer through a port.

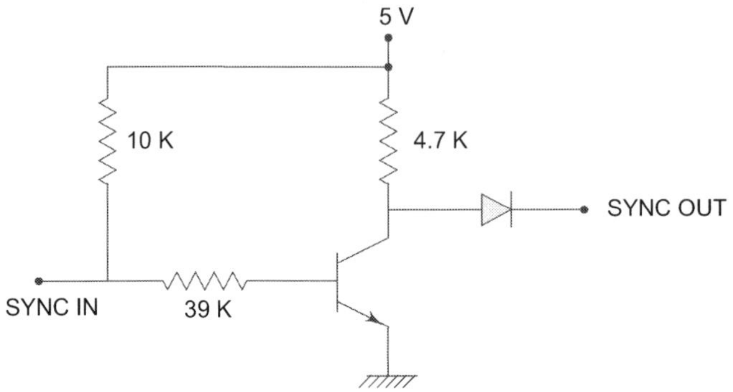

Fig. 15.2 *Level Translator*

Video Level Translation for Off Line Data Storage Since we have 14 rows of photo-diodes, a mod 16-row counter and a 4 to 16-line decoder may be used for selecting the channels sequentially, starting from the zeroth channel (refer to Fig. 15.3). When a channel is selected, serial data in the form of an analog pulse-train signal is obtained at the video output line. A set of FET source followers are connected to the video output lines and the output of the source follower swings between 0.7 V and +2 V corresponding to dark and saturation conditions, respectively. Also the FET source followers enhance the input impedance of each line. Thresholding has been achieved by using a Schmitt trigger in this mode and the scanned data is stored in RAM.

15.3 PROGRAMMED MODE OF OPERATION

In this mode of scanner operation, the generation of a clock signal for the scanner together with the row selection, data storage and initialization operations have been carried out with the aid of a microprocessor system developed around Intel's 8088.

The clock is generated under program control. The 'SYNC' pulse from the scanner, after necessary level translation, is fed to port C of 8255, to be read by the processor for the purpose of initialization of different counters.

Once the 'SYNC' signal is recognized by the processor, the processor branches to storage operation and two additional clock periods elapse before the scanning of a fresh row starts. The on-line interface system is shown in Fig. 15.4.

In the programmed data storage mode, the selection of various channels is achieved by an analog multiplexer designed using JFETs connected in series to each of the video output lines. The 8088 processor, through one of its output ports, provides the input signal to the 4 to 16-line decoder for channel selection as shown in Fig. 15.4. The decoder output is used for switching only one FET switch at a time and the video signal from that output line is fed to the input of ADC through a source follower. The video output is buffered through a source follower whose output swings between 1.2 V and 2V for dark and saturation conditions, respectively. The buffered video signal is fed to an A/D converter with the reference voltage of 1.4 V and 2.1 V set by the three diodes connected across +5 V and grounded with the current limiting resistances. The 8-bit output scanned data corresponding to a pattern pixel is stored in memory through one of the system ports in compact form.

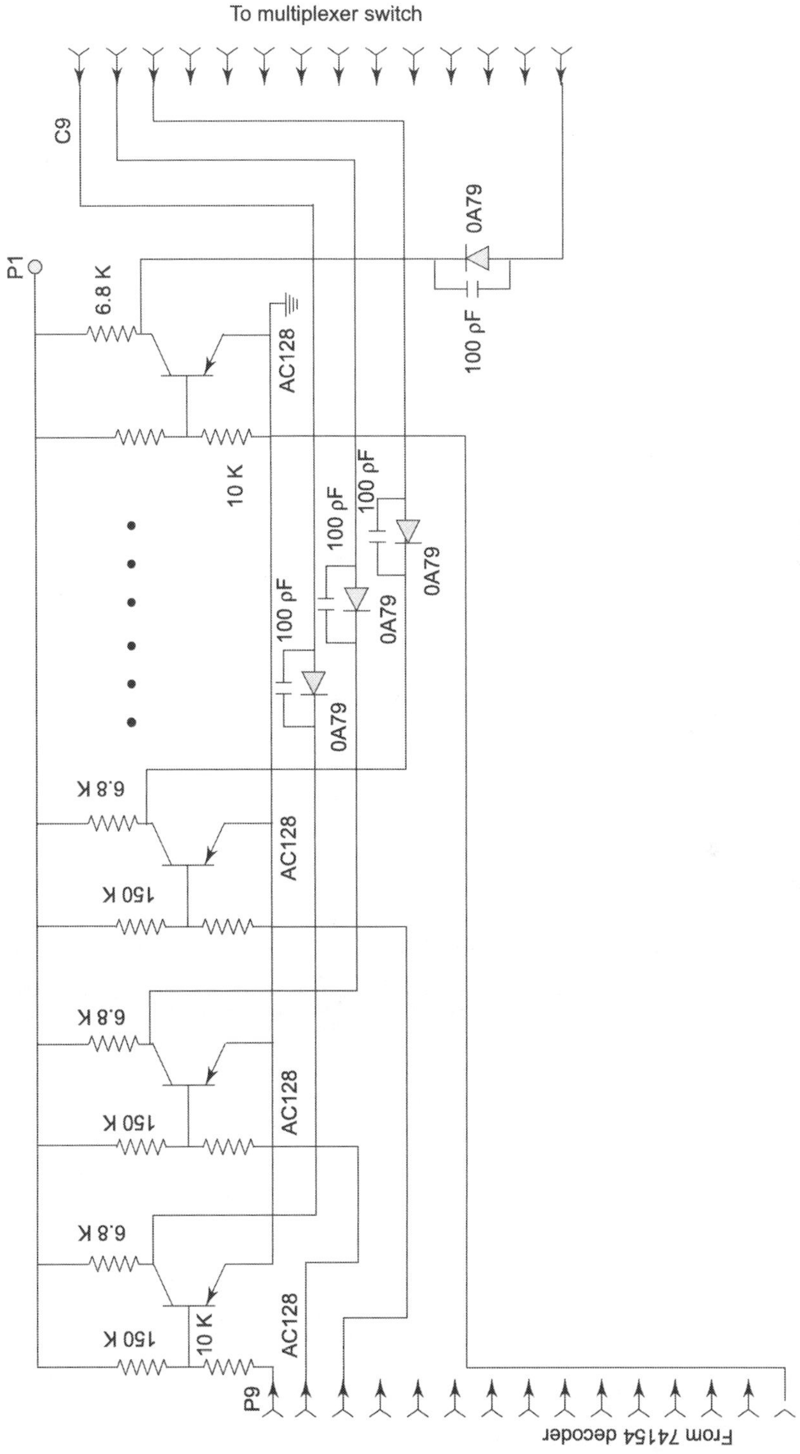

Fig. 15.3 *Multiplexer Driver*

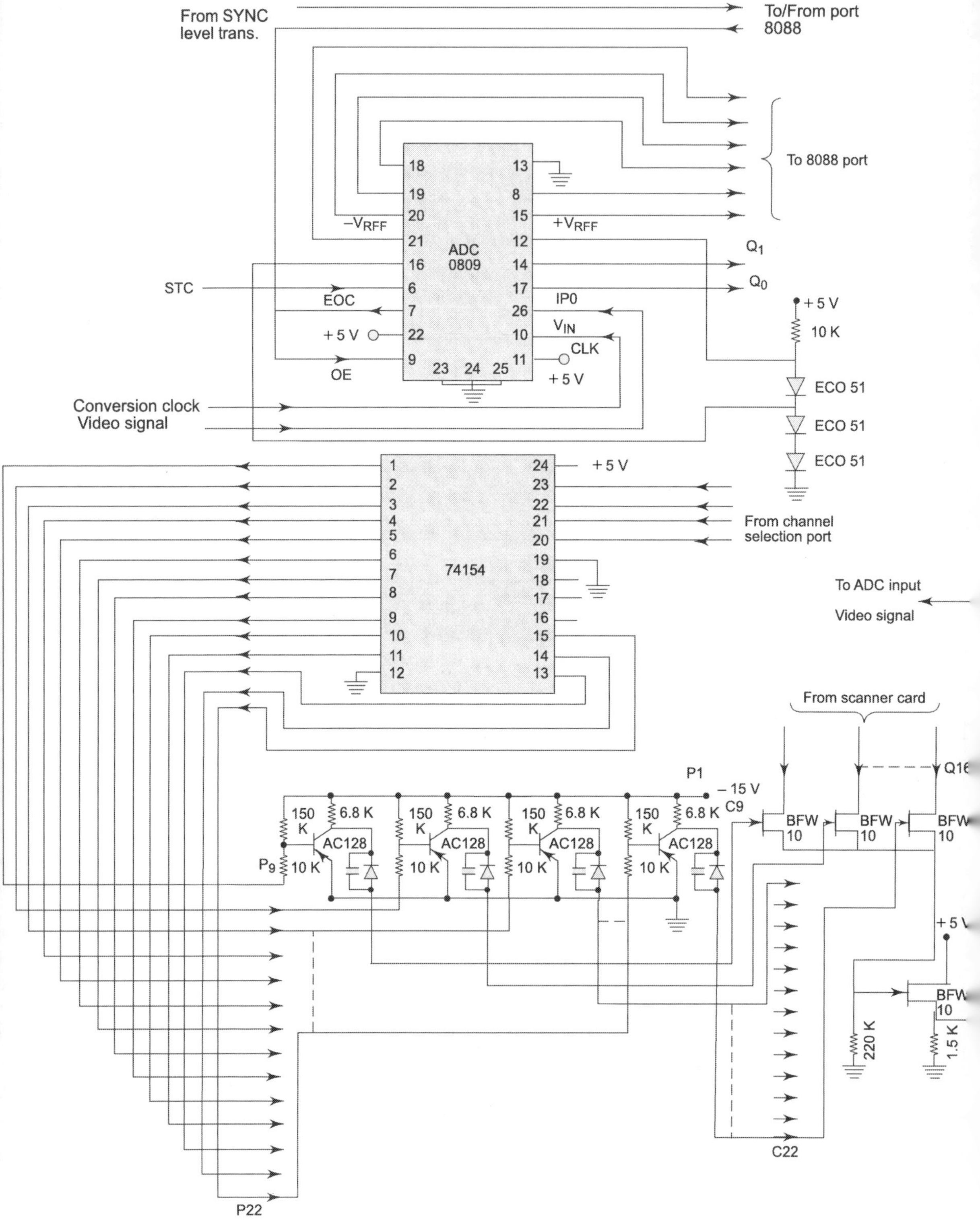

Fig. 15.4 *Converter and Multiplexer Interface*

The following registers and memory locations have been used for the sequence of operations:

Row counter	BL register
Column counter	CL register
Byte counter	DL register
Data pointer	SI register

After initialization, the contents of register BL are fed to the input of a four to 16 line decoder through port A, so as to enable a fresh row to be selected for scanning. The active-low output of the decoder selects a proper driver channel of the analog multiplexer. Once a channel is selected by the decoder, a start of conversion pulse is generated for the A/D converter by a monostable multivibrator in synchronism with the scanner clock and this results in the conduction of a FET switch corresponding to the channel to be scanned. The processor then loops to read the end of conversion signal given out by the A/D converter. As the end of conversion pulse goes high, the validity of the digitized information becomes guaranteed and the processor reads the 8-bit data into register AL. The data is further stored in the memory locations pointed by SI register in compact form when the process of thresholding is over. The overall scanner system diagram is shown in Fig. 15.5.

This process is repeated for 64 elements of a particular row and the register BL is incremented by one. The scanning process is terminated after processing 16 rows and the program then branches to routines to classify the pattern.

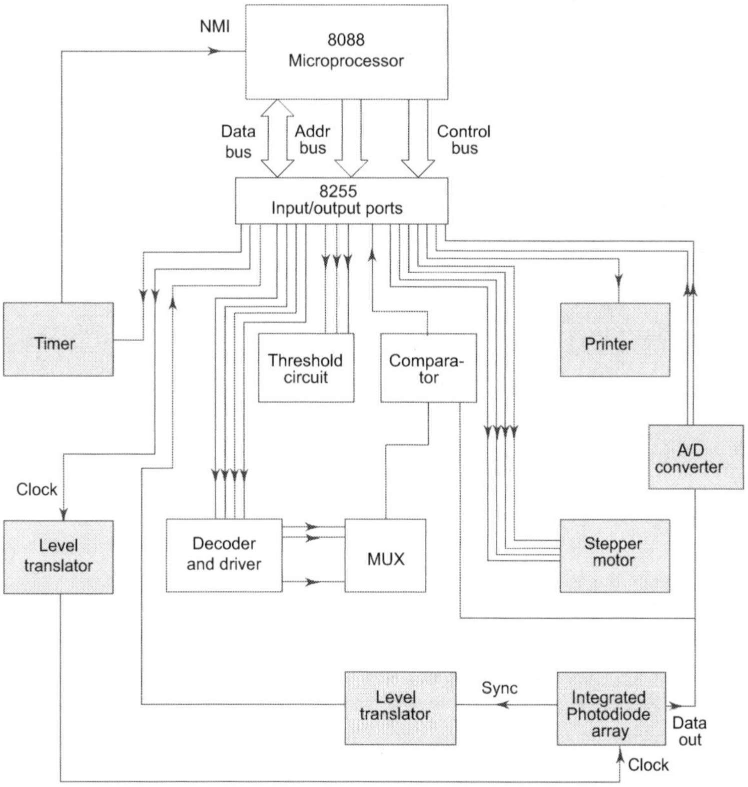

Fig. 15.5 *Overall Scanner System Diagram*

15.4 MEMORY READ/WRITE SYSTEM AND START-UP PROCEDURES

As has already been mentioned, a basic clock is needed for the scanner array, and writing of scanned data in off line memory is performed at the same speed as accessing any photodiode element in the system. This involves the use of address counter, row counter, column counter, etc. A 10-bit address counter may be implemented using three cascaded binary counters, which is incremented when it is enabled, until the content of the counter is less than 560 (14 × 40). This constraint has been imposed by the size of the photosensor array. This facility is used in the off line storage mode for an auto-stop arrangement. The address counter is unutilized by the first SYNC signal after the start of the operation.

A mod-n row counter may be used to keep track of the position of the present row under scan and gets incremented by a level translated 'SYNC' pulse. The output of the counter is fed to a decoder (say 4 to 16-line decoder) to select the rows. A mod-n counter using two cascaded binary counters counts 00 to (n-1) during each scan. The clock input to the address counter is generated by suitably selecting the logic, such that this line remains low during the (n-3)th to the (n-1)th state, which includes the scanning period of the (n-2)th element of a row and two flyback periods. Subsequently, the address counter is incremented only for the relevant clock periods. For transferring the data to a microprocessor port in compact form, the data output from the RAM is fed to 74164 – an 8-bit serial to parallel converter through a tri-state buffer. Another mod-8 counter counts the number of data elements entering the converter in synchronism with the clock. The counter triggers a monoshot to provide the system with a strobe of 10 μsec. The output of the serial to parallel converter is written into the processor system memory through the two tri-state buffers. The outputs of the buffers are kept in a high impedance state except while loading the data. The procedure for loading is:

1. Reset the address counter of the RAM
2. Put mode switch in auto-read mode
3. Enable the strobe output
4. Enable the count by reset switch
5. If the strobe is present, loading continues up to the limit set by the program

The Reticon scanner card does not provide any set/reset arrangement for the internal counters of the scanner array chip. The initialization circuit has been implemented using dual-D flip-flops, where the clock and D inputs of the first flip-flop are triggered by the level translated SYNC signal. The output of the first flip-flop which becomes high at the arrival of the first 'SYNC' pulse, is 'AND'ed with both the address counter and the column counter to provide synchronous operation. The row counter changes state only after the storage of data in the current row is over. The step-wise operations in the write mode are:

(a) Reset address counter, row counter, column counter and initialization flip-flops
(b) Enable all the counters and flip-flops
(c) Enable initialization flip-flop
(d) Writing in RAM stops automatically after storing the scanned data values

15.5 RESULT AND DISCUSSION

The spectral response of the Reticon RA14 × 41 photodiode sensor has been measured using a *Jarrel Ash continuous spectrum grating monochromator* with tungsten iodide source. The relative transmission efficiency of the grating has been considered among the necessary corrections in finding the spectral response. The spectral response is shown in Fig. 15.6. From the spectral response shown in Fig. 15.6, it may be observed that the phototransistor response is maximum at 720 nm, beyond which it falls. Thus, the reliability of the scanning system may be enhanced, if we use a light source at 720 nm wavelength.

Figure 15.7 shows the timing diagrams of the clock generated by 8088 CPU, clock for the scanner, 'SYNC' and the video output signals.

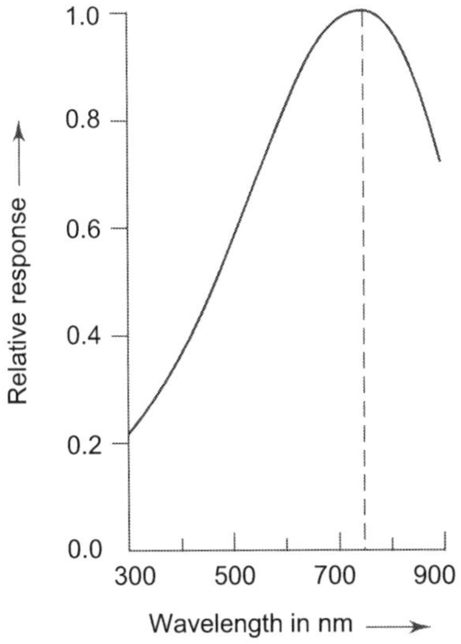

Fig. 15.6 *Spectral Response of the Reticon Array*

The timing diagram of start conversion, end of conversion, level translated 'SYNC', decoder and driver output signals are presented in Fig. 15.8. The digitized numerical character patterns have been subsequently tested for classification. The results of one of the stored digitized patterns are shown in Fig. 15.9.

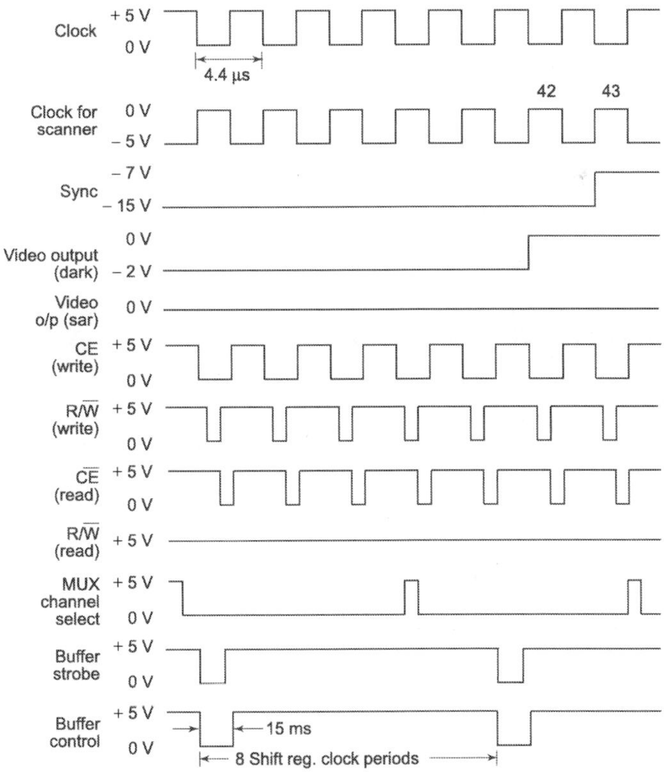

Fig. 15.7 *Timing Diagram*

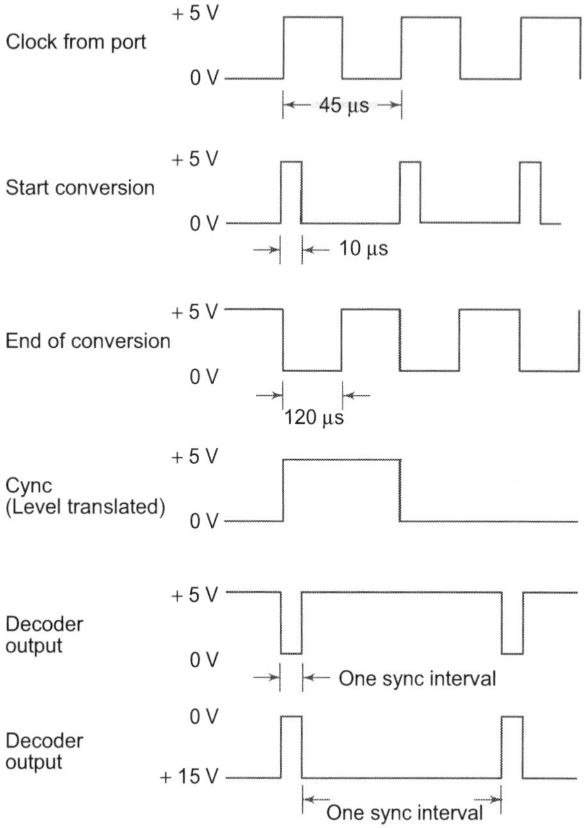

Fig. 15.8 *Timing Diagram*

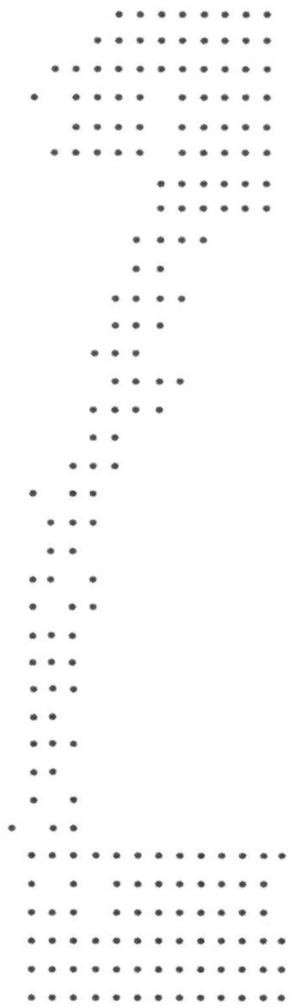

Fig. 15.9 *Digitised Stored Pattern of Numeral '2'*

SUMMARY

The program-controlled data acquisition system is very reliable and of higher precision than systems using other modes of storage. In the first two options of storage mode, as mentioned earlier, a Schmitt trigger has been used with typical threshold levels 1.7 V (positive going) and 0.9 V (negative going). The precision is obtained in program-controlled mode by the use of an A/D converter. However, the conversion time adds to the loop execution time for the clock generation resulting in a decrease of storage speed. The local storage mode is thus faster than the program-controlled mode. 256 grey levels may be obtained between the dark and saturation levels.

16 Design of an Electronic Weighing Bridge

INTRODUCTION

In the industries, which purchase or sell the goods in units of weight, weighing bridges are one of the most important devices. In daily life too, we get most of our domestic goods in the units of weight. Earlier, the shopkeepers used mechanical weighing balances for weighing goods. Nowadays they have been replaced by smart electronic weighing scales. The weighing bridge is nothing but a modified form of a smart weighing scale used to weigh in the range of tonnes. A weighing bridge can weigh a completely loaded truck or train accurately. Previously, these large scale weighing operations were carried out using mechanical weighing bridges which used to function on the principle of leaverage. The complete mechanism of these weighing bridges was located in a pit under the weighing platform. It used to be very bulky, and moreover it was difficult to handle and maintain these pit-type weighing bridges. The electronic weighing bridges have a comparatively light-weight mechanism and do not need a pit for accommodating its mechanism. These are easy to operate and display the weight on 7-segment display units or more advanced display types, like CRTs. Initially, the electronic weighing bridges were designed using microprocessors and thus the system used to have limited capabilities. However, with the advances in the field of computers and the cut-down in their prices, the recent electronic weighing bridges are designed around personal computers. This offered advantages like record maintenance (using floppies or hard disks), advanced and programmable display formats using CRTs, weighing ticket printouts, etc. The advanced electronic weighing bridges have facilities like, tare weighing, automatic calibration, programmable precision and maximum range, etc. This chapter presents an electronic weighing bridge circuit designed by the authors around 8088 with the necessary algorithms.

16.1 DESIGN ISSUES

The main design issues of an electronics weighing bridge are listed below:

1. Foundation of the mechanical structure
2. Mechanical structure design
3. Load cell selection
4. Electronics circuit design
   4.1 Power supply circuit

   4.2 Signal conditioning circuit design
   4.3 Microprocessor system design
5. Algorithms
6. Calibration

All these design issues are briefly discussed in the following text:

16.1.1 Foundation of the Mechanical Structure (Weighing Platform)

A brief description of the weighing platform foundation requirements and its typical structure is presented in this section. The weighing platform may be subjected to a heavy load, in the range of 50,000 kg. Thus the weighing platform itself should be sufficiently strong to bear a weight of such magnitude. Typically, a weighing bridge whose maximum capacity is 40 tonnes, may require a weighing platform of weigh approximately 7 tonnes. In case of a 100 tonnes weighing bridge, the weight of the platform may be up to 20 tonnes. This huge weight remains totally on the foundation and thus the foundation should withstand this weight without any permanent deformation. As the complete mechanical structure, which is further going to carry a huge load, resides on the concrete foundation, it must be designed properly. The design should be carried out keeping in view the type and characteristics of the soil at the site of weighing bridge installation. The foundation, usually is in the form of rectangular concrete pillars, usually four or six in number, depending upon the number of load cells used for the bridge and the concrete ramps on both sides of the weighing platform to provide road to the platform. All the foundation pillars are of exactly equal height to carry the mechanical structure in a single horizontal plane. Even a slight tilt in the plane of the platform may cause a *corner error* (i.e. the same weight placed in the different corners of the platform may show different weight displays). The foundation should be designed considering the types of the soil at the places of the different pillars. The four or six different pillars should preferably have similar type of soil. If the soil type at different pillar locations is different, due consideration should be given to this fact while designing the different foundation pillar bases. If the location of the weighing bridge is be selected so that the pillar base soil is of the same characteristics, it avoids complications in foundation design and the possibility of foundation pillar collapse.

This foundation designed in the form of pillars carries load cells rigidly fixed over it using fixtures known as load cell mountings. The foundation pillars are fixed rigidly with load cell mounting bases. The mechanical structure, in fact, transfers its weight on all the load cells which in turn transfer it to the foundation. There should be a sufficient clearance between the mechanical structure and the foundation so that any moving weight over the structure, if causing any vibration or play should not make it touch or dash the edge of the concrete foundation ramp. The foundation should safely withstand the total weight of the vehicle to be weighed, the weight of the mechanical structure and an additional component due to vibrations and jerks. Usually the capacity of the foundation is described in tonnes per day (just like traffic roads). Figure 16.1 shows a schematic of a typical weighing bridge foundation and a mechanical structure residing on it for a four load cell weighing bridge. In case of a six load cell weighing bridge, two more foundation pillars will be required to carry the two additional load cells as shown in Fig. 16.1.

16.1.2 Mechanical Structure

The mechanical structure that rests over the load cells is a rigid structure that physically carries a vehicle to be weighed over it. Hence it must have adequate strength to bear the weight to be weighed without any permanent deformation or damage in it. If at all any deformation of the structure takes place, it must be within the elastic limits of the material and the platform. A safety factor of 3 is considered while designing the mechanical structure. The mechanical platform rests over the load cells, which are physically quite small as compared to the platform, and thus the platform may topple down the load cells and may get dislodged. Hence the mechanical structure should have some fixing arrangements (or separate fixtures and mountings

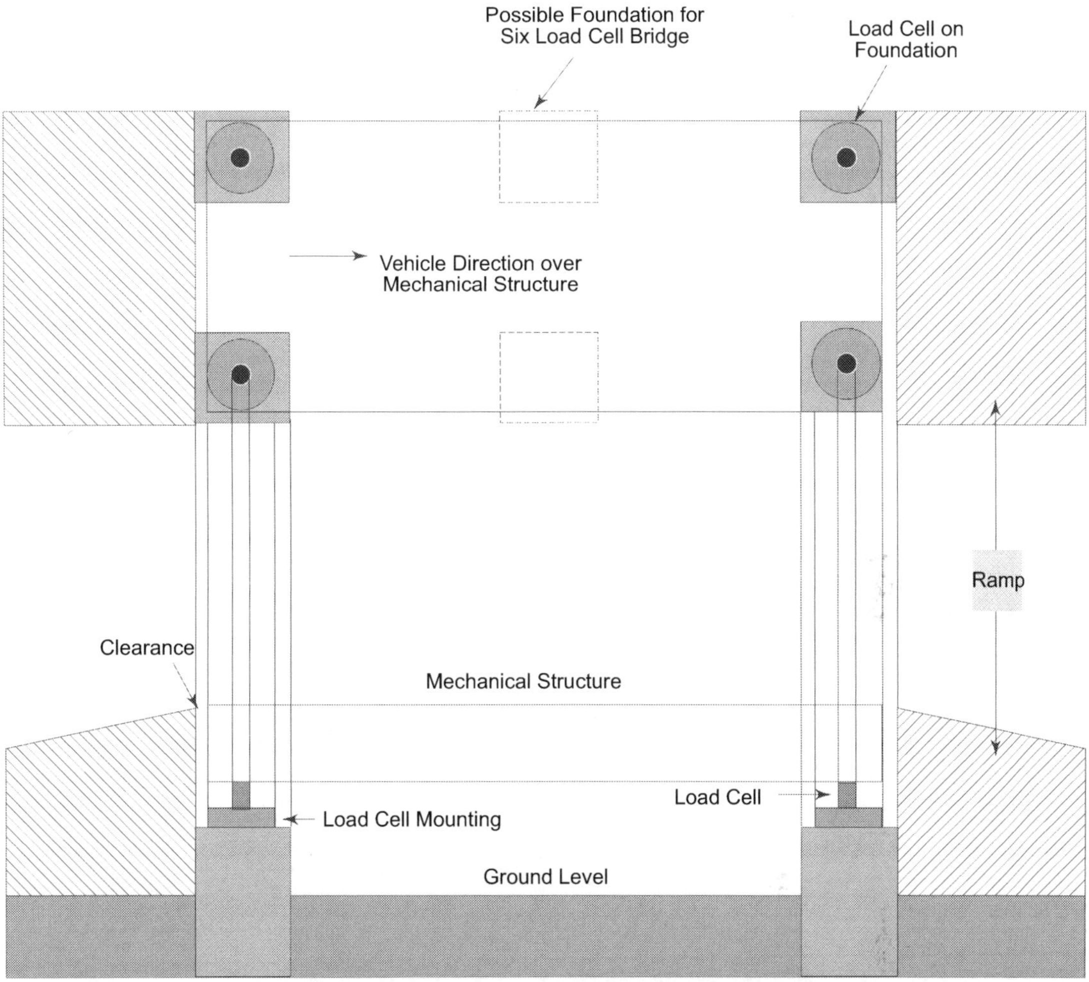

Fig. 16.1 *Schematic of Foundation and Mechanical Structure Resting on it*

may be designed) for fixing the mechanical structure with the load cells. The mechanical structure such mounted should have a sufficient clearance between it and the road ramp, to float the structure laterally between the two ramps. This lateral movement of the structure and the load cell fixtures and mountings prevent the load cells from toppling, due to the lateral forces appearing due to vehicle movement and abrupt braking. The complete mechanical structure must be coplanar to avoid corner error. A typical mechanical structure for a 40 tonnes weigh-bridge is 9 meters in length and 3.1 meters in breadth to carry a full normal size truck vehicle. A number of mechanical structure designs may be suggested, using structural engineering principles to serve the purpose. A simple mechanical structure for a 40 tonnes weigh-bridge is shown in Fig. 16.2.

The mechanical structure should have pipes attached to it along its edges for carrying the load cell wires to the adder circuit, for adding all the load cell signals. The adder circuit is located in a cabinet usually attached with the mechanical structure or mounted near by. The output of the adder circuit is further amplified by the signal processing circuit. During the weighing procedure, the mechanical structure should rest only on the load cells. It should neither touch the road ramp nor any additional support except the load cell fixtures.

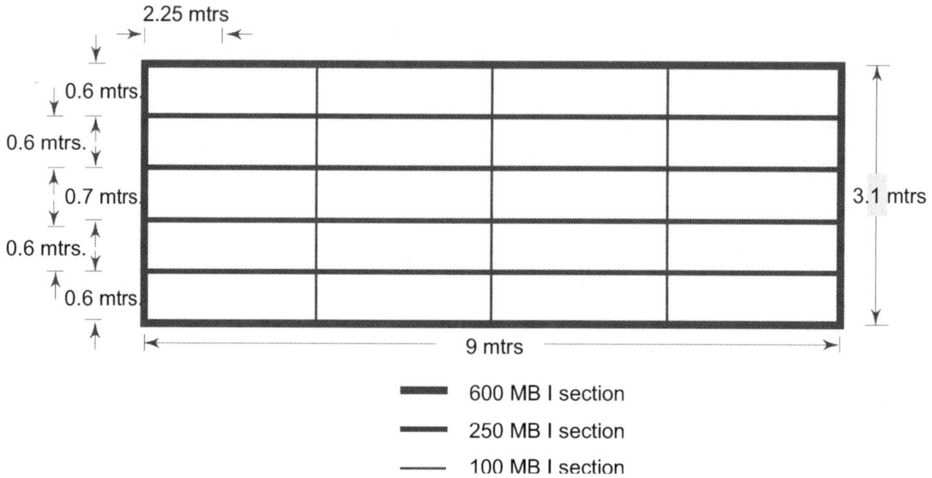

Fig. 16.2 *Mechanical Structure*

16.1.3 Load Cells—Selection and Connections

In the most popular form, a load cell contains a mechanical structure machined out of suitable types of steels or alloys and heat treated to maintain the material characteristics for a long period. This mechanical structure acts as a primary transducer to convert the weight to which it is subjected into its proportional strain. This strain is measured using strain gauges which are usually connected in the form of wheatstone bridge to derive maximum output from the bridge. Additional circuits, like lightning protection, temperature compensation and null adjustment may be incorporated in the bridge. Most of the load cells contain the circuit arrangement shown in Fig. 16.3.

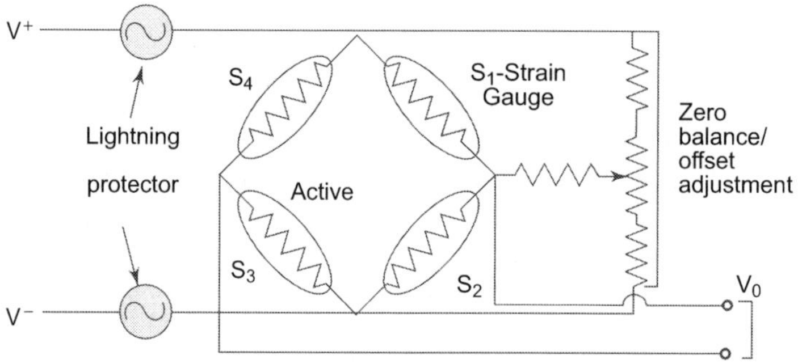

Fig. 16.3 *A Typical Load Cell Circuit*

The offset adjustment arrangement is optional and sometimes it is implemented on a PCB outside the load cell, i.e. in the adder circuit.

As shown in Fig. 16.3, a load cell has two input (supply +V and −V) terminals and to differential output terminals ($+V_0$ and $-V_0$). A cable carrying the differential output signal of the load cell is shielded to protect the signal from external noise. This shield is to be connected with the ground of the circuit.

In case of multipoint measurement systems like weighing bridges, the load cells are connected in parallel to obtain a common signal from all the available load cells in the circuit. This is implemented using a adder circuit. The output of the adder circuit which is a resultant signal of all the load cells is fed to the instrumentation amplifier. The overall arrangement of load cells is shown in Fig. 16.4. The variable resistances added at the input lines of load cells (R_1, R_2, R_3, R_4) are used for the calibration of the individual load cells corners of the bridge.

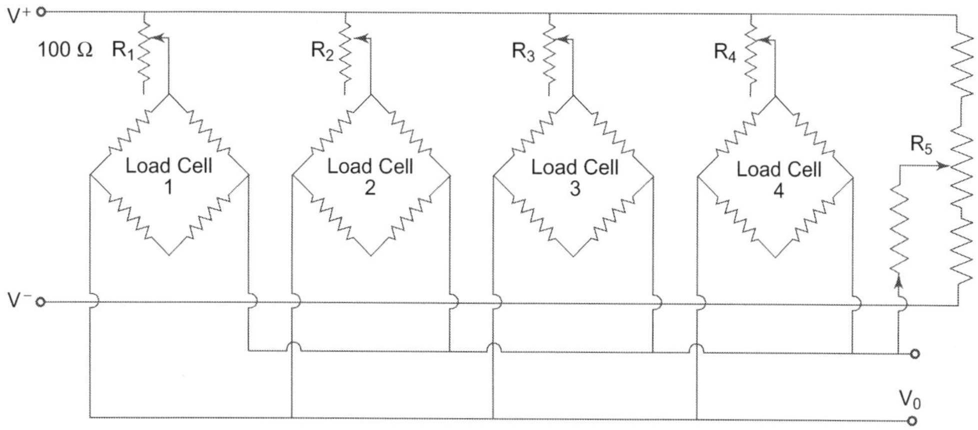

Fig. 16.4 *Arrangement of Load Cells for a Four Load Cell Weighing Bridge*

The selection of load cells generally depends upon the capacity of the weighing-bridge to be designed. For example, for a 40 tonnes weigh-bridge using four load cells, each load cell selected should be at least of 20 tonnes capacity, considering a safety factor of 2. Various types of load cells are available in the market. Previously compression (button, ball or cone) type load cells were generally used. Nowadays, *double ended shear beam type load cells* are used due to their better performance, accuracy and long life.

All the four load cells are connected as shown in Fig. 16.4 to derive a common signal using the adder circuit. The output of a adder circuit is a signal in the range of 0–20 mV. The load cell specifications are usually specified in terms of the output voltage per unit Volt input. For example, a 20 tonnes load cell with parameter 2 mV per Volt will generate 2 mV, if it is excited by a 1 Volt DC source and subjected to its full capacity, i.e. 20 tonnes of load. Practically, a load cell should be used only up to half of its the maximum capacity to ensure its long life and better performance. This output of the adder circuit is amplified using an instrumentation amplifier. An appropriate ADC circuit converts this signal to its digital equivalent. The microprocessor reads the digital equivalent and further manipulates it to compute the equivalent weight to be displayed or printed.

The block diagram of the complete system is shown in Fig. 16.5.

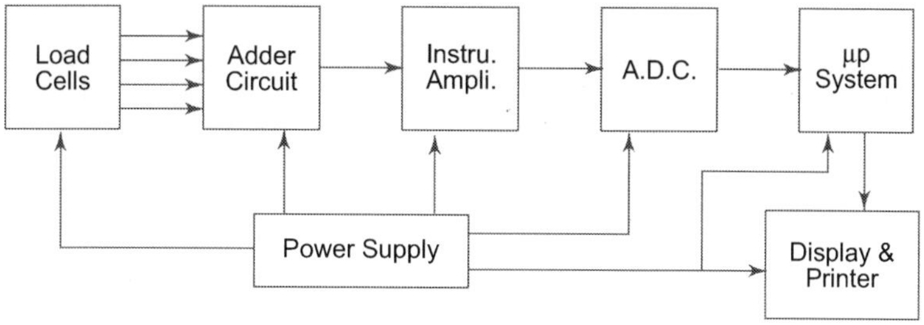

Fig. 16.5 *Block Diagram of the System*

16.1.4 Electronics Circuit Design

The complete electronics circuit is divided into three sections as follows:

1. Power Supply
2. Signal Processing Circuit
3. Microprocessor System

Power Supply Circuit The microprocessor system requires a +5 V regulated supply. This may also be used as +5 V digital supply for the ADC. The ADC requires +5 V (analog) and –5 V supplies for its operation. The instrumentation amplifier requires +5 V and –5 V. All the load cells require +10 V and –10 V supply. Also it is recommended that the supply from which the reference of the ADC is derived should be highly stabilised. Hence one more +5 V supply is obtained from the regulated +10V supply.

There we require three +5 V, two –5 V and one each of +10 V and –10 V for the complete system. The circuit in Fig. 16.6 shows the power supply circuit. Note that all the windings of the transformer are of 500 mA rating. It is recommended that separate supplies should be used for analog and digital sections of the ADC circuit. The 78xx series regulators are sufficiently accurate for deriving all the +5 V and –5 V supplies. The +10 V and –10 V supply may require fine adjustments at the time of calibration. Hence LM317 and LM337 variable voltage regulators are used for deriving these supplies.

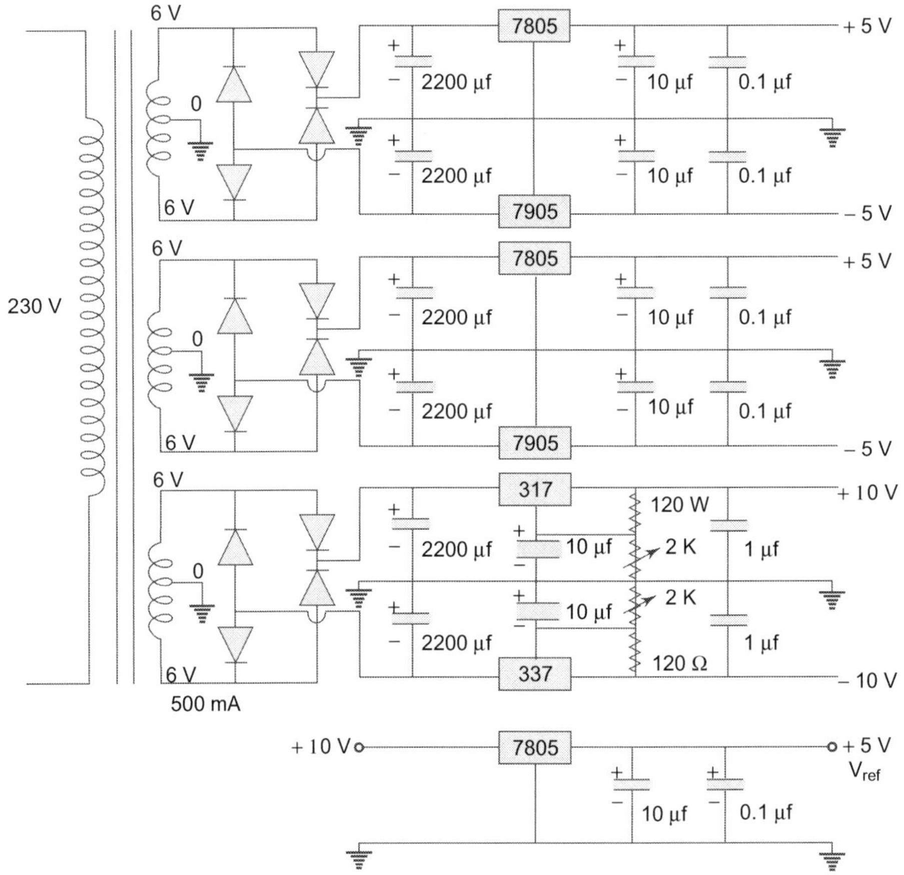

Fig. 16.6 *Power Supply Circuit*

Signal Processing Circuit

Signal Adder Circuit (Adder/Summer) The adder circuit accepts individual outputs of the load cells and derives a common output signal which is further fed to the instrumentation amplifier. The adder circuit has already been shown in Fig. 16.4. The four bridges in Fig. 16.4 represent four load cells. The resistances

R_1, R_2, R_3 and R_4 are used for minute corner adjustments. The resistance R5 is used for zero load adjustment (offset adjustment) of the system.

Instrumentation Amplifier This circuit is the most important and sensitive part of the system which amplifies a signal derived by the adder circuit. A number of single chip instrumentation amplifiers are available commercially. A few of the popular ones are AD625, LM363 and ICL7650, etc. Most of the single chip instrumentation amplifiers are costly components. Hence a comparatively simple and cheaper circuit has been developed as shown in Fig. 16.7. This circuit has been implemented using high precision operational amplifier OP07 and all 1% tolerance resistance values. The three stage filter at the output of the instrumentation amplifier ensures a constant input voltage for the analog to digital converter till the conversion is complete. High quality paper capacitors should be used for the filter circuits.

The adder circuit gives out 0-20mV output. The ADC circuit is designed to accept 4.096 volts as full scale analog input. Hence the required circuit components are selected to provide a gain in the range of 180 to 220. The 200 ohm variable resistance may be trimmed to adjust the gain at an exactly required value. The 50K variable resistance may be trimmed to adjust the offset at minimum possible value. The 1K variable resistance may be adjusted to obtain the equal gain for positive and negative inputs.

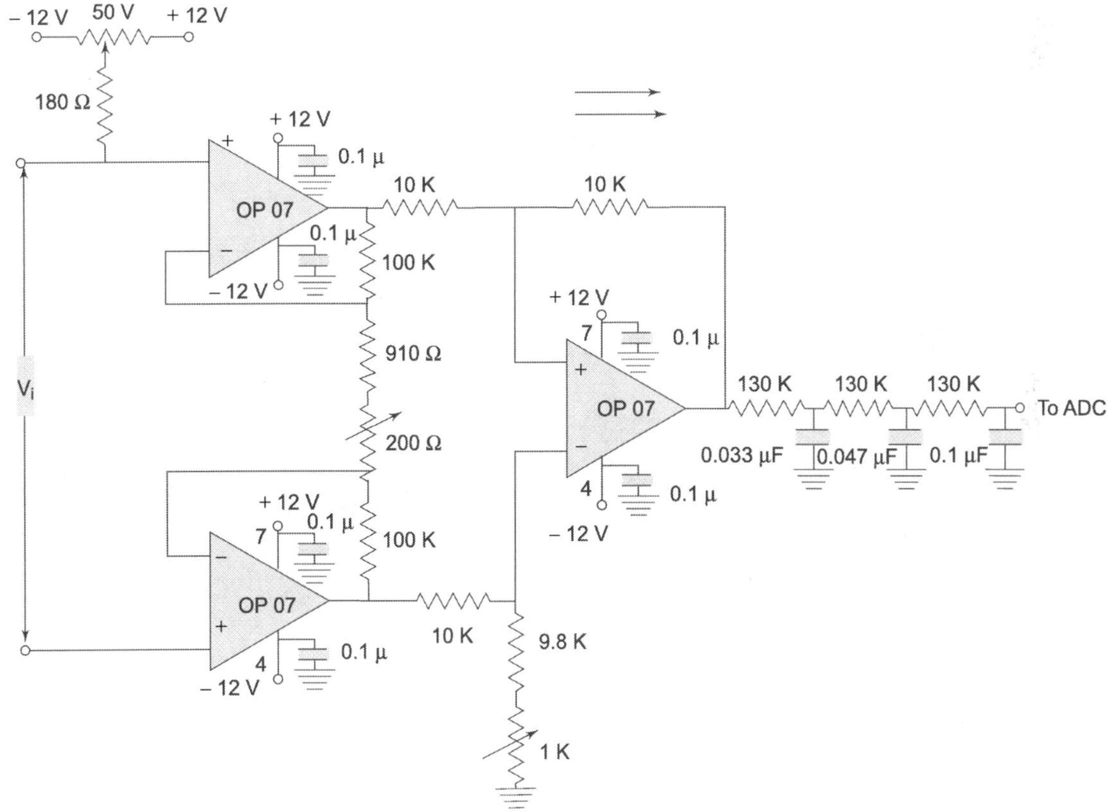

Fig. 16.7 *Instrumentation Amplifier*

Analog to Digital Converter The signal amplified by the instrumentation amplifier is further processed by a three stage RC filter. The output of the filter circuits is given to the input of the ADC for converting it to an equivalent digital count. The count may further be converted to an equivalent decimal number and manipulated using software to obtain the proper weight display. The circuit uses low cost 12-bit Intersil's ICL7109 ADC for this purpose. The circuit parameters are adjusted to give approximately seven samples per second. For a fixed weight input the ADC may give a slightly varying output, and hence one may not get a stable weight display. To overcome this problem average or moving average of samples may be computed and used as an equivalent digital count, to get a stable display. The ADC circuit is shown in Fig. 16.8. The output of the ADC circuit is read by the CPU using an I/O port. The ADC circuit requires a proper software support to function properly. The flowchart and program for ADC operation has already been discussed in Chapter 5.

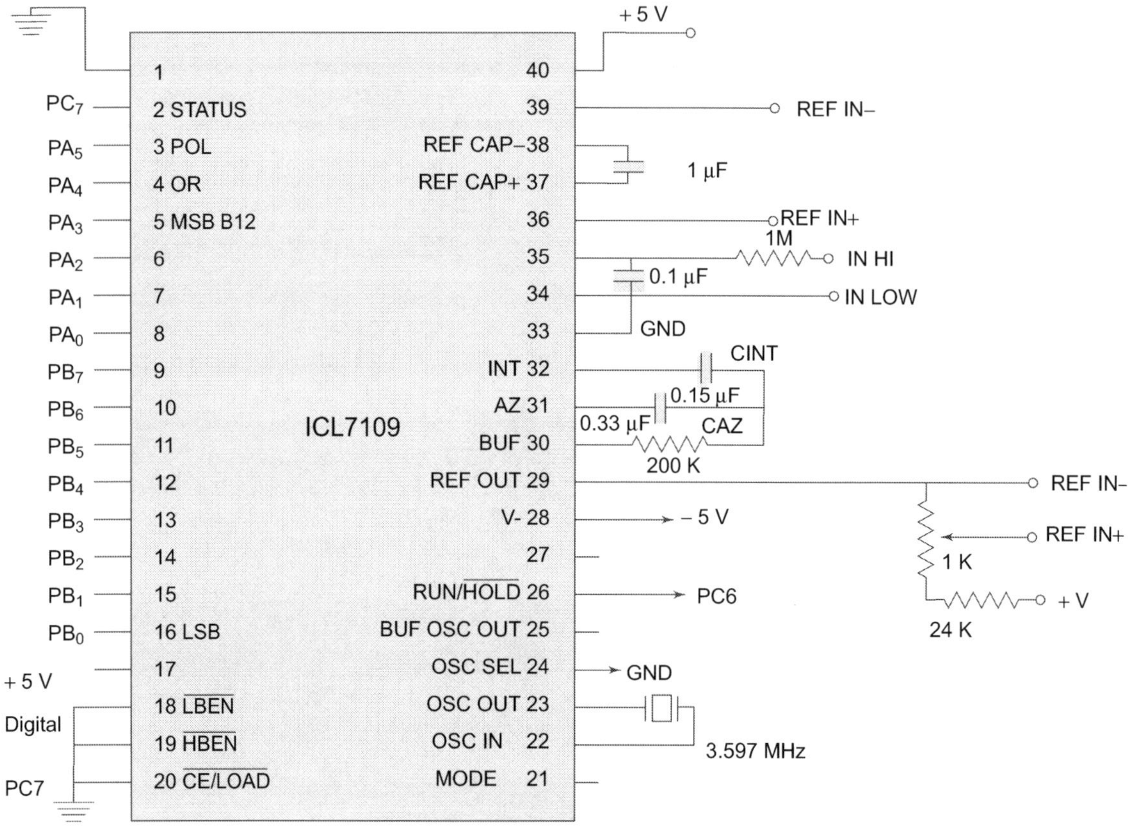

Fig. 16.8 *Analog to Digital Converter*

Microprocessor System The microprocessor system designed for this application is shown in Fig. 16.9. The system is designed around 8088, which offers the simplicity of 8-bit processors for peripheral interfacing and the powerful instruction set of the 16-bit processor 8086. The connector J_1 is a power supply connector. The connector J_2 makes the CPU system bus interrupts and control bus available for external connections. The system is able to address 32 Kbytes of EPROM and 32 Kbytes of RAM available on the board. An additional memory bank of 960 Kbytes, may be designed using thirty 62256 RAM ICs and can be readily connected at socket J_3 which provides the chip select signals for the external 62256 RAM ICs. The chip selects of these additional RAMs are readily designed on the board using two 74154 and are brought out at connector J_3 along with power supply pins.

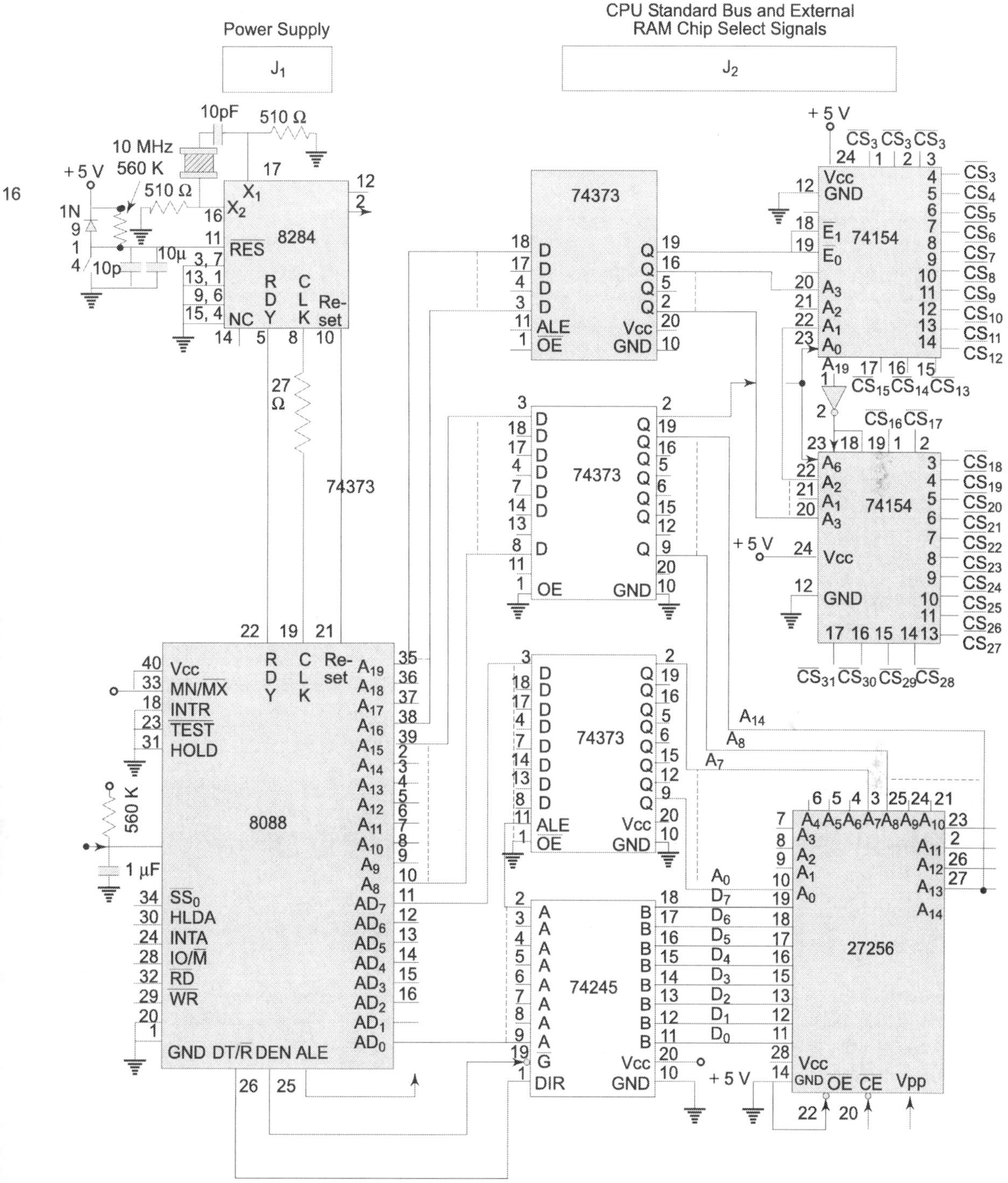

Fig. 16.9 *Microprocessor 8088 Based System Circuit Diagram for the Electronic Weighing Bridge*

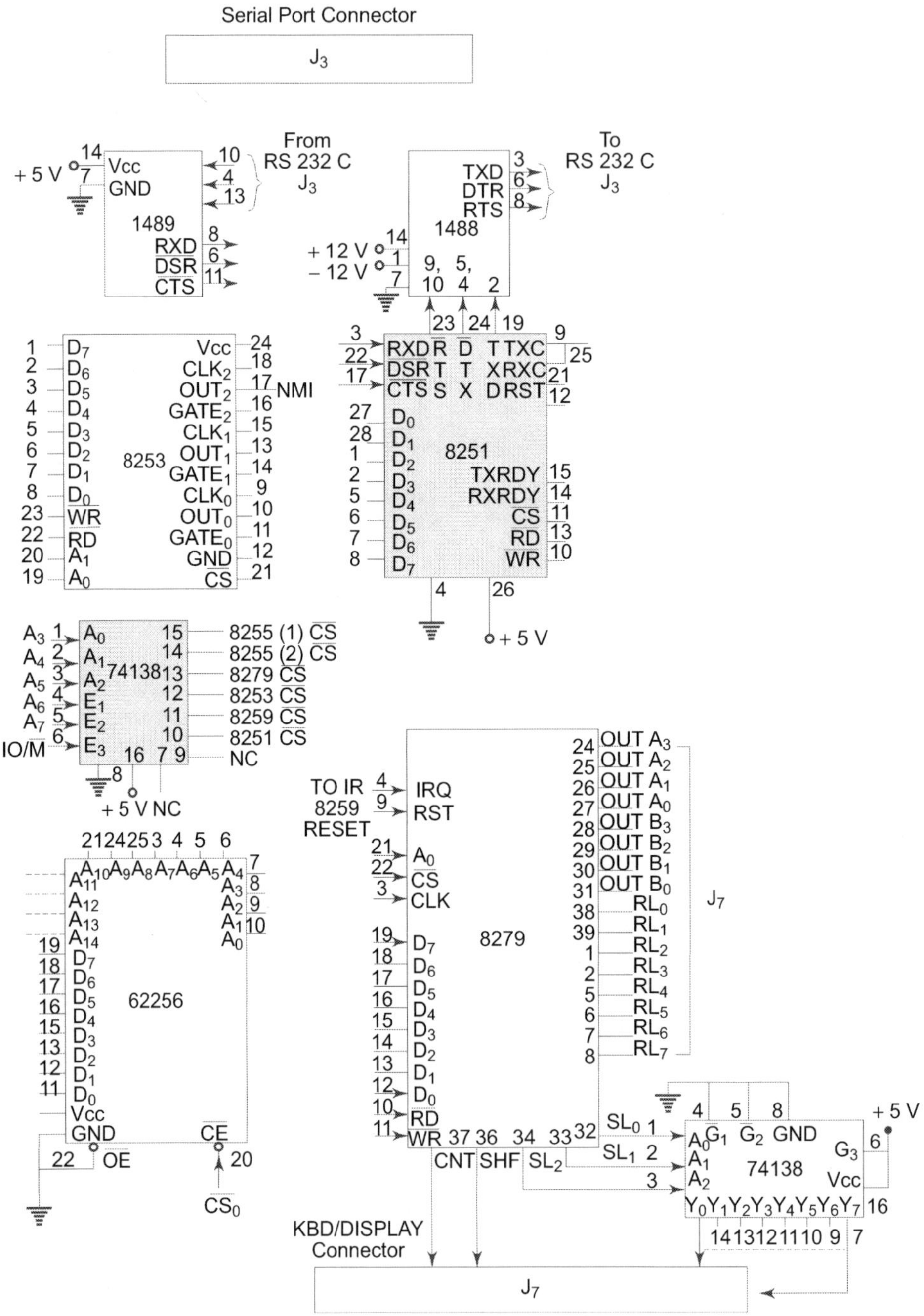

Fig. 16.9 *(Contd.)*

The connector J_4 has the serial communication signals for RS 232C. The RS 232 compatible line drivers are used for their usual purpose along with 8251 for serial communication with a PC. The connector J5 is a 25-pin connector at which a printer may be connected. The printer is interfaced using 8255 as already discussed in Chapter 5. The connector J_6 is a 26-pin 8255 connector and may be used for interfacing a LCD alphanumeric display and driver module, for weighing ticket data entry, like seller's name, purchaser's name, tare weight, etc. The J_6 also interfaces a 12-bit ADC with the CPU. Note that when the data entry on the LCD module is in process the ADC is hold. The connector J_7 presents the signals required for keyboard and display interfacing made available by the on-board 8279.

The microprocessor system contains on-board 32 Kbytes of RAM, 32 Kbytes of EPROM, 8279 keyboard display controller, 8253 programmable timer, 8251 serial communication interface and two 8255's out of which, the first is for a printer interface and the other for a LCD display driver interface. Interfacing techniques of all these peripherals have already been discussed in details in this text except for a LCD driver module.

The latches 74373 and buffers 74245 have been used for latching the addresses and separating the data from the multiplexed address/data signals generated by the CPU. The decoder 74154 is used for generating the chip selects of the 32 Kbytes EPROM and RAM memory chips (either on-board or external). A 3:8 decoder 74138 is used to generate the chip select lines of all the on-board peripheral circuits. Another 74138 is used for decoding the keyboard/display scan lines from the encoded scan output lines generated by 8279. The line receiver 1489 and the line driver 1488 are used for interfacing the 8251 signals with the RS-232 communication standard. The buffers 7407 are used for interfacing the printer data bus and control signals with 8255 I/O lines. Figure 16.9 shows the complete microprocessor system circuit diagram.

The 64-key keyboard is shown along with the key assignments in Fig. 16.10. The keyboard and the five unit 7-segment display are to be connected with the 8279 at connector J_7 using a flat crimped connector. Figure 16.11 shows the 7-segment display unit.

Fig. 16.10 *8 × 8 Keyboard*

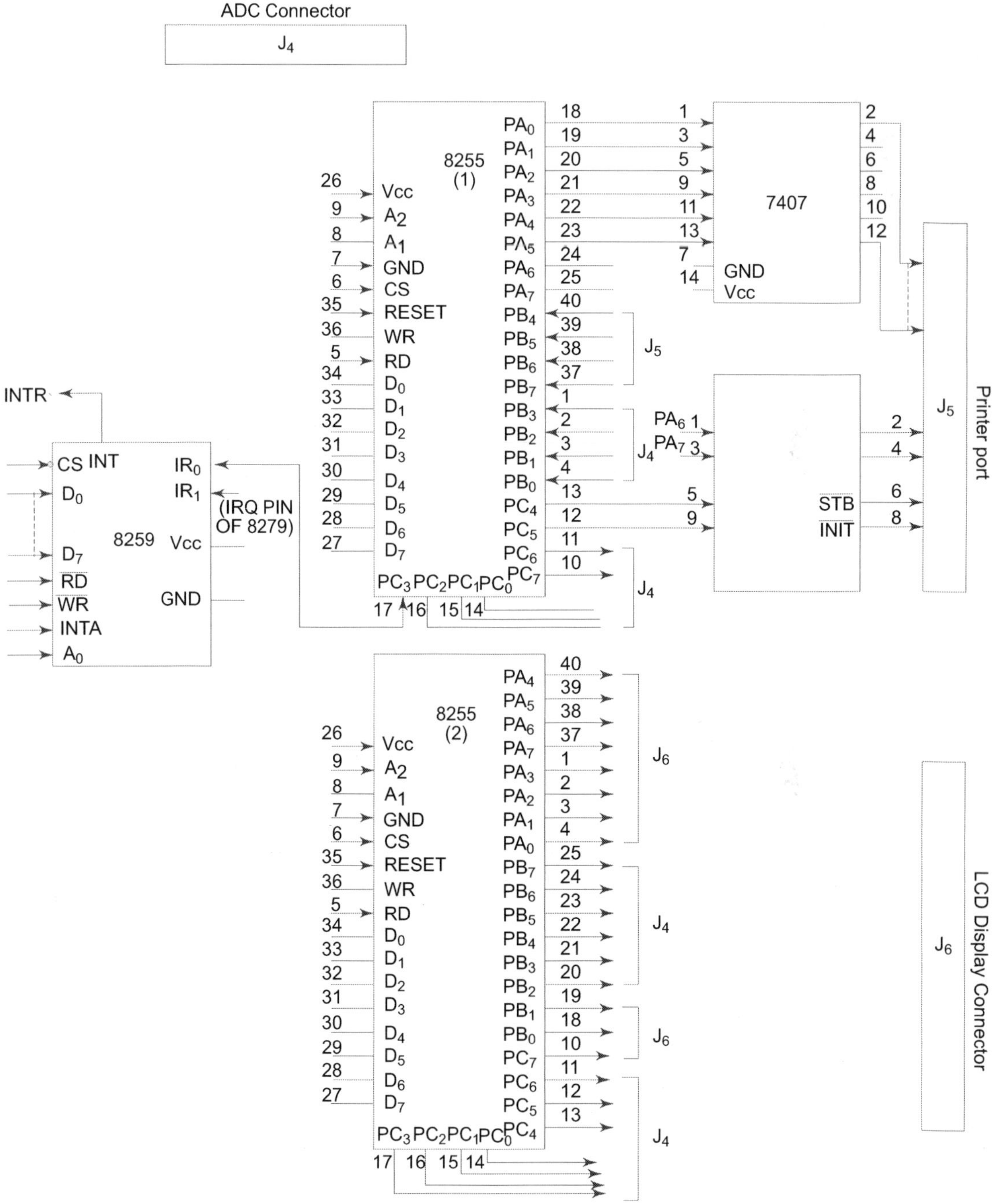

Fig. 16.9 (Contd.)

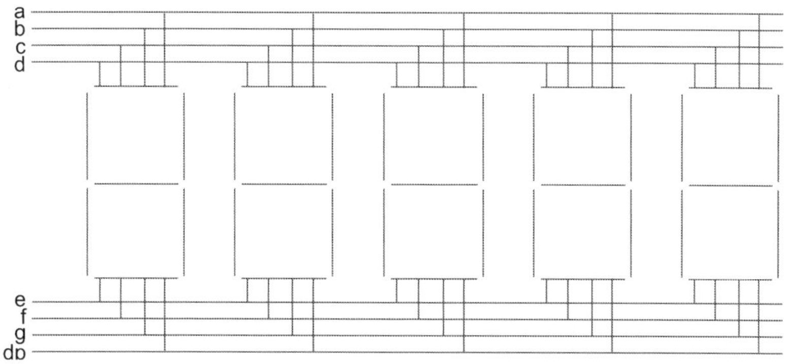

Fig. 16.11 *Multiplexed Display Unit*

Interfacing LCD Module 'ORIOLE' The system provides a LCD dotmatrix 80-character display, organised as two lines, each of 40 characters. A custom built module containing this display with its controller is readily available in the market. Here we have used one such LCD module from 'ORIOLE'. This module can be interfaced with a CPU using I/O ports. Here we have used programmable I/O ports of 8255 for interfacing the LCD module with 8088. The LCD module is to be connected at socket J_6. Figure 16.12 shows the interfacing connections of 8088 with the LCD module using 8255.

The display module has an 80 × 1 byte display buffer with two internal registers namely, instruction and data registers. The eight data lines D0–D7 carry data/control words from/to the CPU to/from the display module. The E (Enable) input line, when high, enables a read/write operation from/to the LCD controller. Once an instruction is written into the instruction register, the internal BUSY status goes high. No further operation is possible with the LCD controller till the BUSY flag is high, i.e. the controller is busy. After the specified busy time, the contents of the address counter that contain the current display pointer can be read by the CPU. The busy status flag can be continuously read, while the controller is in busy status, and whenever it shows NO BUSY status, further address counter read operation can be carried out. The busy state is presented by the D7 line when the E line goes high. The $R/\overline{W}$ line indicates whether it is a read or a write operation. For the write operation, the $R/\overline{W}$ line should be low while for the read operation it should be high. The write operation issues an instruction or a data byte to the

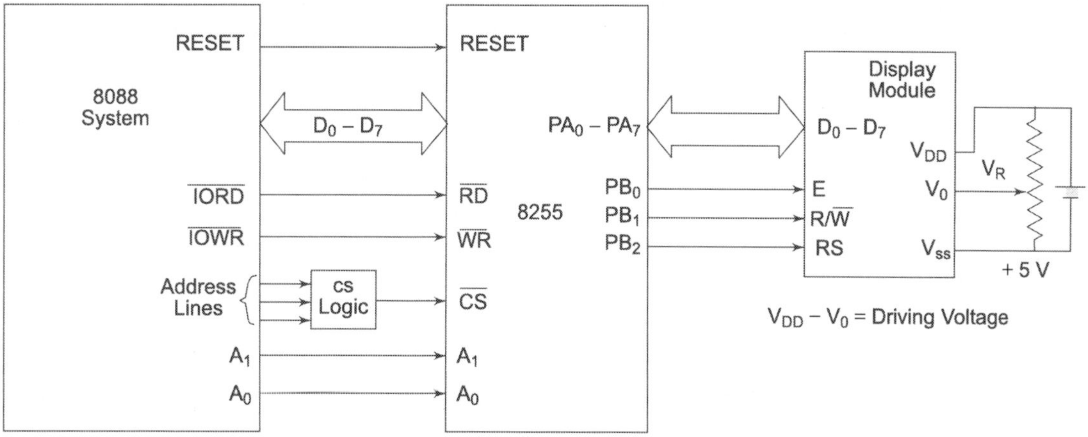

Fig. 16.12 *Interfacing LCD Module with 8088*

controller, while the read operation either reads the busy status or the address counter content. The RS (Register Select line) selects one of the two register, viz. instruction register and data register for the selected read/write operation.

The write and read operations of the LCD controller are presented in Fig. 16.13 and Fig. 16.14 along with the critical timings. The specified timings for the respective operations should be strictly followed, failing which the LCD module and PIO may have permanent damage.

Fig. 16.13 *Write to LCD Controller Timings*

Fig. 16.14 *Read from LCD Controller Timings*

The display module is automatically initialized when the power is turned on. The busy flag BF shows busy status and does not accept any instruction until the initialization is over. The controller is busy for 1ms after the V_{DD} rises to 4.5 V. In the default mode, the display unit is automatically initialized with the following mode specifications.

1. Display Clear
2. Character font 5 × 7 dots (F = low)
3. Number of lines l(80 characters × 1 line) N = low
4. Interface width-8-bits (DL = high)
5. Address counter Increment (I/D = high)
6. Display shift : off (S = low)
7. Display : off (D = low)
8. Cursor : off (C = low)
9. Blink : off (B = low)

Our system uses 5 × 7 dot character size in two lines each containing 40 characters. The display interface width is 8-bits as required for 8088. We have selected a note-book type entry mode, hence the display

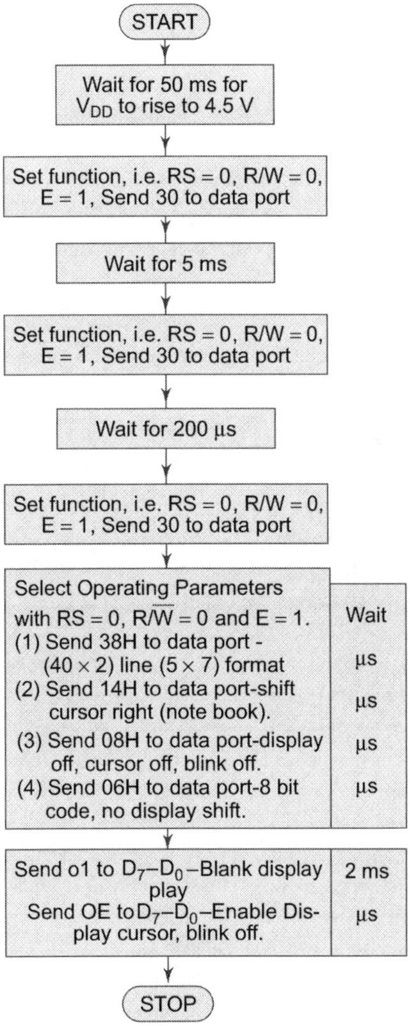

Fig. 16.15 *Initialisation of the LCD Controller*

need not be shifted and the S bit should remain low. We have selected a non-blinking cursor, thus the B bit should remain low. After the initialization is over, the D bit will be set and the cursor will be enabled, i.e. C = 1.

The algorithm in Fig. 16.15 shows the initialization as per our requirement, using the initialization program.

Once the initialization is over, the display unit displays the contents of display RAM, i.e. blank and it waits for a key pressure and its code from the CPU. If it is an alphanumeric key, the corresponding character is displayed on the LCD module at the current cursor position and the control is again transferred to the keyboard monitor, for sensing further keys. The write operation has already been discussed in this chapter. For writing a character to display RAM, RS = 1 and R/W = 0, and the code to be written to the RAM should now be placed on the data bus. While reading display RAM, RS = 1 and $R/\overline{W}$ = 1, the data to be read appears on the data bus and it may be read using I/O read instruction. For displaying a character on the LCD module, the ASCII code of the character is sent to the data port under the control of $R/\overline{W}$, RS and E input pins, as already discussed.

The next section describes the software development of the system in significant detail.

16.2 SOFTWARE DEVELOPMENT

16.2.1 Software Operation

Before we go for actual software development, the function of the complete system must be specified clearly so as to propose the flowcharts. Any system, once power on, displays some message on the display unit to indicate to the operator that it is ready to accept commands from him. The operator then issues suitable commands to the system. This system displays a string 'START' on the 7-segment display unit as well as the LCD module. Before this display appears on dotmatrix LCD unit and 7-segment display unit, the CPU carries out the following functions.

(i) Initialisation of all the Peripherals and CPU Registers Available in the System The peripherals like 8255, 8253, 8251 and 8279 are to be properly initialized before the system starts functioning.

(ii) Building the Necessary Databases for Keycodes and Displays For example, displaying the string 'START' on the 7-segment display unit requires a look-up table of the 7-segment codes which are to be actually sent to the display RAM of 8279. Also the LCD module requires the look up table of ASCII codes for the required alphanumerals' and symbols' display. The CPU generates these type of databases in memory before the 'START' message is displayed. Otherwise, these databases may also be permanently stored in EPROM.

(iii) Allocating Memory Areas for the Required Databases in RAM For the 7-segment display unit, the internal RAM of 8279 is used as a display buffer. However, the LCD display unit, though internally has a display memory of 80-bytes, requires additional memory if more than 80-bytes display data is to be scrolled either up or down. This system is intended to print a weighing ticket that contains the names of the seller and purchaser, material, date of weighing, time of weighing, net weight of the vehicle, gross weight of the vehicle, tare weight of the vehicle and also the vehicle number. This information may require even more than hundred bytes of memory. Hence a buffer of this much size is generated internally and it is scrolled by the 80 byte LCD display unit line by line. The CPU reserves the memory space for this type of structure internally, before any command is received from the operator.

Once the start up message is displayed, the system is ready for accepting further commands from the operator. The operator now has two options. The first, called *direct weighing mode*, is to go for the weighing operation directly wherein the system does not give any chance to the operator to enter the weighing ticket data and the system directly shows the gross weight on the 7-segment display unit and the LCD display. The second option, called weighing with print ticket, allows the operator to enter the weighing ticket data before entering into the weighing mode. After entering the weighing ticket data, the weighing operation calculates and displays the gross weight over the platform at that instant. The print ticket command then prints out the entered data along with the gross and net weight. To calculate the net weight, the tare weight, which is read and stored by the system at the instant the tare key was pressed, is subtracted from the gross weight. In case of the direct weighing mode, if a print operation is attempted, it may print a random weighing ticket.

In the second option, after the weighing ticket is printed, the operator may like to save the weighing operation in memory. Our system has 32 Kbytes of on-board RAM, out of which 2Kbytes are used as scratchpad and stack memory, and the remaining 30Kbytes may be used for maintaining the records of the previous weighings. Thus if a weighing requires 100 bytes, approximately 300 successive weighings can be stored in the 30 Kbytes RAM. The software may implement a first-in-first out structure to save these weighings. In other words, if the capacity of the RAM is of storing 300 weighings then, whenever the 301st weighing is stored, the very first weighing is pushed out of memory and lost. Thus 300 recent most weighings may be stored in the on-board RAM. The option of storing a weighing or neglecting it, is kept in the hands of the operator. A separate 'SW' key is allotted for storing a weighing in the RAM. Once the weighing is over, the system may again be brought back to the 'START' message and prepared for the next weighting operation, using a restart key. To issue all the above discussed commands, the simplest way is to reserve a key for each command. Just pressing the command key executes the respective command.

A list of typical commands for the operation of the system is given as follows. Many more commands may be added to make the system more user friendly, and to offer additional facilities.

1. Restart (RST)
2. Enter in direct weighing mode (DW)
3. Enter in weighing mode with ticket printing (WP)
4. Set date (SD)
5. Set time (ST)
6. Store the weighing in record (SW)
7. Next data field in the ticket record (NXT)
8. Previous field in the ticket record (PRV)
9. Print weighing ticket (PW)
10. Print datewise record (PDR)
11. Print todays record (PTR)
12. Print customer-wise record (PCR)
13. Print seller-wise record (PSR)
14. Print item-wise record (PIR)
15. Print vehicle number-wise record (PVR)
16. Scan the complete record in RAM serially with 'next' key, (Command No. 7) (SCR)
17. Clear record RAM (CRR)
18. Display record status (DRS)
19. Return from a function (RN)

All the commands may be executed at the 'START' message. A number of other commands may be added to this list, of course, putting additional burden on the software designer.

The keyboard has 64 keys. The numbers 0 to 9 require 10 keys. The alphabets require 26 keys. The above 19 commands require 19 keys. Thus the remaining 9 keys are available for expanding the command set. Additional commands like 'Total sales to a customer in the record, 'Today's' total sales to a purchaser', 'Today's' total transport by a vehicle no.' and 'Total sell in record' may be assigned to these keys.

16.2.2 Algorithms

After the initialisation of various peripherals and devices like LCD module and printer, the microprocessor displays the 'START' message, which is an indication to the operator to press any of the command keys. The microprocessor now keeps on waiting for the pressure of a command key. If any other key is pressed, it is ignored and the CPU further waits for a command key. This task is accomplished by a routine called keyboard monitor.

The keyboard monitor routine waits for a key pressure and decides the code of the pressed key and then passes it back to the calling program. The main calling program then compares this key code generated by the keyboard routine with standard predetermined hex codes to identify the pressed key. Then an appropriate subroutine is called, if a match is found, otherwise, an error message is flashed. After this subroutine is executed, the control is returned back to the display of 'START' message and subsequently the system is ready to accept the next command. If the pressed key is not a command key then, the control may not be returned back to the command mode but the necessary action may be completed, and the keyboard monitor may further wait for another alphanumeric key.

The flow chart of the main program is shown in Fig. 16.16. All the command processing routines are written independently and then tested with the main program one by one. Finally, the main program and all the tested subroutines may be transferred to EPROM.

As shown in Fig. 16.16 , the main program may call the 15 command routines. These 15 command routines may further call subroutines like the ADC routine that reads the output of the ADC, HEX-TO-DECIMAL routine that converts the hexadecimal ADC output to the decimal equivalent, calibrate routine that finds out the exact weight to be displayed from the decimal ADC output by multiplying it with a programmable constant or a routine that reads tare weight on the platform of the weighing bridge. An independent routine must be developed to derive the LCD display as already discussed. Also a separate routine may be developed to display the actual weight on a 7-segment display unit using 8279. A print routine that prints the current ticket buffer should also be developed for printing the various print data. In the following discussion, we elaborate the development of each of these routines.

Development of Individual Routines Initialization of all the peripherals—8255, 8253, 8279, 8251 and LCD module have already been discussed in this text. Also the section on 8279 and LCD display interfacing elaborate the routines to display the messages on the respective displays. In this section we discuss other system operation routines.

Direct Weighing Routine In the direct weighing mode, the LCD display and the 7-segment display, display the gross weight on the platform. Once the Direct Weighing mode (DW) is entered by pressing the DW key, the complete system keyboard is disabled. To pull the system out of the direct weighing mode, it must be resetted using the power on key or RST key. All other system functions are disabled in the DW mode. The flow chart of the routine in this mode is shown in Fig. 16.17.

Weighing Mode with Ticket Printing (WP) Routine As soon as the WP key is pressed, the system enters the weighing mode with ticket printing. In this mode, the system first accepts other details of the weighing operation like the name of the seller, name of the purchaser, material, tare weight, etc. The system then calculates the gross weight (like in DW mode), net weight, and then reads the date and time of the weighing and writes all these para-meters in the print buffer. After the P key is pressed, it prints the weighing ticket in the prespecified format. Thus the weighing ticket contains the above specified information. After the weighing ticket is printed, the system again returns to the 'START' message and is ready to accept the next command from the operator. After the weighing ticket is printed and the system is ready to accept the next command, the 'SW' key may be pressed to save the previous weighing operation into the record RAM. Otherwise, the 'WP' key may be pressed to continue the weighing operation.

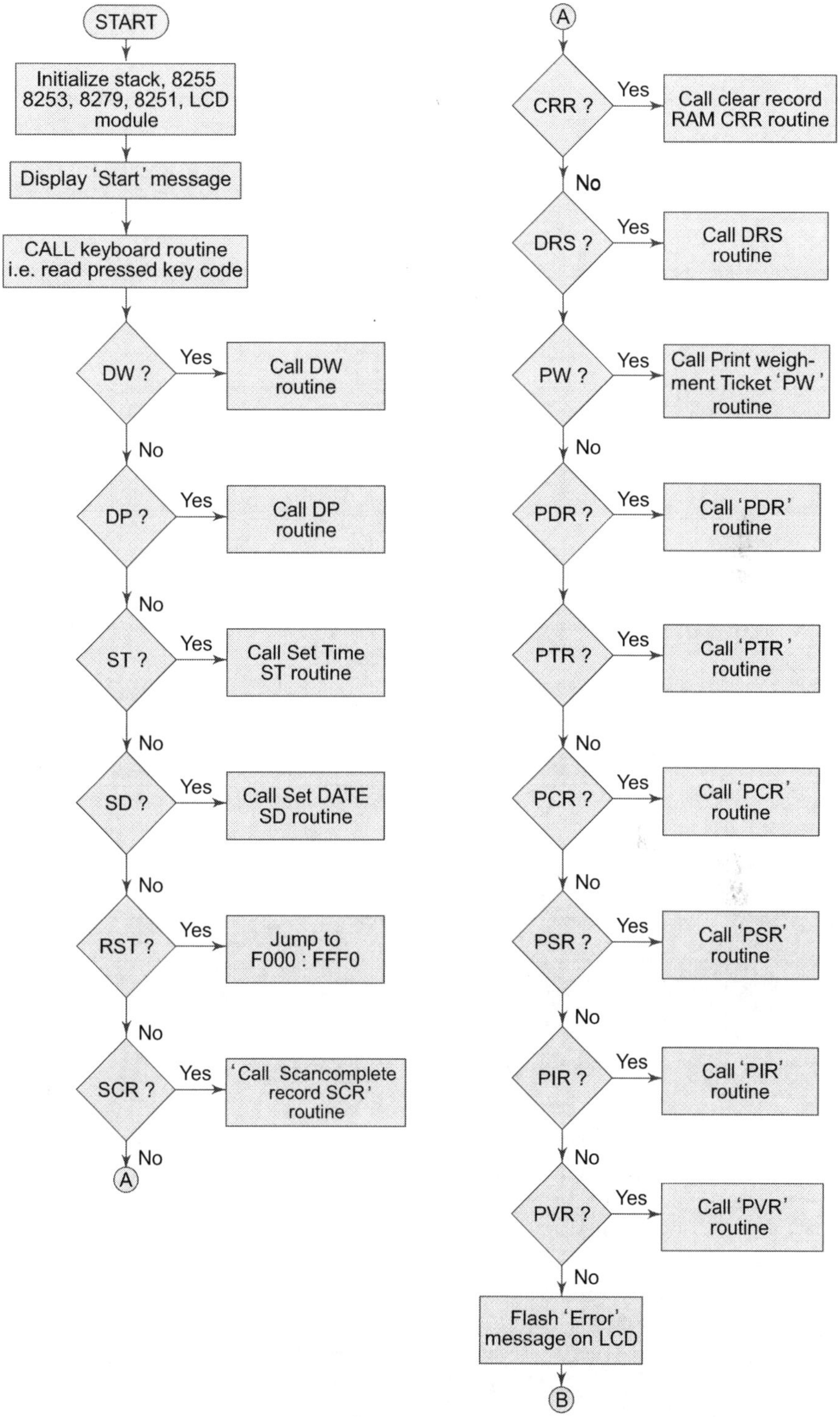

Fig. 16.16 *Complete Flow Chart of the Main Program*

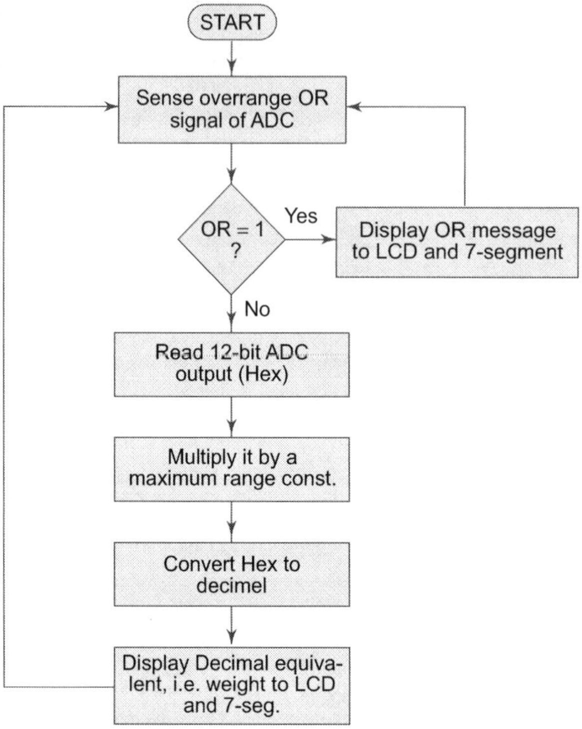

Fig. 16.17 *Flow Chart of DW Routine*

Record No.	-	190 Vehicle no. MH 31–505
Seller's Name	-	Ms Tata Steel Co.
Purchaser's Name.	-	Indian Railways
Date - 1-5-1996		
Time - 12.30 P.M.		
Material	-	Steel EN-21
Tare Weight	-	6000 kg.
Gross Weight	-	20000 kg.
Net Weight	-	14000 kg.

Fig. 16.18 *Typical Weighing Ticket*

This mode internally calls the keyboard routine to accept the alphanumeric weighing ticket data. It is expected that before entering the WP mode the operator sets the system time and date to get the correct system time and date on the weighing ticket. A typical weighing ticket print out is shown in Fig. 16.18.

The record number is the serial number of the weighing on that day and it may be used to find out the weighing at some latter instant from the record RAM. The system clock is expected to upgrade the system time and date appropriately, once they are initialized by the operator. The system date and time may be initialized after every power on operation. This routine calls the other routines like ADC, keyboard monitor (alphanumeric, next record, previous record, return, etc.). Figure 16.19 shows the flow chart of this routine.

The Weighing-Ticket-Data-Entry (WTDE) routine is basically an alphanumeric keyboard monitor that further senses the Next Field (NF), Previous Field (PF) and Return (R) keys. As already described, a weighingticket contains fields for record number, sellers name, purchasers name, etc. While entering each of these

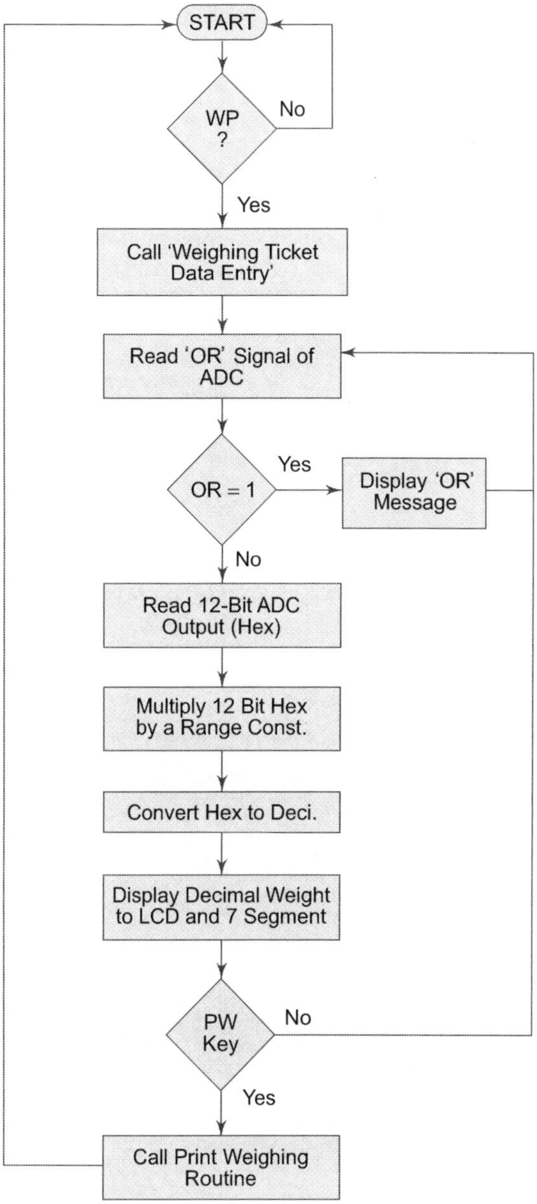

Fig. 16.19 *Flow Chart of WP Routine*

field data, the name of the field is automatically displayed on the LCD display and the user is to type the alphanumeric data. If the data entry for a particular field is over, the user will require to press either the Next Field (NF) or Previous Field (PF) key to go for the data entry of the Next or the Previous Field respectively. After all the fields' data entry is over, the user should press the Return R key to proceed with the weighing. The software internally maintains an image of the weighing ticket with the most recent data entered by the user, in the RAM. The complete weighing ticket can not be displayed on the LCD display and hence it is scrolled field by field. The NF and PF keys are used to scroll the image of the weighing ticket available in the memory over the display buffer of the LCD display unit.

The R key pulls the system out of this data entry mode and pushes it into the weighing mode. In the weighing mode, the system keeps on displaying the gross weight on the platform till the PW key is pressed. Once, the PW key is pressed, the weighing ticket is printed and the system returns to the start message.

Set Date and Set Time Routines These routines are called after the SD and ST keys are pressed. These two routines together implement a date and time calendar. The 8253 in the system is used to implement the clock program that calculates the time in terms of hours and minutes. These routines maintain a buffer in the RAM to store the current date and time. The clock program implements a real time clock that further upgrades the date counter. A look up table of 12 bytes may be defined for storing the days of the 12 months in a complete year. One of the 8253 counters is used for counting seconds and the 8253 counter is used in interrupt on terminal count mode.

An 8253 counter is driven by a 1 μ sec or 1MHz clock. The output of the counter is a 1 second clock (cascading may be required). The set time and set date routines are shown in Fig. 16.20. Figure 16.21 shows the flow chart of the clock routine.

The clock program is invoked as an interrupt service routine and works, in the background to modify the current time buffer, continuously.

Print Routines Overall, the system can execute seven print routines. Each of which is invoked by pressing a specific key. As soon as a key is pressed, the print routine is executed and the system returns to the 'START' message after the print job is over.

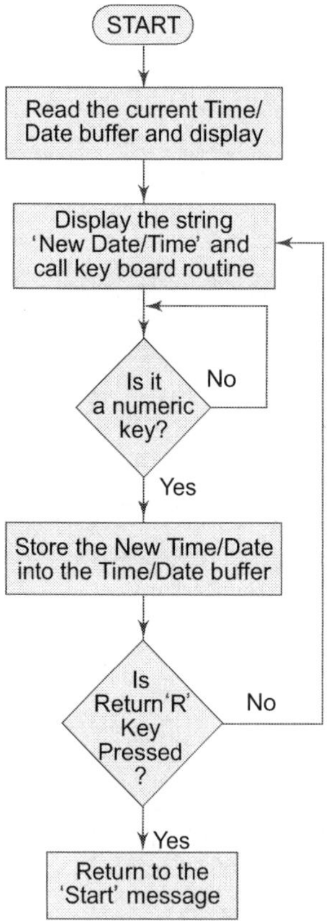

Fig. 16.20 *Flow Chart of SET DATE/TIME Routine*

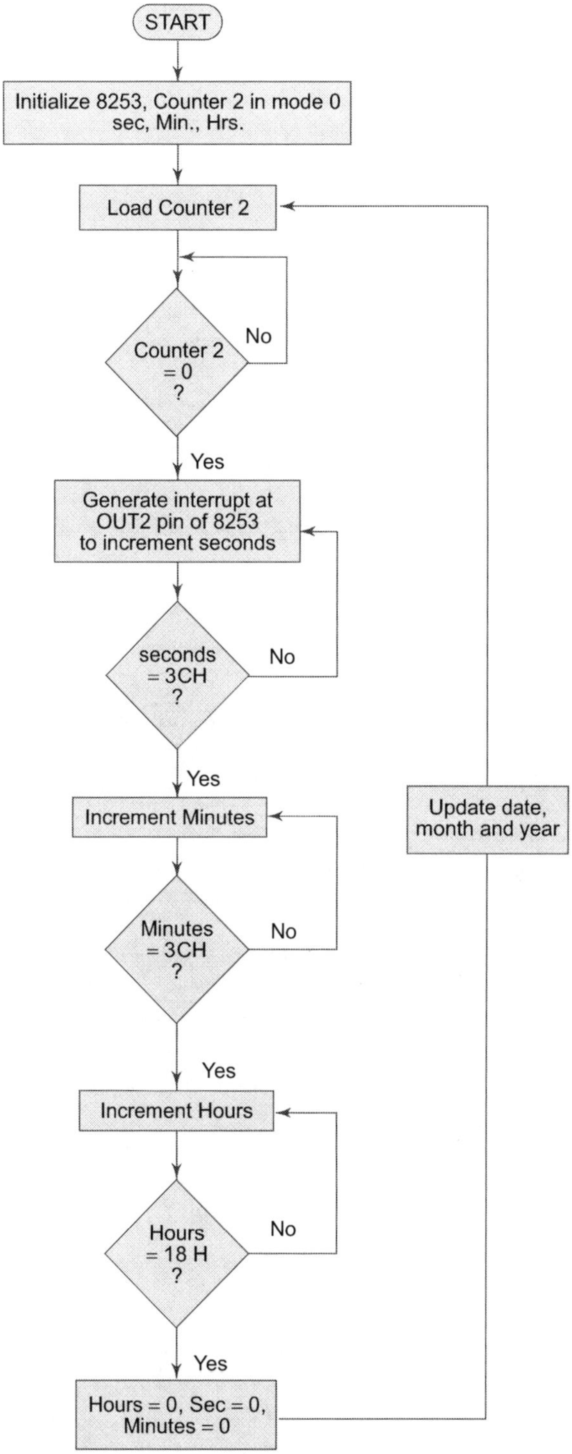

Fig. 16.21 *Flow Chart of the Clock Routine*

The most frequently called print routine is the PW routine. This routine prints the complete current weighing routine buffer. The printer routine has already been discussed for printing a character in Chapter 5. The print character routine is called again and again till the complete buffer has been printed. The flow chart of PW routine is shown in Fig. 16.22.

The other print routines, like, date-wise, customer-wise, item-wise routines etc. scan the record memory and compare the specific field of each record stored with that specified by the command. If it matches, the corresponding record is transferred to the current weighing buffer and then PW (Print Weighing) routine is called.

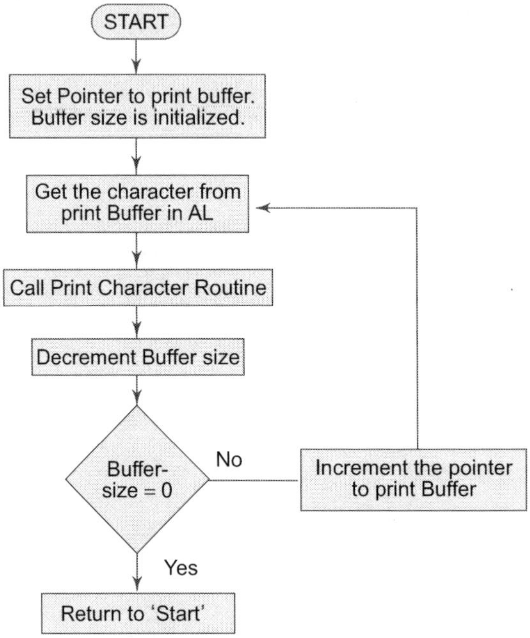

Fig. 16.22 *Flow Chart of PW Routine*

After the weighing is printed, the program compares the specified field with that of the next record. This continues for all the records stored in the record RAM. Flow chart of these routines is given in Fig. 16.23.

Clear Record RAM Routine This routine clears the record pointer and the complete record RAM. The record pointer is reset to zero and the RAM locations are filled by FFH.

Display Record Status This routine displays the number of valid weighing records stored in the record RAM and the number of records that can further be stored in the RAM.

Thus we have discussed all the modules of the weighing bridge software. A number of new facilities can be added to this system, and accordingly, new software modules can be developed.

16.3 CALIBRATION

Once the system is implemented and installed along with the load cells, and the weighing platform is placed over the load cells properly, the system is ready for calibration. As soon as the system is switched on, it displays the 'START' message. Initially, the system is calibrated for the direct weighing mode. In direct weighing mode, it will show some reading that may correspond to the weight of the platform. If this weight is non-zero, adjust the null adjustment potentiometer to obtain zero reading. Then place standard dead weights of say 5 tonnes at the centre of the platform. The display should show a reading near about 5000. If it is showing a slightly less or more reading, adjust the amplifier gain carefully to obtain the display **5000**. This adjustment

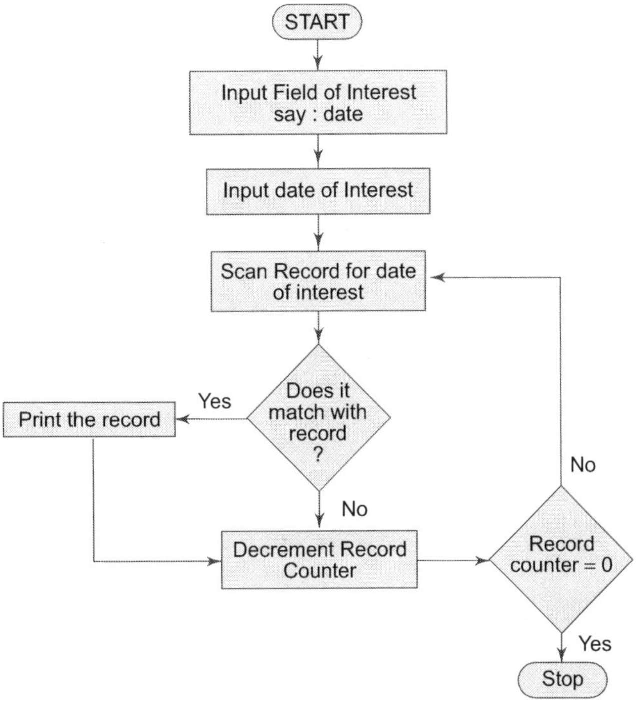

Fig. 16.23 *Itemwise Print Routine*

now disturbs the previous zero adjustment. Thus, the offset adjustment and the gain adjustment are mutually dependent. To achieve both of these adjustments, one will have to repeat these adjustments a few times. Once both of these adjustments are achieved, place the dead weight of 5 tonnes at each corner of the platform one by one and go on adjusting the corresponding variable resistor in the adder circuit connected at the input of the load cell under the corner. After all the four resistors corresponding to the four corners are adjusted properly, you will now get the same display for the same weight placed in the different corners of the weighing platform. Note that this corner adjustment may slightly disturb the offset and gain adjustment. The same procedure is repeated till all the three adjustments, viz. offset, gain and corner are achieved perfectly. Calibration of the bridge is a very important and a critical factor in the proper operation of the weighing bridge.

SUMMARY

In this chapter, we presented different design issues of an electronic weighing bridges right from its foundation, selection of load cells to the hardware and software design. Initially, the required mechanical structure and its foundation has been discussed in significant details. Then load cells, their selection and placement was described in brief. Further, the signal processing circuits like instrumentation amplifier and the analog to digital converter circuits were briefly described . The microprocessor system including LCD interfacing was then presented with necessary details. The keyboard display monitor of this system was then presented module-wise along with flowchart of each module. Further the calibration procedure was presented in brief. This chapter thus presented an overview of the system design procedure of an extremely important industrial weight measurement system—the electronic weighing bridge.

17 An Introduction to Architecture and programming 8051 and 80196

INTRODUCTION

While studying microprocessor based system design, one may note that a stand alone microprocessor is not self-sufficient. It requires other components like memory and input/output devices to form a minimum workable system configuration. Rather, one may infer that in addition to a microprocessor, the memory and I/O ports are integral parts of a practical system. To have all these components in a discrete form and to assemble them on a PCB, is usually not an affordable solution for the following reasons:

1. The overall system cost of a microprocessor based system built around a CPU, memory and other peripherals is high as compared to a microcontroller based system.
2. A large sized PCB is required for assembling all these components, resulting in an enhanced cost of the system.
3. Design of such PCBs require a lot of effort and time and thus the overall product design requires more time.
4. Due to the large size of the PCB and the discrete components used, physical size of the product is big and hence it is not handy.
5. As discrete components are used, the system is not reliable nor is it easy to trouble- shoot such a system.

Considering all these problems, Intel decided to integrate a microprocessor along with I/O ports and minimum memory into a single package. Another frequently used peripheral, a programmable timer, was also integrated to make this device a self-sufficient one. This device which contains a microprocessor and the above mentioned components has been named a *microcontroller*. A microcontroller a microprocessor with integrated peripherals. The introduction of microcontrollers drastically changed the microprocessor based system design concepts, specially in case of small dedicated systems. Design with microcontrollers has the following advantages:

1. As the peripherals are integrated into a single chip, the overall system cost is very low.
2. The size of the product is small as compared to the microprocessor based systems thus very handy.
3. The system design requires very little efforts and is easy to troubleshoot and maintain.

4. As the peripherals are integrated with a microprocessor, the system is more reliable.
5. Though a microcontroller may have on-chip RAM, ROM and I/O ports, additional RAM, ROM and I/O ports may be interfaced externally, if required.
6. The microcontrollers with on-chip ROM provide a software security feature which is not available with microprocessor based systems using ROM/EPROM.
7. All these features are available in a 40 pin package as in an 8-bit processor.

However, in case of a larger system disign, which requires more number of I/O ports and more memory capacity, the system designer may interface external I/O ports and memory with the system. In such cases, the microcontroller based systems are not so attractive as they are in case of the small dedicated systems. Figure 17.1 shows a typical microcontroller internal block diagram.

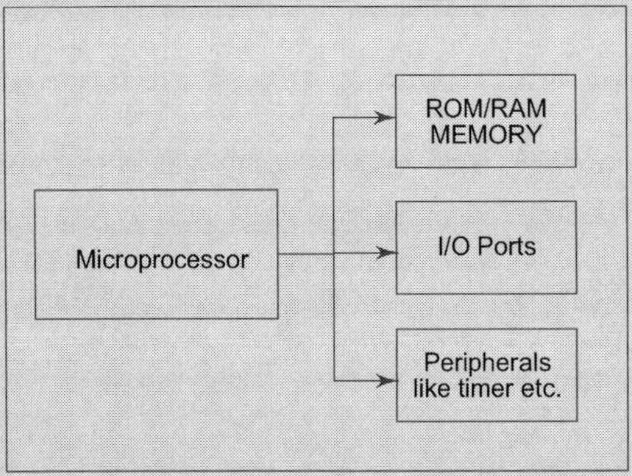

Fig. 17.1 *Microcontroller Internal Block Diagram*

As a microcontroller contains most of the components required to form a microprocessor system, it is sometimes called *a single chip microcomputer*. Since it also has the ability to easily implement simple control functions, it is most frequently called a microcontroller.

In this chapter, we will briefly present Intel's 8-bit microcontroller family, popularly known as MCS-51 family. In the end, we will introduce the architecture and general features of Intel's 16-bit microcontroller family called MCS-96.

17.1 INTEL'S FAMILY OF 8-BIT MICROCONTROLLERS

The earlier versions of Intel's microcontrollers do not have on-chip EPROM. 8031 was one such microcontroller from Intel, followed by the 8051 family. 8751 was the first microcontroller version with on-chip EPROM, followed by a number of 8751 versions with slight modifications. Recently, an electrically programmable and erasable version of 8051, named as 8951, has been introduced. Table 17.1 shows the comparison between different versions of 8051. All these members of the 8051 family have identical instruction set and similar architecture with slight variations as shown in Table 17.1.

Table 17.1 *Intel's MCS51 Family Microcontrollers and their Comparison*

Microprocontroller Version	*EPROM*	*RAM Bytes*	*8-bit I/O Ports*	*Timers 16-bit*	*UART*	*Power Down and Idle Modes*
8031	–	128	4	2	✓	–
8031 AH	–	128	4	2	✓	–
8051	–	128	4	2	✓	–
8051AH	–	128	4	2	✓	–
80C51BH	–	128	4	2	✓	✓
80C51FA	–	256	4	3	✓	✓
80C31BH	–	128	4	2	✓	✓
8751 H	4k	128	4	2	✓	–
8751 BH	4k	128	4	2	✓	–
87C51	4k	128	4	2	✓	✓
87C51FA/83C51FA	8K	256	4	3	✓	✓
87C51FB/83C51FB	16K	256	4	3	✓	✓

17.2 ARCHITECTURE OF 8051

The internal architecture of 8051 is presented in Fig. 17.2. The functional description of each block is presented briefly below.

Accumulator (ACC) The accumulator register (ACC or A) acts as an operand register, in case of some instructions. This may either be implicit or specified in the instruction. The ACC register has been allotted an address in the on-chip special function register bank.

B Register This register is used to store one of the operands for multiply and divide instructions. In other instructions, it may just be used as a scratch pad. This register is considered as a special function register.

Program Status Word (PSW) This set of flags contains the status information and is considered as one of the special function registers.

Stack Pointer (SP) This 8-bit wide register is incremented before the data is stored onto the stack using push or call instructions. This register contains 8-bit stack top address. The stack may be defined anywhere in the on-chip 128-byte RAM. After reset, the SP register is initialised to 07. After each write to stack operation, the 8-bit contents of the operand are stored onto the stack, after incrementing the SP register by one. Thus if SP contains 07 H, the forthcoming PUSH operation will store the data at address 08H in the internal RAM. The SP content will be incremented to 08. The 8051 stack is not a top-down data structure, like other Intel processors. This register has also been allotted an address in the special function register bank.

Data Pointer (DTPR) This 16-bit register contains a higher byte (DPH) and the lower byte (DPL) of a 16-bit external data RAM address. It is accessed as a 16-bit register or two 8-bit registers as specified above. It has been allotted two addresses in the special function register bank, for its two bytes DPH and DPL.

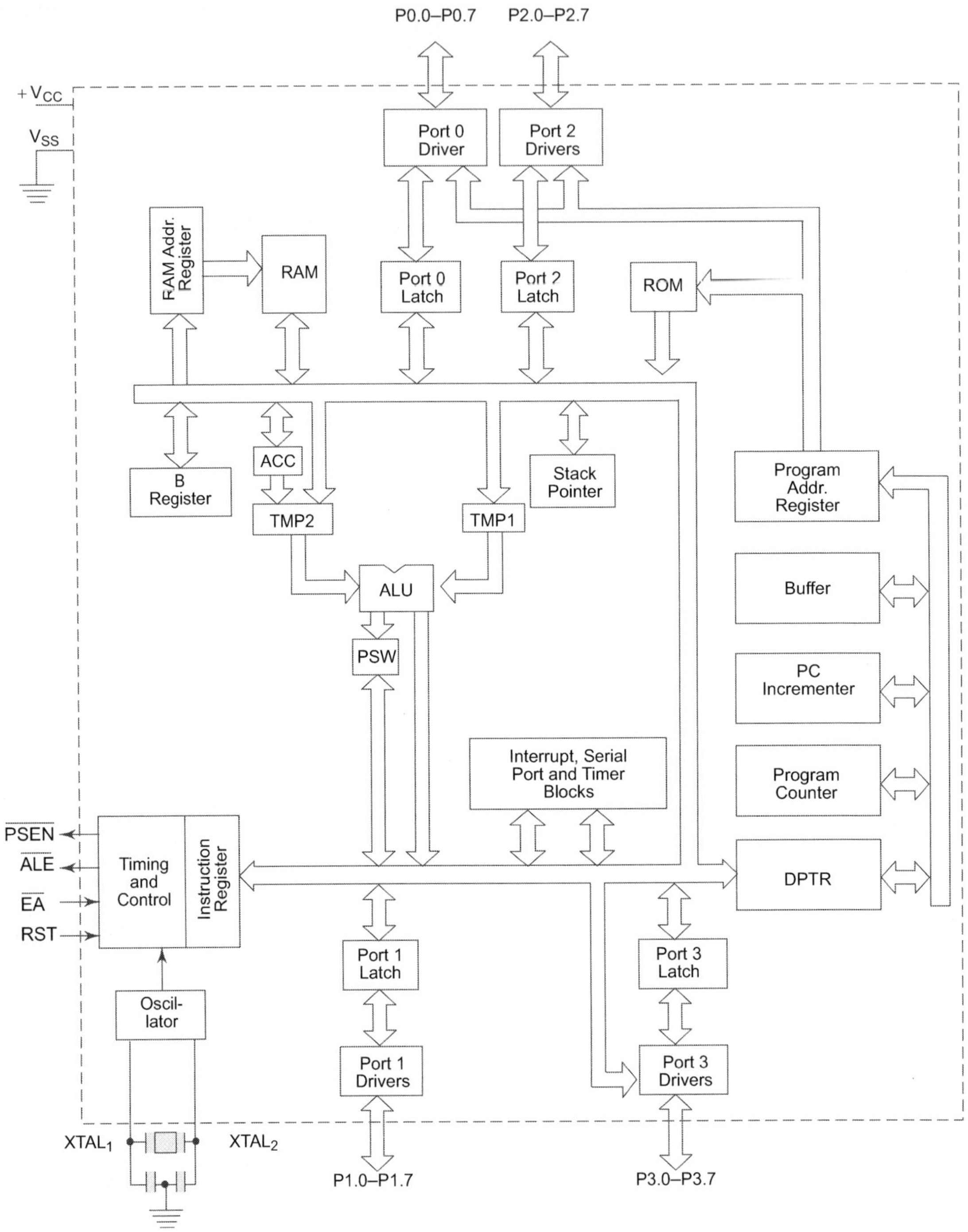

Fig. 17.2 *8051 Block Diagram (Intel Corp.)*

Port 0 to 3 Latches and Drivers These four latches and driver pairs are allotted to each of the four on-chip I/O ports. These latches have been allotted addresses in the special function register bank. Using the allotted addresses, the user can communicate with these ports. These are identified as P0, P1, P2 and P3.

Serial Data Buffer The serial data buffer internally contains two independent registers. One of them is a transmit buffer which is necessarily a parallel-in serial-out register. The other is called receive buffer which is a serial-in parallel-out register. Loading a byte to the transmit buffer initiates serial transmission of that byte. The serial data buffer is identifed as SBUF and is one of the special function registers. If a byte is written to SBUF, it initiates serial transmission and if the SBUF is read, it reads received serial data.

Timer Registers These two 16-bit registers can be accessed as their lower and upper bytes. For example, TL0 represents the lower byte of the timing register 0, while TH0 represents higher bytes of the timing register 0. Similarly, TL1 and TH1 represent lower and higher bytes of timing register 1. All these registers can be accessed using the four addresses allotted to them which lie in the special function registers SFR address range, i.e. 80 H to FF.

Control Registers The special function registers IP, IE, TMOD, TCON, SCON and PCON contain control and status information for interrupts, timers/counters and serial port. These registers will be described later in this chapter. All of these registers have been allotted addresses in the special function register bank of 8051.

Timing and Control Unit This unit derives all the necessary timing and control signals required for the internal operation of the circuit. It also derives control signals required for controlling the external system bus.

Oscillator This circuit generates the basic timing clock signal for the operation of the circuit using crystal oscillator.

Instruction Register This register decodes the opcode of an instruction to be executed and gives information to the timing and control unit to generate necessary signals for the execution of the instruction.

EPROM and Program Address Register These blocks provide an on-chip EPROM and a mechanism to internally address it. Note that EPROM is not available in all 8051 versions.

RAM and RAM Address Register These blocks provide internal 128 bytes of RAM and a mechanism to address it internally.

ALU The arithmetic and logic unit performs 8-bit arithmetic and logical operations over the operands held by the temporary registers TMP1 and TMP2. Users cannot access these temporary registers.

SFR Register Bank This is a set of special function registers, which can be addressed using their respective addresses which lie in the range 80H to FFH.

Finally, the interrupt, serial port and timer units control and perform their specific functions under the control of the timing and control unit.

17.3 SIGNAL DESCRIPTIONS OF 8051

8051 is available in a 40-pin plastic and ceramic DIP packages. The pin diagram of 8051 is shown in Fig. 17.3 followed by description of each pin.

V_{cc} This is a +5 V supply voltage pin

Vss This is a return pin for the supply.

RESET The reset input pin resets the 8051, only when it goes high for two or more machine cycles. For a proper reinitialization after reset, the clock must be running.

ALE/PROG The address latch enable output pulse indicates that the valid address bits are available on their respective pins. This ALE signal is valid only for external memory accesses. Normally, the ALE pulses

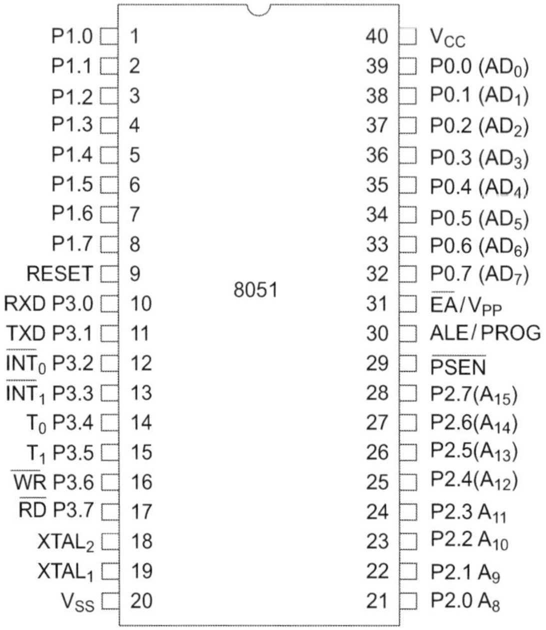

Fig. 17.3 *8051 Pin Configuration (Intel Corp.)*

are emitted at a rate of one-sixth of the oscillator frequency. This pin acts as program pulse input during on-chip EPROM programming. ALE may be used for external timing or clocking purpose. One ALE pulse is skipped during each access to external data memory.

$\overline{EA}/V_{pp}$ External access enable pin, if tied low, indicates that the 8051 can address external program memory. In other words, the 8051 can execute a program in external memory, only if $\overline{EA}$ is tied low. For execution of programs in internal memory, the $\overline{EA}$ must be tied high. This pin also receives 21 volts for programming of the on-chip EPROM.

$\overline{PSEN}$ Program store enable is an active-low output signal that acts as a strobe to read the external program memory. This goes low during external program memory accesses.

Port 0 (P0.0–P0.7) Port 0 is an 8-bit bidirectional bit addressable I/O port. This has been allotted an address in the SFR address range. Port 0 acts as multiplexed address/data lines during external memory access, i.e. when is low and ALE emits a valid signal. In case of controllers with on-chip EPROM, Port 0 receives code bytes during programming of the internal EPROM.

Port 1 (P1.0–P1.7) Port 1 acts as an 8-bit bidirectional bit addressable port. This has been allotted an address in the SFR address range.

Port 2 (P2.0–P2.7) Port 2 acts as 8-bit bidirectional bit addressable I/O port. It has been allotted an address in the SFR address range of 8051. During external memory accesses, port 2 emits higher eight bits of address (A_8–A_{15}) which are valid, if ALE goes high and EA is low. P2 also receives higher order address bits during programming of the on-chip EPROM.

Port 3 (P3.0–P3.7) Port 3 is an 8-bit bidirectional bit addressable I/O port which has been allotted an address in the SFR address range of 8051. The port 3 pins also serve the alternative functions as listed in the Table 17.2.

Table 17.2 *Alternate Functions of Pins of Port 3 (Intel Corp.)*

Port 3 Pin	*Alternative Function*
P3.0	Acts as serial input data pin (RXD)
P3.1	Acts as serial output data pin (TXD)
P3.2	Acts as external interrupt pin 0 ($\overline{INT_0}$)
P3.3	Acts as external interrupt input pin 1 ($\overline{INT_1}$)
P3.4	Acts as external input to timer 0 (T0)
P3.5	Acts as external input to timer 1(T1)
P3.6	Acts as write control signal for external data memory ($\overline{WR}$)
P3.7	Acts as read control signal for external data memory read operation ($\overline{RD}$)

$XTAL_1$ and $XTAL_2$ There is an inbuilt oscillator which derives the necessary clock frequency for the operation of the controller. $XTAL_1$ is the input of amplifier and $XTAL_2$ is the output of the amplifier. A crystal is to be connected externally between these two pins to complete the feedback path to start oscillations. The controller can be operated on an external clock. In this case the external clock is fed to the controller at pin $XTAL_2$ and $XTAL_1$ pin should be grounded. Commercially available versions of 8051 run on 12 MHz to 16 MHz frequency.

17.4 REGISTER SET OF 8051

8051 has two 8-bit registers, registers A and B, which can be used to store operands, as allowed by the instruction set. Internal temporary registers of 8051 are not user accessible. Including these A and B registers, 8051 has a family of special purpose registers known as, Special Function Registers (SFRs). There are, in total, 21-bit addressable, 8-bit registers. ACC (A), B, PSW, P0, P1, P2, P3, IP, IE, TCON and SCON are all 8-bit, bit-addressable registers. The remaining registers, namely, SP, DPH, DPL, TMOD, TH0, TL0, TH1, TL1, SBUF and PCON registers are to be addressed as bytes, i.e. they are not bit-addressable. The registers DPH and DPL are the higher and lower bytes of a 16-bit register DPTR, i.e. data pointer, which is used for accessing external data memory. Starting 32-bytes of on-chip RAM may be used as general purpose registers. They have been allotted addresses in the range from 0000H to 001FH. These 32, 8-bit registers are divided into four groups of 8 registers each, called register banks. At a time only one of these four groups, i.e. banks can be accessed. The register bank to be accessed can be selected using the RS1 and RS0 bits of an internal register called program status word.

The registers TH0 and TL0 form a 16-bit counter/timer register with H indicating the upper byte and L indicating the lower byte of the 16-bit timer register T0. Similarly, TH1 and TL1 form the 16-bit count for the timer T1. The four port latches are represented by P0, P1, P2 and P3. Any communication with these ports is established using the SFR addresses to these registers. Register SP is a stack pointer register. Register PSW is a flag register and contains status information. Register IP can be programmed to control the interrupt priority. Register IE can be programmed to control interrupts, i.e. enable or disable the interrupts. TCON is called timer/counter control register. Some of the bits of this register are used to turn the timers on or off. This register also contains interrupt control flags for external interrupts $\overline{INT_1}$ and $\overline{INT_0}$. The register TMOD is used for programming the modes of operation of the timers/counters. The SCON register is a serial port mode control register and is used to control the operation of the serial port. The SBUF register acts as a serial data buffer for transmit and receive operations. The PCON register is called power control register. This register contains power down bit and idle bit which activate the power down mode and idle mode in 80C51BH. There are two power saving modes of operation provided in the CHMOS version, namely, *idle mode* and *power down mode.*

In the *idle mode*, the oscillator continues to run and the interrupt, serial port and timer blocks are active but the clock to the CPU is disabled. The CPU status is preserved. This mode can be terminated with a hardware interrupt or hardware reset signal. After this, the CPU resumes program execution from where it left off.

In *power down mode*, the on-chip oscillator is stopped. All the functions of the controller are held maintaining the contents of RAM. The only way to terminate this mode is hardware reset. The reset redefines all the SFRs but the RAM contents are left unchanged. Both of these modes can be entered by setting the respective bit in an internal register called PCON register using software.

The PCON register also contains two general purpose flags and a double baud rate bit. All these registers are listed in Table 17.3 along with their SFR addresses and contents after reset.

Table 17.3 *SFR Registers, their Addresses and Contents after Reset*

Register	*Bit Addressable*	*Address (SFR)*	*Content After Reset*
ACC	Y	0E0H	0000 0000
B	Y	0F0H	0000 0000
PSW	Y	0D0H	0000 0000
SP	N	81H	0000 0111
DPH	N	82H	0000 0000
DPL	N	83H	0000 0000
P0	Y	80H	1111 1111
P1	Y	90H	1111 1111
P2	Y	0A0H	1111 1111
P3	Y	0B0H	1111 1111
IP	Y	0B8H	XX0 0000
IE	Y	0A8H	0XX0 0000
TMOD	N	89H	0000 0000
TCON	Y	88H	0000 0000
TH0	N	8CH	0000 0000
TL0	N	8AH	0000 0000
TH1	N	8DH	0000 0000
TL1	N	8BH	0000 0000
SCON	Y	98H	0000 0000
SBUF	N	99H	Indeterminate
PCON	N	87H	HMOS 0XXX XXXX
			CHMOS 0XXX 0000

Y–Yes
N–Nom
X–Undefined

17.5 IMPORTANT OPERATIONAL FEATURES OF 8051—PROGRAM STATUS WORD (PSW)

This bit-addressable register has the following format as shown in Fig. 17.4. The bit descriptions are presented along with the format.

D_7	D_6	D_5	D_4	D_3	D_2	D_1	D_0
CY	AC	F0	RS_1	RS_0	OV	—	P

CY	D_7	Carry Flag.
AC	D_6	Auxiliary carry Flag.
F0	D_5	Flag 0 is available to the user for general purpose.
RS_1	D_4	Register Bank selector bit 1.
RS_0	D_3	Register Bank selector bit 0.

The value presented by RS_0 and RS_1 bits select the corresponding register bank as shown below.

RS_1	RS_0	Register Bank	Address
0	0	0	00H-07H
0	1	1	08H-0FH
1	0	2	10H-17H
1	1	3	18H-1FH

OV	D_2	Overflow Flag.
—	D_1	User definable flags (Reserved for future use)
P	D_0	Parity flag is set/cleared by hardware in each instruction cycle to indicate an odd/even number of '1' bits in the accumulator

Fig. 17.4 *Format of PSW (Intel Corp.)*

17.6 MEMORY AND I/O ADDRESSING BY 8051

17.6.1 Memory Addressing

The total memory of an 8051 system is logically divided into program memory and data memory. Program memory stores the programs to be executed, while data memory stores the data like intermediate results, variables and constants required for the execution of the program. Program memory is invariably implemented using EPROM, because it stores only program code which is to be executed and thus it need not be written into. However, the data memory may be read from or written to and thus it is implemented using RAM.

Further, the program memory and data memory both may be categorized as on-chip (internal) and external memory, depending upon whether the memory physically exists on the chip or it is externally interfaced. The 8051 can address 4 Kbytes on-chip program memory whose map starts from 0000H and ends at 0FFFH. It can address 64 Kbytes of external program memory under the control of $\overline{PSEN}$ signal, whose address map is from 0000H to FFFFH. Here, one may note that the map of internal program memory overlaps with that of the external program memory. However, these two memory spaces can be distinguished using the $\overline{PSEN}$ signal. In case of ROM-less versions of 8051, the $\overline{PSEN}$ signal is used to access the external program memory. Conceptually this is shown in Fig. 17.5.

8051 supports 64 Kbytes of external data memory whose map starts at 0000H and ends at FFFFH. This external data memory can be accessed under the control of register DPTR, which stores the addresses for external data memory accesses. 8051 generates $\overline{RD}$ and $\overline{WR}$ signals during external data memory accesses. The chip select line of the external data memory may be derived from the address lines as in the case of other microprocessors. Internal data memory of 8051 consists of two parts; the first is the RAM block of 128 bytes (256 bytes in case of some versions of 8051) and the second is the set of addresses from 80H to FFH, which includes the addresses allotted to the special function registers.

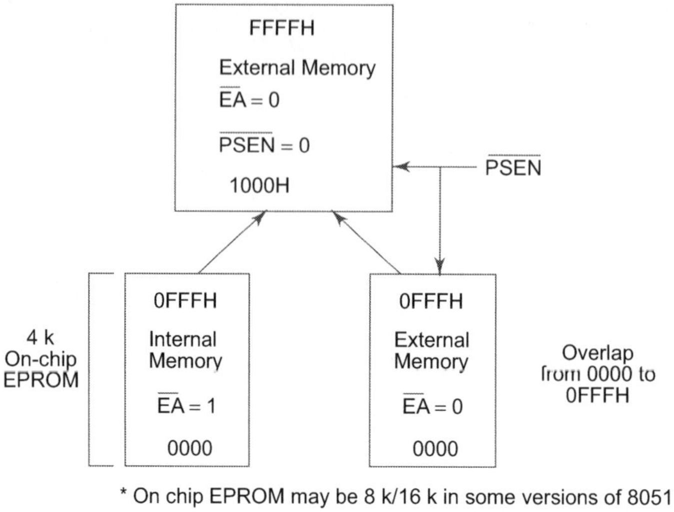

Fig. 17.5 *Program Memory Map of an 8051 System*

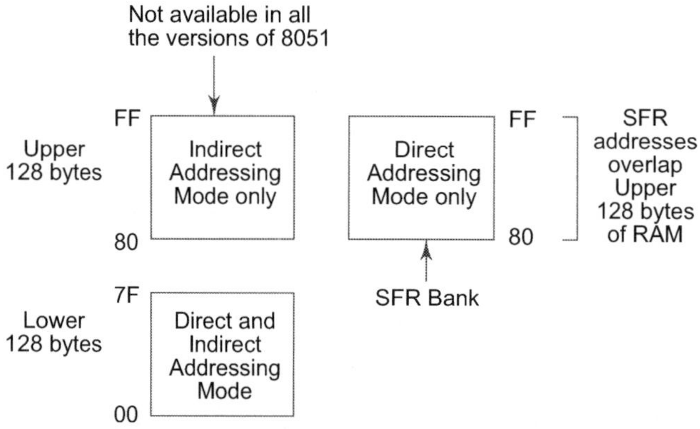

Fig. 17.6 *Internal Data Memory of 8051*

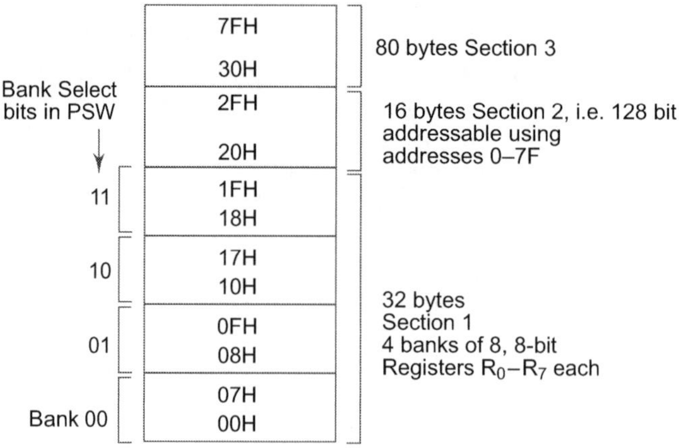

Fig. 17.7 *Functional Description of Internal Lower 128 Bytes of RAM*

The address map of the 8051 internal 128 bytes RAM starts from 00 and ends at 7FH. This RAM can be addressed by using direct or indirect mode of addressing. However, the special function register address map, i.e. from 80H to FFH is accessible only with direct addressing mode. In case of 8051 versions with 256 bytes on-chip RAM, the map starts from 00H and ends at FFH. In this case, it may be noted that the address map of special function registers, i.e. 80H to FFH overlaps with the upper 128 bytes of RAM. However, the way of addressing, i.e. addressing mode, differentiates between these two memory spaces. The upper 128 bytes of the 256 byte on-chip RAM can be accessed only using indirect addressing, while the lower 128 bytes can be accessed using direct or indirect mode of addressing. The special function register address space can only be accessed using direct addressing. The address map of the internal RAM and SFR is shown in Fig. 17.6.

The lower 128 bytes of RAM whose address map is from 00 to 7FH is functionally organised in three sections. The address block from 00 to 1FH, i.e. the lowest 32 bytes which form the first section, is divided into four banks of 8-bit registers, denoted as bank 00,01,10 and 11. Each of these banks contain eight 8-bit registers. The stack pointer gets initialized at address 07H, i.e. the last address of the bank 00, after reset operation. After reset bank 0 is selected by default but the actual stack data is stored from 08H onwards, i.e. bank 01, 10 and 11. These bank addressing bits of the register banks are present in PSW, to select one of these banks at a time. The

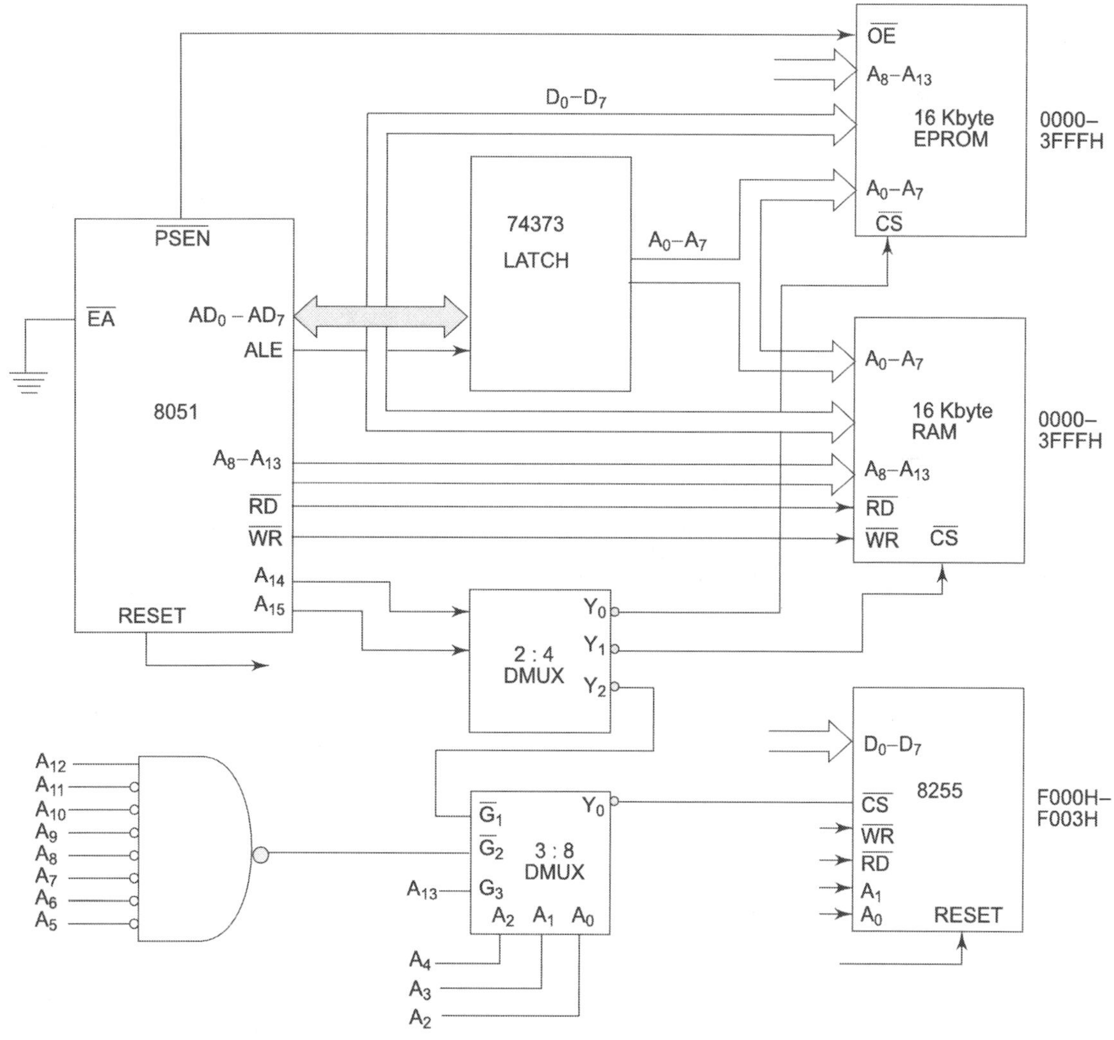

Fig. 17.8 *Interfacing External Memory and I/O with 8051*

second section extends from 20H to 2FH, i.e. 16 bytes, which is a bit-addressable block of memory, containing $16 \times 8 = 128$ bits. Each of these bits can be addressed using the addresses 00 to 7FH. Any of these bits can be accessed in two ways. In the first, its bit number is directly mentioned in the instruction while in the second the bit is mentioned with its position in the respective register byte. For example, the bits 0 to 7 can be referred directly by their numbers, i.e. 0 to 7 or using the notations 20.0 to 20.7 respectively. Note that 20 is the address of the first byte of the on-chip RAM. The third block of internal memory occupies addresses from 30H to 7FH. This block of memory is a byte addressable memory space. In general, this third block of memory is used as stack memory. All the internal data memory locations are accessed using 8-bit addresses under appropriate modes of addressing. Figure 17.7 shows the categorization of 128 bytes of internal RAM into the different sections.

17.6.2 External I/O Interfacing

Internally, 8051 has two timers, one serial input/output port and four 8-bit, bit-addressable ports. Some complex applications may require additional I/O devices to be interfaced with 8051. Such external I/O devices are interfaced with 8051 as external memory-mapped devices. In other words, the devices are treated as external memory locations, and they consume external memory addresses. Figure 17.8 shows a system that has external RAM memory of 16 Kbytes, ROM of 16 Kbytes and one chip of 8255 interfaced externally to an 8051 family microcontroller.

Note that, the maps of external program and data memory may overlap, as the memory spaces are logically separated in an 8051 system. As the 8255 is interfaced in external data memory space its addresses are of 16-bits.

17.7 INTERRUPTS AND STACK OF 8051

8051 provides five sources of interrupts. $\overline{INT_0}$ and $\overline{INT_1}$ are the two external interrupt inputs. These can either be edge-sensitive or level-sensitive, as programmed with bits IT_0 and IT_1 in register TCON. These interrupts are processed internally by the flags IE_0 and IE_1. If the interrupts are programmed as edge-sensitive, these flags are automatically cleared after the control is transferred to the respective vector. On the other hand, if the interrupts are programmed level-sensitive, these flags are controlled by the external interrupts sources themselves. Both timers can be used in timer or counter mode. In counter mode, it counts the pulses at T_0 or T_1 pin. In timer mode, oscillator clock is divided by a prescaler (1/32) and then given to the timer. So clock frequency for timer is 1/32 th of the controller operating frequency. The timer is an up-counter and generates an interrupt when the count has reached FFFFH. It can be operated in four different modes that can be set by TMOD register.

The timer 0 and timer 1 interrupt sources are generated by TF_0 and TF_1 bits of the register TCON, which are set, if a rollover takes place in their respective timer registers, except timer 0 in mode 3. When these interrupts are generated, the respective flags are automatically cleared after the control is transferred to the respective interrupt service routines.

The serial port interrupt is generated, if at least one of the two bits RI and TI is set. Neither of the flags is cleared, after the control is transferred to the interrupt service routine. The RI and TI flags need to be cleared using software, after deciding, which one of these two caused the interrupt. This is accomplished in the interrupt service routine.

In addition to these five interrupts, 8051 also allows single step interrupts to be generated with help of software. The external interrupts, if programmed level-sensitive, should remain high for at least two machine cycles for being sensed. If the external interrupts are programmed edge-sensitive, they should remain high for at least one machine cycle and low for at least one machine cycle, for being sensed.

The interrupt structure of 8051 provides two levels of the interrupt priorities for its sources of interrupt. Each interrupt source can be programmed to have one of these two levels using the interrupt priority register IP. The different sources of interrupts programmed to have the same level of priority, further follow a sequence of priority under that level as shown:

Interrupt Source	Priority within a level	Vectors
IE0 (External INT0)	Highest	0003H
TF0 (Timer 0)	⋮	000BH
IE1 (External INT1)	⋮	0013H
TF1 (Timer 1)	⋮	001BH
RI = TI (Serial Port)	Lowest	0023H

All these interrupts are enabled using a special function register called *interrupt enable register* (IE) and their priorities are programmed using another special function register called *interrupt priority register* (IP), described in Chapter 18.

8051 stack operations are 8-bit wide i.e. in an operation using PUSH or POP instruction one byte of data is stored on to stack or retrieved from the stack. In case of internal 16 bit address push or pop to/from the stack, the operation is implemented byte by byte i.e. lower byte first followed by higher byte. The SP register is an 8-bit register and is initialized to internal RAM address 07H after reset. Obviously, the capabilities of stack in 8051 are limited compared to microprocessors. Fig. 17.9(a) shows operation of PUSH instruction. The SP registers points to stack top. The stack top is always assumed to be preoccupied. So the SP is incremented first. Then 8 bit content of the 8-bit address provided as operand is pushed on to the stack memory address available in SP.

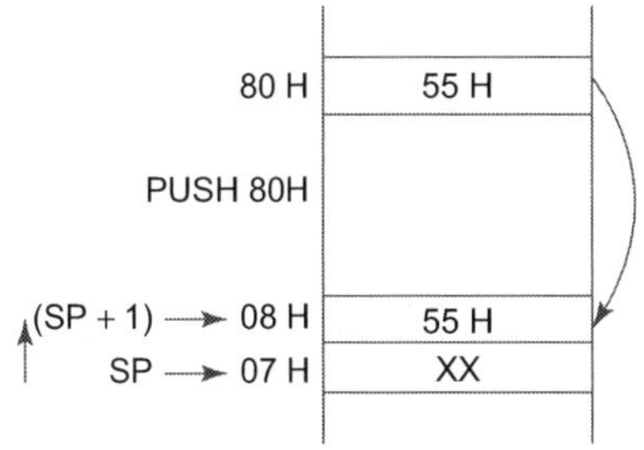

Fig. 17.9 *(a) Storing into Stack Memory*

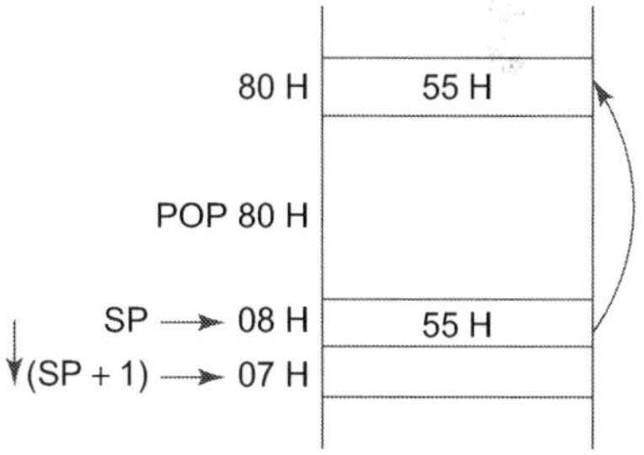

Fig. 17.9 (b) *Retrieving from Stack Memory*

Thus the PUSH instruction has following two steps.

1. Increment stack by 1.
2. Store 8-bit content of the 8-bit address specified in the instruction to the address pointed to by SP.

Complementarily, POP operation has the following two steps as shown in Fig. 17.9(b).

1. Store the content of top of stack pointed to by SP register to the 8 bit memory specified in the instruction.
2. Decrement SP by 1.

It must be kept in mind that as the stack of 8051 is always initialized in internal memory as the SP is only of 8 bits, the stack memory size is very limited. The direction of 8051 stack is opposite to that in 8085 or 8086 i.e. in 8085 it is autodecrement while in 8051 it is auto-increment during push operations. For implementing 16-bit operations two 8-bit operations are cascaded.

17.8 ADDRESSING MODES OF 8051

This section presents an overview of the addressing modes supported by 8051 without going into the details of the instruction set. All the members of MCS-51 family support an identical instruction set which is optimized for control applications.

8051 instruction set supports six addressing modes as listed:

1. Direct Addressing
2. Indirect Addressing

3. Register Instructions
4. Register Specific (Register Implicit)
5. Immediate mode
6. Indexed Addressing

The symbols and their meanings help in understanding the addressing modes of different instructions are given in Table 17.4.

Table 17.4 *Symbols and Meanings of Addressing Modes of 8051*

'R_n'-	Represents one of the registers R_7–R_0 of the currently selected bank.
'Direct'-	Represents 8-bit address of either internal data RAM or SFR register.
'@R_i'-	Represents 8-bit internal data RAM address addressed indirectly using one of the registers R_0 or R_1.
'#data'-	Represents 8-bit immediate data present in an instruction.
'#data 16'-	Represents 16-bit immediate data present in an instruction.
'addr 16'-	Represents 16-bit destination address which is used by LCALL or LJMP instruction to specify the call or jump destination address, within 64 Kbytes program memory. The label of the jump address may even be directly specified in the instruction in place of the address.
'addr 11'-	Represents 11-bit destination address, used by ACALL and AJMP instructions to specify the respective call or jump addresses within the same 2 Kbytes page size of the program memory, in which the first byte of the instruction lies. The label of the jump address may even be directly specified in the instruction in place of the address.
'rel'-	This is a signed 8-bit offset byte in 2's complement form, used by all the conditional jump instructions. It ranges from 128 to 127 from the first byte of the instruction. The negative offset indicates the backward jump while the positive offset indicates a forward jump. The label of the jump address may even be directly specified in the instruction in place of the address.
'bit-	This is a direct accessible bit either in any of the bit addressable special function registers or the bit addressable area of the internal 128 bytes RAM, i.e. (20H to 2FH). The bit addressing methods have been discussed in the previous sections.

The addressing modes supported by 8051 are discussed further in brief.

Direct Addressing In this mode of addressing, the operands are specified using the 8-bit address field, in the instruction format. Only internal data RAM and SFRS can be directly addressed.

Example 17.1 `MOV R0, 89H.`

Here 89H is address of a special function register TMOD.

Indirect Addressing In this mode of addressing, the 8-bit address of an operand is stored in a register and the register, instead of the 8-bit address, is specified in the instruction. The registers R_0 and R_1 of the selected bank of registers or stack pointer can be used as address registers for storing the 8-bit addresses .

The address register for 16-bit addresses can only be 'data pointer' (DPTR).

Example 17.2 `ADD A, @ R0`

Register Instructions In this addressing mode, operands are stored in the registers R_0–R_7 of the selected register bank. One of these eight registers (R_0–R_7) is specified in the instruction using the 3-bit register specification field of the opcode format. A register bank can be selected using the two bank select bits of the PSW.

Example 17.3 `ADD A, R7.`

Register Specific Instructions In this type of instructions, the operand is implicitly specified using one of the registers. Some of the instructions always operate only on a specific register. These type of instructions fall under this category.

Example 17.4 `RLA;` This instruction rotates accumulator left.

Immediate Mode In this mode, an immediate data, i.e. a constant is specified in the instruction, after the opcode byte.

Example 17.5 `ADD A, #100`

Immediate data 100 (decimal) is added to the contents of accumulator. For specifying a hex number in this type of instruction, it should be followed by H.

Indexed Addressing Only program memory can be accessed using this addressing mode. Basically, this mode of addressing is accomplished in 8051 for look-up table manipulations. Program counter or data pointer are the allowed 16-bit address storage registers, in this mode of addressing. These 16-bit registers point to the base of the look-up table and the ACC register contains a code to be converted using the look-up table. In other words, it contains the relative address of the code in the look-up table. The look-up table data address is found out by adding the contents of register ACC with that of the program counter or Data Pointer.

In case of jump instruction, the contents of accumulator are added with one of the specified 16-bit registers to form the jump destination address.

Example 17.6

```
MOVC A,     @ A+DPTR
JMP         @ A+DPTR
```

For details of instruction set readers may reffer to Intel's data book titled **'8-bit Embeded controllers'**: Summary of 8051 instruction set is presented in appendix C.

17.9 8051 INSTRUCTION SET

8051 Instructions can be categorized in the following categories.

1. Data Transfer instructions
2. Arithmetic Instructions
3. Logical Instructions
4. Boolean Instructions
5. Control transfer instructions

The do's and don'ts while using the 8051 instructions are described in brief for the individual group of instructions.

17.9.1 Data Transfer Instructions

- These instructions implement a bit, byte or 16-bit data transfer operations between the 'SRC' (source) and DST 'destination' operands.
- Both operands can be internal direct data memory operands.
- Both cannot be direct and/or indirect register operands R0 to R7.

- Immediate operand can be only a source and not a destination.
- Program counter is not accessible.
- Restricted bit-transfer operations are allowed.
- 'Implicit' indicates not to be specified in the instruction or assumed internally by default, otherwise the operand is to be specified in the instruction. If an operand is not marked implicit, it is explicit.
- Only R0 and R1 are used for indirect addressing mode.

Table 17.5 presents the instructions in brief.

Table 17.5 *8051 Instruction set*

Mnemonic	*Valid Destination Operand (DST)*	*Valid Source Operand (SRC)*	*Operation*	*Affected Flags*
MOV	B, R0….R7, direct internal 8-bit memory address or indirect internal 8-bit memory address using pointer R0 or R1, SFRs	B, R0….R7, direct internal 8-bit memory address or indirect internal 8-bit address using pointer R0 or R1, SFRs and immediate 8-bit data	Copies content of SRC to DST	No flags affected till PSW is not DST
MOV	A	B, R0….R7, direct internal 8-bit memory address or indirect internal 8-bit address using pointer R0 or R1, SFRs and immediate 8 or 16-bit data	Copies content of SRC to DST	No flags affected
MOV	B, R0….R7, direct internal 8-bit memory address or indirect internal 8-bit memory address using pointer R0 or R1, SFRs	A	Copies content of SRC to DST	No flags affected
MOV	DPTR	16-bit immediate data	Copies SRC to DST	No flags affected
MOVX	A,@R(indirect) ,@ DPTR	@R, A,@DPTR.	Copies 8-bit data to/ from external data memory indirectly pointed by @DPTR or @R From/to A.	No flags affected till PSW is not DST
A is compulsory either as destination or as source operand				
MOVC	A	A+@DPTR A+@PC	Copies 8-bit data from internal or external code memory to A	No flags affected till PSW is not DST
MOV	C (Carry flag)	Bit (any bit of bit addressable SFR or bit addressable RAM)	Copies 1-bit data from any bit of bit addressable SFR or bit addressable RAM to C	

(Contd.)

Table 17.5 *(Contd.)*

Mnemonic	*Valid Destination Operand (DST)*	*Valid Source Operand (SRC)*	*Operation*	*Affected Flags*
MOV	Bit (any bit of bit addressable SFR or bit addressable RAM)	C(Carry flag)	Copies 1-bit data to any bit of bit addressable SFR or bit addressable RAM	
	C is compulsory either as destination or source for bit transfer instruction.			
PUSH	Current stack top(SP) +1 (Implicit)	Address of internal 8 bit memory, register or SFR	SP is incremented by 1 and 8-bit content of SRC are pushed to top of Stack	No flags affected
POP	Address of internal 8-bit memory, register or SFR (Implicit)	Current stack top(SP) (Implicit)	8bit content of SRC are stored to DST and SP is decremented by 1.	No flags affected till PSW is not DST
XCH	A	8-bit memory location, register, Indirectly addressed memory location. Immediate operand not allowed.	Content of A and SRC are exchanged using temporary register as an intermediate operand	No flags affected till PSW is an operand
XCHD	A	Only @R0 or @R1	Lower digit (nibble) of A is exchanged with lower nibble of a byte stored at a memory location pointed using indirect addressing with either R0 or R1.	

All the move instructions between any general-purpose register R0–R7 as destination operand and an immediate constant as source operand require 1 machine cycle. All other data transfers including indirect addressing mode and SFRs require 2 machine cycles. PUSH, POP and 16-bit move instruction (to DPTR) also require 2 machine cycles. All other data transfer instructions require one machine cycle. MOV C, bit instruction requires two machine cycles.

17.9.2 Arithmetic Instructions

- These instructions implement arithmetic and logical operations along with increment, decrement and decimal adjust operations.
- Accumulator is a compulsory destination operand for two-operand instructions.
- Immediate operand can be only source and not a destination operand.
- Program counter or its part cannot be an operand.
- Immediate data cannot be an operand for INC/DEC instructions.
- There are no SUB or Compare instructions. Programmer has to implement the subtraction without borrow and comparison instructions using SUBB.

Table 17.6 presents the arithmetic instructions in brief.

Table 17.6 *Arithmetic Instructions of 8051*

Mnemonic	*Valid Destination Operand (DST)*	*Valid Source Operand (SRC)*	*Operation*	*Affected Flags*
ADD	A	B, R0….R7, direct internal 8-bit memory address or indirect internal 8-bit address using pointer R0 or R1, SFRs and immediate 8 bit data	Adds content of SRC with DST and stores the result in A	All status flags
ADDC	A	B, R0….R7, direct internal 8-bit memory address or indirect internal 8-bit address using pointer R0 or R1, SFRs and immediate 8-bit data	Adds content of SRC with A and the carry flag and stores the result in A	All status flags
SUBB	A	B, R0….R7, direct internal 8-bit memory address or indirect internal 8-bit address using pointer R0 or R1, SFRs and immediate 8-bit data	Subtracts content of SRC and borrow flag from A and stores the result in A.	All flags
	Source and destination operands for INC, DEC, MUL, DIV and DAA instructions are the same.			
INC	A, B, R0….R7, direct internal 8-bit memory address or indirect internal 8-bit address using pointer R0 or R1, and SFRs	Decrements the content of the specified operand by 1		All flags excluding carry flag
INC	DPTR	Increments DPTR (16 bit) by 1		No flags
DEC	A, B, R0….R7, direct internal 8-bit memory address or indirect internal 8-bit address using pointer R0 or R1, and SFRs	Decrements the content of the specified operand by 1		All flags excluding carry flag
MUL	AB	Multiplication is carried out considering Multiplicand in A and Multiplier in B. Result lower byte is stored in A and higher byte in B.		No flags affected
DIV	AB	Division is carried out considering 8-bit dividend in A, divisor in B. The resulting quotient is stored in A and remainder in B.		No flags affected
DAA	A	This is used only after an addition instruction of 2 eight bit (2 digit) decimal operands (00-99). If lower nibble is greater than 9 or AF is set 6 is added to the lower nibble. Then again if the upper nibble is greater than 6 or carry flag is set, 6 is added to the upper nibble. This is exactly similar to DAA of 8085/8086		AF and CF affected

INC DPTR instruction requires 2 machine cycles, MUL and DIV require 4 machine cycles. All other instructions require only one machine cycle.

17.9.3 Logical Instructions

- These instructions implement basic logical operations along with rotate and clear operations.
- A is not a compulsory destination operand for logical instructions excluding complement instruction CPL. However, one of the operands must be A.
- Any other DST operand can be a destination operand for logical instructions. Immediate operand can only be a source operand.
- Program counter or its part can't be an operand.
- Immediate data can't be an operand for INC/DEC or any other single operand instruction. instructions.
- There are no SUB or Compare instructions. The programmer has to implement the subtraction without borrow and comparison instructions using SUBB.

Table 17.7 presents a brief elaboration of the logical instructions.

Table 17.7 *Logical Instructions of 8051*

Mnemonic	*Valid Destination Operand (DST)*	*Valid Source Operand (SRC)*	*Operation*	*Affected Flags*
ORL	A	B, R0….R7, direct internal 8-bit memory address or indirect internal 8-bit address using pointer R0 or R1, SFRs and immediate 8 bit data	Logically ORs content of SRC with DST bitwise and stores the result in A.	All status flags excluding carry
ORL	B, R0….R7, direct internal 8-bit memory address or indirect internal 8-bit address using pointer R0 or R1, and SFRs	A	Logically ORs content of SRC with DST bitwise and stores the result in DST operand	All status flags excluding carry
ORL	Internal dada memory or any SFR (R0-R7 can be represented by their addresses)	Immediate 8 bit data	Logically ORs content of SRC with DST bitwise and stores the result in DST operand	All status flags excluding carry
ANL	A	B, R0….R7, direct internal 8-bit memory address or indirect internal 8-bit address using pointer R0 or R1, SFRs and immediate 8 bit data	Logically ANDs content of SRC with DST bitwise and stores the result in A	All status flags excluding carry
ANL	B, R0….R7, direct internal 8-bit memory address or indirect internal 8-bit address using pointer R0 or R1, and SFRs	A	Logically ANDs content of SRC with DST bitwise and stores the result in DST operand	All status flags excluding carry

(*Contd.*)

Table 17.7 *(Contd.)*

Mnemonic	*Valid Destination Operand (DST)*	*Valid Source Operand (SRC)*	*Operation*	*Affected Flags*
ANL	Internal dada memory or any SFR (R0-R7 can be represented by their addresses)	Immediate 8 bit data	Logically ANDs content of SRC with DST bitwise and stores the result in DST operand	All status flags excluding carry
XRL	A	B, R0….R7, direct internal 8-bit memory address or indirect internal 8-bit address using pointer R0 or R1, SFRs and immediate 8 bit data	Logically XORs content of SRC with DST bitwise and stores the result in A	All status flags excluding carry
XRL	B, R0….R7, direct internal 8-bit memory address or indirect internal 8-bit address using pointer R0 or R1, and SFRs	A	Logically XORs content of SRC with DST bitwise and stores the result in DST operand	All status flags excluding carry
XRL	Internal dada memory or any SFR (R0-R7 can be represented by their addresses)	Immediate 8-bit data	Logically XORs content of SRC with DST bitwise and stores the result in DST operand	All status flags excluding carry
	The instructions Clear, Complement, Rotate and Swap are single operand instructions. Accumulator 'A' is the only and compulsory operand for all of them. A works as destination and source operand for all of them			
CLR	A	Accumulator is cleared		No flags affected
CPL	A	Accumulator is complemented bit by bit.		
RL	A	Rotate left A without carry. The MSB of A enters into the LSB and also into the CF. All other bits are shifted by one position left. Carry is not a part of rotation loop.		Only C affected
RLC	A	Rotate left A with carry. The MSB of A enters into C flag. Original C enters into LSB of A. All other bits are shifted by one position left. Carry is a part of rotation loop.		Only C affected
RR	A	Rotate right A without carry. The LSB of A enters into the MSB and also into the CF. All other bits are shifted by one position right. Carry is not a part of rotation loop.		Only C affected
RRC	A	Rotate right A with carry. The LSB of A enters into C flag. Original C enters into MSB of A. All other bits are shifted by one position right. Carry is a part of rotation loop.		Only C affected
SWAP	A	The lower nibble (digit) of A is exchanged with higher nibble of A. This is done by four times left rotation.		No flags affected

Only logical instructions with 8-bit immediate data require 2 machine cycles for execution. All others require only one machine cycle.

17.9.4 Boolean Instructions

- This group implements Boolean bit operations.
- Carry flag (C) as the only allowed destination operand for two operand instructions.
- Immediate bit is not allowed as an operand.
- The ‘Bit flag’ indicates the respective flag of PSW, if it is operand of the respective instruction.

The Boolean instructions of 8051 are presented in Table 17.8

Table 17.8 *Boolean Instructions of 8051*

Mnemonic	*Valid Destination Operand (DST)*	*Valid Source Operand (SRC)*	*Operation*	*Affected Flags*
ANL	C ; Carry flag is the only allowed destination operand for logical operations with bits	Bit Any bit of a bit addressable register or bit addressable internal RAM memory	The Bit is ANDed with C and the result is stored in C flag.	C
ANL	C ; Carry flag is the only allowed destination operand for logical operations with bits	Bit ‘ is the complement of the Bit specified as any bit of a bit addressable register or bit addressable internal RAM memory	Complement of the Bit is ANDed with C and the result is stored in C flag.	C
ORL	C ; Carry flag is the only allowed destination operand for logical operations with bits	Bit ‘ is the complement of the Bit specified as any bit of a bit addressable register or bit addressable internal RAM memory	The Bit is ORed with C and the result is stored in C flag.	C
ORL	C ; Carry flag is the only allowed destination operand for logical operations with bits	Bit ‘ is the complement of the Bit specified as any bit of a bit addressable register or bit addressable internal RAM memory	Complement of the Bit is ORed with C and the result is stored in C flag.	C
Single bit operand instructions require only one bit operand. The same bit works as source and destination operands				
CLR	C		Clears Carry flag	C
SETB	C		Sets Carry flag	C
CPL	C		Complements or inverts Carry flag	C
CLR	Bit		Clears the ‘Bit’of a bit addressable SFR or RAM	‘Bit’ flag
SETB	Bit		Sets the ‘Bit’of a bit addressable SFR or RAM	‘Bit’ Flag
CPL	Bit		Complements or inverts the ‘Bit’of a bit addressable SFR or RAM	‘Bit’ flag

All AND and OR operations with bits require two machine cycles. All others require only one machine cycle. The MOV instructions with bit operands can also be considered as part of this group. However, in our opinion, data transfer is not a Boolean operation hence the instructions have been considered under data transfer group.

17.9.5 Control Transfer Instructions

The control Transfer instructions transfer the control of execution or change the sequence of execution either conditionally or unconditionally. All the jump, call and return instructions come under this group of control transfer instructions. Control transfer instructions of 8051 are significantly different than the respective microprocessor instructions. The control transfer instructions of 8051 as usual can be divided in to two categories; 1) Conditional control transfer and 2) Unconditional control transfer.

Conditional control transfer instructions of 8051 either check a bit condition including any bit of the bit addressable RAM or bit addressable SFRs or content of accumulator for transferring the control to the specified jump location. A few conditional control transfer instructions first execute a decrement or compare operation and then using the result of the operation, transfer the control of execution to the specified address. Depending upon the address space between the first byte of the jump or call instruction and the specified jump or call target address , the conditional instructions can be divided into three categories as below.

Short jump (SJMP 8-bit address) This jump instruction is a two-byte instruction. The first byte represents an opcode byte, while the second byte houses an 8-bit relative address. The relative address is in signed magnitude form. If the most significant sign bit of the relative address byte is 0, it is considered as a forward jump, else it is considered as a back jump. The magnitude of 7 bits represents the address range of –128 to +127 relative to the first byte of the next instruction in the program sequence. All conditional jumps are short jumps.

Absolute jump (AJMP 11-bit address) This jump instruction is intended mainly for a jump within a memory space of 2 K bytes. The instruction has a provision for providing 11-bit jump or call address. Thus it can provide a forward or back jump in a total space of 4 kbytes. This is also a two byte instruction. The first byte houses a five least significant bits op-code and the three most significant bits of the 11-bit address. The next byte carries the least significant 8 bits of the 11 bit address. These 11 bits replace least significant 11 bits of the program counter upon execution of this instruction. The most significant five bits of the program counter remain unaltered. AJMP instruction is always unconditional.

Long jump (LJMP 16 bit address) The long jump instruction is a three-byte instruction. The first byte is opcode. The remaining two bytes point to the subroutine or location to which the control is to be transferred. The second byte is the least significant byte of a 16-bit address while the third byte is the higher or upper byte of the jump location or subroutine. The LJMP instruction is very useful for programming in the external code memory space of 64 KB. LJMP instruction is always unconditional.

It appears that coding these instructions will be quite complex. Thanks to the assemblers for they transparently code these instructions. Programmer can only use the simple JMP instruction without bothering for the type of jump. The assembler will automatically convert it to appropriate SJMP,AJMP or LJMP instruction. The same thing is applicable for CALL instructions.

Conditional CALL instructions are not available in 8051. The available CALL instructions in 8051 are only unconditional. Thus short calls are not available. Only ACALL and LCALL with exactly similar meanings to the AJMP and LJMP respectively are available.

- The control transfer instructions of 8051 can have up to three operands.
- The unconditional jumps only have one operand, i.e. the jump or call address.
- Unconditional jumps with direct as well as indirect addressing are available.
- Conditional jumps are always short while unconditional jumps can be short, long or absolute.
- There are separate instructions for return from a subroutine and interrupt service routine.

The unconditional control transfer instructions are summarized in Table 17.9.

The conditional control transfer instructions those use **status flags or bits of bit addressable Ram and SFRs termed 'bit'** are summarized in Table 17.10. All these jumps are short jumps.

Table 17.9 *Unconditional Control Transfer Instructions*

Mnemonic	*Valid Destination Operand (DST)*	*Operation*	*Affected Flags*
JMP	Address	Jumps to the directly specified address; 8-bit signed relative, if SJMP; 11 bits if AJMP and 16 bit if LJMP.	None
JMP	@A+DPTR	Jumps to the address indirectly specified by the addition of contents of DPTR and A. The address will be always 16 bits.	None
CALL	Address	Address of the next instruction after CALL is pushed to Stack top. Then it calls a subroutine at the specified address; 11 bits if ACALL and 16 bits if LCALL.	None
RET	Implicit SP and Top of stack	Return from a subroutine; Pop the stored address of the next instruction of the calling program from the stack and continue execution of the calling program, SP = SP–2	None
RETI	Implicit SP and Top of stack	Return from a subroutine; Pop the stored address of the next instruction of the calling program from the stack and continue execution of the calling program, SP = SP–2. This also communicates to the internal interrupt unit that the interrupt service is completed.	None

Table 17.10 *Conditional Jump Instructions*

Mnemonic	*Valid Operand (DST)*	*Operation*	*Affected Flags*
JC	Address (8 bits relative)	Jumps to the specified relative address only if C =1, else continues to the next instruction.	None
JNC	Address (8 bits relative)	Jumps to the specified relative address only if C = 0, else continues to the next instruction.	None
JB	Bit, Address (8 bits relative)	Jumps to the specified relative address only if the specified Bit = 1, else continues to the next instruction.	None
JNB	Bit, Address (8 bits relative)	Jumps to the specified relative address only if the specified Bit = 1, else continues to the next instruction.	None
JBC	Bit, Address (8 bits relative)	Jumps to the specified relative address only if the specified Bit = 1, else continues to the next instruction. But before executing the jump the bit is cleared.	None

A last group of a few conditional control transfer instructions compares content of accumulator with zero or carries out some operation like decrement and compare and the jump is taken subject to result of the operation. Table 17.11 highlights such instructions of 8051. The instructions based on the comparison requires three operands; two for comparison and the third being the jump address.

Table 17.11 *Jump Instructions Based on Content of Accumulator, Decrement and Comparison*

Mnemonic	*Valid Operand (DST)*	*Operation*	*Affected Flags*
JZ	Address (8 bits relative)	Jumps to the specified relative address only if content of accumulator is zero, else continues to the next instruction.	None
JNC	Address (8 bits relative)	Jumps to the specified relative address only if, content of accumulator is not zero, else continues to the next instruction.	None
DJNZ	SRC, Address (8 bits relative)	Decrements the specified operand and jumps to the specified relative address only if the content of the specified operand is not zero, else continues to the next instruction. SRC can be B, R0–R7, direct internal 8-bit memory address and SFRs	None
CJNE	A, SRC, Address (8 bits relative)	This performs a subtraction (A-SRC) and jumps to the specified relative address only if the result of subtraction is not zero, else continues to the next instruction. SRC can be an internal memory address or an immediate constant.	None
CJNE	SRC, # 8-bit data, Address (8 bits relative)	This performs a subtraction (SRC-#8-bit) and jumps to the specified relative address only if the result of subtraction is not zero, else continues to the next instruction. SRC can be accumulator, R0–R7, or an indirectly pointed internal memory.	None

All the jump instructions require two machine cycles. Many times, the NOP instruction is also considered a control transfer instruction as it does nothing for one machine cycle and then transfers control to the next instruction. It also does not affect any flag.

17.10 PROGRAMMING EXAMPLES

In this section, we present a few programming examples using 8051 assembly language. Development of algorithms and logic for solving the programming problems have already been discussed in detail for 8086 in Chapter 3 on assembly language programming. In this section, we directly present the programming examples with necessary comments.

Problem 17.1

Write an assembly language program to find whether a given byte is available in the given sequence or not. If it is available, write FF in R3. Otherwise write 00 in R3.

Solution

```
// A program for finding a number in array of numbers stored in data memory
// for example in memory locations {20H,21H,22H,23H,24H}
// the contents are [15,04,06,45,55]
                    ORG 0000H
                    MOV R0,#20H          // 20H is starting address of array
                    MOV R3,#00H          // in R3 register we monitor search
                                         // if R3=00H means number not found
                                         // if R3=FFH means number is found
```

```
                MOV R1,#05H            // This is counter, no of elements are 5 in array
AGAIN:
                MOV A,@R0              // A is stored with contents
                                       // of memory location(@r0)
                DEC R1                 // Counter is decremented
                INC R0                 // Memory address incremented
                CJNE A,#45H,AGAIN      // If number do not match
                                       // with 45H then again
                                       // jump to AGAIN label
                MOV R3,#0FFH           // Store FFH in R3
                                       // indicating 45 is present in array
                END
```

Program 17.1 *Listing for Program 17.1*

Problem 17.2

Write an assembly language program to count the number of 1s and 0s in a given 8-bit number.

Solution

```
// Program to compute number of 1s and 0s in 8 bit number
//  logic: initialize R1 and R2 with 00H
//  initialize R3 as a counter
//  clear carry flag (C ) and rotate A along with carry
//  if C=1, increment  R1, else increment R2 and decrement  the counter
//  if counter=0, store the contents of r1 and r2 and end the program
                ORG 0000H
                SJMP 30H               // Start execution at 30H
                ORG 30H
                MOV A,#05H             // Number is 05H i.e. 00000101
                MOV R1,#00H            // Counter for 1s
                MOV R2,#00H            // Counter for 0s
                MOV R3,#08H            // Counter for total number of bits
                CLR C
UP:             RRC A                  // Rotate right through carry
                JNC DOWN               // If carry is not present goto label down
                INC R1                 // Increment R1 counter
                SJMP EXIT
DOWN:           INC R2
EXIT:           DJNZ R3,UP             // Checking for end of 8 bits, if not, again goto up
                                          label
                INC R0
                MOV A,R1               // for saving status of R1
                MOV A,R2
                MOV @R0,A
                END
```

Program 17.2 *Listing for Program 17.2*

Problem 17.3

Write an assembly language program to compute *x* to the power *n* where both *x* and *n* are 8-bit numbers given by user and the result should not be more than 16 bits.

Solution

The logic of this program is very simple. The *x* is multiplied to itself *n*–1 times.

```
            ORG 0000H
            MOV A,#02H // This is x
            MOV B,#03H // This is n
            MOV R0,B
            MOV R1,A
            MOV R2,#01H
LOOP1:      MOV A,R2
            MOV B,R1
            MUL AB// Multiplication
            DEC R0// Decrementing counter
            MOV R2,A
            CJNE R0,#00H,LOOP1
            MOV A,R2  // Result is stored in accumulator
            END
```

Program 17.3 *Listing for program 17.3*

Problem 17.4

Write an assembly language program to perform addition of two 2 x 2 matrices.

Solution: Let the Contents of A be [5,6;7,8] stored at memory locations {20H,21H,22H,23H}.

Let contents of B are [3,2;1,0] stored in Memory locations {30H,31H,32H,33H}. The result of the addition is to be stored in matrix C=A+B in Memory locations {20H,21H,22H,23H}, i.e. by overwriting the addresses of Matrix A. R0 handles A and R1handles B.

```
        ORG 0000H
        MOV R0,#20H        // Starting address of A in R0
        MOV R1,#30H        // Starting address of B in R1
        MOV R3,#00H        // Clearing R3
        MOV R4,#04H        // Counter=4 (no. of elements)
AGAIN:  MOV A,@R0          // Contents of A matrix stored in A
        MOV R3,A           // Temporarily stored in R3
        MOV A,@R1          // Contents of B matrix stored in A
        ADD A,R3           // Added with R3
        MOV @R0,A          // Result of addition is written at addresses of Matrix A
        DEC R4             // Counter is decremented
        INC R0             // Memory location incremented
        INC R1             // Memory location incremented
        CJNE R4,#00H,AGAIN // until counter becomes 0
                           //(all values added? ) if not, goto label again
        END
```

Program 17.4 *Listing for Program 17.4*

Problem 17.5

Write an assembly language program for finding transpose of a 2x2 matrix.

```
//a program to find transpose of a matrix
    //stored in data memory of 8051
    //content of matrix is a = [10,20;30,50] (2 rows and r columns [A00,A01;A10,A11])
    //stored sequentially at 20H,21H,22H,23H
    //store result at 30H,31H,32H,33H
                ORG 0000H
                MOV R0,#20H
                MOV R1,#30H
                MOV A,@R0
                MOV @R1,A           // A00 to B00 stored
                INC R0
                INC R1
                INC R1
                MOV A,@R0
                MOV @R1,A           // A01 to B10 stored
                INC R0
                DEC R1
                MOV A,@R0
                MOV @R1,A           // A10 to B01 stored
                INC R0
                INC R1
                INC R1
                MOV A,@R0
                MOV @R1,A           // A11 to B11 stored
                                    // Content of transpose matrix is B=[10,30;20,50]
                                    // (2 rows and r columns [B00,B01;B10,B11])
                END
```

Program 17.5 *Listing for Program 17.5*

Problem 17.6

Write an assembly language program for computing square root of an 8 bit number.

Solution: logic: We can calculate square root of a number by using iterative technique

$$x_{j+1} = \frac{x_j + \dfrac{N}{x_j}}{2}$$

where x_{j+1} gives us square root of a number *N*. As *j* increments, we get the result of the next iteration when $x_{j+1} = x_j$, it is the value of the square root.

```
N1 EQU 40H                          // address of the number whose square root
                                    // is to be calculated
N EQU 41H                           // Location where answer is to be stored
          ORG 0000H
STRT:            MOV N1,#0FH        // Store number whose root is to be calculated
```

```
            MOV B,#01H
        MOV R1,B                    // Initialize square root to "01"
        LCALL TRY                   // Call subroutine for next iteration
        JMP STOP
TRY:    MOV A,N1
        MOV B,R1
        DIV AB                      // Calculate N/x_j
        ADD A,R1                    // Calculate x_j + N/x_j
        CLR C
        RRC A                       // Divide by 2
        CLR C
        MOV R2,A
        SUBB A,R1                   // Get x_(j+1) - x_j
        CJNE A,#01H,NOTEQ           // If the difference is zero, square
                                    // has been computed in R2
        SJMP OVER                   // Stop
NOTEQ:  JC OVER                     // Else check for the next number
        MOV A,R2                    // Replace x_j with x_(j+1)
        MOV R1,A
        SJMP TRY                    // Go for the next iteration
OVER:   MOV N,R2                    // Store answer
        RET
STOP:   NOP
        END
```

Program 17.6 *Listing for Program 17.6*

17.11 INTEL'S16-BIT MICROCONTROLLER FAMILY MCS-96

17.11.1 Introduction

As already discussed in this chapter, 8-bit microcontrollers have been designed to facilitate the design of small dedicated control and processing applications, which require general I/O capabilities, and limited processing power. The advantages of the microcontroller based systems have already been discussed. Some advanced applications asked for more processing power, from the computing systems, keeping intact the other advantages of the microcontroller based systems. Keeping in view these type of applications, Intel introduced its MCS-96 family of 16-bit microcontrollers. The MCS-96 family of microprocessors thus caters the needs of applications in the field of closed-loop control, modems, printers, disk drives and medical instrumentation. In this section, we will discuss one of the members of MCS-96 microcontroller family, namely, 80196, which was followed by its different versions and 80197, with similar architecture and instruction set but slightly advanced features. 80196, the 16-bit controller has also been added with a number of enhanced architectural features, peripherals and facilities, which make it the first processor with a set of powerful embedded peripherals, ideally suited for a wide range of applications.

17.11.2 Architecture of 80196

The architecture of 80196 is shown in Fig. 17.10, followed by brief discussion of each unit.

The internal architecture of 80196 may be divided into three sections. The first is a 16-bit CPU which contains memory, ALU and a microcode control unit. The memory of the CPU is organised in two sections, viz. 256 bytes RAM and 232 bytes of special function registers.

The second section is the peripheral section which contains peripherals and on-chip signal processing and conversion circuits. An on-chip ADC unit with a sample and hold circuit and a multiplexer offers 8-bit or 10-bit data logging capability to the microcontroller. The ADC input port is multiplexed with 8-bit I/O port 0. An on-chip pulse width modulator unit provides three PWM outputs. Each of these outputs may provide digital to analog conversion using internal 8-bit PWM registers. Two independent 16-bit timers are available in the microcontroller which may be used to support timing and counting applications.

The high speed inputs HSI_{-0} to HSI_{-3} can be used to capture the contents of the timer 1 when an external event (a transition) is noticed by these input pins. The high speed output pins HSO can generate transitions at the pins when the contents of timer 1 or timer 2 reach the prespecified values for the respective timers. Seven such high speed input events and eight such high speed output events can be stored in their respective FIFO queues. One on-chip serial port works at the rate decided by the baud rate generator. The watch-dog timer register is to be written periodically to prevent automatic reset after every 64K clock cycles. The watch dog feature is actually used to interrupt the CPU to indicate the 'time out', i.e. too much time is taken by the external circuit to complete the external data access initiated by the CPU. At the start of bus cycle DEN# is asserted and the watchdog timer is loaded with FFFF. This goes on decrementing with each clock state. As the CPU keeps on waiting during the bus cycle, for the external access to be completed, the watch dog counter starts decrementing. If the access is not completed, i.e. ready pin does not go high, before the counter reaches zero, a 'time out' interrupt is generated to the CPU.

The third section consists of bus control circuits. The bus control circuit unit consists of a memory controller which controls the external memory accesses and fetches the instructions for execution. The fetched instructions are arranged in a queue. The opcodes from the queue are further sent to the microcode control unit over an internal 8-bit bus, while the data may be sent over the internal 16-bit bus, if required for execution. Thus the queue achieves pipelining which speeds up execution of the programs. The bus hold section, handles the bus requests from other masters, in case of multimaster systems. The interrupt controller and priority resolver unit entertains the interrupt requests from the internal and external sources at the behest of their allotted priority levels. The clock generator generates basic system timings using a crystal of 16 MHz frequency (may differ for different versions).

The ALU of 80196 is called RALU, i.e. *Register Arithmetic Logic Unit* as it is integrated with the special function register bank supported by 80196. The detailed block diagram of the RALU of 80196 KC is shown in Fig. 17.11.

17.11.3 Register Set of 80196KC

80196 has on-chip 256 bytes of RAM which can used as 8-bit scratch pad registers. Besides this, 80196 KC supports 232 bytes of RAM which is called as a *register file* that can be accessed as 8-bit, 16-bit or 32-bit data memory.

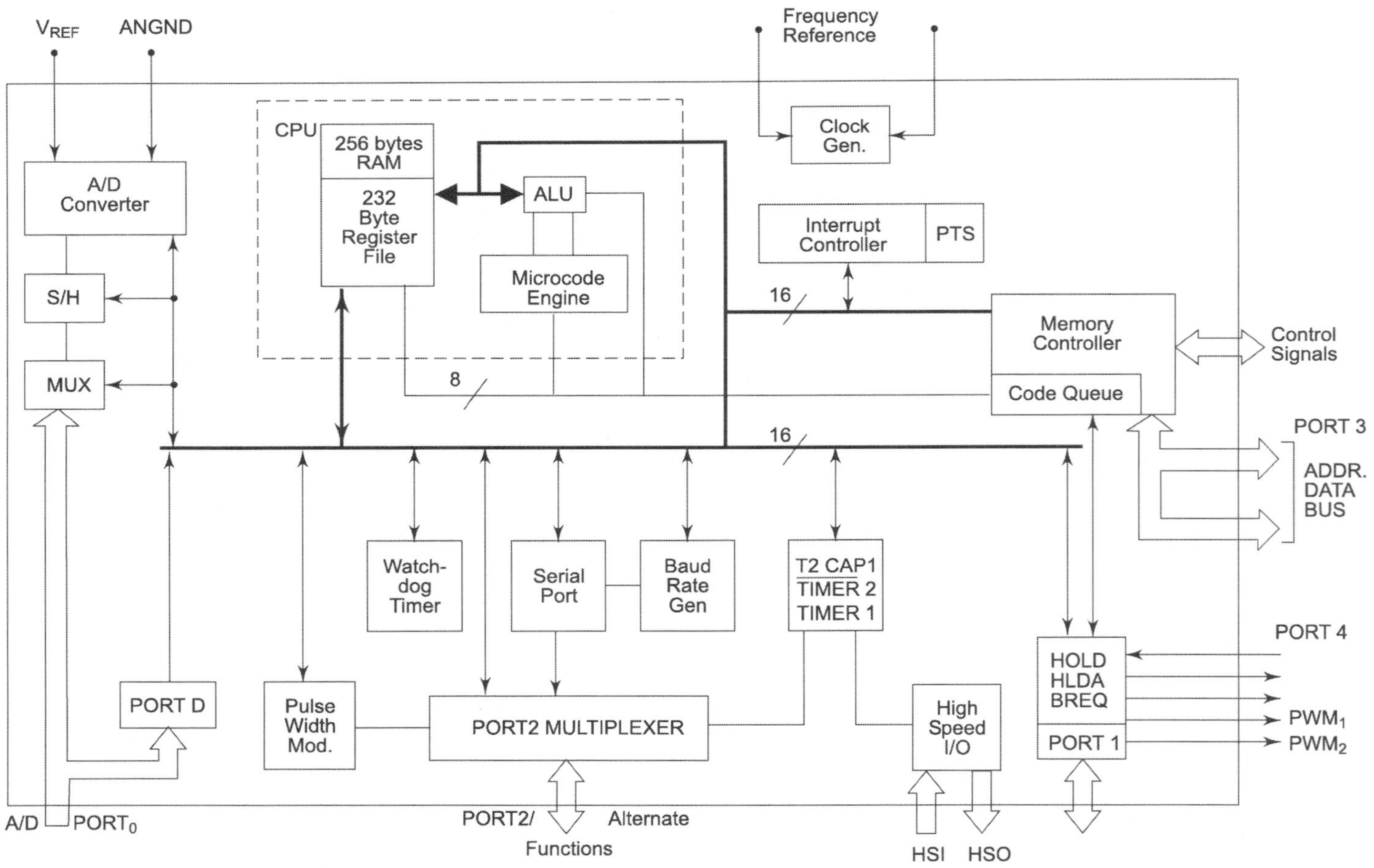

Fig. 17.10 *80196 Block Diagram (Intel Corp.)*

The RALU contain a special function register bank that has 80H (128 bytes) 8-bit registers called as *special function registers*. All these internal memory locations can be addressed under program control using the allotted addresses for them. The 128 special function registers are organized in four banks called as *Hwindows*, namely Hwindow0 to Hwindow3. A window select register selects one of these four windows and then the 20H (32 decimal) registers in each bank can be accessed using their respective addresses. The Hwindows and their respective content SFRs are shown in Fig. 17.12. Table 17.12 shows description of the critical special function registers of 80196KC.

In assembly language, the memory locations designated as registers are represented symbolically using the x86 family register symbols such as AX, BX, CX, etc. for 16-bit registers and AL,BL,CL for the respective 8-bit registers.

The memory map of a typical 80196KC system is shown in Fig. 17.13.

17.11.4 General Features of 80196KC

Addressing Modes The addressing modes supported by 80196KC are presented here with suitable examples.

1. Register Direct The operand lies within the 256 byte on-chip register file. The register file addresses should be allotted with symbolic register names of x86 family.

Example 17.7

```
ADD AX,BX,CX    ; AX ← CX + BX
MUL AX, CX      ; AX ← AX * CX
```

2. Indirect Mode The address of the operand available in memory is in a 16-bit register of the register file.

Example 17.8

```
ADDB AL,BL,[CX]   ; AL ← BL + byte [CX]
ADD AX,[CX]       ; AX ← AX + word [CX]
```

3. Indirect with Autoincrement This mode is similar to the indirect mode except the indirectly specified 16-bit address is incremented appropriately after the data access.

Example 17.9

```
(i)  ADD AX,[CX]+  ; AX ← AX + word[CX]
                   ; CX ← CX + 2
(ii) ADD AL,[BX]+  ; AL ← AL + byte[Bx]
                   ; BX ← BX + 1
```

4. Immediate Mode Immediate or constant data is part of the instruction in this mode.

Example 17.10

```
ADD A,#25H : A ← A + 25H
```

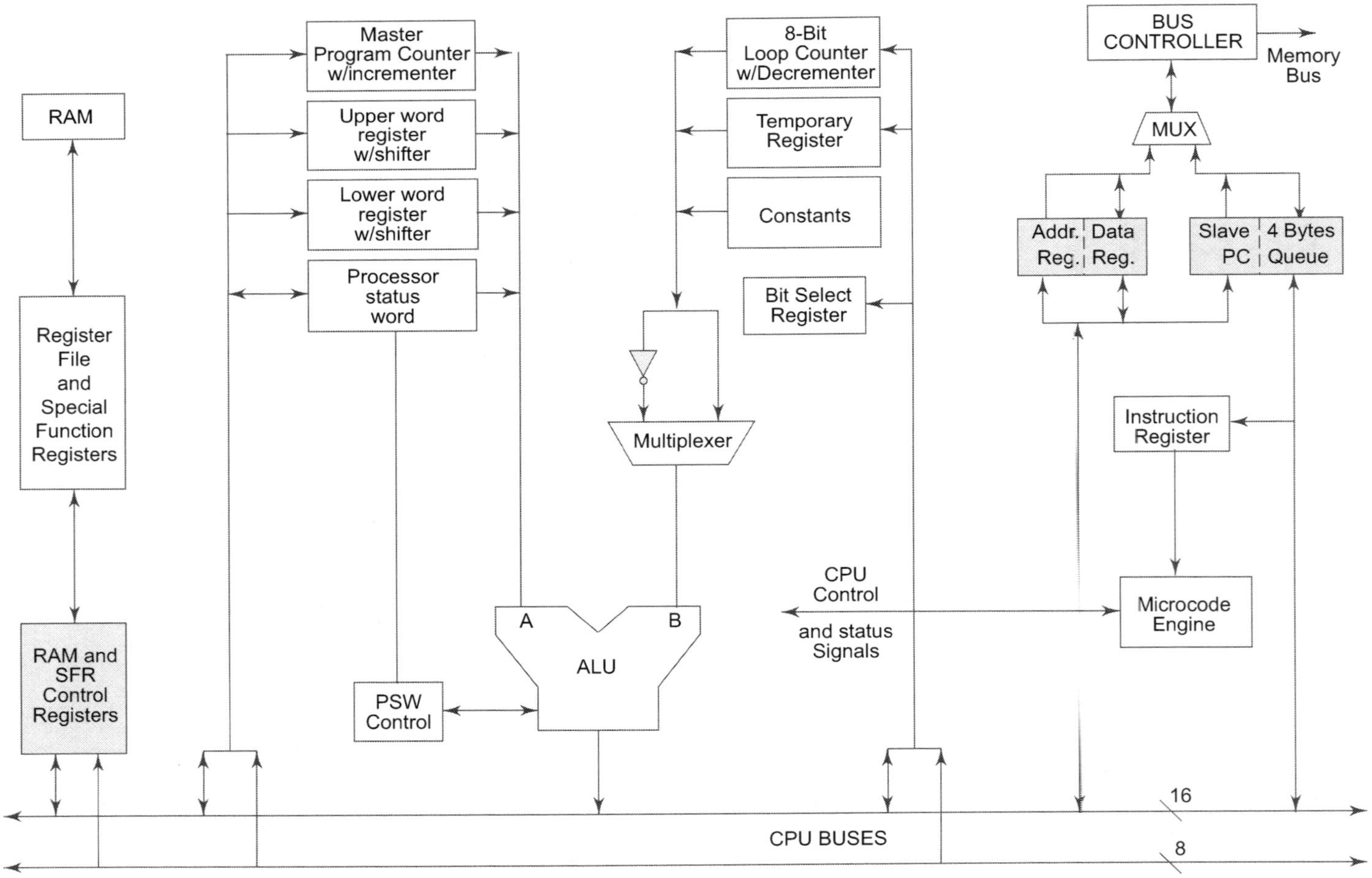

Fig. 17.11 *RALU and Memory Controller Block Diagram*

Table 17.12 *Special Function Register Description of 80C 196KC*

Registers	*Descriptions*
R0	Zero register—Always reads as a zero, useful for a base when indexing and as a constant for calculations and compares.
AD_RESULT	A/D Result Hi/Lo—Low and high order results of the A/D converter.
AD_COMMAND	A/D Command Register—Controls the A/D.
HSI_MODE	HSI Mode Register—Sets the mode of the High Speed Input unit.
HSI_TIME	HSI Time Hi/Lo—Contains the time at which the High Speed Input unit was triggered.
HSO_TIME	HSO Time Hi/Lo—Sets the time or count for the High Speed Output to execute the command in the Command Register.
HSO_COMMAND	HSO Command Register—Determines what will happen at the time loaded into the HSO Time registers.
HSI_STATUS	HSI Status Register—Indicates which HSI pins were detected at the time in the HSI Time registers and the current state of the pins.
SBUF(TX)	Transmit buffer for the serial port, holds contents to be outputted.
SBUF(RX)	Receive buffer for the serial port, holds the byte just received by the serial port.
INT_MASK	Interrupt Mask Register—Enables or disables the individual interrupts.
INT_PEND	Interrupt Pending Register—Indicates that an interrupt signal has occurred on one of the sources and has not been serviced (also INT_PENDING).
WATCHDOG	Watchdog Timer Register—Written periodically to hold off automatic reset every 64K clock state times.
TIMER 1	Timer 1 HI/Lo—Timer 1 high and low bytes.
TIMER 2	Timer 2 HI/Lo—Timer 2 high and low bytes.
IOPORT0	Port 0 Register—Levels on pins of Port 0.
BAUD_RATE	Register which determines the baud rate, is loaded sequentially.
IOPORT1	Port 1 Register—Used to read or write Port 1.
IOPORT2	Port 2 Register—Used to read or write Port 2.
SP_STAT	Serial Port Status—Indicates the status of the serial port.
SP_CON	Serial Port Control—Used to set the mode of the serial port.
IOS0	I/O Status Register 0—Contains information on the HSO status.
IOS1	I/O Status Register 1—Contains information on the status of the timers and of the HSI.
IOC0	I/O Control Register 0—Controls alternate functions of HSI pins, timer interrupts and HSI interrupts.
IOC1	I/O Control Register 1—Controls alternate functions of Port 2 pins, timer interrupts and HSI interrupts.
PWM_CONTROL	Pulse Width Modulation Control Register—Sets the duration of the PWM pulse.
INT_PEND1	Interrupt Pending register for the 8 new interrupt vectors (also INT_PENDING 1).
INT_MASK1	Interrupt Mask register for the 8 new interrupt vectors.
IOC2	I/O Control Register 2.
IOS2	I/O Status Register 2—Contains information on HSO events.
WSR	Window Select Register—Selects register window.
AD_TIME	Determines A/D Conversion Time
IOC3	New 80C196 KC features (T2 internal clocking, PWMs) (Previously T2CONTROL or T2CNTC).
PTSSEL	Individually enables PTS channels.
PTSSRV	End-of-PTS Interrupt Pending Flags.

ADD.	REGISTER	ADD.	REGISTER	ADD.	REGISTER	ADD.	REGISTER
19H	SP(HI)	19H	SP(HI)	19H	SP(HI)	19H	SP(HI)
18H	SP(LO)	18H	SP(LO)	18H	SP(LO)	18H	SP(LO)
17H	IOS2	17H	PWM0-CONTROL	17H	PWM1-CONTROL	17H	
16H	IOS1	16H	IOC1	16H	PWM2-CONTROL	16H	
15H	IOS0	15H	IOC0	15H	RESERVED	15H	
14H	WSR	14H	WSR	14H	WSR	14H	WSR
13H	INT-MASK1	13H	INT-MASK1	13H	INT-MASK1	13H	INT-MASK1
12H	INT-PEND1	12H	INT-PEND1	12H	INT-PEND1	12H	INT-PEND1
11H	SP-STAT	11H	SP-CON	11H	RESERVED	11H	
10H	PORT2	10H	PORT2	10H	RESERVED	10H	RESERVED
0FH	PORT1	0FH	PORT1	0FH	RESERVED	0FH	RESERVED
0EH	PORT0	0EH	BAUD RATE	0EH	RESERVED	0EH	RESERVED
0DH	TIMER2(HI)	0DH	TIMER2(HI)	0DH	RESERVED	0DH	T2CAPT(HI)
0CH	TIMER2(LO)	0CH	TIMER2(LO)	0CH	IOC3(T2CNT)	0CH	T2CAPT(LO)
0BH	TIMER1(HI)	0BH	IOC2	0BH	RESERVED	0BH	
0AH	TIMER1(LO)	0AH	WATCHDOG	0AH	RESERVED	0AH	
09H	INT-PEND	09H	INT-PEND	09H	INT-PEND	09H	INT-PEND
08H	INT-MASK	08H	INT-MASK	08H	INT-MASK	08H	INT-MASK
07H	SBUF(RX)	07H	SBUF(TX)	07H	PTSSRV(HI)	07H	
06H	HSI-STATUS	06H	HSO-COMMAND	06H	PTSSRV(LO)	06H	
05H	HSI-TIME(HI)	05H	HSO-TIME(HI)	05H	PTSSEL(HI)	05H	
04H	HSI-TIME(LO)	04H	HSO-TIME(LO)	04H	PTSSEL(LO)	04H	
03H	AD-RESULT(HI)	03H	HSI(MODE)	03H	AD-TIME	03H	
02H	AD-RESULT(LO)	02H	AD-COMMAND	02H	RESERVED	02H	
01H	ZERO-REG(HI)	01H	ZERO-REG(HI)	01H	ZERO-REG(HI)	01H	ZERO-REG(HI)
00H	ZERO-REG(LO)	00H	ZERO-REG(LO)	00H	ZERO-REG(LO)	00H	ZERO-REG(LO)
	HWINDOW0 WHEN READ		HWINDOW0 WHEN WRITTEN		HWINDOW0 READ/WRITE		HWINDOW 15

Fig. 17.12 *Hwindows and Their Special Function Registers (Intel Corp.)*

5. Short Indexed A 16-bit value in the register file serves as an index address while an 8-bit sign extended immediate data serves as displacement to form the address of the operand.

Example 17.11

```
(i)  ADD AX,15[BX]    ; AX ← AX + word[BX+15]
(ii) LD AX,5[CX]      ; AX ← word [CX+5]
```

6. Long Indexed This mode is similar to the short indexed mode except a 16-bit signed number serves as displacement in this mode.

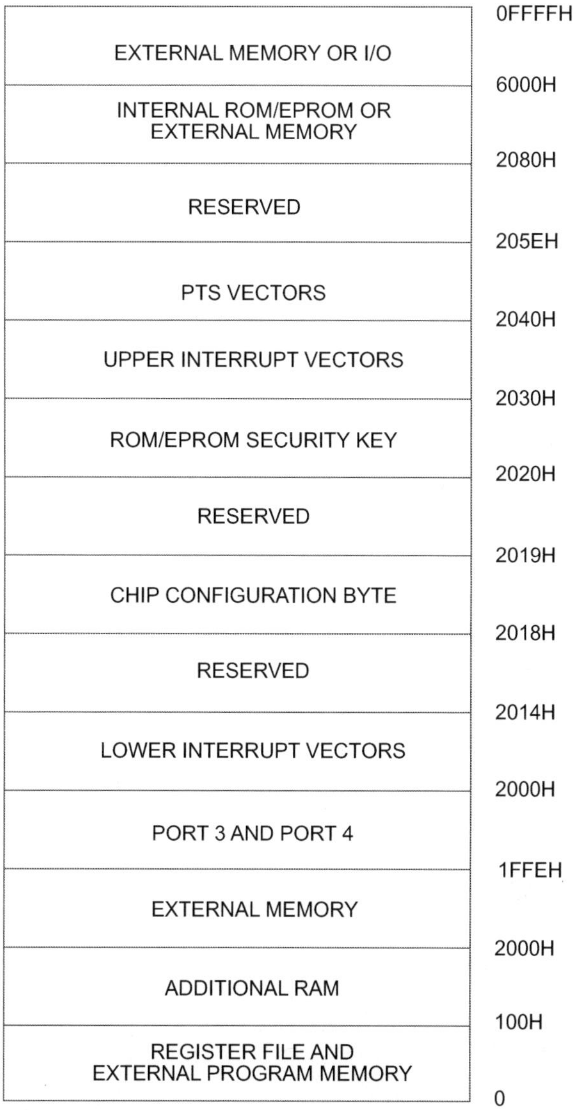

Fig. 17.13 *80C196KC Memory Map*

Example 17.12

```
(i) AND AX,CX,15ABH[BX]        ; AX ← CX AND[15AB+BX]
(ii)ADDB AL,BL,0ABCDH[CX]      ; AX ← BL + Byte [0ABCD+BX]
```

Data Types Supported By 80196KC 80196 KC supports the following data types:

Unsigned data types

1. 8 bit bytes
2. 16-bit words aligned at even addresses.
3. 32-bit double words aligned at addresses divisible by 4.

Signed data types

1. 8-bit short integers
2. 16-bit integers
3. 32-bit long integers aligned at addresses divisible by 4

Minimum Configuration The minimum configuration of 80196 KC is shown in Fig. 17.14.

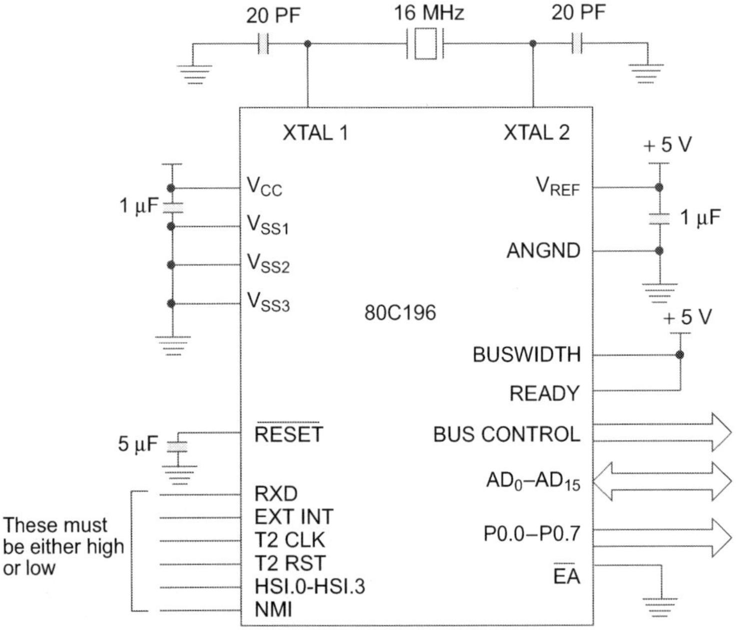

Fig. 17.14 *80C196 Minimum System Connection*

SUMMARY

This chapter started with an introduction to microcontroller systems and their comparison with microprocessor-based systems. Architecture of MCs 51 family was presented in brief with signal descriptions. Instruction set of

8051 was further presented in a very lucid but brief manner. A few simple programming examples along with brief discussion of logic and adequate comments followed the instruction set. The chapter concluded with a brief introduction to the 16-bit microcontroller 80196.

EXERCISES

17.1 Discuss the advantages of microcontroller based systems over microprocessor based systems.
17.2 Enlist the salient features of 8051 family of microcontrollers.
17.3 Discuss the register set of MCS-51 family of microcontrollers .
17.4 Draw and discuss the internal architecture of 8051.
17.5 Discuss the following signal descriptions of 8051.

(i) ALE/PROG	(ii) $\overline{EA}/V_{pp}$	(iii) $\overline{PSEN}$
(iv) RXD	(v) TXD	(vi) $\overline{INT_0}$ and $\overline{INT_1}$
(vii) T_0 and T_1	(viii) $\overline{RD}$	(ix) $\overline{WR}$

17.6 Draw and discuss the formats and bit definitions of the following SFRs of 8051.

(i) PCON	(ii) TCON	(iii) IE	(iv) IP
(v) TMOD	(vi) PSW	(vii) SCON	

17.7 How does 8051 differentiate between the external and internal program memory?
17.8 Draw and discuss the internal architecture of 80196 in detail.
17.9 What is RALU? Draw and discuss its internal block diagram.
17.10 Discuss the register set of 80196.
17.11 What are Hwindows?
17.12 Discuss the addressing modes and the data types supported by 80196.
17.13 Draw the minimum system configuration of 80196.
17.14 Explain all the instructions of 8051 with two examples of each.
17.15 Discuss all the addressing modes of 8051 with two instruction examples each.
17.16 Write an ALP to perform addition of eight 8-byte numbers.
17.17 Write an ALP to perform multiplication of two 3x3 matrices.
17.18 Write an ALP to generate Fibonacci series of 8-bit numbers.
17.19 Write an ALP to perform floating point multiplication of two-four digit floating point numbers with two places after the decimal point.
17.20 Write an ALP to perform floating point division of two four-digit floating point numbers with two places after the decimal point.
17.21 Write an ALP to compute the sin, cos and tan of an angle.(Use series expansion of the functions truncated to five terms.
17.22 Write an ALP to find out factorial of an 8-bit number. The result should be less than 16 bits.
17.23 Write an ALP to find out LCM and GCD of given two 8-bit numbers.
17.24 Write an ALP using internal registers to generate a real-time minutes and hours clock. Assume that the machine cycle clock is 1 MHz.
17.25 Write an ALP to generate a year calendar using R3 for date, R4 for month and DPTR for year. (Use solution of the earlier problem as a subroutine to this program.)

18 8051 Peripherals Interfacing

INTRODUCTION

In the seventeenth chapter a microcontroller was introduced as a microprocessor with on chip integrated peripherals. The MCS 51 architecture and the instruction set was then introduced in brief. This chapter aims at introducing the techniques of initializing and programming the on chip peripherals. However the on chip peripherals have limited capacity; many of them may not be enough for bigger systems. In such cases, external peripherals may also be interfaced and their appropriate interfacing programmes may be developed. But it must be remembered that as we go on interfacing external peripherals with microcontrollers, they go on loosing their advantages of being dedicated, portable, reliable, low power systems. Thus a microcontroller system with many external peripherals and memory chips may not have significant advantages over a microprocessor system of the same capabilities. In other words, a microcontroller may be more suitable for a small, dedicated, portable, limited capability low power application, while a microprocessor may be more suitable for a bigger, general purpose, large capability system without any power consumption constraints.

In this chapter, we also introduce a few external peripherals and their interfacing with 8051.

18.1 INTERFACING WITH 8051 PORTS

As already discussed 8051 has four 8-bit on chip ports. These ports are bit addressable or byte addressable depending upon the instruction used for accessing them. All these ports are considered as special function registers 'SFR's and have 8-bit addresses. Thus a port, for example port 0, can be addressed using its SFR address-80H as an internal RAM memory location and it can also be addressed using its name P0. However the port 0 bits can only be addressed using notations P0.0 for the least significant bit, P0.1 for the next-significant bit and so on up to P0.7 for the most significant bit. The same notations are applicable for addressing the four ports P0 to P3 as bits or bytes. The SFR addresses of the ports P0, P1, P2, and P3 are 80H, 90H, A0H and B0H respectively. All these ports are implemented using low power CMOS technology. Each port line can individually source a current of only up to 0.5 mA, while it can sink a current of around 8 mA individually. Thus 8051 ports may not be able to drive eight LEDs connected to the eight lines of any port in common cathode configuration as each LED requires around 8 mA while the port lines can source only 0.5 mA on each line. So a common anode configuration is preferred, in which each LED receives operating current (8 mA) from power supply while the port lines of 8051 sink the current of 8 mA on each port line. Port 0 is an open drain bidirectional (input or output) port with internal pullups. And when a logic '0' is sent to a port line as an output port, it can sink 8 LS TTL inputs. Port 0 is also used as data bus during external interfacing whenever required.

Port 1 is also an 8 bit bidirectional port with internal pullups. The port 1 lines can drive 4 LS TTL lines when being used as output lines and '1' is written to them. The port 1 lines can also sink current form 4 LS TTL lines when being used as output port and a '0' is written to them. Port 1 lines are also used as lower byte of 16-bit address bus during programming of internal EPROM or EEPROM. Port 1 lines are addresses as P1 as 8-bit port and P1.0 to P1.7 individually.

Port 2 is also an 8-bit bidirectional port, that is also used as higher byte of address bus in case of external memory or peripheral interfacing. It can also source or sink 4 LS TTL input when being used as output port on each of its line. When 8 bit external memory accesses are going on using 8 bit addresses (MOVX A, @ Ri) this port emits content of SFR P2. This also acts as higher byte of address bus during programming of internal EPROM.

Port 3 is also 8 bit bidirectional I/O port with internal pullups. It can also source or sink 4 TTL inputs when being used as output port. Port 3 pins which are externally pulled low when being used as input pins will source current of 500 μA. Port 3 pins also function as different control signals or peripherals pins when programmed for the same, as indicated in chapter 17.

It should be noted that when the port pins are being used for some other functions like memory or other peripheral interfacing, they can not be used as IO ports. Port 0 current sourcing and sinking capacity is double that of other ports and port 0 should be externally pulled up using 10 K registers. All the port lines can be used readily as output ports. When the port lines are to be used as input lines, 'FF' must be written to the port address.

With this primary knowledge about 8051 ports, interfacing of external memory and peripherals is further discussed in this chapter.

18.1.1 Interfacing of External RAM and ROM

It must be noted that for interfacing external program memory $\overline{EA}$ pin must be grounded. Also when external memory is interfaced for designing bigger systems, the microcontroller based system will become bigger in size and may loose its advantages like portability, reliability, upgradability, low power and low cost. The $\overline{EA}$ signal does not have any concern with interfacing of external data memory or RAM. $\overline{EA}$ must be grounded for enabling the 8051 family devices to fetch opcodes for execution from an external EPROM chip. If $\overline{EA}$ is grounded, the execution will directly start from an external 16 bit address 0000H in external program memory. If $\overline{EA} = 1$, the execution starts from an internal EPROM or flash RAM address 000H; can continue up to FFFH (4 KB) address and then for higher addresses it will go into external memory.

During interfacing of external memory with 8051, it must be noted that:

1. Port 0 is used as data bus (D_0–D_7) and lower order address bus (A_0–A_7) can be demultiplexed using a latch like 74373 from AD_0–AD_7 i.e. port 0, as in 8085.
2. Port 2 is used as higher byte of the 16-bit address bus A_8–A_{15}
3. $\overline{PSEN}$ is used for interfacing EPROM i.e. it acts an $\overline{OE}$ input to EPROM while $\overline{RD}$ and $\overline{WR}$ pins are used for interfacing RAM, and are connected to respective pins of RAM. This is how the Harword architecture discriminate between the program memory and data memory addresses.
4. $\overline{EA}$ pin of 8051 must be grounded for interfacing external EPROM.
5. The address decoding and design of the chip select signal is exactly done in the same way as 8085 interfacing.

The procedure of memory interfacing with 8051 is postulated below in precise steps.

1. Ground $\overline{EA}$ is an external EPROM chip is to be interfaced.
2. Connect the data bus (D_0–D_7) i.e. P_0–P_7 to the data lines of the memory chips.
3. Connect $\overline{PSEN}$ to $\overline{OE}$ of EPROM chips and $\overline{RD}$ and $\overline{WR}$ of 8051 to the respective pins of the memory chips.
4. The microcontroller system provides sixteen address lines A_0–A_7 (after demultiplexing) and A_8–A_{15}. Estimate the number of address lines available with memory chip. Observe the size of memory chips available. For practical purposes, it is considered that all the available chips are byte chips i.e. at each memory address they can store 8-bits.

   From the available memory chip size one can compute the available memory address line with the chip. A memory chip with n address lines can address upto $2^n = N$ memory address locations. If each address can store 8 bits or 1 byte, such memory is said to have storing capacity of N bytes. Suppose a memory chip with 12 address lines is available and it is able to store 1 byte at each address then it has $2^{12} = 4096 = 4$ K address locations and each location stores 1 byte so its capacity is 4 K × 8 bits or 4 K bytes (4 KB) or 32 K bits. Or conversely a 4 KB chip will have 12 address lines. Thus an 8 KB chip will have 13 address lines ($2^{13} = 8192 = 8$ K) and a 16 KB chip will have 14 address lines ($2^{14} = 16384 = 16$ K).
5. Connect all the address lines available with the memory chips starting from the least significant address line to the respective address lines of the microcontroller system. For example a 4 KB chip will have 12 address lines (A_0–A_{11}), connect them to least significant 12 address lines of the microcontroller system.
6. After step 5, write address map of the memory chip in bit form and mark the connected lines between the memory chip and microcontroller system.
7. The higher order address lines of the microcontroller system which have so for not been connected with a memory chip are used to derive chip select signal of the memory chip using a combinational logic circuit. The inputs to the combinational logic circuit are the higher order address lines not connected with memory and output of the circuit is the chip select signal for that memory chip. Thus the designed chip select signal is connected with $\overline{CS}$ pin of each memory chip. The logic gates and multiplexers are most commonly used for deriving chip select signals. However advanced circuits like Programable Logic Arrays (PLA) and EPROMS can also be used for deriving the chip select signals. For deriving chip selects of isolated memory or IO devices, NAND and NOT gates are traditionally used.

This process of interfacing memory chips will be clear after the following examples. It should be noted that if 8051 microcontroller is expected to start execution after reset (from the OOOOH address) in external memory, an EPROM must be interfaced at that address. It should also be noted that, unlike 8085. The same 16 bits physical address can be available in program memory as well as data memory in Harward Architectures.

Example 18.1

Interface an EPROM of size 4 KB and RAM of size 8 KB with 8051. The EPROM address starts at 0000H and RAM address starts at 8000H.

Solution

Available EPROM–4 KB = 2^{12}
Address lines with EPROM chip = 12 i.e. A_0–A_{11}
Available RAM–8 KB = 2^{13}
Address lines with RAM chip = 13 i.e. A_0–A_{12}

A_0–A_{11} address lines of EPROM chip and A_0–A_{12} address lines of RAM chip will be directly connected with the respective lines of the microcontrollers. The higher A_{12}–A_{15} lines those are not connected with the EPROM chip will be used for deriving its chip select. Similarly A_{13}–A_{15} lines of microcontroller those are not connected with the RAM chip will be used for deriving its chip select signal. The address maps of the EPROM and RAM are written below.

EPROM Address Map

Hex Address	A_{15}	A_{14}	A_{13}	A_{12}	A_{11}	A_{10}	A_9	A_8	A_7	A_6	A_5	A_4	A_3	A_2	A_1	A_0	size
0000H	0	0	0	0	0	0	0	0	0	0	0	0	0	0	0	0	4 KB
0FFFH	0	0	0	0	1	1	1	1	1	1	1	1	1	1	1	1	

RAM Address Map

Hex Address	A_{15}	A_{14}	A_{13}	A_{12}	A_{11}	A_{10}	A_9	A_8	A_7	A_6	A_5	A_4	A_3	A_2	A_1	A_0
8000H	1	0	0	0	0	0	0	0	0	0	0	0	0	0	0	0
9FFFH	1	0	0	1	1	1	1	1	1	1	1	1	1	1	1	1

The address lines on the right side of the vertical dotted lines in the address map indicate the lines directly connected between the microcontroller and the memory chips. The address lines on the left hand side indicate the lines those are to be used for deriving the chip select signals. After writing the address map as above, a combinational logic circuit called chip select logic will be designed such that when ever the specified address bits are placed on them (higher order address lines), the output of the circuit that is further connected with the chip select of the chip goes low and the chip gets selected. For all other addresses the chip does not get selected. In this example the EPROM chip will get selected only when the higher order address lines A_{15} A_{14} A_{13} A_{12} are 0000. Similarly the RAM Chip will be selected only when the higher order address lines (on the left side of the dotted line in the address map) A_{15} A_{14} A_{13} are 100.

A thumb rule for deriving chip select:

Observe the higher order address lines not connected with the memory chip. Take a NAND gate with as many inputs as the unused higher order address lines. If a particular address line is '1' in the map, connect it directly with an input of the NAND gate. If the address line is '0' connect it to an input of the NAND gate after inverting it (NOT). In this example, for EPROM, A_{15} A_{14} A_{13} A_{12} are 0000 i.e. all are zero; they will be inverted and connected to inputs of an n input NAND gate. The output of the NAND gate will work as the chip select of the EPROM chip as shown in Fig. 18.1 (a).

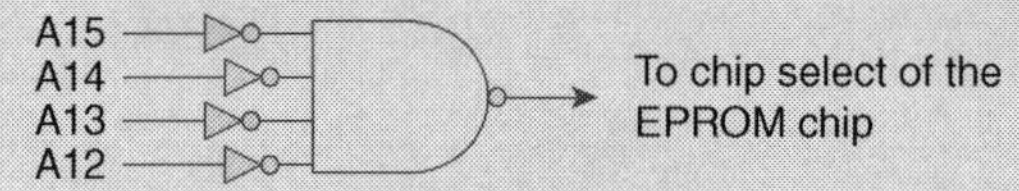

Fig. 18.1 (a) *Chip Select of the EPROM Chip for Example 18.1*

For the RAM chip, the higher order address lines A_{15} A_{14} A_{13} (on the left side of the dotted line) are 100 i.e. $A_{15} = 1$, $A_{14} = 0$ and $A_{13} = 0$. So A_{15} will be directly connected with input of a three input NAND gate while A_{14} and A_{13} are inverted and then connected with inputs of the NAND gate as shown in Fig. 18.1 (b)

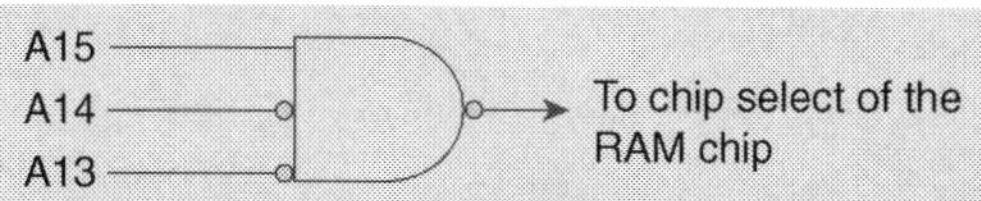

Fig. 18.1 (b) *Chip Select of the RAM Chip for Example 18.1*

The final interfacing diagram of the example is shown below in Fig. 18.2.

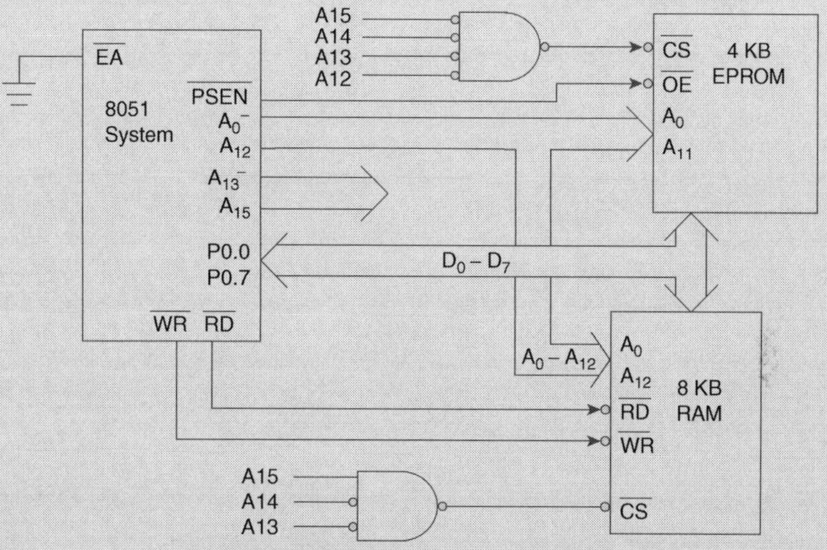

Fig. 18.2 *Interfacing Circuit for Example 18.1*

Note that the bubbles shown at the inputs of NAND gates represent NOT gates. The bubbles shown with the memory chips for $\overline{OE}, \overline{CS}, \overline{RD}$, and $\overline{WR}$ indicate that the respective pins are active low. They do not represent external NOT gates.

Example 18.2

Interface EPROM 2764 and RAM 62128 with 8051 both starting at hexadecimal address 4000H.

NOTE: The nomenclature of static RAM and EPROM chip gives either a 4 digits or 5 digit numbers to the memory chips. The most significant two numbers indicate the series of the chip. For example, in case of EPROM the series no is 27 and in case of RAM the series no are either 61 or 62. The RAM with series no 62 are widely available. Only a 2 KB RAM with series no 61 was introduced initially. All other higher capacity RAM chips are available with series 62. Thus the 2 digit series numbers; 27 for EPROM and 62 for RAM form the most significant two digits of the memory chips. The least significant two or three digits indicate the number of bits or cells available in the memory chip. For example, an 8 KB chip will have 8 K × 8 = 64 K bits in it. Thus an EPROM of 8 KB size will be numbered 2764 while a RAM of 8 KB size will be numbered 6264. A 16 KB memory chip will have an arrangement to store 16 K × 8 = 128 K bits. So an EPROM chip of capacity 16 KB will have its number 27128 while a RAM chip of the same capacity will have its number 62128. Thus given any chip number, one can find its capacity or vice versa.

Solution

chips given ⇒ 1) 2764 = 8 KB EPROM = 2^{13}
Available address lines = 13 (A_0–A_{12})

(2) 62128 = 16KB RAM = 2^{14}
Available address lines = 14 (A_0–A_{13})
Address map of EPROM

Hex Address	A_{15}	A_{14}	A_{13}	A_{12}	A_{11}	A_{10}	A_9	A_8	A_7	A_6	A_5	A_4	A_3	A_2	A_1	A_0	Size
4000H	0	1	0	0	0	0	0	0	0	0	0	0	0	0	0	0	8KB
5FFFH	0	1	0	1	1	1	1	1	1	1	1	1	1	1	1	1	

Address map of RAM

Hex Address	A_{15}	A_{14}	A_{13}	A_{12}	A_{11}	A_{10}	A_9	A_8	A_7	A_6	A_5	A_4	A_3	A_2	A_1	A_0	Size
4000H	0	1	0	0	0	0	0	0	0	0	0	0	0	0	0	0	16KB
7FFFH	0	1	1	1	1	1	1	1	1	1	1	1	1	1	1	1	

The interfacing circuit is presented in Fig. 18.3.

The address lines A_0–A_{12} of EPROM are directly connected with the respective lines of the microcontroller system. The remaining higher address lines A_{13} to A_{15} are used for deriving the chip select. Simillarly A_0–A_{13} of RAM are connected with the respective lines of the microcontroller and $A_{14}A_{15}$ are used for deriving its chip select, using the already discussed thumb rule.

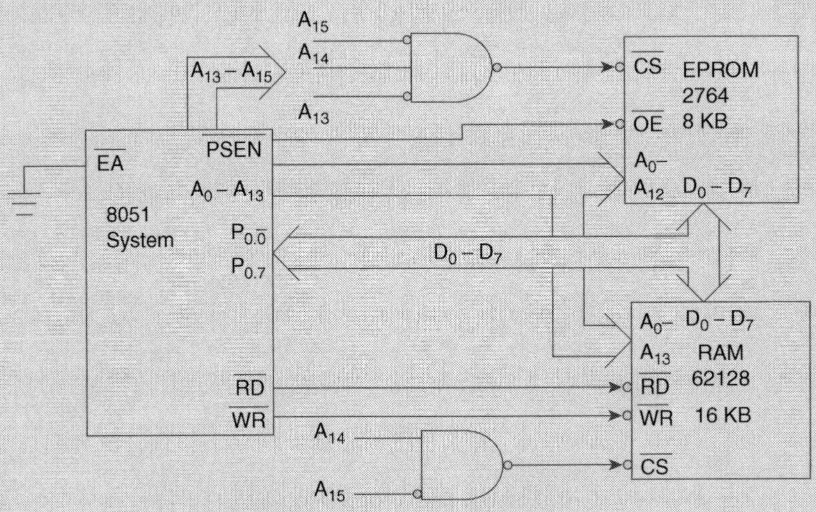

Fig. 18.3 *Interfacing Circuit for Example 18.2*

Example 18.3

Interface an 8 KB RAM chip at address 5000H with 8051.

Solution

Available RAM chip–8 KB = $2^{13} \Rightarrow A_0$–A_{12}
Address map

Hex Address	A_{15}	A_{14}	A_{13}	A_{12}	A_{11}	A_{10}	A_9	A_8	A_7	A_6	A_5	A_4	A_3	A_2	A_1	A_0	Size
5000	0	1	0	1	0	0	0	0	0	0	0	0	0	0	0	0	8 KB
6FFF	0	1	1	0	1	1	1	1	1	1	1	1	1	1	1	1	

In the above address map it can be observed that the address lines on the left side of the dotted lines are not stationary for the complete map like complied 18.1 and 18.2. In such cases, the so presented thumbrule cannot be used as it is. Some complex, combinational logic needs to be implemented for deriving the chip select logic in such cases. One possible solution is presented below.

If the interfacing circuit is observed very carefully, it appears the chip will be selected even for addresses 4000H to 4FFFH and 7000H to 7FFFH. Thus a precise solution to this problem may not be possible. Such address maps are avoided in practical designs as they need complex chip select circuits leading to increased cost without any specific advantage. This can be implemented using gates or de-multiplexers as shown in Fig. 18.4 (a) and (b).

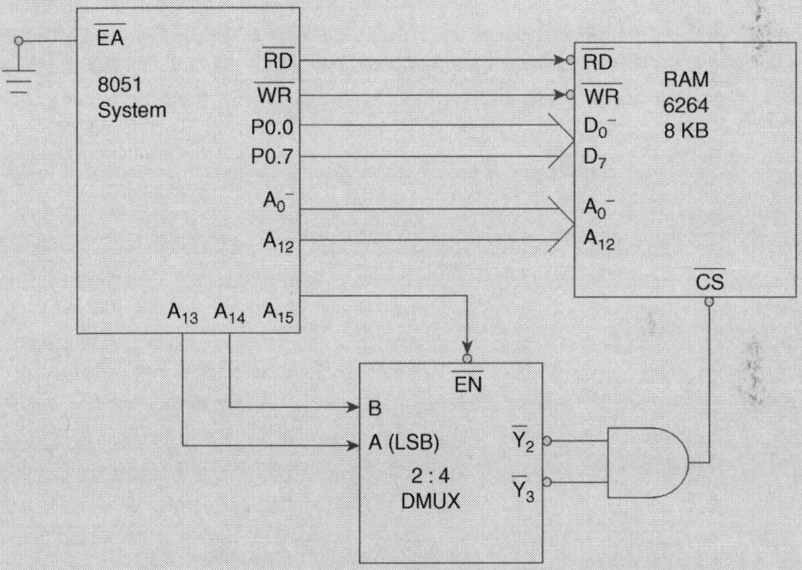

Fig. 18.4 (a) *Interfacing Circuit for Example 18.3*

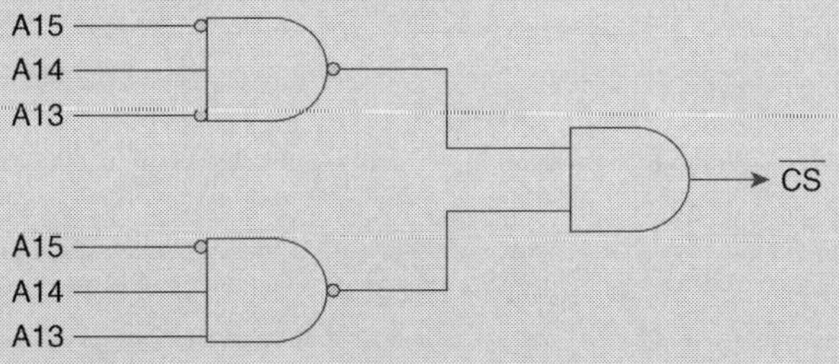

Fig. 18.4 (b) *Alternative Implementation of Chip Select logic for Example 18.3*

Example 18.4

Interface 4 chips of 2764 EPROM and 2 chips of 6264 RAM. EPROM map starts at 0000H and RAM map starts at 8000H.

Solution

In this problem total six memory chips are required to be interfaced. All are 8 KB chips and their map is also continuous i.e. there is no gap (unused address space) in the address map of the system. More number of NAND gate ICs will be required to derive chip select of the six memory chips. In such cases, it is advisable to use a de-multiplexer to derive the chip selects.
Address Maps

EPROM

Hex Add.	A_{15}	A_{14}	A_{13}	A_{12}	A_{11}	A_{10}	A_9	A_8	A_7	A_6	A_5	A_4	A_3	A_2	A_1	A_0	Size of Chip no.
0000H	0	0	0	0	0	0	0	0	0	0	0	0	0	0	0	0	8 K - ① EPROM
1FFFH	0	0	0	1	1	1	1	1	1	1	1	1	1	1	1	1	
2000H	0	0	1	0	0	0	0	0	0	0	0	0	0	0	0	0	8 K - ② EPROM
3FFFH	0	0	1	1	1	1	1	1	1	1	1	1	1	1	1	1	
4000H	0	1	0	0	0	0	0	0	0	0	0	0	0	0	0	0	8 K - ③ EPROM
5FFFH	0	1	0	1	1	1	1	1	1	1	1	1	1	1	1	1	
6000H	0	1	1	0	0	0	0	0	0	0	0	0	0	0	0	0	8 K - ④ EPROM
7FFFH	0	1	1	1	1	1	1	1	1	1	1	1	1	1	1	1	
									TOTAL EPROM								32 KB
RAM																	
8000H	1	0	0	0	0	0	0	0	0	0	0	0	0	0	0	0	8 K - ⑤ RAM
9FFFH	1	0	0	1	1	1	1	1	1	1	1	1	1	1	1	1	
A000H	1	0	1	0	0	0	0	0	0	0	0	0	0	0	0	0	8 K - ⑥ RAM
BFFFH	1	0	1	1	1	1	1	1	1	1	1	1	1	1	1	1	
									TOTAL RAM								16 KB

The interfacing circuit using 3:8 decoder for deriving the chip selects is presented further in Fig. 18.5.

It should be noted that the big interfacing circuits like that of Example 18.4 can be avoided using microcontroller versions those have bigger on chip RAM and ROM memories. Microcontroller 8051 versions with up to 64 KB EPROM and RAM available on chip have been introduced by different manufacturers. Using bigger circuit involving many memory chips adds to the cost of the system and decreases portability and reliability of the system.

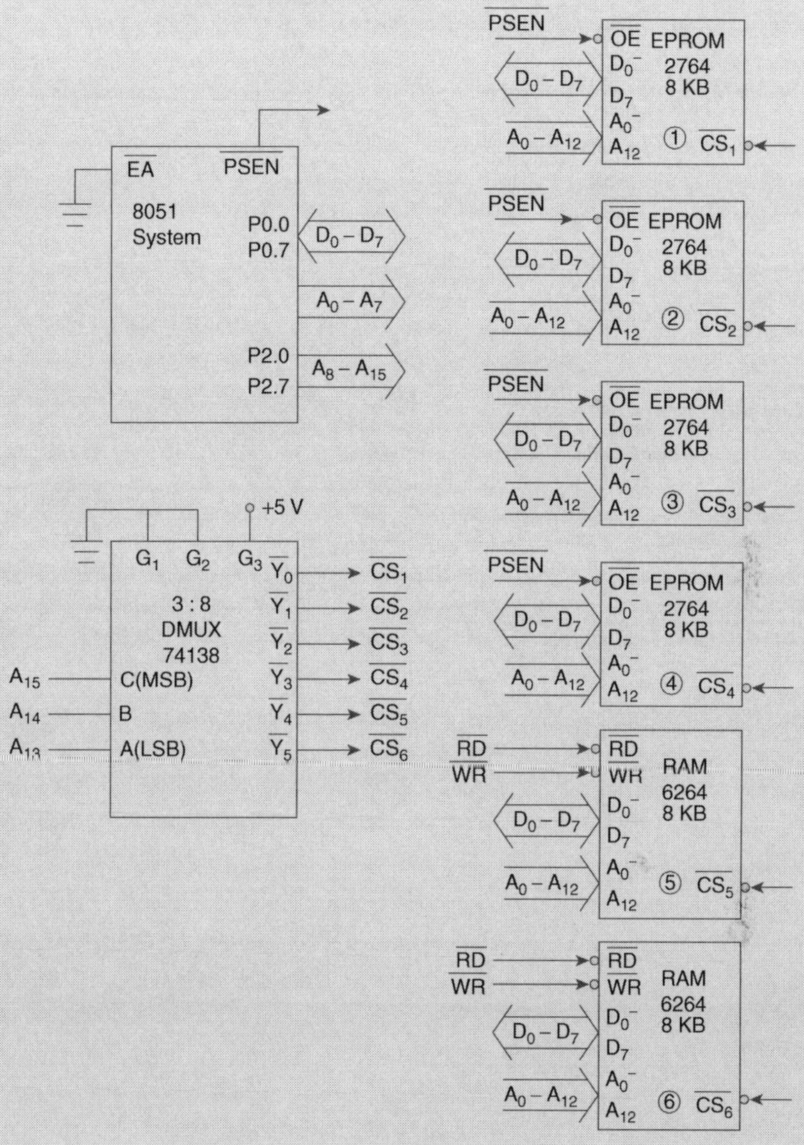

Fig. 18.5 *Interfacing Circuit for Example 18.4.*

Example 18.5

Interface on EPROM chip of 16 KB and a RAM chip of the same size, both at address 8000H using minimum hardware.

Solution

Available chips–16 KB = 2^{14} (A_0–A_{13}) Writing of the maps is left to the users. It is obvious that A_{14} and A_{15} will be used for chip select and as the map for both the chips is the same, a common chip select logic can be used to save the hardware as shown in Fig. 18.6.

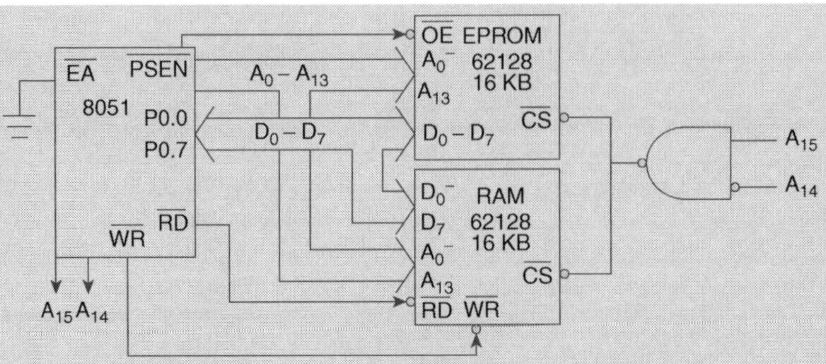

Fig. 18.6 *Interfacing circuit for Example 18.5*

Example 18.6

Interface a RAM chip of size 8 KB with 8051 such that its map will start at address 2000H and it will selected for the above map in program as well as data memory space.

Solution

For selecting the chip is program as well as data memory space (like in 8085), the $\overline{PSEN}$ signal and $\overline{RD}$ signal should be added as shown below in Fig. 18.7. The address map is starting at 2000H and it will end at 3FFFH for 8 KB chip size. The detail address map is left to the readers for practise.

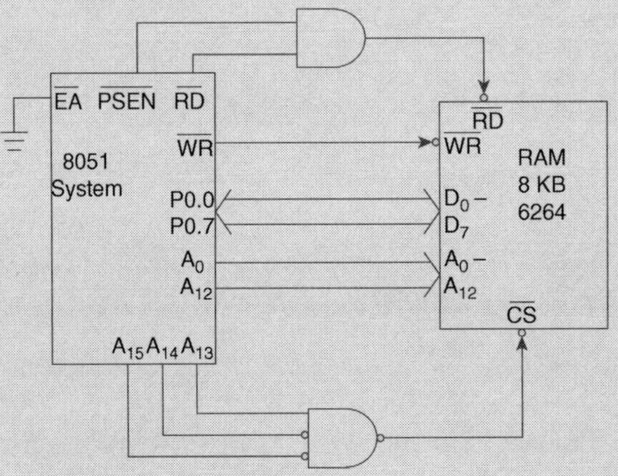

Fig. 18.7 *Interfacing circuit for Example 18.6.*

18.1.2 Interfacing LEDs and 7 Seg Displays

LEDs and 7 segment displays can be interfaced with microcontrollers using the available port lines or using the programmable parallel ports like 8255. In this chapter, interfacing of LEDs and 7 segment displays is presented in brief. LEDs can be connected with the port line (P) in two ways as presented in Fig. 18.8 (a) and (b).

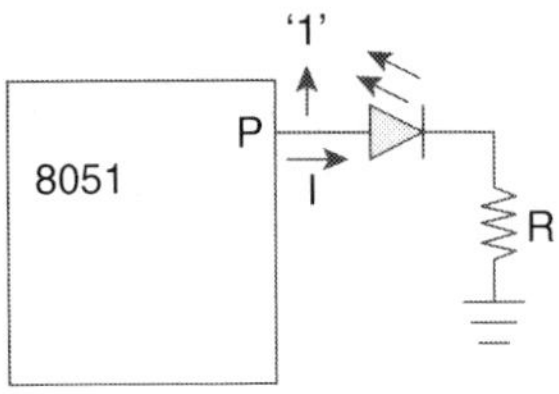

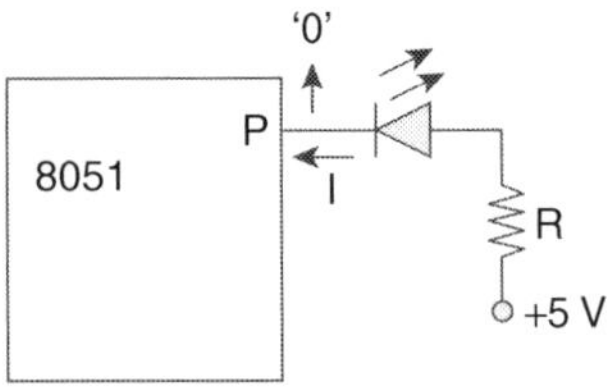

Fig. 18.8 (a) *Connecting a LED with a port line.* **Fig. 18.8 (b)** *Connecting a LED with a port line.*

In Fig. 18.8 (a), a logic level '1' needs to be applied for glowing the LED. The resistance R is a current limiting resistance usually in the range of 270 Ω to 470 Ω. In this configuration, the current required for glowing the LED is sourced by the pin 'P'. In Fig. 18.8 (b) a logic level '0' needs to be applied for glowing the LED. In this condition, the current required for glowing the LED is sourced by the '+5' V supply while it is sinked by the microcontroller pin. For appropriate glow, a LED typically requires 8–10 mA current with around 1.6 Volts across it. For the 8051 architecture family, the port lines individually can source only upto 0.5 mA. Obviously, the circuit configuration in Fig. 18.8 will not be able to drive the LED. However the individual port lines can sink upto 15 mA current as presented in Fig. 18.8. But a total current sinked by an 8 bit port must not exceed 26 mA and all the ports together (4 ports) should not be made to sink more than 71 mA. Thus if 8 LEDs are connected to a port of 8051, and if all are expected to glow simultaneously, the total current sinked by the 8051 port will be 8 × 8 = 64 mA. This is less than 71 mA. So it is acceptable till all other ports together do not sink more than 71–64 = 7 mA. Obviously if 16 LEDs are connected to two ports and if they are expected to glow all at a time, they would need 16 × 8 = 128 mA current to be sinked by 8051 ports. This is more than 71 mA, hence they will not glow properly. Under these limitations 8051 can drive the LEDs connected to its ports. If more current is sourced or sinked by 8051 port lines for a considerable time, the chip may be damaged parmanently.

From the above discussion it is clear that the LEDs or 7 segment displays will always be driven by the 8051 ports, such that the port lines sink currents, i.e. in common anode configuration. Further interfacing examples are presented to explain interfacing of LEDs and 7-segment display.

Problem 18.7

Interface 8 LEDs with 8051 port 0 and write assembly language programs to
a) glow all the LEDs continuously.
b) Flash all the LEDs on and off for 1 second each.
c) Glow alternate LEDs for 1 second and then shift the glowing pattern left continuously

Solution

The interfacing diagram is presented in Fig.18.9.

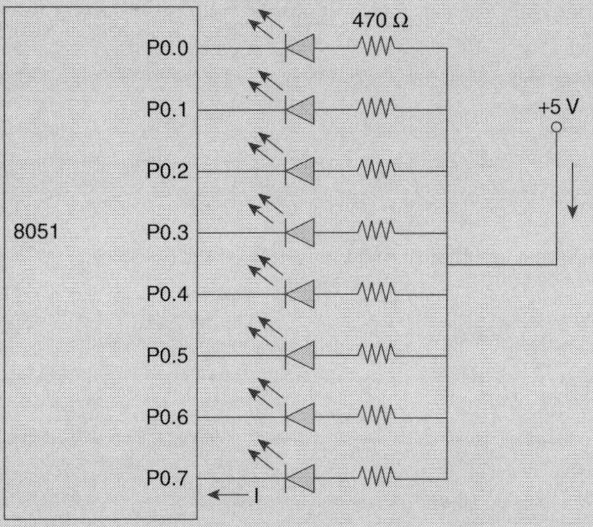

Fig. 18.9 *Interfacing LEDs with port 0 in common anode configuration.*

The assembly language programmes are given below, as programs 18.1 (a), (b) and (c)

```
(a)       Org  000              ; Start Program at internal
                                ; memory address 000 (12 bit)
          MOV  PO,#00H          ; send 00 to all port lines of PO to glow all LEDs
```

Program 18.1 (a) Program for Problem 18.7(a)

```
(b)       Org  000              ; Start program at 000 with a
          JMP  START            ; jump instruction, the 8051
          Org  010              ; compiler will convert the
START:    MOV  PO,#00H          ; jump to appropriate sjmp, ajmp,
                                ; ljmp automatically. The START
          CALL DELAY            ; label is at 010 H. Delay Of 1 sec. is
          MOV  PO,#0FFH         ; assumed available. Glow LEDs
          CALL DELAY            ; wait for 1 sec, make them 0H, wait
          JMP  START            ; for 1 second, continue.
```

Program 18.1 (b) Program for Problem 18.7 (b)

```
c)        Org  000              ; start program at 000
          MOV  ACC,#55H         ; 55H is pattern for glowing alternate
                                ; LEDs, take in Acc
REPEAT:   MOV  PO,ACC           ; Send it to port 0.Wait by
          CALL DELAY            ; Calling delay of 1 sec.
          RL   ACC              ; Rotate glowing LED pattern left.
          JMP  REPEAT           ; Send it to port 0 and continue.
```

Program18.1 (c) Program for Problem 18.7 (c).

Problem18.8

Interface a 7 Segment common anode display with port 3 of 8051 and write assembly language programmes to–

a) Displaying the given one digit hexadecimal number in accumulator.
b) Displaying the decimal numbers 0–9 for 1 seconds each and then stop.
c) Displaying the numbers 0–F for 1 seconds each continuously.

Solution

The Interfacing diagram is presented in Fig.18.10.

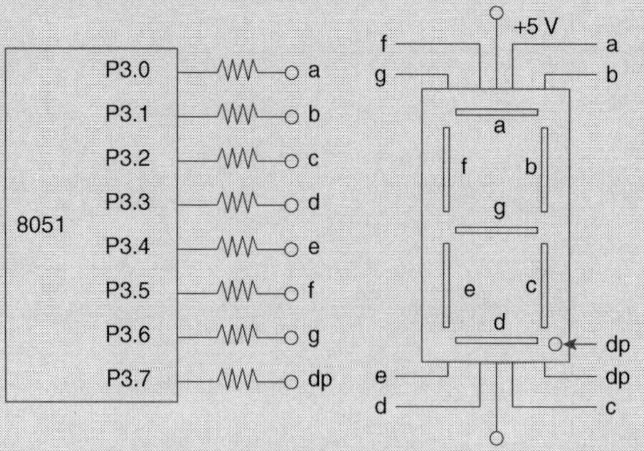

Fig. 18.10 *7-Seg common anode display interfacing with 8051.*

The 7- seg codes of the numbers 0 to F are decided as below. For glowing a segment, cathode of the respective segment must be applied logic '0' and for Keeping it off it must be applied logic '1'.

Num.to Display	7- Seg Display	Port 3 Connections								7 seg code
		P3.7 (dp)	P3.6 (g)	P3.5 (f)	P3.4 (e)	P3.3 (d)	P3.2 (c)	P3.1 (b)	P3.0 (a)	
0	0	1	1	0	0	0	0	0	0	COH
1	1	1	1	1	1	1	0	0	1	F9H
2	2	1	0	1	0	0	1	0	0	A4H
3	3	1	0	1	1	0	0	0	0	B0H
4	4	1	0	0	1	1	0	0	1	99H
5	5	1	0	0	1	0	0	1	0	92H
6	6	1	0	0	0	0	0	1	0	82H
7	7	1	1	1	1	1	0	0	0	F8H
8	8	1	0	0	0	0	0	0	0	80H
9	9	1	0	0	1	0	0	0	0	90H
A	A	1	0	0	0	1	0	0	0	88H
B	B	1	0	0	0	0	0	1	1	83H
C	C	1	1	0	0	0	1	1	0	C6H
D	D	1	0	1	0	0	0	0	1	A1H
E	E	1	0	0	0	0	1	1	0	86H
F	F	1	0	0	0	1	1	1	0	8EH

The above 7- seg codes need to be sent to P3 for displaying the respective number. All the 7 segment codes will be stored in Look-up-table that starts at a known address in program memory. This address will be called base address of the look up table starting from the base address of the LUT. Every address will store one 7- segment code byte in the same sequence as that of the numbers. Thus if the LUT starts at 050H with the code of 0, it will end at 5FH with the code of digit F. For finding 7 segment code of a digit, it will be added with base of the look up table; the 7-seg code byte will be read from the resulting address and sent to the port for display. The program listings for this problem are presented below in programs 18.2(a), (b) and (c).

```
ORG 000                     ; Start code at 000
MOV DPTR,#0050H             ; Base of LUT in DPTR
MOV ACC,#05                 ; Character to be
                            ; displayed in A
                            ; Take 7- seg code of
MOVC ACC,@ACC+DPTR          ; 5 in Acc.
MOV P3, ACC                 ; Send it to P3

ORG 050H
LUT db COH, F9H,A4H, BOH, 99H, 92H, 82H, F8H, 80H, 90H, 88H, 83H, C6H, A1H,
86H, 8EH
end
```

Prog 18.2(a) Prog for problem 18.8(a)

(b) The starting address of the program and the look up table is the Programmer's choice. The Look up table must be defined in the programmer's before the 'end' statement either before starting the instruction sequence or at the end of the instruction sequence. This program starts at 050 and the look up table starts at 020H. The delay of 1 sec is assumed to be available.

```
        ORG 000
        JMP START
        ORG 020H
        LUT DB COH, F9H, A4H, BOH, 99H, 92H, 82H, F8H, 80H, 90H, 88H, 83H,
        C6H, A1H, 86H, 8EH
        ORG 050
START:  MOV DPTR,#0020H          ; Pointer to LUT
        MOV ACC#00               ; 0 for displaying
NEXT:   MOVC ACC,@ACC+DPTR       ; Find 7-seg code
        MOV P3, ACC              ; send to P3
        CALL DELAY               ; Call 1 sec delay
        INC ACC                  ; increment for
                                 ; displaying the next
                                 ; Number
        CJNE ACC,#0AH, NEXT      ; If numbers upto A
                                 ; are displayed, stop
        END                      ; else continue.
```

Prog. 18.2 (b) Program for Problem 18.8 (b).

```
(C)     ORG 000
        JMP START
        ORG 020H
        LUT DB COH, F9H, A4H,-----------
        ORG 050H
START:  MOV DPTR,#020H
AGAIN:  MOV ACC,#00
NEXT:   MOVC ACC, @ ACC+DPTR
        MOV P3, ACC
        CALL DELAY
        INC ACC
        CJNE ACC,#10H, NEXT      ; If the number
                                 ; up to F are not displayed
                                 ; continue to the next
        JMP AGAIN                ; number else start again from 0
        END
```

Prog. 18.2(c) Program for Problem 18.8 (c)

So for we have discussed interfacing of common anode configuration LEDs and 7 segment displays. How-ever in some typical application it may be compulsory to interface LEDs or 7 segment displays in common cathode configuration. In such cases transistor driver circuits as shown in Fig. 18.11(a) and (b) may be used.

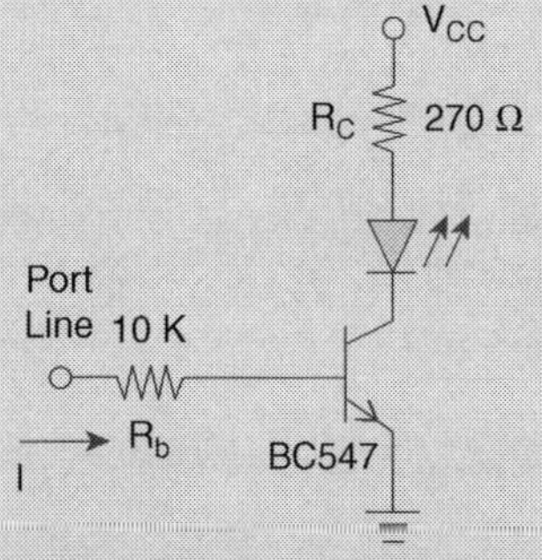

Fig. 18.11 (a) *Current Driver for a LED in sourcing mode.*

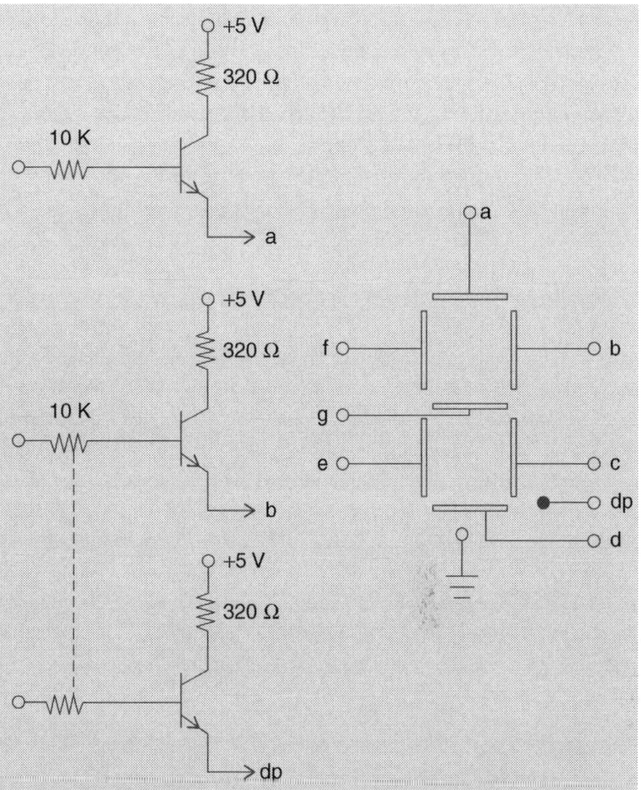

Fig. 18.11 (b) *Current Driver for common cathod 7 seg LED display*

The above driver circuits can be easily designed considering cut in voltage of LED = 1.6 V, current through LED=8 mA, $V_{be} = 0.5$ V, V_{ce}=1 V (transistor is not in saturation) and $I_b = 500$ μA at input voltage 5V (logic 1).

18.1.3 Multiplexed 7-seg Common Anode Display Interfacing

As it is clear from Problem 18.2, for interfacing a 7-segment display one 8-bit input/output port is required. Thus for practical applications requiring many such display units, as many ports may be required. To minimize the required number of ports for interfacing multiple 7-segment display units, the concept of multiplexed 7-segment display was introduced.

Using the concept of multiplexed displays, up to eight 7-segment display units can be interfaced using only two ports of 8 lines each. One of the ports is used as a data port for transmitting 7 segment codes of the digits to be displayed but one at a time. The 7 seg code sent out by this port reaches all the 7 segment display units simultaneously as they are connected in parallel i.e. all 'a's, all 'b's, all 'c's and so on the all 'dp's are connected together. But out of the eight display units only one is selected at a time using another port. Thus the 7 segment code of a digit is transmitted by the first port and while it is latched, the second port selects the display unit at which the digit is to be displayed. As soon as the display is selected by the second port, the digit start glowing on that display position. This unit glows for a duration of around 5 ms (approximately). After 5 ms, the 7 segment code of the glowing display is over written by the 7-segment code of the new digit to be displayed at the next adjuscent position. While the 7 segment code is being latched at the first port, the second port selects the display unit at which it is to be displayed. This display unit also starts glowing as soon as it is selected. Only one display glows at a time. So as soon as the second display starts glowing, the first one is deselected and goes off. Rather the second start glowing, only after the first one is deselected and goes off. In this manner starting from either right most or left most digit every digit glows for 5 ms one by one. Thus one scan of the 8 digit display requires 40 ms. After glowing all the displays once, the procedure is repeated continuously. Thus in one second 25 scans of the complete 8-digit display can be carried out. Due to persistence of vision all 8 display units appear to be glowing continuously.

While interfacing the multiplexed displays units with microcontroller, appropriate care must be taken not to exceed the sourcing or sinking capabilities of the microcontroller chip. Hence it is advisable to always use appropriately designed driver for interfacing common cathode or common anode displays. The following example elaborates the interfacing of common cathode displays.

Problem 18.9

Interface a common cathode 7 segment display unit containing 6 displays with 8051 ports in multiplexed fashion. Use port 1 as data port and port 2 as display select port. Write assembly language programs for;

a. Displaying the number 0 to 5 starting from most significant display.
b. A display buffer starting at 40H in internal RAM contains the 6 digits to be displayed. Display them starting from the least significant digit.

Solution

The 7 segment codes of the digits 0 to 9 can be taken directly from problem 18.8 for the common anode displays, and stored in a look up table from 050H. This look up table can also be stored in the code memory at appropriate address. In that case, MOVC instructions with appropriate operands can be used for accessing the look up table. The multiplexed displays unit containing six common anode displays is shown in Fig. 18.12. It uses port 0 for driving 7- seg data lines a to dp and port 2.0 to port 2.5 for selecting the displays.

It must be noted that though the common anode displays are used here, the display segment a, b, c,......dp will glow only if the respective port 0 line is high and the respective transistors Q conduct Also to glow a digit on a 7 segment display the respective transistor T also must conduct i.e. the respective port 2 line driving the base of T must be high. Thus the transistor Q are segment drivers while the transistors T are display drivers. The program for problem 18.9 are presented further. A delay of 5 ms is assumed to be available.

```
(a)     ORG 000
        JMP START
        ORG 010
        LUT DB (COH, F9H, A4H, ------------)
        ORG 050
START:  MOV DPTR,#0010H          ; Pointer to Look up table
        MOV R2,#00H              ; Number to be displayed
        MOV R3,#01H              ; Starts from 0, Enable
NEXT:   MOV A,R2                 ; display code in R3
        MOVC A,@A+DPTR           ; Code of char. in A
        CPL A
        MOV P0,A                 ; Send it to port 0
        MOV P2,R3                ; Select display.
        CALL DELAY (5 ms)
        INC R2                   ; Next number to display
        MOV A,R3                 ; Select next digit
        RL A                     ; by rotating R3
        MOV R3, A
        CJNE R2,#6, NEXT         ;
        JMP START
        END
```

Prog 18.9(a) A program for Problem 18.9(a)

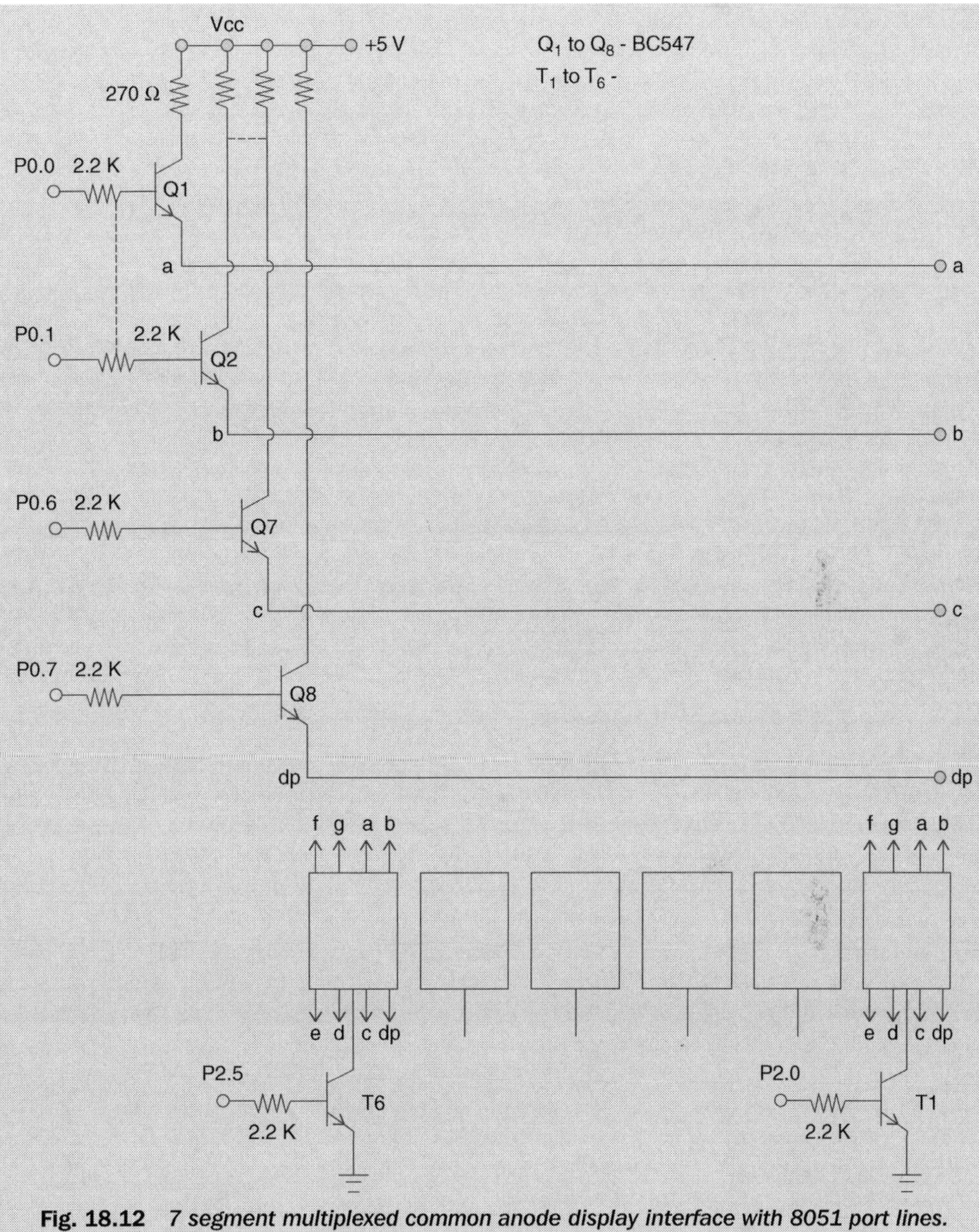

Fig. 18.12 *7 segment multiplexed common anode display interface with 8051 port lines.*

The prog. 18.9 (a) displays only fixed data 0 to 5 on the 7 segment display. The Prog 18.9(b) displays a data available in a display buffer in RAM.

```
(b)     ORG 000
        JMP START
        ORG 010
```

```
        LUT DB (0C0H, 0F9H, -------)
        ORG 050
START:  MOV R0,#050H          ; Display buffer pointer
                              ; in RAM.
        MOV DPTR,#0010H       ; LUT pointer in DPTR
        MOV R3,#01H           ; Display select code in
                              ; R3 for Least significant display
NEXT:   MOV A,@R0             ; Char. in A
        MOVC A,@A+DPTR        ; code in A
        CPL A
        MOV P0,A              ; send 7 seg code to P0
        MOV P2,R3             ; Select display
        CALL DELAY            ; Call delay 5ms
        INC R0                ; Point to the next char.
                              ; in buffer
        MOV A,R3              ; Select the next display
        RL  A                 ;
        MOV R3,A              ; The next digit select code
        CJNE Ro,#56H, NEXT    ; in R3. If all digits are
        JMP START             ; Displayed again start from
        END                   ; 050H else Stop.
```

Prog . 18.9 (b) Program for Problem 18.9 (b)

18.1.4 Keys and Keyboard Interfacing

Individual keys or key matrices called keyboards are important parts of many important appliances. In this section, interfacing of individual keys and keyboards with 8051 ports has been presented in brief. Number of keys are required to be interfaced key matrices called keyboards are used. In principle, a depression of a key is converted into a change in the logic level at a microcontroller input port line. This change is sensosed by the microcontroller by continuously reading the port lines to detect a key closure. Once a key is pressed and detected by the microcontroller, appropriate decision can be taken i.e. the program execution may jump to a specific routine that serves the key. In case of keyboards a pressed key changes the logic level on the row and column driving port lines of the microcontroller. This change in the logic level at the row and column number of the pressed key is used to find out the key code of the specific key. The key code for each key is unique. Thus the key code generated after pressing a key is used to identify the key. Further action like executing a specific routine or even resetting the system can be taken after correctly identifying the key. But appropriate hardware circuit must be designed to yield a perfect logic level transition after closure of a key so that it is identified correctly. Many ready made modules of press keys and touch pad keys keyboards are already available in the market. The interfacing and primary concepts of keys and debouncing have already been discussed in Chapter 5. A few interfacing problems have been considered further.

Problem: 18.10

Interface 8 keys with port 2 of 8051. Also interface 8 LEDs on port 1 of 8051. Interface a 7-segment display on port 0 of 8051. Write ALPs for the following.

(a) Read status of all keys and reflect it on LEDs. ON LED respresents closed key
(b) The LSB port line key is considered key '0' while that at MSB port line is considered key '7' Display the number of the pressed key on the 7 segment display. Assume only 1 key is pressed at a time.
(c) The 7 segment display is displaying numbers 0 to 9 continuously, but if the key '5' is pressed the display will be blanked.

Solution

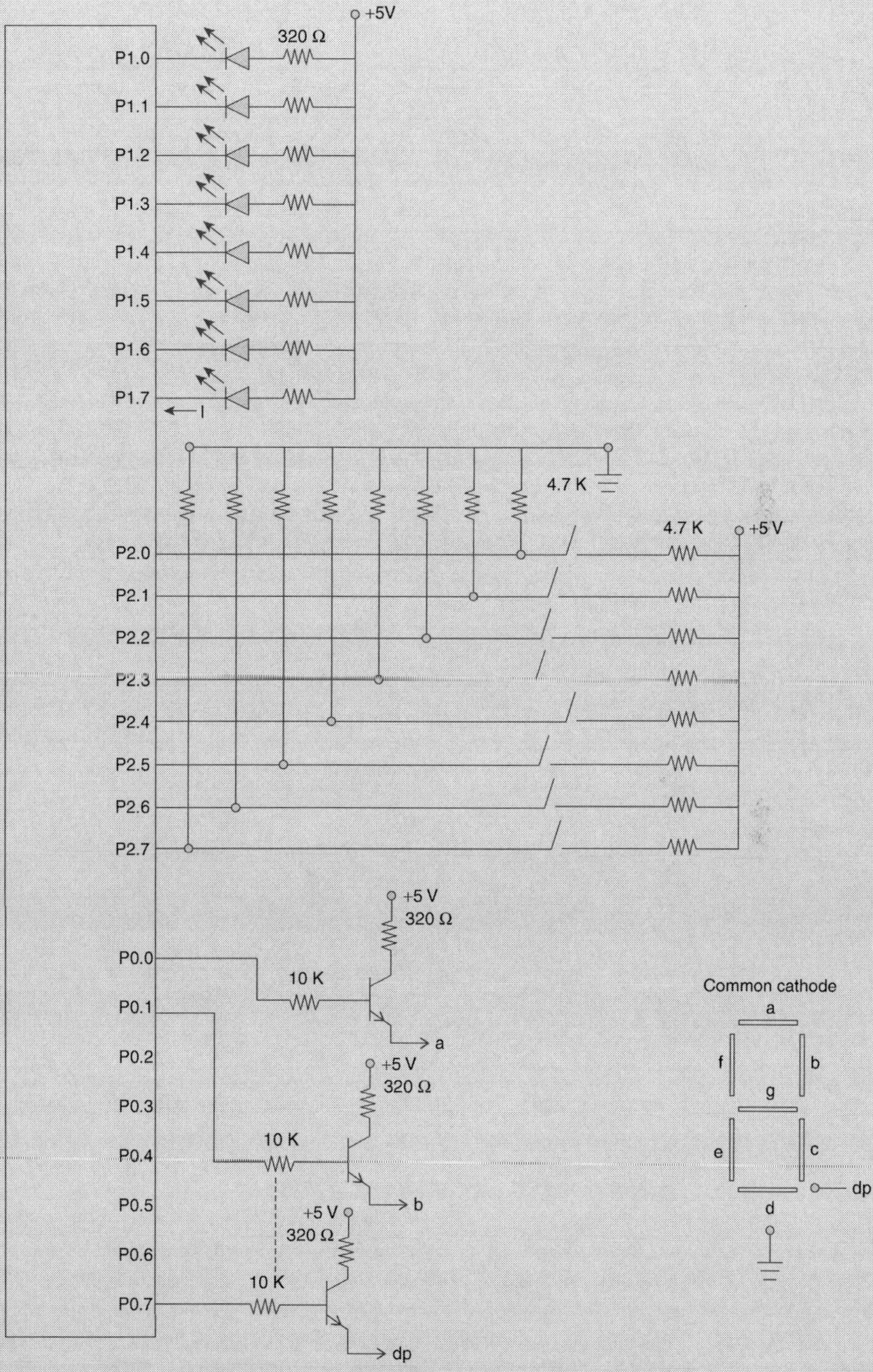

Fig. 18.13 *Interfacing circuit for Problem 18.10.*

Solution

The hardware system of the complete problem is presented in Fig. 18.13. The value of the registers must be appropriately calculated to yield a perfect transition from logic 0(0V) to logic 1 (>2.4V) to represent to the change in status of a key. The driver circuits for the display and the LEDs have already been presented in Fig. 18.11 (a) and (b).

The assembly language programes for this problem have been presented below.

```
(a)     ORG  000
        JMP  START
        ORG  050H
START:  MOV  P2,#0FF H          ; Declare P2 as input port.
        MOV  A, P2              ; Read key status
        CJNE A,#00, LEDS        ; If a key pressed send to LEDS
        JMP  START              ; else wait
LEDS:   CALL DEBOUNCE           ; If a key is pressed wait
        CPL  A                  ; for debounce period
        MOV  P1, A              ; delay (10ms). Glow LEDS
        JMP  START              ; corresponding to pressed
        END                     ; Keys and continue
```

Program. 18.10(a) Program for Problem 18.10 (a)

```
(b)     ORG  000H
START:  MOV  P2,#0FF H
        MOV  A,P2
        CJNE A,#00,KCODE
        JMP  START
KCODE:  MOV  R0,#00             ; counter for key number
        CALL DEBOUNCE           ; wait for debounce
        MOV  DPTR,#050H         ; key pointer to LUT
                                ; send code for display
NEXTK   RRC A
        JC DISP
        INC R0
        JMP NEXTK
DISP:   MOV A, R0               ; The key code (number 0-7)
        MOVC A,@ A+DPTR         ; Get code of the key
        CPL A                   ; convert for common cathode.
        MOV P0, A               ; Send complemented code
                                ; to display port P0.
        JMP START               ; continue
        ORG 050
LUT DB '0C0H', '0FgH'......
```

Program 18.10(b) Program for Problem 18.10 (b)

```
(c)     ORG 000H
        JMP START
        ORG 020H
        LUT DB '0C0H', '0FgH',.......
START:  MOV R0#00H              ; Start display from 0
NEXT1:  MOV DPTR#0020H          ; pointer to LUT.
```

```
        MOV   A, R0
        MOVC  A, @ A+DPTR         ; Get code of char in A
        MOV   P0, A               ; Send for display and
        CALL  DELAY (1SEC)        ; display it for 1 sec.
        INC   R0                  ; Get prepared to display
                                  ; the next number.
        MOV   P2,#0FF H           ; Check it key 5 is
        MOV   A,P2                ; Pressed.
        CJNE  A,#00100000b        ; NEXT ; If key5 is not
        JMP   BLANK               ; Pressed display
                                  ; the next number.
NEXT:   CJNE  R0,#0AH, NEXT1      ; If it is pressed, display
        JMP   START               ; i.e. send 00to po i.e.blank
BLANK:  MOV   A,#00               ; Blank i.e.0 all P0
        MOV   P0, A               ; lines
        END
```

Program .18.10 (c) Program for Problem 18.10 (c)

Problem 18.11

Interface a 4 × 4 keyboard with 8051 ports and get the key number (from 0–15) after a key is pressed in R2.

Solution

The interfacing circuit is presented in Fig. 18.14.

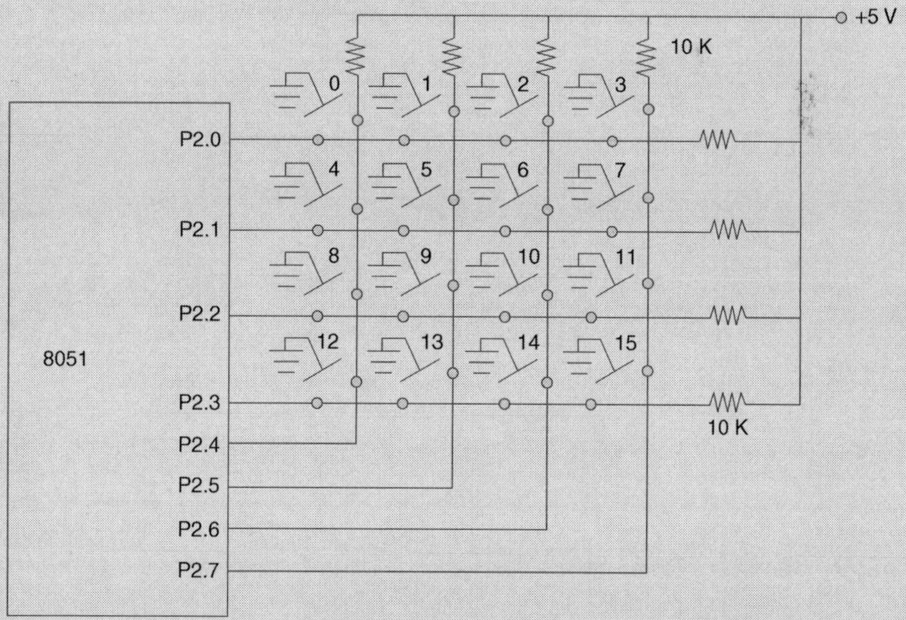

Fig. 18.14 *Interfacing a 4×4 keyboard with 8051 port 2.*

In Fig. 18.14, lines P2.0 to P2.3 are driven by keyboard rows 1 to 4 respectively while the lines P2.4 to P2.7 are driven by columns (1to4)of the keyboard. The key codes (0–15) are shown in the interfacing circuit. When no key is pressed all the port lines are high. Whenever a key is pressed the respective row and column will go low. We are assuming that only one key is going to be pressed at a time. The program for interfacing keyboard is presented is Program 18.11.

```
          ORG  000
          JMPSTART
          Org  050
START:    MOV  R2,#00                ; registers are reserved
          MOV  R1,#03                ; R2 for row info and R1 for column
WAIT:     MOV  P2,#0FF H             ; Initialize P2 as input
          MOV  A, P2                 ; port and read it.
          CJNE A,#0FF H, KEY   ; Key pressed? if Yes
          SJMP WAIT                  ; detect code, if no wait.
KEY:      CALL DEBOUNCE              ;
          MOV  P2,#0FFH              ; Read port again
          MOV  A, P2                 ; (may not be necessary)
          MOV  R3, A                 ; Store in R3.
          ANL  A,#0FH                ; Get row info and
ROW:      RRC  A                     ; convert into code.
          JC   COL                   ; Row detected ? go for
          INC  R2                    ; column detection , if
          JMP  ROW                   ; not continue row detection
COL:      MOV  A, R3                 ; Get column info.
          ANL  A,#FOH                ; Rotate though
COL1:     RLC  A                     ; carry. If column is
          JC   KEYCODE               ; detected go for key
          DEC  R1                    ; code else continue
          JMP  COL1                  ; column detection
KEYCODE:  MOV  A, R2                 ; key code = (row no ) × 4+col. No.
          RLA                        ; shifting left twice is
          RLA                        ; equivalent to multiply by 4.
          ADD  A, R1                 ; add to col. no
          MOV  R0, A                 ;
          END
```

Program. 18.11 Listing for interfacing 4×4 keyboard for Problem 18.11

18.1.5 Interfacing ADC 0808 / 0809

The principle of operation, block diagram and signal descriptions of ADC 0808 / 0809 have already been presented in Chapter 5 in significant details. In this section, the interfacing circuit and related program has been presented directly.

Problem 18.12

Interface an 8-bit ADC 0808 / 0809 with 8051 ports. Further write assembly language programs for:

a) Reading the digital equivalent of the analog inputs applied at channel 0 and channel 5 and store them in R0 and R1.
b) Reading the digital equivalent of all the channels (0–7) and store them starting from address 50 H in internal RAM.

Solution

The ADC 0808/0809 is interfaced using port lines P0 as data port and P1.0, P1.1 and P1.2 are used for ALE, SOC and EC respectively. Port lines P2.0, P2.1 and P2.3 are used for selecting the analog input channel using address lines A, B and C. The address line A is the least significant line. The 8051 interfacing circuit with ADC 0808/0809 is Presented in Fig. 18.15.

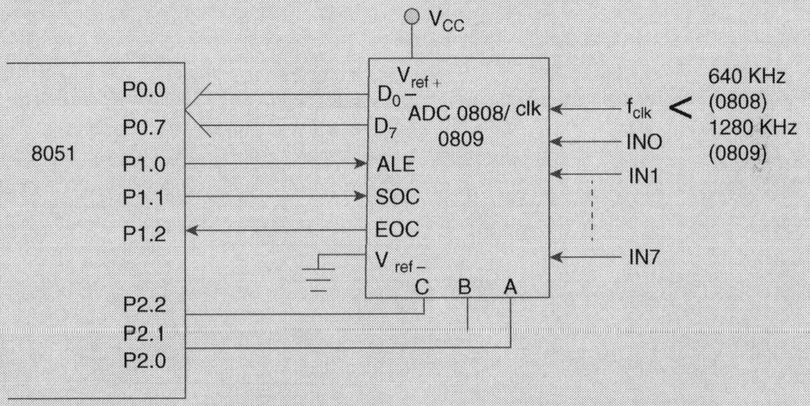

Fig. 18.15 *Interfacing circuit of ADC 0808/0809 with 8051.*

The programs are presented further in programs 18.12 (a) and (b).

```
(a)     ORG  000
        MOV  P0,#0FF H          ; Initialize P0 as input.
        MOV  P2,#00 H           ; select channel address
        CLR  P1.0               ; 000 (CBA) and generate ALE
        SETB P1.0               ; pulse at P1.0
        NOP                     ;
        CLR  P1.0               ; Input channel 0 selected.
        CLR  P1.1               ; Issue soc PULSE at P1.1
        SETB P1.1               ;
        NOP                     ;
        CLR  P1.1               ; SOC pulse issued conversion
                                ; starts. Start checking EOC
                                ; on P1.2. Declare it input
WAIT0:  SETB P.2                ; an input line keep on
        MOVB C, P1.2            ; waiting for EOC (carry).
        JNC  WAIT0              ; If carry is high read
        MOV  R0, P0             ; P0 and store in R0
        MOV  P2,#05             ; set channel address 101= 01
        CLR  P1.0               ; Issue ALE pulse
```

```
          SETB P1.0                    ;
          NOP
          CLR  P1.0                    ;
          CLR  P1.1                    ; Issue SOC pulse
          SETB P1.1
          NOP
          CLR  P1.1                    ; soc pulse issued.
WAIT5:    MOVB P1.2,#1b;
          MOVB C, P1.2
          JNC WAIT5;
          MOV R5, P0                   ; Store digital equivalent in R5.
          END
```

Program 18.12(a) Listing for Problem 18.12(a).

```
(b)       ORG 000
          MOV P0,#0FFH
          MOV R0,#050H                 ; Pointer to memory
          MOV R1,#00H                  ; Channel number
CONTINUE: MOV P2, R1                   ; Channel number to P2
          CLR P1.0                     ; Issue ALE
          SETB P1.0
          NOP
          CLR P1.0
          CLR P1.1
          SETB P1.1
          NOP
          CLR P1.1                     ; SOC pulse issued
WAIT:     MOVB P1.2,#1b                ; Declare line P1.2 as input
          MOVB C, P1.2;
          JNC WAIT;
          MOV @ R0, P0;
          INC R1                       ; Go for the next channel
          INC R0                       ; Increment the memory pointer
          CJNE R1,#08,CONTINUE         ; continue for 8
                                       ; channels then stop
          END
```

Program 18.12(b) Listing for Problem 18.12(b)

18.1.6 Interfacing DAC 0808/0809

The DAC 0808 is an 8 bit, current output digital to analog converter available in 16 pin DIP package. It's accuracy is around ±0.2%.It accepts TTL or CMOS digital inputs. It can operate on power supplies from ±4.5 V to ±18 V. To convert its current output into voltage an external OPAMP is used. The DAC 0808 can be used with reference voltages V_{ref}+ and V_{ref}–up to V_{CC} and V_{EE} respectively. In case of general operations with microprocessors or microcontrollers, V_{CC} and V_{EE} are kept at +5v and 0v respectively. The DAC 0808 uses R-2R ladder with high speed CMOS switches to implement the analog to digital conversion. The signal description of DAC 0808 are similar to that of DAC 0800 as presented in chapter 5. The pin diagram and the application circuit of 0808 are presented in Fig. 18.16(a) and (b).

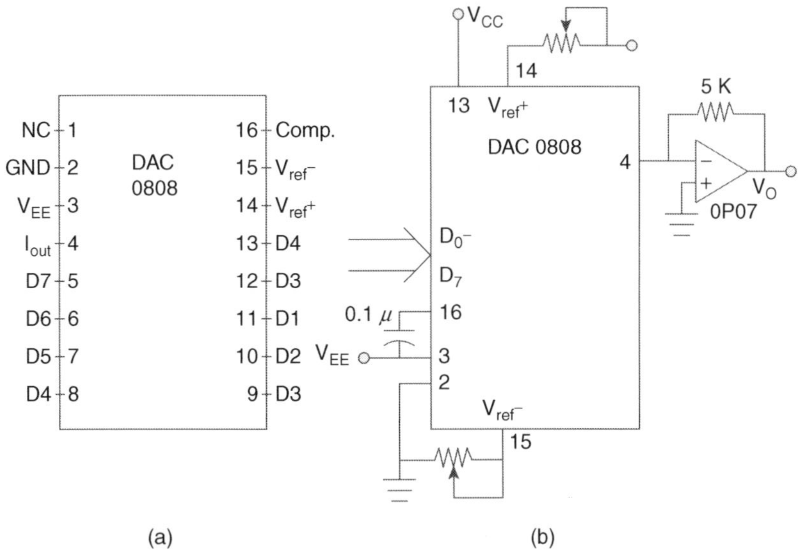

Fig. 18.16 *DAC 0808 and its functional circuit.*

While interfacing DAC 0808 with any processor, only output port lines are to be connected with D_0–D_7 lines of the DAC. After the settling time 100ns the equivalent analog voltage will be available at the output of the OPAMP. By appropriately varying the digital inputs applied to the DAC, some waveforms can be generated, as demonstrated in the following problems.

Problem 18.13

Interface DAC 0808 with 8051 port P1 and write assembly language programs;

(a) To generate a triangular wave of 0 to 3 V with frequency 100 Hz
(b) To generate a square waveform of 0–5 V frequency 500 Hz
(c) To generate the following pattern

Assume appropriate delays are available.

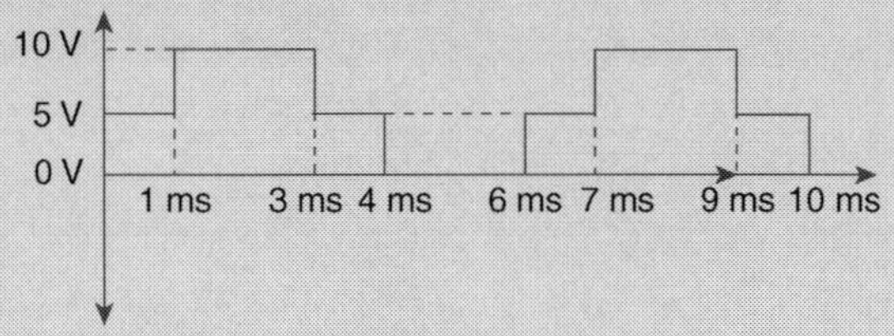

Fig. 18.17 *An irregular waveform.*

Solution

The interfacing circuit for section (a) and (b) of this problem is shown in Fig. 18.18(a).

In the above circuit $V_{ref}+$ and $V_{ref}-$ are directly tied with +5 V and 0 volts respectively. The maximum output swing will be 0 to 5 V. The program for (a) has been presented in 18.13(a)

$$\text{Resolution of DAC} = \frac{5}{2^8 - 1} = \frac{5}{255} = 0.0196 \text{ V} = 19.6 \text{ mV}$$

$$\text{Binary equivalent of 3V} = \frac{3}{19.6\text{mV}} = 153 = 99\text{H}$$

$$T = \frac{1}{100}\ \text{sec} = 10^{-2}\ \text{sec} = 10^{4}\ \mu\text{sec}$$

$$\text{Delay/count} = \frac{5000}{153} = 32.6$$

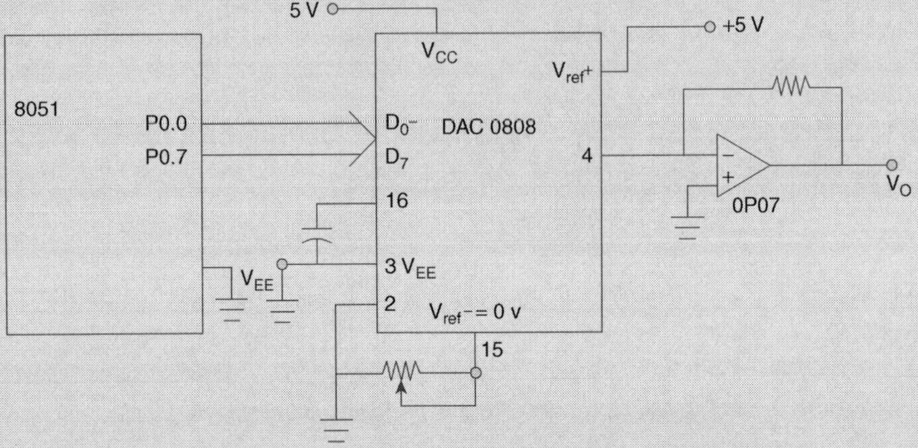

Fig. 18.18(a) *Interfacing DAC 0808 with 8051 (V_{out} = 0–5 V)*

```
           Org 000h
AGAIN:     MOV A,#00H
CONTINUE:  MOV P0, A
           CALL DELAY (32.68 us)
           INC A
           CJNE A,#9AH, CONTINUE
CONTINUE1: DEC A
           MOV P2, A
           CALL DELAY(32.68us)
           CJNE A,#0FFH, CONTINUE1
           SJMP AGAIN
           END
```

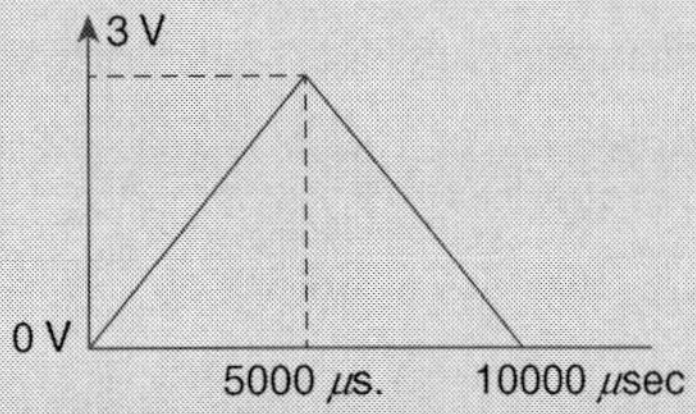

Fig. 18.18(b)

Program 18.13(a) Program for Problem 18.13(a)

```
(b)    ORG 000H                T = 1/500 = 2 ms
       MOV A,#00H              T_Low = 1 ms
AGAIN: MOV P0, A               T_High = 1 ms
       CALL DELAY (1 ms)
       CPL A
       SJMP AGAIN
```

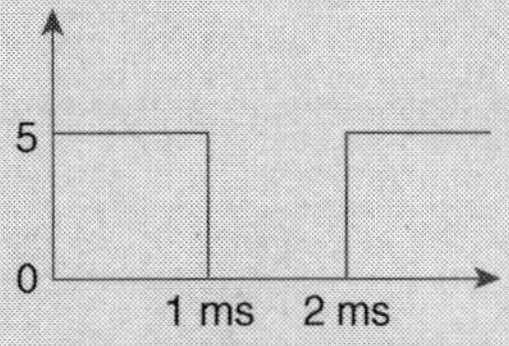

Fig. 18.18(c)

Program 18.13(b) Program for Problem 18.13(b)

(c) For generating the waveform shown in Fig. 18. 17. The circuit shown in Fig. 18.18(a) will be useful with V_{ref}+ tied with V and V_{ref} tied with Gnd, V_{EE} will be connected to Gnd. The assembly language program is presented in program 18.13(c).

```
ORG 000H
MOV A,#00H
MOV P0, A
```

```
REPEAT: MOV A,#80H
        MOV P0, A
        CALL DELAY(1ms)
        MOV A,#0FFH
        MOV P0, A
        CALL DELAY (1ms)
        CALL DELAY (1ms)
        MOV A,#80H
        MOV P0, A
        CALL DELAY (1ms)
        MOV A,#00H
        MOV P0, A
        CALL DELAY (1ms)
        CALL DELAY (1ms)
        JMP REPEAT
        END
```

Program 18.13(c) Program for Problem 18.13(c).

Thus DAC 0808 can also be used to generate voltage waveforms of amplitude bigger than 5 V. But it must be noted that the generated waveforms using this technique are not very accurate and smooth.

18.1.7 Interfacing Stepper Motors

Construction, transistorized driver circuits and interconnections of stepper motor windings have already been presented in Chapter 5. In this section, interfacing of a stepper motor using ULN series drivers has been presented with help of a problem.

Problem 18.14

Interface a 4–ϕ, 200 teeth, 9V stepper motor with 8051 using ULN and write assembly language programs for

(a) Rotating shaft of the stepper motor at a speed of 2 rotations per minute in clockwise direction.
(b) Rotating the shaft 180° anticlockwise in one minute.
(c) Rotating the shaft 90° back and forth in 30 seconds each continuously.

Solution

The interfacing diagram of a stepper motor with 8051 ports using ULN 293 drivers is shown Fig. 18.19.

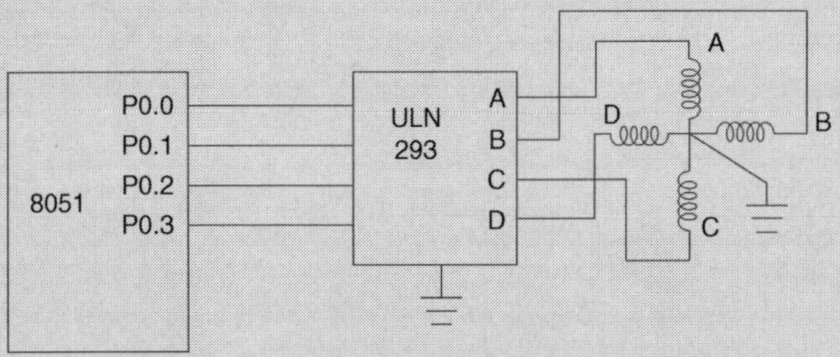

Fig. 18.19 *Interfacing stepper motor using ULN.*

While interfacing a stepper motor two points are very crucial.

1) Sequence of the windings A, B, C, D must be correctly known and connected.
2) Inertial delay of the stepper motor must be known. This delay must be allowed after each digital sequence input for the stepper motor shaft to respond. Stepper motors of inertial delay from 100 ms to 500 ms are generally available. Very fast stepper motors having delay around 20 ms are also available for special applications.

If the sequence of connection of the windings is wrong, the stepper motor shaft may not respond as programmed. If enough delay is not allowed after each input bit sequence, the shaft just slightly jerks at its position independent of the program. While selecting the ULN driver for a specific motor, its current rating per winding must be calculated using its voltage rating and winding resistance. The ULN driver of minimum double the calculated current rating must be used for interfacing the motor.

While writing the programmes for interfacing, either one winding can be energized at a time or two windings can be energized at a time by applying ones on the windings to be energized. The bit pattern is then shifted left or right depending upon the required direction of rotation. As already discussed in chapter 5, if the shaft is to be rotated clockwise i.e A→B→C→D→A, then the field must be rotated anticlockwise i.e. A→D→C→B→A. If the shaft is to be rotated anticlockwise i.e. A→D→C→B→A, the field must be rotated clockwise i.e. A→B→C→D→A. The technique of energizing two windings at a time offers more torque for rotation of the motor shaft as compared to energizing of single winding.

The program listings for problems 18.14(a), (b) and (c) are presented in programs 18.14 (a), (b) and (c) respectively.

(a) No of teeth = 200

Angle for 2 rotations = $2 \times 360^\circ = 720^\circ$

No of teeth to be rotated for 2 rotations = 2×200 = 400

Time available for 2 rotations = 1 min = 60 seconds

$$\text{Time available for 1 teeth rotation} = \frac{60\,\text{seconds}}{400} = 150\ \text{ms}$$

```
          ORG 000H
          MOV A,#11H             ; Bit pattern for energising winding
CONTINUE: MOV P0, A
          CALL DELAY (150 ms) ; Allow for 1 teeth delay
          RR A                   ; Energise the next winding
          SJMP CONTINUE
```

Program 18.14(a) Program for problem 18.14(a)

(b) No of teeth for one rotation 360° = 200

No of teeth for 180° = 100

Time available = 60 sec

$$\text{Time available per teeth} = \frac{60}{100} = 0.6$$

```
          ORG 000H
          MOV R0,#100                ; Count for no of teeth
          MOV A,#11H                 ; Bit pattern for energising
CONTINUE: MOV P0,A                   ; the windings
          CALL DELAY (0.6 sec)       ; Allow for 1 teeth delay
          RL A                       ; Rotate A for anticlockwise rotation
```

```
INC Ro ;  Rotated 100 times? Stop if yes
CINE Ro,#100,CONTINUE          ; continue if no.
END
```

Program 18.14(b) Program for problem 18.14(b)

(C) No of teeth required for 90° rotation $= \dfrac{90^\circ}{360^\circ} \times 200$

$= 50$

Time available for 50 teeth = 30 sec

Time available for rotation of one teeth $= \dfrac{30}{50} = 0.6$ sec

```
              ORG020H
CONTINUE:     MOV RO,#00H              ; Count for 90° rotation
              MOV A,#11H               ; Bit pattern
REPEAT1:      MOV PO, A;
              CALL DELAY (0.6 sec)     ; Allow for idelay for one teeth
              RL A                     ; Rotate for anticlockwise direction
              INC RO                   ; Rotate for 50 teeth.
              CINE Ro,#50,REPEAT1
              MOV Ro,#00H              ; Continue for clockwise
              MOV A,#11H               ; rotation.
REPEAT 2:     MOV PO,A
              CALL DELAY (0.6 sec)     ; Allow for delay per teeth
              RR A                     ; rotate for clockwise direction
              INC RO                   ; for 50 teeth
              CJNE Ro,#50,REPEAT 2
              JMP CONTINUE             ; Continue for ever
```

Program 18.14(c) Program for Problem 18.14(c)

It must be noted here that the motors are electromechanical components. They require sufficient current to flow from the windings to provide enough torque to rotate the shaft. The drivers used for the circuit interfacing must be capable of providing that much current. The inertial delay that must be provided after applying the digital bit pattern for rotation of every teeth depends upon the rotor dynamics of the motor. This parameter is provided by manufacturer of the motor. The inertial delay thus puts limitation on the highest possible speed of rotation of the motor shaft. For example a motor with number of teeth N=200 and inertial delay $T_d = 100$ ms, will require time $T = N \times T_d = 20000$ ms = 20 seconds for one rotation of the motor shaft. Thus it can not be rotated at a speed higher than $1/(N \times T_d)$ rotation per second or $60/(N \times T_d)$ rotation per minute.

18.2 DESIGNING WITH ON CHIP TIMERS

In this section, we initially discuss the on chip timers, their control words and function in details. Further a few problems have been presented to elaborate the design procedure using timers. If the on chip timers are not enough for a specific application, additional 8253 can be interfaced externally. The timer section of 8051 is programmed using a mode control Register (TMOD) and a Timer Operation Control (TCON) Register. The 16-bit SFRs T_0 and T_1; bytewise addressed as TH_0 and TL_0/TH_1 and TL_1 are used as count/timer registers for the respective timers or counters.

MCS 51 family microcontrollers have two on chip timers T_0 and T_1 in the basic version of the architecture. The timers T_0 and T_1 can be operated as either timers or counters separately. Both the timers or counters operate as up counters only. When they are being used as timers, an internal clock that is equivalent to the machine cycle clock of 8051 with frequency equal to $f_{osc}/12$ is used internally to decrement the timers. In the timer mode, T_0 and T_1 are used to derive timing delays. The required delay is given by count × $(12/f_{osc})$. The count thus calculated is subtracted from FFH or FFFFH depending upon 8 bit or 16 bit timer register being used and the resulting subtraction is loaded into the time register for up counting. The counter / timer register is then incremented on each–ve going edge subject to the programmed gate control in TMOD. Whenever it overflows, an overflow flag in the TCON register is set. Also an internal interrupt is generated if enabled. The overflow flag is cleared by software and the interrupt is automatically cleared.

In case of counter mode, the counters T_0 and T_1 are used to count clock pulses appearing at the T_0 and T_1 inputs of the microcontroller respectively. The T_0 and T_1 inputs are actually the clock inputs of the counters and are multiplexed with port lines P3.4 and P3.5 respectively. Thus in the counter mode the T_0 and T_1 are used to count external pulses applied to pins T_0 and T_1 respectively. In this mode, while T_0 and T_1 are counting external pulses, the inputs $\overline{INT0}$ and $\overline{INT1}$ act as respective gate inputs of the respective counters. As already known, if the gate input goes low the counting stops till it goes high again. Thus for uninterrupted counting using counters T_0 and T_1, the interrupts lines $\overline{INT0}$ and $\overline{INT1}$ must be maintained high. In every machine cycle, there are 6 states of operation (S_0, S_1, S_2.....S_5). In every state of operation, there are two cystal clock states (P_1 and P_2). For sensing the external clock, the pins T_0 and T_1 are checked in crystal clock state P2 of operation state S5 of each machine cycle. If it is high, it is again checked in the next machine cycle. And now if it is low, a negative transition is considered at the pin and the corresponding counter register is decremented by 1. Thus to sense one negative edge, two machine cycles are required. Hence the maximum counting frequency in counter mode is $f_{osc}/24$ as against $f_{osc}/12$ for timer mode. The procedure of computing the value of count, loading the counter registers, the upcounting followed by either overflow, or interrupt generation in counter mode is exactly simillar to the timer mode.

The on chip available 16 bit timers or counters can also be used as 8 bit or 16 bit depending upon requirement. As already said the other facets of operation of T_0 and T_1 are programmed or controlled using the TMOD and TCON registers. The registers TMOD and TCON followed by different modes of operation of the timers or counters are presented further.

18.2.1 Mode control register (TMOD;SFR address 89H)

The mode control register TMOD of 8051 allows gating control over the timers, selects each timer for either timer or counter operation and sets one of the four modes of operation of the timers or counters. The bit definitions of the TMOD register are presented in Fig. 18.20 followed by their respective descriptions.

D_7	D_6	D_5	D_4	D_3	D_2	D_1	D_0
GATE1	C/T1	M1	M0	GATE0	C/T0	M1	M0
Timer/Counter 1				Timer/Counter 0			

Fig. 18.20 *Bit Definitions of 8051 TMOD Register.*

The upper nibble of the TMOD register is used for programming Timer 1 configuration while the lower nibble is used for programming Timer 0 configuration.

If a GATE bit is '1' the respective timer or counter will have the GATE function activated. $\overline{INT0}$ will act as GATE input for Timer/Counter0 While $\overline{INT1}$ will act as GATE input for Timer/Counter1. If the GATE bit is one, the respective timer or counter will count up only if the $\overline{INT0}$ or $\overline{INT1}$ (for T_0 or T_1) is high. If INT pin goes low the counting will be withhold till the $\overline{INT}$ pin again goes high. If GATE bit is 0, the respective time/counter will count up independent of the status of $\overline{INT0}$ or $\overline{INT1}$ pin i.e. there will not be any GATE control C/T bit decides whether the timer/counter is to be used as a timer or a counter. If C/T bit is set '1', the corresponding timer/counter will work as a counter and it will count the pulses applied to the clock inputs T_0 or T_1. If C/T is set 0, the respective timer/counter will work as a timer and will be updated using internal machine cycle clock.

The mode control bits M1 and M0 can select one of the four modes of operations. The M1M0 can have binary values 00, 01, 10 and 11 for selecting modes; mode 0–8 bit timer with divided by 32 prescalar,mode 1-16 bit timer, mode 2–8 bit auto reload mode and mode 3- only timer0 as two 8 bit independent timers. The details of all these modes are presented further in the Section 18.2.3.

18.2.2 Timer/Counter Control Register (TCON SFR-88H)

This bit addressable register houses 8-bits. Most significant four bits either control the operation of the respective timers/counters or reflect the overflow condition. The least significant four bits are used to program the operating modes of the external interrupts or to store the received interrupt requests. The bit definitions of this register are presented in Fig.18.21.

D_7	D_6	D_5	D_4	D_3	D_2	D_1	D_0
TF1	TR1	TF0	TR0	IE1	IT1	IE0	IT0
Timer/Counter 1		Timer/Counter 0		$\overline{INT1}$		$\overline{INT0}$	

Fig. 18.21 *Bit Definition of TCON Register.*

TF0/TF1 bits are called overflow bits and are set by the internal hardware when the respective Timer/Counter overflows i.e. the count is incremented from FFFFH (FFH in case of 8-bit timer/counter) to 0000H (00H in case of 8 bit timer/counter). These bits are then reset by program instruction if required. TR0/TR1 bits are called timer run bits and if they are set the respective timer starts up counting, starting from the next–ve edge of the appropriate clock input as discussed earlier. During the counting by timer0 or timer1 if these bits are reset, the counting will stop till they are set again.

IE0/IE1 bits are set by the architecture when an external interrupt is detected on INT0/INT1 pins respectively. These bits are cleared automatically when the control of program execution is transferred to the respective interrupt service routine IT0/IT1 These bits are called interrupt type bits and are used to program the type of interrupts i.e. edge triggered or level triggered. If these bits are 1, the respective interrupts operated as–ve edge triggered interrupts otherwise they operate as low level triggered interrupts.

18.2.3 Modes of Operation

As already said, 8051 timers or counters can operate in the four modes of operations. Each of these modes have been discussed in brief in this section. Mode 0, Mode1 and Mode 2 are equally applicable to both the timer/counters T_0 and T_1, while mode 3 is only applicable to T0. In mode 3, T1 just holds its count and can be used for application like baud rate generation if preprogrammed accordingly.

Mode 0- Both the timers/counters of 8051 can act in mode 0. In mode 0, a timer/counter acts as a 13 bit up counters or timer in a typical way. Both 16-bit timer registers are addressed in terms of their lower and higher bytes using SFRs TL0/TL1 and TH0/TH1. The upper 8 bits i.e TH0 /TH1 are used to store an 8–bit count while the least significant 5 bits of TL0/TL1 are used as a prescaler to divide the input clock by 32. In case of timer the input clock is the machine cycle clock (f_{osc}/12) and in case counter application it can be external clock applied to T_0 or T_1. For dividing the input clock, the least significant bits of TL0/TL1 roll over from 00000H to 11111H and again start rolling from 00000H. Thus the least significant five bits of TL0/TL1 divide input frequency by 32. This divided by 32 frequency is now used to increment the 8 bit counter register TH0/TH1. Thus a 13-bit counter operation is achieved. After the 8 bit counter overflows, the respective overflow flag TF0/TF1 is set. If

Timer0/Timer1 interrupt is enabled and if it is not blocked by other higher priority events, the respective interrupt will be generated. Whenever the interrupt service routine starts execution, the TF0/TF1 flags are cleared. The vector addresses of Timer0 and Timer1 interrupts are 000BH and 001BH respectively. The 8 bit up counter TH0/TH1 continues up counting only if the TR0/TR1 bits are high. If the gate bits for the counters are enabled, then the external interrupt lines $\overline{INT0}/\overline{INT1}$ must be maintained high for the counting to continue. This mode is applicable to timer as well as counter mode. The conceptual operation of this mode is depicted in Fig. 18.22.

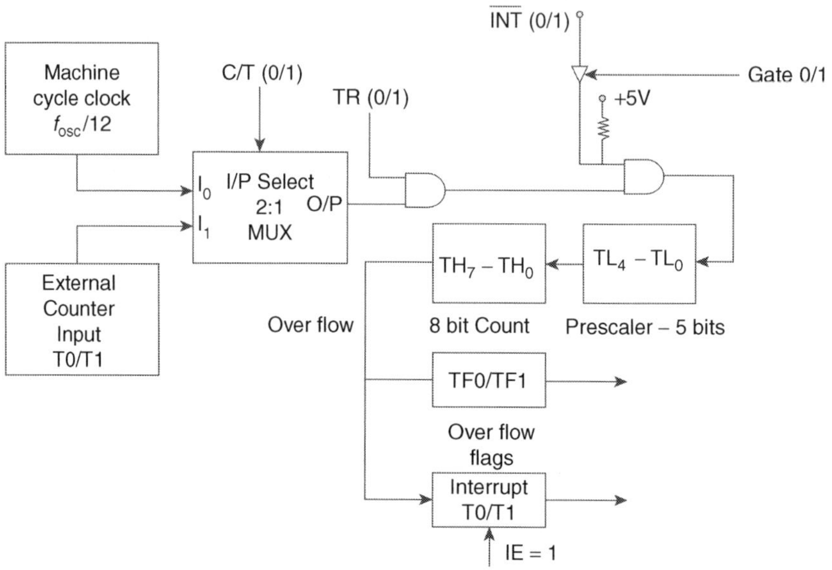

Fig. 18.22 *Operation of Mode 0.*

Mode 1–In this mode of operation, both the timers/counters work as 16 bit timer/counter. The remaining mode operation is exactly similar to that of mode 0. The timer/counter mode, Gate bit significance, $\overline{INT0}/\overline{INT1}$ functions as gates of T0 and T1 are also exactly similar to mode 0. The overflow flags TF0/TF1 and the interrupts of Timer0 and Timer1 with vector addresses 000BH and 001BH are also set in the exactly same manner as mode 0. However this mode will be able to derive bigger delays or count more pulses on T0 or T1 inputs due to 16 bit timer/counter registers. The conceptual mode operation is presented in Fig. 18.23.

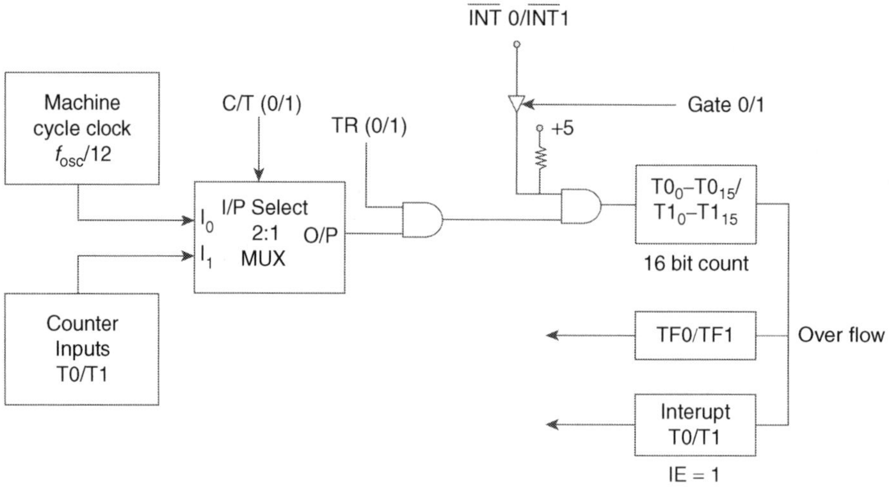

Fig. 18.23 *Operation of Mode 1.*

Mode 2–This mode is also called 8-bit autoreload mode. In this mode, the 16 bit timer counter registers T0 and T1 are considered in terms of their higher bytes TH0/TH1 and lower bytes TL0/TL1. The higher bytes are used to store 8-bit reload values. The lower bytes are used to store the actual 8-bit count that progresses and that starts from the reload value of the count. Thus the lower byte of a counter register and higher byte of a counter register are initially stored the same value. The count stored in the lower byte is updated with every negative edge of either machine cycle clock or external clock connected at inputs T0/T1 depending upon the C/T bit. The count stored in the higher byte remains the same. The count stored in the lower byte goes on increasing and overflows after FFH. After the overflow, the count maintained in the higher byte is copied into the lower byte of the timer register automatically and the upcounting again proceeds further. After each overflow, the reload count stored in the higher byte of the timer/counter register, thus, gets automatically copied into the lower byte, appropriate overflow flags TF0/TF1 are set and the timer interrupts are generated internally if they are enabled and not blocked due to other high priority tasks. The other considerations regarding the C/T, Gate, TR, TF bits and the clock inputs are exactly simillar to mode 0 and mode 1. The timers/counters can be in different modes independent of each other. When the generated interrupts after each overflow are vectored the TF1/TF0 are automatically cleared. If the interrupts are not enabled, the TF0/TF1 need to be cleared using program instructions. The Timer1 in mode 2 with interrupt disabled is used by default for baud rate generation for serial communication applications. The pictorial representation of the mode 2 operation is presented in Fig. 18.24.

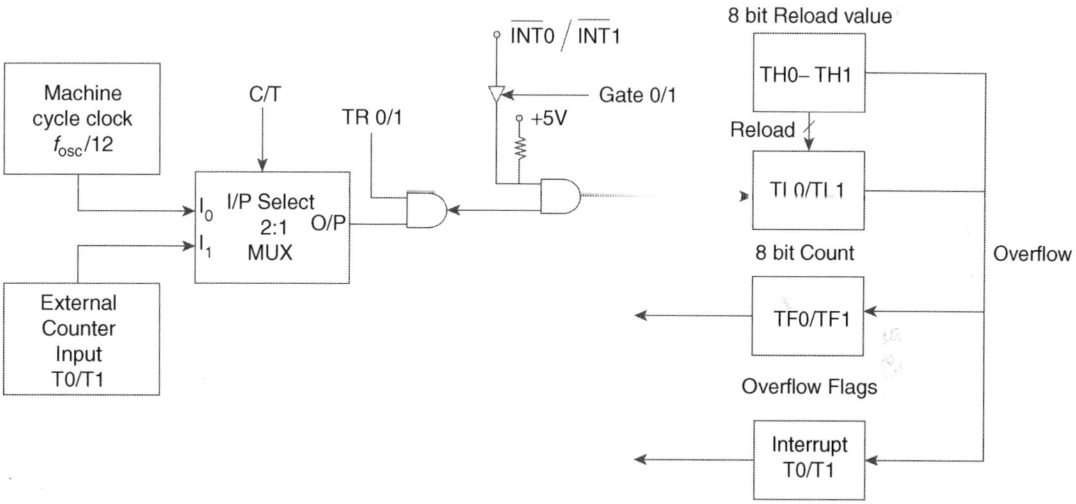

Fig. 18.24 *Operation of Mode 2.*

Mode 3–In mode 3, the timer/counter 0 is used as two independent 8 bit counters while the timer/counter1 just holds its count and is non functional. The lower and higher bytes of T0 i.e. TL0 and TH0 are parallely driven by the internal machine cycle clock ($f_{osc}/12$) or external clock input pin T0 for TH0 respectively depending upon, whether TL0 is used as a timer or a counter.TH0 is only used as a timer. The lower 8 bit timer/counter TL0 is programmed and controlled using the TMOD and TCON bits of timer/counter 0; for example Gate 0, C/T0, M1, M0, TF0,TRO etc. The upper 8 bit timer/counter TH0 is programmed and controlled using the TMOD and TCON bits of the non functional Timer/Counter; for example Gate1, C/T1, M1, M0, TF1, TR1 etc. Obviously the $\overline{INT0}$ and $\overline{INT1}$ functions as gate inputs for the lower 8 bit counter TL0 and upper 8 bit timer TH0 respectively. The upper 8 bit timer TH0 can work as only timer and it can't work as a counter i.e. it can not count pulses on T1. While the timer/counter 0 (T0) is programmed in mode 3, the original timer/counter1 that is non functional in mode 3, can be programmed in mode 0, mode 1 or mode 2. But in this case the original timer 1 will not be able to indicate its overflow as all its (TF1 and Timer 1 interrupt) mechanisms are used by TH0. However the original timer/counter1 can be used for generating serial communication baud rates by programming it in mode 2 as this application does not require any overflow flag or interrupt generation. Thus in mode 3, the Timer/counter 0 offers one 8 bit timer/counter TL0, one additional 8 bit only timer TH0 and original Timer/Counter1 for application like baud rate generation. Mode 3 operation is presented in Fig. 18.25.

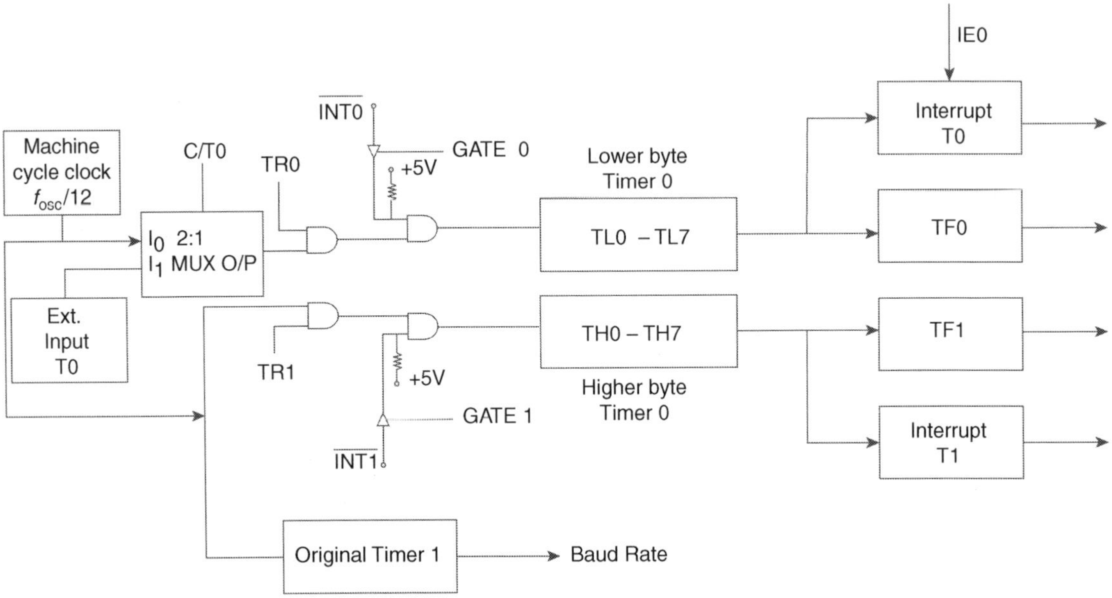

Fig. 18.25 *Operation of Mode 3.*

It must be noted that all the 8051 timers/counters functioning under various modes of operation generate only internal overflow or interrupt generation indications. They do not generate any external signals after overflow. So it is impossible to cascade two timers or counters directly. To solve this problem, a port line of 8051 is used. After overflow of the lower significant timer counter, the port line will be activated by the interrupt service routine and the port line can further drive the clock input of the next counter. The actual programming and design of systems using 8051 timers/counters has been elaborated further with help of the following problems

Problem 18.15

Using appropriate 8051 on chip timers, write assembly language programmes for the following.

(a) Generate a delay of 100 ms using an external frequency of 25 KHz.
(b) Generate a delay of 10 ms using internal machine cycle clock. (f_{osc} = 11.059 MHz)
(c) Generate a frequency of 100 Hz using an external clock of 20KHz at pin P0.0

Solution

The choice of timers or counters for implementing a particular application is totally a choice of the programmer. However for designing specific bigger application, a very thoughtful use of the timers based on the different available modes of operation is required.

a) For writing this assembly language program timer 0 is used as counter in mode 0. In this mode, the external frequency applied at external input T0 is first divided by a prescalar 32 in TL0 and then internally applied as a clock to the 8 bit timer in THO. The arrangement is shown below in Fig. 18.26

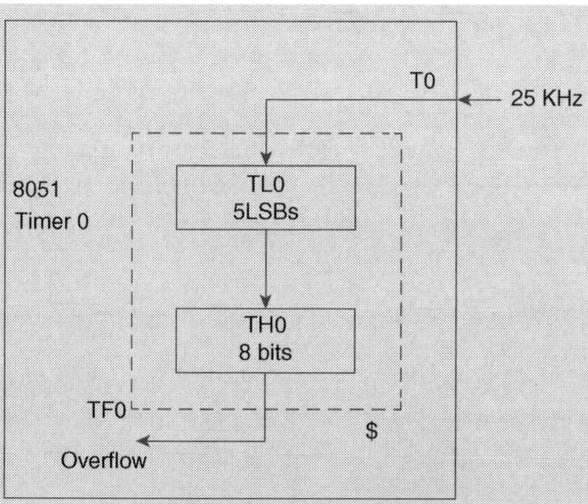

Fig. 18.26 *Implementation of Problem 18.15 (a)*

Available frequency (f_e) = 25 kHz

$$\text{Prescalar output frequency } (f_p) = \frac{25}{32}\text{KHz} = 0.78125 \text{ kHz}$$

$$= 781.25 \text{ Hz}$$

$$\text{Time period } (T_p) = \frac{1}{f_p} = \frac{1}{781.25} = 0.00128 \text{ sec}$$

$$= 1.28 \text{ msec}$$

Required Time delay = 100 ms

$$\text{Count} = \frac{100 \text{ ms}}{1.28 \text{ ms}} = 78.125 \approx 78$$

$$= 4EH$$

Count for loading into up counter = 256–78
= 100–4E
= 0B2 H

TMOD for initializing T0 in counter mode, mode 0 without use of Gate ($\overline{INT0}$) as in Fig. 18.20

0 0 0 0 0 1 0 0 = 04 H

All Timer 1 bits in TMOD are set to 0.
TCON for issuing run command to T0 with all other bits set to 0 in Fig. 18.21.

0 0 0 1 0 0 0 0 = 10 H.

The program listing is provided below in Prog. 18.15(a)

```
ORG  000
SJMP 050H
ORG 050H
START: CLR TCON.5            ; clear overflow TF0 bit
MOV TMOD,#04H                ; Initialize T0
```

```
MOV TLO,#00H                ; start prescalar at 00000.
MOV THO,#0B2H               ; Load up count in THO.
MOV TCON,#10H               ; Issue run command
HERE: JNB TCON.5,HERE       ; to TO and wait for
                            ; TFO to set.
SETB PO.0                   ; Issue external
CLR TCON.5                  ; indication of the delay
                            ; over and then clear
RET                         ; TFO bit (if required).
END
```

Prog. 18.15(a) Program for Problem 18.15(a)

(b) For this program we use time 1 in mode 1, i.e 16-bit timer mode.

$$\text{Available machine cycle clock frequency} = f_m = \frac{f_{osc}}{12} = \frac{11.059\text{ MHz}}{12}$$

$$= 921.583\text{ kHz}$$

$$T = \frac{1}{f_m} = 0.00109\text{ ms}$$

Required Delay = 10 ms

$$\text{Count} = \frac{10\text{ ms}}{0.00109\text{ ms}} = 9174$$

Count for up counter = 65536–9174
= 56362
= DC2AH

TMOD is initialized for T_1 in timer mode, without gate, in mode 1, other bits are kept 0.

0 0 0 1 0 0 0 0 = 10H

TCON for issuing run command to T1 with all other bits set to 0.

0 1 0 0 0 0 0 0 = 40H

The program listing is presented below in prog 18.15(b)

```
ORG 000
SIMP 050
ORG 050
START: CLR TCON.7           ; Clear TFO for setting on overflow.
MOV TMOD,#10H               ; Initialize TO
MOV TL1,#2AH                ; Load lower byte of count
MOV TH1,#0DCH               ; in TLO & higher byte of
                            ; the count in THO
MOV TCON,#40H               ; Issue run command to
                            ; T1
HERE: JNB JCON.7, HERE      ; Issue external indication
SETB PO.0                   ; after overflow, clear
CLR TCON.7                  ; overflow flag i
                            ; required further
END
```

Prog. 18.15(b) program for problem 18.15(b)

(c) For this program we will use Timer /Counter 0 in mode 2 for counting external pulses applied to input T0. The square wave will be generated at pin P0.0. The concept is presented below in Fig. 18.27

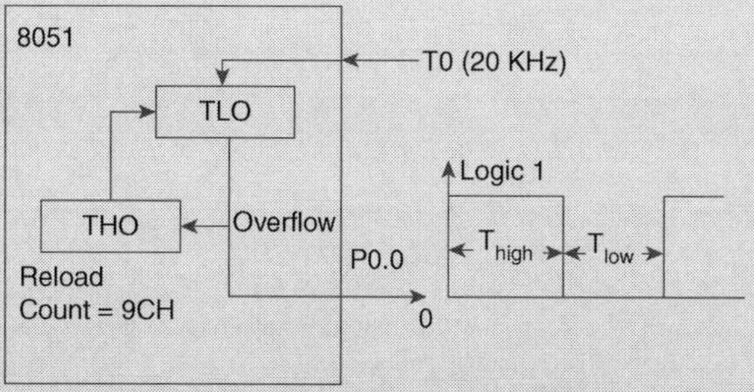

Fig. 18.27 *Implementation of Problem 18.15(c)*

Available external clock $f_e = 20$ kHz

$$T_e = \frac{1}{f_e} = \frac{1}{20} \text{m sec} = 0.05 \text{ m s}$$

Required frequency = $f_r = 100$ Hz

$$T_r = \frac{1}{f_r} = \frac{1}{100} \text{sec} = 0.01 \text{ s}$$

$$\text{Count} = \frac{0.01\text{sec}}{0.05\text{m sec}} = 200$$

For implementing a symmetric square wave the $T_{high} = T_{low}$. Hence the count of 200 must be divided in two equal parts.

Thus $T_{high} + T_{low} \Rightarrow 200$
and $T_{high} = T_{low}$

So $T_{high} = T_{low} \Rightarrow 100$

Count (T_{high}) = 256 – 100 = 156 = 9CH
Count (T_{low}) = 256 – 100 = 156 = 9CH

TMOD for timer 0 in counter mode with gate disabled and operating mode 2. All timer 1 bits are kept 0.

0 1 0 0 0 1 1 0 = 46H

TCON for issuing run command to timer 0. All other bits are kept 0.

0 0 0 1 0 0 0 0 = 10H

The program listing is presented in Program 18.15(c)

```
        ORG 000
        JMP START
        ORG 50H
START: MOV THO,#9CH ; Reload value in THO
```

```
CLR TCON.5                   ; clear overflow flag bit of
MOV TMOD,#46H                ; counter 0, Initialize TMOD
MOV TLO,#9CH                 ; Load counter value in TLO
CONTINUE: MOV TCON,#10H      ; Run timer 0
HERE: JNB TCON.5,HERE        ; If Thigh over change
CPL P0.0                     ; Status of P0.0 clear
CLR TCON.5,                  ; overflow bit and
JMP CONTINUE                 ; continue forever.
END
```

Prog 18.15(c) Program for Problem 18.15(c)

For very big time delays as compared to time period of machine cycle clock ($f_{osc}/12$), a count bigger than 4 digits (16 bits) may be required. In such cases, the two timers T0 and T1 are cascaded using any external port pin. The following problem explains the generation of big time delays.

Program 18.16

Generate a time delay of 1 second using internal machine cycle clock. The 8051 operates at 11.059 MHz. Draw the hardware arrangements

Solution

Available machine cycle freq. $f_m = \frac{f_{osc}}{12}$

$$= \frac{11.059M}{12}$$

$$= 921.583K$$

Time period $T_m = \frac{1}{f_m} = 1.085\ \mu s$

Required Time period = 1 s

$$\text{Count} = \frac{1\text{ s}}{1.085\ \mu s} = 921658.9 = 921659$$

$$= \text{E103BH}$$

Count for up counting = 100000000–000E103B = FFF1EFCS

The lower 4 digits of count 'EFC5H' will be loaded in the count register TH0 and TL0 of timer 0. It will be operated in timer mode mode 1. The higher digits of the count 'i. e 'FFF1' will be loaded in the count register TH1 and TL1 of timer 1. It will be used as counter in mode 1. The overflow of timer 0 will be indicated externally on pin P0.1. The pin P0.1 will further be used for cascading T0 and T1, by connecting it with external counter frequency input T1. The hardware scheme is presented below in Fig. 18.28

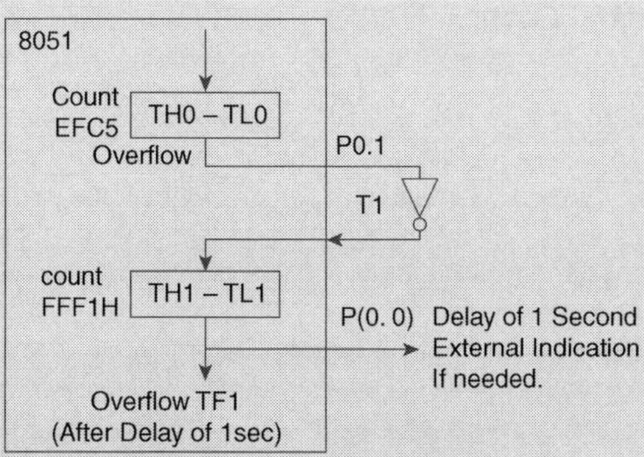

Fig. 18.28 *Implementation Problem 18.16.*

The program listing is presented further as Program. 18.10.

```
           ORG 000
           JMP START
           ORG 050H
START:     CLR P0.1                 ; clear the port bits for
           CLR P0.0                 ; external indication
           CLR TCON.5               ; clear timer overflow flags
           CLR TCON.7               ; for Timer 0 & 1
           MOV TMOD,#51H            ; set mode of timer 0 & counter 1,
           MOV TH0,#0EFH            ; The control byte value computation
           MOV TL0,#0C5H            ; is left to users.
           MOV TH1,#0FFH            ; The count 000E103BH is
           MOV TL1,#0F1H            ; loaded into timer registers T0 & T1
CONTINUE:  MOV TCON,#50H            ; Issue run signal to
           CLR P0.1                 ; both the timers.
HERE:      JNB TCON.5,HERE
           SETB P0.1                ; Set P0.1 on overflow of T0
           MOV TH0,#0EFH            ; Reload count value in
           MOV TL0,#0C5H            ; Timer 0 counter register
           CLR TCON.5               ; clear overflow flag of
           JNB TCON.7, CONTINUE     ; External indication of
                                    ; 1 sec delay on P0.0.
           CLR TCON.7               ; Clear counter 1
                                    ; overflow flag for further
           END                      ; use and stop.
```

Program 18.16 Program for Problem 18.16

A few more timer application problems have been presented in the section on 8051 interrupts and serial communication. Problems 18.14 and 18.15 can also be implemented using interrupts. But in this section, they have been implemented using overflow flags as the interrupts have so far not been discussed. In the next section, interrupt of 8051 have been presented in brief along with adequate problems to elaborate use of interrupts for application design.

18.3 INTERRUPT STRUCTURE OF 8051

The necessity of interrupts, in microprocessor architectures have already been discussed in chapter 4. As already known, an interrupt is an external or internal signal to the processor architecture that temporarily changes the flow of execution of the main program and may execute another program before continuing with the main program. Many big microprocessor architectures and systems support several interrupts. For example, a Pentium based personal computer system supports more than hundred interrupts. These interrupts are either directly supported by the processor architectures or an external peripheral like programmable interrupt controller. In general, only a few interrupts are supported directly by a processor architecture. If a system requires a large number of interrupts, an external interrupt controller is incorporated in the system. Microcontrollers are mainly used in small dedicated systems, so in general less number of interrupts are required.

However, if a specific application demands large number of external hardware interrupts, the programmable interrupt controller can be interfaced and even be cascaded to implement large number of external hardware interrupts. In microprocessor systems, the interrupts may be used for implementing the following applications:

1. Data Communication and IO
2. Task switching , Multitasking, Multiprogramming.
3. Timing & Real time clock, counting.
4. Interfacing peripherals and IO devices.
5. Handling of system faults and errors.
6. Interlinking of external events with system operation and program execution.

18.3.1 8051 Interrupts

8051 architecture supports total five interrupts. Out of these five; two interrupts namely $\overline{INT0}$ and $\overline{INT1}$ and external hardware active low interrupts. They can be enabled and programmed using the least significant four bits of TCON register and the Interrupt Enable and priority registers. The remaining three interrupt are the internal interrupts; Timer 0 overflow, Timer 1 overflow and serial transmission or reception interrupt. In fact, the serial transmission and reception can use only one internal interrupt as signals generated by the serial transmission and reception units are ORed internally. The interrupts available in 8051 are presented below in Table 18.1 in the order of their decreasing default priority and the respective vector addresses.

Table 18.1. *8051 interrupts and vector addresses*

Sr No	*Interrupt*	*Default priority*	*Vector Addreses*
1	$\overline{INT0}$	Higest	0003 H
2	Timer 0	⋮	000B H
3	$\overline{INT1}$	⋮	0013 H
4	Timer 1	⋮	001B H
5	Serial	⋮	0023 H
	Trans./Receive	Lowest	[In code memory]

The individual interrupts presented in Table 18 can be enabled or disabled using the Interrupt enable register bits. The valid interrupt edges detected by the 8051 architecture on the $\overline{INT0}$ and $\overline{INT1}$ pins can be stored using IE flags of the TCON register. The type of these interrupts i.e negative edge triggered or low level triggered, can also be programmed using the respective IT bits. The default priorities of 8051 interrupts are as presented in Table 18. However the default priorities can also be altered using the bits of the Interrupt priority (IP) register. The TCON register bits have already been discussed in Section 18.2.2.

18.3.2 Interrupt Enable Register (IE, SFR address A8H)

The structure of this bit addressable register is presented below in Fig. 18.29.

D7	D6	D5	D4	D3	D2	D1	D0
EA	R	R	ES	ET1	EX1	ET0	EX0

Fig. 18.29 *Bit definitions of IE register*

EA– Enable all–This bit is used to enable the complete interrupt structure of 8051. If EA = 1, the interrupt structure of 8051 is enabled else it is disabled.

R–Reserved– These bits are not used in the architecture rather they are reserved for future use.

ET0 and ET1– These bits are individually set to enable the internal timer interrupt Timer 0 & Timer1 respectively. If they are zero, the respective timer interrupt will be disabled.

EX1 and EX0– These bits individually control the external interrupts $\overline{INT0}$ and $\overline{INT1}$. If $\overline{INT0}$ and $\overline{INT1}$ interrupts are to be enabled the bits EX0 and EX1 must be set respectively. If the EX0 and EX1 bits are reset, the $\overline{INT0}$ and $\overline{INT1}$ interrupts are disabled.

Thus using the EA bit all the interrupts can be enabled or disabled. Using the individual respective bit, the respective interrupt can be enabled or disabled.

18.3.3 Interrupt Priority Register (IP–SFR address B8)

The structure of the IP register along with its bit definitions have been presented further. The priorities of the available interrupts can be configured or altered using different bits of this register and by setting or clearing them.

Each interrupt of 8051 can have two levels of priority: Level 0 and Level 1. Level 1 is considered as a higher priority level compared to Level 0. Each of the five interrupts can be programmed to work at level 0 or level 1 using the respective bit of the IP register. If a specific bit is programmed 0, the respective interrupt will work at level 0 and if the bit is programmed 1, the respective interrupt will work at level 1. In fact, the priority order give in Table 18.1, is actually the sequence of polling of internal interrupt flags. Corresponding to each interrupt, there is internal flip-flop or flag that is set when the interrupt occurs. The internal architecture of 8051 scans or polls the interrupt flags in the order given in Table 18.1. The interrupts are further served in the same order in which the flags are found set during the polling sequence. Thus the order of polling is by default the order of priority. However this default order of priority can be changed by appropriately programming the IP register. For example, the $\overline{INT0}$ has the highest priority while the serial interrupt (SI) has the lowest priority when they are working at equal priority level (Level 0 or Level 1). But if the SI interrupt is programmed for level 1 while the $\overline{INT0}$ is programmed to work at level 0, the SI interrupt will have higher priority than the $\overline{INT0}$ interrupt. At equal level of priority, the interrupts follow the default priority order that is the same as order or sequence of polling. The IP register is presented in Fig. 18.30.

D7	D6	D5	D4	D3	D2	D1	D0
R	R	R	PS	PT1	PX1	PT0	PX0

Fig. 18.30 *Bit definitions of IP register.*

R– Reserved for future use and currently unused

PS– Priority level of serial interrupt–If set to 1, the SI works at level 1 otherwise it works at level 0,

PT1– Priority level of Timer 1 interrupt–If this bit is set, the Timer 1 interrupt works at level 1 otherwise it works at level 0.

PT0– Priority level of Timer 0 interrupt–If this bit set, the Timer 0 interrupt works at level 1 otherwise it works at level 0.

PX0– Priority level of $\overline{INT0}$ - If this bit is set, $\overline{INT0}$ works at level 1, otherwise it works at level 0.

PX1– Priority level of $\overline{INT1}$ - If this bit is set, $\overline{INT1}$ works at level 1, otherwise it works at level 0.

18.3.4 Interrupt Sensing and Response Sequence

The interrupts at level 1 are polled first in the second processor or oscillator clock cycle of the fifth operating (operation) T-state of each machine cycle. It has already been discussed that each machine cycle contains six T-states of operation and each T-state of operation contains two clock cycles. Thus every machine cycle contains $6 \times 2 = 12$ clock cycles. All the interrupts at level 1 are sensed i.e polled in the second clock cycle of the fifth T state (or 9th clock cycle out of 12 clock cycles). Then all the level 0 interrupts are also sensed in the same cycle. The order of sensing or polling is as described in the previous section. Their respective flags are set if they are found high. All these interrupts are again sensed in the second clock cycle of the fifth T–State of operation (9th cycle) of the next machine cycle. If any of the interrupt lines is found zero, that was earlier 1 in the previous machine cycle, a valid interrupt request is considered to be received at such interrupt line. Thus it is obvious that the minimum duration of the active low interrupt pulse should be equal to the duration of one machine cycle for being sensed, else it will be lost. The highest priority level interrupt that is polled first and found to receive a valid interrupt request will be served first. The process of polling continues in every machine cycle even during execution of the interrupt service routine. Hence, if two interrupts occur simultaneously, the one with highest priority level and early polling sequence will receive service. However the other one that is lower in priority level or comes later in polling sequence may get lost as there is no mechanism for storing such interrupt requests.

The received valid interrupt requests will be discarded if the interrupt structure of 8051 is earlier disabled by clearing the EA bit of Interrupt Enable register or if the specific interrupt is disabled by clearing the respective Enable Interrupt bit of the same register. An interrupt service may also be blocked if an equal or higher priority interrupt is already in progress. When an interrupt receives service and its interrupt service routine is to be executed, an additional flag corresponding to its priority level (Level 0 or Level 1) is set indicating that an interrupt at that priority level is in progress. Thus corresponding to the two levels of priority there are two such flags. If a higher priority level interrupt is in progress and its priority level interrupt in progress flag is set, no other equal priority or lower priority interrupt will be sensed or serviced. All such interrupts may be lost. When the interrupt service routine of the in progress interrupt is completely executed and the RETI instruction at the end of the routine completes its execution, it clears the in progress interrupt flag. Thus if an interrupt in progress flag for a priority level is set, other interrupts at the equal priority or lower level can not be serviced or sensed. However if a lower priority level interrupt is in progress and its interrupt in progress flag is set, a higher priority level interrupt can be still serviced.

An interrupt request appearing after the 9th clock cycle of a machine cycle that is the last machine cycle of the currently executed instruction will be sensed during the first machine cycle of the next instruction and served after completion of the next instruction. Thus for an interrupt to be guaranteedly served it should have duration of two machine cycles.

An interrupt appearing before the 9th T-state of any other machine cycle than the last one is immediatly executed after completion of the current instruction. Thus an interrupt occurring in the earlier machine cycles (excluding) the last one will receive service only after completion of the instruction or its service will be delayed till complete execution of the current instruction.

Service to an interrupt will be delayed if it appears during execution of RETI instruction or an instruction that writes to IE/IP registers. The interrupt mechanism is deliberately designed in this way so as to avoid any contention between the writing operation to program counter, Interrupt Enable or Interrupt Priority Registers and normal operation of the interrupt unit of 8051. In such cases, the interrupt is serviced after execution of the next instruction after RETI (i.e the next instruction of the main program after returning from the interrupt service routine) or the instruction after the IE/IP writing instruction.

Finally, if a valid interrupt request is sensed by the architecture and if it is not blocked or discarded for the reasons discussed above, the following sequence of operations is undertaken to serve the interrupt.

1. The current instruction of the main program is completed. If the current instruction is RETI or write to IE/IP register, the next one is also completed.
2. The content of the program counter pointing to the address of the next instruction of the main program to be executed after the interrupt service routine will be pushed on to the stack (data memory) at the current stack top address. The lower byte PCL is pushed first and PCH, the higher byte is pushed later.
3. The overflow flags are cleared if it is a timer interrupt. Corresponding IE0 and IE1 flags are cleared if it is an edge triggered (configured accordingly) interrupt.
4. The interrupt in progress for the priority level flip flop is set.
5. The control of execution is transferred to the interrupt service routine by generating a long call (LCALL). This is also called as vectoring of an interrupt.
6. The execution of the ISR starts. During execution of the ISR, low priority level or equal priority level interrupts are discarded. Only higher priority level interrupts will receive service.
7. At the end of the ISR, RETI instruction is executed. The RETI instruction clears the interrupt in progress flag. The address of the next instruction that was stored on to stack in step2 is popped back from the stack top and loaded into PC. The execution of the main program continues. Other lower or equal priority interrupts can be sensed and serviced further.

18.3.5 Single Stepping using External Interrupts

The main use of single stepping is during debugging of a developed program. The single stepping facility allows the microcontroller to take a break in execution of the program after each instruction to check or change contents of the register and memory. Thus after executing each instruction of the program, the microcontroller gets interrupted. The interrupt service routine allows the user to check or change the contents of the microcontroller registers and memory. After receiving a continue command, the execution returns to the main program, executes one more instruction and again allows a break in execution for checking the register and memory contents. This continues till the last instruction of the program to be debugged.

In 8051 systems, the single stepping is implemented using the external interrupts $\overline{\text{INT0}}$ or $\overline{\text{INT1}}$. The hardware arrangement for the same is shown below in Fig. 18.31.

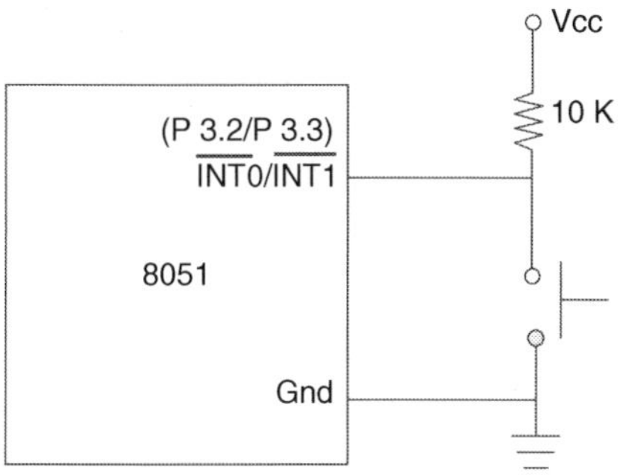

Fig. 18.31 *Single stepping using* $\overline{\text{INT0}}/\overline{\text{INT1}}$

The arrangement in Fig. 18.31 simply generates an active low pulse by pressing the key at the external interrupt pins. It should be noted here that the interrupts $\overline{\text{INT0}}/\overline{\text{INTI}}$ are multiplexed with port pins P 3.2 / P 3.3. Then the pressed key is going to generate an interrupt on $\overline{\text{INT0}}/\overline{\text{INT1}}$ line as well as it is going to pull down the P 3.2 / P 3.3 line. The status on the lines P 3.2 / P 3.3 can be read in the ISR and if it is found low, the execution can continue to the next instruction. But before checking the status of the lines P 3.2 /P3.3, i.e. using them as input lines, the external interrupts must be disabled. However if an interrupt is to generated after the next instruction of the main program, they must be enabled before the RETI instruction. As already discussed, if any interrupt is sensed during the RETI instruction, it will be served after the next instruction of the main program. Once the execution of the ISR starts, the interrupt in progress flag is set and other interrupts will be neglected. In the ISR, the contents of registers or memory can be checked. The interrupt $\overline{INT0} / \overline{INT1}$ will be disabled and the line P 3.2 / P 3.3 will be checked for continue signal. If continue signal is received in the form of a low level on P 3.2 / P 3.3, the interrupts will be enabled again, the RETI instruction will be executed. It will clear the current interrupt will in progress flag. Thus with the same pressure of the key another interrupt will be generated and responded or served after the next instruction of the main program. The scheme in Fig. 18.32 presents the idea more clearly. Before issuing the first interrupt command by pressing the key, the user is expected to provide the correct inputs in the registers and memory locations appropriately. The key issue in implementing single stepping is that the interrupt used for single stepping must be programmed level sensitive or level triggered using appropriate bit of the TCON register. The overall scheme is presented in Fig. 18.32.

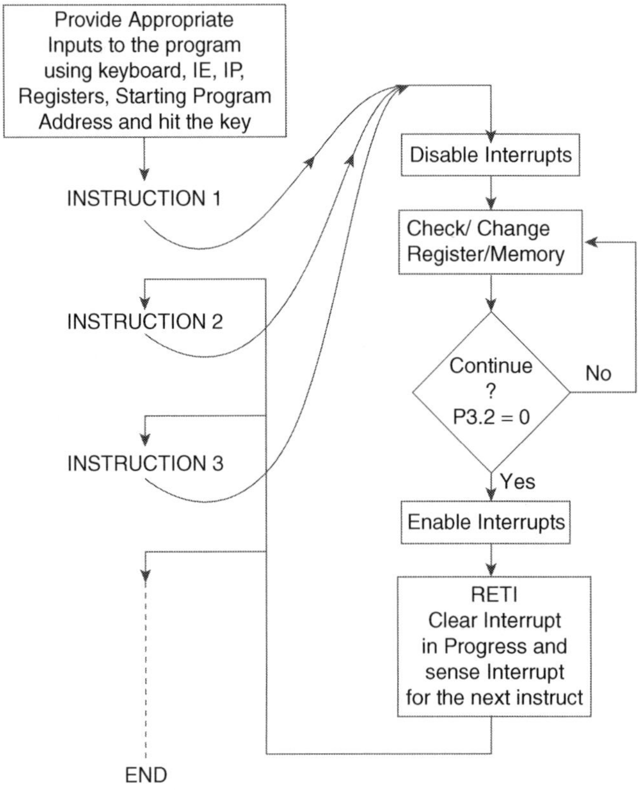

Fig. 18.32 *Conceptual Implementation of Single Stepping Scheme*

However most of the 8051 programmes are developed using advanced simulators and computers. Such systems provide a simulated environment for trouble shooting and debugging. Thus this type of arrangement may not be required for trouble shooting of 8051 programmes using the advanced computer based simulators.

The following problems and programmes elaborate use of interrupts for actual system design.

Problem 18.17

Interface ADC 0809 with 8051 ports. The ALE and SOC signals will be issued using the port line P1.0 and P1.1. The EOC is to be sensed using $\overline{\text{INT0}}$. Write an assembly language program for reading the digital equivalents of all the input channels and storing them from an internal memory address.

Solution

The hardware of the system is presented in Fig. 18.33. Note the connection of EOC pin of the ADC with $\overline{\text{INT0}}$ pin of 8051.

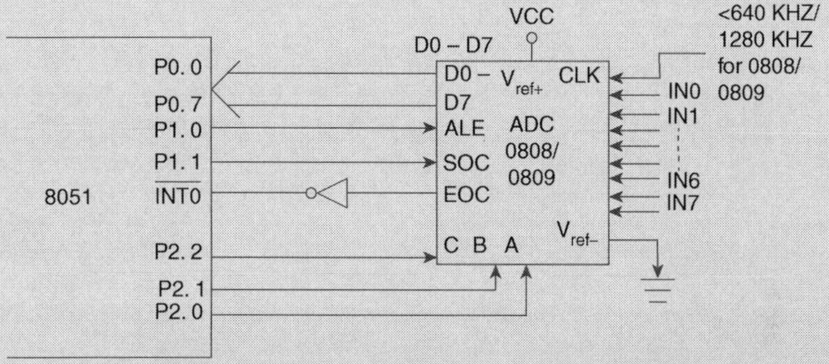

Fig. 18.33 *Interfacing 0808/0809 using Interrupt*

EOC is an active high signal but $\overline{\text{INT0}}$ is an active low signal, so an inverter is connected between them.

Interrupt $\overline{\text{INT0}}$ is configured to operate as edge triggered interrupt at priority level 1. All other unuseful bits of the SFRs are kept 0.

Timer control Register

TF1	TR1	TFO	TRO	IE1	IT1	IE0	IT1	
0	0	0	0	0	0	0	1	= 01H

Interrupt Enable Register

EA	R	R	ES	ET1	EX1	ET0	EX0	
1	0	0	0	0	0	0	1	= 81H

Interrupt Priority Register

R	R	R	PS	PT1	PX1	PT0	PX0	
0	0	0	0	0	0	0	1	= 01H

The interrupt structure of 8051 must be enabled as discussed above and then the program for interfacing the ADC follows. The advantage of this scheme is that while the conversion is going on after issuing the SOC signal, the controller becomes free for executing other tasks. Whenever EOC signal is asserted by ADC, it will interrupt the microcontroller and the ISR will read the digital equivalent and store it in the memory. The microcontroller need not continuously poll the EOC line. The assembly language program along with the ISR is presented below in Program 18.17.

```
ORG 000
JMP START
ORG 003
```

```
          JMP ISR0
          ORG 050H
START:    MOV SP,#07H          ; Initialize SP, IE, IP
          MOV IE,#81H          ;
          MOV IP,#01H          ;
          MOV R0,#050H         ; Pointer to memory
          MOV R1,#00H          ; Channel no in R1 starts at 00.
          MOV P2,R1            ; Select channel using P2
          CLR P1.0             ; Issue ALE pulse
          SETB P1.0
          NOP
          CLR P1.0             ; ALE pulse issued
          CLR P1.1             ; Issue SOC pulse
          SETB P1.1            ;
          NOP
          CLR P1.1             ; SOC pulse issued
HERE:     JMP HERE             ; Wait for the EOC interrupt
ISR0:     MOV P0,#0FFH         ; Interrupt service routine
          MOV A, P0            ; for EOC, Init. P0 as input,
          MOV @ R0, A          ; read P0 in A, store in
          CJNER1,#8,CONII      ; memory. All channels read?
          JMP STOP             ; It yes then stop.
CONTI:    INC R1               ; Else go for the next one
          INC R0               ; Increment memory pointer
          MOV P2, R1           ;
          CLR P1.0             ; Issue ALE
          SETB P1.0
          NOP
          CLR P1.1             ; ALE issued
          CLR P1.1             ; Issue SOC
          SETB P1.1            ;

          NOP
          CLR P1.1             ; SOC issued
          RETI
STOP:     MOV SP, #07
          END
```

Program 18.17 Program for Problem 18.17 including the interrupt service routine ISR0.

Problem 18.18

A 1 MHz crystal clock of high accuracy is available. Using this frequency design an hours - minutes - seconds clock. Suitable external hardware may be used.

Solution

Though 1 MHZ clock is available 8051, can have only 500 kHZ at its external timer frequency inputs. The 1 MHZ frequency needs to be divided to a lower frequency conveniently, we divide it by 10^6 using external hardware chips or circuits. Thus we obtain a 1sec clock. The 8051 has got only two on chip timers. We use T0 for seconds, T1 for minutes and a register R_7 of bank 0 for hours. We use T0 and T1 in auto reload mode with reload value for up counter corresponding to 60 ≡ 3CH ⇒ FF − 3C = 0C3H for obvious reasons. The hours counter R_7 will be reloaded with a value 0 after 12 hours. Gate control is not required.

TMOD

GATE 1	C/T1	M1	M0	GATE 0	C/T0	M1	M0	
0	1	1	0	0	1	1	0	= 66H

TCON

TF1	TR1	TF0	TR0	IE1	IT1	IE0	IT0	
0	1	0	1	0	1	0	1	= 55H

Run command for T0 & T1 with $\overline{INT0}$ & $\overline{INT1}$ both configured as edge triggered.

I E

EA	R	R	ES	ET1	EX1	ET0	EX0	
1	0	0	0	1	1	1	1	= 1FH

All interrupts are enabled except the serial.

I P

R	R	R	PS	PT1	PX1	PT0	PX0	
0	0	0	0	1	1	1	1	= 0FH

All priorities at level 1 except the serial. In this problem interrupt of timers are used instead of overflow flags. The hardware scheme for this problem is presented below in Fig. 18.34.

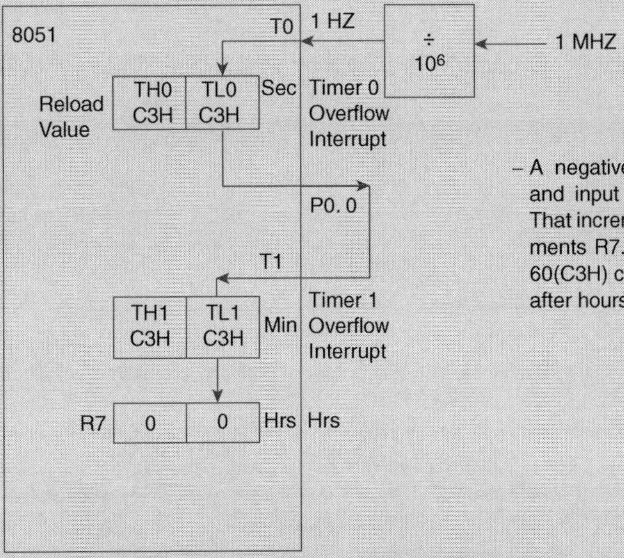

– A negative edge is generated at P0.0 and input T1, every time T0 overflows. That increments T1. Overflow of T1 increments R7. To and T1 are reloaded after 60(C3H) counts and R7 is reloaded by 0 after hours count 12.

Fig. 18.34 *Scheme for Problem 18.18*

A simple flowchart for this scheme is presented below

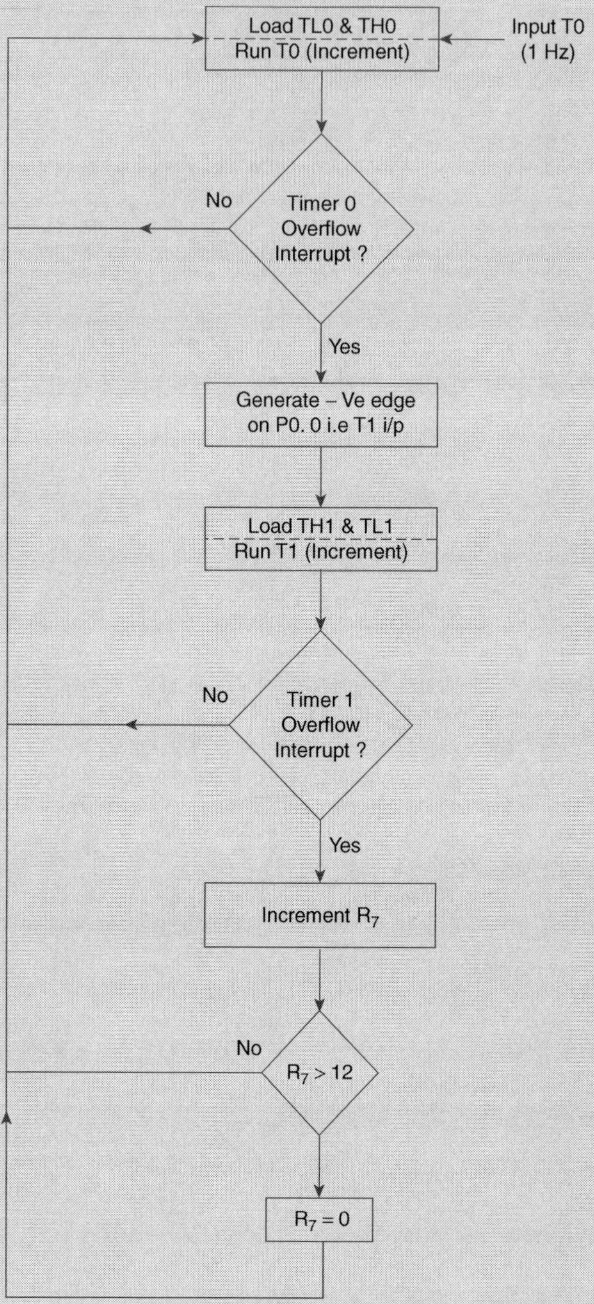

Fig. 18.35 ***Flowchart for problem 18.18***

The program listing for this problem is presented below.

```
ORG 000H
JMP START
ORG 00BH
JMP TIMER0SEC
```

```
            ORG 01BH
            JMP TIMER1MIN
            ORG 050H
START:      MOV IE,#1FH
            MOVIP,#0FH
            MOV TMOD,#66H          ; T1&T0 in autoreload mode
            MOV TL0,#0C3H          ; Load all the counter registers
            MOV TH0,TL0            ; With C3H for seconds &
            MOV TL1,TL0            ; minutes counter
            MOV TH1,TL1            ;
            MOV R7,#00             ; Hours counter
            MOV TCON, #55H         ; Run the counters
            SETB P0.0              ; Wait for interrupts of
HERE        JMP HERE               ; Timer 0 & Timer 1 to be activated
TIMER0SEC:  CLR P0.0               ; After 60 seconds generate
            NOP                    ; increment signal for minute
            CLR TCON.5             ; counter, clear overflow
            SETB P0.0              ; flag and set P0.0 for future
            RETI                   ; Return
TIMER1MIN:  INC R7                 ; After 60 minutes generate
            CLR TCON.7             ; increment for R7, clear
            CJNE R7,#12, LOOP      ; overflow, if hours
            MOV R7,#00             ; have reached 12 make
LOOP:       RETI                   ; them 0 and return
            END
```

Prog 18.18 Program for Problem 18.18 and the Interrupt service routines

A point must be noted here that, the 8051 instruction set does not have any software interrupt instruction. So all the interrupts in 8051 are hardware generated interrupts may be internal or external.

18.4 SERIAL COMMUNICATION UNIT

Serial Communication is more popular for communication over longer distances as it requires less number of conductors and is thus cheaper. However the serial communication becomes slow as the bits are transmitted one by one along with start, stop and parity bits. In this section, the serial communication unit of the 8051 architecture has been discussed with significant details.

mcs 51 architecture supports simultaneous transmission and reception of binary data byte by byte i.e. full duplex mode of communication. It supports serial transmission and reception of data using standard serial communication interface and baud rates. Here the baud rate can be interpreted as the number of bits transmitted or received per second. The serial communication unit of the architecture contains a Transmit control unit and a Receive control unit. The Transmit control unit controls all the operations related to data transmission. The Receive control unit controls all the operations related to data reception. Both these units are autonomous as far as their functions are concerned. Once a byte for transmission is written to the serial buffer (SBUF) register, the transmission unit does not require any assistance from the processor. The task of converting the byte into serial form, transmitting it bit by bit along with the preprogrammed start, stop & parity bits at the preconfigured baud rates is independently carried out by the transmission unit. The receiver unit receives the data bit by bit, separates start, stop and parity bits at the predecided baud rate, converts the bits into a parallel byte; makes it ready for reading by the microcontroller. All these activities of the Receiver unit are carried without any assistance or interference of the architecture. However both units are controlled and programmed using a common Serial Port Control Register (SCON). It is an 8 bit addressable register with SFR address 98H. Also both the units share a common serial Buffer Register (SBUF) with SFR address 99H. This SBUF register is a common 8-bit serial data unit interface, through which the controller interacts with the serial communication unit for to and fro transfer of data. Obviously, the transmission and reception units of 8051 have got their individual 8 bit data buffers in the back ground. When a byte is to be transmitted, it is first loaded int the SBUF register by the controller. It is then transferred to the individual transmitted buffer. When the internal write to SBUF signal goes high, the bit by bit transmission of the byte begins automatically. The SBUF register becomes free and available for the following operations much before the byte is transmitted completely. The process of reception is unique in the sense that it can allow reception of the next byte of serial data and store it before the earlier received byte is read by the controller architecture. Conceptually, the serial communication unit is organized as presented in Fig. 18.36. The processing unit is expected to transmit or receive data from the serial communication unit byte by byte.

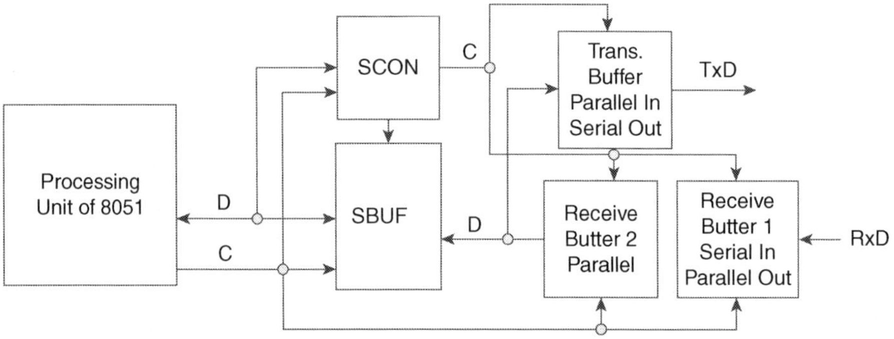

Fig. 18.36 *Conceptual Organization of Serial Unit of 8051.*

During serial reception, the receive buffer 1 receives serial bits and converts to a byte, it then transfers the received parallel byte in receive buffer 2. The receive buffer 1 then becomes free to receive the next serial byte. When the received serial byte is to be read by the processing unit it reads the SBUF register. The data from the Receive buffer 2 is then transferred to SBUF register and it is read by the Processing unit.

18.4.1 Serial Port control Register (SCON–SFR 98)

Bit definitions of this bit addressable register are presented in Fig.18.37.

D7	D6	D5	D4	D3	D2	D1	D0
SM0	SM1	SM2	REN	TB8	RB8	TI	RI

Fig. 18.37 *Bit definitions of SCON Register*

SMO & SMI- These bits decide serial communication mode for transmission and reception as given below.

SM0	SM1	Mode	Brief Description
0	0	mode0	8 bit synchronous shift register.
0	1	mode1	8 - bit asynchronous Transceiver
1	0	mode2	9 - bit asynchronous Transceiver (Baud Rate $f_{osc}/32$)
1	1	mode3	9 - bit asynchronous Transceiver will mode1 baud rates.

All these modes of operation will be discussed in detail in the next section.

SM2–This bit is set if the microcontroller is expected to work or communicate in multiprocessor system. If this bit is cleared the microcontroller disables multiprocessor communication, and operates in single processor mode.

REN–The reception enable bit, if set, starts or enables serial reception under the programmed mode using SM0–SM1 bits. If this bit is cleared reception is disable or with hold.

TB8 –This is the 9th data bit, that is transmitted automatically after the 8 bit (D_0–D_7) of data have been transmitted in mode 2 and mode 3. This is actually used as a parity bit and can be set or reset using appropriate instructions.

RB8 –This is the 9th data bit received after reception of 8 bits of data from the transmitter. As it is obvious from description of TB8, this is the parity bit received from the transmitter. Setting or clearing this using instructions is meaningless as it will be set or reset depending upon the actually received 9th bit from the transmitter side. In mode 0, RB8 is not used. In mode1, if multiprocessor mode is disabled, RB8 bit will work as a stop bit.

TI–A byte is loaded to SBUF register for transmission. The internal write signal goes high and the serial transmission starts bit by bit. The transmission interrupt bit (TI) is set at the end of the transmission of the 8th bit in mode0 or at the start of the 9th bit in other modes. If this bit is set, it indicates to the 8051 architecture that the earlier byte has been transmitted completely and the system is ready to transmit the next byte if required.

RI–After the reception is enabled by setting the REN bit. The reception starts by receiving a start bit followed by bit by bit reception of the serial data. In mode 0, RI bit is set at the end of the 8th bit to indicate that a byte has been completely received by the receive unit and is ready for being read by the controller. In modes 1,2 and 3 it is set at the beginning of the 9th bit. Reception of the next byte starts before the previous byte is read by 8051 architecture.

The TI and RI bits are logically 'OR'ed to generate a common internal interrupt SI.

18.4.2 Serial Communication Modes of 8051

In this section, the modes of serial communication offered by the standard MCS51 architecture have been discussed in necessary details. It should be noted here that in case of asynchronous communication the probability of bit error is higher as compared to synchronous communication. So arrangements like start bit and stop bit must be made for forming data packages in asynchronous communication. Of course the start bit and stop bit can be added even in case of synchronous communication, but they bear less importance as compared to that in asynchronous communication. Another important aspect of serial communication is the speed or baud rate. Higher is the speed of communication i.e. baud rate, higher is the probability of bit error. In case of lower baud rate serial communication, the bit error probability is low. Thus in 8051 serial communication modes; the modes with lower baud rates have been supported with less or no protection or correction mechanism. The modes with higher baud rates have been supported with stronger protection and correction mechanism. It should be noted that the parity error detection and correction system adds to the overhead reducing the speed of communication. If any type of bit error is detected, the byte can either be corrected at the receiving end or retransmitted again by the transmitter. In both the cases the speed will reduce but it is the cost paid for the correct reception of data. Different modes of serial communication available with 8051 are presented further.

Mode 0 In this mode of serial communication, the pin RxD is used to either transmit data or receive data serially. Hence this mode is practically a half- duplex mode. Transmission and Reception both are possible but one at a time. The TxD pin is used to transmit the synchronizing clock that is equal to machine cycle clock ($f_{osc}/12$). In one cycle of this clock one bit is either transmitted or received achieving a fixed baud rate of $f_{osc}/12$ bits per second. A write operation to the SBUF register initiates the transmission operation. LSB of the byte is transmitted first and MSB is transmitted at the end followed by a permanent logic '1' stop bit. The Transmit Interrupt bit is set when all the 8 bits are transmitted. Serial Reception is enabled by setting the 'REN' bit. The reception actually starts only if the RI bit is Zero. Thus it is always advisable to reset the RI bit, if a serial data is expected to be received. Thus a write operation to SCON with REN = 1 & RI = 0 initiates reception. The receive unit samples the RxD line at the center of each clock cycle of the machine cycle and starts placing the received bit at the LSB of the Receive buffer. After receiving each bit the content of Receive buffer are shifted left and a bit position is created at the LSB to store the next bit to be received. In this way, after receiving 8 bits of data, thc RI i.e. receive interrupt bit is set, to indicate the controller architecture that the byte is ready to be received. IP the received stop bit is not '1' it indicates possibility that the received data may be wrong. The stop bit just acts as a separator between MSB of the current byte and LSB of the next byte to be received. The machine cycle clock being continuously transmitted on the TxD pin during the transmission and reception synchronizes both the operations.

Mode I Mode 1 is full duplex mode of serial communication. Under this mode, a serial data byte can be transmitted serially on the TxD pin while another serial data byte can be received on RxD pin simultaneously. Thus the transmit unit and receive unit work totally independent of each other in this mode of operation. However both of them work under the control of the common SCON register and communicate with the controller architecture through a common SBUF register. Transmission of each byte starts with a start bit, followed by 8 data bits starting from LSB and concludes with a stop bit. Thus transmission of the one byte needs 10 bits in this mode. The transmitted stop bit is stored in the bit RB8 of the receiver side SCON. Obviously the transmitter and receiver must act in the same mode of operation. A write operation to the SBUF register initiates transmission process but it is not synchronized with the machine cycle clock ($f_{osc}/12$). Rather it is synchronized to a baud rate clock that is derived using Timer 1, But the clock to the timers 1 is not ($f_{osc}/12$) now, rather it is 16 times less i.e. $f_{osc}/(12 \times 16) = f_{osc}/192$. Thus the maximum baud rate that can be achieved in this mode is $f_{osc}/192$, that is sixteen times less compared to mode 0. Other lower baud rates can be achieved by loading appropriate count to Timer 1 count register. The configuration of appropriate baud rate for serial communication has been discussed further in detail in this section. With the initiation of the transmission process, the TxD line is automatically held high. In synchronism with clock ($f_{osc}/192$), a start bit that is always zero is placed on the TxD pin for a baud duration of ($192/f_{osc}$) sec (baud duration is reciprocal of baud rate). Each bit starting from LSB is placed on TxD line for baud duration. After the MSB, the stop bit'1' is also placed on the TxD line for one baud duration. After a byte is transmitted completely, the TI bit in SCON is set, indicating the microcontroller architecture that the next byte can now be written to SBUF for transmission. As soon as SCON register is written, the Timer 1 is automatically reserved for deriving baud rate. Timer 1 interrupt must be enabled and it must be initialized in autoreload mode 2 timer with gate disabled.

For initiating reception, the SCON and Timer 1 must be properly initialized along with setting of Reception Enable 'REN' bit in SCON; and clearing of 'RI' interrupt bit. The RxD pin is set high initially as it is connected with the TxD pin of the other transmitter that will be momentarily held high before sending a start bit '0'. This '1' to '0' transition on RxD line initiates reception, loads FF into receive buffer and marks the Start bit. Each bit is expected to be on RxD line for one baud duration. But for reading the bit, the baud duration is divided into 16 equal parts in synchronism with $f_{osc}/12$. The RxD line is then sampled in the 7th,8th and 9th part. If the value is either 1 or 0 in at least two of the three parts it is considered as valid bit '1' or '0' respectively. This is done to increase noise immunity of the reception. Thus every bit; start, data or stop must be received through the above process. The received start bit enters into the serial receive shift buffer from the LSB position. On reception of each subsequent bit, the content of serial shift receive buffer goes on shifting to left by one bit Position. As the 8th data bit is received, the start bit is shifted out of the MSB position. The next bit to be received after MSB i.e. stop bit, is directly stored to RB8 and the Receive interrupt bit in SCON is set. It is obvious that for writing the received byte to 'SBUF' and store the stop bit to RB8, the RI must be initially clear. If a valid start bit, transition i.e. 1 to 0 in successive baud durations is not detected, a next valid start bit is searched for. If the received stop bit is not '1', the received byte is not entered into receive buffer for reading. Further RI will also not be set if stop bit is not 1. After generation of 'RI' interrupt, the receiving unit searches for the next valid start bit on the RxD line for receiving the next byte. The transmission and reception processes are synchronized to baud rate derived from a frequency ($f_{osc}/192$).

Configuration of Baud rates for Mode 1–

Though many baud rates can be programmed using the timer as already discussed, only a few standard baud rates are used in general for serial communication to maintain compatibility with other devices. The SMOD bit in PCON register works as baud rate doubler. The baud rate formula for mode 1 is worked out as below.

Let the clock or oscillator frequency = f_{osc}

Machine cycle clock frequency = $f_{osc}/12$

Machine cycle clock scaled down by 16 = $f_{osc}/(12\times16) = f_{osc}/192$ for mode 1 synch clock

Timer 1 up counting count loaded = 100H–TH1 (H) in TLI with reload value in THI = 256 –TH1

The H in bracket indicates hexadecimal value to be loaded in TH1 as an auto reload count. Baud rate doubler value in terms of SMOD bit = $2^{(SMOD - 1)}$

SMOD bit is either '1' or '0'. If its '1' the baud rate remains as it is. But if its '0', baud rate is halved. The formula for baud rate is given as below.

$$B.R. = 2^{(SMOD-1)} \frac{f_{osc}}{12\times16\times(256-TH1)}$$

Thus for different values of TH1, different values of baud rate can be achieved. For SMOD = 1 and TH1 =255 (FFH), maximum baud rate (B_{max}) is achieved, f_{osc} =11.0592 MHz

$$B_{max} = 2^{0} \frac{f_{osc}}{12\ \ 16\ \ (256-255)}$$

$$= \frac{11059200}{192}$$

$$= 57.6 \text{ Kbps}$$

* Minimum Baud rate is achieved with SMOD = 0 and TH1 = 0.

$$B_{min} = 2^{-1} \frac{11059200}{192\ \ 256} = 112.5 \text{ bps}$$

The unit of baud rate is Kbps i.e. kilo bits per second. With Timer 1 configured in mode 2, some of the achieved baud rates for given oscillator frequency are presented below for different values of SMOD.

Baud		*SMOD=0*			*SMOD=1*	
Rates Kbps	*F_{osc}*	*Timer 1 mode*	*Reload Value*	*F_{osc}*	*Timer 1 mode*	*Reload Value*
9.6	11.0592	2	FDH	11.0592	2	FAH
4.8	11.0592	2	FAH	11.0592	2	F4H
2.4	11.0592	2	F4H	11.0592	2	E8H
1.2	11.0592	2	E8H	11.0592	2	D0H

For achieving lower baud rates than the above, the Timer 1 can be operated in mode 1 as a 16 bit timer. In this case the baud rate is given as below.

$$\text{B.R.} = 2^{(\text{SMOD-1})} \frac{\text{fosc}}{12 \times 16 \times (65536 - \text{T1})}$$

T1 is a 16 bit decimal up count. In the ISR of Timer 1 interrupt, the count register must be loaded with the 16-bit count as there is no auto reload mode for 16 bit count. The minimum baud rate achieved with 16 bit count is 0.4394 BPS, though it may be of hardly any practical use.

Mode 2 The mode2 of 8051 serial communication can offer higher baud rates. The baud rate in this mode only depends upon the SMOD bit and the oscillator clock frequency f_{osc} as given below.

$$B = 2^{\text{SMOD}} \frac{\text{fosc}}{64}$$

Thus $B_{max} = \frac{\text{fosc}}{32}$ when SMOD = 1 and $B_{min} = \frac{\text{fosc}}{64}$ when SMOD = 0. Maximum baud rate at f_{osc} = 11.0592 MHz is 345.6 Kbps while the minimum is 172.8 Kbps.

This mode is a full duplex mode. The serial data is transmitted on TxD pin and received on RxD pin. The transmission and reception processes are synchronized with the baud rate clock as already discussed. As already discussed this mode supports higher data rates hence the probability of bit error increases. So to provide immunity to bit error, the parity bit mechanism is introduced in this mode. Before transmission of a byte its parity is computed and the TB8 bit in SCON register is set accordingly. During transmission, a start bit '0' is first transmitted as discussed for mode 1. Then the 8 data bits follow starting from LSB. After the MSB is transmitted, the parity bit as set in TB8 of SCON register is transmitted. Finally the stop bit that is permanently considered '1' is transmitted. Thus for transmitting one byte, 11 bits are transmitted in this mode. Each bit is transmitted for one baud clock period.

The reception of serial data also starts exactly in the same way as mode 1. As soon as a –ve transition is observed on RxD line 1 FFH is loaded into the 9 bits of serial receive buffer. Then the start bit enters the buffer from LSB. As the successive bits are received the contents of the buffer are shifted left by one bit for each received bit. After the MSB, the 10th bit that is parity bit is received and stored into RB8. Using this parity bit a parity check can be carried out by software if required. The received stop bit is just ignored in this mode. Thus mode 2 of 8051 serial communication unit implements a parity enabled serial data transfer.

Mode 3 This is also a full duplex mode. All the functionalities of this mode are exactly similar to Mode 2. This also enables parity enabled serial data communication just like mode 2. But the baud rates of this mode, are configured exactly like mode1. Thus mode3 offers the most secured parity enabled data communication at the lower baud rates of mode 1. The baud rate computation formulae and configuration technique of this mode is exactly similar to that of mode 1.

Thus we have discussed modes of operation of serial communication unit of MCS 51 architecture. Further we present a qualitative comparison of all these modes on achievable baud rates and error protection available

Mode 0 offers synchronous, half duplex data transfer at the fixed highest speed ($f_{osc}/12$) but excluding the byte separator stop bit, no data protection or error correction support is available. In Mode 1, asynchronous full duplex data transfer at variable baud rates much less than that of mode 0 is allowed with start and stop bits. At lower baud rates the probability of bit error is less. Mode 2 offers asynchronous full duplex data transfer at fixed higher baud rates ($f_{osc}/32$, $f_{osc}/64$) as compared to mode 1. With higher baud rates, this mode offers parity enabled data transfer with start and stop bits. Mode 3 combines programmable low baud rate feature of mode 1 with the parity data protection mechanism of mode2. Thus mode 3 can offer most secured data communication at programmable baud rates.

A few design examples have been presented further to elaborate hardware, configuration and programming of serial unit of 8051.

Problem. 18. 19

Design an RS232 PC compatible 8051 system using MAX 232 (TTL to/from RS 232 level converter). The PC is to be configured in 'Hyper Terminal' mode of windows operating system. In the hyper terminal mode PC will transmit a byte entered by keyboard to the 8051 system. The 8051 system will receive the byte from PC and echo it back to PC. The PC screen displays the transmitted and received byte in the 'Hyper Terminal' mode. The 8051 system should be configured as below.

(1) Baud rate = 4.8Kbps
(2) Mode 1
(3) Received byte and the transmitted byte must be indicated by a LED connected with P0.0
(4) The 8051 program will be stored in on chip program memory.
(5) PC should also be appropriately configured in the 'Hyper Terminal' mode.
(6) The 8051 system will be connected to PC RS 232 socket using only 3 core twisted cable. The TxD of 8051–MAX 232 will be connected with RxD of RS 232 socket of the PC and RxD of 8051- MAX 232 will be connected with TxD of the PC. Thus the cable is called twisted cable Ground of both the systems will be shorted together.

Solution

First we discuss configuration of PC in hyper terminal mode using windows XP operating system.

(1) Press 'Start' button on opening screen of window. A pop up Menu appears.
(2) Select 'All Programs' button click it.
(3) The next menu appears. It contains 'Accessories' options. Click it. Again the next menu opens. That contains 'communications' option.
(4) Click the 'Communication' option.
(5) A menu appears containing option 'Hyper terminal'. That is the required option. Click it. It will configure the PC hardware to communicate with a hyper terminal using RS 232 serial communications standard. Our 8051 hardware will operate as a hyper device.
(6) After 'Hyper terminal' is clicked, a setting window titled 'connect to' opens. This asks for country, Region (post code) and hyper terminal connection name. Let us enter 'KMB'. The country and region setting may be left to default or one may appropriately enter them. Further click 'NEXT'.
(7) It will open a new window titled 'connection', and subtitle 'using port'. Set appropriate 'COM' port. One may check, from 'system settings', the availability of RS 232 port assignment to 'COM'. It may be from 'COM 1' to 'COM 7'. In our case, it was found to be 'COM1' Select/type it in the using port entry space. Further click 'Next'.
(8) This will open a new window titled 'COM Properties' Port setting. This asks the following parameters.

Bits per second– [Options from 110 bps to 921.6
Kbps are available]
we select 2.4 Kbps.
Data bits – 8 [By default keep unchanged]
Parity – None [By default keep it unchanged]
Stop – 1 [By default; one can select 1, 1.5 or 2 stop bits; don't Change]
Flow Control – Hardware [Default; don't change]
Press 'OK'

(1) The 'Hyper Terminal' window titled KMB opens. It contains pull down menu options 'File', 'VIEW',---------- 'HELP'. Below that it contains symbol / icon click buttons.

(2) One of the buttons; may be number 3 or 4 from Left shows a 'handle placed telephone symbol' that is disabled. This next button on right of this button is enabled and shows a symbol with 'lifted handset telephone. Click it by mouse. It momentarily disconnects and the earlier button on left side 'handset placed telephone' is enabled.
(3) In the same row of buttons go to the last button. It allows you to enter port settings again. Click it. A window opens with title 'Properties'. This also displays two options 1) Connect to 2) Settings
(4) Click select the 'settings' options. It further enables 'ASCII setup' and 'Echo Typed Character Locally' tick selections. Do not disturb the 'ASCII setup', only tick the 'Echo Typed character Locally' and click Ok/next. This enables display of a character typed on keyboard to the 'Hyper terminal' screen before transmission to the 8051 system.
(5) Thus a typed character using the PC keyboard is displayed on the hyper terminal screen. Then it is sent to the 8051 hard ware connected to the RS 232 COM port. The 8051 hardware and the software as developed further receives the byte from the PC. It gives indication of the received byte using the LED connected to P0.0. Then the received byte is again transmitted back to PC, on the TxD line. The PC receives it on the COM port RxD line and displays it on the hyper terminal screen again. Thus for one key pressed on the keyboard, the same character is displayed twice; the first before transmission to the 8051 hardware (local echo) and the second after getting reflected from 8051 hardware and being received on the COM RS 232 port.

The hardware for this problem is presented further in Fig. 10.38.

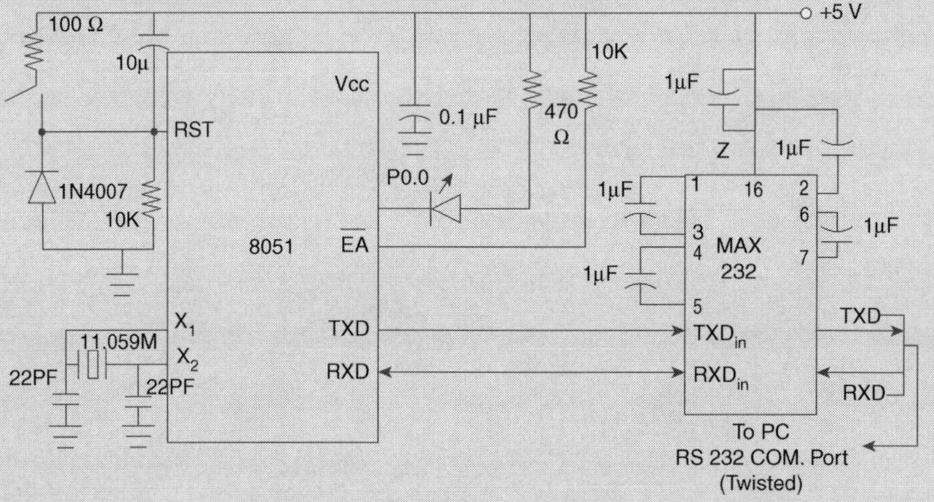

Fig. 18.38 *8051 Hardware for Problem 18.19*

The following Algorithmic steps are to be implemented during implementation of the 8051 program for this problem.

(1) Select SMOD bit and initialize PCON.
(2) Compute reload value for T1 in mode 2 and Load it to T1, Count registers TL1 and TH1.
(3) Decide TMOD and TCON and load them.
(4) Disable interrupt for Timer 1. ET1 = 0
(5) Decide serial communication mode word for loading to SCON. For this problem, the required mode is mode 1, Parity computation is not required.
(6) Clear TB8 & RB8 (In fact they are don't care)
(7) Clear all interrupt flags in SCON (TI & RI)
(8) Set REN = 1. Reception starts.

(9) Go to Hyper terminal mode on PC as discussed earlier. Configure the hyper terminal mode settings.

(10) After a key is pressed, the key is displayed on the hyper terminal screen. It's ASCII code is transmitted from the RS232 PC COM port to 8051 hardware.

(11) After REN = 1, 8051 is waiting for a serial byte on its RxD line. After PC transmits the ASCII code, it is received by 8051. The baud rate configured on PC and 8051 must match. The TxD and RxD lines of PC. COM port and those of 8051- MAX 232 are cross connected. After the byte is received RI is set; The LED is turned on.

(12) The RI is cleared, the receive byte is transmitted back to PC. LED is turned off. The TI is set, after all bits are transmitted. It is also cleared before going for transmission of the next received byte.

(13) PC receives the byte transmitted by 8051. Receives it and displays it to screen. This can be repeated.

The control word bytes are computed as below.

TMOD

Gate1	$C/\overline{T1}$	M1	M0`	Gate 0	$C/\overline{T0}$	M1	M0	
0	0	1	0	0	0	0	0	= 20H

Timer 1
TCON

TF1	TR1	TF0	TR0	IE1	ITI	IE0	IT0	
0	1	0	0	0	0	0	0	= 40H

SCON

SM0	SM1	SM2	REN	TB8	RB8	TI	RI	
0	1	0	0/1	0	0	0	0	= 40/50H

PCON

SMOD	U	U	U	GF1	GF2	PD	IDLE	
1	0	0	0	0	0	0	0	= 80H

Baud rate computation
Let SMOD=1

$$B = 2^{(SMOD-1)} \frac{f_{osc}}{12 \times 16 \times (256 - TH1)}$$

$$4800 = 2^0 \frac{11.0592 \times 10^6}{192 \times (256 - TH1)}$$

TH1 = 244 = F4H
The program is present below in Program. 18.19

```
        ORG 000
        JMP START
        ORG 050H
START:  MOV PCON,#80H        ; Set SMOD = 1
        MOV TMOD,#20H        ; Set Mode of Timer 1
```

```
         MOV TL1,#0F4H          ; Count in TL1
         MOV TH1,TL1            ; Reload value in TH1
         MOV TCON,#40H          ; Start Baud rate generation
         MOV R0,#50H            ; Received bytes are stored from 50H onwards
         SETB P0.0              ; Turn off LED
         MOV SCON,#050H         ; Initialize SCON & start
         CLR RI                 ; reception, clear RI
WAIT1:   JNB RI,WAIT1           ; Wait for a byte from PC
         MOV @ R0,SBUF          ; Store received byte into
         INC R0                 ; memory
         CLR P0.0               ; Glow LED
         CLR RI                 ; Clear reception interrupt
         MOV A,SBUF             ; Byte to be sent to A
         CLR TI                 ; clear transmission interrupt
         MOV SBUF,A             ; Write to transmission buffer
WAIT2:   JNB TI,WAIT2           ; Wait for byte to be sent to PC
         SETB P0.0              ; completely, Turn off LED
         CLR TI                 ;
         CJNE Ro,#60H,
         WAIT1                  ; stop after 16 bytes
         CLR SCON.4             ; stop reception
         END
```

Program 18.19 Program for serial communication with PC under hyperterminal mode.

All high level languages, even assemblers have facility to receive a byte from COM port (RS 232) of a PC. The received byte then can be used as per the application, in the receiver side program in PC. Also similar program can be developed for communication between two microcontrollers. In that case, the same program must be available on both the sides for full duplex communication.

18.5 POWER CONTROL REGISTER (PCON–SFR ADD 87H)

Bits of this non-bit addressable register are mainly used for power saving during 'IDLE' state of the microcontroller and eventual power off to the microcontroller chip. However the most important feature of the PCON register is its 'SMOD' bit. The 'SMOD' bit is used to double the baud rate as discussed in the previous sections. PCON register is presented in Fig. 18.39

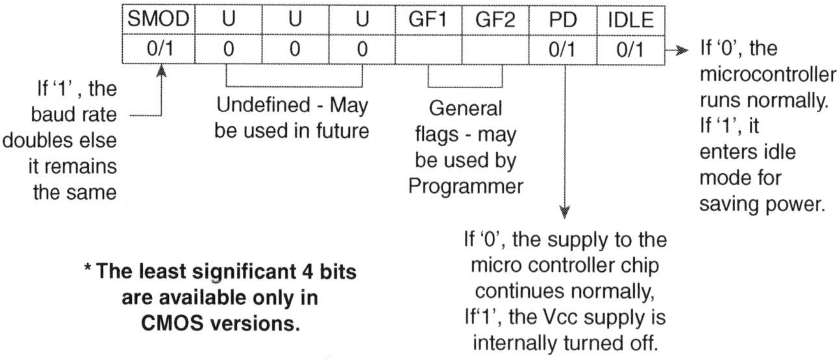

Fig. 18.39 *PCON Register.*

After setting the IDLE bit, clock to the processor section is disabled. Timer, interrupt and serial section receive clock. All the processor and peripheral register, RAM contents, port pin levels are preserved. ALE & $\overline{PSEN}$ remain high in Idle mode. To come out of this mode any external interrupt that is enabled like SI (Serial), $\overline{INT0}$, $\overline{INT1}$ is required. After coming out of idle state, CPU executes the next instruction after the one that (set the Idle'bit. A reset) signal also pulls the microcontroller out of Idle state.

If the PD bit of the PCON register is set, it enters power down mode. In power down mode, clock signal to all the parts of 8051 chip is disabled. All port pins and respective SFRs maintain their logical levels. ALE & $\overline{PSEN}$ are pulled low. Instruction execution is suspended. All other SFR contents are forced to their reset values. But on-chip RAM maintains the contents during the power down mode. The supply voltage can be reduced to a value of around 2 volts, during power down to save battery. But before coming out of the power down mode, it must be retained to its normal value of around 5V for normal operation. Only 'Reset' signal can pull 8051 out of the power down mode. After reset the program execution continues as it would have been in case of any routine reset signal.

18.6 DESIGN OF A MICROCONTROLLER 8051 BASED LENGTH MEASUREMENT SYSTEM FOR CONTINUOUSLY ROLLING CLOTH OR PAPER

18.6.1 Introduction

This simple circuit designed around 8031, which is a ROM-less version of 8051, can be used to measure the length of continuous rolling cloth or paper in the range of few hundreds of meters, with an accuracy of less than 1cm. The principle of the photoelectric tachometer is used to sense the displacement, which is converted into proportional number of votage pulses. These pulses are converted to the form readable by the on-chip timer of 8031. A LM324 based comparator circuit has been used to convert the voltage pulse signal to the appropriate rectangular pulses, which are further counted using the on-chip timer facility of 8031. The counted number of pulses are then converted to the equivalent length by multiplying the count by a calibration constant. The length is then displayed on 7-segment display units interfaced with 8031. Note that, as the circuit design is based on an EPROM-less version of 8051, an external EPROM is required to be interfaced. The same circuit may be implemented as it is, using 8751, i.e. an on-chip EPROM version of 8051.

18.6.2 Transducer

We have used the commonly used device, i.e. a mouse as a displacement transducer, after removing the mouse controller chip. In other words, we have used only the opto-electrical arrangements of the mouse. Thus the mouse keys are of no use. The mouse actually contains two sets of optoelectric arrangements—one for sensing X direction movement and the other for sensing the Y direction movement. Any intermediate direction is obtained from the X and Y direction coordinates. Here we require only one direction, i.e. either X or Y to measure the length of the rolling cloth or paper. The mouse prepared as above is fixed at a position in say X direction. The cloth or paper whose length is to be measured moves below the mouse so as to rotate the mouse ball, which will further activate the optoelectrical arrangement and generate a number of electrical pulses proportional to the length of the cloth which passed below the mouse in X direction. The movement in Y direction is now zero as the mouse is fixed and the cloth is moving only in one direction, i.e. X direction. The internal mouse mechanism is shown in Fig. 18.39(a) and the rolling cloth and mouse installation is shown in Fig. 18.39(b).

18.6.3 Signal Conditioning

The signal generated by the infra-red optoelectrical arrangement needs to be converted into proper rectangular pulse sequence form. This requires a clamping circuit and comparator arrangement (waveshaping circuit) as shown in Fig. 18.40.

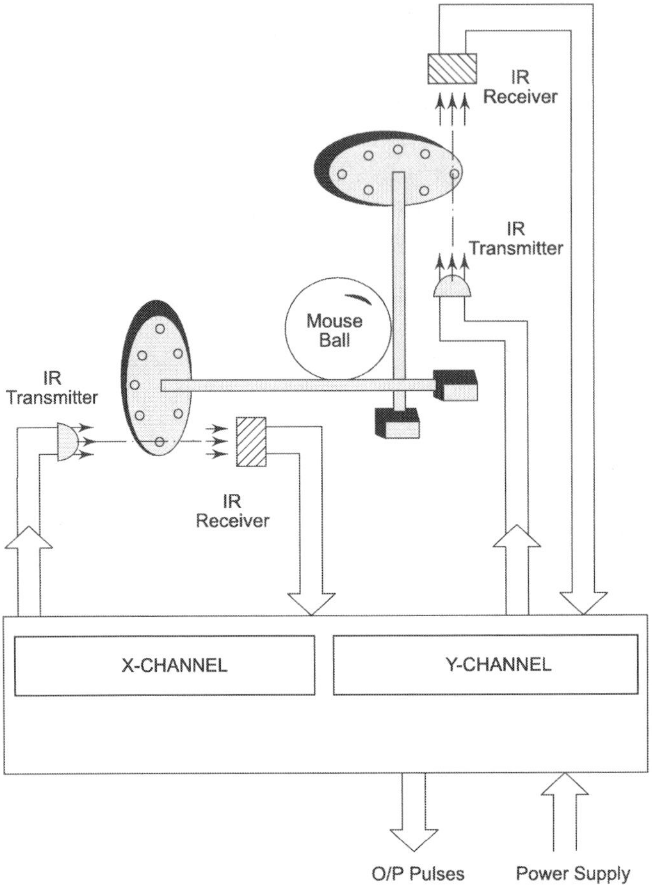

Fig. 18.39(a) *Internal Mechanism of Mouse*

The above circuit first clamps the waveform generated by mouse to zero volts. The comparator further converts it to a rectangular pulse sequence of amplitude 0–5V which is to be fed to timer 0 of 8031.

18.6.4 Microcontroller System

The microcontroller system designed for this application contains the following main functional units:

1. 8031 circuit.
2. EPROM 2732, RAM 6264 and interfacing circuit.
3. Display unit.

The 8031 circuit contains the microcontroller IC 8031, its reset circuit and an octal latch 74373 to separate the multiplexed address and data lines. The rectangular pulses obtained from LM 324 are applied to input T_0 of 8031 via socket C_3. The mouse and the LM 324 circuit get +5 V power supply from the microcontroller board socket C_3. The microcontroller 8031, on its port 1 drives a display unit. Four MSBs of port1, i.e. P1.7 to P1.4 are used to drive the four inputs of BCD to 7-segment converter IC 7448, while the three lines P1.0, P1.1 and P1.2 are used to drive the decoder 74138 which scans the multiplexed display. Thus the single 8-bit port P_1 scans the display using decoder 74138 as well as it drives eight data lines for the 7-segment display using 7448.

The memory and address decoding circuit contain the external program memory IC 2732, external data RAM 6264 and the address decoding circuit. The 4 Kbytes EPROM is interfaced at address 0000, and thus its map extends up to 0FFFH. The ICs 74138 and 7408 are used for address decoding of the EPROM and

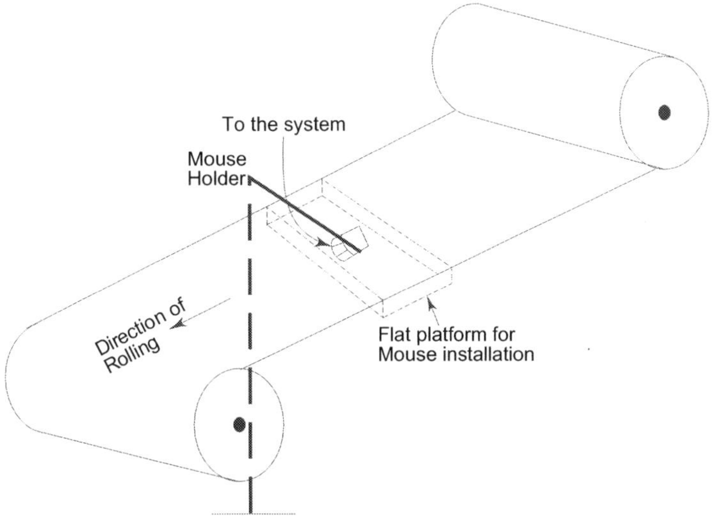

Fig. 18.39(b) *Installation of Mouse over Rolling Cloth for Length Measurement*

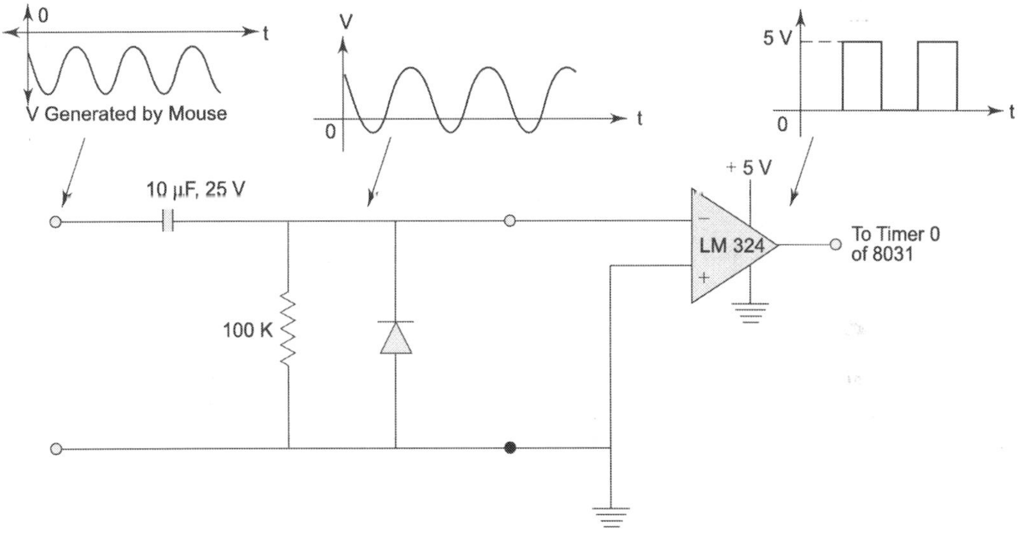

Fig. 18.40 *The Waveshaping Circuit*

RAM. Note here that the RAM 6264 is not necessary for this application but it is added to make a more powerful general 8031 based system. The 8031 on-chip RAM is only of 128 bytes, and may be insufficient for a number of applications. An on-chip version of 8031, say 8751 may directly replace the 8031 in its socket. The serial port socket offers the system a capability to communicate with PCs. The complete system runs at 10 MHz frequency. The circuit diagram of the system is shown in Fig. 18.41.

18.6.5 Algorithm

The algorithm actually counts the pulses at T_0 input. It then converts the number of pulses (hex) to equivalent length by multiplying the number of pulses with the caliberation constant. This hexadecimal multiplication is then converted to the equivalent decimal number that is nothing but the actual length. The maximum range of the system and the minimum measureable length both depend on the caliberation constant. The algorithm is shown in Fig. 18.42.

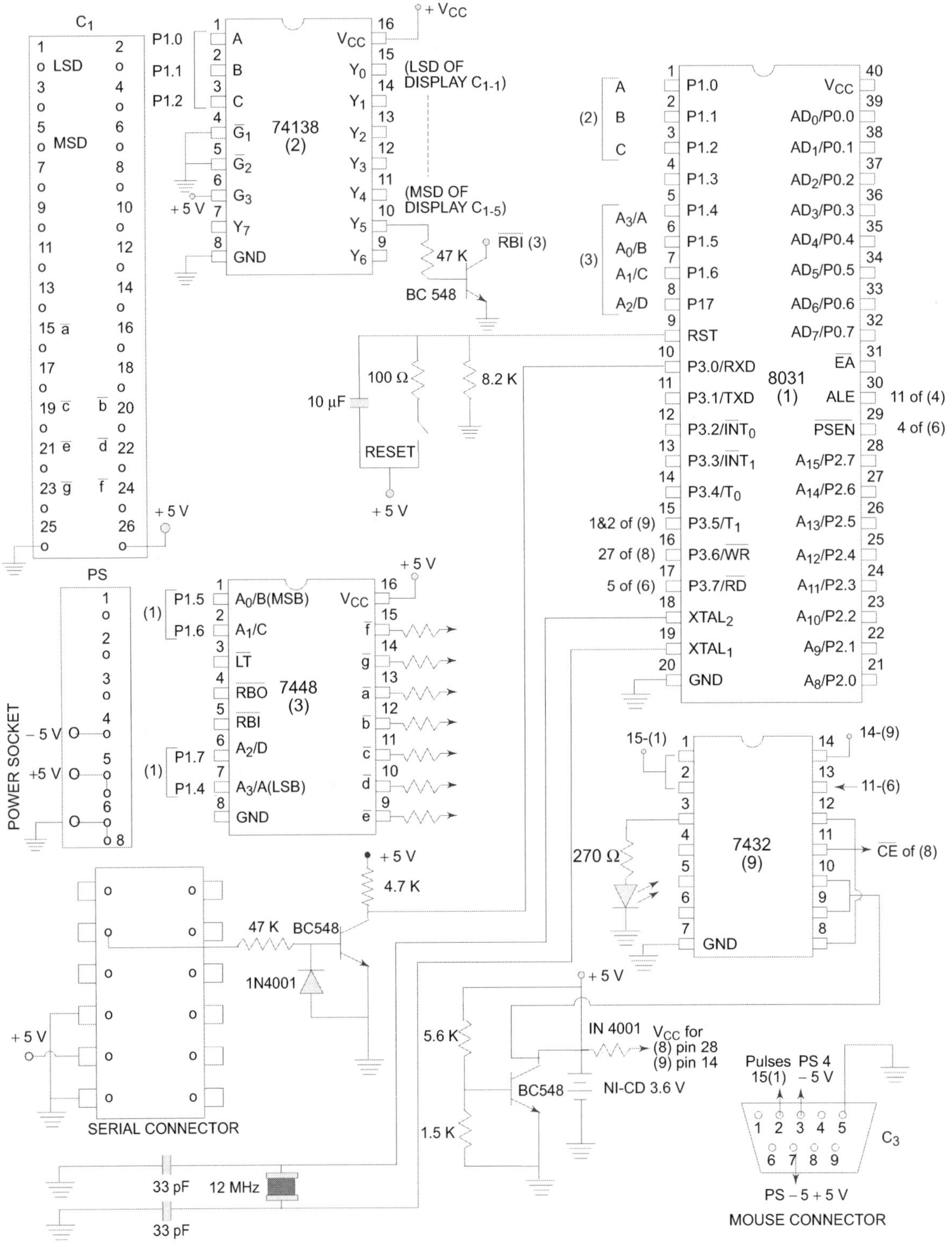

Fig. 18.41 *(Contd.)*

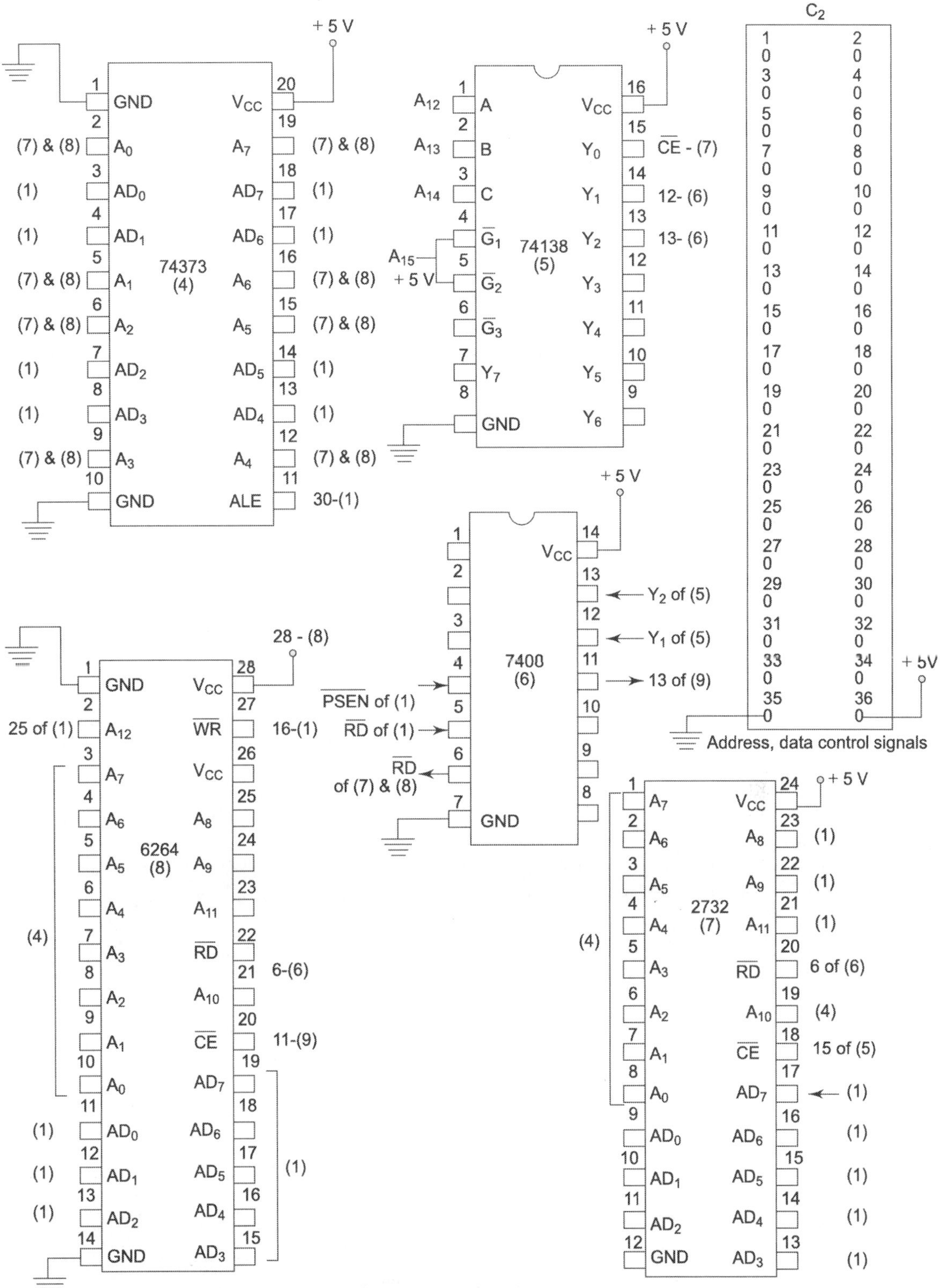

Fig. 18.41 *8031 Based System for Length Measurement of Rolling Cloth*

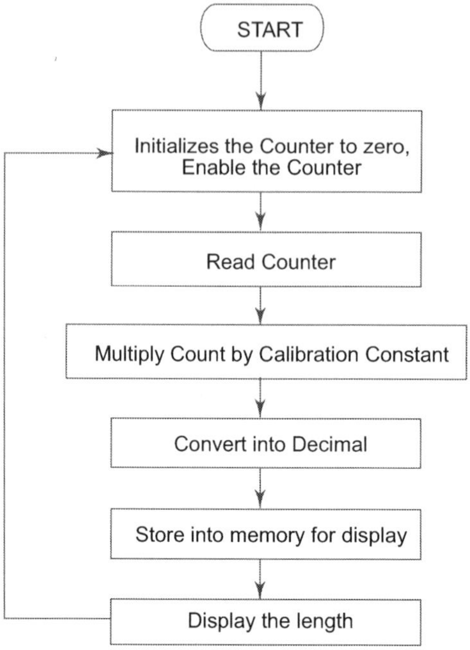

Fig. 18.42 *Algorithm of the Length Measurement System*

SUMMARY

This chapter presents interfacing of on chip and I/O peripherals. Initially, I/O ports of 8051 were discussed in significant details. Then interfacing of LEDs, 7 segment displays, multiplexed displays keys, keyboards, ADC, DAC and stepper motor using 8051 was discussed. Further structure, modes of operation and programming of 8051 on chip timers was presented in significant details alongwith interfacing problems. Interrupt structure of 8051, its programming and initialization of interrupt vector table was further presented in brief. The section on serial communication elaborated the serial communication unit of 8051 along with its programming hardware and interfacing with COM port of PC. The interfacing concepts presented in this chapter are expected to assist the microcontroller system designers in general. Thus this chapter presented an elaborate discussion on structure, interfacing and programming of OFF chip I/O devices and on chip 8051 peripherals.

EXERCISES

18.1 Write short note on port structures of 8051.
18.2 Interface four 8 KB EPROM and four 8 KB RAM chips with 8051. RAM map starts at 0000H. EPROM map starts at 0000 H.
18.3 Repeat Que 2 for RAM map ends at FFFFH & EPROM map ends at FFFFH.
18.4 Interface maximum possible RAM and EPROM with 8051. Select suitable memory maps.

18.5 A family of EPROM memory chips require 25 write cycles for programming each byte. Design suitable EPROM Programmer and write the firmware? How will you interface the EPROM to be programmed?

18.6 Interface 32 KB of RAM with 8051 so that full interrupt vector table is accommodated in it.

18.7 Interface 16 KB of EPROM with 8051 so that the external EPROM will host the monitor program of the complete system.

18.8 Interface 16 CA LEDs with 8051 port 2 and 3 and write a program to

1) Glow alternate three LEDs, shift left the pattern of all sixteen LEDs continuously.
2) Glow alternate two LEDs, shift the pattern of all sixteen LEDs right hundred times.

18.9 Interface 8 common cathode (CC) LEDs with 8051 port 1 and blink them continuously. Use appropriate drivers.

18.10 Interface 8×8 keyboard with 8051 using ports 2 and 3. Write an assembly language program to read the keycode of the pressed key in R0.

18.11 Interface 16 unit common anode (CA) 7 segment. multiplexed display unit with 8051 using only port 0. Write supporting assembly language program to display data available from 40 to 4FH, internal RAM on to it. (Use additional suitable chips)

18.12 Interface two 7 segment CC displays with 8051 port 0 and port 1 (2 lines). Implement a seconds counter on it. 8051 operates at 6 MHz.

18.13 Implement real time clock on hardware on CA 7 segment displays. The 8051 runs on 6 MHz. Appropriate 7 segment LED current drivers may be used.

18.14 Interface ADC 0809 with port 2 of 8051 as data output lines of ADC. The ADC control lines will be implemented using P3 or P1 lines.

1) Draw hardware and write program for the interfacing using polling of EOC signal
2) Draw hardware and write program using $\overline{INT1}$ driven by EOC signal.

18.15 Interface a 12 bit ADC ICL 7109 with 8051 using the ports appropriately. Write an assembly language program to read digital equivalent of analog input (Refer to chapter 5 for details) of ICL 7109 and store it in reg R0.

18.16 Interface DAC 0808 with 8051 and write assembly language program to generate

1) Square wave of 0–6 V frequency 10 Hz
2) Triangular wave of 0–10 V frequency 100 Hz
3) Assymmetric square wave of 1 KHz frequency, 60% Duty cycle and 0–4 V amplitude.
4) To generate the pattern shown below.

Assume suitable delays are available.

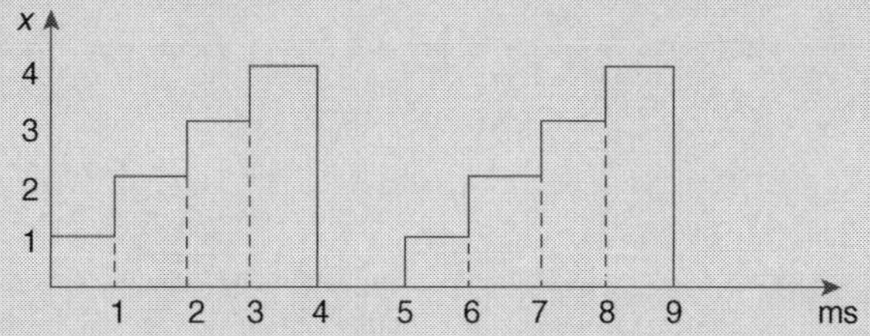

18.17 Interface ADC 0808 with 8051 to convert –5V – 0 +5V analog voltage to digital equivalent, draw hardware and write appropriate program.

18.18 Interface a 9V, 4Φ, 400 teeth stepper motor with 8051 ports using appropriate current drivers of ULN series (search websites for details of ULN series drivers). The resistance of the winding is 25 ohms. The inertial delay of the motor is 400 ms.

(1) Assume suitable delay available.
(2) The 8051 runs on 6 MHz use timers 0/1 for deriving appropriate delay.

18.19 Write appropriate software for Que 8. The 8051 runs on 6 MHz. Cacade timers to achieve seconds, minutes and hours count.

18.20 Using mode 0 of serial communication of a system, that runs on 11.0592 MHz.

i) Transmit 100 bytes available from an external code memory location 5000 H.

ii) Receive 100 bytes from R × D pin and store at external RAM memory location 5000 H.

18.21 Set 8051 serial communication unit in mode 2 and

i) Receive 100 bytes with parity check and store them from external RAM location 8000 H.

ii) Transmit 100 bytes with enable parity. The bytes are given from external RAM location 4000 H.

Select appropriate baud rate and parity arrangements.

18.22 Repeat Que 22 with mode 3 for baud rates given below.

i) 57.6 kbps ii) 0.1375 kbps iii) Any baud rate below 10 bps

18. 23 Implement single stepping system for 8051. The interrupt service routine for $\overline{INT1}$ stores all the R0–R7 registers after execution of the each instruction from 30 H onwards. It maintains track of last 10 instructions.

18.24 Develop a program to exchange blocks of 100 bytes each between two 8051 systems using serial communication protocol RS232 Draw the hardware and write program for both the microcontrollers to implement this transfer using

i) mode 2 ii) mode 3 iii) mode 0

18.25 Interface four 8 Kbyte chips of RAM each and two chips of EPROM, each of 4 Kbyte with 8051 so that it starts execution in the external program memory and the RAM is mapped at the end of the external data memory address map. Also interface two 8255s with the 8051 and write an ALP to initialize the 8255 chips with all ports as input ports in mode 0, read all the 8255 ports and store the data read from the 8255 ports in the external data RAM at addresses starting from D000H.

18.26 Minimise the application circuit given in Fig. 18.41 using an on-chip version of 8051 and write a program for the application using internal RAM locations as scratchpad (assume that the 6264 RAM chip is not used in the new circuit).

Appendix A

Instruction Set Summary*

Possible Flag settings are indicated by following symbols.

'–'	–	Not affected
0	–	Reset
1	–	Set
m	–	Modified according to Result
d	–	Undefined (don't care)
r	–	Restored from previously stored value
AM	–	Addressing Mode

Addressing Mode	No. of Clock Cycles (AM)
Direct Mode	6
Indirect Mode	5
Register Relative	9
Based Indexed	
Base pointer with Destination Index Register Base register with Source Index Register`	7
Base pointer with Source Index Register Base register with Destination Index Register	8
Based indexed relative	
Base pointer with Destination Index Register + Disp Base register with source Index Register + Disp	7 + 4 = 11
Base pointer with source index register + Disp. Base register with destination index register + Disp.	8 + 4 = 12

AM	SI	DI
BP	8	7
BX	7	8

AM	SI	DI
BP	12	11
BX	11	12

* Compiled By Harshad Tambde (B.E. E & T)
Rishikesh Agashe (B.E. E & T)

Table A.1 *Data Copy/Transfer Instructions*

Mnemonic	*Description*	*Clock Cycles*	*Number of bytes*	*Flags*								
				O	*D*	*I*	*T*	*S*	*Z*	*A*	*P*	*C*
MOV	Move			–	–	–	–	–	–	–	–	–
	Accumulator to memory	10	3									
	Memory to accumulator	10	3									
	Register to register	2	2									
	Memory to register	8 + AM	2–4									
	Register to memory	9 + AM	2–4									
	Immediate to register	4	2–3									
	Immediate to memory	10 + AM	3–6									
	Register to SS, DS or ES	2	2									
	Memory to SS, DS or ES	8 + AM	2–4									
	Segment register to register	2	2									
	Segment register to memory	9 + AM	2–4									
PUSH	Push word onto stack			–	–	–	–	–	–	–	–	–
	Register	11	1									
	Segment register	10	1									
	Memory	16 + AM	2–4									
POP	Pop word off stack			–	–	–	–	–	–	–	–	–
	Register	8	1									
	Segment register SS, DS, or ES	8	1									
	Memory	17 + AM	2–4									
XCHG	Exchange			–	–	–	–	–	–	–	–	–
	Register with accumulator	3	1									
	Register with memory	17 + AM	2–4									
	Register with register	4	2									
IN	Input from I/O port			–	–	–	–	–	–	–	–	–
	Fixed port	10	2									
	Variable port	8	1									
OUT	Output to I/O port			–	–	–	–	–	–	–	–	–
	Fixed port	10	2									
	Variable port	8	1									
XLAT/ XLATB	Translate	11	1									
LEA	Load effective address	2 + AM	2–4	–	–	–	–	–	–	–	–	–
LDS/LES	Load pointer using DS/ES	16 + AM	2–4	–	–	–	–	–	–	–	–	–
LAHF	Load AH from flags	4	1	–	–	–	–	–	–	–	–	–
SAHF	Store AH in to flags	4	1	–	–	–	–	r	r	r	r	r
PUSHF	Push flags onto stack	10	1	–	–	–	–	–	–	–	–	–
POPF	Pop flags from stack	8	1	r	r	r	r	r	r	r	r	r

Table A.2 *Arithmetic Instructions*

Mnemonic	*Description*	*Clock Cycles*	*Number of bytes*	*Flags O*	*D*	*I*	*T*	*S*	*Z*	*A*	*P*	*C*
ADD	Addition			m	–	–	–	m	m	m	m	m
	Register to register	3	2									
	Memory to register	9 + AM	2–4									
	Register to memory	16 + AM	2–4									
	Immediate to register	4	3–4									
	Immediate to memory	17 + AM	3–6									
	Immediate to accumulator	4	2–3									
ADC	Add with carry			m	–	–	–	m	m	m	m	m
	Register to register	3	2									
	Memory to register	9 + AM	2–4									
	Register to memory	16 + AM	2–4									
	Immediate to register	4	3–4									
	Immediate to memory	17 + AM	3–6									
	Immediate to accumulator	4	2–3									
INC	Increment by 1			m	–	–	–	m	m	m	m	–
	16-bit register	2	1									
	8-bit register	3	2									
	Memory	15 + AM	2–4									
DEC	Decrement by 1			m	–	–	–	m	m	m	m	
	16-bit register	2	1									
	8-bit register	3	2									
	Memory	15 + AM	2–4									
SUB	Subtraction			m	–	–	–	m	m	m	m	m
	Register from register	3	2									
	Memory from register	9 + AM	2–4									
	Register from memory	16 + AM	2–4									
SUB	Immediate from accumulator	4	2–3									
	Immediate from register	4	3–4									
	Immediate from memory	17 + AM	3–6									
SBB	Subtract with borrow			m	–	–	–	m	m	m	m	m
	Register from register	3	2									
	Memory from register	9 + AM	2–4									
	Register from memory	16 + AM	2–4									
	Immediate from accumulator	4	2–3									
	Immediate from register	4	3–4									
	Immediate from memory	17 + AM	3–6									

(*Contd.*)

Table A.2 (*Contd.*)

Mnemonic	*Description*	*Clock Cycles*	*Number of bytes*	*Flags* O	D	I	T	S	Z	A	P	C
CMP	Compare			m	–	–	–	m	m	m	m	m
	Register to register	3	2									
	Memory to register	9 + AM	2–4									
	Register to memory	16 + AM	2–4									
	Immediate to register	4	3–4									
	Immediate to memory	4	3–6									
	Immediate to accumulator	17 + AM	2–3									
AAA	ASCII adjust after addition	4	1	d	–	–	–	d	d	m	d	m
AAS	ASCII adjust after subtraction	4	1	d	–	–	–	d	d	m	d	m
AAM	ASCII adjust after multiplication	83	2	d	–	–	–	m	m	d	m	d
AAD	ASCII adjust after division	60	2	d	–	–	–	m	m	d	m	d
DAA	Decimal adjust accumulator	4	1	d	–	–	–	m	m	m	m	m
DAS	Decimal adjust subtraction	4	1	d	–	–	–	m	m	m	m	m
NEG	Negate			m	–	–	–	m	m	m	m	m
	Register	3	2									
	Memory	16 + AM	2–4									
MUL	Unsigned multiplication			m	–	–	–	d	d	d	d	m
	8-bit register	70–77	2									
	16-bit register	118–133	2									
	8-bit memory	(76–83) + AM	2–4									
	16-bit memory	(124–139) + AM	2–4									
IMUL	Integer multiplication			m	–	–	–	d	d	d	d	m
	8-bit register	80–98	2									
	16-bit register	128–154	2									
IMUL	8-bit memory	(86–104) + AM	2–4									
	16-bit memory	(134–160) + AM	2–4									
CBW	Convert byte to word	2	1	–	–	–	–	–	–	–	–	–
CWD	Convert word to double word	5	1	–	–	–	–	–	–	–	–	–
DIV	Unsigned division			d	–	–	–	d	d	d	d	d
	8-bit register	80–90	2									
	16-bit register	144–162	2									
	8-bit memory	(86–96) + AM	2–4									
	16-bit memory	(150–168) + AM	2–4									
IDIV	Integer division			d	–	–	–	d	d	d	d	d
	8-bit register	101–112	2									
	16-bit register	165–184	2									
	8-bit memory	(107–118) + AM	2–4									
	16-bit memory	(171–190) + AM	2–4									

Table A.3 *Logical Instructions*

Mnemonic	*Description*	*Clock Cycles*	*Number of bytes*	*Flags*								
				O	*D*	*I*	*T*	*S*	*Z*	*A*	*P*	*C*
AND	Logical AND			0	–	–	–	m	m	d	m	0
	Register to register	3	2									
	Memory to register	9 + AM	2–4									
	Register to memory	16 + AM	2–4									
	Immediate to register	4	3–4									
	Immediate to memory	17 + AM	3–6									
	Immediate to accumulator	4	2–3									
OR	Logical OR			0	–	–	–	m	m	d	m	0
	Register to register	3	2									
	Memory to register	9 + AM	2–4									
	Register to memory	16 + AM	2–4									
	Immediate to accumulator	4	2–3									
	Immediate to register	4	3–4									
	Immediate to memory	17 + AM	3–6									
NOT	Logical NOT			–	–	–	–	–	–	–	–	–
	Register	3	2									
	Memory	16 + AM	2–4									
XOR	Logical exclusive OR			0	–	–	–	m	m	d	m	0
	Register with register	3	2									
	Memory with register	9 + AM	2–4									
	Register with memory	16 + AM	2–4									
	Immediate with accumulator	4	2–3									
	Immediate with register	4	3–4									
	Immediate with memory	17 + AM	3–6									
TEST	TEST			0	–	–	–	m	m	d	m	0
	Register with register	3	2									
	Memory with register	9 + AM	2–4									
	Immediate with accumulator	4	2–3									
	Immediate with register	5	3–4									
	Immediate with memory	11 + AM	3–6									

Table A.4 *Branching Instructions*

Mnemonic	*Description*	*Clock Cycles*	*Number of bytes*	*O*	*D*	*I*	*T*	*S*	*Z*	*A*	*P*	*C*
CALL	Call a procedure			–	–	–	–	–	–	–	–	–
	Intrasegment direct	19	3									
	Intrasegment indirect through register	16	2									
	Intrasegment indirect through memory	21 + AM	2–4									
	Intrasegment direct	28	5									
	Intrasegment indirect	37 + AM	2–4									
RET	Return from a procedure			–	–	–	–	–	–	–	–	–
	Intrasegment	8	1									
	Intrasegment with constant	12	3									
	Intersegment	18	1									
	Intersegment with constant	17	3									
INT N	Interrupt			–	–	0	0	–	–	–	–	–
	Type = 3	52	1									
	Type π 3	51	2									
INTO	Interrupt if overflow			–	–	0	0	–	–	–	–	–
	Interrupt if taken	53										
	Interrupt if not taken	4										
JMP	Jump			–	–	–	–	–	–	–	–	–
	Intrasegment direct short	15	2									
	Intrasegment direct	15	3									
	Intersegment direct	15	5									
	Intrasegment indirect through memory	18 + AM	2–4									
	Intrasegment indirect through register	11	2									
	Intersegment indirect	24 + AM	2–4									
IRET	Return from Interrupt	24	1	r	r	r	r	r	r	r	r	r
JZ/JE	Jump if not zero/ Jump if not equal	16/4	2	–	–	–	–	–	–	–	–	–
JNX/ JNE	Jumps if not zero/ Jumps if not equal	16.4	2	–	–	–	–	–	–	–	–	–
JS	Jump if sign	16/4	2	–	–	–	–	–	–	–	–	–
JNS	Jump if not sign	16/4	2	–	–	–	–	–	–	–	–	–
JO	Jump of overflow	16/4	2	–	–	–	–	–	–	–	–	–
JNO	Jump if not overflow	16/4	2	–	–	–	–	–	–	–	–	–

(*Contd.*)

Table A.4 (*Contd.*)

Mnemonic	*Description*	*Clock Cycles*	*Number of bytes*	*Flags* O	D	I	T	S	Z	A	P	C
JP/JPE	Jump if parity/ Jump if parity even	16/4	2	–	–	–	–	–	–	–	–	–
JNP/JPO	Jump if not parity/Jump if parity odd	16/4	2	–	–	–	–	–	–	–	–	–
JB/ JNAE/JC	Jump if below/Jump if not above or equal/Jump if carry	16/4	2	–	–	–	–	–	–	–	–	–
JNB/JAE/JNC	Jump if not below/Jump if above or equal/Jump if not carry	16/4	2	–	–	–	–	–	–	–	–	–
JBE/JNA	Jump if below or equal/ Jump if not above	16/4	2	–	–	–	–	–	–	–	–	–
JNBE/JA	Jump if not below or equal/ Jump if above	16/4	2	–	–	–	–	–	–	–	–	–
JL/ JNGE	Jump if less/ Jump if not greater or equal	16/4	2	–	–	–	–	–	–	–	–	–
JNL/JGE	Jump if not less/ Jump if greater or equal	16/4	2	–	–	–	–	–	–	–	–	–
JLE/JNG	Jump if less or equal/ Jump if not greater	16/4	2	–	–	–	–	–	–	–	–	–
JNLE/JG	Jump if not less or equal/ Jump if greater	16/4	2	–	–	–	–	–	–	–	–	–
JCXZ	Jump if CX is zero	18/6	2	–	–	–	–	–	–	–	–	–

Table A.5 *Loop Instructions*

Mnemonic	*Description*	*Clock Cycles*	*Number of bytes*	*Flags* O	D	I	T	S	Z	A	P	C
LOOP	Loop	17/5	2	–	–	–	–	–	–	–	–	–
LOOPE/ LOOPZ	Loop if equal/ Loop if zero	18/6	2	–	–	–	–	–	–	–	–	–
LOO- PNZ/ LOOPNE	Loop if not zero/ Loop if not equal	19/5	2	–	–	–	–	–	–	–	–	–

Table A.6 *Machine Control Instructions*

Mnemonic	*Description*	*Clock Cycles*	*Number of bytes*	*Flags*								
				O	*D*	*I*	*T*	*S*	*Z*	*A*	*P*	*C*
NOP	No operation	3	1	–	–	–	–	–	–	–	–	–
HLT	Halt	2	1	–	–	–	–	–	–	–	–	–
WAIT	Wait while $\overline{\text{TEST}}$ pin not asserted	3+5n	1	–	–	–	–	–	–	–	–	–
LOCK	Lock Bus	2	1	–	–	–	–	–	–	–	–	–
ESC	Escape			–	–	–	–	–	–	–	–	–
Register	2	2										
	Memory	8+AM	2–4									

Table A.7 *Flag Manipulation Instruction*

Mnemonic	*Description*	*Clock Cycles*	*Number of bytes*	*Flags*								
				O	*D*	*I*	*T*	*S*	*Z*	*A*	*P*	*C*
CLC	Clear carry flag	2	1	–	–	–	–	–	–	–	–	0
CMC	Complement carry flag	2	1	–	–	–	–	–	–	–	–	m
STC	Set carry flag	2	1	–	–	–	–	–	–	–	–	1
CLD	Clear direction flag	2	1	–	0	–	–	–	–	–	–	–
STD	Set direction flag	2	1	–	1	–	–	–	–	–	–	–
CLI	Clear interrupt flag	2	1	–	–	0	–	–	–	–	–	–
STI	Set interrupt flag	2	1	–	–	1	–	–	–	–	–	–

Table A.8 *Shift and Rotate Instruction*

Mnemonic	*Description*	*Clock Cycles*	*Number of bytes*	*Flags*								
				O	*D*	*I*	*T*	*S*	*Z*	*A*	*P*	*C*
SHL/SAL	Shift Logical Left/ Shift arithmetic Left			m	–	–	–	m	m	d	m	m
	Register with single shift	2	2									
	Register with variable shift	8 + 4/bit	2									
	Memory with single shift	15 + AM	2–4									
	Memory with variable shift	(20 + AM) + 4/bit	2–4									
SHR	Shift logical right			m	–	–	–	m	m	d	m	m
	Register with single shift	2	2									
	Register with variable shift	8 + 4/bit	2									
	Memory with single shift	15 + AM	2–4									
	Memory with variable shift	(20 + AM) + 4/bit	2–4									
SAR	Shift arithmetic right			m	–	–	–	m	m	d	m	m

(*Contd.*)

Table A.8 (*Contd.*)

Mnemonic	*Description*	*Clock Cycles*	*Number of bytes*	*O*	*D*	*I*	*T*	*S*	*Z*	*A*	*P*	*C*
	Register with single shift	2	2									
	Register with variable shift	8 + 4/bit	2									
	Memory with single shift	15+AM	2–4									
	Memory with variable shift	(20+AM) + 4/bit	2–4									
ROR	Rotate right without carry			m	–	–	–	–	–	–	–	m
	Register with single shift	2	2									
	Register with variable shift	8 + 4 bit	2									
	Memory with single shift	15 + AM	2–4									
	Memory with variable shift	(20 + AM) + 4/bit	2–4									
ROL	Rotate left			m	–	–	–	–	–	–	–	m
	Register with single shift	2	2									
	Register with variable shift	8 + 4/bit	2									
	Memory with single shift	15 + AM	2–4									
	Memory with variable shift	(20 + AM) + 4/bit	2–4									
RCR	Rotate right through carry			m	–	–	–	–	–	–	–	m
	Register with single shift	2	2									
	Register with variable shift	8 + 4/bit	2									
	Memory with single shift	15 + AM	2–4									
	Memory with variable shift	(20 + AM) + 4/bit	2–4									
RCL	Rotate left through carry			m	–	–	–	–	–	–	–	m
	Register with single shift	2	2									
	Register with variable shift	8 + 4/bit	2									
	Memory with single shift	15 + AM	2–4									
	Memory with variable shift	(20 + AM) + 4/bit	2–4									

Table A.9 *String Instruction*

Mnemonic	*Description*	*Clock Cycles*	*Number of bytes*	*O*	*D*	*I*	*T*	*S*	*Z*	*A*	*P*	*C*
CMPS/ CMPSB CMPSW	Compare string/compare byte string/compare word string		1	m	–	–	–	m	m	m	m	m
	Not repeated	22										
	Repeated	9 + 22/rep										
MOVS/ MOVSB/ MOVSW	Move string/move byte string/move Word string		1	–	–	–	–	–	–	–	–	–
	Not repeated	18										

(*Contd.*)

Table A.9 (*Contd.*)

Mnemonic	*Description*	*Clock Cycles*	*Number of bytes*	*Flags*								
				O	*D*	*I*	*T*	*S*	*Z*	*A*	*P*	*C*
	Repeated	9 + 17/rep										
LODS/	Load string/Load		1	–	–	–	–	–	–	–	–	
LODSB/	String byte/Load											
LODSW	String word											
	Not repeated	12										
	Repeated	9 + 13/rep										
SCAS/	Scan string/		1									
SCASB/	Scan byte string/											
SCASW	Scan word string											
	Not repeated		15	m	–	–	–	m	m	m	m	m
	Repeated	9 + 15/rep										
STOS/	Store string/		1	–	–	–	–	–	–	–	–	
STOSB/	Store byte string/											
STOSW	Store word string											
	Not repeated		11									
	Repeated	9 + 10/rep										

Appendix

B

DOS Function Calls: INT 21H*

Table B.1

Function Value in AX/AH AL	*Function*	*Register I/P*	*Return O/P*
1. Function 00H (0) Program terminate	Restore termination handler vector from psp: 000AH Restore the ctrl C–vector from psp : 000EH	AH = 00, CS = Segment address of program segment prefix	Nothing
2. Function 01H (1) Character I/P with echo.	Inputs a character from keyboard, then echoes it to display. If no character is ready, waits until one is available.	AH = 01	AL = 8-bit character
3. Function 02H(2) Character output	Output a character to the currently active video display.	AH = 02, DL = 8 bit char. (ASCII code)	Nothing
4. Function 03H(3) Auxiliary input	Reads a character from the first serial port.	AH = 03	AL = 8-bit char.
5. Function 04H(4) Auxiliary output	Output a character to the first serial port.	AH = 04 DL = 8-bit char.	Nothing
6. Function 05H(5) Printer output	Sends a character to the first device (PRN or LPT 1).	AH = 05 DL = 8-bit char.	

(*Contd.*)

* Compiled by Amesha Thaker B. E. (Comp. Tech.)

Function Value in AX/AH AL	*Function*	*Register I/P*	*Return O/P*
7. Function 06H(6) Direct console I/O	Reads a character form keyboard or returns zero if none is ready or writes a character to the display.	AH = 06, DL = Function requested.	If zero flag = clear AL = 8-bit data, else zeroflag = set
8. Function 07H(H) unfiltered char. I/P without zero	Reads a character from keyboard without echoing it to the display. If no character is ready, waits until one is available.	AH = 07	AL = 8-bit char
9. Function 08H(8) Char. I/P without echo.	Reads a character from keyboard without echoing it to the display. If no character is ready, waits until one is available.	AH = 08	AL = 8-bit char.
10. Function 09H(9) Output char. string	Sends a string of characters to the display.	AH = 09, DS: DX = Segment: offset of string	–
11. Function 0AH(10) Buffered input	Reads a string of characters from keyboard and places it in a user–designated buffer.	AH = 0AH, DS: DX = Segment: offset of buffer.	–
12. Function 0BH(11) Get input status	Checks whether a character is available from the keyboard.	AH = 0BH	AL = 00, not available = FFH, available
13. Function 0CH(12) Reset I/P buffer and then input	Clears the type ahead buffer and then invokes one of the keyboard input functions.	AH = 0CH, AL = No. of I/p functions to be after reseting invoked buffer: 01H, 06H, 07H, 08H or 0AH. DS:DX = seg.: offset of I/p buffer	If function is 01H, 06H, 07H, 08H, AL is 8-bit data.
14. Function 0DH(13) Disk reset	Selects drive A as the default, set the disk transfer (DTA) address to DS:0080H, and flushes all file buffers to disk.	AH = 0DH	
15. Function 0EH(14) set default disk drive	Selects a specified drive to be the current, or default, disk drive, and returns the total no. of logical drives in system.	AH = 0EH, DL = Drive code (0 = A, 1 = B ...)	AL = No. of logical drives in system.

(Contd.)

Function Value in AX/AH AL	*Function*	*Register I/P*	*Return O/P*
16. Function 0FH(15) Open File	Opens a file and makes it available for subsequent read/write operation	AH = 0FH, DS:DX = segment: offset of file control block.	fn successful AL = 0. fn failed, AL = 0FFH.
17. Function 10H(16) Close File	Closes a file, and updates the disk directory if the file has been modified or extended.	AH = 10H, DS:DX = segment :offset of File control block	AL = 00–fn successful = 0FFH
18. Function 11H(17) Search for first match	Searches current directory on disk in the designated drive for a matching filename.	AH = 11H, DS:DX = segment: offset of FCB	If file found, AL = 00. File not found, AL = 0FFH
19. Function 12H(18) Search for next match	Given that a previous call to function 11H has been successful, returns next matching filename (if any)	AH = 12H, DS:DX = segment: offset of FCB	File found, AL = 00 Not found, AL = 0FFH
20. Function 13H(19) Delete file	Deletes all matching files from the current subdirectory.	AH = 13H, DS:DX = segment: offset of FCB	File found, AL = 00 File not found, AL = 0FFH
21. Function 14H(20) Sequential read	Reads the next sequential block of data from a file, then increments the file pointer appropriately.	AH = 14H, DS:DX = segment: offset of previously opend FCB	AL = 00 if read, 01 if EOF 02 if seg wrap, 03 if partial record read at EOF.
22. Function 15H(21) Sequential write	Writes the next sequential block of data into a file, then increments file.	AH = 15H, DS:DX = segment: offset of previously opened FCB	AL = 00 if write ok. AL = 01 if disk full. AL = 02 if seg. wrap.
23. Function 16H(22) Create or truncate file.	Creates new directory entry in current subdirectory or truncates any existing file with specified length.	AH = 16H, DS:DX = segment: offset of unopened FCB	AL = 00 file created AL = 0FFH file not created
24. Function 17H(23) Rename file	Alters the name of all watching files in current subdirectory on disk in the specified drive.	AH = 17 H, DS:DX = segment: offset of special FCB	AL = 00 if renamed AL = 0FFH if not found.
25. Function 18H (24)			
26. Function 19H (25) Get default disk drive	Returns drive code of current or default disk drive.	AH = 19H	AL = Drive code

(Contd.)

Function Value in AX/AH AL	*Function*	*Register I/P*	*Return O/P*
27. Function 1A (26) Set DTA address	Specifies memory address to be used for subsequent PCB disk operation.	AH = 1AH, DS:DX = segment: offset of disk transfer area.	
28. Function 1BH(27) Get allocation information for default drive.	The address returned in DS–BX points to the actual FAT.	AL = number of sector per cluster DS:BX = segment: offset of FAT identification byte, CX = Size of physical sector (in bytes), DX = number of clusters for default drive.	AH = 1BH
29. Function 1CH(28) Get allocation information for specified drive.	Obtains selected information about the specified disk drive and a pointer to the identification byte from its file allocation table (FAT)	AL = number of sector per cluster, DS:BX = segment: offset of FAT identification table, CX = Size of physical sector (in bytes), DX = number of clusters for default or specified drive.	AH = 1CH DL = drive code (0 = default, 1 = A, etc.)
30. Function 1DH (29)	Reserved	–	–
31. Function 1EH (30)	Reserved	–	–
32. Function 1FH (31)	Reserved	–	–
33. Function 20H (32)	Reserved	–	–
34. Function 21H (33) Random read	Read a selected record from a file into memory	AH = 21H DS:DX = segment: offset of previously opened file control block.	AL = 00 if read successfully, 01 if end of file, 02 if segment wrap, 03 if partial record read at end of file.
35. Function 22H (34) Random write	Writes data from memory into a selected record in a file.	AH = 22H, DS:DX = segment : offset of previously opened file control block.	AL = 00 if write successfully, 01 if disk full, 02 if segment wrap.
36. Function 23H (35) Get file size in records	Searches for a matching file in the current subdirectory, if one is found, fills a file control block (FCB) with file size information in terms of record count.	AH = 23H, DS:DX = segment: offset of unopened file control block.	If matching file found AL = 0, if not then AL = 0FFH.

(Contd.)

Function Value in AX/AH AL	*Function*	*Register I/P*	*Return O/P*
37. Function 24H (36) Set random record number	Sets the random record field of a file control block (FCB) to correspond to the current file position as recorded in the opened FCB.	AH = 24H, DS:DX = segment: offset of previously opened file control block.	Register contents not affected, Random–record field is modified in file control block.
38. Function 25H (37) Set interrupt vector	Initialize a machine interrupt vector to point to an interrupt handling routine.	AH = 25H, AL = machine interrupt number, DS:DX = segment: offset of interrupt handling routine.	Nothing
39. Function 26H (38) Create program segment prefix	Copies the program segment perfix (PSP) of the current executing program to a specified segment address in free memory, then updates the new PSP to make it usable by another program.	AH = 26H DX = segment of new program segment prefix.	Nothing
40. Function 27H (39) Random block read	Reads one or more sequential records from a file into memory, starting at a designated file location.	AH = 27H CX = number of records to be read, DS:DX = segment:offset of previously opened file control block.	AL = 00 if all requested records read, 01 if end of file, 02 if segment wrap, 03 if partial record read at end of file, CX = actual number of records read.
41. Function 28H (40) Random block write	Writes one or more sequential records from a memory to a file, starting at a designated file location.	AH = 28 H CX = number of records to be written, DS:DX = segment: offset of previously opened FCB	AL = 00 if all requested records are written, 01 if disk full, 02 if segment wrap, CX = actual number of records written.
42. Function 29H (41) Parse filename	Parses a text string into the various fields of the control block.	AH = 29 H, AL = flags to control passing, DS:SI = seg.: offset of text string, ES:DI = segment: string, offset, of file control block.	AL = 00 if no global character encountered, 01 if parsed string contain global character, 0FFH if drive specifier invalid, DS:SI = seg.: offset of 1st char. after parsed filename, ES:DI = seg. : offset of formatted unopened file block.

(Contd.)

Function Value in AX/AH AL	*Function*	*Register I/P*	*Return O/P*
43. Function 2AH (42) Get system date	Obtains the system day of month, day of the week, month, and year.	AH = 2AH	CX = year (1980–2099) DX = month DL = day
44. Function 2BH (43) Set system date	Initialises system—clock driver to a specified date. The system time is not affected.	AH = 2BH CX = year DH = month DL = day	AL = 00 if date set successfully. = 0FFH if date not valid.
45. Function 2CH (44) Get system time	Obtains time of day from system real time clock driver, converted to hour, minutes, seconds and hundredths of seconds.	AH = 2CH	CH–hour CL–minutes DH–seconds DL–1/100th of secs.
46. Function 2DH (45) Set system time	Initialises system real—time clock to a specified hour, min, sec. and hundredth of second. System date is not affected.	AH = 2DH CH = hours CL = minutes DH = seconds DL = 1/100th of secs.	AL = 00 if time set successfully = 0FFH if not valid.
47. Function 2EH (46) Set verify flag	Turns off or turns on o.s. flag for automatic read–after write verification of data.	AH = 2EH AL = 00	
48. Function 2FH (47) Get disk transfer are a addr.	Obtains current address of DTA for FCB file read/write operation.	AH = 2FH	ES:BX = seg.:offset of DTA
49. Function 30H (48) Get MS-DOS version number	Returns version no. of operating system.	AH = 30H no. no.	AL = major version AH = minor version (3.10 = 0AH(10), etc.)
50. Function 31H (49) Terminate and stay resident (KEEP process)	Terminates a process without releasing its memory.	AH = 31H AL = return code = mem. size to reserve	–
51. Function 32H (50) Reserved	–	–	–
52. Function 33H (51) Get/set Ctrl–Break flag	Determines current status of os's Ctrl–break or Ctrl–C checking flag.	AH = 33H if getting status of Ctrl–Break flag AL = 00, if setting AL = 01, DL = 00, DL = 01.	DL = 00 if C–B checking off, DL = 01 if Ctrl–Break checking on.

(Contd.)

Function Value in AX/AH AL	*Function*	*Register I/P*	*Return O/P*
53. Function 34H (52) Reserved	–	–	–
54. Function 35H (53) Get interrupt vector	Obtains address of current interrupt handler routine for specified M/C interrupt.	AH = 35H AL = int. no.	ES:BX = seg.: offset of interrupt handle.
55. Function 36H (54) Get free disk space	Obtains selected info. about a disk drive from which the drive's capacity can be calculated.	AH = 36H DL = drive code.	If drive valid, AX–sectors/cluster BX–no. of clusters CX–bytes/sectors DX–clusters/drive If specified drive invalid AX = FFFFH
56. Function 37H (55) Reserved			
57. Function 38H (56) Get/Set country	Obtains current-country information.	AH = 38H, AL = 00, DS:DX = seg:offset of buffer for returned information. set	If no error occurs, BX = country code DS:DX Bytes 0–1 = date format 2 = currency symbol 3 = zero 4 = thousand, sep. char. 5 = zero 6 = decimal sep. char. 7 = zero 8–31 = reserved. If error occurs, CY flag = set AX = error code If no error while setting current country code CY = clear. If error occurs CY = AX = error code.
58. Function 39H (57) Create sub-directory	Creates sub-directory using specified drive and path.	AH = 39H, DS:DX = seg.: offset of ASCIIZ path specification	If function successful, CY = clear. Function failed, CY = set, AX = error code.

(*Contd.*)

Function Value in AX/AH AL	*Function*	*Register I/P*	*Return O/P*
59. Function 3AH (58) Delete sub-directory	Removes sub-directory using specified disk and path.	AH = 3AH, DS:DX = seg.: offset of ASCIIZ string.	If function successful, CY = clear. Function failed, CY = set, AX = error code.
60. Function 3BH (59) Set current directory	Sets the current or default directory using specified drive and path.	AH = 3BH DS:DX = seg.: offset of ASCIIZ string.	If function successful, CY = clear. Function failed, CY = set, AX = error code.
61. Function 3 CH (60) Create or truncate file	Creates a new file in the designated or default directory on the designated or default disk drive. If specified file already exists it is truncated to zero length. The file is opened and a 16-bit token, or handle is returned, which is used by the program for further access to the file.	AH = 3CH CX = file attribute, 00H if normal, 01H if read only, 02H if hidden, 04H if system. DS:DX = seg.: offset of ASCIIZ file.	If function successful, carry flag = clear, AX = file handle. If not successful, Carry flag = set, AX = error code, 3-if path not found 4-if no handle 5-if access denied.
62. Function 3DH (61) Open file	Given an ASCIIZ file specification opens the specified file in the designated or default directory on the designated or default disk drive.	AH = 3DH AL = access mode DS:DX = seg.:offset of ASCIIZ file specification.	If function successful, Carry flag = clear, AX = file handle. If not successful CY flag = set, AX = error code.
63. Function 3EH (62) Close file	Given a file token or handle that was returned by a previous successful open (function 3DH) or create operation, flushes all internal buffer to disk, closes the file, and releases the handle for reuse. If file was modified or extended, the time and date, stamp and the file size are updated in directory entry.	AH = 3EH BX = file handle.	If function successful, Carry flag = clear. If not successful, Carry flag = set, AX = error code, 6-if handle invalid or not open.

(Contd.)

Function Value in AX/AH AL	*Function*	*Register I/P*	*Return O/P*
64. Function 3FH (63) Read file or device	Given a valid file token or handle from a previous successful open or create operation, a buffer address and a length in bytes, transfers data at the current file-pointer from the file into the buffer and then updates the file pointer position.	AH = 3FH BX = file handle, CX = no. of bytes to be read, DS:DX = seg.:offset of buffer area.	If function successful, CY flag = clear, AX = no. of bytes read. If failed, CY flag = set, AX = error code.
65. Function 40H (64) Write to file or device	Given a file token or handle from a previous successful open or create operation, a buffer address and a length in bytes, transfers data from the buffer into the file and updates the file pointer positions.	AH = 40H BX = file handle, CX = no. of bytes to be written, DS:DX = seg.:offset CY flag = set	If function successful, CY flag = clear, AX = no. of bytes written. If fn failed, AX = error code.
66. Function 41H (65) Delete file	Deletes a file from the specified or default disk and directory.	AH = 41H DS:DX = Seg.:offset	If function successful, CY flag = clear. If function failed, CY = set, AX = error code.
67. Function 42H (66) Move file pointer	Sets file pointer location relative to the start of the file, the end of file or current file position. half of offset	AH = 42H AL = method code BX = file handle CX = most significant half of offset DX = least significant part of new ptr.	If function successful. Carry flag = clear. DX-most significant part of new ptr. location, AX-least significant location, 1-if function no. valid 6-if handle invalid.
68. Function 43H (67) Get or set file attributes	Obtains or alters the attributes of a file.	AH = 43H AL = 00H if getting file attribute, 01H if setting, CX = new attribute DS:DX = seg.:offset	If function successful, CY flag = clear. If AL = 00 on call CX-attribute. If function failed, CY flag = set, AX = error code.

(*Contd.*)

Function Value in AX/AH AL	*Function*	*Register I/P*	*Return O/P*
69. Function 44H (68) Device driver control (IOCTL)	Passes control information directly between an application and a device driver.	AH = 44H AL = 00H if getting device info. 01H- if setting device info 02H-if reading from device control channel to buffer 03H-if writing from buffer to device control channel 04H-same as 02H, but codes using drive no. in BL 05H-same as 03H, but using drive no. in BL 06H-if getting I/p status. 07H-if getting O/p status 08H-if testing whether block device changeable 09H-if testing block device local 0AH -if testing handle local 0BH-if changing sharing retry count.	If function successful CY flag = clear. AX = no of bytes transferred AX = value if function code 08H AL-status if function 06H-07H DX-device into if function code 00H.
70. Function 45H (69) Duplicate handle	Given a handle for a currently open device or file returns a new handle that refers to the same device or file.	AH = 45H BX-file handle	If function successful, CY flag = clear, AX = new file handle. If function failed, CY flag = set, AX = error code, 4-if no handle 6-if handle invalid.
71. Function 46H (70) Force duplicate of handle	Given two handles makes the second handle refer to the same opened file at the same location as first handle.	AH = 46H BX = first file handle CX = second file handle	If function successful, CY flag = clear. If function failed, CY flag = set, AX = error code, 4-if no handle 6-if handle invalid.
72. Function 74H (71) Get current directory	Obtains an ASCIIZ string that describes the path from the root to currently active directory and name of directory.	AH = 47H DL = drive code DS:SI = seg.:offset of 64-byte scratch buffer	If function successful, CY flag = clear. If function failed, CY flag = set, AX = error code.

(*Contd.*)

Function Value in AX/AH AL	*Function*	*Register I/P*	*Return O/P*
73. Function 48H (72) Allocate memory	Allocates a block of memory and returns a pointer to the beginning of the allocated area.	AH = 48H BX = no. of paragraphs of memory needed. available block.	If function successful, CY flag = clear, AX-initial seg. of allocation block. If failed, CY flag = set, AX = error code, BX = size of largest
74. Function 49H (73) Release memory	Release a memory block and makes it available for use by other programs.	AH = 49H ES = seg. or block to be released.	If function successful, Carry flag = clear. It not successful, Carry flag = set, AX = error code, 7-if MCB's destroyed 9-if incorrect segment in ES.
75. Function 4AH (74) Modify memory allocation	Dynamically shrinks or extends a memory block according to the needs of an application program.	AH = 4AH BX = new requested block size in paragraphs ES = seg. block to be modified.	If function successful, Carry flag = clear. If not successful, Carry flag = set, AX = error code, BX = max. block size available.
76. Function 4BH (75) Execute program	Allows an application program to run another program, regaining control when it is finished and optionally examining the child program's return code. Can also be used to load overlays, but this use is uncommon.	AH = 4BH AL = 00 if loading + executing program = 03 if loading overlay ES:BX = seg.:offset of parameter block. DS:DX = seg.:offset of prog. specification (file name)	If function successful, Carry flag = clear, All registers except CS and IP are destroyed including SP. If function failed, Carry flag = set, AX = error code, 1-if function invalid 2-if file not found or path invalid 3-if insufficient memory to load the program 5-if access denied 0AH-if environment invalid 0BH-if format invalid.

(*Contd.*)

Function Value in AX/AH AL	*Function*	*Register I/P*	*Return O/P*
77. Function 4CH (76) Terminate with return code	Performs a final exit to MS-DOS or to a parent task, passing back a return code. DOS then takes following actions: 1. Restores the termination handler vector from PSP:000AH 2. Restores the Ctrl-Break vector from PSP:000EH 3. Restores critical error handler vector from PSP:0012H 4. Flushes file buffers 5.Transfer to termination handler address.	AH = 4CH AL = return code	
78. Function 4DH	Gets return code of child program after its termination.	AH = 4DH	AH = 00-normal termination with function 4CH 01-termination via ^C, INT23H 02-termination due to critical error 03-termination via function 31H. AL = Return code specified while terminating using 4CH or 31H
79. Function 4EH	Search directory for first matching file and report information about it	AH = 4EH, CX = Search attribute, DS:DX = Segment: Offset address of null terminated ASCII string of the filename path or default directory. Before this function user must set DTA (Disk transfer area) using function 1AH.	If function succeeds, CY = 0, i.e. matching filename is found and the following information is reported in DTA- Bytes 00-14H-reserved 15H-Attribute of the file 16H-17H-Time of creation/update

(*Contd.*)

Function value in AX/AH AL	*Function*	*Register I/P*	*Return O/P*
			18H-19H-Date of creation/update 1A-1BH-Least significant word of file size 1C-1DH-Most significant word of file size 1E-2AH-Filename and extension of the matched file if function fails, CY = 1 i.e. a matching filename is not found and AX = 02H-Invalid path 12H-If no file with the matching name is found in the default or specified directory.
80. Function 4FH	Search the default or specified directory for next matching file, following a successful call to function 4EH, and report various information about it.	AH = 4FH, Function 1 AH must be called to set DTA before executing this function.	If function succeeds, CY = 0 i.e. a matching filename is found and the following information is reported in DTA-Bytes 00-14H-reserved 15H-Attribute of the file 16H-17H-Time of creation/update 18H-19H-Date of creation/updated 1A-1BH-Least significant word of file size 1C-1DH-Most

(*Contd.*)

Function Value in AX/AH AL	*Function*	*Register I/P*	*Return O/P*
			significant word of file size 1E-2AH-Filename and extension of the matched file If function fails, CY= 1 i.e. a matching filename is not found and AX = 12 H-If no file with the matching name is found in the default or specified directory
81. Function 50H-53H	RESERVED		
82. Function 54H	Get verified state-Using this function every disk write operation can be verified for correctness of the written data by reading it after the write operation.	AH = 54 H	AL=00-If varify flag is off 01-If varify flag is on
83. Function 55H	RESERVED		
84. Function 56H	Rename the existing file contains Segment: Offset string of the file to be contains Segment: Offset	AH = 56H, DS:DX and the file is of the null terminated CY = 1 and-AX = 02- renamed and ES:DI 03-Invalid Path of the null terminated string of the new filename.	If successful,CY = 0 renamed, else File not found 05-Access denied 11H-for not the same device.
85. Function 57H	Handle type call to get or set the date and time stamp of a previously opened file new time, DX = 16-bit	AH = 57H, BX = file handle of the previously opened file, AL = 00 if getting date and time AL = 01 if setting date and time. If AL = 01, CX = 16-bit is invalid new date information	If function fails, CY= 1 and AX = 01H-If invalid option is and indicated in AL for calling function. 06H-If handle in BX If function successes, CY = 0 For AL = 00, on return CX = 16-bit time stamp of the file DX = 16-bit date

(*Contd.*)

Function Value in AX/AH AL	*Function*	*Register I/P*	*Return O/P*
			stamp of the file For AL = 01, on return time and date fields of the file are modified appropriately.
86. Function 58H	Get or set memory allocation strategy If getting strategy, AL	AH = 58H, 1 and AX = 1 in = 00. If setting strategy, AL = 01. CY = 0 and (a) if	If function fails, CY = dicating invalid option exercised through AL on call. If function succeeds, strategy was being set nothing is returned. (b) if strategy is being read i.e. AL = 00 while calling, AX = current strategy
		code.	
87. Function 59H	Extended error reporting function	AH = 59H, BX = 00H code action for the device where	AX = Extended error BH = Error class BL = Recommended reported error CH = Error locus i.e. error occurrence.
88. Function 5AH	Create temporary file of temp file. 00-normal, string format	AH= 5AH, CX =Attribute Path not found, AX = 01-read-only 02-hidden, 04-system, DS:DX points to null terminated filename path in ASCII temporary filename	If fails CY = 1, AX = 5-Access denied. If succeeds CY = 0, AX = file handle of new file, DS:DX points to the
path.			
89. Function 5BH	Create new file Attribute of temp file. 00-	AH = 5AH, CX = 03-Path not found,	If fails CY = 1, AX =

(*Contd.*)

Function Value in AX/AH AL	*Function*	*Register I/P*	*Return O/P*
	02-hidden, 04-system, in ASCII string format.	normal, 01-read-only available handle, AX DS:DX points to null terminated filename path created already	AX = 04, - No = 05-Access denied, AX = 50H-File to be exists. If succeeds CY = 0, AX = file handle of new file.
90. Function 5CH-5FH	These are intended for use of networking and are not of interest as far as this text is concerned.		
91. Function 60H-61H	RESERVED		
92. Function 62H	Get the address of the current program PSP	AH = 62H	BX = Segment address of the current program PSP
93. Function 63H	This function was used in DOS 2.25 only and is not of interest here.		

N.B.

1. There are number of other DOS interrupt functions. This Appendix enlists only the functions under INT21H in brief. For details of these functions users may refer 'Microsoft DOS Encyclopedia or 'Microsoft DOS Reference Manual'.
2. Besides the DOS interrupts the personal computers also provide a separate family of BIOS interrupts. Their details may be obtained from 'IBMPC Reference Manual'.

Index

Microprocessor

8086/8088

8088

8086 ALP

8086-General Interface

Programmable

8253

USART 8251

Pentium-4

RISC Processor

Made in United States
Orlando, FL
04 November 2026

90218262R00391